Collins
German
Dictionary

HarperCollins Publishers
Westerhill Road
Bishopbriggs
Glasgow
G64 2QT
Great Britain

Seventh Edition 2010

Previously published as
Collins Express German Dictionary
© HarperCollins Publishers 2007

Based on Collins Gem German
Dictionary, 1978, 1988, 1993, 1997, 1999,
2000, 2003, 2006, 2007, 2009

Reprint 10 9 8 7 6 5 4 3 2 1 0

© William Collins Sons & Co. Ltd 1990
© HarperCollins Publishers 1996, 1998,
1999, 2001, 2007, 2010

ISBN 978-0-00-732499-6

Collins® is a registered trademark of
HarperCollins Publishers Limited

www.collinslanguage.com

A catalogue record for this book is available
from the British Library

HarperCollins Publishers, 10 East 53rd
Street, New York, NY 10022

COLLINS GERMAN POCKET DICTIONARY
Fifth US Edition 2010

ISBN 978-0-06-200741-4

www.harpercollins.com

Dictionary text typeset by
RefineCatch Ltd, Bungay, Suffolk

Supplement text typeset by
Davidson Publishing Solutions,
Glasgow

Printed in Italy by
LEGO Spa, Lavis (Trento)

Acknowledgements
We would like to thank those authors and
publishers who kindly gave permission for
copyright material to be used in the Collins
Word Web. We would also like
to thank Times Newspapers Ltd for
providing valuable data.

INHALT

CONTENTS

WARENZEICHEN

NOTE ON TRADEMARKS

GENERAL EDITOR
Gaëlle Amiot-Cadey

CONTRIBUTORS
Daphne Day
Horst Kopleck
Joyce Littlejohn

EDITORIAL COORDINATION
Susanne Reichert

SERIES EDITOR
Rob Scriven

EINFÜHRUNG

Wir freuen uns sehr, dass Sie sich zum Kauf eines Collins Wörterbuchs Deutsch entschlossen haben. Wir wünschen Ihnen viel Spaß beim Gebrauch in der Schule, zu Hause, im Urlaub und im Beruf.

Diese Einführung wird Ihnen einige nützliche Hinweise dazu geben, wie Sie am besten von Ihrem neuen Wörterbuch profitieren. Schließlich bietet Ihnen das Wörterbuch nicht nur Stichwörter und Übersetzungen, sondern auch zahlreiche Zusatzinformationen in jedem einzelnen Eintrag. Mit Hilfe all dieser Informationen können Sie zum einen modernes Deutsch lesen und verstehen, zum anderen auch aktiv auf Deutsch kommunizieren.

Das Collins Wörterbuch Deutsch gibt Ihnen vor dem eigentlichen Wörterbuchtextteil selbst eine Liste aller verwendeten Abkürzungen sowie eine Übersicht zu Aussprache und Gebrauch phonetischer Umschrift. Darüber hinaus finden Sie noch eine Auflistung zu den regelmäßigen deutschen Substantivendungen sowie zu unregelmäßigen englischen und deutschen Verben. Auf den letzten Seiten Ihres Wörterbuchs finden Sie in einem „kleinen Reise-ABC" zahlreiche nützliche Phrasen für verschiedenste Situationen am Urlaubsort.

WIE FINDE ICH WAS?

Die verschiedenen Schriftarten, Schriftgrößen, Symbole, Abkürzungen und Klammern helfen Ihnen dabei, sich innerhalb der Informationen, die das Wörterbuch bietet, zurechtzufinden. Die Konventionen, die diesem Wörterbuch zugrunde liegen, sowie auch der Gebrauch verschiedener Symbole werden im Folgenden näher erläutert.

STICHWÖRTER

Die Wörter, die Sie in Ihrem Wörterbuch nachschlagen, die Stichwörter, sind in alphabetischer Reihenfolge angeordnet. Sie sind **fett** gedruckt und in blauer Farbe, sodass Sie sie schnell finden. Die Stichwörter, die rechts und links oben auf jeder Seite erscheinen, sind das jeweils erste Stichwort einer Seite, wenn es sich dabei um eine linke Seite handelt, bzw. das letzte Stichwort einer Seite, wenn es sich um eine rechte Seite handelt. Informationen zu Form und Gebrauch des jeweiligen Stichworts werden im Anschluss an die Lautschrift in Klammern angegeben. Normalerweise sind diese Angaben in abgekürzter Form und *kursiver Schrift* (z.B. (*fam*) für umgangssprachlich oder (*Comm*) als Sachgebietsangabe für Wirtschaft).

Wo es sich anbietet, werden zusammengehörige Wörter und Wortgruppen in einem Eintrag zusammengefasst (z.B. **gather**, **gathering**; **höflich**, **Höflichkeit**). Hierbei sind die Stichwörter innerhalb des Nests von der Schriftgröße etwas kleiner als das erste Stichwort. Geläufige Ausdrücke, in denen das Stichwort vorkommt, erscheinen ebenfalls **fett**, aber in einer anderen Schriftgröße. Die Tilde (~) steht hierbei für das Hauptstichwort am Anfang eines Eintrags. So steht beispielsweise im Eintrag ‚Mitte' der Ausdruck ‚**~ Juni**' für ‚Mitte Juni'.

PHONETISCHE UMSCHRIFT

Die Aussprache jedes Stichworts findet sich in phonetischer Umschrift in eckigen Klammern jeweils direkt hinter dem Stichwort selbst (z.B. **mountain** ['mauntın]). Eine Liste der Lautschriftzeichen mit Erklärungen finden Sie auf S. xi.

BEDEUTUNGEN

Die Übersetzung der Stichwörter ist in Normalschrift angegeben. Gibt es mehrere Bedeutungen oder Gebrauchsmöglichkeiten, so sind diese durch einen Strichpunkt voneinander zu unterscheiden. Sie finden oft weitere Angaben in Klammern vor den jeweiligen Übersetzungen. Diese zeigen Ihnen typische Kontexte auf, in denen das Stichwort verwendet werden kann (z.B. **breakup** (*of meeting, organisation*)), oder sie liefern Synonyme (z.B. **fit** (*suitable*)).

GRAMMATISCHE HINWEISE

Die Wortartangabe finden Sie als Abkürzung und in *kursiver Schrift* direkt hinter der Ausspracheinformation zum jeweiligen Stichwort (z.B. *vt*, *adj*, *n*).

Die Genusangaben zu deutschen Substantiven werden wie folgt angegeben: *m* für Maskulinum, *f* für Femininum und *nt* für Neutrum. Darüber hinaus finden Sie neben dem Stichwort in Klammern Genitiv- und Pluralform (**Abenteuer** (*-s, -*)).

Die Genusangabe zur deutschen Übersetzung findet sich ebenfalls in *kursiver Schrift* direkt hinter dem Hauptbestandteil der Übersetzung.

INTRODUCTION

We are delighted you have decided to buy the Collins German Dictionary and hope you will enjoy and benefit from using it at school, at home, on holiday or at work.

This introduction gives you a few tips on how to get the most out of your dictionary - not simply from its comprehensive wordlist but also from the information provided in each entry. This will help you to read and understand modern German, as well as to communicate and express yourself in the language.

The Collins German Dictionary begins by listing the abbreviations used in the text and illustrating the sounds shown by the phonetic symbols. Next you will find regular German noun endings and English irregular verbs followed by a section on German irregular verbs. Finally, the new Phrasefinder supplement gives you hundreds of useful phrases which are intended to give you practical help in everyday situations when travelling.

USING YOUR COLLINS DICTIONARY

A wealth of information is presented in the dictionary, using various typefaces, sizes of type, symbols, abbreviations and brackets. The conventions and symbols used are explained in the following sections.

HEADWORDS

The words you look up in the dictionary – 'headwords' – are listed alphabetically. They are printed in **colour** for rapid identification. The headwords appearing at the top of each page indicate the first (if it appears on a left-hand page) and last word (if it appears on a right-hand page) dealt with on the page in question.

Information about the usage or form of certain headwords is given in brackets after the phonetic spelling. This usually appears in abbreviated form and in italics (e.g. *(fam)*, *(Comm)*).

Where appropriate, words related to headwords are grouped in the same entry (**gather, gathering; höflich, Höflichkeit**) in a slightly smaller bold type than the headword. Common expressions in which the headword appears are shown in a different size of bold roman type. The swung dash, ~, represents the main headword at the start of each entry. For example, in the entry for 'Mitte', the phrase '~ Juni' should be read 'Mitte Juni'.

PHONETIC SPELLINGS

The phonetic spelling of each headword (indicating its pronunciation) is given in square brackets immediately after the headword (e.g. **mountain** ['maʊntɪn]). A list of these spellings is given on page xi.

MEANINGS

Headword translations are given in ordinary type and, where more than one meaning or usage exists, they are separated by a semicolon. You will often find other words in italics in brackets before the translations. These offer suggested contexts in which the headword might appear (e.g. **breakup** (*of meeting, organisation*)) or provide synonyms (e.g. **fit** (*suitable*)).

GRAMMATICAL INFORMATION

Parts of speech are given in abbreviated form in italics after the phonetic spellings of headwords (e.g. *vt*, *adj*, *n*).

Genders of German nouns are indicated as follows: *m* for a masculine, *f* for a feminine, and *nt* for a neuter noun. Genitive and plural forms of nouns are also shown next to the headword (**Abenteuer** (*-s, -*)).

The gender of the German translation appears in *italics* immediately following the key element of the translation.

auch	*a.*	also
Abkürzung	*abk, abbr*	abbreviation
Akronym	*acr*	acronym
Adjektiv	*adj*	adjective
Adverb	*adv*	adverb
Landwirtschaft	*Agr*	agriculture
Akkusativ	*akk*	accusative
Akronym	*akr*	acronym
Anatomie	*Anat*	anatomy
Artikel	*art*	article
Bildende Künste	*Art*	fine arts
Astronomie, Astrologie	*Astr*	astronomy, astrology
Auto, Verkehr	*Auto*	automobiles, traffic
Luftfahrt	*Aviat*	aviation
Biologie	*Bio*	biology
Botanik	*Bot*	botany
britisch	*BRIT*	British
schweizerisch	*CH*	Swiss
Chemie	*Chem*	chemistry
Film	*Cine*	cinema
Wirtschaft	*Comm*	commerce
Konjunktion	*conj*	conjunction
Dativ	*dat*	dative
Eisenbahn	*Eisenb*	railways
Elektrizität	*Elek, Elec*	electricity
besonders	*esp*	especially
und so weiter	*etc*	et cetera
etwas	*etw*	
Femininum	*f*	feminine
umgangssprachlich	*fam*	familiar, informal
übertragen	*fig*	figurative
Finanzen, Börse	*Fin*	finance
Fotografie	*Foto*	photography
Gastronomie	*Gastr*	cooking, gastronomy
Genitiv	*gen*	genitive
Geographie, Geologie	*Geo*	geography, geology
Geschichte	*Hist*	history
Imperativ	*imper*	imperative
Imperfekt	*imperf*	past tense
Informatik und Computer	*Inform*	computing
Interjektion, Ausruf	*interj*	interjection
unveränderlich	*inv*	invariable
unregelmäßig	*irr*	irregular
jemand, jemandem	*jd, jdm*	
jemanden, jemandes	*jdn, jds*	
Rechtsprechung	*Jur*	law

German	Abbr	English
Konjunktion	*konj*	conjunction
Bildende Künste	*Kunst*	fine arts
Sprachwissenschaft, Grammatik	*Ling*	linguistics, grammar
Maskulinum	*m*	masculine
Mathematik	*Math*	mathematics
Medizin	*Med*	medicine
Meteorologie	*Meteo*	meteorology
Maskulinum und Femininum	*mf*	masculine and feminine
Militär	*Mil*	military
Musik	*Mus*	music
Substantiv	*n*	noun
Seefahrt	*Naut*	nautical, naval
Neutrum	*nt*	neuter
Zahlwort	*num*	numeral
oder	*o*	or
pejorativ, abwertend	*pej*	pejorative
Physik	*Phys*	physics
Plural	*pl*	plural
Politik	*Pol*	politics
Partizip Perfekt	*pp*	past participle
Präfix	*pref*	prefix
Präposition	*prep*	preposition
Pronomen	*pron*	pronoun
1. Vergangenheit	*pt*	past tense
Eisenbahn	*Rail*	railways
Religion	*Rel*	religion
siehe	*s.*	see
	sb	someone, somebody
schottisch	*Scot*	Scottish
Singular	*sing*	singular
Skisport	*Ski*	skiing
	sth	something
Technik	*Tech*	technology
Nachrichtentechnik	*Tel*	telecommunications
Theater	*Theat*	theatre
Fernsehen	*TV*	television
Typographie, Buchdruck	*Typo*	printing
unpersönlich	*unpers*	impersonal
(nord)amerikanisch	*US*	(North) American
Verb	*vb*	verb
Hilfsverb	*vb aux*	auxiliary verb
intransitives Verb	*vi*	intransitive verb
reflexives Verb	*vr*	reflexive verb
transitives Verb	*vt*	transitive verb
vulgär	*vulg*	vulgar
Zoologie	*Zool*	zoology
ungefähre Entsprechung	≈	cultural equivalent
abtrennbares Präfix	|	separable prefix

LAUTSCHRIFT   PHONETIC SYMBOLS

[:] Längezeichen, length mark
['] Betonung, stress mark
[*] Bindungs-R, 'r' pronounced before a vowel

alle Vokallaute sind nur ungefähre Entsprechungen
all vowel sounds are approximate only

VOKALE UND DIPHTHONGE

plant, arm, father	[ɑ:]	Bahn
fiancé	[ã:]	Ensemble
life	[aɪ]	weit
house	[au]	Haut
man, sad	[æ]	
but, son	[ʌ]	Butler
get, bed	[e]	Metall
name, lame	[eɪ]	
ago, better	[ə]	bitte
bird, her	[ɜ:]	
there, care	[ɛə]	mehr
it, wish	[ɪ]	Bischof
bee, me, beat, belief	[i:]	viel
here	[ɪə]	Bier
no, low	[əʊ]	
not, long	[ɒ]	Post
law, all	[ɔ:]	Mond
boy, oil	[ɔɪ]	Heu
push, look	[ʊ]	Pult
you, do	[u:]	Hut
poor, sure	[ʊə]	

KONSONANTEN

been, blind	[b]	Ball
do, had	[d]	dann
jam, object	[dʒ]	
father, wolf	[f]	Fass
go, beg	[g]	Gast
house	[h]	Herr
youth, Indian	[j]	ja
keep, milk	[k]	kalt
lamp, oil, ill	[l]	Last
man, am	[m]	Mast
no, manner	[n]	Nuss
long, sing	[ŋ]	lang

El Niño	[ɲ]	El Niño
paper, happy	[p]	Pakt
red, dry	[r]	rot
stand, sand, yes	[s]	Rasse
ship, station	[ʃ]	Schal
tell, fat	[t]	Tal
thank, death	[θ]	
this, father	[ð]	
church, catch	[tʃ]	Rutsch
voice, live	[v]	was
water, we, which	[w]	
loch	[x]	Bach
zeal, these, gaze	[z]	Hase
pleasure	[ʒ]	Genie

REGULAR GERMAN NOUN ENDINGS

nominative		genitive	plural
-ade	f	-ade	-aden
-ant	m	-anten	-anten
-anz	f	-anz	-anzen
-ar	m	-ars	-are
-är	m	-ärs	-äre
-at	nt	-at(e)s	-ate
-atte	f	-atte	-atten
-chen	nt	-chens	-chen
-ei	f	-ei	-eien
-elle	f	-elle	-ellen
-ent	m	-enten	-enten
-enz	f	-enz	-enzen
-ette	f	-ette	-etten
-eur	m	-eurs	-eure
-euse	f	-euse	-eusen
-heit	f	-heit	-heiten
-ie	f	-ie	-ien
-ik	f	-ik	-iken
-in	f	-in	-innen
-ine	f	-ine	-inen
-ion	f	-ion	-ionen

nominative		genitive	plural
-ist	m	-isten	-isten
-ium	nt	-iums	-ien
-ius	m	-ius	-iusse
-ive	f	-ive	-iven
-keit	f	-keit	-keiten
-lein	nt	-leins	-lein
-ling	m	-lings	-linge
-ment	nt	-ments	-mente
-mus	m	-mus	-men
-nis	f	-nis	-nisse
-nis	nt	-nisses	-nisse
-nom	m	-nomen	-nomen
-rich	m	-richs	-riche
-schaft	f	-schaft	-schaften
-sel	nt	-sels	-sel
-tät	f	-tät	-täten
-tiv	nt, m	-tivs	-tive
-tor	m	-tors	-toren
-tum	m, nt	-tums	-tümer
-ung	f	-ung	-ungen
-ur	f	-ur	-uren

Substantive, die mit einem geklammerten 'r' oder 's' enden (z.B. **Ange-stellte(r)** *mf*, **Beamte(r)** *m*, **Gute(s)** *nt*) werden wie Adjektive dekliniert:

Nouns listed with an 'r' or an 's' in brackets (eg **Angestellte(r)** *mf*, **Beamte(r)** *m*, **Gute(s)** *nt*) take the same endings as adjectives:

der Angestellte *m*	**die Angestellte** *f*	**die Angestellten** *pl*
ein Angestellter *m*	**eine Angestellte** *f*	**Angestellte** *pl*
der Beamte *m*		**die Beamten** *pl*
ein Beamter *m*		**Beamte** *pl*
das Gute *nt*		
ein Gutes *nt*		

UNREGELMÄßIGE ENGLISCHE VERBEN

present	past tense	past participle	present	past tense	past participle
arise (arising)	arose	arisen	drink	drank	drunk
awake (awaking)	awoke	awaked	drive (driving)	drove	driven
be (am, is, are; being)	was, were	been	eat	ate	eaten
bear	bore	born(e)	fall	fell	fallen
beat	beat	beaten	feed	fed	fed
become (becoming)	became	become	feel	felt	felt
begin (beginning)	began	begun	fight	fought	fought
bend	bent	bent	find	found	found
bet (betting)	bet	bet	flee	fled	fled
bid (bidding)	bid	bid	fling	flung	flung
bind	bound	bound	fly (flies)	flew	flown
bite (biting)	bit	bitten	forbid (forbidding)	forbade	forbidden
bleed	bled	bled	foresee	foresaw	foreseen
blow	blew	blown	forget (forgetting)	forgot	forgotten
break	broke	broken	forgive (forgiving)	forgave	forgiven
breed	bred	bred	freeze (freezing)	froze	frozen
bring	brought	brought	get (getting)	got	got, (US) gotten
build	built	built	give (giving)	gave	given
burn	burnt (o burned)	burnt (o burned)	go (goes)	went	gone
burst	burst	burst	grind	ground	ground
buy	bought	bought	grow	grew	grown
can	could	(been able)	hang	hung (o hanged)	hung (o hanged)
cast	cast	cast	have (has; having)	had	had
catch	caught	caught	hear	heard	heard
choose (choosing)	chose	chosen	hide (hiding)	hid	hidden
cling	clung	clung	hit (hitting)	hit	hit
come (coming)	came	come	hold	held	held
cost	cost	cost	hurt	hurt	hurt
creep	crept	crept	keep	kept	kept
cut (cutting)	cut	cut	kneel	knelt (o kneeled)	knelt (o kneeled)
deal	dealt	dealt			
dig (digging)	dug	dug	know	knew	known
do (does)	did	done	lay	laid	laid
draw	drew	drawn	lead	led	led
dream	dreamed (o dreamt)	dreamed (o dreamt)			

present	past tense	past participle	present	past tense	past participle
lean	leant (o leaned)	leant (o leaned)	shoot	shot	shot
			show	showed	shown
leap	leapt (o leaped)	leapt (o leaped)	shrink	shrank	shrunk
			shut (shutting)	shut	shut
learn	learnt (o learned)	learnt (o learned)	sing	sang	sung
leave (leaving)	left	left	sink	sank	sunk
			sit (sitting)	sat	sat
lend	lent	lent	sleep	slept	slept
let (letting)	let	let	slide (sliding)	slid	slid
lie (lying)	lay	lain			
light	lit (o lighted)	lit (o lighted)	sling	slung	slung
			slit (slitting)	slit	slit
lose (losing)	lost	lost	smell	smelt (o smelled)	smelt (o smelled)
make (making)	made	made			
			sow	sowed	sown (o sowed)
may	might	–	speak	spoke	spoken
mean	meant	meant	speed	sped (o speeded)	sped (o speeded)
meet	met	met			
mow	mowed	mown (o mowed)	spell	spelt (o spelled)	spelt (o spelled)
must	(had to)	(had to)	spend	spent	spent
pay	paid	paid	spin (spinning)	spun	spun
put (putting)	put	put			
quit (quitting)	quit (o quitted)	quit (o quitted)	spit (spitting)	spat	spat
			split (splitting)	split	split
read	read	read			
rid (ridding)	rid	rid	spoil	spoiled (o spoilt)	spoiled (o spoilt)
ride (riding)	rode	ridden			
ring	rang	rung	spread	spread	spread
rise (rising)	rose	risen	spring	sprang	sprung
run (running)	ran	run	stand	stood	stood
saw	sawed	sawn	steal	stole	stolen
say	said	said	stick	stuck	stuck
see	saw	seen	sting	stung	stung
seek	sought	sought	stink	stank	stunk
sell	sold	sold	strike (striking)	struck	struck
send	sent	sent			
set (setting)	set	set	strive (striving)	strove	striven
shake (shaking)	shook	shaken			
			swear	swore	sworn
shall	should	–	sweep	swept	swept
shine (shining)	shone	shone	swell	swelled	swollen (o swelled)

present	past tense	past participle	present	past tense	past participle
swim (swimming)	swam	swum	wake (waking)	woke (o waked)	woken (o waked)
swing	swung	swung	wear	wore	worn
take (taking)	took	taken	weave (weaving)	wove (o weaved)	woven (o weaved)
teach	taught	taught	weep	wept	wept
tear	tore	torn	win (winning)	won	won
tell	told	told			
think	thought	thought	wind	wound	wound
throw	threw	thrown	write (writing)	wrote	written
thrust	thrust	thrust			
tread	trod	trodden			

IRREGULAR GERMAN VERBS

Infinitiv	Präsens 2., 3. Singular	Imperfekt	Partizip Perfekt
backen	bäckst, bäckt	backte o buk	gebacken
befehlen	befiehlst, befiehlt	befahl	befohlen
beginnen	beginnst, beginnt	begann	begonnen
beißen	beißt, beißt	biss	gebissen
bergen	birgst, birgt	barg	geborgen
betrügen	betrügst, betrügt	betrog	betrogen
biegen	biegst, biegt	bog	gebogen
bieten	bietest, bietet	bot	geboten
binden	bindest, bindet	band	gebunden
bitten	bittest, bittet	bat	gebeten
blasen	bläst, bläst	blies	geblasen
bleiben	bleibst, bleibt	blieb	geblieben
braten	brätst, brät	briet	gebraten
brechen	brichst, bricht	brach	gebrochen
brennen	brennst, brennt	brannte	gebrannt
bringen	bringst, bringt	brachte	gebracht
denken	denkst, denkt	dachte	gedacht
dringen	dringst, dringt	drang	gedrungen
dürfen	darfst, darf	durfte	gedurft
erschrecken	erschrickst, erschrickt	erschrak	erschrocken
essen	isst, isst	aß	gegessen
fahren	fährst, fährt	fuhr	gefahren
fallen	fällst, fällt	fiel	gefallen
fangen	fängst, fängt	fing	gefangen
finden	findest, findet	fand	gefunden
fliegen	fliegst, fliegt	flog	geflogen
fließen	fließt, fließt	floss	geflossen
fressen	frisst, frisst	fraß	gefressen
frieren	frierst, friert	fror	gefroren
geben	gibst, gibt	gab	gegeben
gehen	gehst, geht	ging	gegangen
gelingen	–, gelingt	gelang	gelungen
gelten	giltst, gilt	galt	gegolten
genießen	genießt, genießt	genoss	genossen
geschehen	–, geschieht	geschah	geschehen
gewinnen	gewinnst, gewinnt	gewann	gewonnen
gießen	gießt, gießt	goss	gegossen
gleichen	gleichst, gleicht	glich	geglichen
gleiten	gleitest, gleitet	glitt	geglitten
graben	gräbst, gräbt	grub	gegraben
greifen	greifst, greift	griff	gegriffen
haben	hast, hat	hatte	gehabt
halten	hältst, hält	hielt	gehalten
hängen	hängst, hängt	hing	gehangen

Infinitiv	Präsens 2., 3. Singular	Imperfekt	Partizip Perfekt
heben	hebst, hebt	hob	gehoben
heißen	heißt, heißt	hieß	geheißen
helfen	hilfst, hilft	half	geholfen
kennen	kennst, kennt	kannte	gekannt
klingen	klingst, klingt	klang	geklungen
kommen	kommst, kommt	kam	gekommen
können	kannst, kann	konnte	gekonnt
kriechen	kriechst, kriecht	kroch	gekrochen
laden	lädst, lädt	lud	geladen
lassen	lässt, lässt	ließ	gelassen
laufen	läufst, läuft	lief	gelaufen
leiden	leidest, leidet	litt	gelitten
leihen	leihst, leiht	lieh	geliehen
lesen	liest, liest	las	gelesen
liegen	liegst, liegt	lag	gelegen
lügen	lügst, lügt	log	gelogen
mahlen	mahlst, mahlt	mahlte	gemahlen
meiden	meidest, meidet	mied	gemieden
messen	misst, misst	maß	gemessen
mögen	magst, mag	mochte	gemocht
müssen	musst, muss	musste	gemusst
nehmen	nimmst, nimmt	nahm	genommen
nennen	nennst, nennt	nannte	genannt
pfeifen	pfeifst, pfeift	pfiff	gepfiffen
raten	rätst, rät	riet	geraten
reiben	reibst, reibt	rieb	gerieben
reißen	reißt, reißt	riss	gerissen
reiten	reitest, reitet	ritt	geritten
rennen	rennst, rennt	rannte	gerannt
riechen	riechst, riecht	roch	gerochen
rufen	rufst, ruft	rief	gerufen
saufen	säufst, säuft	soff	gesoffen
saugen	saugst, saugt	sog o saugte	gesogen o gesaugt
schaffen	schaffst, schafft	schuf	geschaffen
scheiden	scheidest, scheidet	schied	geschieden
scheinen	scheinst, scheint	schien	geschienen
schieben	schiebst, schiebt	schob	geschoben
schießen	schießt, schießt	schoss	geschossen
schlafen	schläfst, schläft	schlief	geschlafen
schlagen	schlägst, schlägt	schlug	geschlagen
schleichen	schleichst, schleicht	schlich	geschlichen
schließen	schließt, schließt	schloss	geschlossen
schmeißen	schmeißt, schmeißt	schmiss	geschmissen
schmelzen	schmilzt, schmilzt	schmolz	geschmolzen
schneiden	schneidest, schneidet	schnitt	geschnitten

Infinitiv	Präsens 2., 3. Singular	Imperfekt	Partizip Perfekt
schreiben	schreibst, schreibt	schrieb	geschrieben
schreien	schreist, schreit	schrie	geschrie(e)n
schweigen	schweigst, schweigt	schwieg	geschwiegen
schwellen	schwillst, schwillt	schwoll	geschwollen
schwimmen	schwimmst, schwimmt	schwamm	geschwommen
schwören	schwörst, schwört	schwor	geschworen
sehen	siehst, sieht	sah	gesehen
sein	bist, ist	war	gewesen
senden	sendest, sendet	sandte	gesandt
singen	singst, singt	sang	gesungen
sinken	sinkst, sinkt	sank	gesunken
sitzen	sitzt, sitzt	saß	gesessen
sollen	sollst, soll	sollte	gesollt
sprechen	sprichst, spricht	sprach	gesprochen
springen	springst, springt	sprang	gesprungen
stechen	stichst, sticht	stach	gestochen
stehen	stehst, steht	stand	gestanden
stehlen	stiehlst, stiehlt	stahl	gestohlen
steigen	steigst, steigt	stieg	gestiegen
sterben	stirbst, stirbt	starb	gestorben
stinken	stinkst, stinkt	stank	gestunken
stoßen	stößt, stößt	stieß	gestoßen
streichen	streichst, streicht	strich	gestrichen
streiten	streitest, streitet	stritt	gestritten
tragen	trägst, trägt	trug	getragen
treffen	triffst, trifft	traf	getroffen
treiben	treibst, treibt	trieb	getrieben
treten	trittst, tritt	trat	getreten
trinken	trinkst, trinkt	trank	getrunken
tun	tust, tut	tat	getan
verderben	verdirbst, verdirbt	verdarb	verdorben
vergessen	vergisst, vergisst	vergaß	vergessen
verlieren	verlierst, verliert	verlor	verloren
verschwinden	verschwindest, verschwindet	verschwand	verschwunden
verzeihen	verzeihst, verzeiht	verzieh	verziehen
wachsen	wächst, wächst	wuchs	gewachsen
wenden	wendest, wendet	wandte	gewandt
werben	wirbst, wirbt	warb	geworben
werden	wirst, wird	wurde	geworden
werfen	wirfst, wirft	warf	geworfen
wiegen	wiegst, wiegt	wog	gewogen
wissen	weißt, weiß	wusste	gewusst
wollen	willst, will	wollte	gewollt
ziehen	ziehst, zieht	zog	gezogen
zwingen	zwingst, zwingt	zwang	gezwungen

a

à *prep* +*akk* at ... each; **4 Tickets ~ 8 Euro** 4 tickets at 8 euros each
A *abk* = **Autobahn** ≈ M (*Brit*), ≈ I (*US*)
Aal (-(e)s, -e) *m* eel

O SCHLÜSSELWORT

ab *prep* +*dat* from; **Kinder ab 12 Jahren** children from the age of 12; **ab morgen** from tomorrow; **ab sofort** as of now
▷ *adv* **1** off; **links ab** to the left; **der Knopf ist ab** the button has come off; **ab nach Hause!** off you go home
2 (*zeitlich*) **von da ab** from then on; **von heute ab** from today, as of today
3 (*auf Fahrplänen*) **München ab 12.20** leaving Munich 12.20
4 ab und zu *o* **an** now and then *o* again

ab|bauen *vt* (*Zelt*) to take down; (*verringern*) to reduce
ab|beißen *irr vt* to bite off
ab|bestellen *vt* to cancel
ab|biegen *irr vi* to turn off; (*Straße*) to bend; **nach links/rechts ~** to turn left/right
Abbildung *f* illustration
ab|blasen *irr vt* (*fig*) to call off
ab|blenden *vt, vi* (*Auto*) (**die Scheinwerfer**) **~** to dip (*Brit*) (*o* to dim (*US*)) one's headlights; **Abblendlicht** *nt* dipped (*Brit*) (*o* dimmed (*US*)) headlights *pl*
ab|brechen *irr vt* to break off; (*Gebäude*) to pull down; (*aufhören*) to stop; (*Computerprogramm*) to abort
ab|bremsen *vi* to brake, to slow down
ab|bringen *irr vt*: **jdn von einer Idee ~** to talk sb out of an idea; **jdn vom Thema ~** to get sb away from the subject; **davon lasse ich mich nicht ~** nothing will make me change my mind about it
ab|buchen *vt* to debit (*von* to)
ab|danken *vi* to resign
ab|drehen *vt* (*Gas, Wasser*) to turn off; (*Licht*) to switch off ▷ *vi* (*Schiff, Flugzeug*) to change course
Abend (-s, -e) *m* evening; **am ~** in the evening; **zu ~ essen** to have dinner; **heute/morgen/gestern ~** this/tomorrow/yesterday evening; **guten ~!** good evening; **Abendbrot** *nt* supper; **Abendessen** *nt* dinner; **Abendgarderobe** *f* evening dress (*o* gown); **Abendkasse** *f* box office; **Abendkleid** *nt* evening dress (*o* gown); **Abendmahl** *nt*: **das ~** (Holy) Communion; **abends** *adv* in the evening; **montags ~** on Monday evenings
Abenteuer (-s, -) *nt* adventure; **Abenteuerurlaub** *m* adventure

holiday

aber conj but; (jedoch) however; **oder ~** alternatively; **~ ja!** (but) of course; **das ist ~ nett von Ihnen** that's really nice of you

abergläubisch adj superstitious

ab|fahren irr vi to leave (o to depart) (nach for); (Ski) to ski down; **Abfahrt** f departure; (von Autobahn) exit; (Ski) descent; (Piste) run; **Abfahrtslauf** m (Ski) downhill; **Abfahrtszeit** f departure time

Abfall m waste; (Müll) rubbish (Brit), garbage (US); **Abfalleimer** m rubbish bin (Brit), garbage can (US)

abfällig adj disparaging; **~ von jdm sprechen** to make disparaging remarks about sb

ab|färben vi (Wäsche) to run; (fig) to rub off

ab|fertigen vt (Pakete) to prepare for dispatch; (an der Grenze) to clear; **Abfertigungsschalter** m (am Flughafen) check-in desk

ab|finden irr vt to pay off ▷ vr: **sich mit etw ~** to come to terms with sth; **Abfindung** f (Entschädigung) compensation; (von Angestellten) redundancy payment

ab|fliegen irr vi (Flugzeug) to take off; (Passagier a.) to fly off; **Abflug** m departure; (Start) takeoff; **Abflughalle** f departure lounge; **Abflugzeit** f departure time

Abfluss m drain; (am Waschbecken) plughole (Brit); **Abflussrohr** nt waste pipe; (außen) drainpipe

ab|fragen vt to test; (Inform) to call up

ab|führen vi (Med) to have a laxative effect ▷ vt (Steuern, Gebühren) to pay; **jdn ~ lassen** to take sb into custody; **Abführmittel** nt laxative

Abgabe f handing in; (von Ball) pass; (Steuer) tax; (einer Erklärung) making; **abgabenfrei** adj tax-free; **abgabenpflichtig** adj liable to tax

Abgase pl (Auto) exhaust fumes pl; **Abgas(sonder)untersuchung** f exhaust emission test

ab|geben irr vt (Gepäck, Schlüssel) to leave (bei with); (Schularbeit etc) to hand in; (Wärme) to give off; (Erklärung, Urteil) to make ▷ vr: **sich mit jdm ~** to associate with sb; **sich mit etw ~** to bother with sth

abgebildet adj: **wie oben ~** as shown above

ab|gehen irr vi (Post) to go; (Knopf etc) to come off; (abgezogen werden) to be taken off; (Straße) to branch off; **von der Schule ~** to leave school; **sie geht mir ab** I really miss her; **was geht denn hier ab?** (fam) what's going on here?

abgehetzt adj exhausted, shattered

abgelaufen adj (Pass) expired; (Zeit, Frist) up; **die Milch ist ~** the milk is past its sell-by date

abgelegen adj remote

abgemacht interj OK, it's a deal, that's settled, then

abgeneigt adj **einer Sache** (dat) **~ sein** to be averse to sth; **ich wäre nicht ~, das zu tun** I wouldn't mind doing that

Abgeordnete(r) mf Member of Parliament

abgepackt adj prepacked

abgerissen adj: **der Knopf ist ~** the button has come off

abgesehen adj: **es auf jdn/etw ~ haben** to be after sb/sth; **~ von** apart from

abgespannt adj (Person) exhausted, worn out

abgestanden *adj* stale; (*Bier*) flat
abgestorben *adj* (*Pflanze*) dead; (*Finger*) numb
abgestumpft *adj* (*Person*) insensitive
abgetragen *adj* (*Kleidung*) worn
ab|gewöhnen *vt:* **jdm etw ~** to cure sb of sth; **sich etw ~** to give sth up
ab|haken *vt* to tick off; **das (Thema) ist schon abgehakt** that's been dealt with
ab|halten *irr vt* (*Versammlung*) to hold; **jdn von etw ~** (*fernhalten*) to keep sb away from sth; (*hindern*) to keep sb from sth
abhanden *adj:* **~ kommen** to get lost
Abhang *m* slope
ab|hängen *vt* (*Bild*) to take down; (*Anhänger*) to uncouple; (*Verfolger*) to shake off ▷ *irr vi:* **von jdm/etw ~** to depend on sb/sth; **das hängt davon ab, ob …** it depends (on) whether …; **abhängig** *adj* dependent (*von* on)
ab|hauen *irr vt* (*abschlagen*) to cut off ▷ *vi* (*fam: verschwinden*) to clear off; **hau ab!** get lost!, beat it!
ab|heben *irr vt* (*Geld*) to withdraw; (*Telefonhörer, Spielkarte*) to pick up ▷ *vi* (*Flugzeug*) to take off; (*Rakete*) to lift off; (*Karten*) to cut
ab|holen *vt* to collect; (*am Bahnhof etc*) to meet; (*mit dem Auto*) to pick up; **Abholmarkt** *m* cash and carry
ab|horchen *vt* (*Med*) to listen to
ab|hören *vt* (*Vokabeln*) to test; (*Telefongespräch*) to tap; (*Tonband etc*) to listen to
Abitur (*-s, -e*) *nt* German school-leaving examination, ≈ A-levels (*Brit*), ≈ High School Diploma (*US*)

○ **ABITUR**
○
● The **Abitur** is the German
● school-leaving examination
● which is taken at the age of 18
● or 19 by pupils at a **Gymnasium**.
● It is taken in four subjects and is
● necessary for entry to
● university.

ab|kaufen *vt:* **jdm etw ~** to buy sth from sb; **das kauf ich dir nicht ab!** (*fam: glauben*) I don't believe you
ab|klingen *irr vi* (*Schmerz*) to ease; (*Wirkung*) to wear off
ab|kommen *irr vi* to get away; **von der Straße ~** to leave the road; **von einem Plan ~** to give up a plan; **vom Thema ~** to stray from the point
Abkommen (*-s, -*) *nt* agreement
ab|koppeln *vt* (*Anhänger*) to unhitch
ab|kratzen *vt* to scrape off ▷ *vi* (*fam: sterben*) to kick the bucket, to croak
ab|kühlen *vi, vt* to cool down ▷ *vr:* **sich ~** to cool down
ab|kürzen *vt* (*Wort*) to abbreviate; **den Weg ~** to take a short cut; **Abkürzung** *f* (*Wort*) abbreviation; (*Weg*) short cut
ab|laden *irr vt* to unload
Ablage *f* (*für Akten*) tray; (*Aktenordnung*) filing system
Ablauf *m* (*Abfluss*) drain; (*von Ereignissen*) course; (*einer Frist, Zeit*) expiry; **ab|laufen** *irr vi* (*abfließen*) to drain away; (*Ereignisse*) to happen; (*Frist, Zeit, Pass*) to expire
ab|legen *vt* to put down; (*Kleider*) to take off; (*Gewohnheit*) to get out of; (*Prüfung*) to take, to sit; (*Akten*) to file away ▷ *vi* (*Schiff*) to cast off
ab|lehnen *vt* to reject; (*Einladung*) to decline; (*missbilligen*)

to disapprove of; (*Bewerber*) to turn down ▷ *vi* to decline

ab|lenken *vt* to distract; **jdn von der Arbeit ~** to distract sb from their work; **vom Thema ~** to change the subject; **Ablenkung** *f* distraction

ab|lesen *vt* (*Text, Rede*) to read; **das Gas/den Strom ~** to read the gas/electricity meter

ab|liefern *vt* to deliver

ab|machen *vt* (*entfernen*) to take off; (*vereinbaren*) to agree; **Abmachung** *f* agreement

ab|melden *vt* (*Zeitung*) to cancel; (*Auto*) to take off the road ▷ *vr*: **sich ~** to give notice of one's departure; (*im Hotel*) to check out; (*vom Verein*) to cancel one's membership

ab|messen *irr vt* to measure

ab|nehmen *irr vt* to take off, to remove; (*Hörer*) to pick up; (*Führerschein*) to take away; (*Geld*) to get (*jdm out of sb*); (*kaufen, umg: glauben*) to buy (*jdm from sb*) ▷ *vi* to decrease; (*schlanker werden*) to lose weight; (*Tel*) to pick up the phone; **fünf Kilo ~** to lose five kilos

Abneigung *f* dislike (*gegen* of); (*stärker*) aversion (*gegen* to)

ab|nutzen *vt* to wear out ▷ *vr*: **sich ~** to wear out

Abonnement (*-s, -s*) *nt* subscription; **Abonnent(in)** *m(f)* subscriber; **abonnieren** *vt* to subscribe to

ab|raten *irr vi*: **jdm von etw ~** to advise sb against sth

ab|räumen *vt*: **den Tisch ~** to clear the table; **das Geschirr ~** to clear away the dishes; (*Preis etc*) to walk away with

Abrechnung *f* settlement; (*Rechnung*) bill

ab|regen *vr*: **sich ~** (*fam*) to calm

(*o to cool*) down; **reg dich ab!** take it easy

Abreise *f* departure; **ab|reisen** *vi* to leave (*nach* for); **Abreisetag** *m* day of departure

ab|reißen *irr vt* (*Haus*) to pull down; (*Blatt*) to tear off; **den Kontakt nicht ~ lassen** to stay in touch ▷ *vi* (*Knopf etc*) to come off

ab|runden *vt*: **eine Zahl nach oben/unten ~** to round a number up/down

abrupt *adj* abrupt

ABS *nt abk* = **Antiblockiersystem** (*Auto*) ABS

Abs. *abk* = **Absender** from

ab|sagen *vt* to cancel, to call off; (*Einladung*) to turn down ▷ *vi* (*ablehnen*) to decline; **ich muss leider ~** I'm afraid I can't come

Absatz *m* (*Comm*) sales *pl*; (*neuer Abschnitt*) paragraph; (*Schuh*) heel

ab|schaffen *vt* to abolish, to do away with

ab|schalten *vt, vi* (*a. fig*) to switch off

ab|schätzen *vt* to estimate; (*Lage*) to assess

abscheulich *adj* disgusting

ab|schicken *vt* to send off

ab|schieben *irr vt* (*ausweisen*) to deport

Abschied (*-(e)s, -e*) *m* parting; **~ nehmen** to say good-bye (*von jdm* to); **Abschiedsfeier** *f* farewell party

Abschlagszahlung *f* interim payment

Abschleppdienst *m* (*Auto*) breakdown service; **ab|schleppen** *vt* to tow; **Abschleppseil** *nt* towrope; **Abschleppwagen** *m* breakdown truck (*Brit*), tow truck (*US*)

ab|schließen *irr vt* (*Tür*) to lock; (*beenden*) to conclude, to finish; (*Vertrag, Handel*) to conclude;

Abschluss m (*Beendigung*) close, conclusion; (*von Vertrag, Handel*) conclusion

ab|schmecken vt (*kosten*) to taste; (*würzen*) to season

ab|schminken vr: **sich ~** to take one's make-up off ▷ vt (*fam*) **sich** (*dat*) **etw ~** to get sth out of one's mind

ab|schnallen vr: **sich ~** to undo one's seatbelt

ab|schneiden irr vt to cut off ▷ vi: **gut/schlecht ~** to do well/badly

Abschnitt m (*von Buch, Text*) section; (*Kontrollabschnitt*) stub

ab|schrauben vt to unscrew

ab|schrecken vt to deter, to put off

ab|schreiben irr vt to copy (*bei, von* from, off); (*verloren geben*) to write off; (*Comm: absetzen*) to deduct

abschüssig adj steep

ab|schwächen vt to lessen; (*Behauptung, Kritik*) to tone down

ab|schwellen irr vi (*Entzündung*) to go down; (*Lärm*) to die down

absehbar adj foreseeable; **in ~er Zeit** in the foreseeable future;

ab|sehen irr vt (*Ende, Folgen*) to foresee ▷ vi: **von etw ~** to refrain from sth

abseits adv out of the way; (*Sport*) offside ▷ prep +gen away from; **Abseits** nt (*Sport*) offside; **Abseitsfalle** f (*Sport*) offside trap

ab|senden irr vt to send off; (*Post*) to post; **Absender(in)** (-s, -) m(f) sender

ab|setzen vt (*Glas, Brille etc*) to put down; (*aussteigen lassen*) to drop (off); (*Comm*) to sell; (*Fin*) to deduct; (*streichen*) to drop ▷ vr: **sich ~** (*sich entfernen*) to clear off; (*sich ablagern*) to be deposited

Absicht f intention; **mit ~** on purpose; **absichtlich** adj intentional, deliberate

absolut adj absolute

ab|specken vi (*fam*) to lose weight

ab|speichern vt (*Inform*) to save

ab|sperren vt to block (o to close) off; (*Tür*) to lock; **Absperrung** f (*Vorgang*) blocking (o closing) off; (*Sperre*) barricade

ab|spielen vt (*CD etc*) to play ▷ vr: **sich ~** to happen

ab|springen irr vi to jump down/off; (*von etw Geplantem*) to drop out (*von* of)

ab|spülen vt to rinse; (*Geschirr*) to wash (up)

Abstand m distance; (*zeitlich*) interval; **~ halten** to keep one's distance

ab|stauben vt, vi to dust; (*fam: stehlen*) to pinch

Abstecher (-s, -) m detour

ab|steigen irr vi (*vom Rad etc*) to get off, to dismount; (*in Gasthof*) to stay (*in* +dat at)

ab|stellen vt (*niederstellen*) to put down; (*Auto*) to park; (*ausschalten*) to turn (o to switch) off; (*Missstand, Unsitte*) to stop; **Abstellraum** m store room

Abstieg (-(e)s, -e) m (*vom Berg*) descent; (*Sport*) relegation

ab|stimmen vt to vote ▷ vt (*Termine, Ziele*) to fit in (*auf* +akk with); **Dinge aufeinander ~** to coordinate things ▷ vr: **sich ~** to come to an agreement (o arrangement)

abstoßend adj repulsive

abstrakt adj abstract

ab|streiten irr vt to deny

Abstrich m (*Med*) smear; **~e machen** to cut back (*an* +dat on); (*weniger erwarten*) to lower one's sights

Absturz m fall; (*Aviat, Inform*)

crash; **ab|stürzen** *vi* to fall; (*Aviat, Inform*) to crash

absurd *adj* absurd

Abszess (*-es, -e*) *m* abscess

ab|tauen *vt, vi* to thaw; (*Kühlschrank*) to defrost

Abtei (*-, -en*) *f* abbey

Abteil (*-(e)s, -e*) *nt* compartment

Abteilung *f* (*in Firma, Kaufhaus*) department; (*in Krankenhaus*) section

ab|treiben *irr vt* (*Kind*) to abort ▷ *vi* to be driven off course; (*Med: Abtreibung vornehmen*) to carry out an abortion; (*Abtreibung vornehmen lassen*) to have an abortion; **Abtreibung** *f* abortion

ab|trocknen *vt* to dry

ab|warten *vt* to wait for; **das bleibt abzuwarten** that remains to be seen ▷ *vi* to wait

abwärts *adv* down

Abwasch (*-(e)s*) *m* washing-up; **ab|waschen** *irr vt* (*Schmutz*) to wash off; (*Geschirr*) to wash (up)

Abwasser (*-s, Abwässer*) *nt* sewage

ab|wechseln *vr*: **sich ~ to** alternate; **sich mit jdm ~** to take turns with sb; **abwechselnd** *adv* alternately; **Abwechslung** *f* change; **zur ~** for a change

ab|weisen *irr vt* to turn away; (*Antrag*) to turn down; **abweisend** *adj* unfriendly

abwesend *adj* absent; **Abwesenheit** *f* absence

ab|wiegen *irr vt* to weigh (out)

ab|wimmeln *vt* (*fam*) **jdn ~** to get rid of sb, to give sb the elbow

ab|wischen *vt* (*Gesicht, Tisch etc*) to wipe; (*Schmutz*) to wipe off

ab|zählen *vt* to count; (*Geld*) to count out

Abzeichen *nt* badge

ab|zeichnen *vt* to draw, to copy; (*Dokument*) to initial ▷ *vr*: **sich**

~ to stand out; (*fig: bevorstehen*) to loom

ab|ziehen *irr vt* to take off; (*Bett*) to strip; (*Schlüssel*) to take out; (*subtrahieren*) to take away, to subtract ▷ *vi* to go away

Abzug *m* (*Foto*) print; (*Öffnung*) vent; (*Truppen*) withdrawal; (*Betrag*) deduction; **nach ~ der Kosten** charges deducted; **abzüglich** *prep* +*gen* minus; **~ 20% Rabatt** less 20% discount

ab|zweigen *vi* to branch off ▷ *vt* to set aside; **Abzweigung** *f* junction

Accessoires *pl* accessories *pl*

ach *interj* oh; **~ so!** oh, I see; **~ was!** (*Überraschung*) really?; (*Ärger*) don't use nonsense

Achse (*-, -n*) *f* axis; (*Auto*) axle

Achsel (*-, -n*) *f* shoulder; (*Achselhöhle*) armpit

Achsenbruch *m* (*Auto*) broken axle

acht *num* eight; **heute in ~ Tagen** in a week('s time), a week from today

Acht (*-*) *f*: **sich in ~ nehmen** to be careful (*vor* +*dat* of), to watch out (*vor* +*dat* for); **etw außer ~ lassen** to disregard sth

achte(r, s) *adj* eighth; *siehe auch* **dritte**; **Achtel** (*-s, -*) *nt* (*Bruchteil*) eighth; (*Wein etc*) eighth of a litre; (*Glas Wein*) ≈ small glass

achten *vt* to respect ▷ *vi* to pay attention (*auf* +*akk* to)

Achterbahn *f* big dipper, roller coaster

acht|geben *irr vi* to take care (*auf* +*akk* of)

achthundert *num* eight hundred; **achtmal** *adv* eight times

Achtung *f* attention; (*Ehrfurcht*) respect ▷ *interj* look out

achtzehn *num* eighteen;

achtzehnte(r, s) *adj*
eighteenth; *siehe auch* **dritte**;
achtzig *num* eighty; **in den ~er
Jahren** in the eighties;
achtzigste(r, s) *adj* eightieth
Acker (*-s, Äcker*) *m* field
Action (*-, -s*) *f* (*fam*) action;
Actionfilm *m* action film
Adapter (*-s, -*) *m* adapter
addieren *vt* to add (up)
Adel (*-s*) *m* nobility; **adelig** *adj*
noble
Ader (*-, -n*) *f* vein
Adjektiv *nt* adjective
Adler (*-s, -*) *m* eagle
adoptieren *vt* to adopt;
Adoption *f* adoption;
Adoptiveltern *pl* adoptive
parents *pl*; **Adoptivkind** *nt*
adopted child
Adrenalin (*-s*) *nt* adrenalin
Adressbuch *nt* directory;
(*persönliches*) address book;
Adresse (*-, -n*) *f* address;
adressieren *vt* to address (*an*
+akk to)
ADSL *f* ADSL
Advent (*-s, -*) *m* Advent;
Adventskranz *m* Advent
wreath
Adverb *nt* adverb
Aerobic (*-s*) *nt* aerobics *sing*
Affäre (*-, -n*) *f* affair
Affe (*-n, -n*) *m* monkey
Afghanistan (*-s*) *nt*
Afghanistan
Afrika (*-s*) *nt* Africa;
Afrikaner(in) (*-s, -*) *m(f)* African;
afrikanisch *adj* African
After (*-s, -*) *m* anus
Aftershave (*-(s), -s*) *nt*
aftershave
AG (*-, -s*) *f abk =*
Aktiengesellschaft plc (*Brit*),
corp. (*US*)
Agent(in) *m(f)* agent; **Agentur**
f agency

aggressiv *adj* aggressive
Ägypten (*-s*) *nt* Egypt
ah *interj* ah, ooh
aha *interj* I see, aha
ähneln *vi +dat* to be like, to
resemble ▷ *vr:* **sich ~** to be alike (*o*
similar)
ahnen *vt* to suspect; **du ahnst es
nicht!** would you believe it?
ähnlich *adj* similar (*dat* to); **jdm
~ sehen** to look like sb;
Ähnlichkeit *f* similarity
Ahnung *f* idea; (*Vermutung*)
suspicion; **keine ~!** no idea;
ahnungslos *adj* unsuspecting
Ahorn (*-s, -e*) *m* maple
Aids (*-*) *nt* Aids; **aidskrank** *adj*
suffering from Aids; **Aidstest** *m*
Aids test
Airbag (*-s, -s*) *m* (*Auto*) airbag;
Airbus *m* airbus
Akademie (*-, -n*) *f* academy;
Akademiker(in) (*-s, -*) *m(f)*
(university) graduate
akklimatisieren *vr:* **sich ~** to
acclimatize oneself
Akkordeon (*-s, -s*) *nt* accordion
Akku (*-s, -s*) *m* (storage) battery
Akkusativ *m* accusative (case)
Akne (*-, -*) *f* acne
Akrobat(in) (*-s, -en*) *m(f)* acrobat
Akt (*-(e)s, -e*) *m* act; (*Kunst*) nude
Akte (*-, -n*) *f* file; **etw zu den ~n
legen** (*a. fig*) to file sth away;
Aktenkoffer *m* briefcase
Aktie (*-, -n*) *f* share;
Aktiengesellschaft *f* public
limited company (*Brit*),
corporation (*US*)
Aktion *f* (*Kampagne*) campaign;
(*Einsatz*) operation
Aktionär(in) (*-s, -e*) *m(f)*
shareholder
aktiv *adj* active; **aktivieren** *vt*
to activate
aktualisieren *vt* to update;
aktuell *adj* (*Thema*) topical;

(*modern*) up-to-date; (*Problem*) current; **nicht mehr ~** no longer relevant

Akupunktur *f* acupuncture

akustisch *adj* acoustic; **Akustik** *f* acoustics *sing*

akut *adj* acute

AKW (*-s, -s*) *nt abk =* **Atomkraftwerk** nuclear power station

Akzent (*-(e)s, -e*) *m* accent; (*Betonung*) stress; **mit starkem schottischen ~** with a strong Scottish accent

akzeptieren *vt* to accept

Alarm (*-(e)s, -e*) *m* alarm; **Alarmanlage** *f* alarm system; **alarmieren** *vt* to alarm; **die Polizei ~** to call the police

Albanien (*-s*) *nt* Albania

Albatros (*-ses, -se*) *m* albatross

albern *adj* silly

Albtraum *m* nightmare

Album (*-s, Alben*) *nt* album

Algen *pl* algae *pl*; (*Meeresalgen*) seaweed *sing*

Algerien (*-s*) *nt* Algeria

Alibi (*-s, -s*) *nt* alibi

Alimente *pl* maintenance *sing*

Alkohol (*-s, -e*) *m* alcohol; **alkoholfrei** *adj* non-alcoholic; **~es Getränk** soft drink; **Alkoholiker(in)** (*-s, -*) *m(f)* alcoholic; **alkoholisch** *adj* alcoholic; **Alkoholtest** *m* breathalyser® test (*Brit*), alcohol test

All (*-s*) *nt* universe

SCHLÜSSELWORT

alle(r, s) *adj* **1** (*sämtliche*) all; **wir alle** all of us; **alle Kinder waren da** all the children were there; **alle Kinder mögen ...** all children like ...; **alle beide** both of us/them; **sie kamen alle** they all came; **alles Gute** all the best; **alles**

in allem all in all

2 (*mit Zeit- oder Maßangaben*) every; **alle vier Jahre** every four years; **alle fünf Meter** every five metres

▷ *pron* everything; **alles, was er sagt** everything he says, all that he says

▷ *adv* (*zu Ende, aufgebraucht*) finished; **die Milch ist alle** the milk's all gone, there's no milk left; **etw alle machen** to finish sth up

Allee (*-, -n*) *f* avenue

allein *adj, adv* alone; (*ohne Hilfe*) on one's own, by oneself; **nicht ~** (*nicht nur*) not only; **alleinerziehend** *adj*; **~e Mutter** single mother; **Alleinerziehende(r)** *mf* single mother/father/parent; **alleinstehend** *adj* single, unmarried

allerbeste(r, s) *adj* very best

allerdings *adv* (*zwar*) admittedly; (*gewiss*) certainly, sure (*US*)

allererste(r, s) *adj* very first; **zu allererst** first of all

Allergie *f* allergy; **Allergiker(in)** (*-s, -*) *m(f)* allergy sufferer; **allergisch** *adj* allergic (*gegen* to)

allerhand *adj inv* (*fam*) all sorts of; **das ist doch ~!** (*Vorwurf*) that's the limit

Allerheiligen (*-*) *nt* All Saints' Day

allerhöchste(r, s) *adj* very highest; **allerhöchstens** *adv* at the very most; **allerlei** *adj inv* all sorts of; **allerletzte(r, s)** *adj* very last; **allerwenigste(r, s)** *adj* very least

alles *pron* everything; **~ in allem** all in all; *siehe auch* **alle**

Alleskleber (*-s, -*) *m* all-purpose glue

allgemein *adj* general; **im Allgemeinen** in general; **Allgemeinarzt** *m*,

Allgemeinärztin *f* GP (*Brit*), family practitioner (*US*)
Alligator (*-s, -en*) *m* alligator
alljährlich *adj* annual
allmählich *adj* gradual ▷ *adv* gradually
Allradantrieb *m* all-wheel drive
Alltag *m* everyday life; **alltäglich** *adj* everyday; (*gewöhnlich*) ordinary; (*tagtäglich*) daily
allzu *adv* all too
Allzweckreiniger (*-s, -*) *m* multi-purpose cleaner
Alpen *pl:* **die ~** the Alps *pl*
Alphabet (*-(e)s, -e*) *nt* alphabet; **alphabetisch** *adj* alphabetical
Alptraum *m siehe* **Albtraum**

 SCHLÜSSELWORT

als *konj* **1** (*zeitlich*) when; (*gleichzeitig*) as; **damals, als ...** (in the days) when ...; **gerade, als ...** just as ...
2 (*in der Eigenschaft*) than; **als Antwort** as an answer; **als Kind** as a child
3 (*bei Vergleichen*) than; **ich kam später als er** I came later than he (did) *o* later than him; **lieber ... als ...** rather ... than ...; **nichts als Ärger** nothing but trouble
4 als ob/wenn as if

also *konj* (*folglich*) so, therefore ▷ *adv, interj* so; **~ gut** (*o* **schön**)! okay then
alt *adj* old; **wie ~ sind Sie?** how old are you?; **28 Jahre ~** 28 years old; **vier Jahre älter** four years older
Altar (*-(e)s, Altäre*) *m* altar
Alter (*-s, -*) *nt* age; (*hohes*) old age; **im ~ von** at the age of; **er ist in meinem ~** he's my age
alternativ *adj* alternative; (*umweltbewusst*) ecologically

minded; (*Landwirtschaft*) organic;
Alternative *f* alternative
Altersheim *nt* old people's home
Altglas *nt* used glass;
Altglascontainer *m* bottle bank;
altmodisch *adj* old-fashioned;
Altpapier *nt* waste paper;
Altstadt *f* old town
Alt-Taste *f* Alt key
Alufolie *f* tin (*o* kitchen) foil
Aluminium (*-s*) *nt* aluminium (*Brit*), aluminum (*US*)
Alzheimerkrankheit *f* Alzheimer's (disease)
am *kontr von* **an dem**; **~ 2. Januar** on January 2(nd); **~ Morgen** in the morning; **~ Strand** on the beach; **~ Bahnhof** at the station; **was gefällt Ihnen ~ besten?** what do you like best?; **~ besten bleiben wir hier** it would be best if we stayed here
Amateur(in) *m(f)* amateur
ambulant *adj* outpatient; **kann ich ~ behandelt werden?** can I have it done as an outpatient?;
Ambulanz *f* (*Krankenwagen*) ambulance; (*in der Klinik*) outpatients' department
Ameise (*-, -n*) *f* ant
amen *interj* amen
Amerika (*-s*) *nt* America;
Amerikaner(in) (*-s, -*) *m(f)* American; **amerikanisch** *adj* American
Ampel (*-, -n*) *f* traffic lights *pl*
Amphitheater *nt* amphitheatre
Amsel (*-, -n*) *f* blackbird
Amt (*-(e)s, Ämter*) *nt* (*Dienststelle*) office, department; (*Posten*) post; **amtlich** *adj* official;
Amtszeichen *nt* (*Tel*) dialling tone (*Brit*), dial tone (*US*)
amüsant *adj* amusing;
amüsieren *vt* to amuse ▷ *vr:* **sich ~** to enjoy oneself, to have a good time

○ SCHLÜSSELWORT

an prep +dat 1 (räumlich) (wo?) at; (auf, bei) on; (nahe bei) near; **an diesem Ort** at this place; **an der Wand** on the wall; **zu nahe an etw** too near to sth; **unten am Fluss** down by the river; **Köln liegt am Rhein** Cologne is on the Rhine
2 (zeitlich: wann?) on; **an diesem Tag** on this day; **an Ostern** at Easter
3 **arm an Fett** low in fat; **an etw sterben** to die of sth; **an (und für) sich** actually
▷ prep +akk 1 (räumlich: wohin?) to; **er ging ans Fenster** he went (over) to the window; **etw an die Wand hängen/schreiben** to hang/write sth on the wall
2 (woran?) **an etw denken** to think of sth
3 (gerichtet an) to; **ein Gruß/eine Frage an dich** greetings/a question to you
▷ adv 1 (ungefähr) about; **an die hundert** about a hundred
2 (auf Fahrplänen) **Frankfurt an 18.30** arriving Frankfurt 18.30
3 (ab) **von dort/heute an** from there/today onwards
4 (angeschaltet, angezogen) on; **das Licht ist an** the light is on; **ohne etwas an** with nothing on; siehe auch **am**

anal adj anal
analog adj analogous; (Inform) analog
Analyse (-, -n) f analysis; **analysieren** vt to analyse
Ananas (-, - o -se) f pineapple
an|baggern vt (fam) to chat up (Brit), to come on to (US)
Anbau m (Agr) cultivation; (Gebäude) extension; **an|bauen** vt (Agr) to cultivate; (Gebäudeteil) to build on
an|behalten irr vt to keep on
anbei adv enclosed; **~ sende ich ...** please find enclosed ...
an|beten vt to worship
an|bieten irr vt to offer ▷ vr: **sich ~** to volunteer
an|binden irr vt to tie up
Anblick m sight
an|braten irr vt to brown
an|brechen irr vt to start; (Vorräte, Ersparnisse) to break into; (Flasche, Packung) to open ▷ vi to start; (Tag) to break; (Nacht) to fall
an|brennen irr vt, vi to burn; **das Fleisch schmeckt angebrannt** the meat tastes burnt
an|bringen irr vt (herbeibringen) to bring; (befestigen) to fix, to attach
Andacht (-, -en) f devotion; (Gottesdienst) prayers pl
an|dauern vi to continue, to go on; **andauernd** adj continual
Andenken (-s, -) nt memory; (Gegenstand) souvenir
andere(r, s) adj (weitere) other; (verschieden) different; (folgend) next; **am ~n Tag** the next day; **von etw/jmd ~m sprechen** to talk about sth/sb else; **unter ~m** among other things; **andererseits** adv on the other hand
ändern vt to alter, to change ▷ vr: **sich ~** to change
andernfalls adv otherwise
anders adv differently (als from); **jemand/irgendwo ~** someone/somewhere else; **sie ist ~ als ihre Schwester** she's not like her sister; **es geht nicht ~** there's no other way; **anders(he)rum** adv the other way round; **anderswo** adv somewhere else
anderthalb num one and a half

Änderung f change, alteration
an|deuten vt to indicate; (*Wink geben*) to hint at
Andorra (-s) nt Andorra
Andrang m: **es herrschte großer ~** there was a huge crowd
an|drohen vt: **jdm etw ~** to threaten sb with sth
aneinander adv at/on/to one another (*o each other*); **~ denken** think of each other; **sich ~ gewöhnen** to get used to each other; **aneinander|geraten** irr vi to clash; **aneinander|legen** vt to put together
an|erkennen irr vt (*Staat, Zeugnis etc*) to recognize; (*würdigen*) to appreciate; **Anerkennung** f recognition; (*Würdigung*) appreciation
an|fahren irr vt (*fahren gegen*) to run into (*o over*); (*Ort, Hafen*) to stop (*o call*) at; (*liefern*) to deliver; **jdn ~** (*fig: schimpfen*) to jump on sb ▷ vi to start; (*losfahren*) to drive off
Anfall m (*Med*) attack; **anfällig** adj delicate; (*Maschine*) temperamental; **~ für** prone to
Anfang (-(e)s, Anfänge) m beginning, start; **zu/am ~** to start with; **~ Mai** at the beginning of May; **sie ist ~ 20** she's in her early twenties; **an|fangen** irr vt, vi to begin, to start; **damit kann ich nichts ~** that's no use to me; **Anfänger(in)** (-s, -) m(f) beginner; **anfangs** adv at first; **Anfangsbuchstabe** m first (*o initial*) letter
an|fassen vt (*berühren*) to touch ▷ vi: **kannst du mal mit ~?** can you give me a hand?
Anflug m (*Aviat*) approach; (*Hauch*) trace
an|fordern vt to demand; **Anforderung** f request (*von* for); (*Anspruch*) demand

Anfrage f inquiry
an|freunden vr: **sich mit jdm ~** to make (*o to become*) friends with sb
an|fühlen vr: **sich ~** to feel; **es fühlt sich gut an** it feels good
Anführungszeichen pl quotation marks pl
Angabe f (*Tech*) specification; (*fam: Prahlerei*) showing off; (*Tennis*) serve; **~n** pl (*Auskunft*) particulars pl; **die ~n waren falsch** (*Info*) the information was wrong; **an|geben** irr vt (*Name, Grund*) to give; (*zeigen*) to indicate; (*bestimmen*) to set ▷ vi (*fam: prahlen*) to boast; (*Sport*) to serve; **Angeber(in)** (-s, -) m(f) (*fam*) show-off; **angeblich** adj alleged
angeboren adj inborn
Angebot nt offer; (*Comm*) supply (*an +dat* of); **~ und Nachfrage** supply and demand
angebracht adj appropriate
angebunden adj: **kurz ~** curt
angeheitert adj tipsy
an|gehen irr vt to concern; **das geht dich nichts an** that's none of your business; **ein Problem ~** to tackle a problem; **was ihn angeht** as far as he's concerned, as for him ▷ vi (*Feuer*) to catch; (*fam: beginnen*) to begin; **angehend** adj prospective
Angehörige(r) mf relative
Angeklagte(r) mf accused, defendant
Angel (-, -n) f fishing rod; (*an der Tür*) hinge
Angelegenheit f affair, matter
Angelhaken m fish hook; **angeln** vt to catch ▷ vi to fish; **Angeln** (-s) nt angling, fishing; **Angelrute** (-, -n) f fishing rod
angemessen adj appropriate, suitable

angenehm adj pleasant; **~!** (bei Vorstellung) pleased to meet you

angenommen adj assumed ▷ conj: **~, es regnet, was machen wir dann?** suppose it rains, what do we do then?

angesehen adj respected

angesichts prep +gen in view of, considering

Angestellte(r) mf employee

angetan adj: **von jdm/etw ~ sein** to be impressed by (o taken with) sb/sth

angewiesen adj: **auf jdn/etw ~ sein** to be dependent on sb/sth

an|gewöhnen vt: **sich etw ~** to get used to doing sth; **Angewohnheit** f habit

Angina (-, Anginen) f tonsillitis; **Angina Pectoris** (-) f angina

Angler(in) (-s, -) m(f) angler

Angora (-s) adj angora

an|greifen irr vt to attack; (anfassen) to touch; (beschädigen) to damage; **Angriff** m attack; **etw in ~ nehmen** to get started on sth

Angst (-, Ängste) f fear; **~ haben** to be afraid (o scared) (vor +dat of); **jdm ~ machen** to scare sb; **ängstigen** vt to frighten ▷ vr: **sich ~** to worry (um, wegen +dat about); **ängstlich** adj nervous; (besorgt) worried

an|haben irr vt (Kleidung) to have on, to wear; (Licht) to have on

an|halten irr vi to stop; (andauern) to continue; **anhaltend** adj continuous; **Anhalter(in)** (-s, -) m(f) hitch-hiker; **per ~ fahren** to hitch-hike

anhand prep +gen with; **~ von** by means of

an|hängen vt to hang up; (Eisenb: Wagen) to couple; (Zusatz) to add (on); **jdm etw ~** (fam: unterschieben) to pin sth on sb;

eine Datei an eine E-Mail ~ (Inform) to attach a file to an email; **Anhänger** (-s, -) m (Auto) trailer; (am Koffer) tag; (Schmuck) pendant; **Anhänger(in)** (-s, -) m(f) supporter; **Anhängerkupplung** f towbar; **anhänglich** adj affectionate; (pej) clinging

Anhieb m: **auf ~** straight away; **das kann ich nicht auf ~ sagen** I can't say offhand

an|himmeln vt to idolize

an|hören vt to listen to ▷ vr: **sich ~** to sound; **das hört sich gut an** that sounds good

Animateur(in) m(f) host/hostess

Anis (-es, -e) m aniseed

Anker (-s, -) m anchor; **ankern** vt, vi to anchor; **Ankerplatz** m anchorage

an|klicken vt (Inform) to click on

an|klopfen vi to knock (an +akk on)

an|kommen irr vi to arrive; **bei jdm gut ~** to go down well with sb; **es kommt darauf an** it depends (ob on whether); **darauf kommt es nicht an** that doesn't matter

an|kotzen vt (vulg) **es kotzt mich an** it makes me sick

an|kreuzen vt to mark with a cross

an|kündigen vt to announce

Ankunft (-, Ankünfte) f arrival; **Ankunftszeit** f arrival time

Anlage f (Veranlagung) disposition; (Begabung) talent; (Park) gardens pl; (zu Brief etc) enclosure; (Stereoanlage) stereo; (Tech) plant; (Fin) investment

Anlass (-es, Anlässe) m cause (zu for); (Ereignis) occasion; **aus diesem ~** for this reason; **an|lassen** irr vt (Motor) to start; (Licht, Kleidung) to leave on;

Anlasser (-s, -) m (Auto) starter;
anlässlich prep +gen on the occasion of
Anlauf m run-up; **an|laufen** irr vi to begin; (Film) to open; (Fenster) to mist up; (Metall) to tarnish
an|legen vt to put (an +akk against/on); (Schmuck) to put on; (Garten) to lay out; (Geld) to invest; (Gewehr) to aim (auf +akk at); **es auf etw** (akk) **~ to be out for sth** ▷ vi (Schiff) to berth, to dock ▷ vr: **sich mit jdm ~** (fam) to pick a quarrel with sb; **Anlegestelle** f moorings pl
an|lehnen vt to lean (an +akk against); (Tür) to leave ajar ▷ vr: **sich ~** to lean (an +akk against)
an|leiern vt: **etw ~** (fam) to get sth going
Anleitung f instructions pl
Anliegen (-s, -) nt matter; (Wunsch) request
Anlieger(in) (-s, -) m(f) resident; **~ frei** residents only
an|lügen irr vt to lie to
an|machen vt (befestigen) to attach; (einschalten) to switch on; (Salat) to dress; (fam: aufreizen) to turn on; (fam: ansprechen) to chat up (Brit), to come on to (US); (fam: beschimpfen) to have a go at
Anmeldeformular nt application form; (bei Amt) registration form; **an|melden** vt (Besuch etc) to announce ▷ vr: **sich ~** (beim Arzt etc) to make an appointment; (bei Amt, für Kurs etc) to register; **Anmeldeschluss** m deadline for applications, registration deadline; **Anmeldung** f registration; (Antrag) application
an|nähen vt: **einen Knopf (an den Mantel) ~** to sew a button on (one's coat)

annähernd adv roughly; **nicht ~** nowhere near
Annahme (-, -n) f acceptance; (Vermutung) assumption; **annehmbar** adj acceptable; **an|nehmen** irr vt to accept; (Namen) to take; (Kind) to adopt; (vermuten) to suppose, to assume
Annonce (-, -n) f advertisement
an|öden vt (fam) to bore stiff (o silly)
annullieren vt to cancel
anonym adj anonymous
Anorak (-s, -s) m anorak
an|packen vt (Problem, Aufgabe) to tackle; **mit ~** to lend a hand
an|passen vt (fig) to adapt (dat to) ▷ vr: **sich ~** to adapt (an +akk to)
an|pfeifen irr vt (Fußballspiel) **das Spiel ~** to start the game; **Anpfiff** m (Sport) (starting) whistle; (Beginn) kick-off; (fam: Tadel) roasting
an|probieren vt to try on
Anrede f form of address; **an|reden** vt to address
an|regen vt to stimulate; **Anregung** f stimulation; (Vorschlag) suggestion
Anreise f journey; **an|reisen** vi to arrive; **Anreisetag** m day of arrival
Anreiz m incentive
an|richten vt (Speisen) to prepare; (Schaden) to cause
Anruf m call; **Anrufbeantworter** (-s, -) m answering machine, answerphone; **an|rufen** irr vt (Tel) to call, to phone, to ring (Brit)
ans kontr von **an das**
Ansage f announcement; (auf Anrufbeantworter) recorded message; **an|sagen** vt to announce; **angesagt sein** to be recommended; (modisch sein) to be the in thing

an|schaffen vt to buy

an|schauen vt to look at

Anschein m appearance; **dem** (o **allem**) ~ **nach ...** it looks as if ...; **den ~ erwecken, hart zu arbeiten** to give the impression of working hard; **anscheinend** adj apparent ▷ adv apparently

an|schieben irr vt: **könnten Sie mich mal ~?** (Auto) could you give me a push?

Anschlag m notice; (Attentat) attack; **an|schlagen** irr vt (Plakat) to put up; (beschädigen) to chip ▷ vi (wirken) to take effect; **mit etw an etw** (akk) ~ to bang sth against sth

an|schließen irr vt (Elek, Tech) to connect (an +akk to); (mit Stecker) to plug in ▷ vi, vr (sich) **an etw** (akk) ~ (Gebäude etc) to adjoin sth; (zeitlich) to follow sth ▷ vr: **sich ~** to join (jdm/einer Gruppe sb/a group); **anschließend** adj adjacent; (zeitlich) subsequent ▷ adv afterwards; ~ **an** (+akk) following; **Anschluss** m (Elek, Eisenb) connection; (von Wasser, Gas etc) supply; **im ~ an** (+akk) following; **kein ~ unter dieser Nummer** (Tel) the number you have dialled has not been recognized; **Anschlussflug** m connecting flight

an|schnallen vt (Skier) to put on ▷ vr: **sich ~** to fasten one's seat belt

Anschrift f address

an|schwellen irr vi to swell (up)

an|sehen irr vt to look at; (bei etw zuschauen) to watch; **jdn/etw als etw ~** to look on sb/sth as sth; **das sieht man ihm an** he looks it

an sein irr vi siehe **an**

an|setzen vt (Termin) to fix; (zubereiten) to prepare ▷ vi (anfangen) to start, to begin; **zu**

etw ~ to prepare to do sth

Ansicht f (Meinung) view, opinion; (Anblick) sight; **meiner ~ nach** in my opinion; **zur ~** on approval; **Ansichtskarte** f postcard

ansonsten adv otherwise

an|spielen vi **auf etw** (akk) ~ to allude to sth; **Anspielung** f allusion (auf +akk to)

an|sprechen irr vt to speak to; (gefallen) to appeal to ▷ vi **auf etw** (akk) ~ (Patient) to respond to sth; **ansprechend** adj attractive; **Ansprechpartner(in)** m(f) contact

an|springen irr vi (Auto) to start

Anspruch m claim; (Recht) right (auf +akk to); **etw in ~ nehmen** to take advantage of sth; **~ auf etw haben** to be entitled to sth; **anspruchslos** adj undemanding; (bescheiden) modest; **anspruchsvoll** adj demanding

Anstalt (-, -en) f institution

Anstand m decency; **anständig** adj decent; (fig, fam) proper; (groß) considerable

an|starren vt to stare at

anstatt prep +gen instead of

an|stecken vt to pin on; (Med) to infect; **jdn mit einer Erkältung ~** to pass one's cold on to sb ▷ vr: **ich habe mich bei ihm angesteckt** I caught it from him ▷ vi (fig) to be infectious; **ansteckend** adj infectious; **Ansteckungsgefahr** f danger of infection

an|stehen irr vi (in Warteschlange) to queue (Brit), to stand in line (US); (erledigt werden müssen) to be on the agenda

anstelle prep +gen instead of

an|stellen vt (einschalten) to turn on; (Arbeit geben) to employ; (machen) to do; **was hast du**

wieder angestellt? what have you been up to now? ▷ vr: **sich ~** to queue (Brit), to stand in line (US); (fam) **stell dich nicht so an!** stop making such a fuss

Anstoß m impetus; (Sport) kick-off; **an|stoßen** irr vt to push; (mit Fuß) to kick ▷ vi to knock, to bump; (mit Gläsern) to drink (a toast) (auf +akk to); **anstößig** adj offensive; (Kleidung etc) indecent

an|strengen vt to strain ▷ vr: **sich ~** to make an effort; **anstrengend** adj tiring

Antarktis f Antarctic

Anteil m share (an +dat in); **~ nehmen an** (+dat) (mitleidig) to sympathize with; (sich interessieren) to take an interest in

Antenne (-, -n) f aerial

Antibabypille f: **die ~** the pill; **Antibiotikum** (-s, Antibiotika) nt (Med) antibiotic

antik adj antique

Antilope (-, -n) f antelope

Antiquariat nt (für Bücher) second-hand bookshop

Antiquitäten pl antiques pl; **Antiquitätenhändler(in)** m(f) antique dealer

Antiviren- adj (Inform) antivirus; **Antivirensoftware** f antivirus software

an|törnen vt (fam) to turn on

Antrag (-(e)s, Anträge) m proposal; (Pol) motion; (Formular) application form; **einen ~ stellen auf** (+akk) to apply for

an|treffen irr vt to find

an|treiben irr vt (Tech) to drive; (anschwemmen) to wash up; **jdn zur Arbeit ~** to make sb work

an|treten irr vt: **eine Reise ~** to set off on a journey

Antrieb m (Tech) drive; (Motivation) impetus

an|tun irr vt: **jdm etwas ~** to do

sth to sb; **sich** (dat) **etwas ~** (Selbstmord begehen) to kill oneself

Antwort (-, -en) f answer, reply; **um ~ wird gebeten** RSVP (répondez s'il vous plaît); **antworten** vi to answer, to reply; **jdm ~** to answer sb; **auf etw** (akk) **~** to answer sth

an|vertrauen vt: **jdm etw ~** to entrust sb with sth

Anwalt (-s, Anwälte) m, **Anwältin** f lawyer

an|weisen irr vt (anleiten) to instruct; (zuteilen) to allocate (jdm etw sth to sb); **Anweisung** f instruction; (von Geld) money order

an|wenden irr vt to use; (Gesetz, Regel) to apply; **Anwender(in)** (-s, -) m(f) user; **Anwendung** f use; (Inform) application

anwesend adj present; **Anwesenheit** f presence

an|widern vt to disgust

Anwohner(in) (-s, -) m(f) resident

Anzahl f number (an +dat of); **an|zahlen** vt to pay a deposit on; **100 Euro ~** to pay 100 euros as a deposit; **Anzahlung** f deposit

Anzeichen nt sign; (Med) symptom

Anzeige (-, -n) f (Werbung) advertisement; (elektronisch) display; (bei Polizei) report; **an|zeigen** vt (Temperatur, Zeit) to indicate, to show; (elektronisch) to display; (bekannt geben) to announce; **einen Autodiebstahl bei der Polizei ~** to report a stolen car to the police

an|ziehen irr vt to attract; (Kleidung) to put on; (Schraube, Seil) to tighten ▷ vr: **sich ~** to get dressed; **anziehend** adj attractive

Anzug m suit

anzüglich adj suggestive

an|zünden vt to light; (Haus etc)

to set fire to
an|zweifeln vt to doubt
Aperitif (-s, -s (o -e)) m aperitif
Apfel (-s, Äpfel) m apple;
Apfelbaum m apple tree;
Apfelkuchen m apple cake;
Apfelmus nt apple purée;
Apfelsaft m apple juice; **Apfel-
sine** f orange; **Apfelwein** m cider
Apostroph (-s, -e) m apostrophe
Apotheke (-, -n) f chemist's
(shop) (Brit), pharmacy (US);
apothekenpflichtig adj only
available at the chemist's;
Apotheker(in) (-s, -) m(f)
chemist (Brit), pharmacist (US)
Apparat (-(e)s, -e) m (piece of)
apparatus; (Tel) telephone; (Radio,
TV) set; **am ~!** (Tel) speaking; **am
~ bleiben** (Tel) to hold the line
Appartement (-s, -s) nt studio
flat (Brit) (o apartment (US))
Appetit (-(e)s, -e) m appetite;
guten ~! bon appétit; **appetitlich**
adj appetizing
Applaus (-es, -e) m applause
Aprikose (-, -n) f apricot
April (-(s), -e) m April; siehe auch
Juni; ~, ~! April fool!; **Aprilscherz**
(-es, -e) m April fool's joke
apropos adv by the way;
~ Urlaub ... while we're on the
subject of holidays ...
Aquajogging nt aqua jogging;
Aquaplaning (-(s)) nt
aquaplaning
Aquarell (-s, -e) nt watercolour
Aquarium (-s, Aquarien) nt
aquarium
Äquator (-s, -) m equator
Araber(in) (-s, -) m(f) Arab;
arabisch adj Arab; (Ziffer, Sprache)
Arabic; (Meer, Wüste) Arabian
Arbeit (-, -en) f work; (Stelle) job;
(Erzeugnis) piece of work; **arbeiten**
vi to work; **Arbeiter(in)** (-s, -) m(f)
worker; (ungelernt) labourer;

Arbeitgeber(in) (-s, -) m(f) employer;
Arbeitnehmer(in) (-s, -) m(f) employee
Arbeitsagentur f job agency
(Brit), unemployment agency (US);
Arbeitsamt nt job centre (Brit),
employment office (US);
Arbeitserlaubnis f work permit;
arbeitslos adj unemployed;
Arbeitslose(r) mf unemployed
person; **Arbeitslosengeld** nt
(income-related) unemployment
benefit, job-seeker's allowance
(Brit); **Arbeitslosenhilfe** f
(non-income related)
unemployment benefit;
Arbeitslosigkeit f unemploy-
ment; **Arbeitsplatz** m job; (Ort)
workplace; **Arbeitsspeicher** m
(Inform) main memory;
Arbeitszeit f working hours pl;
Arbeitszimmer nt study
Archäologe (-n, -n) m,
Archäologin f archaeologist
Architekt(in) (-en, -en) m(f)
architect; **Architektur** f
architecture
Archiv (-s, -e) nt archives pl
ARD f = **Arbeitsgemeinschaft
der öffentlich-rechtlichen
Rundfunkanstalten der
Bundesrepublik Deutschland**
German broadcasting corporation
arg adj bad; (schrecklich) awful
▷ adv (sehr) terribly
Argentinien (-s) nt Argentina
Ärger (-s) m annoyance;
(stärker) anger; (Unannehmlichkeiten)
trouble; **ärgerlich** adj annoying;
(zornig) angry; **ärgern** vt to annoy
▷ vr: **sich ~** to get annoyed
Argument (-s, -e) nt argument
Arktis (-) f Arctic
arm adj poor
Arm (-(e)s, -e) m arm; (Fluss) branch
Armaturenbrett nt instrument
panel; (Auto) dashboard
Armband nt bracelet;

Armbanduhr f (wrist)watch
Armee (-, -*n*) f army
Ärmel (-*s*, -) m sleeve;
Ärmelkanal m (English) Channel
Armut (-) f poverty
Aroma (-*s*, *Aromen*) nt aroma
arrogant adj arrogant
Arsch (-*es*, *Ärsche*) m (vulg) arse
(Brit), ass (US); **Arschloch** nt
(vulg: Person) arsehole (Brit),
asshole (US)
Art (-, -*en*) f (Weise) way; (Sorte)
kind, sort; (bei Tieren) species;
nach ~ des Hauses à la maison;
auf diese ~ (und Weise) in this
way; **das ist nicht seine ~** that's
not like him
Arterie (-, -*n*) f artery
artig adj good, well-behaved
Artikel (-*s*, -) m (Ware) article,
item; (Zeitung) article
Artischocke (-, -*n*) f artichoke
Artist(in) (-*en*, -*en*) m(f) (circus)
performer
Arznei f medicine; **Arzt** (-*es*,
Ärzte) m doctor; **Arzthelfer(in)**
m(f) doctor's assistant; **Ärztin** f
(female) doctor; **ärztlich** adj
medical; **sich ~ behandeln lassen**
to undergo medical treatment
Asche (-, -*n*) f ashes pl; (von
Zigarette) ash; **Aschenbecher** m
ashtray; **Aschermittwoch** m
Ash Wednesday
Asiat(in) (-*en*, -*en*) m(f) Asian;
asiatisch adj Asian; **Asien** (-*s*) nt
Asia
Aspekt (-(*e*)*s*, -*e*) m aspect
Asphalt (-(*e*)*s*, -*e*) m asphalt
Aspirin® (-*s*, -*e*) nt aspirin
aß imperf von **essen**
Ass (-*es*, -*e*) nt (Karten, Tennis) ace
Assistent(in) m(f) assistant
Ast (-(*e*)*s*, *Äste*) m branch
Asthma (-*s*) nt asthma
Astrologie f astrology;
Astronaut(in) (-*en*, -*en*) m(f)

astronaut; **Astronomie** f
astronomy
ASU (-, -*s*) f abk =
Abgassonderuntersuchung
exhaust emission test
Asyl (-*s*, -*e*) nt asylum; (Heim)
home; (für Obdachlose) shelter;
Asylant(in) m(f), **Asylbe-
werber(in)** m(f) asylum seeker
Atelier (-*s*, -*s*) nt studio
Atem (-*s*) m breath; **atembe-
raubend** adj breathtaking;
Atembeschwerden pl breathing
difficulties pl; **atemlos** adj breath-
less; **Atempause** f breather
Athen nt Athens
Äthiopien (-*s*) nt Ethiopia
Athlet(in) (-*en*, -*en*) m(f) athlete;
Athletik f athletics sing
Atlantik (-*s*) m Atlantic (Ocean)
Atlas (- o Atlasses, Atlanten) m
atlas
atmen vt, vi to breathe; **Atmung**
f breathing
Atom (-*s*, -*e*) nt atom;
Atombombe f atom bomb;
Atomkraftwerk nt nuclear
power station; **Atommüll** m
nuclear waste; **Atomwaffen** pl
nuclear weapons pl
Attentat (-(*e*)*s*, -*e*) nt
assassination (auf +akk of);
(Versuch) assassination attempt
Attest (-(*e*)*s*, -*e*) nt certificate
attraktiv adj attractive
Attrappe (-, -*n*) f dummy
ätzend adj (fam) revolting;
(schlecht) lousy
au interj ouch; **~ ja!** yeah
Aubergine (-, -*n*) f aubergine,
eggplant (US)

 SCHLÜSSELWORT

auch adv **1** (ebenfalls) also, too, as
well; **das ist auch schön** that's
nice too o as well; **er kommt — ich**

auch he's coming — so am I, me too; **auch nicht** not ... either; **ich auch nicht** nor I, me neither; **oder auch** or; **auch das noch!** not that as well!
2 (*selbst, sogar*) even; **auch wenn das Wetter schlecht ist** even if the weather is bad; **ohne auch nur zu fragen** without even asking
3 (*wirklich*) really; **du siehst müde aus—bin ich auch** you look tired—(so) I am; **so sieht es auch aus** it looks like it too
4 (*auch immer*) **wer auch** whoever; **was auch** whatever; **wie dem auch sei** be that as it may; **wie sehr er sich auch bemühte** however much he tried

audiovisuell *adj* audiovisual

O SCHLÜSSELWORT

auf *prep* +*dat* (*wo?*) on; **auf dem Tisch** on the table; **auf der Reise** on the way; **auf der Post/dem Fest** at the post office/party; **auf der Straße** on the road; **auf dem Land/der ganzen Welt** in the country/the whole world
▷ *prep* +*akk* 1 (*wohin?*) on(to); **auf den Tisch** on(to) the table; **auf die Post gehen** to go to the post office; **auf das Land** into the country; **etw auf einen Zettel schreiben** to write sth on a piece of paper
2 **auf Deutsch** in German; **auf Lebenszeit** for my/his lifetime; **bis auf ihn** except for him; **auf einmal** at once; **auf seinen Vorschlag (hin)** at his suggestion
▷ *adv* 1 (*offen*) open; **auf sein** (*fam*) (*Tür, Geschäft*) to be open; **das Fenster ist auf** the window is open

2 (*hinauf*) up; **auf und ab** up and down; **auf und davon** up and away; **auf!** (*los!*) come on!
3 (*aufgestanden*) up; **auf sein** to be up; **ist er schon auf?** is he up yet?
▷ *konj*: **auf dass** (so) that

auf|atmen *vi* to breathe a sigh of relief
auf|bauen *vt* (*errichten*) to put up; (*schaffen*) to build up; (*gestalten*) to construct; (*gründen*) to found, to base (*auf +akk* on); **sich eine Existenz ~** to make a life for oneself
auf|bewahren *vt* to keep, to store
auf|bleiben *irr vi* (*Tür, Laden etc*) to stay open; (*Mensch*) to stay up
auf|blenden *vi, vt*: (**die Scheinwerfer**) **~** to put one's headlights on full beam
auf|brechen *irr vt* to break open ▷ *vi* to burst open; (*gehen*) to leave; (*abreisen*) to set off
auf|drängen *vt*: **jdm etw ~** to force sth on sb ▷ *vr*: **sich ~** to intrude (*jdm* on sb); **aufdringlich** *adj* pushy
aufeinander *adv* (*übereinander*) on top of each other; **~ achten** to look after each other; **~ vertrauen** to trust each other; **aufeinan-der|folgen** *vi* to follow one another; **aufeinander|prallen** *vi* to crash into one another
Aufenthalt *m* stay; (*Zug*) stop; **Aufenthaltsgenehmigung** *f* residence permit; **Aufenthaltsraum** *m* lounge
auf|essen *irr vt* to eat up
auf|fahren *irr vi* (*Auto*) to run (*o* to crash) (*auf +akk* into); (*herankommen*) to drive up; **Auffahrt** *f* (*am Haus*) drive; (*Autobahn*) slip road (*Brit*), ramp (*US*); **Auffahrunfall** *m* rear-end

collision; (*mehrere Fahrzeuge*) pile-up

auf|fallen *irr vi* to stand out; **jdm ~** to strike sb; **das fällt gar nicht auf** nobody will notice; **auffallend** *adj* striking; **auffällig** *adj* conspicuous; (*Kleidung*) striking

auf|fangen *irr vt* (*Ball*) to catch; (*Stoß*) to cushion

auf|fassen *vt* to understand; **Auffassung** *f* view; (*Meinung*) opinion; (*Auslegung*) concept; (*Auffassungsgabe*) grasp

auf|fordern *vt* (*befehlen*) to call upon; (*bitten*) to ask

auf|frischen *vt* to brush up

auf|führen *vt* (*Theat*) to perform; (*in einem Verzeichnis*) to list; (*Beispiel*) to give ▷ *vr*: **sich ~** (*sich benehmen*) to behave; **Aufführung** *f* (*Theat*) performance

Aufgabe *f* job, task; (*Schule*) exercise; (*Hausaufgabe*) homework

Aufgang *m* (*Treppe*) staircase

auf|geben *irr vt* (*verzichten auf*) to give up; (*Paket*) to post; (*Gepäck*) to check in; (*Bestellung*) to place; (*Inserat*) to insert; (*Rätsel, Problem*) to set ▷ *vi* to give up

auf|gehen *irr vi* (*Sonne, Teig*) to rise; (*sich öffnen*) to open; (*klar werden*) to dawn (*jdm* on sb)

aufgelegt *adj*: **gut/schlecht ~** in a good/bad mood

aufgeregt *adj* excited

aufgeschlossen *adj* open(minded)

aufgeschmissen *adj* (*fam*) in a fix

aufgrund, **auf Grund** *prep +gen* on the basis of; (*wegen*) because of

auf|haben *irr vt* (*Hut etc*) to have on; **viel ~** (*Schule*) to have a lot of homework to do ▷ *vi* (*Geschäft*) to be open

auf|halten *irr vt* (*jdn*) to detain; (*Entwicklung*) to stop; (*Tür, Hand*) to hold open; (*Augen*) to keep open ▷ *vr*: **sich ~** (*wohnen*) to live; (*vorübergehend*) to stay

auf|hängen *irr vt* to hang up

auf|heben *irr vt* (*vom Boden etc*) to pick up; (*aufbewahren*) to keep

Aufheiterungen *pl* (*Meteo*) bright periods *pl*

auf|holen *vt* (*Zeit*) to make up ▷ *vi* to catch up

auf|hören *vi* to stop; **~, etw zu tun** to stop doing sth

auf|klären *vt* (*Geheimnis etc*) to clear up; **jdn ~** to enlighten sb; (*sexuell*) to tell sb the facts of life

Aufkleber (*-s, -*) *m* sticker

auf|kommen *irr vi* (*Wind*) to come up; (*Zweifel, Gefühl*) to arise; (*Mode etc*) to appear on the scene; **für den Schaden ~** to pay for the damage

auf|laden *irr vt* to load; (*Handy etc*) to charge; (*Handykarte etc*) to top up; **Aufladegerät** *nt* charger

Auflage *f* edition; (*von Zeitung*) circulation; (*Bedingung*) condition

auf|lassen *vt* (*Hut, Brille*) to keep on; (*Tür*) to leave open

Auflauf *m* (*Menschen*) crowd; (*Speise*) bake

auf|legen *vt* (*CD, Schminke etc*) to put on; (*Hörer*) to put down ▷ *vi* (*Tel*) to hang up

auf|leuchten *vi* to light up

auf|lösen *vt* (*in Flüssigkeit*) to dissolve ▷ *vr*: **sich ~** (*in Flüssigkeit*) to dissolve; **der Stau hat sich aufgelöst** traffic is back to normal; **Auflösung** *f* (*von Rätsel*) solution; (*von Bildschirm*) resolution

auf|machen *vt* to open; (*Kleidung*) to undo ▷ *vr*: **sich ~** to set out (*nach* for)

aufmerksam *adj* attentive; **jdn auf etw** (*akk*) **~ machen** to draw sb's attention to sth;

Aufmerksamkeit f attention; (*Konzentration*) attentiveness; (*Geschenk*) small token

auf|muntern vt (*ermutigen*) to encourage; (*aufheitern*) to cheer up

Aufnahme (-, -n) f (*Foto*) photo(graph); (*einzelne*) shot; (*in Verein, Krankenhaus etc*) admission; (*Beginn*) beginning; (*auf Tonband etc*) recording; **Aufnahmeprüfung** f entrance exam; **auf|nehmen** irr vt (*in Krankenhaus, Verein etc*) to admit; (*Musik*) to record; (*beginnen*) to take up; (*in Liste*) to include; (*begreifen*) to take in; **mit jdm Kontakt ~** to get in touch with sb

auf|passen vi (*aufmerksam sein*) to pay attention; (*vorsichtig sein*) to take care; **auf jdn/etw ~** to keep an eye on sb/sth

Aufprall (-s, -e) m impact; **auf|prallen** vi **auf etw** (*akk*) **~** to hit sth, to crash into sth

Aufpreis m extra charge

auf|pumpen vt to pump up

Aufputschmittel nt stimulant

auf|räumen vt, vi (*Dinge*) to clear away; (*Zimmer*) to tidy up

aufrecht adj upright

auf|regen vt to excite; (*ärgern*) to annoy ▷ vr: **sich ~** to get worked up; **aufregend** adj exciting; **Aufregung** f excitement

auf|reißen irr vt (*Tüte*) to tear open; (*Tür*) to fling open; (*fam: Person*) to pick up

Aufruf m (*Aviat, Inform*) call; (*öffentlicher*) appeal; **auf|rufen** irr vt (*auffordern*) to call upon (*zu* for); (*Namen*) to call out; (*Aviat*) to call; (*Inform*) to call up

auf|runden vt (*Summe*) to round up

aufs kontr von **auf das**

Aufsatz m essay

auf|schieben irr vt (*verschieben*) to postpone; (*verzögern*) to put off; (*Tür*) to slide open

Aufschlag m (*auf Preis*) extra charge; (*Tennis*) service; **auf|schlagen** irr vt (*öffnen*) to open; (*verletzen*) to cut open; (*Zelt*) to pitch, to put up; (*Lager*) to set up ▷ vi (*Tennis*) to serve; **auf etw** (+*akk*) **~** (*aufprallen*) to hit sth

auf|schließen irr vt to unlock, to open up ▷ vi (*aufrücken*) to close up

auf|schneiden irr vt to cut open; (*in Scheiben*) to slice ▷ vi (*angeben*) to boast, to show off

Aufschnitt m (slices pl of) cold meat; (*bei Käse*) (assorted) sliced cheeses pl

auf|schreiben irr vt to write down

Aufschrift f inscription; (*Etikett*) label

Aufschub m (*Verzögerung*) delay; (*Vertagung*) postponement

Aufsehen (-s) nt stir; **großes ~ erregen** to cause a sensation; **Aufseher(in)** (-s, -) m(f) guard; (*im Betrieb*) supervisor; (*im Museum*) attendant; (*im Park*) keeper

auf sein irr vi siehe **auf**

auf|setzen vt to put on; (*Dokument*) to draw up ▷ vi (*Flugzeug*) to touch down

Aufsicht f supervision; (*bei Prüfung*) invigilation; **die ~ haben** to be in charge

auf|spannen vt (*Schirm*) to put up

auf|sperren vt (*Mund*) to open wide; (*aufschließen*) to unlock

auf|springen irr vi to jump (*auf* +*akk* onto); (*hochspringen*) to jump up; (*sich öffnen*) to spring open

auf|stehen irr vi to get up; (*Tür*) to be open

auf|stellen vt (*aufrecht stellen*) to

put up; (*aufreihen*) to line up; (*nominieren*) to put up; (*Liste, Programm*) to draw up; (*Rekord*) to set up

Aufstieg (-(e)s, -e) m (*auf Berg*) ascent; (*Fortschritt*) rise; (*beruflich, im Sport*) promotion

Aufstrich m spread

auf|tanken vt, vi (*Auto*) to tank up; (*Flugzeug*) to refuel

auf|tauchen vi to turn up; (*aus Wasser etc*) to surface; (*Frage, Problem*) to come up

auf|tauen vt (*Speisen*) to defrost ▷ vi to thaw; (*fig: Person*) to unbend

Auftrag (-(e)s, Aufträge) m (*Comm*) order; (*Arbeit*) job; (*Anweisung*) instructions pl; (*Aufgabe*) task; **im ~ von** on behalf of; **auf|tragen** irr vt (*Salbe etc*) to apply; (*Essen*) to serve

auf|treten irr vi to appear; (*Problem*) to come up; (*sich verhalten*) to behave; **Auftritt** m (*des Schauspielers*) entrance; (*fig: Szene*) scene

auf|wachen vi to wake up

auf|wachsen irr vi to grow up

Aufwand (-(e)s) m expenditure; (*Kosten a.*) expense; (*Anstrengung*) effort; **aufwändig** adj costly; **das ist zu ~** that's too much trouble

auf|wärmen vt to warm up ▷ vr: **sich ~** to warm up

aufwärts adv upwards; **mit etw geht es ~** things are looking up for sth

auf|wecken vt to wake up

aufwendig adj siehe **aufwändig**

auf|wischen vt to wipe up; (*Fußboden*) to wipe

auf|zählen vt to list

auf|zeichnen vt to sketch; (*schriftlich*) to jot down; (*auf Band etc*) to record; **Aufzeichnung** f (*schriftlich*) note; (*Tonband etc*) recording; (*Film*) record

auf|ziehen irr vt (*öffnen*) to pull open; (*Uhr*) to wind (up); (*fam: necken*) to tease; (*Kinder*) to bring up; (*Tiere*) to rear ▷ vi (*Gewitter*) to come up

Aufzug m (*Fahrstuhl*) lift (*Brit*), elevator (*US*); (*Kleidung*) get-up; (*Theat*) act

Auge (-s, -n) nt eye; **jdm etw aufs ~ drücken** (fam) to force sth on sb; **ins ~ gehen** (fam) to go wrong; **unter vier ~n** in private; **etw im ~ behalten** to keep sth in mind; **Augenarzt** m, **Augenärztin** f eye specialist, eye doctor (US); **Augenblick** m moment; **im ~** at the moment; **Augenbraue** (-, -n) f eyebrow; **Augenbrauenstift** m eyebrow pencil; **Augenfarbe** f eye colour; **seine ~** the colour of his eyes; **Augenlid** nt eyelid; **Augenoptiker(in)** (-s, -) m(f) optician; **Augentropfen** pl eyedrops pl; **Augenzeuge** m, **Augenzeugin** f eyewitness

August (-(e)s o -, -e) m August; *siehe auch* **Juni**

Auktion f auction

 SCHLÜSSELWORT

aus prep +dat **1** (*räumlich*) out of; (*von … her*) from; **er ist aus Berlin** he's from Berlin; **aus dem Fenster** out of the window
2 (*gemacht/hergestellt aus*) made of; **ein Herz aus Stein** a heart of stone
3 (*auf Ursache deutend*) out of; **aus Mitleid** out of sympathy; **aus Erfahrung** from experience; **aus Spaß** for fun
4 aus ihr wird nie etwas she'll never get anywhere

▷ *adv* **1** (*zu Ende*) finished, over; **aus sein** to be over; **aus und vorbei** over and done with
2 (*ausgeschaltet, ausgezogen*) out; (*Aufschrift an Geräten*) off; **aus sein** (*nicht brennen*) to be out; (*abgeschaltet sein: Radio, Herd*) to be off; **Licht aus!** lights out!
3 (*nicht zu Hause*) **aus sein** to be out
4 (*in Verbindung mit von*) **von Rom aus** from Rome; **vom Fenster aus** out of the window; **von sich aus** (*selbstständig*) of one's own accord; **von ihm aus** as far as he's concerned

Aus (-) *nt* (*Sport*) touch; (*fig*) end
aus|atmen *vi* to breathe out
aus|bauen *vt* (*Haus, Straße*) to extend; (*Motor etc*) to remove
aus|bessern *vt* to repair; (*Kleidung*) to mend
aus|bilden *vt* to educate; (*Lehrling etc*) to train; (*Fähigkeiten*) to develop; **Ausbildung** *f* education; (*von Lehrling etc*) training; (*von Fähigkeiten*) development
Ausblick *m* view; (*fig*) outlook
aus|brechen *irr vi* to break out; **in Tränen ~** to burst into tears; **in Gelächter ~** to burst out laughing
aus|breiten *vt* to spread (out); (*Arme*) to stretch out ▷ *vr*: **sich ~** to spread
Ausbruch *m* (*Krieg, Seuche etc*) outbreak; (*Vulkan*) eruption; (*Gefühle*) outburst; (*von Gefangenen*) escape
aus|buhen *vt* to boo
Ausdauer *f* perseverance; (*Sport*) stamina
aus|dehnen *vt* to stretch; (*fig: Macht*) to extend
aus|denken *irr vt* **sich** (*dat*) **etw ~** to come up with sth

Ausdruck *m* (*Ausdrücke*) expression ▷ *m* (*Ausdrucke, Computerausdruck*) print-out; **aus|drucken** *vt* (*Inform*) to print (out)
aus|drücken *vt* (*formulieren*) to express; (*Zigarette*) to put out; (*Zitrone*) to squeeze ▷ *vr*: **sich ~** to express oneself; **ausdrücklich** *adj* express ▷ *adv* expressly
auseinander *adv* (*getrennt*) apart; **~ schreiben** to write as separate words;
auseinander|gehen *irr vi* (*Menschen*) to separate; (*Meinungen*) to differ; (*Gegenstand*) to fall apart;
auseinander|halten *irr vt* to tell apart; **auseinander|setzen** *vt* (*erklären*) to explain;
auseinander|setzen *vr*: **sich ~** (*sich beschäftigen*) to look (*mit* at); (*sich streiten*) to argue (*mit* with); **Auseinandersetzung** *f* (*Streit*) argument; (*Diskussion*) debate
Ausfahrt *f* (*des Zuges etc*) departure; (*Autobahn, Garage etc*) exit
aus|fallen *irr vi* (*Haare*) to fall out; (*nicht stattfinden*) to be cancelled; (*nicht funktionieren*) to break down; (*Strom*) to be cut off; (*Resultat haben*) to turn out; **groß/klein ~** (*Kleidung, Schuhe*) to be too big/too small
ausfindig machen *vt* to discover
aus|flippen *vi* (*fam*) to freak out
Ausflug *m* excursion, outing; **Ausflugsziel** *nt* destination
Ausfluss *m* (*Med*) discharge
aus|fragen *vt* to question
Ausfuhr (-, -en) *f* export
aus|führen *vt* (*verwirklichen*) to carry out; (*Person*) to take out; (*Comm*) to export; (*darlegen*) to explain

ausführlich *adj* detailed ▷ *adv* in detail

aus|füllen *vt* to fill up; (*Fragebogen etc*) to fill in (*o* out)

Ausgabe *f* (*Geld*) expenditure; (*Inform*) output; (*Buch*) edition; (*Nummer*) issue

Ausgang *m* way out, exit; (*Flugsteig*) gate; (*Ende*) end; (*Ergebnis*) result; „**kein ~**" "no exit"

aus|geben *irr vt* (*Geld*) to spend; (*austeilen*) to distribute; **jdm etw ~** (*spendieren*) to buy sb sth ▷ *vr:* **sich für etw/jdn ~** to pass oneself off as sth/sb

ausgebucht *adj* fully booked

ausgefallen *adj* (*ungewöhnlich*) unusual

aus|gehen *irr vi* (*abends etc*) to go out; (*Benzin, Kaffee etc*) to run out; (*Haare*) to fall out; (*Feuer, Licht etc*) to go out; (*Resultat haben*) to turn out; **davon ~, dass** to assume that; **ihm ging das Geld aus** he ran out of money

ausgelassen *adj* exuberant

ausgeleiert *adj* worn out

ausgenommen *conj, prep +gen o dat* except

ausgerechnet *adv:* **~ du** you of all people; **~ heute** today of all days

ausgeschildert *adj* signposted

ausgeschlafen *adj:* **bist du ~?** have you had enough sleep?

ausgeschlossen *adj* (*unmöglich*) impossible, out of the question

ausgesprochen *adj* (*absolut*) out-and-out; (*unverkennbar*) marked ▷ *adv* extremely; **~ gut** really good

ausgezeichnet *adj* excellent

ausgiebig *adj* (*Gebrauch*) thorough; (*Essen*) substantial

aus|gießen *irr vt* (*Getränk*) to pour out; (*Gefäß*) to empty

aus|gleichen *irr vt* to even out ▷ *vi* (*Sport*) to equalize

Ausguss *m* (*Spüle*) sink; (*Abfluss*) outlet

aus|halten *irr vt* to bear, to stand; **nicht auszuhalten sein** to be unbearable ▷ *vi* to hold out

aus|händigen *vt:* **jdm etw ~** to hand sth over to sb

Aushang *m* notice

Aushilfe *f* temporary help; (*im Büro*) temp

aus|kennen *irr vr:* **sich ~** to know a lot (*bei, mit* about); (*an einem Ort*) to know one's way around

aus|kommen *irr vi:* **gut/schlecht mit jdm ~** to get on well/badly with sb; **mit etw ~** to get by with sth

Auskunft (-, *Auskünfte*) *f* information; (*nähere*) details *pl*; (*Schalter*) information desk; (*Tel*) (directory) enquiries *sing* (*kein Artikel, Brit*), information (*US*)

aus|lachen *vt* to laugh at

aus|laden *irr vt* (*Gepäck etc*) to unload; **jdn ~** (*Gast*) to tell sb not to come

Auslage *f* window display; **~n** *pl* (*Kosten*) expenses

Ausland *nt* foreign countries *pl*; **im/ins ~** abroad; **Ausländer(in)** (-s, -) *m(f)* foreigner;

ausländerfeindlich *adj* hostile to foreigners, xenophobic;

ausländisch *adj* foreign;

Auslandsgespräch *nt* international call; **Auslands-krankenschein** *m* health insurance certificate for foreign countries, ≈ E111 (*Brit*);

Auslandsschutzbrief *m* international (motor) insurance cover (*documents pl*)

aus|lassen *irr vt* to leave out; (*Wort etc a.*) to omit; (*überspringen*) to skip; (*Wut, Ärger*) to vent (*an +dat* on) ▷ vr **sich über etw** (*akk*) ~ to speak one's mind about sth

aus|laufen *irr vi* (*Flüssigkeit*) to run out; (*Tank etc*) to leak; (*Schiff*) to leave port; (*Vertrag*) to expire

aus|legen *vt* (*Waren*) to display; (*Geld*) to lend; (*Text etc*) to interpret; (*technisch ausstatten*) to design (*für, auf +akk* for)

aus|leihen *irr vt* (*verleihen*) to lend; **sich** (*dat*) **etw** ~ to borrow sth

aus|loggen *vi* (*Inform*) to log out (*o off*)

aus|lösen *vt* (*Explosion, Alarm*) to set off; (*hervorrufen*) to cause; **Auslöser** (*-s, -*) *m* (*Foto*) shutter release

aus|machen *vt* (*Licht, Radio*) to turn off; (*Feuer*) to put out; (*Termin, Preis*) to fix; (*vereinbaren*) to agree; (*Anteil darstellen, betragen*) to represent; (*bedeuten*) to matter; **macht es Ihnen etwas aus, wenn ...?** would you mind if ...?; **das macht mir nichts aus** I don't mind

Ausmaß *nt* extent

Ausnahme (*-, -n*) *f* exception; **ausnahmsweise** *adv* as an exception, just this once

aus|nutzen *vt* (*Zeit, Gelegenheit, Einfluss*) to use; (*jdn, Gutmütigkeit*) to take advantage of

aus|packen *vt* to unpack

aus|probieren *vt* to try (out)

Auspuff (*-(e)s, -e*) *m* (*Tech*) exhaust; **Auspuffrohr** *nt* exhaust (pipe); **Auspufftopf** *m* (*Auto*) silencer (*Brit*), muffler (*US*)

aus|rauben *vt* to rob

aus|räumen *vt* (*Dinge*) to clear away; (*Schrank, Zimmer*) to empty; (*Bedenken*) to put aside

aus|rechnen *vt* to calculate, to work out

Ausrede *f* excuse

aus|reden *vi* to finish speaking ▷ *vt*: **jdm etw** ~ to talk sb out of sth

ausreichend *adj* sufficient, satisfactory; (*Schulnote*) ≈ D

Ausreise *f* departure; **bei der** ~ on leaving the country; **Ausreiseerlaubnis** *f* exit visa; **aus|reisen** *vi* to leave the country

aus|reißen *irr vt* to tear out ▷ *vi* to come off; (*fam: davonlaufen*) to run away

aus|renken *vt* **sich** (*dat*) **den Arm** ~ to dislocate one's arm

aus|richten *vt* (*Botschaft*) to deliver; (*Gruß*) to pass on; (*erreichen*) **ich konnte bei ihr nichts** ~ I couldn't get anywhere with her; **jdm etw** ~ to tell sb sth

aus|rufen *irr vt* (*über Lautsprecher*) to announce; **jdn** ~ **lassen** to page sb; **Ausrufezeichen** *nt* exclamation mark

aus|ruhen *vi* to rest ▷ *vr*: **sich** ~ to rest

Ausrüstung *f* equipment

aus|rutschen *vi* to slip

aus|schalten *vt* to switch off; (*fig*) to eliminate

Ausschau *f*: ~ **halten** to look out (*nach* for)

aus|scheiden *irr vt* (*Med*) to give off, to secrete ▷ *vi* to leave (*aus etw* sth); (*Sport*) to be eliminated

aus|schlafen *irr vi* to have a lie-in ▷ *vr*: **sich** ~ to have a lie-in ▷ *vt* to sleep off

Ausschlag *m* (*Med*) rash; **den** ~ **geben** (*fig*) to tip the balance; **aus|schlagen** *irr vt* (*Zahn*) to knock out; (*Einladung*) to turn down ▷ *vi* (*Pferd*) to kick out; **ausschlaggebend** *adj* decisive

aus|schließen *irr vt* to lock out; (*fig*) to exclude; **ausschließlich**

adv exclusively ▷ *prep +gen* excluding

Ausschnitt *m* (*Teil*) section; (*von Kleid*) neckline; (*aus Zeitung*) cutting

Ausschreitungen *pl* riots *pl*

aus|schütten *vt* (*Flüssigkeit*) to pour out; (*Gefäß*) to empty

aus|sehen *irr vi* to look; **krank ~** to look ill; **gut ~** (*Person*) to be good-looking; (*Sache*) to be looking good; **es sieht nach Regen aus** it looks like rain; **es sieht schlecht aus** things look bad

aus sein *irr vi siehe* **aus**

außen *adv* outside; **nach ~** outwards; **von ~** from (the) outside; **Außenbordmotor** *m* outboard motor; **Außenminister(in)** *m(f)* foreign minister, Foreign Secretary (*Brit*); **Außenseite** *f* outside; **Außenseiter(in)** *m(f)* outsider; **Außenspiegel** *m* wing mirror (*Brit*), side mirror (*US*)

außer *prep +dat* (*abgesehen von*) except (for); **nichts ~** nothing but; **~ Betrieb** out of order; **~ sich sein** to be beside oneself (*vor* with); **~ Atem** out of breath ▷ *conj* (*ausgenommen*) except; **~ wenn** unless; **~ dass** except; **außerdem** *conj* besides

äußere(r, s) *adj* outer, external

außergewöhnlich *adj* unusual ▷ *adv* exceptionally; **~ kalt** exceptionally cold; **außerhalb** *prep +gen* outside

äußerlich *adj* external

äußern *vt* to express; (*zeigen*) to show ▷ *vr*: **sich ~** to give one's opinion; (*sich zeigen*) to show itself

außerordentlich *adj* extra-ordinary; **außerplanmäßig** *adj* unscheduled

äußerst *adv* extremely;

äußerste(r, s) *adj* utmost; (*räumlich*) farthest; (*Termin*) last possible

Äußerung *f* remark

aus|setzen *vt* (*Kind, Tier*) to abandon; (*Belohnung*) to offer; **ich habe nichts daran auszusetzen** I have no objection to it ▷ *vi* (*aufhören*) to stop; (*Pause machen*) to drop out; (*beim Spiel*) to miss a turn

Aussicht *f* (*Blick*) view; (*Chance*) prospect; **aussichtslos** *adj* hopeless; **Aussichtsplattform** *f* observation platform; **Aussichtsturm** *m* observation tower

Aussiedler(in) (*-s, -*) *m(f)* émigré (*person of German descent from Eastern Europe*)

aus|spannen *vi* (*erholen*) to relax ▷ *vt*: **er hat ihm die Freundin ausgespannt** (*fam*) he's nicked his girlfriend

aus|sperren *vt* to lock out ▷ *vr*: **sich ~** to lock oneself out

Aussprache *f* (*von Wörtern*) pronunciation; (*Gespräch*) (frank) discussion; **aus|sprechen** *irr vt* to pronounce; (*äußern*) to express ▷ *vr*: **sich ~** to talk (*über +akk* about) ▷ *vi* (*zu Ende sprechen*) to finish speaking

aus|spülen *vt* to rinse (out)

Ausstattung *f* (*Ausrüstung*) equipment; (*Einrichtung*) furnishings *pl*; (*von Auto*) fittings *pl*

aus|stehen *irr vt* to endure; **ich kann ihn nicht ~** I can't stand him ▷ *vi* (*noch nicht da sein*) to be outstanding

aus|steigen *irr vi* to get out (*aus* of); **aus dem Bus/Zug ~** to get off the bus/train; **Aussteiger(in)** *m(f)* dropout

aus|stellen *vt* to display; (*auf Messe, in Museum etc*) to exhibit;

(*fam: ausschalten*) to switch off;
(*Scheck etc*) to make out; (*Pass etc*)
to issue; **Ausstellung** *f*
exhibition
aus|sterben *irr vi* to die out
aus|strahlen *vt* to radiate;
(*Programm*) to broadcast;
Ausstrahlung *f* (*Radio, TV*)
broadcast; (*fig: von Person*)
charisma
aus|strecken *vr*: **sich ~** to
stretch out ▷ *vt* (*Hand*) to reach
out (*nach* for)
aus|suchen *vt* to choose
Austausch *m* exchange;
aus|tauschen *vt* to exchange
(*gegen* for)
aus|teilen *vt* to distribute;
(*aushändigen*) to hand out
Auster (-, -n) *f* oyster;
Austernpilz *m* oyster mushroom
aus|tragen *irr vt* (*Post*) to
deliver; (*Wettkampf*) to hold
Australien (-s) *nt* Australia;
Australier(in) (-s, -) *m(f)*
Australian; **australisch** *adj*
Australian
aus|trinken *irr vt* (*Glas*) to drain;
(*Getränk*) to drink up ▷ *vi* to finish
one's drink
aus|trocknen *vi* to dry out;
(*Fluss*) to dry up
aus|üben *vt* (*Beruf, Sport*) to
practise; (*Einfluss*) to exert
Ausverkauf *m* sale;
ausverkauft *adj* (*Karten, Artikel*)
sold out
Auswahl *f* selection, choice (*an*
+*dat* of); **aus|wählen** *vt* to
select, to choose
aus|wandern *vi* to emigrate
auswärtig *adj* (*nicht am/vom Ort*)
not local; (*ausländisch*) foreign;
auswärts *adv* (*außerhalb der Stadt*)
out of town; (*Sport*) **~ spielen** to
play away; **Auswärtsspiel** *nt*
away match

aus|wechseln *vt* to replace;
(*Sport*) to substitute
Ausweg *m* way out
aus|weichen *irr vi* to get out of
the way; **jdm/einer Sache ~** to
move aside for sb/sth; (*fig*) to
avoid sb/sth
Ausweis (-es, -e) *m*
(*Personalausweis*) identity card, ID;
(*für Bibliothek etc*) card; **aus|weisen**
irr vt to expel ▷ *vr*: **sich ~** to
prove one's identity;
Ausweiskontrolle *f* ID check;
Ausweispapiere *pl* identification documents *pl*
auswendig *adv* by heart
aus|wuchten *vt* (*Auto: Räder*) to
balance
aus|zahlen *vt* (*Summe*) to pay
(out); (*Person*) to pay off ▷ *vr*: **sich**
~ to be worth it
aus|zeichnen *vt* (*ehren*) to
honour; (*Comm*) to price ▷ *vr*: **sich**
~ to distinguish oneself
aus|ziehen *irr vt* (*Kleidung*) to
take off ▷ *vr*: **sich ~** to undress
▷ *vi* (*aus Wohnung*) to move out
Auszubildende(r) *mf* trainee
authentisch *adj* authentic,
genuine
Auto (-s, -s) *nt* car; **~ fahren** to
drive; **Autoatlas** *m* road atlas;
Autobahn *f* motorway (*Brit*),
freeway (*US*); **Autobahnauffahrt**
f motorway access road (*Brit*),
on-ramp (*US*); **Autobahnausfahrt**
f motorway exit (*Brit*), off-ramp
(*US*); **Autobahngebühr** *f* toll;
Autobahnkreuz *nt* motorway
interchange; **Autobahnring** *m*
motorway ring (*Brit*), beltway (*US*);
Autobombe *f* car bomb;
Autofähre *f* car ferry;
Autofahrer(in) *m(f)* driver,
motorist; **Autofahrt** *f* drive
Autogramm (-s, -e) *nt*
autograph

Automarke f make of car
Automat (-en, -en) m vending machine
Automatik (-, -en) f (Auto) automatic transmission; **Automatikschaltung** f automatic gear change (Brit) (o shift (US)); **Automatikwagen** m automatic
automatisch adj automatic ▷ adv automatically
Automechaniker(in) m(f) car mechanic; **Autonummer** f registration (Brit) (o license (US)) number
Autor (-s, -en) m author
Autoradio nt car radio; **Autoreifen** m car tyre; **Autoreisezug** m Motorail train® (Brit), auto train (US); **Autorennen** nt motor racing; (einzelnes Rennen) motor race
Autorin f author(ess)
Autoschlüssel m car key; **Autotelefon** nt car phone; **Autounfall** m car accident; **Autoverleih** m, **Autovermietung** f car hire (Brit) (o rental (US)); (Firma) car hire (Brit) (o rental (US)) company; **Autowaschanlage** f car wash; **Autowerkstatt** f car repair shop, garage; **Autozubehör** nt car accessories pl
Avocado (-, -s) f avocado
Axt (-, Äxte) f axe
Azubi (-s, -s) m (-, -s) f akr = **Auszubildende** trainee

B abk = **Bundesstraße**
Baby (-s, -s) nt baby; **Babybett** nt cot (Brit), crib (US); **Babyfläschchen** nt baby's bottle; **Babynahrung** f baby food; **Babysitter(in)** m(f) babysitter; **Babysitz** m child seat; **Babywickelraum** m baby-changing room
Bach (-(e)s, Bäche) m stream
Backblech nt baking tray (Brit), cookie sheet (US)
Backbord nt port (side)
Backe (-, -n) f cheek
backen (backte, gebacken) vt, vi to bake
Backenzahn m molar
Bäcker(in) (-s, -) m(f) baker; **Bäckerei** f bakery; (Laden) baker's (shop)
Backofen m oven; **Backpulver** nt baking powder
Backspace-Taste f (Inform)

backspace key
Backstein *m* brick
Backwaren *pl* bread, cakes and pastries *pl*
Bad *(-(e)s, Bäder) nt* bath; *(Schwimmen)* swim; *(Ort)* spa; **ein ~ nehmen** to have (*o* take) a bath; **Badeanzug** *m* swimsuit, swimming costume (*Brit*); **Badehose** *f* swimming trunks *pl*; **Badekappe** *f* swimming cap; **Bademantel** *m* bathrobe; **Bademeister(in)** *m(f)* pool attendant; **Bademütze** *f* swimming cap
baden *vi* to have a bath; *(schwimmen)* to swim, to bathe (*Brit*) ▷ *vt* to bath (*Brit*), to bathe (*US*)
Baden-Württemberg *(-s) nt* Baden-Württemberg
Badeort *m* spa; **Badesachen** *pl* swimming things *pl*; **Badeschaum** *m* bubble bath, bath foam; **Badetuch** *nt* bath towel; **Badewanne** *f* bath (tub); **Badezeug** *nt* swimming gear; **Badezimmer** *nt* bathroom
Badminton *nt* badminton
baff *adj* **~ sein** *(fam)* to be flabbergasted (*o* gobsmacked)
Bagger *(-s, -) m* excavator; **Baggersee** *m* artificial lake in quarry etc, used for bathing
Bahamas *pl* **die ~** the Bahamas *pl*
Bahn *(-, -en) f (Eisenbahn)* railway (*Brit*), railroad (*US*); *(Rennbahn)* track; *(für Läufer)* lane; *(Astr)* orbit; **Deutsche ~** Germany's main railway operator; **bahnbrechend** *adj* groundbreaking; **BahnCard®** *(-, -s) f* rail card *(allowing 50% or 25% reduction on tickets)*; **Bahnfahrt** *f* railway (*Brit*) (*o* railroad (*US*)) journey; **Bahnhof** *m* station; **am** (*o* **auf dem**) **~** at the station;

Bahnlinie *f* railway (*Brit*) (*o* railroad (*US*)) line; **Bahnpolizei** *f* railway (*Brit*) (*o* railroad (*US*)) police; **Bahnsteig** *(-(e)s, -e) m* platform; **Bahnstrecke** *f* railway (*Brit*) (*o* railroad (*US*)) line; **Bahnübergang** *m* level crossing (*Brit*), grade crossing (*US*)
Bakterien *pl* bacteria *pl*, germs *pl*
bald *adv (zeitlich)* soon; *(beinahe)* almost; **bis ~!** see you soon (*o* later); **baldig** *adj* quick, speedy
Balkan *(-s) m* **der ~** the Balkans *pl*
Balken *(-s, -) m* beam
Balkon *(-s, -s o -e) m* balcony
Ball *(-(e)s, Bälle) m* ball; *(Tanz)* dance, ball
Ballett *(-s) nt* ballet
Ballon *(-s, -s) m* balloon
Ballspiel *nt* ball game
Ballungsgebiet *nt* conurbation
Baltikum *(-s) nt* **das ~** the Baltic States *pl*
Bambus *(-ses, -se) m* bamboo; **Bambussprossen** *pl* bamboo shoots *pl*
banal *adj* banal; *(Frage, Bemerkung)* trite
Banane *(-, -n) f* banana
band *imperf von* **binden**
Band *(-(e)s, Bände) m (Buch)* volume ▷ *(-(e)s, Bänder) nt (aus Stoff)* ribbon, tape; *(Fließband)* production line; *(Tonband)* tape; *(Anat)* ligament; **etw auf ~ aufnehmen** to tape sth ▷ *(-, -s) f (Musikgruppe)* band
Bandage *(-, -n) f* bandage; **bandagieren** *vt* to bandage
Bande *(-, -n) f (Gruppe)* gang
Bänderriss *m (Med)* torn ligament
Bandscheibe *f (Anat)* disc; **Bandwurm** *m* tapeworm
Bank *(-, Bänke) f (Sitzbank)* bench ▷ *(-, -en) f (Fin)* bank

Bankautomat m cash
dispenser; **Bankkarte** f bank
card; **Bankkonto** nt bank
account; **Bankleitzahl** f bank
sort code; **Banknote** f
banknote; **Bankverbindung** f
banking (o account) details pl
bar adj **~es Geld** cash; **etw (in)**
~ bezahlen to pay sth (in) cash
Bar (-, -s) f bar
Bär (-en, -en) m bear
barfuß adj barefoot
barg imperf von **bergen**
Bargeld nt cash; **bargeldlos** adj
non-cash
Barkeeper (-s, -) m, **Barmann**
m barman, bartender (US)
barock adj baroque
Barometer (-s, -) m barometer
barsch adj brusque
Barsch (-(e)s, -e) m perch
Barscheck m open (o uncrossed)
cheque
Bart (-(e)s, Bärte) m beard; **bärtig**
adj bearded
Barzahlung f cash payment
Basar (-s, -e) m bazaar
Baseballmütze f baseball cap
Basel (-s) nt Basle
Basilikum (-s) nt basil
Basis (-, Basen) f basis
Baskenland nt Basque region
Basketball m basketball
Bass (-es, Bässe) m bass
basta interj **und damit ~!** and
that's that
basteln vt to make ▷ vi to make
things, to do handicrafts; **Bastler**
(-s, -) m do-it-yourselfer
bat imperf von **bitten**
Batterie f battery;
batteriebetrieben adj
battery-powered
Bau (-(e)s) m (Bauen) building,
construction; (Aufbau) structure;
(Baustelle) building site ▷ m (Baue)
(Tier) burrow ▷ m (Bauten)

(Gebäude) building; **Bauarbeiten**
pl construction work sing;
(Straßenbau) roadworks pl (Brit),
roadwork (US); **Bauarbeiter(in)**
m(f) construction worker
Bauch (-(e)s, Bäuche) m stomach;
Bauchnabel m navel;
Bauchredner(in) m(f) ven-
triloquist; **Bauchschmerzen** pl
stomach-ache sing;
Bauchspeicheldrüse f pancreas;
Bauchtanz m belly dance; (das
Tanzen) belly dancing; **Bauchweh**
(-s) nt stomach-ache
bauen vt, vi to build; (Tech) to
construct
Bauer (-n o -s, -n) m farmer;
(Schach) pawn; **Bäuerin** f farmer;
(Frau des Bauern) farmer's wife;
Bauernhof m farm
baufällig adj dilapidated;
Baujahr adj year of construction;
der Wagen ist ~ 2002 the car is a
2002 model, the car was made in
2002
Baum (-(e)s, Bäume) m tree
Baumarkt m DIY centre
Baumwolle f cotton
Bauplatz m building site;
Baustein m (für Haus) stone;
(Spielzeug) brick; (fig) element;
elektronischer ~ chip; **Baustelle**
f building site; (bei Straßenbau)
roadworks pl (Brit), roadwork (US);
Bauteil nt prefabricated part;
Bauunternehmer(in) m(f) building
contractor; **Bauwerk** nt
building
Bayern (-s) nt Bavaria
beabsichtigen vt to intend
beachten vt (Aufmerksamkeit
schenken) to pay attention to;
(Vorschrift etc) to observe; **nicht**
~ to ignore; **beachtlich adj
considerable
Beachvolleyball nt beach
volleyball

Beamte(r) (-n, -n) m, **Beamtin** f official; (*Staatsbeamter*) civil servant

beanspruchen vt to claim; (*Zeit, Platz*) to take up; **jdn ~** to keep sb busy

beanstanden vt to complain about; **Beanstandung** f complaint

beantragen vt to apply for

beantworten vt to answer

bearbeiten vt to work; (*Material, Daten*) to process; (*Chem*) to treat; (*Fall etc*) to deal with; (*Buch etc*) to revise; (*fam: beeinflussen wollen*) to work on; **Bearbeitungsgebühr** f handling (o service) charge

beatmen vt: **jdn ~** to give sb artificial respiration

beaufsichtigen vt to supervise; (*bei Prüfung*) to invigilate

beauftragen vt to instruct; **jdn mit etw ~** to give sb the job of doing sth

Becher (-s, -) m mug; (*ohne Henkel*) tumbler; (*für Jogurt*) pot; (*aus Pappe*) tub

Becken (-s, -) nt basin; (*Spüle*) sink; (*zum Schwimmen*) pool; (*Mus*) cymbal; (*Anat*) pelvis

bedanken vr: **sich ~** to say thank you; **sich bei jdm für etw ~** to thank sb for sth

Bedarf (-(e)s) m need (*an +dat* for); (*Comm*) demand (*an +dat* for); **je nach ~** according to demand; **bei ~** if necessary; **Bedarfshaltestelle** f request stop

bedauerlich adj regrettable; **bedauern** vt to regret; (*bemitleiden*) to feel sorry for; **bedauernswert** adj (*Zustände*) regrettable; (*Mensch*) unfortunate

bedeckt adj covered; (*Himmel*) overcast

bedenken irr vt to consider; **Bedenken** (-s, -) nt (*Überlegen*)

consideration; (*Zweifel*) doubt; (*Skrupel*) scruples pl; **bedenklich** adj dubious; (*Zustand*) serious

bedeuten vt to mean; **jdm nichts/viel ~** to mean nothing/a lot to sb; **bedeutend** adj important; (*beträchtlich*) considerable; **Bedeutung** f meaning; (*Wichtigkeit*) importance

bedienen vt to serve; (*Maschine*) to operate ▷ vr: **sich ~** (*beim Essen*) to help oneself; **Bedienung** f service; (*Kellner/Kellnerin*) waiter/waitress; (*Verkäufer(in)*) shop assistant; (*Zuschlag*) service (charge); **Bedienungsanleitung** f operating instructions pl; **Bedienungshandbuch** nt instruction manual

Bedingung f condition; **unter der ~, dass** on condition that; **unter diesen ~en** under these circumstances

bedrohen vt to threaten

Bedürfnis nt need

Beefsteak (-s, -s) nt steak

beeilen vr: **sich ~** to hurry

beeindrucken vt to impress

beeinflussen vt to influence

beeinträchtigen vt to affect

beenden vt to end; (*fertigstellen*) to finish

beerdigen vt to bury; **Beerdigung** f burial; (*Feier*) funeral

Beere (-, -n) f berry; (*Traubenbeere*) grape

Beet (-(e)s, -e) nt bed

befahl imperf von **befehlen**

befahrbar adj passable; (*Naut*) navigable; **befahren** irr vt (*Straße*) to use; (*Pass*) to drive over; (*Fluss etc*) to navigate ▷ adj: **stark/wenig ~** busy/quiet

Befehl (-(e)s, -e) m order; (*Inform*) command; **befehlen** (*befahl, befohlen*) vt to order; **jdm ~, etw zu tun** to order sb to do sth ▷ vi to give orders

befestigen vt to fix; (mit Schnur, Seil) to attach; (mit Klebestoff) to stick

befeuchten vt to moisten

befinden irr vr: **sich ~** to be

befohlen pp von **befehlen**

befolgen vt (Rat etc) to follow

befördern vt (transportieren) to transport; (beruflich) to promote; **Beförderung** f transport; (beruflich) promotion; **Beförderungsbedingungen** pl conditions pl of carriage

Befragung f questioning; (Umfrage) opinion poll

befreundet adj friendly; **~ sein** to be friends (mit jdm with sb)

befriedigen vt to satisfy; **befriedigend** adj satisfactory; (Schulnote) ≈ C; **Befriedigung** f satisfaction

befristet adj limited (auf +akk to)

befruchten vt to fertilize; (fig) to stimulate

Befund (-(e)s, -e) m findings pl; (Med) diagnosis

befürchten vt to fear

befürworten vt to support

begabt adj gifted, talented; **Begabung** f talent, gift

begann imperf von **beginnen**

begegnen vi to meet (jdm sb), to meet sb (einer Sache dat sth)

begehen irr vt (Straftat) to commit; (Jubiläum etc) to celebrate

begehrt adj sought-after; (Junggeselle) eligible

begeistern vt to fill with enthusiasm; (inspirieren) to inspire ▷ vr: **sich für etw ~** to be/get enthusiastic about sth; **begeistert** adj enthusiastic

Beginn (-(e)s) m beginning; **zu ~** at the beginning; **beginnen** (begann, begonnen) vt, vi to start, to begin

beglaubigen vt to certify; **Beglaubigung** f certification

begleiten vt to accompany; **Begleiter(in)** m(f) companion; **Begleitung** f company; (Mus) accompaniment

beglückwünschen vt to congratulate (zu on)

begonnen pp von **beginnen**

begraben irr vt to bury; **Begräbnis** nt burial; (Feier) funeral

begreifen irr vt to understand

Begrenzung f boundary; (fig) restriction

Begriff (-(e)s, -e) m concept; (Vorstellung) idea; **im ~ sein, etw zu tun** to be on the point of doing sth; **schwer von ~ sein** to be slow on the uptake

begründen vt (rechtfertigen) to justify; **Begründung** f explanation; (Rechtfertigung) justification

begrüßen vt to greet; (willkommen heißen) to welcome; **Begrüßung** f greeting; (Empfang) welcome

behaart adj hairy

behalten irr vt to keep; (im Gedächtnis) to remember; **etw für sich ~** to keep sth to oneself

Behälter (-s, -) m container

behandeln vt to treat; **Behandlung** f treatment

behaupten vt to claim, to maintain ▷ vr: **sich ~** to assert oneself; **Behauptung** f claim

beheizen vt to heat

behelfen irr vr: **sich mit/ohne etw ~** to make do with/without sth

beherbergen vt to accommodate

beherrschen vt (Situation, Gefühle) to control; (Instrument) to master ▷ vr: **sich ~** to control

oneself; **Beherrschung** f control
(*über +akk* of); **die ~ verlieren** to
lose one's self-control
behilflich adj helpful; **jdm ~ sein**
to help sb (*bei* with)
behindern vt to hinder; (*Verkehr,
Sicht*) to obstruct; **Behinderte(r)**
mf disabled person;
behindertengerecht adj suitable
for disabled people
Behörde (-, -n) f authority; **die
~n** pl the authorities pl

SCHLÜSSELWORT

bei prep +dat **1** (*nahe bei*) near; (*zum
Aufenthalt*) at, with; (*unter,
zwischen*) among; **bei München**
near Munich; **bei uns** at our place;
beim Friseur at the hairdresser's;
bei seinen Eltern wohnen to live
with one's parents; **bei einer
Firma arbeiten** to work for a
firm; **etw bei sich haben** to have
sth on one; **jdn bei sich haben** to
have sb with one; **bei Goethe** in
Goethe; **beim Militär** in the army
2 (*zeitlich*) at, on; (*während*) during;
(*Zustand, Umstand*) in; **bei Nacht** at
night; **bei Nebel** in fog; **bei Regen**
if it rains; **bei solcher Hitze** in
such heat; **bei meiner Ankunft** on
my arrival; **bei der Arbeit** when
I'm *etc* working; **beim Fahren**
while driving

bei|behalten irr vt to keep
Beiboot nt dinghy
bei|bringen irr vt: **jdm etw
~** (*mitteilen*) to break sth to sb;
(*lehren*) to teach sb sth
beide(s) pron both; **meine ~n
Brüder** my two brothers, both my
brothers; **wir ~** both (o the two) of
us; **keiner von ~n** neither of them;
alle ~ both (of them); **~s ist sehr
schön** both are very nice; **30**

~ (*beim Tennis*) 30 all
beieinander adv together
Beifahrer(in) m(f) passenger;
Beifahrerairbag m passenger
airbag; **Beifahrersitz** m
passenger seat
Beifall (-(e)s) m applause
beige adj inv beige
Beigeschmack m aftertaste
Beil (-(e)s, -e) nt axe
Beilage f (*Gastr*) side dish;
(*Gemüse*) vegetables pl; (*zu Buch etc*)
supplement
beiläufig adj casual ▷ adv
casually
Beileid nt condolences pl; (**mein**)
herzliches ~ please accept my
sincere condolences
beiliegend adj enclosed
beim kontr von **bei dem**
Bein (-(e)s, -e) nt leg
beinah(e) adv almost, nearly
beinhalten vt to contain
Beipackzettel m instruction
leaflet
beisammen adv together;
Beisammensein (-s) nt
get-together
beiseite adv aside;
beiseite|legen vt: **etw ~** (*sparen*)
to put sth by
Beispiel (-(e)s, -e) nt example;
sich (*dat*) **an jdm/etw ein
~ nehmen** to take sb/sth as an
example; **zum ~** for example
beißen (*biss, gebissen*) vt to bite
▷ vi to bite; (*stechen: Rauch, Säure*)
to sting ▷ vr: **sich ~** (*Farben*) to
clash
Beitrag (-(e)s, Beiträge) m
contribution; (*für Mitgliedschaft*)
subscription; (*Versicherung*)
premium; **bei|tragen** irr vt, vi to
contribute (*zu* to)
bekannt adj well-known; (*nicht
fremd*) familiar; **mit jdm ~ sein** to
know sb; **~ geben** to announce;

jdn mit jdm ~ machen to introduce sb to sb; **Bekannte(r)** *mf* friend; (*entfernter*) acquaintance; **bekanntlich** *adv* as everyone knows; **Bekanntschaft** *f* acquaintance
bekiffen *vr*: **sich ~** (*fam*) to get stoned
beklagen *vr*: **sich ~** to complain
Bekleidung *f* clothing
bekommen *irr vt* to get; (*erhalten*) to receive; (*Kind*) to have; (*Zug, Grippe*) to catch, to get; **wie viel ~ Sie dafür?** how much is that? ▷ *vi*: **jdm ~** (*Essen*) to agree with sb; **wir ~ schon** (*bedient werden*) we're being served
beladen *irr vt* to load
Belag (*-(e)s, Beläge*) *m* coating; (*auf Zähnen*) plaque; (*auf Zunge*) fur
belasten *vt* to load; (*Körper*) to strain; (*Umwelt*) to pollute; (*fig: mit Sorgen etc*) to burden; (*Comm: Konto*) to debit; (*Jur*) to incriminate
belästigen *vt* to bother; (*stärker*) to pester; (*sexuell*) to harass; **Belästigung** *f* annoyance; **sexuelle ~** sexual harassment
belebt *adj* (*Straße etc*) busy
Beleg (*-(e)s, -e*) *m* (*Comm*) receipt; (*Beweis*) proof; **belegen** *vt* (*Brot*) to spread; (*Platz*) to reserve; (*Kurs, Vorlesung*) to register for; (*beweisen*) to prove
belegt *adj* (*Tel*) engaged (*Brit*), busy (*US*); (*Hotel*) full; (*Zunge*) coated; **~es Brötchen** sandwich; **der Platz ist ~** this seat is taken; **Belegtzeichen** *nt* (*Tel*) engaged tone (*Brit*), busy tone (*US*)
beleidigen *vt* to insult; (*kränken*) to offend; **Beleidigung** *f* insult; (*Jur*) slander; (*schriftliche*) libel
beleuchten *vt* to light; (*bestrahlen*) to illuminate; (*fig*) to examine; **Beleuchtung** *f* lighting; (*Bestrahlung*) illumination

Belgien (*-s*) *nt* Belgium; **Belgier(in)** (*-s, -*) *m(f)* Belgian; **belgisch** *adj* Belgian
belichten *vt* to expose; **Belichtung** *f* exposure; **Belichtungsmesser** (*-s, -*) *m* light meter
Belieben *nt*: (**ganz**) **nach ~** (just) as you wish
beliebig *adj*: **jedes ~e Muster** any pattern; **jeder ~e** anyone ▷ *adv*: **~ lange** as long as you like; **~ viel** as many (*o much*) as you like
beliebt *adj* popular; **sich bei jdm ~ machen** to make oneself popular with sb
beliefern *vt* to supply
bellen *vi* to bark
Belohnung *f* reward
Belüftung *f* ventilation
belügen *irr vt* to lie to
bemerkbar *adj* noticeable; **sich ~ machen** (*Mensch*) to attract attention; (*Zustand*) to become noticeable; **bemerken** *vt* (*wahrnehmen*) to notice; (*sagen*) to remark; **bemerkenswert** *adj* remarkable; **Bemerkung** *f* remark
bemitleiden *vt* to pity
bemühen *vr*: **sich ~** to try (hard), to make an effort; **Bemühung** *f* effort
bemuttern *vt* to mother
benachbart *adj* neighbouring
benachrichtigen *vt* to inform; **Benachrichtigung** *f* notification
benachteiligen *vt* to (put at a) disadvantage; (*wegen Rasse etc*) to discriminate against
benehmen *irr vr*: **sich ~** to behave; **Benehmen** (*-s*) *nt* behaviour
beneiden *vt* to envy; **jdn um etw ~** to envy sb sth
Beneluxländer *pl* Benelux countries *pl*

benommen | 34

benommen *adj* dazed
benötigen *vt* to need
benutzen *vt* to use;
Benutzer(in) (-s, -) *m(f)* user;
benutzerfreundlich *adj* user-friendly; **Benutzerhandbuch** *nt*
user's guide; **Benutzerkennung** *f*
user ID; **Benutzeroberfläche** *f*
(*Inform*) user/system interface;
Benutzung *f* use;
Benutzungsgebühr *f* (hire)
charge
Benzin (-s, -e) *nt* (*Auto*) petrol
(*Brit*), gas (*US*); **Benzingutschein**
m petrol (*Brit*) (*o* gas (*US*)) coupon;
Benzinkanister *m* petrol (*Brit*) (*o*
gas (*US*)) can; **Benzinpumpe** *f*
petrol (*Brit*) (*o* gas (*US*)) pump;
Benzintank *m* petrol (*Brit*) (*o* gas
(*US*)) tank; **Benzinuhr** *f* fuel
gauge
beobachten *vt* to observe;
Beobachtung *f* observation
bequem *adj* comfortable;
(*Ausrede*) convenient; (*faul*) lazy;
machen Sie es sich ~ make
yourself at home; **Bequemlichkeit**
f comfort; (*Faulheit*) laziness
beraten *irr vt* to advise;
(*besprechen*) to discuss ▷ *vr:* **sich
~** to consult; **Beratung** *f* advice;
(*bei Arzt etc*) consultation
berauben *vt* to rob
berechnen *vt* to calculate;
(*Comm*) to charge; **berechnend**
adj (*Mensch*) calculating
berechtigen *vt* to entitle (*zu* to);
(*fig*) to justify; **berechtigt** *adj*
justified; **zu etw ~ sein** to be
entitled to sth
bereden *vt* (*besprechen*) to discuss
Bereich (-(e)s, -e) *m* area;
(*Ressort, Gebiet*) field
bereisen *vt* to travel through
bereit *adj* ready; **zu etw ~ sein** to
be ready for sth; **sich ~ erklären,
etw zu tun** to agree to do sth

bereiten *vt* to prepare; (*Kummer*)
to cause; (*Freude*) to give
bereit|legen *vt* to lay out
bereit|machen *vr:* **sich ~** to get
ready
bereits *adv* already
Bereitschaft *f* readiness;
~ haben (*Arzt*) to be on call
bereit|stehen *vi* to be ready
bereuen *vt* to regret
Berg (-(e)s, -e) *m* mountain;
(*kleiner*) hill; **in die ~e fahren** to go
to the mountains; **bergab** *adv*
downhill; **bergauf** *adv* uphill;
Bergbahn *f* mountain railway
(*Brit*) (*o* railroad (*US*))
bergen (*barg, geborgen*) *vt* (*retten*)
to rescue; (*enthalten*) to contain
Bergführer(in) *m(f)* mountain
guide; **Berghütte** *f* mountain hut;
bergig *adj* mountainous;
Bergschuh *m* climbing boot;
Bergsteigen (-s) *nt*
mountaineering; **Bergsteiger(in)**
(-s, -) *m(f)* mountaineer;
Bergtour *f* mountain hike
Bergung *f* (*Rettung*) rescue; (*von
Toten, Fahrzeugen*) recovery
Bergwacht (-, -en) *f* mountain
rescue service; **Bergwerk** *nt*
mine
Bericht (-(e)s, -e) *m* report;
berichten *vt, vi* to report
berichtigen *vt* to correct
Bermudadreieck *nt* Bermuda
triangle; **Bermudainseln** *pl*
Bermuda *sing*; **Bermudashorts**
pl Bermuda shorts *pl*
Bernstein *m* amber
berüchtigt *adj* notorious,
infamous
berücksichtigen *vt* to take into
account; (*Antrag, Bewerber*) to
consider
Beruf (-(e)s, -e) *m* occupation;
(*akademischer*) profession;
(*Gewerbe*) trade; **was sind Sie von**

~? what do you do (for a living)?;
beruflich adj professional
Berufsausbildung f vocational
training; **Berufsschule** f
vocational college; **berufstätig**
adj employed; **Berufsverkehr** m
commuter traffic
beruhigen vt to calm ▷ vr: **sich
~** (Mensch, Situation) to calm down;
beruhigend adj reassuring;
Beruhigungsmittel nt sedative
berühmt adj famous
berühren vt to touch;
(gefühlsmäßig bewegen) to move;
(betreffen) to affect; (flüchtig
erwähnen) to mention, to touch on
▷ vr: **sich ~** to touch
besaufen irr vr: **sich ~** (fam) to
get plastered
beschädigen vt to damage
beschäftigen vt to occupy;
(beruflich) to employ ▷ vr: **sich mit
etw ~** to occupy oneself with sth;
(sich befassen) to deal with sth;
beschäftigt adj busy, occupied;
Beschäftigung f (Beruf)
employment; (Tätigkeit)
occupation; (geistige)
preoccupation (mit with)
Bescheid (-(e)s, -e) m
information; **~ wissen** to be
informed (o know) (über +akk
about); **ich weiß ~** I know; **jdm
~ geben** (o sagen) to let sb know
bescheiden adj modest
bescheinigen vt to certify;
(bestätigen) to acknowledge;
Bescheinigung f certificate;
(Quittung) receipt
bescheißen irr vt (vulg) to cheat
(um out of)
bescheuert adj (fam, pej) crazy
beschimpfen vt (mit
Kraftausdrücken) to swear at
Beschiss (-es) m: **das ist ~** (vulg)
that's a rip-off; **beschissen** adj
(vulg) shitty

beschlagnahmen vt to
confiscate
Beschleunigung f acceleration;
Beschleunigungsspur f
acceleration lane
beschließen irr vt to decide on;
(beenden) to end; **Beschluss** m
decision
beschränken vt to limit, to
restrict (auf +akk to) ▷ vr: **sich ~** to
restrict oneself (auf +akk to);
Beschränkung f limitation,
restriction
beschreiben irr vt to describe;
(Papier) to write on; **Beschreibung**
f description
beschuldigen vt to accuse (gen
of); **Beschuldigung** f
accusation
beschummeln vt, vi (fam) to
cheat (um out of)
beschützen vt to protect (vor
+dat from)
Beschwerde (-, -n) f complaint;
~n pl (Leiden) trouble sing;
beschweren vt to weight down;
(fig) to burden ▷ vr: **sich ~** to
complain
beschwipst adj tipsy
beseitigen vt to remove;
(Problem) to get rid of; (Müll) to
dispose of; **Beseitigung** f
removal; (von Müll) disposal
Besen (-s, -) m broom
besetzen vt (Haus, Land) to
occupy; (Platz) to take; (Posten) to
fill; (Rolle) to cast; **besetzt** adj
full; (Tel) engaged (Brit), busy (US);
(Platz) taken; (WC) engaged;
Besetztzeichen nt engaged tone
(Brit), busy tone (US)
besichtigen vt (Museum) to visit;
(Sehenswürdigkeit) to have a look at;
(Stadt) to tour
besiegen vt to defeat
Besitz (-es) m possession;
(Eigentum) property; **besitzen** irr

vt to own; (*Eigenschaft*) to have;
Besitzer(in) (-s, -) *m(f)* owner
besoffen *adj* (*fam*) plastered
besondere(r, s) *adj* special;
(*bestimmt*) particular;
(*eigentümlich*) peculiar; **nichts ~s**
nothing special; **Besonderheit** *f*
special feature; (*besondere
Eigenschaft*) peculiarity; **besonders**
adv especially, particularly;
(*getrennt*) separately
besorgen *vt* (*beschaffen*) to get
(*jdm for sb*); (*kaufen a.*) to purchase;
(*erledigen: Geschäfte*) to deal with
besprechen *irr vt* to discuss;
Besprechung *f* discussion;
(*Konferenz*) meeting; **Besprechungsraum** *m* consultation
room
besser *adj* better; **es geht ihm
~** he feels better; **~ gesagt** or
rather; **~ werden** to improve;
bessern *vt* to improve ▷ *vr:* **sich
~** to improve; (*Mensch*) to mend
one's ways; **Besserung** *f*
improvement; **gute ~!** get well
soon
beständig *adj* constant; (*Wetter*)
settled
Bestandteil *m* component
bestätigen *vt* to confirm;
(*Empfang, Brief*) to acknowledge;
Bestätigung *f* confirmation; (*von
Brief*) acknowledgement
beste(r, s) *adj* best; **das ~ wäre,
wir ...** it would be best if we ...
▷ *adv:* **sie singt am ~n** she sings
best; **so ist es am ~n** it's best that
way; **am ~n gehst du gleich** you'd
better go at once
bestechen *irr vt* to bribe;
Bestechung *f* bribery
Besteck (-(e)s, -e) *nt* cutlery
bestehen *irr vi* to be, to exist;
(*andauern*) to last; **~ auf** (+*dat*) to
insist on; **~ aus** to consist of ▷ *vt*
(*Probe, Prüfung*) to pass; (*Kampf*) to

win
bestehlen *irr vt* to rob
bestellen *vt* to order; (*reservieren*)
to book; (*Grüße, Auftrag*) to pass on
(*jdm to sb*); (*kommen lassen*) to send
for; **Bestellnummer** *f* order
number; **Bestellung** *f* (*Comm*)
order; (*das Bestellen*) ordering
bestens *adv* very well
bestimmen *vt* to determine;
(*Regeln*) to lay down; (*Tag, Ort*) to
fix; (*ernennen*) to appoint;
(*vorsehen*) to mean (*für for*);
bestimmt *adj* definite; (*gewiss*)
certain; (*entschlossen*) firm ▷ *adv*
definitely; (*wissen*) for sure;
Bestimmung *f* (*Verordnung*)
regulation; (*Zweck*) purpose
Best.-Nr. *abk* = **Bestellnummer**
order number
bestrafen *vt* to punish
bestrahlen *vt* to illuminate;
(*Med*) to treat with radiotherapy
bestreiten *irr vt* (*leugnen*) to
deny
Bestseller (-s, -) *m* bestseller
bestürzt *adj* dismayed
Besuch (-(e)s, -e) *m* visit; (*Mensch*)
visitor; **~ haben** to have visitors/a
visitor; **besuchen** *vt* to visit;
(*Schule, Kino etc*) to go to;
Besucher(in) (-s, -) *m(f)* visitor;
Besuchszeit *f* visiting hours *pl*
betäuben *vt* (*Med*) to
anaesthetize; **Betäubung** *f*
anaesthetic; **örtliche ~** local
anaesthetic; **Betäubungsmittel**
nt anaesthetic
Bete (-, -n) *f:* **Rote ~** beetroot
beteiligen *vr* **sich an etw** (*dat*)
~ to take part in sth, to participate
in sth ▷ *vt* **jdn an etw** (*dat*) **~** to
involve sb in sth; **Beteiligung** *f*
participation; (*Anteil*) share;
(*Besucherzahl*) attendance
beten *vi* to pray
Beton (-s, -s) *m* concrete

betonen vt to stress; (*hervorheben*) to emphasize; **Betonung** f stress; (*fig*) emphasis

Betr. *abk* = **Betreff** re

Betracht m: **in ~ ziehen** to take into consideration; **in ~ kommen** to be a possibility; **nicht in ~ kommen** to be out of the question; **betrachten** vt to look at; **~ als** to regard as; **beträchtlich** *adj* considerable

Betrag (-(e)s, *Beträge*) m amount, sum; **betragen** *irr* vt to amount (*o come*) to ▷ vr: **sich ~** to behave

betreffen *irr* vt to concern; (*Regelung etc*) to affect; **was mich betrifft** as for me; **betreffend** *adj* relevant, in question

betreten *irr* vt to enter; (*Bühne etc*) to step onto; „**Betreten verboten**" "keep off/out"

betreuen vt to look after; (*Reisegruppe, Abteilung*) to be in charge of; **Betreuer(in)** (-s, -) m(f) (*Pfleger*) carer; (*von Kind*) child minder; (*von Reisegruppe*) groupleader

Betrieb (-(e)s, -e) m (*Firma*) firm; (*Anlage*) plant; (*Tätigkeit*) operation; (*Treiben*) bustle; **außer ~ sein** to be out of order; **in ~ sein** to be in operation; **betriebsbereit** *adj* operational; **Betriebsrat** m (*Gremium*) works council; **Betriebssystem** nt (*Inform*) operating system

betrinken *irr* vr: **sich ~** to get drunk

betroffen *adj* (*bestürzt*) shaken; **von etw ~ werden/sein** to be affected by sth

betrog *imperf von* **betrügen**; **betrogen** *pp von* **betrügen**

Betrug (-(e)s) m deception; (*Jur*) fraud; **betrügen** (*betrog, betrogen*) vt to deceive; (*Jur*) to defraud; (*Partner*) to cheat on; **Betrüger(in)** (-s, -) m(f) cheat

betrunken *adj* drunk

Bett (-(e)s, -en) nt bed; **ins** (*o zu*) **~ gehen** to go to bed; **das ~ machen** to make the bed; **Bettbezug** m duvet cover; **Bettdecke** f blanket

betteln vi to beg

Bettlaken nt sheet

Bettler(in) (-s, -) m(f) beggar

Bettsofa nt sofa bed; **Betttuch** nt sheet; **Bettwäsche** f bed linen; **Bettzeug** nt bedding

beugen vt to bend ▷ vr: **sich ~** to bend; (*sich fügen*) to submit (*dat* to)

Beule (-, -n) f (*Schwellung*) bump; (*Delle*) dent

beunruhigen vt to worry ▷ vr: **sich ~** to worry

beurteilen vt to judge

Beute (-) f (*von Dieb*) booty, loot; (*von Tier*) prey

Beutel (-s, -) m bag

Bevölkerung f population

bevollmächtigt *adj* authorized (*zu etw* to do sth)

bevor *conj* before; **bevor|stehen** *irr* vi (*Schwierigkeiten*) to lie ahead; (*Gefahr*) to be imminent; **jdm ~** (*Überraschung etc*) to be in store for sb; **bevorstehend** *adj* forthcoming; **bevorzugen** vt to prefer

bewachen vt to guard; **bewacht** *adj*: **~er Parkplatz** supervised car park (*Brit*), guarded parking lot (*US*)

bewegen vt to move; **jdn dazu ~, etw zu tun** to get sb to do sth ▷ vr: **sich ~** to move; **es bewegt sich etwas** (*fig*) things are beginning to happen; **Bewegung** f movement; (*Phys*) motion; (*innere*) emotion; (*körperlich*) exercise; **Bewegungsmelder** (-s, -) m sensor (*which reacts to* *movement)*

Beweis (*-es, -e*) *m* proof; (*Zeugnis*) evidence; **beweisen** *irr vt* to prove; (*zeigen*) to show

bewerben *irr vr:* **sich ~** to apply (*um* for); **Bewerbung** *f* application; **Bewerbungsunterlagen** *pl* application documents *pl*

bewilligen *vt* to allow; (*Geld*) to grant

bewirken *vt* to cause, to bring about

bewohnen *vt* to live in; **Bewohner(in)** (*-s, -*) *m(f)* inhabitant; (*von Haus*) resident

bewölkt *adj* cloudy, overcast; **Bewölkung** *f* clouds *pl*

bewundern *vt* to admire; **bewundernswert** *adj* admirable

bewusst *adj* conscious; (*absichtlich*) deliberate; **sich** (*dat*) **einer Sache** (*gen*) **~ sein** to be aware of sth ▷ *adv* consciously; (*absichtlich*) deliberately; **bewusstlos** *adj* unconscious; **Bewusstlosigkeit** *f* unconsciousness; **Bewusstsein** (*-s*) *nt* consciousness; **bei ~** conscious

bezahlen *vt* to pay; (*Ware, Leistung*) to pay for; **kann ich bar/mit Kreditkarte ~?** can I pay cash/by credit card?; **sich bezahlt machen** to be worth it; **Bezahlung** *f* payment

bezeichnen *vt* (*kennzeichnen*) to mark; (*nennen*) to call; (*beschreiben*) to describe; **Bezeichnung** *f* (*Name*) name; (*Begriff*) term

beziehen *irr vt* (*Bett*) to change; (*Haus, Position*) to move into; (*erhalten*) to receive; (*Zeitung*) to take; **einen Standpunkt ~** (*fig*) to take up a position ▷ *vr:* **sich ~** to refer (*auf +akk* to); **Beziehung** *f* (*Verbindung*) connection; (*Verhältnis*) relationship; **~en**

haben (*vorteilhaft*) to have connections (*o contacts*); **in dieser ~** in this respect; **beziehungsweise** *adv* or; (*genauer gesagt*) or rather

Bezirk (*-(e)s, -e*) *m* district

Bezug (*-(e)s, Bezüge*) *m* (*Überzug*) cover; (*von Kopfkissen*) pillowcase; **in ~ auf** (*+akk*) with regard to; **bezüglich** *prep +gen* concerning

bezweifeln *vt* to doubt

BH (*-s, -s*) *m* bra

Bhf. *abk* = **Bahnhof** station

Biathlon (*-s, -s*) *m* biathlon

Bibel (*-, -n*) *f* Bible

Biber (*-s, -*) *m* beaver

Bibliothek (*-, -en*) *f* library

biegen (*bog, gebogen*) *vt* to bend ▷ *vr:* **sich ~** to bend ▷ *vi* to turn (*in +akk* into); **Biegung** *f* bend

Biene (*-, -n*) *f* bee

Bier (*-(e)s, -e*) *nt* beer; **helles ~** ≈ lager (*Brit*), beer (*US*); **dunkles ~** ≈ brown ale (*Brit*), dark beer (*US*); **zwei ~, bitte!** two beers, please; **Biergarten** *m* beer garden; **Bierzelt** *nt* beer tent

bieten (*bot, geboten*) *vt* to offer; (*bei Versteigerung*) bid; **sich** (*dat*) **etw ~ lassen** to put up with sth ▷ *vr:* **sich ~** (*Gelegenheit*) to present itself (*dat* to)

Bikini (*-s, -s*) *m* bikini

Bild (*-(e)s, -er*) *nt* picture; (*gedankliches*) image; (*Foto*) photo

bilden *vt* to form; (*geistig*) to educate; (*ausmachen*) to constitute ▷ *vr:* **sich ~** (*entstehen*) to form; (*lernen*) to educate oneself

Bilderbuch *nt* picture book

Bildhauer(in) (*-s, -*) *m(f)* sculptor

Bildschirm *m* screen; **Bildschirmschoner** (*-s, -*) *m* screensaver; **Bildschirmtext** *m* viewdata, videotext

Bildung *f* formation; (*Wissen,*

Benehmen) education;
Bildungsurlaub m educational
holiday; *(von Firma)* study leave
Billard nt billiards *sing*
billig *adj* cheap; *(gerecht)* fair
Billigflieger m budget airline
Billigflug m cheap flight
Binde (-, -n) f bandage;
(Armbinde) band; *(Damenbinde)*
sanitary towel *(Brit)*, sanitary
napkin *(US)*
Bindehautentzündung f
conjunctivitis
binden *(band, gebunden)* vt to tie;
(Buch) to bind; *(Soße)* to thicken
Bindestrich m hyphen
Bindfaden m string
Bindung f bond, tie; *(Skibindung)*
binding
Bio- in zW bio-; **Biokost** f health
food

○ **BIOLADEN**
○
○ A **Bioladen** is a shop which
○ specializes in selling
○ environmentally friendly
○ products such as
○ phosphate-free washing
○ powders, recycled paper and
○ organically grown vegetables.

Biologie f biology; **biologisch**
adj biological; *(Anbau)* organic
Birke (-, -n) f birch
Birne (-, -n) f *(Obst)* pear; *(Elek)*
(light) bulb

 SCHLÜSSELWORT

bis *prep* +akk, *adv* **1** *(zeitlich)* till,
until; *(bis spätestens)* by; **Sie haben
bis Dienstag Zeit** you have until o
till Tuesday; **bis Dienstag muss es
fertig sein** it must be ready by
Tuesday; **bis auf Weiteres** until
further notice; **bis in die Nacht**

into the night; **bis bald/gleich** see
you later/soon
2 *(räumlich)* (up) to; **ich fahre bis
Köln** I'm going to o I'm going as far
as Cologne; **bis an unser
Grundstück** (right o up) to our
plot; **bis hierher** this far
3 *(bei Zahlen)* up to; **bis zu** up to
4 bis auf etw *akk (außer)* except
sth; *(einschließlich)* including sth
▷ *konj* **1** *(mit Zahlen)* to; **10 bis 20** 10
to 20
2 *(zeitlich)* till, until; **bis es dunkel
wird** till o until it gets dark; **von ...
bis ...** from ... to ...

Bischof (-s, *Bischöfe*) m bishop
bisher *adv* up to now, so far
Biskuit (-(e)s, -s o -e) nt sponge
biss *imperf von* **beißen**
Biss (-es, -e) m bite
bisschen *adj*: **ein ~** a bit of; **ein
~ Salz/Liebe** a bit of salt/love; **ich
habe kein ~ Hunger** I'm not a bit
hungry ▷ *adv*: **ein ~** a bit; **kein
~** not at all
bissig *adj (Hund)* vicious;
(Bemerkung) cutting
Bit (-s, -s) nt *(Inform)* bit
bitte *interj* please; **(wie) ~?** (I beg
your) pardon?; **~** (**schön** o **sehr**)!
(als Antwort auf Dank) you're
welcome; **hier, ~** here you are;
Bitte (-, -n) f request; **bitten**
(bat, gebeten) vt, vi to ask (**um** for)
bitter *adj* bitter
Blähungen pl *(Med)* wind *sing*
blamieren vr: **sich ~** to make a
fool of oneself ▷ vt: **jdn ~** to make
sb look a fool
Blankoscheck m blank cheque
Blase (-, -n) f bubble; *(Med)*
blister; *(Anat)* bladder
blasen *(blies, geblasen)* vi to blow;
jdm einen ~ *(vulg)* to give sb a
blow job
Blasenentzündung f cystitis

blass adj pale

Blatt (-(e)s, Blätter) nt leaf; (von Papier) sheet; **blättern** vi (Inform) to scroll; **in etw** (dat) ~ to leaf through sth; **Blätterteig** m puff pastry; **Blattsalat** m green salad; **Blattspinat** m spinach

blau adj blue; (fam: betrunken) plastered; (Gastr) boiled; ~**es Auge** black eye; ~**er Fleck** bruise; **Blaubeere** f bilberry, blueberry; **Blaulicht** nt flashing blue light; **blau|machen** vi to skip work o school; **Blauschimmelkäse** m blue cheese

Blazer (-s, -) m blazer

Blech (-(e)s, -e) nt sheet metal; (Backblech) baking tray (Brit), cookie sheet (US); **Blechschaden** m (Auto) damage to the bodywork

Blei (-(e)s, -e) nt lead

bleiben (blieb, geblieben) vi to stay; **lass das ~!** stop it; **das bleibt unter uns** that's (just) between ourselves; **mir bleibt keine andere Wahl** I have no other choice

bleich adj pale; **bleichen** vt to bleach

bleifrei adj (Benzin) unleaded; **bleihaltig** adj (Benzin) leaded

Bleistift m pencil

Blende (-, -n) f (Foto) aperture

Blick (-(e)s, -e) m look; (kurz) glance; (Aussicht) view; **auf den ersten** ~ at first sight; **einen** ~ **auf etw** (akk) **werfen** to have a look at sth; **blicken** vi to look; **sich** ~ **lassen** to show up

blieb imperf von **bleiben**

blies imperf von **blasen**

blind adj blind; (Glas etc) dull; **Blinddarm** m appendix; **Blinddarmentzündung** f appendicitis; **Blinde(r)** mf blind person/man/woman; **die ~n** pl the blind pl; **Blindenhund** m guide dog; **Blindenschrift** f braille

blinken vi (Stern, Lichter) to twinkle; (aufleuchten) to flash; (Auto) to indicate; **Blinker** (-s, -) m (Auto) indicator (Brit), turn signal (US)

blinzeln vi (mit beiden Augen) to blink; (mit einem Auge) to wink

Blitz (-es, -e) m (flash of) lightning; (Foto) flash; **blitzen** vi (Foto) to use a/the flash; **es blitzte und donnerte** there was thunder and lightning; **Blitzlicht** nt flash

Block (-(e)s, Blöcke) m (a. fig) block; (von Papier) pad; **Blockflöte** f recorder; **Blockhaus** nt log cabin; **blockieren** vt to block ▷ vi to jam; (Räder) to lock; **Blockschrift** f block letters pl

blöd adj stupid; **blödeln** vi (fam) to fool around

Blog (-s, -s) nt (Inform) blog; **bloggen** vi to blog

blond adj blond; (Frau) blonde

◯ SCHLÜSSELWORT

bloß adj 1 (unbedeckt) bare; (nackt) naked; **mit der bloßen Hand** with one's bare hand; **mit bloßem Auge** with the naked eye
2 (alleinig, nur) mere; **der bloße Gedanke** the very thought; **bloßer Neid** sheer envy
▷ adv only, merely; **lass das bloß!** just don't do that!; **wie ist das bloß passiert?** how on earth did that happen?

blühen vi to bloom; (fig) to flourish

Blume (-, -n) f flower; (von Wein) bouquet; **Blumenbeet** nt flower bed; **Blumengeschäft** nt florist's (shop); **Blumenkohl** m cauliflower; **Blumenladen** m flower shop; **Blumenstrauß** m

bunch of flowers; **Blumentopf** m flowerpot; **Blumenvase** f vase
Bluse (-, -n) f blouse
Blut (-(e)s) nt blood; **Blutbild** nt blood count; **Blutdruck** m blood pressure; **Blutorange** f blood orange
Blüte (-, -n) f (Pflanzenteil) flower, bloom; (Baumblüte) blossom; (fig) prime
bluten vi to bleed
Blütenstaub m pollen
Bluter (-s, -) m (Med) haemophiliac; **Bluterguss** m haematoma; (blauer Fleck) bruise; **Blutgruppe** f blood group; **blutig** adj bloody; **Blutkonserve** f unit of stored blood; **Blutprobe** f blood sample; **Blutspende** f blood donation; **Bluttransfusion** f blood transfusion; **Blutung** f bleeding; **Blutvergiftung** f blood poisoning; **Blutwurst** f black pudding (Brit), blood sausage (US)
BLZ abk = **Bankleitzahl**
Bob (-s, -s) m bob(sleigh)
Bock (-(e)s, Böcke) m (Reh) buck; (Schaf) ram; (Gestell) trestle; (Sport) vaulting horse; **ich hab keinen ~ (drauf)** (fam) I don't feel like it
Boden (-s, Böden) m ground; (Fußboden) floor; (von Meer, Fass) bottom; (Speicher) attic; **Bodennebel** m ground mist; **Bodenpersonal** nt ground staff; **Bodenschätze** pl mineral resources pl
Bodensee m: **der ~** Lake Constance
Body (-s, -s) m body; **Bodybuilding** (-s) nt bodybuilding
bog imperf von **biegen**
Bogen (-s, -) m (Biegung) curve; (in der Architektur) arch; (Waffe, Instrument) bow; (Papier) sheet

Bohne (-, -n) f bean; **grüne ~n** pl green (o French (Brit)) beans pl; **weiße ~n** pl haricot beans pl; **Bohnenkaffee** m real coffee; **Bohnensprosse** f bean sprout
bohren vt to drill; **Bohrer** (-s, -) m drill
Boiler (-s, -) m water heater
Boje (-, -n) f buoy
Bolivien (-s) nt Bolivia
Bombe (-, -n) f bomb
Bon (-s, -s) m (Kassenzettel) receipt; (Gutschein) voucher, coupon
Bonbon (-s, -s) nt sweet (Brit), candy (US)
Bonus (- o -ses, -se o Boni) m bonus; (Punktvorteil) bonus points pl; (Schadenfreiheitsrabatt) no-claims bonus
Boot (-(e)s, -e) nt boat; **Bootsverleih** m boat hire (Brit) (o rental (US))
Bord (-(e)s, -e) m: **an ~ (eines Schiffes)** on board (a ship); **an ~ gehen** (Schiff) to go on board; (Flugzeug) to board; **von ~ gehen** to disembark; **Bordcomputer** m dashboard computer
Bordell (-s, -e) nt brothel
Bordkarte f boarding card
Bordstein m kerb (Brit), curb (US)
borgen vt to borrow; **jdm etw ~** to lend sb sth; **sich** (dat) **etw ~** to borrow sth
Börse (-, -n) f stock exchange; (Geldbörse) purse
bös adj siehe **böse**; **bösartig** adj malicious; (Med) malignant
Böschung f slope; (Uferböschung) embankment
böse adj bad; (stärker) evil; (Wunde) nasty; (zornig) angry; **bist du mir ~?** are you angry with me?
boshaft adj malicious
Bosnien (-s) nt Bosnia; **Bosnien-Herzegowina** (-s) nt

Bosnia-Herzegovina
böswillig adj malicious
bot imperf von **bieten**
botanisch adj: **~er Garten**
botanical gardens pl
Botschaft f message; (Pol)
embassy; **Botschafter(in)** m(f)
ambassador
Botsuana (-s) nt Botswana
Bouillon (-, -s) f stock
Boutique (-, -n) f boutique
Bowle (-, -n) f punch
Box (-, -en) f (Behälter, Pferdebox)
box; (Lautsprecher) speaker; (bei
Autorennen) pit
boxen vi to box; **Boxer** (-s, -) m
(Hund, Sportler) boxer;
Boxershorts pl boxer shorts pl;
Boxkampf m boxing match
Boykott (-s, -e) m boycott
brach imperf von **brechen**
brachte imperf von **bringen**
Brainstorming (-s) nt
brainstorming
Branchenverzeichnis nt
yellow pages® pl
Brand (-(e)s, Brände) m fire; **einen
~ haben** (fam) to be parched
Brandenburg (-s) nt
Brandenburg
Brandsalbe f ointment for burns
Brandung f surf
Brandwunde f burn
brannte imperf von **brennen**
Brasilien (-s) nt Brazil
braten (briet, gebraten) vt to
roast; (auf dem Rost) to grill; (in der
Pfanne) to fry; **Braten** (-s, -) m
roast; (roher) joint; **Bratensoße** f
gravy; **Brathähnchen** nt roast
chicken; **Bratkartoffeln** pl fried
potatoes pl; **Bratpfanne** f frying
pan; **Bratspieß** m spit;
Bratwurst f fried sausage;
(gegrillte) grilled sausage
Brauch (-s, Bräuche) m custom
brauchen vt (nötig haben) to need

(für, zu for); (erfordern) to require;
(Zeit) to take; (gebrauchen) to use;
wie lange wird er ~? how long will
it take him?; **du brauchst es nur
zu sagen** you only need to say;
das braucht (seine) Zeit it takes
time; **ihr braucht es nicht zu tun**
you don't have (o need) to do it; **sie
hätte nicht zu kommen ~** she
needn't have come
brauen vt to brew; **Brauerei** f
brewery
braun adj brown; (von Sonne)
tanned; **Bräune** (-, -n) f
brownness; (von Sonne) tan;
Bräunungsstudio nt tanning
studio
Brause (-, -n) f (Dusche) shower;
(Getränk) fizzy drink (Brit), soda
(US)
Braut (-, Bräute) f bride;
Bräutigam (-s, -e) m bridegroom
brav adj (artig) good,
well-behaved
bravo interj well done
BRD (-) f abk = **Bundesrepublik
Deutschland** FRG

- **BRD**
-
- The **BRD** is the official name for
- the Federal Republic of
- Germany. It comprises 16
- **Länder** (see **Land**). It was the
- name given to the former West
- Germany as opposed to East
- Germany (the **DDR**). The two
- Germanies were reunited on 3rd
- October 1990.

brechen (brach, gebrochen) vt to
break; (erbrechen) to bring up; **sich**
(dat) **den Arm ~** to break one's arm
▷ vi to break; (erbrechen) to vomit,
to sick; **Brechreiz** m nausea
Brei (-(e)s, -e) m (Breimasse) mush,
pulp; (Haferbrei) porridge; (für

Kinder) pap

breit *adj* wide; *(Schultern)* broad; **zwei Meter ~** two metres wide; **Breite** (-, -*n*) *f* breadth; *(bei Maßangaben)* width; *(Geo)* latitude; **der ~ nach** widthways; **Breitengrad** *m* (degree of) latitude

Bremen (-*s*) *nt* Bremen

Bremsbelag *m* brake lining; **Bremse** (-, -*n*) *f* brake; *(Zool)* horsefly; **bremsen** *vi* to brake ▷ *vt (Auto)* to brake; *(fig)* to slow down; **Bremsflüssigkeit** *f* brake fluid; **Bremslicht** *nt* brake light; **Bremspedal** *nt* brake pedal; **Bremsspur** *f* tyre marks *pl*; **Bremsweg** *m* braking distance

brennen *(brannte, gebrannt) vi* to burn; *(in Flammen stehen)* to be on fire; **es brennt!** fire!; **mir ~ die Augen** my eyes are smarting; **das Licht ~ lassen** to leave the light on; **Brennholz** *nt* firewood; **Brennnessel** *f* stinging nettle; **Brennspiritus** *m* methylated spirits *pl*; **Brennstab** *m* fuel rod; **Brennstoff** *m* fuel

Brett (-*(e)s*, -*er*) *nt* board; *(länger)* plank; *(Regal)* shelf; *(Spielbrett)* board; **Schwarzes ~** notice board, bulletin board *(US)*; **~er** *pl (ski)* skis *pl*; **Brettspiel** *nt* board game

Brezel (-, -*n*) *f* pretzel

Brief (-*(e)s*, -*e*) *m* letter; **Briefbombe** *f* letter bomb; **Brieffreund(in)** *m(f)* penfriend, pen pal; **Briefkasten** *m* letterbox *(Brit)*, mailbox *(US)*; **elektronischer ~** electronic mailbox; **Briefmarke** *f* stamp; **Briefpapier** *nt* writing paper; **Brieftasche** *f* wallet; **Briefträger(in)** *m(f)* postman/-woman; **Briefumschlag** *m* envelope; **Briefwaage** *f* letter scales *pl*

briet *imperf von* **braten**

Brille (-, -*n*) *f* glasses *pl*; *(Schutzbrille)* goggles *pl*; **Brillenetui** *nt* glasses case

bringen *(brachte, gebracht) vt (herbringen)* to bring; *(mitnehmen, vom Sprecher weg)* to take; *(holen, herbringen)* to get, to fetch; *(Theat, Cine)* to show; *(Radio, TV)* to broadcast; **~ Sie mir bitte noch ein Bier** could you bring me another beer, please?; **jdn nach Hause ~** to take sb home; **jdn dazu ~, etw zu tun** to make sb do sth; **jdn auf eine Idee ~** to give sb an idea

Brise (-, -*n*) *f* breeze

Brite (-*n*, -*n*) *m*, **Britin** *f* British person, Briton; **er ist ~** he is British; **die ~n** the British; **britisch** *adj* British

Brocken (-*s*, -) *m* bit; *(größer)* lump, chunk

Brokkoli *m* broccoli

Brombeere *f* blackberry

Bronchitis (-) *f* bronchitis

Bronze (-, -*n*) *f* bronze

Brosche (-, -*n*) *f* brooch

Brot (-*(e)s*, -*e*) *nt* bread; *(Laib)* loaf; **Brotaufstrich** *m* spread; **Brötchen** *nt* roll; **Brotzeit** *f (Pause)* break; *(Essen)* snack; **~ machen** to have a snack

Browser (-*s*, -) *m (Inform)* browser

Bruch (-*(e)s*, *Brüche*) *m (Brechen)* breaking; *(Bruchstelle; mit Partei, Tradition etc)* break; *(Med: Eingeweidebruch)* rupture, hernia; *(Knochenbruch)* fracture; *(Math)* fraction; **brüchig** *adj* brittle

Brücke (-, -*n*) *f* bridge

Bruder (-*s*, *Brüder*) *m* brother

Brühe (-, -*n*) *f (Suppe)* (clear) soup; *(Grundlage)* stock; *(pej: Getränk)* muck; **Brühwürfel** *m* stock cube

brüllen vi to roar; (*Stier*) to bellow; (*vor Schmerzen*) to scream (with pain)

brummen vi (*Bär, Mensch*) to growl; (*brummeln*) to mutter; (*Insekt*) to buzz; (*Motor, Radio*) to drone ▷ vt to growl

brünett adj brunette

Brunnen (-s, -) m fountain; (*tief*) well; (*natürlich*) spring

Brust (-, *Brüste*) f breast; (*beim Mann*) chest; **Brustschwimmen** (-s) nt breaststroke; **Brustwarze** f nipple

brutal adj brutal

brutto adv gross

BSE (-) nt abk = **bovine spongiforme Enzephalopathie** BSE

Bube (-n, -n) m boy, lad; (*Karten*) jack

Buch (-(e)s, *Bücher*) nt book

Buche (-, -n) f beech (tree)

buchen vt to book; (*Betrag*) to enter

Bücherei f library

Buchfink m chaffinch

Buchhalter(in) m(f) accountant

Buchhandlung f bookshop

Büchse (-, -n) f tin (*Brit*), can

Buchstabe (-ns, -n) m letter; **buchstabieren** vt to spell

Bucht (-, -en) f bay

Buchung f booking; (*Comm*) entry

Buckel (-s, -) m hump

bücken vr: **sich ~** to bend down

Buddhismus (-) m Buddhism

Bude (-, -en) f (*auf Markt*) stall; (*fam: Wohnung*) pad, place

Büfett (-s, -s) nt sideboard; **kaltes ~** cold buffet

Büffel (-s, -) m buffalo

Bügel (-s, -) m (*Kleidung*) hanger; (*Steigbügel*) stirrup; (*Brille*) sidepiece; (*von Skilift*) T-bar; **Bügelbrett** nt ironing board;

Bügeleisen nt iron; **Bügelfalte** f crease; **bügelfrei** adj non-iron; **bügeln** vt, vi to iron

buh interj boo

Bühne (-, -n) f stage; **Bühnenbild** nt set

Bulgare (-n, -n) m, **Bulgarin** f Bulgarian; **Bulgarien** (-s) nt Bulgaria; **bulgarisch** adj Bulgarian; **Bulgarisch** nt Bulgarian

Bulimie f bulimia

Bulle (-n, -n) m bull; (*fam: Polizist*) cop

Bummel (-s, -) m stroll; **bummeln** vi to stroll; (*trödeln*) to dawdle; (*faulenzen*) to loaf around; **Bummelzug** m slow train

bums interj bang

bumsen vi (*vulg*) to screw

Bund (-(e)s, *Bünde*) m (*von Hose, Rock*) waistband; (*Freundschaftsbund*) bond; (*Organisation*) association; (*Pol*) confederation; **der ~** (*fam: Bundeswehr*) the army ▷ (-(e)s, -e) nt bunch; (*von Stroh etc*) bundle

Bundes- in zW Federal; (*auf Deutschland bezogen a.*) German; **Bundeskanzler(in)** m(f) Chancellor; **Bundesland** nt state, Land; **Bundesliga** f: **erste/zweite ~** First/Second Division; **Bundespräsident(in)** m(f) President; **Bundesrat** m (*in Deutschland*) Upper House (of the German Parliament); (*in der Schweiz*) Council of Ministers; **Bundesregierung** f Federal Government; **Bundesrepublik** f Federal Republic; **~ Deutschland** Federal Republic of Germany; **Bundesstraße** f ≈ A road (*Brit*), ≈ state highway (*US*); **Bundestag** m Lower House (of the German Parliament); **Bundeswehr** f (German) armed forces pl

● **BUNDESWEHR**
●
● The **Bundeswehr** is the name
● for the German armed forces. It
● was established in 1955, first of
● all for volunteers, but since 1956
● there has been compulsory
● military service for all
● able-bodied young men of 18. In
● peacetime the Defence Minister
● is the head of the 'Bundeswehr',
● but in wartime the
● **Bundeskanzler** takes over. The
● 'Bundeswehr' comes under the
● jurisdiction of NATO.

Bündnis nt alliance
Bungalow (-s, -s) m bungalow
Bungeejumping (-s) nt bungee
  jumping
bunt adj colourful; (von Programm
  etc) varied; **~e Farben** bright
  colours ▷ adv (anstreichen) in
  bright colours; **Buntstift** m
  crayon, coloured pencil
Burg (-, -en) f castle
Bürger(in) (-s, -) m(f) citizen;
  bürgerlich adj (Rechte, Ehe etc)
  civil; (vom Mittelstand)
  middle-class; (pej) bourgeois;
  Bürgermeister(in) m(f) mayor;
  Bürgersteig (-(e)s, -e) m
  pavement (Brit), sidewalk (US)
Büro (-s, -s) nt office;
  Büroklammer f paper clip
Bürokratie f bureaucracy
Bursche (-n, -n) m lad; (Typ) guy
Bürste (-, -n) f brush; **bürsten**
  vt to brush
Bus (-ses, -se) m bus; (Reisebus)
  coach (Brit), bus; **Busbahnhof** m
  bus station
Busch (-(e)s, Büsche) m bush;
  (Strauch) shrub
Busen (-s, -) m breasts pl, bosom
Busfahrer(in) m(f) bus driver;
  Bushaltestelle f bus stop

Businessclass (-) f business
  class
Buslinie f bus route; **Busreise** f
  coach tour (Brit), bus tour
Bußgeld nt fine
Büstenhalter (-s, -) m bra
Busverbindung f bus
  connection
Butter (-) f butter; **Butterbrot**
  nt slice of bread and butter;
  Butterkäse m type of mild, full-fat
  cheese; **Buttermilch** f
  buttermilk; **Butterschmalz** nt
  clarified butter
Button (-s, -s) m badge (Brit),
  button (US)
b. w. abk = **bitte wenden** pto
Byte (-s, -s) nt byte
bzw. adv abk = **beziehungsweise**

C

ca. adv abk = **circa** approx
Cabrio (-s, -s) nt convertible
Café (-s, -s) nt café
Cafeteria (-, -s) f cafeteria
Call-Center (-s, -) nt call centre
campen vi to camp; **Camping** (-s) nt camping; **Campingbus** m camper; **Campingplatz** m campsite, camping ground (US)
Cappuccino (-s, -) m cappuccino
Carving (-s) nt (Ski) carving; **Carvingski** m carving ski
CD (-, -s) f abk = **Compact Disc** CD; **CD-Brenner** (-s, -) m CD burner, CD writer; **CD-Player** (-s, -) m CD player; **CD-ROM** (-, -s) f abk = **Compact Disc Read Only Memory** CD-ROM; **CD-ROM-Laufwerk** nt CD-ROM drive, **CD-Spieler** m CD player
Cello (-s, -s o Celli) nt cello
Celsius nt celsius; **20 Grad ~** 20 degrees Celsius, 68 degrees Fahrenheit
Cent (-, -s) m (von Dollar und Euro) cent
Chamäleon (-s, -s) nt chameleon
Champagner (-s, -) m champagne
Champignon (-s, -s) m mushroom
Champions League (-, -s) f Champions League
Chance (-, -n) f chance; **die ~n stehen gut** the prospects are good
Chaos (-) nt chaos; **Chaot(in)** (-en, -en) m(f) (fam) disorganized person, scatterbrain; **chaotisch** adj chaotic
Charakter (-s, -e) m character; **charakteristisch** adj characteristic (für of)
Charisma (-s, Charismen o Charismata) nt charisma
charmant adj charming
Charterflug m charter flight; **chartern** vt to charter
Chat (-s, -s) m (Inform) chat; **chatten** vi (Inform) to chat
checken vt (überprüfen) to check; (fam: verstehen) to get
Check-in (-s, -s) m check-in; **Check-in-Schalter** m check-in desk
Chef(in) (-s, -s) m(f) boss; **Chefarzt**, **Chefärztin** f senior consultant (Brit), medical director (US)
Chemie (-) f chemistry; **chemisch** adj chemical; **~e Reinigung** dry cleaning
Chemotherapie f chemotherapy
Chicoree (-s) m chicory
Chiffre (-, -n) f (Geheimzeichen) cipher; (in Zeitung) box number
Chile (-s) nt Chile
Chili (-s, -s) m chilli

China (-s) nt China; **Chinakohl**
m Chinese leaves pl (Brit), bok
choy (US); **Chinarestaurant** nt
Chinese restaurant; **Chinese** (-n,
-n) m Chinese; **Chinesin** (-, -nen)
f Chinese (woman); **sie ist ~** she's
Chinese; **chinesisch** adj
Chinese; **Chinesisch** nt Chinese

Chip (-s, -s) m (Inform) chip;
Chipkarte f smart card

Chips pl (Kartoffelchips) crisps pl
(Brit), chips pl (US)

Chirurg(in) (-en, -en) m(f)
surgeon

Chlor (-s) nt chlorine

Choke (-s, -s) m choke

Cholera (-) f cholera

Cholesterin (-s) nt cholesterol

Chor (-(e), Chöre) m choir; (Theat)
chorus

Choreografie f choreography

Christ(in) (-en, -en) m(f)
Christian; **Christbaum** m
Christmas tree; **Christi ·**
Himmelfahrt f the Ascension (of
Christ); **Christkind** nt baby
Jesus; (das Geschenke bringt) ≈
Father Christmas, Santa Claus;
christlich adj Christian

Chrom (-s) nt chrome; (Chem)
chromium

chronisch adj chronic

chronologisch adj chronological ▷ adv in
chronological order

Chrysantheme (-, -n) f
chrysanthemum

circa adv about, approximately

City (-) f city centre, downtown
(US)

Clementine (-, -n) f clementine

clever adj clever, smart

Clique (-, -n) f group; (pej) clique;
David und seine ~ David and his
lot o crowd

Clown (-s, -s) m clown

Club (-s, -s) m club; **Cluburlaub**
m club holiday (Brit), club
vacation (US)

Cocktail (-s, -s) m cocktail;
Cocktailtomate f cherry tomato

Cognac (-s) m cognac

Cola (-, -s) f Coke®, cola

Comic (-s, -s) m comic strip;
(Heft) comic

Compact Disc (-, -s) f compact
disc

Computer (-s, -) m computer;
Computerfreak m computer
nerd; **computergesteuert** adj
computer-controlled; **Computer-**
grafik f computer graphics pl;
computerlesbar adj machine-
readable; **Computerspiel** nt
computer game; **Computer-**
tomografie f computer
tomography, scan; **Computer-**
virus m computer virus

Container (-s, -) m (zum
Transport) container; (für Bauschutt
etc) skip

Control-Taste f control key

Cookie (-s, -s) nt (Inform) cookie

cool adj (fam) cool

Cornflakes pl cornflakes pl

Couch (-, -en) f couch;
Couchtisch m coffee table

Coupé (-s, -s) nt coupé

Coupon (-s, -s) m coupon

Cousin (-s, -s) m cousin; **Cousine**
f cousin

Crack (-s) nt (Droge) crack

Creme (-, -s) f cream; (Gastr)
mousse

Creutzfeld-Jakob-Krankheit f
Creutzfeld-Jakob disease, CJD

Croissant (-s, -s) nt croissant

Curry (-s) m curry powder ▷ (-s)
nt (indisches Gericht) curry;
Currywurst f fried sausage with
ketchup and curry powder

Cursor (-s, -) m (Inform) cursor

Cybercafé nt cybercafé;
Cyberspace (-) m cyberspace

d

even though he has no idea; **ich finde nichts ~** I don't see anything wrong with it; **es bleibt ~** that's settled; **~ sein** (*anwesend*) to be present; (*beteiligt*) to be involved; **ich bin ~!** count me in; **er war gerade ~ zu gehen** he was just (*o* on the point of) leaving

dabei|bleiben *irr vi* to stick with it; **ich bleibe dabei** I'm not changing my mind

dabei|haben *irr vt*: **er hat seine Schwester dabei** he's brought his sister; **ich habe kein Geld dabei** I haven't got any money on me

Dach (*-(e)s, Dächer*) *nt* roof; **Dachboden** *m* attic, loft; **Dachgepäckträger** *m* roofrack; **Dachrinne** *f* gutter

Dachs (*-es, -e*) *m* badger

dachte *imperf von* **denken**

Dackel (*-s, -*) *m* dachshund

dadurch *adv* (*räumlich*) through it; (*durch diesen Umstand*) in that way; (*deshalb*) because of that, for that reason ▷ *conj*: **~, dass** because; **~, dass er hart arbeitete** (*indem*) by working hard

dafür *adv* for it; (*anstatt*) instead; **~ habe ich 50 Euro bezahlt** I paid 50 euros for it; **ich bin ~ zu bleiben** I'm for (*o* in favour of) staying; **~ ist er ja da** that's what he's there for; **er kann nichts ~** he can't help it

dagegen *adv* against it; (*im Vergleich damit*) in comparison; (*bei Tausch*) for it; **ich habe nichts ~** I don't mind

daheim *adv* at home

daher *adv* (*räumlich*) from there; (*Ursache*) that's why ▷ *conj* (*deshalb*) that's why

dahin *adv* (*räumlich*) there; (*zeitlich*) then; (*vergangen*) gone; **bis ~** (*zeitlich*) till then; (*örtlich*) up to there; **bis ~ muss die Arbeit fertig**

da *adv* **1** (*örtlich*) there; (*hier*) here; **da draußen** out there; **da sein** to be there; **da bin ich** here I am; **da, wo** where; **ist noch Milch da?** is there any milk left?
2 (*zeitlich*) then; (*folglich*) so
3 da haben wir Glück gehabt we were lucky there; **da kann man nichts machen** nothing can be done about it
▷ *konj* (*weil*) as, since

dabei *adv* (*räumlich*) close to it; (*zeitlich*) at the same time; (*obwohl, doch*) though; **sie hörte Radio und rauchte ~** she was listening to the radio and smoking (at the same time); **~ fällt mir ein ...** that reminds me ...; **~ kam es zu einem Unfall** this led to an accident; **... und ~ hat er gar keine Ahnung ...**

sein the work must be finished by then

dahinter adv behind it; **~ kommen** to find out

Dahlie f dahlia

Dalmatiner (-s, -) m dalmatian

damals adv at that time, then

Dame (-, -n) f lady; (Karten) queen; (Spiel) draughts sing (Brit), checkers sing (US); **Damenbinde** f sanitary towel (Brit), sanitary napkin (US); **Damenkleidung** f ladies' wear; **Damentoilette** f ladies' toilet (o restroom (US))

damit adv with it; (begründend) by that; **was meint er ~?** what does he mean by that?; **genug ~!** that's enough ▷ conj so that

Damm (-(e)s, Dämme) m dyke; (Staudamm) dam; (am Hafen) mole; (Bahn-, Straßendamm) embankment

Dämmerung f twilight; (am Morgen) dawn; (am Abend) dusk

Dampf (-(e)s, Dämpfe) m steam; (Dunst) vapour; **Dampfbad** nt Turkish bath; **Dampfbügeleisen** nt steam iron; **dampfen** vi to steam

dämpfen vt (Gastr) to steam; (Geräusch) to deaden; (Begeisterung) to dampen

Dampfer (-s, -) m steamer

Dampfkochtopf m pressure cooker

danach adv after that; (zeitlich a.) afterwards; (demgemäß) accordingly; **mir ist nicht ~** I don't feel like it; **~ sieht es aus** that's what it looks like

Däne (-n, -n) m Dane

daneben adv beside it; (im Vergleich) in comparison

Dänemark (-s) nt Denmark; **Dänin** f Dane, Danish woman/girl; **dänisch** adj Danish; **Dänisch** nt Danish

dank prep +dat o gen thanks to; **Dank** (-(e)s) m thanks pl; **vielen ~!** thank you very much; **jdm ~ sagen** to thank sb; **dankbar** adj grateful; (Aufgabe) rewarding; **danke** interj thank you, thanks; **~ schön** (o sehr) thank you very much; **nein ~!** no, thank you; **~, gerne!** yes, please; **~, gleichfalls!** thanks, and the same to you; **danken** vi: **jdm für etw ~** to thank sb for sth; **nichts zu ~!** you're welcome

dann adv then; **bis ~!** see you (later); **~ eben nicht** okay, forget it, suit yourself

daran adv (räumlich) on it; (befestigen) to it; (stoßen) against it; **es liegt ~, dass ...** it's because ...

darauf adv (räumlich) on it; (zielgerichtet) towards it; (danach) afterwards; **es kommt ganz ~ an, ob ...** it all depends whether ...; **ich freue mich ~** I'm looking forward to it; **am Tag ~** the next day; **~ folgend** (Tag, Jahr) next, following

darauffolgend adj (Tag, Jahr) next, following

daraus adv from it; **was ist ~ geworden?** what became of it?

darin adv in it; **das Problem liegt ~, dass ...** the basic problem is that ...

Darlehen (-s, -) nt loan

Darm (-(e)s, Därme) m intestine; (Wurstdarm) skin; **Darmgrippe** f gastroenteritis

dar|stellen vt to represent; (Theat) to play; (beschreiben) to describe; **Darsteller(in)** m(f) actor/actress; **Darstellung** f representation; (Beschreibung) description

darüber adv (räumlich) above it, over it; (fahren) over it; (mehr) more; (*währenddessen*) meanwhile; (*sprechen, streiten, sich freuen*) about it

darum *adv* (*deshalb*) that's why; **es geht ~, dass ...** the point (*o* thing) is that ...

darunter *adv* (*räumlich*) under it; (*dazwischen*) among them; (*weniger*) less; **was verstehen Sie ~?** what do you understand by that?; **~ fallen** to be included

darunterfallen *vi* to be included

das *art* the; **~ Auto da** that car; **er hat sich ~ Bein gebrochen** he's broken his leg; **vier Euro ~ Kilo** four euros a kilo ▷ *pron* that (one), this (one); (*relativ, Sache*) that, which; (*relativ, Person*) who, that; (*demonstrativ*) this/that one; **~ Auto da** that car; **ich nehme ~ da** I'll take that one; **~ Auto, ~ er kaufte** the car (that (*o* which)) he bought; **~ Mädchen, ~ nebenan wohnt** the girl who (*o* that) lives next door; **~ heißt** that is; **~ sind Amerikaner** they're American

da sein *irr vi siehe* **da**

dass *conj* that; **so ~** so that; **es sei denn, ~** unless; **ohne ~ er grüßte** without saying hello

dasselbe *pron* the same

Datei *f* (*Inform*) file; **Dateimanager** *m* file manager

Daten *pl* data *pl*; **Datenbank** *f* database; **Datenmissbrauch** *m* misuse of data; **Datenschutz** *m* data protection; **Datenträger** *m* data carrier; **Datenverarbeitung** *f* data processing

datieren *vt* to date

Dativ *m* dative (case)

Dattel (-, -n) *f* date

Datum (-s, *Daten*) *nt* date

Dauer (-, -n) *f* duration; (*Länge*) length; **auf die ~** in the long run; **für die ~ von zwei Jahren** for (a

period of) two years; **Dauerauftrag** *m* (*Fin*) standing order; **dauerhaft** *adj* lasting; (*Material*) durable; **Dauerkarte** *f* season ticket; **dauern** *vi* to last; (*Zeit benötigen*) to take; **es hat sehr lange gedauert, bis er ...** it took him a long time to ...; **wie lange dauert es denn noch?** how much longer will it be?; **das dauert mir zu lange** I can't wait that long; **dauernd** *adj* lasting; (*ständig*) constant ▷ *adv* always, constantly; **er lachte ~** he kept laughing; **unterbrich mich nicht ~** stop interrupting me; **Dauerwelle** *f* perm (*Brit*), permanent (*US*)

Daumen (-s, -) *m* thumb

Daunendecke *f* eiderdown

davon *adv* of it; (*räumlich*) away; (*weg von*) from it; (*Grund*) because of it; **ich hätte gerne ein Kilo ~** I'd like one kilo of that; **~ habe ich gehört** I've heard of it; (*Geschehen*) I've heard about it; **das kommt ~, wenn ...** that's what happens when ...; **was habe ich ~?** what's the point?; **auf und ~** up and away; **davon|laufen** *irr vi* to run away

davor *adv* (*räumlich*) in front of it; (*zeitlich*) before; **ich habe Angst ~** I'm afraid of it

dazu *adv* (*zusätzlich*) on top of that, as well; (*zu diesem Zweck*) for it, for that purpose; **ich möchte Reis ~** I'd like rice with it; **und ~ noch** and in addition; **~ fähig sein, etw zu tun** to be capable of doing sth; **wie kam es ~?** how did it happen?; **dazu|gehören** *vi* to belong to it; **dazu|kommen** *irr vi* (*zu jdm ~*) to join sb; **kommt noch etwas dazu?** anything else?

dazwischen *adv* in between; (*Unterschied etc*) between them; (*in einer Gruppe*) among them

dazwischen|kommen *irr vi*: **wenn nichts dazwischenkommt** if all goes well; **mir ist etwas dazwischengekommen** something has cropped up

DDR (-) *f abk* = **Deutsche Demokratische Republik** (*Hist*) GDR

dealen *vi* (*fam*: mit Drogen) to deal in drugs; **Dealer(in)** (-s, -) *m(f)* (*fam*) dealer, pusher

Deck (-(e)s, -s o -e) *nt* deck

Decke (-, -n) *f* cover; (*für Bett*) blanket; (*für Tisch*) tablecloth; (*von Zimmer*) ceiling

Deckel (-s, -) *m* lid

decken *vt* to cover; (*Tisch*) to lay, to set ▷ *vr*: **sich ~** (*Interessen*) to coincide; (*Aussagen*) to correspond ▷ *vi* (*den Tisch decken*) to lay (*o* set) the table

Decoder (-s, -) *m* decoder

defekt *adj* faulty; **Defekt** (-(e)s, -e) *m* fault, defect

definieren *vt* to define; **Definition** (-, -en) *f* definition

deftig *adj* (*Preise*) steep; **ein ~es Essen** a good solid meal

dehnbar *adj* flexible, elastic; **dehnen** *vt* to stretch ▷ *vr*: **sich ~** to stretch

Deich (-(e)s, -e) *m* dyke

dein *pron* (*adjektivisch*) your; **deine(r, s)** *pron* (*substantivisch*) yours, of you; **deiner** *pron gen von* **du**; of you; **deinetwegen** *adv* (*wegen dir*) because of you; (*dir zuliebe*) for your sake; (*um dich*) about you

deinstallieren *vt* (*Programm*) to uninstall

Dekolleté (-s, -s) *nt* low neckline

Dekoration *f* decoration; (*in Laden*) window dressing; **dekorativ** *adj* decorative; **dekorieren** *vt* to decorate; (*Schaufenster*) to dress

Delfin (-s, -e) *m* dolphin

delikat *adj* (*lecker*) delicious; (*heikel*) delicate

Delikatesse (-, -n) *f* delicacy

Delle (-, -en) *f* (*fam*) dent

Delphin (-s, -e) *m* dolphin

dem *dat sing von* **der/das**; **wie ~ auch sein mag** be that as it may

demnächst *adv* shortly, soon

Demo (-, -s) *f* (*fam*) demo

Demokratie (-, -n) *f* democracy; **demokratisch** *adj* democratic

demolieren *vt* to demolish

Demonstration *f* demonstration; **demonstrieren** *vt, vi* to demonstrate

den *art akk sing, dat pl von* **der**; **sie hat sich ~ Arm gebrochen** she's broken her arm ▷ *pron* him; (*Sache*) that one; (*relativ: Person*) who, that, whom; (*relativ: Sache*) which, that; **~ hab ich schon ewig nicht mehr gesehen** I haven't seen him in ages ▷ *pron* (*Person*) who, that, whom; (*Sache*) which, that; **der Typ, auf ~ sie steht** the guy (who) she fancies; **der Berg, auf ~ wir geklettert sind** the mountain (that) we climbed

denkbar *adj*: **das ist ~** that's possible ▷ *adv*: **~ einfach** extremely simple; **denken** (*dachte, gedacht*) *vt, vi* to think (*über +akk* about); **an jdn/etw ~** to think of sb/sth; (*sich erinnern, berücksichtigen*) to remember sb/sth; **woran denkst Du?** what are you thinking about?; **denk an den Kaffee!** don't forget the coffee ▷ *vr*: **sich ~** (*sich vorstellen*) to imagine; **das kann ich mir ~** I can (well) imagine

Denkmal (-s, Denkmäler) *nt* monument; **Denkmalschutz** *m* monument preservation; **unter ~ stehen** to be listed

denn *conj* for, because ▷ *adv*

then; (*nach Komparativ*) than; **was ist ~?** what's wrong?; **ist das ~ so schwierig?** is it really that difficult?

dennoch *conj* still, nevertheless

Deo (-s, -s) *nt*, **Deodorant** (-s, -s) *nt* deodorant; **Deoroller** *m* roll-on deodorant; **Deospray** *m o nt* deodorant spray

Deponie (-, -n) *f* waste disposal site, tip

Depressionen *pl*: **an ~ leiden** to suffer from depression *sing*; **deprimieren** *vt* to depress

○ SCHLÜSSELWORT

der (*f* **die**, *nt* **das**, *gen* **des, der, des,** *dat* **dem, der, dem,** *akk* **den, die, das,** *pl* **die**) *def art* the; **der Rhein** the Rhine; **der Klaus** (*fam*) Klaus; **die Frau** (*im Allgemeinen*) women; **der Tod/das Leben** death/life; **der Fuß des Berges** the foot of the hill; **gib es der Frau** give it to the woman; **er hat sich die Hand verletzt** he has hurt his hand

▷ *relativ pron* (*bei Menschen*) who, that; (*bei Tieren, Sachen*) which, that; **der Mann, den ich gesehen habe** the man who *o* whom *o* that I saw

▷ *demonstrativ pron* he/she/it (*jener, dieser*) that; (*pl*) those; **der/die war es** it was him/her; **der mit der Brille** the one with glasses; **ich will den (da)** I want that one

derart *adv* so; (*solcher Art*) such; **derartig** *adj*: **ein ~er Fehler** such a mistake, a mistake like that

deren *gen von* **die** ▷ *pron* (*Person*) her; (*Sache*) its; (*Plural*) their ▷ *pron* (*Person*) whose; (*Sache*) of which; **meine Freundin und ~ Mutter** my friend and her mother; **das sind ~ Sachen** that's their stuff; **die Frau, ~ Tochter ...** the woman whose daughter ...; **ich bin mir ~ bewusst** I'm aware of that

dergleichen *pron*: **und ~ mehr** and the like, and so on; **nichts ~** no such thing

derjenige *pron* the one; **~, der** (*relativ*) the one who (*o* that)

dermaßen *adv* so much; (*mit Adj*) so

derselbe *pron* the same (person/thing)

deshalb *adv* therefore; **~ frage ich ja** that's why I'm asking

Design (-s, -s) *nt* design; **Designer(in)** (-s, -) *m(f)* designer

Desinfektionsmittel *nt* disinfectant; **desinfizieren** *vt* to disinfect

dessen *gen von* **der, das** ▷ *pron* (*Person*) his; (*Sache*) its; **ich bin mir ~ bewusst** I'm aware of that ▷ *pron* (*Person*) whose; (*Sache*) of which; **mein Freund und ~ Mutter** my friend and his mother; **der Mann, ~ Tochter ...** the man whose daughter ...; **ich bin mir ~ bewusst** I'm aware of that

Dessert (-s, -s) *nt* dessert; **zum** (*o* **als**) **~** for dessert

destilliert *adj* distilled

desto *adv*: **je eher, ~ besser** the sooner, the better

deswegen *conj* therefore

Detail (-s, -s) *nt* detail; **ins ~ gehen** to go into detail

Detektiv(in) (-s, -e) *m(f)* detective

deutlich *adj* clear; (*Unterschied*) distinct

deutsch *adj* German; **Deutsch** *nt* German; **auf ~** in German; **ins ~e übersetzen** to translate into German; **Deutsche(r)** *mf*

German; **Deutschland** nt Germany

Devise (-, -n) f motto; **~n** pl (Fin) foreign currency sing; **Devisenkurs** m exchange rate

Dezember (-(s), -) m December; siehe auch **Juni**

dezent adj discreet

d.h. abk von **das heißt** i.e. (gesprochen: i.e. oder that is)

Dia (-s, -s) nt slide

Diabetes (-, -) m (Med) diabetes; **Diabetiker(in)** (-s, -) m(f) diabetic

Diagnose (-, -n) f diagnosis

diagonal adj diagonal

Dialekt (-(e)s, -e) m dialect

Dialog (-(e)s, -e) m dialogue; (Inform) dialog

Dialyse (-, -n) f (Med) dialysis

Diamant m diamond

Diaprojektor m slide projector

Diät (-, -en) f diet; **eine ~ machen** to be on a diet; (anfangen) to go on a diet

dich pron akk von **du** you; **~ (selbst)** (reflexiv) yourself; **pass auf ~ auf** look after yourself; **reg ~ nicht auf** don't get upset

dicht adj dense; (Nebel) thick; (Gewebe) close; (wasserdicht) watertight; (Verkehr) heavy ▷ adv: **~ an/bei** close to; **~ bevölkert** densely populated

Dichter(in) (-s, -) m(f) poet; (Autor) writer

Dichtung f (Auto) gasket; (Dichtungsring) washer; (Gedichte) poetry

Dichtungsring m (Tech) washer

dick adj thick; (Person) fat; **jdn ~ haben** to be sick of sb; **Dickdarm** m colon; **Dickkopf** m stubborn (o pig-headed) person; **Dickmilch** f sour milk

die art the; **~ arme Sarah** poor Sarah ▷ pron (sing, Person, als Subjekt) she; (Person, als Subjekt, Plural) they; (Person, als Objekt) her; (Person, als Objekt, Plural) them; (Sache) that (one), this (one); (Plural) those (ones); (Sache, Plural) those (ones); (relativ, auf Person) who, that; (relativ, auf Sache) which, that; **~ mit den langen Haaren** the one (o her) with the long hair; **sie war ~ erste, ~ es erfuhr** she was the first to know; **ich nehme ~ da** I'll take that one/those ▷ pl von **der, die, das**

Dieb(in) (-(e)s, -e) m(f) thief; **Diebstahl** (-(e)s, Diebstähle) m theft; **Diebstahlsicherung** f burglar alarm

diejenige pron the one; **~, die** (relativ) the one who (o that); **~n** pl those pl, the ones

Diele (-, -n) f hall

Dienst (-(e)s, -e) m service; **außer ~** retired; **~ haben** to be on duty

Dienstag m Tuesday; siehe auch **Mittwoch**; **dienstags** adv on Tuesdays; siehe auch **mittwochs**

Dienstbereitschaft f: **~ haben** (Arzt) to be on call; **diensthabend** adj: **der ~e Arzt** the doctor on duty; **Dienstleistung** f service; **dienstlich** adj official; **er ist ~ unterwegs** he's away on business; **Dienstreise** f business trip; **Dienststelle** f department; **Dienstwagen** m company car; **Dienstzeit** f office hours pl; (Mil) period of service

diesbezüglich adj (formell) on this matter

diese(r, s) pron this (one); pl these; **~ Frau** this woman; **~r Mann** this man; **~s Mädchen** this girl; **~ Leute** these people; **ich nehme ~/~n/~s** (hier) I'll take this one; (dort) I'll take that one; **ich nehme ~** pl (hier) I'll take these (ones); (dort) I'll take those (ones)

Diesel (-s, -) m (Auto) diesel
dieselbe pron the same; **es sind immer ~n** it's always the same people
Dieselmotor m diesel engine; **Dieselöl** nt diesel (oil)
diesig adj hazy, misty
diesmal adv this time
Dietrich (-s, -e) m skeleton key
Differenz (-, -en) f difference
digital adj digital; **Digital-** in zW (Anzeige etc) digital; **Digitalfernsehen** nt digital television, digital TV; **Digitalkamera** f digital camera
Diktat (-(e)s, -e) nt dictation
Diktatur f dictatorship
Dill (-s) m dill
DIN abk = **Deutsche Industrienorm** DIN; **~ A4** A4
Ding (-(e)s, -e) nt thing; **vor allen ~en** above all; **der Stand der ~e** the state of affairs; **das ist nicht mein ~** (fam) it's not my sort of thing (o cup of tea); **Dingsbums** (-) nt (fam) thingy, thingummybob
Dinkel (-s, -) m (Bot) spelt
Dinosaurier (-s, -) m dinosaur
Diphtherie (-, -n) f diphtheria
Diplom (-(e)s, -e) nt diploma
Diplomat(in) (-en, -en) m(f) diplomat
dir pron dat von **du** (to) you; **hat er ~ geholfen?** did he help you?; **ich werde es ~ erklären** I'll explain it to you; (reflexiv) **wasch ~ die Hände** go and wash your hands; **ein Freund von ~** a friend of yours
direkt adj direct; (Frage) straight; **~e Verbindung** through service ▷ adv directly; (sofort) immediately; **~ am Bahnhof** right next to the station; **Direktflug** m direct flight
Direktor(in) m(f) director; (Schule) headmaster/-mistress

(Brit), principal (US)
Direktübertragung f live broadcast
Dirigent(in) m(f) conductor; **dirigieren** vt to direct; (Mus) to conduct
Discman® (-s, -s) m Discman®
Diskette f disk, diskette; **Diskettenlaufwerk** nt disk drive
Diskjockey (-s, -s) m disc jockey; **Disko** (-, -s) f (fam) disco, club; **Diskothek** (-, -en) f discotheque, club
diskret adj discreet
diskriminieren vt to discriminate against
Diskussion f discussion; **diskutieren** vt, vi to discuss
Display (-s, -s) nt display
disqualifizieren vt to disqualify
Distanz f distance
Distel (-, -n) f thistle
Disziplin (-, -en) f discipline
divers adj various
dividieren vt to divide (durch by); **8 dividiert durch 2 ist 4** 8 divided by 2 is 4
DJ (-s, -s) m abk = **Diskjockey** DJ

🔵 **SCHLÜSSELWORT**

doch adv 1 (dennoch) after all; (sowieso) anyway; **er kam doch noch** he came after all; **du weißt es ja doch besser** you know better than I do anyway; **und doch ...** and yet ...
2 (als bejahende Antwort) yes I do/it does etc; **das ist nicht wahr — doch!** that's not true — yes it is!
3 (auffordernd) **komm doch** do come; **lass ihn doch** just leave him; **nicht doch!** oh no!
4 **sie ist doch noch so jung** but she's still so young; **Sie wissen doch, wie das ist** you know how

it is(, don't you?); **wenn doch** if only
▷ *konj (aber)* but; *(trotzdem)* all the same; **und doch hat er es getan** but still he did it

Doktor(in) *m(f)* doctor
Dokument *nt* document;
Dokumentarfilm *m* documentary (film); **dokumentieren** *vt* to document;
Dokumentvorlage *f (Inform)* document template
Dolch *(-(e)s, -e)* *m* dagger
Dollar *(-(s), -s)* *m* dollar
dolmetschen *vt, vi* to interpret;
Dolmetscher(in) *(-s, -)* *m(f)* interpreter
Dolomiten *pl* Dolomites *pl*
Dom *(-(e)s, -e)* *m* cathedral
Domäne *(-, -n)* *f* domain, province; *(Inform: Domain)* domain
Dominikanische Republik *f* Dominican Republic
Domino *(-s, -s)* *nt* dominoes *sing*
Donau *(-)* *f* Danube
Döner *(-s, -s)* *m*, **Döner Kebab** *(-(s), -s)* *m* doner kebab
Donner *(-s, -)* *m* thunder;
donnern *vi*: **es donnert** it's thundering
Donnerstag *m* Thursday; *siehe auch* **Mittwoch**; **donnerstags** *adv* on Thursdays; *siehe auch* **mittwochs**
doof *adj (fam)* stupid
dopen *vt* to dope; **Doping** *(-s)* *nt* doping; **Dopingkontrolle** *f* drugs test
Doppel *(-s, -)* *nt* duplicate; *(Sport)* doubles *sing*; **Doppelbett** *nt* double bed; **Doppeldecker** *m* double-decker; **Doppelhaushälfte** *f* semi-detached house *(Brit)*, duplex *(US)*; **doppelklicken** *vi* to double-click; **Doppelname** *m* double-barrelled name;

Doppelpunkt *m* colon;
Doppelstecker *m* two-way adaptor; **doppelt** *adj* double; **in ~er Ausführung** in duplicate;
Doppelzimmer *nt* double room
Dorf *(-(e)s, Dörfer)* *nt* village
Dorn *(-(e)s, -en)* *m (Bot)* thorn
Dörrobst *nt* dried fruit
Dorsch *(-(e)s, -e)* *m* cod
dort *adv* there; **~ drüben** over there; **dorther** *adv* from there;
dorthin *adv* there
Dose *(-, -n)* *f* box; *(Blechdose)* tin *(Brit)*, can; *(Bierdose)* can
dösen *vi* to doze
Dosenbier *nt* canned beer;
Dosenmilch *f* canned milk, tinned milk *(Brit)*; **Dosenöffner** *m* tin opener *(Brit)*, can opener
Dotter *(-s, -)* *m* (egg) yolk
downloaden *vt* to download
Downsyndrom *(-(e)s, -e)* *nt* *(Med)* Down's syndrome
Dozent(in) *m(f)* lecturer
Dr. *abk* = **Doktor**
Drache *(-n, -n)* *m* dragon;
Drachen *(-s, -)* *m (Spielzeug)* kite; *(Sport)* hang-glider;
Drachenfliegen *(-s)* *nt* hang-gliding; **Drachenflieger(in)** *(-s, -)* *m(f)* hang-glider
Draht *(-(e)s, Drähte)* *m* wire;
Drahtseilbahn *f* cable railway
Drama *(-s, Dramen)* *nt* drama;
dramatisch *adj* dramatic
dran *adv (fam) kontr von* **daran**; **gut ~ sein** *(reich)* to be well-off; *(glücklich)* to be fortunate; *(gesundheitlich)* to be well; **schlecht ~ sein** to be in a bad way; **wer ist ~?** whose turn is it?; **ich bin ~** it's my turn; **bleib ~!** *(Tel)* hang on
drang *imperf von* **dringen**
Drang *(-(e)s, Dränge)* *m (Trieb)* urge *(nach* for); *(Druck)* pressure
drängeln *vt, vi* to push
drängen *vt (schieben)* to push;

(*antreiben*) to urge ▷ *vi* (*eilig sein*)
to be urgent; (*Zeit*) to press; **auf
etw** (*akk*) **~** to press for sth

dran|kommen *irr vi*: **wer
kommt dran?** who's turn is it?,
who's next?

drauf (*fam*) *kontr von* **darauf**;
gut/schlecht ~ sein to be in a
good/bad mood

Draufgänger(in) (*-s, -*) *m(f)*
daredevil

drauf|kommen *irr vi* to
remember; **ich komme nicht
drauf** I can't think of it

drauf|machen *vi* (*fam*) **einen
~** to go on a binge

draußen *adv* outside

Dreck (*-(e)s*) *m* dirt, filth; **dreckig**
adj dirty, filthy

drehen *vt, vi* to turn; (*Zigaretten*)
to roll; (*Film*) to shoot ▷ *vr*: **sich
~** to turn; (*um Achse*) to rotate; **sich
~ um** (*handeln von*) to be about

Drehstrom *m* three-phase
current; **Drehtür** *f* revolving
door; **Drehzahlmesser** *m* rev
counter

drei *num* three; **~ viertel voll**
three-quarters full; **es ist ~ viertel
neun** it's a quarter to nine; **Drei**
(*-, -en*) *f* three; (*Schulnote*) ≈ C;
Dreieck *nt* triangle; **dreieckig**
adj triangular; **dreifach** *adj*
triple ▷ *adv* three times;
dreihundert *num* three hundred;
Dreikönigstag *m* Epiphany;
dreimal *adv* three times; **Dreirad**
nt tricycle; **dreispurig** *adj*
three-lane

dreißig *num* thirty; **dreißigste(r,
s)** *adj* thirtieth; *siehe auch* **dritte**

Dreiviertelstunde *f*: **eine
~** three quarters of an hour

dreizehn *num* thirteen;
dreizehnte(r, s) *adj* thirteenth;
siehe auch **dritte**

dressieren *vt* to train

Dressing (*-s, -s*) *nt* (*salad*)
dressing

Dressman (*-s, Dressmen*) *m* (male)
model

Dressur (*-, -en*) *f* training

drin (*fam*) *kontr von* **darin** in it;
mehr war nicht ~ that was the
best I could do

dringen (*drang, gedrungen*) *vi*
(*Wasser, Licht, Kälte*) to penetrate
(*durch* through, *in +akk* into); **auf
etw** (*akk*) **~** to insist on sth;
dringend, dringlich *adj* urgent

drinnen *adv* inside

dritt *adv*: **wir sind zu ~** there are
three of us; **dritte(r, s)** *adj* third;
die Dritte Welt the Third World; **7.
Juni** 7(th) June (*gesprochen: the
seventh of June*); **am 7. Juni** on 7(th)
June, on June 7(th) (*gesprochen: on
the seventh of June*); **München, den
7. Juni** Munich, June 7(th); **Drittel**
(*-s, -*) *nt* (*Bruchteil*) third; **drittens**
adv thirdly

Droge (*-, -n*) *f* drug;
drogenabhängig, drogensüchtig
adj addicted to drugs

Drogerie *f* chemist's (*Brit*),
drugstore (*US*); **Drogeriemarkt**
m discount chemist's (*Brit*) (*o
drugstore* (*US*))

- **DROGERIE**
-
- The **Drogerie** as opposed to the
- **Apotheke** sells medicines not
- requiring a prescription. It
- tends to be cheaper and also
- sells cosmetics, perfume and
- toiletries.

drohen *vi* to threaten (*jdm* sb);
mit etw ~ to threaten to do sth

dröhnen *vi* (*Motor*) to roar;
(*Stimme, Musik*) to boom; (*Raum*) to
resound

Drohung *f* threat

Drossel (-, -n) f thrush
drüben adv over there; (auf der anderen Seite) on the other side
drüber (fam) kontr von **darüber**
Druck (-(e)s, Drücke) m (Phys) pressure; (fig: Belastung) stress; **jdn unter ~ setzen** to put sb under pressure ▷ (-(e)s, -e) m (Typo: Vorgang) printing; (Produkt, Schriftart) print; **Druckbuchstabe** m block letter; **in ~n schreiben** to print; **drucken** vt, vi to print
drücken vt, vi (Knopf, Hand) to press; (zu eng sein) to pinch; (fig: Preise) to keep down; **jdm etw in die Hand ~** to press sth into sb's hand ▷ vr **sich vor etw** (dat) **~** to get out of sth; **drückend** adj oppressive
Drucker (-s, -) m (Inform) printer; **Druckertreiber** m printer driver
Druckknopf m press stud (Brit), snap fastener (US); **Drucksache** f printed matter; **Druckschrift** f block letters pl
drunten adv down there
drunter (fam) kontr von **darunter**
Drüse (-, -n) f gland
Dschungel (-s, -) m jungle
du pron you; **bist ~ es?** is it you?; **wir sind per ~** we're on first-name terms
Dübel (-s, -) m Rawlplug®
ducken vt to duck ▷ vr: **sich ~** to duck
Dudelsack m bagpipes pl
Duett (-s, -e) nt duet
Duft (-(e)s, Düfte) m scent; **duften** vi to smell nice; **es duftet nach ...** it smells of ...
dulden vt to tolerate
dumm adj stupid; **Dummheit** f stupidity; (Tat) stupid thing; **Dummkopf** m idiot
dumpf adj (Ton) muffled; (Erinnerung) vague; (Schmerz) dull
Düne (-, -n) f dune

Dünger (-s, -) m fertilizer
dunkel adj dark; (Stimme) deep; (Ahnung) vague; (rätselhaft) obscure; (verdächtig) dubious; **im Dunkeln tappen** (fig) to be in the dark; **dunkelblau** adj dark blue; **dunkelblond** adj light brown; **dunkelhaarig** adj dark-haired; **Dunkelheit** f darkness
dünn adj thin; (Kaffee) weak
Dunst (-es, Dünste) m haze; (leichter Nebel) mist; (Chem) vapour
dünsten vt (Gastr) to steam
Duo (-s, -s) nt duo
Dur (-) nt (Mus) major (key); **in G-~** in G major

⬤ SCHLÜSSELWORT

durch prep +akk **1** (hindurch) through; **durch den Urwald** through the jungle; **durch die ganze Welt reisen** to travel all over the world
2 (mittels) through, by (means of); (aufgrund) due to, owing to; **Tod durch Herzschlag/den Strang** death from a heart attack/by hanging; **durch die Post** by post; **durch seine Bemühungen** through his efforts
▷ adv **1** (hindurch) through; **die ganze Nacht durch** all through the night; **den Sommer durch** during the summer; **8 Uhr durch** past 8 o'clock; **durch und durch** completely
2 (durchgebraten etc) **(gut) durch** well-done

durchaus adv absolutely; **~ nicht** not at all
Durchblick m view; **den ~ haben** (fig) to know what's going on; **durch|blicken** vi to look through; (fam: verstehen) to understand (bei etw sth); **etw**

~ lassen (fig) to hint at sth
Durchblutung f circulation
durch|brennen irr vi (Sicherung) to blow; (Draht) to burn through; (fam: davonlaufen) to run away
durchdacht adv: **gut ~** well thought-out
durch|drehen vt (Fleisch) to mince ▷ vi (Räder) to spin; (fam: nervlich) to crack up
durcheinander adv in a mess; (fam: verwirrt) confused; **Durcheinander** (-s) nt (Verwirrung) confusion; (Unordnung) mess; **durcheinander|bringen** irr vt to mess up; (verwirren) to confuse; **durcheinander|reden** vi to talk all at the same time; **durcheinander|trinken** irr vi to mix one's drinks
Durchfahrt f way through; **„~ verboten!"** "no thoroughfare"
Durchfall m (Med) diarrhoea
durch|fallen irr vi to fall through; (in Prüfung) to fail
durch|fragen vr: **sich ~** to ask one's way
durch|führen vt to carry out
Durchgang m passage; (Sport) round; (bei Wahl) ballot; **Durchgangsverkehr** m through traffic
durchgebraten adj well done
durchgefroren adj frozen to the bone
durch|gehen irr vi to go through (durch etw sth); (ausreißen: Pferd) to break loose; (Mensch) to run away; **durchgehend** adj (Zug) through; **~ geöffnet** open all day
durch|halten irr vi to hold out ▷ vt (Tempo) to keep up; **etw ~** (bis zum Schluss) to see sth through
durch|kommen irr vi to get through; (Patient) to pull through

durch|lassen irr vt (jdn) to let through; (Wasser) to let in
durch|lesen irr vt to read through
durchleuchten vt to X-ray
durch|machen vt to go through; (Entwicklung) to undergo; **die Nacht ~** to make a night of it, to have an all-nighter
Durchmesser (-s, -) m diameter
Durchreise f journey through; **auf der ~** passing through; (Güter) in transit; **Durchreisevisum** nt transit visa
durch|reißen irr vt, vi to tear (in two)
durchs kontr von **durch das**
Durchsage (-, -n) f announcement
durchschauen vt (jdn, Lüge) to see through
durch|schlagen irr vr: **sich ~** to struggle through
durch|schneiden irr vt to cut (in two)
Durchschnitt m (Mittelwert) average; **im ~** on average; **durchschnittlich** adj average ▷ adv (im Durchschnitt) on average; **Durchschnittsgeschwindigkeit** f average speed
durch|setzen vt to get through ▷ vr: **sich ~** (Erfolg haben) to succeed; (sich behaupten) to get one's way
durchsichtig adj transparent, see-through
durch|stellen vt (Tel) to put through
durch|streichen irr vt to cross out
durchsuchen vt to search (nach for); **Durchsuchung** f search
durchwachsen adj (Speck) streaky; (fig: mittelmäßig) so-so
Durchwahl f direct dialling; (Nummer) extension

durch|ziehen *irr vt* (*Plan*) to
carry through
Durchzug *m* draught

O SCHLÜSSELWORT

dürfen *unreg vi* **1** (*Erlaubnis haben*)
to be allowed to; **ich darf das** I'm
allowed to (do that); **darf ich?** may
I?; **darf ich ins Kino?** can o may I
go to the cinema?; **es darf
geraucht werden** you may smoke
2 (*in Verneinungen*) **er darf das
nicht** he's not allowed to (do that);
das darf nicht geschehen that
must not happen; **da darf sie sich
nicht wundern** that shouldn't
surprise her
3 (*in Höflichkeitsformeln*) **darf ich
Sie bitten, das zu tun?** may o
could I ask you to do that?; **was
darf es sein?** what can I do for
you?
4 (*können*) **das dürfen Sie mir
glauben** you can believe me
5 (*Möglichkeit*) **das dürfte genug
sein** that should be enough; **es
dürfte Ihnen bekannt sein,
dass ...** as you will probably
know ...

dürftig *adj* (*ärmlich*) poor;
(*unzulänglich*) inadequate
dürr *adj* dried-up; (*Land*) arid;
(*mager*) skinny
Durst (-*(e)s*) *m* thirst; **~ haben** to
be thirsty; **durstig** *adj* thirsty
Dusche (-, -*n*) *f* shower; **duschen**
vi to have a shower ▷ *vr*: **sich ~** to
have a shower; **Duschgel** *nt*
shower gel; **Duschvorhang** *m*
shower curtain
Düse (-, -*n*) *f* nozzle; (*Tech*) jet;
Düsenflugzeug *nt* jet (aircraft)
Dussel (-*s*, -) *m* (*fam*) dope;
duss(e)lig *adj* (*fam*) stupid

düster *adj* dark; (*Gedanken,
Zukunft*) gloomy
Dutyfreeshop (-*s*, -*s*) *m* duty-
-free shop
Dutzend (-*s*, -*e*) *nt* dozen
duzen *vt to address as "du"* ▷ *vr*:
sich ~ (**mit jdm**) *to address each
other as "du"*, to be on first-name
terms
DVD (-, -*s*) *f abk =* **Digital
Versatile Disk** DVD; **DVD-Player**
(-*s*, -) *m* DVD player;
DVD-Rekorder (-*s*, -) *m* DVD
recorder
dynamisch *adj* dynamic
Dynamo (-*s*, -*s*) *m* dynamo
D-Zug *m* fast train

e

Ebbe (-, -n) *f* low tide
eben *adj* level; (*glatt*) smooth
▷ *adv* just; (*bestätigend*) exactly
Ebene (-, -n) *f* plain; (*fig*) level
ebenfalls *adv* also, as well;
(*Antwort: gleichfalls!*) you too;
ebenso *adv* just as; **~ gut** just as
well; **~ viel** just as much
Eber (-s, -) *m* boar
EC (-, -s) *m abk* = **Eurocityzug**
Echo (-s, -s) *nt* echo
echt *adj* (*Leder, Gold*) real, genuine;
ein ~er Verlust a real loss
EC-Karte *f* ≈ debit card
Ecke (-, -n) *f* corner; (*Math*) angle;
an der ~ at the corner; **gleich um
die ~** just round the corner; **eckig**
adj rectangular; **Eckzahn** *m*
canine
Economyclass (-) *f* coach
(class), economy class
Ecstasy (-) *f* (*Droge*) ecstasy
edel *adj* noble; **Edelstein** *m*
precious stone
EDV (-) *f abk* = **elektronische
Datenverarbeitung** EDP
Efeu (-s) *m* ivy
Effekt (-s, -e) *m* effect
egal *adj*: **das ist ~** it doesn't
matter; **das ist mir ~** I don't care,
it's all the same to me; **~ wie teuer**
no matter how expensive
egoistisch *adj* selfish
ehe *conj* before
Ehe (-, -n) *f* marriage; **Ehefrau** *f*
wife; (*verheiratete Frau*) married
woman; **Eheleute** *pl* married
couple *sing*
ehemalig *adj* former; **ehemals**
adv formerly
Ehemann *m* husband;
(*verheirateter Mann*) married man;
Ehepaar *nt* married couple
eher *adv* (*früher*) sooner; (*lieber*)
rather, sooner; (*mehr*) more; **je ~,
desto besser** the sooner the
better
Ehering *m* wedding ring
eheste(r, s) *adj* (*früheste*) first
▷ *adv*: **am ~n** (*am
wahrscheinlichsten*) most likely
Ehre (-, -n) *f* honour; **ehren** *vt*
to honour; **ehrenamtlich** *adj*
voluntary; **Ehrengast** *m* guest
of honour; **Ehrenwort** *nt* word
of honour; **~!** I promise; **ich gebe
dir mein ~** I give you my word
ehrgeizig *adj* ambitious
ehrlich *adj* honest
Ei (-(e)s, -er) *nt* egg; **hart
gekochtes/weiches
~** hard-boiled/soft-boiled egg
Eiche (-, -n) *f* oak (tree); **Eichel**
(-, -n) *f* acorn
Eichhörnchen *nt* squirrel
Eid (-(e)s, -e) *m* oath
Eidechse (-, -n) *f* lizard
Eierbecher *m* eggcup; **Eierstock**
m ovary; **Eieruhr** *f* egg timer
Eifersucht *f* jealousy;

eifersüchtig *adj* jealous (*auf +akk* of)

Eigelb (-(e)s, -) *nt* egg yolk

eigen *adj* own; (*typisch*) characteristic (*jdm* of sb); (*eigenartig*) peculiar; **eigenartig** *adj* peculiar; **Eigenschaft** *f* quality; (*Chem, Phys*) property; (*Merkmal*) characteristic

eigentlich *adj* actual, real ▷ *adv* actually, really; **was denken Sie sich ~ dabei?** what on earth do you think you're doing?

Eigentum *nt* property; **Eigentümer(in)** *m(f)* owner; **Eigentumswohnung** *f* owner-occupied flat (*Brit*), condominium (*US*)

eignen *vr*: **sich ~ für** to be suited for; **er würde sich als Lehrer ~** he'd make a good teacher

Eilbrief *m* express letter, special-delivery letter; **Eile** (-) *f* hurry; **eilen** *vi* (*dringend sein*) to be urgent; **es eilt nicht** there's no hurry; **eilig** *adj* hurried; (*dringlich*) urgent; **es ~ haben** to be in a hurry

Eimer (-s, -) *m* bucket

ein *adv*: **nicht ~ noch aus wissen** not to know what to do; **~ - aus** (*Schalter*) on - off

ein(e) *art* a; (*vor gesprochenem Vokal*) an; **~ Mann** a man; **~ Apfel** an apple; **~e Stunde** an hour; **~ Haus** a house; **~ (gewisser) Herr Miller** a (certain) Mr Miller; **~es Tages** one day

einander *pron* one another, each other

ein|arbeiten *vt* to train ▷ *vr*: **sich ~** to get used to the work

ein|atmen *vt, vi* to breathe in

Einbahnstraße *f* one-way street

ein|bauen *vt* to build in; (*Motor etc*) to install, to fit; **Einbauküche** *f* fitted kitchen

ein|biegen *irr vi* to turn (*in +akk* into)

ein|bilden *vt* **sich** (*dat*) **etw ~** to imagine sth

ein|brechen *irr vi* (*in Haus*) to break in; (*Dach etc*) to fall in, to collapse; **Einbrecher(in)** (-s, -) *m(f)* burglar

ein|bringen *irr vt* (*Ernte*) to bring in; (*Gewinn*) to yield; **jdm etw ~** to bring (*o earn*) sb sth ▷ *vr* **sich in** (*akk*) **etw ~** to make a contribution to sth

Einbruch *m* (*Haus*) break-in, burglary; **bei ~ der Nacht** at nightfall

Einbürgerung *f* naturalization

ein|checken *vt* to check in

ein|cremen *vt* to put some cream on ▷ *vr*: **sich ~** to put some cream on

eindeutig *adj* clear, obvious ▷ *adv* clearly; **~ falsch** clearly wrong

ein|dringen *irr vi* (*gewaltsam*) to force one's way in (*in +akk* -to); (*in Haus*) to break in (*in +akk* -to); (*Gas, Wasser*) to get in (*in +akk* -to)

Eindruck *m* impression; **großen ~ auf jdn machen** to make a big impression on sb

eine(r, s) *pron* one; (*jemand*) someone; **~r meiner Freunde** one of my friends; **~r nach dem andern** one after the other

eineiig *adj* (*Zwillinge*) identical

eineinhalb *num* one and a half

einerseits *adv* on the one hand

einfach *adj* (*nicht kompliziert*) simple; (*Mensch*) ordinary; (*Essen*) plain; (*nicht mehrfach*) single; **~e Fahrkarte** single ticket (*Brit*), one-way ticket (*US*) ▷ *adv* simply; (*nicht mehrfach*) once

Einfahrt *f* (*Vorgang*) driving in; (*eines Zuges*) arrival; (*Ort*) entrance

Einfall m (*Idee*) idea; **ein|fallen** *irr*
vi (*Licht etc*) to fall in; (*einstürzen*)
to collapse; **ihm fiel ein, dass ...** it
occurred to him that ...; **ich werde
mir etwas ~ lassen** I'll think of
something; **was fällt Ihnen ein!**
what do you think you're doing?
Einfamilienhaus nt detached
house
einfarbig adj all one colour; (*Stoff
etc*) self-coloured
Einfluss m influence
ein|frieren *irr* vt, vi to freeze
ein|fügen vt to fit in; (*zusätzlich*)
to add; (*Inform*) to insert;
Einfügetaste f (*Inform*) insert key
Einfuhr (-, -en) f import;
Einfuhrbestimmungen pl import
regulations pl
ein|führen vt to introduce;
(*Ware*) to import; **Einführung** f
introduction
Eingabe f (*Dateneingabe*) input;
Eingabetaste f (*Inform*) return (*o*
enter) key
Eingang m entrance;
Eingangshalle f entrance hall,
lobby (*US*)
ein|geben *irr* vt (*Daten etc*) to
enter, to key in
eingebildet adj imaginary; (*eitel*)
arrogant
Eingeborene(r) mf native
ein|gehen *irr* vi (*Sendung, Geld*) to
come in, to arrive; (*Tier, Pflanze*) to
die; (*Stoff*) to shrink; **auf etw** (*akk*)
~ to agree to sth; **auf jdn ~** to
respond to sb ▷ vt (*Vertrag*) to
enter into; (*Wette*) to make; (*Risiko*)
to take
eingelegt adj (*in Essig*) pickled
eingeschaltet adj (switched) on
eingeschlossen adj locked in;
(*inklusive*) included
ein|gewöhnen vr: **sich ~** to
settle in
ein|gießen *irr* vt to pour

ein|greifen *irr* vi to intervene;
Eingriff m intervention;
(*Operation*) operation
ein|halten *irr* vt (*Versprechen etc*)
to keep
einheimisch adj (*Produkt,
Mannschaft*) local; **Einheimische(r)**
mf local
Einheit f (*Geschlossenheit*) unity;
(*Maß*) unit; **einheitlich** adj
uniform
ein|holen vt (*Vorsprung aufholen*)
to catch up with; (*Verspätung*) to
make up for; (*Rat, Erlaubnis*) to ask
for
Einhorn nt unicorn
einhundert num one (*o* a)
hundred
einig adj (*vereint*) united; **sich**
(*dat*) **~ sein** to agree
einige pron pl some; (*mehrere*)
several ▷ adj some; **nach ~er Zeit**
after some time; **~e hundert Euro**
some hundred euros
einigen vr: **sich ~** to agree (*auf*
+*akk* on)
einigermaßen adv fairly, quite;
(*leidlich*) reasonably
einiges pron something; (*ziemlich
viel*) quite a bit; (*mehreres*) a few
things; **es gibt noch ~ zu tun**
there's still a fair bit to do
Einkauf m purchase; **Einkäufe**
(**machen**) (to do one's) shopping;
ein|kaufen vt to buy ▷ vi to go
shopping; **Einkaufsbummel** m
shopping trip; **Einkaufstasche** f,
Einkaufstüte f shopping bag;
Einkaufswagen m shopping
trolley (*Brit*) (*o* cart (*US*));
Einkaufszentrum nt shopping
centre (*Brit*) (*o* mall (*US*))
ein|klemmen vt to jam; **er hat
sich** (*dat*) **den Finger
eingeklemmt** he got his finger
caught
Einkommen (-s, -) nt income

ein|laden irr vt (jdn) to invite; (Gegenstände) to load; **jdn zum Essen ~** to take sb out for a meal; **ich lade dich ein** (bezahle) it's my treat; **Einladung** f invitation

Einlass (-es, Einlässe) m admittance; **~ ab 18 Uhr** doors open at 6 pm; **ein|lassen** irr vr **sich mit jdm/auf etw** (akk) **~ to** get involved with sb/sth

ein|leben vr: **sich ~** to settle down

ein|legen vt (Film etc) to put in; (marinieren) to marinate; **eine Pause ~** to take a break

ein|leiten vt to start; (Maßnahmen) to introduce; (Geburt) to induce; **Einleitung** f introduction; (von Geburt) induction

ein|leuchten vi: **jdm ~** to be (o become) clear to sb; **einleuchtend** adj clear

ein|loggen vi (Inform) to log on (o in)

ein|lösen vt (Scheck) to cash; (Gutschein) to redeem; (Versprechen) to keep

einmal adv once; (früher) before; (in Zukunft) some day; (erstens) first; **~ im Jahr** once a year; **noch ~** once more, again; **ich war schon ~ hier** I've been here before; **warst du schon ~ in London?** have you ever been to London?; **nicht ~** not even; **auf ~** suddenly; (gleichzeitig) at once; **einmalig** adj unique; (einmal geschehend) single; (prima) fantastic

ein|mischen vr: **sich ~** to interfere (in +akk with)

Einnahme (-, -n) f (Geld) takings pl; (von Medizin) taking; **ein|nehmen** irr vt (Medizin) to take; (Geld) to take in; (Standpunkt, Raum) to take up; **jdn für sich ~** to win sb over

ein|ordnen vt to put in order; (klassifizieren) to classify; (Akten) to file ▷ vr: **sich ~** (Auto) to get in lane; **sich rechts/links ~** to get into the right/left lane

ein|packen vt to pack (up)

ein|parken vt, vi to park

ein|planen vt to allow for

ein|prägen vt **sich** (dat) **etw ~** to remember (o memorize) sth

ein|räumen vt (Bücher, Geschirr) to put away; (Schrank) to put things in

ein|reden vt: **jdm/sich etw ~** to talk sb/oneself into (believing) sth

ein|reiben irr vt: **sich mit etw ~** to rub sth into one's skin

ein|reichen vt to hand in; (Antrag) to submit

Einreise f entry; **Einreisebestimmungen** pl entry regulations pl; **Einreiseerlaubnis** f, **Einreisegenehmigung** f entry permit; **ein|reisen** vi to enter (in ein Land a country); **Einreisevisum** nt entry visa

ein|renken vt (Arm, Bein) to set

ein|richten vt (Wohnung) to furnish; (gründen) to establish, to set up; (arrangieren) to arrange ▷ vr: **sich ~** (in Haus) to furnish one's home; (sich vorbereiten) to prepare oneself (auf +akk for); (sich anpassen) to adapt (auf +akk to); **Einrichtung** f (Wohnung) furnishings pl; (öffentliche Anstalt) institution; (Schwimmbad etc) facility

eins num one; **Eins** (-, -en) f one; (Schulnote) ≈ A

einsam adj lonely

ein|sammeln vt to collect

Einsatz m (Teil) insert; (Verwendung) use; (Spieleinsatz) stake; (Risiko) risk; (Mus) entry

ein|schalten vt (Elek) to switch on

ein|schätzen vt to estimate, to assess

ein|schenken vt to pour

ein|schiffen vr: **sich ~** to embark (*nach* for)

ein|schlafen irr vi to fall asleep, to drop off; **mir ist der Arm eingeschlafen** my arm's gone to sleep

ein|schlagen irr vt (*Fenster*) to smash; (*Zähne, Schädel*) to smash in; (*Weg, Richtung*) to take ▷ vi to hit (*in etw akk* sth, *auf jdn* sb); (*Blitz*) to strike; (*Anklang finden*) to be a success

ein|schließen irr vt (*jdn*) to lock in; (*Gegenstand*) to lock away; (*umgeben*) to surround; (*fig: beinhalten*) to include;
einschließlich adv inclusive ▷ prep +gen including; **von Montag bis ~ Freitag** from Monday up to and including Friday, Monday through Friday (US)

ein|schränken vt to limit, to restrict; (*verringern*) to cut down on ▷ vr: **sich ~** to cut down (on expenditure)

ein|schreiben irr vr: **sich ~** to register; (*Schule*) to enrol; **Einschreiben** (*-s, -*) nt registered letter; **etw per ~ schicken** to send sth by special delivery

ein|schüchtern vt to intimidate

ein|sehen irr vt (*verstehen*) to see; (*Fehler*) to recognize; (*Akten*) to have a look at

einseitig adj one-sided

ein|senden irr vt to send in

ein|setzen vt to put in; (*in Amt*) to appoint; (*Geld*) to stake; (*verwenden*) to use ▷ vi (*beginnen*) to set in; (*Mus*) to enter, to come in ▷ vr: **sich ~** to work hard; **sich für jdn/etw ~** to support sb/sth

Einsicht f insight; **zu der**

~ kommen, dass ... to come to realize that ...

ein|sperren vt to lock up

ein|spielen vt (*Geld*) to bring in

ein|springen irr vi (*aushelfen*) to step in (*für* for)

Einspruch m objection (*gegen* to)

einspurig adj single-lane

Einstand m (*Tennis*) deuce

ein|stecken vt to pocket; (*Elek: Stecker*) to plug in; (*Brief*) to post, to mail (US); (*mitnehmen*) to take; (*hinnehmen*) to swallow

ein|steigen irr vi (*in Auto*) to get in; (*in Bus, Zug, Flugzeug*) to get on; (*sich beteiligen*) to get involved

ein|stellen vt (*beenden*) to stop; (*Geräte*) to adjust; (*Kamera*) to focus; (*Sender, Radio*) to tune in; (*unterstellen*) to put; (*in Firma*) to employ, to take on ▷ vr: **sich auf jdn/etw ~** to adapt to sb/prepare oneself for sth; **Einstellung** f (*von Gerät*) adjustment; (*von Kamera*) focusing; (*von Arbeiter*) taking on; (*Meinung*) attitude

ein|stürzen vi to collapse

eintägig adj one-day

ein|tauschen vt to exchange (*gegen* for)

eintausend num one (*o a*) thousand

ein|teilen vt (*in Teile*) to divide (up) (*in +akk* into); (*Zeit*) to organize

eintönig adj monotonous

Eintopf m stew

ein|tragen irr vt (*in eine Liste*) to put down, to enter ▷ vr: **sich ~** to put one's name down, to register

ein|treffen irr vi to happen; (*ankommen*) to arrive

ein|treten irr vi (*hineingehen*) to enter (*in etw akk* sth); (*in Klub, Partei*) to join (*in etw akk* sth); (*sich ereignen*) to occur; **~ für** to support; **Eintritt** m admission; **„~ frei"**

"admission free"; **Eintrittskarte** f (entrance) ticket; **Eintrittspreis** m admission charge

einverstanden interj okay, all right ▷ adj: **mit etwas ~ sein** to agree to sth, to accept sth

Einwanderer m, **Einwanderin** f immigrant; **ein|wandern** vi to immigrate

einwandfrei adj perfect, flawless

Einwegflasche f non-returnable bottle

ein|weichen vt to soak

ein|weihen vt (Gebäude) to inaugurate, to open; **jdn in etw** (akk) **~** to let sb in on sth; **Einweihungsparty** f house-warming party

ein|werfen irr vt (Ball, Bemerkung etc) to throw in; (Brief) to post, to mail (US); (Geld) to put in, to insert; (Fenster) to smash

ein|wickeln vt to wrap up; (fig) **jdn ~** to take sb in

Einwohner(in) (-s, -) m(f) inhabitant; **Einwohnermeldeamt** nt registration office for residents

Einwurf m (Öffnung) slot; (Sport) throw-in

Einzahl f singular

ein|zahlen vt to pay in (auf ein Konto -to an account)

Einzel (-s, -) nt (Tennis) singles sing; **Einzelbett** nt single bed; **Einzelfahrschein** m single ticket (Brit), one-way ticket (US); **Einzelgänger(in)** m(f) loner; **Einzelhandel** m retail trade; **Einzelkind** nt only child

einzeln adj individual; (getrennt) separate; (einzig) single; **~e ...** several ..., some ...; **der/die Einzelne** the individual; **im Einzelnen** in detail ▷ adv separately; (verpacken, aufführen) individually; **~ angeben** to specify; **~ eintreten** to enter one

by one

Einzelzimmer nt single room; **Einzelzimmerzuschlag** m single-room supplement

ein|ziehen irr vt: **den Kopf ~** to duck ▷ vi (in ein Haus) to move in

einzig adj only; (einzeln) single; (einzigartig) unique; **kein ~er Fehler** not a single mistake; **das Einzige** the only thing; **der/die Einzige** the only person ▷ adv only; **die ~ richtige Lösung** the only correct solution; **einzigartig** adj unique

Eis (-es, -) nt ice; (Speiseeis) ice-cream; **Eisbahn** f ice(skating) rink; **Eisbär** m polar bear; **Eisbecher** m (ice-cream) sundae; **Eisberg** m iceberg; **Eisbergsalat** m iceberg lettuce; **Eiscafé** nt, **Eisdiele** f ice-cream parlour

Eisen (-s, -) nt iron; **Eisenbahn** f railway (Brit), railroad (US); **eisern** adj iron

eisgekühlt adj chilled; **Eishockey** nt ice hockey; **Eiskaffee** m iced coffee; **eiskalt** adj ice-cold; (Temperatur) freezing; **Eiskunstlauf** m figure skating; **eis|laufen** irr vi to skate; **Eisschokolade** f iced chocolate; **Eisschrank** m fridge, ice-box (US); **Eistee** m iced tea; **Eiswürfel** m ice cube; **Eiszapfen** m icicle

eitel adj vain

Eiter (-s) m pus

Eiweiß (-es, -e) nt egg white; (Chem, Bio) protein

ekelhaft, **ek(e)lig** adj disgusting, revolting; **ekeln** vr: **sich ~** to be disgusted (vor +dat at)

EKG (-s, -s) nt abk = **Elektrokardiogramm** ECG

Ekzem (-s, -e) nt (Med) eczema

elastisch adj elastic

Elch (-(e)s, -e) m elk; (nordamerikanischer) moose
Elefant m elephant
elegant adj elegant
Elektriker(in) (-s, -) m(f) electrician; **elektrisch** adj electric; **Elektrizität** f electricity; **Elektroauto** nt electric car; **Elektrogerät** nt electrical appliance; **Elektrogeschäft** nt electrical shop; **Elektroherd** m electric cooker; **Elektromotor** m electric motor; **Elektronik** f electronics sing; **elektronisch** adj electronic; **Elektrorasierer** (-s, -) m electric razor
Element (-s, -e) nt element
elend adj miserable; **Elend** (-(e)s) nt misery
elf num eleven; **Elf** (-, -en) f (Sport) eleven
Elfenbein nt ivory
Elfmeter m (Sport) penalty (kick)
elfte(r, s) adj eleventh; siehe auch **dritte**
Ell(en)bogen m elbow
Elster (-, -n) f magpie
Eltern pl parents pl; **Elternteil** m parent
EM f abk = **Europameisterschaft** European Championship(s)
E-Mail (-, -s) f (Inform) e-mail; **jdm eine ~ schicken** to e-mail sb, to send sb an e-mail; **jdm etwas per ~ schicken** to e-mail sth to sb; **E-Mail-Adresse** f e-mail address; **e-mailen** vt to e-mail
Emoticon (-s, -s) nt emoticon
emotional adj emotional
empfahl imperf von **empfehlen**
empfand imperf von **empfinden**
Empfang (-(e)s, Empfänge) m reception; (Erhalten) receipt; **in ~ nehmen** to receive; **empfangen** (empfing, empfangen) vt to receive; **Empfänger(in)** (-s, -) m(f) recipient; (Adressat) addressee ▷ m

(Tech) receiver; **Empfängnisverhütung** f contraception; **Empfangshalle** f reception area
empfehlen (empfahl, empfohlen) vt to recommend; **Empfehlung** f recommendation
empfinden (empfand, empfunden) vt to feel; **empfindlich** adj (Mensch) sensitive; (Stelle) sore; (reizbar) touchy; (Material) delicate
empfing imperf von **empfangen**
empfohlen pp von **empfehlen**
empfunden pp von **empfinden**
empört adj indignant (über +akk at)
Ende (-s, -n) nt end; (Film, Roman) ending; **am ~** at the end; (schließlich) in the end; **~ Mai** at the end of May; **~ der Achtzigerjahre** in the late eighties; **sie ist ~ zwanzig** she's in her late twenties; **zu ~** over, finished; **enden** vi to end; **der Zug endet hier** this service (o train) terminates here; **endgültig** adj final; (Beweis) conclusive
Endivie f endive
endlich adv at last, finally; (am Ende) eventually; **Endspiel** nt final; (Endrunde) finals pl; **Endstation** f terminus; **Endung** f ending
Energie f energy; **~ sparend** energy-saving; **Energiebedarf** m energy requirement; **Energieverbrauch** m energy consumption
energisch adj (entschlossen) forceful
eng adj narrow; (Kleidung) tight; (fig: Freundschaft, Verhältnis) close; **das wird ~** (fam: zeitlich) we're running out of time, it's getting tight ▷ adv: **~ befreundet sein** to be close friends
engagieren vt to engage ▷ vr: **sich ~** to commit oneself, to be

committed (*für* to)

Engel (-s, -) *m* angel

England *nt* England;
Engländer(in) (-s, -) *m(f)*
Englishman/ -woman; **die ~** *pl* the
English *pl*; **englisch** *adj* English;
(*Gastr*) rare; **Englisch** *nt* English;
ins ~e übersetzen to translate
into English

Enkel (-s, -) *m* grandson; **Enkelin**
f granddaughter

enorm *adj* enormous; (*fig*)
tremendous

Entbindung *f* (*Med*) delivery

entdecken *vt* to discover;
Entdeckung *f* discovery

Ente (-, -n) *f* duck

Enter-Taste *f* (*Inform*) enter (*o*
return) key

entfernen *vt* to remove; (*Inform*)
to delete ▷ *vr*: **sich ~** to go away;
entfernt *adj* distant; **15 km von X
~** 15 km away from X; **20 km
voneinander ~** 20 km apart;
Entfernung *f* distance; **aus der
~** from a distance

entführen *vt* to kidnap;
Entführer(in) *m(f)* kidnapper;
Entführung *f* kidnapping

entgegen *prep* +dat contrary to
▷ *adv* towards; **dem Wind
~** against the wind;
entgegengesetzt *adj* (*Richtung*)
opposite; (*Meinung*) opposing;
entgegen|kommen *irr vi*: **jdm
~** to come to meet sb; (*fig*) to
accommodate sb;
entgegenkommend *adj* (*Verkehr*)
oncoming; (*fig*) obliging

entgegnen *vt* to reply (*auf* +akk
to)

entgehen *irr vi*: **jdm ~** to escape
sb's notice; **sich** (*dat*) **etw ~ lassen**
to miss sth

entgleisen *vi* (*Eisenb*) to be
derailed; (*fig: Mensch*) to
misbehave

Enthaarungscreme *f* hair
remover

enthalten *irr vt* (*Behälter*) to
contain; (*Preis*) to include ▷ *vr*:
sich ~ to abstain (*gen* from)

entkoffeiniert *adj*
decaffeinated

entkommen *irr vi* to escape

entkorken *vt* to uncork

entlang *prep* +akk o dat **~ dem
Fluss, den Fluss ~** along the river;
entlang|gehen *irr vi* to walk
along

entlassen *irr vt* (*Patient*) to
discharge; (*Arbeiter*) to dismiss

entlasten *vt*: **jdn ~** (*Arbeit
abnehmen*) to relieve sb of some of
his/her work

entmutigen *vt* to discourage

entnehmen *vt* to take (*dat* from)

entrahmt *adj* (*Milch*) skimmed

entschädigen *vt* to
compensate; **Entschädigung** *f*
compensation

entscheiden *irr vt, vi* to decide
▷ *vr*: **sich ~** to decide; **sich
für/gegen etw ~** to decide
on/against sth; **wir haben uns
entschieden, nicht zu gehen** we
decided not to go; **das
entscheidet sich morgen** that'll
be decided tomorrow;
entscheidend *adj* decisive;
(*Stimme*) casting; (*Frage, Problem*)
crucial; **Entscheidung** *f*
decision

entschließen *irr vr*: **sich ~** to
decide (*zu, für* on), to make up
one's mind; **Entschluss** *m*
decision

entschuldigen *vt* to excuse
▷ *vr*: **sich ~** to apologize; **sich bei
jdm für etw ~** to apologize to sb
for sth ▷ *vi*: **entschuldige!, ~ Sie!**
(*vor einer Frage*) excuse me;
(*Verzeihung!*) (I'm) sorry, excuse me
(*US*); **Entschuldigung** *f* apology;

(*Grund*) excuse; **jdn um ~ bitten** to apologize to sb; **~!** (*bei Zusammenstoß*) (I'm) sorry, excuse me (*US*); (*vor einer Frage*) excuse me; (*wenn man etw nicht verstanden hat*) (I beg your) pardon?

entsetzlich *adj* dreadful, appalling

entsorgen *vt* to dispose of

entspannen *vt* (*Körper*) to relax; (*Pol: Lage*) to ease ▷ *vr*: **sich ~** to relax; (*fam*) to chill out; **Entspannung** *f* relaxation

entsprechen *irr vi +dat* to correspond to; (*Anforderungen, Wünschen etc*) to comply with; **entsprechend** *adj* appropriate ▷ *adv* accordingly ▷ *prep +dat* according to, in accordance with

entstehen *vi* (*Schwierigkeiten*) to arise; (*gebaut werden*) to be built; (*hergestellt werden*) to be created

enttäuschen *vt* to disappoint; **Enttäuschung** *f* disappointment

entweder *conj*: **~ ... oder ...** either ... or ...; **~ oder!** take it or leave it

entwerfen *irr vt* (*Möbel, Kleider*) to design; (*Plan, Vertrag*) to draft

entwerten *vt* to devalue; (*Fahrschein*) to cancel; **Entwerter** (*-s, -*) *m* ticket-cancelling machine

entwickeln *vt* (*a. Foto*) to develop; (*Mut, Energie*) to show, to display ▷ *vr*: **sich ~** to develop; **Entwicklung** *f* development; (*Foto*) developing; **Entwicklungs-helfer(in)** (*-s, -*) *m(f)* development worker; **Entwicklungsland** *nt* developing country

Entwurf *m* outline; (*Design*) design; (*Vertragsentwurf*) draft

entzückend *adj* delightful, charming

Entzug *m* withdrawal; (*Behandlung*) detox;

Entzugserscheinung *f* withdrawal symptom

entzünden *vr*: **sich ~** to catch fire; (*Med*) to become inflamed; **Entzündung** *f* (*Med*) inflammation

Epidemie (*-, -n*) *f* epidemic

Epilepsie (*-, -n*) *f* epilepsy

epilieren *vt* to remove body hair, to depilate; **Epiliergerät** *nt* Ladyshave®

er *pron* (*Person*) he; (*Sache*) it; **er ist's** it's him; **wo ist mein Mantel? — ~ ist ...** where's my coat? — it's ...

Erbe (*-n, -n*) *m* heir ▷ (*-s*) *nt* inheritance; (*fig*) heritage; **erben** *vt* to inherit; **Erbin** *f* heiress; **erblich** *adj* hereditary

erblicken *vt* to catch sight of

erbrechen *irr vt* to vomit ▷ *vr*: **sich ~** to vomit; **Erbrechen** *nt* vomiting

Erbschaft *f* inheritance

Erbse (*-, -n*) *f* pea

Erdapfel *m* potato; **Erdbeben** *nt* earthquake; **Erdbeere** *f* strawberry; **Erde** (*-, -n*) *f* (*Planet*) earth; (*Boden*) ground; **Erdgas** *nt* natural gas; **Erdgeschoss** *nt* ground floor (*Brit*), first floor (*US*); **Erdkunde** *f* geography; **Erdnuss** *f* peanut; **Erdöl** *nt* (mineral) oil; **Erdrutsch** *m* landslide; **Erdteil** *m* continent

ereignen *vr*: **sich ~** to happen, to take place; **Ereignis** *nt* event

erfahren *irr vt* to learn, to find out; (*erleben*) to experience ▷ *adj* experienced; **Erfahrung** *f* experience

erfinden *irr vt* to invent; **erfinderisch** *adj* inventive, creative; **Erfindung** *f* invention

Erfolg (*-(e)s, -e*) *m* success; (*Folge*) result; **~ versprechend** promising; **viel ~!** good luck;

erfolglos adj unsuccessful; **erfolgreich** adj successful
erforderlich adj necessary
erforschen vt to explore; (untersuchen) investigate
erfreulich adj pleasing, pleasant; (Nachricht) good; **erfreulicherweise** adv fortunately
erfrieren irr vi to freeze to death; (Pflanzen) to be killed by frost
Erfrischung f refreshment
erfüllen vt (Raum) to fill; (Bitte, Wunsch etc) to fulfil ▷ vr: **sich ~** to come true
ergänzen vt (hinzufügen) to add; (vervollständigen) to complete ▷ vr: **sich ~** to complement one another; **Ergänzung** f completion; (Zusatz) supplement
ergeben irr vt (Betrag) to come to; (zum Ergebnis haben) to result in ▷ irr vr: **sich ~** to surrender; (folgen) to result (aus from) ▷ adj devoted; (demütig) humble
Ergebnis nt result
ergreifen irr vt to seize; (Beruf) to take up; (Maßnahme, Gelegenheit) to take; (rühren) to move
erhalten irr vt (bekommen) to receive; (bewahren) to preserve; **gut ~ sein** to be in good condition; **erhältlich** adj available
erheblich adj considerable
erhitzen vt to heat (up)
erhöhen vt to raise; (verstärken) to increase ▷ vr: **sich ~** to increase
erholen vr: **sich ~** to recover; (sich ausruhen) to have a rest; **erholsam** adj restful; **Erholung** f recovery; (Entspannung) relaxation, rest
erinnern vt to remind (an +akk of) ▷ vr: **sich ~** to remember (an etw akk sth); **Erinnerung** f memory; (Andenken) souvenir;

(Mahnung) reminder
erkälten vr: **sich ~** to catch a cold; **erkältet** adj: (**stark**) **~ sein** to have a (bad) cold; **Erkältung** f cold
erkennen irr vt to recognize; (sehen, verstehen) to see; **~, dass ...** to realize that ...; **erkenntlich** adj: **sich ~ zeigen** to show one's appreciation
Erker (-s, -) m bay
erklären vt to explain; (kundtun) to declare; **Erklärung** f explanation; (Aussage) declaration
erkundigen vr: **sich ~** to enquire (nach about)
erlauben vt to allow, to permit; **jdm ~, etw zu tun** to allow (o permit) sb to do sth; **sich** (dat) **etw ~** to permit oneself sth; **~ Sie**(, **dass ich rauche**)**?** do you mind (if I smoke)?; **was ~ Sie sich?** what do you think you're doing?; **Erlaubnis** f permission
Erläuterung f explanation; (zu Text) comment
erleben vt to experience; (schöne Tage etc) to have; (Schlimmes) to go through; (miterleben) to witness; (noch miterleben) to live to see; **Erlebnis** nt experience
erledigen vt (Angelegenheit, Aufgabe) to deal with; (fam: ruinieren) to finish; **erledigt** adj (beendet) finished; (gelöst) dealt with; (fam: erschöpft) whacked, knackered (Brit)
erleichtert adj relieved
Erlös (-es, -e) m proceeds pl
ermahnen vt (warnend) to warn
ermäßigt adj reduced; **Ermäßigung** f reduction
ermitteln vt to find out; (Täter) to trace ▷ vi (Jur) to investigate
ermöglichen vt to make possible (dat for)
ermorden vt to murder

ermüdend adj tiring
ermutigen vt to encourage
ernähren vt to feed; (Familie) to support ▷ vr: **sich ~ to** support oneself; **sich ~ von** to live on; **Ernährung** f (Essen) food; **Ernährungsberater(in)** m(f) nutritional (o dietary) adviser
erneuern vt to renew; (restaurieren) to restore; (renovieren) to renovate; (auswechseln) to replace
ernst adj serious ▷ adv: **jdn/etw ~ nehmen** take sb/sth seriously; **Ernst** (-es) m seriousness; **das ist mein ~** I'm quite serious; **im ~?** seriously?; **ernsthaft** adj serious ▷ adv seriously
Ernte (-, -n) f harvest; **Erntedankfest** nt harvest festival (Brit), Thanksgiving (Day) (US: 4. Donnerstag im November); **ernten** vt to harvest; (Lob etc) to earn
erobern vt to conquer
eröffnen vt to open; **Eröffnung** f opening
erogen adj erogenous
erotisch adj erotic
erpressen vt (jdn) to blackmail; (Geld etc) to extort; **Erpressung** f blackmail; (von Geld) extortion
erraten irr vt to guess
erregen vt to excite; (sexuell) to arouse; (ärgern) to annoy; (hervorrufen) to arouse ▷ vr: **sich ~ to** get worked up; **Erreger** (-s, -) m (Med) germ; (Virus) virus
erreichbar adj: **~ sein** to be within reach; (Person) to be available; **das Stadtzentrum ist zu Fuß/mit dem Wagen leicht ~** the city centre is within easy walking/driving distance; **erreichen** vt to reach; (Zug etc) to catch
Ersatz (-es) m replacement; (auf

Zeit) substitute; (Ausgleich) compensation; **Ersatzreifen** m (Auto) spare tyre; **Ersatzteil** nt spare (part)
erscheinen irr vi to appear; (wirken) to seem
erschöpft adj exhausted; **Erschöpfung** f exhaustion
erschrecken vt to frighten ▷ (erschrak, erschrocken) vi to get a fright; **erschreckend** adj alarming; **erschrocken** adj frightened
erschwinglich adj affordable
ersetzen vt to replace; (Auslagen) to reimburse

🅞 SCHLÜSSELWORT

erst adv **1** first; **mach erst mal die Arbeit fertig** finish your work first; **wenn du das erst mal hinter dir hast** once you've got that behind you
2 (nicht früher als, nur) only; (nicht bis) not till; **erst gestern** only yesterday; **erst morgen** not until tomorrow; **erst als** only when, not until; **wir fahren erst später** we're not going until later; **er ist (gerade) erst angekommen** he's only just arrived
3 wäre er doch erst zurück! if only he were back!

erstatten vt (Kosten) to refund; **Bericht ~** to report (über +akk on); **Anzeige gegen jdn ~** to report sb to the police
erstaunlich adj astonishing; **erstaunt** adj surprised
erstbeste(r, s) adj: **das ~ Hotel** any old hotel; **der Erstbeste** just anyone
erste(r, s) adj first; siehe auch **dritte**; **zum ~n Mal** for the first time; **er wurde Erster** he came

first; **auf den ~n Blick** at first sight

erstens adv first(ly), in the first place

ersticken vi (Mensch) to suffocate; **in Arbeit ~** to be snowed under with work

erstklassig adj first-class; **erstmals** adv for the first time

erstrecken vr: **sich ~** to extend, to stretch (auf +akk to; über +akk over)

ertappen vt to catch

erteilen vt (Rat, Erlaubnis) to give

Ertrag (-(e)s, Erträge) m yield; (Gewinn) proceeds pl; **ertragen** irr vt (Schmerzen) to bear, to stand; (dulden) to put up with; **erträglich** adj bearable; (nicht zu schlecht) tolerable

ertrinken irr vi to drown

erwachsen adj grown-up; **~ werden** to grow up; **Erwachsene(r)** mf adult, grown-up

erwähnen vt to mention

erwarten vt to expect; (warten auf) to wait for; **ich kann den Sommer kaum ~** I can hardly wait for the summer

erwerbstätig adj employed

erwidern vt to reply; (Gruß, Besuch) to return

erwischen vt (fam) to catch (bei etw doing sth)

erwünscht adj desired; (willkommen) welcome

Erz (-es, -e) nt ore

erzählen vt to tell (jdm etw sb sth); **Erzählung** f story, tale

erzeugen vt to produce; (Strom) to generate; **Erzeugnis** nt product

erziehen irr vt to bring up; (geistig) to educate; (Tier) to train; **Erzieher(in)** (-s, -) m(f) educator; (Kindergarten) (nursery school)

teacher; **Erziehung** f upbringing; (Bildung) education

es pron (Sache, im Nom und Akk) it; (Baby, Tier) he/she; **ich bin ~** it's me; **~ ist kalt** it's cold; **~ gibt ...** there is .../there are ...; **ich hoffe ~** I hope so; **ich kann ~** I can do it

Escape-Taste f (Inform) escape key

Esel (-s, -) m donkey

Espresso (-s, -) m espresso

essbar adj edible; **essen** (aß, gegessen) vt, vi to eat; **zu Mittag/Abend ~** to have lunch/dinner; **was gibt's zu ~?** what's for lunch/dinner?; **~ gehen** to eat out; **gegessen sein** (fig, fam) to be history; **Essen** (-s, -) nt (Mahlzeit) meal; (Nahrung) food

Essig (-s, -e) m vinegar

Esslöffel m dessert spoon; **Esszimmer** nt dining room

Estland nt Estonia

Etage (-, -n) f floor, storey; **in** (o **auf**) **der ersten ~** on the first (Brit) (o second (US)) floor; **Etagenbett** nt bunk bed

Etappe (-, -n) f stage

ethnisch adj ethnic

Etikett (-(e)s, -e) nt label

etliche pron pl several, quite a few; **etliches** pron quite a lot

etwa adv (ungefähr) about; (vielleicht) perhaps; (beispielsweise) for instance

etwas pron something; (verneinend, fragend) anything; (ein wenig) a little; **~ Neues** something/anything new; **~ zu essen** something to eat; **~ Salz** some salt; **wenn ich noch ~ tun kann ...** if I can do anything else ... ▷ adv a bit, a little; **~ mehr** a little more

EU (-) f abk = **Europäische Union** EU

euch pron akk, dat von **ihr**; you, (to)

you; **~ (selbst)** (*reflexiv*) yourselves; **wo kann ich ~ treffen?** where can I meet you?; **sie schickt es ~** she'll send it to you; **ein Freund von ~** a friend of yours; **setzt ~ bitte** please sit down; **habt ihr ~ amüsiert?** did you enjoy yourselves?

euer *pron* (*adjektivisch*) your; **~ David** (*am Briefende*) Yours, David ▷ *pron gen von* **ihr**; of you; **euere(r, s)** *pron siehe* **eure**

Eule (-, -n) *f* owl

eure(r, s) *pron* (*substantivisch*) yours; **das ist ~** that's yours; **euretwegen** *adv* (*wegen euch*) because of you; (*euch zuliebe*) for your sake; (*um euch*) about you

Euro (-, -) *m* (*Währung*) euro; **Eurocent** *m* eurocent; **Eurocity** (-(*s*), -*s*) *m*, **Eurocityzug** *m* European Intercity train; **Europa** (-*s*) *nt* Europe; **Europäer(in)** (-*s*, -) *m(f)* European; **europäisch** *adj* European; **Europäische Union** European Union; **Europameister(in)** *m(f)* European champion; (*Mannschaft*) European champions *pl*; **Europaparlament** *nt* European Parliament

Euter (-*s*, -) *nt* udder

evangelisch *adj* Protestant

eventuell *adj* possible ▷ *adv* possibly, perhaps

ewig *adj* eternal; **er hat ~ gebraucht** it took him ages; **Ewigkeit** *f* eternity

Ex *mf* ex

Ex- *in zW* ex-, former; **~frau** ex-wife; **~freund** *m* ex-boyfriend; **~minister** former minister

exakt *adj* precise

Examen (-*s*, -) *nt* exam

Exemplar (-*s*, -*e*) *nt* specimen; (*Buch*) copy

Exil (-*s*, -*e*) *nt* exile

Existenz *f* existence; (*Unterhalt*) livelihood, living; **existieren** *vi* to exist

exklusiv *adj* exclusive; **exklusive** *adv, prep* +*gen* excluding

exotisch *adj* exotic

Experte (-*n*, -*n*) *m*, **Expertin** *f* expert

explodieren *vi* to explode; **Explosion** *f* explosion

Export (-(*e*)*s*, -*e*) *m* export; **exportieren** *vt* to export

Express (-*es*) *m*, **Expresszug** *m* express (train)

extra *adj inv* (*fam: gesondert*) separate; (*zusätzlich*) extra ▷ *adv* (*gesondert*) separately; (*speziell*) specially; (*absichtlich*) on purpose; **Extra** (-*s*, -*s*) *nt* extra

extrem *adj* extreme ▷ *adv* extremely; **~ kalt** extremely cold

exzellent *adj* excellent

Eyeliner (-*s*, -) *m* eyeliner

f

fabelhaft *adj* fabulous, marvellous

Fabrik *f* factory

Fach (-(e)s, *Fächer*) *nt* compartment; (*Schulfach, Sachgebiet*) subject; **Facharzt** *m*, **Fachärztin** *f* specialist; **Fachausdruck** (-s, *Fachausdrücke*) *m* technical term

Fächer (-s, -) *m* fan

Fachfrau *f* specialist, expert; **Fachmann** (-*leute*) *m* specialist, expert; **Fachwerkhaus** *nt* half-timbered house

Fackel (-, -n) *f* torch

fad(e) *adj* (*Essen*) bland; (*langweilig*) dull

Faden (-s, *Fäden*) *m* thread

fähig *adj* capable (*zu, gen* of); **Fähigkeit** *f* ability

Fahndung *f* search

Fahne (-, -n) *f* flag

Fahrausweis *m* ticket

Fahrbahn *f* road; (*Spur*) lane

Fähre (-, -n) *f* ferry

fahren (*fuhr, gefahren*) *vt* to drive; (*Rad*) to ride; (*befördern*) to drive, to take; **50 km/h ~** to drive at (*o do*) 50 kph ▷ *vi* (*sich bewegen*) to go; (*Autofahrer*) to drive; (*Schiff*) to sail; (*abfahren*) to leave; **mit dem Auto/Zug ~** to go by car/train; **rechts ~!** keep to the right; **Fahrer(in)** (-s, -) *m(f)* driver; **Fahrerairbag** *m* driver airbag; **Fahrerflucht** *f*: **~ begehen** to fail to stop after an accident; **Fahrersitz** *m* driver's seat

Fahrgast *m* passenger; **Fahrgeld** *nt* fare; **Fahrgemeinschaft** *f* car pool; **Fahrkarte** *f* ticket; **Fahrkartenautomat** *m* ticket machine; **Fahrkartenschalter** *m* ticket office

fahrlässig *adj* negligent

Fahrlehrer(in) *m(f)* driving instructor; **Fahrplan** *m* timetable; **Fahrplanauszug** *m* individual timetable; **fahrplanmäßig** *adj* (*Eisenb*) scheduled; **Fahrpreis** *m* fare; **Fahrpreisermäßigung** *f* fare reduction; **Fahrrad** *nt* bicycle; **Fahrradschlauch** *m* bicycle tube; **Fahrradschloss** *nt* bicycle lock; **Fahrradverleih** *m* cycle hire (*Brit*) (*o rental* (*US*)); **Fahrradweg** *m* cycle path; **Fahrschein** *m* ticket; **Fahrscheinautomat** *m* ticket machine; **Fahrscheinentwerter** *m* ticket-cancelling machine; **Fahrschule** *f* driving school; **Fahrschüler(in)** *m(f)* learner (driver) (*Brit*), student driver (*US*); **Fahrspur** *f* lane; **Fahrstreifen** *m* lane; **Fahrstuhl** *m* lift (*Brit*), elevator (*US*)

Fahrt (-, -en) *f* journey; (*kurz*) trip; (*Auto*) drive; **auf der ~ nach London** on the way to London; **nach drei Stunden ~** after

travelling for three hours; **gute ~!**
have a good trip; **Fahrtkosten** pl
travelling expenses pl;
Fahrtrichtung f direction of
travel
fahrtüchtig f (Person) fit to
drive; (Fahrzeug) roadworthy
Fahrtunterbrechung f break
in the journey, stop
Fahrverbot nt: **~ erhalten/
haben** to be banned from
driving; **Fahrzeug** nt vehicle;
Fahrzeugbrief m (vehicle)
registration document;
Fahrzeughalter(in) m(f) registered owner; **Fahrzeugpapiere**
pl vehicle documents pl
fair adj fair
Fakultät f faculty
Falke (-n, -n) m falcon
Fall (-(e)s, Fälle) m (Sturz) fall;
(Sachverhalt, juristisch) case; **auf
jeden ~, auf alle Fälle** in any
case; (bestimmt) definitely; **auf
keinen ~** on no account; **für den ~,
dass ...** in case ...
Falle (-, -n) f trap
fallen (fiel, gefallen) vi to fall; **etw
~ lassen** to drop sth
fällig adj due
falls adv if; (für den Fall, dass) in
case
Fallschirm m parachute;
Fallschirmspringen nt
parachuting, parachute jumping;
Fallschirmspringer(in) m(f)
parachutist
falsch adj (unrichtig) wrong;
(unehrlich, unecht) false; (Schmuck)
fake; **~ verbunden** sorry, wrong
number; **fälschen** vt to forge;
Falschfahrer(in) m(f) person
driving the wrong way on the
motorway; **Falschgeld** nt
counterfeit money; **Fälschung** f
forgery, fake
Faltblatt nt leaflet

Falte (-, -n) f (Knick) fold; (Haut)
wrinkle; (Rock) pleat; (Bügel)
crease; **falten** vt to fold; **faltig**
adj (zerknittert) creased; (Haut,
Gesicht) wrinkled
Familie f family; **Familien-
angehörige(r)** mf family
member; **Familienname** m
surname; **Familienstand** m
marital status
Fan (-s, -s) m fan
fand imperf von **finden**
fangen (fing, gefangen) vt to
catch ▷ vr: **sich ~** (nicht fallen) to
steady oneself; (fig) to compose
oneself
Fantasie f imagination
fantastisch adj fantastic
Farbdrucker m colour printer;
Farbe (-, -n) f colour; (zum Malen
etc) paint; (für Stoff) dye; **färben**
vt to colour; (Stoff, Haar) to dye;
Farbfernsehen nt colour
television; **Farbfilm** m colour
film; **farbig** adj coloured;
Farbkopierer m colour copier;
farblos adj colourless; **Farbstoff**
m dye; (für Lebensmittel) colouring
Farn (-(e)s, -e) m fern
Fasan (-(e)s, -e(n)) m pheasant
Fasching (-s, -e) m carnival,
Mardi Gras (US); **Faschings-
dienstag** (-s, -e) m Shrove
Tuesday, Mardi Gras (US)
Faschismus m fascism
Faser (-, -n) f fibre
Fass (-es, Fässer) nt barrel; (Öl)
drum
fassen vt (ergreifen) to grasp;
(enthalten) to hold; (Entschluss) to
take; (verstehen) to understand;
nicht zu ~! unbelievable ▷ vr:
sich ~ to compose oneself;
Fassung f (Umrahmung) mount;
(Brille) frame; (Lampe) socket;
(Wortlaut) version; (Beherrschung)
composure; **jdn aus der ~ bringen**

to throw sb; **die ~ verlieren** to
lose one's cool
fast adv almost, nearly
fasten vi to fast; **Fastenzeit** f:
die ~ (christlich) Lent; (muslimisch)
Ramadan
Fast Food (-s) nt fast food
Fastnacht f (Fasching) carnival
fatal adj (verhängnisvoll)
disastrous; (peinlich) embarrassing
faul adj (Obst, Gemüse) rotten;
(Mensch) lazy; (Ausreden) lame;
faulen vi to rot
faulenzen vi to do nothing, to
hang around; **Faulheit** f laziness
faulig adj rotten; (Geruch,
Geschmack) foul
Faust (-, Fäuste) f fist;
Fausthandschuh m mitten
Fax (-, -(e)) nt fax; **faxen** vi, vt to
fax; **Faxgerät** nt fax machine;
Faxnummer f fax number
FCKW (-, -s) nt abk =
Fluorchlorkohlenwasserstoff
CFC
Februar (-(s), -e) m February;
siehe auch **Juni**
Fechten nt fencing
Feder (-, -n) f feather;
(Schreibfeder) (pen-)nib; (Tech)
spring; **Federball** m (Ball)
shuttlecock; (Spiel) badminton;
Federung f suspension
Fee (-, -n) f fairy
fegen vi, vt to sweep
fehl adj: **~ am Platz** (o Ort) out of
place
fehlen vi (abwesend sein) to be
absent; **etw fehlt jdm** sb lacks sth;
was fehlt ihm? what's wrong with
him?; **du fehlst mir** I miss you; **es
fehlt an ...** there's no...
Fehler (-s, -) m mistake, error;
(Mangel, Schwäche) fault;
Fehlerbeseitigung f (Inform)
debugging; **Fehlermeldung** f
(Inform) error message

Fehlzündung f (Auto) misfire
Feier (-, -n) f celebration; (Party)
party; **Feierabend** m end of the
working day; **~ haben** to finish
work; **nach ~** after work; **feierlich**
adj solemn; **feiern** vt, vi to
celebrate, to have a party;
Feiertag m holiday; **gesetzlicher
~** public holiday
feige(e) adj cowardly
Feige (-, -n) f fig
Feigling m coward
Feile (-, -n) f file
fein adj fine; (vornehm) refined; **~!**
great!; **das schmeckt ~** that tastes
delicious
Feind(in) (-(e)s, -e) m(f) enemy;
feindlich adj hostile
Feinkost (-) f delicacies pl;
Feinkostladen m delicatessen;
Feinschmecker(in) (-s, -) m(f)
gourmet; **Feinstaub** m
particulate matter;
Feinwaschmittel nt washing
powder for delicate fabrics
Feld (-(e)s, -er) nt field; (Schach)
square; (Sport) pitch; **Feldsalat** m
lamb's lettuce; **Feldweg** m path
across the fields
Felge (-, -n) f (wheel) rim
Fell (-(e)s, -e) nt fur; (von Schaf)
fleece
Fels (-en, -en) m, **Felsen** (-s, -) m
rock; (Klippe) cliff; **felsig** adj rocky
feminin adj feminine;
Femininum (-s, Feminina) nt (Ling)
feminine noun
feministisch adj feminist
Fenchel (-s, -) m fennel
Fenster (-s, -) nt window;
Fensterbrett nt windowsill;
Fensterladen m shutter;
Fensterplatz m windowseat;
Fensterscheibe f windowpane
Ferien pl holidays pl (Brit),
vacation sing (US); **~ haben/
machen** to be/go on holiday (Brit)

(*o* vacation (*US*)); **Ferienhaus** *nt*
holiday (*Brit*) (*o* vacation (*US*))
home; **Ferienkurs** *m* holiday
(*Brit*) (*o* vacation (*US*)) course;
Ferienlager *nt* holiday camp
(*Brit*), vacation camp (*US*); (*für
Kinder im Sommer*) summer camp;
Ferienort *m* holiday (*Brit*) (*o*
vacation (*US*)) resort;
Ferienwohnung *f* holiday flat
(*Brit*), vacation apartment (*US*)
Ferkel (*-s, -*) *nt* piglet
fern *adj* distant, far-off; **von**
~ from a distance; **Fernabfrage** *f*
remote-control access;
Fernbedienung *f* remote control;
Ferne *f* distance; **aus der ~** from
a distance
ferner *adj, adv* further; (*außerdem*)
besides
Fernflug *m* long-distance flight;
Ferngespräch *nt* long-distance
call; **ferngesteuert** *adj*
remote-controlled; **Fernglas** *nt*
binoculars *pl*; **Fernlicht** *nt* full
beam (*Brit*), high beam (*US*)
Fernsehapparat *m* TV (set);
fern|sehen *irr vi* to watch
television; **Fernsehen** *nt*
television; **im ~** on television;
Fernseher *m* TV (set);
Fernsehkanal *m* TV channel;
Fernsehprogramm *nt* (*Sendung*)
TV programme; (*Zeitschrift*) TV
guide; **Fernsehserie** *f* TV series
sing; **Fernsehturm** *m* TV tower;
Fernsehzeitschrift *f* TV guide
Fernstraße *f* major road;
Ferntourismus *m* long-haul
tourism; **Fernverkehr** *m*
long-distance traffic
Ferse (*-, -n*) *f* heel
fertig *adj* (*bereit*) ready; (*beendet*)
finished; (*gebrauchsfertig*)
ready-made; **~ machen** (*beenden*)
to finish; **sich ~ machen** to get
ready; **mit etw ~ werden** to be

able to cope with sth; **auf die**
Plätze, ~, los! on your marks, get
set, go!; **Fertiggericht** *nt* ready
meal; **fertig|machen** *vt* (*jdn
kritisieren*) to give sb hell; (*jdn zur
Verzweiflung bringen*) to drive sb
mad; (*jdn deprimieren*) to get sb
down
fest *adj* firm; (*Nahrung*) solid;
(*Gehalt*) regular; (*Schuhe*) sturdy;
(*Schlaf*) sound
Fest (*-(e)s, -e*) *nt* party; (*Rel*)
festival
Festbetrag *m* fixed amount
fest|binden *irr vt* to tie (*an +dat*
to); **fest|halten** *irr vt* to hold
onto ▷ *vr:* **sich ~** to hold on (*an
+dat* to)
Festiger (*-s, -*) *m* setting lotion
Festival (*-s, -s*) *nt* festival
Festland *nt* mainland; **das**
europäische ~ the (European)
continent
fest|legen *vt* to fix ▷ *vr:* **sich**
~ to commit oneself
festlich *adj* festive
fest|machen *vt* to fasten;
(*Termin etc*) to fix; **fest|nehmen** *irr*
vt to arrest; **Festnetz** *nt* (*Tel*)
fixed-line network; **Festplatte** *f*
(*Inform*) hard disk
fest|setzen *vt* to fix
Festspiele *pl* festival *sing*
fest|stehen *irr vi* to be fixed
fest|stellen *vt* to establish;
(*sagen*) to remark
Feststelltaste *f* shift lock
Festung *f* fortress
Festzelt *nt* marquee
Fete (*-, -n*) *f* party
fett *adj* (*dick*) fat; (*Essen etc*)
greasy; (*Schrift*) bold; **Fett** (*-(e)s,
-e*) *nt* fat; (*Tech*) grease; **fettarm**
adj low-fat; **fettig** *adj* fatty;
(*schmierig*) greasy
feucht *adj* damp; (*Luft*) humid;
Feuchtigkeit *f* dampness;

(*Luftfeuchtigkeit*) humidity; **Feuchtigkeitscreme** *f* moisturizing cream

Feuer (*-s, -*) *nt* fire; **haben Sie ~?** have you got a light?; **Feueralarm** *m* fire alarm; **feuerfest** *adj* fireproof; **Feuerlöscher** (*-s, -*) *m* fire extinguisher; **Feuermelder** (*-s, -*) *m* fire alarm; **Feuertreppe** *f* fire escape; **Feuerwehr** (*-, -en*) *f* fire brigade; **Feuerwehrfrau** *f* firewoman, fire fighter; **Feuerwehrmann** *m* fireman, fire fighter; **Feuerwerk** *nt* fireworks *pl*; **Feuerzeug** *nt* (cigarette) lighter

Fichte (*-, -n*) *f* spruce

ficken *vt, vi* (*vulg*) to fuck

Fieber (*-s, -*) *nt* temperature, fever; **~ haben** to have a high temperature; **Fieberthermometer** *nt* thermometer

fiel *imperf von* **fallen**

fies *adj* (*fam*) nasty

Figur (*-, -en*) *f* figure; (*im Schach*) piece

Filet (*-s, -s*) *nt* fillet; **filetieren** *vt* to fillet; **Filetsteak** *nt* fillet steak

Filiale (*-, -n*) *f* (*Comm*) branch

Film (*-(e)s, -e*) *m* film, movie; **filmen** *vt, vi* to film

Filter (*-s, -*) *m* filter; **Filterkaffee** *m* filter coffee; **filtern** *vt* to filter; **Filterpapier** *nt* filter paper

Filz (*-es, -e*) *m* felt; **Filzschreiber** *m*, **Filzstift** *m* felt(-tip) pen, felt-tip

Finale (*-s, -*) *nt* (*Sport*) final

Finanzamt *nt* tax office; **finanziell** *adj* financial; **finanzieren** *vt* to finance

finden (*fand, gefunden*) *vt* to find; (*meinen*) to think; **ich finde nichts dabei, wenn ...** I don't see what's

wrong if ...; **ich finde es gut/schlecht** I like/don't like it ▷ *vr*: **es fanden sich nur wenige Helfer** there were only a few helpers

fing *imperf von* **fangen**

Finger (*-s, -*) *m* finger; **Fingerabdruck** *m* fingerprint; **Fingerhandschuh** *m* glove; **Fingernagel** *m* fingernail

Fink (*-en, -en*) *m* finch

Finne (*-n, -n*) *m*, **Finnin** *f* Finn, Finnish man/woman; **finnisch** *adj* Finnish; **Finnisch** *nt* Finnish; **Finnland** *nt* Finland

finster *adj* dark; (*verdächtig*) dubious; (*verdrossen*) grim; (*Gedanke*) dark; **Finsternis** *f* darkness

Firewall (*-, -s*) *f* (*Inform*) firewall

Firma (*-, Firmen*) *f* firm

Fisch (*-(e)s, -e*) *m* fish; **~e** *pl* (*Astr*) Pisces *sing*; **fischen** *vt, vi* to fish; **Fischer(in)** (*-s, -*) *m(f)* fisherman/-woman; **Fischerboot** *nt* fishing boat; **Fischgericht** *nt* fish dish; **Fischhändler(in)** *m(f)* fishmonger; **Fischstäbchen** *nt* fish finger (*Brit*) (o stick (*US*))

Fisole (*-, -n*) *f* French bean

fit *adj* fit; **Fitness** (*-*) *f* fitness; **Fitnesscenter** (*-s, -*) *nt* fitness centre; **Fitnesstrainer(in)** *m(f)* fitness trainer, personal trainer

fix *adj* (*schnell*) quick; **~ und fertig** exhausted

fixen *vi* (*fam*) to shoot up; **Fixer(in)** (*-s, -*) *m(f)* (*fam*) junkie

FKK *f abk* = **Freikörperkultur** nudism; **FKK-Strand** *m* nudist beach

flach *adj* flat; (*Gewässer; Teller*) shallow; **~er Absatz** low heel; **Flachbildschirm** *m* flat screen

Fläche (*-, -n*) *f* area; (*Oberfläche*) surface

Flagge (*-, -n*) *f* flag

flambiert adj flambé(ed)
Flamme (-, -n) f flame
Flanell (-s) m flannel
Flasche (-, -n) f bottle; **eine ~ sein** (fam) to be useless;
Flaschenbier nt bottled beer;
Flaschenöffner m bottle opener;
Flaschenpfand nt deposit;
Flaschentomate f plum tomato
flatterhaft adj fickle; **flattern** vi to flutter
flauschig adj fluffy
Flausen pl (fam) daft ideas pl
Flaute (-, -n) f calm; (Comm) recession
Flechte (-, -n) f plait; (Med) scab; (Bot) lichen; **flechten** (flocht, geflochten) vt to plait; (Kranz) to bind
Fleck (-(e)s, -e) m, **Flecken** (-s, -) m spot; (Schmutz) stain; (Stoff~) patch; (Makel) blemish;
Fleckentferner (-s, -) m stain remover; **fleckig** adj spotted; (mit Schmutzflecken) stained
Fledermaus f bat
Fleisch (-(e)s) nt flesh; (Essen) meat; **Fleischbrühe** f meat stock; **Fleischer(in)** (-s, -) m(f) butcher; **Fleischerei** f butcher's (shop); **Fleischtomate** f beef tomato
fleißig adj diligent, hard-working
flennen vi (fam) to cry, to howl
flexibel adj flexible
flicken vt to mend; **Flickzeug** nt repair kit
Flieder (-s, -) m lilac
Fliege (-, -n) f fly; (Krawatte) bow tie
fliegen (flog, geflogen) vt, vi to fly
Fliese (-, -n) f tile
Fließband nt conveyor belt; (als Einrichtung) production (o assembly) line; **fließen** (floss, geflossen) vi to flow; **fließend** adj fluent; (Übergänge) smooth; **~(es) Wasser** running water

Flipper (-s, -) m pinball machine; **flippern** vi to play pinball
flippig adj (fam) eccentric
flirten vi to flirt
Flitterwochen pl honeymoon sing
flocht imperf von **flechten**
Flocke (-, -n) f flake
flog imperf von **fliegen**
Floh (-(e)s, Flöhe) m flea; **Flohmarkt** m flea market
Flop (-s, -s) m flop
Floskel (-, -n) f empty phrase
floss imperf von **fließen**
Floß (-es, Flöße) nt raft
Flosse (-, -n) f fin; (Schwimmflosse) flipper
Flöte (-, -n) f flute; (Blockflöte) recorder
flott adj lively; (elegant) smart; (Naut) afloat
Fluch (-(e)s, Flüche) m curse; **fluchen** vi to swear, to curse
Flucht (-, -en) f flight; **flüchten** vi to flee (vor +dat from); **flüchtig** adj: **ich kenne ihn nur ~** I don't know him very well at all; **Flüchtling** m refugee
Flug (-(e)s, Flüge) m flight; **Flugbegleiter(in)** (-s, -) m(f) flight attendant; **Flugblatt** nt leaflet
Flügel (-s, -) m wing; (Mus) grand piano
Fluggast m passenger (on a plane); **Fluggesellschaft** f airline; **Flughafen** m airport; **Flugkarte** f airline ticket; **Fluglotse** m air-traffic controller; **Flugnummer** f flight number; **Flugplan** m flight schedule; **Flugplatz** m airport; (klein) airfield; **Flugschein** m plane ticket; **Flugschreiber** m flight recorder, black box; **Flugsteig** (-s, -e) m gate; **Flugstrecke** f air route; **Flugticket** nt plane ticket; **Flugverbindung** f flight

connection; **Flugverkehr** m air traffic; **Flugzeit** f flying time; **Flugzeug** nt plane; **Flugzeugentführung** f hijacking

Flunder (-, -n) f flounder

Fluor (-s) nt fluorine

Flur (-(e)s, -e) m hall

Fluss (-es, Flüsse) m river; (Fließen) flow

flüssig adj liquid; **Flüssigkeit** (-, -en) f liquid; **Flüssigseife** f liquid soap

flüstern vt, vi to whisper

Flut (-, -en) f (a. fig) flood; (Gezeiten) high tide; **Flutlicht** nt floodlight

Fohlen (-s, -) nt foal

Föhn (-(e)s, -e) m hairdryer; (Wind) foehn; **föhnen** vt to dry; (beim Friseur) to blow-dry

Folge (-, -n) f (Reihe, Serie) series sing; (Aufeinanderfolge) sequence; (Fortsetzung eines Romans) instalment; (Fortsetzung einer Fernsehserie) episode; (Auswirkung) result; **etw zur ~ haben** to result in sth; **~n haben** to have consequences; **folgen** vi to follow (jdm sb); (gehorchen) to obey (jdm sb); **jdm ~ können** (fig) to be able to follow sb; **folgend** adj following; **folgendermaßen** adv as follows; **folglich** adv consequently

Folie f foil; (für Projektor) transparency

Fön® m siehe **Föhn**

Fondue (-s, -s) nt fondue

fönen vt siehe **föhnen**

fordern vt to demand

fördern vt to promote; (unterstützen) to help

Forderung f demand

Forelle f trout

Form (-, -en) f form; (Gestalt) shape; (Gussform) mould; (Backform) baking tin (Brit) (o pan

(US)); **in ~ sein** to be in good form; **Formalität** f formality; **Format** nt format; **von internationalem ~** of international standing; **formatieren** vt (Diskette) to format; (Text) to edit

Formblatt nt form; **formen** vt to form, to shape; **förmlich** adj formal; (buchstäblich) real; **formlos** adj informal; **Formular** (-s, -e) nt form; **formulieren** vt to formulate

forschen vi to search (nach for); (wissenschaftlich) to (do) research; **Forscher(in)** m(f) researcher; **Forschung** f research

Förster(in) (-s, -) m(f) forester; (für Wild) gamekeeper

fort adv away; (verschwunden) gone; **fort|bewegen** vt to move away ▷ vr: **sich ~** to move; **Fortbildung** f further education; (im Beruf) further training; **fort|fahren** irr vi to go away; (weitermachen) to continue; **fort|gehen** irr vi to go away; **fortgeschritten** adj advanced; **Fortpflanzung** f reproduction

Fortschritt m progress; **~e machen** to make progress; **fortschrittlich** adj progressive

fort|setzen vt to continue; **Fortsetzung** f continuation; (folgender Teil) instalment; **~ folgt** to be continued

Foto (-s, -s) nt photo ▷ (-s, -s) m (Fotoapparat) camera; **Fotograf(in)** (-en, -en) m(f) photographer; **Fotografie** f photography; (Bild) photograph; **fotografieren** vt to photograph ▷ vi to take photographs; **Fotohandy** nt camera phone; **Fotokopie** f photocopy; **fotokopieren** vt to photocopy

Foul (-s, -s) nt foul

Foyer (-s, -s) nt foyer

Fr. f abk = **Frau** Mrs; (unverheiratet, neutral) Ms

Fracht (-, -en) f freight; (Naut) cargo; (Preis) carriage; **Frachter** (-s, -) m freighter

Frack (-(e)s, Fräcke) m tails pl

Frage (-, -n) f question; **das ist eine ~ der Zeit** that's a matter (o question) of time; **das kommt nicht in ~** that's out of the question; **Fragebogen** m questionnaire; **fragen** vt, vi to ask; **Fragezeichen** nt question mark; **fragwürdig** adj dubious

Franken (-s, -) m (Schweizer Währung) Swiss franc ▷ (-s) nt (Land) Franconia

frankieren vt to stamp; (maschinell) to frank

Frankreich (-s) nt France; **Franzose** (-n, -n) m, **Französin** f Frenchman/-woman; **die ~n** pl the French pl; **französisch** adj French; **Französisch** nt French

fraß imperf von **fressen**

Frau (-, -en) f woman; (Ehefrau) wife; (Anrede) Mrs; (unverheiratet, neutral) Ms; **Frauenarzt** m, **Frauenärztin** f gynaecologist; **Frauenbewegung** f women's movement; **frauenfeindlich** adj misogynous; **Frauenhaus** nt refuge (for battered women)

Fräulein nt (junge Dame) young lady; (veraltet als Anrede) Miss

Freak (-s, -s) m (fam) freak

frech adj cheeky; **Frechheit** f cheek; **so eine ~!** what a cheek

Freeclimbing (-s) nt free climbing

frei adj free; (Straße) clear; (Mitarbeiter) freelance; **ein ~er Tag** a day off; **~e Arbeitsstelle** vacancy; **Zimmer ~** room(s) to let (Brit), room(s) for rent (US); **im Freien** in the open air; **Freibad** nt open-air (swimming) pool;

freiberuflich adj freelance; **freig(i)ebig** adj generous; **Freiheit** f freedom; **Freikarte** f free ticket; **frei|lassen** irr vt to (set) free

freilich adv of course

Freilichtbühne f open-air theatre; **frei|machen** vr: **sich ~** to undress; **frei|nehmen** irr vt **sich** (dat) **einen Tag ~** to take a day off; **Freisprechanlage** f hands-free phone; **Freistoß** m free kick

Freitag m Friday; siehe auch **Mittwoch**; **freitags** adv on Fridays; siehe auch **mittwochs**

freiwillig adj voluntary

Freizeichen nt (Tel) ringing tone

Freizeit f spare (o free) time; **Freizeithemd** nt sports shirt; **Freizeitkleidung** f leisure wear; **Freizeitpark** m leisure park

fremd adj (nicht vertraut) strange; (ausländisch) foreign; (nicht eigen) someone else's; **Fremde(r)** mf (Unbekannter) stranger; (Ausländer) foreigner; **fremdenfeindlich** adj anti-foreigner, xenophobic; **Fremdenführer(in)** m(f) (tourist) guide; **Fremdenverkehr** m tourism; **Fremdenverkehrsamt** nt tourist information office; **Fremdenzimmer** nt (guest) room; **Fremdsprache** f foreign language; **Fremdsprachen-kenntnisse** pl knowledge sing of foreign languages; **Fremdwort** nt foreign word

Frequenz f (Radio) frequency

fressen (fraß, gefressen) vt, vi (Tier) to eat; (Mensch) to guzzle

Freude (-, -n) f joy, delight; **freuen** vt to please; **es freut mich, dass ...** I'm pleased that ... ▷ vr: **sich ~** to be pleased (über +akk about); **sich auf etw** (akk) **~** to look forward to sth

Freund (-(e)s, -e) m friend; (in Beziehung) boyfriend; **Freundin** f friend; (in Beziehung) girlfriend; **freundlich** adj friendly; (liebenswürdig) kind; **freundlicherweise** adv kindly; **Freundlichkeit** f friendliness; (Liebenswürdigkeit) kindness; **Freundschaft** f friendship

Frieden (-s, -) m peace; **Friedhof** m cemetery; **friedlich** adj peaceful

frieren (fror, gefroren) vt, vi to freeze; **ich friere, es friert mich** I'm freezing

Frikadelle f rissole

Frisbee® nt, **Frisbeescheibe**® f frisbee®

frisch adj fresh; (lebhaft) lively; „**~ gestrichen**" "wet paint"; **sich ~ machen** to freshen up; **Frischhaltefolie** f clingfilm® (Brit), plastic wrap (US); **Frischkäse** m cream cheese

Friseur(in) (-s, -e) m(f) hairdresser; **frisieren** vt: **jdn ~** to do sb's hair ▷ vr: **sich ~** to do one's hair

Frist (-, -en) f period; (Zeitpunkt) deadline; **innerhalb einer ~ von zehn Tagen** within a ten-day period; **eine ~ einhalten** to meet a deadline; **die ~ ist abgelaufen** the deadline has expired; **fristgerecht** adj, adv within the specified time; **fristlos** adj: **~e Entlassung** dismissal without notice

Frisur f hairdo, hairstyle

frittieren vt to deep-fry

Frl. f abk = **Fräulein** Miss

froh adj happy; **~e Weihnachten!** Merry Christmas

fröhlich adj happy, cheerful

Fronleichnam (-(e)s) m Corpus Christi

frontal adj frontal

fror imperf von **frieren**

Frosch (-(e)s, Frösche) m frog

Frost (-(e)s, Fröste) m frost; **bei ~** in frosty weather; **Frostschutzmittel** nt anti-freeze

Frottee nt terry(cloth); **Frottier(hand)tuch** nt towel

Frucht (-, Früchte) f (a. fig) fruit; (Getreide) corn; **Fruchteis** nt fruit-flavoured ice-cream; **Früchtetee** m fruit tea; **fruchtig** adj fruity; **Fruchtpresse** f juicer; **Fruchtsaft** m fruit juice; **Fruchtsalat** m fruit salad

früh adj, adv early; **heute ~** this morning; **um fünf Uhr ~** at five (o'clock) in the morning; **~ genug** soon enough; **früher** adj earlier; (ehemalig) former ▷ adv formerly, in the lead ▷ at the earliest; **frühestens** adv at the earliest

Frühjahr nt, **Frühling** m spring; **Frühlingsrolle** f spring roll; **Frühlingszwiebel** f spring onion (Brit), scallion (US)

frühmorgens adv early in the morning

Frühstück nt breakfast; **frühstücken** vi to have breakfast; **Frühstücksbüfett** nt breakfast buffet; **Frühstücksfernsehen** nt breakfast television; **Frühstücksspeck** m bacon

frühzeitig adj early

Frust (-s) m (fam) frustration; **frustrieren** vt to frustrate

Fuchs (-es, Füchse) m fox

fühlen vt, vi to feel ▷ vr: **sich ~** to feel

fuhr imperf von **fahren**

führen vt to lead; (Geschäft) to run; (Name) to bear; (Buch) to keep ▷ vi to lead, to be in the lead ▷ vr: **sich ~** to behave; **Führerschein** m driving licence (Brit), driver's license (US); **Führung** f leadership; (eines Unternehmens) management; (*Mil*) command; (*in Museum, Stadt*) guided tour; **in ~ liegen** to be in the lead

füllen *vt* to fill; (*Gastr*) to stuff ▷ *vr*: **sich ~** to fill

Füller (*-s, -*) *m*, **Füllfederhalter** (*-s, -*) *m* fountain pen

Füllung *f* filling

Fund (*-(e)s, -e*) *m* find; **Fundbüro** *nt* lost property office (*Brit*), lost and found (*US*); **Fundsachen** *pl* lost property *sing*

fünf *num* five; **Fünf** (*-, -en*) *f* five; (*Schulnote*) ≈ E; **fünfhundert** *num* five hundred; **fünfmal** *adv* five times; **fünfte(r, s)** *adj* fifth; *siehe auch* **dritte**; **Fünftel** (*-s, -*) *nt* (*Bruchteil*) fifth; **fünfzehn** *num* fifteen; **fünfzehnte(r, s)** *adj* fifteenth; *siehe auch* **dritte**; **fünfzig** *num* fifty; **fünfzigste(r, s)** *adj* fiftieth

Funk (*-s*) *m* radio; **über ~** by radio

Funke (*-ns, -n*) *m* spark; **funkeln** *vi* to sparkle

Funkgerät *nt* radio set; **Funktaxi** *nt* radio taxi, radio cab

Funktion *f* function; **funktionieren** *vi* to work, to function; **Funktionstaste** *f* (*Inform*) function key

für *prep* +*akk* for; **was ~ (ein) ...?** what kind (*o* sort) of ...?; **Tag ~ Tag** day after day

Furcht (*-*) *f* fear; **furchtbar** *adj* terrible; **fürchten** *vt* to be afraid of, to fear ▷ *vr*: **sich ~** to be afraid (*vor* +*dat* of); **fürchterlich** *adj* awful

füreinander *adv* for each other

fürs *kontr von* **für das**

Fürst(in) (*-en, -en*) *m(f)* prince/princess; **Fürstentum** *nt* principality; **fürstlich** *adj* (*fig*) splendid

Furunkel (*-s, -*) *nt* boil

Furz (*-es, -e*) *m* (*vulg*) fart; **furzen** *vi* (*vulg*) to fart

Fuß (*-es, Füße*) *m* foot; (*von Glas, Säule etc*) base; (*von Möbel*) leg; **zu ~** on foot; **zu ~ gehen** to walk; **Fußball** *m* football (*Brit*), soccer; **Fußballmannschaft** *f* football (*Brit*) (*o* soccer) team; **Fußballplatz** *m* football pitch (*Brit*), soccer field (*US*); **Fußballspiel** *nt* football (*Brit*) (*o* soccer) match; **Fußballspieler(in)** *m(f)* footballer (*Brit*), soccer player; **Fußboden** *m* floor; **Fußgänger(in)** (*-s, -*) *m(f)* pedestrian; **Fußgängerüberweg** *m* pedestrian crossing (*Brit*), crosswalk (*US*); **Fußgängerzone** *f* pedestrian precinct (*Brit*) (*o* zone (*US*)); **Fußgelenk** *nt* ankle; **Fußpilz** *m* athlete's foot; **Fußtritt** *m* kick; **jdm einen ~ geben** to give sb a kick, to kick sb; **Fußweg** *m* footpath

Futon (*-s, -s*) *m* futon

Futter (*-s, -*) *nt* feed; (*Heu etc*) fodder; (*Stoff*) lining; **füttern** *vt* to feed; (*Kleidung*) to line

Futur (*-s, -e*) *nt* (*Ling*) future (tense)

Fuzzi (*-s, -s*) *m* (*fam*) guy

g

gab imperf von **geben**
Gabe (-, -n) f gift
Gabel (-, -n) f fork; **Gabelung** f
fork
gaffen vi to gape
Gage (-, -n) f fee
gähnen vi to yawn
Galerie f gallery
Galle (-, -n) f gall; (Organ) gall
bladder; **Gallenstein** m
gallstone
Galopp (-s) m gallop;
galoppieren vi to gallop
galt imperf von **gelten**
Gameboy® (-s, -s) m Gameboy®
Gameshow f game show
gammeln vi to loaf around;
Gammler(in) (-s, -) m(f) layabout
gang adj: **~ und gäbe sein** to be
quite normal
Gang (-(e)s, Gänge) m walk; (im
Flugzeug) aisle; (Essen, Ablauf)
course; (Flur etc) corridor;
(Durchgang) passage; (Auto) gear;
den zweiten ~ einlegen to
change into second (gear); **etw in
~ bringen** to get sth going;
Gangschaltung f gears pl;
Gangway (-, -s) f (Aviat) steps pl;
(Naut) gangway
Gans (-, Gänse) f goose;
Gänseblümchen nt daisy;
Gänsehaut f goose pimples pl
(Brit), goose bumps pl (US)
ganz adj whole; (vollständig)
complete; **~ Europa** all of Europe;
sein ~es Geld all his money; **den
~en Tag** all day; ▷ adv quite;
(völlig) completely; **es hat mir
~ gut gefallen** I quite liked it;
~ schön viel quite a lot; **~ und gar
nicht** not at all; **das ist etwas
~ anderes** that's a completely
different matter; **ganztägig** adj
all-day; (Arbeit, Stelle) full-time;
ganztags adv (arbeiten) full-time;
Ganztagsschule f all-day school;
Ganztagsstelle f full-time job
gar adj done, cooked ▷ adv at all;
~ nicht/nichts not/nothing at all;
~ nicht schlecht not bad at all
Garage (-, -n) f garage
Garantie f guarantee;
garantieren vt to guarantee
Garderobe (-, -n) f (Kleidung)
wardrobe; (Abgabe) cloakroom
Gardine f curtain
Garn (-(e)s, -e) nt thread
Garnele (-, -n) f shrimp
garnieren vt to decorate;
(Speisen) to garnish
Garten (-s, Gärten) m garden;
Gärtner(in) (-s, -) m(f) gardener;
Gärtnerei f nursery;
(Gemüsegärtnerei) market garden
(Brit), truck farm (US)
Gas (-es, -e) nt gas; **~ geben** (Auto)
to accelerate; (fig) to get a move
on; **Gasanzünder** m gas lighter;
Gasbrenner m gas burner;

Gasflasche f gas bottle;
Gasheizung f gas heating;
Gasherd m gas stove, gas cooker
(Brit); **Gaskocher** (-s, -) m
camping stove; **Gaspedal** nt
accelerator, gas pedal (US)
Gasse (-, -n) f alley
Gast (-es, Gäste) m guest; **Gäste
haben** to have guests;
Gastarbeiter(in) m(f) foreign
worker; **Gästebett** nt spare bed;
Gästebuch nt visitors' book;
Gästehaus nt guest house;
Gästezimmer nt guest room;
gastfreundlich adj hospitable;
Gastfreundschaft f hospitality;
Gastgeber(in) (-s, -) m(f) host/
hostess; **Gasthaus** nt, **Gasthof** m
inn; **Gastland** nt host country
Gastritis (-) f gastritis
Gastronomie f catering trade
Gastspiel nt (Sport) away game;
Gaststätte f restaurant;
(Trinklokal) pub (Brit), bar;
Gastwirt(in) m(f) landlord/-lady
GAU (-s, -s) m akr = **größter
anzunehmender Unfall** MCA
Gaumen (-s, -) m palate
Gaze (-, -n) f gauze
geb. adj abk = **geboren** b. ▷ adj
abk = **geborene** née; siehe **geboren**
Gebäck (-(e)s, -e) nt pastries pl;
(Kekse) biscuits pl (Brit), cookies pl
(US)
gebacken pp von **backen**
Gebärdensprache f sign
language
Gebärmutter f womb
Gebäude (-s, -) nt building
geben (gab, gegeben) vt, vi to give
(jdm etw sb sth, sth to sb); (Karten)
to deal; **lass dir eine Quittung
~** ask for a receipt ▷ vt impers: **es
gibt** there is/are; (in Zukunft) there
will be; **das gibt's nicht** I don't
believe it ▷ vr: **sich ~** (sich
verhalten) to behave, to act; **das**

gibt sich wieder it'll sort itself out
Gebet (-(e)s, -e) nt prayer
gebeten pp von **bitten**
Gebiet (-(e)s, -e) nt area;
(Hoheitsgebiet) territory; (fig) field
gebildet adj educated; (belesen)
well-read
Gebirge (-s, -) nt mountains pl;
gebirgig adj mountainous
Gebiss (-es, -e) nt teeth pl;
(künstlich) dentures pl; **gebissen**
pp von **beißen**; **Gebissreiniger** m
denture tablets pl
Gebläse (-s, -) nt fan, blower
geblasen pp von **blasen**
geblieben pp von **bleiben**
gebogen pp von **biegen**
geboren pp von **gebären** ▷ adj
born; **Andrea Jordan, geborene
Christian** Andrea Jordan, née
Christian
geborgen pp von **bergen** ▷ adj
secure, safe
geboten pp von **bieten**
gebracht pp von **bringen**
gebrannt pp von **brennen**
gebraten pp von **braten**
gebrauchen vt to use;
Gebrauchsanweisung f direc-
tions pl for use; **gebrauchsfertig**
adj ready to use; **gebraucht** adj
used; **etw ~ kaufen** to buy sth
secondhand; **Gebrauchtwagen**
m secondhand (o used) car
gebräunt adj tanned
gebrochen pp von **brechen**
Gebühr (-, -en) f charge; (Maut)
toll; (Honorar) fee; **Gebühren-
einheit** f (Tel) unit;
gebührenfrei adj free of charge;
(Telefonnummer) freefone® (Brit),
toll-free (US); **gebührenpflichtig**
adj subject to charges; **~e Straße**
toll road
gebunden pp von **binden**
Geburt (-, -en) f birth; **gebürtig**
adj: **er ist ~er Schweizer** he is

Swiss by birth; **Geburtsdatum** nt date of birth; **Geburtsjahr** nt year of birth; **Geburtsname** m birth name; (einer Frau) maiden name; **Geburtsort** m birthplace; **Geburtstag** m birthday; **herzlichen Glückwunsch zum ~!** Happy Birthday; **Geburtsurkunde** f birth certificate

Gebüsch (-(e)s, -e) nt bushes pl

gedacht pp von **denken**

Gedächtnis nt memory; **im ~ behalten** to remember

Gedanke (-ns, -n) m thought; **sich** (dat) **über etw** (akk) **~n machen** to think about sth; (besorgt) to be worried about sth; **Gedankenstrich** m dash

Gedeck (-(e)s, -e) nt place setting; (Speisenfolge) set meal

Gedenkstätte f memorial; **Gedenktafel** f commemorative plaque

Gedicht (-(e)s, -e) nt poem

Gedränge (-s) nt crush, crowd

gedrungen pp von **dringen**

Geduld (-) f patience; **geduldig** adj patient

gedurft pp von **dürfen**

geehrt adj: **Sehr ~er Herr Young** Dear Mr Young

geeignet adj suitable

Gefahr (-, -en) f danger; **auf eigene ~** at one's own risk; **außer ~ sein** out of danger; **gefährden** vt to endanger

gefahren pp von **fahren**

gefährlich adj dangerous

Gefälle (-s, -) nt gradient, slope

gefallen pp von **fallen** ▷ irr vi: **jdm ~** to please sb; **er/es gefällt mir** I like him/it; **sich** (dat) **etw ~ lassen** to put up with sth

Gefallen (-s, -) m favour; **jdm einen ~ tun** to do sb a favour

gefälligst adv ..., will you!; **sei ~ still!** be quiet, will you!

gefangen pp von **fangen**

Gefängnis nt prison

Gefäß (-es, -e) nt (Behälter) container, receptacle; (Anat, Bot) vessel

gefasst adj composed, calm; **auf etw** (akk) **~ sein** to be prepared (o ready) for sth

geflochten pp von **flechten**

geflogen pp von **fliegen**

geflossen pp von **fließen**

Geflügel (-s) nt poultry

gefragt adj in demand

gefressen pp von **fressen**

Gefrierbeutel m freezer bag; **gefrieren** irr vi to freeze; **Gefrierfach** nt freezer compartment; **Gefrierschrank** m (upright) freezer; **Gefriertruhe** f (chest) freezer

gefroren pp von **frieren**

Gefühl (-(e)s, -e) nt feeling

gefunden pp von **finden**

gegangen pp von **gehen**

gegeben pp von **geben**; **gegebenenfalls** adv if need be

 SCHLÜSSELWORT

gegen prep +akk **1** against; **nichts gegen jdn haben** to have nothing against sb; **X gegen Y** (Sport, Jur) X versus Y; **ein Mittel gegen Schnupfen** something for colds **2** (in Richtung auf) towards; **gegen Osten** to(wards) the east; **gegen Abend** towards evening; **gegen einen Baum fahren** to drive into a tree **3** (ungefähr) round about; **gegen 3 Uhr** around 3 o'clock **4** (gegenüber) towards; (ungefähr) around; **gerecht gegen alle** fair to all **5** (im Austausch für) for; **gegen bar** for cash; **gegen Quittung** against

a receipt
6 (*verglichen mit*) compared with

Gegend (-, -en) f area; **hier in der ~** around here
gegeneinander adv against one another
Gegenfahrbahn f opposite lane; **Gegenmittel** nt remedy (*gegen* for); **Gegenrichtung** f opposite direction; **Gegensatz** m contrast; **im ~ zu** in contrast to; **gegensätzlich** adj conflicting; **gegenseitig** adj mutual; **sich ~ helfen** to help each other
Gegenstand m object; (*Thema*) subject
Gegenteil nt opposite; **im ~** on the contrary; **gegenteilig** adj opposite, contrary
gegenüber prep +dat opposite; (*zu jdm*) to(wards); (*angesichts*) in the face of ▷ adv opposite; **gegenüber|stehen** vt to face; (*Problemen*) to be faced with; **gegenüber|stellen** vt to confront (*dat* with); (*fig*) compare (*dat* with)
Gegenverkehr m oncoming traffic; **Gegenwart** (-) f present (tense)
Gegenwind m headwind
gegessen pp von **essen**
geglichen pp von **gleichen**
geglitten pp von **gleiten**
Gegner(in) (-s, -) m(f) opponent
gegolten pp von **gelten**
gegossen pp von **gießen**
gegraben pp von **graben**
gegriffen pp von **greifen**
gehabt pp von **haben**
Gehackte(s) nt mince(d meat) (*Brit*), ground meat (*US*)
Gehalt (-(e)s, -e) m content ▷ (-(e)s, Gehälter) nt salary
gehalten pp von **halten**
gehangen pp von **hängen**

gehässig adj spiteful, nasty
gehauen pp von **hauen**
gehbehindert adj: **sie ist ~** she can't walk properly
geheim adj secret; **etw ~ halten** to keep sth secret; **Geheimnis** nt secret; (*rätselhaft*) mystery; **geheimnisvoll** adj mysterious; **Geheimnummer** f, **Geheimzahl** f (*von Kreditkarte*) PIN number
geheißen pp von **heißen**
gehen (ging, gegangen) vt, vi to go; (*zu Fuß*) to walk; (*funktionieren*) to work; **über die Straße ~** to cross the street; **~ nach** (*Fenster*) to face ▷ vi impers: **wie geht es (dir)?** how are you? (o things)?; **mir/ihm geht es gut** I'm/he's (doing) fine; **geht das?** is that possible?; **geht's noch?** can you still manage?; **es geht** not too bad, OK; **das geht nicht** that's not on; **es geht um ...** it's about ...
Gehirn (-(e)s, -e) nt brain; **Gehirnerschütterung** f concussion
gehoben pp von **heben**
geholfen pp von **helfen**
Gehör (-(e)s) nt hearing
gehorchen vi to obey (*jdm* sb)
gehören vi to belong (*jdm* to sb); **wem gehört das Buch?** whose book is this?; **gehört es dir?** is it yours? ▷ vr impers: **das gehört sich nicht** it's not done
gehörlos adj deaf
gehorsam adj obedient
Gehsteig m, **Gehweg** (-s, -e) m pavement (*Brit*), sidewalk (*US*)
Geier (-s, -) m vulture
Geige (-, -n) f violin
geil adj randy (*Brit*), horny (*US*); (*fam: toll*) fantastic
Geisel (-, -n) f hostage
Geist (-(e)s, -er) m spirit; (*Gespenst*) ghost; (*Verstand*) mind; **Geisterbahn** f ghost train, tunnel

of horror (US); **Geisterfahrer(in)** m(f) person driving the wrong way on the motorway

geizig adj stingy

gekannt pp von **kennen**

geklungen pp von **klingen**

geknickt adj (fig) dejected

gekniffen pp von **kneifen**

gekommen pp von **kommen**

gekonnt pp von **können** ▷ adj skilful

gekrochen pp von **kriechen**

Gel (-s, -s) nt gel

Gelächter (-s, -) nt laughter

geladen pp von **laden** ▷ adj loaded; (Elek) live; (fig) furious

gelähmt adj paralysed

Gelände (-s, -) nt land, terrain; (Fabrik, Sportgelände) grounds pl; (Baugelände) site

Geländer (-s, -) nt railing; (Treppengeländer) banister

Geländewagen m off-road vehicle

gelang imperf von **gelingen**

gelassen pp von **lassen** ▷ adj calm, composed

Gelatine f gelatine

gelaufen pp von **laufen**

gelaunt adj: **gut/schlecht ~** in a good/bad mood

gelb adj yellow; (Ampel) amber, yellow (US); **gelblich** adj yellowish; **Gelbsucht** f jaundice

Geld (-(e)s, -er) nt money; **Geldautomat** m cash machine (o dispenser (Brit)), ATM (US); **Geldbeutel** m, **Geldbörse** f purse; **Geldbuße** f fine; **Geldschein** m (bank)note (Brit), bill (US); **Geldstrafe** f fine; **Geldstück** nt coin; **Geldwechsel** m exchange of money; (Ort) bureau de change; **Geldwechselautomat** m, **Geldwechsler** (-s, -) m change machine

Gelee (-s, -s) nt jelly

gelegen pp von **liegen** ▷ adj situated; (passend) convenient; **etw kommt jdm ~** sth is convenient for sb

Gelegenheit f opportunity; (Anlass) occasion

gelegentlich adj occasional ▷ adv occasionally; (bei Gelegenheit) some time (or other)

Gelenk (-(e)s, -e) nt joint

gelernt adj skilled

gelesen pp von **lesen**

geliehen pp von **leihen**

gelingen (gelang, gelungen) vi to succeed; **es ist mir gelungen, ihn zu erreichen** I managed to get hold of him

gelitten pp von **leiden**

gelockt adj curly

gelogen pp von **lügen**

gelten (galt, gegolten) vt (wert sein) to be worth; **jdm viel/wenig ~** to mean a lot/not to mean much to sb ▷ vi (gültig sein) to be valid; (erlaubt sein) to be allowed; **jdm ~** (gemünzt sein auf) to be meant for (o aimed at) sb; **etw ~ lassen** to accept sth; **als etw ~** to be considered to be sth; **Geltungsdauer** f: **eine ~ von fünf Tagen haben** to be valid for five days

gelungen pp von **gelingen**

gemahlen pp von **mahlen**

Gemälde (-s, -) nt painting, picture

gemäß prep +dat in accordance with ▷ adj appropriate (dat to)

gemein adj (niederträchtig) mean, nasty; (gewöhnlich) common

Gemeinde (-, -n) f district, community; (Pfarrgemeinde) parish; (Kirchengemeinde) congregation

gemeinsam adj joint, common ▷ adv together, jointly; **das Haus**

g

gehört uns beiden ~ the house belongs to both of us

Gemeinschaft f community; **~ Unabhängiger Staaten** Commonwealth of Independent States

gemeint pp von **meinen**; **das war nicht so ~** I didn't mean it like that

gemessen pp von **messen**

gemieden pp von **meiden**

gemischt adj mixed

gemocht pp von **mögen**

Gemüse (-s, -) nt vegetables pl; **Gemüsehändler(in)** m(f) greengrocer

gemusst pp von **müssen**

gemustert adj patterned

gemütlich adj comfortable, cosy; (Mensch) good-natured, easy-going; **mach es dir ~** make yourself at home

genannt pp von **nennen**

genau adj exact, precise ▷ adv exactly, precisely; **~ in der Mitte** right in the middle; **es mit etw ~ nehmen** to be particular about sth; **~ genommen** strictly speaking; **ich weiß es ~** I know for certain (o for sure); **genauso** adv exactly the same (way); **~ gut/viel/viele Leute** just as well/much/many people (wie as)

genehmigen vt to approve; **sich** (dat) **etw ~** to indulge in sth; **Genehmigung** f approval

Generalkonsulat nt consulate general

Generation f generation

Genf (-s) nt Geneva; **~er See** Lake Geneva

Genforschung f genetic research

genial adj brilliant

Genick (-(e)s, -e) nt (back of the) neck

Genie (-s, -s) nt genius

genieren vr: **sich ~** to feel awkward; **ich geniere mich vor ihm** he makes me feel embarrassed

genießen (genoss, genossen) vt to enjoy

Genitiv m genitive (case)

genmanipuliert adj genetically modified, GM

genommen pp von **nehmen**

genoss imperf von **genießen**

genossen pp von **genießen**

Gentechnik f genetic technology; **gentechnisch** adv: **~ verändert** genetically modified, GM

genug adv enough

genügen vi to be enough (jdm for sb); **danke, das genügt** thanks, that's enough (o that will do)

Genuss (-es, Genüsse) m pleasure; (Zusichnehmen) consumption

geöffnet adj (Geschäft etc) open

Geografie f geography

Geologie f geology

Georgien (-s) nt Georgia

Gepäck (-(e)s) nt luggage (Brit), baggage; **Gepäckabfertigung** f luggage (Brit) (o baggage) check-in; **Gepäckablage** f luggage (Brit) (o baggage) rack; **Gepäckannahme** f (zur Beförderung) luggage (Brit) (o baggage) office; (zur Aufbewahrung) left-luggage office (Brit), baggage checkroom (US); **Gepäckaufbewahrung** f left-luggage office (Brit), baggage checkroom (US); **Gepäckausgabe** f luggage (Brit) (o baggage) office; (am Flughafen) baggage reclaim; **Gepäckband** nt luggage (Brit) (o baggage) conveyor; **Gepäckkontrolle** f luggage (Brit) (o baggage) check; **Gepäckstück** nt item of luggage (Brit) (o baggage (US)); **Gepäckträger** m porter; (an Fahrrad) carrier;

Gepäckversicherung f luggage (Brit) (o baggage) insurance; **Gepäckwagen** m luggage van (Brit), baggage car (US)
gepfiffen pp von **pfeifen**
gepflegt adj well-groomed; (Park) well looked after
gequollen pp von **quellen**

🔵 SCHLÜSSELWORT

gerade adj straight; (aufrecht) upright; **eine gerade Zahl** an even number
▷ adv 1 (genau) just, exactly; (speziell) especially; **gerade deshalb** that's just o exactly why; **das ist es ja gerade!** that's just it!; **gerade du** you especially; **warum gerade ich?** why me (of all people)?; **jetzt gerade nicht!** not now!; **gerade neben** right next to
2 (eben, soeben) just; **er wollte gerade aufstehen** he was just about to get up; **gerade erst** only just; **gerade noch** (only) just

geradeaus adv straight ahead
gerannt pp von **rennen**
geraspelt adj grated
Gerät (-(e)s, -e) nt device, gadget; (Werkzeug) tool; (Radio, Fernseher) set; (Zubehör) equipment
geraten pp von **raten** ▷ irr vi to turn out; **gut/schlecht ~** to turn out well/badly; **an jdn ~** to come across sb; **in etw** (akk) **~** to get into sth
geräuchert adj smoked
geräumig adj roomy
Geräusch (-(e)s, -e) nt sound; (unangenehm) noise
gerecht adj fair; (Strafe, Belohnung) just; **jdm/einer Sache ~ werden** to do justice to sb/sth
gereizt adj irritable

Gericht (-(e)s, -e) nt (Jur) court; (Essen) dish
gerieben pp von **reiben**
gering adj small; (unbedeutend) slight; (niedrig) low; (Zeit) short; **geringfügig** adj slight, minor
▷ adv slightly
gerissen pp von **reißen**
geritten pp von **reiten**
gern(e) adv willingly, gladly; **etw ~ tun** to like doing sth; **~ geschehen** you're welcome; **gern|haben, gern mögen** irr vt to like
gerochen pp von **riechen**
Gerste (-, -n) f barley; **Gerstenkorn** nt (im Auge) stye
Geruch (-(e)s, Gerüche) m smell
Gerücht (-(e)s, -e) nt rumour
gerufen pp von **rufen**
Gerümpel (-s) nt junk
gerungen pp von **ringen**
Gerüst (-(e)s, -e) nt (auf Bau) scaffolding; (Gestell) trestle; (fig) framework (zu of)
gesalzen pp von **salzen**
gesamt adj whole, entire; (Kosten) total; (Werke) complete; **Gesamtschule** f ≈ comprehensive school
gesandt pp von **senden**
Gesäß (-es, -e) nt bottom
geschaffen pp von **schaffen**
Geschäft (-(e)s, -e) nt business; (Laden) shop; (Geschäftsabschluss) deal; **geschäftlich** adj commercial ▷ adv on business; **Geschäftsfrau** f businesswoman; **Geschäftsführer(in)** m(f) managing director; (von Laden) manager; **Geschäftsleitung** f executive board; **Geschäftsmann** m businessman; **Geschäftsreise** f business trip; **Geschäftsstraße** f shopping street; **Geschäftszeiten** pl business (o opening) hours pl

g

geschehen (*geschah, geschehen*) *vi* to happen

Geschenk (*-(e)s, -e*) *nt* present, gift; **Geschenkgutschein** *m* gift voucher; **Geschenkpapier** *nt* gift-wrapping paper, giftwrap

Geschichte (*-, -n*) *f* story; (*Sache*) affair; (*Hist*) history

geschickt *adj* skilful

geschieden *pp von* **scheiden**
▷ *adj* divorced

geschienen *pp von* **scheinen**

Geschirr (*-(e)s, -e*) *nt* crockery; (*zum Kochen*) pots and pans *pl*; (*von Pferd*) harness; **~ spülen** to do (*o* wash) the dishes, to do the washing-up (*Brit*); **Geschirrspülmaschine** *f* dishwasher; **Geschirrspülmittel** *nt* washing-up liquid (*Brit*), dishwashing liquid (*US*); **Geschirrtuch** *nt* tea towel (*Brit*), dish towel (*US*)

geschissen *pp von* **scheißen**

geschlafen *pp von* **schlafen**

geschlagen *pp von* **schlagen**

Geschlecht (*-(e)s, -er*) *nt* sex; (*Ling*) gender; **Geschlechtskrankheit** *f* sexually transmitted disease, STD; **Geschlechtsorgan** *nt* sexual organ; **Geschlechtsverkehr** *m* sexual intercourse

geschlichen *pp von* **schleichen**

geschliffen *pp von* **schleifen**

geschlossen *adj* closed

Geschmack (*-(e)s, Geschmäcke*) *m* taste; **geschmacklos** *adj* tasteless; **Geschmack(s)sache** *f*: **das ist ~** that's a matter of taste; **geschmackvoll** *adj* tasteful

geschmissen *pp von* **schmeißen**

geschmolzen *pp von* **schmelzen**

geschnitten *pp von* **schneiden**

geschoben *pp von* **schieben**

Geschoss (*-es, -e*) *nt* (*Stockwerk*) floor

geschossen *pp von* **schießen**

Geschrei (*-s*) *nt* cries *pl*; (*fig*) fuss

geschrieben *pp von* **schreiben**

geschrie(e)n *pp von* **schreien**

geschützt *adj* protected

Geschwätz (*-es*) *nt* chatter; (*Klatsch*) gossip; **geschwätzig** *adj* talkative, gossipy

geschweige *adv*: **~ (denn)** let alone

geschwiegen *pp von* **schweigen**

Geschwindigkeit *f* speed; (*Phys*) velocity; **Geschwindigkeitsbegrenzung** *f* speed limit

Geschwister *pl* brothers and sisters *pl*

geschwollen *adj* (*angeschwollen*) swollen; (*Rede*) pompous

geschwommen *pp von* **schwimmen**

geschworen *pp von* **schwören**

Geschwulst (*-, Geschwülste*) *f* growth

Geschwür (*-(e)s, -e*) *nt* ulcer

gesehen *pp von* **sehen**

gesellig *adj* sociable; **Gesellschaft** *f* society; (*Begleitung*) company; (*Abend~*) party; **~ mit beschränkter Haftung** limited company (*Brit*), limited corporation (*US*)

gesessen *pp von* **sitzen**

Gesetz (*-es, -e*) *nt* law; **gesetzlich** *adj* legal; **~er Feiertag** public (*o* bank (*Brit*) *o* legal (*US*)) holiday; **gesetzwidrig** *adj* illegal

Gesicht (*-(e)s, -er*) *nt* face; (*Miene*) expression; **mach doch nicht so ein ~!** stop pulling such a face; **Gesichtscreme** *f* face cream; **Gesichtswasser** *nt* toner

gesoffen *pp von* **saufen**

gesogen *pp von* **saugen**

gespannt *adj* tense; (*begierig*) eager; **ich bin ~, ob ...** I wonder if ...; **auf etw/jdn ~ sein** to look

forward to sth/to seeing sb
Gespenst (-(e)s, -er) nt ghost
gesperrt adj closed
gesponnen pp von **spinnen**
Gespräch (-(e)s, -e) nt talk,
conversation; (Diskussion)
discussion; (Anruf) call
gesprochen pp von **sprechen**
gesprungen pp von **springen**
Gestalt (-, -en) f form, shape;
(Mensch) figure
gestanden pp von **stehen,
gestehen**
Gestank (-(e)s) m stench
gestatten vt to permit, to allow;
~ **Sie?** may I?
Geste (-, -n) f gesture
gestehen irr vt to confess
gestern adv yesterday;
~ **Abend/Morgen** yesterday
evening/morning
gestiegen pp von **steigen**
gestochen pp von **stechen**
gestohlen pp von **stehlen**
gestorben pp von **sterben**
gestört adj disturbed; (Empfang)
poor
gestoßen pp von **stoßen**
gestreift adj striped
gestrichen pp von **streichen**
gestritten pp von **streiten**
gestunken pp von **stinken**
gesund adj healthy; **wieder
~ werden** to get better;
Gesundheit f health; **~!** bless
you!; **gesundheitsschädlich** adj
unhealthy
gesungen pp von **singen**
gesunken pp von **sinken**
getan pp von **tun**
getragen pp von **tragen**
Getränk (-(e)s, -e) nt drink;
Getränkeautomat m drinks
machine; **Getränkekarte** f list
of drinks
Getreide (-s, -) nt cereals pl,
grain

getrennt adj separate; **~ leben**
to live apart; **~ zahlen** to pay
separately
getreten pp von **treten**
Getriebe (-s, -) nt (Auto) gearbox
getrieben pp von **treiben**
Getriebeschaden m gearbox
damage
getroffen pp von **treffen**
getrunken pp von **trinken**
Getue nt fuss
geübt adj experienced
gewachsen pp von **wachsen**
▷ adj: **jdm/einer Sache ~ sein** to
be a match for sb/up to sth
Gewähr (-) f guarantee; **keine
~ übernehmen für** to accept no
responsibility for
Gewalt (-, -en) f (Macht) power;
(Kontrolle) control; (große Kraft)
force; (~taten) violence; **mit aller
~** with all one's might; **gewaltig**
adj tremendous; (Irrtum) huge
gewandt pp von **wenden** ▷ adj
(flink) nimble; (geschickt) skilful
gewann imperf von **gewinnen**
gewaschen pp von **waschen**
Gewebe (-s, -) nt (Stoff) fabric;
(Bio) tissue
Gewehr (-(e)s, -e) nt rifle, gun
Geweih (-(e)s, -e) nt antlers pl
gewellt adj (Haare) wavy
gewendet pp von **wenden**
Gewerbe (-s, -) nt trade;
Gewerbegebiet nt industrial
estate (Brit) (o park (US));
gewerblich adj commercial
Gewerkschaft f trade union
gewesen pp von **sein**
Gewicht (-(e)s, -e) nt weight;
(fig) importance
gewiesen pp von **weisen**
Gewinn (-(e)s, -e) m profit; (bei
Spiel) winnings pl; **gewinnen**
(gewann, gewonnen) vt to win;
(erwerben) to gain; (Kohle, Öl) to
extract ▷ vi to win; (profitieren) to

gain; **Gewinner(in)** (-s, -) m(f) winner

gewiss adj certain ▷ adv certainly

Gewissen (-s, -) nt conscience; **ein gutes/schlechtes ~ haben** to have a clear/bad conscience

Gewitter (-s, -) nt thunderstorm; **gewittern** vi impers: **es gewittert** it's thundering

gewogen pp von **wiegen**

gewöhnen vt **jdn an etw** (akk) **~** to accustom sb to sth ▷ vr: **sich an jdn/etw ~** to get used (o accustomed) to sb/sth; **Gewohnheit** f habit; (Brauch) custom; **gewöhnlich** adj usual; (durchschnittlich) ordinary; (pej) common; **wie ~** as usual; **gewohnt** adj usual; **etw ~ sein** to be used to sth

Gewölbe (-s, -) nt (Deckengewölbe) vault

gewonnen pp von **gewinnen**

geworben pp von **werben**

geworden pp von **werden**

geworfen pp von **werfen**

Gewürz (-es, -e) nt spice; **Gewürznelke** f clove; **gewürzt** adj seasoned

gewusst pp von **wissen**

Gezeiten pl tides pl

gezogen pp von **ziehen**

gezwungen pp von **zwingen**

Gibraltar (-s) nt Gibraltar

Gicht (-) f gout

Giebel (-s, -) m gable

gierig adj greedy

gießen (goss, gegossen) vt to pour; (Blumen) to water; (Metall) to cast; **Gießkanne** f watering can

Gift (-(e)s, -e) nt poison; **giftig** adj poisonous

Gigabyte nt gigabyte

Gin (-s, -s) m gin

ging imperf von **gehen**

Gin Tonic (-(s), -s) m gin and tonic

Gipfel (-s, -) m summit, peak; (Pol) summit; (fig: Höhepunkt) height

Gips (-es, -e) m (a. Med) plaster; **Gipsbein** nt: **sie hat ein ~** she's got her leg in plaster; **Gipsverband** m plaster cast

Giraffe (-, -n) f giraffe

Girokonto nt current account (Brit), checking account (US)

Gitarre (-, -n) f guitar

Gitter (-s, -) nt bars pl

glänzen vi (a. fig) to shine; **glänzend** adj shining; (fig) brilliant

Glas (-es, Gläser) nt glass; (Marmelade) jar; **zwei ~ Wein** two glasses of wine; **Glascontainer** m bottle bank; **Glaser(in)** m(f) glazier; **Glasscheibe** f pane (of glass); **Glassplitter** m splinter of glass

Glasur f glaze; (Gastr) icing

glatt adj smooth; (rutschig) slippery; (Lüge) downright; **Glatteis** nt (black) ice

Glatze (-, -n) f bald head; (fam: Skinhead) skinhead

glauben vt, vi to believe (an +akk in); (meinen) to think; **jdm ~** to believe sb

gleich adj equal; (identisch) same, identical; **alle Menschen sind ~** all people are the same; **es ist mir ~** it's all the same to me ▷ adv equally; (sofort) straight away; (bald) in a minute; **~ groß/alt** the same size/age; **~ nach/an** right after/at; **Gleichberechtigung** f equal rights pl; **gleichen** (glich, geglichen) vi: **jdm/einer Sache ~** to be like sb/sth ▷ vr: **sich ~** to be alike; **gleichfalls** adv likewise; **danke ~!** thanks, and the same to you; **gleichgültig** adj indifferent; **gleichmäßig** adj regular; (Verteilung) even, equal;

gleichzeitig *adj* simultaneous ▷ *adv* at the same time

Gleis (*-es, -e*) *nt* track, rails *pl*; (*Bahnsteig*) platform

gleiten (*glitt, geglitten*) *vi* to glide; (*rutschen*) to slide; **Gleitschirmfliegen** (*-s*) *nt* paragliding

Gletscher (*-s, -*) *m* glacier; **Gletscherskifahren** *nt* glacier skiing; **Gletscherspalte** *f* crevasse

glich *imperf von* **gleichen**

Glied (*-(e)s, -er*) *nt* (*Arm, Bein*) limb; (*von Kette*) link; (*Penis*) penis; **Gliedmaßen** *pl* limbs *pl*

glitschig *adj* slippery

glitt *imperf von* **gleiten**

glitzern *vi* to glitter; (*Sterne*) to twinkle

Glocke (*-, -n*) *f* bell; **Glockenspiel** *nt* chimes *pl*

Glotze (*-, -n*) *f* (*fam: TV*) box; **glotzen** *vi* (*fam*) to stare

Glück (*-(e)s*) *nt* luck; (*Freude*) happiness; **~ haben** to be lucky; **viel ~!** good luck; **zum ~** fortunately; **glücklich** *adj* lucky; (*froh*) happy; **glücklicherweise** *adj* fortunately; **Glückwunsch** *m* congratulations *pl*; **herzlichen ~ zur bestandenen Prüfung** congratulations on passing your exam; **herzlichen ~ zum Geburtstag!** Happy Birthday

Glühbirne *f* light bulb; **glühen** *vi* to glow; **Glühwein** *m* mulled wine

GmbH (*-, -s*) *f abk* = **Gesellschaft mit beschränkter Haftung** ≈ Ltd (*Brit*), ≈ Inc (*US*)

Gokart (*-(s), -s*) *m* go-kart

Gold (*-(e)s*) *nt* gold; **golden** *adj* gold; (*fig*) golden; **Goldfisch** *m* goldfish; **Goldmedaille** *f* gold medal; **Goldschmied(in)** *m(f)* goldsmith

Golf (*-(e)s, -e*) *m* gulf; **der ~ von Biskaya** the Bay of Biscay ▷ (*-s*) *nt* golf; **Golfplatz** *m* golf course; **Golfschläger** *m* golf club

Gondel (*-, -n*) *f* gondola; (*Seilbahn*) cable-car

gönnen *vt*: **ich gönne es ihm** I'm really pleased for him; **sich** (*dat*) **etw ~** to allow oneself sth

goss *imperf von* **gießen**

gotisch *adj* Gothic

Gott (*-es, Götter*) *m* God; (*Gottheit*) god; **Gottesdienst** *m* service; **Göttin** *f* goddess

Grab (*-(e)s, Gräber*) *nt* grave

graben (*grub, gegraben*) *vt* to dig; **Graben** (*-s, Gräben*) *m* ditch

Grabstein *m* gravestone

Grad (*-(e)s, -e*) *m* degree; **wir haben 30 ~ Celsius** it's 30 degrees Celsius, it's 86 degrees Fahrenheit; **bis zu einem gewissen ~** up to a certain extent

Graf (*-en, -en*) *m* count; (*in Großbritannien*) earl

Graffiti *pl* graffiti *sing*

Grafik (*-, -en*) *f* graph; (*Kunstwerk*) graphic; (*Illustration*) diagram; **Grafikkarte** *f* (*Inform*) graphics card; **Grafikprogramm** *nt* (*Inform*) graphics software

Gräfin (*-, -nen*) *f* countess

Gramm (*-s*) *nt* gram(me)

Grammatik *f* grammar

Grapefruit (*-, -s*) *f* grapefruit

Graphik *f siehe* **Grafik**

Gras (*-es, Gräser*) *nt* grass

grässlich *adj* horrible

Gräte (*-, -n*) *f* (fish)bone

gratis *adj, adv* free (of charge)

gratulieren *vi*: **jdm** (**zu etw**) **~** to congratulate sb (on sth); (**ich**) **gratuliere!** congratulations!

grau *adj* grey, gray (*US*); **grauhaarig** *adj* grey-haired

grausam *adj* cruel

g

gravierend adj (Fehler) serious
greifen (griff, gegriffen) vt to
seize; **zu etw ~** (fig) to resort to
sth ▷ vi (Regel etc) to have an
effect (bei on)
grell adj harsh
Grenze (-, -n) f boundary; (Staat)
border; (Schranke) limit; **grenzen**
vi to border (an +akk on);
Grenzkontrolle f border control;
Grenzübergang m border
crossing point; **Grenzverkehr** m
border traffic
Grieche (-n, -n) m Greek;
Griechenland nt Greece;
Griechin f Greek; **griechisch** adj
Greek; **Griechisch** nt Greek
griesgrämig adj grumpy
Grieß (-es, -e) m (Gastr) semolina
griff imperf von **greifen**
Griff (-(e)s, -e) m grip; (Tür etc)
handle; **griffbereit** adj handy
Grill (-s, -s) m grill; (im Freien)
barbecue
Grille (-, -n) f cricket
grillen vt to grill ▷ vi to have a
barbecue; **Grillfest** nt, **Grillfete** f
barbecue; **Grillkohle** f charcoal
grinsen vi to grin; (höhnisch) to
sneer
Grippe (-, -n) f flu;
Grippeschutzimpfung f flu
vaccination
grob adj coarse; (Fehler, Verstoß)
gross; (Einschätzung) rough
Grönland (-s) nt Greenland
groß adj big, large; (hoch) tall;
(fig) great; (Buchstabe) capital;
(erwachsen) grown-up; **im Großen
und Ganzen** on the whole ▷ adv
greatly; **großartig** adj
wonderful
Großbritannien (-s) nt (Great)
Britain
Großbuchstabe m capital letter
Größe (-, -n) f size; (Länge)
height; (fig) greatness; **welche**

~ haben Sie? what size do you
take?
Großeltern pl grandparents pl;
Großhandel m wholesale trade;
Großmarkt m hypermarket;
Großmutter f grandmother;
Großraum m: **der ~ Manchester**
Greater Manchester;
groß|schreiben irr vt to write
with a capital letter; **Großstadt** f
city; **Großvater** m grandfather;
großzügig adj generous;
(Planung) on a large scale
Grotte (-, -n) f grotto
grub imperf von **graben**
Grübchen nt dimple
Grube (-, -n) f pit
grüezi interj (schweizerisch) hello
Gruft (-, -en) f vault
grün adj green; **~er Salat** lettuce;
~e Bohnen French beans; **der ~e
Punkt** symbol for recyclable
packaging; **im ~en Bereich**
hunky-dory

● GRÜNER PUNKT
●
● The **grüner Punkt** is the green
● spot symbol which appears on
● packaging, indicating that the
● packaging should not be
● thrown into the normal
● household refuse but kept
● separate to be recycled through
● the **DSD** (Duales System
● Deutschland) system. The
● recycling is financed by licences
● bought by the manufacturer
● from the 'DSD' and the cost of
● this is often passed on to the
● consumer.

Grünanlage f park
Grund (-(e)s, Gründe) m (Ursache)
reason; (Erdboden) ground; (See,
Gefäß) bottom; (Grundbesitz) land,
property; **aus gesundheitlichen**

Gründen for health reasons; **im ~e** basically; **aus diesem ~** for this reason

gründen vt to found; **Gründer(in)** m(f) founder

Grundgebühr f basic charge; **Grundgesetz** nt (German) Constitution

gründlich adj thorough

Gründonnerstag m Maundy Thursday

grundsätzlich adj fundamental, basic; **sie kommt ~ zu spät** she's always late; **Grundschule** f primary school; **Grundstück** nt plot; (Anwesen) estate; (Baugrundstück) site; **Grundwasser** nt ground water

Grüne(r) mf (Pol) Green; **die ~n** the Green Party

Gruppe (-, -n) f group; **Gruppenermäßigung** f group discount; **Gruppenreise** f group tour

Gruselfilm m horror film

Gruß (-es, Grüße) m greeting; **viele Grüße** best wishes; **Grüße an** (+akk) regards to; **mit freundlichen Grüßen** Yours sincerely (Brit), Sincerely yours (US); **sag ihm einen schönen ~ von mir** give him my regards; **grüßen** vt to greet; **grüß deine Mutter von mir** give your mother my regards; **Julia lässt (euch) ~** Julia sends (you) her regards

gucken vi to look

Gulasch (-(e)s, -e) nt goulash

gültig adj valid

Gummi (-s, -s) m o nt rubber; **Gummiband** nt rubber (o elastic (Brit)) band; **Gummibärchen** pl gums pl (in the shape of a bear) (Brit), gumdrops pl (in the shape of a bear) (US); **Gummihandschuhe** pl rubber gloves pl; **Gummistiefel** m wellington (boot) (Brit), rubber

boot (US)

günstig adj favourable; (Preis) good

gurgeln vi to gurgle; (im Mund) to gargle

Gurke (-, -n) f cucumber; **saure ~** gherkin

Gurt (-(e)s, -e) m belt

Gürtel (-s, -) m belt; (Geo) zone; **Gürtelrose** f shingles sing

GUS (-) f akr = **Gemeinschaft Unabhängiger Staaten** CIS

g

⭕ SCHLÜSSELWORT

gut adj good; **alles Gute** all the best; **also gut** all right then
▷ adv well; **gut gehen** to work, to come off; **es geht jdm gut** sb's doing fine; **gut gemeint** well meant; **gut schmecken** to taste good; **jdm guttun** to do sb good; **gut, aber ...** OK, but ...; **(na) gut, ich komme** all right, I'll come; **gut drei Stunden** a good three hours; **das kann gut sein** that may well be; **lass es gut sein** that'll do

Gutachten (-s, -) nt report; **Gutachter(in)** (-s, -) m(f) expert

gutartig adj (Med) benign

Güter pl goods pl; **Güterbahnhof** m goods station; **Güterzug** m goods train

gutgläubig adj trusting; **Guthaben** (-s) nt (credit) balance

gutmütig adj good-natured

Gutschein m voucher; **Gutschrift** f credit

Gymnasium nt ≈ grammar school (Brit), ≈ high school (US)

Gymnastik f exercises pl, keep-fit

Gynäkologe m, **Gynäkologin** f gynaecologist

Gyros (-, -) nt doner kebab

h

you mind if ...?; **was hast du denn?** what's the matter (with you)?

Haben nt (Comm) credit

Habicht (-(e)s, -e) m hawk

Hacke (-, -n) f (im Garten) hoe; (Ferse) heel; **hacken** vt to chop; (Loch) to hack; (Erde) to hoe; **Hacker(in)** (-s, -) m(f) (Inform) hacker; **Hackfleisch** nt mince(d meat) (Brit), ground meat (US)

Hafen (-s, Häfen) m harbour; (großer) port; **Hafenstadt** f port

Hafer (-s, -) m oats pl; **Haferflocken** pl rolled oats pl

Haft (-) f custody; **haftbar** adj liable, responsible; **haften** vi to stick; **~ für** to be liable (o responsible) for; **Haftnotiz** f Post-it®; **Haftpflichtversicherung** f third party insurance; **Haftung** f liability

Hagebutte (-, -n) f rose hip

Hagel (-s) m hail; **hageln** vi impers to hail

Hahn (-(e)s, Hähne) m cock; (Wasserhahn) tap (Brit), faucet (US); **Hähnchen** nt cockerel; (Gastr) chicken

Hai(fisch) (-(e)s, -e) m shark

häkeln vi, vt to crochet; **Häkelnadel** f crochet hook

Haken (-s, -) m hook; (Zeichen) tick

Haar (-(e)s, -e) nt hair; **um ein ~** nearly; **sich** (dat) **die ~e schneiden lassen** to have one's hair cut; **Haarbürste** f hairbrush; **Haarfestiger** m setting lotion; **Haargel** nt hair gel; **haarig** adj hairy; (fig) nasty; **Haarschnitt** m haircut; **Haarspange** f hair slide (Brit), barrette (US); **Haarspliss** m split ends pl; **Haarspray** nt hair spray; **Haartrockner** (-s, -) m hairdryer; **Haarwaschmittel** nt shampoo; **Haarwasser** nt hair tonic

haben (hatte, gehabt) vt, vaux to have; **Hunger/Angst ~** to be hungry/afraid; **Ferien ~** to be on holiday (Brit) (o vacation (US)); **welches Datum ~ wir heute?** what's the date today?; **ich hätte gerne ...** I'd like ...; **hätten Sie etwas dagegen, wenn ...?** would

halb adj half; **~ eins** half past twelve; (fam) half twelve; **eine ~e Stunde** half an hour; **~ offen** half-open; **Halbfinale** nt semifinal; **halbieren** vt to halve; **Halbinsel** f peninsula; **Halbjahr** nt half-year; **halbjährlich** adj half-yearly; **Halbmond** m (Astr) half-moon; (Symbol) crescent; **Halbpension** f half board; **halbseitig** adj: **~ gelähmt** paralyzed on one side; **halbtags**

adv (*arbeiten*) part-time; **halbwegs**
adv (*leidlich*) reasonably; **Halbzeit**
f half; (*Pause*) half-time
half *imperf von* **helfen; Hälfte**
(-, -n) *f* half
Halle (-, -n) *f* hall; **Hallenbad** *nt*
indoor (swimming) pool
hallo *interj* hello, hi
Halogenlampe *f* halogen lamp;
Halogenscheinwerfer *m* halogen headlight
Hals (-es, Hälse) *m* neck; (*Kehle*)
throat; **Halsband** *nt* (*für Tiere*)
collar; **Halsentzündung** *f* sore
throat; **Halskette** *f* necklace;
Hals-Nasen-Ohren-Arzt *m*,
Hals-Nasen-Ohren-Ärztin *f* ear,
nose and throat specialist;
Halsschmerzen *pl* sore throat
sing; **Halstuch** *nt* scarf
halt *interj* stop ▷ *adv:* **das ist ~ so**
that's just the way it is; **Halt** (-(e)s,
-e) *m* stop; (*fester*) hold; (*innerer*)
stability
haltbar *adj* durable; (*Lebensmittel*)
non-perishable; **Haltbar-**
keitsdatum *nt* best-before
date
halten (*hielt, gehalten*) *vt* to keep;
(*festhalten*) to hold; **~ für** to regard
as; **~ von** to think of; **den**
Elfmeter ~ to save the penalty;
eine Rede ~ to give (o make) a
speech ▷ *vi* to hold; (*frisch bleiben*)
to keep; (*stoppen*) to stop; **zu jdm**
~ to stand by sb ▷ *vr:* **sich ~** (*frisch*
bleiben) to keep; (*sich behaupten*) to
hold out
Haltestelle *f* stop; **Halteverbot**
nt: **hier ist ~** you can't stop here
Haltung *f* (*Körper*) posture; (*fig*)
attitude; (*Selbstbeherrschung*)
composure; **~ bewahren** to keep
one's composure
Hamburg (-s) *nt* Hamburg;
Hamburger (-s, -) *m* (*Gastr*)
hamburger

Hammelfleisch *nt* mutton
Hammer (-s, Hämmer) *m* hammer; (*fig, fam: Fehler*) howler; **das**
ist der ~ (*unerhört*) that's a bit
much
Hämorr(ho)iden *pl* haemorrhoids *pl,* piles *pl*
Hamster (-s, -) *m* hamster
Hand (-, Hände) *f* hand; **jdm die**
~ geben to shake hands with sb;
jdn bei der ~ nehmen to take sb
by the hand; **eine ~ voll**
Reis/Leute a handful of
rice/people; **zu Händen von**
attention; **Handarbeit** *f*
(*Schulfach*) handicraft; **~ sein** to be
handmade; **Handball** *m*
handball; **Handbremse** *f*
handbrake; **Handbuch** *nt*
handbook, manual; **Handcreme**
f hand cream; **Händedruck** *m*
handshake
Handel (-s) *m* trade; (*Geschäft*)
transaction; **handeln** *vi* to act;
(*Comm*) to trade; **~ von** to be
about ▷ *vr impers:* **sich ~ um** to
be about; **es handelt sich um ...**
it's about ...; **Handelskammer** *f*
chamber of commerce;
Handelsschule *f* business school
Handfeger (-s, -) *m* brush;
Handfläche *f* palm; **Handgelenk**
nt wrist; **handgemacht** *adj*
handmade; **Handgepäck** *nt*
hand luggage (*Brit*) (o baggage)
Händler(in) (-s, -) *m(f)* dealer
handlich *adj* handy
Handlung *f* act, action; (*von*
Roman, Film) plot
Handschellen *pl* handcuffs *pl;*
Handschrift *f* handwriting;
Handschuh *m* glove;
Handschuhfach *nt* glove
compartment; **Handtasche** *f*
handbag, purse (*US*); **Handtuch**
nt towel; **Handwerk** *nt* trade;
(*Kunst~*) craft; **Handwerker** (-s, -)

m workman

Handy (-s, -s) *nt* mobile (phone) (*Brit*), cell phone (*US*); **Handynummer** *f* mobile number (*Brit*), cell phone number (*US*)

Hanf (-(e)s) *m* hemp

Hang (-(e)s, Hänge) *m* (*Abhang*) slope; (*fig*) tendency

Hängebrücke *f* suspension bridge; **Hängematte** *f* hammock

hängen (hing, gehangen) *vi* to hang; **an der Wand/an der Decke ~** to hang on the wall/from the ceiling; **an jdm ~** (*fig*) to be attached to sb; **~ bleiben** to get caught (*an +dat* on); (*fig*) to get stuck ▷ *vt* to hang (*an +akk* on)

Hantel (-, -n) *f* dumbbell

Hardware (-, -s) *f* (*Inform*) hardware

Harfe (-, -n) *f* harp

harmlos *adj* harmless

harmonisch *adj* harmonious

Harn (-(e)s, -e) *m* urine; **Harnblase** *f* bladder

Harpune (-, -n) *f* harpoon

hart *adj* hard; (*fig*) harsh; **zu jdm ~ sein** to be hard on sb; **~ gekocht** (*Ei*) hard-boiled; **hartnäckig** *adj* stubborn

Haschee (-s, -s) *nt* hash

Haschisch (-) *nt* hashish

Hase (-n, -n) *m* hare

Haselnuss *f* hazelnut

Hasenscharte *f* (*Med*) harelip

Hass (-es) *m* hatred (*auf, gegen +akk* of), hate; **einen ~ kriegen** (*fam*) to see red; **hassen** *vt* to hate

hässlich *adj* ugly; (*gemein*) nasty

Hast (-) *f* haste, hurry; **hastig** *adj* hasty

hatte *imperf von* **haben**

Haube (-, -n) *f* hood; (*Mütze*) cap; (*Auto*) bonnet (*Brit*), hood (*US*)

Hauch (-(e)s, -e) *m* breath; (*Luft~*)

breeze; (*fig*) trace; **hauchdünn** *adj* (*Schicht, Scheibe*) wafer-thin

hauen (haute, gehauen) *vt* to hit

Haufen (-s, -) *m* pile; **ein ~ Geld** (*viel Geld*) a lot of money

häufig *adj* frequent ▷ *adv* frequently, often

Haupt- *in zW* main; **Hauptbahnhof** *m* central (*o* main) station; **Hauptdarsteller(in)** *m(f)* leading actor/lady; **Haupteingang** *m* main entrance; **Hauptgericht** *nt* main course; **Hauptgeschäftszeiten** *pl* peak shopping hours *pl*; **Hauptgewinn** *m* first prize

Häuptling *m* chief

Hauptquartier *nt* headquarters *pl*; **Hauptreisezeit** *f* peak tourist season; **Hauptrolle** *f* leading role; **Hauptsache** *f* main thing; **hauptsächlich** *adv* mainly, chiefly; **Hauptsaison** *f* high (*o* peak) season; **Hauptsatz** *m* main clause; **Hauptschule** *f* ≈ secondary school (*Brit*), ≈ junior high school (*US*); **Hauptspeicher** *m* (*Inform*) main storage (*o* memory); **Hauptstadt** *f* capital; **Hauptstraße** *f* main road; (*im Stadtzentrum*) main street; **Hauptverkehrszeit** *f* rush hour

Haus (-es, Häuser) *nt* house; **nach ~e** home; **zu ~e** at home; **jdn nach ~e bringen** to take sb home; **bei uns zu ~e** (*Heimat*) where we come from; (*Familie*) in my family; (*Haus*) at our place; **Hausarbeit** *f* housework; **Hausaufgabe** *f* (*Schule*) homework; **~n** *pl* homework *sing*; **Hausbesitzer(in)** (-s, -) *m(f)* house owner; (*Vermieter*) landlord/-lady; **Hausbesuch** *m* home visit; **Hausbewohner(in)** (-s, -) *m(f)* occupa **Hausflur** *m* hall; **Hausfrau** *f*

housewife; **hausgemacht** adj
homemade; **Haushalt** m
household; (Pol) budget;
Hausherr(in) m(f) host/hostess;
(Vermieter) landlord/-lady
häuslich adj domestic
Hausmann m house-husband;
Hausmannskost f good plain
cooking; **Hausmeister(in)** m(f)
caretaker (Brit), janitor (US);
Hausnummer f house number;
Hausordnung f (house) rules pl;
Hausschlüssel m front-door key;
Hausschuh m slipper; **Haustier**
nt pet; **Haustür** f front door
Haut (-, Häute) f skin; (Tier) hide;
Hautarzt m, **Hautärztin** f
dermatologist; **Hautausschlag**
m skin rash; **Hautcreme** f skin
cream; **Hautfarbe** f skin colour;
Hautkrankheit f skin disease
Hawaii (-s) nt Hawaii
Hbf. abk = **Hauptbahnhof** central
station
Hebamme (-, -n) f midwife
Hebel (-s, -) m lever
heben (hob, gehoben) vt to raise,
to lift
Hebräisch (-) nt Hebrew
Hecht (-(e)s, -e) m pike
Heck (-(e)s, -e) nt (von Boot) stern;
(von Auto) rear; **Heckantrieb** m
rear-wheel drive
Hecke (-, -n) f hedge
Heckklappe f tailgate;
Hecklicht nt tail-light;
Heckscheibe f rear window
Hefe (-, -n) f yeast
Heft (-(e)s, -e) nt notebook,
exercise book; (Ausgabe) issue
heftig adj violent; (Kritik, Streit)
fierce
Heftklammer f paper clip;
Heftpflaster nt plaster (Brit),
Band-Aid® (US)
Heide (-, -n) f heath, moor;
Heidekraut nt heather

Heidelbeere f bilberry, blueberry
heidnisch adj (Brauch) pagan
heikel adj (Angelegenheit)
awkward; (wählerisch) fussy
heil adj (Sache) in one piece,
intact; (Person) unhurt; **heilbar**
adj curable
Heilbutt (-(e)s, -e) m halibut
heilen vt to cure ▷ vi to heal
heilig adj holy; **Heiligabend** m
Christmas Eve; **Heilige(r)** mf
saint
Heilmittel nt remedy, cure (gegen
for); **Heilpraktiker(in)** (-s, -) m(f)
non-medical practitioner
heim adv home; **Heim** (-(e), -e) nt
home
Heimat (-, -en) f home
(town/country); **Heimatland** nt
home country
heim|fahren irr vi to drive
home; **Heimfahrt** f journey
home; **heimisch** adj
(Bevölkerung, Brauchtum) local;
(Tiere, Pflanzen) native;
heim|kommen irr vi to come (o
return) home
heimlich adj secret
Heimreise f journey home;
Heimspiel nt (Sport) home game;
Heimvorteil m (Sport) home
advantage; **Heimweg** m way
home; **Heimweh** (-s) nt
homesickness; **~ haben** to be
homesick; **Heimwerker(in)** m(f)
DIY enthusiast
Heirat (-, -en) f marriage;
heiraten vi to get married ▷ vt
to marry; **Heiratsantrag** m
proposal; **er hat ihr einen
~ gemacht** he proposed to her
heiser adj hoarse
heiß adj hot; (Diskussion) heated;
mir ist ~ I'm hot
heißen (hieß, geheißen) vi to be
called; (bedeuten) to mean; **ich
heiße Tom** my name is Tom; **wie**

h

~ Sie? what's your name?; **wie heißt sie mit Nachnamen?** what's her surname?; **wie heißt das auf Englisch?** what's that in English? ▷ *vi impers:* **es heißt** (*man sagt*) it is said; **es heißt in dem Brief ...** it says in the letter ...; **das heißt** that is

Heißluftherd *m* fan-assisted oven

heiter *adj* cheerful; (*Wetter*) bright

heizen *vt* to heat; **Heizkissen** *m* (*Med*) heated pad; **Heizkörper** *m* radiator; **Heizöl** *nt* fuel oil; **Heizung** *f* heating

Hektar (*-s, -*) *nt* hectare

Hektik (*-, -en*) *f:* **nur keine ~!** take it easy; **hektisch** *adj* hectic

Held (*-en, -en*) *m* hero; **Heldin** *f* heroine

helfen (*half, geholfen*) *vi* to help (*jdm bei etw* sb with sth); (*nützen*) to be of use; **sie weiß sich** (*dat*) **zu ~** she can manage ▷ *vi impers:* **es hilft nichts, du musst ...** it's no use, you have to ...; **Helfer(in)** *m(f)* helper; (*Mitarbeiter*) assistant

Helikopter-Skiing (*-s*) *nt* heliskiing, helicopter skiing

hell *adj* bright; (*Farbe*) light; (*Hautfarbe*) fair; **hellblau** *adj* light blue; **hellblond** *adj* ash-blond; **hellgelb** *adj* pale yellow; **hellgrün** *adj* light green; **Hellseher(in)** *m(f)* clairvoyant

Helm (*-(e)s, -e*) *m* helmet; **Helmpflicht** *f* compulsory wearing of helmets

Hemd (*-(e)s, -en*) *nt* shirt; (*Unter~*) vest

hemmen *vt* to check; (*behindern*) to hamper; **gehemmt sein** to be inhibited; **Hemmung** *f* (*psychisch*) inhibition; **sie hatte keine ~, ihn zu betrügen** she had no scruples about deceiving him; (*moralisch*) scruple

Henkel (*-s, -*) *m* handle

Henna (*-s*) *nt* henna

Henne (*-, -n*) *f* hen

Hepatitis (*-, Hepatitiden*) *f* hepatitis

 SCHLÜSSELWORT

her *adv* 1 (*Richtung*) **komm her zu mir** come here (to me); **von England her** from England; **von weit her** from a long way away; **her damit!** hand it over!; **wo hat er das her?** where did he get that from?; **wo bist du her?** where do you come from?
2 (*Blickpunkt*) **von der Form her** as far as the form is concerned
3 (*zeitlich*) **das ist 5 Jahre her** that was 5 years ago; **ich kenne ihn von früher her** I know him from before

herab *adv* down; **herablassend** *adj* (*Bemerkung*) condescending; **herab|sehen** *irr vt:* **auf jdn ~** to look down on sb; **herab|setzen** *vt* to reduce; (*fig*) to disparage

heran *adv:* **näher ~!** come closer; **heran|kommen** *irr vi* to approach; **~ an** (*+akk*) to be able to get at; (*fig*) to be able to get hold of; **heran|wachsen** *irr vi* to grow up

herauf *adv* up; **herauf|beschwören** *irr vt* to evoke; (*verursachen*) to cause; **herauf|ziehen** *irr vt* to pull up ▷ *vi* to approach; (*Sturm*) to gather

heraus *adv* out; **heraus|bekommen** *irr vt* (*Geheimnis*) to find out; (*Rätsel*) to solve; **ich bekomme noch zwei Euro heraus** I've got two euros change to come; **heraus|bringen** *irr vt* to bring out; **heraus|finden**

irr vt to find out; **heraus|fordern**
vt to challenge; **Herausforderung**
f challenge; **heraus|geben** *irr vt*
(*Buch*) to edit; (*veröffentlichen*) to
publish; **jdm zwei Euro ~** to give
sb two euros change; **geben Sie
mir bitte auf 20 Euro heraus**
could you give me change for 20
euros, please?; **heraus|holen** *vt*
to get out (*aus* of); **heraus|-
kommen** *irr vi* to come
out; **dabei kommt nichts heraus**
nothing will come of it;
heraus|stellen *vr*: **sich ~** to turn
out (*als* to be); **heraus|ziehen** *irr
vt* to pull out
Herbergseltern *pl* (youth hostel)
wardens *pl*
Herbst (*-(e)s, -e*) *m* autumn, fall
(*US*)
Herd (*-(e)s, -e*) *m* cooker, stove
Herde (*-, -n*) *f* herd; (*Schafe*) flock
herein *adv* in; **~!** come in;
herein|fallen *irr vi*: **wir sind auf
einen Betrüger hereingefallen**
we were taken in by a swindler;
herein|legen *vt*: **jdn ~** (*fig*) to
take sb for a ride
Herfahrt *f* journey here; **auf der
~** on the way here
Hergang *m* course (of events);
schildern Sie mir den ~ tell me
what happened
Hering (*-s, -e*) *m* herring
her|kommen *irr vi* to come; **wo
kommt sie her?** where does she
come from?
Heroin (*-s*) *nt* heroin
Herpes (*-*) *m* (*Med*) herpes
Herr (*-(e)n, -en*) *m* (*vor Namen*) Mr;
(*Mann*) gentleman; (*Adliger, Gott*)
Lord; **mein ~!** sir; **meine ~en!**
gentlemen; **Sehr geehrte Damen
und ~en** Dear Sir or Madam;
herrenlos *adj* (*Gepäck*) abandoned;
(*Tier*) stray; **Herrentoilette** *f*
men's toilet, gents

her|richten *vt* to prepare
herrlich *adj* marvellous, splendid
Herrschaft *f* rule; (*Macht*) power;
meine ~en! ladies and gentlemen!
herrschen *vi* to rule; (*bestehen*) to
be
her|stellen *vt* to make;
(*industriell*) to manufacture; **Her-
steller(in)** *m(f)* manufacturer;
Herstellung *f* production
herüber *adv* over
herum *adv* around; (*im Kreis*)
round; **um etw ~** around sth; **du
hast den Pulli falsch ~ an** your
sweater's inside out; **anders ~** the
other way round; **herum|fahren**
irr vi to drive around; **herum|
führen** *vt*: **jdn in der Stadt ~** to
show sb around the town ▷ *vi*:
**die Straße führt um das Zentrum
herum** the road goes around the
city centre; **herum|kommen** *irr
vi*: **sie ist viel in der Welt
herumgekommen** she's been
around the world; **um etw
~** (*vermeiden*) to get out of sth;
herum|kriegen *vt* to talk round;
herum|treiben *irr vr*: **sich ~** to
hang around
herunter *adv* down;
heruntergekommen *adj* (*Gebäude,
Gegend*) run-down; (*Person*)
down-at-heel; **herunter|handeln**
vt to get down; **herunter|holen**
vt to bring down;
herunter|kommen *irr vi* to come
down; **herunterladbar** *adj*
(*Inform*) downloadable;
herunter|laden *irr vt* (*Inform*) to
download
hervor *adv* out; **hervor|bringen**
irr vt to produce; (*Wort*) to utter;
hervor|heben *irr vt* to
emphasize; **hervorragend** *adj*
excellent; **hervor|rufen** *irr vt* to
cause, to give rise to
Herz (*-ens, -en*) *nt* heart; (*Karten*)

hearts pl; **von ganzem ~en**
wholeheartedly; **sich** (dat) **etw zu
~en nehmen** to take sth to heart;
Herzanfall m heart attack;
Herzbeschwerden pl heart
trouble sing; **Herzfehler** m heart
defect; **herzhaft** adj (Essen)
substantial; **~ lachen** to have a
good laugh; **Herzinfarkt** m
heart attack; **Herzklopfen** (-s) nt
(Med) palpitations pl; **ich hatte
~** (vor Aufregung) my heart was
pounding (with excitement);
herzkrank adj: **sie ist ~** she's got
a heart condition; **herzlich** adj
(Empfang, Mensch) warm; **~en
Glückwunsch** congratulations
Herzog(in) (-s, Herzöge) m(f)
duke/duchess
Herzschlag m heartbeat;
(Herzversagen) heart failure;
Herzschrittmacher m pacemaker; **Herzstillstand** m
cardiac arrest
Hessen (-s) nt Hessen
heterosexuell adj heterosexual;
Heterosexuelle(r) mf
heterosexual
Hetze (-, -n) f (Eile) rush; **hetzen**
vt to rush ▷ vr: **sich ~** to rush
Heu (-(e)s) nt hay
heuer adv this year
heulen vi to howl; (weinen) to cry
Heuschnupfen m hay fever;
Heuschrecke (-, -n) f grasshopper; (größer) locust
heute adv today; **~ Abend/früh**
this evening/morning; **~ Morgen**
this morning; **~ Nacht** tonight;
(letzte Nacht) last night; **~ in acht
Tagen** a week (from) today; **sie
hat bis ~ nicht bezahlt** she hasn't
paid to this day; **heutig** adj: **die
~e Zeitung/Generation** today's
paper/generation; **heutzutage**
adv nowadays
Hexe (-, -n) f witch;

Hexenschuss m lumbago
hielt imperf von **halten**
hier adv here; **~ entlang** this way;
ich bin auch nicht von ~ I'm a
stranger here myself; **hier|bleiben**
irr vi to stay here; **hier|lassen** irr
vt to leave here; **hierher** adv
here; **das gehört nicht ~** that
doesn't belong here; **hiermit** adv
with this; **hierzulande** adv in
this country
hiesig adj local
hieß imperf von **heißen**
Hi-Fi-Anlage f hi-fi (system)
high adj (fam) high; **Highlife** (-s)
nt high life; **~ machen** to live it
up; **Hightech** (-s) nt high tech
Hilfe (-, -n) f help; (für Notleidende,
finanziell) aid; **~!** help!; **Erste
~ leisten** to give first aid; **um
~ bitten** to ask for help; **hilflos**
adj helpless; **hilfsbereit** adj
helpful; **Hilfsmittel** nt aid
Himbeere f raspberry
Himmel (-s, -) m sky; (Rel)
heaven; **Himmelfahrt** f
Ascension; **Himmelsrichtung** f
direction; **himmlisch** adj
heavenly

○ SCHLÜSSELWORT

hin adv 1 (Richtung) **hin und zurück**
there and back; **hin und her** to
and fro; **bis zur Mauer hin** up to
the wall; **wo ist er hin?** where has
he gone?; **Geld hin, Geld her**
money or no money
2 (auf ... hin) **auf meine Bitte hin**
at my request; **auf seinen Rat hin**
on the basis of his advice
3 **mein Glück ist hin** my happiness
has gone

hinab adv down; **hinab|gehen** irr
vi to go down
hinauf adv up; **hinauf|gehen** irr

vi, vt to go up; **hinauf|steigen** *irr vi* to climb (up)

hinaus *adv* out; **hinaus|gehen** *irr vi* to go out; **das Zimmer geht auf den See hinaus** the room looks out onto the lake; **~ über** (+*akk*) to exceed; **hinaus|laufen** *irr vi* to run out; **~ auf** (+*akk*) to come to, to amount to; **hinaus|schieben** *irr vi* to put off, to postpone; **hinaus|werfen** *irr vt* to throw out; (*aus Firma*) to fire, to sack (*Brit*); **hinaus|zögern** *vr*: **sich ~** to take longer than expected

Hinblick *m* **in** (*o* **im**) **~ auf** (+*akk*) with regard to; (*wegen*) in view of

hin|bringen *irr vt*: **ich bringe Sie hin** I'll take you there

hindern *vt* to prevent; **jdn daran ~, etw zu tun** to stop (*o* prevent) sb from doing sth; **Hindernis** *nt* obstacle

Hinduismus *m* Hinduism

hindurch *adv* through; **das ganze Jahr ~** throughout the year, all year round; **die ganze Nacht ~** all night (long)

hinein *adv* in; **hinein|gehen** *irr vi* to go in; **~ in** (+*akk*) to go into, to enter; **hinein|passen** *vi* to fit in; **~ in** (+*akk*) to fit into

hin|fahren *irr vi* to go there ▷ *vt* to take there; **Hinfahrt** *f* outward journey

hin|fallen *irr vi* to fall (down)

Hinflug *m* outward flight

hing *imperf von* **hängen**

hin|gehen *irr vi* to go there; (*Zeit*) to pass; **hin|halten** *irr vt* to hold out; (*warten lassen*) to put off

hinken *vi* to limp; **der Vergleich hinkt** the comparison doesn't work

hin|knien *vr*: **sich ~** to kneel down; **hin|legen** *vt* to put down ▷ *vr*: **sich ~** to lie down; **hin|nehmen** *irr vt* (*fig*) to put up

with, to take; **Hinreise** *f* outward journey; **hin|setzen** *vr*: **sich ~** to sit down; **hinsichtlich** *prep* +*gen* with regard to; **hin|stellen** *vt* to put (down) ▷ *vr*: **sich ~** to stand

hinten *adv* at the back; (*im Auto*) in the back; (*dahinter*) behind

hinter *prep* +*dat o akk* behind; (*nach*) after; **~ jdm her sein** to be after sb; **etw ~ sich** (*akk*) **bringen** to get sth over (and done) with; **Hinterachse** *f* rear axle; **Hinterausgang** *m* rear exit; **Hinterbein** *nt* hind leg; **Hinterbliebene(r)** *mf* dependant; **hintere(r, s)** *adj* rear, back; **hintereinander** *adv* (*in einer Reihe*) one behind the other; (*hintereinander her*) one after the other; **drei Tage ~** three days running (*o* in a row); **Hintereingang** *m* rear entrance; **Hintergedanke** *m* ulterior motive; **hintergehen** *irr vt* to deceive; **Hintergrund** *m* background; **hinterher** *adv* (*zeitlich*) afterwards; **los, ~!** come on, after him/her/them; **Hinterkopf** *m* back of the head; **hinterlassen** *vt* to leave; **jdm eine Nachricht ~** to leave a message for sb; **hinterlegen** *vt* to leave (*bei* with)

Hintern (-, -) *m* (*fam*) backside, bum

Hinterradantrieb *m* (*Auto*) rear-wheel drive; **Hinterteil** *nt* back (part); (*Hintern*) behind; **Hintertür** *f* back door

hinüber *adv* over; **~ sein** (*fam*: *kaputt*) to be ruined; (*verdorben*) to have gone bad; **hinüber|gehen** *irr vi* to go over

hinunter *adv* down; **hinunter|gehen** *irr vi, vt* to go down; **hinunter|schlucken** *vt* (*a. fig*) to swallow

Hinweg *m* outward journey

hinweg|setzen *vr* **sich über etw** (*akk*) ~ to ignore sth

Hinweis (*-es, -e*) *m* (*Andeutung*) hint; (*Anweisung*) instruction; (*Verweis*) reference; **hin|weisen** *irr vi* **jdn auf etw** (*acc*) ~ to point sth out to sb; **jdn nochmal auf etw** ~ to remind sb of sth

hinzu *adv* in addition; **hinzu|fügen** *vt* to add; **hinzu|kommen** *irr vi*: **zu jdm** ~ to join sb; **es war kalt, hinzu kam, dass es auch noch regnete** it was cold, and on top of that it was raining

Hirn (*-(e)s, -e*) *nt* brain; (*Verstand*) brains *pl*; **Hirnhautentzündung** *f* meningitis

Hirsch (*-(e)s, -e*) *m* deer; (*als Speise*) venison

Hirte (*-n, -n*) *m* shepherd

historisch *adj* historical

Hit (*-s, -s*) *m* (*fig, Mus, Inform*) hit; **Hitliste** *f*, **Hitparade** *f* charts *pl*

Hitze (*-*) *f* heat; **hitzebeständig** *adj* heat-resistant; **Hitzewelle** *f* heatwave; **hitzig** *adj* hot-tempered; (*Debatte*) heated; **Hitzschlag** *m* heatstroke

HIV (*-(s), -(s)*) *nt abk* = **Human Immunodeficiency Virus** HIV; **HIV-negativ** *adj* HIV-negative; **HIV-positiv** *adj* HIV-positive

H-Milch *f* long-life milk

hob *imperf von* **heben**

Hobby (*-s, -s*) *nt* hobby

Hobel (*-s, -*) *m* plane

hoch *adj* high; (*Baum*) tall; (*Schnee*) deep; **der Zaun ist drei Meter** ~ the fence is three metres high; ~ **auflösend** high-resolution; ~ **begabt** extremely gifted; **das ist mir zu** ~ that's above my head; ~ **soll sie leben!, sie lebe** ~! three cheers for her; **4 ~ 2 ist 16** 4 squared

is 16; **4 ~ 5** 4 to the power of 5

Hoch (*-s, -s*) *nt* (*Ruf*) cheer; (*Meteo*) high; **hochachtungsvoll** *adv* (*in Briefen*) Yours faithfully; **Hochbetrieb** *m*: **es herrscht** ~ they/we are extremely busy; **Hochdeutsch** *nt* High German; **Hochgebirge** *nt* high mountains *pl*; **Hochgeschwindigkeitszug** *m* high-speed train; **Hochhaus** *nt* high rise; **hoch|heben** *irr vt* to lift (up); **hochprozentig** *adj* (*Alkohol*) high-proof; **Hochsaison** *f* high season; **Hochschule** *f* college; (*Universität*) university; **Hochschulreife** *f* **er hat (die)** ~ he's got his A-levels (*Brit*), he's graduated from high school (*US*); **Hochsommer** *m* midsummer; **Hochspannung** *f* great tension; (*Elek*) high voltage; **Hochsprung** *m* high jump

höchst *adv* highly, extremely; **höchste(r, s)** *adj* highest; (*äußerste*) extreme; **höchstens** *adv* at the most; **Höchstform** *f* (*Sport*) top form; **Höchstgeschwindigkeit** *f* maximum speed; **Höchstparkdauer** *f* maximum stay

Hochstuhl *m* high chair

höchstwahrscheinlich *adv* very probably

Hochwasser *nt* high water; (*Überschwemmung*) floods *pl*; **hochwertig** *adj* high-quality

Hochzeit (*-, -en*) *f* wedding; **Hochzeitsnacht** *f* wedding night; **Hochzeitsreise** *f* honeymoon; **Hochzeitstag** *m* wedding day; (*Jahrestag*) wedding anniversary

hocken *vi* to squat, to crouch

Hocker (*-s, -*) *m* stool

Hockey (*-s*) *nt* hockey

Hoden (*-s, -*) *m* testicle

Hof (*-(e)s, Höfe*) *m* (*Hinterhof*) yard;

(*Innenhof*) courtyard; (*Bauernhof*) farm; (*Königshof*) court

hoffen *vi* to hope (*auf +akk* for); **ich hoffe es** I hope so; **hoffentlich** *adv* hopefully; **~ nicht** I hope not; **Hoffnung** *f* hope; **hoffnungslos** *adj* hopeless

höflich *adj* polite; **Höflichkeit** *f* politeness

hohe(r, s) *adj* siehe **hoch**

Höhe (-, -n) *f* height; (*Anhöhe*) hill; (*einer Summe*) amount; **in einer ~ von 5000 Metern** at an altitude of 5,000 metres; (*Flughöhe*) altitude; **Höhenangst** *f* vertigo

Höhepunkt *m* (*einer Reise*) high point; (*einer Veranstaltung*) highlight; (*eines Films; sexuell*) climax

höher *adj, adv* higher

hohl *adj* hollow

Höhle (-, -n) *f* cave

holen *vt* to get, to fetch; (*abholen*) to pick up; (*Atem*) to catch; **die Polizei ~** to call the police; **jdn/etw ~ lassen** to send for sb/sth

Holland *nt* Holland; **Holländer(in)** (-s, -) *m(f)* Dutchman/-woman; **holländisch** *adj* Dutch

Hölle (-, -n) *f* hell

Hologramm *nt* hologram

holperig *adj* bumpy

Holunder (-s, -) *m* elder

Holz (-es, *Hölzer*) *nt* wood; **Holzboden** *m* wooden floor; **hölzern** *adj* wooden; **holzig** *adj* (*Stängel*) woody; **Holzkohle** *f* charcoal

Homebanking (-s) *nt* home banking, online banking; **Homepage** (-, -s) *f* home page; **Hometrainer** *m* exercise machine

Homoehe *f* (*fam*) gay marriage

homöopathisch *adj* homeopathic

homosexuell *adj* homosexual; **Homosexuelle(r)** *mf* homosexual

Honig (-s, -e) *m* honey; **Honigmelone** *f* honeydew melon

Honorar (-s, -e) *nt* fee

Hopfen (-s, -) *m* (*Bot*) hop; (*beim Brauen*) hops *pl*

hoppla *interj* whoops, oops

horchen *vi* to listen (*auf +akk* to); (*an der Tür*) to eavesdrop

hören *vt, vi* (*passiv, mitbekommen*) to hear; (*zufällig*) to overhear; (*aufmerksam zuhören; Radio, Musik*) to listen to; **ich habe schon viel von Ihnen gehört** I've heard a lot about you; **Hörer** *m* (*Tel*) receiver; **Hörer(in)** *m(f)* listener; **Hörgerät** *nt* hearing aid

Horizont (-(*e*)*s*, -e) *m* horizon; **das geht über meinen ~** that's beyond me

Hormon (-s, -e) *nt* hormone

Hornhaut *f* hard skin; (*des Auges*) cornea

Hornisse (-, -n) *f* hornet

Horoskop (-s, -e) *nt* horoscope

Hörsaal *m* lecture hall; **Hörsturz** *m* acute hearing loss; **Hörweite** *f*: **in/außer ~** within/out of earshot

Höschenwindel (-, -n) *f* nappy (*Brit*), diaper (*US*)

Hose (-, -n) *f* trousers *pl* (*Brit*), pants *pl* (*US*); (*Unterhose*) (under)pants *pl*; **eine ~** a pair of trousers/pants; **kurze ~** (pair of) shorts *pl*; **Hosenanzug** *m* trouser suit (*Brit*), pantsuit (*US*); **Hosenschlitz** *m* fly, flies (*Brit*); **Hosentasche** *f* trouser pocket (*Brit*), pant pocket (*US*); **Hosenträger** *m* braces *pl* (*Brit*), suspenders *pl* (*US*)

Hospital (-s, *Hospitäler*) *nt* hospital

Hotdog (-s, -s) *nt o m* hot dog

h

Hotel (-s, -s) nt hotel; **in welchem ~ seid ihr?** which hotel are you staying at?; **Hoteldirektor(in)** m(f) hotel manager; **Hotelkette** f hotel chain; **Hotelzimmer** nt hotel room

Hotline (-, -s) f hot line; **Hotspot** m (wireless) hotspot

Hubraum m cubic capacity

hübsch adj (Mädchen, Kind, Kleid) pretty; (gutaussehend; Mann, Frau) good-looking, cute

Hubschrauber (-s, -) m helicopter

Huf (-(e)s, -e) m hoof; **Hufeisen** nt horseshoe

Hüfte (-, -n) f hip

Hügel (-s, -) m hill; **hügelig** adj hilly

Huhn (-(e)s, Hühner) nt hen; (Gastr) chicken; **Hühnchen** nt chicken; **Hühnerauge** nt corn; **Hühnerbrühe** f chicken broth

Hülle (-, -n) f cover; (für Ausweis) case; (Zellophan) wrapping

Hummel (-, -n) f bumblebee

Hummer (-s, -) m lobster; **Hummerkrabbe** f king prawn

Humor (-s) m humour; **~ haben** to have a sense of humour; **humorlos** adj humourless; **humorvoll** adj humorous

humpeln vi hobble

Hund (-(e)s, -e) m dog; **Hundeleine** f dog lead (Brit), dog leash (US)

hundert num hundred; **Hundertjahrfeier** f centenary; **hundertprozentig** adj, adv one hundred per cent; **hundertste(r, s)** adj hundredth

Hündin f bitch

Hunger (-s) m hunger; **~ haben/bekommen** to be/get hungry; **hungern** vi to go hungry; (ernsthaft, dauernd) to starve

Hupe (-, -n) f horn; **hupen** vi to sound one's horn

Hüpfburg f bouncy castle®; **hüpfen** vi to hop; (springen) to jump

Hürde (-, -n) f hurdle

Hure (-, -n) f whore

hurra interj hooray

husten vi to cough; **Husten** (-s) m cough; **Hustenbonbon** nt cough sweet; **Hustensaft** m cough mixture

Hut (-(e)s, Hüte) m hat

hüten vt to look after ▷ vr: **sich ~** to watch out; **sich ~, etw zu tun** to take care not to do sth; **sich ~ vor** (+dat) to beware of

Hütte (-, -n) f hut, cottage; **Hüttenkäse** m cottage cheese

Hyäne (-, -n) f hyena

Hydrant m hydrant

hygienisch adj hygienic

Hyperlink (-s, -s) m hyperlink

Hypnose (-, -n) f hypnosis; **Hypnotiseur(in)** m(f) hypnotist; **hypnotisieren** vt to hypnotize

Hypothek (-, -en) f mortgage

hysterisch adj hysterical

I

Igel (-s, -) m hedgehog

ignorieren vt to ignore

ihm pron dat sing von **er/es**; (to) him, (to) it; **wie geht es ~?** how is he?; **ein Freund von ~** a friend of his ▷ pron dat von **es**; (to) it

ihn pron akk sing von **er**; (Person) him; (Sache) it

ihnen pron dat pl von **sie**; (to) them; **wie geht es ~?** how are they?; **ein Freund von ~** a friend of theirs

Ihnen pron dat sing u pl von **Sie**; (to) you; **wie geht es ~?** how are you?; **ein Freund von ~** a friend of yours

  SCHLÜSSELWORT

i. A. abk = **im Auftrag** pp

IC (-, -s) m abk = **Intercityzug** Intercity (train)

ICE (-, -s) m abk = **Intercityexpresszug** German high-speed train

ich pron I; **~ bin's** it's me; **~ nicht** not me; **du und ~** you and me; **hier bin ~!** here I am; **~ Idiot!** stupid me

Icon (-s, -s) nt (Inform) icon

IC-Zuschlag m Intercity supplement

ideal adj ideal; **Ideal** (-s, -e) nt ideal

Idee (-, -n) f idea

identifizieren vt to identify ▷ vr: **sich mit jdm/etw ~** to identify with sb/sth

identisch adj identical

Idiot(in) (-en, -en) m(f) idiot; **idiotisch** adj idiotic

Idol (-s, -e) nt idol

Idylle f idyll; **idyllisch** adj idyllic

ihr pron 1 (nom pl) you; **ihr seid es** it's you
2 (dat von sie) to her; **gib es ihr** give it to her; **er steht neben ihr** he is standing beside her
▷ possessiv pron 1 (sg) her; (bei Tieren, Dingen) its; **ihr Mann** her husband
2 (pl) their; **die Bäume und ihre Blätter** the trees and their leaves

Ihr pron von **Sie**; (adjektivisch) your; **~(e) XY** (am Briefende) Yours, XY

ihre(r, s) pron (substantivisch, sing) hers; (pl) theirs; **das ist ~/~r/ihr(e)s** that's hers; (pl) that's theirs

Ihre(r, s) pron (substantivisch) yours; **das ist ~/~r/Ihr(e)s** that's yours

ihretwegen adv (wegen ihr) because of her; (ihr zuliebe) for her sake; (um sie) about her; (von ihr aus) as far as she is concerned ▷ adv (wegen ihnen) because of them; (ihnen zuliebe) for their sake; (um sie) about them; (von ihnen aus)

as far as they are concerned;
Ihretwegen adv (wegen Ihnen)
because of you; (Ihnen zuliebe) for
your sake; (um Sie) about you; (von
Ihnen aus) as far as you are
concerned

Ikone (-, -n) f icon

illegal adj illegal

Illusion f illusion; **sich** (dat) **~en
machen** to delude oneself;
illusorisch adj illusory

Illustration f illustration

Illustrierte (-n, -n) f (glossy)
magazine

im kontr von **in dem**; **~ Bett** in bed;
~ Fernsehen on TV; **~ Radio** on
the radio; **~ Bus/Zug** on the
bus/train; **~ Januar** in January;
~ Stehen (while) standing up

Imbiss (-es, -e) m snack;
Imbissbude f, **Imbissstube** f
snack bar

Imbusschlüssel m hex key

immer adv always; **~ mehr** more
and more; **~ wieder** again and
again; **~ noch** still; **~ noch nicht**
still not; **für ~** forever; **~ wenn
ich ...** every time I ...; **~ schöner/
trauriger** more and
more beautiful/sadder and
sadder; **was/wer/wo/wann
(auch) ~** whatever/whoever/
wherever/whenever; **immerhin**
adv after all; **immerzu** adv all the
time

Immigrant(in) m(f) immigrant

Immobilien pl property sing, real
estate sing; **Immobilien-
makler(in)** m(f) estate
agent (Brit), realtor (US)

immun adj immune (gegen to);
Immunschwäche f immunodeficiency; **Immun-
schwächekrankheit** f immune
deficiency syndrome;
Immunsystem nt immune
system

impfen vt to vaccinate; **ich muss
mich gegen Pocken ~ lassen** I've
got to get myself vaccinated
against smallpox; **Impfpass** m
vaccination card; **Impfstoff** m
vaccine; **Impfung** f vaccination

imponieren vi to impress (jdm
sb)

Import (-(e)s, -e) m import;
importieren vt to import

impotent adj impotent

imstande adj: **~ sein** to be
in a position; (fähig) to be
able

⭕   SCHLÜSSELWORT

in prep +akk 1 (räumlich: wohin?) in,
into; **in die Stadt** into town; **in die
Schule gehen** to go to school
2 (zeitlich) **bis ins 20. Jahrhundert**
into o up to the 20th century
▷ prep +dat 1 (räumlich: wo?) in; **in
der Stadt** in town; **in der Schule
sein** to be at school
2 (zeitlich: wann?) **in diesem Jahr**
this year; (in jenem Jahr) in that
year; **heute in zwei Wochen** two
weeks today

inbegriffen adj included

indem conj: **sie gewann, ~ sie
mogelte** she won by cheating

Inder(in) (-s, -) m(f) Indian

Indianer(in) (-s, -) m(f)
American Indian, Native
American; **indianisch** adj
American Indian, Native American

Indien (-s) nt India

indirekt adj indirect

indisch adj Indian

indiskret adj indiscreet

individuell adj individual

Indonesien (-s) nt Indonesia

Industrie f industry; **Industrie-
in** zW industrial; **Industriegebiet**
nt industrial area; **industriell** adj

industrial

ineinander *adv* in(to) one another (*o* each other)

Infarkt (-(e)s, -e) *m* (*Herzinfarkt*) heart attack

Infektion *f* infection; **Infektionskrankheit** *f* infectious disease; **infizieren** *vt* to infect ▷ *vr*: **sich ~** to be infected

Info (-, -s) *f* (*fam*) info

infolge *prep* +*gen* as a result of, owing to; **infolgedessen** *adv* consequently

Infomaterial *nt* (*fam*) bumf, info

Informatik *f* computer science; **Informatiker(in)** (-s, -) *m(f)* computer scientist

Information *f* information; **Informationsschalter** *m* information desk; **informieren** *vt* to inform; **falsch ~** to misinform ▷ *vr*: **sich ~** to find out (*über* +*akk* about)

infrage *adv*: **das kommt nicht ~** that's out of the question; **etw ~ stellen** to question sth

Infrastruktur *f* infrastructure

Infusion *f* infusion

Ingenieur(in) *m(f)* engineer

Ingwer (-s) *m* ginger

Inhaber(in) (-s, -) *m(f)* owner; (*Haus~*) occupier; (*von Lizenz*) holder; (*Fin*) bearer

Inhalt (-(e)s, -e) *m* contents *pl*; (*eines Buchs etc*) content; (*Math*) volume; (*Flächeninhalt*) area; **Inhaltsangabe** *f* summary; **Inhaltsverzeichnis** *nt* table of contents

Initiative *f* initiative; **die ~ ergreifen** to take the initiative

Injektion *f* injection

inklusive *adv*, *prep* inclusive (*gen* of)

inkonsequent *adj* inconsistent

Inland *nt* (*Pol*, *Comm*) home; **im ~** at home; (*Geo*) inland;

inländisch *adj* domestic; **Inlandsflug** *m* domestic flight; **Inlandsgespräch** *nt* national call

Inliner *pl*, **Inlineskates** *pl* (*Sport*) Rollerblades® *pl*, in-line skates *pl*

innen *adv* inside; **Innenarchitekt(in)** *m(f)* interior designer; **Innenhof** *m* (inner) courtyard; **Innenminister(in)** *m(f)* minister of the interior, Home Secretary (*Brit*); **Innenseite** *f* inside; **Innenspiegel** *m* rearview mirror; **Innenstadt** *f* town centre; (*von Großstadt*) city centre

innere(r, s) *adj* inner; (*im Körper, inländisch*) internal; **Innere(s)** *nt* inside; (*Mitte*) centre; (*fig*) heart

Innereien *pl* innards *pl*

innerhalb *adv*, *prep* +*gen* within; (*räumlich*) inside

innerlich *adj* internal; (*geistig*) inner

innerste(r, s) *adj* innermost

Innovation *f* innovation; **innovativ** *adj* innovative

inoffiziell *adj* unofficial; (*zwanglos*) informal

ins *kontr von* **in das**

Insasse (-n, -n) *m*, **Insassin** *f* (*Auto*) passenger; (*Anstalt*) inmate

insbesondere *adv* particularly, in particular

Inschrift *f* inscription

Insekt (-(e)s, -en) *nt* insect, bug (*US*); **Insektenschutzmittel** *nt* insect repellent; **Insektenstich** *m* insect bite

Insel (-, -n) *f* island

Inserat *nt* advertisement

insgesamt *adv* altogether, all in all

Insider(in) (-s, -) *m(f)* insider

insofern *adv* in that respect; (*deshalb*) (and) so ▷ *conj* if; **~ als** in so far as

Installateur(in) *m(f)* (*Klempner*)
plumber; (*Elektroinstallateur*)
electrician; **installieren** *vt*
(*Inform*) to install
Instinkt (*-(e)s, -e*) *m* instinct
Institut (*-(e)s, -e*) *nt* institute
Institution *f* institution
Instrument *nt* instrument
Insulin (*-s*) *nt* insulin
Inszenierung *f* production
intakt *adj* intact
intellektuell *adj* intellectual
intelligent *adj* intelligent;
Intelligenz *f* intelligence
intensiv *adj* (*gründlich*) intensive;
(*Gefühl, Schmerz*) intense;
Intensivkurs *m* crash course;
Intensivstation *f* intensive care
unit
interaktiv *adj* interactive
Intercityexpress(zug) *m German*
high-speed train; **Intercityzug** *m*
Intercity (train); **Intercityzuschlag**
m Intercity supplement
interessant *adj* interesting;
Interesse (*-s, -n*) *nt* interest;
~ haben an (+*dat*) to be interested
in; **interessieren** *vt* to interest
▷ *vr*: **sich ~** to be interested (*für in*)
Interface (*-, -s*) *nt* (*Inform*)
interface
Internat *nt* boarding school
international *adj* international
Internet (*-s*) *nt* internet, net; **im**
~ on the internet; **im ~ surfen** to
surf the net; **Internetanschluss**
m internet connection;
Internetauktion *f* internet
auction; **Internetcafé** *nt*
internet café, cybercafé;
Internetfirma *f* dotcom
company; **Internethandel** *m*
e-commerce; **Internetseite** *f*
web page; **Internetzugang** *m*
internet access
interpretieren *vt* to interpret
(*als* as)

Interpunktion *f* punctuation
Interview (*-s, -s*) *nt* interview;
interviewen *vt* to interview
intim *adj* intimate
intolerant *adj* intolerant
investieren *vt* to invest
inwiefern *adv* in what way; (*in*
welchem Ausmaß) to what extent;
inwieweit *adv* to what extent
inzwischen *adv* meanwhile
iPod® *m* iPod®
Irak (*-(s)*) *m*: (**der**) **~** Iraq
Iran (*-(s)*) *m*: (**der**) **~** Iran
Ire (*-n, -n*) *m* Irishman
irgend *adv*: **~ so ein Idiot** some
idiot; **wenn ~ möglich** if at all
possible; **irgendein** *pron*,
irgendeine(r, s) *adj* some;
(*fragend, im Bedingungssatz; beliebig*)
any; **irgendetwas** *pron*
something; (*fragend, im*
Bedingungssatz) anything;
irgendjemand *pron* somebody;
(*fragend, im Bedingungssatz*)
anybody; **irgendwann** *adv*
sometime; (*zu beliebiger Zeit*) any
time; **irgendwie** *adv* somehow;
irgendwo *adv* somewhere;
(*fragend, im Bedingungssatz*)
anywhere
Irin *f* Irishwoman; **irisch** *adj*
Irish; **Irland** *nt* Ireland
ironisch *adj* ironic
irre *adj* crazy, mad; (*toll*) terrific;
Irre(r) *mf* lunatic; **irreführen** *irr*
vt to mislead; **irremachen** *vt* to
confuse; **irren** *vi* to be mistaken;
(*umherirren*) to wander ▷ *vr*: **sich**
~ to be mistaken; **wenn ich mich**
nicht irre if I'm not mistaken; **sich**
in der Nummer ~ (*Telefon*) to get
the wrong number; **irrsinnig** *adj*
mad, crazy; **Irrtum** (*-s, -tümer*) *m*
mistake, error; **irrtümlich** *adj*
mistaken ▷ *adv* by mistake
ISBN (*-*) *nt* *abk* = **industrial**
standard business network ISBN

▷ (-) *f abk* = **Internationale Standard Buchnummer** ISBN
Ischias (-) *m* sciatica
ISDN (-) *nt abk* = **integrated services digital network** ISDN
Islam (-s) *m* Islam; **islamisch** *adj* Islamic
Island *nt* Iceland; **Isländer(in)** (-s, -) *m(f)* Icelander; **isländisch** *adj* Icelandic; **Isländisch** *nt* Icelandic
Isolierband *nt* insulating tape; **isolieren** *vt* to isolate; (*Elek*) to insulate
Isomatte *f* thermomat, karrymat®
Israel (-s) *nt* Israel; **Israeli** (-(s), -(s)) *m* (-, -(s)) *f* Israeli; **israelisch** *adj* Israeli
IT (-) *f abk* = **Informationstechnologie** IT
Italien (-s) *nt* Italy; **Italiener(in)** (-s, -) *m(f)* Italian; **italienisch** *adj* Italian; **Italienisch** *nt* Italian

j

ja *adv* **1** yes; **haben Sie das gesehen? — ja** did you see it? — yes(, I did); **ich glaube ja** (yes,) I think so
2 (*fragend*) really?; **ich habe gekündigt — ja?** I've quit — have you?; **du kommst, ja?** you're coming, aren't you?
3 sei ja vorsichtig do be careful; **Sie wissen ja, dass ...** as you know, ...; **tu das ja nicht!** don't do that!; **ich habe es ja gewusst** I just knew it; **ja, also ...** well you see ...
Jacht (-, -en) *f* yacht; **Jachthafen** *m* marina
Jacke (-, -n) *f* jacket; (*Wolljacke*) cardigan
Jackett (-s, -s *o* -e) *nt* jacket
Jagd (-, -en) *f* hunt; (*Jagen*) hunting; **jagen** *vi* to hunt ▷ *vt* to

hunt; (*verfolgen*) to chase; **Jäger(in)** *m(f)* hunter

Jaguar (-s, -e) *m* jaguar

Jahr (-(e)s, -e) *nt* year; **ein halbes ~** six months *pl*; **Anfang der neunziger ~e** in the early nineties; **mit sechzehn ~en** at (the age of) sixteen; **Jahrestag** *m* anniversary; **Jahreszahl** *f* date, year; **Jahreszeit** *f* season; **Jahrgang** *m* (*Wein*) year, vintage; **der ~ 1989** (*Personen*) those born in 1989; **Jahrhundert** (-s, -e) *nt* century; **jährlich** *adj* yearly, annual; **Jahrmarkt** *m* fair; **Jahrtausend** *nt* millennium; **Jahrzehnt** *nt* decade

jähzornig *adj* hot-tempered

Jakobsmuschel *f* scallop

Jalousie *f* (venetian) blind

Jamaika (-s) *nt* Jamaica

jämmerlich *adj* pathetic

jammern *vi* to moan

Januar (-(s), -e) *m* January; *siehe auch* **Juni**

Japan (-s) *nt* Japan; **Japaner(in)** (-s, -) *m(f)* Japanese; **japanisch** *adj* Japanese; **Japanisch** *nt* Japanese

jaulen *vi* to howl

jawohl *adv* yes (of course)

Jazz (-) *m* jazz

⭕ SCHLÜSSELWORT

je *adv* 1 (*jemals*) ever; **hast du so was je gesehen?** did you ever see anything like it?
2 (*jeweils*) every, each; **sie zahlten je 3 Euro** they paid 3 euros each
▷ *konj* 1 **je nach** depending on; **je nachdem** it depends; **je nachdem, ob ...** depending on whether ...
2 **je eher, desto** *o* **umso besser** the sooner the better

Jeans (-, -) *f* jeans *pl*

jede(r, s) *unbest Zahlwort* (*insgesamt gesehen*) every; (*einzeln gesehen*) each; (*jede(r, s) beliebige*) any; **~s Mal** every time, each time; **~n zweiten Tag** every other day; **sie hat an ~m Finger einen Ring** she's got a ring on each finger; **~r Computer reicht aus** any computer will do; **bei ~m Wetter** in any weather ▷ *pron* everybody; (*jeder Einzelne*) each; **~r von euch/uns** each of you/us; **jedenfalls** *adv* in any case; **jederzeit** *adv* at any time; **jedesmal** *adv* every time

jedoch *adv* however

jemals *adv* ever

jemand *pron* somebody; (*in Frage und Verneinung*) anybody

Jemen (-(s)) *m* Yemen

jene(r, s) *adj* that, those *pl* ▷ *pron* that (one), those *pl*

jenseits *adv* on the other side ▷ *prep* +*gen* on the other side of; (*fig*) beyond

Jetlag (-s) *m* jet lag

jetzig *adj* present

jetzt *adv* now; **erst ~** only now; **~ gleich** right now; **bis ~** so far, up to now; **von ~ an** from now on

jeweils *adv*: **~ zwei zusammen** two at a time; **zu ~ 5 Euro** at 5 euros each

Job (-s, -s) *m* job; **jobben** *vi* (*fam*) to work, to have a job

Jod (-(e)s) *nt* iodine

joggen *vi* to jog; **Jogging** (-s) *nt* jogging; **Jogginganzug** *m* jogging suit, tracksuit; **Jogginghose** *f* jogging pants *pl*

Jog(h)urt (-s, -s) *m* o *nt* yoghurt

Johannisbeere *f*: **Schwarze ~** blackcurrant; **Rote ~** redcurrant

Joint (-s, -s) *m* (*fam*) joint

jonglieren *vi* to juggle

Jordanien (-s) *nt* Jordan

Journalist(in) *m(f)* journalist

Joystick (-s, -s) m (Inform) joystick

jubeln vi to cheer

Jubiläum (-s, Jubiläen) nt jubilee; (Jahrestag) anniversary

jucken vi to itch ▷ vt: **es juckt mich am Arm** my arm is itching; **das juckt mich nicht** (fam) I couldn't care less; **Juckreiz** m itch

Jude (-n, -n) m, **Jüdin** f Jew; **sie ist Jüdin** she's Jewish; **jüdisch** adj Jewish

Judo (-(s)) nt judo

Jugend (-) f youth; **jugendfrei** adj: **ein ~er Film** a U-rated film (Brit), a G-rated film (US); **ein nicht ~er Film** an X-rated film; **Jugendgruppe** f youth group; **Jugendherberge** (-, -n) f youth hostel; **Jugendherbergsausweis** m youth hostel card; **jugendlich** adj youthful; **Jugendliche(r)** mf young person; **Jugendstil** m art nouveau; **Jugendzentrum** nt youth centre

Jugoslawien (-s) nt (Hist) Yugoslavia; **das ehemalige ~** the former Yugoslavia

Juli (-(s), -s) m July; siehe auch **Juni**

jung adj young

Junge (-n, -n) m boy

Junge(s) (-n, -n) nt young animal; **die ~n** pl the young pl

Jungfrau f virgin; (Astr) Virgo

Junggeselle (-n, -n) m bachelor; **Junggesellin** f single woman

Juni (-(s), -s) m June; **im ~** in June; **am 4. ~** on 4(th) June, on June 4(th) (gesprochen: on the fourth of June); **Anfang/Mitte/Ende ~** at the beginning/in the middle/at the end of June; **letzten/nächsten ~** last/next June

Jupiter (-s) m Jupiter

Jura ohne Artikel (Studienfach) law; **~ studieren** to study law; **Jurist(in)** m(f) lawyer; **juristisch** adj legal

Justiz (-) f justice; **Justizminister(in)** m(f) minister of justice

Juwel (-s, -en) nt jewel; **Juwelier(in)** (-s, -e) m(f) jeweller

k

Kabel (-s, -) nt (Elek) wire; (stark) cable; **Kabelfernsehen** nt cable television

Kabeljau (-s, -e o -s) m cod

Kabine f cabin; (im Schwimmbad) cubicle

Kabrio (-s, -s) nt convertible

Kachel (-, -n) f tile; **Kachelofen** m tiled stove

Käfer (-s, -) m beetle, bug (US)

Kaff (-s, -s) nt dump, hole

Kaffee (-s, -s) m coffee; **~ kochen** to make some coffee; **Kaffeefilter** m coffee filter; **Kaffeekanne** f coffeepot; **Kaffeeklatsch** (-(e)s, -e) m chat over coffee and cakes, coffee klatch (US); **Kaffeelöffel** m coffee spoon; **Kaffeemaschine** f coffee maker (o machine); **Kaffeetasse** f coffee cup

Käfig (-s, -e) m cage

kahl adj bald; (Baum, Wand) bare

Kahn (-(e)s, Kähne) m boat; (Lastkahn) barge

Kai (-s, -e o -s) m quay

Kaiser (-s, -) m emperor; **Kaiserin** f empress; **Kaiserschnitt** m (Med) caesarean (section)

Kajak (-s, -s) nt kayak; **Kajakfahren** nt kayaking

Kajal (-s) m kohl

Kajüte (-, -n) f cabin

Kakao (-s, -s) m cocoa; (Getränk) (hot) chocolate

Kakerlake (-, -n) f cockroach

Kaki (-, -s) f kaki

Kaktee (-, -n) f, **Kaktus** (-, -se) m cactus

Kalb (-(e)s, Kälber) nt calf; **Kalbfleisch** nt veal; **Kalbsbraten** m roast veal; **Kalbsschnitzel** nt veal cutlet; (paniert) escalope of veal

Kalender (-s, -) m calendar; (Taschenkalender) diary

Kalk (-(e)s, -e) m lime; (in Knochen) calcium

Kalorie f calorie; **kalorienarm** adj low-calorie

kalt adj cold; **mir ist (es) ~** I'm cold; **kaltblütig** adj cold-blooded; **Kälte** (-) f cold; (fig) coldness

kam imperf von **kommen**

Kambodscha (-s) nt Cambodia

Kamel (-(e)s, -e) nt camel

Kamera (-, -s) f camera

Kamerad(in) (-en, -en) m(f) friend; (als Begleiter) companion

Kamerafrau f camerawoman; **Kamerahandy** nt cameraphone; **Kameramann** m cameraman

Kamille (-, -n) f camomile; **Kamillentee** m camomile tea

Kamin (-s, -e) m (außen) chimney; (innen) fireplace

Kamm (-(e)s, Kämme) m comb; (Berg) ridge; (Hahn) crest; **kämmen** vr **sich ~, sich** (dat) **die Haare ~** to

comb one's hair; **Kammermusik**
f chamber music
Kampf (-(e)s, Kämpfe) m fight;
(Schlacht) battle; (Wettbewerb)
contest; (fig: Anstrengung)
struggle; **kämpfen** vi to fight
(für, um for); **Kampfsport** m
martial art
Kanada (-s) nt Canada;
Kanadier(in) (-s, -) m(f) Cana-
dian; **kanadisch** adj Canadian
Kanal (-s, Kanäle) m (Fluss) canal;
(Rinne, TV) channel; (für Abfluss)
drain; **der ~** (Ärmelkanal) the
(English) Channel; **Kanalinseln**
pl Channel Islands pl;
Kanalisation f sewerage system;
Kanaltunnel m Channel Tunnel
Kanarienvogel m canary
Kandidat(in) (-en, -en) m(f)
candidate
Kandis(zucker) (-) m rock
candy
Känguru (-s, -s) nt kangaroo
Kaninchen nt rabbit
Kanister (-s, -) m can
Kännchen nt pot; **ein
~ Kaffee/Tee** a pot of coffee/tea;
Kanne (-, -n) f (Krug) jug;
(Kaffeekanne) pot; (Milchkanne)
churn; (Gießkanne) can
kannte imperf von **kennen**
Kante (-, -n) f edge
Kantine f canteen
Kanton (-s, -e) m canton
Kanu (-s, -s) nt canoe
Kanzler(in) (-s, -) m(f)
chancellor
Kap (-s, -s) nt cape
Kapazität f capacity; (Fachmann)
authority
Kapelle f (Gebäude) chapel; (Mus)
band
Kaper (-, -n) f caper
kapieren vt, vi (fam) to
understand; **kapiert?** got it?
Kapital (-s, -e o -ien) nt capital

Kapitän (-s, -e) m captain
Kapitel (-s, -) nt chapter
Kappe (-, -n) f cap
Kapsel (-, -n) f capsule
kaputt adj (fam) broken; (Mensch)
exhausted; **kaputt|gehen** irr vi
to break; (Schuhe) to fall apart;
(Firma) to go bust; (Stoff) to wear
out; **kaputt|machen** vt to
break; (jdn) to wear out
Kapuze (-, -n) f hood
Kap Verde (-s) nt Cape Verde
Karaffe (-, -n) f carafe; (mit
Stöpsel) decanter
Karamell (-s) m caramel, toffee
Karaoke (-(s)) nt karaoke
Karat (-s, -e) nt carat
Karate (-s) nt karate
Kardinal (-s, Kardinäle) m
cardinal
Karfreitag m Good Friday
kariert adj checked; (Papier)
squared
Karies (-) f (tooth) decay
Karikatur f caricature
Karneval (-s, -e o -s) m carnival

○ **KARNEVAL**
○
○
○ **Karneval** is the name given to
○ the days immediately before
○ Lent when people gather to
○ sing, dance, eat, drink and
○ generally make merry before the
○ fasting begins. **Rosenmontag**,
○ the day before Shrove Tuesday,
○ is the most important day of
○ 'Karneval' on the Rhine. Most
○ firms take a day's holiday on
○ that day to enjoy the parades
○ and revelry. In South Germany
○ 'Karneval' is called **Fasching**.

Kärnten (-s) nt Carinthia
Karo (-s, -s) nt square; (Karten)
diamonds pl
Karosserie f (Auto) body(work)

Karotte (-, -n) f carrot
Karpfen (-s, -) m carp
Karriere (-, -n) f career
Karte (-, -n) f card; (*Landkarte*) map; (*Speisekarte*) menu; (*Eintrittskarte, Fahrkarte*) ticket; **mit ~ bezahlen** to pay by credit card; **~n spielen** to play cards; **die ~n mischen/geben** to shuffle/deal the cards
Kartei f card index; **Karteikarte** f index card
Kartenspiel nt card game; **Kartentelefon** nt cardphone; **Kartenvorverkauf** m advance booking
Kartoffel (-, -n) f potato; **Kartoffelbrei** m mashed potatoes pl; **Kartoffelchips** pl crisps pl (*Brit*), chips pl (*US*); **Kartoffelpuffer** m potato cake (*made from grated potatoes*); **Kartoffelpüree** nt mashed potatoes pl; **Kartoffelsalat** m potato salad
Karton (-s, -s) m cardboard; (*Schachtel*) (cardboard) box
Kartusche (-, -n) f cartridge
Karussell (-s, -s) nt roundabout (*Brit*), merry-go-round
Kaschmir (-s, e) m (*Stoff*) cashmere
Käse (-s, -) m cheese; **Käsekuchen** m cheesecake; **Käseplatte** f cheeseboard
Kasino (-s, -s) nt (*Spielkasino*) casino
Kaskoversicherung f comprehensive insurance
Kasper(l) (-s, -) m Punch; (*fig*) clown; **Kasperl(e)theater** nt (*Vorstellung*) Punch and Judy show; (*Gebäude*) Punch and Judy theatre
Kasse (-, -n) f (*in Geschäft*) till, cash register; (*im Supermarkt*) checkout; (*Geldkasten*) cashbox;

(*Theater*) box office; (*Kino*) ticket office; (*Krankenkasse*) health insurance; (*Spar~*) savings bank; **Kassenbon** (-s, -s) m, **Kassenzettel** m receipt
Kassette f (small) box; (*Tonband*) cassette; **Kassettenrekorder** m cassette recorder
kassieren vt to take ▷ vi: **darf ich ~?** would you like to pay now?; **Kassierer(in)** m(f) cashier
Kastanie f chestnut
Kasten (-s, Kästen) m (*Behälter*) box; (*Getränkekasten*) crate
Kat m abk = **Katalysator**
Katalog (-(e)s, -e) m catalogue
Katalysator m (*Auto*) catalytic converter; (*Phys*) catalyst
Katar (-s) nt Qatar
Katarr(h) (-s, -e) m catarrh
Katastrophe (-, -n) f catastrophe, disaster
Kategorie (-, -n) f category
Kater (-s, -) m tomcat; (*fam: nach zu viel Alkohol*) hangover
Kathedrale (-, -n) f cathedral
Katholik(in) m(f) Catholic; **katholisch** adj Catholic
Katze (-, -n) f cat
Kauderwelsch (-(s)) nt (*unverständlich*) gibberish; (*Fachjargon*) jargon
kauen vt, vi to chew
Kauf (-(e)s, Käufe) m purchase; (*Kaufen*) buying; **ein guter ~** a bargain; **etw in ~ nehmen** to put up with sth; **kaufen** vt to buy; **Käufer(in)** m(f) buyer; **Kauffrau** f businesswoman; **Kaufhaus** nt department store; **Kaufmann** m businessman; (*im Einzelhandel*) shopkeeper (*Brit*), storekeeper (*US*); **Kaufpreis** m purchase price; **Kaufvertrag** m purchase agreement
Kaugummi m chewing gum
Kaulquappe (-, -n) f tadpole

kaum adv hardly, scarcely
Kaution f deposit; (Jur) bail
Kaviar m caviar
KB (-, -) nt, **Kbyte** (-, -) nt abk = **Kilobyte** KB
Kebab (-(s), -s) m kebab
Kegel (-s, -) m skittle; (beim Bowling) pin; (Math) cone; **Kegelbahn** f bowling alley; **kegeln** vi to play skittles; (bowlen) to bowl
Kehle (-, -n) f throat; **Kehlkopf** m larynx
Kehre (-, -n) f sharp bend
kehren vt (fegen) to sweep
Keilriemen m (Auto) fan belt
kein pron no, not ... any; **ich habe ~ Geld** I have no money, I don't have money; **~ Mensch** no one; **du bist ~ Kind mehr** you're not a child any more; **keine(r, s)** pron (Person) no one, nobody; (Sache) not ... any, none; **~r von ihnen** none of them; (bei zwei Personen/Sachen) neither of them; **ich will keins von beiden** I don't want either (of them); **keinesfalls** adv on no account, under no circumstances
Keks (-es, -e) m biscuit (Brit), cookie (US); **jdm auf den ~ gehen** (fam) to get on sb's nerves
Keller (-s, -) m cellar; (Geschoss) basement
Kellner (-s, -) m waiter; **Kellnerin** f waitress
Kenia (-s) nt Kenya
kennen (kannte, gekannt) vt to know; **wir ~ uns seit 1990** we've known each other since 1990; **wir ~ uns schon** we've already met; **kennst du mich noch?** do you remember me?; **kennen|lernen** vt to get to know; **sich ~** to get to know each other; (zum ersten Mal) to meet
Kenntnis f knowledge; **seine ~se** his knowledge

Kennwort nt (a. Inform) password; **Kennzeichen** nt mark, sign; (Auto) number plate (Brit), license plate (US); **besondere ~** distinguishing marks
Kerl (-s, -e) m guy, bloke (Brit)
Kern (-(e)s, -e) m (Obst) pip; (Pfirsich, Kirsche etc) stone; (Nuss) kernel; (Atomkern) nucleus; (fig) heart, core
Kernenergie f nuclear energy; **Kernkraft** f nuclear power; **Kernkraftwerk** nt nuclear power station
Kerze (-, -n) f candle; (Zündkerze) plug
Ket(s)chup (-(s), -s) m o nt ketchup
Kette (-, -n) f chain; (Halskette) necklace
keuchen vi to pant; **Keuchhusten** m whooping cough
Keule (-, -n) f club; (Gastr) leg; (von Hähnchen a.) drumstick
Keyboard (-s, -s) nt (Mus) keyboard
Kfz nt abk = **Kraftfahrzeug**
Kfz-Brief m ≈ logbook
Kfz-Steuer f ≈ road tax (Brit), vehicle tax (US)
KG (-, -s) f abk = **Kommanditgesellschaft** limited partnership
Kichererbse f chick pea
kichern vi to giggle
Kickboard® (-s, -s) nt micro scooter
Kicker (-s, -) m (Spiel) table football (Brit), foosball (US)
kidnappen vt to kidnap
Kidney-Bohne f kidney bean
Kiefer (-s, -) m jaw ▷ (-, -n) f pine; **Kieferchirurg(in)** m(f) oral surgeon

Kieme (-, -n) f gill
Kies (-es, -e) m gravel; **Kiesel**
(-s, -) m, **Kieselstein** m pebble
Kilo (-s, -(s)) nt kilo; **Kilobyte** nt
kilobyte; **Kilogramm** nt
kilogram; **Kilometer** m
kilometre; **Kilometerstand** m
≈ mileage; **Kilometerzähler** m
≈ mileometer; **Kilowatt** nt
kilowatt
Kind (-(e)s, -er) nt child; **sie
bekommt ein ~** she's having a
baby; **Kinderarzt** m,
Kinderärztin f paediatrician;
Kinderbetreuung f childcare;
Kinderbett nt cot (Brit), crib (US);
Kinderfahrkarte f child's ticket;
Kindergarten m nursery school,
kindergarten; **Kindergärtner(in)**
m(f) nursery-school teacher;
Kindergeld nt child benefit;
Kinderkrippe f crèche (Brit),
daycare center (US);
Kinderlähmung f polio;
Kindermädchen nt nanny (Brit),
nurse(maid); **kindersicher** adj
childproof; **Kindersicherung** f
childproof safety catch; (an Flasche)
childproof cap; **Kindersitz** m
child seat; **Kindertagesstätte** nt
day nursery; **Kinderteller** m (im
Restaurant) children's portion;
Kinderwagen m pram (Brit),
baby carriage (US); **Kinderzimmer**
nt children's (bed)room; **Kindheit**
f childhood; **kindisch** adj
childish; **kindlich** adj childlike
Kinn (-(e)s, -e) nt chin
Kino (-s, -s) nt cinema (Brit),
movie theater (US); **ins ~ gehen** to
go to the cinema (Brit) (o to the
movies (US))
Kiosk (-(e)s, -e) m kiosk
Kippe f (fam: Zigarettenstummel)
cigarette end, fag end (Brit)
kippen vi to tip over ▷ vt to tilt;
(Regierung, Minister) to topple

Kirche (-, -n) f church;
Kirchturm m church tower; (mit
Spitze) steeple; **Kirchweih** f fair
Kirmes (-, -sen) f fair
Kirsche (-, -n) f cherry;
Kirschtomate f cherry tomato
Kissen (-s, -) nt cushion;
(Kopfkissen) pillow; **Kissenbezug**
m cushion cover; (für Kopfkissen)
pillowcase
Kiste (-, -n) f box; (Truhe) chest
KITA (-, -s) f abk =
Kindertagesstätte day-care
centre (Brit), day-care center (US)
kitschig adj kitschy, cheesy
kitzelig adj (a. fig) ticklish;
kitzeln vt, vi to tickle
Kiwi (-, -s) f (Frucht) kiwi (fruit)
Klage (-, -n) f complaint; (Jur)
lawsuit; **klagen** vi to complain
(über +akk about, bei to); **kläglich**
adj wretched
Klammer (-, -n) f (in Text)
bracket; (Büroklammer) clip;
(Wäscheklammer) peg (Brit),
clothespin (US); (Zahnklammer)
brace; **Klammeraffe** m (fam)
at-sign, @; **klammern** vr: **sich
~ to** cling (an +akk to)
Klamotten pl (fam: Kleider)
clothes pl
klang imperf von **klingen**
Klang (-(e)s, Klänge) m sound
Klappbett nt folding bed
klappen vi impers (gelingen) to
work; **es hat gut geklappt** it went
well
klappern vi to rattle; (Geschirr) to
clatter; **Klapperschlange** f
rattlesnake
Klappfahrad nt folding bicycle;
Klappstuhl m folding chair
klar adj clear; **sich** (dat) **im Klaren
sein** to be clear (über +akk about);
alles ~? everything okay?
klären vt (Flüssigkeit) to purify;
(Probleme, Frage) to clarify ▷ vr:

sich ~ to clear itself up
Klarinette (-, -n) f clarinet
klar|kommen irr vi: **mit etw ~** to cope with something; **kommst du klar?** are you managing all right?; **mit jdm ~** to get along with sb; **klar|machen** vt: **jdm etw ~** to make sth clear to sb; **klar|stellen** vt to clarify
Klärung f (von Frage, Problem) clarification
klasse adj inv (fam) great, brilliant
Klasse (-, -n) f class; (Schuljahr) form (Brit), grade (US); **erster ~ reisen** to travel first class; **in welche ~ gehst du?** which form (Brit) (o grade (US)) are you in?; **Klassenarbeit** f test; **Klassenlehrer(in)** m(f) class teacher; **Klassenzimmer** nt classroom
Klassik f (Zeit) classical period; (Musik) classical music
Klatsch (-(e)s, -e) m (Gerede) gossip; **klatschen** vi (schlagen) to smack; (Beifall) to applaud, to clap; (reden) to gossip; **Klatschmohn** m (corn) poppy; **klatschnass** adj soaking (wet)
Klaue (-, -n) f claw; (fam: Schrift) scrawl; **klauen** vt (fam) to pinch
Klavier (-s, -e) nt piano
Klebeband nt adhesive tape; **kleben** vt to stick (an +akk to) ▷ vi (klebrig sein) to be sticky; **klebrig** adj sticky; **Klebstoff** m glue; **Klebstreifen** m adhesive tape
Klecks (-es, -e) m blob; (Tinte) blot
Klee (-s) m clover
Kleid (-(e)s, -er) nt (Frauen~) dress; **~er** pl (Kleidung) clothes pl; **Kleiderbügel** m coat hanger; **Kleiderschrank** m wardrobe (Brit), closet (US); **Kleidung** f clothing
klein adj small, little; (Finger) little; **mein ~er Bruder** my little (o

younger) brother; **als ich noch ~ war** when I was a little boy/girl; **etw ~ schneiden** to chop sth up; **Kleinanzeige** f classified ad; **Kleinbuchstabe** m small letter; **Kleinbus** m minibus; **Kleingeld** nt change; **Kleinigkeit** f trifle; (Zwischenmahlzeit) snack; **Kleinkind** nt toddler; **klein|schreiben** vt (mit kleinem Anfangsbuchstaben) to write with a small letter; **Kleinstadt** f small town
Kleister (-s, -) m paste
Klempner(in) m(f) plumber
klettern vi to climb
Klettverschluss m Velcro® fastening
klicken vi (a. Inform) to click
Klient(in) (-en, -en) m(f) client
Klima (-s, -s) nt climate; **Klimaanlage** f air conditioning; **klimatisiert** adj air-conditioned
Klinge (-, -n) f blade
Klingel (-, -n) f bell; **klingeln** vi to ring
klingen (klang, geklungen) vi to sound
Klinik f clinic; (Krankenhaus) hospital
Klinke (-, -n) f handle
Klippe (-, -n) f cliff; (im Meer) reef; (fig) hurdle
Klischee (-s, -s) nt (fig) cliché
Klo (-s, -s) nt (fam) loo (Brit), john (US); **Klobrille** f toilet seat; **Klopapier** nt toilet paper
klopfen vt, vi to knock; (Herz) to thump
Kloß (-es, Klöße) m (im Hals) lump; (Gastr) dumpling
Kloster (-s, Klöster) nt (für Männer) monastery; (für Frauen) convent
Klub (-s, -s) m club
klug adj clever
knabbern vt, vi to nibble

k

Knäckebrot nt crispbread
knacken vt, vi to crack
Knall (-(e)s, -e) m bang; **knallen**
vi to bang
knapp adj (kaum ausreichend)
scarce; (Sieg) narrow; **~ bei Kasse
sein** to be short of money; **~ zwei
Stunden** just under two hours
Knauf (-s, Knäufe) m knob
kneifen (kniff, gekniffen) vt, vi to
pinch; (sich drücken) to back out
(vor +dat of); **Kneifzange** f
pincers pl
Kneipe (-, -n) f (fam) pub (Brit),
bar
Knete (-) f (fam: Geld) dough;
kneten vt to knead; (formen) to
mould
knicken vt, vi (brechen) to break;
(Papier) to fold; **geknickt sein** (fig)
to be downcast
Knie (-s, -) nt knee; **in die
~ gehen** to bend one's knees;
Kniebeuge f knee bend;
Kniegelenk nt knee joint;
Kniekehle f back of the knee;
knien vi to kneel; **Kniescheibe** f
kneecap; **Knieschoner** (-s, -) m,
Knieschützer (-s, -) m knee pad;
Kniestrumpf m knee-length sock
kniff imperf von **kneifen**
knipsen vt to punch; (Foto) to
snap ▷ vi (Foto) to take snaps
knirschen vi to crunch; **mit den
Zähnen ~** to grind one's teeth
knitterfrei adj non-crease;
knittern vi to crease
Knoblauch m garlic;
Knoblauchbrot nt garlic bread;
Knoblauchzehe f clove of garlic
Knöchel (-s, -) m (Finger)
knuckle; (Fuß) ankle
Knochen (-s, -) m bone;
Knochenbruch m fracture;
Knochenmark nt marrow
Knödel (-s, -) m dumpling
Knollensellerie m celeriac

Knopf (-(e)s, Knöpfe) m button;
Knopfdruck m: **auf ~** at the
touch of a botton; **Knopfloch** nt
buttonhole
Knospe (-, -n) f bud
knoten vt to knot; **Knoten** (-s, -)
m knot; (Med) lump
Know-how (-(s)) nt know-how,
expertise
knurren vi (Hund) to growl;
(Magen) to rumble; (Mensch) to
grumble
knusprig adj crisp; (Keks) crunchy
knutschen vi (fam) to smooch
k. o. adj inv (Sport) knocked out;
(fig) knackered
Koalition f coalition
Koch (-(e)s, Köche) m cook;
Kochbuch nt cookery book,
cookbook; **kochen** vt, vi to cook;
(Wasser) to boil; (Kaffee, Tee) to
make; **Köchin** f cook;
Kochlöffel m wooden spoon;
Kochnische f kitchenette;
Kochplatte f hotplate;
Kochrezept nt recipe; **Kochtopf**
m saucepan
Kode (-s, -s) m code
Köder (-s, -) m bait
Koffein (-s) nt caffeine;
koffeinfrei adj decaffeinated
Koffer (-s, -) m (suit)case;
Kofferraum m (Auto) boot (Brit),
trunk (US)
Kognak (-s, -s) m brandy
Kohl (-(e)s, -e) m cabbage
Kohle (-, -n) f coal; (Holzkohle)
charcoal; (Chem) carbon; (fam:
Geld) cash, dough; **Kohlehydrat**
nt carbohydrate; **Kohlendioxid**
nt carbon dioxide; **Kohlensäure**
f (in Getränken) fizz; **ohne ~** still,
non-carbonated (US); **mit
~** sparkling, carbonated (US);
Kohletablette f charcoal tablet
Kohlrabi (-(s), -(s)) m kohlrabi
Koje (-, -n) f cabin; (Bett) bunk

Kokain (-s) nt cocaine
Kokosnuss f coconut
Kolben (-s, -) m (Tech) piston; (Mais~) cob
Kolik (-, -en) f colic
Kollaps (-es, -e) m collapse
Kollege (-n, -n) m, **Kollegin** f colleague
Köln (-s) nt Cologne; **Kölnischwasser** nt eau du cologne
Kolonne (-, -n) f convoy
Kölsch (-, -) nt (Bier) (strong) lager (from the Cologne region)
Kolumbien (-s) nt Columbia
Koma (-s, -s) nt coma
Kombi (-(s), -s) m estate (car) (Brit), station wagon (US); **Kombination** f combination; (Folgerung) deduction; (Hemdhose) combinations pl; (Aviat) flying suit; **kombinieren** vt to combine ▷ vi to reason; (vermuten) to guess; **Kombizange** f (pair of) pliers pl
Komfort (-s) m conveniences pl; (Bequemlichkeit) comfort
Komiker(in) m(f) comedian, comic; **komisch** adj funny
Komma (-s, -s) nt comma
Kommanditgesellschaft f limited partnership
kommen (kam, gekommen) vi to come; (näher kommen) to approach; (passieren) to happen; (gelangen, geraten) to get; (erscheinen) to appear; (in die Schule, das Gefängnis etc) to go; **~ lassen** to send for; **zu sich ~** to come round (o to); **zu etw ~** (bekommen) to acquire sth; (Zeit dazu finden) to get round to sth; **wer kommt zuerst?** who's first?; **kommend** adj coming; **~e Woche** next week; **in den ~en Jahren** in the years to come
Kommentar m commentary; **kein ~** no comment
Kommilitone (-n, -n) m,

Kommilitonin f fellow student
Kommissar(in) m(f) inspector
Kommode (-, -n) f chest of drawers
Kommunikation f communication
Kommunion f (Rel) communion
Kommunismus m communism
Komödie f comedy
kompakt adj compact
Kompass (-es, -e) m compass
kompatibel adj compatible
kompetent adj competent
komplett adj complete
Kompliment nt compliment; **jdm ein ~ machen** to pay sb a compliment; **~!** congratulations
Komplize (-n, -n) m accomplice
kompliziert adj complicated
Komponist(in) m(f) composer
Kompost (-(e)s, -e) m compost; **Komposthaufen** m compost heap; **kompostierbar** adj biodegradable
Kompott (-(e)s, -e) nt stewed fruit
Kompresse (-, -n) f compress
Kompromiss (-es, -e) m compromise
Kondensmilch f condensed milk, evaporated milk
Kondition f (Leistungsfähigkeit) condition; **sie hat eine gute ~** she's in good shape
Konditorei f cake shop; (mit Café) café
Kondom (-s, -e) nt condom
Konfektionsgröße f size
Konferenz f conference
Konfession f religion; (christlich) denomination
Konfetti (-(s)) nt confetti
Konfirmation f (Rel) confirmation
Konfitüre (-, -n) f jam
Konflikt (-(e)s, -e) m conflict
konfrontieren vt to confront

k

Kongress (-es, -e) m conference;
der ~ (Parlament der USA)
Congress
König (-(e)s, -e) m king; **Königin**
f queen; **königlich** adj royal;
Königreich nt kingdom
Konkurrenz f competition

⬤ SCHLÜSSELWORT

können (pt **konnte**, pp **gekonnt** o
(als Hilfsverb) **können**) vt, vi **1** to be
able to; **ich kann es machen** I can
do it, I am able to do it; **ich kann
es nicht machen** I can't do it, I'm
not able to do it; **ich kann nicht ...**
I can't ..., I cannot ...; **ich kann
nicht mehr** I can't go on
2 (wissen, beherrschen) to know;
können Sie Deutsch? can you
speak German?; **er kann gut
Englisch** he speaks English well;
sie kann keine Mathematik she
can't do mathematics
3 (dürfen) to be allowed to; **kann
ich gehen?** can I go?; **könnte ich
...?** could I ...?; **kann ich mit?** (fam)
can I come with you?
4 (möglich sein) **Sie könnten recht
haben** you may be right; **das kann
sein** that's possible; **kann sein**
maybe

konsequent adj consistent;
Konsequenz f consequence
konservativ adj conservative
Konserven pl tinned food sing
(Brit), canned food sing;
Konservendose f tin (Brit), can
konservieren vt to preserve;
Konservierungsmittel nt
preservative
Konsonant m consonant
Konsul(in) (-s, -n) m(f) consul;
Konsulat nt consulate
Kontakt (-(e)s, -e) m contact;
kontaktarm adj: **er ist ~** he lacks

contact with other people;
kontaktfreudig adj sociable;
Kontaktlinsen pl contact lenses
pl
Kontinent m continent
Konto (-s, Konten) nt account;
Kontoauszug m (bank)
statement;
Kontoauszugsdrucker m
bank-statement machine;
Kontoinhaber(in) m(f) account
holder; **Kontonummer** f
account number; **Kontostand** m
balance
Kontrabass m double bass
Kontrast (-(e)s, -e) m contrast
Kontrolle (-, -n) f control;
(Aufsicht) supervision;
(Passkontrolle) passport control;
kontrollieren vt to control;
(nachprüfen) to check
Konzentration f concentra-
tion; **Konzentrationslager** nt
(Hist) concentration camp;
konzentrieren vt to concentrate
▷ vr: **sich ~** to concentrate
Konzept (-(e)s, -e) nt rough draft;
jdn aus dem ~ bringen to put sb
off
Konzern (-(e)s, -e) m firm
Konzert (-(e)s, -e) nt concert;
(Stück) concerto; **Konzertsaal** m
concert hall
koordinieren vt to coordinate
Kopf (-(e)s, Köpfe) m head; **pro
~** per person; **sich den
~ zerbrechen** to rack one's brains;
Kopfhörer m headphones pl;
Kopfkissen nt pillow; **Kopfsalat**
m lettuce; **Kopfschmerzen** pl
headache sing; **Kopfstütze** f
headrest; **Kopftuch** nt
headscarf; **kopfüber** adv
headfirst
Kopie f copy; **kopieren** vt (a.
Inform) to copy; **Kopierer** (-s, -) m,
Kopiergerät nt copier

Kopilot(in) *m(f)* co-pilot
Koralle (-, -n) *f* coral
Koran (-s) *m* (Rel) Koran
Korb (-(e)s, Körbe) *m* basket; **jdm einen ~ geben** (fig) to turn sb down
Kord (-(e)s, -e) *m* corduroy
Kordel (-, -n) *f* cord
Kork (-(e)s, -e) *m* cork; **Korken** (-s, -) *m* cork; **Korkenzieher** (-s, -) *m* corkscrew
Korn (-(e)s, Körner) *nt* grain; **Kornblume** *f* cornflower
Körper (-s, -) *m* body; **Körperbau** *m* build; **Körpergeruch** *m* body odour; **Körpergröße** *f* height; **körperlich** *adj* physical; **Körperteil** *m* part of the body; **Körperverletzung** *f* physical injury
korrekt *adj* correct
Korrespondent(in) *m(f)* correspondent; **Korrespondenz** *f* correspondence
korrigieren *vt* to correct
Kosmetik *f* cosmetics *pl*; **Kosmetikkoffer** *m* vanity case; **Kosmetiksalon** *m* beauty parlour; **Kosmetiktuch** *nt* paper tissue
Kost (-) *f* (Nahrung) food; (Verpflegung) board
kostbar *adj* precious; (teuer) costly, expensive
kosten *vt* to cost ▷ *vt, vi* (versuchen) to taste; **Kosten** *pl* costs *pl*, cost; (Ausgaben) expenses *pl*; **auf ~ von** at the expense of; **kostenlos** *adj* free (of charge); **Kostenvoranschlag** *m* estimate
köstlich *adj* (Essen) delicious; (Einfall) delightful; **sich ~ amüsieren** to have a marvellous time
Kostprobe *f* taster; (fig) sample; **kostspielig** *adj* expensive
Kostüm (-s, -e) *m* costume; (Damenkostüm) suit
Kot (-(e)s) *m* excrement
Kotelett (-(e)s, -e o -s) *nt* chop, cutlet
Koteletten *pl* sideboards *pl* (Brit), sideburns *pl* (US)
Kotflügel *m* (Auto) wing
kotzen *vi* (vulg) to puke, to throw up
Krabbe (-, -n) *f* shrimp; (größer) prawn; (Krebs) crab
krabbeln *vi* to crawl
Krach (-(e)s, -s o -e) *m* crash; (andauernd) noise; (fam: Streit) row
Kraft (-, Kräfte) *f* strength; (Pol, Phys) force; (Fähigkeit) power; (Arbeits~) worker; **in ~ treten** to come into effect; **Kraftausdruck** *m* swearword; **Kraftfahrzeug** *nt* motor vehicle; **Kraftfahrzeugbrief** *m* ≈ logbook; **Kraftfahrzeugschein** *m* vehicle registration document; **Kraftfahrzeugsteuer** *f* ≈ road tax (Brit), vehicle tax (US); **Kraftfahrzeugversicherung** *f* car insurance; **kräftig** *adj* strong; (gesund) healthy; (Farben) intense, strong; **Kraftstoff** *m* fuel; **Kraftwerk** *nt* power station
Kragen (-s, -) *m* collar
Krähe (-, -n) *f* crow
Kralle (-, -n) *f* claw; (Parkkralle) wheel clamp
Kram (-(e)s) *m* stuff
Krampf (-(e)s, Krämpfe) *m* cramp; (zuckend) spasm; **Krampfader** *f* varicose vein
Kran (-(e)s, Kräne) *m* crane
Kranich (-s, -e) *m* (Zool) crane
krank *adj* ill, sick
kränken *vt* to hurt
Krankengymnastik *f* physiotherapy; **Krankenhaus** *nt* hospital; **Krankenkasse** *f* health insurance; **Krankenpfleger** (-s, -) *m* (male) nurse;

k

Krankenschein m *health insurance certificate*; **Krankenschwester** f nurse; **Krankenversicherung** f health insurance; **Krankenwagen** m ambulance; **Krankheit** f illness; *(durch Infektion hervorgerufen)* disease

Kränkung f insult

Kranz *(-es, Kränze)* m wreath

krass *adj* crass; *(fam: toll)* wicked

kratzen *vt, vi* to scratch; **Kratzer** *(-s, -)* m scratch

kraulen *vi (schwimmen)* to do the crawl ▷ *vt (streicheln)* to pet

Kraut *(-(e)s, Kräuter)* nt plant; *(Gewürz)* herb; *(Gemüse)* cabbage; **Kräuter** *pl* herbs *pl*; **Kräuterbutter** f herb butter; **Kräutertee** m herbal tea; **Krautsalat** m coleslaw

Krawatte f tie

kreativ *adj* creative

Krebs *(-es, -e)* m *(Zool)* crab; *(Med)* cancer; *(Astr)* Cancer

Kredit *(-(e)s, -e)* m credit; **auf ~** on credit; **einen ~ aufnehmen** to take out a loan; **Kreditkarte** f credit card

Kreide *(-, -n)* f chalk

Kreis *(-es, -e)* m circle; *(Bezirk)* district

kreischen *vi* to shriek; *(Bremsen, Säge)* to screech

Kreisel *(-s, -)* m *(Spielzeug)* top; *(Verkehrskreisel)* roundabout *(Brit)*, traffic circle *(US)*

Kreislauf m *(Med)* circulation; *(fig: der Natur etc)* cycle; **Kreislaufstörungen** *pl (Med)* **ich habe ~** I've got problems with my circulation; **Kreisverkehr** m roundabout *(Brit)*, traffic circle *(US)*

Kren *(-s)* m horseradish

Kresse *(-, -n)* f cress

Kreuz *(-es, -e)* nt cross; *(Anat)* small of the back; *(Karten)* clubs *pl*; **mir tut das ~ weh** I've got backache; **Kreuzband** m cruciate ligament; **kreuzen** *vt* to cross ▷ *vr:* **sich ~** to cross ▷ *vi (Naut)* to cruise; **Kreuzfahrt** f cruise; **Kreuzgang** m cloisters *pl*; **Kreuzotter** *(-, -n)* f adder; **Kreuzschlitzschraubenzieher** m Phillips® screwdriver; **Kreuzschlüssel** m *(Auto)* wheel brace; **Kreuzschmerzen** *pl* backache *sing*; **Kreuzung** f *(Verkehrskreuzung)* crossroads *sing*, intersection; *(Züchtung)* cross; **Kreuzworträtsel** nt crossword (puzzle)

kriechen *(kroch, gekrochen)* vi to crawl; *(unauffällig)* to creep; *(fig, pej)* **(vor jdm) ~** to crawl (to sb); **Kriechspur** f crawler lane

Krieg *(-(e)s, -e)* m war

kriegen *vt (fam)* to get; *(erwischen)* to catch; **sie kriegt ein Kind** she's having a baby; **ich kriege noch Geld von dir** you still owe me some money

Krimi *(-s, -s)* m *(fam)* thriller; **Kriminalität** f criminality; **Kriminalpolizei** f detective force, ≈ CID *(Brit)*, ≈ FBI *(US)*; **Kriminalroman** m detective novel; **kriminell** *adj* criminal

Krippe *(-, -n)* f *(Futterkrippe)* manger; *(Weihnachtskrippe)* crib *(Brit)*, crèche *(US)*; *(Kinderkrippe)* crèche *(Brit)*, daycare center *(US)*

Krise *(-, -n)* f crisis

Kristall *(-s, -e)* m crystal ▷ *(-s)* nt *(Glas)* crystal

Kritik f criticism; *(Rezension)* review; **Kritiker(in)** *m(f)* critic; **kritisch** *adj* critical

kritzeln *vt, vi* to scribble, to scrawl

Kroate *(-n, -n)* m Croat; **Kroatien** *(-s)* nt Croatia; **Kroatin** f Croat; **kroatisch** *adj* Croatian;

Kroatisch nt Croatian
kroch imperf von **kriechen**
Krokodil (-s, -e) nt crocodile
Krokus (-, - o -se) m crocus
Krone (-, -n) f crown;
Kronleuchter m chandelier
Kropf (-(e)s, Kröpfe) m (Med)
goitre; (von Vogel) crop
Kröte (-, -n) f toad
Krücke (-, -n) f crutch
Krug (-(e)s, Krüge) m jug;
(Bierkrug) mug
Krümel (-s, -) m crumb
krumm adj crooked
Krüppel (-s, -) m cripple
Kruste (-, -n) f crust
Kruzifix (-es, -e) nt crucifix
Kuba (-s) nt Cuba
Kübel (-s, -) m tub; (Eimer) bucket
Kubikmeter m cubic metre
Küche (-, -n) f kitchen; (Kochen)
cooking
Kuchen (-s, -) m cake; (mit
Teigdeckel) pie; **Kuchengabel** f
cake fork
Küchenmaschine f food
processor; **Küchenpapier** nt
kitchen roll; **Küchenschrank** m
(kitchen) cupboard
Kuckuck (-s, -e) m cuckoo
Kugel (-, -n) f ball; (Math) sphere;
(Mil) bullet; (Weihnachtskugel)
bauble; **Kugellager** nt ball
bearing; **Kugelschreiber** m
(ball-point) pen, biro® (Brit);
Kugelstoßen (-s) nt shot put
Kuh (-, Kühe) f cow
kühl adj cool; **Kühlakku** (-s, -s) m
ice pack; **Kühlbox** f cool box;
kühlen vt to cool; **Kühler** (-s, -)
m (Auto) radiator; **Kühlerhaube**
f (Auto) bonnet (Brit), hood (US);
Kühlschrank m fridge,
refrigerator; **Kühltasche** f cool
bag; **Kühltruhe** f freezer;
Kühlwasser nt (Auto) radiator
water

Kuhstall m cowshed
Küken (-s, -) nt chick
Kuli (-s, -s) m (fam: Kugelschreiber)
pen, biro® (Brit)
Kulisse (-, -n) f scenery
Kult (-(e)s, -e) m cult; **Kultfigur** f
cult figure
Kultur f culture; (Lebensform)
civilization; **Kulturbeutel** m
toilet bag (Brit), washbag;
kulturell adj cultural
Kümmel (-s, -) m caraway
seeds pl
Kummer (-s) m grief, sorrow
kümmern vr: **sich um jdn ~** to
look after sb; **sich um etw ~** to see
to sth ▷ vt to concern; **das
kümmert mich nicht** that doesn't
worry me
Kumpel (-s, -) m (fam) mate, pal
Kunde (-n, -n) m customer;
Kundendienst m after-sales (o
customer) service;
Kunden(kredit)karte f storecard, chargecard; **Kunden-
nummer** f customer number
kündigen vi to hand in one's
notice; (Mieter) to give notice that
one is moving out; **jdm ~** to give
sb his/her notice; (Vermieter) to
give sb notice to quit ▷ vt to
cancel; (Vertrag) to terminate; **jdm
die Stellung ~** to give sb his/her
notice; **jdm die Wohnung ~** to
give sb notice to quit; **Kündigung**
f (Arbeitsverhältnis) dismissal;
(Vertrag) termination;
(Abonnement) cancellation; (Frist)
notice; **Kündigungsfrist** f
period of notice
Kundin f customer; **Kundschaft**
f customers pl
künftig adj future
Kunst (-, Künste) f art; (Können)
skill; **Kunstausstellung** f art
exhibition; **Kunstgewerbe** nt arts
and crafts pl; **Künstler(in)** (-s, -)

k

m(f) artist; **künstlerisch** *adj* artistic

künstlich *adj* artificial

Kunststoff *m* synthetic material; **Kunststück** *nt* trick; **Kunstwerk** *nt* work of art

Kupfer (*-s, -*) *nt* copper

Kuppel (*-, -n*) *f* dome

kuppeln *vi* (*Auto*) to operate the clutch; **Kupplung** *f* coupling; (*Auto*) clutch

Kur (*-, -en*) *f* course of treatment; (*am Kurort*) cure

Kür (*-, -en*) *f* (*Sport*) free programme

Kurbel (*-, -n*) *f* crank; (*von Rollo, Fenster*) winder

Kürbis (*-ses, -se*) *m* pumpkin

Kurierdienst *m* courier service

kurieren *vt* to cure

Kurort *m* health resort

Kurs (*-es, -e*) *m* course; (*Fin*) rate; (*Wechselkurs*) exchange rate

kursiv *adj* italic ▷ *adv* in italics

Kursleiter(in) *m(f)* course tutor; **Kursteilnehmer(in)** *m(f)* (course) participant; **Kurswagen** *m* (*Eisenb*) through carriage

Kurve (*-, -n*) *f* curve; (*Straßenkurve*) bend; **kurvenreich** *adj* (*Straße*) winding

kurz *adj* short; (*zeitlich a.*) brief; **~ vorher/darauf** shortly before/after; **kannst du ~ kommen?** could you come here for a minute?; **~ gesagt** in short; **kurzärmelig** *adj* short-sleeved; **kürzen** *vt* to cut short; (*in der Länge*) to shorten; (*Gehalt*) to reduce; **kurzerhand** *adv* on the spot; **kurzfristig** *adj* short-term; **das Konzert wurde ~ abgesagt** the concert was called off at short notice; **Kurzgeschichte** *f* short story; **kurzhaarig** *adj* short-haired; **kürzlich** *adv* recently; **Kurzparkzone** *f*

short-stay (*Brit*) (*o* short-term (*US*)) parking zone; **Kurzschluss** *m* (*Elek*) short circuit; **kurzsichtig** *adj* short-sighted; **Kurztrip** *m* trip, break; **Kurzurlaub** *m* short holiday (*Brit*), short vacation (*US*); **Kurzwelle** *f* short wave

Kusine *f* cousin

Kuss (*-es, Küsse*) *m* kiss; **küssen** *vt* to kiss ▷ *vr:* **sich ~** to kiss

Küste (*-, -n*) *f* coast; (*Ufer*) shore; **Küstenwache** *f* coastguard

Kutsche (*-, -n*) *f* carriage; (*geschlossene*) coach

Kuvert (*-s, -s*) *nt* envelope

Kuvertüre (*-, -n*) *f* coating

Kuwait (*-s*) *nt* Kuwait

KZ (*-s, -s*) *nt abk =* **Konzentrationslager** (*Hist*) concentration camp

I

Labor (-s, -e o -s) nt lab
Labyrinth (-s, -e) nt maze
Lache (-, -n) f (Pfütze) puddle; (Blut~, Öl~) pool
lächeln vi to smile; **Lächeln** (-s) nt smile; **lachen** vi to laugh; **lächerlich** adj ridiculous
Lachs (-es, -e) m salmon
Lack (-(e)s, -e) m varnish; (Farblack) lacquer; (an Auto) paint; **lackieren** vt to varnish; (Auto) to spray; **Lackschaden** m scratch (on the paintwork)
Ladegerät nt (battery) charger; **laden** (lud, geladen) vt (a. Inform) to load; (einladen) to invite; (Handy etc) to charge
Laden (-s, Läden) m shop; (Fensterladen) shutter; **Ladendieb(in)** m(f) shoplifter; **Ladendiebstahl** m shoplifting; **Ladenschluss** m closing time
Ladung f load; (Naut, Aviat)

cargo; (Jur) summons sing
lag imperf von **liegen**
Lage (-, -n) f position, situation; (Schicht) layer; **in der ~ sein zu** to be in a position to
Lager (-s, -) nt camp; (Comm) warehouse; (Tech) bearing; **Lagerfeuer** nt campfire; **lagern** vi (Dinge) to be stored; (Menschen) to camp ▷ vt to store
Lagune f lagoon
lahm adj lame; (langweilig) dull; **lähmen** vt to paralyse; **Lähmung** f paralysis
Laib (-s, -e) m loaf
Laie (-n, -n) m layman
Laken (-s, -) nt sheet
Lakritze (-, -n) f liquorice
Lamm (-(e)s, Lämmer) nt lamb
Lampe (-, -n) f lamp; (Glühbirne) bulb; **Lampenfieber** nt stage fright; **Lampenschirm** m lampshade
Lampion (-s, -s) m Chinese lantern
Land (-(e)s, Länder) nt (Gelände) land; (Nation) country; (Bundesland) state, Land; **auf dem ~(e)** in the country

○ **LAND**
○
○ A **Land** (plural **Länder**) is a
○ member state of the **BRD**. There
○ are 16 **Länder**, namely
○ Baden-Württemberg, Bayern,
○ Berlin, Brandenburg, Bremen,
○ Hamburg, Hessen,
○ Mecklenburg-Vorpommern,
○ Niedersachsen,
○ Nordrhein-Westfalen,
○ Rheinland-Pfalz, Saarland,
○ Sachsen, Sachsen-Anhalt,
○ Schleswig-Holstein and
○ Thüringen. Each "Land" has its
○ own parliament and
○ constitution.

Landebahn f runway; **landen** vt, vi to land; (Schiff) to dock

Länderspiel nt international (match)

Landesgrenze f national border, frontier; **Landesinnere** nt interior; **landesüblich** adj customary; **Landeswährung** f national currency; **landesweit** adj nationwide

Landhaus nt country house; **Landkarte** f map; **Landkreis** m administrative region, ≈ district

ländlich adj rural

Landschaft f countryside; (schöne) scenery; (Kunst) landscape; **Landstraße** f country road, B road (Brit)

Landung f landing; **Landungsbrücke** f, **Landungssteg** m gangway

Landwirt(in) m(f) farmer; **Landwirtschaft** f agriculture, farming; **landwirtschaftlich** adj agricultural

lang adj long; (Mensch) tall; **ein zwei Meter ~er Tisch** a table two metres long; **den ganzen Tag ~** all day long; **die Straße ~** along the street; **langärmelig** adj long-sleeved; **lange** adv for a long time; **ich musste ~ warten** I had to wait (for) a long time; **ich bleibe nicht ~** I won't stay long; **es ist ~ her, dass wir uns gesehen haben** it's a long time since we saw each other; **Länge** (-, -n) f length; (Geo) longitude

langen vi (fam: ausreichen) to be enough; (fam: fassen) to reach (nach for); **mir langt's** I've had enough

Langeweile f boredom

langfristig adj long-term ▷ adv in the long term

Langlauf m cross-country skiing

längs prep +gen **die Bäume ~ der Straße** the trees along(side) the road ▷ adv: **die Streifen laufen ~ über das Hemd** the stripes run lengthways down the shirt

langsam adj slow ▷ adv slowly

Langschläfer(in) (-s, -) m(f) late riser

längst adv: **das ist ~ fertig** that was finished a long time ago; **sie sollte ~ da sein** she should have been here long ago; **als sie kam, waren wir ~ weg** when she arrived we had long since left

Langstreckenflug m long-haul flight

Languste (-, -n) f crayfish, crawfish (US)

langweilen vt to bore; **ich langweile mich** I'm bored; **langweilig** adj boring; **Langwelle** f long wave

Laos (-) nt Laos

Lappen (-s, -) m cloth, rag; (Staublappen) duster

läppisch adj silly; (Summe) ridiculous

Laptop (-s, -s) m laptop

Lärche (-, -n) f larch

Lärm (-(e)s) m noise

las imperf von **lesen**

Lasche (-, -n) f flap

Laser (-s, -) m laser; **Laserdrucker** m laser printer

SCHLÜSSELWORT

lassen (pt **ließ**, pp **gelassen** o (als Hilfsverb) **lassen**) vt **1** (unterlassen) to stop; (momentan) to leave; **lass das (sein)!** don't (do it)!; (hör auf!) stop it!; **lass mich!** leave me alone; **lassen wir das!** let's leave it; **er kann das Trinken nicht lassen** he can't stop drinking

2 (zurücklassen) to leave; **etw lassen, wie es ist** to leave sth (just) as it is

3 (*überlassen*) **jdn ins Haus lassen** to let sb into the house
▷ *vi* ; **lass mal, ich mache das schon** leave it, I'll do it
▷ *Hilfsverb* 1 (*veranlassen*) **etw machen lassen** to have *o* get sth done; **sich dat etw schicken lassen** to have sth sent (to one) 2 (*zulassen*) **jdn etw wissen lassen** to let sb know sth; **das Licht brennen lassen** to leave the light on; **jdn warten lassen** to keep sb waiting; **das lässt sich machen** that can be done
3 **lass uns gehen** let's go

lässig *adj* casual
Last (-, -en) *f* load; (*Bürde*) burden; (*Naut, Aviat*) cargo
Laster (-s, -) *nt* vice; (*fam*) truck, lorry (*Brit*)
lästern *vi*: **über jdn/etw ~** to make nasty remarks about sb/sth
lästig *adj* annoying; (*Person*) tiresome
Last-Minute-Angebot *nt* last-minute offer; **Last-Minute-Flug** *m* last-minute flight; **Last-Minute-Ticket** *nt* last-minute ticket
Lastwagen *m* truck, lorry (*Brit*)
Latein (-s) *nt* Latin
Laterne (-, -n) *f* lantern; (*Straßenlaterne*) streetlight
Latte (-, -n) *f* slat; (*Sport*) bar
Latz (-es, Lätze) *m* bib; **Lätzchen** *nt* bib; **Latzhose** *f* dungarees *pl*
lau *adj* (*Wind, Luft*) mild
Laub (-(e)s) *nt* foliage; **Laubfrosch** *m* tree frog; **Laubsäge** *f* fretsaw
Lauch (-(e)s, -e) *m* leeks *pl*; **eine Stange ~** a leek; **Lauchzwiebel** *f* spring onions *pl* (*Brit*), scallions *pl* (*US*)
Lauf (-(e)s, Läufe) *m* run; (*Wettlauf*) race; (*Entwicklung*) course; (*von*

Gewehr) barrel; **Laufbahn** *f* career;
laufen (*lief, gelaufen*) *vi, vt* to run; (*gehen*) to walk; (*funktionieren*) to work; **mir läuft die Nase** my nose is running; **was läuft im Kino?** what's on at the cinema?; **wie läuft's so?** how are things?;
laufend *adj* running; (*Monat, Ausgaben*) current; **auf dem Laufenden sein/halten** to be/to keep up-to-date; **Läufer** (-s, -) *m* (*Teppich*) rug; (*Schach*) bishop; **Läufer(in)** *m(f)* (*Sport*) runner; **Laufmasche** *f* ladder (*Brit*), run (*US*); **Laufwerk** *nt* (*Inform*) drive
Laune (-, -n) *f* mood; **gute/schlechte ~ haben** to be in a good/bad mood; **launisch** *adj* moody
Laus (-, Läuse) *f* louse
lauschen *vi* to listen; (*heimlich*) to eavesdrop
laut *adj* loud ▷ *adv* loudly; (*lesen*) aloud ▷ *prep* +*gen o dat* according to
läuten *vt, vi* to ring
lauter *adv* (*fam: nichts als*) nothing but
Lautsprecher *m* loudspeaker; **Lautstärke** *f* loudness; (*Radio, TV*) volume
lauwarm *adj* lukewarm
Lava (-, Laven) *f* lava
Lavendel (-s, -) *m* lavender
Lawine *f* avalanche
LCD-Anzeige *f* LCD-display
leasen *vt* to lease; **Leasing** (-s) *nt* leasing
leben *vt, vi* to live; (*am Leben sein*) to be alive; **wie lange ~ Sie schon hier?** how long have you been living here?; **von ... ~** (*Nahrungsmittel etc*) to live on ...; (*Beruf, Beschäftigung*) to make one's living from ...; **Leben** (-s, -) *nt* life; **lebend** *adj* living; **lebendig** *adj* alive; (*lebhaft*) lively;

lebensgefährlich adj very dangerous; (Verletzung) critical; **Lebensgefährte** m, **Lebensgefährtin** f partner; **Lebenshaltungskosten** pl cost sing of living; **lebenslänglich** adj for life; **~ bekommen** to get life; **Lebenslauf** m curriculum vitae (Brit), CV (Brit), resumé (US); **Lebensmittel** pl food sing; **Lebensmittelgeschäft** nt grocer's (shop); **Lebensmittelvergiftung** f food poisoning; **lebensnotwendig** adj vital; **Lebensretter(in)** m(f) rescuer; **Lebensstandard** m standard of living; **Lebensunterhalt** m livelihood; **Lebensversicherung** f life insurance (o assurance (Brit)); **Lebenszeichen** nt sign of life

Leber (-, -n) f liver; **Leberfleck** m mole; **Leberpastete** f liver pâté

Lebewesen nt living being

lebhaft adj lively; (Erinnerung, Eindruck) vivid; **Lebkuchen** m gingerbread; **ein ~** a piece of gingerbread; **leblos** adj lifeless

Leck nt leak

lecken vi (Loch haben) to leak ▷ vt, vi (schlecken) to lick

lecker adj delicious, tasty

Leder (-s, -) nt leather

ledig adj single

leer adj empty; (Seite) blank; (Batterie) dead; **leeren** vt to empty ▷ vr: **sich ~** to empty; **Leerlauf** m (Gang) neutral; **Leertaste** f space bar; **Leerung** f emptying; (Briefkasten) collection; **Leerzeichen** nt blank, space

legal adj legal, lawful

legen vt to put, to place; (Eier) to lay ▷ vr: **sich ~** to lie down; (Sturm, Begeisterung) to die down; (Schmerz, Gefühl) to wear off

Legende (-, -n) f legend

leger adj casual

Lehm (-(e)s, -e) m loam; (Ton) clay

Lehne (-, -n) f arm(rest); (Rückenlehne) back(rest); **lehnen** vt to lean ▷ vr: **sich ~** to lean (an/gegen +akk against); **Lehnstuhl** m armchair

Lehrbuch nt textbook; **Lehre** (-, -n) f teaching; (beruflich) apprenticeship; (moralisch) lesson; **lehren** vt to teach; **Lehrer(in)** (-s, -) m(f) teacher; **Lehrgang** m course; **Lehrling** m apprentice; **lehrreich** adj instructive

Leib (-(e)s, -er) m body; **Leibgericht** nt, **Leibspeise** f favourite dish; **Leibwächter(in)** m(f) bodyguard

Leiche (-, -n) f corpse; **Leichenhalle** f mortuary; **Leichenwagen** m hearse

leicht adj light; (einfach) easy, simple; (Erkrankung) slight; **es sich** (dat) **~ machen** to take the easy way out ▷ adv (mühelos, schnell) easily; (geringfügig) slightly; **Leichtathletik** f athletics sing; **leicht|fallen** irr vi: **jdm ~** to be easy for sb; **leichtsinnig** adj careless; (stärker) reckless

leid adj: **jdn/etw ~ sein** to be tired of sb/sth; **Leid** (-(e)s) nt grief, sorrow; **leiden** (litt, gelitten) vi, vt to suffer (an, unter +dat from); **ich kann ihn/es nicht ~** I can't stand him/it; **Leiden** (-s, -) nt suffering; (Krankheit) illness

Leidenschaft f passion; **leidenschaftlich** adj passionate

leider adv unfortunately; **wir müssen jetzt ~ gehen** I'm afraid we have to go now; **~ ja/nein** I'm afraid so/not

leid|tun irr vi: **es tut mir/ihm leid** I'm/he's sorry; **er tut mir leid** I'm sorry for him

Leihbücherei f lending library
leihen (lieh, geliehen) vt: **jdm etw ~** to lend sb sth; **sich** (dat) **etw von jdm ~** to borrow sth from sb; **Leihfrist** f lending period; **Leihgebühr** f hire charge; (für Buch) lending charge; **Leihwagen** m hire car (Brit), rental car (US)
Leim (-(e)s, -e) m glue
Leine (-, -n) f cord; (für Wäsche) line; (Hundeleine) lead (Brit), leash (US)
Leinen (-s, -) nt linen; **Leintuch** nt (für Bett) sheet; **Leinwand** f (Kunst) canvas; (Cine) screen
leise adj quiet; (sanft) soft ▷ adv quietly
Leiste (-, -n) f ledge; (Zierleiste) strip; (Anat) groin
leisten vt (Arbeit) to do; (vollbringen) to achieve; **jdm Gesellschaft ~** to keep sb company; **sich** (dat) **etw ~** (gönnen) to treat oneself to sth; **ich kann es mir nicht ~** I can't afford it
Leistenbruch m hernia
Leistung f performance; (gute) achievement
Leitartikel m leading article (Brit), editorial (US)
leiten vt to lead; (Firma) to run; (in eine Richtung) to direct; (Elek) to conduct
Leiter (-, -n) f ladder
Leiter(in) (-s, -) m(f) (von Geschäft) manager
Leitplanke (-, -n) f crash barrier
Leitung f (Führung) direction; (Tel) line; (von Firma) management; (Wasserleitung) pipe; (Kabel) cable; **eine lange ~ haben** to be slow on the uptake; **Leitungswasser** nt tap water
Lektion f lesson
Lektüre (-, -n) f (Lesen) reading; (Lesestoff) reading matter

Lende (-, -n) f (Speise) loin; (vom Rind) sirloin; **die ~n** pl (Med) the lumbar region sing
lenken vt to steer; (Blick) to direct (auf +akk towards); **jds Aufmerksamkeit auf etw** (akk) **~** to draw sb's attention to sth; **Lenker** m (von Fahrrad, Motorrad) handlebars pl; **Lenkrad** nt steering wheel; **Lenkradschloss** nt steering lock; **Lenkstange** f handlebars pl
Leopard (-en, -en) m leopard
Lepra (-) f leprosy
Lerche (-, -n) f lark
lernen vt, vi to learn; (für eine Prüfung) to study, to revise
lesbisch adj lesbian
Lesebuch nt reader; **lesen** (las, gelesen) vi, vt to read; (ernten) to pick; **Leser(in)** m(f) reader; **Leserbrief** m letter to the editor; **leserlich** adj legible; **Lesezeichen** nt bookmark
Lettland nt Latvia
letzte(r, s) adj last; (neueste) latest; (endgültig) final; **zum ~n Mal** for the last time; **am ~n Montag** last Monday; **in ~r Zeit** lately, recently; **letztens** adv (vor kurzem) recently; **letztere(r, s)** adj the latter
Leuchtanzeige f illuminated display; **Leuchte** (-, -n) f lamp, light; **leuchten** vi to shine; (Feuer, Zifferblatt) to glow; **Leuchter** (-s, -) m candlestick; **Leuchtfarbe** f fluorescent colour; (Anstrichfarbe) luminous paint; **Leuchtreklame** f neon sign; **Leuchtstoffröhre** f strip light; **Leuchtturm** m lighthouse
leugnen vt to deny ▷ vi to deny everything
Leukämie f leukaemia (Brit), leukemia (US)

Leukoplast® (-(e)s, -e) nt
  Elastoplast® (Brit), Band-Aid®
  (US)
Leute pl people pl
Lexikon (-s, Lexika) nt encyclo-
  paedia (Brit), encyclopedia (US);
  (Wörterbuch) dictionary
Libanon (-s) m: **der ~** Lebanon
Libelle f dragonfly
liberal adj liberal
Libyen (-s) nt Libya
Licht (-(e)s, -er) nt light;
  Lichtblick m ray of hope;
  lichtempfindlich adj sensitive to
  light; **Lichtempfindlichkeit** f
  (Foto) speed; **Lichthupe** f: **die
  ~ betätigen** to flash one's lights;
  Lichtjahr nt light year;
  Lichtmaschine f dynamo;
  Lichtschalter m light switch;
  Lichtschranke f light barrier;
  Lichtschutzfaktor m sun
  protection factor, SPF
Lichtung f clearing
Lid (-(e)s, -er) nt eyelid;
  Lidschatten m eyeshadow
lieb adj (nett) nice; (teuer, geliebt)
  dear; (liebenswert) sweet; **das ist
  ~ von dir** that's nice of you; **Lieber
  Herr X** Dear Mr X; **Liebe** (-, -n) f
  love; **lieben** vt to love; (sexuell) to
  make love to; **liebenswürdig** adj
  kind; **lieber** adv rather; **ich
  möchte ~ nicht** I'd rather not;
  welches ist dir ~? which one do
  you prefer?; siehe auch **gern, lieb**;
  Liebesbrief m love letter;
  Liebeskummer m: **~ haben** to be
  lovesick; **Liebespaar** nt lovers pl;
  liebevoll adj loving;
  Liebhaber(in) (-s, -) m(f) lover;
  lieblich adj lovely; (Wein) sweet;
  Liebling m darling; (Günstling)
  favourite; **Lieblings-** in zW
  favourite; **liebste(r, s)** adj
  favourite; **liebsten** adv: **am
  ~ esse ich …** my favourite food

is …; **am ~ würde ich bleiben** I'd
  really like to stay
Liechtenstein (-s) nt
  Liechtenstein
Lied (-(e)s, -er) nt song; (Rel) hymn
lief imperf von **laufen**
Lieferant(in) m(f) supplier
lieferbar adj available
liefern vt to deliver; (beschaffen)
  to supply
Lieferschein m delivery note;
  Lieferung f delivery;
  Lieferwagen m delivery van
Liege (-, -n) f (beim Arzt) couch;
  (Notbett) campbed; (Gartenliege)
  lounger; **liegen** (lag, gelegen) vi to
  lie; (sich befinden) to be; **mir liegt
  nichts/viel daran** it doesn't
  matter to me/it matters a lot to
  me; **woran liegt es nur, dass …?**
  why is it that …?; **~ bleiben**
  (Mensch) to stay lying down; (im
  Bett) to stay in bed; (Ding) to be left
  (behind); **~ lassen** (vergessen) to
  leave behind; **Liegestuhl** m deck
  chair; **Liegestütz** m press-up
  (Brit), push-up (US); **Liegewagen**
  m (Eisenb) couchette car
lieh imperf von **leihen**
ließ imperf von **lassen**
Lift (-(e)s, -e o -s) m lift, elevator
  (US)
Liga (-, Ligen) f league, division
light adj (Cola) diet; (fettarm)
  low-fat; (kalorienarm) low-calorie;
  (Zigaretten) mild
Likör (-s, -e) m liqueur
lila adj inv purple
Lilie f lily
Limette (-, -n) f lime
Limo (-, -s) f (fam) fizzy drink
  (Brit), soda (US); **Limonade** f
  fizzy drink (Brit), soda (US); (mit
  Zitronengeschmack) lemonade
Limone (-, -n) f lime
Limousine (-, -n) f saloon (car)
  (Brit), sedan (US); (fam) limo

Linde (-, -n) f lime tree
lindern vt to relieve, to soothe
Lineal (-s, -e) nt ruler
Linie f line; **Linienflug** m
scheduled flight; **liniert** adj
ruled, lined
Link (-s, -s) m (Inform) link
Linke (-n, -n) f left-hand side;
(Hand) left hand; (Pol) left (wing);
linke(r, s) adj left; **auf der ~n
Seite** on the left, on the left-hand
side; **links** adv on the left;
~ abbiegen to turn left; **~ von** to
the left of; **~ oben** at the top left;
Linkshänder(in) (-s, -) m(f) left-
hander; **linksherum** adv to the
left, anticlockwise; **Linksverkehr**
m driving on the left
Linse (-, -n) f lentil; (optisch) lens
Lippe (-, -n) f lip; **Lipgloss** nt lip
gloss; **Lippenstift** m lipstick
lispeln vi to lisp
List (-, -en) f cunning; (Trick)
trick
Liste (-, -n) f list
Litauen (-s) nt Lithuania
Liter (-s, -) m o nt litre
literarisch adj literary; **Literatur**
f literature
Litschi (-, -s) f lychee, litchi
litt imperf von **leiden**
live adv (Radio, TV) live
Lizenz f licence
Lkw (-(s), -(s)) m abk =
Lastkraftwagen truck, lorry (Brit);
Lkw-Maut f heavy goods vehicle
toll
Lob (-(e)s) nt praise; **loben** vt to
praise
Loch (-(e)s, Löcher) nt hole;
lochen vt to punch; **Locher** (-s, -)
m (hole) punch
Locke (-, -n) f curl; **locken** vt
(anlocken) to lure; (Haare) to curl;
Lockenstab m curling tongs pl
(Brit), curling irons pl (US);
Lockenwickler (-s, -) m curler

locker adj (Schraube, Zahn) loose;
(Haltung) relaxed; (Person)
easy-going; **das schaffe ich
~** (fam) I'll manage it, no problem;
lockern vt to loosen ▷ vr: **sich
~** to loosen
lockig adj curly
Löffel (-s, -) m spoon; **einen
~ Mehl zugeben** add a spoonful of
flour; **Löffelbiskuit** (-s, -s) m
sponge finger
log imperf von **lügen**
Loge (-, -n) f (Theat) box
logisch adj logical
Logo (-s, -s) nt logo
Lohn (-(e)s, Löhne) m reward;
(Arbeitslohn) pay, wages pl
lohnen vr: **sich ~** to be worth it;
es lohnt sich nicht zu warten it's
no use waiting
Lohnerhöhung f pay rise (Brit),
pay raise (US); **Lohnsteuer** f
income tax
Lokal (-(e)s, -e) nt (Gaststätte)
restaurant; (Kneipe) pub (Brit), bar
Lokomotive f locomotive
London (-s) nt London
Lorbeer (-s, -en) m laurel;
Lorbeerblatt nt (Gastr) bay leaf
los adj loose; **~!** go on!; **jdn/etw
~ sein** to be rid of sb/sth; **was ist
~?** what's the matter?, what's up?;
dort ist nichts/viel ~ there's
nothing/a lot going on there
Los (-es, -e) nt (Schicksal) lot, fate;
(Lotterie etc) ticket
los|binden irr vt to untie
löschen vt (Feuer, Licht) to put
out, to extinguish; (Durst) to
quench; (Tonband) to erase; (Daten,
Zeile) to delete; **Löschtaste** f
delete key
lose adj loose
Lösegeld nt ransom
losen vi to draw lots
lösen vt (lockern) to loosen;
(Rätsel) to solve; (Chem) to

dissolve; (*Fahrkarte*) to buy ▷ vr:
sich ~ (*abgehen*) to come off;
(*Zucker etc*) to dissolve; (*Problem,
Schwierigkeit*) to (re)solve itself
los|fahren *irr vi* to leave;
los|gehen *irr vi* to set out;
(*anfangen*) to start; **los|lassen** *irr
vt* to let go
löslich *adj* soluble
Lösung *f* (*eines Rätsels, Problems,
Flüssigkeit*) solution
los|werden *irr vt* to get rid of
Lotterie *f* lottery; **Lotto** (*-s*) *nt*
National Lottery; **~ spielen** to play
the lottery
Löwe (*-n, -n*) *m* (*Zool*) lion; (*Astr*)
Leo; **Löwenzahn** *m* dandelion
Luchs (*-es, -e*) *m* lynx
Lücke (*-, -n*) *f* gap;
Lückenbüßer(in) (*-s, -*) *m(f)*
stopgap
lud *imperf von* **laden**
Luft (*-, Lüfte*) *f* air; (*Atem*) breath;
Luftballon *m* balloon; **Luftblase**
f (air) bubble; **luftdicht** *adj*
airtight; **Luftdruck** *m* (*Meteo*)
atmospheric pressure; (*in Reifen*)
air pressure
lüften *vt* to air; (*Geheimnis*) to
reveal
Luftfahrt *f* aviation;
Luftfeuchtigkeit *f* humidity;
Luftfilter *m* air filter; **Luftfracht**
f air freight; **Luftkissenboot** *nt*,
Luftkissenfahrzeug *nt* hovercraft;
Luftlinie *f*: **10 km ~** 10 km as the
crow flies; **Luftmatratze** *f* airbed;
Luftpirat(in) *m(f)* hijacker;
Luftpost *f* airmail; **Luftpumpe** *f*
(bicycle) pump; **Luftröhre** *f*
windpipe
Lüftung *f* ventilation
Luftveränderung *f* change of
air; **Luftverschmutzung** *f* air
pollution; **Luftwaffe** *f* air force;
Luftzug *m* draught (*Brit*), draft
(*US*)

Lüge (*-, -n*) *f* lie; **lügen** (*log,
gelogen*) *vi* to lie; **Lügner(in)** (*-s, -*)
m(f) liar
Luke (*-, -n*) *f* hatch
Lumpen (*-s, -*) *m* rag
Lunchpaket *nt* packed lunch
Lunge (*-, -n*) *f* lungs *pl*;
Lungenentzündung *f*
pneumonia
Lupe (*-, -n*) *f* magnifying glass;
etw unter die ~ nehmen (*fig*) to
have a close look at sth
Lust (*-, Lüste*) *f* joy, delight;
(*Neigung*) desire; **~ auf etw** (*akk*)
haben to feel like sth; **~ haben,
etw zu tun** to feel like doing sth
lustig *adj* (*komisch*) amusing,
funny; (*fröhlich*) cheerful
lutschen *vt* to suck ▷ *vi* **~ an**
(*+dat*) to suck; **Lutscher** (*-s, -*) *m*
lollipop
Luxemburg (*-s*) *nt* Luxembourg
luxuriös *adj* luxurious
Luxus (*-*) *m* luxury
Lymphdrüse *f* lymph gland;
Lymphknoten *m* lymph node
Lyrik (*-*) *f* poetry

m

does that make?
5 was macht die Arbeit? how's the work going?; **was macht dein Bruder?** how is your brother doing?; **das Auto machen lassen** to have the car done; **mach's gut!** take care!; (*viel Glück*) good luck!
▷ *vi*: **mach schnell!** hurry up!; **Schluss machen** to finish (off); **mach schon!** come on!; **das macht müde** it makes you tired; **in etw** *dat* **machen** to be o deal in sth
▷ *vr* to come along (nicely); **sich an etw** *akk* **machen** to set about sth; **sich verständlich machen** to make o.s. understood; **sich** *dat* **viel aus jdm/etw machen** to like sb/sth

Macho (-*s*, -*s*) *m* (*fam*) macho (type)
Macht (-*s*, *Mächte*) *f* power; **mächtig** *adj* powerful; (*fam: ungeheuer*) enormous; **machtlos** *adj* powerless; **da ist man ~** there's nothing you can do (about it)
Mädchen *nt* girl; **Mädchenname** *m* maiden name
Made (-, -*n*) *f* maggot
Magazin (-*s*, -*e*) *nt* magazine
Magen (-*s*, - o *Mägen*) *m* stomach; **Magenbeschwerden** *pl* stomach trouble *sing*; **Magen-Darm-Infektion** *f* gastroenteritis; **Magengeschwür** *nt* stomach ulcer; **Magenschmerzen** *pl* stomach-ache *sing*
mager *adj* (*Fleisch, Wurst*) lean; (*Person*) thin; (*Käse, Joghurt*) low-fat; **Magermilch** *f* skimmed milk; **Magersucht** *f* anorexia; **magersüchtig** *adj* anorexic
magisch *adj* magical
Magnet (-*s* o -*en*, -*en*) *m* magnet
mähen *vt, vi* to mow

machbar *adj* feasible

○ SCHLÜSSELWORT

machen *vt* **1** to do; (*herstellen, zubereiten*) to make; **was machst du da?** what are you doing (there)?; **das ist nicht zu machen** that can't be done; **das Radio leiser machen** to turn the radio down; **aus Holz gemacht** made of wood
2 (*verursachen, bewirken*) to make; **jdm Angst machen** to make sb afraid; **das macht die Kälte** it's the cold that does that
3 (*ausmachen*) to matter; **das macht nichts** that doesn't matter; **die Kälte macht mir nichts** I don't mind the cold
4 (*kosten, ergeben*) to be; **3 und 5 macht 8** 3 and 5 is o are 8; **was** o **wie viel macht das?** how much

mahlen *(mahlte, gemahlen)* vt to grind

Mahlzeit f meal; *(für Baby)* feed ▷ *interj (guten Appetit)* enjoy your meal

Mähne *(-, -n)* f mane

mahnen vt to urge; **jdn schriftlich ~** to send sb a reminder; **Mahngebühr** f fine; **Mahnung** f warning; *(schriftlich)* reminder

Mai *(-(s), -e)* m May; *siehe auch* **Juni**; **Maifeiertag** m May Day; **Maiglöckchen** nt lily of the valley; **Maikäfer** m cockchafer

Mail *(-, -s)* f e-mail; **jdm eine~ schicken** to mail sb, to e-mail sb; **Mailbox** f *(Inform)* mailbox; **mailen** vi, vt to e-mail

Mais *(-es, -e)* m maize, corn *(US)*; **Maiskolben** m corn cob; *(Gastr)* corn on the cob

Majestät *(-, -en)* f Majesty

Majonäse *(-, -n)* f mayonnaise

Majoran *(-s, -e)* m marjoram

makaber adj macabre

Make-up *(-s, -s)* nt make-up

Makler(in) *(-s, -)* m(f) broker; *(Immobilienmakler)* estate agent *(Brit)*, Realtor® *(US)*

Makrele *(-, -n)* f mackerel

Makro *(-s, -s)* nt *(Inform)* macro

Makrone *(-, -n)* f macaroon

mal adv *(beim Rechnen)* times, multiplied by; *(beim Messen)* by; *(fam: einmal = früher)* once; *(einmal = zukünftig)* some day; **4 ~ 3 ist 12** 4 times 3 is *(o equals)* twelve; **da habe ich ~ gewohnt** I used to live there; **irgendwann ~ werde ich dort hinfahren** I'll go there one day; **das ist nun ~ so** well, that's just the way it is *(o goes)*; **Mal** *(-(e)s, -e)* nt *(Zeitpunkt)* time; *(Markierung)* mark; **jedes ~** every time; **ein paar ~** a few times; **ein einziges ~** just once

Malaria *(-)* f malaria

Malaysia *(-s)* nt Malaysia

Malbuch nt colouring book

Malediven pl Maldives pl

malen vt, vi to paint; **Maler(in)** *(-s, -)* m(f) painter; **Malerei** f painting; **malerisch** adj picturesque

Mallorca *(-s)* nt Majorca, Mallorca

mal|nehmen irr vt to multiply *(mit* by)

Malta *(-s)* nt Malta

Malventee m mallow tea

Malz *(-es)* nt malt; **Malzbier** nt malt beer

Mama *(-, -s)* f mum(my) *(Brit)*, mom(my) *(US)*

man pron you; *(förmlich)* one; *(jemand)* someone, somebody; *(die Leute)* they, people pl; **wie schreibt ~ das?** how do you spell that?; **~ hat ihr das Fahrrad gestohlen** someone stole her bike; **~ sagt, dass ...** they *(o people)* say that ...

managen vt *(fam)* to manage; **Manager(in)** *(-s, -)* m(f) manager

manche(r, s) adj many a; *(mit pl)* a number of, some ▷ pron *(einige)* some; *(viele)* many; **~ Politiker** many politicians pl, many a politician; **manchmal** adv sometimes

Mandant(in) m(f) client

Mandarine f mandarin, tangerine

Mandel *(-, -n)* f almond; **~n** *(Anat)* tonsils pl; **Mandelentzündung** f tonsillitis

Manege *(-, -n)* f ring

Mangel *(-s, Mängel)* m *(Fehlen)* lack; *(Knappheit)* shortage *(an +dat* of); *(Fehler)* defect, fault; **mangelhaft** adj *(Ware)* faulty; *(Schulnote)* ≈ E

Mango *(-, -s)* f mango

Mangold *(-s)* m mangel(wurzel)

Manieren pl manners pl

Maniküre (-, -n) f manicure

manipulieren vt to manipulate

Manko (-s, -s) nt deficiency

Mann (-(e)s, Männer) m man; (Ehemann) husband; **Männchen** nt: **es ist ein ~** (Tier) it's a he; **männlich** adj masculine; (Bio) male

Mannschaft f (Sport, fig) team; (Naut, Aviat) crew

Mansarde (-, -n) f attic

Manschettenknopf m cufflink

Mantel (-s, Mäntel) m coat; (Tech) casing, jacket

Mappe (-, -n) f briefcase; (Aktenmappe) folder

Maracuja (-, -s) f passion fruit

Marathon (-s, -s) m marathon

Märchen nt fairy tale

Marder (-s, -) m marten

Margarine f margarine

Marienkäfer m ladybird (Brit), ladybug (US)

Marihuana (-s) nt marijuana

Marille (-, -n) f apricot

Marinade f marinade

Marine f navy

marinieren vt to marinate

Marionette f puppet

Mark (-(e)s) nt (Knochenmark) marrow; (Fruchtmark) pulp

Marke (-, -n) f (Warensorte) brand; (Fabrikat) make; (Briefmarke) stamp; (Essenmarke) voucher, ticket; (aus Metall etc) disc; (Messpunkt) mark; **Markenartikel** m branded item, brand name product; **Markenzeichen** nt trademark

markieren vt to mark; **Markierung** f marking; (Zeichen) mark

Markise (-, -n) f awning

Markt (-(e)s, Märkte) m market; **auf den ~ bringen** to launch; **Markthalle** f covered market;

Marktlücke f gap in the market; **Marktplatz** m market place; **Marktwirtschaft** f market economy

Marmelade f jam; (Orangenmarmelade) marmalade

Marmor (-s, -e) m marble; **Marmorkuchen** m marble cake

Marokko (-s) nt Morocco

Marone (-, -n) f chestnut

Mars (-) m Mars

Marsch (-(e)s, Märsche) m march

Märtyrer(in) (-s, -) m(f) martyr

März (-(es), -e) m March; siehe auch **Juni**

Marzipan (-s, -e) nt marzipan

Maschine f machine; (Motor) engine; **maschinell** adj mechanical, machine-; **Maschinenbau** m mechanical engineering

Masern pl (Med) measles sing

Maske (-, -n) f mask; **Maskenball** m fancy-dress ball; **maskieren** vr: **sich ~** (Maske aufsetzen) to put on a mask; (verkleiden) to dress up

Maskottchen nt mascot

maß imperf von **messen**

Maß (-es, -e) nt measure; (Mäßigung) moderation; (Grad) degree, extent; **~e** (Person) measurements; (Raum) dimensions; **in gewissem/hohem ~e** to a certain/high degree; **in zunehmendem ~e** increasingly

Mass (-, -(en)) f (Bier) litre of beer

Massage (-, -n) f massage

Masse (-, -n) f mass; (von Menschen) crowd; (Großteil) majority; **massenhaft** adv masses (o loads) of; **am See sind ~ Mücken** there are masses of mosquitoes at the lake; **Massenkarambolage** f pile-up; **Massenmedien** pl mass media pl; **Massenproduktion** f mass

m

production; **Massentourismus**
m mass tourism
Masseur(in) *m(f)*
masseur/masseuse
maßgeschneidert *adj* (*Kleidung*) made-to-measure
massieren *vt* to massage
mäßig *adj* moderate
massiv *adj* solid; (*fig*) massive
maßlos *adj* extreme
Maßnahme (-, -n) *f* measure,
step
Maßstab *m* rule, measure; (*fig*)
standard; **im ~ von 1:5** on a scale
of 1:5
Mast (-(*e*)*s*, -*e*(*n*)) *m* mast; (*Elek*)
pylon
Material (-*s*, -*ien*) *nt* material;
(*Arbeitsmaterial*) materials *pl*;
materialistisch *adj* materialistic
Materie *f* matter; **materiell** *adj*
material
Mathe (-) *f* (*fam*) maths (*Brit*),
math (*US*); **Mathematik** *f*
mathematics *sing*; **Mathe-
matiker(in)** *m(f)* mathematician
Matinee (-, -*n*) *f* ≈ matinee
Matratze (-, -*n*) *f* mattress
Matrose (-*n*, -*n*) *m* sailor
Matsch (-(*e*)*s*) *m* mud; (*Schnee*)
slush; **matschig** *adj* muddy;
(*Schnee*) slushy; (*Obst*) mushy
matt *adj* weak; (*glanzlos*) dull;
(*Foto*) matt; (*Schach*) mate
Matte (-, -*n*) *f* mat
Matura (-) *f* Austrian
school-leaving examination; ≈
A-levels (*Brit*), ≈ High School
Diploma (*US*)
Mauer (-, -*n*) *f* wall
Maul (-(*e*)*s*, *Mäuler*) *nt* mouth;
(*fam*) gob; **halt's ~!** shut your face
(*o* gob); **Maulbeere** *f* mulberry;
Maulesel *m* mule; **Maulkorb** *m*
muzzle; **Maul- und Klauenseuche**
f foot-and-mouth disease;
Maulwurf *m* mole

Maurer(in) (-*s*, -) *m(f)* bricklayer
Mauritius (-) *nt* Mauritius
Maus (-, *Mäuse*) *f* mouse;
Mausefalle *f* mousetrap;
Mausklick (-*s*, -*s*) *m* mouse click;
Mauspad (-*s*, -*s*) *nt* mouse mat (*o*
pad); **Maustaste** *f* mouse key (*o*
button)
Maut (-, -*en*) *f* toll; **Mautgebühr**
f toll; **mautpflichtig** *adj*: **~e**
Straße toll road, turnpike (*US*);
Mautstelle *f* tollbooth, tollgate;
Mautstraße *f* toll road, turnpike
(*US*)
maximal *adv*: **ihr habt ~ zwei**
Stunden Zeit you've got two
hours at (the) most; **~ vier Leute** a
maximum of four people
Mayonnaise *f siehe* **Majonäse**
Mazedonien (-*s*) *nt* Macedonia
MB (-, -) *nt*, **Mbyte** (-, -) *nt abk* =
Megabyte MB
Mechanik *f* mechanics *sing*;
(*Getriebe*) mechanics *pl*;
Mechaniker(in) (-*s*, -) *m(f)* mechanic;
mechanisch *adj* mechanical;
Mechanismus *m* mechanism
meckern *vi* (*Ziege*) to bleat; (*fam*:
schimpfen) to moan
Mecklenburg-Vorpommern
(-*s*) *nt* Mecklenburg-Western
Pomerania
Medaille (-, -*n*) *f* medal
Medien *pl* media *pl*
Medikament *nt* medicine
Meditation *f* meditation;
meditieren *vi* to meditate
medium *adj* (*Steak*) medium
Medizin (-, -*en*) *f* medicine (*gegen*
for); **medizinisch** *adj* medical
Meer (-(*e*)*s*, -*e*) *nt* sea; **am ~** by
the sea; **Meerenge** *f* straits *pl*;
Meeresfrüchte *pl* seafood *sing*;
Meeresspiegel *m* sea level;
Meerrettich *m* horseradish;
Meerschweinchen *nt* guinea
pig; **Meerwasser** *nt* seawater

Megabyte nt megabyte;
Megahertz nt megahertz
Mehl (-(e)s, -e) nt flour;
Mehlspeise f sweet dish made from flour, eggs and milk
mehr pron, adv more; **~ will ich nicht ausgeben** I don't want to spend any more, that's as much as I want to spend; **was willst du ~?** what more do you want? ▷ adv: **immer ~** (**Leute**) more and more (people); **~ als fünf Minuten** more than five minutes; **je ~ ..., desto besser** the more ..., the better; **ich kann nicht ~ stehen** I can't stand any more (o longer); **es ist kein Brot ~ da** there's no bread left; **nie ~** never again; **mehrdeutig** adj ambiguous; **mehrere** pron several; **mehreres** pron several things; **mehrfach** adj multiple; (wiederholt) repeated;
Mehrfachstecker m multiple plug; **Mehrheit** f majority; **mehrmals** adv repeatedly; **mehrsprachig** adj multilingual; **Mehrwegflasche** f returnable bottle, deposit bottle; **Mehrwertsteuer** f value added tax, VAT; **Mehrzahl** f majority; (Plural) plural
meiden (mied, gemieden) vt to avoid
Meile (-, -n) f mile
mein pron (adjektivisch) my; **meine(r, s)** pron (substantivisch) mine
meinen vt, vi (glauben, der Ansicht sein) to think; (sagen) to say; (sagen wollen, beabsichtigen) to mean; **das war nicht so gemeint** I didn't mean it like that
meinetwegen adv (wegen mir) because of me; (mir zuliebe) for my sake; (von mir aus) as far as I'm concerned
Meinung f opinion; **meiner**

~ nach in my opinion;
Meinungsumfrage f opinion poll; **Meinungsverschiedenheit** f disagreement (über +akk about)
Meise (-, -n) f tit; **eine ~ haben** (fam) to be crazy
Meißel (-s, -) m chisel
meist adv mostly; **meiste(r, s)** pron (adjektivisch) most; **die ~n** (**Leute**) most people; **die ~ Zeit** most of the time; **das ~** (davon) most of it; **die ~n von ihnen** most of them; (substantivisch) most of them; **am ~n** (the) most; **meistens** adv mostly; (zum größten Teil) for the most part
Meister(in) (-s, -) m(f) master; (Sport) champion; **Meisterschaft** f championship; **Meisterwerk** nt masterpiece
melden vt to report ▷ vr: **sich ~** to report (bei to); (Schule) to put one's hand up; (freiwillig) to volunteer; (auf etw, am Telefon) to answer; **Meldung** f announcement; (Bericht) report; (Inform) message
Melodie f tune, melody
Melone (-, -n) f melon
Memoiren pl memoirs pl
Menge (-, -n) f quantity; (Menschen) crowd; **eine ~** (große Anzahl) a lot (gen of); **Mengenrabatt** m bulk discount
Meniskus (-, Menisken) m meniscus
Mensa (-, Mensen) f canteen, cafeteria (US)
Mensch (-en, -en) m human being, man; (Person) person; **kein ~** nobody; **~!** (bewundernd) wow!; (verärgert) bloody hell!; **Menschenmenge** f crowd; **Menschenrechte** pl human rights pl; **Menschenverstand** m: **gesunder ~** common sense; **Menschheit** f humanity,

mankind; **menschlich** *adj* human; (*human*) humane

Menstruation *f* menstruation

Mentalität *f* mentality, mindset

Menthol (-s) *nt* menthol

Menü (-s, -s) *nt* set meal; (*Inform*) menu; **Menüleiste** *f* (*Inform*) menu bar

Merkblatt *nt* leaflet; **merken** *vt* (*bemerken*) to notice; **sich** (*dat*) **etw ~** to remember sth; **Merkmal** *nt* feature

Merkur (-s) *m* Mercury

merkwürdig *adj* odd

Messbecher *m* measuring jug

Messe (-, -n) *f* fair; (*Rel*) mass; **Messebesucher(in)** *m(f)* visitor to a/the fair; **Messegelände** *nt* exhibition site

messen (*maß, gemessen*) *vt* to measure; (*Temperatur, Puls*) to take ▷ *vr*: **sich ~** to compete; **sie kann sich mit ihm nicht ~** she's no match for him

Messer (-s, -) *nt* knife

Messgerät *nt* measuring device, gauge

Messing (-s) *nt* brass

Metall (-s, -e) *nt* metal

Meteorologe *m*, **Meteorologin** *f* meteorologist

Meter (-s, -) *m o nt* metre; **Metermaß** *nt* tape measure

Methode (-, -n) *f* method

Metzger(in) (-s, -) *m(f)* butcher; **Metzgerei** *f* butcher's (shop)

Mexiko (-s) *nt* Mexico

MEZ *f abk* = **mitteleuropäische Zeit** CET

miau *interj* miaow

mich *pron akk von* **ich** me; **~** (**selbst**) (*reflexiv*) myself; **stell dich hinter ~** stand behind me; **ich fühle ~ wohl** I feel fine

mied *imperf von* **meiden**

Miene (-, -n) *f* look, expression

mies *adj* (*fam*) lousy

Miesmuschel *f* mussel

Mietauto *nt siehe* **Mietwagen**; **Miete** (-, -n) *f* rent; **mieten** *vt* to rent; (*Auto*) to hire (*Brit*), to rent (*US*); **Mieter(in)** (-s, -) *m(f)* tenant; **Mietshaus** *nt* block of flats (*Brit*), apartment house (*US*); **Mietvertrag** *m* rental agreement; **Mietwagen** *m* hire car (*Brit*), rental car (*US*); **sich** (*dat*) **einen ~ nehmen** to hire (*Brit*) (*o* rent (*US*)) a car

Migräne (-, -n) *f* migraine

Migrant(in) (-en, -en) *m(f)* migrant (worker)

Mikrofon (-s, -e) *nt* microphone

Mikrowelle (-, -n) *f*, **Mikrowellenherd** *m* microwave (oven)

Milch (-) *f* milk; **Milcheis** *nt* ice-cream (*made with milk*); **Milchglas** *nt* (*dickes, trübes Glas*) frosted glass; **Milchkaffee** *m* milky coffee; **Milchprodukte** *pl* dairy products *pl*; **Milchpulver** *nt* powdered milk; **Milchreis** *m* rice pudding; **Milchshake** *m* milk shake; **Milchstraße** *f* Milky Way

mild *adj* mild; (*Richter*) lenient; (*freundlich*) kind

Militär (-s) *nt* military, army

Milliarde (-, -n) *f* billion; **Milligramm** *nt* milligram; **Milliliter** *m* millilitre; **Millimeter** *m* millimetre; **Million** *f* million; **Millionär(in)** *m(f)* millionaire

Milz (-, -en) *f* spleen

Mimik *f* facial expression(s)

Minderheit *f* minority

minderjährig *adj* underage

minderwertig *adj* inferior; **Minderwertigkeitskomplex** *m* inferiority complex

Mindest- *in zW* minimum; **mindeste(r, s)** *adj* least; **mindestens** *adv* at least; **Mindesthaltbarkeitsdatum** *nt*

best-before date, sell-by date (*Brit*)

Mine (-, -n) f mine; (*Bleistift*) lead; (*Kugelschreiber*) refill

Mineralwasser nt mineral water

Minibar f minibar; **Minigolf** nt miniature golf, crazy golf (*Brit*)

minimal adj minimal

Minimum (-s, Minima) nt minimum

Minirock m miniskirt

Minister(in) (-s, -) m(f) minister; **Ministerium** nt ministry; **Ministerpräsident(in)** m(f) (*von Bundesland*) Minister President (*Prime Minister of a Bundesland*)

minus adv minus; **Minus** (-, -) nt deficit; **im ~ sein** to be in the red; (*Konto*) to be overdrawn

Minute (-, -n) f minute

Minze (-, -n) f mint

Mio. nt abk von **Million(en)** m

mir pron dat von **ich** (to) me; **kannst du ~ helfen?** can you help me?; **kannst du es ~ erklären?** can you explain it to me?; **ich habe ~ einen neuen Rechner gekauft** I bought (myself) a new computer; **ein Freund von ~** a friend of mine

Mirabelle (-, -n) f mirabelle (*small yellow plum*)

mischen vt to mix; (*Karten*) to shuffle; **Mischmasch** m (*fam*) hotchpotch; **Mischung** f mixture (*aus* of)

missachten vt to ignore; **Missbrauch** m abuse; (*falscher Gebrauch*) misuse; **missbrauchen** vt to misuse (*zu* for); (*sexuell*) to abuse; **Misserfolg** m failure; **Missgeschick** nt (*Panne*) mishap; **misshandeln** vt to ill-treat

Mission f mission

misslingen (misslang, misslungen) vi to fail; **der Versuch ist mir misslungen** my attempt failed;

misstrauen vt +dat to distrust; **Misstrauen** (-s) nt mistrust, suspicion (*gegenüber* of); **misstrauisch** adj distrustful; (*argwöhnisch*) suspicious;

Missverständnis nt misunderstanding; **missverstehen** irr vt to misunderstand

Mist (-(e)s) m (*fam*) rubbish; (*von Kühen*) dung; (*als Dünger*) manure

Mistel (-, -n) f mistletoe

mit prep +dat with; (*mittels*) by; **~ der Bahn** by train; **~ der Kreditkarte bezahlen** to pay by credit card; **~ 10 Jahren** at the age of 10; **wie wärs ~ ...?** how about ...? ▷ adv along, too; **wollen Sie ~?** do you want to come along?

Mitarbeiter(in) m(f) (*Angestellter*) employee; (*an Projekt*) collaborator; (*freier*) freelancer

mit|bekommen irr vt (*fam: aufschnappen*) to catch; (*hören*) to hear; (*verstehen*) to get

mit|benutzen vt to share

Mitbewohner(in) m(f) (*in Wohnung*) flatmate (*Brit*), roommate (*US*)

mit|bringen irr vt to bring along; **Mitbringsel** (-s, -) nt small present

miteinander adv with one another; (*gemeinsam*) together

mit|erleben vt to see (with one's own eyes)

Mitesser (-s, -) m blackhead

Mitfahrgelegenheit f ≈ lift, ride (*US*); **Mitfahrzentrale** f *agency for arranging lifts*

mit|geben irr vt: **jdm etw ~** to give sb sth (to take along)

Mitgefühl nt sympathy

mit|gehen irr vi to go/come along

mitgenommen adj worn out, exhausted

Mitglied nt member

m

mithilfe *prep +gen* **~ von** with the help of

mit|kommen *irr vi* to come along; (*verstehen*) to follow

Mitleid *nt* pity; **~ haben mit** to feel sorry for

mit|machen *vt* to take part in ▷ *vi* to take part

mit|nehmen *irr vt* to take along; (*anstrengen*) to wear out, to exhaust

mit|schreiben *irr vi* to take notes ▷ *vt* to take down

Mitschüler(in) *m(f)* schoolmate

mit|spielen *vi* (*in Mannschaft*) to play; (*bei Spiel*) to join in; **in einem Film/Stück ~** to act in a film/play

Mittag *m* midday; **gestern ~** at midday yesterday, yesterday lunchtime; **über ~ geschlossen** closed at lunchtime; **zu ~ essen** to have lunch; **Mittagessen** *nt* lunch; **mittags** *adv* at lunchtime, at midday; **Mittagspause** *f* lunch break

Mitte (-, *-n*) *f* middle; **~ Juni** in the middle of June; **sie ist ~ zwanzig** she's in her mid-twenties

mit|teilen *vt*: **jdm etw ~** to inform sb of sth; **Mitteilung** *f* notification

Mittel (-*s* -) *nt* means *sing*; (*Maßnahme, Methode*) method; (*Med*) remedy (*gegen* for); **das ist ein gutes ~, (um) junge Leute zu erreichen** that's a good way of engaging with young people

Mittelalter *nt* Middle Ages *pl*; **mittelalterlich** *adj* medieval; **Mittelamerika** *nt* Central America; **Mitteleuropa** *nt* Central Europe; **Mittelfeld** *nt* midfield; **Mittelfinger** *m* middle finger; **mittelmäßig** *adj* mediocre; **Mittelmeer** *nt* Mediterranean (Sea);

Mittelohrentzündung *f* inflammation of the middle ear; **Mittelpunkt** *m* centre; **im ~ stehen** to be the centre of attention

mittels *prep +gen* by means of

Mittelstreifen *m* central reservation (*Brit*), median (*US*); **Mittelstürmer(in)** *m(f)* striker, centre-forward; **Mittelwelle** *f* medium wave

mitten *adv* in the middle; **~ auf der Straße/in der Nacht** in the middle of the street/night

Mitternacht *f* midnight

mittlere(r, s) *adj* middle; (*durchschnittlich*) average

mittlerweile *adv* meanwhile

Mittwoch (-*s*, *-e*) *m* Wednesday; (**am**) **~** on Wednesday; (**am**) **~ Morgen/Nachmittag/Abend** (on) Wednesday morning/afternoon/evening; **diesen/letzten/nächsten ~** this/last/next Wednesday; **jeden ~** every Wednesday; **~ in einer Woche** a week on Wednesday, Wednesday week; **mittwochs** *adv* on Wednesdays; **~ abends** (*jeden Mittwochabend*) on Wednesday evenings

mixen *vt* to mix; **Mixer** (-*s*, -) *m* (*Küchengerät*) blender

MKS *f abk* = **Maul- und Klauenseuche** FMD

mobben *vt* to harass (*o* to bully) (at work)

Mobbing (-*s*) *nt* workplace bullying (*o* harassment)

Möbel (-*s*, -) *nt* piece of furniture; **die ~** *pl* the furniture *sing*; **Möbelwagen** *m* removal van

mobil *adj* mobile

Mobilfunknetz *nt* cellular network; **Mobiltelefon** *nt* mobile phone

möblieren *vt* to furnish

mochte *imperf von* **mögen**
Mode (-, -*n*) *f* fashion
Model (-*s*, -*s*) *nt* model
Modell (-*s*, -*e*) *nt* model
Modem (-*s*, -*s*) *nt* (*Inform*)
modem
Mode(n)schau *f* fashion show
Moderator(in) *m(f)* presenter
modern *adj* modern; (*modisch*)
fashionable
Modeschmuck *m* costume
jewellery; **modisch** *adj*
fashionable
Modus (-, *Modi*) *m* (*Inform*) mode;
(*fig*) way
Mofa (-*s*, -*s*) *nt* moped
mogeln *vi* to cheat

 SCHLÜSSELWORT

mögen (*pt* **mochte**, *pp* **gemocht** *o*
(*als Hilfsverb*) **mögen**) *vt, vi* to like;
magst du/mögen Sie ihn? do you
like him?; **ich möchte ...** I would
like ..., I'd like ...; **er möchte in die
Stadt** he'd like to go into town;
ich möchte nicht, dass du ... I
wouldn't like you to ...; **ich mag
nicht mehr** I've had enough
▷ *Hilfsverb* to like to; (*wollen*) to
want; **möchtest du etwas essen?**
would you like something to
eat?; **sie mag nicht bleiben** she
doesn't want to stay; **das mag
wohl sein** that may well be; **was
mag das heißen?** what might
that mean?; **Sie möchten zu
Hause anrufen** could you please
call home?

möglich *adj* possible; **so bald
wie ~** as soon as possible;
möglicherweise *adv* possibly;
Möglichkeit *f* possibility;
möglichst *adv* as ... as possible
Mohn (-(*e*)*s*, -*e*) *m* (*Blume*) poppy;
(*Samen*) poppy seed

Möhre (-, -*n*) *f*, **Mohrrübe** *f*
carrot
Mokka (-*s*, -*s*) *m* mocha
Moldawien (-*s*) *nt* Moldova
Molkerei (-, -*en*) *f* dairy
Moll (-) *nt* minor (key); **a-~** A
minor
mollig *adj* cosy; (*dicklich*)
plump
Moment (-(*e*)*s*, -*e*) *m* moment;
im ~ at the moment; **einen
~ bitte!** just a minute; **momentan**
adj momentary ▷ *adv* at the
moment
Monaco (-*s*) *nt* Monaco
Monarchie *f* monarchy
Monat (-(*e*)*s*, -*e*) *m* month; **sie ist
im dritten ~** (*schwanger*) she's
three months pregnant;
monatlich *adj, adv* monthly;
~ 100 Euro zahlen to pay 100
euros a month (*o* every month);
Monatskarte *f* monthly season
ticket
Mönch (-*s*, -*e*) *m* monk
Mond (-(*e*)*s*, -*e*) *m* moon;
Mondfinsternis *f* lunar eclipse
Mongolei (-) *f*: **die ~** Mongolia
Monitor *m* (*Inform*) monitor
monoton *adj* monotonous
Monsun (-*s*, -*e*) *m* monsoon
Montag *m* Monday; *siehe auch*
Mittwoch; **montags** *adv* on
Mondays; *siehe auch* **mittwochs**
Montenegro (-*s*) *nt*
Montenegro
Monteur(in) (-*s*, -*e*) *m(f)* fitter;
montieren *vt* to assemble, to set
up
Monument *nt* monument
Moor (-(*e*)*s*, -*e*) *nt* moor
Moos (-*es*, -*e*) *nt* moss
Moped (-*s*, -*s*) *nt* moped
Moral (-) *f* (*Werte*) morals *pl*; (*einer
Geschichte*) moral; **moralisch** *adj*
moral
Mord (-(*e*)*s*, -*e*) *m* murder;

m

Mörder(in) (-s, -) m(f) murderer/murderess

morgen adv tomorrow; **~ früh** tomorrow morning

Morgen (-s, -) m morning; **am ~** in the morning; **Morgenmantel** m, **Morgenrock** m dressing gown; **Morgenmuffel** m: **er ist ein ~** he's not a morning person; **morgens** adv in the morning; **um 3 Uhr ~** at 3 (o'clock) in the morning, at 3 am

Morphium (-s) nt morphine

morsch adj rotten

Mosaik (-s, -e(n)) nt mosaic

Mosambik (-s) nt Mozambique

Moschee (-, -n) f mosque

Moskau (-s) nt Moscow

Moskito (-s, -s) m mosquito; **Moskitonetz** nt mosquito net

Moslem (-s, -s) m, **Moslime** (-, -n) f Muslim

Most (-(e)s, -e) m (unfermented) fruit juice; (Apfelwein) cider

Motel (-s, -s) nt motel

motivieren vt to motivate

Motor m engine; (Elek) motor; **Motorboot** nt motorboat; **Motorenöl** nt engine oil; **Motorhaube** f bonnet (Brit), hood (US); **Motorrad** nt motorbike, motorcycle; **Motorradfahrer(in)** m(f) motorcyclist; **Motorroller** m (motor) scooter; **Motorschaden** m engine trouble

Motte (-, -n) f moth

Motto (-s, -s) nt motto

Mountainbike (-s, -s) nt mountain bike

Möwe (-, -n) f (sea)gull

MP3-Player (-s, -) m MP3 player

Mrd. f abk = **Milliarde(n)**

MS (-) f abk = **multiple Sklerose** MS

Mücke (-, -n) f midge; (tropische) mosquito; **Mückenstich** m mosquito bite

müde adj tired

muffig adj (Geruch) musty; (Gesicht, Mensch) grumpy

Mühe (-, -n) f trouble, pains pl; **sich** (dat) **große ~ geben** to go to a lot of trouble

muhen vi to moo

Mühle (-, -n) f mill; (Kaffeemühle) grinder

Müll (-(e)s) m rubbish (Brit), garbage (US); **Müllabfuhr** f rubbish (Brit) (o garbage (US)) disposal

Mullbinde f gauze bandage

Müllcontainer m waste container; **Mülldeponie** f rubbish (Brit) (o garbage (US)) dump; **Mülleimer** m rubbish bin (Brit), garbage can (US); **Mülltonne** f dustbin (Brit), garbage can (US); **Mülltrennung** f sorting and collecting household waste according to type of material; **Müllverbrennungsanlage** f incineration plant; **Müllwagen** m dustcart (Brit), garbage truck (US)

multikulturell adj multicultural

Multimedia- in zW multimedia

Multiple-Choice-Verfahren nt multiple choice

multiple Sklerose (-n, -n) f multiple sclerosis

Multiplexkino nt multiplex (cinema)

multiplizieren vt to multiply (mit by)

Mumie f mummy

Mumps (-) m mumps sing

München (-s) nt Munich

Mund (-(e)s, Münder) m mouth; **halt den ~!** shut up; **Mundart** f dialect; **Munddusche** f dental water jet

münden vi to flow (in +akk into)

Mundgeruch m bad breath; **Mundharmonika** (-, -s) f mouth organ

mündlich *adj* oral
Mundschutz *m* mask;
  Mundwasser *nt* mouthwash
Munition *f* ammunition
Münster (*-s, -*) *nt* minster,
  cathedral
munter *adj* lively
Münzautomat *m* vending
  machine; **Münze** (*-, -n*) *f* coin;
  Münzeinwurf *m* slot;
  Münzrückgabe *f* coin return;
  Münztelefon *nt* pay phone;
  Münzwechsler *m* change
  machine
murmeln *vt, vi* to murmur, to
  mutter
Murmeltier *nt* marmot
mürrisch *adj* sullen, grumpy
Mus (*-es, -e*) *nt* puree
Muschel (*-, -n*) *f* mussel; (*~schale*)
  shell
Museum (*-s, Museen*) *nt*
  museum
Musical (*-s, -s*) *nt* musical
Musik *f* music; **musikalisch** *adj*
  musical; **Musiker(in)** (*-s, -*) *m(f)*
  musician; **Musikinstrument** *nt*
  musical instrument; **musizieren**
  vi to play music
Muskat (*-(e)s*) *m* nutmeg
Muskel (*-s, -n*) *m* muscle;
  Muskelkater *m*: **~ haben** to be
  stiff; **Muskelriss** *m* torn muscle;
  Muskelzerrung *f* pulled muscle;
  muskulös *adj* muscular
Müsli (*-s, -*) *nt* muesli
Muslim(in) (*-s, -s*) *m(f)* Muslim
Muss (*-*) *nt* must

 SCHLÜSSELWORT

müssen (*pt* **musste**, *pp* **gemusst**
o (als Hilfsverb) **müssen**) *vi*
1 (*Zwang*) must; (*nur im Präsens*) to
have to; **ich muss es tun** I must do
it, I have to do it; **ich musste es
tun** I had to do it; **er muss es**

nicht tun he doesn't have to do it;
muss ich? must I?, do I have to?;
wann müsst ihr zur Schule?
when do you have to go to
school?; **er hat gehen müssen** he
(has) had to go; **muss das sein?** is
that really necessary?; **ich muss
mal** (*fam*) I need the toilet
2 (*sollen*) **das musst du nicht tun!**
you oughtn't to *o* shouldn't do
that; **Sie hätten ihn fragen
müssen** you should have asked
him
3 **es muss geregnet haben** it
must have rained; **es muss nicht
wahr sein** it needn't be true

Muster (*-s, -*) *nt* (*Dessin*) pattern,
design; (*Probe*) sample; (*Vorbild*)
model; **mustern** *vt* to have a
close look at; **jdn ~** to look sb up
and down
Mut (*-(e)s*) *m* courage; **jdm
~ machen** to encourage sb; **mutig**
adj brave, courageous
Mutter (*-, Mütter*) *f* mother
  ▷ (*-, -n*) *f* (*Schraubenmutter*) nut;
  Muttersprache *f* mother
  tongue; **Muttertag** *m* Mother's
  Day; **Mutti** *f* mum(my) (*Brit*),
  mom(my) (*US*)
mutwillig *adj* deliberate
Mütze (*-, -n*) *f* cap
MwSt. *abk* = **Mehrwertsteuer**
  VAT
Myanmar (*-s*) *nt* Myanmar

m

n

N *abk* = **Nord** N

na *interj* **~ also!, ~ bitte!** see?, what did I tell you?; **~ ja** well; **~ und?** so what?

Nabel (-s, -) *m* navel

SCHLÜSSELWORT

nach *prep* +*dat* **1** (*örtlich*) to; **nach Berlin** to Berlin; **nach links/rechts** (to the) left/right; **nach oben/hinten** up/back **2** (*zeitlich*) after; **einer nach dem anderen** one after the other; **nach Ihnen!** after you!; **zehn (Minuten) nach drei** ten (minutes) past three **3** (*gemäß*) according to; **nach dem Gesetz** according to the law; **dem Namen nach** judging by his/her name; **nach allem, was ich weiß** as far as I know ▷ *adv*: **ihm nach!** after him!; **nach**

und nach gradually, little by little; **nach wie vor** still

nach|ahmen *vt* to imitate

Nachbar(in) (-*n*, -*n*) *m(f)* neighbour; **Nachbarschaft** *f* neighbourhood

nach|bestellen *vt* to order some more

nachdem *conj* after; (*weil*) since; **je ~ (ob/wie)** depending on (whether/how)

nach|denken *irr vi* to think (*über* +*akk* about); **nachdenklich** *adj* thoughtful

nacheinander *adv* one after another (*o* the other)

Nachfolger(in) (-*s*, -) *m(f)* successor

nach|forschen *vt* to investigate

Nachfrage *f* inquiry; (*Comm*) demand; **nach|fragen** *vi* to inquire

nach|geben *irr vi* to give in (*jdm* to sb)

Nachgebühr *f* surcharge; (*für Briefe etc*) excess postage

nach|gehen *irr vi* to follow (*jdm* sb); (*erforschen*) to inquire (*einer Sache dat* into sth); **die Uhr geht (zehn Minuten) nach** this watch is (ten minutes) slow

nachher *adv* afterwards; **bis ~!** see you later

Nachhilfe *f* extra tuition

nach|holen *vt* to catch up with; (*Versäumtes*) to make up for

nach|kommen *irr vi* to follow; **einer Verpflichtung** (*dat*) **~ to** fulfil an obligation

nach|lassen *irr vt* (*Summe*) to take off ▷ *vi* to decrease, to ease off; (*schlechter werden*) to deteriorate; **nachlässig** *adj* negligent, careless

nach|laufen *irr vi* to run after, to chase (*jdm* sb)

nach|lösen vt: **eine Fahrkarte ~** to buy a ticket on the bus/train

nach|machen vt to imitate, to copy (jdm etw sth from sb); (fälschen) to counterfeit

Nachmittag m afternoon; **heute ~** this afternoon; **am ~** in the afternoon; **nachmittags** adv in the afternoon; **um 3 Uhr ~** at 3 (o'clock) in the afternoon, at 3 pm

Nachnahme (-, -n) f cash on delivery; **per ~** COD

Nachname m surname

nach|prüfen vt to check

nach|rechnen vt to check

Nachricht (-, -en) f (piece of) news sing; (Mitteilung) message; **Nachrichten** pl news sing

Nachsaison f off-season

nach|schauen vi: **jdm ~** to gaze after sb ▷ vt (prüfen) to check

nach|schicken vt to forward

nach|schlagen irr vt to look up

nach|sehen irr vt (prüfen) to check

Nachspeise f dessert

nächstbeste(r, s) adj: **der ~ Zug/Job** the first train/job that comes along; **nächste(r, s)** adj next; (nächstgelegen) nearest

Nacht (-, Nächte) f night; **in der ~** during the night; (bei Nacht) at night; **Nachtclub** m nightclub; **Nachtdienst** m night duty; **~ haben** (Apotheke) to be open all night

Nachteil m disadvantage

Nachtflug m night flight; **Nachtfrost** m overnight frost; **Nachthemd** nt (für Damen) nightdress; (für Herren) nightshirt

Nachtigall (-, -en) f nightingale

Nachtisch m dessert, sweet (Brit), pudding (Brit); **Nachtleben** nt nightlife

nach|tragen irr vt: **jdm etw ~** (übel nehmen) to hold sth against sb

nachträglich adv: **~ alles Gute zum Geburtstag!** Happy belated birthday

nachts adv at night; **um 11 Uhr ~** at 11 (o'clock) at night, at 11 pm; **um 2 Uhr ~** at 2 (o'clock) in the morning, at 2 am; **Nachtschicht** f night shift; **Nachttarif** m off-peak rate; **Nachttisch** m bedside table; **Nachtzug** m night train

Nachweis (-es, -e) m proof

Nachwirkung f after-effect

nach|zahlen vi to pay extra ▷ vt: **20 Euro ~** to pay 20 euros extra

nach|zählen vt to check

Nacken (-s, -) m (nape of the) neck

nackt adj naked; (Tatsachen) plain, bare; **Nacktbadestrand** m nudist beach

Nadel (-, -n) f needle; (Stecknadel) pin; **Nadelstreifen** pl pinstripes pl

Nagel (-s, Nägel) m nail; **Nagelbürste** f nail brush; **Nagelfeile** f nail-file; **Nagellack** m nail varnish (o polish); **Nagellackentferner** (-s, -) m nail-varnish (o nail-polish) remover; **Nagelschere** f nail scissors pl

nah(e) adj, adv (räumlich) near(by); (zeitlich) near; (Verwandte, Freunde) close; **Nähe** (-) f (Umgebung) vicinity; **in der ~** nearby; **in der ~ von** near to; **nahe|gehen** vi: **jdm ~** to upset sb; **nahe|legen** vt: **jdm etw ~** to suggest sth to sb; **nahe|liegen** irr vi to be obvious ▷ prep +dat near (to), close to

nähen vt, vi to sew

nähere(r, s) adj (Erklärung, Erkundigung) more detailed; **die ~ Umgebung** the immediate area;

Nähere(s) nt details pl; **nähern** vr: **sich ~** to approach

nahezu adv virtually, almost

nahm imperf von **nehmen**

Nähmaschine f sewing machine

nahrhaft adj nourishing, nutritious; **Nahrung** f food; **Nahrungsmittel** nt food

Naht (-, **Nähte**) f seam; (Med) stitches pl, suture; (Tech) join

Nahverkehr m local traffic; **Nahverkehrszug** m local train

Nähzeug nt sewing kit

naiv adj naive

Name (-ns, -n) m name

nämlich adv that is to say, namely; (denn) since

nannte imperf von **nennen**

Napf (-(e)s, **Näpfe**) m bowl, dish

Narbe (-, -n) f scar

Narkose (-, -n) f anaesthetic

Narzisse (-, -n) f narcissus

naschen vi to nibble; **Naschkatze** f (fam) nibbler; **eine ~ sein** to have a sweet tooth

Nase (-, -n) f nose; **Nasenbluten** (-s) nt nosebleed; **~ haben** to have a nosebleed; **Nasenloch** nt nostril; **Nasentropfen** pl nose drops pl

Nashorn nt rhinoceros

nass adj wet; **Nässe** (-) f wetness; **nässen** vi (Wunde) to weep

Nation (-, -en) f nation; **national** adj national; **Nationalfeiertag** m national holiday; **Nationalhymne** (-, -n) f national anthem; **Nationalität** f nationality; **Nationalmannschaft** f national team; **Nationalpark** m National Park; **Nationalspieler(in)** m(f) international (player)

NATO (-) f abk = **North Atlantic Treaty Organization** NATO, Nato

Natur f nature; **Naturkost** f health food; **natürlich** adj natural ▷ adv naturally; (selbstverständlich) of course; **Naturpark** m nature reserve; **naturrein** adj natural, pure; **Naturschutz** m conservation; **Naturschutzgebiet** nt nature reserve; **Naturwissenschaft** f (natural) science; **Naturwissenschaftler(in)** m(f) scientist

Navigationssystem nt (Auto) navigation system

n. Chr. abk = **nach Christus** AD

Nebel (-s, -) m fog, mist; **nebelig** adj foggy, misty; **Nebelscheinwerfer** m foglamp; **Nebelschlussleuchte** f (Auto) rear foglight

neben prep +akk o dat next to; (außer) apart from, besides; **nebenan** adv next door; **Nebenausgang** m side exit; **nebenbei** adv at the same time; (außerdem) additionally; (beiläufig) incidentally; **nebeneinander** adv side by side; **Nebeneingang** m side entrance; **Nebenfach** nt subsidiary subject

nebenher adv (zusätzlich) besides; (gleichzeitig) at the same time; (daneben) alongside

Nebenkosten pl extra charges pl, extras pl; **Nebensache** f minor matter; **nebensächlich** adj minor; **Nebensaison** f low season; **Nebenstraße** f side street; **Nebenwirkung** f side effect

neblig adj foggy, misty

necken vt to tease

Neffe (-n, -n) m nephew

negativ adj negative; **Negativ** nt (Foto) negative

nehmen (nahm, genommen) vt to take; **wie man's nimmt** it depends on how you look at it; **den Bus/Zug ~** to take the bus/train; **jdn/etw ernst ~** to

take sb/sth seriously; **etw zu sich ~** to eat sth; **jdn zu sich ~** to have sb come and live with one; **jdn an die Hand ~** to take sb by the hand
neidisch *adj* envious
neigen *vi*: **zu etw ~** to tend towards sth; **Neigung** *f* (*des Geländes*) slope; (*Tendenz*) inclination; (*Vorliebe*) liking
nein *adv* no
Nektarine *f* nectarine
Nelke (-, -n) *f* carnation; (*Gewürz*) clove
nennen (*nannte, genannt*) *vt* to name; (*mit Namen*) to call
Neonazi (-s, -s) *m* neo-Nazi
Nepal (-s) *nt* Nepal
Neptun (-s) *m* Neptune
Nerv (-s, -en) *m* nerve; **jdm auf die ~en gehen** to get on sb's nerves; **nerven** *vt*: **jdn ~** (*fam*) to get on sb's nerves; **Nerven-zusammenbruch** *m* nervous breakdown; **nervös** *adj* nervous
Nest (-(e)s, -er) *nt* nest; (*pej: Ort*) dump
nett *adj* nice; (*freundlich*) kind; **sei so ~ und ...** do me a favour and ...
netto *adv* net
Netz (-es, -e) *nt* net; (*für Einkauf*) string bag; (*System*) network; (*Stromnetz*) mains, power (*US*); **Netzanschluss** *m* mains connection; **Netzbetreiber(in)** *m(f)* network operator; (*Inform*) Internet operator; **Netzgerät** *nt* power pack; **Netzkarte** *f* season ticket; **Netzwerk** *nt* (*Inform*) network; **Netzwerken** *nt* (*social*) networking; **Netzwerkkarte** *f* network card
neu *adj* new; (*Sprache, Geschichte*) modern; **die ~esten Nachrichten** the latest news; **Neubau** *m* new building; **neuerdings** *adv* recently; **Neueröffnung** *f*

new business; **Neuerung** *f* innovation; (*Reform*) reform
Neugier *f* curiosity; **neugierig** *adj* curious (*auf +akk* about); **ich bin ~, ob ...** I wonder whether (*o* if) ...; **ich bin ~, was du dazu sagst** I'll be interested to hear what you have to say about it
Neuheit *f* novelty; **Neuigkeit** *f* news *sing*; **eine ~** a piece of news; **Neujahr** *nt* New Year; **prosit ~!** Happy New Year; **neulich** *adv* recently, the other day; **Neumond** *m* new moon
neun *num* nine; **neunhundert** *num* nine hundred; **neunmal** *adv* nine times; **neunte(r, s)** *adj* ninth; *siehe auch* **dritte**; **Neuntel** (-s, -) *nt* ninth; **neunzehn** *num* nineteen; **neunzehnte(r, s)** *adj* nineteenth; *siehe auch* **dritte**; **neunzig** *num* ninety; **in den ~er Jahren** in the nineties; **Neunzigerjahre** *pl* nineties *pl*; **neunzigste(r, s)** *adj* ninetieth
neureich *adj* nouveau riche
Neurologe *m*, **Neurologin** *f* neurologist; **Neurose** (-, -n) *f* neurosis; **neurotisch** *adj* neurotic
Neuseeland *nt* New Zealand
Neustart *m* (*Inform*) restart, reboot
neutral *adj* neutral
neuwertig *adj* nearly new
Nicaragua (-s) *nt* Nicaragua

 SCHLÜSSELWORT

nicht *adv* **1** (*Verneinung*) not; **er ist es nicht** it's not him, it isn't him; **er raucht nicht** (*gerade*) he isn't smoking; (*gewöhnlich*) he doesn't smoke; **ich kann das nicht — ich auch nicht** I can't do it — neither *o* nor can I; **es regnet nicht mehr** it's not raining any more; **nicht rostend** stainless

n

2 (*Bitte, Verbot*) **nicht!** don't!, no!;
nicht berühren! do not touch!;
nicht doch! don't!

3 (*rhetorisch*) **du bist müde, nicht
(wahr)?** you're tired, aren't you?;
das ist schön, nicht (wahr)? it's
nice, isn't it?

4 was du nicht sagst! the things
you say!

Nichte (-, -n) f niece
Nichtraucher(in) m(f) non-
smoker; **Nichtraucherabteil** nt
non-smoking compartment;
Nichtraucherzone f non-
smoking area
nichts pron nothing; **für ~ und
wieder ~** for nothing at all; **ich
habe ~ gesagt** I didn't say
anything; **macht ~** never mind
Nichtschwimmer(in) m(f)
non-swimmer
nichtssagend adj meaningless
nicken vi to nod
Nickerchen nt nap
nie adv never; **~ wieder** (o **mehr**)
never again; **fast ~** hardly ever
nieder adj (*niedrig*) low; (*gering*)
inferior ▷ adv down;
niedergeschlagen adj depressed;
Niederlage f defeat
Niederlande pl Netherlands pl;
Niederländer(in) m(f) Dutch-
man/Dutchwoman;
niederländisch adj Dutch;
Niederländisch nt Dutch
Niederlassung f branch
Niederösterreich nt Lower
Austria; **Niedersachsen** nt
Lower Saxony
Niederschlag m (*Meteo*)
precipitation; (*Regen*) rainfall
niedlich adj sweet, cute
niedrig adj low; (*Qualität*)
inferior
niemals adv never
niemand pron nobody, no one;

ich habe ~en gesehen I haven't
seen anyone; **~ von ihnen** none of
them
Niere (-, -n) f kidney;
Nierenentzündung f kidney
infection; **Nierensteine** pl
kidney stones pl
nieseln vi impers to drizzle;
Nieselregen m drizzle
niesen vi to sneeze
Niete (-, -n) f (*Los*) blank; (*Reinfall*)
flop; (*pej: Mensch*) failure; (*Tech*) rivet
Nigeria (-s) nt Nigeria
Nikotin (-s) nt nicotine
Nilpferd nt hippopotamus
nippen vi to sip; **an etw** (*dat*) **~** to
sip sth
nirgends adv nowhere
Nische (-, -n) f niche
Niveau (-s, -s) nt level; **sie hat
~** she's got class
nobel adj (*großzügig*) generous;
(*fam: luxuriös*) classy, posh;
Nobelpreis m Nobel Prize

O SCHLÜSSELWORT

noch adv **1** (*weiterhin*) still; **noch
nicht** not yet; **noch nie** never
(yet); **noch immer** o **immer noch**
still; **bleiben Sie doch noch** stay a
bit longer

2 (*in Zukunft*) still, yet; **das kann
noch passieren** that might still
happen; **er wird noch kommen**
he'll come (yet)

3 (*nicht später als*) **noch vor einer
Woche** only a week ago; **noch am
selben Tag** the very same day;
noch im 19. Jahrhundert as late
as the 19th century; **noch heute**
today

4 (*zusätzlich*) **wer war noch da?**
who else was there?; **noch einmal**
once more, again; **noch dreimal**
three more times; **noch einer**
another one

5 (*bei Vergleichen*) **noch größer** even bigger; **das ist noch besser** that's better still; **und wenn es noch so schwer ist** however hard it is

6 Geld noch und noch heaps (and heaps) of money; **sie hat noch und noch versucht, ...** she tried again and again to ...

▷ *konj:* **weder A noch B** neither A nor B

nochmal(s) *adv* again, once more
Nominativ *m* nominative (case)
Nonne (-, -n) *f* nun
Nonstop-Flug *m* nonstop flight
Nord north; **Nordamerika** *nt* North America; **Norddeutschland** *nt* Northern Germany; **Norden** (-s) *m* north; **im ~ Deutschlands** in the north of Germany; **Nordeuropa** *nt* Northern Europe
Nordic Walking *nt* (*Sport*) Nordic Walking
Nordirland *nt* Northern Ireland; **nordisch** *adj* (*Völker, Sprache*) Nordic; **Nordkorea** (-s) *nt* North Korea; **nördlich** *adj* northern; (*Kurs, Richtung*) northerly; **Nordost(en)** *m* northeast; **Nordpol** *m* North Pole; **Nordrhein-Westfalen** (-s) *nt* North Rhine-Westphalia; **Nordsee** *f* North Sea; **nordwärts** *adv* north, northwards; **Nordwest(en)** *m* northwest; **Nordwind** *m* north wind
nörgeln *vi* to grumble
Norm (-, -en) *f* norm; (*Größenvorschrift*) standard
normal *adj* normal; **Normalbenzin** *nt* regular (petrol (*Brit*) o gas (*US*)); **normalerweise** *adv* normally
normen *vt* to standardize
Norwegen (-s) *nt* Norway;

Norweger(in) *m(f)* Norwegian; **norwegisch** *adj* Norwegian; **Norwegisch** *nt* Norwegian
Not (-, *Nöte*) *f* need; (*Armut*) poverty; (*Elend*) hardship; (*Bedrängnis*) trouble; (*Mangel*) want; (*Mühe*) trouble; (*Zwang*) necessity; **zur ~** if necessary; (*gerade noch*) just about
Notar(in) *m(f)* public notary; **notariell** *adj:* **~ beglaubigt** attested by a notary
Notarzt *m*, **Notärztin** *f* emergency doctor; **Notarztwagen** *m* emergency ambulance; **Notaufnahme** *f* A&E, casualty (*Brit*), emergency room (*US*); **Notausgang** *m* emergency exit; **Notbremse** *f* emergency brake; **Notdienst** *m* emergency service, after-hours service; **notdürftig** *adj* scanty; (*behelfsmäßig*) makeshift
Note (-, -n) *f* note; (*in Schule*) mark, grade (*US*); (*Mus*) note
Notebook (-(s), -s) *nt* (*Inform*) notebook
Notfall *m* emergency; **notfalls** *adv* if necessary
notieren *vt* to note down
nötig *adj* necessary; **etw ~ haben** to need sth
Notiz (-, -en) *f* note; (*Zeitungs~*) item; **Notizblock** *m* notepad; **Notizbuch** *nt* notebook
Notlage *f* crisis; (*Elend*) plight; **notlanden** *vi* to make a forced (o emergency) landing; **Notlandung** *f* emergency landing; **Notruf** *m* emergency call; **Notrufnummer** *f* emergency number; **Notrufsäule** *f* emergency telephone
notwendig *adj* necessary
Nougat (-s, -s) *m od nt* nougat
November (-(s), -) *m* November; *siehe auch* **Juni**

n

Nr. *abk* = **Nummer** No., no.

Nu *m*: **im ~** in no time

nüchtern *adj* sober; (*Magen*) empty

Nudel (-, -n) *f* noodle; **~n** *pl* (*italienische*) pasta *sing*

null *num* zero; (*Tel*) O (*Brit*), zero (*US*); **~ Fehler** no mistakes; **~ Uhr** midnight; **Null** (-, -en) *f* nought, zero; (*pej: Mensch*) dead loss; **Nulltarif** *m*: **zum ~** free of charge

Numerus clausus (-) *m* restriction on the number of students allowed to study a particular subject

Nummer (-, -n) *f* number; **nummerieren** *vt* to number; **Nummernschild** *nt* (*Auto*) number plate (*Brit*), license plate (*US*)

nun *adv* now; **von ~ an** from now on ▷ *interj* well; **~ gut!** all right, then; **es ist ~ mal so** that's the way it is

nur *adv* only; **nicht ~ ..., sondern auch ...** not only ..., but also ...; **~ Anna nicht** except Anna

Nürnberg (-s) *nt* Nuremberg

Nuss (-, *Nüsse*) *f* nut; **Nussknacker** (-s, -) *m* nutcracker; **Nuss-Nougat-Creme** *f* chocolate nut cream

Nutte (-, -n) *f* (*fam*) tart

nutz, nütze *adj*: **zu nichts ~ sein** to be useless; **nutzen, nützen** *vt* to use (*zu etw* for sth); **was nützt es?** what use is it? ▷ *vi* to be of use; **das nützt nicht viel** that doesn't help much; **es nützt nichts...** it's no use (doing it); **Nutzen** (-s, -) *m* usefulness; (*Gewinn*) profit; **nützlich** *adj* useful

Nylon (-s) *nt* nylon

O

o *interj* oh

O *abk* = **Ost** E

Oase (-, -n) *f* oasis

ob *conj* if, whether; **so als ~** as if; **er tut so, als ~ er krank wäre** he's pretending to be sick; **und ~!** you bet

obdachlos *adj* homeless

oben *adv* (*am oberen Ende*) at the top; (*obenauf*) on (the) top; (*im Haus*) upstairs; (*in einem Text*) above; **~ erwähnt** (*o genannt*) above-mentioned; **mit dem Gesicht nach ~** face up; **da ~** up there; **von ~ bis unten** from top to bottom; **siehe ~** see above

Ober (-s, -) *m* waiter

obere(r, s) *adj* upper, top

Oberfläche *f* surface; **oberflächlich** *adj* superficial; **Obergeschoss** *nt* upper floor

oberhalb *adv, prep* +*gen* above

Oberhemd *nt* shirt; **Oberkörper**

m upper body; **Oberlippe** *f* upper lip; **Oberösterreich** *nt* Upper Austria; **Oberschenkel** *m* thigh
oberste(r, s) *adj* very top, topmost
Oberteil *nt* top; **Oberweite** *f* bust/chest measurement
obig *adj* above(-mentioned)
Objekt (-(e)s, -e) *nt* object
objektiv *adj* objective; **Objektiv** *nt* lens
obligatorisch *adj* compulsory, obligatory
Oboe (-, -n) *f* oboe
Observatorium *nt* observatory
Obst (-(e)s) *nt* fruit; **Obstkuchen** *m* fruit tart; **Obstsalat** *m* fruit salad
obszön *adj* obscene
obwohl *conj* although
Ochse (-n, -n) *m* ox; **Ochsenschwanzsuppe** *f* oxtail soup
ocker *adj* ochre
öd(e) *adj* waste; (*unbebaut*) barren; (*fig*) dull
oder *conj* or; **~ aber** or else; **er kommt doch, ~?** he's coming, isn't he?
Ofen (-s, Öfen) *m* oven; (*Heizofen*) heater; (*Kohleofen*) stove; (*Herd*) cooker, stove; **Ofenkartoffel** *f* baked (*o* jacket) potato
offen *adj* open; (*aufrichtig*) frank; (*Stelle*) vacant ▷ *adv* frankly; **~ gesagt** to be honest
offenbar *adj* obvious; **offensichtlich** *adj* evident, obvious
öffentlich *adj* public; **Öffentlichkeit** *f* (*Leute*) public; (*einer Versammlung etc*) public nature
offiziell *adj* official
offline *adv* (*Inform*) offline
öffnen *vt* to open ▷ *vr*: **sich ~** to open; **Öffner** (-s, -) *m* opener;

Öffnung *f* opening; **Öffnungszeiten** *pl* opening times *pl*
oft *adv* often; **schon ~** many times; **öfter** *adv* more often (*o* frequently); **öfters** *adv* often, frequently
ohne *conj, prep* +*akk* without; **~ weiteres** without a second thought; (*sofort*) immediately; **~ ein Wort zu sagen** without saying a word; **~ mich** count me out
Ohnmacht (-machten) *f* unconsciousness; (*Hilflosigkeit*) helplessness; **in ~ fallen** to faint; **ohnmächtig** *adj* unconscious; **sie ist ~** she has fainted
Ohr (-(e)s, -en) *nt* ear; (*Gehör*) hearing
Öhr (-(e)s, -e) *nt* eye
Ohrenarzt *m*, **Ohrenärztin** *f* ear specialist; **Ohrenschmerzen** *pl* earache; **Ohrentropfen** *pl* ear drops *pl*; **Ohrfeige** *f* slap (in the face); **Ohrläppchen** *nt* earlobe; **Ohrringe** *pl* earrings *pl*
oje *interj* oh dear
okay *interj* OK, okay
Ökoladen *m* health food store; **ökologisch** *adj* ecological; **~e Landwirtschaft** organic farming
ökonomisch *adj* economic; (*sparsam*) economical
Ökosystem *nt* ecosystem
Oktanzahl *f* (*bei Benzin*) octane rating
Oktober (-(s), -) *m* October; *siehe auch* **Juni**

○ **OKTOBERFEST**
○
○ The annual October beer
○ festival, the **Oktoberfest**,
○ takes place in Munich on a
○ huge field where beer tents,
○ roller coasters and many other

- amusements are set up. People
- sit at long wooden tables, drink
- beer from enormous litre beer
- mugs, eat pretzels and listen
- to brass bands. It is a great
- attraction for tourists and locals
- alike.

Öl (-(e)s, -e) nt oil; **Ölbaum** m
olive tree; **ölen** vt to oil; (Tech) to
lubricate; **Ölfarbe** f oil paint;
Ölfilter m oil filter; **Ölgemälde**
nt oil painting; **Ölheizung** f
oil-fired central heating; **ölig** adj
oily

oliv adj inv olive-green; **Olive**
(-, -n) f olive; **Olivenöl** nt olive
oil

Ölmessstab m dipstick; **Ölofen**
m oil stove; **Ölpest** f oil
pollution; **Ölsardine** f sardine in
oil; **Ölstandanzeiger** m (Auto)
oil gauge; **Ölteppich** m oil slick;
Ölwechsel m oil change

Olympiade f Olympic Games pl;
olympisch adj Olympic

Oma f, **Omi** (-s, -s) f grandma,
gran(ny)

Omelett (-(e)s, -s) nt, **Omelette**
f omelette

Omnibus m bus

onanieren vi to masturbate

Onkel (-s, -) m uncle

online adv (Inform) online;
Onlinedienst m (Inform) online
service

OP (-s, -s) m abk =
Operationssaal operating
theatre (Brit) (o room (US))

Opa m, **Opi** (-s, -s) m grandpa,
grandad

Open-Air-Konzert nt open-air
concert

Oper (-, -n) f opera; (Gebäude)
opera house

Operation f operation

Operette f operetta

operieren vi to operate ▷ vt to
operate on

Opernhaus nt opera house,
opera; **Opernsänger(in)** m(f)
opera singer

Opfer (-s, -) nt sacrifice; (Mensch)
victim; **ein ~ bringen** to make a
sacrifice

Opium (-s) nt opium

Opposition f opposition

Optiker(in) (-s, -) m(f) optician

optimal adj optimal, optimum

optimistisch adj optimistic

oral adj oral; **Oralverkehr** m
oral sex

orange adj inv orange; **Orange**
(-, -n) f orange; **Orangenmarmelade** f marmalade;
Orangensaft m orange juice

Orchester (-s, -) nt orchestra

Orchidee (-, -n) f orchid

Orden (-s, -) m (Rel) order; (Mil)
decoration

ordentlich adj (anständig)
respectable; (geordnet) tidy, neat;
(fam: annehmbar) not bad; (fam:
tüchtig) proper ▷ adv properly

ordinär adj common, vulgar;
(Witz) dirty

ordnen vt to sort out; **Ordner**
(-s, -) m (bei Veranstaltung)
steward; (Aktenordner) file;
Ordnung f order; (Geordnetsein)
tidiness; **(geht) in ~!** (that's) all
right; **mit dem Drucker ist etwas
nicht in ~** there's something
wrong with the printer

Oregano (-s) m oregano

Organ (-s, -e) nt organ; (Stimme)
voice

Organisation f organization;
organisieren vt to organize;
(fam: beschaffen) to get hold of
▷ vr: **sich ~** to organize

Organismus m organism

Orgasmus m orgasm

Orgel (-, -n) f organ

Orgie f orgy
orientalisch adj oriental
orientieren vr: **sich ~** to get
one's bearings; **Orientierung** f
orientation; **Orientierungssinn**
m sense of direction
original adj original; (echt)
genuine; **Original** (-s, -e) nt
original
originell adj original; (komisch)
witty
Orkan (-(e)s, -e) m hurricane
Ort (-(e)s, -e) m place; (Dorf)
village; **an ~ und Stelle, vor ~** on
the spot
Orthopäde (-n, -n) m,
Orthopädin f orthopaedist
örtlich adj local; **Ortschaft** f
village, small town; **Ortsgespräch**
nt local call; **Ortstarif** m local
rate; **Ortszeit** f local time

○ ossi
○
○ **Ossi** is a colloquial and rather
○ derogatory word used to
○ describe a German from the
○ former **DDR**.

Ost east; **Ostdeutschland** nt
(als Landesteil) Eastern Germany;
(Hist) East Germany; **Osten** (-s) m
east
Osterei nt Easter egg;
Osterglocke f daffodil;
Osterhase m Easter bunny;
Ostermontag m Easter Monday;
Ostern (-, -) nt Easter; **an** (o **zu**)
~ at Easter; **frohe ~** Happy Easter
Österreich (-s) nt Austria;
Österreicher(in) (-s, -) m(f) Austrian;
österreichisch adj Austrian
Ostersonntag m Easter Sunday
Osteuropa nt Eastern Europe;
Ostküste f east coast; **östlich**
adj eastern; (Kurs, Richtung)
easterly; **Ostsee** f: **die ~** the

Baltic (Sea); **Ostwind** m
east(erly) wind
OSZE (-) f abk = **Organisation für**
Sicherheit und Zusammenarbeit
in Europa OSCE
Otter (-s, -) m otter
out adj (fam) out; **outen** vt to
out
oval adj oval
Overheadprojektor m overhead projector
Ozean (-s, -e) m ocean; **der Stille**
~ the Pacific (Ocean)
Ozon (-s) nt ozone;
Ozonbelastung f ozone level;
Ozonloch nt hole in the ozone
layer; **Ozonschicht** f ozone
layer; **Ozonwerte** pl ozone
levels pl

o

P

vi to paddle

Paket (-(e)s, -e) *nt* packet; (*Postpaket*) parcel; (*Inform*) package; **Paketbombe** *f* parcel bomb; **Paketkarte** *f* dispatch form (*to be filled in with details of the sender and the addressee when handing in a parcel at the post office*)

Pakistan (-s) *nt* Pakistan

Palast (-es, Paläste) *m* palace

Palästina (-s) *nt* Palestine; **Palästinenser(in)** (-s, -) *m(f)* Palestinian

Palatschinken *pl* filled pancakes *pl*

Palette *f* (*von Maler*) palette; (*Ladepalette*) pallet; (*Vielfalt*) range

Palme (-, -n) *f* palm (tree); **Palmsonntag** *m* Palm Sunday

Pampelmuse (-, -n) *f* grapefruit

pampig *adj* (*fam: frech*) cheeky; (*breiig*) gooey

Panda(bär) (-s, -s) *m* panda

Pandemie (-, -n) *f* pandemic

panieren *vt* (*Gastr*) to coat with breadcrumbs; **paniert** *adj* breaded

Panik *f* panic

Panne (-, -n) *f* (*Auto*) breakdown; (*Missgeschick*) slip; **Pannendienst** *m*, **Pannenhilfe** *f* breakdown (*o* rescue) service

Pant(h)er (-s, -) *m* panther

Pantomime (-, -n) *f* mime

Panzer (-s, -) *m* (*Panzerung*) armour (plating); (*Mil*) tank

Papa (-s, -s) *m* dad(dy), pa (*US*)

Papagei (-s, -en) *m* parrot

Papaya (-, -s) *f* papaya

Papier (-s, -e) *nt* paper; **~e** *pl* (*Ausweispapiere*) papers *pl*; (*Dokumente, Urkunden*) papers *pl*, documents *pl*; **Papiercontainer** *m* paper bank; **Papierformat** *nt* paper size; **Papiergeld** *nt* paper money; **Papierkorb** *m* wastepaper basket; (*Inform*)

paar *adj inv* **ein ~** a few; **ein ~ Mal** a few times; **ein ~ Äpfel** some apples

Paar (-(e)s, -e) *nt* pair; (*Ehepaar*) couple; **ein ~ Socken** a pair of socks

pachten *vt* to lease

Päckchen *nt* package; (*Zigaretten*) packet; (*zum Verschicken*) small parcel; **packen** *vt* to pack; (*fassen*) to grasp, to seize; (*fam: schaffen*) to manage; (*fig: fesseln*) to grip; **Packpapier** *nt* brown paper; **Packung** *f* packet, pack (*US*); **Packungsbeilage** *f* package insert, patient information leaflet

Pädagoge (-n, -n) *m*, **Pädagogin** *f* teacher; **pädagogisch** *adj* educational; **~e Hochschule** college of education

Paddel (-s, -) *nt* paddle; **Paddelboot** *nt* canoe; **paddeln**

recycle bin; **Papiertaschentuch** nt (paper) tissue; **Papiertonne** f paper bank

Pappbecher m paper cup; **Pappe** (-, -n) f cardboard; **Pappkarton** m cardboard box; **Pappteller** m paper plate

Paprika (-s, -s) m (Gewürz) paprika; (Schote) pepper

Papst (-(e)s, Päpste) m pope

Paradeiser (-s, -) m tomato

Paradies (-es, -e) nt paradise

Paragliding (-s) nt paragliding

Paragraph (-en, -en) m paragraph; (Jur) section

parallel adj parallel

Paranuss f Brazil nut

Parasit (-en, -en) m parasite

parat adj ready; **etw ~ haben** to have sth ready

Pärchen nt couple

Parfüm (-s, -s o -e) nt perfume; **Parfümerie** f perfumery; **parfümieren** vt to scent, to perfume

Pariser (-s, -) m (fam: Kondom) rubber

Park (-s, -s) m park

Park-and-ride-System nt park-and-ride system; **Parkbank** f park bench; **Parkdeck** nt parking level; **parken** vt, vi to park

Parkett (-s, -e) nt parquet flooring; (Theat) stalls pl (Brit), parquet (US)

Parkhaus nt multi-storey car park (Brit), parking garage (US)

parkinsonsche Krankheit f Parkinson's disease

Parkkralle f (Auto) wheel clamp; **Parklicht** nt parking light; **Parklücke** f parking space; **Parkplatz** m (für ein Auto) parking space; (für mehrere Autos) car park (Brit), parking lot (US); **Parkscheibe** f parking disc; **Parkscheinautomat** m pay

point; (Parkscheinausgabegerät) ticket machine; **Parkuhr** f parking meter; **Parkverbot** nt (Stelle) no-parking zone; **hier ist ~** you can't park here

Parlament nt parliament

Parmesan (-s) m Parmesan (cheese)

Partei f party

Parterre (-s, -s) nt ground floor (Brit), first floor (US)

Partie f part; (Spiel) game; (Mann, Frau) catch; **mit von der ~ sein** to be in on it

Partitur f (Mus) score

Partizip (-s, -ien) nt participle

Partner(in) (-s, -) m(f) partner; **Partnerschaft** f partnership; **eingetragene ~** civil partnership; **Partnerstadt** f twin town

Party (-, -s) f party; **Partymuffel** (-s, -) m party pooper; **Partyservice** f catering service

Pass (-es, Pässe) m pass; (Ausweis) passport

passabel adj reasonable

Passagier (-s, -e) m passenger

Passamt nt passport office

Passant(in) m(f) passer-by; **Passbild** nt passport photo

passen vi (Größe) to fit; (Farbe, Stil) to go (zu with); (auf Frage) to pass; **passt (es) dir morgen?** does tomorrow suit you?; **das passt mir gut** that suits me fine; **passend** adj suitable; (zusammenpassend) matching; (angebracht) fitting; (Zeit) convenient; **haben Sie es nicht ~?** (Kleingeld) have you got the right change?

passieren vi to happen

passiv adj passive

Passkontrolle f passport control

Passwort nt password

Paste (-, -n) f paste

Pastellfarbe f pastel colour
Pastete (-, -n) f (warmes Gericht) pie; (Pastetchen) vol-au-vent; (ohne Teig) pâté
Pastor, in (-s, -en) m(f) minister, vicar
Pate (-n, -n) m godfather; **Patenkind** nt godchild
Patient(in) m(f) patient
Patin f godmother
Patrone (-, -n) f cartridge
patsch interj splat; **patschnass** adj soaking wet
pauschal adj (Kosten) inclusive; (Urteil) sweeping; **Pauschale** (-, -n) f, **Pauschalgebühr** f flat rate (charge); **Pauschalpreis** m flat rate; (für Hotel, Reise) all-inclusive price; **Pauschalreise** f package tour
Pause (-, -n) f break; (Theat) interval; (Kino etc) intermission; (Innehalten) pause
Pavian (-s, -e) m baboon
Pavillon (-s, -s) m pavilion
Pay-TV (-s) nt pay-per-view television, pay TV
Pazifik (-s) m Pacific (Ocean)
PC (-s, -s) m abk = **Personal Computer** PC
Pech (-s, -e) nt (fig) bad luck; **~ haben** to be unlucky; **~ gehabt!** tough (luck)
Pedal (-s, -e) nt pedal
Pediküre (-, -en) f pedicure
Peeling (-s, -s) nt (facial/body) scrub
peinlich adj (unangenehm) embarrassing, awkward; (genau) painstaking; **es war mir sehr ~** I was totally embarrassed
Peitsche (-, -n) f whip
Pelikan (-s, -e) m pelican
Pellkartoffeln pl potatoes pl boiled in their skins
Pelz (-es, -e) m fur; **pelzig** adj (Zunge) furred

pendeln vi (Zug, Bus) to shuttle; (Mensch) to commute; **Pendelverkehr** m shuttle traffic; (für Pendler) commuter traffic; **Pendler(in)** (-s, -) m(f) commuter
penetrant adj sharp; (Mensch) pushy
Penis (-, -se) m penis
Pension f (Geld) pension; (Ruhestand) retirement; (für Gäste) guesthouse, B&B; **pensioniert** adj retired; **Pensionsgast** m guest (in a guesthouse)
Peperoni (-, -) f chilli
per prep +akk by, per; (pro) per; (bis) by
perfekt adj perfect
Pergamentpapier nt grease-proof paper
Periode (-, -n) f period
Perle (-, -n) f (a. fig) pearl
perplex adj dumbfounded
Person (-, -en) f person; **ein Tisch für drei ~en** a table for three; **Personal** (-s) nt staff, personnel; (Bedienung) servants pl; **Personalausweis** m identity card; **Personalien** pl particulars pl; **Personenschaden** m injury to persons; **Personenwaage** f (bathroom) scales pl; **Personenzug** m passenger train; **persönlich** adj personal; (auf Briefen) private ▷ adv personally; (selbst) in person; **Persönlichkeit** f personality
Peru (-s) nt Peru
Perücke (-, -n) f wig
pervers adj perverted
pessimistisch adj pessimistic
Pest (-) f plague
Petersilie f parsley
Petroleum (-s) nt paraffin (Brit), kerosene (US)
Pfad (-(e)s, -e) m path; **Pfadfinder** (-s, -) m boy scout;

Pfadfinderin f girl guide
Pfahl (-(e)s, Pfähle) m post, stake
Pfand (-(e)s, Pfänder) nt security; (Flaschenpfand) deposit; (im Spiel) forfeit; **Pfandflasche** f returnable bottle
Pfanne (-, -n) f (frying) pan
Pfannkuchen m pancake
Pfarrei f parish; **Pfarrer(in)** (-s, -) m(f) priest
Pfau (-(e)s, -en) m peacock
Pfeffer (-s, -) m pepper; **Pfefferkuchen** m gingerbread; **Pfefferminze** (-e) f peppermint; **Pfefferminztee** m peppermint tea; **Pfeffermühle** f pepper mill; **pfeffern** vt to put pepper on/in; **Pfefferstreuer** (-s, -) m pepper pot
Pfeife (-, -n) f whistle; (für Tabak, von Orgel) pipe; **pfeifen** (pfiff, gepfiffen) vt, vi to whistle
Pfeil (-(e)s, -e) m arrow
Pfeiltaste f (Inform) arrow key
Pferd (-(e)s, -e) nt horse; **Pferdeschwanz** m (Frisur) ponytail; **Pferdestall** m stable; **Pferdestärke** f horsepower
pfiff imperf von **pfeifen**
Pfifferling m chanterelle
Pfingsten (-, -) nt Whitsun, Pentecost (US); **Pfingstmontag** m Whit Monday; **Pfingstsonntag** m Whit Sunday, Pentecost (US)
Pfirsich (-s, -e) m peach
Pflanze (-, -n) f plant; **pflanzen** vt to plant; **Pflanzenfett** nt vegetable fat
Pflaster (-s, -) nt (für Wunde) plaster, Band Aid® (US); (Straßenpflaster) road surface, pavement (US)
Pflaume (-, -n) f plum
Pflege (-, -n) f care; (Krankenpflege) nursing; (von Autos, Maschinen) maintenance; **pflegebedürftig** adj in need of

care; **pflegeleicht** adj easy-care; (fig) easy to handle; **pflegen** vt to look after; (Kranke) to nurse; (Beziehungen) to foster; (Fingernägel, Gesicht) to take care of; (Daten) to maintain; **Pflegepersonal** nt nursing staff; **Pflegeversicherung** f long-term care insurance
Pflicht (-, -en) f duty; (Sport) compulsory section; **pflicht-bewusst** adj conscientious; **Pflichtfach** nt (Schule) compulsory subject; **Pflicht-versicherung** f compulsory insurance
pflücken vt to pick
Pforte (-, -n) f gate; **Pförtner(in)** (-s, -) m(f) porter
Pfosten (-s, -) m post
Pfote (-, -n) f paw
pfui interj ugh
Pfund (-(e)s, -e) nt pound
pfuschen vi (fam) to be sloppy
Pfütze (-, -n) f puddle
Phantasie f siehe **Fantasie**; **phantastisch** adj siehe **fantastisch**
Phase (-, -n) f phase
Philippinen pl Philippines pl
Philosophie f philosophy
Photo nt siehe **Foto**
pH-neutral adj pH-balanced; **pH-Wert** m pH-value
Physalis (-, Physalen) f physalis
Physik f physics sing
physisch adj physical
Pianist(in) (-en, -en) m(f) pianist
Pickel (-s, -) m pimple; (Werkzeug) pickaxe; (Berg~) ice-axe
Picknick (-s, -e o -s) nt picnic; **ein ~ machen** to have a picnic
piepsen vi to chirp
piercen vt: **sich die Nase ~ lassen** to have one's nose pierced; **Piercing** (-s) nt (body) piercing
pieseln vi (fam) to pee

P

Pik (-, -) nt (Karten) spades pl
pikant adj spicy
Pilates nt (Sport) Pilates
Pilger(in) m(f) pilgrim;
Pilgerfahrt f pilgrimage
Pille (-, -n) f pill; **sie nimmt die
~** she's on the pill
Pilot(in) (-en, -en) m(f) pilot
Pils (-, -) nt (Pilsner) lager
Pilz (-es, -e) m (essbar) mushroom;
(giftig) toadstool; (Med) fungus
PIN (-, -s) f PIN (number)
pingelig adj (fam) fussy
Pinguin (-s, -e) m penguin
Pinie f pine; **Pinienkern** m pine
nut
pink adj shocking pink
pinkeln vi (fam) to pee
Pinsel (-s, -) m (paint)brush
Pinzette f tweezers pl
Pistazie f pistachio
Piste (-, -n) f (Ski) piste; (Aviat)
runway
Pistole (-, -n) f pistol
Pixel (-s) nt (Inform) pixel
Pizza (-, -s) f pizza; **Pizzaservice**
m pizza delivery service; **Pizzeria**
(-, Pizzerien) f pizzeria
Pkw (-(s), -(s)) m abk =
Personenkraftwagen car
Plakat nt poster
Plakette f (Schildchen) badge;
(Aufkleber) sticker
Plan (-(e)s, Pläne) m plan; (Karte)
map; **planen** vt to plan
Planet (-en, -en) m planet;
Planetarium nt planetarium
planmäßig adj scheduled
Plan(t)schbecken nt paddling
pool; **plan(t)schen** vi to splash
around
Planung f planning
Plastik f sculpture ▷ (-s) nt
plastic; **Plastikfolie** f plastic film;
Plastiktüte f plastic bag
Platin (-s) nt platinum
platsch interj splash

platt adj flat; (fam: überrascht)
flabbergasted; (fig: geistlos) flat,
boring
Platte (-, -n) f (Foto, Tech, Gastr)
plate; (Steinplatte) flag;
(Schallplatte) record;
Plattenspieler m record player
Plattform f platform; **Plattfuß**
m flat foot; (Reifen) flat (tyre)
Platz (-es, Plätze) m place;
(Sitzplatz) seat; (freier Raum) space,
room; (in Stadt) square; (Sportplatz)
playing field; **nehmen Sie ~** please
sit down, take a seat; **ist dieser
~ frei?** is this seat taken?;
Platzanweiser(in) m(f)
usher/usherette
Plätzchen nt spot; (Gebäck)
biscuit
platzen vi to burst; (Bombe) to
explode
Platzkarte f seat reservation;
Platzreservierung f seat
reservation; **Platzverweis** m: **er
erhielt einen ~** he was sent off;
Platzwunde f laceration, cut
plaudern vi to chat, to talk
pleite adj (fam) broke; **Pleite**
(-, -n) f (Bankrott) bankruptcy;
(fam: Reinfall) flop
Plombe (-, -n) f lead seal;
(Zahnplombe) filling; **plombieren**
vt (Zahn) to fill
plötzlich adj sudden ▷ adv suddenly,
all at once
plump adj clumsy; (Hände)
ungainly; (Körper) shapeless
plumps interj thud; (in Flüssigkeit)
plop
Plural (-s, -e) m plural
plus adv plus; **fünf ~ sieben ist
zwölf** five plus seven is (o are)
twelve; **zehn Grad ~** ten degrees
above zero; **Plus** (-, -) nt plus;
(Fin) profit; (Vorteil) advantage
Plüsch (-(e)s, -e) m plush
Pluto (-) m Pluto

PLZ *abk* = **Postleitzahl** postcode (Brit), zip code (US)

Po (-s, -s) m (fam) bottom, bum

Pocken pl smallpox sing

Podcast (-s, -s) m podcast

poetisch adj poetic

Pointe (-, -n) f punch line

Pokal (-s, -e) m goblet; (Sport) cup

pökeln vt to pickle

Pol (-s, -e) m pole

Pole (-n, -n) m Pole; **Polen** (-s) nt Poland

Police (-, -n) f (insurance) policy

polieren vt to polish

Polin f Pole, Polish woman

Politik f politics sing; (eine bestimmte) policy; **Politiker(in)** m(f) politician; **politisch** adj political

Politur f polish

Polizei f police pl; **Polizeibeamte(r)** m, **Polizeibeamtin** f police officer; **polizeilich** adj police; **sie wird ~ gesucht** the police are looking for her; **Polizeirevier** nt, **Polizeiwache** f police station; **Polizeistunde** f closing time; **Polizeiwache** f police station; **Polizist(in)** m(f) policeman/-woman

Pollen (-s, -) m pollen; **Pollenflug** (-s) m pollen count

polnisch adj Polish; **Polnisch** nt Polish

Polo (-s) nt polo; **Polohemd** nt polo shirt

Polster (-s, -) nt cushion; (Polsterung) upholstery; (in Kleidung) padding; (fig: Geld) reserves pl; **Polstergarnitur** f living-room suite; **Polstermöbel** pl upholstered furniture sing; **polstern** vt to upholster; (Kleidung) to pad

Polterabend m party prior to a wedding, at which old crockery is smashed to bring good luck

poltern vi (Krach machen) to crash; (schimpfen) to rant

Polyester (-s, -) m polyester

Polypen pl (Med) adenoids pl

Pommes frites pl chips pl (Brit), French fries pl (US)

Pony (-s, -s) m (Frisur) fringe (Brit), bangs pl (US) ▷ (-s, -s) nt (Pferd) pony

Popcorn (-s) nt popcorn

Popmusik f pop (music)

populär adj popular

Pore (-, -n) f pore

Pornografie f pornography

Porree (-s, -s) m leeks pl; **eine Stange ~** a leek

Portemonnaie, **Portmonee** (-s, -s) nt purse

Portier (-s, -s) m porter

Portion f portion, helping

Porto (-s, -s) nt postage

Portrait, **Porträt** (-s, -s) nt portrait

Portugal (-s) nt Portugal; **Portugiese** (-n, -n) m Portuguese; **Portugiesin** (-, -nen) f Portuguese; **portugiesisch** adj Portuguese; **Portugiesisch** nt Portuguese

Portwein (-s, -e) m port

Porzellan (-s, -e) nt china

Posaune (-, -n) f trombone

Position f position

positiv adj positive

Post® (-, -en) f post office; (Briefe) post (Brit), mail; **Postamt** nt post office; **Postanweisung** f postal order (Brit), money order (US); **Postbank** f German post office bank; **Postbote** m, **-botin** f postman/-woman

Posten (-s, -) m post, position; (Comm) item; (auf Liste) entry

Poster (-s, -) nt poster

Postfach nt post-office box, PO box; **Postkarte** f postcard;

postlagernd adv poste restante;
Postleitzahl f postcode (Brit), zip
code (US)
postmodern adj postmodern
Postsparkasse f post office
savings bank; **Poststempel** m
postmark; **Postweg** m: **auf dem**
~ by mail
Potenz f (Math) power; (eines
Mannes) potency
PR (-, -s) f abk = **Public Relations**
PR
prächtig adj splendid
prahlen vi to boast, to brag
Praktikant(in) m(f) trainee;
Praktikum (-s, Praktika) nt prac-
tical training; **praktisch** adj
practical; **~er Arzt** general
practitioner
Praline f chocolate
Prämie f (bei Versicherung)
premium; (Belohnung) reward; (von
Arbeitgeber) bonus
Präparat nt (Med) medicine; (Bio)
preparation
Präservativ nt condom
Präsident(in) m(f) president
Praxis (-, Praxen) f practice;
(Behandlungsraum) surgery; (von
Anwalt) office; **Praxisgebühr** f
surgery surcharge
präzise adj precise, exact
predigen vt, vi to preach; **Predigt**
(-, -en) f sermon
Preis (-es, -e) m (zu zahlen) price;
(bei Sieg) prize; **den ersten**
~ gewinnen to win first prize;
Preisausschreiben nt
competition
Preiselbeere f cranberry
preisgünstig adj inexpensive;
Preislage f price range; **Preisliste**
f price list; **Preisschild** nt price
tag; **Preisträger(in)** m(f)
prizewinner; **preiswert** adj
inexpensive
Prellung f bruise

Premiere (-, -n) f premiere, first
night
Premierminister(in) m(f) prime
minister, premier
Prepaidhandy nt prepaid
mobile (Brit), prepaid cell phone
(US); **Prepaidkarte** f prepaid
card
Presse (-, -n) f press
pressen vt to press
prickeln vi to tingle
Priester(in) (-s, -) m(f) priest/(woman)
priest
Primel (-, -n) f primrose
primitiv adj primitive
Prinz (-en, -en) m prince;
Prinzessin f princess
Prinzip (-s, -ien) nt principle; **im**
~ basically; aus ~ on principle
Priorität f priority
privat adj private;
Privatfernsehen nt commercial
television; **Privatgrundstück** nt
private property; **privatisieren**
vt to privatize
pro prep +akk per; **5 Euro**
~ Stück/Person 5 euros each/per
person; **Pro** (-s) nt pro
Probe (-, -n) f test; (Teststück)
sample; (Theat) rehearsal;
Probefahrt f test drive; **eine**
~ machen to go for a test drive;
Probezeit f trial period;
probieren vt, vi to try; (Wein,
Speise) to taste, to sample
Problem (-s, -e) nt problem
Produkt (-(e)s, -e) nt product;
Produktion f production;
(produzierte Menge) output;
produzieren vt to produce
Professor(in) (-s, -en) m(f)
professor
Profi (-s, -s) m pro
Profil (-s, -e) nt profile; (von
Reifen, Schuhsohle) tread
Profit (-(e)s, -e) m profit;
profitieren vi to profit (von from)

Prognose (-, -n) f prediction; (Wetter) forecast

Programm (-s, -e) nt programme; (Inform) program; (TV) channel; **Programmheft** nt programme; **programmieren** vt to program; **Programmierer(in)** (-s, -) m(f) programmer; **Programmkino** nt arts (o repertory (US)) cinema

Projekt (-(e)s, -e) nt project

Projektor m projector

Promenade (-, -n) f promenade

Promille (-(s), -) nt (blood) alcohol level; **0,8 ~** 0,08 per cent; **Promillegrenze** f legal alcohol limit

prominent adj prominent; **Prominenz** f VIPs pl, prominent figures pl; (fam: Stars) the glitterati pl

Propeller (-s, -) m propeller

prosit interj cheers

Prospekt (-(e)s, -e) m leaflet, brochure

prost interj cheers

Prostituierte(r) mf prostitute

Protest (-(e)s, -e) m protest

Protestant(in) m(f) Protestant; **protestantisch** adj Protestant

protestieren vi to protest (gegen against)

Prothese (-, -n) f artificial arm/leg; (Gebiss) dentures pl

Protokoll (-s, -e) nt (bei Sitzung) minutes pl; (diplomatisch, Inform) protocol; (bei Polizei) statement

protzen vi to show off; **protzig** adj flashy

Proviant (-s, -e) m provisions pl

Provider (-s, -) m (Inform) (service) provider

Provinz (-, -en) f province

Provision f (Comm) commission

provisorisch adj provisional; **Provisorium** (-s, Provisorien) nt stopgap; (Zahn) temporary filling

provozieren vt to provoke

Prozent (-(e)s, -e) nt per cent

Prozess (-es, -e) m (Vorgang) process; (Jur) trial; (Rechtsfall) (court) case; **prozessieren** vi to go to law (mit against)

Prozession f procession

Prozessor (-s, -en) m (Inform) processor

prüde adj prudish

prüfen vt to test; (nachprüfen) to check; **Prüfung** f (Schule) exam; (Überprüfung) check; **eine ~ machen** (Schule) to take an exam

Prügelei f fight; **prügeln** vt to beat ▷ vr: **sich ~** to fight

PS abk = **Pferdestärke** hp; = **Postskript(um)** PS

pseudo- präf pseudo; **Pseudokrupp** (-s) m (Med) pseudocroup; **Pseudonym** (-s, -e) nt pseudonym

pst interj ssh

Psychiater(in) (-s, -) m(f) psychiatrist; **psychisch** adj psychological; (Krankheit) mental; **Psychoanalyse** f psychoanalysis; **Psychologe** (-n, -n) m, **Psychologin** f psychologist; **Psychologie** f psychology

Psychopharmaka pl mind-affecting drugs pl, psychotropic drugs pl; **psychosomatisch** adj psychosomatic; **Psychoterror** m psychological intimidation; **Psychotherapie** f psychotherapy

Pubertät f puberty

Publikum (-s) nt audience; (Sport) crowd

Pudding (-s, -e o -s) m blancmange

Pudel (-s, -) m poodle

Puder (-s, -) m powder; **Puderzucker** m icing sugar

Puerto Rico (-s) nt Puerto Rico

Pulli (-s, -s) m, **Pullover** (-s, -) m sweater, pullover, jumper (Brit)

Puls (-es, -e) m pulse
Pulver (-s, -) nt powder;
  Pulverkaffee m instant coffee;
  Pulverschnee m powder snow
pummelig adj chubby
Pumpe (-, -n) f pump; **pumpen**
  vt to pump; (fam: verleihen) to lend;
  (fam: sich ausleihen) to borrow
Pumps pl court shoes pl (Brit),
  pumps pl (US)
Punk (-s, -s) m (Musik, Mensch)
  punk
Punkt (-(e)s, -e) m point; (bei
  Muster) dot; (Satzzeichen) full stop
  (Brit), period (US); **~ zwei Uhr** at
  two o'clock sharp
pünktlich adj punctual, on time;
  Pünktlichkeit f punctuality
Punsch (-(e)s, -e) m punch
Pupille (-, -n) f pupil
Puppe (-, -n) f doll
pur adj pure; (völlig) sheer;
  (Whisky) neat
Püree (-s, -s) nt puree;
  (Kartoffelpüree) mashed potatoes pl
Puste (-) f (fam) puff; **außer
  ~ sein** to be puffed
Pustel (-, -n) f pustule; (Pickel)
  pimple; **pusten** vi to blow;
  (keuchen) to puff
Pute (-, -n) f turkey;
  Putenschnitzel nt turkey
  escalope
Putsch (-es, -e) m putsch
Putz (-es) m (Mörtel) plaster
putzen vt to clean; **sich** (dat) **die
  Nase ~** to blow one's nose; **sich**
  (dat) **die Zähne ~** to brush one's
  teeth; **Putzfrau** f cleaner;
  Putzlappen m cloth, **Putzmann**
  m cleaner; **Putzmittel** nt
  cleaning agent, cleaner
Puzzle (-s, -s) nt jigsaw (puzzle)
Pyjama (-s, -s) m pyjamas pl
Pyramide (-, -n) f pyramid
Python (-s, -s) m python

q

Quadrat nt square; **quadratisch**
  adj square; **Quadratmeter** m
  square metre
quaken vi (Frosch) to croak; (Ente)
  to quack
Qual (-, -en) f pain, agony;
  (seelisch) anguish; **quälen** vt to
  torment ▷ vr: **sich ~** to struggle;
  (geistig) to torment oneself;
  Quälerei f torture, torment
qualifizieren vt to qualify;
  (einstufen) to label ▷ vr: **sich ~** to
  qualify
Qualität f quality
Qualle (-, -n) f jellyfish
Qualm (-(e)s) m thick smoke;
  qualmen vt, vi to smoke
Quantität f quantity
Quarantäne (-, -n) f quarantine
Quark (-s) m quark; (fam: Unsinn)
  rubbish
Quartett (-s, -e) nt quartet;
  (Kartenspiel) happy families sing

Quartier (-s, -e) nt accommodation

quasi adv more or less

Quatsch (-es) m (fam) rubbish; **quatschen** vi (fam) to chat

Quecksilber nt mercury

Quelle (-, -n) f spring; (eines Flusses) source

quellen vi to pour

quer adv crossways, diagonally; (rechtwinklig) at right angles; **~ über die Straße** straight across the street; **querfeldein** adv across country; **Querflöte** f flute; **Querschnitt** m cross section; **querschnittsgelähmt** adj paraplegic; **Querstraße** f side street

quetschen vt to squash, to crush; (Med) to bruise; **Quetschung** f bruise

Queue (-s, -s) m (billiard) cue

quietschen vi to squeal; (Tür, Bett) to squeak; (Bremsen) to screech

quitt adj quits, even

Quitte (-, -n) f quince

Quittung f receipt

Quiz (-, -) nt quiz

Quote (-, -n) f rate; (Comm) quota

r

Rabatt (-(e)s, -e) m discount

Rabbi (-(s), -s) m rabbi; **Rabbiner** (-s, -) m rabbi

Rabe (-n, -n) m raven

Rache (-) f revenge, vengeance

Rachen (-s, -) m throat

rächen vt to avenge ▷ vr: **sich ~** to take (one's) revenge (an +dat on)

Rad (-(e)s, Räder) nt wheel; (Fahrrad) bike; **~ fahren** to cycle; **mit dem ~ fahren** to go by bike

Radar (-s) m o nt radar; **Radarfalle** f speed trap; **Radarkontrolle** f radar speed check

radeln vi (fam) to cycle; **Radfahrer(in)** m(f) cyclist; **Radfahrweg** m cycle track (o path)

Radicchio (-s) m (Salatsorte) radicchio

radieren vt to rub out, to erase; **Radiergummi** m rubber (Brit), eraser; **Radierung** f (Kunst) etching

Radieschen nt radish

radikal adj radical

Radio (-s, -s) nt radio; **im ~** on the radio

radioaktiv adj radioactive

Radiologe (-n, -n) m, **Radiologin** f radiologist

Radiorekorder m radio cassette recorder; **Radiosender** m radio station; **Radiowecker** m radio alarm (clock)

Radkappe f (Auto) hub cap

Radler(in) (-s, -) m(f) cyclist

Radler (-s, -) nt ≈ shandy

Radlerhose f cycling shorts pl; **Radrennen** nt cycle racing; (einzelnes Rennen) cycle race; **Radtour** f cycling tour; **Radweg** m cycle track (o path)

raffiniert adj crafty, cunning; (Zucker) refined

Rafting (-s) nt white water rafting

Ragout (-s, -s) nt ragout

Rahm (-s) m cream

rahmen vt to frame; **Rahmen** (-s, -) m frame

Rakete (-, -n) f rocket

rammen vt to ram

Rampe (-, -n) f ramp

ramponieren vt (fam) to damage, to batter

Ramsch (-(e)s, -e) m junk

ran (fam) kontr von **heran**

Rand (-(e)s, Ränder) m edge; (von Brille, Tasse etc) rim; (auf Papier) margin; (Schmutzrand, unter Augen) ring; (fig) verge, brink

randalieren vi to (go on the) rampage; **Randalierer(in)** (-s, -) m(f) hooligan

Randstein m kerb (Brit), curb (US); **Randstreifen** m shoulder

rang imperf von **ringen**

Rang (-(e)s, Ränge) m rank; (in Wettbewerb) place; (Theat) circle

rannte imperf von **rennen**

ranzig adj rancid

Rap (-(s), -s) m (Mus) rap; **rappen** vi (Mus) to rap; **Rapper(in)** (-s, -) m(f) (Mus) rapper

rar adj rare, scarce

rasant adj quick, rapid

rasch adj quick

rascheln vi to rustle

rasen vi (sich schnell bewegen) to race; (toben) to rave; **gegen einen Baum ~** to crash into a tree

Rasen (-s, -) m lawn

rasend adj (vor Wut) furious

Rasenmäher (-s, -) m lawnmower

Rasierapparat m razor; (elektrischer) shaver; **Rasiercreme** f shaving cream; **rasieren** vt to shave ▷ vr: **sich ~** to shave; **Rasierer** m shaver; **Rasiergel** nt shaving gel; **Rasierklinge** f razor blade; **Rasiermesser** nt (cutthroat) razor; **Rasierpinsel** m shaving brush; **Rasierschaum** m shaving foam; **Rasierzeug** nt shaving tackle, shaving equipment

Rasse (-, -n) f race; (Tiere) breed

Rassismus m racism; **Rassist(in)** m(f) racist; **rassistisch** adj racist

Rast (-, -en) f rest, break; **~ machen** to have a rest (o break); **rasten** vi to rest; **Rastplatz** m (Auto) rest area; **Raststätte** f (Auto) service area; (Gaststätte) motorway (Brit) (o highway (US)) restaurant

Rasur f shave

Rat (-(e)s, Ratschläge) m (piece of) advice; **sie hat mir einen ~ gegeben** she gave me some advice; **um ~ fragen** to ask for advice

Rate (-, -n) f instalment; **etw auf ~n kaufen** to buy sth in instalments (Brit), to buy sth on the instalment plan (US)

raten (riet, geraten) vt, vi to guess; (empfehlen) to advise (jdm sb)

Rathaus nt town hall

Ration f ration

ratlos adj at a loss, helpless; **ratsam** adj advisable

Rätsel (-s, -) nt puzzle; (Worträtsel) riddle; **das ist mir ein ~** it's a mystery to me; **rätselhaft** adj mysterious

Ratte (-, -n) f rat

rau adj rough, coarse; (Wetter) harsh

Raub (-(e)s) m robbery; (Beute) loot, booty; **rauben** vt to steal; **jdm etw ~** to rob sb of sth; **Räuber(in)** (-s, -) m(f) robber; **Raubfisch** m predatory fish; **Raubkopie** f pirate copy; **Raubmord** m robbery with murder; **Raubtier** nt predator; **Raubüberfall** m mugging; **Raubvogel** m bird of prey

Rauch (-(e)s) m smoke; (Abgase) fumes pl; **rauchen** vt, vi to smoke; **Raucher(in)** (-s, -) m(f) smoker; **Raucherabteil** nt smoking compartment

Räucherlachs m smoked salmon; **räuchern** vt to smoke

rauchig adj smoky; **Rauchmelder** m smoke detector; **Rauchverbot** nt smoking ban; **hier ist ~** there's no smoking here

rauf (fam) kontr von **herauf**

rauh adj siehe **rau**; **Rauhreif** m siehe **Raureif**

Raum (-(e)s, Räume) m space; (Zimmer, Platz) room; (Gebiet) area

räumen vt to clear; (Wohnung, Platz) to vacate; (wegbringen) to shift, to move; (in Schrank etc) to put away

Raumfähre f space shuttle; **Raumfahrt** f space travel; **Raumschiff** nt spacecraft, spaceship; **Raumsonde** f space probe; **Raumstation** f space station

Raumtemperatur f room temperature

Räumungsverkauf m clearance sale, closing-down sale

Raupe (-, -n) f caterpillar

Raureif m hoarfrost

raus (fam) kontr von **heraus, hinaus**; **~!** (get) out!

Rausch (-(e)s, Räusche) m intoxication; **einen ~ haben/kriegen** to be/get drunk

rauschen vi (Wasser) to rush; (Baum) to rustle; (Radio etc) to hiss; **Rauschgift** nt drug; **Rauschgiftsüchtige(r)** mf drug addict

raus|fliegen irr vi (fam) to be kicked out

raus|halten irr vr (fam) **halt du dich da raus!** you (just) keep out of it

räuspern vr: **sich ~** to clear one's throat

raus|schmeißen irr vt (fam) to throw out

Razzia (-, Razzien) f raid

reagieren vi to react (auf +akk to); **Reaktion** f reaction

real adj real; **realisieren** vt (merken) to realize; (verwirklichen) to implement; **realistisch** adj realistic; **Realität** (-, -en) f reality; **Reality-TV** (-s) nt reality TV

Realschule f ≈ secondary school, junior high (school) (US)

Rebe (-, -n) f vine

rebellieren vi to rebel

Rebhuhn nt partridge

r

rechnen *vt, vi* to calculate; **~ mit**
to expect; (*bauen auf*) to count on
▷ *vr:* **sich ~** to pay off, to turn out
to be profitable; **Rechner** (*-s, -*) *m*
calculator; (*Computer*) computer;
Rechnung *f* calculation(s);
(*Comm*) bill (*Brit*), check (*US*); **die ~,
bitte!** can I have the bill, please?;
das geht auf meine ~ this is on
me

recht *adj* (*richtig, passend*) right;
~ haben to be right; **jdm ~ geben**
to agree with sb; **mir soll's ~ sein**
it's alright by me; **mir ist es ~** I
don't mind ▷ *adv* really, quite;
(*richtig*) right(ly); **ich weiß nicht
~** I don't really know; **es geschieht
ihm ~** it serves him right

Recht (*-(e)s, -e*) *nt* right; (*Jur*)
law

Rechte (*-n, -n*) *f* right-hand side;
(*Hand*) right hand; (*Pol*) right
(wing); **rechte(r, s)** *adj* right;
auf der ~n Seite on the right, on
the right-hand side; **Rechte(s)**
nt right thing; **etwas/nichts ~s**
something/nothing proper

Rechteck (*-s, -e*) *nt* rectangle;
rechteckig *adj* rectangular

rechtfertigen *vt* to justify ▷ *vr:*
sich ~ to justify oneself

rechtlich *adj* legal; **rechtmäßig**
adj legal, lawful

rechts *adv* on the right;
~ abbiegen to turn right; **~ von** to
the right of; **~ oben** at the top
right

Rechtsanwalt *m*, **-anwältin** *f*
lawyer

Rechtschreibung *f* spelling

Rechtshänder(in) (*-s, -*) *m(f)*
right-hander; **rechtsherum** *adv*
to the right, clockwise;
rechtsradikal *adj* (*Pol*) extreme
right-wing

Rechtsschutzversicherung *f*
legal costs insurance

Rechtsverkehr *m* driving on
the right

rechtswidrig *adj* illegal

rechtwinklig *adj* right-angled;
rechtzeitig *adj* timely ▷ *adv* in
time

recycelbar *adj* recyclable;
recyceln *vt* to recycle; **Recycling**
(*-s*) *nt* recycling; **Recyclingpapier**
nt recycled paper

Redakteur(in) *m(f)* editor;
Redaktion *f* editing; (*Leute*)
editorial staff; (*Büro*) editorial
office(s)

Rede (*-, -n*) *f* speech; (*Gespräch*)
talk; **eine ~ halten** to make a
speech; **reden** *vi* to talk, to speak
▷ *vt* to say; (*Unsinn etc*) to talk;
Redewendung *f* idiom;
Redner(in) *m(f)* speaker

reduzieren *vt* to reduce

Referat (*-s, -e*) *nt* paper; **ein
~ halten** to give a paper (*über +akk*
on)

reflektieren *vt* to reflect

Reform (*-, -en*) *f* reform;
Reformhaus *nt* health food
shop; **reformieren** *vt* to
reform

Regal (*-s, -e*) *nt* shelf; (*Möbelstück*)
shelves *pl*

Regel (*-, -n*) *f* rule; (*Med*) period;
regelmäßig *adj* regular; **regeln**
vt to regulate, to control;
(*Angelegenheit*) to settle ▷ *vr:* **sich
von selbst ~** to sort itself out;
Regelung *f* regulation

Regen (*-s, -*) *m* rain;
Regenbogen *m* rainbow;
Regenmantel *m* raincoat;
Regenrinne *f* gutter;
Regenschauer *m* shower;
Regenschirm *m* umbrella;
Regenwald *m* rainforest;
Regenwurm *m* earthworm

Regie *f* direction

regieren *vt, vi* to govern, to rule;

Regierung f government; (von Monarch) reign

Region f region; **regional** adj regional

Regisseur(in) m(f) director

registrieren vt to register; (bemerken) to notice

regnen vi impers to rain; **regnerisch** adj rainy

regulär adj regular; **regulieren** vt to regulate, to adjust

Reh (-(e)s, -e) nt deer; (Fleisch) venison

Rehabilitationszentrum nt (Med) rehabilitation centre

Reibe (-, -n) f, **Reibeisen** nt grater; **reiben** (rieb, gerieben) vt to rub; (Gastr) to grate; **reibungslos** adj smooth

reich adj rich

Reich (-(e)s, -e) nt empire; (eines Königs) kingdom

reichen vi to reach; (genügen) to be enough, to be sufficient (jdm for sb) ▷ vt to hold out; (geben) to pass, to hand; (anbieten) to offer

reichhaltig adj ample, rich; **reichlich** adj (Trinkgeld) generous; (Essen) ample; ~ **Zeit** plenty of time; **Reichtum** (-s, -tümer) m wealth

reif adj ripe; (Mensch, Urteil) mature

Reif (-(e)s) m (Raureif) hoarfrost ▷ (-(e)s, -e) m (Ring) ring, hoop

reifen vi to mature; (Obst) to ripen

Reifen (-s, -) m ring, hoop; (von Auto) tyre; **Reifendruck** m tyre pressure; **Reifenpanne** m puncture; **Reifenwechsel** m tyre change

Reihe (-, -n) f row; (von Tagen etc, fam: Anzahl) series sing; **der** ~ **nach** one after the other; **er ist an der** ~ it's his turn; **Reihenfolge** f order, sequence; **Reihenhaus** nt terraced house (Brit), row house (US)

Reiher (-s, -) m heron

rein (fam) kontr von **herein, hinein** ▷ adj pure; (sauber) clean

Reinfall m (fam) letdown; **rein|fallen** irr vi (fam) **auf etw** (akk) ~ to fall for sth

reinigen vt to clean; **Reinigung** f cleaning; (Geschäft) (dry) cleaner's; **Reinigungsmittel** nt cleaning agent, cleaner

rein|legen vt: **jdn** ~ to take sb for a ride

Reis (-es, -e) m rice

Reise (-, -n) f journey; (auf Schiff) voyage; **Reiseapotheke** f first-aid kit; **Reisebüro** nt travel agent's; **Reisebus** m coach; **Reiseführer(in)** m(f) (Mensch) courier; (Buch) guide(book); **Reisegepäck** nt luggage (Brit), baggage; **Reisegesellschaft** f (Veranstalter) tour operator; **Reisegruppe** f tourist party; (mit Reisebus) coach party; **Reiseleiter(in)** m(f) courier; **reisen** vi to travel; ~ **nach** to go to; **Reisende(r)** mf traveller; **Reisepass** m passport; **Reiseroute** f route, itinerary; **Reiserücktrittversicherung** f holiday cancellation insurance; **Reisescheck** m traveller's cheque; **Reisetasche** f holdall (Brit), carryall (US); **Reiseveranstalter** m tour operator; **Reiseverkehr** m holiday traffic; **Reiseversicherung** f travel insurance; **Reiseziel** nt destination

Reiskocher (-s, -) m rice steamer

reißen (riss, gerissen) vt, vi to tear; (ziehen) to pull, to drag; (Witz) to crack

Reißnagel m drawing pin (*Brit*), thumbtack (*US*); **Reißverschluss** m zip (*Brit*), zipper (*US*); **Reißzwecke** f drawing pin (*Brit*), thumbtack (*US*)

reiten (*ritt, geritten*) vt, vi to ride; **Reiter(in)** m(f) rider; **Reithose** f riding breeches pl; **Reitsport** m riding; **Reitstiefel** m riding boot

Reiz (*-es, -e*) m stimulus; (*angenehm*) charm; (*Verlockung*) attraction; **reizen** vt to stimulate; (*unangenehm*) to annoy; (*verlocken*) to appeal to, to attract; **reizend** adj charming; **Reizgas** nt irritant gas; **Reizung** f irritation

Reklamation f complaint

Reklame (*-, -n*) f advertising; (*Einzelwerbung*) advertisement; (*im Fernsehen*) commercial

reklamieren vi to complain (*wegen* about)

Rekord (*-(e)s, -e*) m record

relativ adj relative ▷ adv relatively

relaxen vi to relax, to chill out

Religion f religion; **religiös** adj religious

Remoulade (*-, -n*) f tartar sauce

Renaissance f renaissance, revival; (*Hist*) Renaissance

Rennbahn f racecourse; (*Auto*) racetrack; **rennen** (*rannte, gerannt*) vt, vi to run; **Rennen** (*-s, -*) nt running; (*Wettbewerb*) race; **Rennfahrer(in)** m(f) racing driver; **Rennrad** nt racing bike; **Rennwagen** m racing car

renommiert adj famous, noted (*wegen, für* for)

renovieren vt to renovate; **Renovierung** f renovation

rentabel adj profitable

Rente (*-, -n*) f pension; **Rentenversicherung** f pension scheme

Rentier nt reindeer

rentieren vr: **sich ~** to pay, to be profitable

Rentner(in) (*-s, -*) m(f) pensioner, senior citizen

Reparatur f repair; **Reparaturwerkstatt** f repair shop; (*Auto*) garage; **reparieren** vt to repair

Reportage f report; **Reporter(in)** (*-s, -*) m(f) reporter

Reptil (*-s, -ien*) nt reptile

Republik f republic

Reservat (*-s, -e*) nt nature reserve; (*für Ureinwohner*) reservation; **Reserve** (*-, -n*) f reserve; **Reservekanister** m spare can; **Reserverad** nt (*Auto*) spare wheel; **reservieren** vt to reserve; **Reservierung** f reservation

resignieren vi to give up; **resigniert** adj resigned

Respekt (*-(e)s*) m respect; **respektieren** vt to respect

Rest (*-(e)s, -e*) m rest, remainder; (*Überreste*) remains pl; **der ~ ist für Sie** keep the change

Restaurant (*-s, -s*) nt restaurant

restaurieren vt to restore

Restbetrag m balance; **restlich** adj remaining; **restlos** adj complete; **Restmüll** m non-recyclable waste

Resultat nt result

retten vt to save, to rescue

Rettich (*-s, -e*) m radish (*large white or red variety*)

Rettung f rescue; (*Hilfe*) help; (*Rettungsdienst*) ambulance service; **Rettungsboot** nt lifeboat; **Rettungshubschrauber** m rescue helicopter; **Rettungsring** m lifebelt, life preserver (*US*); **Rettungswagen** m ambulance

Reue (*-*) f remorse; (*Bedauern*)

regret; **reuen** vt: **es reut ihn** he regrets it

revanchieren vr: **sich ~** (sich rächen) to get one's own back, to get one's revenge; (für Hilfe etc) to return the favour

Revolution f revolution

Rezept (-(e)s, -e) nt (Gastr) recipe; (Med) prescription; **rezeptfrei** adj over-the-counter, non-prescription

Rezeption f (im Hotel) reception

rezeptpflichtig adj available only on prescription

R-Gespräch nt reverse-charge (Brit) (o collect (US)) call

Rhabarber (-s) m rhubarb

Rhein (-s) m Rhine; **Rheinland-Pfalz** (-) nt Rhineland-Palatinate

Rheuma (-s) nt rheumatism

Rhythmus m rhythm

richten vt (lenken) to direct (auf +akk to); (Waffe, Kamera) to point (auf +akk at); (Brief, Anfrage) to address (an +akk to); (einstellen) to adjust; (instand setzen) to repair; (zurechtmachen) to prepare ▷ vr: **sich ~ nach** (Regel etc) to keep to; (Mode, Beispiel) to follow; (abhängen von) to depend on

Richter(in) (-s, -) m(f) judge

Richtgeschwindigkeit f recommended speed

richtig adj right, correct; (echt) proper ▷ adv (fam: sehr) really; **richtig**|**stellen** vt: **etw ~** (berichtigen) to correct sth

Richtlinie f guideline

Richtung f direction; (Tendenz) tendency; **Richtungstaste** f arrow key

rieb imperf von **reiben**

riechen (roch, gerochen) vt, vi to smell; **nach etw ~** to smell of sth; **an etw** (dat) **~** to smell sth

rief imperf von **rufen**

Riegel (-s, -) m bolt; (Gastr) bar

Riemen (-s, -) m strap; (Gürtel) belt

Riese (-n, -n) m giant; **Riesengarnele** f king prawn; **riesengroß** adj gigantic, huge; **Riesenrad** nt big wheel; **riesig** adj enormous, huge

riet imperf von **raten**

Riff (-(e)s, -e) nt reef

Rind (-(e)s, -er) nt cow; (Bulle) bull; (Gastr) beef; **~er** pl cattle pl

Rinde (-, -n) f (Baum) bark; (Käse) rind; (Brot) crust

Rinderbraten m roast beef; **Rinderwahn(sinn)** m mad cow disease; **Rindfleisch** nt beef

Ring (-(e)s, -e) m ring; (Straße) ring road; **Ringbuch** nt ring binder

ringen (rang, gerungen) vi to wrestle; **Ringer(in)** m(f) wrestler; **Ringfinger** m ring finger; **Ringkampf** m wrestling match; **ringsherum** adv round about

Rippe (-, -n) f rib; **Rippenfellentzündung** f pleurisy

Risiko (-s, -s o Risiken) nt risk; **auf eigenes ~** at one's own risk; **riskant** adj risky; **riskieren** vt to risk

riss imperf von **reißen**

Riss (-es, -e) m tear; (in Mauer, Tasse etc) crack; **rissig** adj cracked; (Haut) chapped

ritt imperf von **reiten**

Ritter (-s, -) m knight

Rivale (-n, -n) m, **Rivalin** f rival

Rizinusöl nt castor oil

Robbe (-, -n) f seal

Roboter (-s, -) m robot

robust adj robust

roch imperf von **riechen**

Rock (-(e)s, Röcke) m skirt

Rockband f (Musikgruppe) rock band; **Rockmusik** f rock (music)

Rodelbahn f toboggan run;
rodeln vi to toboggan
Roggen (-s, -) m rye;
Roggenbrot nt rye bread
roh adj raw; (Mensch) coarse,
crude; **Rohkost** f raw vegetables
and fruit pl
Rohr (-(e)s, -e) nt pipe; (Bot) cane;
(Schilf) reed; **Röhre** (-, -n) f tube;
(Leitung) pipe; (Elek) valve;
(Backröhre) oven; **Rohrzucker** m
cane sugar
Rohstoff m raw material
Rokoko (-s) nt rococo
Rollbrett nt skateboard
Rolle (-, -n) f (etw
Zusammengerolltes) roll; (Theat) role
rollen vt, vi to roll
Roller (-s, -) m scooter
Rollerblades® pl Rollerblades®
pl; **Rollerskates** pl roller skates pl
Rollkragenpullover m polo-
neck (Brit) (o turtleneck (US))
sweater; **Rollladen** m, **Rollo**
(-s, -s) m (roller) shutters pl;
Rollschuh m roller skate;
Rollstuhl m wheelchair;
rollstuhlgerecht adj suitable
for wheelchairs; **Rolltreppe** f
escalator
Roman (-s, -e) m novel
Romantik f romance;
romantisch adj romantic
römisch-katholisch adj Roman
Catholic
röntgen vt to X-ray;
Röntgenaufnahme f,
Röntgenbild nt X-ray;
Röntgenstrahlen pl X-rays pl
rosa adj inv pink
Rose (-, -n) f rose
Rosenkohl m (Brussels) sprouts
pl
Rosé(wein) m rosé (wine)
rosig adj rosy
Rosine f raisin
Rosmarin (-s) m rosemary

Rosskastanie f horse chestnut
Rost (-(e)s, -e) m rust; (zum Braten)
grill, gridiron; **Rostbratwurst** f
grilled sausage; **rosten** vi to
rust; **rösten** vt to roast, to grill;
(Brot) to toast; **rostfrei** adj
rustproof; (Stahl) stainless; **rostig**
adj rusty; **Rostschutz** m
rustproofing
rot adj red; **~ werden** to blush;
Rote Karte red card; **Rote Bete**
beetroot; **bei Rot über die Ampel
fahren** to jump the lights; **das
Rote Kreuz** the Red Cross
Röteln pl German measles sing
röten vt to redden ▷ vr: **sich ~** to
redden
rothaarig adj red-haired
rotieren vi to rotate; **am
Rotieren sein** (fam) to be rushing
around like a mad thing
Rotkehlchen nt robin; **Rotkohl**
m, **Rotkraut** nt red cabbage;
Rotlichtviertel nt red-light
district; **Rotwein** m red wine
Rouge (-s, -s) nt rouge
Route (-, -n) f route
Routine f experience; (Trott)
routine
Rubbellos nt scratchcard;
rubbeln vt to rub
Rübe (-, -n) f turnip; **Gelbe
~** carrot; **Rote ~** beetroot
rüber (fam) kontr von **herüber,
hinüber**
rückbestätigen vt (Flug etc) to
reconfirm
rücken vt, vi to move; **könntest
du ein bisschen ~?** could you
move over a bit?
Rücken (-s, -) m back;
Rückenlehne f back(rest);
Rückenmark nt spinal cord;
Rückenschmerzen pl backache
sing; **Rückenschwimmen** (-s) nt
backstroke; **Rückenwind** m
tailwind

Rückerstattung f refund;
Rückfahrkarte f return ticket
(Brit), round-trip ticket (US);
Rückfahrt f return journey;
Rückfall m relapse; **Rückflug** m
return flight; **Rückgabe** f return;
rückgängig adj: **etw ~ machen**
to cancel sth; **Rückgrat** (-(e)s, -e)
nt spine, backbone; **Rückkehr**
(-, -en) f return; **Rücklicht** nt
rear light; **Rückreise** f return
journey; **auf der ~** on the way
back

Rucksack m rucksack, backpack;
Rucksacktourist(in) m(f)
backpacker

Rückschritt m step back;
Rückseite f back; (hinterer Teil)
rear; **siehe ~** see overleaf;
Rücksicht f consideration;
~ nehmen auf (+akk) to show
consideration for; **rücksichtslos**
adj inconsiderate; (Fahren)
reckless; (unbarmherzig) ruthless;
rücksichtsvoll adj considerate;
Rücksitz m back seat;
Rückspiegel m (Auto) rear-view
mirror; **Rückstand** m: **sie sind
zwei Tore im ~** they're two goals
down; **im ~ sein mit** (Arbeit, Miete)
to be behind with; **Rücktaste** f
backspace key; **Rückvergütung**
f refund; **rückwärts** adv
backwards, back; **Rückwärtsgang** m (Auto) reverse (gear);
Rückweg m return journey, way
back; **Rückzahlung** f repayment

Ruder (-s, -) nt oar; (Steuer)
rudder; **Ruderboot** nt rowing
boat (Brit), rowboat (US); **rudern**
vt, vi to row

Ruf (-(e)s, -e) m call, cry; (Ansehen)
reputation; **rufen** (rief, gerufen) vt,
vi to call; (schreien) to cry;
Rufnummer f telephone number

Ruhe (-) f rest; (Ungestörtheit)
peace, quiet; (Gelassenheit, Stille)
calm; (Schweigen) silence; **lass
mich in ~!** leave me alone; **ruhen**
vi to rest; **Ruhestand** m
retirement; **im ~ sein** to be retired;
Ruhestörung f disturbance of
the peace; **Ruhetag** m closing
day; **montags ~ haben** to be
closed on Mondays

ruhig adj quiet; (bewegungslos)
still; (Hand) steady; (gelassen) calm

Ruhm (-(e)s) m fame, glory

Rührei nt scrambled egg(s);
rühren vt to move; (umrühren) to
stir ▷ vr: **sich ~** to move; (sich
bemerkbar machen) to say
something; **rührend** adj
touching, moving; **Rührung** f
emotion

Ruine (-, -n) f ruin; **ruinieren** vt
to ruin

rülpsen vi to burp, to belch

rum (fam) kontr von **herum**

Rum (-s, -s) m rum

Rumänien (-s) nt Romania

Rummel (-s) m (Trubel) hustle
and bustle; (Jahrmarkt) fair;
(Medienrummel) hype;
Rummelplatz m fairground

rumoren vi: **es rumort in
meinem Bauch/Kopf** my
stomach is rumbling/my head is
spinning

Rumpf (-(e)s, Rümpfe) m (Anat)
trunk; (Aviat) fuselage; (Naut)
hull

rümpfen vt: **die Nase ~** to turn
one's nose up (über at)

Rumpsteak nt rump steak

rund adj round ▷ adv (etwa)
around; **~ um etw** (a)round sth;
Runde (-, -n) f round; (in Rennen)
lap; **Rundfahrt** f tour (durch of);
Rundfunk m broadcasting;
(Rundfunkanstalt) broadcasting
service; **im ~** on the radio;
Rundgang m tour (durch of); (von
Wächter) round

r

rundlich *adj* plump; **Rundreise**
f tour (*durch* of)
runter (*fam*) *kontr von* **herunter,
hinunter**; **runterscrollen** *vt*
(*Inform*) to scroll down
runzeln *vt*: **die Stirn ~** to frown;
runzelig *adj* wrinkled
ruppig *adj* gruff
Rüsche (-, -n) *f* frill
Ruß (-es) *m* soot
Russe (-n, -n) *m* Russian
Rüssel (-s, -) *m* (*Elefant*) trunk;
(*Schwein*) snout
Russin *f* Russian; **russisch** *adj*
Russian; **Russisch** *nt* Russian;
Russland *nt* Russia
Rüstung *f* (*mit Waffen*) arming;
(*Ritterrüstung*) armour; (*Waffen*)
armaments *pl*
Rutsch (-(e)s, -e) *m*: **guten ~ (ins
neue Jahr)!** Happy New Year;
Rutschbahn *f*, **Rutsche** *f* slide;
rutschen *vi* to slide; (*ausrutschen*)
to slip; **rutschig** *adj* slippery
rütteln *vt, vi* to shake

S

S *abk* = **Süd** S
s. *abk* = **siehe** see; = **Seite** p.
Saal (-(e)s, *Säle*) *m* hall; (*für
Sitzungen*) room
Saarland *nt* Saarland
sabotieren *vt* to sabotage
Sache (-, -n) *f* thing;
(*Angelegenheit*) affair, business;
(*Frage*) matter; **bei der ~ bleiben**
to keep to the point; **sachkundig**
adj competent; **Sachlage** *f*
situation; **sachlich** *adj* (*objektiv*)
objective; (*nüchtern*)
matter-of-fact; (*inhaltlich*) factual;
sächlich *adj* (*Ling*) neuter;
Sachschaden *m* material
damage
Sachsen (-s) *nt* Saxony;
Sachsen-Anhalt (-s) *nt*
Saxony-Anhalt
sacht(e) *adv* softly, gently
Sachverständige(r) *mf* expert
Sack (-(e)s, *Säcke*) *m* sack; (*pej*:

Mensch) bastard, bugger;
Sackgasse f dead end, cul-de-sac
Safe (-s, -s) m safe
Safer Sex m safe sex
Safran (-s, -e) m saffron
Saft (-(e)s, Säfte) m juice; **saftig** adj juicy
Sage (-, -n) f legend
Säge (-, -n) f saw; **Sägemehl** nt sawdust
sagen vt, vi to say (*jdm* to sb), to tell (*jdm* sb); **wie sagt man ... auf Englisch?** what's ... in English?
sägen vt, vi to saw
sagenhaft adj legendary; (*fam: großartig*) fantastic
sah imperf von **sehen**
Sahne (-) f cream
Saison (-, -s) f season; **außerhalb der ~** out of season
Saite (-, -n) f string
Sakko (-s, -s) nt jacket
Salami (-, -s) f salami
Salat (-(e)s, -e) m salad; (*Kopfsalat*) lettuce; **Salatbar** f salad bar; **Salatschüssel** f salad bowl; **Salatsoße** f salad dressing
Salbe (-, -n) f ointment
Salbei (-s) m sage
Salmonellenvergiftung f salmonella (poisoning)
salopp adj (*Kleidung*) casual; (*Sprache*) slangy
Salsamusik f salsa (music)
Salto (-s, -s) m somersault
Salz (-es, -e) nt salt; **salzarm** adj low-salt; **salzen** (*salzte, gesalzen*) vt to salt; **Salzgurke** f pickled gherkin; **Salzhering** m pickled herring; **salzig** adj salty; **Salzkartoffeln** pl boiled potatoes pl; **Salzstange** f pretzel stick; **Salzstreuer** m salt cellar (*Brit*) (o shaker (*US*)); **Salzwasser** nt salt water

Samba (-, -s) f samba
Samen (-s, -) m seed; (*Sperma*) sperm
sammeln vt to collect; **Sammler(in)** m(f) collector; **Sammlung** f collection; (*Ansammlung, Konzentration*) concentration
Samstag m Saturday; *siehe auch* **Mittwoch**; **samstags** adv on Saturdays; *siehe auch* **mittwochs**
samt prep +dat (along) with, together with
Samt (-(e)s, -e) m velvet
sämtliche(r, s) adj all (the)
Sanatorium (-s, Sanatorien) nt sanatorium (*Brit*), sanitarium (*US*)
Sand (-(e)s, -e) m sand
Sandale (-, -n) f sandal
sandig adj sandy; **Sandkasten** m sandpit (*Brit*), sandbox (*US*); **Sandpapier** nt sandpaper; **Sandstrand** m sandy beach
sandte imperf von **senden**
sanft adj soft, gentle
sang imperf von **singen**; **Sänger(in)** (-s, -) m(f) singer
Sangria (-, -s) f sangria
sanieren vt to redevelop; (*Gebäude*) to renovate; (*Betrieb*) to restore to profitability
sanitär adj sanitary; **~e Anlagen** pl sanitation
Sanitäter(in) (-s, -) m(f) ambulance man/woman, paramedic
sank imperf von **sinken**
Sankt Gallen (-s) nt St Gallen
Saphir (-s, -e) m sapphire
Sardelle f anchovy
Sardine f sardine
Sarg (-(e)s, Särge) m coffin
saß imperf von **sitzen**
Satellit (-en, -en) m satellite; **Satellitenfernsehen** nt satellite TV; **Satellitenschüssel** f (*fam*) satellite dish
Satire (-, -n) f satire (*auf* +akk on)

satt *adj* full; (*Farbe*) rich, deep;
~ sein (*gesättigt*) to be full;
~ machen to be filling; **jdn/etw**
~ sein to be fed up with sb/sth
Sattel (*-s, Sättel*) *m* saddle
satt|haben *irr vt*: **jdn/etw**
~ (*nicht mehr mögen*) to be fed up
with sb/sth
Saturn (*-s*) *m* Saturn
Satz (*-es, Sätze*) *m* (*Ling*) sentence;
(*Mus*) movement; (*Tennis*) set;
(*Kaffee*) grounds *pl*; (*Comm*) rate;
(*Sprung*) jump; (*Comm*) rate
Satzzeichen *nt* punctuation
mark
Sau (*-, Säue*) *f* sow; (*pej: Mensch*)
dirty bugger
sauber *adj* clean; (*ironisch*) fine;
~ machen to clean; **Sauberkeit** *f*
cleanness; (*von Person*) cleanliness;
säubern *vt* to clean
saublöd *adj* (*fam*) really stupid,
dumb
Sauce (*-, -n*) *f* sauce; (*zu Braten*)
gravy
Saudi-Arabien (*-s*) *nt* Saudi
Arabia
sauer *adj* sour; (*Chem*) acid; (*fam:*
verärgert) cross; **saurer Regen** acid
rain; **Sauerkirsche** *f* sour
cherry; **Sauerkraut** *nt*
sauerkraut; **säuerlich** *adj*
slighthly sour; **Sauermilch** *f*
sour milk; **Sauerrahm** *m* sour
cream; **Sauerstoff** *m* oxygen
saufen (*soff, gesoffen*) *vt* to drink;
(*fam: Mensch*) to knock back ▷ *vi*
to drink; (*fam: Mensch*) to booze
saugen (*sog o saugte, gesogen o*
gesaugt) *vt, vi* to suck; (*mit*
Staubsauger) to vacuum, to hoover
(*Brit*); **Sauger** (*-s, -*) *m* (*auf Flasche*)
teat; **Säugetier** *nt* mammal;
Säugling *m* infant, baby
Säule (*-, -n*) *f* column, pillar
Saum (*-s, Säume*) *m* hem; (*Naht*)
seam

Sauna (*-, -s*) *f* sauna
Säure (*-, -n*) *f* acid
sausen *vi* (*Ohren*) to buzz; (*Wind*)
to howl; (*Mensch*) to rush
Saustall *m* pigsty; **Sauwetter**
nt: **was für ein ~** (*fam*) what lousy
weather
Saxophon (*-s, -e*) *nt* saxophone
S-Bahn *f* suburban railway;
S-Bahn-Haltestelle *f*, **S-Bahnhof**
m suburban (train) station
scannen *vt* to scan; **Scanner**
(*-s, -*) *m* scanner
schäbig *adj* shabby
Schach (*-s, -s*) *nt* chess; (*Stellung*)
check; **Schachbrett** *nt*
chessboard; **Schachfigur** *f*
chess piece; **schachmatt** *adj*
checkmate
Schacht (*-(e)s, Schächte*) *m* shaft
Schachtel (*-, -n*) *f* box
schade *interj* what a pity
Schädel (*-s, -*) *m* skull;
Schädelbruch *m* fractured skull
schaden *vi* to damage, to harm
(*jdm sb*); **das schadet nichts** it
won't do any harm; **Schaden**
(*-s, Schäden*) *m* damage;
(*Verletzung*) injury; (*Nachteil*)
disadvantage; **einen**
~ verursachen to cause damage;
Schadenersatz *m* compensation, damages *pl*; **schadhaft** *adj*
faulty; (*beschädigt*) damaged;
schädigen *vt* to damage; (*jdn*) to
do harm to, to harm; **schädlich**
adj harmful (*für to*); **Schadstoff**
m harmful substance;
schadstoffarm *adj* low-emission
Schaf (*-(e)s, -e*) *nt* sheep;
Schafbock *m* ram; **Schäfer** (*-s, -*)
m shepherd; **Schäferhund** *m*
Alsatian (*Brit*), German shepherd;
Schäferin *f* shepherdess
schaffen (*schuf, geschaffen*) *vt* to
create; (*Platz*) to make ▷ *vt*
(*erreichen*) to manage, to do;

(*erledigen*) to finish; (*Prüfung*) to pass; (*transportieren*) to take; **jdm zu ~ machen** to cause sb trouble

Schaffner(in) (*-s, -*) *m(f)* (*in Bus*) conductor/conductress; (*Eisenb*) guard

Schafskäse *m* sheep's (milk) cheese

schal *adj* (*Getränk*) flat

Schal (*-s, -e o -s*) *m* scarf

Schälchen *nt* (small) bowl

Schale (*-, -n*) *f* skin; (*abgeschält*) peel; (*Nuss, Muschel, Ei*) shell; (*Geschirr*) bowl, dish

schälen *vt* to peel; (*Tomate, Mandel*) to skin; (*Erbsen, Eier, Nüsse*) to shell; (*Getreide*) to husk ▷ *vr*: **sich ~** to peel

Schall (*-(e)s, -e*) *m* sound; **Schalldämpfer** (*-s, -*) *m* (*Auto*) silencer (*Brit*), muffler (*US*); **Schallplatte** *f* record

Schalotte (*-, -n*) *f* shallot

schalten *vt* to switch ▷ *vi* (*Auto*) to change gear; (*fam: begreifen*) to catch on; **Schalter** (*-s, -*) *m* (*auf Post, Bank*) counter; (*an Gerät*) switch; **Schalterhalle** *f* main hall; **Schalteröffnungszeiten** *pl* business hours *pl*

Schaltfläche *f* (*Inform*) button; **Schalthebel** *m* gear lever (*Brit*) (*o* shift (*US*)); **Schaltjahr** *nt* leap year; **Schaltknüppel** *m* gear lever (*Brit*) (*o* shift (*US*)); **Schaltung** *f* gear change (*Brit*), gearshift (*US*)

Scham (*-*) *f* shame; (*Schamgefühl*) modesty; **schämen** *vr*: **sich ~** to be ashamed

Schande (*-*) *f* disgrace

Schanze (*-, -n*) *f* ski jump

Schar (*-, -en*) *f* (*von Vögeln*) flock; (*Menge*) crowd; **in ~en** in droves

scharf *adj* (*Messer, Kritik*) sharp; (*Essen*) hot; **auf etw** (*akk*) **~ sein** (*fam*) to be keen on sth

Schärfe (*-, -n*) *f* sharpness; (*Strenge*) rigour; (*Foto*) focus

Scharlach (*-s*) *m* (*Med*) scarlet fever

Scharnier (*-s, -e*) *nt* hinge

Schaschlik (*-s, -s*) *m o nt* (shish) kebab

Schatten (*-s, -*) *m* shadow; **30 Grad im ~** 30 degrees in the shade; **schattig** *adj* shady

Schatz (*-es, Schätze*) *m* treasure; (*Mensch*) love

schätzen *vt* (*abschätzen*) to estimate; (*Gegenstand*) to value; (*würdigen*) to value, to esteem; (*vermuten*) to reckon; **Schätzung** *f* estimate; (*das Schätzen*) estimation; (*von Wertgegenstand*) valuation; **schätzungsweise** *adv* roughly, approximately

Schau (*-, -en*) *f* show; (*Ausstellung*) exhibition

schauen *vi* to look; **ich schau mal, ob ...** I'll go and have a look whether ...; **schau, dass ...** see (to it) that ...

Schauer (*-s, -*) *m* (*Regen*) shower; (*Schreck*) shudder

Schaufel (*-, -n*) *f* shovel; **~ und Besen** dustpan and brush; **schaufeln** *vt* to shovel; **Schnee ~** to clear the snow away

Schaufenster *nt* shop window; **Schaufensterbummel** *m* window-shopping expedition

Schaukel (*-, -n*) *f* swing; **schaukeln** *vi* to rock; (*mit Schaukel*) to swing

Schaulustige(r) *mf* gawper (*Brit*), rubbernecker (*US*)

Schaum (*-(e)s, Schäume*) *m* foam; (*Seifenschaum*) lather; (*Bierschaum*) froth; **Schaumbad** *nt* bubble bath; **schäumen** *vi* to foam; **Schaumfestiger** (*-s, -*) *m* styling mousse; **Schaumgummi** *m*

foam (rubber); **Schaumwein** *m* sparkling wine

Schauplatz *m* scene; **Schauspiel** *nt* spectacle; (*Theat*) play; **Schauspieler(in)** *m(f)* actor/actress

Scheck (*-s, -s*) *m* cheque; **Scheckheft** *nt* chequebook; **Scheckkarte** *f* cheque card

Scheibe (*-, -n*) *f* disc; (*von Brot, Käse etc*) slice; (*Glasscheibe*) pane; **Scheibenbremse** *f* (*Auto*) disc brake; **Scheibenwaschanlage** *f* (*Auto*) windscreen (*Brit*) (*o* windshield (*US*)) washer unit; **Scheibenwischer** (*-s, -*) *m* (*Auto*) windscreen (*Brit*) (*o* windshield (*US*)) wiper

Scheich (*-s, -s*) *m* sheik(h)

Scheide (*-, -n*) *f* (*Anat*) vagina

scheiden (*schied, geschieden*) *vt* (*trennen*) to separate; (*Ehe*) to dissolve; **sich ~ lassen** to get a divorce; **sie hat sich von ihm ~ lassen** she divorced him; **Scheidung** *f* divorce

Schein (*-(e)s, -e*) *m* light; (*Anschein*) appearance; (*Geld*) (bank)note; **scheinbar** *adj* apparent; **scheinen** (*schien, geschienen*) *vi* (*Sonne*) to shine; (*den Anschein haben*) to seem; **Scheinwerfer** (*-s, -*) *m* floodlight; (*Theat*) spotlight; (*Auto*) headlight

Scheiß- *in zW* (*vulg*) damned, bloody (*Brit*); **Scheiße** (*-*) *f* (*vulg*) shit, crap; **scheißegal** *adj* (*vulg*) **das ist mir ~** I don't give a damn (*o* toss); **scheißen** (*schiss, geschissen*) *vi* (*vulg*) to shit

Scheitel (*-s, -*) *m* parting (*Brit*), part (*US*)

scheitern *vi* to fail (*an +dat* because of)

Schellfisch *m* haddock

Schema (*-s, -s o Schemata*) *nt*

scheme, plan; (*Darstellung*) diagram

Schenkel (*-s, -*) *m* thigh

schenken *vt* to give; **er hat es mir geschenkt** he gave it to me (as a present); **sich** (*dat*) **etw ~** (*fam: weglassen*) to skip sth

Scherbe (*-, -n*) *f* broken piece, fragment

Schere (*-, -n*) *f* scissors *pl*; (*groß*) shears *pl*; **eine ~** a pair of scissors/shears

Scherz (*-es, -e*) *m* joke

scheu *adj* shy

scheuen *vr* **sich ~ vor** (*+dat*) to be afraid of, to shrink from ▷ *vt* to shun ▷ *vi* (*Pferd*) to shy

scheuern *vt* to scrub; **jdm eine ~** (*fam*) to slap sb in the face

Scheune (*-, -n*) *f* barn

scheußlich *adj* dreadful

Schi (*-s, -er*) *m siehe* **Ski**

Schicht (*-, -en*) *f* layer; (*in Gesellschaft*) class; (*in Fabrik etc*) shift

schick *adj* stylish, chic

schicken *vt* to send ▷ *vr*: **sich ~** (*sich beeilen*) to hurry up

Schickimicki (*-(s), -s*) *m* (*fam*) trendy

Schicksal (*-s, -e*) *nt* fate

Schiebedach *nt* (*Auto*) sunroof; **schieben** (*schob, geschoben*) *vt, vi* to push; **die Schuld auf jdn ~** to put the blame on sb; **Schiebetür** *f* sliding door

schied *imperf von* **scheiden**

Schiedsrichter(in) *m(f)* referee; (*Tennis*) umpire; (*Schlichter*) arbitrator

schief *adj* crooked; (*Blick*) funny ▷ *adv* crooked(ly); **schief|gehen** *irr vi* (*fam: misslingen*) to go wrong

schielen *vi* to squint

schien *imperf von* **scheinen**

Schienbein *nt* shin

Schiene (*-, -n*) *f* rail; (*Med*) splint

schier adj pure; (fig) sheer ▷ adv nearly, almost

schießen (schoss, geschossen) vt to shoot; (Ball) to kick; (Tor) to score; (Foto) to take ▷ vi to shoot (auf +akk at)

Schiff (-(e)s, -e) nt ship; (in Kirche) nave; **Schifffahrt** f shipping; **Schiffsreise** f voyage

schikanieren vt to harass; (Schule) to bully

Schild (-(e)s, -e) m (Schutz) shield ▷ (-(e)s, -er) nt sign; **was steht auf dem ~?** what does the sign say?

Schilddrüse f thyroid gland

schildern vt to describe

Schildkröte f tortoise; (Wasserschildkröte) turtle

Schimmel (-s, -) m mould; (Pferd) white horse; **schimmeln** vi to go mouldy

schimpfen vt to tell off ▷ vi (sich beklagen) to complain; **mit jdm ~** to tell sb off; **Schimpfwort** nt swearword

Schinken (-s, -) m ham

Schirm (-(e)s, -e) m (Regenschirm) umbrella; (Sonnenschirm) parasol, sunshade

schiss imperf von **scheißen**

Schlacht (-, -en) f battle; **schlachten** vt to slaughter; **Schlachter(in)** (-s, -) m(f) butcher

Schlaf (-(e)s) m sleep; **Schlafanzug** m pyjamas pl; **Schlafcouch** f bed settee

Schläfe (-, -n) f temple

schlafen (schlief, geschlafen) vi to sleep; **schlaf gut!** sleep well; **hast du gut geschlafen?** did you sleep all right?; **er schläft noch** he's still asleep; **~ gehen** to go to bed

schlaff adj slack; (kraftlos) limp; (erschöpft) exhausted

Schlafgelegenheit f place to sleep; **Schlaflosigkeit** f

sleeplessness; **Schlafmittel** nt sleeping pill; **schläfrig** adj sleepy

Schlafsaal m dormitory; **Schlafsack** m sleeping bag; **Schlaftablette** f sleeping pill; **er ist eine richtige ~** (fam: langweilig) he's such a bore; **Schlafwagen** m sleeping car, sleeper; **Schlafzimmer** nt bedroom

Schlag (-(e)s, Schläge) m blow; (Puls) beat; (Elek) shock; (fam: Portion) helping; (Art) kind, type; **Schlagader** f artery; **Schlaganfall** m (Med) stroke; **schlagartig** adj sudden

schlagen (schlug, geschlagen) vt to hit; (besiegen) to beat; (Sahne) to whip; **jdn zu Boden ~** to knock sb down ▷ vi (Herz) to beat; (Uhr) to strike; **mit dem Kopf gegen etw ~** to bang one's head against sth ▷ vr: **sich ~** to fight

Schläger (-s, -) m (Sport) bat; (Tennis) racket; (Golf) (golf) club; (Hockey) hockey stick; (Mensch) brawler; **Schlägerei** f fight, brawl

schlagfertig adj quick-witted; **Schlagloch** nt pothole; **Schlagsahne** f whipping cream; (geschlagen) whipped cream; **Schlagzeile** f headline; **Schlagzeug** nt drums pl; (in Orchester) percussion

Schlamm (-(e)s, -e) m mud

schlampig adj (fam) sloppy

schlang imperf von **schlingen**

Schlange (-, -n) f snake; (von Menschen) queue (Brit), line (US); **~ stehen** to queue (Brit), to stand in line (US); **Schlangenlinie** f wavy line; **in ~n fahren** to swerve about

schlank adj slim

schlapp adj limp; (locker) slack

Schlappe (-, -n) f (fam) setback

schlau adj clever, smart; (raffiniert) crafty, cunning

Schlauch (-(e)s, Schläuche) m hose; (in Reifen) inner tube; **Schlauchboot** nt rubber dinghy

schlecht adj bad; **mir ist ~** I feel sick; **die Milch ist ~** the milk has gone off ▷ adv badly; **es geht ihm ~** he's having a hard time; (gesundheitlich) he's not feeling well; (finanziell) he's pretty hard up; **schlecht|machen** vt: **jdn ~** (herabsetzen) to run sb down

schleichen (schlich, geschlichen) vi to creep

Schleier (-s, -) m veil

Schleife (-, -n) f (Inform, Aviat, Elek) loop; (Band) bow

schleifen (ziehen, schleppen) to drag ▷ (schliff, geschliffen) vt (schärfen) to grind; (Edelstein) to cut

Schleim (-(e)s, -e) m slime; (Med) mucus; **Schleimer** (-s, -) m (fam) creep; **Schleimhaut** f mucous membrane

schlendern vi to stroll

schleppen vt to drag; (Auto, Schiff) to tow; (tragen) to lug; **Schlepplift** m ski tow

Schleswig-Holstein (-s) nt Schleswig-Holstein

Schleuder (-, -n) f catapult; (für Wäsche) spin-dryer; **schleudern** vt to hurl; (Wäsche) to spin-dry ▷ vi (Auto) to skid; **Schleudersitz** m ejector seat

schlich imperf von **schleichen**

schlicht adj simple, plain

schlichten vt (Streit) to settle

schlief imperf von **schlafen**

schließen (schloss, geschlossen) vt, vi to close, to shut; (beenden) to close; (Freundschaft, Ehe) to enter into; (folgern) to infer (aus from) ▷ vr: **sich ~** to close, to shut; **Schließfach** nt locker

schließlich adv finally; (schließlich doch) after all

schliff imperf von **schleifen**

schlimm adj bad; **schlimmer** adj worse; **schlimmste(r, s)** adj worst; **schlimmstenfalls** adv at (the) worst

Schlinge (-, -n) f loop; (Med) sling

Schlips (-es, -e) m tie

Schlitten (-s, -) m sledge, toboggan; (mit Pferden) sleigh; **Schlittenfahren** (-s) nt tobogganing

Schlittschuh m ice skate; **~ laufen** to ice-skate

Schlitz (-es, -e) m slit; (für Münze) slot; (an Hose) flies pl

schloss imperf von **schließen**

Schloss (-es, Schlösser) nt lock; (Burg) castle

Schlosser(in) m(f) mechanic

Schlucht (-, -en) f gorge, ravine

schluchzen vi to sob

Schluck (-(e)s, -e) m swallow; **Schluckauf** (-s) m hiccups pl; **schlucken** vt, vi to swallow

schludern vi (fam) to do sloppy work

schlug imperf von **schlagen**

Schlüpfer (-s, -) m panties pl

schlürfen vt, vi to slurp

Schluss (-es, Schlüsse) m end; (Schlussfolgerung) conclusion; **am ~** at the end; **mit jdm ~ machen** to finish (o split up) with sb

Schlüssel (-s, -) m (a. fig) key; **Schlüsselbein** nt collarbone; **Schlüsselbund** m bunch of keys; **Schlüsseldienst** m key-cutting service; **Schlüsselloch** nt keyhole

Schlussfolgerung f conclusion; **Schlusslicht** nt tail-light; (fig) tail-ender; **Schlussverkauf** m clearance sale

schmächtig adj frail

schmal adj narrow; (Mensch, Buch etc) slim; (karg) meagre

Schmalz (-es, -e) nt dripping, lard; (fig: Sentimentalitäten) schmaltz
schmatzen vi to eat noisily
schmecken vt, vi to taste (nach of); **es schmeckt ihm** he likes it; **lass es dir ~!** bon appétit
Schmeichelei f flattery; **schmeichelhaft** adj flattering; **schmeicheln** vi: **jdm ~** to flatter sb
schmeißen (schmiss, geschmissen) vt (fam) to chuck, to throw
schmelzen (schmolz, geschmolzen) vt, vi to melt; (Metall, Erz) to smelt; **Schmelzkäse** m cheese spread
Schmerz (-es, -en) m pain; (Trauer) grief; **~en haben** to be in pain; **~en im Rücken haben** to have a pain in one's back; **schmerzen** vt, vi to hurt; **Schmerzensgeld** nt compensation; **schmerzhaft, schmerzlich** adj painful; **schmerzlos** adj painless; **Schmerzmittel** nt painkiller; **schmerzstillend** adj painkilling; **Schmerztablette** f painkiller
Schmetterling m butterfly
Schmied(in) (-(e)s, -e) m(f) blacksmith; **schmieden** vt to forge; (Pläne) to make
schmieren vt to smear; (ölen) to lubricate, to grease; (bestechen) to bribe ▷ vt, vi (unsauber schreiben) to scrawl; **Schmiergeld** nt (fam) bribe; **schmierig** adj greasy; **Schmierseife** f soft soap
Schminke (-, -n) f make-up; **schminken** vr: **sich ~** to put one's make-up on
schmiss imperf von **schmeißen**
schmollen vi to sulk; **schmollend** adj sulky
schmolz imperf von **schmelzen**
Schmuck (-(e)s, -e) m jewellery (Brit), jewelry (US); (Verzierung) decoration; **schmücken** vt to decorate
schmuggeln vt, vi to smuggle
schmunzeln vi to smile
schmusen vi to (kiss and) cuddle
Schmutz (-es) m dirt, filth; **schmutzig** adj dirty
Schnabel (-s, Schnäbel) m beak, bill; (Ausguss) spout
Schnake (-, -n) f mosquito
Schnalle (-, -n) f buckle
Schnäppchen nt (fam) bargain; **schnappen** vt (fangen) to catch ▷ vi: **nach Luft ~** to gasp for breath; **Schnappschuss** m (Foto) snap(shot)
Schnaps (-es, Schnäpse) m schnapps
schnarchen vi to snore
schnaufen vi to puff, to pant
Schnauzbart m moustache; **Schnauze** (-, -n) f snout, muzzle; (Ausguss) spout; (fam: Mund) trap; **die ~ voll haben** to have had enough
schnäuzen vr: **sich ~** to blow one's nose
Schnecke (-, -n) f snail; **Schneckenhaus** nt snail's shell
Schnee (-s) m snow; **Schneeball** m snowball; **Schneebob** m snowmobile; **Schneebrille** f snow goggles pl; **Schneeflocke** f snowflake; **Schneegestöber** (-s, -) nt snow flurry; **Schneeglöckchen** nt snowdrop; **Schneegrenze** f snowline; **Schneekanone** f snow thrower; **Schneekette** f (Auto) snow chain; **Schneemann** m snowman; **Schneepflug** m snowplough; **Schneeregen** m sleet; **Schneeschmelze** f thaw; **Schneesturm** m snowstorm, blizzard; **Schneetreiben** nt light blizzards pl; **Schneewehe** f snowdrift

Schneide (-, -n) f edge; (Klinge) blade; **schneiden** (schnitt, geschnitten) vt to cut; **sich** (dat) **die Haare ~ lassen** to have one's hair cut ▷ vr: **sich ~** to cut oneself; **Schneider(in)** (-s, -) m(f) tailor; (für Damenmode) dressmaker; **Schneiderin** f dressmaker; **Schneidezahn** m incisor

schneien vi impers to snow

schnell adj quick, fast ▷ adv quickly, fast; **mach ~!** hurry up; **Schnelldienst** m express service; **Schnellhefter** m loose-leaf binder; **Schnellimbiss** m snack bar; **Schnellkochtopf** m pressure cooker; **Schnellreinigung** f express dry cleaning; (Geschäft) express (dry) cleaner's; **Schnellstraße** f expressway; **Schnellzug** m fast train

schneuzen vr siehe **schnäuzen**

schnitt imperf von **schneiden**

Schnitt (-(e)s, -e) m cut; (Schnittpunkt) intersection; (Querschnitt) (cross) section; (Durchschnitt) average; (eines Kleides) style; **Schnitte** (-, -n) f slice; (belegt) sandwich; **Schnittkäse** m cheese slices pl; **Schnittlauch** m chives pl; **Schnittmuster** nt pattern; **Schnittstelle** f (Inform, fig) interface; **Schnittwunde** f cut, gash

Schnitzel (-s, -) nt (Papier) scrap; (Gastr) escalope

schnitzen vt to carve

Schnorchel (-s, -) m snorkel; **schnorcheln** vi to go snorkelling, to snorkel

schnüffeln vi to sniff

Schnuller (-s, -) m dummy (Brit), pacifier (US)

Schnulze (-, -n) f (Film, Roman) weepie

Schnupfen (-s, -) m cold

schnuppern vi to sniff

Schnur (-, Schnüre) f string, cord; (Elek) lead; **schnurlos** adj (Telefon) cordless

Schnurrbart m moustache

schnurren vi to purr

Schnürsenkel (-s, -) m shoelace

schob imperf von **schieben**

Schock (-(e)s, -e) m shock; **unter ~ stehen** to be in a state of shock; **schockieren** vt to shock

Schokolade f chocolate; **Schokoriegel** m chocolate bar

Scholle (-, -n) f (Fisch) plaice; (Eis) ice floe

SCHLÜSSELWORT

schon adv 1 (bereits) already; **er ist schon da** he's there already, he's already there; **ist er schon da?** is he there yet?; **warst du schon einmal da?** have you ever been there?; **ich war schon einmal da** I've been there before; **das war schon immer so** that has always been the case; **schon oft** often; **hast du schon gehört?** have you heard?

2 (bestimmt) all right; **du wirst schon sehen** you'll see (all right); **das wird schon noch gut** that'll be OK

3 (bloß) just; **allein schon das Gefühl ...** just the very feeling ...; **schon der Gedanke** the very thought; **wenn ich das schon höre** I only have to hear that

4 (einschränkend) **ja schon, aber ...** yes (well), but ...

5 (überhaupt) possible; **schon gut!** OK!; **du weißt schon** you know; **komm schon!** come on!

schön adj beautiful; (nett) nice; (Frau) beautiful, pretty; (Mann) beautiful, handsome; (*Wetter*) fine; **~e Grüße** best wishes; **~es Wochenende** have a nice weekend

schonen *vt* (*pfleglich behandeln*) to look after ▷ *vr:* **sich ~** to take it easy

Schönheit *f* beauty

Schonkost *f* light diet

schöpfen *vt* to scoop; (*mit Kelle*) to ladle; **Schöpfkelle** *f*, **Schöpflöffel** *m* ladle

Schöpfung *f* creation

Schoppen (*-s, -*) *m* glass (of wine)

Schorf (*-(e)s, -e*) *m* scab

Schorle (*-, -n*) *f* spritzer

Schornstein *m* chimney; **Schornsteinfeger(in)** (*-s, -*) *m(f)* chimney sweep

schoss *imperf von* **schießen**

Schoß (*-es, Schöße*) *m* lap

Schotte (*-n, -n*) *m* Scot, Scotsman; **Schottin** *f* Scot, Scotswoman; **schottisch** *adj* Scottish, Scots; **Schottland** *nt* Scotland

schräg *adj* slanting; (*Dach*) sloping; (*Linie*) diagonal; (*fam: unkonventionell*) wacky

Schrank (*-(e)s, Schränke*) *m* cupboard; (*Kleiderschrank*) wardrobe (*Brit*), closet (*US*)

Schranke (*-, -n*) *f* barrier

Schrankwand *f* wall unit

Schraube (*-, -n*) *f* screw; **schrauben** *vt* to screw; **Schraubendreher** (*-s, -*) *m* screwdriver; **Schraubenschlüssel** *m* spanner; **Schraubenzieher** (*-s, -*) *m* screwdriver; **Schraubverschluss** *m* screw top, screw cap

Schreck (*-(e)s, -e*) *m*, **Schrecken** (*-s, -*) *m* terror; (*Angst*) fright; **jdm einen ~ einjagen** to give sb a fright; **schreckhaft** *adj* jumpy; **schrecklich** *adj* terrible, dreadful

Schrei (*-(e)s, -e*) *m* scream; (*Ruf*) shout

Schreibblock *m* writing pad; **schreiben** (*schrieb, geschrieben*) *vt, vi* to write; (*buchstabieren*) to spell; **wie schreibt man ...?** how do you spell ...?; **Schreiben** (*-s, -*) *nt* writing; (*Brief*) letter; **Schreibfehler** *m* spelling mistake; **schreibgeschützt** *adj* (*Diskette*) write-protected; **Schreibtisch** *m* desk; **Schreibwaren** *pl* stationery *sing*; **Schreibwarenladen** *m* stationer's

schreien (*schrie, geschrie(e)n*) *vt, vi* to scream; (*rufen*) to shout

Schreiner(in) *m(f)* joiner; **Schreinerei** *f* joiner's workshop

schrie *imperf von* **schreien**

schrieb *imperf von* **schreiben**

Schrift (*-, -en*) *f* writing; (*Handschrift*) handwriting; (*Schriftart*) typeface; (*Schrifttyp*) font; **schriftlich** *adj* written ▷ *adv* in writing; **würden Sie uns das bitte ~ geben?** could we have that in writing, please?; **Schriftsteller(in)** (*-s, -*) *m(f)* writer

Schritt (*-(e)s, -e*) *m* step; **~ für ~** step by step; **~e gegen etw unternehmen** to take steps against sth; **Schrittgeschwindigkeit** *f* walking speed; **Schrittmacher** *m* (*Med*) pacemaker

Schrott (*-(e)s, -e*) *m* scrap metal; (*fig*) rubbish

schrubben *vi, vt* to scrub; **Schrubber** (*-s, -*) *m* scrubbing brush

schrumpfen *vi* to shrink

Schubkarren (*-s, -*) *m* wheelbarrow; **Schublade** *f* drawer

schubsen *vt* to shove, to push

schüchtern *adj* shy

schuf *imperf von* **schaffen**

Schuh (-(e)s, -e) m shoe;
Schuhcreme f shoe polish;
Schuhgeschäft nt shoe shop;
Schuhgröße f shoe size;
Schuhlöffel m shoehorn
Schulabschluss m school-
leaving qualification
schuld adj: **wer ist ~ daran?**
whose fault is it?; **er ist ~** it's his
fault, he's to blame; **Schuld** (-) f
guilt; (Verschulden) fault; **~ haben**
to be to blame (an +dat for); **er hat
~** it's his fault; **sie gibt mir die
~ an dem Unfall** she blames me
for the accident; **schulden** vt to
owe (jdm etw sb sth); **Schulden** pl
debts pl; **~ haben** to be in debt;
~ machen to run up debts; **seine
~ bezahlen** to pay off one's debts;
schuldig adj guilty (an +dat of);
(gebührend) due; **jdm etw ~ sein** to
owe sb sth
Schule (-, -n) f school; **in der ~** at
school; **in die ~ gehen** to go to
school; **Schüler(in)** (-s, -) m(f)
(jüngerer) pupil; (älterer) student;
Schüleraustausch m school
exchange; **Schulfach** nt subject;
Schulferien pl school holidays pl
(Brit) (o vacation (US)); **schulfrei**
adj: **morgen ist ~** there's no school
tomorrow; **Schulfreund(in)** m(f)
schoolmate; **Schuljahr** nt school
year; **Schulkenntnisse** pl: **~ in
Französisch** school(-level) French;
Schulklasse f class; **Schul-
leiter(in)** m(f) headmaster/
headmistress (Brit), principal (US)
Schulter (-, -n) f shoulder;
Schulterblatt nt shoulder blade
Schulung f training;
(Veranstaltung) training course
schummeln vi (fam) to cheat
Schuppe (-, -n) f (von Fisch) scale;
schuppen vt to scale ▷ vr: **sich
~** to peel; **Schuppen** pl (im Haar)
dandruff sing

Schürfwunde f graze
Schürze (-, -n) f apron
Schuss (-es, Schüsse) m shot; **mit
einem ~ Wodka** with a dash of
vodka
Schüssel (-, -n) f bowl
Schuster(in) (-s, -) m(f)
shoemaker
Schutt (-(e)s) m rubble
Schüttelfrost m shivering fit;
schütteln vt to shake ▷ vr: **sich
~** to shake
schütten vt to pour; (Zucker, Kies
etc) to tip ▷ vi impers to pour
(down)
Schutz (-es) m protection (gegen,
vor against, from); (Unterschlupf)
shelter; **jdn in ~ nehmen** to stand
up for sb; **Schutzblech** nt
mudguard; **Schutzbrief** m travel
insurance document for drivers;
Schutzbrille f (safety) goggles pl
Schütze (-n, -n) m (beim Fußball)
scorer; (Astr) Sagittarius
schützen vt: **jdn gegen/vor etw
~** to protect sb against/from sth;
Schutzimpfung f inoculation,
vaccination
schwach adj weak; **~e Augen**
poor eyesight sing; **Schwäche**
(-, -n) f weakness; **Schwachstelle**
f weak point; **Schwachstrom** m
low-voltage current
Schwager (-s, Schwäger) m
brother-in-law; **Schwägerin** f
sister-in-law
Schwalbe (-, -n) f swallow; (beim
Fußball) dive
schwamm imperf von
schwimmen
Schwamm (-(e)s, Schwämme) m
sponge; **~ drüber!** (fam) let's forget
it!
Schwan (-(e)s,
Schwäne) m swan
schwanger adj pregnant; **im
vierten Monat ~ sein** to be four

months pregnant; **Schwanger-schaft** f pregnancy; **Schwanger-schaftsabbruch** m abortion; **Schwangerschaftstest** m pregnancy test

schwanken vi to sway; (*Preise, Zahlen*) to fluctuate; (*zögern*) to hesitate; (*taumeln*) to stagger; **ich schwanke zwischen A und B** I can't decide between A and B

Schwanz (*-es, Schwänze*) m tail; (*vulg: Penis*) cock

Schwarm (*-(e)s, Schwärme*) m swarm; (*fam: angehimmelte Person*) heartthrob; **schwärmen** vi to swarm; **~ für** to be mad about

schwarz adj black; **mir wurde ~ vor Augen** everything went black; **Schwarzarbeit** f illicit work; **Schwarzbrot** nt black bread; **schwarz|fahren** irr vi to travel without a ticket; (*ohne Führerschein*) to drive without a licence; **Schwarzfahrer(in)** m(f) fare-dodger; **Schwarzmarkt** m black market; **schwarz|sehen** irr vi (*fam: pessimistisch sein*) to be pessimistic (*für* about); **Schwarzwald** m Black Forest; **schwarzweiß** adj black and white; **Schwarzwurzel** f black salsify

schwatzen vi to chatter; **Schwätzer(in)** (*-s, -*) m(f) chatterbox; (*Schwafler*) gasbag; (*Klatschmaul*) gossip

Schwebebahn f suspension railway; **schweben** vi to float; (*hoch*) to soar

Schwede (*-n, -n*) m Swede; **Schweden** (*-s*) nt Sweden; **Schwedin** f Swede; **schwedisch** adj Swedish; **Schwedisch** nt Swedish

Schwefel (*-s*) m sulphur

schweigen (*schwieg, geschwiegen*) vi to be silent; (*nicht mehr reden*) to

stop talking; **Schweigen** (*-s*) nt silence; **Schweigepflicht** f duty of confidentiality; **die ärztliche ~** medical confidentiality

Schwein (*-(e)s, -e*) nt pig; (*fam: Glück*) luck; (*fam: gemeiner Mensch*) swine; **Schweinebraten** m roast pork; **Schweinefleisch** nt pork; **Schweinerei** f mess; (*Gemeinheit*) dirty trick

Schweiß (*-es*) m sweat

schweißen vt, vi to weld

Schweiz (*-*) f: **die ~** Switzerland; **Schweizer(in)** (*-s, -*) m(f) Swiss; **Schweizerdeutsch** nt Swiss German; **schweizerisch** adj Swiss

Schwelle (*-, -n*) f doorstep; (*a. fig*) threshold

schwellen vi to swell (up); **Schwellung** f swelling

schwer adj heavy; (*schwierig*) difficult, hard; (*schlimm*) serious, bad; **er ist ~ zu verstehen** it's difficult to understand what he's saying ▷ adv (*sehr*) really; (*verletzt etc*) seriously, badly; **etw ~ nehmen** to take sth hard; **Schwerbehinderte(r)** mf severely disabled person; **schwer|fallen** irr vi (*Schwierigkeiten bereiten*) **jdm ~** to be difficult for sb; **schwerhörig** adj hard of hearing

Schwert (*-(e)s, -er*) nt sword; **Schwertlilie** f iris

Schwester (*-, -n*) f sister; (*Med*) nurse

schwieg imperf von **schweigen**

Schwiegereltern pl parents-in-law pl; **Schwiegermutter** f mother-in-law; **Schwiegersohn** m son-in-law; **Schwiegertochter** f daughter-in-law; **Schwiegervater** m father-in-law

schwierig adj difficult, hard; **Schwierigkeit** f difficulty; **in ~en kommen** to get into trouble; **jdm**

~en machen to make things difficult for sb

Schwimmbad nt swimming pool; **Schwimmbecken** nt swimming pool; **schwimmen** (*schwamm, geschwommen*) vi to swim; (*treiben*) to float; (*fig: unsicher sein*) to be all at sea; **Schwimmer(in)** m(f) swimmer; **Schwimmflosse** f flipper; **Schwimmflügel** m water wing; **Schwimmreifen** m rubber ring; **Schwimmweste** f life jacket

Schwindel (-s) m dizziness; (*Anfall*) dizzy spell; (*Betrug*) swindle; **schwindelfrei** adj: **nicht ~ sein** to suffer from vertigo; **~ sein** to have a head for heights; **schwindlig** adj dizzy; **mir ist ~** I feel dizzy

Schwips m: **einen ~ haben** to be tipsy

schwitzen vi to sweat

schwoll imperf von **schwellen**

schwor imperf von **schwören**

schwören (*schwor, geschworen*) vt, vi to swear; **einen Eid ~** to take an oath

schwul adj gay

schwül adj close

Schwung (-(e)s, Schwünge) m swing; (*Triebkraft*) momentum; (*fig: Energie*) energy; (*fam: Menge*) batch; **in ~ kommen** to get going

Schwur (-s, Schwüre) m oath

scrollen vi (*Inform*) to scroll

sechs num six; **Sechs** (-, -en) f six; (*Schulnote*) ≈ F; **Sechserpack** m sixpack; **sechshundert** num six hundred; **sechsmal** adv six times; **sechste(r, s)** adj sixth; *siehe auch* **dritte**; **Sechstel** (-s, -) nt sixth; **sechzehn** num sixteen; **sechzehnte(r, s)** adj sixteenth; *siehe auch* **dritte**; **sechzig** num sixty; **in den ~er Jahren** in the

sixties; **sechzigste(r, s)** adj sixtieth

Secondhandladen m second-hand shop

See (-, -n) f sea; **an der ~** by the sea ▷ (-s, -n) m lake; **am ~** by the lake; **Seegang** m waves; **hoher/schwerer/leichter ~** rough/heavy/calm seas pl; **Seehund** m seal; **Seeigel** m sea urchin; **seekrank** adj seasick

Seele (-, -n) f soul

Seeleute pl seamen pl, sailors pl

seelisch adj mental, psychological

Seelöwe m sea lion; **Seemann** m sailor, seaman; **Seemeile** f nautical mile; **Seemöwe** f seagull; **Seenot** f distress (at sea); **Seepferdchen** nt sea horse; **Seerose** f water lily; **Seestern** m starfish; **Seezunge** f sole

Segel (-s, -) nt sail; **Segelboot** nt yacht; **Segelfliegen** (-s) nt gliding; **Segelflugzeug** nt glider; **segeln** vt, vi to sail; **Segelschiff** nt sailing ship

sehbehindert adj partially sighted

sehen (*sah, gesehen*) vt, vi to see; (*in bestimmte Richtung*) to look; **gut/schlecht ~** to have good/bad eyesight; **auf die Uhr ~** to look at one's watch; **kann ich das mal ~?** can I have a look at it?; **wir ~ uns morgen!** see you tomorrow; **ich kenne sie nur vom Sehen** I only know her by sight; **Sehenswürdigkeiten** pl sights pl

Sehne (-, -n) f tendon; (*an Bogen*) string

sehnen vr: **sich ~** to long (*nach* for)

Sehnenscheidenentzündung f (*Med*) tendovaginitis;

Sehnenzerrung f (Med) pulled tendon
Sehnsucht f longing;
sehnsüchtig adj longing
sehr adv (vor Adjektiv, Adverb) very;
(mit Verben) a lot, very much; **zu ~** too much
seicht adj shallow
Seide (-, -n) f silk
Seife (-, -n) f soap; **Seifenoper** f soap (opera); **Seifenschale** f soap dish
Seil (-(e)s, -e) nt rope; (Kabel) cable; **Seilbahn** f cable railway

⭕ SCHLÜSSELWORT

sein¹ (pt **war**, pp **gewesen**) vi **1** to be; **ich bin** I am; **du bist** you are; **er/sie/es ist** he/she/it is; **wir sind/ihr seid/sie sind** we/you/they are; **wir waren** we were; **wir sind gewesen** we have been

2 seien Sie nicht böse don't be angry; **sei so gut und ...** be so kind as to ...; **das wäre gut** that would o that'd be a good thing; **wenn ich Sie wäre** if I were o was you; **das wär's** that's all, that's it; **morgen bin ich in Rom** tomorrow I'll o I will o I shall be in Rome; **waren Sie mal in Rom?** have you ever been to Rome?

3 wie ist das zu verstehen? how is that to be understood?; **er ist nicht zu ersetzen** he cannot be replaced; **mit ihr ist nicht zu reden** you can't talk to her

4 mir ist kalt I'm cold; **was ist?** what's the matter?, what is it?; **ist was?** is something the matter?; **es sei denn, dass ...** unless ...; **wie dem auch sei** be that as it may; **wie wäre es mit ...?** how o what about ...?; **lass das sein!** stop that!

sein² pron possessiv von **er**;
(adjektivisch) his ▷ pron possessiv von **es** (adjektivisch) its;
(adjektivisch, männlich) his;
(weiblich) her; (sächlich) its; **das ist ~e Tasche** that's his bag; **jeder hat ~e Sorgen** everyone has their problems; **seine(r, s)** pron possessiv von **er**; (substantivisch) his ▷ pron possessiv von **es**;
(substantivisch) its; (substantivisch, männlich) his; (weiblich) hers; **das ist ~r/~/~s** that's his/hers;
seiner pron gen von **er**; of him ▷ pron gen von **es**; of it;
seinetwegen adv (wegen ihm) because of him; (ihm zuliebe) for his sake; (um ihn) about him; (von ihm aus) as far as he is concerned
seit conj (bei Zeitpunkt) since; (bei Zeitraum) for; **er ist ~ Montag hier** he's been here since Monday; **er ist ~ einer Woche hier** he's been here for a week; **~ langem** for a long time; **seitdem** adv, conj since
Seite (-, -n) f side; (in Buch) page; **zur ~ gehen** to step aside;
Seitenairbag m side-impact airbag; **Seitenaufprallschutz** m (Auto) side-impact protection;
Seitensprung m affair;
Seitenstechen (-s) nt: **~ haben/ bekommen** to have/get a stitch;
Seitenstraße f side street;
Seitenstreifen m hard shoulder (Brit), shoulder (US); **Seitenwind** m crosswind
seither adv since (then)
seitlich adj side
Sekretär(in) m(f) secretary;
Sekretariat (-s, -e) nt secretary's office
Sekt (-(e)s, -e) m sparkling wine (similar to champagne)
Sekte (-, -n) f sect

Sekunde (-, -*n*) *f* second;
Sekundenkleber (-*s*, -) *m* superglue; **Sekundenschnelle** *f*: **es
geschah alles in ~** it was all over
in a matter of seconds

 SCHLÜSSELWORT

selbst *pron* **1 ich/er/wir selbst** I
myself/he himself/we ourselves;
sie ist die Tugend selbst she's
virtue itself; **er braut sein Bier
selbst** he brews his own beer; **wie
geht's? — gut, und selbst?** how
are things? — fine, and yourself?
2 (*ohne Hilfe*) alone, on
my/his/one's *etc* own; **von selbst**
by itself; **er kam von selbst** he
came of his own accord; **selbst
gemacht** home-made
▷ *adv* even; **selbst wenn** even if;
selbst Gott even God (himself)

selbständig *adj siehe*
selbstständig
Selbstauslöser (-*s*, -) *m* (*Foto*)
self-timer; **Selbstbedienung** *f*
self-service; **Selbstbefriedigung** *f*
masturbation;
Selbstbeherrschung *f*
self-control; **Selbstbeteiligung** *f*
(*einer Versicherung*) excess;
selbstbewusst *adj*
(self-)confident; **Selbstbräuner**
(-*s*, -) *m* self-tanning lotion;
selbstgemacht *adj* self-made;
selbstklebend *adj* self-adhesive;
Selbstlaut *m* vowel; **Selbstmord**
m suicide; **Selbstmordattentat**
nt suicide bombing; **Selbstmord-
attentäter(in)** *m(f)* suicide
bomber; **selbstsicher** *adj*
self-assured; **selbstständig** *adj*
independent; (*arbeitend*)
self-employed; **Selbstverpflegung**
f self-catering;
selbstverständlich *adj* obvious;

ich halte das für ~ I take that for
granted ▷ *adv* naturally;
Selbstvertrauen *nt*
self-confidence
Sellerie (-*s*, -(*s*)) *m* (-, -*n*) *f* (*Knollensellerie*) celeriac; (*Stangensellerie*)
celery
selten *adj* rare ▷ *adv* seldom,
rarely
seltsam *adj* strange;
~ schmecken/riechen to
taste/smell strange
Semester (-*s*, -) *nt* semester;
Semesterferien *pl* vacation *sing*
Semikolon (-*s*, *Semikola*) *nt*
semicolon
Seminar (-*s*, -*e*) *nt* seminar
Semmel (-, -*n*) *f* roll;
Semmelbrösel *pl* breadcrumbs
Senat (-(*e*)*s*, -*e*) *m* senate
senden (*sandte, gesandt*) *vt* to
send ▷ *vt, vi* (*Radio, TV*) to
broadcast; **Sender** (-*s*, -) *m* (*TV*)
channel; (*Radio*) station; (*Anlage*)
transmitter; **Sendung** *f* (*Radio,
TV*) broadcasting; (*Programm*)
programme
Senf (-(*e*)*s*, -*e*) *m* mustard
Senior(in) *m(f)* senior citizen;
Seniorenpass *m* senior citizen's
travel pass
senken *vt* to lower ▷ *vr*: **sich
~** to sink
senkrecht *adj* vertical
Sensation (-, -*en*) *f* sensation
sensibel *adj* sensitive
sentimental *adj* sentimental
separat *adj* separate
September (-(*s*), -) *m*
September; *siehe auch* **Juni**
Serbien (-*s*) *nt* Serbia
Serie *f* series *sing*
seriös *adj* (*ernsthaft*) serious;
(*anständig*) respectable
Serpentine *f* hairpin (bend)
Serum (-*s*, *Seren*) *nt* serum
Server (-*s*, -) *m* (*Inform*) server

Service (-(s), -) nt (Geschirr)
service ▷ (-, -s) m service
servieren vt, vi to serve
Serviette f napkin, serviette
Servolenkung f (Auto) power
steering
Sesam (-s, -s) m sesame seeds pl
Sessel (-s, -) m armchair;
Sessellift m chairlift
Set (-s, -s) m o nt set; (Tischset)
tablemat
setzen vt to put; (Baum etc) to
plant; (Segel) to set ▷ vr: **sich ~** to
settle; (hinsetzen) to sit down; **~ Sie
sich doch** please sit down
Seuche (-, -n) f epidemic
seufzen vt, vi to sigh
Sex (-(es)) m sex; **Sexismus** m
sexism; **sexistisch** adj sexist;
Sextourismus m sex tourism;
Sexualität f sexuality; **sexuell**
adj sexual
Seychellen pl Seychelles pl
sfr abk = **Schweizer Franken** Swiss
franc(s)
Shampoo (-s, -s) nt shampoo
Shareware (-, -s) f (Inform)
shareware
Shorts pl shorts pl
Shuttlebus m shuttle bus

 SCHLÜSSELWORT

sich pron **1** (akk) **er/sie/es ... sich**
he/she/it ... himself/herself/itself;
sie pl/**man ... sich** they/one ...
themselves/oneself; **Sie ... sich**
you ... yourself/yourselves pl; **sich
wiederholen** to repeat
oneself/itself
2 (dat) **er/sie/es ... sich** he/she/it
... to himself/herself/itself; **sie**
pl/**man ... sich** they/one ... to
themselves/oneself; **Sie ... sich**
you ... to yourself/yourselves pl;
**sie hat sich einen Pullover
gekauft** she bought herself a

jumper; **sich die Haare waschen**
to wash one's hair
3 (mit Präposition) **haben Sie Ihren
Ausweis bei sich?** do you have
your pass on you?; **er hat nichts
bei sich** he's got nothing on him;
sie bleiben gern unter sich they
keep themselves to themselves
4 (einander) each other, one
another; **sie bekämpfen sich** they
fight each other o one another
5 dieses Auto fährt sich gut this
car drives well; **hier sitzt es sich
gut** it's good to sit here

sicher adj safe (vor +dat from);
(gewiss) certain (gen of);
(zuverlässig) reliable; (selbstsicher)
confident; **aber ~!** of course, sure;
Sicherheit f safety; (Aufgabe von
Sicherheitsbeamten) (Fin) security;
(Gewissheit) certainty;
(Selbstsicherheit) confidence; **mit
~** definitely; **Sicherheitsabstand**
m safe distance; **Sicherheitsgurt**
m seat belt; **sicherheitshalber**
adv just to be on the safe side;
Sicherheitsnadel f safety pin;
Sicherheitsvorkehrung f safety
precaution; **sicherlich** adv
certainly; (wahrscheinlich) probably
sichern vt to secure (gegen
against); (schützen) to protect;
(Daten) to back up; **Sicherung** f
(Sichern) securing; (Vorrichtung)
safety device; (an Waffen) safety
catch; (Elek) fuse; (Inform) backup;
die ~ ist durchgebrannt the fuse
has blown
Sicht (-) f sight; (Aussicht) view;
sichtbar adj visible; **sichtlich**
adj evident, obvious;
Sichtverhältnisse pl visibility
sing; **Sichtweite** f: **in/außer
~** within/out of sight
sie pron (3. Person sing) she; (3.
Person pl) they; (akk von sing) her;

(*akk von pl*) them; (*für eine Sache*) it; **da ist ~ ja** there she is; **da sind ~ ja** there they are; **ich kenne ~** (*Frau*) I know her; (*mehrere Personen*) I know them; **~ lag gerade noch hier** (*meine Jacke, Uhr*) it was here just a minute ago; **ich hab ~ gefunden** (*meine Jacke, Uhr*) I've found it; **hast du meine Brille/Hose gesehen? — ich kann ~ nirgends finden** have you seen my glasses/trousers? — I can't find them anywhere

Sie *pron* (*Höflichkeitsform, Nom und Akk*) you

Sieb (*-(e)s, -e*) *nt* sieve; (*Teesieb*) strainer

sieben *num* seven; **siebenhundert** *num* seven hundred; **siebenmal** *adv* seven times; **siebte(r, s)** *adj* seventh; *siehe auch* **dritte**; **Siebtel** (*-s, -*) *nt* seventh; **siebzehn** *num* seventeen; **siebzehnte(r, s)** *adj* seventeenth; *siehe auch* **dritte**; **siebzig** *num* seventy; **in den ~er Jahren** in the seventies; **siebzigste(r, s)** *adj* seventieth

Siedlung (*-, -en*) *f* (*Wohngebiet*) housing estate (*Brit*) (*o* development (*US*))

Sieg (*-(e)s, -e*) *m* victory; **siegen** *vi* to win; **Sieger(in)** (*-s, -*) *m(f)* winner; **Siegerehrung** *f* presentation ceremony

siehe *imper* see

siezen *vt* to address as "Sie"

Signal (*-s, -e*) *nt* signal

Silbe (*-, -n*) *f* syllable

Silber (*-s*) *nt* silver; **Silberhochzeit** *f* silver wedding; **Silbermedaille** *f* silver medal

Silikon (*-s, -e*) *nt* silicone

Silvester (*-s, -*) *nt*, **Silvesterabend** *m* New Year's Eve, Hogmanay (*Scot*)

● **SILVESTER**
●
● **Silvester** is the German name
● for New Year's Eve. Although
● not an official holiday, most
● businesses close early and
● shops shut at midday. Most
● Germans celebrate in the
● evening and at midnight they
● let off fireworks and rockets;
● the revelry usually lasts until the
● early hours of the morning.

Simbabwe (*-s*) *nt* Zimbabwe

SIM-Karte *f* SIM card

simpel *adj* simple

simultan *adj* simultaneous

simsen *vt, vi* (*fam*) to text

Sinfonie (*-, -n*) *f* symphony; **Sinfonieorchester** *nt* symphony orchestra

Singapur (*-s*) *nt* Singapore

singen (*sang, gesungen*) *vt, vi* to sing; **richtig/falsch ~** to sing in tune/out of tune

Single (*-, -s*) *f* (*CD*) single ▷ (*-s, -s*) *m* (*Mensch*) single

Singular *m* singular

sinken (*sank, gesunken*) *vi* to sink; (*Preise etc*) to fall, to go down

Sinn (*-(e)s, -e*) *m* (*Denken*) mind; (*Wahrnehmung*) sense; (*Bedeutung*) sense, meaning; **~ machen** to make sense; **das hat keinen ~** it's no use; **sinnlich** *adj* sensuous; (*erotisch*) sensual; (*Wahrnehmung*) sensory; **sinnlos** *adj* (*unsinnig*) stupid; (*Verhalten*) senseless; (*zwecklos*) pointless; (*bedeutungslos*) meaningless; **sinnvoll** *adj* meaningful; (*vernünftig*) sensible

Sirup (*-s, -e*) *m* syrup

Sitte (*-, -n*) *f* custom

Situation *f* situation

Sitz (*-es, -e*) *m* seat; **sitzen** (*saß, gesessen*) *vi* to sit; (*Bemerkung, Schlag*) to strike home; (*Gelerntes*) to have sunk in; **der Rock sitzt**

gut the skirt is a good fit;
~ bleiben (*Schule*) to have to repeat
a year; **Sitzgelegenheit** *f* place to
sit down; **Sitzplatz** *m* seat;
Sitzung *f* meeting
Sizilien (-s) *nt* Sicily
Skandal (-s, -e) *m* scandal
Skandinavien (-s) *nt*
Scandinavia
Skateboard (-s, -s) *nt*
skateboard: **skateboarden** *vi* to
skateboard
Skelett (-s, -e) *nt* skeleton
skeptisch *adj* sceptical
Ski (-s, -er) *m* ski; **~ laufen** (*o*
fahren) to ski; **Skianzug** *m* ski
suit; **Skibrille** *f* ski goggles *pl*;
Skifahren (-s) *nt* skiing; **Skigebiet**
(-s, -e) *nt* skiing area; **Skihose** *f*
skiing trousers *pl*; **Skikurs** *m*
skiing course; **Skilanglauf** *m*
cross-country skiing; **Skiläufer(in)**
m(f) skier; **Skilehrer(in)** *m(f)* ski
instructor; **Skilift** *m* ski-lift
Skinhead (-s, -s) *m* skinhead
Skipiste *f* ski run; **Skischanze**
(-, -n) *f* ski jump; **Skischuh** *m*
ski boot; **Skischule** *f* ski school;
Skispringen (-s, -n) *nt* ski jumping;
Skistiefel (-s, -) *m* ski boot;
Skistock *m* ski pole; **Skiträger** *m*
ski rack; **Skiurlaub** *m* skiing
holiday (*Brit*) (*o* vacation (*US*))
Skizze (-, -n) *f* sketch
Skonto (-s, -s) *m o nt* discount
Skorpion (-s, -e) *m* (*Zool*)
scorpion; (*Astr*) Scorpio
Skulptur (-, -en) *f* sculpture
S-Kurve *f* double bend
Slalom (-s, -s) *m* slalom
Slip (-s, -s) *m* (pair of) briefs *pl*;
Slipeinlage *f* panty liner
Slowakei (-) *f* Slovakia;
slowakisch *adj* Slovakian;
S~ Republik Slovak Republic;
Slowakisch *nt* Slovakian
Slowenien (-s) *nt* Slovenia;

slowenisch *adj* Slovenian;
Slowenisch *nt* Slovenian
Smiley (-s, -s) *m* smiley
Smog (-s) *m* smog; **Smogalarm**
m smog alert
Smoking (-s, -s) *m* dinner jacket
(*Brit*), tuxedo (*US*)
SMS *nt abk* = **Short Message**
Service ▷ *f* (*Nachricht*) text
message; **ich schicke dir eine ~** I'll
text you, I'll send you a text
Snowboard (-s, -s) *nt* snow-
board; **snowboarden** *vi* to
snowboard; **Snowboardfahren**
(-s) *nt* snowboarding;
Snowboardfahrer(in) *m(f)*
snowboarder

SCHLÜSSELWORT

so *adv* **1** (*so sehr*) so; **so groß/schön**
etc so big/nice *etc*; **so groß/schön**
wie ... as big/nice as ...; **so viel**
(wie) as much as; **rede nicht so**
viel don't talk so much; **so weit**
sein to be ready; **so weit wie** *o* **als**
möglich as far as possible; **ich bin**
so weit zufrieden by and large I'm
quite satisfied; **so wenig (wie)** as
little (as); **das hat ihn so**
geärgert, dass ... that annoyed
him so much that ...; **so einer wie**
ich somebody like me; **na so was!**
well, well!
2 (*auf diese Weise*) like this; **mach**
es nicht so don't do it like that; **so**
oder so in one way or the other;
und so weiter and so on; **... oder**
so was ... or something like that;
das ist gut so that's fine
3 (*fam*) (*umsonst*) **ich habe es so**
bekommen I got it for nothing
▷ *konj*: **sodass** so that; **so wie es**
jetzt ist as things are at the
moment
▷ *excl*: **so?** really?; **so, das wär's**
so, that's it then

S

s. o. *abk = **siehe oben** see above
sobald *conj* as soon as
Socke (-, -n) *f* sock
Sodbrennen (-s) *nt* heartburn
Sofa (-s, -s) *nt* sofa
sofern *conj* if, provided (that)
soff *imperf von* **saufen**
sofort *adv* immediately, at once;
  Sofortbildkamera *f* instant
  camera
Softeis *nt* soft ice-cream
Software (-, -s) *f* software
sog *imperf von* **saugen**
sogar *adv* even; **kalt, ~ sehr kalt**
  cold, in fact very cold
sogenannt *adj* so-called
Sohle (-, -n) *f* sole
Sohn (-(e)s, Söhne) *m* son
Soja (-, Sojen) *f* soya;
  Sojasprossen *pl* bean sprouts *pl*
solang(e) *conj* as long as
Solarium *nt* solarium
Solarzelle *f* solar cell
solche(r, s) *pron* such; **eine**
  ~ Frau, solch eine Frau such a
  woman, a woman like that;
  ~ Sachen things like that, such
  things; **ich habe ~ Kopfschmerz-**
  en I've got such a headache; **ich**
  habe ~n Hunger I'm so hungry
Soldat(in) (-en, -en) *m(f)* soldier
solidarisch *adj* showing
  solidarity; **sich ~ erklären mit** to
  declare one's solidarity with
solid(e) *adj* solid; (*Leben, Mensch*)
  respectable
Soll (-(s), -(s)) *nt* (*Fin*) debit;
  (*Arbeitsmenge*) quota, target

 SCHLÜSSELWORT

sollen (*pt* **sollte**, *pp* **gesollt** *o* (*als
  Hilfsverb*) **sollen**) *Hilfsverb* **1** (*Pflicht,
  Befehl*) to be supposed to; **du**
  hättest nicht gehen sollen you
  shouldn't have gone, you oughtn't
  to have gone; **soll ich?** shall I?; **soll**

ich dir helfen? shall I help you?;
  sag ihm, er soll warten tell him
  he's to wait; **was soll ich**
  machen? what should I do?
  2 (*Vermutung*) **sie soll verheiratet**
  sein she's said to be married; **was**
  soll das heißen? what's that
  supposed to mean?; **man sollte**
  glauben, dass ... you would think
  that ...; **sollte das passieren, ...** if
  that should happen ...
  ▷ *vt, vi*: **was soll das?** what's all
  this?; **das sollst du nicht** you
  shouldn't do that; **was soll's?**
  what the hell!

Solo (-s, -) *nt* solo
Sommer (-s, -) *m* summer;
  Sommerfahrplan *m* summer
  timetable; **Sommerferien** *pl*
  summer holidays *pl* (*Brit*) (*o*
  vacation *sing* (*US*)); **sommerlich**
  adj summery; (*Sommer-*) summer;
  Sommerreifen *m* normal tyre;
  Sommersprossen *pl* freckles *pl*;
  Sommerzeit *f* summertime;
  (*Uhrzeit*) daylight saving
  time
Sonderangebot *nt* special
  offer; **sonderbar** *adj* strange,
  odd; **Sondermarke** *f* special
  stamp; **Sondermaschine** *f*
  special plane; **Sondermüll** *m*
  hazardous waste
sondern *conj* but; **nicht nur ...,**
  ~ auch not only ..., but also
Sonderpreis *m* special price;
  Sonderschule *f* special school;
  Sonderzeichen *nt* (*Inform*)
  special character; **Sonderzug** *m*
  special train
Song (-s, -s) *m* song
Sonnabend *m* Saturday; *siehe*
  auch **Mittwoch**; **sonnabends** *adv*
  on Saturdays; **~ morgens** on
  Saturday mornings; *siehe auch*
  mittwochs

Sonne (-, -n) f sun; **sonnen** vr:
sich ~ to sunbathe;
Sonnenallergie f sun allergy;
Sonnenaufgang m sunrise;
Sonnenblume f sunflower;
Sonnenblumenkern m sunflower seed; **Sonnenbrand** m
sunburn; **Sonnenbrille** f
sunglasses pl, shades pl;
Sonnencreme f sun cream;
Sonnendach nt (an Haus)
awning; (Auto) sunroof; **Sonnen-
deck** nt sun deck; **Sonnenmilch** f
suntan lotion; **Sonnenöl** nt
suntan oil; **Sonnenschein** m
sunshine; **Sonnenschirm** m
parasol, sunshade; **Sonnenschutz-
creme** f sunscreen; **Sonnenstich**
m sunstroke; **Sonnenstudio** nt
solarium; **Sonnenuhr** f sundial;
Sonnenuntergang m sunset;
sonnig adj sunny
Sonntag m Sunday; siehe auch
Mittwoch; **sonntags** adv on
Sundays; siehe auch **mittwochs**
sonst adv, conj (außerdem) else;
(andernfalls) otherwise, (or) else;
(mit Pron, in Fragen) else;
(normalerweise) normally, usually;
~ noch etwas? anything else?;
~ nichts nothing else
sooft conj whenever
Sopran (-s, -e) m soprano
Sorge (-, -n) f worry; (Fürsorge)
care; **sich** (dat) **um jdn ~n machen**
to be worried about sb; **sorgen**
vi: **für jdn ~** to look after sb; **für
etw ~** to take care of sth, to see to
sth ▷ vr: **sich ~** to worry (um
about); **sorgfältig** adj careful
sortieren vt to sort (out)
Sortiment nt assortment
sosehr conj however much
Soße (-, -n) f sauce; (zu Braten)
gravy
Soundkarte f (Inform) sound
card

Souvenir (-s, -s) nt souvenir
soviel conj as far as
soweit conj as far as
sowie conj (wie auch) as well as;
(sobald) as soon as
sowohl conj: **~ ... als** (o **wie**) **auch**
both ... and
sozial adj social; **~er
Wohnungsbau** public-sector
housing (programme); **Sozialhilfe**
f income support (Brit), welfare
(aid) (US); **Sozialismus** m
socialism; **Sozialkunde** f social
studies pl; **Sozialversicherung** f
social security; **Sozialwohnung** f
council flat (Brit), state-subsidized
apartment (US)
Soziologie f sociology
sozusagen adv so to speak
Spachtel (-s, -) m spatula
Spag(h)etti pl spaghetti sing
Spalte (-, -n) f crack; (Gletscher)
crevasse; (in Text) column
spalten vt to split
Spam (-s, -s) nt (Inform) spam
Spange (-, -n) f clasp; (Haarspange) slide (Brit), barrette (US)
Spanien (-s) nt Spain;
Spanier(in) (-s, -) m(f) Spaniard;
spanisch adj Spanish; **Spanisch**
nt Spanish
spann imperf von **spinnen**
spannen vt (straffen) to tighten;
(befestigen) to brace ▷ vi to be tight;
spannend adj exciting, gripping;
Spannung f tension; (Elek)
voltage; (fig) suspense
Sparbuch nt savings book;
(Konto) savings account; **sparen**
vt, vi to save
Spargel (-s, -) m asparagus
Sparkasse f savings bank;
Sparkonto nt savings account
spärlich adj meagre; (Bekleidung)
scanty
sparsam adj economical;
Sparschwein nt piggy bank

s

Spaß (-es, Späße) m joke; (Freude) fun; **es macht mir ~** I enjoy it, it's (great) fun; **viel ~!** have fun

spät adj, adv late; **zu ~ kommen** to be late

Spaten (-s, -) m spade

später adj, adv later; **spätestens** adv at the latest; **Spätlese** f late vintage (wine); **Spätvorstellung** f late-night performance

Spatz (-en, -en) m sparrow

spazieren vi to stroll, to walk; **~ gehen** to go for a walk; **Spaziergang** m walk

Specht (-(e)s, -e) m woodpecker

Speck (-(e)s, -e) m bacon fat; (durchwachsen) bacon

Spedition f (für Umzug) removal firm

Speiche (-, -n) f spoke

Speichel (-s) m saliva

Speicher (-s, -) m storehouse; (Dachboden) attic; (Inform) memory; **speichern** vt (Inform) to store; (sichern) to save

Speise (-, -n) f food; (Gericht) dish; **Speisekarte** f menu; **Speiseröhre** f gullet, oesophagus; **Speisesaal** m dining hall; **Speisewagen** m dining car

Spende (-, -n) f donation; **spenden** vt to donate, to give

spendieren vt: **jdm etw ~** to treat sb to sth

Sperre (-, -n) f barrier; (Verbot) ban; **sperren** vt to block; (Sport) to suspend; (verbieten) to ban

Sperrgepäck m bulky luggage; **Sperrmüll** m bulky refuse; **Sperrstunde** f closing time; **Sperrung** f closing

Spesen pl expenses pl

spezialisieren vr: **sich ~** to specialize (auf +akk in); **Spezialist(in)** m(f) specialist; **Spezialität** f speciality (Brit),

specialty (US); **speziell** adj special ▷ adv especially

Spiegel (-s, -) m mirror; **Spiegelei** nt fried egg (sunny-side up (US)); **spiegelglatt** adj very slippery; **Spiegelreflexkamera** f reflex camera

Spiel (-(e)s, -e) nt game; (Tätigkeit) play(ing); (Karten) pack, deck; (Tech) (free) play; **Spielautomat** m (ohne Geldgewinn) gaming machine; (mit Geldgewinn) slot machine; **spielen** vt, vi to play; (um Geld) to gamble; (Theat) to perform, to act; **Klavier ~** to play the piano; **spielend** adv easily; **Spieler(in)** (-s, -) m(f) player; (um Geld) gambler; **Spielfeld** nt (für Fußball, Hockey) field; (für Basketball) court; **Spielfilm** m feature film; **Spielkasino** nt casino; **Spielplatz** m playground; **Spielraum** m room to manoeuvre; **Spielregel** f rule; **sich an die ~n halten** to stick to the rules; **Spielsachen** pl toys pl; **Spielzeug** nt toys pl; (einzelnes) toy

Spieß (-es, -e) m spear; (Bratspieß) spit; **Spießer(in)** (-s, -) m(f) square, stuffy type; **spießig** adj square, uncool

Spikes pl (Sport) spikes pl; (Auto) studs pl

Spinat (-(e)s, -e) m spinach

Spinne (-, -n) f spider; **spinnen** (spann, gesponnen) vt, vi to spin; (fam: Unsinn reden) to talk rubbish; (verrückt sein) to be crazy; **du spinnst!** you must be mad; **Spinnwebe** (-, -n) f cobweb

Spion(in) (-s, -e) m(f) spy; **spionieren** vi to spy; (fig) to snoop around

Spirale (-, -n) f spiral; (Med) coil

Spirituosen pl spirits pl, liquor sing (US)

Spiritus (-, -se) m spirit
spitz adj (Nase, Kinn) pointed;
(Bleistift, Messer) sharp; (Winkel)
acute; **Spitze** (-, -n) f point; (von
Finger, Nase) tip; (Bemerkung) taunt,
dig; (erster Platz) lead; (Gewebe)
lace; **Spitzer** (-s, -) m pencil
sharpener; **Spitzname** m
nickname
Spliss (-) m split ends pl
sponsern vt to sponsor;
Sponsor(in) (-s, -en) m(f)
sponsor
spontan adj spontaneous
Sport (-(e)s, -e) m sport;
~ treiben to do sport;
Sportanlage f sports grounds pl;
Sportart f sport;
Sportbekleidung f sportswear;
Sportgeschäft nt sports shop;
Sporthalle f gymnasium, gym;
Sportlehrer(in) (-s, -) m(f) sports
instructor; (Schule) PE teacher;
Sportler(in) (-s, -) m(f) sports-
man/-woman; **sportlich** adj
sporting; (Mensch) sporty;
Sportplatz m playing field;
Sporttauchen nt (skin-)diving;
(mit Gerät) scuba-diving;
Sportverein m sports club;
Sportwagen m sports car
sprach imperf von **sprechen**
Sprache (-, -n) f language;
(Sprechen) speech;
Sprachenschule f language
school; **Sprachführer** m
phrasebook; **Sprachkenntnisse**
pl knowledge sing of languages;
gute englische ~ haben to have a
good knowledge of English;
Sprachkurs m language course;
Sprachunterricht m language
teaching
sprang imperf von **springen**
Spray (-s, -s) m o nt spray
Sprechanlage f intercom;
sprechen (sprach, gesprochen) vt, vi

to speak (jdn, mit jdm to sb); (sich
unterhalten) to talk (mit to, über, von
about); **~ Sie Deutsch?** do you
speak German?; **kann ich bitte
mit David ~?** (am Telefon) can I
speak to David, please?;
Sprecher(in) m(f) speaker;
(Ansager) announcer;
Sprechstunde f consultation;
(Arzt) surgery hours pl; (Anwalt etc)
office hours pl; **Sprechzimmer**
nt consulting room
Sprengstoff m explosive
Sprichwort nt proverb
Springbrunnen m fountain
springen (sprang, gesprungen) vi
to jump; (Glas) to crack; (mit
Kopfsprung) to dive
Sprit (-(e)s, -e) m (fam: Benzin)
petrol (Brit), gas (US)
Spritze (-, -n) f (Gegenstand)
syringe; (Injektion) injection; (an
Schlauch) nozzle; **spritzen** vt to
spray; (Med) to inject ▷ vi to
splash; (Med) to give injections
Spruch (-(e)s, Sprüche) m saying
Sprudel (-s, -) m sparkling
mineral water; (süßer) fizzy drink
(Brit), soda (US); **sprudeln** vi to
bubble
Sprühdose f aerosol (can);
sprühen vt, vi to spray; (fig) to
sparkle; **Sprühregen** m drizzle
Sprung (-(e)s, Sprünge) m jump;
(Riss) crack; **Sprungbrett** nt
springboard; **Sprungschanze** f
ski jump; **Sprungturm** m diving
platforms pl
Spucke (-) f spit; **spucken** vt, vi
to spit; (fam: sich erbrechen) to
vomit; **Spucktüte** f sick bag
spuken vi (Geist) to walk; **hier
spukt es** this place is haunted
Spülbecken nt sink
Spule (-, -n) f spool; (Elek) coil
Spüle (-, -n) f sink; **spülen** vt, vi
to rinse; (Geschirr) to wash up;

S

(*Toilette*) to flush; **Spülmaschine** f dishwasher; **Spülmittel** nt washing-up liquid (*Brit*), dishwashing liquid (*US*); **Spültuch** nt dishcloth; **Spülung** f (*von WC*) flush

Spur (-, -en) f trace; (*Fußspur, Radspur*) track; (*Fährte*) trail; (*Fahrspur*) lane; **die ~ wechseln** to change lanes pl

spüren vt to feel; (*merken*) to notice; **Spürhund** m sniffer dog

Squash (-) nt squash; **Squashschläger** m squash racket

Sri Lanka (-s) nt Sri Lanka

Staat (-(e)s, -en) m state; **staatlich** adj state(-); (*vom Staat betrieben*) state-run; **Staatsangehörigkeit** f nationality; **Staatsanwalt** m, **-anwältin** f prosecuting counsel (*Brit*), district attorney (*US*); **Staatsbürger(in)** m(f) citizen; **Staatsbürgerschaft** f nationality; **doppelte ~** dual nationality; **Staatsexamen** nt final exam taken by trainee teachers, medical and law students

Stab (-(e)s, Stäbe) m rod; (*Gitter*) bar; **Stäbchen** nt (*Essstäbchen*) chopstick; **Stabhochsprung** m pole vault

stabil adj stable; (*Möbel*) sturdy

stach imperf von **stechen**

Stachel (-s, -n) m spike; (*von Tier*) spine; (*von Insekten*) sting; **Stachelbeere** f gooseberry; **Stacheldraht** m barbed wire; **stachelig** adj prickly

Stadion (-s, Stadien) nt stadium

Stadt (-, Städte) f town; (*groß*) city; **in der ~** in town; **Stadtautobahn** f urban motorway (*Brit*) (o expressway (*US*)); **Stadtbummel** (-s, -) m: **einen ~ machen** to go round town; **Stadtführer** m (*Heft*) city

guide; **Stadtführung** f city sightseeing tour; **Stadthalle** f municipal hall; **städtisch** adj municipal; **Stadtmauer** f city wall(s); **Stadtmitte** f town/city centre, downtown (*US*); **Stadtplan** m (*street*) map; **Stadtrand** m outskirts pl; **Stadtrundfahrt** f city tour; **Stadtteil** m, **Stadtviertel** nt district, part of town; **Stadtzentrum** nt town/city centre, downtown (*US*)

stahl imperf von **stehlen**

Stahl (-(e)s, Stähle) m steel

Stall (-(e)s, Ställe) m stable; (*Kaninchen*) hutch; (*Schweine*) pigsty; (*Hühner*) henhouse

Stamm (-(e)s, Stämme) m (*Baum*) trunk; (*von Menschen*) tribe; **stammen** vi: **~ aus** to come from; **Stammgast** m regular (guest); **Stammkunde** m, **Stammkundin** f regular (customer); **Stammtisch** m table reserved for regulars

stampfen vt, vi to stamp; (*mit Werkzeug*) to pound; (*stapfen*) to tramp

stand imperf von **stehen**

Stand (-(e)s, Stände) m (*Wasser, Benzin*) level; (*Stehen*) standing position; (*Zustand*) state; (*Spielstand*) score; (*auf Messe etc*) stand; (*Klasse*) class; **im ~e sein** to be in a position; (*fähig*) to be able

Stand-by-Betrieb m stand-by; **Stand-by-Ticket** nt stand-by ticket

Ständer (-s, -) m (*Gestell*) stand; (*fam: Erektion*) hard-on

Standesamt nt registry office

ständig adj permanent; (*ununterbrochen*) constant, continual

Standlicht nt sidelights pl (*Brit*), parking lights pl (*US*); **Standort** m position; **Standpunkt** m

standpoint; **Standspur** f (Auto)
hard shoulder (Brit), shoulder
(US)
Stange (-, -n) f stick; (Stab) pole;
(Metall) bar; (Zigaretten) carton;
Stangenbohne f runner (Brit) (o
string (US)) bean; **Stangenbrot**
nt French stick; **Stangensellerie**
m celery
stank imperf von **stinken**
Stapel (-s, -) m pile
Star (-(e)s, -e) m (Vogel) starling;
(Med) cataract ▷ (-s, -s) m (in Film
etc) star
starb imperf von **sterben**
stark adj strong; (heftig, groß)
heavy; (Maßangabe) thick; **Stärke**
(-, -n) f strength; (Dicke)
thickness; (Wäschestärke,
Speisestärke) starch; **stärken** vt
to strengthen; (Wäsche) to starch;
Starkstrom m high-voltage
current; **Stärkung** f
strengthening; (Essen)
refreshment
starr adj stiff; (unnachgiebig) rigid;
(Blick) staring
starren vi to stare
Start (-(e)s, -e) m start; (Aviat)
takeoff; **Startautomatik** f
automatic choke; **Startbahn** f
runway; **starten** vt, vi to start;
(Aviat) to take off; **Starthilfekabel**
nt jump leads pl (Brit), jumper
cables pl (US); **Startmenü** nt
(Inform) start menu
Station f (Haltestelle) stop;
(Bahnhof) station; (im Krankenhaus)
ward; **stationär** adj stationary;
~e Behandlung in-patient
treatment; **jdn ~ behandeln** to
treat sb as an in-patient
Statistik f statistics pl
Stativ nt tripod
statt conj, prep +gen o dat instead
of; **~ zu arbeiten** instead of
working

statt|finden irr vi to take place
Statue (-, -n) f statue
Statusleiste f, **Statuszeile** f
(Inform) status bar
Stau (-(e)s, -e) m (im Verkehr)
(traffic) jam; **im ~ stehen** to be
stuck in a traffic jam
Staub (-(e)s) m dust; **~ wischen**
to dust; **staubig** adj dusty;
staubsaugen vt, vi to vacuum, to
hoover (Brit); **Staubsauger** m
vacuum cleaner, Hoover® (Brit);
Staubtuch nt duster
Staudamm m dam
staunen vi to be astonished (über
+akk at)
Stausee m reservoir; **Stauung** f
(von Wasser) damming-up; (von
Blut, Verkehr) congestion;
Stauwarnung f traffic report
Std. abk = **Stunde** h
Steak (-s, -s) nt steak
stechen (stach, gestochen) vt, vi
(mit Nadel etc) to prick; (mit Messer)
to stab; (mit Finger) to poke; (Biene)
to sting; (Mücke) to bite; (Sonne) to
burn; (Kartenspiel) to trump;
Stechen (-s, -) nt sharp pain,
stabbing pain; **Stechmücke** f
mosquito
Steckdose f socket; **stecken** vt
to put; (Nadel) to stick; (beim
Nähen) to pin ▷ vi (festsitzen) to be
stuck; (Nadeln) to be (sticking); **der
Schlüssel steckt** the key is in the
door; **Stecker** (-s, -) m plug;
Steckrübe f swede (Brit),
rutabaga (US)
Steg (-s, -e) m bridge
stehen (stand, gestanden) vi to
stand (zu by); (sich befinden) to be;
(stillstehen) to have stopped; **was
steht im Brief?** what does it say in
the letter?; **jdm (gut) ~** to suit sb;
~ bleiben (Uhr) to stop; **~ lassen**
to leave ▷ vi impers: **wie steht's?**
(Sport) what's the score?

stehlen (*stahl, gestohlen*) *vt* to steal

Stehplatz *m* (*im Konzert etc*) standing ticket

Steiermark (-) *f* Styria

steif *adj* stiff

steigen (*stieg, gestiegen*) *vi* (*Preise, Temperatur*) to rise; (*klettern*) to climb; **~ in/auf** (*+akk*) to get in/on

steigern *vt* to increase ▷ *vr*: **sich ~** to increase

Steigung *f* incline, gradient

steil *adj* steep; **Steilhang** *m* steep slope; **Steilküste** *f* steep coast

Stein (-(*e*)*s, -e*) *m* stone; **Steinbock** *m* (*Zool*) ibex; (*Astr*) Capricorn; **steinig** *adj* stony; **Steinschlag** *m* falling rocks *pl*

Stelle (-, -*n*) *f* place, spot; (*Arbeit*) post, job; (*Amt*) office; **ich an deiner ~** if I were you; **auf der ~** straightaway; **stellen** *vt* to put; (*Uhr etc*) to set (*auf +akk* to); (*zur Verfügung stellen*) to provide ▷ *vr*: **sich ~** (*bei Polizei*) to give oneself up; **sich schlafend ~** to pretend to be asleep; **Stellenangebot** *nt* job offer, vacancy; **stellenweise** *adv* in places; **Stellenwert** *m* (*fig*) status; **einen hohen ~ haben** to play an important role; **Stellplatz** *m* parking space; **Stellung** *f* position; **zu etw ~ nehmen** to comment on sth; **Stellvertreter(in)** *m(f)* representative; (*amtlich*) deputy; (*von Arzt*) locum (*Brit*), locum tenens (*US*)

Stempel (-*s, -*) *m* stamp; **stempeln** *vt* to stamp; (*Briefmarke*) to cancel

sterben (*starb, gestorben*) *vi* to die

Stereoanlage *f* stereo (system)

steril *adj* sterile; **sterilisieren** *vt* to sterilize

Stern (-(*e*)*s, -e*) *m* star; **ein Hotel mit vier ~en** a four-star hotel; **Sternbild** *nt* constellation; (*Sternzeichen*) star sign, sign of the zodiac; **Sternfrucht** *f* star fruit; **Sternschnuppe** (-, -*n*) *f* shooting star; **Sternwarte** (-*e, -n*) *f* observatory; **Sternzeichen** *nt* star sign, sign of the zodiac; **welches ~ bist du?** what's your star sign?

stets *adv* always

Steuer (-*s, -*) *nt* (*Auto*) steering wheel ▷ (-, -*n*) *f* tax; **Steuerberater(in)** *m(f)* tax adviser; **Steuerbord** *nt* starboard; **Steuererklärung** *f* tax declaration; **steuerfrei** *adj* tax-free; (*Waren*) duty-free; **Steuerknüppel** *m* control column; (*Aviat, Inform*) joystick; **steuern** *vt*, to steer; (*Flugzeug*) to pilot; (*Entwicklung, Tonstärke*) (*Inform*) to control; **steuerpflichtig** *adj* taxable; **Steuerung** *f* (*Auto*) steering; (*Vorrichtung*) controls *pl*; (*Aviat*) piloting; (*fig*) control; **Steuerungstaste** *f* (*Inform*) control key

Stich (-(*e*)*s, -e*) *m* (*von Insekt*) sting; (*von Mücke*) bite; (*durch Messer*) stab; (*beim Nähen*) stitch; (*Färbung*) tinge; (*Kartenspiel*) trick; (*Kunst*) engraving

sticken *vt, vi* to embroider

Sticker (-*s, -*) *m* sticker

Stickerei *f* embroidery

stickig *adj* stuffy, close

Stiefbruder *m* stepbrother

Stiefel (-*s, -*) *m* boot

Stiefmutter *f* stepmother

Stiefmütterchen *nt* pansy

Stiefschwester *f* stepsister; **Stiefsohn** *m* stepson; **Stieftochter** *f* stepdaughter; **Stiefvater** *m* stepfather

stieg *imperf von* **steigen**

Stiege (-, -n) f steps pl
Stiel (-(e)s, -e) m handle; (Bot) stalk; **ein Eis am ~** an ice lolly (Brit), a Popsicle® (US)
Stier (-(e)s, -e) m (Zool) bull; (Astr) Taurus; **Stierkampf** m bullfight
stieß imperf von **stoßen**
Stift (-(e)s, -e) m (aus Holz) peg; (Nagel) tack; (zum Schreiben) pen; (Farbstift) crayon; (Bleistift) pencil
Stil (-s, -e) m style
still adj quiet; (unbewegt) still
stillen vt (Säugling) to breast-feed
still|halten irr vi to keep still; **still|stehen** irr vi to stand still
Stimme (-, -n) f voice; (bei Wahl) vote
stimmen vi to be right; **stimmt!** that's right; **hier stimmt was nicht** there's something wrong here; **stimmt so!** (beim Bezahlen) keep the change
Stimmung f mood; (Atmosphäre) atmosphere
Stinkefinger m (fam) **jdm den ~ zeigen** to give sb the finger (o bird (US))
stinken (stank, gestunken) vi to stink (nach of)
Stipendium (-s, -(e)s) nt scholarship; (als Unterstützung) grant
Stirn (-, -en) f forehead; **Stirnhöhle** f sinus
Stock (-(e)s, Stöcke) m stick; (Bot) stock ▷ m (Stockwerke) floor, storey; **Stockbett** nt bunk bed; **Stöckelschuhe** pl high-heels; **Stockwerk** nt floor; **im ersten ~** on the first floor (Brit), on the second floor (US)
Stoff (-(e)s, -e) m (Gewebe) material; (Materie) matter; (von Buch etc) subject (matter); (fam: Rauschgift) stuff
stöhnen vi to groan (vor with)
stolpern vi to stumble, to trip
stolz adj proud

stopp interj hold it; (Moment mal!) hang on a minute; **stoppen** vt, vi to stop; (mit Uhr) to time; **Stoppschild** nt stop sign; **Stoppuhr** f stopwatch
Stöpsel (-s, -) m plug; (für Flaschen) stopper
Storch (-(e)s, Störche) m stork
stören vt to disturb; (behindern) to interfere with; **darf ich dich kurz ~?** can I trouble you for a minute?; **stört es dich, wenn ...?** do you mind if ...?
stornieren vt to cancel; **Stornogebühr** f cancellation fee
Störung f disturbance; (in der Leitung) fault
Stoß (-es, Stöße) m (Schub) push; (Schlag) blow; (mit Fuß) kick; (Haufen) pile; **Stoßdämpfer** (-s, -) m shock absorber
stoßen (stieß, gestoßen) vt (mit Druck) to shove, to push; (mit Schlag) to knock; (mit Fuß) to kick; (anstoßen) to bump; (zerkleinern) to pulverize ▷ vr: **sich ~** to bang oneself; **sich ~ an** (+dat) (fig) to take exception to
Stoßstange f (Auto) bumper
stottern vt, vi to stutter
Str. abk von **Straße** St, Rd
Strafe (-, -n) f punishment; (Sport) penalty; (Gefängnisstrafe) sentence; (Geldstrafe) fine; **strafen** vt to punish; **Straftat** f (criminal) offence; **Strafzettel** m ticket
Strahl (-s, -en) m ray, beam; (Wasser) jet; **strahlen** vi to radiate; (fig) to beam
Strähne (-, -n) f strand; (weiß, gefärbt) streak
Strand (-(e)s, Strände) m beach; **am ~** on the beach; **Strandcafé** nt beach café; **Strandkorb** m wicker beach chair with a hood; **Strandpromenade** f promenade

strapazieren vt (*Material*) to be hard on; (*Mensch, Kräfte*) to be a strain on

Straße (-, -n) f road; (*in der Stadt*) street; **Straßenarbeiten** pl roadworks pl (*Brit*), road repairs pl (*US*); **Straßenbahn** f tram (*Brit*), streetcar (*US*); **Straßencafé** nt pavement café (*Brit*), sidewalk café (*US*); **Straßenfest** nt street party; **Straßenglätte** f slippery roads pl; **Straßenkarte** f road map; **Straßenrand** m: **am ~** at the roadside; **Straßenschild** nt street sign; **Straßensperre** f roadblock; **Straßenverhältnisse** pl road conditions pl

Strategie (-, -n) f strategy

Strauch (-(e)s, Sträucher) m bush, shrub; **Strauchtomate** f vine-ripened tomato

Strauß (-es, Sträuße) m bunch; (*als Geschenk*) bouquet ▷ m (*Strauße*) (*Vogel*) ostrich

Strecke (-, -n) f route; (*Entfernung*) distance; (*Eisenb*) line

strecken vt to stretch ▷ vr: **sich ~** to stretch

streckenweise adv (*teilweise*) in parts; (*zeitweise*) at times

Streich (-(e)s, -e) m trick, prank

streicheln vt to stroke

streichen (*strich, gestrichen*) vt (*anmalen*) to paint; (*berühren*) to stroke; (*auftragen*) to spread; (*durchstreichen*) to delete; (*nicht genehmigen*) to cancel

Streichholz nt match; **Streichholzschachtel** f matchbox; **Streichkäse** m cheese spread

Streifen (-s, -) m (*Linie*) stripe; (*Stück*) strip; (*Film*) film

Streifenwagen m patrol car

Streik (-(e)s, -s) m strike; **streiken** vi to be on strike

Streit (-(e)s, -e) m argument (*um, wegen* about, over); **streiten** (*stritt, gestritten*) vi to argue (*um, wegen* about, over) ▷ vr: **sich ~** to argue (*um, wegen* about, over)

streng adj (*Blick*) severe; (*Lehrer*) strict; (*Geruch*) sharp

Stress (-es) m stress; **stressen** vt to stress (out); **stressig** adj (*fam*) stressful

Stretching (-s) nt (*Sport*) stretching exercises pl

streuen vt to scatter; **die Straßen ~** to grit the roads; (*mit Salz*) to put salt down on the roads; **Streufahrzeug** nt gritter lorry (*Brit*), salt truck (*US*)

strich imperf von **streichen**

Strich (-(e)s, -e) m (*Linie*) line; **Stricher** m (*fam: Strichjunge*) rent boy (*Brit*), boy prostitute; **Strichkode** (-s, -s) m bar code; **Stricherin** f (*fam: Strichmädchen*) hooker; **Strichpunkt** m semicolon

Strick (-(e)s, -e) m rope

stricken vt, vi to knit; **Strickjacke** f cardigan; **Stricknadel** f knitting needle

String (-s, -s) m, **Stringtanga** m G-string

Stripper(in) m(f) stripper; **Striptease** (-) m striptease

stritt imperf von **streiten**

Stroh (-(e)s) nt straw; **Strohdach** nt thatched roof; **Strohhalm** m (drinking) straw

Strom (-(e)s, Ströme) m river; (*fig*) stream; (*Elek*) current; **Stromanschluss** m connection; **Stromausfall** m power failure

strömen vi to stream, to pour; **Strömung** f current

Stromverbrauch m power consumption; **Stromzähler** m electricity meter

Strophe (-, -n) f verse

Strudel (-s, -) m (in Fluss) whirlpool; (Gebäck) strudel

Struktur f structure; (von Material) texture

Strumpf (-(e)s, Strümpfe) m (Damenstrumpf) stocking; (Socke) sock; **Strumpfhose** f (pair of) tights pl (Brit), pantyhose (US)

Stück (-(e)s, -e) nt piece; (von Zucker) lump; (etwas) bit; (Zucker) lump; (Theat) play; **ein ~ Käse** a piece of cheese

Student(in) m(f) student; **Studentenausweis** m student card; **Studentenwohnheim** nt hall of residence (Brit), dormitory (US); **Studienabschluss** m qualification (at the end of a course of higher education); **Studienfahrt** f study trip; **Studienplatz** m university/college place; **studieren** vt, vi to study; **Studium** nt studies pl; **während seines ~s** while he is/was studying

Stufe (-, -n) f step; (Entwicklungsstufe) stage

Stuhl (-(e)s, Stühle) m chair

stumm adj silent; (Med) dumb

stumpf adj blunt; (teilnahmslos, glanzlos) dull; **stumpfsinnig** adj dull

Stunde (-, -n) f hour; (Unterricht) lesson; **eine halbe ~** half an hour; **Stundenkilometer** m: **80 ~** 80 kilometres an hour; **stundenlang** adv for hours; **Stundenlohn** m hourly wage; **Stundenplan** m timetable; **stündlich** adj hourly

Stuntman (-s, Stuntmen) m stuntman; **Stuntwoman** (-, Stuntwomen) f stuntwoman

stur adj stubborn; (stärker) pigheaded

Sturm (-(e)s, Stürme) m storm; **stürmen** vi (Wind) to blow hard; (rennen) to storm; **Stürmer(in)** m(f) striker, forward; **Sturmflut** f storm tide; **stürmisch** adj stormy; (fig) tempestuous; (Zeit) turbulent; (Liebhaber) passionate; (Beifall, Begrüßung) tumultuous; **Sturmwarnung** f gale warning

Sturz (-es, Stürze) m fall; (Pol) overthrow; **stürzen** vt (werfen) to hurl; (Pol) to overthrow; (umkehren) to overturn ⊳ vi to fall; (rennen) to dash; **Sturzhelm** m crash helmet

Stute (-, -n) f mare

Stütze (-, -n) f support; (Hilfe) help; (fam: Arbeitslosenunterstützung) dole (Brit), welfare (US)

stützen vt to support; (Ellbogen) to prop

stutzig adj perplexed, puzzled; (misstrauisch) suspicious

Styropor® (-s) nt polystyrene (Brit), styrofoam (US)

subjektiv adj subjective

Substanz (-, -en) f substance

subtrahieren vt to subtract

Subvention f subsidy; **subventionieren** vt to subsidize

Suche f search (nach for); **auf der ~ nach etw sein** to be looking for sth; **suchen** vt to look for; (Inform) to search ⊳ vi to look, to search (nach for); **Suchmaschine** f (Inform) search engine

Sucht (-, Süchte) f mania; (Med) addiction; **süchtig** adj addicted; **Süchtige(r)** mf addict

Süd south; **Südafrika** nt South Africa; **Südamerika** nt South America; **Süddeutschland** nt Southern Germany; **Süden** (-s) m south; **im ~ Deutschlands** in the south of Germany; **Südeuropa** nt Southern Europe; **Südkorea** (-s) nt South Korea; **südlich** adj southern; (Kurs, Richtung) southerly; **Verkehr in ~er**

Richtung southbound traffic;
Südost(en) m southeast; **Südpol**
m South Pole; **Südstaaten** pl
(*der USA*) the Southern States pl,
the South *sing*; **südwärts** *adv*
south, southwards; **Südwest(en)**
m southwest; **Südwind** m south
wind
Sülze (-, -n) f jellied meat
Summe (-, -n) f sum;
(*Gesamtsumme*) total
summen *vi, vt* to hum; (*Insekt*) to
buzz
Sumpf (-(e)s, Sümpfe) m marsh;
(*subtropischer*) swamp; **sumpfig**
adj marshy
Sünde (-, -n) f sin
super *adj* (*fam*) super, great;
Super (-s) nt (*Benzin*) four star
(petrol) (*Brit*), premium (*US*);
Supermarkt m supermarket
Suppe (-, -n) f soup; **Suppengrün**
nt bunch of herbs and vegetables for
flavouring soup; **Suppenlöffel** m
soup spoon; **Suppenschüssel** f
soup tureen; **Suppentasse** f
soup cup; **Suppenteller** m soup
plate; **Suppenwürfel** m stock
cube
Surfbrett nt surfboard; **surfen** *vi*
to surf; **im Internet ~** to surf the
Internet; **Surfer(in)** (-s, -) m(f)
surfer
Surrealismus m surrealism
Sushi (-s, -s) nt sushi
süß *adj* sweet; **süßen** *vt* to
sweeten; **Süßigkeit** f (*Bonbon
etc*) sweet (*Brit*), candy (*US*);
Süßkartoffel f sweet potato
(*Brit*), yam (*US*); **süßsauer** *adj*
sweet-and-sour; **Süßspeise** f
dessert; **Süßstoff** m sweetener;
Süßwasser nt fresh water
Sweatshirt (-s, -s) nt sweatshirt
Swimmingpool (-s, -s) m
(swimming) pool
Sylvester nt *siehe* **Silvester**

Symbol (-s, -e) nt symbol;
Symbolleiste f (*Inform*) toolbar
Symmetrie (-, -n) f symmetry;
symmetrisch *adj* symmetrical
sympathisch *adj* nice; **jdn
~ finden** to like sb
Symphonie (-, -n) f symphony
Symptom (-s, -e) nt symptom
(*für of*)
Synagoge (-, -n) f synagogue
synchronisiert *adj* (*Film*)
dubbed; **Synchronstimme** f
dubbing voice
Synthetik (-, -en) f synthetic
(fibre); **synthetisch** *adj*
synthetic
Syrien (-s) nt Syria
System (-s, -e) nt system;
systematisch *adj* systematic;
Systemsteuerung f (*Inform*)
control panel
Szene (-, -n) f scene

t

Tabak (-s, -e) m tobacco;
Tabakladen m tobacconist's
Tabelle f table
Tablett (-s, -s) nt tray
Tablette f tablet, pill
Tabulator m tabulator, tab
Tacho(meter) (-s, -) m (Auto)
speedometer
Tafel (-, -n) f (a. Math) table;
(Anschlagtafel) board; (Wandtafel)
blackboard; (Schiefer~) slate;
(Gedenktafel) plaque; **eine
~ Schokolade** a bar of chocolate;
Tafelwasser nt table water;
Tafelwein m table wine
Tag (-(e)s, -e) m day; (Tageslicht)
daylight; **guten ~!** good
morning/afternoon; **am ~** during
the day; **sie hat ihre ~e** she's got
her period; **eines ~es** one day;
~ der Arbeit Labour Day;
Tagebuch nt diary; **tagelang**
adj for days (on end);

Tagesanbruch m daybreak;
Tagesausflug m day trip;
Tagescreme f day cream;
Tagesdecke f bedspread;
Tagesgericht nt dish of the day;
Tageskarte f (Fahrkarte) day
ticket; **die ~** (Speisekarte) today's
menu; **Tageslicht** nt daylight;
Tagesmutter f child minder;
Tagesordnung f agenda;
Tagestour f day trip;
Tageszeitung f daily newspaper;
täglich adj, adv daily; **tags(über)**
adv during the day; **Tagung** f
conference
Tai Chi (-) nt tai chi
Taille (-, -n) f waist
Taiwan (-s) nt Taiwan
Takt (-(e)s, -e) m (Taktgefühl) tact;
(Mus) time
Taktik (-, -en) f tactics pl
taktlos adj tactless; **taktvoll** adj
tactful
Tal (-(e)s, Täler) nt valley
Talent (-(e)s, -e) nt talent;
talentiert adj talented
Talkmaster(in) (-s, -) m(f) talk-show
host; **Talkshow** (-, -s) f talkshow
Tampon (-s, -s) m tampon
Tandem (-s, -s) nt tandem
Tang (-s, -e) m seaweed
Tanga (-s, -s) m thong
Tank (-s, -s) m tank;
Tankanzeige f fuel gauge;
Tankdeckel m fuel cap; **tanken** vi
to get some petrol (Brit) (o gas
(US)); (Aviat) to refuel; **Tanker**
(-s, -) m (oil) tanker; **Tankstelle** f
petrol station (Brit), gas station
(US); **Tankwart(in)** (-s, -e) m(f)
petrol pump attendant (Brit), gas
station attendant (US)
Tanne (-, -n) f fir; **Tannenzapfen**
m fir cone
Tansania (-s) nt Tanzania
Tante (-, -n) f aunt;
Tante-Emma-Laden m corner

shop (Brit), grocery store (US)

Tanz (-es, Tänze) m dance; **tanzen**
vt, vi to dance; **Tänzer(in)** m(f)
dancer; **Tanzfläche** f dance floor;
Tanzkurs m dancing course;
Tanzlehrer(in) m(f) dancing
instructor; **Tanzstunde** f
dancing lesson

Tapete (-, -n) f wallpaper;
tapezieren vt, vi to wallpaper

Tarantel (-, -n) f tarantula

Tarif (-s, -e) m tariff, (scale of)
fares/charges pl

Tasche (-, -n) f bag; (Hosentasche)
pocket; (Handtasche) bag (Brit),
purse (US)

Taschen- in zW pocket;
Taschenbuch nt paperback;
Taschendieb(in) m(f) pick-
pocket; **Taschengeld** nt pocket
money; **Taschenlampe** f torch
(Brit), flashlight (US);
Taschenmesser nt penknife;
Taschenrechner m pocket
calculator; **Taschentuch** nt
handkerchief

Tasse (-, -n) f cup; **eine ~ Kaffee**
a cup of coffee

Tastatur f keyboard; **Taste**
(-, -n) f button; (von Klavier,
Computer) key; **Tastenkombi-
nation** f (Inform) shortcut

tat imperf von **tun**

Tat (-, -en) f action

Tatar (-s, -s) nt raw minced beef

Täter(in) (-s, -) m(f) culprit

tätig adj active; **in einer Firma
~ sein** to work for a firm;
Tätigkeit f activity; (Beruf)
occupation

tätowieren vt to tattoo;
Tätowierung f tattoo (an +dat
on)

Tatsache f fact; **tatsächlich** adj
actual ▷ adv really

Tau (-(e)s, -e) nt (Seil) rope ▷ (-(e)s)
m dew

taub adj deaf; (Füße etc) numb (vor
Kälte with cold)

Taube (-, -n) f pigeon; (Turtel~,
fig: Friedenssymbol) dove

taubstumm adj deaf-and-dumb;
Taubstumme(r) mf deaf-mute

tauchen vt to dip ▷ vi to dive;
(Naut) to submerge; **Tauchen** (-s)
nt diving; **Taucher(in)** (-s, -) m(f)
diver; **Taucheranzug** m diving
(o wet) suit; **Taucherbrille** f
diving goggles pl; **Tauchermaske**
f diving mask; **Tauchkurs** m
diving course; **Tauchsieder** (-s, -)
m portable immersion coil for heating
water

tauen vi impers to thaw

Taufe (-, -n) f baptism; **taufen**
vt to baptize; (nennen) to christen

taugen vi to be suitable (für for);
nichts ~ to be no good

Tausch (-(e)s, -e) m exchange;
tauschen vt to exchange, to
swap

täuschen vt to deceive ▷ vi to
be deceptive ▷ vr: **sich ~** to be
wrong; **täuschend** adj
deceptive; **Täuschung** f
deception; (optisch) illusion

tausend num a thousand;
vier~ four thousand; **~ Dank!**
thanks a lot; **tausendmal** adv a
thousand times; **tausendste(r, s)**
adj thousandth; **Tausendstel**
(-s, -) nt (Bruchteil) thousandth

Taxi nt taxi; **Taxifahrer(in)** m(f)
taxi driver; **Taxistand** m taxi
rank (Brit), taxi stand (US)

Team (-s, -s) nt team;
Teamarbeit f team work;
teamfähig adj able to work in a
team

Technik f technology;
(angewandte) engineering;
(Methode) technique;
Techniker(in) (-s, -) m(f) engineer; (Sport, Mus) technician;

technisch *adj* technical
Techno (-s) *m* (*Mus*) techno
Teddybär *m* teddy bear
TEE *abk* = **Trans-Europ-Express**
Trans-Europe-Express
Tee (-s, -s) *m* tea; **Teebeutel** *m*
teabag; **Teekanne** *f* teapot;
Teelöffel *m* teaspoon
Teer (-(e)s, -e) *m* tar
Teesieb *nt* tea strainer; **Teetasse**
f teacup
Teich (-(e)s, -e) *m* pond
Teig (-(e)s, -e) *m* dough;
Teigwaren *pl* pasta *sing*
Teil (-(e)s, -e) *m* part; (*Anteil*)
share; **zum ~** partly ▷ (-(e)s, -e) *nt*
part; (*Bestandteil*) component;
teilen *vt* to divide; (*mit jdm*) to
share (*mit* with); **20 durch 4 ~** to
divide 20 by 4 ▷ *vr*: **sich ~** to
divide
Teilkaskoversicherung *f* third
party, fire and theft insurance
teilmöbliert *adj* partly furnished
Teilnahme (-, -n) *f* participation
(*an* +*dat* in); **teilnehmen** *irr vi* to
take part (*an* +*dat* in); **Teilneh-
mer(in)** (-s, -) *m(f)* participant
teils *adv* partly; **teilweise** *adv*
partially, in part; **Teilzeit** *f*:
~ arbeiten to work part-time
Teint (-s, -s) *m* complexion
Tel. *abk von* **Telefon** tel.
Telefon (-s, -e) *nt* telephone;
Telefonanruf *m*, **Telefonat** *nt*
(tele)phone call;
Telefonanschluss *m* telephone
connection; **Telefonauskunft** *f*
directory enquiries *pl* (*Brit*),
directory assistance (*US*);
Telefonbuch *nt* telephone
directory; **Telefongebühren** *pl*
telephone charges *pl*;
Telefongespräch *nt* telephone
conversation; **telefonieren** *vi*:
ich telefoniere gerade (mit ...)
I'm on the phone (to ...);

telefonisch *adj* telephone;
(*Benachrichtigung*) by telephone;
Telefonkarte *f* phonecard;
Telefonnummer *f* (tele)phone
number; **Telefonrechnung** *f*
phone bill; **Telefonverbindung** *f*
telephone connection;
Telefonzelle *f* phone box (*Brit*),
phone booth; **Telefonzentrale** *f*
switchboard; **über die ~** through
the switchboard
Telegramm *nt* telegram;
Teleobjektiv *nt* telephoto lens;
Teleshopping (-s) *nt* teleshopping; **Teleskop** (-s, -e) *nt*
telescope
Teller (-s, -) *m* plate
Tempel (-s, -) *m* temple
Temperament *nt* temperament; (*Schwung*) liveliness;
temperamentvoll *adj* lively
Temperatur *f* temperature; **bei
~en von 30 Grad** at temperatures
of 30 degrees; **~ haben** to have a
temperature; **~ bei jdm messen** to
take sb's temperature
Tempo (-s, -s) *nt* (*Geschwindigkeit*)
speed; **Tempolimit** (-s, -s) *nt*
speed limit
Tempotaschentuch® *nt*
(*Papiertaschentuch*) (paper) tissue
Tendenz *f* tendency; (*Absicht*)
intention
Tennis (-) *nt* tennis; **Tennisball**
m tennis ball; **Tennisplatz** *m*
tennis court; **Tennisschläger** *m*
tennis racket; **Tennisspieler(in)**
m(f) tennis player
Tenor (-s, Tenöre) *m* tenor
Teppich (-s, -e) *m* carpet;
Teppichboden *m* (fitted) carpet
Termin (-s, -e) *m* (*Zeitpunkt*) date;
(*Frist*) deadline; (*Arzttermin etc*)
appointment
Terminal (-s, -s) *nt* (*Inform, Aviat*)
terminal
Terminkalender *m* diary;

t

Terminplaner m (in Buchform) personal organizer, Filofax®; (Taschencomputer) personal digital assistant, PDA

Terpentin (-s, -e) nt turpentine, turps sing

Terrasse (-, -n) f terrace; (hinter einem Haus) patio

Terror (-s) m terror; **Terroranschlag** m terrorist attack; **terrorisieren** vt to terrorize; **Terrorismus** m terrorism; **Terrorist(in)** m(f) terrorist

Tesafilm® m ≈ sellotape® (Brit), ≈ Scotch tape® (US)

Test (-s, -s) m test

Testament nt will; **das Alte/Neue ~** the Old/New Testament

testen vt to test; **Testergebnis** nt test results pl

Tetanus (-) m tetanus; **Tetanusimpfung** f (anti-)tetanus injection

teuer adj expensive, dear (Brit)

Teufel (-s, -) m devil; **was/wo zum ~** what/where the devil; **Teufelskreis** m vicious circle

Text (-(e)s, -e) m text; (Liedertext) words pl, lyrics pl; **Textmarker** (-s, -) m highlighter; **Textverarbeitung** f word processing; **Textverarbeitungsprogramm** nt word processing program

Thailand nt Thailand

Theater (-s, -) nt theatre; (fam) fuss; **ins ~ gehen** to go to the theatre; **Theaterkasse** f box office; **Theaterstück** nt (stage) play; **Theatervorstellung** f (stage) performance

Theke (-, -n) f (Schanktisch) bar; (Ladentisch) counter

Thema (-s, Themen) nt subject, topic; **kein ~!** no problem

Themse (-) f Thames

Theologie f theology

theoretisch adj theoretical; **~ stimmt das** that's right in theory; **Theorie** f theory

Therapeut(in) m(f) therapist; **Therapie** f therapy; **eine ~ machen** to undergo therapy

Thermalbad nt thermal bath; (Ort) thermal spa; **Thermometer** (-s, -) nt thermometer

Thermosflasche® f, **Thermoskanne®** f Thermos® (flask); **Thermostat** (-(e)s, -e) m thermostat

These (-, -n) f theory

Thron (-(e)s, -e) m throne

Thunfisch m tuna

Thüringen (-s) nt Thuringia

Thymian (-s, -e) m thyme

Tick (-(e)s, -s) m tic; (Eigenart) quirk; (Fimmel) craze; **ticken** vi to tick; **er tickt nicht ganz richtig** he's off his rocker

Ticket (-s, -s) nt (plane) ticket

tief adj deep; (Ausschnitt, Ton, Sonne) low; **2 Meter ~** 2 metres deep; **Tief** (-s, -s) nt (Meteo) low; (seelisch) depression; **Tiefdruck** m (Meteo) low pressure; **Tiefe** (-, -n) f depth; **Tiefgarage** f underground car park (Brit) (o garage (US)); **tiefgekühlt** adj frozen; **Tiefkühlfach** nt freezer compartment; **Tiefkühlkost** f frozen food; **Tiefkühltruhe** f freezer; **Tiefpunkt** m low

Tier (-(e)s, -e) nt animal; **Tierarzt** m, **Tierärztin** f vet; **Tiergarten** m zoo; **Tierhandlung** f pet shop; **Tierheim** nt animal shelter; **tierisch** adj animal ▷ adv (fam) really; **~ ernst** deadly serious; **ich hatte ~ Angst** I was dead scared; **Tierkreiszeichen** nt sign of the zodiac; **Tierpark** m zoo; **Tierquälerei** f cruelty to animals;

Tierschützer(in) *(-s, -)* *m(f)* animal rights campaigner; **Tierversuch** *m* animal experiment
Tiger *(-s, -)* *m* tiger
timen *vt* to time; **Timing** *(-s)* *nt* timing
Tinte *(-, -n)* *f* ink; **Tintenfisch** *m* cuttlefish; *(klein)* squid; *(achtarmig)* octopus; **Tintenfischringe** *pl* calamari *pl*; **Tintenstrahldrucker** *m* ink-jet printer
Tipp *(-s, -s)* *m* tip; **tippen** *vt, vi* to tap; *(fam: schreiben)* to type; *(fam: raten)* to guess
Tirol *(-s)* *nt* Tyrol
Tisch *(-(e)s, -e)* *m* table; **Tischdecke** *f* tablecloth; **Tischlerei** *f* joiner's workshop; *(Arbeit)* joinery; **Tischtennis** *nt* table tennis; **Tischtennisschläger** *m* table-tennis bat
Titel *(-s, -)* *m* title; **Titelbild** *nt* cover picture
Toast *(-(e)s, -s)* *m* toast; **toasten** *vt* to toast; **Toaster** *(-s, -)* *m* toaster
Tochter *(-, Töchter)* *f* daughter
Tod *(-(e)s, -e)* *m* death; **Todesopfer** *nt* casualty; **Todesstrafe** *f* death penalty; **todkrank** *adj* terminally ill; *(sehr krank)* seriously ill; **tödlich** *adj* deadly, fatal; **er ist ~ verunglückt** he was killed in an accident; **todmüde** *adj (fam)* dead tired; **todsicher** *adj (fam)* dead certain
Tofu *(-(s))* *m* tofu, bean curd
Toilette *f* toilet, restroom *(US)*; **Toilettenpapier** *nt* toilet paper
toi, toi, toi *interj* good luck
tolerant *adj* tolerant *(gegen* of)
toll *adj* mad; *(Treiben)* wild; *(fam: großartig)* great; **Tollkirsche** *f* deadly nightshade; **Tollwut** *f* rabies *sing*

Tomate *(-, -n)* *f* tomato; **Tomatenmark** *nt* tomato purée *(Brit)* *(o* paste *(US))*; **Tomatensaft** *m* tomato juice
Tombola *(-, -s)* *f* raffle, tombola *(Brit)*
Ton *(-(e)s, -e)* *m (Erde)* clay ▷ *m* *(Töne; Laut)* sound; *(Mus)* note; *(Redeweise)* tone; *(Farbton, Nuance)* shade; **Tonband** *nt* tape; **Tonbandgerät** *nt* tape recorder
tönen *vi* to sound ▷ *vt* to shade; *(Haare)* to tint
Toner *(-s, -)* *m* toner; **Tonerkassette** *f* toner cartridge
Tonne *(-, -n)* *f (Fass)* barrel; *(Gewicht)* tonne, metric ton
Tontechniker(in) *m(f)* sound engineer
Tönung *f* hue; *(für Haar)* rinse
Top *(-s, -s)* *nt* top
Topf *(-(e)s, Töpfe)* *m* pot
Töpfer(in) *(-s, -)* *m(f)* potter; **Töpferei** *f* pottery; *(Gegenstand)* piece of pottery
Tor *(-(e)s, -e)* *nt* gate; *(Sport)* goal; **ein ~ schießen** to score a goal; **Torhüter(in)** *m(f)* goalkeeper
torkeln *vi* to stagger
Tornado *(-s, -s)* *m* tornado
Torschütze *m*, **Torschützin** *f* (goal)scorer
Torte *(-, -n)* *f* cake; *(Obsttorte)* flan; *(Sahnetorte)* gateau
Torwart(in) *(-s, -e)* *m(f)* goalkeeper
tot *adj* dead; **~er Winkel** blind spot
total *adj* total, complete; **Totalschaden** *m* complete write-off
Tote(r) *mf* dead man/woman; *(Leiche)* corpse; **töten** *vt, vi* to kill; **Totenkopf** *m* skull
tot|lachen *vr*: **sich ~** to kill oneself laughing
Toto *(-s, -s)* *m o nt* pools *pl*

tot|schlagen *irr vt* to beat to death; **die Zeit ~** to kill time
Touchscreen (-s, -s) *m* touch screen
Tour (-, -en) *f* trip; (*Rundfahrt*) tour; **eine ~ nach York machen** to go on a trip to York; **Tourenski** *m* touring ski
Tourismus *m* tourism; **Tourist(in)** *m(f)* tourist; **Touristenklasse** *f* tourist class; **touristisch** *adj* tourist; (*pej*) touristy
traben *vi* to trot
Tournee (-, -n) *f* tour
Tracht (-, -en) *f* (*Kleidung*) traditional costume
Trackball (-s, -s) *m* (*Inform*) trackball
Tradition *f* tradition; **traditionell** *adj* traditional
traf *imperf von* **treffen**
Trafik (-, -en) *f* tobacconist's
Tragbahre (-, -n) *f* stretcher
tragbar *adj* portable
träge *adj* sluggish, slow
tragen (trug, getragen) *vt* to carry; (*Kleidung, Brille, Haare*) to wear; (*Namen, Früchte*) to bear; **Träger** (-s, -) *m* (*an Kleidung*) strap; (*Hosen~*) braces *pl* (*Brit*), suspenders *pl* (*US*); (*in der Architektur*) beam; (*Stahl~, Eisen~*) girder
Tragfläche *f* wing; **Tragflügelboot** *nt* hydrofoil
tragisch *adj* tragic; **Tragödie** *f* tragedy
Trainer(in) (-s, -) *m(f)* trainer, coach; **trainieren** *vt, vi* to train; (*jdn a.*) to coach; (*Übung*) to practise; **Training** (-s, -s) *nt* training; **Trainingsanzug** *m* tracksuit
Traktor *m* tractor
Trambahn *f* tram (*Brit*), streetcar (*US*)

trampen *vi* to hitchhike; **Tramper(in)** *m(f)* hitchhiker
Träne (-, -n) *f* tear; **tränen** *vi* to water; **Tränengas** *nt* teargas
trank *imperf von* **trinken**
Transfusion *f* transfusion
Transitverkehr *m* transit traffic; **Transitvisum** *nt* transit visa
Transplantation *f* transplant; (*Hauttransplantation*) graft
Transport (-(e)s, -e) *m* transport; **transportieren** *vt* to transport; **Transportmittel** *nt* means *sing of* transport; **Transportunternehmen** *nt* haulage firm
Transvestit (-en, -en) *m* transvestite
trat *imperf von* **treten**
Traube (-, -n) *f* (*einzelne Beere*) grape; (*ganze Frucht*) bunch of grapes; **Traubensaft** *m* grape juice; **Traubenzucker** *m* glucose
trauen *vi*: **jdm/einer Sache ~** to trust sb/sth; **ich traute meinen Ohren nicht** I couldn't believe my ears ▷ *vr*: **sich ~** to dare ▷ *vt* to marry; **sich ~ lassen** to get married
Trauer (-) *f* sorrow; (*für Verstorbenen*) mourning
Traum (-(e)s, Träume) *m* dream; **träumen** *vt, vi* to dream (*von of, about*); **traumhaft** *adj* dreamlike; (*fig*) wonderful
traurig *adj* sad (*über +akk about*)
Trauschein *m* marriage certificate; **Trauung** *f* wedding ceremony; **Trauzeuge** *m*, **Trauzeugin** *f* witness (*at wedding ceremony*), ≈ best man/maid of honour
Travellerscheck *m* traveller's cheque
treffen (traf, getroffen) *vr*: **sich ~** to meet ▷ *vt, vi* to hit; (*Bemerkung*) to hurt; (*begegnen*) to

meet; (*Entscheidung*) to make; (*Maßnahmen*) to take; **Treffen** (-s, -) *nt* meeting; **Treffer** (-s, -) *m* (*Tor*) goal; **Treffpunkt** *m* meeting place

treiben (*trieb, getrieben*) *vt* to drive; (*Sport*) to do ▷ *vi* (*im Wasser*) to drift; (*Pflanzen*) to sprout; (*Tee, Kaffee*) to be diuretic; **Treiber** (-s, -) *m* (*Inform*) driver

Treibgas *nt* propellant; **Treibhaus** *nt* greenhouse; **Treibstoff** *m* fuel

trennen *vt* to separate; (*teilen*) to divide ▷ *vr*: **sich ~** to separate; **sich von jdm ~** to leave sb; **sich von etw ~** to part with sth; **Trennung** *f* separation

Treppe (-, -n) *f* stairs *pl*; (*im Freien*) steps *pl*; **Treppengeländer** *nt* banister; **Treppenhaus** *nt* staircase

Tresen (-s, -) *m* (*in Kneipe*) bar; (*in Laden*) counter

Tresor (-s, -e) *m* safe

Tretboot *nt* pedal boat; **treten** (*trat, getreten*) *vi* to step; **mit jdm in Verbindung ~** to get in contact with sb ▷ *vt* to kick; (*nieder~*) to tread

treu *adj* (*gegenüber Partner*) faithful; (*Kunde, Fan*) loyal; **Treue** (-) *f* (*eheliche*) faithfulness; (*von Kunde, Fan*) loyalty

Triathlon (-s, -s) *m* triathlon

Tribüne (-, -n) *f* stand; (*Rednertribüne*) platform

Trick (-s, -e *o* -s) *m* trick; **Trickfilm** *m* cartoon

trieb *imperf von* **treiben**

Trieb (-(e)s, -e) *m* urge; (*Instinkt*) drive; (*Neigung*) inclination; (*an Baum etc*) shoot; **Triebwerk** *nt* engine

Trikot (-s, -s) *nt* shirt, jersey

Trimm-Dich-Pfad *m* fitness trail

trinkbar *adj* drinkable; **trinken** (*trank, getrunken*) *vt, vi* to drink; **einen ~ gehen** to go out for a drink; **Trinkgeld** *nt* tip; **Trinkhalm** *m* (drinking) straw; **Trinkwasser** *nt* drinking water

Trio (-s, -s) *nt* trio

Tripper (-s, -) *m* gonorrhoea

Tritt (-(e)s, -e) *m* (*Schritt*) step; (*Fußtritt*) kick; **Trittbrett** *nt* running board

Triumph (-(e)s, -e) *m* triumph; **triumphieren** *vi* to triumph (*über* +*akk* over)

trivial *adj* trivial

trocken *adj* dry; **Trockenhaube** *f* hair-dryer; **Trockenheit** *f* dryness; **trocken|legen** *vt* (*Baby*) to change; **trocknen** *vt, vi* to dry; **Trockner** (-s, -) *m* dryer

Trödel (-s) *m* (*fam*) junk; **Trödelmarkt** *m* flea market

trödeln *vi* (*fam*) to dawdle

Trommel (-, -n) *f* drum; **Trommelfell** *nt* eardrum; **trommeln** *vt, vi* to drum

Trompete (-, -n) *f* trumpet

Tropen *pl* tropics *pl*

Tropf (-(e)s, -e) *m* (*Med*) drip; **am ~ hängen** to be on a drip; **tröpfeln** *vi* to drip; **es tröpfelt** it's drizzling; **tropfen** *vt, vi* to drip; **Tropfen** (-s, -) *m* drop; **tropfenweise** *adv* drop by drop; **tropfnass** *adj* dripping wet; **Tropfsteinhöhle** *f* stalactite cave

tropisch *adj* tropical

Trost (-es) *m* consolation, comfort; **trösten** *vt* to console, to comfort; **trostlos** *adj* bleak; (*Verhältnisse*) wretched; **Trostpreis** *m* consolation prize

Trottoir (-s, -s) *nt* pavement (*Brit*), sidewalk (*US*)

trotz *prep* +*gen o dat* in spite of; **Trotz** (-es) *m* defiance; **trotzdem** *adv* nevertheless ▷ *conj* although;

trotzig *adj* defiant

trüb *adj* dull; *(Flüssigkeit, Glas)* cloudy; *(fig)* gloomy

Trüffel (-, -n) *f* truffle

trug *imperf von* **tragen**

trügerisch *adj* deceptive

Truhe (-, -n) *f* chest

Trümmer *pl* wreckage *sing*; *(Bau~)* ruins *pl*

Trumpf (-(e)s, Trümpfe) *m* trump

Trunkenheit *f* intoxication; **~ am Steuer** drink driving *(Brit)*, drunk driving *(US)*

Truthahn *m* turkey

Tscheche (-n, -n) *m*, **Tschechin** *f* Czech; **Tschechien** (-s) *nt* Czech Republic; **tschechisch** *adj* Czech; **Tschechische Republik** Czech Republic; **Tschechisch** *nt* Czech

Tschetschenien (-s) *nt* Chechnya

tschüs(s) *interj* bye

T-Shirt (-s, -s) *nt* T-shirt

Tube (-, -n) *f* tube

Tuberkulose (-, -n) *f* tuberculosis, TB

Tuch (-(e)s, Tücher) *nt* cloth; *(Halstuch)* scarf; *(Kopftuch)* headscarf

tüchtig *adj* competent; *(fleißig)* efficient; *(fam: kräftig)* good

Tugend (-, -en) *f* virtue; **tugendhaft** *adj* virtuous

Tulpe (-, -n) *f* tulip

Tumor (-s, -en) *m* tumour

tun (tat, getan) *vt* (machen) to do; *(legen)* to put; **was tust du da?** what are you doing?; **das tut man nicht** you shouldn't do that; **jdm etw ~** *(antun)* to do sth to sb; **das tut es auch** that'll do ▷ *vi* to act; **so ~, als ob** to act as if ▷ *vr impers*: **es tut sich etwas/viel** something/a lot is happening

Tuner (-s, -) *m* tuner

Tunesien (-s) *nt* Tunisia

Tunfisch *m siehe* **Thunfisch** tuna

Tunnel (-s, -s o -) *m* tunnel

Tunte (-, -n) *f* (pej, fam) fairy

tupfen *vt, vi* to dab; *(mit Farbe)* to dot; **Tupfen** (-s, -) *m* dot

Tür (-, -en) *f* door; **vor/an der ~** at the door; **an die ~ gehen** to answer the door

Türke (-n, -n) *m* Turk; **Türkei** (-) *f*: **die ~** Turkey; **Türkin** *f* Turk

Türkis (-es, -e) *m* turquoise

türkisch *adj* Turkish; **Türkisch** *nt* Turkish

Turm (-(e)s, Türme) *m* tower; *(spitzer Kirchturm)* steeple; *(Sprung~)* diving platform; *(Schach)* rook, castle

turnen *vi* to do gymnastics; **Turnen** (-s) *nt* gymnastics *sing*; *(Schule)* physical education, PE; **Turner(in)** *m(f)* gymnast; **Turnhalle** *f* gym(nasium); **Turnhose** *f* gym shorts *pl*

Turnier (-s, -e) *nt* tournament

Turnschuh *m* gym shoe, sneaker *(US)*

Türschild *nt* doorplate; **Türschloss** *nt* lock

tuscheln *vt, vi* to whisper

Tussi (-, -s) *f* (pej, fam) chick

Tüte (-, -n) *f* bag

TÜV (-s, -s) *m akr* = **Technischer Überwachungsverein** ≈ MOT *(Brit)*, vehicle inspection *(US)*

- **TÜV**
-
- The **TÜV** is the organization
- responsible for checking the
- safety of machinery, particularly
- vehicles. Cars over three years
- old have to be examined every
- two years for their safety and
- for their exhaust emissions.
- **TÜV** is also the name given to
- the test itself.

TÜV-Plakette *f badge attached to a vehicle's numberplate, indicating that it has passed the "TÜV"*
Tweed (*-s, -s*) *m* tweed
Typ (*-s, -en*) *m* type; (*Auto*) model; (*Mann*) guy, bloke
Typhus (*-*) *m* typhoid
typisch *adj* typical (*für* of); **ein ~er Fehler** a common mistake; **~ Marcus!** that's just like Marcus; **~ amerikanisch!** that's so American

u. *abk* = **und**
u. a. *abk* = **und andere(s)** and others; = **unter anderem, unter anderen** among other things
u. A. w. g. *abk* = **um Antwort wird gebeten** RSVP
U-Bahn *f* underground (*Brit*), subway (*US*)
übel *adj* bad; (*moralisch*) wicked; **mir ist ~** I feel sick; **diese Bemerkung hat er mir ~ genommen** he took offence at my remark; **Übelkeit** *f* nausea
üben *vt, vi* to practise

○ **SCHLÜSSELWORT**

über *prep +dat* **1** (*räumlich*) over, above; **zwei Grad über null** two degrees above zero
2 (*zeitlich*) over; **über der Arbeit einschlafen** to fall asleep over one's work

▷ prep +akk **1** (räumlich) over; (hoch über auch) above; (quer über auch) across
2 (zeitlich) over; **über Weihnachten** over Christmas; **über kurz oder lang** sooner or later
3 (mit Zahlen) **Kinder über 12 Jahren** children over o above 12 years of age; **ein Scheck über 200 Euro** a cheque for 200 euros
4 (auf dem Wege) via; **nach Köln über Aachen** to Cologne via Aachen; **ich habe es über die Auskunft erfahren** I found out from information
5 (betreffend) about; **ein Buch über ...** a book about o on ...; **über jdn/etw lachen** to laugh about o at sb/sth
6 Macht über jdn haben to have power over sb; **sie liebt ihn über alles** she loves him more than everything
▷ adv over; **über und über** over and over; **den ganzen Tag über** all day long; **jdm in etw** dat **über sein** to be superior to sb in sth

überall adv everywhere
überanstrengen vr: **sich ~** to overexert oneself
überbacken adj: (mit Käse) **~ au** gratin; **überbelichten** vt (Foto) to overexpose; **überbieten** irr vt to outbid; (übertreffen) to surpass; (Rekord) to break
Überbleibsel (-s, -) nt remnant
Überblick m overview; (fig: in Darstellung) survey; (Fähigkeit zu verstehen) grasp (über +akk of)
überbuchen vt to overbook; **Überbuchung** f overbooking
überdurchschnittlich adj above average
übereinander adv on top of each other; (sprechen etc) about each other

überein|stimmen vi to agree (mit with)
überempfindlich adj hypersensitive
überfahren irr vt (Auto) to run over; **Überfahrt** f crossing
Überfall m (Banküberfall) robbery; (Mil) raid; (auf jdn) assault; **überfallen** irr vt to attack; (Bank) to raid
überfällig adj overdue
überfliegen irr vt to fly over; (Buch) to skim through
Überfluss m overabundance, excess (an +dat of); **überflüssig** adj superfluous
überfordern vt to demand too much of; (Kräfte) to overtax; **da bin ich überfordert** (bei Antwort) you've got me there
Überführung f (Brücke) flyover (Brit), overpass (US)
überfüllt adj overcrowded
Übergabe f handover
Übergang m crossing; (Wandel, Überleitung) transition; **Übergangslösung** f temporary solution, stopgap
übergeben irr vt to hand over
▷ vr: **sich ~** to be sick, to vomit
Übergepäck nt excess baggage
Übergewicht nt excess weight; (10 Kilo) **~ haben** to be (10 kilos) overweight
überglücklich adj overjoyed; (fam) over the moon
Übergröße f outsize
überhaupt adv at all; (im Allgemeinen) in general; (besonders) especially; **was willst du ~?** what is it you want?
überheblich adj arrogant
überholen vt to overtake; (Tech) to overhaul; **Überholspur** f overtaking (Brit) (o passing (US)) lane; **überholt** adj outdated

Überholverbot nt: **hier herrscht ~** you can't overtake here
überhören vt to miss, not to catch; (absichtlich) to ignore;
überladen irr vt to overload ▷ adj (fig) cluttered; **überlassen** irr vt: **jdm etw ~** to leave sth to sb; **über|laufen** irr vi (Flüssigkeit) to overflow
überleben vt, vi to survive; **Überlebende(r)** mf survivor
überlegen vt to consider; **sich** (dat) **etw ~** to think about sth; **er hat es sich** (dat) **anders überlegt** he's changed his mind ▷ adj superior (dat to); **Überlegung** f consideration
überm kontr von **über dem**
übermäßig adj excessive
übermorgen adv the day after tomorrow
übernächste(r, s) adj: **~ Woche** the week after next
übernachten vi to spend the night (bei jdm at sb's place); **übernächtigt** adj bleary-eyed, very tired; **Übernachtung** f overnight stay; **~ mit Frühstück** bed and breakfast
übernehmen irr vt to take on; (Amt, Geschäft) to take over ▷ vr: **sich ~** to take on too much
überprüfen vt to check; **Überprüfung** f check; (Überprüfen) checking
überqueren vt to cross
überraschen vt to surprise; **Überraschung** f surprise
überreden vt to persuade; **er hat mich überredet** he talked me into it
überreichen vt to hand over
übers kontr von **über das**
überschätzen vt to overestimate; **überschlagen** irr vt (berechnen) to estimate; (auslassen: Seite) to skip ▷ vr: **sich**

~ to somersault; (Auto) to overturn; (Stimme) to crack;
überschneiden irr vr: **sich ~** (Linien etc) to intersect; (Termine) to clash
Überschrift f heading
Überschwemmung f flood
Übersee f: **nach/in ~** overseas
übersehen irr vt (Gelände) to look (out) over; (nicht beachten) to overlook
übersetzen vt to translate (aus from, in +akk into); **Übersetzer(in)** (-s, -) m(f) translator; **Übersetzung** f translation
Übersicht f overall view; (Darstellung) survey; **übersichtlich** adj clear
überstehen irr vt (durchstehen) to get over; (Winter etc) to get through
Überstunden pl overtime sing
überstürzt adj hasty
überteuert adj overpriced
übertragbar adj transferable; (Med) infectious; **übertragen** irr vt to transfer (auf +akk to); (Radio) to broadcast; (Krankheit) to transmit ▷ vr to spread (auf +akk to) ▷ adj figurative; **Übertragung** f (Radio) broadcast; (von Daten) transmission
übertreffen irr vt to surpass
übertreiben irr vt, vi to exaggerate, to overdo; **Übertreibung** f exaggeration; **übertrieben** adj exaggerated, overdone
überwachen vt to supervise; (Verdächtigen) to keep under surveillance
überwand imperf von **überwinden**
überweisen irr vt to transfer; (Patienten) to refer (an +akk to); **Überweisung** f transfer; (von Patienten) referral

u

überwiegend adv mainly
überwinden (überwand, überwunden) vt to overcome ▷ vr: **sich ~** to make an effort, to force oneself; **überwunden** pp von **überwinden**
Überzelt nt flysheet
überzeugen vt to convince; **Überzeugung** f conviction
überziehen irr vt (bedecken) to cover; (Jacke etc) to put on; (Konto) to overdraw; **die Betten frisch ~** to change the sheets
üblich adj usual
übrig adj remaining; **ist noch Saft ~?** is there any juice left?; **die Übrigen** pl the rest pl; **im Übrigen** besides; **~ bleiben** to be left (over); **mir blieb nichts anderes ~(, als zu gehen)** I had no other choice (but to go); **übrigens** adv besides; (nebenbei bemerkt) by the way; **übrig|haben** irr vt: **für jdn etwas ~** (fam: jdn mögen) to have a soft spot for sb
Übung f practice; (im Sport, Aufgabe etc) exercise
Ufer (-s, -) nt (Fluss) bank; (Meer, See) shore; **am ~** on the bank/shore
Ufo (-(s), -s) nt akr = **unbekanntes Flugobjekt** UFO
Uhr (-, -en) f clock; (am Arm) watch; **wie viel ~ ist es?** what time is it?; **1 ~** 1 o'clock; **20 ~** 8 o'clock, 8 pm; **Uhrzeigersinn** m: **im ~** clockwise; **gegen den ~** anticlockwise (Brit), counterclockwise (US); **Uhrzeit** f time (of day)
Ukraine (-) f: **die ~** the Ukraine
UKW abk = **Ultrakurzwelle** VHF
Ulme (-, -n) f elm
Ultrakurzwelle f very high frequency; **Ultraschallaufnahme** f (Med) scan

○ SCHLÜSSELWORT

um prep +akk 1 (um herum) (a)round; **um Weihnachten** around Christmas; **er schlug um sich** he hit about him
2 (mit Zeitangabe) at; **um acht (Uhr)** at eight (o'clock)
3 (mit Größenangabe) by; **etw um 4 cm kürzen** to shorten sth by 4 cm; **um 10% teurer** 10% more expensive; **um vieles besser** better by far; **um so besser** so much the better
4 **der Kampf um den Titel** the battle for the title; **um Geld spielen** to play for money; **Stunde um Stunde** hour after hour; **Auge um Auge** an eye for an eye
▷ prep +gen: **um ... willen** for the sake of ...; **um Gottes willen** for goodness' o (stärker) God's sake
▷ konj: **um ... zu** (in order) to ...; **zu klug, um zu ...** too clever to ...; siehe **umso**
▷ adv 1 (ungefähr) about; **um (die) 30 Leute** about o around 30 people
2 (vorbei) **die 2 Stunden sind um** the two hours are up

umarmen vt to embrace
Umbau m rebuilding; (zu etwas) conversion (zu into); **um|bauen** vt to rebuild; (zu etwas) to convert (zu into)
um|blättern vt, vi to turn over
um|bringen irr vt to kill
um|buchen vi to change one's reservation/flight
um|drehen vt to turn (round); (obere Seite nach unten) to turn over ▷ vr: **sich ~** to turn (round); **Umdrehung** f turn; (Phys, Auto) revolution
um|fahren irr vt to knock down

um|fallen irr vi to fall over
Umfang m (Ausmaß) extent; (von Buch) size; (Reichweite) range; (Math) circumference; **umfangreich** adj extensive
Umfeld nt environment
Umfrage f survey
Umgang m company; (mit jdm) dealings pl; **umgänglich** adj sociable; **Umgangssprache** f colloquial language, slang
Umgebung f surroundings pl; (Milieu) environment; (Personen) people around one
umgehen irr vi (Gerücht) to go round; ~ (**können**) **mit** (know how to) handle ▷ irr vt to avoid; (Schwierigkeit, Verbot) to get round
um|gehen irr vi: **mit etw ~** to handle sth; **Umgehungsstraße** f bypass
umgekehrt adj reverse; (gegenteilig) opposite ▷ adv the other way round; **und ~** and vice versa
um|hören vr: **sich ~** to ask around; **um|kehren** vi to turn back ▷ vt to reverse; (Kleidungsstück) to turn inside out; **um|kippen** vt to tip over ▷ vi to overturn; (fig) to change one's mind; (fam: ohnmächtig werden) to pass out
Umkleidekabine f changing cubicle (Brit), dressing room (US); **Umkleideraum** m changing room
Umkreis m neighbourhood; **im ~ von** within a radius of
um|leiten vt to divert; **Umleitung** f diversion
um|rechnen vt to convert (in +akk into); **Umrechnung** f conversion; **Umrechnungskurs** m rate of exchange
Umriss m outline
um|rühren vi, vt to stir

ums kontr von **um das**
Umsatz m turnover
um|schalten vi to turn over
Umschlag m cover; (Buch) jacket; (Med) compress; (Brief) envelope
Umschulung f retraining
um|sehen irr vr: **sich ~** to look around; (suchen) to look out (nach for)
umso adv all the; **~ mehr** all the more; **~ besser** so much the better
umsonst adv (vergeblich) in vain; (gratis) for nothing
Umstand m circumstance; **Umstände** (pl) (fig) fuss; **in anderen Umständen sein** to be pregnant; **jdm Umstände machen** to cause sb a lot of trouble; **machen Sie bitte keine Umstände** please, don't put yourself out; **unter diesen/ keinen Umständen** under these/no circumstances; **unter Umständen** possibly;
umständlich adj (Methode) complicated; (Ausdrucksweise) long-winded; (Mensch) ponderous; **Umstandsmode** f maternity wear
um|steigen irr vi to change (trains/buses)
um|stellen vt (an anderen Ort) to change round; (Tech) to convert ▷ vr: **sich ~** to adapt (auf +akk to); **Umstellung** f change; (Umgewöhnung) adjustment; (Tech) conversion
Umtausch m exchange; **um|tauschen** vt to exchange; (Währung) to change
Umweg m detour
Umwelt f environment; **Umweltbelastung** f ecological damage; **umweltbewusst** adj environmentally aware;

u

umweltfreundlich *adj*
environment-friendly;
Umweltpapier *nt* recycled paper;
umweltschädlich *adj* harmful to
the environment; **Umweltschutz**
m environmental protection;
Umweltschützer(in) (*-s, -*) *m(f)*
environmentalist;
Umweltverschmutzung *f*
pollution; **umweltverträglich** *adj*
environment-friendly

um|werfen *irr vt* to knock over;
(*fig: ändern*) to upset; (*fig, fam: jdn*)
to flabbergast

um|ziehen *irr vt* to change ▷ *vr:*
sich ~ to change ▷ *vi* to move
(house); **Umzug** *m*
(*Straßenumzug*) procession;
(*Wohnungsumzug*) move

unabhängig *adj* independent;
Unabhängigkeitstag *m*
Independence Day, Fourth of July
(*US*)

unabsichtlich *adv*
unintentionally

unangenehm *adj* unpleasant;
Unannehmlichkeit *f* inconvenience;
~en *pl* trouble *sing*

unanständig *adj* indecent;
unappetitlich *adj* (*Essen*)
unappetizing; (*abstoßend*)
off-putting; **unbeabsichtigt** *adj*
unintentional; **unbedeutend** *adj*
insignificant, unimportant;
(*Fehler*) slight

unbedingt *adj* unconditional
▷ *adv* absolutely

unbefriedigend *adj* unsatisfactory; **unbegrenzt** *adj*
unlimited; **unbekannt** *adj*
unknown; **unbeliebt** *adj*
unpopular; **unbemerkt** *adj*
unnoticed; **unbequem** *adj*
(*Stuhl, Mensch*) uncomfortable;
(*Regelung*) inconvenient;
unbeständig *adj* (*Wetter*)
unsettled; (*Lage*) unstable;

(*Mensch*) unreliable; **unbestimmt**
adj indefinite; **unbeteiligt** *adj*
(*nicht dazugehörig*) uninvolved;
(*innerlich nicht berührt*) indifferent,
unconcerned; **unbewacht** *adj*
unguarded; **unbewusst** *adj*
unconscious; **unbezahlt** *adj*
unpaid; **unbrauchbar** *adj*
useless

und *conj* and; **~ so weiter** and so
on; **na ~?** so what?

undankbar *adj* (*Person*)
ungrateful; (*Aufgabe*) thankless;
undenkbar *adj* inconceivable;
undeutlich *adj* indistinct;
undicht *adj* leaky; **uneben** *adj*
uneven; **unecht** *adj* (*Schmuck etc*)
fake; **unehelich** *adj* (*Kind*)
illegitimate; **unendlich** *adj*
endless; (*Math*) infinite;
unentbehrlich *adj* indispensable;
unentgeltlich *adj* free (of charge)

unentschieden *adj* undecided;
~ enden (*Sport*) to end in a draw

unerfreulich *adj* unpleasant

unerhört *adj* unheard-of; (*Bitte*)
outrageous; **unerlässlich** *adj*
indispensable; **unerträglich** *adj*
unbearable; **unerwartet** *adj*
unexpected

unerwünscht *adj* unwelcome;
(*Eigenschaften*) undesirable;
unfähig *adj* incompetent; **~ sein,
etw zu tun** to be incapable of
doing sth; **unfair** *adj* unfair

Unfall *m* accident; **Unfallbericht**
m accident report; **Unfallflucht** *f*
failure to stop after an accident;
Unfallhergang *m:* **den
~ schildern** to give details of the
accident; **Unfallstation** *f*
casualty ward; **Unfallstelle** *f*
scene of the accident;
Unfallversicherung *f* accident
insurance

unfreundlich *adj* unfriendly

Ungarn (*-s*) *nt* Hungary

Ungeduld f impatience; **ungeduldig** adj impatient
ungeeignet adj unsuitable
ungefähr adj approximate ▷ adv approximately; **~ 10 Kilometer** about 10 kilometres; **wann ~?** about what time?; **wo ~?** whereabouts?
ungefährlich adj harmless; (sicher) safe
ungeheuer adj huge ▷ adv (fam) enormously; **Ungeheuer** (-s, -) nt monster
ungehorsam adj disobedient (gegenüber to)
ungelegen adj inconvenient; **ungemütlich** adj unpleasant; (Mensch) disagreeable; **ungenießbar** adj inedible; (Getränk) undrinkable; **ungenügend** adj unsatisfactory; (Schulnote) ≈ F; **ungepflegt** adj (Garten) untended; (Aussehen) unkempt; (Hände) neglected; **ungerade** adj odd
ungerecht adj unjust; **ungerechtfertigt** adj unjustified; **Ungerechtigkeit** f injustice, unfairness
ungern adv reluctantly; **ungeschickt** adj clumsy; **ungeschminkt** adj without make-up; **ungesund** adj unhealthy; **ungewiss** adj uncertain; **ungewöhnlich** adj unusual
Ungeziefer (-s) nt vermin pl
ungezogen adj ill-mannered
ungezwungen adj relaxed
ungiftig adj non-toxic
unglaublich adj incredible
Unglück (-(e)s, -e) nt (Unheil) misfortune; (Pech) bad luck; (Unglücksfall) disaster; (Verkehrs~) accident; **das bringt ~** that's unlucky; **unglücklich** adj unhappy; (erfolglos) unlucky;

(unerfreulich) unfortunate; **unglücklicherweise** adv unfortunately
ungültig adj invalid
ungünstig adj inconvenient
unheilbar adj incurable; **~ krank sein** to be terminally ill
unheimlich adj eerie ▷ adv (fam) incredibly
unhöflich adj impolite
uni adj plain
Uni (-, -s) f uni
Uniform (-, -en) f uniform
Universität f university
Unkenntnis f ignorance
unklar adj unclear
Unkosten pl expenses pl; **Unkostenbeitrag** m contribution (towards expenses)
Unkraut nt weeds pl, ~art, weed
unlogisch adj illogical
unmissverständlich adj unambiguous
unmittelbar adj immediate; **~ darauf** immediately afterwards
unmöbliert adj unfurnished
unmöglich adj impossible
unnahbar adj unapproachable
unnötig adj unnecessary
UNO (-) f akr = **United Nations Organization** UN
unordentlich adj untidy; **Unordnung** f disorder
unpassend adj inappropriate; (Zeit) inconvenient; **unpersönlich** adj impersonal; **unpraktisch** adj impractical
Unrecht nt wrong; **zu ~** wrongly; **im ~ sein** to be wrong; **unrecht** adj wrong; **~ haben** to be wrong
unregelmäßig adj irregular; **unreif** adj unripe; **unruhig** adj restless; **~ schlafen** to have a bad night
uns pron akk, dat von **wir**; us, (to) us; **~ (selbst)** (reflexiv) ourselves;

sehen Sie ~? can you see us?; **er schickte es ~** he sent it to us; **lasst ~ in Ruhe** leave us alone; **ein Freund von ~** a friend of ours; **wir haben ~ hingesetzt** we sat down; **wir haben ~ amüsiert** we enjoyed ourselves; **wir mögen ~** we like each other

unscharf *adj* (*Foto*) blurred, out of focus

unscheinbar *adj* insignificant; (*Aussehen*) unprepossessing

unschlüssig *adj* undecided

unschuldig *adj* innocent

unser *pron* (*adjektivisch*) our ▷ *pron gen von* **wir**; of us; **unsere(r, s)** *pron* (*substantivisch*) ours; **unseretwegen** *adv* (*wegen uns*) because of us; (*uns zuliebe*) for our sake; (*um uns*) about us; (*von uns aus*) as far as we are concerned

unseriös *adj* dubious; **unsicher** *adj* (*ungewiss*) uncertain; (*Person, Job*) insecure

Unsinn *m* nonsense

unsterblich *adj* immortal; **~ verliebt** madly in love

unsympathisch *adj* unpleasant; **er ist mir ~** I don't like him

unten *adv* below; (*im Haus*) downstairs; (*an der Treppe etc*) at the bottom; **nach ~** down

○ SCHLÜSSELWORT

unter *prep* +*dat* **1** (*räumlich, mit Zahlen*) under; (*drunter*) underneath, below; **unter 18 Jahren** under 18 years
2 (*zwischen*) among(st); **sie waren unter sich** they were by themselves; **einer unter ihnen** one of them; **unter anderem** among other things
▷ *prep* +*akk* under, below

Unterarm *m* forearm

unterbelichtet *adj* (*Foto*) underexposed

Unterbewusstsein *nt* subconscious

unterbrechen *irr vt* to interrupt; **Unterbrechung** *f* interruption; **ohne ~** nonstop

unterdrücken *vt* to suppress; (*Leute*) to oppress

unterdurchschnittlich *adj* below average

untere(r, s) *adj* lower

untereinander *adv* (*räumlich*) one below the other; (*gegenseitig*) each other; (*miteinander*) among themselves/yourselves/ourselves

Unterführung *f* underpass

unter|gehen *irr vi* to go down; (*Sonne*) to set; (*Volk*) to perish; (*Welt*) to come to an end; (*im Lärm*) to be drowned out

Untergeschoss *nt* basement; **Untergewicht** *nt*: (**3 Kilo**) **~ haben** to be (3 kilos) underweight; **Untergrund** *m* foundation; (*Pol*) underground; **Untergrundbahn** *f* underground (*Brit*), subway (*US*)

unterhalb *adv*, *prep* +*gen* below; **~ von** below

Unterhalt *m* maintenance; **unterhalten** *irr vt* to maintain; (*belustigen*) to entertain ▷ *vr*: **sich ~** to talk; (*sich belustigen*) to enjoy oneself; **Unterhaltung** *f* (*Belustigung*) entertainment; (*Gespräch*) talk, conversation

Unterhemd *nt* vest (*Brit*), undershirt (*US*); **Unterhose** *f* underpants *pl*; (*für Damen*) briefs *pl*

unterirdisch *adj* underground

Unterkiefer *m* lower jaw

Unterkunft (-, -*künfte*) *f* accommodation

Unterlage *f* (*Beleg*) document; (*Schreibunterlage*) pad

unterlassen *irr vt*: **es ~, etw zu tun** (*versäumen*) to fail to do sth; (*bleiben lassen*) to refrain from doing sth

unterlegen *adj* inferior (*dat* to); (*besiegt*) defeated

Unterleib *m* abdomen

Unterlippe *f* lower lip

Untermiete *f*: **zur ~ wohnen** to be a subtenant; **Untermieter(in)** *m(f)* subtenant

unternehmen *irr vt* (*Reise*) to go on; (*Versuch*) to make; **etwas ~ to** do something (*gegen* about); **Unternehmen** (*-s, -*) *nt* undertaking; (*Comm*) company; **Unternehmensberater(in)** (*-s, -*) *m(f)* management consultant; **Unternehmer(in)** (*-s, -*) *m(f)* entrepreneur

Unterricht (*-(e)s, -e*) *m* lessons *pl*; **unterrichten** *vt* to teach

unterschätzen *vt* to underestimate

unterscheiden *irr vt* to distinguish (*von* from, *zwischen +dat* between); ▷ *vr*: **sich ~ to** differ (*von* from)

Unterschenkel *m* lower leg

Unterschied (*-(e)s, -e*) *m* difference; **im ~ zu dir** unlike you; **unterschiedlich** *adj* different

unterschreiben *irr vt* to sign; **Unterschrift** *f* signature

Untersetzer (*-s, -*) *m* tablemat; (*für Gläser*) coaster

unterste(r, s) *adj* lowest, bottom

unter|stellen *vr*: **sich ~ to** take shelter

unterstellen *vt* (*rangmäßig*) to subordinate (*dat* to); (*fig*) to impute (*jdm etw* sth to sb)

unterstreichen *irr vt* (*a. fig*) to underline

Unterstrich *m* (*Inform*) underscore

unterstützen *vt* to support; **Unterstützung** *f* support

untersuchen *vt* (*Med*) to examine; (*Polizei*) to investigate; **Untersuchung** *f* examination; (*polizeiliche*) investigation

untertags *adv* during the day

Untertasse *f* saucer

Unterteil *nt* lower part, bottom

Untertitel *m* subtitle

untervermieten *vt* to sublet

Unterwäsche *f* underwear

unterwegs *adv* on the way

unterzeichnen *vt* to sign

untreu *adj* unfaithful

untröstlich *adj* inconsolable; **unüberlegt** *adj* ill-considered ▷ *adv* without thinking; **unüblich** *adj* unusual; **unverantwortlich** *adj* irresponsible; (*unentschuldbar*) inexcusable

unverbindlich *adj* not binding; (*Antwort*) noncommittal ▷ *adv* (*Comm*) without obligation

unverbleit *adj* unleaded; **unverheiratet** *adj* unmarried, single; **unvermeidlich** *adj* unavoidable; **unvernünftig** *adj* silly; **unverschämt** *adj* impudent; **unverständlich** *adj* incomprehensible; **unverträglich** *adj* (*Person*) quarrelsome; (*Essen*) indigestible

unverwüstlich *adj* indestructible; (*Mensch*) irrepressible

unverzeihlich *adj* unpardonable; **unverzüglich** *adj* immediate; **unvollständig** *adj* incomplete; **unvorsichtig** *adj* careless

unwahrscheinlich *adj* improbable, unlikely ▷ *adv* (*fam*) incredibly

Unwetter *nt* thunderstorm

unwichtig *adj* unimportant

unwiderstehlich *adj* irresistible

unwillkürlich *adj* involuntary
▷ *adv* instinctively; **ich musste
~ lachen** I couldn't help laughing
unwohl *adj* unwell, ill
unzählig *adj* innumerable,
countless
unzerbrechlich *adj* unbreak-
able; **unzertrennlich** *adj*
inseparable; **unzufrieden** *adj*
dissatisfied; **unzugänglich** *adj*
inaccessible; **unzumutbar** *adj*
unacceptable
unzusammenhängend *adj*
disconnected; (*Äußerung*)
incoherent; **unzutreffend** *adj*
inapplicable; (*unwahr*) incorrect;
unzuverlässig *adj* unreliable
Update (*-s, -s*) *nt* (*Inform*) update
üppig *adj* (*Essen*) lavish;
(*Vegetation*) lush
uralt *adj* ancient, very old
Uran (*-s*) *nt* uranium
Uranus (*-*) *m* Uranus
Uraufführung *f* premiere
Urenkel *m* great-grandson;
Urenkelin *f* great-grand-
daughter; **Urgroßeltern** *pl*
great-grandparents *pl*;
Urgroßmutter *f* great-grandmother; **Urgroßvater** *m*
great-grandfather
Urheber(in) (*-s, -*) *m(f)* origin-
ator; (*Autor*) author
Urin (*-s, -e*) *m* urine; **Urinprobe**
f urine specimen
Urkunde (*-, -n*) *f* document
Urlaub (*-(e)s, -e*) *m* holiday (*Brit*),
vacation (*US*); **im ~** on holiday
(*Brit*), on vacation (*US*); **in ~ fahren**
to go on holiday (*Brit*) (*o* vacation
(*US*)); **Urlauber(in)** (*-s, -*) *m(f)*
holiday-maker (*Brit*), vacationer
(*US*); **Urlaubsort** *m* holiday
resort; **urlaubsreif** *adj* ready for
a holiday (*Brit*) (*o* vacation (*US*));
Urlaubszeit *f* holiday season
(*Brit*), vacation period (*US*)

Urne (*-, -n*) *f* urn
Urologe *m*, **Urologin** *f*
urologist
Ursache *f* cause (*für* of); **keine ~!**
not at all; (*bei Entschuldigung*) that's
all right
Ursprung *m* origin; (*von Fluss*)
source; **ursprünglich** *adj*
original ▷ *adv* originally;
Ursprungsland *adj* country of
origin
Urteil (*-s, -e*) *nt* (*Meinung*)
opinion; (*Jur*) verdict; (*Strafmaß*)
sentence; **urteilen** *vi* to judge
Uruguay (*-s*) *nt* Uruguay
Urwald *m* jungle
USA *pl* USA *sing*
User(in) (*-s, -*) *m(f)* (*Inform*) user
usw. *abk* = **und so weiter** etc
Utensilien *pl* utensils *pl*

V

vage adj vague
Vagina (-, Vaginen) f vagina
Valentinstag m St Valentine's Day
Vandalismus m vandalism
Vanille (-) f vanilla
variieren vt, vi to vary
Vase (-, -n) f vase
Vaseline (-) f Vaseline®
Vater (-s, Väter) m father; **väterlich** adj paternal; **Vaterschaft** f fatherhood; (Jur) paternity; **Vatertag** m Father's Day; **Vaterunser** nt: **das ~** (**beten**) (to say) the Lord's Prayer
V-Ausschnitt m V-neck
v. Chr. abk = **vor Christus** BC
Veganer(in) (-s, -) m(f) vegan; **Vegetarier(in)** (-s, -) m(f) vegetarian; **vegetarisch** adj vegetarian
Veilchen nt violet
Velo (-s, -s) nt (schweizerisch) bicycle

Vene (-, -n) f vein
Venedig (-s) nt Venice
Venezuela (-s) nt Venezuela
Ventil (-s, -e) nt valve
Ventilator m ventilator
Venus (-) f Venus
Venusmuschel f clam
verabreden vt to arrange ▷ vr: **sich ~** to arrange to meet (mit jdm sb); **ich bin schon verabredet** I'm already meeting someone; **Verabredung** f arrangement; (Termin) appointment; (zum Ausgehen) date
verabschieden vt (Gäste) to say goodbye to; (Gesetz) to pass ▷ vr: **sich ~** to say goodbye
verachten vt to despise; **verächtlich** adj contemptuous; (verachtenswert) contemptible; **Verachtung** f contempt
verallgemeinern vt to generalize
Veranda (-, Veranden) f veranda, porch (US)
veränderlich adj changeable; **verändern** vt to change ▷ vr: **sich ~** to change; **Veränderung** f change
veranlassen vt to cause
veranstalten vt to organize; **Veranstalter(in)** (-s, -) m(f) organizer; **Veranstaltung** f event; **Veranstaltungsort** m venue
verantworten vt to take responsibility for ▷ vr: **sich für etw ~** to answer for sth; **verantwortlich** adj responsible (für for); **Verantwortung** f responsibility (für for)
verärgern vt to annoy
verarschen vt (fam) to take the piss out of (Brit), to make a sucker out of (US)
Verb (-s, -en) nt verb

Verband m (Med) bandage; (Bund) association; **Verband(s)kasten** m first-aid box; **Verband(s)zeug** nt dressing material

verbergen irr vt to hide (vor +dat from) ▷ vr: **sich ~** to hide (vor +dat from)

verbessern vt to improve; (berichtigen) to correct ▷ vr: **sich ~** to improve; (berichtigen) to correct oneself; **Verbesserung** f improvement; (Berichtigung) correction

verbiegen irr vi to bend ▷ vr: **sich ~** to bend

verbieten irr vt to forbid; **jdm ~, etw zu tun** to forbid sb to do sth

verbinden irr vt to connect; (kombinieren) to combine; (Med) to bandage; **können Sie mich mit ... ~?** (Tel) can you put me through to ...?; **ich verbinde** (Tel) I'm putting you through ▷ vr (Chem) **sich ~** to combine

verbindlich adj binding; (freundlich) friendly; **Verbindung** f connection

verbleit adj leaded

verblüffen vt to amaze

verblühen vi to fade

verborgen adj hidden

Verbot (-(e)s, -e) nt ban (für, von on); **verboten** adj forbidden; **es ist ~** it's not allowed; **es ist ~, hier zu parken** you're not allowed to park here; **Rauchen ~** no smoking

verbrannt adj burnt

Verbrauch (-(e)s) m consumption; **verbrauchen** vt to use up; **Verbraucher(in)** (-s, -) m(f) consumer

Verbrechen (-s, -) nt crime; **Verbrecher(in)** (-s, -) m(f) criminal

verbreiten vt to spread ▷ vr: **sich ~** to spread

verbrennen irr vt to burn; **Verbrennung** f burning; (in Motor) combustion

verbringen irr vt to spend

verbunden adj: **falsch ~** sorry, wrong number

Verdacht (-(e)s) m suspicion; **verdächtig** adj suspicious; **verdächtigen** vt to suspect

verdammt interj (fam) damn

verdanken vt: **jdm etw ~** to owe sth to sb

verdarb imperf von **verderben**

verdauen vt (a. fig) to digest; **verdaulich** adj digestible; **das ist schwer ~** that is hard to digest; **Verdauung** f digestion

Verdeck (-(e)s, -e) nt top

verderben (verdarb, verdorben) vt to spoil; (schädigen) to ruin; (moralisch) to corrupt; **es sich** (dat) **mit jdm ~** to get into sb's bad books; **ich habe mir den Magen verdorben** I've got an upset stomach ▷ vi (Lebensmittel) to go off

verdienen vt to earn; (moralisch) to deserve; **Verdienst** (-(e)s, -e) m earnings pl ▷ (-(e)s, -e) nt merit; (Leistung) service (um to)

verdoppeln vt to double

verdorben pp von **verderben** ▷ adj spoilt; (geschädigt) ruined; (moralisch) corrupt

verdrehen vt to twist; (Augen) to roll; **jdm den Kopf ~** (fig) to turn sb's head

verdünnen vt to dilute

verdunsten vi to evaporate

verdursten vi to die of thirst

verehren vt to admire; (Rel) to worship; **Verehrer(in)** (-s, -) m(f) admirer

Verein (-(e)s, -e) m association; (Klub) club

vereinbar adj compatible

vereinbaren *vt* to arrange; **Vereinbarung** *f* agreement, arrangement

vereinigen *vt* to unite ▷ *vr*: **sich ~** to unite; **Vereinigtes Königreich** *nt* United Kingdom; **Vereinigte Staaten (von Amerika)** *pl* United States *sing* (of America); **Vereinigung** *f* union; (*Verein*) association; **Vereinte Nationen** *pl* United Nations *pl*

vereisen *vi* (*Straße*) to freeze over; (*Fenster*) to ice up ▷ *vt* (*Med*) to freeze

vererben *vt*: **jdm etw ~** to leave sth to sb; (*Bio*) to pass sth on to sb ▷ *vr*: **sich ~** to be hereditary; **vererblich** *adj* hereditary

verfahren *irr vi* to proceed ▷ *vr*: **sich ~** to get lost; **Verfahren** (*-s, -*) *nt* procedure; (*Tech*) method; (*Jur*) proceedings *pl*

verfallen *irr vi* to decline; (*Haus*) to be falling apart; (*Fin*) to lapse; (*Fahrkarte etc*) to expire; **~ in** (*+akk*) to lapse into; **Verfallsdatum** *nt* expiry (*Brit*) (*o* expiration (*US*)) date; (*von Lebensmitteln*) best-before date

verfärben *vr*: **sich ~** to change colour; (*Wäsche*) to discolour

Verfasser(in) (*-s, -*) *m(f)* author, writer; **Verfassung** *f* (*gesundheitlich*) condition; (*Pol*) constitution

verfaulen *vi* to rot

verfehlen *vt* to miss

verfeinern *vt* to refine

Verfilmung *f* film (*o* screen) version

verfluchen *vt* to curse

verfolgen *vt* to pursue; (*Pol*) to persecute

verfügbar *adj* available; **verfügen** *vi* **über etw** (*akk*) **~** to have sth at one's disposal;

Verfügung *f* order; **jdm zur ~ stehen** to be at sb's disposal; **jdm etw zur ~ stellen** to put sth at sb's disposal

verführen *vt* to tempt; (*sexuell*) to seduce; **verführerisch** *adj* seductive

vergangen *adj* past; **~e Woche** last week; **Vergangenheit** *f* past

Vergaser (*-s, -*) *m* (*Auto*) carburettor

vergaß *imperf von* **vergessen**

vergeben *irr vt* to forgive (*jdm etw* sb for sth); (*weggeben*) to award, to allocate; **vergebens** *adv* in vain; **vergeblich** *adv* in vain ▷ *adj* vain, futile

vergehen *irr vi* to pass ▷ *vr*: **sich an jdm ~** to indecently assault sb; **Vergehen** (*-s, -*) *nt* offence

Vergeltung *f* retaliation

vergessen (*vergaß, vergessen*) *vt* to forget; **vergesslich** *adj* forgetful

vergeuden *vt* to squander, to waste

vergewaltigen *vt* to rape; **Vergewaltigung** *f* rape

vergewissern *vr*: **sich ~** to make sure

vergiften *vt* to poison; **Vergiftung** *f* poisoning

Vergissmeinnicht (*-(e)s, -e*) *nt* forget-me-not

Vergleich (*-(e)s, -e*) *m* comparison; (*Jur*) settlement; **im ~ zu** compared to (*o* with); **vergleichen** *irr vt* to compare (*mit* to, with)

Vergnügen (*-s, -*) *nt* pleasure; **viel ~!** enjoy yourself; **vergnügt** *adj* cheerful; **Vergnügungspark** *m* amusement park

vergoldet *adj* gold-plated

vergriffen *adj* (*Buch*) out of print; (*Ware*) out of stock

vergrößern vt to enlarge; (Menge) to increase; (mit Lupe) to magnify; **Vergrößerung** f enlargement; (Menge) increase; (mit Lupe) magnification; **Vergrößerungsglas** nt magnifying glass

verh. adj abk = **verheiratet** married

verhaften vt to arrest

verhalten irr vr: **sich ~** (sich benehmen) to behave; (Sache) to be; **Verhalten** (-s) nt behaviour

Verhältnis nt relationship (zu with); (Math) ratio; **~se** pl circumstances pl, conditions pl; **im ~ von 1 zu 2** in a ratio of 1 to 2; **verhältnismäßig** adj relative ▷ adv relatively

verhandeln vi to negotiate (über etw akk sth); **Verhandlung** f negotiation

verheimlichen vt to keep secret (jdm from sb)

verheiratet adj married

verhindern vt to prevent; **sie ist verhindert** she can't make it

Verhör (-(e)s, -e) nt interrogation; (gerichtlich) examination; **verhören** vt to interrogate; (bei Gericht) to examine ▷ vr: **sich ~** to mishear

verhungern vi to starve to death

verhüten vt to prevent; **Verhütung** f prevention; (mit Pille, Kondom etc) contraception; **Verhütungsmittel** nt contraceptive

verirren vr: **sich ~** to get lost

Verkauf m sale; **verkaufen** vt to sell; **zu ~** for sale; **Verkäufer(in)** m(f) seller; (beruflich) salesperson; (in Laden) shop assistant (Brit), salesperson (US); **verkäuflich** adj for sale

Verkehr (-s, -e) m traffic; (Sex) intercourse; (Umlauf) circulation; **verkehren** vi (Bus etc) to run; **~ in** to frequent; **~ mit** to associate (o mix) with; **Verkehrsampel** f traffic lights pl; **Verkehrsamt** nt tourist information office; **verkehrsfrei** adj traffic-free; **Verkehrsfunk** m travel news sing; **Verkehrsinsel** f traffic island; **Verkehrsmeldung** f traffic report; **Verkehrsmittel** nt means sing of transport; **öffentliche ~** pl public transport sing; **Verkehrsschild** nt traffic sign; **Verkehrstote(r)** mf road casualty; **die Zahl der ~n** the number of deaths on the road; **Verkehrsunfall** m road accident; **Verkehrszeichen** nt traffic sign

verkehrt adj wrong; (verkehrt herum) the wrong way round; (Pullover etc) inside out; **du machst es ~** you're doing it wrong

verklagen vt to take to court

verkleiden vt to dress up (als as) ▷ vr: **sich ~** to dress up (als as); (um unerkannt zu bleiben) to disguise oneself; **Verkleidung** f (Karneval) fancy dress; (um nicht erkannt zu werden) disguise

verkleinern vt to reduce; (Zimmer, Gebiet etc) to make smaller

verkneifen irr vt **sich** (dat) **etw ~** (Lachen) to stifle sth; (Schmerz) to hide sth; (sich versagen) to do without sth; **verkommen** irr vi to deteriorate; (Mensch) to go downhill ▷ adj (Haus) dilapidated; (moralisch) depraved; **verkraften** vt to cope with

verkratzt adj scratched

verkühlen vr: **sich ~** to get a chill

verkürzen vt to shorten

Verlag (-(e)s, -e) m publishing company

verlangen vt (fordern) to

demand; (*wollen*) to want; (*Preis*) to ask; (*Qualifikation*) to require; (*erwarten*) to ask (*von* of); (*fragen nach*) to ask for; (*Pass etc*) to ask to see; **~ Sie Herrn X** ask for Mr X ▷ *vi:* **~ nach** to ask for

verlängern *vt* to extend; (*Pass, Erlaubnis*) renew; **Verlängerung** *f* extension; (*Sport*) extra time; (*von Pass, Erlaubnis*) renewal; **Verlängerungsschnur** *f* extension cable; **Verlängerungswoche** *f* extra week

verlassen *irr vt* to leave ▷ *irr vr:* **sich ~** to rely (*auf +akk* on) ▷ *adj* desolate; (*Mensch*) abandoned; **verlässlich** *adj* reliable

Verlauf *m* course; **verlaufen** *irr vi* (*Weg, Grenze*) to run (*entlang* along); (*zeitlich*) to pass; (*Farben*) to run ▷ *vr:* **sich ~** to get lost; (*Menschenmenge*) to disperse

verlegen *vt* to move; (*verlieren*) to mislay; (*Buch*) to publish ▷ *adj* embarrassed; **Verlegenheit** *f* embarrassment; (*Situation*) difficulty

Verleih (-*(e)s, -e*) *m* (*Firma*) hire company (*Brit*), rental company (*US*); **verleihen** *irr vt* to lend; (*vermieten*) to hire (out) (*Brit*), to rent (out) (*US*); (*Preis, Medaille*) to award

verleiten *vt:* **jdn dazu ~, etw zu tun** to induce sb to do sth

verlernen *vt* to forget

verletzen *vt* to injure; (*fig*) to hurt; **Verletzte(r)** *mf* injured person; **Verletzung** *f* injury; (*Verstoß*) violation

verlieben *vr:* **sich ~** to fall in love (*in jdn* with sb); **verliebt** *adj* in love

verlieren (*verlor, verloren*) *vt, vi* to lose

verloben *vr:* **sich ~** to get engaged (*mit* to); **Verlobte(r)** *mf*

fiancé/fiancée; **Verlobung** *f* engagement

verlor *imperf von* **verlieren**

verloren *pp von* **verlieren** ▷ *adj* lost; (*Eier*) poached; **~ gehen** to go missing

verlosen *vt* to raffle; **Verlosung** *f* raffle

Verlust (-*(e)s, -e*) *m* loss

vermehren *vt* to multiply; (*Menge*) to increase ▷ *vr:* **sich ~** to multiply; (*Menge*) to increase

vermeiden *irr vt* to avoid

vermeintlich *adj* supposed

vermieten *vt* to rent (out), to let (out) (*Brit*); (*Auto*) to hire (out) (*Brit*), to rent (out) (*US*); **Vermieter(in)** *m(f)* landlord/-lady

vermischen *vt* to mix ▷ *vr:* **sich ~** to mix

vermissen *vt* to miss; **vermisst** *adj* missing; **jdn als ~ melden** to report sb missing

Vermittlung *f* (*bei Streit*) mediation; (*Herbeiführung*) arranging; (*Stelle*) agency

Vermögen (-*s, -*) *nt* fortune

vermuten *vt* to suppose; (*argwöhnen*) to suspect; **vermutlich** *adj* probable ▷ *adv* probably; **Vermutung** *f* supposition; (*Verdacht*) suspicion

vernachlässigen *vt* to neglect

vernichten *vt* to destroy; **vernichtend** *adj* (*fig*) crushing; (*Blick*) withering; (*Kritik*) scathing

Vernunft (-) *f* reason; **ich kann ihn nicht zur ~ bringen** I can't make him see reason; **vernünftig** *adj* sensible; (*Preis*) reasonable

veröffentlichen *vt* to publish

verordnen *vt* (*Med*) to prescribe; **Verordnung** *f* order; (*Med*) prescription

verpachten *vt* to lease (out) (*an +akk* to)

v

verpacken vt to pack; (*einwickeln*) to wrap up

Verpackung f packaging; **Verpackungskosten** pl packing charges pl

verpassen vt to miss

verpflegen vt to feed; **Verpflegung** f feeding; (*Kost*) food; (*in Hotel*) board

verpflichten vt to oblige; (*anstellen*) to engage ▷ vr: **sich ~** to commit oneself (*etw zu tun* to doing sth)

verprügeln vt to beat up

verraten irr vt to betray; (*Geheimnis*) to divulge; **aber nicht ~!** but don't tell anyone ▷ vr: **sich ~** to give oneself away

verrechnen vt: **~ mit** to set off against ▷ vr: **sich ~** to miscalculate; **Verrechnungsscheck** m crossed cheque (*Brit*), check for deposit only (*US*)

verregnet adj rainy

verreisen vi to go away (*nach* to); **sie ist (geschäftlich) verreist** she's away (on business); **verrenken** vt to contort; (*Med*) to dislocate; **sich** (*dat*) **den Knöchel ~** to sprain (o twist) one's ankle; **verringern** vt to reduce

verrostet adj rusty

verrückt adj mad, crazy; **es macht mich ~** it's driving me mad

versagen vi to fail; **Versagen** (-s) nt failure; **Versager(in)** (-s, -) m(f) failure

versalzen irr vt to put too much salt in/on

versammeln vt to assemble, to gather ▷ vr: **sich ~** to assemble, to gather; **Versammlung** f meeting

Versand (-(e)s) m dispatch; (*Abteilung*) dispatch department; **Versandhaus** nt mail-order company

versäumen vt to miss; (*unterlassen*) to neglect; **~, etw zu tun** to fail to do sth

verschätzen vr: **sich ~** to miscalculate

verschenken vt to give away; (*Chance*) to waste

verschicken vt to send off

verschieben vt irr (*auf später*) to postpone, to put off; (*an anderen Ort*) to move

verschieden adj (*unterschiedlich*) different; (*mehrere*) various; **sie sind ~ groß** they are of different sizes; **Verschiedene** pl various people/things pl; **Verschiedenes** various things pl

verschimmelt adj mouldy

verschlafen irr vt to sleep through; (*fig*) to miss ▷ vi to oversleep

verschlechtern vr: **sich ~** to deteriorate, to get worse; **Verschlechterung** f deterioration

Verschleiß (-es) m wear and tear

verschließbar adj lockable; **verschließen** vt irr to close; (*mit Schlüssel*) to lock

verschlimmern vt to make worse ▷ vr: **sich ~** to get worse

verschlossen adj locked; (*fig*) reserved

verschlucken vt to swallow ▷ vr: **sich ~** to choke (*an +dat* on)

Verschluss m lock; (*von Kleid*) fastener; (*Foto*) shutter; (*Stöpsel*) stopper

verschmutzen vt to get dirty; (*Umwelt*) to pollute

verschnaufen vi: **ich muss mal ~** I need to get my breath back

verschneit adj snow-covered

verschnupft adj: **~ sein** to have a cold; (*fam: beleidigt*) to be peeved

verschonen vt to spare (*jdn mit etw* sb sth)

verschreiben irr vt (Med) to prescribe;
verschreibungspflichtig adj available only on prescription
verschwand imperf von **verschwinden**
verschweigen irr vt to keep secret; **jdm etw ~** to keep sth from sb
verschwenden vt to waste; **Verschwendung** f waste
verschwiegen adj discreet; (Ort) secluded
verschwinden (verschwand, verschwunden) vi to disappear, to vanish; **verschwinde!** get lost!; **verschwunden** pp von **verschwinden**
Versehen (-s, -) nt: **aus ~** by mistake; **versehentlich** adv by mistake
versenden irr vt to send off
versessen adj **~ auf** (+akk) mad about
versetzen vt to transfer; (verpfänden) to pawn; (fam: bei Verabredung) to stand up ⊳ vr: **sich in jdn** (o **jds Lage**) **~** to put oneself in sb's place
verseuchen vt to contaminate
versichern vt to insure; (bestätigen) to assure; **versichert sein** to be insured;
Versichertenkarte f health-insurance card; **Versicherung** f insurance; **Versicherungskarte** f: **grüne ~** green card (Brit), insurance document for driving abroad; **Versicherungspolice** f insurance policy
versilbert adj silver-plated
versinken irr vi to sink
Version f version
versöhnen vt to reconcile ⊳ vr: **sich ~** to become reconciled
versorgen vt to provide, to supply (mit with); (Familie) to look

after ⊳ vr: **sich ~** to look after oneself; **Versorgung** f provision; (Unterhalt) maintenance; (für Alter etc) benefit
verspäten vr: **sich ~** to be late; **verspätet** adj late; **Verspätung** f delay; (**eine Stunde**) **~ haben** to be (an hour) late
versprechen irr vt to promise ⊳ vr: **ich habe mich versprochen** I didn't mean to say that
Verstand m mind; (Vernunft) (common) sense; **den ~ verlieren** to lose one's mind; **verständigen** vt to inform ⊳ vr: **sich ~** to communicate; (sich einigen) to come to an understanding; **Verständigung** f communication; **verständlich** adj understandable; **Verständnis** nt understanding (für of); (Mitgefühl) sympathy; **verständnisvoll** adj understanding
verstauchen vt to sprain; **verstaucht** pp von **verstauchen** sprained
Versteck (-(e)s, -e) nt hiding place; **~ spielen** to play hide-and-seek; **verstecken** vt to hide (vor +dat from) ⊳ vr: **sich ~** to hide (vor +dat from)
verstehen irr vt to understand; **falsch ~** to misunderstand ⊳ vr: **sich ~** to get on (mit with)
Versteigerung f auction
verstellbar adj adjustable; **verstellen** vt to move; (Uhr) to adjust; (versperren) to block; (Stimme, Handschrift) to disguise ⊳ vr: **sich ~** to pretend, to put on an act
verstopfen vt to block up; (Med) to constipate; **Verstopfung** f obstruction; (Med) constipation
Verstoß m infringement, violation (gegen of)

V

Versuch (-(e)s, -e) m attempt; (wissenschaftlich) experiment; **versuchen** vt to try

vertauschen vt to exchange; (versehentlich) to mix up

verteidigen vt to defend; **Verteidiger(in)** (-s, -) m(f) (Sport) defender; (Jur) defence counsel; **Verteidigung** f defence

verteilen vt to distribute

Vertrag (-(e)s, Verträge) m contract; (Pol) treaty

vertragen irr vt to stand, to bear ▷ vr: **sich ~** to get along (with each other); (sich aussöhnen) to make it up

verträglich adj (Mensch) good-natured; (Speisen) digestible

vertrauen vi: **jdm/einer Sache ~** to trust sb/sth; **Vertrauen** (-s) nt trust (in +akk in, zu in); **ich habe kein ~ zu ihm** I don't trust him; **ich hab's ihm im ~ gesagt** I told him in confidence; **vertraulich** adj (geheim) confidential; **vertraut** adj: **sich mit etw ~ machen** to familiarize oneself with sth

vertreten irr vt to represent; (Ansicht) to hold; **Vertreter(in)** (-s, -) m(f) representative

Vertrieb (-(e)s, -e) m (Abteilung) sales department

vertrocknen vi to dry up

vertun irr vr: **sich ~** to make a mistake

vertuschen vt to cover up

verunglücken vi to have an accident; **tödlich ~** to be killed in an accident

verunsichern vt to make uneasy

verursachen vt to cause

verurteilen vt to condemn

vervielfältigen vt to make copies of

verwählen vr: **sich ~** to dial the wrong number

verwalten vt to manage; (behördlich) to administer; **Verwalter(in)** (-s, -) m(f) manager; (Vermögens~) trustee; **Verwaltung** f management; (amtlich) administration

verwandt adj related (mit to); **Verwandte(r)** mf relative, relation; **Verwandtschaft** f relationship; (Menschen) relations pl

verwarnen vt to warn; (Sport) to caution

verwechseln vt to confuse (mit with); (halten für) to mistake (mit for)

verweigern vt to refuse

verwenden vt to use; (Zeit) to spend; **Mühe auf etw** (akk) **~** to take trouble over sth; **Verwendung** f use

verwirklichen vt to realize; **sich selbst ~** to fulfil oneself

verwirren vt to confuse; **Verwirrung** f confusion

verwitwet adj widowed

verwöhnen vt to spoil

verwunderlich adj surprising; **Verwunderung** f astonishment

verwüsten vt to devastate

verzählen vr: **sich ~** to miscount

verzehren vt to consume

Verzeichnis nt (Liste) list; (Katalog) catalogue; (in Buch) index; (Inform) directory

verzeihen (verzieh, verziehen) vt, vi to forgive (jdm etw sb for sth); **~ Sie bitte, ...** (vor Frage etc) excuse me, ...; **~ Sie die Störung** sorry to disturb you; **Verzeihung** f: **~!** sorry; **~, ...** (vor Frage etc) excuse me, ...; **(jdn) um ~ bitten** to apologize (to sb)

verzichten vi: **auf etw** (akk) **~** to do without sth; (aufgeben) to give sth up

verzieh *imperf von* **verzeihen**
verziehen *pp von* **verzeihen**
verziehen *irr vt* (*Kind*) to spoil;
das Gesicht ~ to pull a face ▷ *vr*:
sich ~ to go out of shape; (*Gesicht*)
to contort; (*verschwinden*) to
disappear
verzieren *vt* to decorate
verzögern *vt* to delay ▷ *vr*: **sich
~** to be delayed; **Verzögerung** *f*
delay
verzweifeln *vi* to despair (*an
+dat* of); **verzweifelt** *adj*
desperate; **Verzweiflung** *f*
despair
Veterinär(in) (*-s, -e*) *m(f)* veter-
inary surgeon (*Brit*), veterinarian
(*US*)
Vetter (*-s, -n*) *m* cousin
vgl. *abk* = **vergleiche** cf
Viagra® (*-s*) *nt* Viagra®
Vibrator (*-s, -en*) *m* vibrator;
vibrieren *vi* to vibrate
Video (*-s, -s*) *nt* video; **auf
~ aufnehmen** to video; **Videoclip**
(*-s, -s*) *m* video clip; **Videofilm**
m video; **Videogerät** *nt* video
(recorder); **Videokamera** *f* video
camera; **Videokassette** *f* video
(cassette); **Videorekorder** *m*
video recorder; **Videospiel** *nt*
video game; **Videothek** (*-, -en*) *f*
video library
Vieh (*-(e)s*) *nt* cattle
viel *pron* a lot (of), lots of; **~ Arbeit**
a lot of work, lots of work; **~e
Leute** a lot of people, lots of
people, many people; **zu ~** too
much; **zu ~e** too many; **sehr ~** a
great deal of; **sehr ~e** a great
many; **ziemlich ~/~e** quite a lot
of; **nicht ~** not much, not a lot of;
nicht ~e not many, not a lot of
▷ *pron* a lot; **sie sagt nicht ~** she
doesn't say a lot; **nicht ~** not
much, not a lot of; **nicht ~e** not
many, not a lot of; **gibt es ~?** is

there much?, is there a lot?; **gibt
es ~e?** are there many?, are there a
lot? ▷ *adv* a lot; **er geht ~ ins Kino**
he goes a lot to the cinema; **sehr
~** a great deal; **ziemlich ~** quite a
lot; **~ besser** much better;
~ teurer much more expensive;
~ zu ~ far too much
vielleicht *adv* perhaps; **~ ist sie
krank** perhaps she's ill, she might
be ill; **weißt du ~, wo er ist?** do
you know where he is (by any
chance)?
vielmal(s) *adv* many times;
danke ~s many thanks; **vielmehr**
adv rather; **vielseitig** *adj* very
varied; (*Mensch, Gerät*) versatile
vier *num* four; **auf allen ~en** on all
fours; **unter ~ Augen** in private,
privately; **Vier** (*-, -en*) *f* four;
(*Schulnote*) ≈ D; **Vierbettzimmer**
nt four-bed room; **Viereck** (*-(e)s,
-e*) *nt* four-sided figure; (*Quadrat*)
square; **viereckig** *adj* four-sided;
(*quadratisch*) square; **vierfach**
adj: **die ~e Menge** four times the
amount; **vierhundert** *num* four
hundred; **viermal** *adv* four
times; **vierspurig** *adj* four-lane
viert *adv*: **wir sind zu ~** there are
four of us; **vierte(r, s)** *adj* fourth;
siehe auch **dritte**
Viertel (*-s, -*) *nt* (*Stadtviertel*)
quarter, district; (*Bruchteil*)
quarter; (*Viertelliter*) quarter-litre;
(*Uhrzeit*) quarter; **~ vor/nach drei**
a quarter to/past three; **viertel
drei** a quarter past two; **drei
viertel drei** a quarter to three;
Viertelfinale *nt* quarter-final;
vierteljährlich *adj* quarterly;
Viertelstunde *f* quarter of an
hour
vierzehn *num* fourteen; **in
~ Tagen** in two weeks, in a
fortnight (*Brit*); **vierzehntägig** *adj*
two-week, fortnightly (*Brit*);

vierzehnte(r, s) adj fourteenth;
siehe auch **dritte**; **vierzig** num
forty; **vierzigste(r, s)** adj
fortieth

Vietnam (-s) nt Vietnam

Vignette f (Autobahn~)
motorway (Brit) (o freeway (US))
permit

Villa (-, Villen) f villa

violett adj purple

Violine f violin

Virus (-, Viren) m o nt virus

Visitenkarte f card

Visum (-s, Visa o Visen) nt visa

Vitamin (-s, -e) nt vitamin

Vitrine (-, -n) f (glass) cabinet;
(Schaukasten) display case

Vogel (-s, Vögel) m bird;
Vogelgrippe f bird flu, avian flu;
vögeln vi, vt (vulg) to screw

Voicemail (-, -s) f voice mail

Vokal (-s, -e) m vowel

Volk (-(e)s, Völker) nt people pl;
(Nation) nation; **Volksfest** nt
festival; (Jahrmarkt) funfair;
Volkshochschule f adult
education centre; **Volkslied** nt
folksong; **Volksmusik** f folk
music; **volkstümlich** adj (einfach
und beliebt) popular; (herkömmlich)
traditional; (Kunst) folk

voll adj full (von of); **voll|machen**
vt to fill (up); **voll|tanken** vi to
fill up

Vollbart m beard; **Vollbremsung**
f: **eine ~ machen** to slam on
the brakes; **vollends** adv
completely

Volleyball m volleyball

Vollgas nt: **mit ~** at full throttle;
~ geben to step on it

völlig adj complete ▷ adv
completely

volljährig adj of age;
Vollkaskoversicherung f fully
comprehensive insurance;
vollklimatisiert adj fully

air-conditioned; **vollkommen**
adj perfect; **~er Unsinn** complete
rubbish ▷ adv completely

Vollkornbrot nt wholemeal
(Brit) (o whole wheat (US)) bread

Vollmacht (-, -en) f authority;
(Urkunde) power of attorney

Vollmilch f full-fat milk (Brit),
whole milk (US);
Vollmilchschokolade f milk
chocolate; **Vollmond** m full
moon; **Vollnarkose** f general
anaesthetic; **Vollpension** f full
board

vollständig adj complete

Volltreffer m direct hit;
Vollwertkost f wholefood;
vollzählig adj complete

Volt (-, -) nt volt

Volumen (-s, -) nt volume

vom kontr von **von dem** (räumlich,
zeitlich, Ursache) from; **ich kenne
sie nur ~ Sehen** I only know her by
sight

⊙ SCHLÜSSELWORT

von prep +dat 1 (Ausgangspunkt)
from; **von ... bis** from ... to; **von
morgens bis abends** from
morning till night; **von ... nach ...**
from ... to ...; **von ... an** from ...;
von ... aus from ...; **von dort aus**
from there; **etw von sich aus tun**
to do sth of one's own accord; **von
mir aus** (fam) if you like, I don't
mind; **von wo/wann ...?**
where/when ... from?
2 (Ursache, im Passiv) by; **ein
Gedicht von Schiller** a poem by
Schiller; **von etw müde** tired from
sth
3 (als Genitiv) of; **ein Freund von
mir** a friend of mine; **nett von dir**
nice of you; **jeweils zwei von zehn**
two out of every ten
4 (über) about; **er erzählte vom**

Urlaub he talked about his holiday
5 von wegen! (*fam*) no way!

voneinander *adv* from each
other

O   SCHLÜSSELWORT

vor *prep* +*dat* **1** (*räumlich*) in front
of; **vor der Kirche links abbiegen**
turn left before the church
2 (*zeitlich*) before; **ich war vor ihm
da** I was there before him; **vor 2
Tagen** 2 days ago; **5 (Minuten) vor
4** 5 (minutes) to 4; **vor Kurzem** a
little while ago
3 (*Ursache*) with; **vor Wut/Liebe**
with rage/love; **vor Hunger
sterben** to die of hunger; **vor
lauter Arbeit** because of work
4 vor allem, vor allen Dingen
most of all
▷ *prep* +*akk* (*räumlich*) in front of
▷ *adv*: **vor und zurück** backwards
and forwards

voran|gehen *irr vi* to go ahead;
einer Sache (*dat*) **~** to precede sth;
voran|kommen *irr vi* to make
progress
Vorarlberg (-s) *nt* Vorarlberg
voraus *adv* ahead ; **im Voraus** in
advance; **voraus|fahren** *irr vi* to
drive on ahead; **vorausgesetzt**
conj provided (that); **Voraussage**
f prediction; (*Wetter*) forecast;
voraus|sagen *vt* to predict;
voraus|sehen *irr vt* to foresee;
voraus|sein *vi*: **jdm ~** to be
ahead of sb; **voraus|setzen** *vt* to
assume; **Voraussetzung** *f*
requirement, prerequisite;
voraussichtlich *adj* expected
▷ *adv* probably; **voraus|zahlen**
vt to pay in advance
Vorbehalt (-(*e*)*s*, -*e*) *m*
reservation; **vor|behalten** *irr vt*:

sich/jdm etw ~ to reserve sth (for
oneself)/for sb
vorbei *adv* past, over, finished;
vorbei|bringen *irr vt* to drop by
(*o* in); **vorbei|fahren** *irr vi* to
drive past; **vorbei|gehen** *irr vi* to
pass by, to go past; (*verstreichen,
aufhören*) to pass; **vorbei|kommen**
irr vi to drop by; **vorbei|lassen** *irr
vt*: **kannst du die Leute ~?** would
you let these people pass?; **lässt
du mich bitte mal vorbei?** can I
get past, please?; **vorbei|reden**
vi: **aneinander ~** to talk at
cross-purposes
vor|bereiten *vt* to prepare ▷ *vr*:
sich ~ to get ready (*auf* +*akk*, **für**
for); **Vorbereitung** *f* preparation
vor|bestellen *vt* to book in
advance; (*Essen*) to order in
advance; **Vorbestellung** *f*
booking, reservation
vor|beugen *vi* to prevent (*dat*
sth); **vorbeugend** *adj* preven-
tive; **Vorbeugung** *f* prevention
Vorbild *nt* (role) model;
vorbildlich *adj* model, ideal
Vorderachse *f* front axle;
vordere(r, s) *adj* front;
Vordergrund *m* foreground;
Vorderradantrieb *m* (*Auto*)
front-wheel drive; **Vorderseite** *f*
front; **Vordersitz** *m* front seat;
Vorderteil *m o nt* front (part)
Vordruck *m* form
voreilig *adj* hasty, rash; **~e
Schlüsse ziehen** to jump to
conclusions; **voreingenommen**
adj biased
vor|enthalten *irr vt*: **jdm etw
~** to withhold sth from sb
vorerst *adv* for the moment
vor|fahren *irr vi* (*vorausfahren*) to
drive on ahead; **vor das Haus ~** to
drive up to the house; **fahren Sie
bis zur Ampel vor** drive as far as
the traffic lights

v

Vorfahrt f (Auto) right of way;
~ achten give way (Brit), yield
(US); **Vorfahrtsschild** nt give
way (Brit) (o yield (US)) sign;
Vorfahrtsstraße f major road

Vorfall m incident

vor|führen vt to demonstrate;
(Film) to show; (Theaterstück, Trick)
to perform

Vorgänger(in) m(f) predecessor

vor|gehen irr vi (vorausgehen) to
go on ahead; (nach vorn) to go
forward; (handeln) to act, to
proceed; (Uhr) to be fast; (Vorrang
haben) to take precedence;
(passieren) to go on; **Vorgehen** (-s)
nt procedure

Vorgesetzte(r) mf superior

vorgestern adv the day before
yesterday

vor|haben irr vt to plan; **hast du
schon was vor?** have you got
anything on?; **ich habe vor, nach
Rom zu fahren** I'm planning to go
to Rome

vor|halten irr vt: **jdm etw ~** to
accuse sb of sth

Vorhand f forehand

vorhanden adj existing;
(erhältlich) available

Vorhang m curtain

Vorhaut f foreskin

vorher adv before; **zwei Tage
~** two days before; **~ essen wir**
we'll eat first; **Vorhersage** f
forecast; **vorher|sehen** irr vt to
foresee

vorhin adv just now, a moment
ago

Vorkenntnisse pl previous
knowledge sing

vor|kommen irr vi (nach vorne
kommen) to come forward;
(geschehen) to happen; (sich finden)
to occur; (scheinen) to seem (to
be); **sich** (dat) **dumm ~** to feel
stupid

Vorlage f model

vor|lassen irr vt: **jdn ~** to let sb
go first

vorläufig adj temporary

vor|lesen irr vt to read out

Vorlesung f lecture

vorletzte(r, s) adj last but one;
am ~n Samstag (on) the Saturday
before last

Vorliebe f preference

vor|machen vt: **kannst du es
mir ~?** can you show me how to do
it?; **jdm etwas ~** (fig: täuschen) to
fool sb

vor|merken vt to note down;
(Plätze) to book

Vormittag m morning; **am ~** in
the morning; **heute ~** this
morning; **vormittags** adv in the
morning; **um 9 Uhr ~** at 9 (o'clock)
in the morning, at 9 am

vorn(e) adv in front; **von
~ anfangen** to start at the
beginning; **nach ~** to the front;
weiter ~ further up; **von ~ bis
hinten** from beginning to end

Vorname m first name; **wie
heißt du mit ~** what's your first
name?

vornehm adj (von Rang)
distinguished; (Benehmen) refined;
(fein, elegant) elegant

vor|nehmen irr vt **sich** (dat) **etw
~** to start on sth; **sich** (dat) **~, etw
zu tun** (beschließen) to decide to do
sth

vornherein adv: **von ~** from the
start

Vorort m suburb

vorrangig adj priority

Vorrat m stock, supply; **vorrätig**
adj in stock

Vorrecht nt privilege

Vorruhestand m early
retirement

Vorsaison f early season

Vorsatz m intention; (Jur) intent;

vorsätzlich *adj* intentional; (*Jur*) premeditated

Vorschau *f* preview; (*Film*) trailer

Vorschlag *m* suggestion, proposal; **vorschlagen** *irr vt* to suggest, to propose; **ich schlage vor, dass wir gehen** I suggest we go

vor|schreiben *irr vt* (*befehlen*) to stipulate; **jdm etw ~** to dictate sth to sb

Vorschrift *f* regulation, rule; (*Anweisung*) instruction; **vorschriftsmäßig** *adj* correct

Vorschule *f* nursery school, pre-school (*US*)

Vorsicht *f* care; **~!** look out; (*Schild*) caution; **~ Stufe!** mind the step; **vorsichtig** *adj* careful; **vorsichtshalber** *adv* just in case

Vorsorge *f* precaution; (*Vorbeugung*) prevention; **Vorsorgeuntersuchung** *f* checkup; **vorsorglich** *adv* as a precaution

Vorspann (*-(e)s, -e*) *m* credits *pl*

Vorspeise *f* starter

Vorsprung *m* projection; (*Abstand*) lead

vor|stellen *vt* (*bekannt machen*) to introduce; (*vor*) to put forward; (*vor etw*) to put in front; **sich** (*dat*) **etw ~** to imagine sth; **Vorstellung** *f* (*Bekanntmachen*) introduction; (*Theat*) performance; (*Gedanke*) idea; **Vorstellungsgespräch** *nt* interview

vor|täuschen *vt* to feign

Vorteil *m* advantage (*gegenüber* over); **die Vor- und Nachteile** the pros and cons; **vorteilhaft** *adj* advantageous

Vortrag (*-(e)s, Vorträge*) *m* talk (*über +akk* on); (*akademisch*) lecture; **einen ~ halten** to give a talk

vorüber *adv* over; **vorüber|gehen** *irr vi* to pass; **vorübergehend** *adj* temporary

▷ *adv* temporarily, for the time being

Vorurteil *nt* prejudice

Vorverkauf *m* advance booking

vor|verlegen *vt* to bring forward

Vorwahl *f* (*Tel*) dialling code (*Brit*), area code (*US*)

Vorwand (*-(e)s, Vorwände*) *m* pretext, excuse; **unter dem ~, dass** with the excuse that

vorwärts *adv* forward; **vorwärts|gehen** *irr vi* (*fig*) to progress

vorweg *adv* in advance; **vorweg|nehmen** *irr vt* to anticipate

Vorweihnachtszeit *f* pre-Christmas period, run-up to Christmas (*Brit*)

vor|werfen *irr vt*: **jdm etw ~** to accuse sb of sth

vorwiegend *adv* mainly

Vorwort *nt* preface

Vorwurf *m* reproach; **sich** (*dat*) **Vorwürfe machen** to reproach oneself; **jdm Vorwürfe machen** to accuse sb; **vorwurfsvoll** *adj* reproachful

vor|zeigen *vt* to show

vorzeitig *adj* premature, early

vor|ziehen *irr vt* (*lieber haben*) to prefer

Vorzug *m* preference; (*gute Eigenschaft*) merit; (*Vorteil*) advantage

vorzüglich *adj* excellent

vulgär *adj* vulgar

Vulkan (*-s, -e*) *m* volcano; **Vulkanausbruch** *m* volcanic eruption

W

W *abk* = **West** W

Waage (-, -n) *f* scales *pl*; (*Astr*) Libra; **waagerecht** *adj* horizontal

wach *adj* awake; **~ werden** to wake up; **Wache** (-, -n) *f* guard

Wachs (-es, -e) *nt* wax

wachsen (*wuchs*, *gewachsen*) *vi* to grow

wachsen *vt* (*Skier*) to wax

Wachstum *nt* growth

Wachtel (-, -n) *f* quail

Wächter(in) (-s, -) *m(f)* guard; (*auf Parkplatz*) attendant

wackelig *adj* wobbly; (*fig*) shaky; **Wackelkontakt** *m* loose connection; **wackeln** *vi* (*Stuhl*) to be wobbly; (*Zahn, Schraube*) to be loose; **mit dem Kopf ~** to waggle one's head

Wade (-, -n) *f* (*Anat*) calf

Waffe (-, -n) *f* weapon

Waffel (-, -n) *f* waffle; (*Keks, Eiswaffel*) wafer

wagen *vt* to risk; **es ~, etw zu tun** to dare to do sth

Wagen (-s, -) *m* (*Auto*) car; (*Eisenb*) carriage; **Wagenheber** (-s, -) *m* jack; **Wagentyp** *m* model, make

Wahl (-, -en) *f* choice; (*Pol*) election

wählen *vt* to choose; (*Tel*) to dial; (*Pol*) to vote for; (*durch Wahl ermitteln*) to elect ▷ *vi* to choose; (*Tel*) to dial; (*Pol*) to vote; **Wähler(in)** (-s, -) *m(f)* voter; **wählerisch** *adj* choosy

Wahlkampf *m* election campaign; **wahllos** *adv* at random; **Wahlwiederholung** *f* redial

Wahnsinn *m* madness; **~!** amazing!; **wahnsinnig** *adj* insane, mad ▷ *adv* (*fam*) incredibly

wahr *adj* true; **das darf doch nicht ~ sein!** I don't believe it; **nicht ~?** that's right, isn't it?

während *prep* +*gen* during ▷ *conj* while; **währenddessen** *adv* meanwhile, in the meantime

Wahrheit *f* truth

wahrnehmbar *adj* noticeable, perceptible; **wahr|nehmen** *irr vt* to perceive

Wahrsager(in) (-s, -) *m(f)* fortune-teller

Waise (-, -n) *f* orphan

Wal (-(e)s, -e) *m* whale

Wald (-(e)s, *Wälder*) *m* wood; (*groß*) forest; **Waldbrand** *m* forest fire; **Waldsterben** (-s) *nt* forest dieback

wahrscheinlich *adj* probable, likely ▷ *adv* probably; **ich komme ~ zu spät** I'll probably be late; **Wahrscheinlichkeit** *f* probability

Währung *f* currency

Wahrzeichen *nt* symbol

Wales (-) *nt* Wales; **Waliser(in)** *m(f)* Welshman/Welshwoman; **walisisch** *adj* Welsh; **Walisisch** *nt* Welsh

Walkie-Talkie (-(s), -s) *nt* walkie-talkie

Walkman® (-s, -s) *m* walkman®, personal stereo

Wall (-(e)s, Wälle) *m* embankment

Wallfahrt *f* pilgrimage; **Wallfahrtsort** *m* place of pilgrimage

Walnuss *f* walnut

Walross (-es, -e) *nt* walrus

wälzen *vt* to roll; (*Bücher*) to pore over; (*Probleme*) to deliberate on ▷ *vr*: **sich ~** to wallow; (*vor Schmerzen*) to roll about; (*im Bett*) to toss and turn

Walzer (-s, -) *m* waltz

Wand (-, Wände) *f* wall; (*Trenn~*) partition; (*Berg~*) (rock) face

Wandel (-s) *m* change; **wandeln** *vt* to change ▷ *vr*: **sich ~** to change

Wanderer (-s, -) *m*, **Wanderin** *f* hiker; **Wanderkarte** *f* hiking map; **wandern** *vi* to hike; (*Blick*) to wander; (*Gedanken*) to stray; **Wanderschuh** *m* walking shoe; **Wanderstiefel** *m* hiking boot; **Wanderung** *f* hike; **eine ~ machen** to go on a hike; **Wanderweg** *m* walking (*o* hiking) trail

Wandleuchte *f* wall lamp; **Wandmalerei** *f* mural; **Wandschrank** *m* built-in cupboard (*Brit*), closet (*US*)

wandte *imperf von* **wenden**

Wange (-, -n) *f* cheek

wann *adv* when; **seit ~ ist sie da?** how long has she been here?; **bis ~ bleibt ihr?** how long are you staying?

Wanne (-, -n) *f* (bath) tub

Wappen (-s, -) *nt* coat of arms

war *imperf von* **sein**

warb *imperf von* **werben**

Ware (-, -n) *f* product; **~n** goods *pl*; **Warenhaus** *nt* department store; **Warenprobe** *f* sample; **Warenzeichen** *nt* trademark

warf *imperf von* **werfen**

warm *adj* warm; (*Essen*) hot; **~ laufen** to warm up; **mir ist es zu ~** I'm too warm; **Wärme** (-, -n) *f* warmth; **wärmen** *vt* to warm; (*Essen*) to warm (*o* to heat) up ▷ *vi* (*Kleidung, Sonne*) to be warm ▷ *vr*: **sich ~** to warm up; (*gegenseitig*) to keep each other warm; **Wärmflasche** *f* hot-water bottle; **Warmstart** *m* (*Inform*) warm start

Warnblinkanlage *f* (*Auto*) warning flasher; **Warndreieck** *nt* (*Auto*) warning triangle; **warnen** *vt* to warn (*vor +dat* about, of); **Warnung** *f* warning

Warteliste *f* waiting list; **warten** *vi* to wait (*auf +akk* for); **warte mal!** wait (*o* hang on) a minute ▷ *vt* (*Tech*) to service

Wärter(in) *m(f)* attendant

Wartesaal *m*, **Wartezimmer** *nt* waiting room

Wartung *f* service; (*das Warten*) servicing

warum *adv* why

Warze (-, -n) *f* wart

was *pron* what; (*fam: etwas*) something; **~ kostet das?** what does it cost? how much is it?; **~ für ein Auto ist das?** what kind of car is that?; **~ für eine Farbe/Größe?** what colour/size?; **~?** (*fam: wie bitte?*) what?; **~ ist/gibt's?** what is it? what's up? **du weißt, ~ ich meine** you know what I mean; **~ (auch) immer** whatever; **soll ich dir ~ mitbringen?** do you want me to bring you anything?; **alles, ~ er hat** everything he's got

w

Waschanlage f (*Auto*) car wash;
waschbar adj washable;
Waschbär m raccoon;
Waschbecken nt washbasin
Wäsche (-, -n) f washing;
(*schmutzig*) laundry; (*Bettwäsche*)
linen; (*Unterwäsche*) underwear; **in
der ~** in the wash;
Wäscheklammer f clothes peg
(*Brit*) (*o* pin (*US*)); **Wäscheleine** f
clothesline
waschen (*wusch, gewaschen*) vt, vi
to wash; **Waschen und Legen**
shampoo and set ▷ vr: **sich ~** to
(have a) wash; **sich** (*dat*) **die Haare
~** to wash one's hair
Wäscherei f laundry;
Wäscheständer m clothes horse;
Wäschetrockner m tumble-drier
Waschgelegenheit f washing
facilities pl; **Waschlappen** m
flannel (*Brit*), washcloth (*US*); (*fam:
Mensch*) wet blanket;
Waschmaschine f washing
machine; **Waschmittel** nt,
Waschpulver nt washing
powder; **Waschraum** m
washroom; **Waschsalon** (-s, -s) m
launderette (*Brit*), laundromat
(*US*); **Waschstraße** f car wash
Wasser (-s, -) nt water;
fließendes ~ running water;
Wasserball m (*Sport*) water polo;
Wasserbob m jet ski;
wasserdicht adj watertight; (*Uhr
etc*) waterproof; **Wasserfall** m
waterfall; **Wasserfarbe** f
watercolour; **wasserfest** adj
watertight, waterproof;
Wasserhahn m tap (*Brit*), faucet
(*US*); **wässerig** adj watery;
Wasserkessel (-s, -) m kettle;
Wasserkocher (-s, -) m electric
kettle; **Wasserleitung** f water
pipe; **wasserlöslich** adj
water-soluble; **Wassermann** m
(*Astr*) Aquarius; **Wassermelone** f

water melon; **Wasserrutschbahn**
f water chute; **Wasserschaden**
m water damage; **wasserscheu**
adj scared of water; **Wasserski**
nt water-skiing; **Wasserspiegel**
m surface of the water;
(*Wasserstand*) water level;
Wassersport m water sports pl;
wasserundurchlässig adj
watertight, waterproof;
Wasserverbrauch m water
consumption;
Wasserversorgung f water
supply; **Wasserwaage** f spirit
level; **Wasserwerk** nt
waterworks pl
waten vi to wade
Watt (-(e)s, -en) nt (*Geo*) mud flats
pl ▷ (-s, -) nt (*Elek*) watt
Watte (-, -n) f cotton wool;
Wattepad (-s, -s) m cotton pad;
Wattestäbchen nt cotton bud,
Q-tip® (*US*)
WC (-s, -s) nt toilet, restroom
(*US*); **WC-Reiniger** m toilet
cleaner
Web (-s) nt (*Inform*) Web;
Webseite f (*Inform*) web page
Wechsel (-s, -) m change;
(*Spieler~: Sport*) substitution;
Wechselgeld nt change;
wechselhaft adj (*Wetter*)
changeable; **Wechseljahre** pl
menopause sing; **Wechselkurs** m
exchange rate; **wechseln** vt to
change; (*Blicke*) to exchange; **Geld
~** to change some money; (*in
Kleingeld*) to get some change;
Euro in Pfund ~ to change euros
into pounds ▷ vi to change;
kannst du ~? can you change
this?; **Wechselstrom** m
alternating current, AC;
Wechselstube f bureau de
change
Weckdienst m wake-up call
service; **wecken** vt to wake (up);

Wecker (-s, -) m alarm clock;
Weckruf m wake-up call
wedeln vi (Ski) to wedel; **mit etw
~** to wave sth; **mit dem Schwanz
~** to wag its tail; **der Hund
wedelte mit dem Schwanz** the
dog wagged its tail
weder conj: **~ ... noch ...** neither
... nor ...
weg adv (entfernt, verreist) away;
(los, ab) off; **er war schon ~** he had
already left (o gone); **Hände ~!**
hands off; **weit ~** a long way away
(o off)
Weg (-(e)s, -e) m way; (Pfad) path;
(Route) route; **jdn nach dem
~ fragen** to ask sb the way; **auf
dem ~ sein** to be on the way
weg|bleiben irr vi to stay away;
weg|bringen irr vt to take away
wegen prep +gen o dat because of
weg|fahren irr vi to drive away;
(abfahren) to leave; (in Urlaub) to go
away; **Wegfahrsperre** f (Auto)
(engine) immobilizer; **weg|gehen**
irr vi to go away; **weg|kommen**
irr vi to get away; (fig)
gut/schlecht ~ to come off
well/badly; **weg|lassen** irr vt to
leave out; **weg|laufen** irr vi to
run away; **weg|legen** vt to put
aside; **weg|machen** vt (fam) to
get rid of; **weg|müssen** irr vi: **ich
muss weg** I've got to go;
weg|nehmen irr vt to take away;
weg|räumen vt to clear away;
weg|rennen irr vi to run away;
weg|schicken vt to send away;
weg|schmeißen irr vt to throw
away; **weg|sehen** irr vi to look
away; **weg|tun** irr vt to put away
Wegweiser (-s, -) m signpost
weg|werfen irr vt to throw
away; **weg|wischen** vt to wipe
off; **weg|ziehen** irr vi to move
(away)
weh adj sore; siehe auch **wehtun**

wehen vt, vi to blow; (Fahne) to
flutter
Wehen pl labour pains pl
Wehrdienst m military service
wehren vr: **sich ~** to defend
oneself
weh|tun irr vi to hurt; **jdm/sich
~** to hurt sb/oneself
Weibchen nt: **es ist ein ~** (Tier)
it's a she; **weiblich** adj feminine;
(Bio) female
weich adj soft; **~ gekocht** (Ei)
soft-boiled
Weichkäse m soft cheese;
(Streichkäse) cheese spread;
weichlich adj soft; (körperlich)
weak; **Weichspüler** (-s, -) m (für
Wäsche) (fabric) softener
Weide (-, -n) f (Baum) willow;
(Grasfläche) meadow
weigern vr: **sich ~** to refuse;
Weigerung f refusal
Weiher (-s, -) m pond
Weihnachten (-, -) nt Christ-
mas; **Weihnachtsabend** m
Christmas Eve; **Weihnachtsbaum**
m Christmas tree;
Weihnachtsfeier f Christmas
party; **Weihnachtsferien** pl
Christmas holidays pl (Brit),
Christmas vacation sing (US);
Weihnachtsgeld nt Christmas
bonus; **Weihnachtsgeschenk** nt
Christmas present;
Weihnachtskarte f Christmas
card; **Weihnachtslied** nt
Christmas carol;
Weihnachtsmann m Father
Christmas, Santa (Claus)

● **WEIHNACHTSMARKT**
●
● The **Weihnachtsmarkt** is a
● market held in most large
● towns in Germany in the weeks
● prior to Christmas. People visit
● it to buy presents, toys and

- Christmas decorations, and to
- enjoy the festive atmosphere.
- Food and drink associated with
- the Christmas festivities can
- also be eaten and drunk there,
- for example, gingerbread and
- mulled wine.

Weihnachtsstern m (Bot)
poinsettia; **Weihnachtstag** m:
erster ~ Christmas Day; **zweiter
~** Boxing Day; **Weihnachtszeit** f
Christmas season
weil conj because
Weile (-) f while, short time; **es
kann noch eine ~ dauern** it could
take some time
Wein (-(e)s, -e) m wine; (Pflanze)
vine; **Weinbeere** f grape;
Weinberg m vineyard;
Weinbergschnecke f snail;
Weinbrand m brandy
weinen vt, vi to cry
Weinglas nt wine glass;
Weinkarte f wine list;
Weinkeller m wine cellar;
Weinlese (-, -n) f vintage;
Weinprobe f wine tasting;
Weintraube f grape
weise adj wise
Weise (-, -n) f manner, way; **auf
diese** (Art und) **~** this way
weisen (wies, gewiesen) vt to
show
Weisheit f wisdom;
Weisheitszahn m wisdom
tooth
weiß adj white; **Weißbier** nt ≈
wheat beer; **Weißbrot** nt white
bread; **weißhaarig** adj
white-haired; **Weißkohl** m,
Weißkraut nt (white) cabbage;
Weißwein m white wine
weit adj wide; (Begriff) broad;
(Reise, Wurf) long; (Kleid) loose; **wie
~ ist es …?** how far is it …?; **so
~ sein** to be ready ▷ adv far;

~ verbreitet widespread;
~ gereist widely travelled; **~ offen**
wide open; **das geht zu ~** that's
going too far, that's pushing it
weiter adj wider; (~ weg) farther
(away); (zusätzlich) further; **~e
Informationen** further
information sing ▷ adv further; **~!**
go on; (weitergehen!) keep moving;
~ nichts/niemand
nothing/nobody else; **und so
~** and so on; **weiter|arbeiten** vi
to carry on working;
Weiterbildung f further training
(o education); **weiter|empfehlen**
irr vt to recommend;
weiter|erzählen vt: **nicht ~!**
don't tell anyone; **weiter|fahren**
irr vi to go on (nach to, bis as far
as); **weiter|geben** irr vt to pass
on; **weiter|gehen** irr vi to go on;
weiter|helfen irr vi: **jdm ~** to
help sb; **weiterhin** adv: **etw
~ tun** to go on doing sth;
weiter|machen vt, vi to
continue; **weiter|reisen** vi to
continue one's journey
weitgehend adj considerable
▷ adv largely; **weitsichtig** adj
long-sighted; (fig) far-sighted;
Weitsprung m long jump;
Weitwinkelobjektiv nt (Foto)
wide-angle lens
Weizen (-s, -) m wheat;
Weizenbier nt ≈ wheat beer

 SCHLÜSSELWORT

welche(r, s) interrogativ pron
which; **welcher von beiden?**
which (one) of the two?; **welchen
hast du genommen?** which (one)
did you take?; **welche eine …!**
what a …!; **welche Freude!** what
joy! ▷ indef pron some; (in Fragen)
any; **ich habe welche** I have some;
haben Sie welche? do you have

any? ▷ *relativ pron* (*bei Menschen*) who; (*bei Sachen*) which, that; **welche(r, s) auch immer** whoever/whichever/whatever

welk *adj* withered; **welken** *vi* to wither

Welle (-, -n) *f* wave; **Wellengang** *m* waves *pl*; **starker ~** heavy seas *pl*; **Wellenlänge** *f* (*a. fig*) wavelength; **Wellenreiten** *nt* surfing; **Wellensittich** (-s, -e) *m* budgerigar, budgie; **wellig** *adj* wavy

Wellness *f* health and beauty (*Brit*), wellness (*US*)

Welpe (-n, -n) *m* puppy

Welt (-, -en) *f* world; **auf der ~** in the world; **auf die ~ kommen** to be born; **Weltall** *nt* universe; **weltbekannt, weltberühmt** *adj* world-famous; **Weltkrieg** *m* world war; **Weltmacht** *f* world power; **Weltmeister(in)** *m(f)* world champion; **Weltmeisterschaft** *f* world championship; (*im Fußball*) World Cup; **Weltraum** *m* space; **Weltreise** *f* trip round the world; **Weltrekord** *m* world record; **Weltstadt** *f* metropolis; **weltweit** *adj* worldwide, global

wem *pron dat von* **wer** who ... to, (to) whom; **~ hast du's gegeben?** who did you give it to?; **~ gehört es?** who does it belong to?, whose is it?; **~ auch immer es gehört** whoever it belongs to

wen *pron akk von* **wer** who, whom; **~ hast du besucht?** who did you visit?; **~ möchten Sie sprechen?** who would you like to speak to?

Wende (-, -n) *f* turning point; (*Veränderung*) change; **die ~** (*Hist*) the fall of the Berlin Wall; **Wendekreis** *m* (*Auto*) turning circle

Wendeltreppe *f* spiral staircase

wenden (wendete o wandte, gewendet o gewandt) *vt, vi* to turn (round); (*um 180°*) to make a U-turn; **sich an jdn ~** to turn to sb; **bitte ~!** please turn over, PTO ▷ *vr*: **sich ~** to turn; **sich an jdn ~** to turn to sb

wenig *pron, adv* little; **~(e)** *pl* few; (**nur**) **ein (klein) ~** (just) a little (bit); **ein ~ Zucker** a little bit of sugar, a little sugar; **wir haben ~ Zeit** we haven't got much time; **zu ~** too little; *pl* too few; **nur ~ wissen** only a few know ▷ *adv*: **er spricht ~** he doesn't talk much; **~ bekannt** little known; **wenige** *pron pl* few *pl*; **wenigste(r, s)** *adj* least; **wenigstens** *adv* at least

○ SCHLÜSSELWORT

wenn *konj* **1** (falls, bei Wünschen) if; **wenn auch ..., selbst wenn ...** even if ...; **wenn ich doch ...** if only I ...
2 (zeitlich) when; **immer wenn** whenever

wennschon *adv*: **na ~** so what?

wer *pron* who; **~ war das?** who was that?; **~ von euch?** which (one) of you? ▷ *pron* anybody who, anyone who; **~ das glaubt, ist dumm** anyone who believes that is stupid; **~ auch immer** whoever ▷ *pron* somebody, someone; (*in Fragen*) anybody, anyone; **ist da ~?** is (there) anybody there?

Werbefernsehen *nt* TV commercials *pl*; **Werbegeschenk** *nt* promotional gift; **werben** (warb, geworben) *vt* to win; (*Mitglied*) to recruit ▷ *vi* to advertise; **Werbespot** (-s, -s) *m* commercial; **Werbung** *f* advertising

w

◐ SCHLÜSSELWORT

werden (pt **wurde**, pp **geworden** o (bei Passiv) **worden**) vi to become; **was ist aus ihm/aus der Sache geworden?** what became of him/it?; **es ist nichts/gut geworden** it came to nothing/turned out well; **es wird Nacht/Tag** it's getting dark/light; **mir wird kalt** I'm getting cold; **mir wird schlecht** I feel ill; **Erster werden** to come o be first; **das muss anders werden** that'll have to change; **rot/zu Eis werden** to turn red/to ice; **was willst du (mal) werden?** what do you want to be?; **die Fotos sind gut geworden** the photos have come out nicely

▷ als Hilfsverb **1** (bei Futur) **er wird es tun** he will o he'll do it; **er wird das nicht tun** he will not o he won't do it; **es wird gleich regnen** it's going to rain

2 (bei Konjunktiv) **ich würde ...** I would ...; **er würde gern ...** he would o he'd like to ...; **ich würde lieber ...** I would o I'd rather ...

3 (bei Vermutung) **sie wird in der Küche sein** she will be in the kitchen

4 (bei Passiv) **gebraucht werden** to be used; **er ist erschossen worden** he has o he's been shot; **mir wurde gesagt, dass ...** I was told that ...

werfen (warf, geworfen) vt to throw

Werft (-, -en) f shipyard, dockyard

Werk (-(e)s, -e) nt (Kunstwerk, Buch etc) work; (Fabrik) factory; (Mechanismus) works pl; **Werkstatt** (-, -stätten) f workshop; (Auto)

garage; **Werktag** m working day; **werktags** adv on weekdays, during the week; **Werkzeug** nt tool; **Werkzeugkasten** m toolbox

wert adj worth; **es ist etwa 50 Euro ~** it's worth about 50 euros; **das ist nichts ~** it's worthless; **Wert** (-(e)s, -e) m worth; (Zahlen~) (Fin) value; **~ legen auf** (+akk) to attach importance to; **es hat doch keinen ~** (Sinn) it's pointless; **Wertangabe** f declaration of value; **Wertbrief** m insured letter; **Wertgegenstand** m valuable object; **wertlos** adj worthless; **Wertmarke** f token; **Wertpapiere** pl securities pl; **Wertsachen** pl valuables pl; **Wertstoff** m recyclable waste; **wertvoll** adj valuable

Wesen (-s, -) nt being; (Natur, Charakter) nature

wesentlich adj significant; (beträchtlich) considerable ▷ adv considerably

weshalb adv why

Wespe (-, -n) f wasp; **Wespenstich** m wasp sting

wessen pron gen von **wer**; whose

◦ WESSI
◦
◦ A **Wessi** is a colloquial and often
◦ derogatory word used to
◦ describe a German from the
◦ former West Germany. The
◦ expression 'Besserwessi' is used
◦ by East Germans to describe a
◦ West German who is considered
◦ to be a know-all.

West west; **Westdeutschland** nt (als Landesteil) Western Germany; (Hist) West Germany

Weste (-, -n) f waistcoat (Brit), vest (US); (Wollweste) cardigan

Westen (-s) m west; **im
~ Englands** in the west of
England; **der Wilde ~** the Wild
West; **Westeuropa** nt Western
Europe; **Westküste** f west
coast; **westlich** adj western;
(Kurs, Richtung) westerly;
Westwind m west(erly) wind
weswegen adv why
Wettbewerb m competition;
Wettbüro nt betting office;
Wette (-, -n) f bet; **eine
~ abschließen** to make a bet;
die ~ gilt! you're on; **wetten** vt, vi
to bet (auf +akk on); **ich habe mit
ihm gewettet, dass ...** I bet him
that ...; **ich wette mit dir um 50
Euro** I'll bet you 50 euros; **~, dass?**
wanna bet?
Wetter (-s, -) nt weather;
Wetterbericht m,
Wettervorhersage f weather
forecast; **Wetterkarte** f
weather map; **Wetterlage** f
weather situation;
Wettervorhersage f weather
forecast
Wettkampf m contest;
Wettlauf m race; **Wettrennen**
nt race
WG (-, -s) f abk =
Wohngemeinschaft
Whirlpool® (-s, -s) m jacuzzi®
Whisky (-s, -s) m (schottisch)
whisky; (irisch, amerikanisch)
whiskey
wichtig adj important
wickeln vt (Schnur) to wind (um
round); (Schal, Decke) to wrap (um
round); **ein Baby ~** to change a
baby's nappy (Brit) (o diaper (US));
Wickelraum m baby-changing
room; **Wickeltisch** m
baby-changing table
Widder (-s, -) m (Zool) ram; (Astr)
Aries sing
wider prep +akk against

widerlich adj disgusting
widerrufen irr vt to withdraw;
(Auftrag, Befehl etc) to cancel
widersprechen irr vi to
contradict (jdm sb); **Widerspruch**
m contradiction
Widerstand m resistance;
widerstandsfähig adj resistant
(gegen to)
widerwärtig adj disgusting
widerwillig adj unwilling
widmen vt to dedicate ▷ vr: **sich
jdm/etw ~** to devote oneself to
sb/sth; **Widmung** f dedication

O SCHLÜSSELWORT

wie adv how; **wie groß/schnell?**
how big/fast?; **wie wär's?** how
about it?; **wie ist er?** what's he
like?; **wie gut du das kannst!**
you're very good at it; **wie bitte?**
pardon?; (entrüstet) I beg your
pardon!; **und wie!** and how!; **wie
viel** how much; **wie viele
Menschen** how many people; **wie
weit** to what extent
▷ konj 1 (bei Vergleichen) **so schön
wie ...** as beautiful as ...; **wie ich
schon sagte** as I said; **wie du** like
you; **singen wie ein ...** to sing like
a ...; **wie (zum Beispiel)** such as
(for example)
2 (zeitlich) **wie er das hörte, ging
er** when he heard that he left; **er
hörte, wie der Regen fiel** he
heard the rain falling

wieder adv again; **~ ein(e) ...**
another ...; **~ erkennen** to
recognize; **etw ~ gutmachen** to
make up for sth; **~ verwerten**
to recycle
wieder|bekommen irr vt to
get back
wiederbeschreibbar adj (CD,
DVD) rewritable

w

wiederholen vt to repeat;
Wiederholung f repetition
Wiederhören nt (Tel) **auf**
~ goodbye
wieder|kommen irr vi to come
back
wieder|sehen irr vt to see
again; (wieder treffen) to meet
again; **Wiedersehen** (-s) nt
reunion; **auf ~!** goodbye
Wiedervereinigung f
reunification
Wiege (-, -n) f cradle; **wiegen**
(wog, gewogen) vt, vi to weigh
Wien (-s) nt Vienna
wies imperf von **weisen**
Wiese (-, -n) f meadow
Wiesel (-s, -) nt weasel
wieso adv why
wievielmal adv how often;
wievielte(r, s) adj: **zum ~n Mal?**
how many times?; **den**
Wievielten haben wir heute?
what's the date today?; **am**
Wievielten hast du Geburtstag?
which day is your birthday?
wieweit conj to what extent
Wi-Fi nt Wi-Fi
wild adj wild
Wild (-(e)s) nt game
wildfremd adj (fam) **ein ~er**
Mensch a complete (o total)
stranger; **Wildleder** nt suede;
Wildpark m game park;
Wildschwein nt (wild) boar;
Wildwasserfahren (-s) nt
whitewater rafting
Wille (-ns, -n) m will
willen prep +gen **um ... ~** for the
sake of ...; **um Himmels ~!**
(vorwurfsvoll) for heaven's sake;
(betroffen) goodness me
willkommen adj welcome; **jdn**
~ heißen to welcome sb
Wimper (-, -n) f eyelash;
Wimperntusche f mascara
Wind (-(e)s, -e) m wind

Windel (-, -n) f nappy (Brit),
diaper (US)
windgeschützt adj sheltered
from the wind; **windig** adj windy;
(fig) dubious; **Windjacke** f
windcheater; **Windmühle** f
windmill; **Windpark** m wind
farm; **Windpocken** pl chickenpox
sing; **Windschutzscheibe** f (Auto)
windscreen (Brit), windshield (US);
Windstärke f wind force;
Windsurfen (-s) nt windsurfing;
Windsurfer(in) m(f) windsurfer
Winkel (-s, -) m (Math) angle;
(Gerät) set square; (in Raum)
corner; **im rechten ~ zu** at right
angles to
winken vt, vi to wave
Winter (-s, -) m winter;
Winterausrüstung f (Auto)
winter equipment;
Winterfahrplan m winter
timetable; **winterlich** adj
wintry; **Wintermantel** m winter
coat; **Winterreifen** m winter
tyre; **Winterschlussverkauf** m
winter sales pl; **Wintersport** m
winter sports pl
Winterzeit f (Uhrzeit) winter
time (Brit), standard time (US)
winzig adj tiny
wir pron we; **~ selbst** we
ourselves; **~ alle** all of us; **~ drei**
the three of us; **~ sind's** it's us;
~ nicht not us
Wirbel (-s, -) m whirl; (Trubel)
hurly-burly; (Aufsehen) fuss; (Anat)
vertebra; **Wirbelsäule** f spine
wirken vi to be effective;
(erfolgreich sein) to work; (scheinen)
to seem
wirklich adj real; **Wirklichkeit** f
reality
wirksam adj effective; **Wirkung**
f effect
wirr adj confused; **Wirrwarr** (-s)
m confusion

Wirsing (-s) m savoy cabbage
Wirt (-(e)s, -e) m landlord; **Wirtin** f landlady
Wirtschaft f (Comm) economy; (Gaststätte) pub; **wirtschaftlich** adj (Pol, Comm) economic; (sparsam) economical
Wirtshaus nt pub
wischen vt, vi to wipe; **Wischer** (-s, -) m wiper
wissen (wusste, gewusst) vt to know; **weißt du schon, ...?** did you know ...?; **woher weißt du das?** how do you know?; **das musst du selbst ~** that's up to you; **Wissen** (-s) nt knowledge
Wissenschaft f science; **Wissenschaftler(in)** (-s, -) m(f) scientist; (Geisteswissenschaftler) academic; **wissenschaftlich** adj scientific; (geisteswissenschaftlich) academic
Witwe (-, -n) f widow; **Witwer** (-s, -) m widower
Witz (-(e)s, -e) m joke; **mach keine ~e!** you're kidding!; **das soll wohl ein ~ sein** you've got to be joking; **witzig** adj funny
wo adv where; **zu einer Zeit, ~ ...** at a time when ...; **überall, ~ ich hingehe** wherever I go ▷ conj: **jetzt, ~ du da bist** now that you're here; **~ ich dich gerade spreche** while I'm talking to you; **woanders** adv somewhere else
wobei adv: **~ mir einfällt ...** which reminds me ...
Woche (-, -n) f week; **während** (o unter) der **~** during the week; **einmal die ~** once a week; **Wochenende** nt weekend; **am ~** at (Brit) (o on (US)) the weekend; **wir fahren übers ~ weg** we're going away for the weekend; **Wochenendhaus** nt weekend cottage; **Wochenendtrip** m weekend trip; **Wochenendurlaub**

m weekend break; **Wochenkarte** f weekly (season) ticket; **wochenlang** adv for weeks (on end); **Wochenmarkt** m weekly market; **Wochentag** m weekday; **wöchentlich** adj, adv weekly
Wodka (-s, -s) m vodka
wodurch adv: **~ unterscheiden sie sich?** what's the difference between them?; **~ hast du es gemerkt?** how did you notice?; **wofür** adv (relativ) for which; (Frage) what ... for; **~ brauchst du das?** what do you need that for?
wog imperf von **wiegen**
woher adv where ... from; **wohin** adv where ... to

 SCHLÜSSELWORT

wohl adv 1 **wohl oder übel** whether one likes it or not 2 (wahrscheinlich) probably; (gewiss) certainly; (vielleicht) perhaps; **sie ist wohl zu Hause** she's probably at home; **das ist doch wohl nicht dein Ernst!** surely you're not serious; **das mag wohl sein** that may well be; **ob das wohl stimmt?** I wonder if that's true; **er weiß das sehr wohl** he knows that perfectly well

Wohl (-(e)s) nt: **zum ~!** cheers; **wohlbehalten** adv safe and sound; **wohl|fühlen** vr: **sich ~** (zufrieden) to feel happy; (gesundheitlich) to feel well; **Wohlstand** m prosperity, affluence; **wohl|tun** irr vi: **jdm ~** to do sb good; **Wohlwollen** nt goodwill
Wohnblock m block of flats (Brit), apartment house (US); **wohnen** vi to live; **Wohngemeinschaft** f shared flat

(*Brit*) (*o* apartment (*US*)); **ich wohne in einer ~** I share a flat (*o* apartment); **wohnhaft** *adj* resident; **Wohnküche** *f* kitchen-cum-living-room; **Wohnmobil** (*-s, -e*) *nt* camper, RV (*US*); **Wohnort** *m* place of residence; **Wohnsitz** *m* place of residence; **Wohnung** *f* flat (*Brit*), apartment (*US*); **Wohnungstür** *f* front door; **Wohnwagen** *m* caravan; **Wohnzimmer** *nt* living room

Wolf (*-(e)s, Wölfe*) *m* wolf

Wolke (*-, -n*) *f* cloud; **Wolkenkratzer** *m* skyscraper; **wolkenlos** *adj* cloudless; **wolkig** *adj* cloudy

Wolldecke *f* (woollen) blanket; **Wolle** (*-, -n*) *f* wool

 SCHLÜSSELWORT

wollen (*pt* **wollte**, *pp* **gewollt** *o* (*als Hilfsverb*) **wollen**) *vt, vi* to want; **ich will nach Hause** I want to go home; **er will nicht** he doesn't want to; **er wollte das nicht** he didn't want it; **wenn du willst** if you like; **ich will, dass du mir zuhörst** I want you to listen to me ▷ *Hilfsverb:* **er will ein Haus kaufen** he wants to buy a house; **ich wollte, ich wäre ...** I wish I were ...; **etw gerade tun wollen** to be going to do sth

Wolljacke *f* cardigan

womit *adv* what ... with; **~ habe ich das verdient?** what have I done to deserve that?

womöglich *adv* possibly

woran *adv:* **~ denkst du?** what are you thinking of?; **~ ist er gestorben?** what did he die of?; **~ sieht man das?** how can you tell?

worauf *adv:* **~ wartest du?** what are you waiting for?

woraus *adv:* **~ ist das gemacht?** what is it made of?

Workshop (*-s, -s*) *m* workshop

World Wide Web *nt* World Wide Web

Wort (*-(e)s, Wörter*) *nt* (*Vokabel*) word ▷ (*-(e)s, -e*) *nt* (*Äußerung*) word; **mit anderen ~en** in other words; **jdn beim ~ nehmen** to take sb at his/her word; **Wörterbuch** *nt* dictionary; **wörtlich** *adj* literal

worüber *adv:* **~ redet sie?** what is she talking about?

worum *adv:* **~ gehts?** what is it about?

worunter *adv:* **~ leidet er?** what is he suffering from?

wovon *adv* (*relativ*) from which; **~ redest du?** what are you talking about?; **wozu** *adv* (*relativ*) to/for which; (*interrogativ*) what ... for/to; (*warum*) why; **~?** what for?; **~ brauchst du das?** what do you need it for?; **~ soll das gut sein?** what's it for?; **~ hast du Lust?** what do you feel like doing?

Wrack (*-(e)s, -s*) *nt* wreck

Wucher (*-s*) *m* profiteering; **das ist ~!** that's daylight robbery!

wuchs *imperf von* **wachsen**

wühlen *vi* to rummage; (*Tier*) to root; (*Maulwurf*) to burrow

Wühltisch *m* bargain counter

wund *adj* sore; **Wunde** (*-, -n*) *f* wound

Wunder (*-s, -*) *nt* miracle; **es ist kein ~** it's no wonder; **wunderbar** *adj* wonderful, marvellous; **Wunderkerze** *f* sparkler; **Wundermittel** *nt* wonder cure; **wundern** *vr:* **sich ~** to be surprised (*über +akk* at) ▷ *vt* to surprise; **wunderschön** *adj* beautiful; **wundervoll** *adj* wonderful

Wundsalbe *f* antiseptic ointment; **Wundstarrkrampf** *m* tetanus

Wunsch *(-(e)s, Wünsche)* *m* wish (*nach* for); **wünschen** *vt* to wish; **sich** *(dat)* **etw ~** to want sth; **ich wünsche dir alles Gute** I wish you all the best; **wünschenswert** *adj* desirable

wurde *imperf von* **werden**

Wurf *(-s, Würfe)* *m* throw; *(Zool)* litter

Würfel *(-s, -)* *m* dice; *(Math)* cube; **würfeln** *vi* to throw (the dice); *(Würfel spielen)* to play dice ▷ *vt (Zahl)* to throw; *(Gastr)* to dice; **Würfelzucker** *m* lump sugar

Wurm *(-(e)s, Würmer)* *m* worm

Wurst *(-, Würste)* *f* sausage; **das ist mir ~** *(fam)* I couldn't care less

Würstchen *nt* frankfurter

Würze *(-, -n)* *f* seasoning, spice

Wurzel *(-, -n)* *f* root; **Wurzelbehandlung** *f* root canal treatment

würzen *vt* to season, to spice; **würzig** *adj* spicy

wusch *imperf von* **waschen**

wusste *imperf von* **wissen**

wüst *adj (unordentlich)* chaotic; *(ausschweifend)* wild; *(öde)* desolate; *(fam: heftig)* terrible

Wüste *(-, -n)* *f* desert

Wut *(-)* *f* rage, fury; **ich habe eine ~ auf ihn** I'm really mad at him; **wütend** *adj* furious

WWW *(-)* *nt abk =* **World Wide Web** WWW

X-Beine *pl* knock-knees *pl*; **x-beinig** *adj* knock-kneed

x-beliebig *adj*: **ein ~es Buch** any book (you like)

x-mal *adv* umpteen times

Xylophon *(-s, -e)* *nt* xylophone

Y Z

Yoga (-(s)) *m o nt* yoga
Yuppie (-s, -s) *m* (-, -s) *f* yuppie

zackig *adj* (*Linie etc*) jagged; (*fam: Tempo*) brisk
zaghaft *adj* timid
zäh *adj* tough; (*Flüssigkeit*) thick
Zahl (-, -en) *f* number; **zahlbar** *adj* payable; **zahlen** *vt, vi* to pay; **~ bitte!** could I have the bill (*Brit*) (*o* check (*US*)) please?; **bar ~** to pay cash; **zählen** *vt, vi* to count (**auf** +*akk* on); **~ zu** to be one of; **Zahlenschloss** *nt* combination lock; **Zähler** (-s, -) *m* (*Gerät*) counter; (*für Strom, Wasser*) meter; **zahlreich** *adj* numerous; **Zahlung** *f* payment; **Zahlungsanweisung** *f* money order; **Zahlungsbedingungen** *pl* terms *pl* of payment
zahm *adj* tame; **zähmen** *vt* to tame
Zahn (-(e)s, *Zähne*) *m* tooth; **Zahnarzt** *m*, **Zahnärztin** *f* dentist; **Zahnbürste** *f*

toothbrush; **Zahncreme** f toothpaste; **Zahnersatz** m dentures pl; **Zahnfleisch** nt gums pl; **Zahnfleischbluten** nt bleeding gums pl; **Zahnfüllung** f filling; **Zahnklammer** f brace; **Zahnpasta** f, **Zahnpaste** f toothpaste; **Zahnradbahn** f rack railway (Brit) (o railroad (US)); **Zahnschmerzen** pl toothache sing; **Zahnseide** f dental floss; **Zahnspange** f brace; **Zahnstocher** (-s, -) m toothpick
Zange (-, -n) f pliers pl; (Zuckerzange) tongs pl; (Beißzange, Zool) pincers pl; (Med) forceps pl
zanken vi to quarrel
Zäpfchen nt (Anat) uvula; (Med) suppository
zapfen vt (Bier) to pull; **Zapfsäule** f petrol (Brit) (o gas (US)) pump
zappeln vi to wriggle; (unruhig sein) to fidget
zappen vi to zap, to channel-hop
zart adj (weich, leise) soft; (Braten etc) tender; (fein, schwächlich) delicate; **zartbitter** adj (Schokolade) plain, dark
zärtlich adj tender, affectionate; **Zärtlichkeit** f tenderness; **~en** pl hugs and kisses pl
Zauber (-s, -) m magic; (Bann) spell; **Zauberei** f magic; **Zauberer** (-s, -) m magician; (Künstler) conjuror; **Zauberformel** f (magic) spell; **zauberhaft** adj enchanting; **Zauberin** f sorceress; **Zauberkünstler(in)** m(f) magician, conjuror; **Zaubermittel** nt magic cure; **zaubern** vi to do magic; (Künstler) to do conjuring tricks; **Zauberspruch** m (magic) spell
Zaun (-(e)s, Zäune) m fence
z. B. abk = **zum Beispiel** e.g., eg
ZDF nt = **Zweites Deutsches Fernsehen** second German television channel

Zebra (-s, -s) nt zebra; **Zebrastreifen** m zebra crossing (Brit), crosswalk (US)
Zecke (-, -n) f tick
Zehe (-, -n) f toe; (Knoblauch) clove; **Zehennagel** m toenail; **Zehenspitze** f tip of the toes
zehn num ten; **Zehnerkarte** f ticket valid for ten trips; **Zehnkampf** m decathlon; **Zehnkämpfer(in)** m(f) decathlete; **zehnmal** adv ten times; **zehntausend** num ten thousand; **zehnte(r, s)** adj tenth; siehe auch **dritte**; **Zehntel** (-s, -) nt tenth; **Zehntelsekunde** f tenth of a second
Zeichen (-s, -) nt sign; (Schriftzeichen) character; **Zeichenblock** m sketch pad; **Zeichenerklärung** f key; **Zeichensetzung** f punctuation; **Zeichensprache** f sign language; **Zeichentrickfilm** m cartoon
zeichnen vt, vi to draw; **Zeichnung** f drawing
Zeigefinger m index finger; **zeigen** vt to show; **sie zeigte uns die Stadt** she showed us around the town; **zeig mal!** let me see ▷ vi to point (auf +akk to, at) ▷ vr: **sich ~** to show oneself; **es wird sich ~** time will tell; **Zeiger** (-s, -) m pointer; (Uhr) hand
Zeile (-, -n) f line
Zeit (-, -en) f time; **ich habe keine ~** I haven't got time; **lass dir ~** take your time; **das hat ~** there's no rush; **von ~ zu ~** from time to time; **Zeitansage** f (Tel) speaking clock (Brit), correct time (US); **Zeitarbeit** f temporary work; **zeitgenössisch** adj contemporary, modern; **zeitgleich** adj simultaneous ▷ adv at exactly the same time; **zeitig** adj early; **Zeitkarte** f season ticket; **zeitlich** adj (Reihenfolge)

z

chronological; **es passt ~ nicht** it isn't a convenient time; **ich schaff es ~ nicht** I'm not going to make it; **Zeitlupe** f slow motion; **Zeitplan** m schedule; **Zeitpunkt** m point in time; **Zeitraum** m period (of time); **Zeitschrift** f magazine; (*wissenschaftliche*) periodical

Zeitung f newspaper; **es steht in der ~** it's in the paper(s); **Zeitungsanzeige** f newspaper advertisement; **Zeitungsartikel** m newspaper article; **Zeitungskiosk** m, **Zeitungsstand** m newsstand

Zeitunterschied m time difference; **Zeitverschiebung** f time lag; **Zeitvertreib** (*-(e)s, -e*) m: **zum ~** to pass the time; **zeitweise** adv occasionally; **Zeitzone** f time zone

Zelle (*-, -n*) f cell

Zellophan® (*-s*) nt cellophane®

Zelt (*-(e)s, -e*) nt tent; **zelten** vi to camp, to go camping; **Zeltplatz** m campsite, camping site

Zement (*-(e)s, -e*) m cement

Zentimeter m o nt centimetre

Zentner (*-s, -*) m (metric) hundredweight; (*in Deutschland*) fifty kilos; (*in Österreich und der Schweiz*) one hundred kilos

zentral adj central; **Zentrale** (*-, -n*) f central office; (*Tel*) exchange; **Zentralheizung** f central heating; **Zentralverriegelung** f (*Auto*) central locking; **Zentrum** (*-s, Zentren*) nt centre

zerbrechen irr vt, vi to break; **zerbrechlich** adj fragile

Zeremonie (*-, -n*) f ceremony

zergehen irr vi to dissolve; (*schmelzen*) to melt

zerkleinern vt to cut up; (*zerhacken*) to chop (up);

zerkratzen vt to scratch;

zerlegen vt to take to pieces; (*Fleisch*) to carve; (*Gerät, Maschine*) to dismantle; **zerquetschen** vt to squash; **zerreißen** irr vt to tear to pieces ▷ vi to tear

zerren vt to drag; **sich** (*dat*) **einen Muskel ~** to pull a muscle ▷ vi to tug (*an +dat* at); **Zerrung** f (*Med*) pulled muscle

zerschlagen irr vt to smash ▷ vr: **sich ~** to come to nothing

zerschneiden irr vt to cut up

zerstören vt to destroy; **Zerstörung** f destruction

zerstreuen vt to scatter; (*Menge*) to disperse; (*Zweifel etc*) to dispel ▷ vr: **sich ~** (*Menge*) to disperse; **zerstreut** adj scattered; (*Mensch*) absent-minded; (*kurzfristig*) distracted

zerteilen vt to split up

Zertifikat (*-(e)s, -e*) nt certificate

Zettel (*-s, -*) m piece of paper; (*Notizzettel*) note

Zeug (*-(e)s, -e*) nt (*fam*) stuff; (*Ausrüstung*) gear; **dummes ~** nonsense

Zeuge (*-n, -n*) m, **Zeugin** f witness

Zeugnis nt certificate; (*Schule*) report; (*Referenz*) reference

z. H(d). abk = **zu Händen von** attn

zickig adj (*fam*) touchy, bitchy

Zickzack (*-(e)s, -e*) m: **im ~ fahren** to zigzag (across the road)

Ziege (*-, -n*) f goat

Ziegel (*-s, -*) m brick; (*Dach*) tile

Ziegenkäse m goat's cheese; **Ziegenpeter** m mumps

ziehen (*zog, gezogen*) vt to draw; (*zerren*) to pull; (*Spielfigur*) to move; (*züchten*) to rear ▷ vi (*zerren*) to pull; (*sich bewegen*) to move; (*Rauch, Wolke etc*) to drift; **den Tee**

~ lassen to let the tea stand ▷ *vi impers*: **es zieht** there's a draught ▷ *vr*: **sich ~** (*Treffen, Rede*) to drag on

Ziel (*-(e)s, -e*) *nt* (*Reise*) destination; (*Sport*) finish; (*Absicht*) goal, aim; **zielen** *vi* to aim (*auf +akk* at); **Zielgruppe** *f* target group; **ziellos** *adj* aimless; **Zielscheibe** *f* target

ziemlich *adj* considerable; **ein ~es Durcheinander** quite a mess; **mit ~er Sicherheit** with some certainty ▷ *adv* rather, quite; **~ viel** quite a lot

zierlich *adj* dainty; (*Frau*) petite

Ziffer (*-, -n*) *f* figure; **arabische/römische ~n** *pl* Arabic/Roman numerals *pl*; **Zifferblatt** *nt* dial, face

zig *adj* (*fam*) umpteen

Zigarette *f* cigarette; **Zigarettenautomat** *m* cigarette machine; **Zigarettenpapier** *nt* cigarette paper; **Zigarettenschachtel** *f* cigarette packet; **Zigarettenstummel** *m* cigarette end; **Zigarillo** (*-s, -s*) *m* cigarillo; **Zigarre** (*-, -n*) *f* cigar

Zigeuner(in) (*-s, -*) *m(f)* gipsy

Zimmer (*-s, -*) *nt* room; **haben Sie ein ~ für zwei Personen?** do you have a room for two?; **Zimmerlautstärke** *f* reasonable volume; **Zimmermädchen** *nt* chambermaid; **Zimmermann** *m* carpenter; **Zimmerpflanze** *f* house plant; **Zimmerschlüssel** *m* room key; **Zimmerservice** *m* room service; **Zimmervermittlung** *f* accommodation agency

Zimt (*-(e)s, -e*) *m* cinnamon; **Zimtstange** *f* cinnamon stick

Zink (*-(e)s*) *nt* zinc

Zinn (*-(e)s*) *nt* (*Element*) tin; (*legiertes*) pewter

Zinsen *pl* interest *sing*

Zipfel (*-s, -*) *m* corner; (*spitz*) tip; (*Hemd*) tail; (*Wurst*) end; **Zipfelmütze** *f* pointed hat

zirka *adv* about, approximately

Zirkel (*-s, -*) *m* (*Math*) (pair of) compasses *pl*

Zirkus (*-, -se*) *m* circus

zischen *vi* to hiss

Zitat (*-(e)s, -e*) *nt* quotation (*aus* from); **zitieren** *vt* to quote

Zitronat *nt* candied lemon peel; **Zitrone** (*-, -n*) *f* lemon; **Zitronenlimonade** *f* lemonade; **Zitronensaft** *m* lemon juice

zittern *vi* to tremble (*vor +dat* with)

zivil *adj* civilian; (*Preis*) reasonable; **Zivil** (*-s*) *nt* plain clothes *pl*; (*Mil*) civilian clothes *pl*; **Zivildienst** *m* community service (*for conscientious objectors*)

zocken *vi* (*fam*) to gamble

Zoff (*-s*) *m* (*fam*) trouble

zog *imperf von* **ziehen**

zögerlich *adj* hesitant; **zögern** *vi* to hesitate

Zoll (*-(e)s, Zölle*) *m* customs *pl*; (*Abgabe*) duty; **Zollabfertigung** *f* customs clearance; **Zollamt** *nt* customs office; **Zollbeamte(r)** *m*, **-beamtin** *f* customs official; **Zollerklärung** *f* customs declaration; **zollfrei** *adj* duty-free; **Zollgebühren** *pl* customs duties *pl*; **Zollkontrolle** *f* customs check; **Zöllner(in)** *m(f)* customs officer; **zollpflichtig** *adj* liable to duty

Zone (*-, -n*) *f* zone

Zoo (*-s, -s*) *m* zoo

Zoom (*-s, -s*) *nt* zoom (shot); (*Objektiv*) zoom (lens)

Zopf (*-(e)s, Zöpfe*) *m* plait (*Brit*), braid (*US*)

Zorn (*-(e)s*) *m* anger; **zornig** *adj* angry (*über etw akk* about sth, *auf jdn* with sb)

○ SCHLÜSSELWORT

zu *prep +dat* **1** (*örtlich*) to; **zum Bahnhof/Arzt gehen** to go to the station/doctor; **zur Schule/Kirche gehen** to go to school/church; **sollen wir zu euch gehen?** shall we go to your place?; **sie sah zu ihm hin** she looked towards him; **zum Fenster herein** through the window; **zu meiner Linken** to *o* on my left

2 (*zeitlich*) at; **zu Ostern** at Easter; **bis zum 1. Mai** until May 1st; (*nicht später als*) by May 1st; **zu meiner Zeit** in my time

3 (*Zusatz*) with; **Wein zum Essen trinken** to drink wine with one's meal; **sich zu jdm setzen** to sit down beside sb; **setz dich doch zu uns** (come and) sit with us; **Anmerkungen zu etw** notes on sth

4 (*Zweck*) for; **Wasser zum Waschen** water for washing; **Papier zum Schreiben** paper to write on; **etw zum Geburtstag bekommen** to get sth for one's birthday

5 (*Veränderung*) into; **zu etw werden** to turn into sth; **jdn zu etw machen** to make sb (into) sth; **zu Asche verbrennen** to burn to ashes

6 (*mit Zahlen*) **3 zu 2** (*Sport*) 3-2; **das Stück zu 5 Euro** at 5 euros each; **zum ersten Mal** for the first time

7 zu meiner Freude *etc* to my joy *etc*; **zum Glück** luckily; **zu Fuß** on foot; **es ist zum Weinen** it's enough to make you cry

▷ *konj* to; **etw zu essen** sth to eat; **um besser sehen zu können** in order to see better; **ohne es zu wissen** without knowing it; **noch zu bezahlende Rechnungen** bills that are still to be paid

▷ *adv* **1** (*allzu*) too; **zu sehr** too much; **zu viel** too much; **zu wenig** too little

2 (*örtlich*) toward(s); **er kam auf mich zu** he came up to me

3 (*geschlossen*) shut, closed; **die Geschäfte haben zu** the shops are closed; „**auf/zu**" (*Wasserhahn etc*) "on/off"

4 (*fam*) (*los*) **nur zu!** just keep on!; **mach zu!** hurry up!

zuallererst *adv* first of all; **zuallerletzt** *adv* last of all
Zubehör (-(e)s, -e) *nt* accessories *pl*
zu|bereiten *vt* to prepare; **Zubereitung** *f* preparation
zu|binden *irr vt* to do (*o* tie) up
Zucchini *pl* courgettes *pl* (*Brit*), zucchini *pl* (*US*)
züchten *vt* (*Tiere*) to breed; (*Pflanzen*) to grow
zucken *vi* to jerk; (*krampfhaft*) to twitch; (*Strahl etc*) to flicker; **mit den Schultern ~** to shrug (one's shoulders)
Zucker (-s, -) *m* sugar; (*Med*) diabetes *sing*; **Zuckerdose** *f* sugar bowl; **zuckerkrank** *adj* diabetic; **Zuckerrohr** *nt* sugar cane; **Zuckerrübe** *f* sugar beet; **Zuckerwatte** *f* candy-floss (*Brit*), cotton candy (*US*)
zu|decken *vt* to cover up
zu|drehen *vt* to turn off
zueinander *adv* to one another; (*mit Verb*) together; **zueinander|halten** *irr vi* to stick together
zuerst *adv* first; (*zu Anfang*) at first; **~ einmal** first of all
Zufahrt *f* access; (*Einfahrt*) drive(way); **Zufahrtsstraße** *f* access road; (*Autobahn*) slip road (*Brit*), ramp (*US*)

Zufall *m* chance; (*Ereignis*) coincidence; **durch ~** by accident; **so ein ~!** what a coincidence; **zufällig** *adj* chance ▷ *adv* by chance; **weißt du ~, ob ...?** do you happen to know whether ...?

zufrieden *adj* content(ed); (*befriedigt*) satisfied; **lass sie ~** leave her alone; **zufrieden|geben** *irr vr:* **sich mit etw ~** to settle for sth; **Zufriedenheit** *f* contentment; (*Befriedigtsein*) satisfaction; **zufrieden|stellen** *vt:* **sie ist schwer zufriedenzustellen** she is hard to please

zu|fügen *vt* to add (*dat* to); **jdm Schaden/Schmerzen ~** to cause sb harm/pain

Zug (*-(e)s, Züge*) *m* (*Eisenb*) train; (*Luft*) draught; (*Ziehen*) pull; (*Gesichtszug*) feature; (*Schach*) move; (*Charakterzug*) trait; (*an Zigarette*) puff, drag; (*Schluck*) gulp

Zugabe *f* extra; (*in Konzert etc*) encore

Zugabteil *nt* train compartment

Zugang *m* access; **„kein ~!"** "no entry!"

Zugauskunft *f* (*Stelle*) train information office/desk; **Zugbegleiter(in)** *m(f)* guard (*Brit*), conductor (*US*)

zu|geben *irr vt* to admit; **zugegeben** *adv* admittedly

zu|gehen *irr vi* (*schließen*) to shut; **auf jdn/etw ~** to walk towards sb/sth; **dem Ende ~** to be coming to a close ▷ *vi impers* (*sich ereignen*) to happen; **es ging lustig zu** we/they had a lot of fun; **dort geht es streng zu** it's strict there

Zügel (*-s, -*) *m* rein

Zugführer(in) *m(f)* guard (*Brit*), conductor (*US*)

zugig *adj* draughty

zügig *adj* speedy

zugleich *adv* (*zur gleichen zeit*) at the same time; (*ebenso*) both

Zugluft *f* draught

Zugpersonal *nt* train staff

zu|greifen *irr vi* (*fig*) to seize the opportunity; (*beim Essen*) to help oneself; **~ auf** (+*akk*) (*Inform*) to access

Zugrestauraunt *nt* dining car, diner (*US*)

Zugriffsberechtigung *f* (*Inform*) access right

zugrunde *adv:* **~ gehen** to perish; **~ gehen an** (+*dat*) (*sterben*) to die of

Zugschaffner(in) *m(f)* ticket inspector; **Zugunglück** *nt* train crash

zugunsten *prep* +*gen o dat* in favour of

Zugverbindung *f* train connection

zu|haben *irr vi* to be closed

zu|halten *irr vt* **sich** (*dat*) **die Nase ~** to hold one's nose; **sich** (*dat*) **die Ohren ~** to hold one's hands over one's ears; **die Tür ~** to hold the door shut

Zuhause (*-s*) *nt* home

zu|hören *vi* to listen (*dat* to); **Zuhörer(in)** *m(f)* listener

zu|kleben *vt* to seal

zu|kommen *irr vi* to come up (*auf* +*akk* to); **jdm etw ~ lassen** to give/send sb sth; **etw auf sich** (*akk*) **~ lassen** to take sth as it comes

zu|kriegen *vt:* **ich krieg den Koffer nicht zu** I can't shut the case

Zukunft (*-, Zukünfte*) *f* future; **zukünftig** *adj* future ▷ *adv* in future

zu|lassen *irr vt* (*hereinlassen*) to admit; (*erlauben*) to permit; (*Auto*) to license; (*fam: nicht öffnen*) to keep shut; **zulässig** *adj* permissible, permitted

zuletzt *adv* finally, at last

zuliebe *adv*: **jdm ~** for sb's sake

zum *kontr von* **zu dem**; **~ dritten Mal** for the third time; **~ Scherz** as a joke; **~ Trinken** for drinking

zu|machen *vt* to shut; (*Kleidung*) to do up ▷ *vi* to shut

zumindest *adv* at least

zu|muten *vt*: **jdm etw ~** to expect sth of sb ▷ *vr*: **sich** (*dat*) **zu viel ~** to overdo things

zunächst *adv* first of all; **~ einmal** to start with

Zunahme (-, -n) *f* increase

Zuname *m* surname, last name

zünden *vt, vi* (*Auto*) to ignite, to fire; **Zündkabel** *f* (*Auto*) ignition cable; **Zündkerze** *f* (*Auto*) spark plug; **Zündschloss** *nt* ignition lock; **Zündschlüssel** *m* ignition key; **Zündung** *f* ignition

zu|nehmen *irr vi* to increase; (*Mensch*) to put on weight ▷ *vt*: **5 Kilo ~** to put on 5 kilos

Zunge (-, -n) *f* tongue

Zungenkuss *m* French kiss

zunichte|machen *vt* (*zerstören*) to ruin

zunutze *adv* **sich** (*dat*) **etw ~ machen** to make use of sth

zu|parken *vt* to block

zur *kontr von* **zu der**

zurecht|finden *irr vr*: **sich ~** to find one's way around; **zurecht|kommen** *irr vi* to cope (*mit etw* with sth); **zurecht|machen** *vt* to prepare ▷ *vr*: **sich ~** to get ready

Zürich (-s) *nt* Zurich

zurück *adv* back

zurück|bekommen *irr vt* to get back; **zurück|blicken** *vi* to look back (*auf +akk* at); **zurück|bringen** *irr vt* (*hierhin*) to bring back; (*woandershin*) to take back; **zurück|erstatten** *vt* to refund; **zurück|fahren** *irr vi* to go back;

zurück|geben *irr vt* to give back; (*antworten*) to answer;

zurück|gehen *irr vi* to go back; (*zeitlich*) to date back (*auf +akk* to)

zurück|halten *irr vt* to hold back; (*hindern*) to prevent ▷ *vr*: **sich ~** to hold back; **zurückhaltend** *adj* reserved

zurück|holen *vt* to fetch back; **zurück|kommen** *irr vi* to come back; **auf etw** (*akk*) **~** to return (o get back) to sth; **zurück|lassen** *vt* to leave behind; **zurück|legen** *vt* to put back; (*Geld*) to put by; (*reservieren*) to keep back; (*Strecke*) to cover; **zurück|nehmen** *irr vt* to take back; **zurück|rufen** *irr vt* to call back; **zurück|schicken** *vt* to send back; **zurück|stellen** *vt* to put back; **zurück|treten** *irr vi* to step back; (*von Amt*) to retire; **zurück|verlangen** *vt*: **etw ~** to ask for sth back; **zurück|zahlen** *vt* to pay back

zurzeit *adv* at present

Zusage *f* promise; (*Annahme*) acceptance; **zu|sagen** *vt* to promise ▷ *vi* to accept; **jdm ~** (*gefallen*) to appeal to sb

zusammen *adv* together

Zusammenarbeit *f* collaboration; **zusammen|arbeiten** *vi* to work together

zusammen|brechen *irr vi* to collapse; (*psychisch*) to break down; **Zusammenbruch** *m* collapse; (*psychischer*) breakdown

zusammen|fassen *vt* to summarize; (*vereinigen*) to unite; **zusammenfassend** *adj* summarizing ▷ *adv* to summarize; **Zusammenfassung** *f* summary

zusammen|gehören *vi* to belong together; **zusammen|halten** *irr vi* to stick together

Zusammenhang *m* connection; **im/aus dem ~** in/out of context; **zusammen|hängen** *irr vi* to be connected; **zusammenhängend** *adj* coherent; **zusammenhang(s)los** *adj* incoherent

zusammen|klappen *vi, vt* to fold up

zusammen|knüllen *vt* to screw up

zusammen|kommen *irr vi* to meet; *(sich ereignen)* to happen together; **zusammen|legen** *vt* to fold up ▷ *vi (Geld sammeln)* to club together; **zusammen|nehmen** *irr vt* to summon up; **alles zusammengenommen** all in all ▷ *vr:* **sich ~** to pull oneself together; *(fam)* to get a grip, to get one's act together; **zusammen|passen** *vi* to go together; *(Personen)* to be suited; **zusammen|rechnen** *vt* to add up

Zusammensein (*-s*) *nt* get-together

zusammen|setzen *vt* to put together ▷ *vr:* **sich ~ aus** to be composed of; **Zusammensetzung** *f* composition

Zusammenstoß *m* crash, collision; **zusammen|stoßen** *irr vi* to crash *(mit into)*

zusammen|zählen *vt* to add up

zusammen|ziehen *irr vi (in Wohnung etc)* to move in together

Zusatz *m* addition; **zusätzlich** *adj* additional ▷ *adv* in addition

zu|schauen *vi* to watch; **Zuschauer(in)** (*-s, -*) *m(f)* spectator; **die ~** (*pl*) *(Theat)* the audience *sing*; **Zuschauertribüne** *f* stand

zu|schicken *vt* to send

Zuschlag *m* extra charge; *(Fahrkarte)* supplement

zuschlagpflichtig *adj* subject to an extra charge; *(Eisenb)* subject to a supplement

zu|schließen *irr vt* to lock up

zu|sehen *irr vi* to watch *(jdm sb)*; **~, dass** *(dafür sorgen)* to make sure that

zu|sichern *vt:* **jdm etw ~** to assure sb of sth

Zustand *m* state, condition; **sie bekommt Zustände, wenn sie das sieht** *(fam)* she'll have a fit if she sees that

zustande *adv:* **~ bringen** to bring about; **~ kommen** to come about

zuständig *adj (Behörde)* relevant; **~ für** responsible for

Zustellung *f* delivery

zu|stimmen *vi* to agree *(einer Sache dat* to sth, *jdm* with sb); **Zustimmung** *f* approval

zu|stoßen *irr vi (fig)* to happen *(jdm* to sb)

Zutaten *pl* ingredients *pl*

zu|trauen *vt:* **jdm etw ~** to think sb is capable of sth; **das hätte ich ihm nie zugetraut** I'd never have thought he was capable of it; **ich würde es ihr ~** *(etw Negatives)* I wouldn't put it past her; **Zutrauen** (*-s*) *nt* confidence *(zu in)*; **zutraulich** *adj* trusting; *(Tier)* friendly

zu|treffen *irr vi* to be correct; **~ auf** *(+akk)* to apply to; **Zutreffendes bitte streichen** please delete as applicable

Zutritt *m* entry; *(Zugang)* access; **~ verboten!** no entry

zuverlässig *adj* reliable; **Zuverlässigkeit** *f* reliability

Zuversicht *f* confidence; **zuversichtlich** *adj* confident

zuvor *adv* before; *(zunächst)* first; **zuvor|kommen** *irr vi:* **jdm ~** to

z

beat sb to it; **zuvorkommend**
adj obliging
Zuwachs *(-es, Zuwächse) m*
increase, growth; *(fam: Baby)*
addition to the family
zuwider *adv*: **es ist mir ~** I hate (*o*
detest) it
zu|winken *vi*: **jdm ~** to wave to
sb
zuzüglich *prep +gen* plus
zwang *imperf von* **zwingen**
Zwang *(-(e)s, Zwänge) m (innerer)*
compulsion; *(Gewalt)* force
zwängen *vt* to squeeze (*in +akk*
into) ▷ *vr*: **sich ~** to squeeze (*in*
+akk into)
zwanglos *adj* informal
zwanzig *num* twenty;
zwanzigste(r, s) *adj* twentieth;
siehe auch **dritte**
zwar *adv*: **und ~ ...** (*genauer*) ...,
to be precise; **das ist ~ schön,**
aber ... it is nice, but ...; **ich kenne**
ihn ~, aber ... I know him all right,
but ...
Zweck *(-(e)s, -e) m* purpose;
zwecklos *adj* pointless
zwei *num* two; **Zwei** (*-, -en*) *f*
two; (*Schulnote*) ≈ B;
Zweibettzimmer *nt* twin room;
zweideutig *adj* ambiguous;
(*unanständig*) suggestive;
zweifach *adj, adv* double
Zweifel (*-s, -*) *m* doubt;
zweifellos *adv* undoubtedly;
zweifeln *vi* to doubt (*an etw dat*
sth); **Zweifelsfall** *m*: **im ~** in case
of doubt
Zweig (*-(e)s, -e*) *m* branch
Zweigstelle *f* branch
zweihundert *num* two hundred;
zweimal *adv* twice; **zweisprachig**
adj bilingual; **zweispurig** *adj*
(*Auto*) two-lane; **zweit** *adv*: **wir**
sind zu ~ there are two of us;
zweite(r, s) *adj* second; *siehe*
auch **dritte eine ~ Portion** a

second helping; **zweitens** *adv*
secondly; (*bei Aufzählungen*)
second; **zweitgrößte(r, s)** *adj*
second largest; **Zweitschlüssel**
m spare key
Zwerchfell *nt* diaphragm
Zwerg(in) (*-(e)s, -e*) *m(f)* dwarf
Zwetschge (*-, -n*) *f* plum
zwicken *vt* to pinch
Zwieback (*-(e)s, -e*) *m* rusk
Zwiebel (*-, -n*) *f* onion; (*von*
Blume) bulb; **Zwiebelsuppe** *f*
onion soup
Zwilling (*-s, -e*) *m* twin; **~e** (*pl*)
(*Astr*) Gemini *sing*
zwingen (*zwang, gezwungen*) *vt*
to force
zwinkern *vi* to blink; (*absichtlich*)
to wink
zwischen *prep +akk o dat*
between
Zwischenablage *f* (*Inform*)
clipboard
zwischendurch *adv* in between
Zwischenfall *m* incident
Zwischenlandung *f* stopover
zwischenmenschlich *adj*
interpersonal
Zwischenraum *m* space
Zwischenstopp (*-s, -s*) *m*
stopover
Zwischensumme *f* subtotal
Zwischenzeit *f*: **in der ~** in the
meantime
zwitschern *vt, vi* to twitter, to
chirp
zwölf *num* twelve; **zwölfte(r, s)**
adj twelfth; *siehe auch* **dritte**
Zylinder (*-s, -*) *m* cylinder; (*Hut*)
top hat
zynisch *adj* cynical
Zypern (*-s*) *nt* Cyprus
Zyste (*-, -n*) *f* cyst

German in focus

Introduction

German in focus gives you an introduction to various aspects of Germany, Austria and other German-speaking areas. The following pages help you get to know the countries where the language is spoken and the people who speak it.

Practical language tips and helpful notes on common translation difficulties will enable you to become a more confident German speaker. A useful correspondence section gives you all the information you need to be able to communicate effectively.

We've also included a number of links to useful websites, which will give you the opportunity to read more about German-speaking Europe and the German language.

We hope you will enjoy using your *German in focus* supplement. We are sure it will help you find out more about German and German speakers and become more confident in writing and speaking German.

Los gehts!

Germany and its regions

Germany and its regions

The ten biggest German cities

City	Name of inhabitants	Population
Berlin	die Berliner	3,275,000
Hamburg	die Hamburger	1,686,000
München	die Münchner	1,185,400
Köln	die Kölner	965,300
Frankfurt	die Frankfurter	648,400
Essen	die Essener	588,800
Dortmund	die Dortmunder	587,600
Stuttgart	die Stuttgarter	581,100
Düsseldorf	die Düsseldorfer	568,900
Bremen	die Bremer	527,900

Berlin was the capital of Germany between 1871 and 1945. After the second world war, until 1990, Germany was divided into West Germany and East Germany. This division was mirrored in Berlin, which was divided by a wall into western and eastern sectors. Germany (including Berlin) was reunified in 1990, and in 1999 Berlin again became the capital of the whole country.

Germany is a republic made up of 16 federal states (*Länder*). Many of these states have long histories. Three cities have Land status: Berlin and the Free Hanseatic Cities of Bremen and Hamburg. The other 13 Länder are regions: Baden-Württemberg, Bavaria, Brandenburg, Hesse, Mecklenburg-Pomerania, North Rhine-Westphalia, Rhineland-Palatinate, Saarland, Saxony, Saxony Anhalt, Lower Saxony, Schleswig-Holstein, Thuringia.

The head of the German state is the President (*der Bundespräsident*) and the head of government is the Chancellor (*der Bundeskanzler*). The feminine form of this word (*die Bundeskanzlerin*) was used for the first time in 2005, when Germany got a woman chancellor.

A useful link is:
 www.tatsachen-ueber-deutschland.de
Federal Foreign Office – Facts about Germany

A snapshot of Germany

- In area, Germany (357,045 km²) is a third bigger than the UK (244,110 km²).

- The population of Germany is about 82.5 million, a third more than that of the UK. The birth rate is low (1.4 children per woman).

- The German economy is the biggest in the EU and one of the biggest in the world.

- The Rhine, which rises in Switzerland and flows into the North Sea in Holland is 1,320 km long. Most of this great river is in Germany (865 km).

- There are almost equal numbers of Roman Catholics and Protestants in Germany.

- Germany's highest mountain is the Zugspitze (2962 m).

- Germany has borders with nine other countries: Denmark, Holland, Belgium, Luxembourg, France, Switzerland, Austria, the Czech Republic and Poland.

- German beer is famous for its purity and high quality. There are hundreds of small independent breweries which produce distinctive beers. The Oktoberfest in Munich is a two-week beer festival attended by 6 million people.

Some useful links are:
www.destatis.de
Federal statistical office
www.muenchen.de
Munich tourist office

Austria and its regions

Switzerland and its regions

A snapshot of Austria and Switzerland

- German is the main language in Austria, and is spoken by 65% of the population in Switzerland.

- Austria has an area of 83,870 km². A quarter of the 8 million inhabitants live in or around the capital, Vienna (Wien).

- Austria is a member of the EU, and uses the euro, while Switzerland remains outside the EU and retains the Swiss franc as its currency.

- Austria is a federal republic consisting of nine states. Switzerland too is a federal state, made up of 26 cantons. Its official name is the Swiss Confederation. The letters CH on the back of Swiss cars stand for the Latin version: Confoederatio Helvetica.

- Austria's highest mountain is the Großglockner (3 797m).

- Switzerland's highest mountain is the Dufourspitze (4 643m): it's just within Switzerland's boundary with Italy.

- Switzerland has an area of only 41,290 km², about half that of Austria, but its population is only slightly less than that of Austria – about 7.5m.

- There are three official languages in Switzerland – German, French and Italian. 21% of the population speak French, and 7% Italian. There is a fourth national language, Romansch, which is spoken by less than 1% of the Swiss population. The population also includes a large number of foreign workers.

- Switzerland's biggest city is Zürich, (about 1.3 million), but the capital is Bern (just under a million).

- Banking is one of Switzerland's most important industries. The secrecy of Swiss banks is legendary.

Some useful links are:
www.bfs.admin.ch
Swiss Federal Statistical Office
www. austria.org
Austrian Press and Information Service

Varieties of German

The type of German we are taught is Standard German or *Hochdeutsch*.
There are many regional dialects, though, no more so than in Austria and
Switzerland where you may encounter a variety of words and expressions
which do not correspond to Standard German. Here are a few examples:

Austrian German (Österreichisch)	English	Standard German
die Aschanti	peanut	*die Erdnuss*
das Beisel	(small) pub	*das Wirtshaus*
das Best	prize	*der Preis*
die Bim	tram	*die Straßenbahn*
der Karfiol	cauliflower	*der Blumenkohl*
die Marille	apricot	*die Aprikose*
das Obers	cream	*die Sahne*
der Paradeiser	tomato	*die Tomate*
die Ribisel	(red)currant	*die Johannisbeere*

Some of the words listed below are used both by people speaking
Standard German in Switzerland and by people speaking *Schweizerdeutsch*.
This is a spoken dialect, while Standard German is the written language of
German-speaking Switzerland.

Swiss German (Schweizerdeutsch)	English	Standard German
der Abwart	caretaker	*der Hausmeister*
das Bébé	baby	*das Baby*
das Billett	ticket	*die (Fahr)karte*
der Goalie	goalkeeper	*der Torwart*
grüezi!	hello!	*guten Tag!*
das Morgenessen	breakfast	*das Frühstück*
parkieren	to park	*parken*
die Serviertochter	waitress	*die Kellnerin*
salü!	hi!	*hallo!*
das Velo	bicycle	*das Fahrrad*

German words used in English

English was originally a Germanic language, and many of the oldest words in English are the same as, or very similar to, German words, for example, hand (*Hand*), man (*Mann*), house (*Haus*), garden (*Garten*), father (*Vater*), mother (*Mutter*), to have (*haben*), to sing (*singen*), to bring (*bringen*), to run (*rennen*).

In more recent times English has borrowed words from German such as delicatessen, kindergarten, blitz, angst, schadenfreude, lager, hamburger, rucksack.

It is often possible to work out how these words came about. For example, in German lager means 'storeroom',

and Lagerbier was so called because it was kept for a while. Rucksacks are carried on your back, the German for back being *der Rücken*. Schadenfreude combines the words for misfortune (*der Schaden*) and pleasure (*die Freude*), and is a neat way of describing enjoyment of someone else's misfortune.

As in other languages some very familiar words used in English are the names of German inventors and scientists, for example Rudolf Diesel who invented the diesel engine, Daniel Fahrenheit who invented the alcohol thermometer and Hans Geiger, a nuclear physicist.

English words used in German

With the spread of English as a global means of communication, English terms have become very common in the German language.

Many of these terms mean the same in both languages:

das Baby	die Software
der Computer	der Stress
die Hardware	das T-Shirt
die Hitparade	das WC
das Internet	der Western
das Interview	der Yuppie

But be careful – others often have either totally different meanings in German and English, or they sound English but aren't proper English at all:

der Beamer	digital projector
die Box	(stereo) speaker
das Handy	mobile phone
der Oldtimer	vintage car
der Pullunder	tank top
der Slip	briefs, panties
der Smoking	dinner jacket
der Talkmaster	talk-show host
der Twen	twentysomething

Some informal German

We all use different language styles depending on the situation we find ourselves in.

When you visit a German-speaking country, you're sure to hear some informal expressions in everyday situations.

Here are some examples of informal German words:

Informal language is marked very clearly in the dictionary to help you choose the appropriate word or phrase.

> *Be careful!*
> Be careful when using items marked 'informal' (*fam*) in your dictionary, and avoid ones marked 'offensive' (*vulg*) altogether.

bescheuert	crazy
flennen	to cry
geil	fantastic
die Glotze	television
das Klo	toilet
der Knast	prison
die Kneipe	pub
die Kohle	money
quatschen	to talk
schummeln	to cheat
tschüs(s)	bye bye
der Typ	guy
der Zoff	trouble

Improving your pronunciation

There are a number of different methods you can use to improve your pronunciation and increase your confidence in speaking German:

- listen to German radio
- watch German-language films
- chat with German speakers

Some useful links are:
www.ard.de/radio/
A choice of German radio stations, plus information about cultural events.
www.dw-world.de/
Deutsche Welle, the equivalent of the BBC World Service.

Some points to help you with your pronunciation

Letters which are peculiar to German:

- **ä** is pronounced like English 'a' in 'b**a**re'.

- **ö** is pronounced similar to English 'ea' in '**ea**rn'.

- **ü** is pronounced like French 'u' – round your lips and say 'ee'.

- **ß** is pronounced like English 's' in '**s**ing'.

Also note the following:

- **j** is usually pronounced like English 'y' in '**y**et'

- **v** is usually pronounced like 'f'.

- **w** is pronounced like 'v'.

Improving your fluency

Conversational words and phrases

In English we insert lots of words and phrases, such as *so, then, by the way*, into our conversation, to give our thoughts a structure and often to show our attitude. The German words below do the same thing. If you use them they will make you sound more fluent and natural.

- *also*
  Kommst du **also** mit (ja oder nein)?
  (=so, then)
  Also, wie ich schon sagte, ... (=well)

- *übrigens*
  Übrigens, du schuldest mir Geld.
  (=by the way)
  Ich habe sie **übrigens** gestern getroffen.
  (=by the way)

- *schließlich*
  Er hat es mir **schließlich** doch gesagt.
  (=eventually)
  Sie ist **schließlich** erst drei Jahre alt.
  (=after all)

- *stimmt!, stimmts?*
  Er ist doch in Australien. – **Stimmt!**
  (=correct!, that's right!)
  Du hast mich belogen, **stimmts?**
  (=right?)

- *wirklich*
  Bist du mir böse? – Nicht **wirklich**.
  (=really)
  Das hat mich **wirklich** geärgert.
  (=really)

- *jedenfalls*
  Es ist **jedenfalls** schon zu spät.
  (=anyhow)
  Er hat nichts gesagt, **jedenfalls** nichts Neues. (=anyway)

- *eigentlich*
  Wer hat das Spiel **eigentlich** gewonnen? (=actually)
  Bist du müde? – **Eigentlich** nicht.
  (=really)

- *nämlich*
  Wir bleiben zu Hause, es ist **nämlich** sehr regnerisch. (=since)
  Er ist **nämlich** mein bester Freund.
  (=you see)

- *überhaupt*
  Hörst du mir **überhaupt** zu? (=at all)
  Ich habe **überhaupt** keinen Grund dazu. (=whatsoever)

Improving your fluency

Varying the words you use to get your message across will make you sound more fluent in German. For example, you already know *Ich mag diesen Film*, but for a change you could say *Dieser Film gefällt mir* to mean the same thing. Here are some other suggestions:

Saying what you like or dislike

Die CD *hat mir sehr gut gefallen*.	I loved …
Der Englandurlaub *hat uns Spaß gemacht*.	We enjoyed …
Ich mag ihn.	I like …
Ich mag keinen Fisch.	I don't like …
Ich hasse Fußball.	I hate …
Ich kann ihn *nicht ausstehen*.	I can't stand …

Expressing your opinion

Ich denke, dass wir gehen sollten.	I think …
Ich glaube, er hat richtig gehandelt.	I think …
Ich meine, wir sollten es versuchen.	I think …
Ich bin sicher, dass er gelogen hat.	I'm sure …
Meiner Meinung nach hat er einen Fehler gemacht.	In my opinion …

Agreeing or disagreeing

Du hast recht.	You're right.
Ich stimme Ihnen zu.	I agree with you.
Ich bin ganz Ihrer Meinung.	I totally agree with you.
Er hat unrecht.	He's wrong.
Ich bin anderer Meinung.	I disagree.

Correspondence

The following section on correspondence has been designed to help you communicate confidently in written as well as spoken German. Sample letters, emails and sections on text messaging and making telephone calls will ensure that you have all the vocabulary you need to correspond successfully in German.

Text messaging

Abbreviation	German	English
8ung	*Achtung*	look out
akla	*alles klar*	okay
bb	*bis bald*	see you soon
DaD	*denk an dich*	thinking of you
div	*danke im Voraus*	thanks in advance
GA	*Gruß an*	love/greetings to
GiE	*Ganz im Ernst*	seriously
GLG	*Ganz liebe Grüße*	love
gn8	*gute Nacht*	good night
GuK, G&K	*Gruß und Kuss*	love and kisses
ild	*Ich liebe dich*	I love you
mediwi	*melde dich wieder*	get in touch
mfg	*mit freundlichen Grüßen*	yours
rumian	*ruf mich an*	call me
sfh	*Schluss für heute*	enough for today
siw	*soweit ich weiß*	as far as I know
sTn	*schönen Tag noch*	have a nice day
sz	*schreib zurück*	write back
vlg	*viele Grüße*	love/greetings
vv	*viel Vergnügen*	have fun
wamaduheu?	*was machst du heute?*	what are you up to today?

Writing an email

| Datei | Bearbeiten | Ansicht | Extras | **Verfassen** | Hilfe | Senden |

An:	markus.mueller@euronet.de		Nachricht erstellen
Cc:			Antworten
			Allen antworten
Bcc:			Weiterleiten
			Anlage
Betreff:	Unsere Verabredung

> In German, when you tell someone your email address, you say:
> *markus punkt mueller at euronet punkt day-ay*

Hallo Markus,

hattest du vergessen, dass wir uns gestern treffen wollten? Anke und ich waren da und haben über eine Stunde lang auf dich gewartet. Bitte melde dich so bald wie möglich bei mir, sodass wir einen neuen Termin vereinbaren können.
Viele Grüße
Thomas

Datei (f)	file	*Allen antworten*	reply to all
Bearbeiten	to edit	*Weiterleiten*	to forward
Ansicht (f)	to view	*Anlage (f)*	attachment
Extras (ntpl)	tools	*An*	to
Verfassen	to compose	*Cc*	cc (carbon copy)
Hilfe (f)	help	*Bcc*	bcc (blind carbon copy)
Senden	to send	*Betreff (m)*	subject
Neue Nachricht (f)	new message	*Von*	from
Antworten	reply to sender	*Datum (nt)*	date

17

Here is some additional useful Internet vocabulary:

abmelden	to sign off		*klicken*	to click
anmelden	to sign in		*Links (mpl)*	links
ausloggen	to log off		*Menü (nt)*	menu
ausschneiden	to cut		*Monitor (m)*	monitor
Breitband (nt)	broadband		*Ordner (m)*	folder
Browser (m)	browser		*Papierkorb (m)*	recycle bin
chatten	to chat		*Pfeiltasten (fpl)*	arrow keys
Datenbank (f)	database		*speichern*	to save
doppelklicken	to double-click		*suchen*	to search
drucken	to print		*Suchmaschine (f)*	search engine
einfügen	to paste		*(im Internet) surfen*	to surf (the Net)
einloggen	to log on		*Tabellenkalkulation (f)*	spreadsheet
ersetzen	to replace		*Tastatur (f)*	keyboard
FAQ (nt)	FAQ		*Verzeichnis (nt)*	directory
Favoriten (mpl)	favourites		*Webseite (f)*	web page
Fenster (nt)	window		*Website (f)*	website
herunterladen	to download		*weiter*	forward
Homepage (f)	home page		*(WorldWide)Web (nt)*	the (World-Wide) Web
Icon (nt)	icon		*zurück*	back
Internet (nt)	Internet			
Internetprovider (m)	Internet Service Provider			

Writing a personal letter

→ Köln, 24. September 2010

Liebe Tante Erika,

ich möchte mich ganz herzlich für dein tolles Geburtstagsgeschenk bedanken. Diese DVD habe ich mir schon seit langem gewünscht. Colin Farrell war schon immer mein Lieblingsschauspieler, und ich habe mir den Film bereits zweimal angesehen.

Den Sommerurlaub habe ich mit meiner Freundin in Frankreich verbracht. Aber in den nächsten Monaten muss ich mich intensiv auf mein Abitur vorbereiten. Ich hoffe, dass ich danach in München Medizin studieren kann. Vielleicht gehe ich aber zuvor noch für ein Jahr ins Ausland.

Ich habe gehört, dass Onkel Heinz vor kurzem krank war. Ich hoffe, es geht ihm inzwischen besser, und meine Eltern und ich freuen uns auf unseren Besuch bei euch im Oktober.

Viele Grüße

Jens

Writing a personal letter

Other ways of starting a personal letter	Other ways of ending a personal letter
Liebe Freunde	*Herzliche Grüße*
Liebe Anita, lieber Andreas	*Alles Gute*
Liebe Eltern	*Viele Grüße auch von …*

Some useful phrases

Vielen Dank für deinen Brief.	Thank you for your letter.
Es war schön, von dir zu hören.	It was great to hear from you.
Tut mir Leid, dass ich erst jetzt antworte.	I'm sorry I didn't reply sooner.
Bitte grüße Silvia von mir.	Give my love to Silvia.
Mutti sendet viele Grüße.	Mum sends her best wishes.
Bitte schreib mir bald.	Please write soon.

Writing a formal letter

Ina Grünewald
Augustinstr. 24
69321 Heidelberg
→ Your own name and address

Heidelberg,
14. August 2010
→ Town/city you are writing from, and the date

Fuhrmann GmbH
Personalabteilung
Friedrich-Schiller-Str. 10
70569 Stuttgart
→ Name and address of the person/company you are writing to

Sehr geehrte Damen und Herren,

ich beziehe mich auf Ihr Stellenangebot in der Stuttgarter Zeitung vom 12. August und möchte mich als Fremdsprachenkorrespondentin in Ihrer Firma bewerben.

Ich verfüge über ausgezeichnete Englisch- und Französischkenntnisse sowie Grundkenntnisse in den Sprachen Spanisch und Portugiesisch. Darüber hinaus habe ich gute Erfahrung bei der Texterfassung am PC (ca. 220 Anschläge pro Minute).

Weitere Einzelheiten entnehmen Sie bitte dem beigefügten Lebenslauf.

Mit freundlichen Grüßen

Ina Grünewald

Writing a formal letter

Other ways of starting a formal letter	Other ways of ending a formal letter
Sehr geehrter Herr Franzen, *Sehr geehrte Frau Meinhardt,* *Sehr geehrter Herr Dr. Bleibtreu,* *Sehr geehrter Herr Professor,*	*... und verbleibe mit freundlichen Grüßen* *Mit freundlichem Gruß* *Hochachtungsvoll*

Some useful phrases

Vielen Dank für Ihr Schreiben vom ...	Thank you for your letter of ...
Mit Bezug auf ...	With reference to ...
Anbei schicke ich Ihnen ...	Please find enclosed ...
Ich würde mich freuen, von Ihnen zu hören.	I look forward to hearing from you ...
Ich danke Ihnen im Voraus für ...	Thank you in advance for ...

This is the dative form of "Herr" – the word "an" (=to) is assumed. If writing to a woman, use "Frau".

Herrn
Prof. Günter Seiffarth
Salamanderstr. 57
04989 Leipzig
DEUTSCHLAND

The house number comes after the street name, and the postcode comes before the name of the town.

Making a call

Asking for information

Was ist die Vorwahl für Freiburg?	What's the code for Freiburg?
Wie bekomme ich eine Amtsleitung?	How do I get an outside line?
Können Sie mir die Durchwahl für Herrn Faltermeier geben?	Could you give me the extension number for Mr Faltermeier?

When your number answers

Hallo! Ist Barbara da?	Hello! Is Barbara there?
Kann ich bitte mit Peter Martin sprechen?	Could I speak to Peter Martin, please?
Spreche ich mit Frau Schuster?	Is that Ms/Mrs Schuster?
Könnten Sie sie bitten, mich zurückzurufen?	Could you ask her to call me back?
Ich rufe in einer halben Stunde wieder an.	I'll call back in half an hour.
Kann ich bitte eine Nachricht hinterlassen?	Could I leave a message, please?

When you answer the telephone

Wer spricht bitte?	Who's speaking?
Hier ist Marion.	It's Marion speaking.
Am Apparat.	Speaking.

What you may hear

Wer ist am Apparat?	Who shall I say is calling?
Ich stelle durch.	I'm putting you through now.
Bitte bleiben Sie am Apparat.	Please hold.
Es meldet sich niemand.	There's no reply.
Es ist besetzt.	The line is engaged (*Brit*)/busy (*US*).
Möchten Sie eine Nachricht hinterlassen?	Would you like to leave a message?

If you have a problem

Tut mir Leid, ich habe mich verwählt.	Sorry, I dialled the wrong number.
Die Verbindung ist sehr schlecht.	This is a very bad line.
Ich kann Sie nur schlecht verstehen.	You're breaking up.
Mein Akku ist fast leer.	My battery's low.
Ich kann Sie nicht verstehen.	I can't hear you.

Saying your phone number

To tell someone your phone number in German, you usually divide the number up into pairs instead of saying each digit separately. For example:

0180 45 23 12

null-eins / achtzig / fünfundvierzig / dreiundzwanzig / zwölf

If there's an extra number, you say that first. For example:

238 47 32 94

zwei / achtunddreißig / siebenundvierzig / zweiunddreißig / vierundneunzig

German phrases and sayings

In German, as in many languages, people use vivid expressions based on images from their experience of real life. We've grouped the common expressions below according to the type of image they use. For fun, we have given you the word-for-word translation as well as the true English equivalent.

Fruit and vegetables

für einen Apfel und ein Ei
    word for word:
→ dirt cheap, as a bargain
for an apple and an egg

mit ihm ist nicht gut Kirschen essen
    word for word:
→ it's best not to tangle with him
you can't eat cherries with him

das macht den Kohl nicht fett
    word for word:
→ that won't be much help
it won't fatten the cabbage

sich die Radieschen von unten ansehen
    word for word:
→ to be pushing up the daisies
to look at the radishes from below

Animals and birds

da liegt der Hund begraben
    word for word:
→ that's the real problem
that's where the dog is buried

die Spatzen pfeifen es von den Dächern
    word for word:
→ it's common knowledge
the sparrows are whistling it from the rooftops

wo sich Hase und Fuchs gute Nacht sagen
    word for word:
→ in the middle of nowhere
where hare and fox bid each other good night

German phrases and sayings

die Katze im Sack kaufen
    word for word:
→ to buy a pig in a poke
    to buy the cat in the bag

die Sau rauslassen
    word for word:
→ to let one's hair down
    to let the sow go

The weather

das ist Schnee von gestern
    word for word:
→ it's old hat
    it's yesterday's snow

ein Gesicht wie drei Tage Regenwetter
    word for word:
→ a miserable face
    a face like three days' rain

ein Sturm im Wasserglas
    word for word:
→ a storm in a teacup
    a storm in a glass of water

etwas in den Wind schreiben
    word for word:
→ to give something up for lost
    to write something in the wind

es regnet Bindfäden
    word for word:
→ it's bucketing down
    it's raining pieces of string

Parts of the body

sich den Kopf zerbrechen
    word for word:
→ to rack one's brains
    to break one's head

Hals über Kopf
    word for word:
→ head over heels
    neck over head

sich kein Bein ausreißen
    word for word:
→ not to overstrain oneself
    not to tear one's leg off

es brennt mir auf der Zunge
    word for word:
→ I'm dying to say it
    it burns on my tongue

auf großem Fuß leben
    word for word:
→ to live the high life
    to live on a big foot

German phrases and sayings

Clothes

mir platzt der Kragen → this is the last straw for me
    word for word: *my collar is bursting*

das ist Jacke wie Hose → it doesn't make the slightest difference

    word for word: *it's like jacket like trousers*

jemandem auf den Schlips treten → to tread on somebody's toes
    word for word: *to step on somebody's tie*

das sind zwei Paar Stiefel → they are two completely different things

    word for word: *they are two pairs of boots*

eine weiße Weste haben → to have a clean record
    word for word: *to have a white waistcoat*

Colours

das Blaue vom Himmel versprechen → to promise the moon
    word for word: *to promise the blue off the sky*

sie sind sich nicht grün → there's no love lost between them

    word for word: *they are not green to each other*

du kannst warten, bis du schwarz wirst → you can wait till the cows come home

    word for word: *you can wait till you go black*

eine Fahrt ins Blaue → a mystery tour
    word for word: *a journey into the blue*

sich eine goldene Nase verdienen → to make a mint
    word for word: *to earn a golden nose*

Some common translation difficulties

On the following pages we have shown some of the translation difficulties that you are most likely to come across. We hope that the tips we have given will help you to avoid these common pitfalls when writing and speaking German.

Du or Sie?

In German the word for 'you' depends on who you are talking to:

• To a person you know well, or to a child, use **du**:

Will **you** lend me this CD? → *Kannst **du** mir diese CD leihen?*

• To more than one person you know well, or a group of children, use **ihr**:

Do **you** understand, children? → *Versteht **ihr** das, Kinder?*

• To a person or people you do not know so well, use **Sie**:

Have **you** met my wife? → *Kennen **Sie** meine Frau?*

> **Getting friendly**
> When you get to know someone, they may ask you:
> *Wollen wir uns duzen?* → Shall we use '**du**' to each other?

Singular versus plural

A word that is singular in English may be plural in German, and vice versa. Check in the dictionary if you are not sure:

Singular:	*Plural:*
headache	→ ***die** Kopfschmerz**en***
Plural:	*Singular:*
my trouser**s**	→ ***meine** Hose*

Some common translation difficulties

'There is' and 'there are'

In German, when meaning 'to exist', these are both translated by **es gibt**:

There is no God.	→ **Es gibt** keinen Gott.
There are two reasons for this.	→ **Es gibt** zwei Gründe dafür.

In other contexts the most appropriate German verb is used – note that this is not necessarily **sein** (to be):

There is someone at the door.	→ Jemand **ist** an der Tür.
There are five books on the table.	→ Fünf Bücher **liegen** auf dem Tisch.

Word order

Word order in German sentences is much more variable than in English. If, for example, a German sentence begins with something other than the subject, the position of subject and verb will change:

Today **we** don't **have** any lessons.	→ Heute **haben wir** keinen Unterricht.
At 3 o'clock **my uncle** will **come** for a visit.	→ Um 3 Uhr **kommt mein Onkel** zu Besuch.

This applies in particular to questions:

Why **are**n't **you** at school?	→ Warum **bist du** nicht in der Schule?
Where **did he** go?	→ Wohin **ist er** gegangen?

It is also worth noting the word order in clauses beginning with words like that, if, because and so on, where in German the verb always comes last:

I know that **she is** a teacher.	→ Ich weiß, dass **sie** Lehrerin **ist**.
I like him because **he** always **buys** me presents.	→ Ich mag ihn, weil **er** mir immer Geschenke **kauft**.

Some common translation difficulties

The translation of 'to' varies a lot in German:

• When indicating a direction, 'to' is translated by **nach**:

the train **to** London	→ *der Zug **nach** London*
to the left	→ ***nach** links*

• But when you are talking about the time, **nach** would in fact mean 'past' – for 'to' you must use **vor**:

five **to** ten	→ *fünf **vor** zehn*

• When talking about going to a particular place or visiting a particular person, use **zu**:

We drove **to** the station.	→ *Wir fuhren **zum** Bahnhof.*
I'm going **to** Anne's house.	→ *Ich gehe **zu** Anne.*

• When you mean 'in order to', use **um...zu**:

He's going into town **(in order)** **to** buy a present.	→ *Er geht in die Stadt, **um** ein Geschenk **zu** kaufen.*

• In front of verbs, it is shown by the verb ending (**-en** or **-n**):

to eat	→ *ess**en***
to fish	→ *angel**n***

'To be' usually corresponds to **sein**, but remember:

• In phrases describing how you feel, you sometimes use **haben**:

to be hungry/thirsty	→ *Hunger/Durst **haben***
to be afraid	→ *Angst **haben***

• To talk about your health, use **gehen**:

I'**m** very well, thank you	→ *Es **geht** mir sehr gut, danke.*

Some common translation difficulties

Translating 'to have'

'To have' usually corresponds to **haben**, but remember that while in English 'to have' is always used to form the perfect tense, in German many verbs take **sein** instead:

They **have** arrived	→ *Sie **sind** angekommen.*
She **has** gone to Berlin.	→ *Sie **ist** nach Berlin gegangen.*

Translating 'to go'

'To go' is normally translated by **gehen**, but if you are talking about various modes of transport, this may change:

• When talking about going by car, train or boat, use **fahren**:

We're **going** to Calais tomorrow.	→ *Morgen **fahren** wir nach Calais.*
My car won't **go**.	→ *Mein Auto **fährt** nicht.*

• When talking about going by plane, use **fliegen**:

This plane **goes** to Toronto.	→ *Dieses Flugzeug **fliegt** nach Toronto.*

Translating 'to know'

In German, there are two ways of translating 'to know'. It is important not to get them confused:

• When talking about knowing facts, use **wissen**:

Do you **know** how this works?	→ ***Weißt** du, wie das funktioniert?*
I don't **know**.	→ *Ich **weiß** nicht.*

• When talking about knowing people and places, use **kennen**:

I **know** Berlin well.	→ *Ich **kenne** Berlin gut.*
Do you **know** her?	→ ***Kennst** du sie?*

Some common translation difficulties

Translating 'to put'

German tends to be a lot more specific than English when talking about putting things in certain places:

- When putting something down flat, use *legen*:

    Put the book in the drawer. → *Leg das Buch in die Schublade.*
    Where shall I **put** my things? → *Wohin soll ich meine Sachen legen?*

- When putting something upright, use *stellen*:

    Put the book on the shelf. → *Stell das Buch ins Regal.*
    She **put** the vase on the table. → *Sie stellte die Vase auf den Tisch.*

- When 'to put' means 'to sit' or 'to place', use *setzen*:

    She **put** the child on the chair. → *Sie setzte das Kind auf den Stuhl.*
    Put the red ball behind the → *Setz die rote Kugel hinter die schwarze.*
    black one.

Translating '-ing'

Unlike English, German does not distinguish between the simple and continuous form of verbs. The simple form is used for both:

    He smok**es** cigarettes. → *Er raucht Zigaretten.*
    He is smok**ing** a cigarette. → *Er raucht eine Zigarette.*

If you want to emphasize that somebody is doing something at this very moment, you have to add the word ***gerade***.

    He is smok**ing** a cigarette. → *Er raucht gerade eine Zigarette.*

a

abandon [ə'bændən] *vt* (*desert*) verlassen; (*give up*) aufgeben

abbey ['æbɪ] *n* Abtei *f*

abbreviate [əbri:vɪ'eɪt] *vt* abkürzen; **abbreviation** [əbri:vɪ'eɪʃən] *n* Abkürzung *f*

ABC ['eɪbiː'siː] *n* (*a. fig*) Abc *nt*

abdicate ['æbdɪkeɪt] *vi* (*king*) abdanken; **abdication** [æbdɪ'keɪʃən] *n* Abdankung *f*

abdomen ['æbdəmən] *n* Unterleib *m*

ability [ə'bɪlɪtɪ] *n* Fähigkeit *f*; **able** ['eɪbl] *adj* fähig; **to be ~ to do sth** etw tun können

abnormal [æb'nɔːml] *adj* anormal

aboard [ə'bɔːd] *adv, prep* an Bord +*gen*

abolish [ə'bɒlɪʃ] *vt* abschaffen

aborigine [æbə'rɪdʒiniː] *n* Ureinwohner(in) *m(f)* (Australiens)

abort [ə'bɔːt] *vt* (*Med: foetus*) abtreiben; (*Space: mission*) abbrechen; **abortion** [ə'bɔːʃən] *n* Abtreibung *f*

KEYWORD

a [eɪ, ə; æn, ən] (*before vowel or silent h*: **an**) *indef art* **1** ein, eine; **a woman** eine Frau; **a book** ein Buch; **an eagle** ein Adler; **she's a doctor** sie ist Ärztin

2 (*instead of the number "one"*) ein, eine; **a year ago** vor einem Jahr; **a hundred/thousand** *etc* **pounds** (ein) hundert/(ein) tausend *etc* Pfund

3 (*in expressing ratios, prices etc*) pro; **3 a day/week** 3 pro Tag/Woche, 3 am Tag/in der Woche; **10 km an hour** 10 km pro Stunde/in der Stunde

AA *abbr* = **Automobile Association** *britischer Automobilklub*, ≈ ADAC *m*

aback *adv*: **taken ~** erstaunt

KEYWORD

about [ə'baʊt] *adv* **1** (*approximately*) etwa, ungefähr; **about a hundred/thousand** *etc* etwa hundert/tausend *etc*; **at about 2 o'clock** etwa um 2 Uhr; **I've just about finished** ich bin gerade fertig

2 (*referring to place*) herum, umher; **to leave things lying about** Sachen herumliegen lassen; **to run/walk** *etc* **about** herumrennen/gehen *etc*

3 to be about to do sth im Begriff sein, etw zu tun; **he was about to go to bed** er wollte gerade ins Bett gehen

▷ *prep* **1** (*relating to*) über +*akk*; **a book about London** ein Buch über London; **what is it about?** worum geht es?; (*book etc*) wovon handelt es?; **we talked about it** wir haben darüber geredet; **what** o **how about doing this?** wollen wir das machen?
2 (*referring to place*) um (... herum); **to walk about the town** in der Stadt herumgehen; **her clothes were scattered about the room** ihre Kleider waren über das ganze Zimmer verstreut

above [ə'bʌv] *adv* oben; **children aged 8 and ~** Kinder ab 8 Jahren; **on the floor ~** ein Stockwerk höher ▷ *prep* über; **~ 40 degrees** über 40 Grad; **~ all** vor allem ▷ *adj* obig

abroad [ə'brɔːd] *adv* im Ausland; **to go ~** ins Ausland gehen

abrupt [ə'brʌpt] *adj* (*sudden*) plötzlich, abrupt

abscess ['æbsɪs] *n* Geschwür *nt*

absence ['æbsəns] *n* Abwesenheit *f*; **absent** ['æbsənt] *adj* abwesend; **to be ~** fehlen; **absent-minded** *adj* zerstreut

absolute ['æbsəluːt] *adj* absolut; (*power*) unumschränkt; (*rubbish*) vollkommen, total; **absolutely** *adv* absolut; (*true, stupid*) vollkommen; **~!** genau!; **you're ~ right** du hast/Sie haben völlig recht

absorb [əb'zɔːb] *vt* absorbieren; (*fig: information*) in sich aufnehmen; **absorbed** *adj*: **~ in sth** in etw vertieft; **absorbent** *adj* absorbierend; **~ cotton** (*US*) Watte *f*; **absorbing** *adj* (*fig*) faszinierend, fesselnd

abstain [əb'steɪn] *vi*: **to ~ (from voting)** sich (der Stimme) enthalten

abstract ['æbstrækt] *adj* abstrakt

absurd [əb'sɜːd] *adj* absurd

abundance [ə'bʌndəns] *n* Reichtum *m* (*of* an +*dat*)

abuse [ə'bjuːs] *n* (*rude language*) Beschimpfungen *pl*; (*mistreatment*) Missbrauch *m* ▷ [ə'bjuːz] *vt* (*misuse*) missbrauchen; **abusive** [ə'bjuːsɪv] *adj* beleidigend

AC *abbr* = **alternating current** Wechselstrom *m* ▷ *abbr* = **air conditioning** Klimaanlage

a/c *abbr* = **account** Kto.

academic [ækə'demɪk] *n* Wissenschaftler(in) *m(f)* ▷ *adj* akademisch, wissenschaftlich

accelerate [æk'seləreɪt] *vi* (*car etc*) beschleunigen; (*driver*) Gas geben; **acceleration** [əksela'reɪʃən] *n* Beschleunigung *f*; **accelerator** [ək'seləreɪtə°] *n* Gas(pedal) *nt*

accent ['æksent] *n* Akzent *m*

accept [ək'sept] *vt* annehmen; (*agree to*) akzeptieren; (*responsibility*) übernehmen; **acceptable** [ək'septəbl] *adj* annehmbar

access ['ækses] *n* Zugang *m*; (*Inform*) Zugriff *m*; **accessible** [æk'sesəbl] *adj* (*leicht*) zugänglich/erreichbar; (*place*) (leicht) erreichbar

accessory [æk'sesərɪ] *n* Zubehörteil *nt*

access road *n* Zufahrtsstraße *f*

accident ['æksɪdənt] *n* Unfall *m*; **by ~** zufällig; **accidental** [æksɪ'dentl] *adj* unbeabsichtigt; (*meeting*) zufällig; (*death*) durch Unfall; **~ damage** Unfallschaden *m*; **accident-prone** *adj* vom Pech verfolgt

acclimatize [ə'klaɪmətaɪz] *vt*: **to ~ oneself** sich gewöhnen (*to* an +*akk*)

accommodate [əˈkɒmədeɪt] vt
unterbringen;
accommodation(s)
[əkɒməˈdeɪʃən(z)] n Unterkunft f
accompany [əˈkʌmpənɪ] vt
begleiten
accomplish [əˈkʌmplɪʃ] vt
erreichen
accord [əˈkɔːd] n: **of one's own
~** freiwillig; **according to** prep
nach, laut +dat
account [əˈkaʊnt] n (in bank etc)
Konto nt; (narrative) Bericht m; **on
~ of** wegen; **on no ~** auf keinen
Fall; **to take into ~**
berücksichtigen, in Betracht
ziehen; **accountant** [əˈkaʊntənt]
n Buchhalter(in) m(f); **account for**
vt (explain) erklären; (expenditure)
Rechenschaft ablegen für;
account number n
Kontonummer f
accumulate [əˈkjuːmjʊleɪt] vt
ansammeln ▷ vi sich ansammeln
accuracy [ˈækjʊrəsɪ] n
Genauigkeit f; **accurate** [ˈækjʊrɪt]
adj genau
accusation [ækjʊˈzeɪʃən] n
Anklage f, Beschuldigung f
accusative [əˈkjuːzətɪv] n
Akkusativ m
accuse [əˈkjuːz] vt beschuldigen;
(Jur) anklagen (of wegen +gen); **~ sb
of doing sth** jdn beschuldigen,
etw getan zu haben; **accused** n
(Jur) Angeklagte(r) mf
accustom [əˈkʌstəm] vt
gewöhnen (to an +akk);
accustomed adj gewohnt; **to get
~ to sth** sich an etw akk gewöhnen
ace [eɪs] n Ass nt ▷ adj Star-
ache [eɪk] n Schmerz m ▷ vi
wehtun
achieve [əˈtʃiːv] vt erreichen;
achievement n Leistung f
acid [ˈæsɪd] n Säure f ▷ adj sauer;
~ rain saurer Regen

acknowledge [əkˈnɒlɪdʒ] vt
(recognize) anerkennen; (admit)
zugeben; (receipt of letter etc)
bestätigen; **acknowledgement** n
Anerkennung f; (of letter)
Empfangsbestätigung f
acne [ˈæknɪ] n Akne f
acorn [ˈeɪkɔːn] n Eichel f
acoustic [əˈkuːstɪk] adj akustisch; **acoustics** [əˈkuːstɪks] npl
Akustik f
acquaintance [əˈkweɪntəns] n
(person) Bekannte(r) mf
acquire [əˈkwaɪəʳ] vt erwerben,
sich aneignen; **acquisition**
[ækwɪˈzɪʃn] n (of skills etc) Erwerb
m; (object) Anschaffung f
acrobat [ˈækrəbæt] n Akrobat(in)
m(f)
across [əˈkrɒs] prep über +akk; **he
lives ~ the street** er wohnt auf der
anderen Seite der Straße ▷ adv
hinüber, herüber; **100m ~** 100m
breit
act [ækt] n (deed) Tat f; (Jur: law)
Gesetz nt; (Theat) Akt m; (fig:
pretence) Schau f; **it's all an ~** es ist
alles nur Theater; **to be in the ~ of
doing sth** gerade dabei sein, etw
zu tun ▷ vi (take action) handeln;
(behave) sich verhalten; (Theat) spielen;
to ~ as (person) fungieren als; (thing)
dienen als ▷ vt (a part) spielen
action [ˈækʃən] n (of play, novel
etc) Handlung f; (in film etc) Action
f; (Mil) Kampf m; **to take ~** etwas
unternehmen; **out of ~** (machine)
außer Betrieb; **to put a plan into
~** einen Plan in die Tat umsetzen;
action replay n (Sport, TV)
Wiederholung f
activate [ˈæktɪveɪt] vt aktivieren;
active [ˈæktɪv] adj aktiv; (child)
lebhaft; **activity** [ækˈtɪvɪtɪ] n
Aktivität f; (occupation)
Beschäftigung f; (organized event)
Veranstaltung f

actor ['æktə°] n Schauspieler(in) m(f); **actress** ['æktrıs] n Schauspielerin f
actual ['æktjʊəl] adj wirklich; **actually** adv eigentlich; (said in surprise) tatsächlich
acupuncture ['ækjʊpʌŋktʃə°] n Akupunktur f
acute [ə'kju:t] adj (pain) akut; (sense of smell) fein; (Math: angle) spitz
ad [æd] abbr = **advertisement**
AD abbr = **Anno Domini** nach Christi, n. Chr.
adapt [ə'dæpt] vi sich anpassen (to +dat) ▷ vt anpassen (to +dat); (rewrite) bearbeiten (for für); **adaptable** adj anpassungsfähig; **adaptation** n (of book etc) Bearbeitung f; **adapter** n (Elec) Zwischenstecker m, Adapter m
add [æd] vt (ingredient) hinzufügen; (numbers) addieren; **add up** vi (make sense) stimmen ▷ vt (numbers) addieren
addict ['ædıkt] n Süchtige(r) mf; **addicted** [ə'dıktıd] adj: **~ to alcohol/drugs** alkohol-/drogensüchtig
addition [ə'dıʃən] n Zusatz m; (to bill) Aufschlag m; (Math) Addition f; **in ~** außerdem, zusätzlich (to zu); **additional** adj zusätzlich, weiter; **additive** ['ædıtıv] n Zusatz m; **add-on** ['ædɒn] n Zusatzgerät nt
address [ə'dres] n Adresse f ▷ vt (letter) adressieren; (person) anreden
adequate ['ædıkwıt] adj (appropriate) angemessen; (sufficient) ausreichend; (time) genügend
adhesive [əd'hi:sıv] n Klebstoff m; **adhesive tape** n Klebstreifen m
adjacent [ə'dʒeısənt] adj benachbart

adjective ['ædʒəktıv] n Adjektiv nt
adjoining [ə'dʒɔınıŋ] adj benachbart, Neben-
adjust [ə'dʒʌst] vt einstellen; (put right also) richtig stellen; (speed, flow) regulieren; (in position) verstellen ▷ vi sich anpassen (to +dat); **adjustable** adj verstellbar
admin [əd'mın] n (fam) Verwaltung f; **administration** [ədmınıs'treıʃən] n Verwaltung f; (Pol) Regierung f
admirable ['ædmərəbl] adj bewundernswert; **admiration** [ædmı'reıʃən] n Bewunderung f; **admire** [əd'maıə°] vt bewundern
admission [əd'mıʃən] n (entrance) Zutritt m; (to university etc) Zulassung f; (fee) Eintritt m; (confession) Eingeständnis nt; **admission charge, admission fee** n Eintrittspreis m; **admit** [əd'mıt] vt (let in) hereinlassen (to in +akk); (to university etc) zulassen; (confess) zugeben, gestehen; **to be ~ted to hospital** ins Krankenhaus eingeliefert werden
adolescent [ædə'lesnt] n Jugendliche(r) mf
adopt [ə'dɒpt] vt (child) adoptieren; (idea) übernehmen; **adoption** [ə'dɒpʃn] n (of child) Adoption f; (of idea) Übernahme f
adorable [ə'dɔ:rəbl] adj entzückend; **adore** [ə'dɔ:°] vt anbeten; (person) über alles lieben, vergöttern
ADSL abbr = **asymmetric digital subscriber line** ADSL f
adult ['ædʌlt] adj erwachsen; (film etc) für Erwachsene ▷ n Erwachsene(r) mf
adultery [ə'dʌltərı] n Ehebruch m
advance [əd'vɑ:ns] n (money) Vorschuss m; (progress) Fortschritt

m; **in ~** im Voraus; **to book in ~**
vorbestellen ▷ vi (*move forward*)
vorrücken ▷ vt (*money*)
vorschießen; **advance booking** n
Reservierung f; (*Theat*) Vorverkauf
m; **advanced** adj (*modern*)
fortschrittlich; (*course, study*) für
Fortgeschrittene; **advance**
payment n Vorauszahlung f
advantage [əd'vɑːntɪdʒ] n
Vorteil m; **to take ~ of** (*exploit*)
ausnutzen; (*profit from*) Nutzen
ziehen aus; **it's to your ~** es ist in
deinem/Ihrem Interesse
adventure [əd'ventʃə*] n
Abenteuer nt; **adventure holiday**
n Abenteuerurlaub m; **adventure**
playground n Abenteuerspiel-
platz m; **adventurous**
[əd'ventʃərəs] adj (*person*)
abenteuerlustig
adverb ['ædvɜːb] n Adverb nt
adverse ['ædvɜːs] adj (*conditions*
etc) ungünstig; (*effect, comment etc*)
negativ
advert ['ædvɜːt] n Anzeige f;
advertise ['ædvətaɪz] vt werben
für; (*in newspaper*) inserieren; (*job*)
ausschreiben ▷ vi Reklame
machen; (*in newspaper*)
annoncieren (*for* für);
advertisement [əd'vɜːtɪsmənt]
n Werbung f; (*announcement*)
Anzeige f; **advertising** n
Werbung f
advice [əd'vaɪs] n Rat(schlag) m;
word o **piece of ~** Ratschlag m;
take my ~ hör auf mich;
advisable [əd'vaɪzəbl] adj ratsam; **advise** [əd'vaɪz] vt raten
(*sb* jdm); **to ~ sb to do sth/not to**
do sth jdm zuraten/abraten, etw
zu tun
Aegean [iː'dʒiːən] n: **the ~ (Sea)**
die Ägäis
aerial ['ɛərɪəl] n Antenne f ▷ adj
Luft-

aerobatics [ɛərəʊ'bætɪks] npl
Kunstfliegen nt
aerobics [ɛə'rəʊbɪks] nsing
Aerobic nt
aeroplane ['ɛərəpleɪn] n
Flugzeug nt
afaik abbr = **as far as I know**;
(*SMS*) ≈ soweit ich weiß
affair [ə'fɛə*] n (*matter, business*)
Sache f, Angelegenheit f; (*scandal*)
Affäre f; (*love affair*) Verhältnis nt
affect [ə'fekt] vt (*influence*)
(ein)wirken auf +akk; (*health,*
organ) angreifen; (*move deeply*)
berühren; (*concern*) betreffen;
affection [ə'fekʃən] n Zuneigung
f; **affectionate** [ə'fekʃənɪt] adj
liebevoll
affluent ['æfluənt] adj
wohlhabend
afford [ə'fɔːd] vt sich leisten; **I**
can't ~ it ich kann es mir nicht
leisten; **affordable** [ə'fɔːdəbl]
adj erschwinglich
Afghanistan [æf'gænɪstæn] n
Afghanistan nt
aforementioned
[əfɔː'menʃənd] adj oben genannt
afraid [ə'freɪd] adj: **to be ~** Angst
haben (*of* vor +dat); **to be ~ that ...**
fürchten, dass ...; **I'm ~ I don't**
know das weiß ich leider nicht
Africa ['æfrɪkə] n Afrika nt;
African adj afrikanisch ▷ n
Afrikaner(in) m(f); **African**
American, **Afro-American** n
Afroamerikaner(in) m(f)
after ['ɑːftə*] prep nach; **ten**
~ five (*US*) zehn nach fünf; **to be**
~ sb/sth (*following, seeking*) hinter
jdm/etw her sein; **~ all**
schließlich; (*in spite of everything*)
(schließlich) doch ▷ conj
nachdem ▷ adv: **soon ~** bald
danach; **aftercare** n
Nachbehandlung f; **after-effect** n
Nachwirkung f

afternoon n Nachmittag m; **~, good ~** guten Tag!; **in the ~** nachmittags

afters npl Nachtisch m; **after-sales service** n Kundendienst m; **after-shave (lotion)** n Rasierwasser nt; **aftersun** n After-Sun-Lotion f; **afterwards** adv nachher; (after that) danach

again [ə'gen] adv wieder; (one more time) noch einmal; **not ~!** (nicht) schon wieder; **~ and ~** immer wieder; **the same ~ please** das Gleiche noch mal bitte

against [ə'genst] prep gegen; **~ my will** wider Willen; **~ the law** unrechtmäßig, illegal

age [eɪdʒ] n Alter nt; (period of history) Zeitalter nt; **at the ~ of four** im Alter von vier (Jahren); **what ~ is she?, what is her ~?** wie alt ist sie?; **to come of ~** volljährig werden; **under ~** minderjährig ▷ vi altern, alt werden; **aged** adj: **~ thirty** dreißig Jahre alt; **a son ~ twenty** ein zwanzigjähriger Sohn ▷ adj ['eɪdʒɪd] (elderly) betagt; **age group** n Altersgruppe f; **ageism** n Diskriminierung f aufgrund des Alters; **age limit** n Altersgrenze f

agency ['eɪdʒənsɪ] n Agentur f

agenda [ə'dʒendə] n Tagesordnung f

agent ['eɪdʒənt] n (Comm) Vertreter(in) m(f); (for writer, actor etc) Agent(in) m(f)

aggression [ə'greʃn] n Aggression f; **aggressive** [ə'gresɪv] adj aggressiv

agitated adj aufgeregt; **to get ~** sich aufregen

AGM abbr = **Annual General Meeting** JHV f

ago [ə'gəʊ] adv: **two days ~** heute vor zwei Tagen; **not long ~** (erst) vor Kurzem

agonize ['ægənaɪz] vi sich den Kopf zerbrechen (over über dat); **agonizing** adj qualvoll; **agony** ['ægənɪ] n Qual f

agree [ə'griː] vt (date, price etc) vereinbaren; **to ~ to do sth** sich bereit erklären, etw zu tun; **to ~ that ...** sich dat einig sein, dass ...; (decide) beschließen, dass ...; (admit) zugeben, dass ... ▷ vi (have same opinion, correspond) übereinstimmen (with mit); (consent) zustimmen; (come to an agreement) sich einigen (about, on auf +akk); (food) **not to ~ with sb** jdm nicht bekommen; **agreement** n (agreeing) Übereinstimmung f; (contract) Abkommen nt, Vereinbarung f

agricultural [ægrɪ'kʌltʃərəl] adj landwirtschaftlich, Landwirtschafts-; **agriculture** ['ægrɪkʌltʃə°] n Landwirtschaft f

ahead [ə'hed] adv: **to be ~** führen, vorne liegen; **~ of** vor +dat; **to be ~ of sb** (person) jdm voraus sein; (thing) vor jdm liegen; **to be 3 metres ~** 3 Meter Vorsprung haben

aid [eɪd] n Hilfe f; **in ~ of** zugunsten +gen; **with the ~ of** mithilfe +gen ▷ vt helfen +dat; (support) unterstützen

Aids [eɪdz] n acr = **acquired immune deficiency syndrome** Aids nt

aim [eɪm] vt (gun, camera) richten (at auf +akk) ▷ vi: **to ~ at** (with gun etc) zielen auf +akk; (fig) abzielen auf +akk; **to ~ to do sth** beabsichtigen, etw zu tun ▷ n Ziel nt

air [eə°] n Luft f; **in the open ~** im Freien; (Radio, TV) **to be on the ~** (programme) auf Sendung sein;

(station) senden ▷ vt lüften;
airbag n (Auto) Airbag m;
air-conditioned adj mit
Klimaanlage; **air-conditioning** n
Klimaanlage f; **aircraft** n
Flugzeug nt; **airfield** n Flugplatz
m; **air force** n Luftwaffe f;
airgun n Luftgewehr nt; **airline** n Fluggesellschaft f;
airmail n Luftpost f; **by ~** mit
Luftpost; **airplane** n (US)
Flugzeug nt; **air pollution** n
Luftverschmutzung f; **airport** n
Flughafen m; **airsick** adj
luftkrank; **airtight** adj luftdicht;
air-traffic controller n Fluglotse
m, Fluglotsin f; **airy** adj luftig;
(manner) lässig
aisle [aɪl] n Gang m; (in church)
Seitenschiff nt; **~ seat** Sitz m am
Gang
ajar [ə'dʒɑː*] adj (door) angelehnt
alarm [ə'lɑːm] n (warning) Alarm
m; (bell etc) Alarmanlage f ▷ vt
beunruhigen; **alarm clock** n
Wecker m; **alarmed** adj (protected)
alarmgesichert; **alarming** adj
beunruhigend
Albania [æl'beɪnɪə] n Albanien
nt; **Albanian** adj albanisch ▷ n
(person) Albaner(in) m(f); (language)
Albanisch nt
album ['ælbəm] n Album nt
alcohol ['ælkəhɒl] n Alkohol m;
alcohol-free adj alkoholfrei;
alcoholic [ælkə'hɒlɪk] adj (drink)
alkoholisch ▷ n Alkoholiker(in)
m(f); **alcoholism** n Alkoholismus
m
ale [eɪl] n Ale nt (helles englisches
Bier)
alert [ə'lɜːt] adj wachsam ▷ n
Alarm m ▷ vt warnen (to vor +dat)
algebra ['ældʒɪbrə] n Algebra f
Algeria [æl'dʒɪərɪə] n Algerien nt
alibi ['ælɪbaɪ] n Alibi nt
alien ['eɪlɪən] n (foreigner)

Ausländer(in) m(f); (from space)
Außerirdische(r) mf
align [ə'laɪn] vt ausrichten (with
auf +akk)
alike [ə'laɪk] adj, adv gleich;
(similar) ähnlich
alive [ə'laɪv] adj lebendig; **to
keep sth ~** etw am Leben
erhalten; **he's still ~** er lebt noch

O **KEYWORD**

all [ɔːl] adj alle(r, s); **all day/night**
den ganzen Tag/die ganze Nacht;
all men are equal alle Menschen
sind gleich; **all five came** alle fünf
kamen; **all the books/food** die
ganzen Bücher/das ganze Essen;
all the time die ganze Zeit (über);
all his life sein ganzes Leben
(lang)
▷ pron 1 alles; **I ate it all, I ate all of
it** ich habe alles gegessen; **all of
us/the boys went** wir gingen
alle/alle Jungen gingen; **we all sat
down** wir setzten uns alle
2 (in phrases) **above all** vor allem;
after all schließlich; **at all**: **not at
all** (in answer to question)
überhaupt nicht; (in answer to
thanks) gern geschehen; **I'm not at
all tired** ich bin überhaupt nicht
müde; **anything at all will do** es
ist egal, welche(r, s); **all in all** alles
in allem
▷ adv ganz; **all alone** ganz allein;
it's not as hard as all that so
schwer ist es nun auch wieder
nicht; **all the more/the better**
umso mehr/besser; **all but** fast;
the score is 2 all es steht 2 zu 2

allegation [ælɪ'geɪʃən] n
Behauptung f; **alleged** adj
angeblich
allergic [ə'lɜːdʒɪk] adj allergisch

(*to* gegen); **allergy** ['ælədʒɪ] *n*
Allergie *f*
alleviate [ə'liːvɪeɪt] *vt* (*pain*)
lindern
alley ['ælɪ] *n* (enge) Gasse;
(*passage*) Durchgang *m*; (*bowling*)
Bahn *f*
alliance [ə'laɪəns] *n* Bündnis *nt*
alligator ['ælɪgeɪtə*] *n* Alligator
m
all-night *adj* (*café, cinema*) die
ganze Nacht geöffnet
allocate ['æləkeɪt] *vt* zuweisen,
zuteilen (*to dat*)
allotment *n* (*plot*)
Schrebergarten *m*
allow [ə'laʊ] *vt* (*permit*) erlauben
(*sb* jdm); (*grant*) bewilligen; (*time*)
einplanen; **allow for** *vt*
berücksichtigen; (*cost etc*)
einkalkulieren; **allowance** *n* (*from
state*) Beihilfe *f*; (*from parent*)
Unterhaltsgeld *nt*
all right ['ɔːl'raɪt] *adj* okay, in
Ordnung; **I'm ~** mir geht's gut
▷ *adv* (*satisfactorily*) ganz gut
▷ *interj* okay
all-time *adj* (*record, high*) aller
Zeiten
allusion [ə'luːʒn] *n* Anspielung *f*
(*to* auf +*akk*)
ally ['ælaɪ] *n* Verbündete(r) *mf*;
(*Hist*) Alliierte(r) *mf*
almond ['ɑːmənd] *n* Mandel *f*
almost ['ɔːlməʊst] *adv* fast
alone [ə'ləʊn] *adj, adv* allein
along [ə'lɒŋ] *prep* entlang
+*akk*; **~ the river** den Fluss
entlang; (*position*) am Fluss
entlang ▷ *adv* (*onward*) weiter;
~ with zusammen mit; **all ~** die
ganze Zeit, von Anfang an;
alongside *prep* neben +*dat* ▷ *adv*
(*walk*) nebenher
aloud [ə'laʊd] *adv* laut
alphabet ['ælfəbet] *n* Alphabet
nt

alpine ['ælpaɪn] *adj* alpin; **Alps**
[ælps] *npl*: **the ~** die Alpen
already [ɔːl'redɪ] *adv* schon,
bereits
Alsace ['ælsæs] *n* Elsass *nt*;
Alsatian [æl'seɪʃən] *adj*
elsässisch ▷ *n* Elsässer(in) *m(f)*;
(*Brit: dog*) Schäferhund *m*
also ['ɔːlsəʊ] *adv* auch
altar ['ɔːltə*] *n* Altar *m*
alter ['ɔːltə*] *vt* ändern;
alteration [ɔːltə'reɪʃən] *n*
Änderung *f*; **~s** (*to building*) Umbau
m
alternate [ɔːl'tɜːnət] *adj*
abwechselnd ▷ [ɔːl'tɜːneɪt] *vi*
abwechseln (*with* mit);
alternating current *n*
Wechselstrom *m*
alternative [ɔːl'tɜːnətɪv] *adj*
Alternativ- ▷ *n* Alternative *f*
although [ɔːl'ðəʊ] *conj* obwohl
altitude ['æltɪtjuːd] *n* Höhe *f*
altogether [ɔːltə'geðə*] *adv* (*in
total*) insgesamt; (*entirely*) ganz
und gar
aluminium, **aluminum** (*US*)
[æljʊ'mɪnɪəm, ə'luːmɪnəm] *n*
Aluminium *nt*
always ['ɔːlweɪz] *adv* immer
am [æm] *present of* **be**; bin
am, **a.m.** *abbr* = **ante meridiem**
vormittags, vorm.
amateur ['æmətə*] *n* Ama-
teur(in) *m(f)* ▷ *adj* Amateur-;
(*theatre, choir*) Laien-
amaze [ə'meɪz] *vt* erstaunen;
amazed *adj* erstaunt (*at* über
+*akk*); **amazing** *adj* erstaunlich
Amazon ['æməzən] *n*: **~** (**river**)
Amazonas *m*
ambassador [æm'bæsədə*] *n*
Botschafter *m*
amber ['æmbə*] *n* Bernstein *m*
ambiguity [æmbɪ'gjʊɪtɪ] *n*
Zweideutigkeit *f*; **ambiguous**
[æm'bɪgjʊəs] *adj* zweideutig

ambition [æm'bɪʃən] n Ambition f; (ambitious nature) Ehrgeiz m; **ambitious** [æm'bɪʃəs] adj ehrgeizig

ambulance ['æmbjʊləns] n Krankenwagen m

amend [ə'mend] vt (law etc) ändern

America [ə'merɪkə] n Amerika nt; **American** adj amerikanisch ▷ n Amerikaner(in) m(f); **native ~** Indianer(in) m(f)

amiable ['eɪmɪəbl] adj liebenswürdig

amicable ['æmɪkəbl] adj freundlich; (relations) freundschaftlich; (Jur: settlement) gütlich

amnesia [æm'niːzɪə] n Gedächtnisverlust m

among(st) [ə'mʌŋ(st)] prep unter +dat

amount [ə'maʊnt] n (quantity) Menge f; (of money) Betrag m; **a large/small ~ of ...** ziemlich viel/wenig ... ▷ vi: **to ~ to** (total) sich belaufen auf +akk

amp, ampere [æmp, 'æmpeə°] n Ampere nt

amplifier ['æmplɪfaɪə°] n Verstärker m

amputate ['æmpjʊteɪt] vt amputieren

Amtrak® ['æmtræk] n amerikanische Eisenbahngesellschaft

amuse [ə'mjuːz] vt amüsieren; (entertain) unterhalten; **amused** adj: **I'm not ~** das finde ich gar nicht lustig; **amusement** n (enjoyment) Vergnügen nt; (recreation) Unterhaltung f; **amusement arcade** n Spielhalle f; **amusement park** n Vergnügungspark m; **amusing** adj amüsant

an [æn, ən] art ein(e)

anaemic [ə'niːmɪk] adj blutarm

anaesthetic [ænɪs'θetɪk] n Narkose f; (substance) Narkosemittel nt

analyse, analyze ['ænəlaɪz] vt analysieren; **analysis** [ə'nælɪsɪs] n Analyse f

anatomy [ə'nætəmɪ] n Anatomie f; (structure) Körperbau m

ancestor ['ænsestə°] n Vorfahr m

anchor ['æŋkə°] n Anker m ▷ vt verankern; **anchorage** n Ankerplatz m

anchovy ['æntʃəvɪ] n Sardelle f

ancient ['eɪnʃənt] adj alt; (fam: person, clothes etc) uralt

and [ænd, ənd] conj und

Andorra [æn'dɔːrə] n Andorra nt

anemic adj (US) see **anaemic**

anesthetic n (US) see **anaesthetic**

angel ['eɪndʒəl] n Engel m

anger ['æŋgə°] n Zorn m ▷ vt ärgern

angina, angina pectoris [æn'dʒaɪnə('pektərɪs)] n Angina Pectoris f

angle ['æŋgl] n Winkel m; (fig) Standpunkt m

angler ['æŋglə°] n Angler(in) m(f); **angling** ['æŋglɪŋ] n Angeln nt

angry ['æŋgrɪ] adj verärgert; (stronger) zornig; **to be ~ with sb** auf jdn böse sein

angular ['æŋgjʊlə°] adj eckig; (face) kantig

animal ['ænɪməl] n Tier nt; **animal rights** npl Tierrechte pl

animated ['ænɪmeɪtɪd] adj lebhaft; **~ film** Zeichentrickfilm m

aniseed ['ænɪsiːd] n Anis m

ankle ['æŋkl] n (Fuß)knöchel m

annex ['æneks] n Anbau m

anniversary [ænɪ'vɜːsərɪ] n Jahrestag m

announce [ə'naʊns] vt bekannt geben; (officially) bekannt machen; (on radio, TV etc) (Radio,

TV) ansagen; **announcement** n
Bekanntgabe f; (official)
Bekanntmachung f; (Radio, TV)
Ansage f; **announcer** n (Radio, TV)
Ansager(in) m(f)
annoy [əˈnɔɪ] vt ärgern;
annoyance n Ärger m; **annoyed**
adj ärgerlich; **to be ~ with sb**
(**about sth**) sich über jdn (über
etw) ärgern; **annoying** adj
ärgerlich; (person) lästig, nervig
annual [ˈænjʊəl] adj jährlich
▷ n Jahrbuch nt
anonymous [əˈnɒnɪməs] adj
anonym
anorak [ˈænəræk] n Anorak m
anorexia [ænəˈreksɪə] n Magersucht f; **anorexic** adj
magersüchtig
another [əˈnʌðə°] adj, pron
(different) ein(e) andere(r, s);
(additional) noch eine(r, s); **let me
put it ~ way** lass es mich anders
sagen
answer [ˈɑːnsə°] n Antwort f (to
auf +akk); (solution) Lösung f +gen
▷ vi antworten; (on phone) sich
melden ▷ vt (person) antworten
+dat; (letter, question) beantworten;
(telephone) gehen an +akk,
abnehmen; (door) öffnen; **answer
back** vi widersprechen;
answering machine,
answerphone n Anrufbeant-
worter m
ant [ænt] n Ameise f
Antarctic [æntˈɑːktɪk] n
Antarktis f; **Antarctic Circle** n
südlicher Polarkreis
antelope [ˈæntɪləʊp] n Antilope f
antenna [ænˈtenə] (pl **antennae**)
n (Zool) Fühler m; (Radio) Antenne f
anti- [ˈæntɪ] pref Anti-, anti-;
antibiotic [ˈæntɪbaɪˈɒtɪk] n
Antibiotikum nt
anticipate [ænˈtɪsɪpeɪt] vt (expect:
trouble, question) erwarten,

rechnen mit; **anticipation**
[æntɪsɪˈpeɪʃən] n Erwartung f
anticlimax [æntɪˈklaɪmæks] n
Enttäuschung f; **anticlockwise**
[æntɪˈklɒkwaɪz] adv entgegen
dem Uhrzeigersinn
antidote [ˈæntɪdəʊt] n Gegenmittel nt; **antifreeze** n
Frostschutzmittel nt
Antipodes [ænˈtɪpədiːz] npl
Australien und Neuseeland
antiquarian [æntɪˈkweərɪən]
adj: **~ bookshop** Antiquariat nt
antique [ænˈtiːk] n Antiquität f
▷ adj antik; **antique shop** n
Antiquitätengeschäft nt
anti-Semitism [æntɪˈsemɪtɪzm]
n Antisemitismus m; **antiseptic**
[æntɪˈseptɪk] n Antiseptikum nt
▷ adj antiseptisch; **antisocial** adj
(person) ungesellig; (behaviour)
unsozial, asozial; **antivirus** adj
(Inform) Antiviren-; **antivirus
software** n Antinvirensoftware f
antlers [ˈæntləz] npl Geweih nt
anxiety [æŋˈzaɪətɪ] n Sorge f
(about um); **anxious** [ˈæŋkʃəs] adj
besorgt (about um); (apprehensive)
ängstlich

⊙ **KEYWORD**

any [ˈenɪ] adj **1** (in questions etc)
have you any butter? haben Sie
(etwas) Butter?; **have you any
children?** haben Sie Kinder?; **if
there are any tickets left** falls
noch Karten da sind
2 (with negative) **I haven't any
money** ich habe kein Geld
3 (no matter which) jede(r, s)
(beliebige); **any colour (at all)**
jede beliebige Farbe; **choose any
book you like** nehmen Sie ein
beliebiges Buch
4 (in phrases) **in any case** in jedem

Fall; **any day now** jeden Tag; **at any moment** jeden Moment; **at any rate** auf jeden Fall
▷ *pron* 1 (*in questions etc*) **have you got any?** haben Sie welche?; **can any of you sing?** kann (irgend)einer von euch singen?
2 (*with negative*) **I haven't any (of them)** ich habe keinen/keines (davon)
3 (*no matter which one(s)*): **take any of those books (you like)** nehmen Sie irgendeines dieser Bücher
▷ *adv* 1 (*in questions etc*) **do you want any more soup/ sandwiches?** möchten Sie noch Suppe/Brote?; **are you feeling any better?** fühlen Sie sich etwas besser?
2 (*with negative*) **I can't hear him any more** ich kann ihn nicht mehr hören

anybody *pron* (*whoever one likes*) irgendjemand; (*everyone*) jeder; (*in question*) jemand; **anyhow** *adv*: **I don't want to talk about it, not now ~** ich möchte nicht darüber sprechen, jedenfalls nicht jetzt; **they asked me not to go, but I went ~** sie baten mich, nicht hinzugehen, aber ich bin trotzdem hingegangen; **anyone** *pron* (*whoever one likes*) irgendjemand; (*everyone*) jeder; (*in question*) jemand; **isn't there ~ you can ask?** gibt es denn niemanden, den du fragen kannst/den Sie fragen können?; **anyplace** *adv* (*US*) irgendwo; (*direction*) irgendwohin; (*everywhere*) überall

○ **KEYWORD**

anything ['enɪθɪŋ] *pron* 1 (*in questions etc*) (irgend)etwas; **can**

you see anything? können Sie etwas sehen?
2 (*with negative*) **I can't see anything** ich kann nichts sehen
3 (*no matter what*) **you can say anything you like** Sie können sagen, was Sie wollen; **anything will do** irgendetwas (wird genügen), irgendeine(r, s) (wird genügen); **he'll eat anything** er isst alles

anytime *adv* jederzeit; **anyway** *adv*: **I didn't want to go there ~** ich wollte da sowieso nicht hingehen; **thanks ~** trotzdem danke; **~, as I was saying, ...** jedenfalls, wie ich schon sagte, ...;
anywhere *adv* irgendwo; (*direction*) irgendwohin; (*everywhere*) überall

apart [ə'pɑːt] *adv* auseinander; **~ from** außer; **live ~** getrennt leben
apartment [ə'pɑːtmənt] *n* (*esp US*) Wohnung *f*; **apartment block** *n* (*esp US*) Wohnblock *m*
ape [eɪp] *n* (Menschen)affe *m*
aperitif [ə'perɪtɪf] *n* Aperitif *m*
aperture ['æpətjʊə°] *n* Öffnung *f*; (*Foto*) Blende *f*
apologize [ə'pɒlədʒaɪz] *vi* sich entschuldigen; **apology** *n* Entschuldigung *f*
apostrophe [ə'pɒstrəfɪ] *n* Apostroph *m*
appalled [ə'pɔːld] *adj* entsetzt (*at* über +*akk*); **appalling** *adj* entsetzlich
apparatus [æpə'reɪtəs] *n* Apparat *m*; (*piece of apparatus*) Gerät *nt*
apparent [ə'pærənt] *adj* (*obvious*) offensichtlich (*to* für); (*seeming*) scheinbar; **apparently** *adv* anscheinend
appeal [ə'piːl] *vi* (dringend)

bitten (for um, to +akk); (Jur)
Berufung einlegen; **to ~ to sb** (be
attractive) jdm zusagen ▷ n Aufruf
m (to an +akk); (Jur) Berufung f;
(attraction) Reiz m; **appealing** adj
ansprechend, attraktiv

appear [əˈpɪə*] vi erscheinen;
(Theat) auftreten; (seem) scheinen;
appearance n Erscheinen nt;
(Theat) Auftritt m; (look) Aussehen
nt

appendicitis [əpendɪˈsaɪtɪs] n
Blinddarmentzündung f;
appendix [əˈpendɪks] n Blinddarm m; (to book) Anhang m

appetite [ˈæpɪtaɪt] n Appetit m;
(fig: desire) Verlangen nt; (sexual)
Lust f; **appetizing** [ˈæpɪtaɪzɪŋ]
adj appetitlich, appetitanregend

applause [əˈplɔːz] n Beifall m,
Applaus m

apple [ˈæpl] n Apfel m; **apple
crumble** n mit Streuseln bestreutes
Apfeldessert; **apple juice** n
Apfelsaft m; **apple pie** n
gedeckter Apfelkuchen m; **apple
puree**, **apple sauce** n Apfelmus
nt; **apple tart** n Apfelkuchen m;
apple tree n Apfelbaum m

appliance [əˈplaɪəns] n Gerät nt;
applicable [əˈplɪkəbl] adj
anwendbar; (on forms) zutreffend;
applicant [ˈæplɪkənt] n Bewer-
ber(in) m(f); **application**
[æplɪˈkeɪʃən] n (request) Antrag m
(for auf +akk); (for job) Bewerbung f
(for um); **application form** n
Anmeldeformular nt; **apply**
[əˈplaɪ] vi (be relevant) zutreffen (to
auf +akk); (for job etc) sich
bewerben (for um) ▷ vt (cream,
paint etc) auftragen; (put into
practice) anwenden; (brakes)
betätigen

appoint [əˈpɔɪnt] vt (to post)
ernennen; **appointment** n
Verabredung f; (at doctor, hairdresser

etc, in business) Termin m; **by
~** nach Vereinbarung

appreciate [əˈpriːʃɪeɪt] vt (value)
zu schätzen wissen; (understand)
einsehen; **to be much ~d** richtig
gewürdigt werden ▷ vi (increase in
value) im Wert steigen;
appreciation [əpriːʃɪˈeɪʃən] n
(esteem) Anerkennung f,
Würdigung f; (of person also)
Wertschätzung f

apprehensive [æprɪˈhensɪv] adj
ängstlich

apprentice [əˈprentɪs] n Lehrling m

approach [əˈprəʊtʃ] vi sich
nähern ▷ vt (place) sich nähern
+dat; (person) herantreten an +akk;
(problem) angehen

appropriate [əˈprəʊprɪət] adj
passend; (to occasion) angemessen;
(remark) treffend; **appropriately**
adv passend; (expressed) treffend

approval [əˈpruːvəl] n (show of
satisfaction) Anerkennung f;
(permission) Zustimmung f (of zu);
approve [əˈpruːv] vt billigen
▷ vi: **to ~ of sth/sb** etw
billigen/von jdm etwas halten; **I
don't ~** ich missbillige das

approx [əˈprɒks] abbr =
approximately ca.; **approximate**
[əˈprɒksɪmɪt] adj ungefähr;
approximately adv ungefähr,
circa

apricot [ˈeɪprɪkɒt] n Aprikose f

April [ˈeɪprəl] n April m; see also
September

apron [ˈeɪprən] n Schürze f

aptitude [ˈæptɪtjuːd] n Begabung
f

aquaplaning [ˈækwəpleɪnɪŋ] n
(Auto) Aquaplaning nt

aquarium [əˈkweərɪəm] n
Aquarium nt

Aquarius [əˈkweərɪəs] n (Astr)
Wassermann m

Arab ['ærəb] n Araber(in) m(f); (horse) Araber m; **Arabian** [ə'reɪbɪən] adj arabisch; **Arabic** ['ærəbɪk] n (language) Arabisch nt ▷ adj arabisch

arbitrary ['ɑːbɪtrərɪ] adj willkürlich

arcade [ɑː'keɪd] n Arkade f; (shopping arcade) Einkaufspassage f

arch [ɑːtʃ] n Bogen m

archaeologist, **archeologist** (US) [ɑːkɪ'ɒlədʒɪst] n Archäologe m, Archäologin f; **archaeology**, **archeology** (US) [ɑːkɪ'ɒlədʒɪ] n Archäologie f

archaic [ɑː'keɪɪk] adj veraltet

archbishop [ɑːtʃ'bɪʃəp] n Erzbischof m

archery ['ɑːtʃərɪ] n Bogenschießen nt

architect ['ɑːkɪtekt] n Architekt(in) m(f); **architecture** [ɑːkɪ'tektʃə] n Architektur f

archive(s) ['ɑːkaɪv(z)] n(pl) Archiv nt

archway ['ɑːtʃweɪ] n Torbogen m

Arctic ['ɑːktɪk] n Arktis f; **Arctic Circle** n nördlicher Polarkreis

are [ə, unstressed ɑː*] present of be

area ['ɛərɪə] n (region, district) Gebiet nt, Gegend f; (amount of space) Fläche f; (part of building etc) Bereich m, Zone f; (fig: field) Bereich m; **the London ~** der Londoner Raum; **area code** n (US) Vorwahl f

aren't [ɑːnt] contr of are not

Argentina [ɑːdʒən'tiːnə] n Argentinien nt

argue ['ɑːgjuː] vi streiten (about, over über +akk); **to ~ that ...** behaupten, dass ...; **to ~ for/against ...** sprechen für/gegen ...; **argument** n (reasons) Argument nt; (quarrel)

Streit m; **to have an ~** sich streiten

Aries ['ɛəriːz] nsing (Astr) Widder m

arise [ə'raɪz] (**arose, arisen**) vi sich ergeben, entstehen; (problem, question, wind) aufkommen

aristocracy [ærɪs'tɒkrəsɪ] n (class) Adel m; **aristocrat** ['ærɪstəkræt] n Adlige(r) mf; **aristocratic** [ærɪstə'krætɪk] adj aristokratisch, adlig

arm [ɑːm] n Arm m; (sleeve) Ärmel m; (of armchair) Armlehne f ▷ vt bewaffnen; **armchair** ['ɑːmtʃɛə*] n Lehnstuhl m

armed [ɑːmd] adj bewaffnet

armpit ['ɑːmpɪt] n Achselhöhle f

arms [ɑːmz] npl Waffen pl

army ['ɑːmɪ] n Armee f, Heer nt

A road ['eɪrəʊd] n (Brit) ≈ Bundesstraße f

aroma [ə'rəʊmə] n Duft m, Aroma nt; **aromatherapy** [ərəʊmə'θerəpɪ] n Aromatherapie f

arose [ə'rəʊz] pt of arise

around [ə'raʊnd] adv herum, umher; (present) hier (irgendwo); (approximately) ungefähr; (with time) gegen; **he's ~ somewhere** er ist hier irgendwo in der Nähe ▷ prep (surrounding) um ... (herum); (about in) in ... herum

arr. abbr = **arrival**, **arrives** Ank.

arrange [ə'reɪndʒ] vt (put in order) (an)ordnen; (alphabetically) ordnen; (artistically) arrangieren; (agree to: meeting etc) vereinbaren, festsetzen; (holidays) festlegen; (organize) planen; **to ~ that ...** es so einrichten, dass ...; **we ~d to meet at eight o'clock** wir haben uns für acht Uhr verabredet; **it's all ~d** es ist alles arrangiert; **arrangement** n (layout) Anordnung f; (agreement)

Vereinbarung f, Plan m; **make ~s** Vorbereitungen treffen

arrest [ə'rest] vt (person) verhaften ▷ n Verhaftung f; **under ~** verhaftet

arrival [ə'raɪvəl] n Ankunft f; **new ~** (person) Neuankömmling m; **arrivals** n (airport) Ankunftshalle f; **arrive** [ə'raɪv] vi ankommen (at bei, in +dat); **to ~ at a solution** eine Lösung finden

arrogant ['ærəgənt] adj arrogant

arrow ['ærəʊ] n Pfeil m

arse [ɑːs] n (vulg) Arsch m

art [ɑːt] n Kunst f, **the ~s** (pl) Geisteswissenschaften pl

artery ['ɑːtərɪ] n Schlagader f, Arterie f

art gallery n Kunstgalerie f, Kunstmuseum nt

arthritis [ɑː'θraɪtɪs] n Arthritis f

artichoke ['ɑːtɪtʃəʊk] n Artischocke f

article ['ɑːtɪkl] n Artikel m; (object) Gegenstand m

artificial [ɑːtɪ'fɪʃəl] adj künstlich, Kunst-; (smile etc) gekünstelt

artist ['ɑːtɪst] n Künstler(in) m(f); **artistic** [ɑː'tɪstɪk] adj künstlerisch

○ **KEYWORD**

as [æz, əz] conj 1 (referring to time) als; **as the years went by** mit den Jahren; **he came in as I was leaving** als er hereinkam, ging ich gerade; **as from tomorrow** ab morgen
2 (in comparisons) **as big as** so groß wie; **twice as big as** zweimal so groß wie; **as much/many as** so viel/so viele wie; **as soon as** sobald
3 (since, because) da; **he left early as he had to be home by 10** er

ging früher, da er um 10 zu Hause sein musste
4 (referring to manner, way) wie; **do as you wish** mach was du willst; **as she said** wie sie sagte
5 (concerning) **as for o to that** was das betrifft o angeht
6 **as if** o **though** als ob
▷ prep als; see also **long**; **he works as a driver** er arbeitet als Fahrer; see also **such**; **he gave it to me as a present** er hat es mir als Geschenk gegeben; see also **well**

asap [eɪeseɪ'piː, 'eɪsæp] acr = **as soon as possible** möglichst bald

ascertain [æsə'teɪn] vt feststellen

ash [æʃ] n (dust) Asche f; (tree) Esche f

ashamed [ə'ʃeɪmd] adj beschämt; **to be ~ (of sb/sth)** sich (für jdn/etw) schämen

ashore [ə'ʃɔː°] adv an Land

ashtray ['æʃtreɪ] n Aschenbecher m

Asia ['eɪʃə] n Asien nt; **Asian** adj asiatisch ▷ n Asiat(in) m(f)

aside [ə'saɪd] adv beiseite, zur Seite; **~ from** (esp US) außer

ask [ɑːsk] vt, vi fragen; (question) stellen; (request) bitten um; (invite) einladen; **to ~ sb the way** jdn nach dem Weg fragen; **to ~ sb to do sth** jdn darum bitten, etw zu tun; **ask for** vt bitten um

asleep [ə'sliːp] adj, adv: **to be ~** schlafen; **to fall ~** einschlafen

asparagus [əs'pærəgəs] n Spargel m

aspect ['æspekt] n Aspekt m

aspirin ['æsprɪn] n Aspirin® nt

ass [æs] n (a. fig) Esel m; (US vulg) Arsch m

assassinate [ə'sæsɪneɪt] vt ermorden; **assassination**

[ə'sæsɪneɪʃn] n Ermordung f;
~ attempt Attentat nt

assault [ə'sɔːlt] n Angriff m; (Jur)
Körperverletzung f ▷ vt
überfallen, herfallen über +akk

assemble [ə'sembl] vt (parts)
zusammensetzen; (people)
zusammenrufen ▷ vi sich
versammeln; **assembly**
[ə'semblɪ] n (of people)
Versammlung f; (putting together)
Zusammensetzen nt; **assembly
hall** n Aula f

assert [ə'sɜːt] vt behaupten;
assertion [ə'sɜːʃən] n Behauptung f

assess [ə'ses] vt einschätzen;
assessment n Einschätzung f

asset ['æset] n Vermögenswert
m; (fig) Vorteil m; **~s** pl Vermögen
nt

assign [ə'saɪn] vt zuweisen;
assignment n Aufgabe f;
(mission) Auftrag m

assist [ə'sɪst] vt helfen +dat;
assistance n Hilfe f; **assistant** n
Assistent(in) m(f), Mitarbeiter(in)
m(f); (in shop) Verkäufer(in) m(f);
assistant referee n (Sport)
Schiedsrichterassistent(in) m(f)

associate [ə'səʊʃɪeɪt] vt
verbinden (with mit); **association**
[əsəʊsɪ'eɪʃən] n (organization)
Verband m, Vereinigung f; **in
~ with ...** in Zusammenarbeit
mit ...

assorted [ə'sɔːtɪd] adj gemischt;
assortment n Auswahl f (of an
+dat); (of sweets) Mischung f

assume [ə'sjuːm] vt annehmen
(that ... dass ...); (role, responsibility)
übernehmen; **assumption**
[ə'sʌmpʃən] n Annahme f

assurance [ə'ʃʊərəns] n Versicherung f; (confidence) Zuversicht
f; **assure** [ə'ʃʊəʳ] vt (say
confidently) versichern +dat; **to**

~ sb of sth jdm etw zusichern; **to
be ~d of sth** einer Sache sicher
sein

asterisk ['æstərɪsk] n Sternchen
nt

asthma ['æsmə] n Asthma nt

astonish [əs'tɒnɪʃ] vt erstaunen;
astonished adj erstaunt (at
über); **astonishing** adj
erstaunlich; **astonishment** n
Erstaunen nt

astound [ə'staʊnd] vt sehr
erstaunen; **astounding** adj
erstaunlich

astray [ə'streɪ] adv: **to go ~**
(letter etc) verloren gehen;
(person) vom Weg abkommen; **to
lead ~** irreführen, verführen

astrology [əs'trɒlədʒɪ] n
Astrologie f

astronaut ['æstrənɔːt] n Astro-
naut(in) m(f)

astronomy [əs'trɒnəmɪ] n
Astronomie f

asylum [ə'saɪləm] n (home)
Anstalt f; (political asylum) Asyl nt;
asylum seeker n
Asylbewerber(in) m(f)

KEYWORD

at [æt] prep **1** (referring to position,
direction) an +dat; (with) in +dat; (with
place) in +dat; **at the top** an der
Spitze; **at home/school** zu Hause,
zuhause (österreichisch,
schweizerisch)/in der Schule; **at the
baker's** beim Bäcker; **to look at
sth** auf etw akk blicken; **to throw
sth at sb** etw nach jdm werfen
2 (referring to time) **at 4 o'clock** um
4 Uhr; **at night** bei Nacht; **at
Christmas** zu Weihnachten; **at
times** manchmal
3 (referring to rates, speed etc) **at £1 a
kilo** zu £1 pro Kilo; **two at a time**

zwei auf einmal; **at 50 km/h** mit 50 km/h
4 (referring to manner) **at a stroke** mit einem Schlag; **at peace** in Frieden
5 (referring to activity) **to be at work** bei der Arbeit sein; **to play at cowboys** Cowboy spielen; **to be good at sth** gut in etw dat sein
6 (referring to cause) **surprised/ annoyed at sth** überrascht/ verärgert über etw akk; **I went at his suggestion** ich ging auf seinen Vorschlag hin
7 (@ symbol) At-Zeichen nt

ate [et, eɪt] pt of **eat**
athlete ['æθliːt] n Athlet(in) m(f); (track and field) Leichtathlet(in) m(f); (sportsman) Sportler(in) m(f); **~'s foot** Fußpilz m; **athletic** [æθ'letɪk] adj sportlich; (build) athletisch; **athletics** npl Leichtathletik f
Atlantic [ət'læntɪk] n: **the ~ (Ocean)** der Atlantik
atlas ['ætləs] n Atlas m
ATM abbr = **automated teller machine** Geldautomat m
atmosphere ['ætməsfɪə°] n Atmosphäre f; (fig) Stimmung f
atom ['ætəm] n Atom nt; **atomic** [ə'tɒmɪk] adj Atom-; **~ energy** Atomenergie f; **~ power** Atomkraft f
A to Z® ['eɪtə'zed] n Stadtplan m (in Buchform)
atrocious [ə'trəʊʃəs] adj grauenhaft; **atrocity** [ə'trɒsɪtɪ] n Grausamkeit f; (deed) Gräueltat f
attach [ə'tætʃ] vt befestigen, anheften (to an +dat); **to ~ importance to sth** Wert auf etw akk legen; **to be ~ed to sb/sth** an jdm/etw hängen; **to ~ a file to an email** eine Datei an eine E-mail anhängen; **attachment** n

(affection) Zuneigung f; (Inform) Attachment nt, Anhang m, Anlage f
attack [ə'tæk] vt, vi angreifen ⊳ n Angriff m (on auf +akk); (Med) Anfall m
attempt [ə'tempt] n Versuch m; **to make an ~ to do sth** versuchen, etw zu tun ⊳ vt versuchen
attend [ə'tend] vt (go to) teilnehmen an +dat; (lectures, school) besuchen ⊳ vi (be present) anwesend sein; **attend to** vt sich kümmern um; (customer) bedienen; **attendance** n (presence) Anwesenheit f; (people present) Teilnehmerzahl f; **attendant** n (in car park etc) Wächter(in) m(f); (in museum) Aufseher(in) m(f)
attention [ə'tenʃən] n Aufmerksamkeit f; **(your) ~ please** Achtung!; **to pay ~ to sth** etw beachten; **to pay ~ to sb** jdm aufmerksam zuhören; (listen) jdm/etw aufmerksam zuhören; **for the ~ of ...** zu Händen von ...; **attentive** [ə'tentɪv] adj aufmerksam
attic ['ætɪk] n Dachboden m; (lived in) Mansarde f
attitude ['ætɪtjuːd] n (mental) Einstellung f (to, towards zu); (more general, physical) Haltung f
attorney [ə'tɜːnɪ] n (US: lawyer) Rechtsanwalt m, Rechtsanwältin f
attract [ə'trækt] vt anziehen; (attention) erregen; **to be ~ed to o by sb** sich zu jdm hingezogen fühlen; **attraction** [ə'trækʃən] n Anziehungskraft f; (thing) Attraktion f; **attractive** adj attraktiv; (thing, idea) reizvoll
aubergine ['əʊbəʒiːn] n Aubergine f
auction ['ɔːkʃən] n Versteigerung f, Auktion f ⊳ vt versteigern

audible [ˈɔːdɪbl] *adj* hörbar
audience [ˈɔːdɪəns] *n* Publikum *nt*; (*Radio*) Zuhörer *pl*; (*TV*) Zuschauer *pl*
audio [ˈɔːdɪəʊ] *adj* Ton-
audition [ɔːˈdɪʃən] *n* Probe *f* ▷ *vi* (*Theat*) vorspielen, vorsingen
auditorium [ɔːdɪˈtɔːrɪəm] *n* Zuschauerraum *m*
Aug *abbr* = **August**
August [ˈɔːgəst] *n* August *m*; *see also* **September**
aunt [ɑːnt] *n* Tante *f*
au pair [əʊˈpɛəʳ] *n* Aupairmädchen *nt*, Aupairjunge *m*
Australia [ɒˈstreɪlɪə] *n* Australien *nt*; **Australian** *adj* australisch ▷ *n* Australier(in) *m(f)*
Austria [ˈɒstrɪə] *n* Österreich *nt*; **Austrian** *adj* österreichisch ▷ *n* Österreicher(in) *m(f)*
authentic [ɔːˈθentɪk] *adj* echt; (*signature*) authentisch; **authenticity** [ɔːθenˈtɪsɪtɪ] *n* Echtheit *f*
author [ˈɔːθəʳ] *n* Autor(in) *m(f)*; (*of report etc*) Verfasser(in) *m(f)*
authority [ɔːˈθɒrɪtɪ] *n* (*power, expert*) Autorität *f*; **an ~ on sth** eine Autorität auf dem Gebiet einer Sache; **the authorities** (*pl*) die Behörden *pl*; **authorize** [ˈɔːθəraɪz] *vt* (*permit*) genehmigen; **to be ~d to do sth** offiziell berechtigt sein, etw zu tun
auto [ˈɔːtəʊ] (*pl* **-s**) *n* (*US*) Auto *nt*
autobiography [ɔːtəʊbaɪˈɒgrəfɪ] *n* Autobiographie *f*; **autograph** [ˈɔːtəgrɑːf] *n* Autogramm *nt*
automatic [ɔːtəˈmætɪk] *adj* automatisch; **~ gear change** (*Brit*), **~ gear shift** (*US*) Automatikschaltung *f* ▷ *n* (*car*) Automatikwagen *m*
automobile [ˈɔːtəməbiːl] *n* (*US*) Auto(mobil) *nt*; **autotrain**

[ˈɔːtəʊtreɪn] *n* (*US*) Autoreisezug *m*
autumn [ˈɔːtəm] *n* (*Brit*) Herbst *m*
auxiliary [ɔːgˈzɪlɪərɪ] *adj* Hilfs-; **~ verb** Hilfsverb *nt* ▷ *n* Hilfskraft *f*
availability [əveɪləˈbɪlɪtɪ] *n* (*of product*) Lieferbarkeit *f*; (*of resources*) Verfügbarkeit *f*; **available** *adj* erhältlich; (*existing*) vorhanden; (*product*) lieferbar; (*person*) erreichbar; **to be/make ~ to sb** jdm zur Verfügung stehen/stellen; **they're only ~ in black** es gibt sie nur in Schwarz, sie sind nur in Schwarz erhältlich
avalanche [ˈævəlɑːnʃ] *n* Lawine *f*
Ave *abbr* = **avenue**
avenue [ˈævənjuː] *n* Allee *f*
average [ˈævrɪdʒ] *n* Durchschnitt *m*; **on ~** im Durchschnitt ▷ *adj* durchschnittlich; **~ speed** Durchschnittsgeschwindigkeit *f*; **of ~ height** von mittlerer Größe
avian flu [ˈeɪvɪənˈfluː] *n* Vogelgrippe *f*
aviation [eɪvɪˈeɪʃən] *n* Luftfahrt *f*
avocado [ævəˈkɑːdəʊ] (*pl* **-s**) *n* Avocado *f*
avoid [əˈvɔɪd] *vt* vermeiden; **to ~ sb** jdm aus dem Weg gehen; **avoidable** *adj* vermeidbar
awake [əˈweɪk] (**awoke, awoken**) *vi* aufwachen ▷ *adj* wach
award [əˈwɔːd] *n* (*prize*) Preis *m*; (*for bravery etc*) Auszeichnung *f* ▷ *vt* zuerkennen (*to sb* jdm); (*present*) verleihen (*to sb* jdm)
aware [əˈwɛəʳ] *adj* bewusst; **to be ~ of sth** sich *dat* einer Sache *gen* bewusst sein; **I was not ~ that ...** es war mir nicht klar, dass ...
away [əˈweɪ] *adv* weg; **to look ~** wegsehen; **he's ~** er ist nicht da; (*on a trip*) er ist verreist; (*from school, work*) er fehlt; (*Sport*) **they**

are (playing) ~ sie spielen
auswärts; (*with distance*) **three
miles** ~ drei Meilen (von hier)
entfernt; **to work** ~ drauflos
arbeiten
awful ['ɔːfʊl] *adj* schrecklich,
furchtbar; **awfully** *adv* furchtbar
awkward ['ɔːkwəd] *adj* (*clumsy*)
ungeschickt; (*embarrassing*)
peinlich; (*difficult*) schwierig
awning ['ɔːnɪŋ] *n* Markise *f*
awoke [ə'wəʊk] *pt of* **awake**;
awoken [ə'wəʊkən] *pp of* **awake**
ax (*US*), **axe** [æks] *n* Axt *f*
axle ['æksl] *n* (*Tech*) Achse *f*

BA *abbr* = **Bachelor of Arts**
BSc *abbr* = **Bachelor of Science**
babe [beɪb] *n* (*fam*) Baby *nt*;
(*fam: affectionate*) Schatz *m*,
Kleine(r) *mf*
baby ['beɪbɪ] *n* Baby *nt*; (*of animal*)
Junge(s) *nt*; (*fam: affectionate*)
Schatz *m*, Kleine(r) *mf*; **to have a**
~ ein Kind bekommen; **it's your**
~ (*fam: responsibility*) das ist dein
Bier; **baby carriage** *n* (*US*)
Kinderwagen *m*; **baby food** *n*
Babynahrung *f*; **babyish** *adj*
kindisch; **baby shower** *n* (*US*)
Party für die werdende Mutter;
baby-sit *irr vi* babysitten;
baby-sitter *n* Babysitter(in) *m(f)*
bachelor ['bætʃələ°] *n* Junggeselle *m*; **Bachelor of
Arts/Science** *erster akademischer
Grad*, ≈ Magister/Diplom;
bachelorette *n* Junggesellin *f*;
bachelorette party *n* (*US*)

Junggesellinnenabschied; **bachelor party** *n* (US) *Junggesellenabschied*
back [bæk] *n* (of person, animal) Rücken *m;* (of house, coin etc) Rückseite *f;* (of chair) Rückenlehne *f;* (of car) Rücksitz *m;* (of train) Ende *nt;* (Sport: defender) Verteidiger(in) *m(f);* **at the ~ of ...**, (US) **in ~ of** (inside) hinten in ...; (outside) hinter ...; **~ to front** verkehrt herum ▷ *vt* (support) unterstützen; (car) rückwärtsfahren ▷ *vi* (go backwards) rückwärtsgehen *o* rückwärtsfahren ▷ *adj* Hinter-; **~ wheel** Hinterrad *nt* ▷ *adv* zurück; **they're ~** sie sind wieder da; **back away** *vi* sich zurückziehen; **back down** *vi* nachgeben; **back up** *vi* (car etc) zurücksetzen ▷ *vt* (support) unterstützen; (Inform) sichern; (car) zurückfahren
backache *n* Rückenschmerzen *pl;* **backbone** *n* Rückgrat *nt;* **backdate** *vt* zurückdatieren; **backdoor** *n* Hintertür *f;* **backfire** *vi* (plan) fehlschlagen; (Auto) fehlzünden; **background** *n* Hintergrund *m;* **backhand** *n* (Sport) Rückhand *f;* **backlog** *n* (of work) Rückstand *m;* **backpack** *n* (US) Rucksack *m;* **backpacker** *n* Rucksacktourist(in) *m(f);* **backpacking** *n* Rucksacktourismus *m;* **back seat** *n* Rücksitz *m;* **backside** *n* (fam) Po *m;* **back street** *n* Seitensträßchen *nt;* **backstroke** *n* Rückenschwimmen *nt;* **back-up** *n* (support) Unterstützung *f;* **~ (copy)** (Inform) Sicherungskopie *f;* **backward** *adj* (child) zurückgeblieben; (region) rückständig; **~ movement** Rückwärtsbewegung *f;* **backwards** *adv* rückwärts; **backyard** *n* Hinterhof *m*

bacon ['beɪkən] *n* Frühstücksspeck *m*
bacteria [bæk'tɪərɪə] *npl* Bakterien *pl*
bad [bæd] (**worse, worst**) *adj* schlecht, schlimm; (smell) übel; **I have a ~ back** mir tut der Rücken weh; **I'm ~ at maths/sport** ich bin schlecht in Mathe/Sport; **to go ~** schlecht werden, verderben
badge [bædʒ] *n* Abzeichen *nt*
badger ['bædʒə°] *n* Dachs *m*
badly ['bædlɪ] *adv* schlecht; **~ wounded** schwer verwundet; **to need sth ~** etw dringend brauchen; **bad-tempered** ['bæd'tempəd] *adj* schlecht gelaunt
bag [bæg] *n* (small) Tüte *f;* (larger) Beutel *m;* (handbag) Tasche *f;* **my ~s** (luggage) mein Gepäck
baggage ['bægɪdʒ] *n* Gepäck *nt;* **baggage allowance** *n* Freigepäck *nt;* **baggage (re)claim** *n* Gepäckrückgabe *f*
baggy ['bægɪ] *adj* (zu) weit; (trousers, suit) ausgebeult
bag lady ['bægleɪdɪ] *n* Stadtstreicherin *f*
bagpipes ['bægpaɪps] *npl* Dudelsack *m*
Bahamas [bə'hɑːməz] *npl:* **the ~** die Bahamas *pl*
bail [beɪl] *n* (money) Kaution *f*
bait [beɪt] *n* Köder *m*
bake [beɪk] *vt, vi* backen; **baked beans** *npl* weiße Bohnen in Tomatensoße; **baked potato** (pl **-es**) *n* in der Schale gebackene Kartoffel, Ofenkartoffel *f;* **baker** *n* Bäcker(in) *m(f);* **bakery** ['beɪkərɪ] *n* Bäckerei *f;* **baking powder** *n* Backpulver *nt*
balance ['bæləns] *n* (equilibrium) Gleichgewicht *nt* ▷ *vt* (make up for) ausgleichen; **balanced** *adj*

ausgeglichen; **balance sheet** n
Bilanz f
balcony ['bælkənɪ] n Balkon m
bald [bɔːld] adj kahl; **to be ~** eine
Glatze haben
Balkans ['bɔːlkənz] npl: **the ~**
der Balkan, die Balkanländer pl
ball [bɔːl] n Ball m; **to have a ~**
(fam) sich prima amüsieren
ballet ['bæleɪ] n Ballett nt; **ballet
dancer** n Balletttänzer(in) m(f)
balloon [bə'luːn] n (Luft)ballon
m
ballot ['bælət] n (geheime)
Abstimmung; **ballot box** n
Wahlurne f; **ballot paper** n
Stimmzettel m
ballpoint (pen) ['bɔːlpɔɪnt] n
Kugelschreiber m
ballroom ['bɔːlruːm] n Tanzsaal
m
Baltic ['bɔːltɪk] adj: **~ Sea** Ostsee
f; **the ~ States** die baltischen
Staaten
Baltics ['bɔːltɪks] n: **the ~** das
Baltikum nt
bamboo [bæm'buː] n Bambus m;
bamboo shoots npl
Bambussprossen pl
ban [bæn] n Verbot nt ▷ vt
verbieten
banana [bə'nɑːnə] n Banane f;
he's ~s er ist völlig durchgeknallt;
banana split n Bananensplit nt
band [bænd] n (group) Gruppe f;
(of criminals) Bande f; (Mus) Kapelle
f; (pop, rock etc) Band f; (strip) Band
nt
bandage ['bændɪdʒ] n Verband
m; (elastic) Bandage f ▷ vt
verbinden
B & B abbr = **bed and breakfast**
bang [bæŋ] n (noise) Knall m;
(blow) Schlag m ▷ vt, vi knallen;
(door) zuschlagen, zuknallen;
banger [bæŋə°] n (Brit fam:
firework) Knallkörper m; (sausage)

Würstchen nt; (fam: old car)
Klapperkiste f
bangs [bæŋz] npl (US: of hair)
Pony m
banish ['bænɪʃ] vt verbannen
banister(s) ['bænɪstə°] n (Treppen)geländer nt
bank [bæŋk] n (Fin) Bank f; (of
river etc) Ufer nt; **bank account** n
Bankkonto nt; **bank balance** n
Kontostand m; **bank card** n
Bankkarte f; **bank code** n
Bankleitzahl f; **bank holiday** n
gesetzlicher Feiertag

● **BANK HOLIDAY**
●
● Als **bank holiday** wird in
● Großbritannien ein gesetzlicher
● Feiertag bezeichnet, an dem die
● Banken geschlossen sind. Die
● meisten dieser Feiertage,
● abgesehen von Weihnachten
● und Ostern, fallen auf Montage
● im Mai und August. An diesen
● langen Wochenenden (bank
● holiday weekends) fahren viele
● Briten in Urlaub, sodass dann
● auf den Straßen, Flughäfen und
● bei der Bahn sehr viel Betrieb
● ist.

---

bank manager n Filialleiter(in)
m(f); **banknote** n Banknote f
bankrupt vt ruinieren; **to go
~** Pleite gehen
bank statement n
Kontoauszug m
baptism ['bæptɪzəm] n Taufe f;
baptize ['bæptaɪz] vt taufen
bar [bɑː°] n (for drinks) Bar f; (less
smart) Lokal nt; (rod) Stange f; (of
chocolate etc) Riegel m, Tafel f; (of
soap) Stück nt; (counter) Theke f
▷ prep außer; **~ none** ohne
Ausnahme
barbecue ['bɑːbɪkjuː] n (device)

Grill *m*; (*party*) Barbecue *nt*, Grillfete *f*; **to have a ~** grillen

barbed wire ['bɑːbd'waɪə*] *n* Stacheldraht *m*

barber ['bɑːbə*] *n* (Herren)friseur *m*

bar code ['bɑːkəʊd] *n* Strichkode *m*

bare [beə*] *adj* nackt; **~ patch** kahle Stelle; **barefoot** *adj, adv* barfuß; **bareheaded** *adj, adv* ohne Kopfbedeckung; **barely** *adv* kaum; (*with age*) knapp

bargain ['bɑːgɪn] *n* (*cheap offer*) günstiges Angebot, Schnäppchen *nt*; (*transaction*) Geschäft *nt*; **what a ~** das ist aber günstig! ▷ *vi* (ver)handeln

barge [bɑːdʒ] *n* (*for freight*) Lastkahn *m*; (*unpowered*) Schleppkahn *m*

bark [bɑːk] *n* (*of tree*) Rinde *f*; (*of dog*) Bellen *nt* ▷ *vi* (*dog*) bellen

barley ['bɑːlɪ] *n* Gerste *f*

barmaid ['bɑːmeɪd] *n* Barkeeperin *f*; **barman** ['bɑːmən] (*pl* **-men**) *n* Barkeeper *m*

barn [bɑːn] *n* Scheune *f*

barometer [bə'rɒmɪtə*] *n* Barometer *nt*

baroque [bə'rɒk] *adj* barock, Barock-

barracks ['bærəks] *npl* Kaserne *f*

barrel ['bærəl] *n* Fass *nt*; **barrel organ** *n* Drehorgel *f*

barricade [bærɪ'keɪd] *n* Barrikade *f*

barrier ['bærɪə*] *n* (*obstruction*) Absperrung *f*, Barriere *f*; (*across road etc*) Schranke *f*

barrow ['bærəʊ] *n* (*cart*) Schubkarren *m*

bartender ['bɑːtendə*] *n* (*US*) Barkeeper(in) *m(f)*

base [beɪs] *n* Basis *f*; (*of lamp, pillar etc*) Fuß *m*; (*Mil*) Stützpunkt *m* ▷ *vt* gründen (*on* auf +*akk*); **to be ~d on sth** auf etw *dat* basieren; **baseball** *n* Baseball *m*; **baseball cap** *n* Baseballmütze *f*; **basement** *n* Kellergeschoss *nt*

bash [bæʃ] (*fam*) *n* Schlag *m*; (*fam*) Party *f* ▷ *vt* hauen

basic ['beɪsɪk] *adj* einfach; (*fundamental*) Grund-; (*importance, difference*) grundlegend; (*in principle*) grundsätzlich; **the accomodation is very ~** die Unterkunft ist sehr bescheiden; **basically** *adv* im Grunde; **basics** *npl*: **the ~** das Wesentliche

basil ['bæzl] *n* Basilikum *nt*

basin ['beɪsn] *n* (*for washing, valley*) (Wasch)becken *nt*

basis ['beɪsɪs] *n* Basis *f*; **on the ~ of** aufgrund +*gen*; **on a monthly ~** monatlich

basket ['bɑːskɪt] *n* Korb *m*; **basketball** *n* Basketball *m*

Basque [bæsk] *n* (*person*) Baske *m*, Baskin *f*; (*language*) Baskisch *nt* ▷ *adj* baskisch

bass [beɪs] *n* (*Mus*) Bass *m*; (*Zool*) Barsch *m* ▷ *adj* (*Mus*) Bass-

bastard ['bɑːstəd] *n* (*vulg: awful person*) Arschloch *nt*

bat [bæt] *n* (*Zool*) Fledermaus *f*; (*Sport: cricket, baseball*) Schlagholz *nt*; (*table tennis*) Schläger *m*

batch [bætʃ] *n* Schwung *m*; (*fam: of letters, books etc*) Stoß *m*

bath [bɑːθ] *n* Bad *nt*; (*tub*) Badewanne *f*; **to have a ~** baden ▷ *vt* (*child etc*) baden

bathe [beɪð] *vt, vi* (*wound etc*) baden; **bath foam** ['bɑːθfəʊm] *n* Badeschaum *m*; **bathing cap** *n* Badekappe *f*; **bathing costume**, **bathing suit** (*US*) *n* Badeanzug *m*

bathmat ['bɑːθmæt] *n* Badevorleger *m*; **bathrobe** *n* Bademantel *m*; **bathroom** *n* Bad(ezimmer) *nt*; **baths** [bɑːðz] *npl* (Schwimm)bad

nt; **bath towel** n Badetuch nt;
bathtub n Badewanne f
baton ['bætən] n (Mus) Taktstock
m; (police) Schlagstock m
batter ['bætə*] n Teig m ▷ vt
heftig schlagen; **battered** adj
übel zugerichtet; (hat, car)
verbeult; (wife, baby) misshandelt
battery ['bætərɪ] n (Elec) Batterie
f; **battery charger** n Ladegerät nt
battle ['bætl] n Schlacht f; (fig)
Kampf m (for um +akk); **battlefield**
n Schlachtfeld nt; **battlements**
npl Zinnen pl
Bavaria [bə'veərɪə] n Bayern nt;
Bavarian adj bay(e)risch ▷ n
Bayer(in) m(f)
bay [beɪ] n (of sea) Bucht f; (on
house) Erker m; (tree) Lorbeerbaum
m; **bay leaf** n Lorbeerblatt nt; **bay
window** n Erkerfenster nt
BBC abbr = **British Broadcasting
Corporation** BBC f
BC abbr = **before Christ** vor Christi
Geburt, v. Chr.

 KEYWORD

be [bi:] (pt **was**, **were**, pp **been**) vb
aux **1** (with present participle: forming
continuous tenses): **what are you
doing?** was machst du (gerade)?;
it is raining es regnet; **I've been
waiting for you for hours** ich
warte schon seit Stunden auf dich
2 (with pp: forming passives): **to be
killed** getötet werden; **the thief
was nowhere to be seen** der Dieb
war nirgendwo zu sehen
3 (in tag questions) **it was fun,
wasn't it?** es hat Spaß gemacht,
nicht wahr?
4 (+to +infin) **the house is to be
sold** das Haus soll verkauft
werden; **he's not to open it** er darf
es nicht öffnen
▷ vb +complement **1** (usu) sein; **I'm

tired** ich bin müde; **I'm hot/cold**
mir ist heiß/kalt; **he's a doctor** er
ist Arzt; **2 and 2 are 4** 2 und 2 ist o
sind 4; **she's tall/pretty** sie ist
groß/hübsch; **be careful/quiet**
sei vorsichtig/ruhig
2 (of health) **how are you?** wie geht
es dir?; **he's very ill** er ist sehr
krank; **I'm fine now** jetzt geht es
mir gut
3 (of age) **how old are you?** wie alt
bist du?; **I'm sixteen (years old)**
ich bin sechzehn (Jahre alt)
4 (cost) **how much was the meal?**
was o wie viel hat das Essen
gekostet?; **that'll be £5.75, please**
das macht £5.75, bitte
▷ vi **1** (exist, occur etc) sein; **is there
a God?** gibt es einen Gott?; **be
that as it may** wie dem auch sei;
so be it also gut
2 (referring to place) sein; **I won't be
here tomorrow** ich werde morgen
nicht hier sein
3 (referring to movement) **where
have you been?** wo bist du
gewesen?; **I've been in the
garden** ich war im Garten
▷ impers vb **1** (referring to time,
distance, weather) sein; **it's 5
o'clock** es ist 5 Uhr; **it's 10 km to
the village** es sind 10 km bis zum
Dorf; **it's too hot/cold** es ist zu
heiß/kalt
2 (emphatic) **it's me** ich bin's; **it's
the postman** es ist der Briefträger

beach [bi:tʃ] n Strand m;
beachwear n Strandkleidung f
bead [bi:d] n (of glass, wood etc)
Perle f; (drop) Tropfen m
beak [bi:k] n Schnabel m
beam [bi:m] n (of wood etc) Balken
m; (of light) Strahl m ▷ vi (smile etc)
strahlen
bean [bi:n] n Bohne f; **bean curd**
n Tofu m

bear [bɛə*] (**bore, borne**) vt
(*carry*) tragen; (*tolerate*) ertragen
▷ n Bär m; **bearable** adj
erträglich
beard [bɪəd] n Bart m
beast [biːst] n Tier nt; (*brutal
person*) Bestie f; (*disliked person*)
Biest nt
beat [biːt] (**beat, beaten**) vt
schlagen; (*as punishment*) prügeln;
to ~ sb at tennis jdn im Tennis
schlagen ▷ n (*of heart, drum etc*)
Schlag m; (*Mus*) Takt m; (*type of
music*) Beat m; **beat up** vt
zusammenschlagen
beaten ['biːtn] pp of **beat**; **off the
~ track** abgelegen
beautiful ['bjuːtɪfʊl] adj schön;
(*splendid*) herrlich; **beauty** ['bjuːtɪ]
n Schönheit f; **beauty spot** n
(*place*) lohnendes Ausflugsziel
beaver ['biːvə*] n Biber m
became [bɪ'keɪm] pt of **become**
because [bɪ'kɒz] adv, conj weil
▷ prep: **~ of** wegen +gen o dat
become [bɪ'kʌm] (**became,
become**) vt werden; **what's ~ of
him?** was ist aus ihm geworden?
bed [bɛd] n Bett nt; (*in garden*)
Beet nt; **bed and breakfast** n
Übernachtung f mit Frühstück;
bedclothes npl Bettwäsche f;
bedding n Bettzeug nt; **bed linen**
n Bettwäsche f; **bedroom** n
Schlafzimmer nt; **bed-sit(ter)** n
(*fam*) möblierte
Einzimmerwohnung; **bedspread**
n Tagesdecke f; **bedtime** n
Schlafenszeit f
bee [biː] n Biene f
beech [biːtʃ] n Buche f
beef [biːf] n Rindfleisch nt;
beefburger n Hamburger m; **beef
tomato** (*pl* **-es**) n Fleischtomate
f
beehive ['biːhaɪv] n Bienenstock
m

been [biːn] pp of **be**
beer [bɪə*] n Bier nt; **beer garden**
n Biergarten m
beetle ['biːtl] n Käfer m
beetroot ['biːtruːt] n Rote Bete
before [bɪ'fɔː*] prep vor; **the year
~ last** vorletztes Jahr; **the day
~ yesterday** vorgestern ▷ conj
bevor ▷ adv (*of time*) vorher; **have
you been there ~?** waren
Sie/warst du schon einmal dort?;
beforehand adv vorher
beg [bɛg] vt: **to ~ sb to do sth** jdn
inständig bitten, etw zu tun ▷ vi
(*beggar*) betteln (*for* um +akk)
began [bɪ'gæn] pt of **begin**
beggar ['bɛgə*] n Bettler(in) m(f)
begin [bɪ'gɪn] (**began, begun**) vt,
vi anfangen, beginnen; **to ~ to do
sth** anfangen, etw zu tun;
beginner n Anfänger(in) m(f);
beginning n Anfang m
begun [bɪ'gʌn] pp of **begin**
behalf [bɪ'hɑːf] n: **on ~ of, in ~ of**
(*US*) im Namen/Auftrag von; **on
my ~** für mich
behave [bɪ'heɪv] vi sich
benehmen; **~ yourself!** benimm
dich!; **behavior** (*US*), **behaviour**
[bɪ'heɪvjə*] n Benehmen nt
behind [bɪ'haɪnd] prep hinter;
to be ~ time Verspätung haben
▷ adv hinten; **to be ~ with one's
work** mit seiner Arbeit im
Rückstand sein ▷ n (*fam*)
Hinterteil nt
beige [beɪʒ] adj beige
being ['biːɪŋ] n (*existence*) Dasein
nt; (*person*) Wesen nt
Belarus [bɛlə'rʊs] n Weißruss-
land nt
belch [bɛltʃ] n Rülpser m ▷ vi
rülpsen
belfry ['bɛlfrɪ] n Glockenturm m
Belgian ['bɛldʒən] adj belgisch
▷ n Belgier(in) m(f); **Belgium**
['bɛldʒəm] n Belgien nt

belief [bɪ'liːf] n Glaube m (in an +akk); (conviction) Überzeugung f; **it's my ~ that ...** ich bin der Überzeugung, dass ...; **believe** [bɪ'liːv] vt glauben; **believe in** vi glauben an +akk; **believer** n (Rel) Gläubige(r) mf

bell [bel] n (church) Glocke f; (bicycle, door) Klingel f; **bellboy** ['belbɔɪ] n (esp US) Page m

bellows ['beləʊz] npl (for fire) Blasebalg m

belly ['belɪ] n Bauch m; **bellyache** n Bauchweh nt ▷ vi (fam) meckern; **belly button** n (fam) Bauchnabel m; **bellyflop** n (fam) Bauchklatscher m

belong [bɪ'lɒŋ] vi gehören (to sb jdm); (to club) angehören +dat; **belongings** npl Habe f

below [bɪ'ləʊ] prep unter ▷ adv unten

belt [belt] n (round waist) Gürtel m; (safety belt) Gurt m; **below the ~** unter der Gürtellinie ▷ vi (fam: go fast) rasen, düsen; **beltway** n (US) Umgehungsstraße f

bench [bentʃ] n Bank f

bend [bend] n Biegung f; (in road) Kurve f ▷ vt (**bent, bent**) (curve) biegen; (head, arm) beugen ▷ vi sich biegen; (person) sich beugen; **bend down** vi sich bücken

beneath [bɪ'niːθ] prep unter ▷ adv darunter

beneficial [benɪ'fɪʃl] adj gut, nützlich (to für); **benefit** ['benɪfɪt] n (advantage) Vorteil m; (profit) Nutzen m; **for your/his ~** deinetwegen/seinetwegen; **unemployment ~** Arbeitslosengeld nt ▷ vt guttun +dat ▷ vi Nutzen ziehen (from aus)

benign [bɪ'naɪn] adj (person) gütig; (climate) mild; (Med) gutartig

bent [bent] pt, pp of **bend** ▷ adj krumm; (fam) korrupt

beret ['bereɪ] n Baskenmütze f

Bermuda [bə'mjuːdə] n **the ~s** pl die Bermudas pl ▷ adj **~ shorts** pl Bermudashorts pl; **the ~ triangle** das Bermudadreieck

berry ['berɪ] n Beere f

berth [bɜːθ] n (for ship) Ankerplatz m; (in ship) Koje f; (in train) Bett nt ▷ vt am Kai festmachen ▷ vi anlegen

beside [bɪ'saɪd] prep neben; **~ the sea/lake** am Meer/See; **besides** [bɪ'saɪdz] prep außer ▷ adv außerdem

besiege [bɪ'siːdʒ] vt belagern

best [best] adj beste(r, s); **my ~ friend** mein bester Freund; **the ~ thing (to do) would be to ...** das Beste wäre zu ...; (on food packaging) **~ before ...** mindestens haltbar bis ... ▷ n der/die/das Beste; **all the ~** alles Gute; **to make the ~ of it** das Beste daraus machen ▷ adv am besten; **I like this ~** das mag ich am liebsten; **best-before date** n Mindesthaltbarkeitsdatum nt; **best man** ['best'mæn] (pl **men**) n Trauzeuge m; **bestseller** ['bestselə*] n Bestseller m

bet [bet] (**bet, bet**) vt, vi wetten (on auf +akk); **I ~ him £5 that ...** ich habe mit ihm um 5 Pfund gewettet, dass ...; **you ~** (fam) und ob!; **I ~ he'll be late** er kommt mit Sicherheit zu spät ▷ n Wette f

betray [bɪ'treɪ] vt verraten; **betrayal** n Verrat m

better ['betə*] adj, adv besser; **to get ~** (healthwise) sich erholen, wieder gesund werden; (improve) sich verbessern; **I'm much ~ today** es geht mir heute viel besser; **you'd ~ go** du solltest/Sie sollten lieber gehen; **a change for the ~** eine Wendung zum Guten

betting [ˈbetɪŋ] n Wetten nt; **betting shop** n Wettbüro nt

between [bɪˈtwiːn] prep zwischen; (among) unter; **~ you and me, ...** unter uns gesagt, ...
▷ adv: (in) ~ dazwischen

beverage [ˈbevərɪdʒ] n (formal) Getränk nt

beware [bɪˈweə*] vt: **to ~ of sth** sich vor etw +dat hüten; **"~ of the dog"** „Vorsicht, bissiger Hund!"

bewildered [bɪˈwɪldəd] adj verwirrt

beyond [bɪˈjɒnd] prep (place) jenseits +gen; (time) über ... hinaus; (out of reach) außerhalb +gen; **it's ~ me** da habe ich keine Ahnung, da bin ich überfragt
▷ adv darüber hinaus

bias [ˈbaɪəs] n (prejudice) Vorurteil nt, Voreingenommenheit f

bias(s)ed adj voreingenommen

bib [bɪb] n Latz m

Bible [ˈbaɪbl] n Bibel f

bicycle [ˈbaɪsɪkl] n Fahrrad nt

bid [bɪd] (bid, bid) vt (offer) bieten
▷ n (attempt) Versuch m; (offer) Gebot nt

big [bɪɡ] adj groß; **it's no ~ deal** (fam) es ist nichts Besonderes; **big dipper** n (Brit) Achterbahn f; **big-headed** [bɪɡˈhedɪd] adj eingebildet

bike [baɪk] n (fam) Rad nt

bikini [bɪˈkiːnɪ] n Bikini m

bilberry [ˈbɪlbərɪ] n Heidelbeere f

bilingual [baɪˈlɪŋɡwəl] adj zweisprachig

bill [bɪl] n (account) Rechnung f; (US: banknote) Banknote f; (Pol) Gesetzentwurf m; (Zool) Schnabel m; **billfold** [ˈbɪlfəʊld] n (US) Brieftasche f

billiards [ˈbɪlɪədz] nsing Billard nt; **billiard table** Billardtisch m

billion [ˈbɪlɪən] n Milliarde f

bin [bɪn] n Behälter m; (rubbish bin) (Müll)eimer m; (for paper) Papierkorb m

bind [baɪnd] (**bound, bound**) vt binden; (bind together) zusammenbinden; (wound) verbinden; **binding** n (ski) Bindung f; (book) Einband m

binge [bɪndʒ] n (fam: drinking) Sauferei f; **to go on a ~** auf Sauftour gehen

bingo [ˈbɪŋɡəʊ] n Bingo nt

binoculars [bɪˈnɒkjʊləz] npl Fernglas nt

biodegradable [ˌbaɪəʊdɪˈɡreɪdəbl] adj biologisch abbaubar

biography [baɪˈɒɡrəfɪ] n Biografie f

biological [baɪəˈlɒdʒɪkəl] adj biologisch; **biology** [baɪˈɒlədʒɪ] n Biologie f

birch [bɜːtʃ] n Birke f

bird [bɜːd] n Vogel m; (Brit fam: girl, girlfriend) Tussi f; **bird flu** n Vogelgrippe f; **bird watcher** n Vogelbeobachter(in) m(f)

birth [bɜːθ] n Geburt f; **birth certificate** n Geburtsurkunde f; **birth control** n Geburtenkontrolle f; **birthday** n Geburtstag m; **happy ~** herzlichen Glückwunsch zum Geburtstag; **birthday card** n Geburtstagskarte f; **birthday party** n Geburtstagsfeier f; **birthplace** n Geburtsort m

biscuit [ˈbɪskɪt] n (Brit) Keks m

bisexual [baɪˈseksjʊəl] adj bisexuell

bishop [ˈbɪʃəp] n Bischof m; (in chess) Läufer m

bit [bɪt] pt of **bite** ▷ n (piece) Stück(chen) nt; (Inform) Bit nt; **a ~ (of ...)** (small amount) ein bisschen ...; **a ~ tired** etwas müde;

~ by ~ allmählich; (*time*) **for a ~** ein Weilchen; **quite a ~** (*a lot*) ganz schön viel

bitch [bɪtʃ] n (*dog*) Hündin f; (*pej: woman*) Miststück nt, Schlampe f; **son of a ~** (*US: vulg*) Hurensohn m, Scheißkerl m; **bitchy** adj gemein, zickig

bite [baɪt] (**bit, bitten**) vt, vi beißen ▷ n Biss m; (*mouthful*) Bissen m; (*insect*) Stich m; **to have a ~** eine Kleinigkeit essen; **bitten** pp of **bite**

bitter ['bɪtə°] adj bitter; (*memory etc*) schmerzlich ▷ n (*Brit: beer*) halbdunkles Bier; **bitter lemon** n Bitter Lemon nt

bizarre [bɪ'zɑː°] adj bizarr

black [blæk] adj schwarz; **blackberry** n Brombeere f; **blackbird** n Amsel f; **blackboard** n (*Wand*)tafel f; **black box** n (*Aviat*) Flugschreiber m; **blackcurrant** n Schwarze Johannisbeere; **black eye** n blaues Auge; **Black Forest** n Schwarzwald m; **Black Forest gateau** n Schwarzwälder Kirschtorte f; **blackmail** n Erpressung f ▷ vt erpressen; **black market** n Schwarzmarkt m; **blackout** n (*Med*) Ohnmacht f; **to have a ~** ohnmächtig werden; **black pudding** n ≈ Blutwurst f; **Black Sea** n: **the ~** das Schwarze Meer; **blacksmith** n Schmied(in) m(f); **black tie** n Abendanzug m, Smoking m; **is it ~?** ist/besteht da Smokingzwang?

bladder ['blædə°] n Blase f

blade [bleɪd] n (*of knife*) Klinge f; (*of propeller*) Blatt nt; (*of grass*) Halm m

blame [bleɪm] n Schuld f ▷ vt: **to ~ sth on sb** jdm die Schuld an etw dat geben; **he is to ~** er ist daran schuld

bland [blænd] adj (*taste*) fade; (*comment*) nichtssagend

blank [blæŋk] adj (*page, space*) leer, unbeschrieben; (*look*) ausdruckslos; **~ cheque** Blankoscheck m

blanket ['blæŋkɪt] n (*Woll*)decke f

blast [blɑːst] n (*of wind*) Windstoß m; (*of explosion*) Druckwelle f ▷ vt (*blow up*) sprengen; **~!** (*fam*) Mist!, verdammt!

blatant ['bleɪtənt] adj (*undisguised*) offen; (*obvious*) offensichtlich

blaze [bleɪz] vi lodern; (*sun*) brennen ▷ n (*building*) Brand m; (*other fire*) Feuer nt; **a ~ of colour** eine Farbenpracht

blazer ['bleɪzə°] n Blazer m

bleach [bliːtʃ] n Bleichmittel nt ▷ vt bleichen

bleak [bliːk] adj öde, düster; (*future*) trostlos

bleary ['blɪərɪ] adj (*eyes*) trübe, verschlafen

bleed [bliːd] (**bled, bled**) vi bluten

blend [blend] n Mischung f ▷ vt mischen ▷ vi sich mischen; **blender** n Mixer m

bless [bles] vt segnen; **~ you!** Gesundheit!; **blessing** n Segen m

blew [bluː] pt of **blow**

blind [blaɪnd] adj blind; (*corner*) unübersichtlich; **to turn a ~ eye to sth** bei etw ein Auge zudrücken ▷ n (*for window*) Rollo nt ▷ vt blenden; **blind alley** n Sackgasse f; **blind spot** n (*Auto*) toter Winkel; (*fig*) schwacher Punkt

blink [blɪŋk] vi blinzeln; (*light*) blinken

bliss [blɪs] n (*Glück*)seligkeit f

blister ['blɪstə°] n Blase f

blizzard ['blɪzəd] n Schneesturm m

bloated ['bləʊtɪd] adj aufgedunsen

block [blɒk] n (of wood, stone, ice) Block m, Klotz m; (of buildings) Häuserblock m; **~ of flats** (Brit) Wohnblock m ▷ vt (road etc) blockieren; (pipe, nose) verstopfen; **blockage** ['blɒkɪdʒ] n Verstopfung f; **blockbuster** ['blɒkbʌstə*] n Knüller m; **block letters** npl Blockschrift f

blog [blɒg] n (Inform) Blog m, Weblog m ▷ vi bloggen

bloke [bləʊk] n (Brit fam) Kerl m, Typ m

blond(e) [blɒnd] adj blond ▷ n (person) Blondine f, blonder Typ

blood [blʌd] n Blut nt; **blood count** n Blutbild nt; **blood donor** n Blutspender(in) m(f); **blood group** n Blutgruppe f; **blood orange** n Blutorange f; **blood poisoning** n Blutvergiftung f; **blood pressure** n Blutdruck m; **blood sample** n Blutprobe f; **bloodsports** npl Sportarten, bei denen Tiere getötet werden; **bloodthirsty** adj blutrünstig; **bloody** adj (Brit fam) verdammt, Scheiß-; (literal sense) blutig

bloom [bluːm] n Blüte f ▷ vi blühen

blossom ['blɒsəm] n Blüte f ▷ vi blühen

blot ['blɒt] n (of ink) Klecks m; (fig) Fleck m

blouse [blaʊz] n Bluse f; **big girl's ~** (fam) Schwächling m

blow [bləʊ] n Schlag m ▷ vi, vt (**blew, blown**) (wind) wehen, blasen; (person: trumpet etc) blasen; **to ~ one's nose** sich dat die Nase putzen; **blow out** vt (candle etc) ausblasen; **blow up** vi explodieren ▷ vt sprengen;

(balloon, tyre) aufblasen; (Foto: enlarge) vergrößern; **blow-dry** vt föhnen; **blowjob** n (fam) **to give sb a ~** jdm einen blasen; **blown** [bləʊn] pp of **blow**; **blow-out** n (Auto) geplatzter Reifen

BLT n abbr = **bacon, lettuce and tomato sandwich** mit Frühstücksspeck, Kopfsalat und Tomaten belegtes Sandwich

blue [bluː] adj blau; (fam: unhappy) trübsinnig, niedergeschlagen; (film) pornografisch; (joke) anzüglich; (language) derb; **bluebell** n Glockenblume f; **blueberry** n Blaubeere f; **blue cheese** n Blauschimmelkäse m; **blues** npl: **the ~** (Mus) der Blues; **to have the ~** (fam) niedergeschlagen sein

blunder ['blʌndə*] n Schnitzer m

blunt [blʌnt] adj (knife) stumpf; (fig) unverblümt; **bluntly** adv geradeheraus

blurred [blɜːd] adj verschwommen, unklar

blush [blʌʃ] vi erröten

board [bɔːd] n (of wood) Brett nt; (committee) Ausschuss m; (of firm) Vorstand m; **~ and lodging** Unterkunft und Verpflegung; **on ~** an Bord ▷ vt (train, bus) einsteigen in +akk; (ship) an Bord +gen gehen; **boarder** n Pensionsgast m; (school) Internatsschüler(in) m(f); **board game** n Brettspiel nt; **boarding card, boarding pass** n Bordkarte f, Einsteigekarte f; **boarding school** n Internat nt; **board meeting** n Vorstandssitzung f; **boardroom** n Sitzungssaal m (des Vorstands)

boast [bəʊst] vi prahlen (about mit) ▷ n Prahlerei f

boat [bəʊt] n Boot nt; (ship) Schiff nt; **boatman** n (hirer)

Bootsverleiher m; **boat race** n
Regatta f; **boat train** n Zug m mit
Schiffsanschluss
bob(sleigh) ['bɒbsleɪ] n Bob m
bodily ['bɒdɪlɪ] adj körperlich
▷ adv (forcibly) gewaltsam; **body**
['bɒdɪ] n Körper m; (dead) Leiche f;
(of car) Karosserie f; **bodybuilding**
n Bodybuilding nt; **bodyguard** n
Leibwächter m; (group) Leibwache
f; **body jewellery** n
Intimschmuck m; **body odour** n
Körpergeruch m; **body piercing** n
Piercing nt; **bodywork** n
Karosserie f
boil [bɔɪl] vt, vi kochen ▷ n (Med)
Geschwür nt; **boiler** n Boiler m;
boiling adj (water etc) kochend
(heiß); **I was ~** (hot) mir war
fürchterlich heiß; (with rage) ich
kochte vor Wut; **boiling point** n
Siedepunkt m
bold [bəʊld] adj kühn, mutig;
(colours) kräftig; (type) fett
Bolivia [bə'lɪvɪə] n Bolivien nt
bolt [bəʊlt] n (lock) Riegel m;
(screw) Bolzen m ▷ vt verriegeln
bomb [bɒm] n Bombe f ▷ vt
bombardieren
bond [bɒnd] n (link) Bindung f;
(Fin) Obligation f
bone [bəʊn] n Knochen m; (of
fish) Gräte f; **boner** n (US fam)
Schnitzer m; (vulg: erection) Ständer
m
bonfire ['bɒnfaɪə°] n Feuer nt
(im Freien)
bonnet ['bɒnɪt] n (Brit Auto)
Haube f; (for baby) Häubchen nt
bonny ['bɒnɪ] adj (esp Scottish)
hübsch
bonus ['bəʊnəs] n Bonus m,
Prämie f
boo [buː] vt auspfeifen,
ausbuhen ▷ vi buhen ▷ n Buhruf
m
book [bʊk] n Buch nt; (of tickets,

stamps) Heft nt ▷ vt (ticket etc)
bestellen; (hotel, flight etc) buchen;
(Sport) verwarnen; **fully ~ed** (up)
ausgebucht; (performance)
ausverkauft; **book in** vt
eintragen; **to be ~ed in at a hotel**
ein Zimmer in einem Hotel
bestellt haben; **bookcase** n
Bücherregal nt; **booking** n
Buchung f; **booking office** n
(Rail) Fahrkartenschalter m; (Theat)
Vorverkaufsstelle f; **book-keeping**
n Buchhaltung f; **booklet** n
Broschüre f; **bookmark** n (a.
Inform) Lesezeichen nt; **bookshelf**
n Bücherbord nt; **bookshelves**
Bücherregal nt; **bookshop**,
bookstore n (esp US)
Buchhandlung f
boom [buːm] n (of business)
Boom m; (noise) Dröhnen nt ▷ vi
(business) boomen; (fam) florieren;
(voice etc) dröhnen
boomerang ['buːməræŋ] n
Bumerang m
boost [buːst] n Auftrieb m ▷ vt
(production, sales) ankurbeln;
(power, profits etc) steigern;
booster (injection) n
Wiederholungsimpfung f
boot [buːt] n Stiefel m; (Brit Auto)
Kofferraum m ▷ vt (Inform) laden,
booten
booth [buːð] n (at fair etc) Bude f;
(at trade fair etc) Stand m
booze [buːz] n (fam) Alkohol m
▷ vi (fam) saufen
border ['bɔːdə°] n Grenze f; (edge)
Rand m; **north/south of the
Border** in Schottland/England;
borderline n Grenze f
bore [bɔː°] pt of **bear** ▷ vt (hole
etc) bohren; (person) langweilen
▷ n (person) Langweiler(in) m(f),
langweiliger Mensch; (thing)
langweilige Sache; **bored** adj: **to
be ~** sich langweilen; **boredom** n

Langeweile f; **boring** adj
langweilig
born [bɔːn] adj: **he was ~ in
London** er ist in London geboren
borne [bɔːn] pp of **bear**
borough ['bʌrə] n Stadtbezirk m
borrow ['bɒrəʊ] vt borgen
Bosnia-Herzegovina
['bɒznɪəhɜːtsəgəʊ'viːnə] n
Bosnien-Herzegowina nt; **Bosnian**
['bɒznɪən] adj bosnisch ▷ n
Bosnier(in) m(f)
boss [bɒs] n Chef(in) m(f), Boss
m; **boss around** vt
herumkommandieren; **bossy** adj
herrisch
botanical [bə'tænɪkəl] adj botanisch; **~ garden(s)** botanischer
Garten
both [bəʊθ] adj beide; **~ the
books** beide Bücher ▷ pron
(people) beide; (things) beides;
~ (of) the boys die beiden Jungs; **I
like ~ of them** ich mag sie (alle)
beide ▷ adv: **~ X and Y** sowohl X
als auch Y
bother ['bɒðə°] vt ärgern,
belästigen; **it doesn't ~ me** das
stört mich nicht; **he can't be ~ed
with details** mit Details gibt er
sich nicht ab; **I'm not ~ed** das ist
mir egal ▷ vi sich kümmern
(about um); **don't ~** (das ist) nicht
nötig, lass es! ▷ n (trouble) Mühe f;
(annoyance) Ärger m
bottle ['bɒtl] n Flasche f ▷ vt (in
Flaschen) abfüllen; **bottle out** vi
(fam) den Mut verlieren, aufgeben;
bottle bank n Altglascontainer
m; **bottled** adj in Flaschen; **~ beer**
Flaschenbier nt; **bottleneck** n
(fig) Engpass m; **bottle opener** n
Flaschenöffner m
bottom ['bɒtəm] n (of container)
Boden m; (underside) Unterseite f;
(fam: of person) Po m; **at the ~ of
the sea/table/page** auf dem

Meeresgrund/am Tabellen-
ende/unten auf der Seite ▷ adj
unterste(r, s); **to be ~ of the
class/league** Klassen-
letzte(r)/Tabellenletzte(r) sein;
~ gear (Auto) erster Gang
bought [bɔːt] pt, pp of **buy**
bounce [baʊns] vi (ball)
springen, aufprallen; (cheque)
platzen; **~ up and down** (person)
herumhüpfen; **bouncy** adj (ball)
gut springend; (person) munter;
bouncy castle® n Hüpfburg f
bound [baʊnd] pt, pp of **bind**
▷ adj (tied up) gebunden; (obliged)
verpflichtet; **to be ~ to do sth** (sure
to) etw bestimmt tun (werden);
(have to) etw tun müssen; **it's ~ to
happen** es muss so kommen; **to
be ~ for ...** auf dem Weg nach ...
sein; **boundary** ['baʊndərɪ] n
Grenze f
bouquet [bʊ'keɪ] n (flowers)
Strauß m; (of wine) Blume f
boutique [buː'tiːk] n Boutique f
bow [bəʊ] n (ribbon) Schleife f;
(instrument, weapon) Bogen m
▷ [baʊ] vi sich verbeugen ▷ [baʊ]
n (with head) Verbeugung f; (of
ship) Bug m
bowels ['baʊəlz] npl Darm m
bowl [bəʊl] n (basin) Schüssel f;
(shallow) Schale f; (for animal) Napf
m ▷ vt, vi (in cricket) werfen
bowler ['bəʊlə°] n (in cricket)
Werfer(in) m(f); (hat) Melone f
bowling ['bəʊlɪŋ] n Kegeln nt;
bowling alley n Kegelbahn f;
bowling green n Rasen m zum
Bowling-Spiel; **bowls** [bəʊlz]
nsing (game) Bowling-Spiel nt
bow tie [bəʊ'taɪ] n Fliege f
box [bɒks] n Schachtel f;
(cardboard) Karton m; (bigger)
Kasten m; (space on form) Kästchen
nt; (Theat) Loge f; **boxer** n
Boxer(in) m(f); **boxers, boxer**

shorts npl Boxershorts pl; **boxing** n (Sport) Boxen nt; **Boxing Day** n zweiter Weihnachtsfeiertag

boxing gloves npl Boxhandschuhe pl; **boxing ring** n Boxring m
box number n Chiffre f
box office n (cinema, theatre) Kasse f
boy [bɔɪ] n Junge m
boycott ['bɔɪkɒt] n Boykott m ▷ vt boykottieren
boyfriend ['bɔɪfrend] n (fester) Freund m; **boy scout** n Pfadfinder m
bra [brɑː] n BH m
brace [breɪs] n (on teeth) Spange f
bracelet ['breɪslɪt] n Armband nt
braces ['breɪsɪz] npl (Brit) Hosenträger pl
bracket ['brækɪt] n (in text) Klammer f; (Tech) Träger m ▷ vt einklammern
brag [bræg] vi angeben
Braille [breɪl] n Blindenschrift f
brain [breɪn] n (Anat) Gehirn nt; (mind) Verstand m; **~s** (pl) (intelligence) Grips m; **brainwave** n Geistesblitz m; **brainy** adj schlau, clever
braise [breɪz] vt schmoren
brake [breɪk] n Bremse f ▷ vi

bremsen; **brake fluid** n Bremsflüssigkeit f; **brake light** n Bremslicht nt; **brake pedal** n Bremspedal nt
branch [brɑːntʃ] n (of tree) Ast m; (of family, subject) Zweig m; (of firm) Filiale f, Zweigstelle f; **branch off** vi (road) abzweigen
brand [brænd] n (Comm) Marke f
brand-new ['brænd'njuː] adj (funkel)nagelneu
brandy ['brændɪ] n Weinbrand m
brass [brɑːs] n Messing nt; (Brit fam: money) Knete f; **brass band** n Blaskapelle f
brat [bræt] n (pej, fam) Gör nt
brave [breɪv] adj tapfer, mutig; **bravery** ['breɪvərɪ] n Mut m
brawl [brɔːl] n Schlägerei f
brawn [brɔːn] n (strength) Muskelkraft f; (Gastr) Sülze f; **brawny** adj muskulös
Brazil [brə'zɪl] n Brasilien nt; **Brazilian** adj brasilianisch ▷ n Brasilianer(in) m(f); **brazil nut** n Paranuss f
bread [bred] n Brot nt; **breadbin** (Brit), **breadbox** (US) n Brotkasten m; **breadcrumbs** npl Brotkrumen pl; (Gastr) Paniermehl nt; **breaded** adj paniert; **breadknife** n Brotmesser nt
breadth [bredθ] n Breite f
break [breɪk] n (fracture) Bruch m; (rest) Pause f; (short holiday) Kurzurlaub m; **give me a ~** gib mir eine Chance, hör auf damit! ▷ vt (**broke, broken**) (fracture) brechen; (in pieces) zerbrechen; (toy, device) kaputt machen; (promise) nicht halten; (silence) brechen; (law) verletzen; (journey) unterbrechen; (news) mitteilen (to sb jdm); **I broke my leg** ich habe mir das Bein gebrochen; **he broke it to her gently** er hat es ihr schonend beigebracht ▷ vi (come apart)

(auseinander)brechen; (in pieces) zerbrechen; (toy, device) kaputtgehen; (person) zusammenbrechen; (day, dawn) anbrechen; (news) bekannt werden; **break down** vi (car) eine Panne haben; (machine) versagen; (person) zusammenbrechen; **break in** vi (burglar) einbrechen; **break into** vt einbrechen in +akk; **break off** vi, vt abbrechen; **break out** vi ausbrechen; **to ~ in a rash** einen Ausschlag bekommen; **break up** vi aufbrechen; (meeting, organisation) sich auflösen; (marriage) in die Brüche gehen; (couple) sich trennen; **school breaks up on Friday** am Freitag beginnen die Ferien ▷ vt aufbrechen; (marriage) zerstören; (meeting) auflösen; **breakable** adj zerbrechlich; **breakage** n Bruch m; **breakdown** n (of car) Panne f; (of machine) Störung f; (of person, relations, system) Zusammenbruch m; **breakdown service** n Pannendienst m; **breakdown truck** n Abschleppwagen m

breakfast ['brɛkfəst] n Frühstück nt; **to have ~** frühstücken; **breakfast cereal** n Cornflakes, Muesli etc; **breakfast television** n Frühstücksfernsehen nt

break-in ['breɪkɪn] n Einbruch m; **breakup** ['breɪkʌp] n (of meeting, organization) Auflösung f; (of marriage) Zerrüttung f

breast [brɛst] n Brust f; **breastfeed** vt stillen; **breaststroke** n Brustschwimmen nt

breath [brɛθ] n Atem m; **out of ~** außer Atem; **breathalyse**, **breathalyze** ['brɛθəlaɪz] vt (ins Röhrchen) blasen lassen; **breathalyser**, **breathalyzer** n Promillemesser m; **breathe** [briːð] vt, vi atmen; **breathe in** vt, vi einatmen; **breathe out** vt, vi ausatmen; **breathless** ['brɛθlɪs] adj atemlos; **breathtaking** ['brɛθteɪkɪŋ] adj atemberaubend

bred [brɛd] pt, pp of **breed**

breed [briːd] n (race) Rasse f ▷ vi (**bred, bred**) sich vermehren ▷ vt züchten; **breeder** n Züchter(in) m(f); (fam) Hetero m; **breeding** n (of animals) Züchtung f; (of person) (gute) Erziehung

breeze [briːz] n Brise f

brevity ['brɛvɪtɪ] n Kürze f

brew [bruː] vt (beer) brauen; (tea) kochen; **brewery** n Brauerei f

bribe ['braɪb] n Bestechungsgeld nt ▷ vt bestechen; **bribery** ['braɪbərɪ] n Bestechung f

brick [brɪk] n Backstein m; **bricklayer** n Maurer(in) m(f)

bride [braɪd] n Braut f; **bridegroom** n Bräutigam m; **bridesmaid** n Brautjungfer f

bridge [brɪdʒ] n Brücke f; (cards) Bridge nt

brief [briːf] adj kurz ▷ vt instruieren (on über +akk); **briefcase** n Aktentasche f; **briefs** npl Slip m

bright [braɪt] adj hell; (colour) leuchtend; (cheerful) heiter; (intelligent) intelligent; (idea) glänzend; **brighten up** vt aufhellen; (person) aufheitern ▷ vi sich aufheitern; (person) fröhlicher werden

brilliant ['brɪljənt] adj (sunshine, colour) strahlend; (person) brillant; (idea) glänzend; (Brit fam) **it was ~** es war fantastisch

brim [brɪm] n Rand m

bring [brɪŋ] (**brought, brought**) vt bringen; (with one) mitbringen; **bring about** vt herbeiführen, bewirken; **bring back** vt zurückbringen; (memories) wecken; **bring down** vt (reduce) senken; (*government etc*) zu Fall bringen; **bring in** vt hereinbringen; (*introduce*) einführen; **bring out** vt herausbringen; **bring round**, **bring to** vt wieder zu sich bringen; **bring up** vt (*child*) aufziehen; (*question*) zur Sprache bringen

brisk [brɪsk] adj (*trade*) lebhaft; (*wind*) frisch

bristle ['brɪsl] n Borste f

Brit [brɪt] n (*fam*) Brite m, Britin f; **Britain** ['brɪtn] n Großbritannien nt; **British** ['brɪtɪʃ] adj britisch; **the ~ Isles** (*pl*) die Britischen Inseln pl ▷ n **the ~** (*pl*) die Briten pl

brittle ['brɪtl] adj spröde

broad [brɔːd] adj breit; (*accent*) stark; **in ~ daylight** am helllichten Tag ▷ (*US fam*) Frau f

B road ['biːrəʊd] n (*Brit*) ≈ Landstraße f

broadcast ['brɔːdkɑːst] n Sendung f ▷ irr vt, vi senden; (*event*) übertragen

broaden ['brɔːdn] vt: **to ~ the mind** den Horizont erweitern; **broad-minded** adj tolerant

broccoli ['brɒkəlɪ] n Brokkoli pl

brochure ['brəʊʃʊə*] n Prospekt m, Broschüre f

broke [brəʊk] pt of **break** ▷ adj (*Brit fam*) pleite; **broken** ['brəʊkən] pp of **break**; **broken-hearted** adj untröstlich

broker ['brəʊkə*] n Makler(in) m(f)

brolly ['brɒlɪ] n (*Brit*) Schirm m

bronchitis [brɒŋ'kaɪtɪs] n Bronchitis f

bronze [brɒnz] n Bronze f

brooch [brəʊtʃ] n Brosche f

broom [bruːm] n Besen m

Bros [brɒs] abbr = **brothers** Gebr.

broth [brɒθ] n Fleischbrühe f

brothel ['brɒθl] n Bordell nt

brother ['brʌðə*] n Bruder m; **~s** (*pl*) (*Comm*) Gebrüder pl; **brother-in-law** (*pl* **brothers-in-law**) n Schwager m

brought [brɔːt] pt, pp of **bring**

brow [braʊ] n (*eyebrow*) (Augen)braue f; (*forehead*) Stirn f

brown [braʊn] adj braun; **brown bread** n Mischbrot nt; (*wholemeal*) Vollkornbrot nt; **brownie** ['braʊnɪ] n (*Gastr*) Brownie m; (*Brit*) junge Pfadfinderin; **brown paper** n Packpapier nt; **brown rice** n Naturreis m; **brown sugar** n brauner Zucker

browse [braʊz] vi (*in book*) blättern; (*in shop*) schmökern, herumschauen; **browser** n (*Inform*) Browser m

bruise [bruːz] n blauer Fleck ▷ vt: **to ~ one's arm** sich dat einen blauen Fleck (am Arm) holen

brunette [bruː'net] n Brünette f

brush [brʌʃ] n Bürste f; (*for sweeping*) Handbesen m; (*for painting*) Pinsel m ▷ vt bürsten; (*sweep*) fegen; **to ~ one's teeth** sich dat die Zähne putzen; **brush up** vt (*French etc*) auffrischen

Brussels sprouts [brʌsl'spraʊts] npl Rosenkohl m, Kohlsprossen pl

brutal ['bruːtl] adj brutal; **brutality** [bruː'tælɪtɪ] n Brutalität f

BSE abbr = **bovine spongiform encephalopathy** BSE f

bubble ['bʌbl] n Blase f; **bubble bath** n Schaumbad nt, Badeschaum m; **bubbly** ['bʌblɪ] adj sprudelnd; (*person*) temperamentvoll ▷ n (*fam*) Schampus m

buck [bʌk] n (*animal*) Bock m; (*US fam*) Dollar m

bucket ['bʌkɪt] n Eimer m

● **BUCKINGHAM PALACE**

Der **Buckingham Palace** ist die offizielle Londoner Residenz der britischen Monarchen und liegt am St James's Park. Der Palast wurde 1703 für den Herzog von Buckingham erbaut, 1762 von George III gekauft, zwischen 1821 und 1836 von John Nash umgebaut und Anfang des 20. Jahrhunderts teilweise neu gestaltet. Teile des Buckingham Palace sind heute der Öffentlichkeit zugänglich.

buckle [ˈbʌkl] n Schnalle f ▷ vi (Tech) sich verbiegen ▷ vt zuschnallen
bud [bʌd] n Knospe f
Buddhism [ˈbʊdɪzəm] n Buddhismus m; **Buddhist** adj buddhistisch ▷ n Buddhist(in) m(f)
buddy [ˈbʌdɪ] n (fam) Kumpel m
budget [ˈbʌdʒɪt] n Budget nt ▷ adj preisgünstig; **budget airline** n Billigflieger m
budgie [ˈbʌdʒɪ] n Wellensittich m
buff [bʌf] adj (US) muskulös; **in the ~** nackt ▷ n (enthusiast) Fan m
buffalo [ˈbʌfələʊ] (pl **-es**) n Büffel m
buffer [ˈbʌfə°] n (a. Inform) Puffer m
buffet [ˈbʊfeɪ] n (food) (kaltes) Büfett nt
bug [bʌg] n (Inform) Bug m, Programmfehler m; (listening device) Wanze f; (US: insect) Insekt nt; (fam: illness) Infektion f ▷ vt (fam) nerven
bugger [ˈbʌgə°] n (vulg) Scheißkerl m ▷ interj (vulg) Scheiße f; **bugger off** vi (vulg) abhauen, Leine ziehen
buggy® [ˈbʌgɪ] n (for baby) Buggy® m

build [bɪld] (**built, built**) vt bauen; **build up** vt aufbauen; **builder** n Bauunternehmer(in) m(f); **building** n Gebäude nt; **building site** n Baustelle f; **building society** n Bausparkasse f
built pt, pp of **build**; **built-in** adj (cupboard) Einbau-, eingebaut
bulb [bʌlb] n (Bot) (Blumen)zwiebel f; (Elec) Glühbirne f
Bulgaria [bʌlˈgɛərɪə] n Bulgarien nt; **Bulgarian** adj bulgarisch ▷ n (person) Bulgare m, Bulgarin f; (language) Bulgarisch nt
bulimia [bəˈlɪmɪə] n Bulimie f
bulk [bʌlk] n (size) Größe f; (greater part) Großteil m (of +gen): **in ~** en gros; **bulky** adj (goods) sperrig; (person) stämmig
bull [bʊl] n Stier m; **bulldog** n Bulldogge f; **bulldoze** [ˈbʊldəʊz] vt planieren; **bulldozer** n Planierraupe f
bullet [ˈbʊlɪt] n Kugel f
bulletin [ˈbʊlɪtɪn] n Bulletin nt; (announcement) Bekanntmachung f; (Med) Krankenbericht m; **bulletin board** n (US: Inform) schwarzes Brett
bullfight [ˈbʊlfaɪt] n Stierkampf m; **bullshit** n (fam) Scheiß m
bully [ˈbʊlɪ] n Tyrann m
bum [bʌm] n (Brit fam: backside) Po m; (US: vagrant) Penner m; (worthless person) Rumtreiber m; **bum around** vi herumgammeln
bumblebee [ˈbʌmblbiː] n Hummel f
bumf [bʌmf] (fam) n Infomaterial nt, Papierkram m
bump [bʌmp] n (fam: swelling) Beule f; (road) Unebenheit f; (blow) Stoß m ▷ vt stoßen; **to ~ one's head** sich dat den Kopf anschlagen (on an +dat); **bump into** vt stoßen gegen; (fam: meet)

(zufällig) begegnen +dat; **bumper**
n (Auto) Stoßstange f ▷ adj
(edition etc) Riesen-; (crop etc)
Rekord-; **bumpy** ['bʌmpɪ] adj
holp(e)rig

bun [bʌn] n süßes Brötchen

bunch [bʌntʃ] n (of flowers)
Strauß m; (fam: of people) Haufen m;
~ of keys Schlüsselbund m; **~ of
grapes** Weintraube f

bundle ['bʌndl] n Bündel nt

bungalow ['bʌŋgələʊ] n Bungalow m

bungee jumping ['bʌndʒɪ-
dʒʌmpɪŋ] n Bungeejumping nt

bunk [bʌŋk] n Koje f; **bunk
bed(s)** n(pl) Etagenbett nt

bunker ['bʌŋkə°] n (Mil) Bunker
m

bunny ['bʌnɪ] n Häschen nt

buoy [bɔɪ] n Boje f; **buoyant**
['bɔɪənt] adj (floating)
schwimmend

BUPA ['buːpə] abbr (Brit) private
Krankenkasse

burden ['bɜːdn] n Last f

bureau ['bjʊərəʊ] n Büro nt;
(government department) Amt nt;
bureaucracy [bjʊˈrɒkrəsɪ] n
Bürokratie f; **bureaucratic**
[bjuːrəˈkrætɪk] adj bürokratisch;
bureau de change ['bjuːrəʊ də
ˈʃɑ̃ʒ] n Wechselstube f

burger ['bɜːgə°] n Hamburger m

burglar ['bɜːglə°] n Einbre-
cher(in) m(f); **burglar alarm** n
Alarmanlage f; **burglarize** vt (US)
einbrechen in +akk; **burglary** n
Einbruch m; **burgle** ['bɜːgl] vt
einbrechen in +akk

burial ['berɪəl] n Beerdigung f

burn [bɜːn] (burnt o burned,
burnt o burned) vt verbrennen;
(food, slightly) anbrennen; **to
~ one's hand** sich dat die Hand
verbrennen ▷ vi brennen ▷ n
(injury) Brandwunde f; (on material)

verbrannte Stelle; **burn down** vt,
vi abbrennen

burp [bɜːp] vi rülpsen ▷ vt (baby)
aufstoßen lassen

bursary ['bɜːsərɪ] n Stipendium nt

burst [bɜːst] (burst, burst) vt
platzen lassen ▷ vi platzen;
to ~ into tears in Tränen
ausbrechen

bury ['berɪ] vt begraben; (in grave)
beerdigen; (hide) vergraben

bus [bʌs] n Bus m; **bus driver** n
Busfahrer(in) m(f)

bush [bʊʃ] n Busch m

business ['bɪznɪs] n Geschäft nt;
(enterprise) Unternehmen nt;
(concern, affair) Sache f; **I'm here on
~** ich bin geschäftlich hier; **it's
none of your ~** das geht dich
nichts an; **business card** n
Visitenkarte f; **business class** n
(Aviat) Businessclass f;
businessman (pl **-men**) n
Geschäftsmann m; **business
studies** npl Betriebswirtschaft-
slehre f; **businesswoman** (pl
-women) n Geschäftsfrau f

bus service n Busverbindung f;
bus shelter n Wartehäuschen nt;
bus station n Busbahnhof m; **bus
stop** n Bushaltestelle f

bust [bʌst] n Büste f ▷ adj
(broken) kaputt; **to go ~** Pleite
gehen; **bust-up** n (fam) Krach m

busy ['bɪzɪ] adj beschäftigt;
(street, place) belebt; (esp US:
telephone) besetzt; **~ signal** (US)
Besetztzeichen nt

○ **KEYWORD**

but [bʌt, bət] conj 1 (yet) aber; **not
X but Y** nicht X sondern Y
2 (however) **I'd love to come, but
I'm busy** ich würde gern kommen,
bin aber beschäftigt
3 (showing disagreement, surprise etc)

but that's fantastic! (aber) das ist
ja fantastisch!
▷ *prep* (*apart from, except*): **nothing
but trouble** nichts als Ärger;
no-one but him can do it
niemand außer ihm kann es
machen; **but for you/your help**
ohne dich/deine Hilfe; **anything
but that** alles, nur das nicht
▷ *adv* (*just, only*) **she's but a child**
sie ist noch ein Kind; **had I but
known** wenn ich es nur gewusst
hätte; **I can but try** ich kann es
immerhin versuchen; **all but
finished** so gut wie fertig

butcher ['bʊtʃə*] *n* Fleischer(in)
  m(f), Metzger(in) *m(f)*
butler ['bʌtlə*] *n* Butler *m*
butt [bʌt] (*US fam*) *n* Hintern *m*
butter ['bʌtə*] *n* Butter *f* ▷ *vt*
  buttern; **buttercup** *n*
  Butterblume *f*; **butterfly** *n*
  Schmetterling *m*
buttocks ['bʌtəks] *npl* Gesäß *nt*
button ['bʌtn] *n* Knopf *m*; (*badge*)
  Button *m* ▷ *vt* zuknöpfen;
  buttonhole *n* Knopfloch *nt*
buy [baɪ] *n* Kauf *m* ▷ *vt* (**bought,
  bought**) kaufen (*from* von); **he
  bought me a ring** er hat mir einen
  Ring gekauft; **buyer** *n* Käufer(in)
  m(f)
buzz [bʌz] *n* Summen *nt*; **to give
  sb a ~** (*fam*) jdn anrufen ▷ *vi*
  summen; **buzzer** *n* ['bʌzə*] *n*
  Summer *m*; **buzz word** *n* (*fam*)
  Modewort *nt*

KEYWORD

by [baɪ] *prep* **1** (*referring to cause,
  agent*) von, durch; **killed by
  lightning** vom Blitz getötet; **a
  painting by Picasso** ein Gemälde
  von Picasso
2 (*referring to method, manner*) **by**
bus/car/train mit dem
Bus/Auto/Zug; **to pay by cheque**
per Scheck bezahlen; **by
moonlight** bei Mondschein; **by
saving hard, he ...** indem er
eisern sparte, ... er ...
3 (*via, through*) über +akk; **he came
in by the back door** er kam durch
die Hintertür herein
4 (*close to, past*) bei, an +dat; **a
holiday by the sea** ein Urlaub am
Meer; **she rushed by me** sie eilte
an mir vorbei
5 (*not later than*) **by 4 o'clock** bis 4
Uhr; **by this time tomorrow**
morgen um diese Zeit; **by the
time I got here it was too late** als
ich hier ankam, war es zu spät
6 (*during*) **by day** bei Tag
7 (*amount*) **by the kilo/metre**
kiloweise/meterweise; **paid by
the hour** stundenweise bezahlt
8 (*math, measure*) **to divide by 3**
durch 3 teilen; **to multiply by 3**
mit 3 malnehmen; **a room 3
metres by 4** ein Zimmer 3 mal 4
Meter; **it's broader by a metre** es
ist (um) einem Meter breiter
9 (*according to*) nach; **it's all right
by me** von mir aus gern
10 (**all**) **by oneself** *etc* ganz allein
11 **by the way** übrigens
▷ *adv* **1** *see* **go**; **pass** *etc*
2 **by and by** irgendwann; (*with
past tenses*) nach einiger Zeit; **by
and large** (*on the whole*) im Großen
und Ganzen

bye-bye ['baɪ'baɪ] *interj* (*fam*)
  Wiedersehen, tschüss
by-election *n* Nachwahl *f*;
  bypass *n* Umgehungsstraße *f*;
  (*Med*) Bypass *m*; **byproduct** *n*
  Nebenprodukt *nt*; **byroad** *n*
  Nebenstraße *f*; **bystander** *n*
  Zuschauer(in) *m(f)*
byte [baɪt] *n* Byte *nt*

C

C [si:] *abbr* = **Celsius** C

c *abbr* = **circa** ca

cab [kæb] *n* Taxi *nt*

cabbage ['kæbɪdʒ] *n* Kohl *m*

cabin ['kæbɪn] *n* (*Naut*) Kajüte *f*;
(*Aviat*) Passagierraum *m*; (*wooden house*) Hütte *f*; **cabin crew** *n*
Flugbegleitpersonal *nt*; **cabin cruiser** *n* Kajütboot *nt*

cabinet ['kæbɪnɪt] *n* Schrank *m*;
(*for display*) Vitrine *f*; (*Pol*) Kabinett *nt*

cable ['keɪbl] *n* (*Elec*) Kabel *nt*;
cable-car *n* Seilbahn *f*; **cable railway** *n* Drahtseilbahn *f*; **cable television**, **cablevision** (*US*) *n*
Kabelfernsehen *nt*

cactus ['kæktəs] *n* Kaktus *m*

CAD *abbr* = **computer-aided design** CAD *nt*

Caesarean [si:'zɛərɪən] *adj*:
~ (**section**) Kaiserschnitt *m*

café ['kæfeɪ] *n* Café *nt*; **cafeteria**
[kæfɪ'tɪərɪə] *n* Cafeteria *f*;
cafetiere [kæfə'tjɛə*] *n* Kaffeebereiter *m*

cage [keɪdʒ] *n* Käfig *m*

Cairo ['kaɪərəʊ] *n* Kairo *nt*

cake [keɪk] *n* Kuchen *m*; **cake shop** *n* Konditorei *f*

calamity [kə'læmɪtɪ] *n* Katastrophe *f*

calculate ['kælkjʊleɪt] *vt*
berechnen; (*estimate*) kalkulieren;
calculating *adj* berechnend;
calculation [kælkjʊ'leɪʃən] *n*
Berechnung *f*; (*estimate*)
Kalkulation *f*; **calculator**
['kælkjʊleɪtə*] *n* Taschenrechner *m*

calendar ['kælɪndə*] *n* Kalender *m*

calf [kɑːf] (*pl* **calves**) *n* Kalb *nt*;
(*Anat*) Wade *f*

California [kælɪ'fɔːnɪə] *n* Kalifornien *nt*

call [kɔːl] *vt* rufen; (*name, describe as*) nennen; (*Tel*) anrufen;
(*Inform, Aviat*) aufrufen; **what's this ~ed?** wie heißt das?; **that's what I ~ service** das nenne ich guten Service ▷ *vi* (*shout*) rufen
(*for help* um Hilfe); (*visit*)
vorbeikommen; **to ~ at the doctor's** beim Arzt vorbeigehen;
(*of train*) **to ~ at ...** in ... halten ▷ *n*
(*shout*) Ruf *m*; (*Tel*) Anruf *m*; (*Inform, Aviat*) Aufruf *m*; **to make a ~** telefonieren; **to give sb a ~** jdn anrufen; **to be on ~** Bereitschaftsdienst haben; **call back** *vt*, *vi* zurückrufen; **call for** *vt* (*come to pick up*) abholen;
(*demand, require*) verlangen; **call off** *vt* absagen

call centre *n* Callcenter *nt*; **caller** *n* Besucher(in) *m(f)*; (*Tel*)
Anrufer(in) *m(f)*

calm [kɑːm] *n* Stille *f*; (*also of person*) Ruhe *f*; (*of sea*) Flaute *f* ▷ *vt* beruhigen ▷ *adj* ruhig; **calm down** *vi* sich beruhigen

calorie [ˈkælərɪ] *n* Kalorie *f*

calves [kɑːvz] *pl of* **calf**

Cambodia [kæmˈbəʊdɪə] *n* Kambodscha *nt*

camcorder [ˈkæmkɔːdə*] *n* Camcorder *m*

came [keɪm] *pt of* **come**

camel [ˈkæməl] *n* Kamel *nt*

camera [ˈkæmərə] *n* Fotoapparat *m*, Kamera *f*; **camera phone** [ˈkæmərəfəʊn] *n* Fotohandy *nt*

camomile [ˈkæməmaɪl] *n* Kamille *f*

camouflage [ˈkæməflɑːʒ] *n* Tarnung *f*

camp [kæmp] *n* Lager *nt*; (*camping place*) Zeltplatz *m* ▷ *vi* zelten, campen ▷ *adj* (*fam*) theatralisch, tuntig

campaign [kæmˈpeɪn] *n* Kampagne *f*; (*Pol*) Wahlkampf *m* ▷ *vi* sich einsetzen (*for/against* für/gegen)

campbed [ˈkæmpbed] *n* Campingliege *f*; **camper** [ˈkæmpə*] *n* (*person*) Camper(in) *m(f)*; (*van*) Wohnmobil *nt*; **camping** [ˈkæmpɪŋ] *n* Zelten *nt*, Camping *nt*; **campsite** [ˈkæmpsaɪt] *n* Zeltplatz *m*, Campingplatz *m*

campus [ˈkæmpəs] *n* (*of university*) Universitätsgelände *nt*, Campus *m*

⭕ **KEYWORD**

can [kæn] (*negative* **cannot, can't**, *conditional* **could**) *vb aux* **1** (*be able to, know how to*) können; **I can see you tomorrow, if you like** ich könnte Sie morgen sehen, wenn Sie wollen; **I can swim** ich kann schwimmen; **can you speak German?** sprechen Sie Deutsch?

2 (*may*) können, dürfen; **could I have a word with you?** könnte ich Sie kurz sprechen?

Canada [ˈkænədə] *n* Kanada *nt*; **Canadian** [kəˈneɪdjən] *adj* kanadisch ▷ *n* Kanadier(in) *m(f)*

canal [kəˈnæl] *n* Kanal *m*

canary [kəˈnɛərɪ] *n* Kanarienvogel *m*

cancel [ˈkænsəl] *vt* (*plans*) aufgeben; (*meeting, event*) absagen; (*Comm: order etc*) stornieren; (*contract*) kündigen; (*Inform*) löschen; (*Aviat: flight*) streichen; **to be ~led** (*event, train, bus*) ausfallen; **cancellation** [kænsəˈleɪʃən] *n* Absage *f*; (*Comm*) Stornierung *f*; (*Aviat*) gestrichener Flug

cancer [ˈkænsə*] *n* (*Med*) Krebs *m*; **Cancer** *n* (*Astr*) Krebs *m*

candid [ˈkændɪd] *adj* (*person, conversation*) offen

candidate [ˈkændɪdət] *n* (*for post*) Bewerber(in) *m(f)*; (*Pol*) Kandidat(in) *m(f)*

candle [ˈkændl] *n* Kerze *f*; **candlelight** *n* Kerzenlicht *nt*; **candlestick** *n* Kerzenhalter *m*

candy [ˈkændɪ] *n* (*US*) Bonbon *nt*; (*quantity*) Süßigkeiten *pl*; **candy-floss** *n* (*Brit*) Zuckerwatte *f*

cane [keɪn] *n* Rohr *nt*; (*stick*) Stock *m*

cannabis [ˈkænəbɪs] *n* Cannabis *m*

canned [kænd] *adj* Dosen-

cannot [ˈkænɒt] *contr of* **can not**

canny [ˈkænɪ] *adj* (*shrewd*) schlau

canoe [kəˈnuː] *n* Kanu *nt*; **canoeing** *n* Kanufahren *nt*

can opener [ˈkænəʊpnə*] *n* Dosenöffner *m*

canopy [ˈkænəpɪ] *n* Baldachin *m*; (*awning*) Markise *f*; (*over entrance*) Vordach *nt*

can't [kɑːnt] *contr of* **can not**
canteen [kæn'tiːn] *n* (*in factory*) Kantine *f*; (*in university*) Mensa *f*
canvas ['kænvəs] *n* (*for sails, shoes*) Segeltuch *nt*; (*for tent*) Zeltstoff *m*; (*for painting*) Leinwand *f*
canvass ['kænvəs] *vi* um Stimmen werben (*for* für)
canyon ['kænjən] *n* Felsenschlucht *f*; **canyoning** ['kænjənɪŋ] *n* Canyoning *nt*
cap [kæp] *n* Mütze *f*; (*lid*) Verschluss *m*, Deckel *m*
capability [keɪpə'bɪlɪtɪ] *n* Fähigkeit *f*; **capable** ['keɪpəbl] *adj* fähig; **to be ~ of sth** zu etw fähig (*o* imstande) sein; **to be ~ of doing sth** etw tun können
capacity [kə'pæsɪtɪ] *n* (*of building, container*) Fassungsvermögen *nt*; (*ability*) Fähigkeit *f*; (*function*) **in his ~ as ...** in seiner Eigenschaft als ...
cape [keɪp] *n* (*garment*) Cape *nt*, Umhang *m*; (*Geo*) Kap *nt*
caper ['keɪpə*] *n* (*for cooking*) Kaper *f*
capital ['kæpɪtl] *n* (*Fin*) Kapital *nt*; (*letter*) Großbuchstabe *m*; **~ (city)** Hauptstadt *f*; **capitalism** *n* Kapitalismus *m*; **capital punishment** *n* die Todesstrafe
Capricorn ['kæprɪkɔːn] *n* (*Astr*) Steinbock *m*
capsize [kæp'saɪz] *vi* kentern
capsule ['kæpsjuːl] *n* Kapsel *f*
captain ['kæptɪn] *n* Kapitän *m*; (*army*) Hauptmann *m*
caption ['kæpʃən] *n* Bildunterschrift *f*
captive ['kæptɪv] *n* Gefangene(r) *mf*; **capture** ['kæptʃə*] *vt* (*person*) fassen, gefangen nehmen; (*town etc*) einnehmen; (*Inform: data*) erfassen ▷ *n* Gefangennahme *f*; (*Inform*) Erfassung *f*
car [kɑː*] *n* Auto *nt*; (*US Rail*)

Wagen *m*
carafe [kə'ræf] *n* Karaffe *f*
caramel ['kærəmel] *n* Karamelle *f*
caravan ['kærəvæn] *n* Wohnwagen *m*; **caravan site** *n* Campingplatz *m* für Wohnwagen
caraway (seed) ['kærəweɪ] *n* Kümmel *m*
carbohydrate [kɑːbəʊ'haɪdreɪt] *n* Kohle(n)hydrat *nt*
car bomb *n* Autobombe *f*
carbon ['kɑːbən] *n* Kohlenstoff *m*; **carbon footprint** *n* ökologischer Fußabdruck
car boot sale *n* auf einem Parkplatz stattfindender Flohmarkt
carburettor, **carburetor** (*US*) ['kɑːbjʊretə*] *n* Vergaser *m*
card [kɑːd] *n* Karte *f*; (*material*) Pappe *f*; **cardboard** *n* Pappe *f*; **~ (box)** Karton *m*; (*smaller*) Pappschachtel *f*; **card game** *n* Kartenspiel *m*
cardigan ['kɑːdɪgən] *n* Strickjacke *f*
card index *n* Kartei *f*; **cardphone** ['kɑːdfəʊn] *n* Kartentelefon *nt*
care [keə*] *n* (*worry*) Sorge *f*; (*carefulness*) Sorgfalt *f*; (*looking after things, people*) Pflege *f*; **with ~** sorgfältig; (*cautiously*) vorsichtig; **to take ~** (*watch out*) vorsichtig sein; (*in address*) **~ of** bei; **to take ~ of** sorgen für, sich kümmern um ▷ *vi*: **I don't ~** es ist mir egal; **to ~ about sth** Wert auf etw *akk* legen; **he ~s about her** sie liegt ihm am Herzen; **care for** *vt* (*look after*) sorgen für, sich kümmern um; (*like*) mögen
career [kə'rɪə*] *n* Karriere *f*, Laufbahn *f*; **career woman** (*pl* **women**) *n* Karrierefrau *f*; **careers adviser** *n* Berufsberater(in) *m(f)*
carefree ['keəfriː] *adj* sorgenfrei; **careful**, **carefully** *adj*, *adv* sorgfältig; (*cautious, cautiously*)

vorsichtig; **careless, carelessly**
adj, adv nachlässig; (*driving etc*)
leichtsinnig; (*remark*)
unvorsichtig; **carer** ['kɛərə°] *n*
Betreuer(in) *m(f)*, Pfleger(in) *m(f)*;
caretaker ['kɛəteɪkə°] *n* Haus-
meister(in) *m(f)*; **careworker** *n*
Pfleger(in) *m(f)*

car-ferry ['kɑːferɪ] *n* Autofähre *f*

cargo ['kɑːgəʊ] (*pl* **-(e)s**) *n*
Ladung *f*

car hire, car hire company *n*
Autovermietung *f*

Caribbean [kærɪˈbiːən] *n* Karibik
f ▷ *adj* karibisch

caring ['kɛərɪŋ] *adj* mitfühlend;
(*parent, partner*) liebevoll; (*looking
after sb*) fürsorglich

car insurance *n*
Kraftfahrzeugversicherung *f*

carnation [kɑːˈneɪʃən] *n* Nelke *f*

carnival ['kɑːnɪvəl] *n* Volksfest
nt; (*before Lent*) Karneval *m*

carol ['kærəl] *n* Weihnachtslied *nt*

carp [kɑːp] *n* (*fish*) Karpfen *m*

car park *n* (*Brit*) Parkplatz *m*;
(*multi-storey car park*) Parkhaus *nt*

carpenter ['kɑːpəntə°] *n* Zimmermann *m*

carpet ['kɑːpɪt] *n* Teppich *m*

car phone *n* Autotelefon *nt*;
carpool *n* Fahrgemeinschaft *f*;
(*vehicles*) Fuhrpark *m* ▷ *vi* eine
Fahrgemeinschaft bilden; **car
rental** *n* Autovermietung *f*

carriage ['kærɪdʒ] *n* (*Brit Rail:
coach*) Wagen *m*; (*compartment*)
Abteil *nt*; (*horse-drawn*) Kutsche *f*;
(*transport*) Beförderung *f*;
carriageway *n* (*Brit: on road*)
Fahrbahn *f*

carrier ['kærɪə°] *n* (*Comm*)
Spediteur(in) *m(f)*; **carrier bag** *n*
Tragetasche *f*

carrot ['kærət] *n* Karotte *f*

carry ['kærɪ] *vt* tragen; (*in vehicle*)
befördern; (*have on one*) bei sich

haben; **carry on** *vi* (*continue*)
weitermachen; (*fam: make a scene*)
ein Theater machen ▷ *vt*
(*continue*) fortführen; **to ~ on
working** weiter arbeiten; **carry
out** *vt* (*orders, plan*) ausführen,
durchführen

carrycot *n* Babytragetasche *f*

carsick ['kɑːsɪk] *adj*: **he gets
~** ihm wird beim Autofahren übel

cart [kɑːt] *n* Wagen *m*, Karren *m*;
(*US: shopping trolley*)
Einkaufswagen *m*

carton ['kɑːtən] *n* (*Papp*)karton
m; (*of cigarettes*) Stange *f*

cartoon [kɑːˈtuːn] *n* Cartoon *m* o
nt; (*one drawing*) Karikatur *f*; (*film*)
(Zeichen)trickfilm *m*

cartridge ['kɑːtrɪdʒ] *n* (*for film*)
Kassette *f*; (*for gun, pen, printer*)
Patrone *f*; (*for copier*) Kartusche *f*

carve [kɑːv] *vt, vi* (*wood*)
schnitzen; (*stone*) meißeln; (*meat*)
schneiden, tranchieren; **carving** *n*
(*in wood*) Schnitzerei *f*; (*in stone*)
Skulptur *f*; (*Ski*) Carving *nt*

car wash *n* Autowaschanlage *f*

case [keɪs] *n* (*crate*) Kiste *f*; (*box*)
Schachtel *f*; (*for jewels*) Schatulle *f*;
(*for spectacles*) Etui *nt*; (*Jur, matter*)
Fall *m*; **in ~ falls; in that ~** in dem
Fall; **in ~ of fire** bei Brand; **it's a
~ of ...** es handelt sich hier um ...

cash [kæʃ] *n* Bargeld *nt*; **in ~** bar;
~ on delivery per Nachnahme
▷ *vt* (*cheque*) einlösen; **cash desk**
n Kasse *f*; **cash dispenser** *n*
Geldautomat *m*; **cashier** [kæˈʃɪə°]
n Kassierer(in) *m(f)*; **cash
machine** *n* (*Brit*) Geldautomat *m*

cashmere ['kæʃmɪə°] *n* Kasch-
mirwolle *f*

cash payment *n* Barzahlung *f*;
cashpoint *n* (*Brit*) Geldautomat *m*

casing ['keɪsɪŋ] *n* Gehäuse *nt*

casino [kəˈsiːnəʊ] (*pl* **-s**) *n*
Kasino *nt*

cask [kɑ:sk] n Fass nt
casserole ['kæsərəʊl] n Kasserole f; (food) Schmortopf m
cassette [kæ'set] n Kassette f; **cassette recorder** n Kassettenrekorder m
cast [kɑ:st] (**cast, cast**) vt (throw) werfen; (Theat, Cine) besetzen; (roles) verteilen ▷ n (Theat, Cine) Besetzung f; (Med) Gipsverband m; **cast off** vi (Naut) losmachen
caster ['kɑ:stə*] n: ~ **sugar** Streuzucker m
castle ['kɑ:sl] n Burg f
castrate [kæs'treɪt] vt kastrieren
casual ['kæʒjʊəl] adj (arrangement, remark) beiläufig; (attitude, manner) (nach)lässig, zwanglos; (dress) leger; (work, earnings) Gelegenheits-; (look, glance) flüchtig; ~ **wear** Freizeitkleidung f; ~ **sex** Gelegenheitssex m; **casually** adv (remark, say) beiläufig; (meet) zwanglos; (dressed) leger
casualty ['kæʒjʊəltɪ] n Verletzte(r) mf; (dead) Tote(r) mf; (department in hospital) Notaufnahme f
cat [kæt] n Katze f; (male) Kater m
catalog (US), **catalogue** ['kætəlɒg] n Katalog m ▷ vt katalogisieren
cataract ['kætərækt] n Wasserfall m; (Med) grauer Star
catarrh [kə'tɑ:*] n Katarr(h) m
catastrophe [kə'tæstrəfɪ] n Katastrophe f
catch [kætʃ] n (fish etc) Fang m ▷ vt (**caught, caught**) fangen; (thief) fassen; (train, bus etc) nehmen; (not miss) erreichen; **to ~ a cold** sich erkälten; **to ~ fire** Feuer fangen; **I didn't ~ that** das habe ich nicht verstanden; **catch on** vi (become popular) Anklang finden; **catch up** vt, vi: **to ~ with**

sb jdn einholen; **to ~ on sth** etw nachholen; **catching** adj ansteckend
category ['kætɪgərɪ] n Kategorie f
cater ['keɪtə*] vi die Speisen und Getränke liefern (for für); **cater for** vt (have facilities for) eingestellt sein auf +akk; **catering** n Versorgung f mit Speisen und Getränken, Gastronomie f; **catering service** n Partyservice m
caterpillar ['kætəpɪlə*] n Raupe f
cathedral [kə'θi:drəl] n Kathedrale f, Dom m
Catholic ['kæθəlɪk] adj katholisch ▷ Katholik(in) m(f)
cat nap n (Brit) kurzer Schlaf; **cat's eyes** ['kætsaɪz] npl (in road) Katzenaugen pl, Reflektoren pl
catsup ['kætsəp] n (US) Ketschup nt o m
cattle ['kætl] npl Vieh nt
caught [kɔ:t] pt, pp of **catch**
cauliflower ['kɒlɪflaʊə*] n Blumenkohl m; **cauliflower cheese** n Blumenkohl m in Käsesoße
cause [kɔ:z] n (origin) Ursache f (of für); (reason) Grund m (for zu); (purpose) Sache f; **for a good ~** für wohltätige Zwecke; **no ~ for alarm/complaint** kein Grund zur Aufregung/Klage ▷ vt verursachen
causeway ['kɔ:zweɪ] n Damm m
caution ['kɔ:ʃən] n Vorsicht f; (Jur, Sport) Verwarnung f ▷ vt (ver)warnen; **cautious** ['kɔ:ʃəs] adj vorsichtig
cave [keɪv] n Höhle f; **cave in** vi einstürzen
cavity ['kævɪtɪ] n Hohlraum m; (in tooth) Loch nt
cayenne (pepper) [keɪ'en] n Cayennepfeffer m

CCTV *abbr* = **closed circuit television** Video-überwachungsanlage *f*

CD *abbr* = **Compact Disc** CD *f*; **CD player** *n* CD-Spieler *m*; **CD-ROM** *abbr* = **Compact Disc Read Only Memory** CD-ROM *f*; **CD-RW** *abbr* = **Compact Disc Rewritable** CD-RW *f*

cease [siːs] *vi* aufhören ▷ *vt* beenden; **to ~ doing sth** aufhören, etw zu tun; **cease fire** *n* Waffenstillstand *m*

ceiling ['siːlɪŋ] *n* Decke *f*

celebrate ['selɪbreɪt] *vt, vi* feiern; **celebrated** *adj* gefeiert; **celebration** [selɪ'breɪʃən] *n* Feier *f*; **celebrity** [sɪ'lebrɪtɪ] *n* Berühmtheit *f*, Star *m*

celeriac [sə'lerɪæk] *n* (Knollen)sellerie *m o f*; **celery** ['selərɪ] *n* (Stangen)sellerie *m o f*

cell [sel] *n* Zelle *f*; (US) see **cellphone**

cellar ['selə*] *n* Keller *m*

cello ['tʃeləʊ] (*pl* -s) *n* Cello *nt*

cellphone ['selfəʊn], **cellular phone** ['seljʊlə* 'fəʊn] *n* Mobiltelefon *nt*, Handy *nt*

Celt [kelt] *n* Kelte *m*, Keltin *f*; **Celtic** ['keltɪk] *adj* keltisch ▷ *n* (language) Keltisch *nt*

cement [sɪ'ment] *n* Zement *m*

cemetery ['semɪtrɪ] *n* Friedhof *m*

censorship ['sensəʃɪp] *n* Zensur *f*

cent [sent] *n* (of dollar, euro etc) Cent *m*

center *n* (US) see **centre**

centiliter (US), **centilitre** ['sentiliːtə*] *n* Zentiliter *m*; **centimeter** (US), **centimetre** ['sentimiːtə*] *n* Zentimeter *m*

central ['sentrəl] *adj* zentral; **Central America** *n* Mittelamerika *nt*; **Central Europe** *n* Mitteleuropa *nt*; **central heating** *n* Zentralheizung *f*; **centralize** *vt* zentralisieren; **central locking** *n* (Auto) Zentralverriegelung *f*; **central reservation** *n* (Brit) Mittelstreifen *m*; **central station** *n* Hauptbahnhof *m*

centre ['sentə*] *n* Mitte *f*; (building, of city) Zentrum *nt* ▷ *vt* zentrieren; **centre forward** *n* (Sport) Mittelstürmer *m*

century ['sentjʊrɪ] *n* Jahrhundert *nt*

ceramic [sɪ'ræmɪk] *adj* keramisch

cereal ['sɪərɪəl] *n* (any grain) Getreide *nt*; (breakfast cereal) Frühstücksflocken *pl*

ceremony ['serɪmənɪ] *n* Feier *f*, Zeremonie *f*

certain ['sɜːtən] *adj* sicher (of +gen); (particular) bestimmt; **for ~** mit Sicherheit; **certainly** *adv* sicher; (without doubt) bestimmt; **~!** aber sicher!; **~ not** ganz bestimmt nicht!

certificate [sə'tɪfɪkɪt] *n* Bescheinigung *f*; (in school, of qualification) Zeugnis *nt*; **certify** ['sɜːtɪfaɪ] *vt, vi* bescheinigen

cervical smear ['sɜːvɪkəl smɪə*] *n* Abstrich *m*

CFC *abbr* = **chlorofluorocarbon** FCKW *nt*

chain [tʃeɪn] *n* Kette *f* ▷ *vt*: **to ~ (up)** anketten; **chain reaction** *n* Kettenreaktion *f*; **chain store** *n* Kettenladen *m*

chair [tʃeə*] *n* Stuhl *m*; (university) Lehrstuhl *m*; (armchair) Sessel *m*; (chairperson) Vorsitzende(r) *mf*; **chairlift** *n* Sessellift *m*; **chairman** (*pl* -men) *n* Vorsitzende(r) *m*; (of firm) Präsident *m*; **chairperson** *n* Vorsitzende(r) *mf*; (of firm) Präsident(in) *m(f)*; **chairwoman**

(pl **-women**) n Vorsitzende f; (of firm) Präsidentin f
chalet [ˈʃæleɪ] n (in mountains) Berghütte f; (holiday dwelling) Ferienhäuschen nt
chalk [tʃɔːk] n Kreide f
challenge [ˈtʃælɪndʒ] n Herausforderung f ▷ vt (person) herausfordern; (statement) bestreiten
chambermaid [ˈtʃeɪmbəˀmeɪd] n Zimmermädchen nt
chamois leather [ˈʃæmwɑːˈleðəˀ] n (for windows) Fensterleder nt
champagne [ʃæmˈpeɪn] n Champagner m
champion [ˈtʃæmpɪən] n (Sport) Meister(in) m(f); **championship** n Meisterschaft f
chance [tʃɑːns] n (fate) Zufall m; (possibility) Möglichkeit f; (opportunity) Gelegenheit f; (risk) Risiko nt; **by ~** zufällig; **he doesn't stand a ~ (of winning)** er hat keinerlei Chance(, zu gewinnen)
chancellor [ˈtʃɑːnsələˀ] n Kanzler(in) m(f)
chandelier [ʃændɪˈlɪəˀ] n Kronleuchter m
change [tʃeɪndʒ] vt verändern; (alter) ändern; (money, wheel, nappy) wechseln; (exchange) (um)tauschen; **to ~ one's clothes** sich umziehen; **to ~ trains** umsteigen; **to ~ gear** (Auto) schalten ▷ vi sich ändern; (esp outwardly) sich verändern; (get changed) sich umziehen ▷ n Veränderung f; (alteration) Änderung f; (money) Wechselgeld nt; (coins) Kleingeld nt; **for a ~** zur Abwechslung; **can you give me ~ for £10?** können Sie mir auf 10 Pfund herausgeben?; **change down** vi (Brit Auto) herunterschalten; **change over** vi

sich umstellen (to auf +akk); **change up** vi (Brit Auto) hochschalten
changeable adj (weather) veränderlich, wechselhaft; **change machine** n Geldwechsler m; **changing room** n Umkleideraum m
channel [ˈtʃænl] n Kanal m; (Radio, TV) Kanal m, Sender m; **the (English) Channel** der Ärmelkanal; **the Channel Islands** die Kanalinseln; **the Channel Tunnel** der Kanaltunnel; **channel-hopping** n Zappen nt
chaos [ˈkeɪɒs] n Chaos nt; **chaotic** [keɪˈɒtɪk] adj chaotisch
chap [tʃæp] n (Brit fam) Bursche m, Kerl m
chapel [ˈtʃæpəl] n Kapelle f
chapped [tʃæpt] adj (lips) aufgesprungen
chapter [ˈtʃæptəˀ] n Kapitel nt
character [ˈkærəktəˀ] n Charakter m, Wesen nt; (in a play, novel etc) Figur f; (Typo) Zeichen nt; **he's a real ~** er ist ein echtes Original; **characteristic** [kærəktəˈrɪstɪk] n typisches Merkmal
charcoal [ˈtʃɑːkəʊl] n Holzkohle f
charge [tʃɑːdʒ] n (cost) Gebühr f; (Jur) Anklage f; **free of ~** gratis, kostenlos; **to be in ~ of** verantwortlich sein für ▷ vt (money) verlangen; (Jur) anklagen; (battery) laden; **charge card** n Kundenkreditkarte f
charity [ˈtʃærɪtɪ] n (institution) wohltätige Organisation f; **a collection for ~** eine Sammlung für wohltätige Zwecke; **charity shop** n Geschäft einer 'charity', in dem freiwillige Helfer gebrauchte Kleidung, Bücher etc verkaufen
charm [tʃɑːm] n Charme m ▷ vt bezaubern; **charming** adj reizend, charmant

chart [tʃɑːt] n Diagramm nt; (map) Karte f; **the ~s** pl die Charts, die Hitliste

charter ['tʃɑːtə*] n Urkunde f ▷ vt (Naut, Aviat) chartern; **charter flight** n Charterflug m

chase [tʃeɪs] vt jagen, verfolgen ▷ n Verfolgungsjagd f; (hunt) Jagd f

chassis ['ʃæsɪ] n (Auto) Fahrgestell nt

chat [tʃæt] vi plaudern; (Inform) chatten ▷ n Plauderei f; (Inform) Chat m; **chat up** vt anmachen, anbaggern; **chatroom** n (Inform) Chatroom m; **chat show** n Talkshow f; **chatty** adj geschwätzig

chauffeur ['ʃəʊfə*] n Chauffeur(in) m(f), Fahrer(in) m(f)

cheap [tʃiːp] adj billig; (of poor quality) minderwertig

cheat [tʃiːt] vt, vi betrügen; (in school, game) mogeln

Chechen ['tʃetʃen] adj tschetschenisch ▷ n Tschetschene m, Tschetschenin f; **Chechnya** ['tʃetʃnɪə] n Tschetschenien nt

check [tʃek] vt (examine) überprüfen (for auf +akk); (Tech: adjustment etc) kontrollieren; (US: tick) abhaken; (Aviat: luggage) einchecken; (US: coat) abgeben ▷ n (examination, restraint) Kontrolle f; (US: restaurant bill) Rechnung f; (pattern) Karo(muster) nt; (US) see **cheque**; **check in** vt, vi (Aviat) einchecken; (into hotel) sich anmelden; **check out** vi sich abmelden, auschecken; **check up** vi nachprüfen; **to ~ on sb** Nachforschungen über jdn anstellen

checkers ['tʃekəz] nsing (US) Damespiel nt

check-in ['tʃekɪn] n (airport) Check-in m; (hotel) Anmeldung f; **check-in desk** n

Abfertigungsschalter m; **checking account** n (US) Scheckkonto nt; **check list** n Kontrollliste f; **checkout** n (supermarket) Kasse f; **checkout time** n (hotel) Abreise(zeit) f; **checkpoint** n Kontrollpunkt m; **checkroom** n (US) Gepäckaufbewahrung f; **checkup** n (Med) (ärztliche) Untersuchung

cheddar ['tʃedə*] n Cheddarkäse m

cheek [tʃiːk] n Backe f, Wange f; (insolence) Frechheit f; **what a ~** so eine Frechheit!; **cheekbone** n Backenknochen m; **cheeky** adj frech

cheer [tʃɪə*] n Beifallsruf m; **~s** (when drinking) prost!; (Brit fam: thanks) danke; (Brit: goodbye) tschüs ▷ vt zujubeln +dat ▷ vi jubeln; **cheer up** vt aufmuntern ▷ vi fröhlicher werden; **~!** Kopf hoch!; **cheerful** ['tʃɪəfʊl] adj fröhlich

cheese [tʃiːz] n Käse m; **cheeseboard** n Käsebrett nt; (as course) (gemischte) Käseplatte; **cheesecake** n Käsekuchen m

chef [ʃef] n Koch m; (in charge of kitchen) Küchenchef(in) m(f)

chemical ['kemɪkəl] adj chemisch ▷ Chemikalie f; **chemist** ['kemɪst] n (pharmacist) Apotheker(in) m(f); (industrial chemist) Chemiker(in) m(f); **~'s** (**shop**) Apotheke f; **chemistry** n Chemie f

cheque [tʃek] n (Brit) Scheck m; **cheque account** n (Brit) Girokonto nt; **cheque book** n (Brit) Scheckheft nt; **cheque card** n (Brit) Scheckkarte f

chequered ['tʃekəd] adj kariert

cherish ['tʃerɪʃ] vt (look after) liebevoll sorgen für; (hope) hegen; (memory) bewahren

cherry ['tʃerɪ] n Kirsche f; **cherry tomato** (pl **-es**) n Kirschtomate f

chess [tʃes] n Schach nt; **chessboard** n Schachbrett nt

chest [tʃest] n Brust f; (box) Kiste f; **~ of drawers** Kommode f

chestnut ['tʃesnʌt] n Kastanie f

chew [tʃuː] vt, vi kauen; **chewing gum** n Kaugummi m

chick [tʃɪk] n Küken nt; **chicken** n Huhn nt; (food: roast) Hähnchen nt; (coward) Feigling m; **chicken breast** n Hühnerbrust f; **chicken Kiev** n paniertes Hähnchen, mit Knoblauchbutter gefüllt; **chickenpox** n Windpocken pl; **chickpea** n Kichererbse f

chicory ['tʃɪkərɪ] n Chicorée f

chief [tʃiːf] n (of department etc) Leiter(in) m(f); (boss) Chef(in) m(f); (of tribe) Häuptling m ▷ adj Haupt-; **chiefly** adv hauptsächlich

child [tʃaɪld] (pl **children**) n Kind nt; **child abuse** n Kindesmisshandlung f; **child allowance**, **child benefit** (Brit) n Kindergeld nt; **childbirth** n Geburt f, Entbindung f; **childhood** n Kindheit f; **childish** adj kindisch; **child lock** n Kindersicherung f; **childproof** adj kindersicher; **children** ['tʃɪldrən] pl of **child**; **child seat** n Kindersitz m

Chile ['tʃɪlɪ] n Chile nt

chill [tʃɪl] n Kühle f; (Med) Erkältung f ▷ vt (wine) kühlen; **chill out** vi (fam) chillen, relaxen; **chilled** adj gekühlt

chilli ['tʃɪlɪ] n Pepperoni pl; (spice) Chili m; **chilli con carne** ['tʃɪlɪkɔn'kaːnɪ] n Chili con carne nt

chilly ['tʃɪlɪ] adj kühl, frostig

chimney ['tʃɪmnɪ] n Schornstein m; **chimneysweep** n Schornsteinfeger(in) m(f)

chimpanzee [tʃɪmpæn'ziː] n Schimpanse m

chin [tʃɪn] n Kinn nt

china ['tʃaɪnə] n Porzellan nt

China ['tʃaɪnə] n China nt; **Chinese** [tʃaɪ'niːz] adj chinesisch ▷ n (person) Chinese m, Chinesin f; (language) Chinesisch nt; **Chinese leaves** npl Chinakohl m

chip [tʃɪp] n (of wood etc) Splitter m; (damage) angeschlagene Stelle; (Inform) Chip m; **~s** (Brit: potatoes) Pommes (frites) pl; (US: crisps) Kartoffelchips pl ▷ vt anschlagen, beschädigen; **chippie** (fam), **chip shop** n Frittenbude f

chiropodist [kɪ'rɒpədɪst] n Fußpfleger(in) m(f)

chirp [tʃɜːp] vi zwitschern

chisel ['tʃɪzl] n Meißel m

chitchat ['tʃɪttʃæt] n Gerede nt

chives [tʃaɪvz] npl Schnittlauch m

chlorine ['klɔːriːn] n Chlor nt

chocaholic, **chocoholic** [tʃɒkə'hɒlɪk] n Schokoladenfreak m; **choc-ice** ['tʃɒkaɪs] n Eis nt mit Schokoladenüberzug; **chocolate** ['tʃɒklɪt] n Schokolade f; (chocolate-coated sweet) Praline f; **a bar of ~** eine Tafel Schokolade; **a box of ~s** eine Schachtel Pralinen; **chocolate cake** n Schokoladenkuchen m; **chocolate sauce** n Schokoladensoße f

choice [tʃɔɪs] n Wahl f; (selection) Auswahl f ▷ adj auserlesen; (product) Qualitäts-

choir ['kwaɪə°] n Chor m

choke [tʃəuk] vi sich verschlucken; (Sport) die Nerven verlieren ▷ vt erdrosseln ▷ n (Auto) Choke m

cholera ['kɒlərə] *n* Cholera *f*

cholesterol [kə'lestərəl] *n* Cholesterin *nt*

choose [tʃuːz] (**chose, chosen**) *vt* wählen; (*pick out*) sich aussuchen; **there are three to ~ from** es stehen drei zur Auswahl

chop [tʃɒp] *vt* (zer)hacken; (*meat etc*) klein schneiden ▷ *n* (*meat*) Kotelett *nt*; **to get the ~** gefeuert werden; **chopper** *n* Hackbeil *nt*; (*fam: helicopter*) Hubschrauber *m*; **chopsticks** *npl* Essstäbchen *pl*

chorus ['kɔːrəs] *n* Chor *m*; (*in song*) Refrain *m*

chose, chosen [tʃəʊz, 'tʃəʊzn] *pt, pp of* **choose**

chowder ['tʃaʊdə*] *n* (*US*) *dicke Suppe mit Meeresfrüchten*

christen ['krɪsn] *vt* taufen; **christening** *n* Taufe *f*; **Christian** ['krɪstɪən] *adj* christlich ▷ *n* Christ(in) *m(f)*; **Christian name** *n* (*Brit*) Vorname *m*

Christmas ['krɪsməs] *n* Weihnachten *pl*; **Christmas bonus** *n* Weihnachtsgeld *nt*; **Christmas card** *n* Weihnachtskarte *f*; **Christmas carol** *n* Weihnachtslied *nt*; **Christmas Day** *n* der erste Weihnachtstag; **Christmas Eve** *n* Heiligabend *m*; **Christmas pudding** *n* Plumpudding *m*; **Christmas tree** *n* Weihnachtsbaum *m*

chronic ['krɒnɪk] *adj* (*Med, fig*) chronisch; (*fam: very bad*) miserabel

chrysanthemum [krɪ'sænθɪməm] *n* Chrysantheme *f*

chubby ['tʃʌbɪ] *adj* (*child*) pummelig; (*adult*) rundlich

chuck [tʃʌk] *vt* (*fam*) schmeißen; **chuck in** *vt* (*fam: job*) hinschmeißen; **chuck out** *vt* (*fam*) rausschmeißen; **chuck up** *vi* (*fam*) kotzen

chunk [tʃʌŋk] *n* Klumpen *m*; (*of bread*) Brocken *m*; (*of meat*) Batzen *m*; **chunky** *adj* (*person*) stämmig

Chunnel ['tʃʌnəl] *n* (*fam*) Kanaltunnel *m*

church [tʃɜːtʃ] *n* Kirche *f*; **churchyard** *n* Kirchhof *m*

chute [ʃuːt] *n* Rutsche *f*

chutney ['tʃʌtnɪ] *n* Chutney *m*

CIA *abbr* = **Central Intelligence Agency** (*US*) CIA *f*

CID *abbr* = **Criminal Investigation Department** (*Brit*) ≈ Kripo *f*

cider ['saɪdə*] *n* ≈ Apfelmost *m*

cigar [sɪ'gɑː*] *n* Zigarre *f*; **cigarette** [sɪgə'ret] *n* Zigarette *f*

cinema ['sɪnəmə] *n* Kino *nt*

cinnamon ['sɪnəmən] *n* Zimt *m*

circle ['sɜːkl] *n* Kreis *m* ▷ *vi* kreisen; **circuit** ['sɜːkɪt] *n* Rundfahrt *f*; (*on foot*) Rundgang *m*; (*for racing*) Rennstrecke *f*; (*Elec*) Stromkreis *m*; **circular** ['sɜːkjʊlə*] *adj* (kreis)rund, kreisförmig ▷ *n* Rundschreiben *nt*; **circulation** [sɜːkjʊ'leɪʃən] *n* (*of blood*) Kreislauf *m*; (*of newspaper*) Auflage *f*

circumstances ['sɜːkəmstənsəz] *npl* (*facts*) Umstände *pl*; (*financial condition*) Verhältnisse *pl*; **in/under the ~** unter den Umständen; **under no ~** auf keinen Fall

circus ['sɜːkəs] *n* Zirkus *m*

cissy ['sɪsɪ] *n* (*fam*) Weichling *m*

cistern ['sɪstən] *n* Zisterne *f*; (*of WC*) Spülkasten *m*

citizen ['sɪtɪzn] *n* Bürger(in) *m(f)*; (*of nation*) Staatsangehörige(r) *mf*; **citizenship** *n* Staatsangehörigkeit *f*

city ['sɪtɪ] *n* Stadt *f*; (*large*) Großstadt *f*; **the ~** (*London's financial centre*) die (Londoner)

City; **city centre** n Innenstadt f,
Zentrum nt
civil ['sɪvil] adj (of town) Bürger-;
(of state) staatsbürgerlich; (not
military) zivil; **civil ceremony** n
standesamtliche Hochzeit; **civil
engineering** n Hoch- und Tiefbau
m, Bauingenieurwesen nt; **civilian**
[sɪ'vɪljən] n Zivilist(in) m(f);
civilization [sɪvɪlaɪ'zeɪʃən] n
Zivilisation f, Kultur f; **civilized**
['sɪvɪlaɪzd] adj zivilisiert,
kultiviert; **civil partnership** n
eingetragene Partnerschaft; **civil
rights** npl Bürgerrechte pl; **civil
servant** n (Staats)beamte(r) m,
(Staats)beamtin f; **civil service** n
Staatsdienst m; **civil war** n
Bürgerkrieg m
CJD abbr = **Creutzfeld-Jakob
disease** Creutzfeld-
Jakob-Krankheit f
cl abbr = **centilitre(s)** cl
claim [kleɪm] vt beanspruchen;
(apply for) beantragen; (demand)
fordern; (assert) behaupten (that
dass) ▷ n (demand) Forderung f
(for für); (right) Anspruch m (to auf
+akk); **~ for damages**
Schadenersatzforderung f; **to
make** o **put in a ~** (insurance)
Ansprüche geltend machen;
claimant n Antragsteller(in) m(f)
clam [klæm] n Venusmuschel f;
clam chowder n (US) dicke
Muschelsuppe (mit Sellerie, Zwiebeln
etc)
clap [klæp] vi (Beifall) klatschen
claret ['klærɪt] n roter
Bordeaux(wein)
clarify ['klærɪfaɪ] vt klären
clarinet [klærɪ'net] n Klarinette f
clarity ['klærɪtɪ] n Klarheit f
clash [klæʃ] vi (physically)
zusammenstoßen (with mit);
(argue) sich auseinandersetzen
(with mit); (fig: colours) sich beißen

▷ n Zusammenstoß m; (argument)
Auseinandersetzung f
clasp [klɑːsp] n (on belt) Schnalle f
class [klɑːs] n Klasse f ▷ vt
einordnen, einstufen
classic ['klæsɪk] adj (mistake,
example etc) klassisch ▷ n
Klassiker m; **classical** ['klæsɪkəl]
adj (music, ballet etc) klassisch
classification [klæsɪfɪ'keɪʃn] n
Klassifizierung f; **classify**
['klæsɪfaɪ] vt klassifizieren;
classified advertisement
Kleinanzeige f
classroom ['klɑːsrʊm] n Klassenzimmer nt
classy ['klɑːsɪ] adj (fam) nobel,
exklusiv
clatter ['klætə°] vi klappern
clause [klɔːz] n (Ling) Satz m; (Jur)
Klausel f
claw [klɔː] n Kralle f
clay [kleɪ] n Lehm m; (for pottery)
Ton m
clean [kliːn] adj sauber;
~ driving licence Führerschein
ohne Strafpunkte ▷ vt sauber
machen; (carpet etc) reinigen;
(window, shoes, vegetables) putzen;
(wound) säubern; **clean up** vt
sauber machen ▷ vi aufräumen;
cleaner n (person) Putzmann m,
Putzfrau f; (substance) Putzmittel
nt; **~'s** (firm) Reinigung f
cleanse [klenz] vt reinigen;
(wound) säubern; **cleanser** n
Reinigungsmittel nt
clear ['klɪə°] adj klar; (distinct)
deutlich; (conscience) rein; (free,
road etc) frei; **to be ~ about sth**
sich über etw im Klaren sein
▷ adv: **to stand ~** zurücktreten
▷ vt (road, room etc) räumen; (table)
abräumen; (Jur: find innocent)
freisprechen (of von) ▷ vi (fog,
mist) sich verziehen; (weather)
aufklaren; **clear away** vt

wegräumen; (*dishes*) abräumen; **clear off** *vi* (*fam*) abhauen; **clear up** *vi* (*tidy up*) aufräumen; (*weather*) sich aufklären ▷ *vt* (*room*) aufräumen; (*litter*) wegräumen; (*matter*) klären

clearance sale *n* Räumungsverkauf *m*; **clearing** *n* Lichtung *f*; **clearly** *adv* klar; (*speak, remember*) deutlich; (*obviously*) eindeutig; **clearout** *n* Entrümpelungsaktion *f*; **clearway** *n* (*Brit*) Straße *f* mit Halteverbot *nt*

clench [klɛntʃ] *vt* (*fist*) ballen; (*teeth*) zusammenbeißen

clergyman [ˈklɜːdʒɪmæn] (*pl* **-men**) *n* Geistliche(r) *m*; **clergywoman** [ˈklɜːdʒɪwʊmən] (*pl* **-women**) *n* Geistliche *f*

clerk [klɑːk], (*US*) [klɜːk] *n* (*in office*) Büroangestellte(r) *mf*; (*US: salesperson*) Verkäufer(in) *m(f)*

clever [ˈklɛvə°] *adj* schlau, klug; (*idea*) clever

cliché [ˈkliːʃeɪ] *n* Klischee *nt*

click [klɪk] *n* Klicken *nt*; (*Inform*) Mausklick *m* ▷ *vi* klicken; **to ~ on sth** (*Inform*) etw anklicken; **it ~ed** (*fam*) ich hab's/er hat's etc geschnallt, es hat gefunkt, es hat Klick gemacht; **they ~ed** sie haben sich gleich verstanden; **click on** *vt* (*Inform*) anklicken

client [ˈklaɪənt] *n* Kunde *m*, Kundin *f*; (*Jur*) Mandant(in) *m(f)*

cliff [klɪf] *n* Klippe *f*

climate [ˈklaɪmɪt] *n* Klima *nt*

climax [ˈklaɪmæks] *n* Höhepunkt *m*

climb [klaɪm] *vi* (*person*) klettern; (*aircraft, sun*) steigen; (*road*) ansteigen ▷ *vt* (*mountain*) besteigen; (*tree etc*) klettern auf +*akk* ▷ *n* Aufstieg *m*; **climber** *n* (*mountaineer*) Bergsteiger(in) *m(f)*; **climbing** *n* Klettern *nt*,

Bergsteigen *nt*; **climbing frame** *n* Klettergerüst *nt*

cling [klɪŋ] (**clung, clung**) *vi* sich klammern (*to an +akk*); **cling film®** *n* Frischhaltefolie *f*

clinic [ˈklɪnɪk] *n* Klinik *f*; **clinical** *adj* klinisch

clip [klɪp] *n* Klammer *f* ▷ *vt* (*fix*) anklemmen (*to an +akk*); (*fingernails*) schneiden; **clipboard** *n* Klemmbrett *nt*; **clippers** *npl* Schere *f*; (*for nails*) Zwicker *m*

cloak [kləʊk] *n* Umhang *m*; **cloakroom** *n* (*for coats*) Garderobe *f*

clock [klɒk] *n* Uhr *f*; (*Auto: fam*) Tacho *m*; **round the ~** rund um die Uhr; **clockwise** *adv* im Uhrzeigersinn

clog [klɒg] *n* Holzschuh *m* ▷ *vt* verstopfen

cloister [ˈklɔɪstə°] *n* Kreuzgang *m*

clone [kləʊn] *n* Klon *m* ▷ *vt* klonen

close [kləʊs] *adj* nahe (*to +dat*); (*friend, contact*) eng; (*resemblance*) groß; **~ to the beach** in der Nähe des Strandes; **~ win** knapper Sieg; **on ~r examination** bei näherer o genauerer Untersuchung ▷ *adv* [kləʊs] dicht; **he lives ~ by** er wohnt ganz in der Nähe ▷ *vt* [kləʊz] schließen; (*road*) sperren; (*discussion, matter*) abschließen ▷ *vi* [kləʊz] schließen rtri; *n* [kləʊz] Ende *nt*; **close down** *vi* schließen; (*factory*) stillgelegt werden ▷ *vt* (*shop*) schließen; (*factory*) stilllegen; **closed** *adj* (*road*) gesperrt; (*shop etc*) geschlossen; **closed circuit television** *n* Videoüberwachungsanlage *f*; **closely** *adv* (*related*) eng, nah; (*packed, follow*) dicht; (*attentively*) genau

closet ['klɒzɪt] n (esp US) Schrank m

close-up ['kləʊsʌp] n Nahaufnahme f

closing ['kləʊzɪŋ] adj: ~ **date** letzter Termin; (for competition) Einsendeschluss m; ~ **time** (of shop) Ladenschluss m; (Brit: of pub) Polizeistunde f

closure ['kləʊʒə°] n Schließung f; Abschluss m; **to look for ~** mit etw abschließen wollen

clot [klɒt] (**blood**) ~ Blutgerinnsel nt; (fam: idiot) Trottel m ▷ vi (blood) gerinnen

cloth [klɒθ] n (material) Tuch nt; (for cleaning) Lappen m

clothe [kləʊð] vt kleiden; **clothes** [kləʊðz] npl Kleider pl, Kleidung f; **clothes line** n Wäscheleine f; **clothes peg**, **clothespin** (US) n Wäscheklammer f; **clothing** ['kləʊðɪŋ] n Kleidung f

clotted ['klɒtɪd] adj: ~ **cream** dicke Sahne (aus erhitzter Milch)

cloud [klaʊd] n Wolke f; **cloudy** adj (sky) bewölkt; (liquid) trüb

clove [kləʊv] n Gewürznelke f; ~ **of garlic** Knoblauchzehe f

clover ['kləʊvə°] n Klee m; **cloverleaf** (pl **-leaves**) n Kleeblatt nt

clown [klaʊn] n Clown m

club [klʌb] n (weapon) Knüppel m; (society) Klub m, Verein m; (nightclub) Disko f; (golf club) Golfschläger m; ~**s** (Cards) Kreuz nt; **clubbing** n: **to go** ~ in die Disko gehen; **club class** n (Aviat) Businessclass f

clue [kluː] n Anhaltspunkt m, Hinweis m; **he hasn't a** ~ er hat keine Ahnung

clumsy ['klʌmzɪ] adj unbeholfen, ungeschickt

clung [klʌŋ] pt, pp of **cling**

clutch [klʌtʃ] n (Auto) Kupplung f ▷ vt umklammern; (book etc) an sich akk klammern

cm abbr = **centimetre(s)** cm

c/o abbr = **care of** bei

Co abbr = **company** Co

coach [kəʊtʃ] n (Brit: bus) Reisebus m; (Rail) (Personen)wagen m; (Sport: trainer) Trainer(in) m(f) ▷ vt Nachhilfeunterricht geben +dat; (Sport) trainieren; **coach (class)** n (Aviat) Economyclass f; **coach driver** n Busfahrer(in) m(f); **coach party** n Reisegruppe f (Bus) ; **coach station** n Busbahnhof m; **coach trip** n Busfahrt f; (tour) Busreise f

coal [kəʊl] n Kohle f

coalition [kəʊə'lɪʃən] n (Pol) Koalition f

coalmine ['kəʊlmaɪn] n Kohlenbergwerk nt; **coalminer** n Bergarbeiter m

coast [kəʊst] n Küste f; **coastguard** n Küstenwache f; **coastline** n Küste f

coat [kəʊt] n Mantel m; (jacket) Jacke f; (on animals) Fell nt, Pelz m; (of paint) Schicht f; ~ **of arms** Wappen nt; **coathanger** n Kleiderbügel m; **coating** n Überzug m; (layer) Schicht f

cobble(stone)s ['kɒbl(stəʊn)z] npl Kopfsteine pl; (surface) Kopfsteinpflaster nt

cobweb ['kɒbweb] n Spinnennetz nt

cocaine [kə'keɪn] n Kokain nt

cock [kɒk] n Hahn m; (vulg: penis) Schwanz m; **cock up** vt (Brit fam) vermasseln, versauen; **cockerel** ['kɒkərəl] n junger Hahn

cockle ['kɒkl] n Herzmuschel f

cockpit ['kɒkpɪt] n (in plane, racing car) Cockpit nt; **cockroach** ['kɒkrəʊtʃ] n Kakerlake f; **cocktail**

['kɒkteɪl] *n* Cocktail *m*; **cock-up** *n* (*Brit fam*) **to make a ~ of sth** bei etw Mist bauen; **cocky** ['kɒkɪ] *adj* großspurig, von sich selbst überzeugt

cocoa ['kəʊkəʊ] *n* Kakao *m*

coconut ['kəʊkənʌt] *n* Kokosnuss *f*

cod [kɒd] *n* Kabeljau *m*

COD *abbr* = **cash on delivery** per Nachnahme

code [kəʊd] *n* Kode *m*

coeducational [kəʊedjʊ'keɪʃənl] *adj* (*school*) gemischt

coffee ['kɒfɪ] *n* Kaffee *m*; **coffee bar** *n* Café *nt*; **coffee break** *n* Kaffeepause *f*; **coffee maker** *n* Kaffeemaschine *f*; **coffee pot** *n* Kaffeekanne *f*; **coffee shop** *n* Café *nt*; **coffee table** *n* Couchtisch *m*

coffin ['kɒfɪn] *n* Sarg *m*

coil [kɔɪl] *n* Rolle *f*; (*Elec*) Spule *f*; (*Med*) Spirale *f*

coin [kɔɪn] *n* Münze *f*

coincide [kəʊɪn'saɪd] *vi* (*happen together*) zusammenfallen (*with* mit); **coincidence** [kəʊ'ɪnsɪdəns] *n* Zufall *m*

coke [kəʊk] *n* Koks *m*; **Coke®** Cola *f*

cola ['kəʊlə] *n* Cola *f*

cold [kəʊld] *adj* kalt; **I'm ~** mir ist kalt, ich friere ▷ *n* Kälte *f*; (*illness*) Erkältung *f*, Schnupfen *m*; **to catch a ~** sich erkälten; **cold box** *n* Kühlbox *f*; **cold sore** *n* Herpes *m*; **cold turkey** *n* (*fam*) Totalentzug *m*; (*symptoms*) Entzugserscheinungen *pl*

coleslaw ['kəʊlslɔː] *n* Krautsalat *m*

collaborate [kə'læbəreɪt] *vi* zusammenarbeiten (*with* mit); **collaboration** [kəlæbə'reɪʃən] *n* Zusammenarbeit *f*; (*of one party*) Mitarbeit *f*

collapse [kə'læps] *vi* zusammenbrechen; (*building etc*) einstürzen ▷ *n* Zusammenbruch *m*; (*of building*) Einsturz *m*; **collapsible** [kə'læpsəbl] *adj* zusammenklappbar, Klapp-

collar ['kɒlə*] *n* Kragen *m*; (*for dog, cat*) Halsband *nt*; **collarbone** *n* Schlüsselbein *nt*

colleague ['kɒliːg] *n* Kollege *m*, Kollegin *f*

collect [kə'lekt] *vt* sammeln; (*fetch*) abholen ▷ *vi* sich sammeln; **collect call** *n* (*US*) R-Gespräch *nt*; **collected** *adj* (*works*) gesammelt; (*person*) gefasst; **collector** *n* Sammler(in) *m(f)*; **collection** [kə'lekʃən] *n* Sammlung *f*; (*Rel*) Kollekte *f*; (*from postbox*) Leerung *f*

college ['kɒlɪdʒ] *n* (*residential*) College *nt*; (*specialist*) Fachhochschule *f*; (*vocational*) Berufsschule *f*; (*US: university*) Universität *f*; **to go to ~** (*US*) studieren

collide [kə'laɪd] *vi* zusammenstoßen; **collision** [kə'lɪʒən] *n* Zusammenstoß *m*

colloquial [kə'ləʊkwɪəl] *adj* umgangssprachlich

Cologne [kə'ləʊn] *n* Köln *nt*

colon ['kəʊlən] *n* (*punctuation mark*) Doppelpunkt *m*

colonial [kə'ləʊnɪəl] *adj* Kolonial-; **colonize** ['kɒlənaɪz] *vt* kolonisieren; **colony** ['kɒlənɪ] *n* Kolonie *f*

color *n* (*US*), **colour** ['kʌlə*] *n* Farbe *f*; (*of skin*) Hautfarbe *f* ▷ *vt* anmalen; (*bias*) färben; **colour-blind** *adj* farbenblind; **coloured** *adj* farbig; (*biased*) gefärbt; **colour film** *n* Farbfilm *m*; **colourful** *adj* (*lit, fig*) bunt; (*life, past*) bewegt; **colouring** *n* (*in food etc*) Farbstoff *m*; (*complexion*) Gesichtsfarbe *f*; **colourless** *adj* (*lit, fig*) farblos; **colour photo(graph)** *n* Farbfoto *nt*; **colour television** *n* Farbfernsehen *nt*

column ['kɒləm] *n* Säule *f*; (*of print*) Spalte *f*

comb [kəʊm] *n* Kamm *m* ▷ *vt* kämmen; **to ~ one's hair** sich kämmen

combination [kɒmbɪ'neɪʃən] *n* Kombination *f*; (*mixture*) Mischung *f* (*of* aus); **combine** [kəm'baɪn] *vt* verbinden (*with* mit); (*two things*) kombinieren

come [kʌm] (**came, come**) *vi* kommen; (*arrive*) ankommen; (*on list, in order*) stehen; (*with adjective: become*) werden; **~ and see us** besuchen Sie uns mal; **coming** ich komm ja schon!; **to ~ first/second** erster/zweiter werden; **to ~ true** wahr werden; **to ~ loose** sich lockern; **the years to ~** die kommenden Jahre; **there's one more to ~** es kommt noch eins/noch einer; **how ~ ...?** (*fam*) wie kommt es, dass ...?; **~ to think of it** (*fam*) wo es mir gerade einfällt; **come across** *vt* (*find*) stoßen auf +*akk*; **come back** *vi* zurückkommen; **I'll ~ to that** ich komme darauf zurück; **come down** *vi* herunterkommen; (*rain, snow, price*) fallen; **come from** *vt* (*result*) kommen von; **where do you ~?** wo kommen Sie her?; **I ~ London** ich komme aus London; **come in** *vi* hereinkommen; (*arrive*) ankommen; (*in race*) **to ~ fourth** Vierter werden; **come off** *vi* (*button, handle etc*) abgehen; (*succeed*) gelingen; **to ~ well/badly** gut/schlecht wegkommen; **come on** *vi* (*progress*) vorankommen; **~!** komm!; (*hurry*) beeil dich!; (*encouraging*) los!; **come out** *vi*

herauskommen; (*photo*) was werden; (*homosexual*) sich outen; **come round** *vi* (*visit*) vorbeikommen; (*regain consciousness*) wieder zu sich kommen; **come to** *vi* (*regain consciousness*) wieder zu sich kommen ▷ *vt* (*sum*) sich belaufen auf +*akk*; **when it comes to ...** wenn es um ... geht; **come up** *vi* hochkommen; (*sun, moon*) aufgehen; **to ~ (for discussion)** zur Sprache kommen; **come up to** *vt* (*approach*) zukommen auf +*akk*; (*water*) reichen bis zu; (*expectations*) entsprechen +*dat*; **come up with** *vt* (*idea*) haben; (*solution, answer*) kommen auf +*akk*; **to ~ a suggestion** einen Vorschlag machen

comedian [kə'miːdɪən] *n* Komiker(in) *m(f)*

comedown ['kʌmdaʊn] *n* Abstieg *m*

comedy ['kɒmədɪ] *n* Komödie *f*, Comedy *f*

comfort ['kʌmfət] *n* Komfort *m*; (*consolation*) Trost *m* ▷ *vt* trösten; **comfortable** *adj* bequem; (*income*) ausreichend; (*temperature, life*) angenehm; **comforting** *adj* tröstlich

comic ['kɒmɪk] *n* (*magazine*) Comic(heft) *nt*; (*comedian*) Komiker(in) *m(f)* ▷ *adj* komisch

coming ['kʌmɪŋ] *adj* kommend; (*event*) bevorstehend

comma ['kɒmə] *n* Komma *nt*

command [kə'mɑːnd] *n* Befehl *m*; (*control*) Führung *f*; (*Mil*) Kommando *nt* ▷ *vt* befehlen +*dat*

commemorate [kə'meməreɪt] *vt* gedenken +*gen*; **commemoration** [kəmemə'reɪʃən] *n*: **in ~ of** in Gedenken an +*akk*

comment ['kɒment] *n* (*remark*)

Bemerkung f; (note) Anmerkung f; (official) Kommentar m (on zu); **no ~** kein Kommentar ▷ vi sich äußern (on zu); **commentary** ['kɒməntrɪ] n Kommentar m (on zu); (TV, Sport) Livereportage f; **commentator** ['kɒmənteɪtə*] n Kommentator(in) m(f); (TV, Sport) Reporter(in) m(f)

commerce ['kɒmɜ:s] n Handel m; **commercial** [kə'mɜ:ʃəl] adj kommerziell; (training) kaufmännisch; **~ break** Werbepause f; **~ vehicle** Lieferwagen m ▷ n (TV) Werbespot m

commission [kə'mɪʃən] n Auftrag m; (fee) Provision f; (reporting body) Kommission f ▷ vt beauftragen

commit [kə'mɪt] vt (crime) begehen ▷ vr: **to ~ oneself** (undertake) sich verpflichten (to zu); **commitment** n Verpflichtung f; (Pol) Engagement nt

committee [kə'mɪtɪ] n Ausschuss m, Komitee nt

commodity [kə'mɒdɪtɪ] n Ware f

common ['kɒmən] adj (experience) allgemein, alltäglich; (shared) gemeinsam; (widespread, frequent) häufig; (pej) gewöhnlich, ordinär; **to have sth in ~** etw gemein haben ▷ n (Brit: land) Gemeindewiese f; **commonly** adv häufig, allgemein; **commonplace** adj alltäglich; (pej) banal; **commonroom** n Gemeinschaftsraum m; **Commons** n (Brit Pol) **the (House of) ~** das Unterhaus; **common sense** n gesunder Menschenverstand; **Commonwealth** n Commonwealth nt; **~ of Independent States** Gemeinschaft f Unabhängiger Staaten

communal ['kɒmjʊnl] adj gemeinsam; (of a community) Gemeinschafts-, Gemeinde-

communicate [kə'mju:nɪkeɪt] vi kommunizieren (with mit); **communication** [kəmju:nɪ'keɪʃən] n Kommunikation f, Verständigung f; **communications satellite** n Nachrichtensatellit m; **communications technology** n Nachrichtentechnik f; **communicative** adj gesprächig

communion [kə'mju:nɪən] n: **(Holy) Communion** Heiliges Abendmahl; (Catholic) Kommunion f

communism ['kɒmjʊnɪzəm] n Kommunismus m; **communist** ['kɒmjʊnɪst] adj kommunistisch ▷ n Kommunist(in) m(f)

community [kə'mju:nɪtɪ] n Gemeinschaft f; **community centre** n Gemeindezentrum nt; **community service** n (Jur) Sozialdienst m

commutation ticket [kɒmjʊ'teɪʃəntɪkɪt] n (US) Zeitkarte f; **commute** [kə'mju:t] vi pendeln; **commuter** n Pendler(in) m(f)

compact [kəm'pækt] adj kompakt ▷ ['kɒmpækt] n (for make-up) Puderdose f; (US: car) ≈ Mittelklassewagen m; **compact camera** n Kompaktkamera f; **compact disc** n Compact Disc f, CD f

companion [kəm'pænɪən] n Begleiter(in) m(f)

company ['kʌmpənɪ] n Gesellschaft f; (Comm) Firma f; **to keep sb ~** jdm Gesellschaft leisten; **company car** n Firmenauto nt

comparable ['kɒmpərəbl] *adj* vergleichbar (*with, to* mit)

comparative [kəm'pærətɪv] *adj* relativ ▷ *n* (*Ling*) Komparativ *m*; **comparatively** *adv* verhältnismäßig

compare [kəm'pɛəᵇ] *vt* vergleichen (*with, to* mit); **~d with** *o* **to** im Vergleich zu; **beyond ~** unvergleichlich; **comparison** [kəm'pærɪsn] *n* Vergleich *m*; **in ~ with** im Vergleich mit (*o* zu)

compartment [kəm'pɑːtmənt] *n* (*Rail*) Abteil *nt*; (*in desk etc*) Fach *nt*

compass ['kʌmpəs] *n* Kompass *m*; **~es** *pl* Zirkel *m*

compassion [kəm'pæʃən] *n* Mitgefühl *nt*

compatible [kəm'pætɪbl] *adj* vereinbar (*with* mit); (*Inform*) kompatibel; **we're not ~** wir passen nicht zueinander

compensate ['kɒmpenseɪt] *vt* (*person*) entschädigen (*for* für) ▷ *vi*: **to ~ for sth** Ersatz für etw leisten; (*make up for*) etw ausgleichen; **compensation** [kɒmpen'seɪʃən] *n* Entschädigung *f*; (*money*) Schadenersatz *m*; (*Jur*) Abfindung *f*

compete [kəm'piːt] *vi* konkurrieren (*for* um); (*Sport*) kämpfen (*for* um); (*take part*) teilnehmen (*in* an +*dat*)

competence ['kɒmpɪtəns] *n* Fähigkeit *f*; (*Jur*) Zuständigkeit *f*; **competent** *adj* fähig; (*Jur*) zuständig

competition [kɒmpɪ'tɪʃən] *n* (*contest*) Wettbewerb *m*; (*Comm*) Konkurrenz *f* (*for* um); **competitive** [kəm'petɪtɪv] *adj* (*firm, price, product*) konkurrenzfähig; **competitor** [kəm'petɪtəᵇ] *n* (*Comm*) Konkurrent(in) *m(f)*; (*Sport*) Teilnehmer(in) *m(f)*

complain [kəm'pleɪn] *vi* klagen; (*formally*) sich beschweren (*about* über +*akk*); **complaint** *n* Klage *f*; Beanstandung *f*; (*formal*) Beschwerde *f*; (*Med*) Leiden *nt*

complement *vt* ergänzen

complete [kəm'pliːt] *adj* vollständig; (*finished*) fertig; (*failure, disaster*) total; (*happiness*) vollkommen; **are we ~?** sind wir vollzählig? ▷ *vt* vervollständigen; (*finish*) beenden; (*form*) ausfüllen; **completely** *adv* völlig; **not ~ ...** nicht ganz ...

complex ['kɒmpleks] *adj* komplex; (*task, theory etc*) kompliziert ▷ *n* Komplex *m*

complexion [kəm'plekʃən] *n* Gesichtsfarbe *f*, Teint *m*

complicated ['kɒmplɪkeɪtɪd] *adj* kompliziert; **complication** ['kɒmplɪkeɪʃən] *n* Komplikation *f*

compliment ['kɒmplɪmənt] *n* Kompliment *nt*; **complimentary** [kɒmplɪ'mentərɪ] *adj* lobend; (*free of charge*) Gratis-; **~ ticket** Freikarte *f*

comply [kəm'plaɪ] *vi*: **to ~ with the regulations** den Vorschriften entsprechen

component [kəm'pəʊnənt] *n* Bestandteil *m*

compose [kəm'pəʊz] *vt* (*music*) komponieren; **to ~ oneself** sich zusammennehmen; **composed** *adj* gefasst; **to be ~ of** bestehen aus; **composer** *n* Komponist(in) *m(f)*; **composition** [kɒmpə'zɪʃən] *n* (*of a group*) Zusammensetzung *f*; (*Mus*) Komposition *f*

comprehend [kɒmprɪ'hend] *vt* verstehen; **comprehension** [kɒmprɪ'henʃən] *n* Verständnis *nt*

comprehensive [kɒmprɪ'hensɪv] *adj* umfassend; **~ school** Gesamtschule *f*

compress [kəm'pres] *vt* komprimieren

comprise [kəm'praɪz] *vt* umfassen, bestehen aus

compromise ['kɒmprəmaɪz] *n* Kompromiss *m* ▷ *vi* einen Kompromiss schließen

compulsory [kəm'pʌlsərɪ] *adj* obligatorisch; **~ subject** Pflichtfach *nt*

computer [kəm'pju:tə°] *n* Computer *m*; **computer-aided** *adj* computergestützt; **computer-controlled** *adj* rechnergesteuert; **computer game** *n* Computerspiel *nt*; **computer-literate** *adj*: **to be ~** mit dem Computer umgehen können; **computer scientist** *n* Informatiker(in) *m(f)*; **computing** *n* (*subject*) Informatik *f*

con [kɒn] (*fam*) *n* Schwindel *m* ▷ *vt* betrügen (*out of* um)

conceal [kən'si:l] *vt* verbergen (*from* vor +*dat*)

conceivable [kən'si:vəbl] *adj* denkbar, vorstellbar; **conceive** [kən'si:v] *vt* (*imagine*) sich vorstellen; (*child*) empfangen

concentrate ['kɒnsəntreɪt] *vi* sich konzentrieren (*on* auf +*akk*); **concentration** [kɒnsən'treɪʃən] *n* Konzentration *f*

concept ['kɒnsept] *n* Begriff *m*

concern [kən's3:n] *n* (*affair*) Angelegenheit *f*; (*worry*) Sorge *f*; (*Comm: firm*) Unternehmen *nt*; **it's not my ~** das geht mich nichts an; **there's no cause for ~** kein Grund zur Beunruhigung ▷ *vt* (*affect*) angehen; (*have connection with*) betreffen; (*be about*) handeln von; **those ~ed** die Betroffenen; **as far as I'm ~ed** was mich betrifft; **concerned** *adj* (*anxious*) besorgt; **concerning** *prep* bezüglich, hinsichtlich +*gen*

concert ['kɒnsət] *n* Konzert *nt*; **~ hall** Konzertsaal *m*

concession [kən'seʃən] *n* Zugeständnis *nt*; (*reduction*) Ermäßigung *f*

concise [kən'saɪs] *adj* knapp gefasst, prägnant

conclude [kən'klu:d] *vt* (*end*) beenden, (ab)schließen; (*infer*) folgern (*from* aus); **to ~ that ...** zu dem Schluss kommen, dass ...; **conclusion** [kən'klu:ʒən] *n* Schluss *m*, Schlussfolgerung *f*

concrete ['kɒnkri:t] *n* Beton *m* ▷ *adj* konkret

concussion [kɒn'kʌʃən] *n* Gehirnerschütterung *f*

condemn [kən'dem] *vt* verdammen; (*esp Jur*) verurteilen

condensed milk *n* Kondensmilch *f*, Dosenmilch *f*

condition [kən'dɪʃən] *n* (*state*) Zustand *m*; (*requirement*) Bedingung *f*; **on ~ that ...** unter der Bedingung, dass ...; **~s** *pl* (*circumstances, weather*) Verhältnisse *pl*; **conditional** *adj* bedingt; (*Ling*) Konditional-; **conditioner** *n* Weichspüler *m*; (*for hair*) Pflegespülung *f*

condo ['kɒndəʊ] (*pl* -s) *n see* **condominium**

condolences [kən'dəʊlənsɪz] *npl* Beileid *nt*

condom ['kɒndəm] *n* Kondom *nt*

condominium [kɒndə'mɪnɪəm] *n* (*US: apartment*) Eigentumswohnung *f*

conduct ['kɒndʌkt] *n* (*behaviour*) Verhalten *nt* ▷ [kən'dʌkt] *vt* führen, leiten; (*orchestra*) dirigieren; **conductor** [kən'dʌktə°] *n* (*of orchestra*) Dirigent(in) *m(f)*; (*Brit: in bus*) Schaffner(in) *m(f)*; (*US: on train*) Zugführer(in) *m(f)*

cone [kəʊn] n Kegel m; (for ice cream) Waffeltüte f; (fir cone) (Tannen)zapfen m

conference ['kɒnfərəns] n Konferenz f

confess [kən'fes] vt, vi: **to ~ that ...** gestehen, dass ...; **confession** [kən'feʃən] n Geständnis nt; (Rel) Beichte f

confetti [kən'feti] n Konfetti nt

confidence ['kɒnfɪdəns] n Vertrauen nt (in zu); (assurance) Selbstvertrauen nt; **confident** adj (sure) zuversichtlich (that ... dass ...), überzeugt (of von); (self-assured) selbstsicher; **confidential** [kɒnfɪ'denʃəl] adj vertraulich

confine [kən'faɪn] vt beschränken (to auf +akk)

confirm [kən'fɜːm] vt bestätigen; **confirmation** [kɒnfə'meɪʃən] n Bestätigung f; (Rel) Konfirmation f; **confirmed** adj überzeugt; (bachelor) eingefleischt

confiscate ['kɒnfɪskeɪt] vt beschlagnahmen, konfiszieren

conflict ['kɒnflɪkt] n Konflikt m

confuse [kən'fjuːz] vt verwirren; (sth with sth) verwechseln (with mit); (several things) durcheinanderbringen; **confused** adj (person) konfus, verwirrt; (account) verworren; **confusing** adj verwirrend; **confusion** [kən'fjuːʒən] n Verwirrung f; (of two things) Verwechslung f; (muddle) Chaos nt

congested [kən'dʒestɪd] adj verstopft; (overcrowded) überfüllt; **congestion** [kən'dʒestʃən] n Stau m

congratulate [kən'grætjʊleɪt] vt gratulieren (on zu); **congratulations** [kəngrætjʊ'leɪʃənz] npl Glückwünsche pl; **~!** gratuliere!, herzlichen Glückwunsch!

congregation [kɒngrɪ'geɪʃən] n (Rel) Gemeinde f

congress ['kɒngres] n Kongress m; (US) **Congress** der Kongress; **congressman** (pl **-men**), **congresswoman** (pl **-women**) n (US) Mitglied nt des Repräsentantenhauses

conifer ['kɒnɪfə*] n Nadelbaum m

conjunction [kən'dʒʌŋkʃən] n (Ling) Konjunktion f; **in ~ with** in Verbindung mit

conk out [kɒŋk 'aʊt] vi (fam: appliance, car) den Geist aufgeben, streiken; (person: die) ins Gras beißen

connect [kə'nekt] vt verbinden (with, to mit); (Elec, Tech: appliance etc) anschließen (to an +akk) ▷ vi (train, plane) Anschluss haben (with an +akk); **~ing flight** Anschlussflug m; **~ing train** Anschlusszug m; **connection** [kə'nekʃən] n Verbindung f; (link) Zusammenhang m; (for train, plane, electrical appliance) Anschluss m (with, to an +akk); (business etc) Beziehung f; **in ~ with** in Zusammenhang mit; **bad ~** (Tel) schlechte Verbindung; (Elec) Wackelkontakt m; **connector** n (Inform: computer) Stecker m

conscience ['kɒnʃəns] n Gewissen nt; **conscientious** [kɒnʃɪ'enʃəs] adj gewissenhaft

conscious ['kɒnʃəs] adj (act) bewusst; (Med) bei Bewusstsein; **to be ~** bei Bewusstsein sein; **consciousness** n Bewusstsein nt

consecutive [kən'sekjʊtɪv] adj aufeinanderfolgend

consent [kən'sent] n Zustimmung f ▷ vi zustimmen (to dat)

consequence ['kɒnsɪkwəns] n
Folge f, Konsequenz f;
consequently ['kɒnsɪkwəntlɪ]
adv folglich, deshalb

conservation [kɒnsə'veɪʃən] n
Erhaltung f; (nature conservation)
Naturschutz m; **conservation
area** n Naturschutzgebiet nt

conservative, (Pol) **Conservative**
[kən'sɜːvətɪv] adj konservativ

conservatory [kən'sɜːvətrɪ] n
(greenhouse) Gewächshaus nt;
(room) Wintergarten m

consider [kən'sɪdə°] vt (reflect
on) nachdenken über, sich
überlegen; (take into account) in
Betracht ziehen; (regard) halten
für; **he is ~ed (to be) ...** er gilt als
...; **considerable** [kən'sɪdərəbl]
adj beträchtlich; **considerate**
[kən'sɪdərɪt] adj aufmerksam,
rücksichtsvoll; **consideration**
[kənsɪdə'reɪʃən] n (thoughtfulness)
Rücksicht f; (thought) Überlegung
f; **to take sth into ~** etw in
Betracht ziehen; **considering**
[kən'sɪdərɪŋ] prep in Anbetracht
+gen ▷ conj da

consist [kən'sɪst] vi: **to ~ of ...**
bestehen aus ...

consistent [kən'sɪstənt] adj
(behaviour, process etc)
konsequent; (statements)
übereinstimmend; (argument)
folgerichtig; (performance, results)
beständig

consolation [kɒnsə'leɪʃən] n
Trost m; **console** [kən'səʊl] vt
trösten

consolidate [kən'sɒlɪdeɪt] vt
festigen

consonant ['kɒnsənənt] n
Konsonant m

conspicuous [kən'spɪkjʊəs] adj
auffällig, auffallend

conspiracy [kən'spɪrəsɪ] n
Komplott nt; **conspire**

[kən'spaɪə°] vi sich verschwören
(against gegen)

constable ['kʌnstəbl] n (Brit)
Polizist(in) m(f)

Constance ['kɒnstəns] n Kon-
stanz nt; **Lake ~** der Bodensee

constant ['kɒnstənt] adj (continual) ständig, dauernd;
(unchanging: temperature etc)
gleichbleibend; **constantly** adv
dauernd

consternation [kɒnstə'neɪʃən]
n (dismay) Bestürzung f

constituency [kən'stɪtjʊənsɪ]
n Wahlkreis m

constitution [kɒnstɪ'tjuːʃən] n
Verfassung f; (of person)
Konstitution f

construct [kən'strʌkt] vt bauen;
construction [kən'strʌkʃən] n
(process, result) Bau m; (method)
Bauweise f; **under ~** im Bau
befindlich; **construction site** n
Baustelle f; **construction worker**
n Bauarbeiter(in) m(f)

consulate ['kɒnsjʊlət] n Konsulat nt

consult [kən'sʌlt] vt um Rat
fragen; (doctor) konsultieren;
(book) nachschlagen in +dat;
consultant n (Med) Facharzt m,
Fachärztin f; **consultation**
[kɒnsəl'teɪʃən] n Beratung f;
(Med) Konsultation f; **~ room**
Besprechungsraum;
Sprechzimmer

consume [kən'sjuːm] vt verbrauchen; (food) konsumieren;
consumer n Verbraucher(in)
m(f); **consumer-friendly** adj
verbraucherfreundlich

contact ['kɒntækt] n (touch)
Berührung f; (communication)
Kontakt m; (person) Kontaktperson
f; **to be/keep in ~ (with sb)** (mit
jdm) in Kontakt sein/bleiben ▷ vt
sich in Verbindung setzen mit;

contact lenses npl Kontaktlinsen pl

contagious [kən'teɪdʒəs] adj ansteckend

contain [kən'teɪn] vt enthalten; **container** n Behälter m; (for transport) Container m

contaminate [kən'tæmɪneɪt] vt verunreinigen; (chemically) verseuchen; **~d by radiation** strahlenverseucht, verstrahlt; **contamination** [kəntæmɪ'neɪʃən] n Verunreinigung f; (by radiation) Verseuchung f

contemporary [kən'tempərərɪ] adj zeitgenössisch

contempt [kən'tempt] n Verachtung f; **contemptuous** adj verächtlich; **to be ~** voller Verachtung sein (of für)

content [kən'tent] adj zufrieden

content(s) ['kɒntent(s)] n pl Inhalt m

contest ['kɒntest] n (Wett)kampf m (for um); (competition) Wettbewerb m ▷ [kən'test] vt kämpfen um +akk; (dispute) bestreiten; **contestant** [kən'testənt] n Teilnehmer(in) m(f)

context ['kɒntekst] n Zusammenhang m; **out of ~** aus dem Zusammenhang gerissen

continent ['kɒntɪnənt] n Kontinent m, Festland nt; **the Continent** (Brit) das europäische Festland, der Kontinent; **continental** [kɒntɪ'nentl] adj kontinental; **~ breakfast** kleines Frühstück mit Brötchen und Marmelade, Kaffee oder Tee

continual [kən'tɪnjʊəl] adj (endless) ununterbrochen; (constant) dauernd, ständig; **continually** adv dauernd; (again and again) immer wieder; **continuation** [kəntɪnjʊ'eɪʃən] n

Fortsetzung f; **continue** [kən'tɪnjuː] vi weitermachen (with mit); (esp talking) fortfahren (with mit); (travelling) weiterfahren; (state, conditions) fortdauern, anhalten ▷ vt fortsetzen; **to be ~d** Fortsetzung folgt; **continuous** [kən'tɪnjʊəs] adj (endless) ununterbrochen; (constant) ständig

contraceptive [kɒntrə'septɪv] n Verhütungsmittel nt

contract ['kɒntrækt] n Vertrag m

contradict [kɒntrə'dɪkt] vt widersprechen +dat; **contradiction** [kɒntrə'dɪkʃən] n Widerspruch m

contrary ['kɒntrərɪ] n Gegenteil nt; **on the ~** im Gegenteil ▷ adj: **~ to** entgegen +dat

contrast ['kɒntrɑːst] n Kontrast m, Gegensatz m; **in ~ to** im Gegensatz zu ▷ [kən'trɑːst] vt entgegensetzen

contribute [kən'trɪbjuːt] vt, vi beitragen (to zu); (money) spenden (to für); **contribution** [kɒntrɪ'bjuːʃən] n Beitrag m

control [kən'trəʊl] vt (master) beherrschen; (temper etc) im Griff haben; (esp Tech) steuern; **to ~ oneself** sich beherrschen ▷ n Kontrolle f; (mastery) Beherrschung f; (esp Tech) Steuerung f; **~s** pl (knobs, switches etc) Bedienungselemente pl; (collectively) Steuerung f; **to be out of ~** außer Kontrolle sein; **control knob** n Bedienungsknopf m; **control panel** n Schalttafel f

controversial [kɒntrə'vɜːʃəl] adj umstritten

convalesce [kɒnvə'les] vi gesund werden; **convalescence** n Genesung f

convenience [kən'viːnɪəns] n (quality, thing) Annehmlichkeit f; **at**

your ~ wann es Ihnen passt; **with all modern ~s** mit allem Komfort; **convenience food** n Fertiggericht nt; **convenient** adj günstig, passend
convent ['kɒnvənt] n Kloster nt
convention [kən'venʃən] n (custom) Konvention f; (meeting) Konferenz f; **the Geneva Convention** die Genfer Konvention; **conventional** adj herkömmlich, konventionell
conversation [kɒnvə'seɪʃən] n Gespräch nt, Unterhaltung f
conversion [kən'vɜ:ʃən] n Umwandlung f (into in +akk); (of building) Umbau m (into zu); (calculation) Umrechnung f; **conversion table** n Umrechnungstabelle f; **convert** [kən'vɜ:t] vt umwandeln; (person) bekehren; (Inform) konvertieren; **to ~ into euros** in Euro umrechnen; **convertible** n (Auto) Kabrio nt ▷ adj umwandelbar
convey [kən'veɪ] vt (carry) befördern; (feelings) vermitteln; **conveyor belt** n Förderband nt, Fließband nt
convict [kən'vɪkt] vt verurteilen (of wegen) ▷ ['kɒnvɪkt] n Strafgefangene(r) mf; **conviction** n (Jur) Verurteilung f; (strong belief) Überzeugung f
convince [kən'vɪns] vt überzeugen (of von); **convincing** adj überzeugend
cook [kʊk] vt, vi kochen ▷ n Koch m, Köchin f; **cookbook** n Kochbuch nt; **cooker** n Herd m; **cookery** n Kochkunst f; **~ book** Kochbuch nt; **cookie** n (US) Keks m; **cooking** n Kochen nt; (style of cooking) Küche f
cool [ku:l] adj kühl, gelassen; (fam: brilliant) cool, stark ▷ vt, vi (ab)kühlen; **~ it** reg dich ab! ▷ n:

to keep/lose one's ~ (fam) ruhig bleiben/durchdrehen; **cool down** vi abkühlen; (calm down) sich beruhigen
cooperate [kəʊ'ɒpəreɪt] vi zusammenarbeiten, kooperieren; **cooperation** [kəʊɒpə'reɪʃən] n Zusammenarbeit f, Kooperation f; **cooperative** [kəʊ'ɒpərətɪv] adj hilfsbereit ▷ n Genossenschaft f
coordinate [kəʊ'ɔ:dɪneɪt] vt koordinieren
cop [kɒp] n (fam: policeman) Bulle m
cope [kəʊp] vi zurechtkommen, fertig werden (with mit)
Copenhagen [kəʊpən'heɪgən] n Kopenhagen nt
copier ['kɒpɪəʳ] n Kopierer m
copper ['kɒpəʳ] n Kupfer nt; (Brit fam: policeman) Bulle m; (fam: coin) Kupfermünze f; **~s** Kleingeld nt
copy ['kɒpɪ] n Kopie f; (of book) Exemplar nt ▷ vt kopieren; (imitate) nachahmen; **copyright** n Urheberrecht nt
coral ['kɒrəl] n Koralle f
cord [kɔ:d] n Schnur f; (material) Kordsamt m; **cordless** ['kɔ:dlɪs] adj (phone) schnurlos
core [kɔ:ʳ] n (a. fig) Kern m; (of apple, pear) Kerngehäuse nt; **core business** n Kerngeschäft nt
cork [kɔ:k] n (material) Kork m; (stopper) Korken m; **corkscrew** ['kɔ:kskru:] n Korkenzieher m
corn [kɔ:n] n Getreide nt, Korn nt; (US: maize) Mais m; (on foot) Hühnerauge nt; **~ on the cob** (gekochter) Maiskolben; **corned beef** n Cornedbeef nt
corner ['kɔ:nəʳ] n Ecke f; (on road) Kurve f; (Sport) Eckstoß m ▷ vt in die Enge treiben; **corner shop** n Laden m an der Ecke
cornflakes ['kɔ:fleɪks] npl Cornflakes pl

Cornish ['kɔːnɪʃ] *adj* kornisch;
~ pasty *mit Fleisch und Kartoffeln
gefüllte Pastete*; **Cornwall**
['kɔːnwəl] *n* Cornwall *nt*

coronation [kɒrə'neɪʃən] *n*
Krönung *f*

corporation [kɔːpə'reɪʃən] *n*
(*US Comm*) Aktiengesellschaft *f*

corpse [kɔːps] *n* Leiche *f*

correct [kə'rekt] *adj* (*accurate*)
richtig; (*proper*) korrekt ▷ *vt*
korrigieren, verbessern;
correction *n* (*esp written*)
Korrektur *f*

correspond [kɒrɪ'spɒnd] *vi*
entsprechen (*to dat*); (*two things*)
übereinstimmen; (*exchange letters*)
korrespondieren; **corresponding**
adj entsprechend

corridor ['kɒrɪdɔː°] *n* (*in building*)
Flur *m*; (*in train*) Gang *m*

corrupt [kə'rʌpt] *adj* korrupt

cosmetic [kɒz'metɪk] *adj* kos-
metisch; **cosmetics** *npl*
Kosmetika *pl*; **cosmetic surgeon**
n Schönheitschirurg(in) *m(f)*;
cosmetic surgery *n*
Schönheitschirurgie *f*

cosmopolitan [kɒzmə'pɒlɪtən]
adj international; (*attitude*)
weltoffen

cost [kɒst] (**cost, cost**) *vt* kosten
▷ *n* Kosten *pl*; **at all ~s, at any
~** um jeden Preis; **~ of living**
Lebenshaltungskosten *pl*; **costly**
adj kostspielig

costume ['kɒstjuːm] *n* (*Theat*)
Kostüm *nt*

cosy ['kəʊzɪ] *adj* gemütlich

cot [kɒt] *n* (*Brit*) Kinderbett *nt*;
(*US*) Campingliege *f*

cottage ['kɒtɪdʒ] *n* kleines Haus;
(*country cottage*) Landhäuschen *nt*;
cottage cheese *n* Hüttenkäse *m*;
cottage pie *n* Hackfleisch mit
Kartoffelbrei überbacken

cotton ['kɒtn] *n* Baumwolle *f*;

cotton candy *n* (*US*) Zuckerwatte
f; **cotton wool** *n* (*Brit*) Watte *f*

couch [kaʊtʃ] *n* Couch *f*; (*sofa*)
Sofa *nt*; **couchette** [kuːʃet] *n*
Liegewagen(platz) *m*

cough [kɒf] *vi* husten ▷ *n* Hus-
ten *m*; **cough mixture** *n*
Hustensaft *m*; **cough sweet** *n*
Hustenbonbon *nt*

could [kʊd] *pt of* **can** konnte;
conditional könnte; **~ you come
earlier?** könntest du/könnten Sie
früher kommen?

couldn't *contr of* **could not**

council ['kaʊnsl] *n* (*Pol*) Rat *m*;
(*local ~*) Gemeinderat *m*; (*town ~*)
Stadtrat *m*; **council estate** *n*
Siedlung *f* des sozialen
Wohnungsbaus; **council house** *n*
Sozialwohnung *f*; **councillor**
['kaʊnsɪlə°] *n* Gemeinderat *m*,
Gemeinderätin *f*; **council tax** *n*
Gemeindesteuer *f*

count [kaʊnt] *vt, vi* zählen;
(*include*) mitrechnen ▷ *n* Zählung
f; (*noble*) Graf *m*; **count on** *vt* (*rely
on*) sich verlassen auf +*akk*; (*expect*)
rechnen mit

counter ['kaʊntə°] *n* (*in shop*)
Ladentisch *m*; (*in café*) Theke *f*; (*in
bank, post office*) Schalter *m*;
counter attack *n* Gegenangriff *m*
▷ *vi* zurückschlagen;
counter-clockwise *adv* (*US*)
entgegen dem Uhrzeigersinn

counterpart ['kaʊntəpɔːt] *n*
Gegenstück *nt* (*of zu*)

countess *n* Gräfin *f*

countless ['kaʊntlɪs] *adj* zahl-
los, unzählig

country ['kʌntrɪ] *n* Land *nt*; **in
the ~** auf dem Land(e); **in this
~** hierzulande; **country cousin** *n*
(*fam*) Landei *nt*; **country dancing**
n Volkstanz *m*; **country house** *n*
Landhaus *nt*; **countryman** *n*
(*compatriot*) Landsmann *m*;

country music n Countrymusic f;
country road n Landstraße f;
countryside n Landschaft f; (*rural area*) Land nt
county ['kaʊntɪ] n (*Brit*) Grafschaft f; (*US*) Verwaltungsbezirk m; **county town** n (*Brit*) ≈ Kreisstadt f
couple ['kʌpl] n Paar nt; **a ~ of** ein paar
coupon ['kuːpɒn] n (*voucher*) Gutschein m
courage ['kʌrɪdʒ] n Mut m; **courageous** [kə'reɪdʒəs] adj mutig
courgette [kʊə'ʒet] n (*Brit*) Zucchini f
courier ['kʊrɪə°] n (*for tourists*) Reiseleiter(in) m(f); (*messenger*) Kurier m
course [kɔːs] n (*of study*) Kurs m; (*for race*) Strecke f; (*Naut, Aviat*) Kurs m; (*at university*) Studiengang m; (*in meal*) Gang m; **of ~** natürlich; **in the ~ of** während
court [kɔːt] n (*Sport*) Platz m; (*Jur*) Gericht nt
courteous ['kɜːtɪəs] adj höflich; **courtesy** ['kɜːtəsɪ] n Höflichkeit f; **~ bus/coach** (gebührenfreier) Zubringerbus
courthouse ['kɔːthaʊs] n (*US*) Gerichtsgebäude nt; **court order** n Gerichtsbeschluss m; **courtroom** n Gerichtssaal m
courtyard ['kɔːtjɑːd] n Hof m
cousin ['kʌzn] n (*male*) Cousin m; (*female*) Cousine f
cover ['kʌvə°] vt bedecken (*in, with* mit); (*distance*) zurücklegen; (*loan, costs*) decken ▷ n (*for bed etc*) Decke f; (*of cushion*) Bezug m; (*lid*) Deckel m; (*of book*) Umschlag m; (**insurance**) ~ Versicherungsschutz m; **cover up** vt zudecken; (*error etc*) vertuschen; **coverage** n Berichterstattung f (*of* über +akk);

cover charge n Kosten pl für ein Gedeck; **covering** n Decke f; **covering letter** n Begleitbrief m; **cover story** n (*newspaper*) Titelgeschichte f
cow [kaʊ] n Kuh f
coward ['kaʊəd] n Feigling m; **cowardly** adj feig(e)
cowboy ['kaʊbɔɪ] n Cowboy m
coy [kɔɪ] adj gespielt schüchtern, kokett
cozy ['kəʊzɪ] adj (*US*) gemütlich
CPU abbr = **central processing unit** Zentraleinheit f
crab [kræb] n Krabbe f
crabby ['kræbɪ] adj mürrisch, reizbar
crack [kræk] n Riss m; (*in pottery, glass*) Sprung m; (*drug*) Crack nt; **to have a ~ at sth** etw ausprobieren ▷ vi (*pottery, glass*) einen Sprung bekommen; (*wood, ice etc*) einen Riss bekommen; **to get ~ing** (*fam*) loslegen ▷ vt (*bone*) anbrechen; (*nut, code*) knacken
cracker ['krækə°] n (*biscuit*) Kräcker m; (*Christmas ~*) Knallbonbon nt; **crackers** adj (*fam*) verrückt, bekloppt; **he's ~** er hat nicht alle Tassen im Schrank
crackle ['krækl] vi knistern; (*telephone, radio*) knacken; **crackling** n (*Gastr*) Kruste f (*des Schweinebratens*)
cradle ['kreɪdl] n Wiege f
craft [krɑːft] n Handwerk nt; (*art*) Kunsthandwerk nt; (*Naut*) Boot nt; **craftsman** (pl **-men**) n Handwerker m; **craftsmanship** n Handwerkskunst f; (*ability*) handwerkliches Können
crafty ['krɑːftɪ] adj schlau
cram [kræm] vt stopfen (*into* in +akk); **to be ~med with …** mit … vollgestopft sein ▷ vi (*revise for exam*) pauken (*for* für)
cramp [kræmp] n Krampf m

cranberry ['krænbərɪ] n Preiselbeere f
crane [kreɪn] n (machine) Kran m;
(bird) Kranich m
crap [kræp] n (vulg) Scheiße f;
(rubbish) Mist m ▷ adj beschissen,
Scheiß-
crash [kræʃ] vi einen Unfall
haben; (two vehicles)
zusammenstoßen; (plane,
computer) abstürzen; (economy)
zusammenbrechen; **to ~ into sth**
gegen etw knallen ▷ vt einen
Unfall haben mit ▷ n (car) Unfall
m; (train) Unglück nt; (collision)
Zusammenstoß m; (Aviat, Inform)
Absturz m; (noise) Krachen nt;
crash barrier n Leitplanke f;
crash course n Intensivkurs m;
crash helmet n Sturzhelm m;
crash landing n Bruchlandung f
crate [kreɪt] n Kiste f; (of beer)
Kasten m
crater ['kreɪtə*] n Krater m
craving [kreɪvɪŋ] n starkes
Verlangen, Bedürfnis nt
crawl [krɔːl] vi kriechen; (baby)
krabbeln ▷ n (swimming) Kraul nt;
crawler lane n Kriechspur f
crayfish ['kreɪfɪʃ] n Languste f
crayon ['kreɪən] n Buntstift m
crazy ['kreɪzɪ] adj verrückt (about
nach)
cream [kriːm] n (from milk)
Sahne f, Rahm m; (polish, cosmetic)
Creme f ▷ adj cremefarben;
cream cake n (small)
Sahnetörtchen nt; (big) Sahnetorte
f; **cream cheese** n Frischkäse m;
creamer n Kaffeeweißer m;
cream tea n (Brit) Nachmittagstee
mit Törtchen, Marmelade und
Schlagsahne; **creamy** adj sahnig
crease [kriːs] n Falte f ▷ vt
falten; (untidy) zerknittern
create [kriˈeɪt] vt schaffen;
(cause) verursachen; **creative**

[kriˈeɪtɪv] adj schöpferisch;
(person) kreativ; **creature**
['kriːtʃə*] n Geschöpf nt
crèche [kreɪʃ] n Kinderkrippe f
credible ['kredɪbl] adj (person)
glaubwürdig; **credibility** n
Glaubwürdigkeit f
credit ['kredɪt] n (Fin: amount
allowed) Kredit m; (amount
possessed) Guthaben nt;
(recognition) Anerkennung f; **~s** (of
film) Abspann m; **credit card** n
Kreditkarte f; **credit crunch** n
Kreditklemme f
creep [kriːp] (**crept, crept**) vi
kriechen; **creeps** n: **he gives me
the ~** er ist mir nicht ganz
geheuer; **creepy** ['kriːpɪ] adj
(frightening) gruselig, unheimlich
crept [krept] pt, pp of **creep**
cress [kres] n Kresse f
crest [krest] n Kamm m; (coat of
arms) Wappen nt
crew [kruː] n Besatzung f,
Mannschaft f
crib [krɪb] n (US) Kinderbett nt
cricket ['krɪkɪt] n (insect) Grille f;
(game) Kricket nt
crime [kraɪm] n Verbrechen nt;
criminal ['krɪmɪnl] n Verbre-
cher(in) m(f) ▷ adj kriminell,
strafbar
cripple ['krɪpl] n Krüppel m ▷ vt
verkrüppeln, lähmen
crisis ['kraɪsɪs] (pl **crises**) n Krise f
crisp [krɪsp] adj knusprig; **crisps**
npl (Brit) Chips pl; **crispbread** n
Knäckebrot nt
criterion [kraɪˈtɪərɪən] n Krite-
rium nt
critic ['krɪtɪk] n Kritiker(in) m(f);
critical adj kritisch; **critically** adv
kritisch; **~ ill/injured** schwer
krank/verletzt; **criticism**
['krɪtɪsɪzəm] n Kritik f; **criticize**
['krɪtɪsaɪz] vt kritisieren
Croat [ˈkrəʊæt] n Kroate m,

Kroatin f; **Croatia** [krəʊ'eɪʃə] n Kroatien nt; **Croatian** [krəʊ'eɪʃən] adj kroatisch

crockery ['krɒkərɪ] n Geschirr nt

crocodile ['krɒkədaɪl] n Krokodil nt

crocus ['krəʊkəs] n Krokus m

crop [krɒp] n (harvest) Ernte f; **crops** npl Getreide nt; **crop up** vi auftauchen

croquette [krə'ket] n Krokette f

cross [krɒs] n Kreuz nt; **to mark sth with a ~** etw ankreuzen ▷ vt (road, river etc) überqueren; (legs) übereinanderschlagen; **it ~ed my mind** es fiel mir ein; **to ~ one's fingers** die Daumen drücken ▷ adj ärgerlich, böse; **cross out** vt durchstreichen

crossbar n (of bicycle) Stange f; (Sport) Querlatte f; **cross-country** adj: **~ running** Geländelauf m; **~ skiing** Langlauf m; **cross-examination** n Kreuzverhör nt; **cross-eyed** adj: **to be ~** schielen; **crossing** n (crossroads) (Straßen)kreuzung f; (for pedestrians) Fußgängerüberweg m; (on ship) Überfahrt f; **crossroads** nsing o pl Straßenkreuzung f; **cross section** n Querschnitt m; **crosswalk** n (US) Fußgängerüberweg m; **crossword (puzzle)** n Kreuzworträtsel nt

crouch [kraʊtʃ] vi hocken

crouton ['kru:tɒn] n Croûton m

crow [krəʊ] n Krähe f

crowbar [krəʊbɑ:ʳ] n Brecheisen nt

crowd [kraʊd] n Menge f ▷ vi sich drängen (into in +akk; round um); **crowded** adj überfüllt

crown [kraʊn] n Krone f ▷ vt krönen; (fam) **and to ~ it all ...** und als Krönung ...

crucial ['kru:ʃəl] adj entscheidend

crude [kru:d] adj primitiv; (humour, behaviour) derb, ordinär ▷ n: **~ (oil)** Rohöl nt

cruel ['krʊəl] adj grausam (to zu, gegen); (unfeeling) gefühllos; **cruelty** n Grausamkeit f; **~ to animals** Tierquälerei f

cruise [kru:z] n Kreuzfahrt f ▷ vi (ship) kreuzen; (car) mit Reisegeschwindigkeit fahren; **cruise liner** n Kreuzfahrtschiff nt; **cruise missile** n Marschflugkörper m; **cruising speed** n Reisegeschwindigkeit f

crumb [krʌm] n Krume f

crumble ['krʌmbl] vt, vi zerbröckeln ▷ n mit Streuseln überbackenes Kompott

crumpet ['krʌmpɪt] n weiches Hefegebäck zum Toasten; (fam: attractive woman) Schnecke f

crumple ['krʌmpl] vt zerknittern

crunchy ['krʌntʃɪ] adj (Brit) knusprig

crusade [kru:'seɪd] n Kreuzzug m

crush [krʌʃ] vt zerdrücken; (finger etc) quetschen; (spices, stone) zerstoßen ▷ n: **to have a ~ on sb** in jdn verknallt sein; **crushing** adj (defeat, remark) vernichtend

crust [krʌst] n Kruste f; **crusty** adj knusprig

crutch [krʌtʃ] n Krücke f

cry [kraɪ] vi (call) rufen; (scream) schreien; (weep) weinen ▷ n (call) Ruf m; (louder) Schrei m

crypt [krɪpt] n Krypta f

crystal ['krɪstl] n Kristall m

cu abbr = **see you** (SMS, e-mail) bis bald

Cuba ['kju:bə] n Kuba nt

cube [kju:b] n Würfel m

cubic ['kju:bɪk] adj Kubik-

cubicle ['kju:bɪkl] n Kabine f

cuckoo ['kʊkuː] *n* Kuckuck *m*

cucumber ['kjuːkʌmbəʳ] *n* Salatgurke *f*

cuddle ['kʌdl] *vt* in den Arm nehmen; (*amorously*) schmusen mit ▷ *n* Liebkosung *f*, Umarmung *f*; **to have a ~** schmusen; **cuddly** *adj* verschmust; **cuddly toy** *n* Plüschtier *nt*

cuff [kʌf] *n* Manschette *f*; (*US: trouser ~*) Aufschlag *m*; **off the ~** aus dem Stegreif; **cufflink** *n* Manschettenknopf *m*

cuisine [kwɪˈziːn] *n* Kochkunst *f*, Küche *f*

cul-de-sac ['kʌldəsæk] *n* (*Brit*) Sackgasse *f*

culprit ['kʌlprɪt] *n* Schuldige(r) *mf*; (*fig*) Übeltäter(in) *m(f)*

cult [kʌlt] *n* Kult *m*

cultivate ['kʌltɪveɪt] *vt* (*Agr: land*) bebauen; (*crop*) anbauen; **cultivated** *adj* (*person*) kultiviert, gebildet

cultural ['kʌltʃərəl] *adj* kulturell, Kultur-; **culture** ['kʌltʃəʳ] *n* Kultur *f*; **cultured** *adj* gebildet, kultiviert; **culture vulture** (*Brit fam*) *n* Kulturfanatiker(in) *m(f)*

cumbersome ['kʌmbəsəm] *adj* (*object*) unhandlich

cumin ['kʌmɪn] *n* Kreuzkümmel *m*

cunning ['kʌnɪŋ] *adj* schlau; (*person a.*) gerissen

cup [kʌp] *n* Tasse *f*; (*prize*) Pokal *m*; **it's not his ~ of tea** das ist nicht sein Fall; **cupboard** ['kʌbəd] *n* Schrank *m*; **cup final** *n* Pokalendspiel *nt*; **cup tie** *n* Pokalspiel *nt*

cupola ['kjuːpələ] *n* Kuppel *f*

curable ['kjʊərəbəl] *adj* heilbar

curb [kɜːb] *n* (*US*) *see* **kerb**

curd [kɜːd] *n*: **~ cheese**, **~s** ≈ Quark *m*

cure [kjʊəʳ] *n* Heilmittel *nt* (*for*

gegen); (*process*) Heilung *f* ▷ *vt* heilen; (*Gastr*) pökeln; (*smoke*) räuchern

curious ['kjʊərɪəs] *adj* neugierig; (*strange*) seltsam

curl [kɜːl] *n* Locke *f* ▷ *vi* sich kräuseln; **curly** *adj* lockig

currant ['kʌrənt] *n* (*dried*) Korinthe *f*; (*red, black*) Johannisbeere *f*

currency ['kʌrənsɪ] *n* Währung *f*; **foreign ~**·Devisen *pl*

current ['kʌrənt] *n* (*in water*) Strömung *f*; (*electric ~*) Strom *m* ▷ *adj* (*issue, affairs*) aktuell, gegenwärtig; (*expression*) gängig; **current account** *n* Girokonto *nt*; **currently** *adv* zur Zeit

curriculum [kəˈrɪkjʊləm] *n* Lehrplan *m*; **curriculum vitae** [kəˈrɪkjʊləmˈviːtaɪ] *n* (*Brit*) Lebenslauf *m*

curry ['kʌrɪ] *n* Currygericht *nt*; **curry powder** *n* Curry(pulver) *nt*

curse [kɜːs] *vi* (*swear*) fluchen (*at* auf +*akk*) ▷ *n* Fluch *m*

cursor ['kɜːsəʳ] *n* (*Inform*) Cursor *m*

curt [kɜːt] *adj* schroff, kurz angebunden

curtain ['kɜːtn] *n* Vorhang *m*; **it was ~s for Benny** für Benny war alles vorbei

curve [kɜːv] *n* Kurve *f* ▷ *vi* einen Bogen machen; **curved** *adj* gebogen

cushion ['kʊʃən] *n* Kissen *nt*

custard ['kʌstəd] *n* *dicke Vanillesoße, die warm oder kalt zu vielen englischen Nachspeisen gegessen wird*

custom ['kʌstəm] *n* Brauch *m*; (*habit*) Gewohnheit *f*; **customary** ['kʌstəmrɪ] *adj* üblich; **custom-built** *adj* nach Kundenangaben gefertigt; **customer** ['kʌstəməʳ] *n* Kunde

m, Kundin f; **customer loyalty card** n Kundenkarte f; **customer service** n Kundendienst m
customs ['kʌstəmz] npl (*organization, location*) Zoll m; **to pass through ~** durch den Zoll gehen; **customs officer** n Zollbeamte(r) m, Zollbeamtin f
cut [kʌt] (**cut, cut**) vt schneiden; (*cake*) anschneiden; (*wages, benefits*) kürzen; (*prices*) heruntersetzen; **I ~ my finger** ich habe mir in den Finger geschnitten ▷ n Schnitt m; (*wound*) Schnittwunde f; (*reduction*) Kürzung f (*in gen*); **price/tax ~** Preissenkung/Steuersenkung f; **to be a ~ above the rest** eine Klasse besser als die anderen sein; **cut back** vt (*workforce etc*) reduzieren; **cut down** vt (*tree*) fällen; **to ~ on sth** etwas einschränken; **cut in** vi (*Auto*) scharf einscheren; **to ~ on sb** jdn schneiden; **cut off** vt abschneiden; (*gas, electricity*) abdrehen, abstellen; (*Tel*) **I was ~** ich wurde unterbrochen
cutback n Kürzung f
cute [kjuːt] adj putzig, niedlich; (*US: shrewd*) clever
cutlery ['kʌtləri] n Besteck nt
cutlet ['kʌtlit] n (*pork*) Kotelett nt; (*veal*) Schnitzel nt
cut-price adj verbilligt
cutting ['kʌtɪŋ] n (*from paper*) Ausschnitt m; (*of plant*) Ableger m ▷ adj (*comment*) verletzend
CV abbr = **curriculum vitae**
cwt abbr = **hundredweight** ≈ Zentner, Ztr.
cybercafé [saɪbə'kæfeɪ] n Internetcafé nt; **cyberspace** n Cyberspace m
cycle ['saɪkl] n Fahrrad nt ▷ vi Rad fahren; **cycle lane**, **cycle path** n Radweg m; **cycling** n

Radfahren nt; **cyclist** ['saɪklɪst] n Radfahrer(in) m(f)
cylinder ['sɪlɪndə°] n Zylinder m
cynical ['sɪnɪkəl] adj zynisch
cypress ['saɪprɪs] n Zypresse f
Cypriot ['sɪprɪət] adj zypriotisch ▷ n Zypriote m, Zypriotin f; **Cyprus** ['saɪprəs] n Zypern nt
czar [zɑː°] n Zar m; **czarina** [zɑ'riːnə] n Zarin f
Czech [tʃek] adj tschechisch ▷ n (*person*) Tscheche m, Tschechin f; (*language*) Tschechisch nt; **Czech Republic** n Tschechische Republik, Tschechien nt

d

dab [dæb] vt (wound, nose etc) betupfen (with mit)

dachshund ['dækshʊnd] n Dackel m

dad(dy) ['dæd(ɪ)] adj, adv täglich ⊳ n Papa m, Vati m; **daddy-longlegs** nsing (Brit) Schnake; (US) Weberknecht m

daffodil ['dæfədɪl] n Osterglocke f

daft [dɑːft] adj (fam) blöd, doof

dahlia ['deɪlɪə] n Dahlie f

daily ['deɪlɪ] adj, adv täglich ⊳ n (paper) Tageszeitung f

dairy ['dɛərɪ] n (on farm) Molkerei f; **dairy products** npl Milchprodukte pl

daisy ['deɪzɪ] n Gänseblümchen nt

dam [dæm] n Staudamm m ⊳ vt stauen

damage ['dæmɪdʒ] n Schaden m; **~s** pl (Jur) Schadenersatz m ⊳ vt beschädigen; (reputation, health) schädigen, schaden +dat

damn [dæm] adj (fam) verdammt ⊳ vt (condemn) verurteilen; **~ (it)!** verflucht! ⊳ n: **he doesn't give a ~** es ist ihm völlig egal

damp [dæmp] adj feucht ⊳ n Feuchtigkeit f; **dampen** ['dæmpən] vt befeuchten

dance [dɑːns] n Tanz m; (event) Tanzveranstaltung f ⊳ vi tanzen; **dance floor** n Tanzfläche f; **dancer** n Tänzer(in) m(f); **dancing** n Tanzen nt

dandelion ['dændɪlaɪən] n Löwenzahn m

dandruff ['dændrəf] n Schuppen pl

Dane [deɪn] n Däne m, Dänin f

danger ['deɪndʒə°] n Gefahr f; **~ (sign)** Achtung!; **to be in ~** in Gefahr sein; **dangerous** adj gefährlich

Danish ['deɪnɪʃ] adj dänisch ⊳ n (language) Dänisch nt; **the ~** pl die Dänen; **Danish pastry** n Plundergebäck nt

Danube ['dænjuːb] n Donau f

dare [dɛə°] vi: **to ~ (to) do sth** es wagen, etw zu tun; **I didn't ~ ask** ich traute mich nicht, zu fragen; **how ~ you** was fällt dir ein!; **daring** adj (person) mutig; (film, clothes etc) gewagt

dark [dɑːk] adj dunkel; (gloomy) düster, trübe; (sinister) finster; **~ chocolate** Bitterschokolade f; **~ green/blue** dunkelgrün/dunkelblau ⊳ n Dunkelheit f; **in the ~** im Dunkeln; **dark glasses** npl Sonnenbrille f; **darkness** n Dunkelheit nt

darling ['dɑːlɪŋ] n Schatz m; (also favourite) Liebling m

darts [dɑːts] nsing (game) Darts nt

dash [dæʃ] vi stürzen, rennen

▷ vt: **to ~ hopes** Hoffnungen zerstören ▷ n (in text) Gedankenstrich m; (of liquid) Schuss m; **dashboard** n Armaturenbrett nt

data ['deɪtə] npl Daten pl; **data bank**, **data base** n Datenbank f; **data capture** n Datenerfassung f; **data processing** n Datenverarbeitung f; **data protection** n Datenschutz m

date [deɪt] n Datum nt; (for meeting, delivery etc) Termin m; (with person) Verabredung f; (with girlfriend/boyfriend etc) Date nt; (fruit) Dattel f; **what's the ~ (today)?** der Wievielte ist heute?; **out of ~** adj veraltet; **up to ~** adj (news) aktuell; (fashion) zeitgemäß ▷ vt (letter etc) datieren; (person) gehen mit; **dated** adj altmodisch; **date of birth** n Geburtsdatum nt; **dating agency** n Partnervermittlung f

dative ['deɪtɪv] n Dativ m

daughter ['dɔːtə°] n Tochter f; **daughter-in-law** (pl **daughters-in-law**) n Schwiegertochter f

dawn [dɔːn] n Morgendämmerung f ▷ vi dämmern; **it ~ed on me** mir ging ein Licht auf

day [deɪ] n Tag m; **one ~** eines Tages; **by ~** bei Tage; **~ after ~**, **~ by ~** Tag für Tag; **the ~ after/before** am Tag danach/zuvor; **the ~ before yesterday** vorgestern; **the ~ after tomorrow** übermorgen; **these ~s** heutzutage; **in those ~s** damals; **let's call it a ~** Schluss für heute!; **daybreak** n Tagesanbruch m; **day-care center** (US), **day-care centre** n (Brit) Kita f (Kindertagesstätte); **daydream** n Tagtraum m ▷ vi (mit offenen Augen) träumen; **daylight** n

Tageslicht nt; **in ~** bei Tage; **day nursery** n Kita f (Kindertagesstätte); **day return** n (Brit Rail) Tagesrückfahrkarte f; **daytime** n: **in the ~** bei Tage, tagsüber; **daytrip** n Tagesausflug m

dazed [deɪzd] adj benommen

dazzle ['dæzl] vt blenden; **dazzling** adj blendend, glänzend

dead [ded] adj tot; (limb) abgestorben ▷ adv genau; (fam) total, völlig; **~ tired** adj todmüde; **~ slow** (sign) Schritt fahren; **dead end** n Sackgasse f; **deadline** n Termin m; (period) Frist f; **~ for applications** Anmeldeschluss m; **deadly** adj tödlich ▷ adv: **~ dull** todlangweilig

deaf [def] adj taub; **deafen** vt taub machen; **deafening** adj ohrenbetäubend

deal [diːl] (**dealt, dealt**) vt, vi (cards) geben, austeilen ▷ n (business ~) Geschäft nt; (agreement) Abmachung f; **it's a ~** abgemacht!; **a good/great ~ of** ziemlich/sehr viel; **deal in** vt handeln mit; **deal with** vt (matter) sich beschäftigen mit; (book, film) behandeln; (successfully: person, problem) fertig werden mit; (matter) erledigen; **dealer** n (Comm) Händler(in) m(f); (drugs) Dealer(in) m(f); **dealings** npl (Comm) Geschäfte pl

dealt [delt] pt, pp of **deal**

dear [dɪə°] adj lieb, teuer; **Dear Sir or Madam** Sehr geehrte Damen und Herren; **Dear David** Lieber David ▷ n Schatz m; (as address) mein Schatz, Liebling; **dearly** adv (love) (heiß und) innig; (pay) teuer

death [deθ] n Tod m; (of project, hopes) Ende nt; (in accident etc) Todesfall m, Todesopfer nt; **death certificate** n Totenschein m;

death penalty n Todesstrafe f;
death toll n Zahl f der Todesopfer; **death trap** n Todesfalle f
debatable [dɪ'beɪtəbl] adj
fraglich; (question) strittig; **debate**
[dɪ'beɪt] n Debatte f ▷ vt
debattieren
debauched [dɪ'bɔːtʃt] adj
ausschweifend
debit ['debɪt] n Soll nt ▷ vt
(account) belasten; **debit card** n
Geldkarte f
debris ['debriː] n Trümmer pl
debt [det] n Schuld f; **to be in**
~ verschuldet sein
debug [diː'bʌg] vt (Inform) Fehler
beseitigen in +dat
decade ['dekeɪd] n Jahrzehnt nt
decadent ['dekədənt] adj
dekadent
decaff ['diːkæf] n (fam) koffein-
freier Kaffee; **decaffeinated**
[diː'kæfɪneɪtɪd] adj koffeinfrei
decanter [dɪ'kæntə*] n Dekanter
m, Karaffe f
decay [dɪ'keɪ] n Verfall m;
(rotting) Verwesung f; (of tooth)
Karies f ▷ vi verfallen; (rot)
verwesen; (wood) vermodern;
(teeth) faulen; (leaves) verrotten
deceased [dɪ'siːst] n: **the** ~
der/die Verstorbene
deceit [dɪ'siːt] n Betrug m;
deceive [dɪ'siːv] vt täuschen
December [dɪ'sembə*] n
Dezember m; see also **September**
decent ['diːsənt] adj anständig
deception [dɪ'sepʃən] n Betrug
m; **deceptive** [dɪ'septɪv] adj
täuschend, irreführend
decide [dɪ'saɪd] vt (question)
entscheiden; (body of people)
beschließen; **I can't** ~ **what to do**
ich kann mich nicht entscheiden,
was ich tun soll ▷ vi sich
entscheiden; **to** ~ **on sth** (in favour
of sth) sich für etw entscheiden,

sich zu etw entschließen; **decided**
adj entschieden; (clear) deutlich;
decidedly adv entschieden
decimal ['desɪməl] adj Dezimal-;
decimal system n
Dezimalsystem nt
decipher [dɪ'saɪfə*] vt entziffern
decision [dɪ'sɪʒən] n Entscheidung f (on über +akk); (of committee,
jury etc) Beschluss m; **to make a**
~ eine Entscheidung treffen;
decisive [dɪ'saɪsɪv] adj entscheidend; (person)
entscheidungsfreudig
deck [dek] n (Naut) Deck nt; (of
cards) Blatt nt; **deckchair** n
Liegestuhl m
declaration [deklə'reɪʃən] n
Erklärung f; **declare** [dɪ'kleə*] vt
erklären; (state) behaupten (that
dass); (at customs) **have you**
anything to ~? haben Sie etwas
zu verzollen?
decline [dɪ'klaɪn] n Rückgang m
▷ vt (invitation, offer) ablehnen ▷ vi
(become less) sinken, abnehmen;
(health) sich verschlechtern
decode [diː'kəʊd] vt
entschlüsseln
decompose [diːkəm'pəʊz] vi sich
zersetzen
decontaminate
[diːkən'tæmɪneɪt] vt entgiften;
(from radioactivity) entseuchen
decorate ['dekəreɪt] vt
(aus)schmücken; (wallpaper)
tapezieren; (paint) anstreichen;
decoration [dekə'reɪʃən] n
Schmuck m; (process) Schmücken
nt; (wallpapering) Tapezieren nt;
(painting) Anstreichen nt;
Christmas ~s Weihnachts-
schmuck m; **decorator** n
Maler(in) m(f)
decrease ['diːkriːs] n Abnahme f
▷ [diː'kriːs] vi abnehmen
dedicate ['dedɪkeɪt] vt widmen

(*to sb* jdm); **dedicated** adj (*person*) engagiert; **dedication** [dedɪ'keɪʃən] n Widmung f; (*commitment*) Hingabe f, Engagement nt

deduce [dɪ'djuːs] vt folgern, schließen (*from* aus, *that* dass)

deduct [dɪ'dʌkt] vt abziehen (*from* von); **deduction** [dɪ'dʌkʃən] n (*of money*) Abzug m; (*conclusion*) (Schluss)folgerung f

deed [diːd] n Tat f

deep [diːp] adj tief; **deepen** vt vertiefen; **deep-freeze** n Tiefkühltruhe f; (*upright*) Gefrierschrank m; **deep-fry** vt frittieren

deer [dɪə°] n Reh nt; (*with stag*) Hirsch m

defeat [dɪ'fiːt] n Niederlage f; **to admit ~** sich geschlagen geben ▷ vt besiegen

defect [di:'fekt] n Defekt m, Fehler m; **defective** [dɪ'fektɪv] adj fehlerhaft

defence [dɪ'fens] n Verteidigung f; **defend** [dɪ'fend] vt verteidigen; **defendant** [dɪ'fendənt] n (*Jur*) Angeklagte(r) mf; **defender** n (*Sport*) Verteidiger(in) m(f); **defensive** [dɪ'fensɪv] adj defensiv

deficiency [dɪ'fɪʃənsɪ] n Mangel m; **deficient** adj mangelhaft; **deficit** ['defɪsɪt] n Defizit nt

define [dɪ'faɪn] vt (*word*) definieren; (*duties, powers*) bestimmen; **definite** ['defɪnɪt] adj (*clear*) klar, eindeutig; (*certain*) sicher; **it's ~** es steht fest; **definitely** adv bestimmt; **definition** [defɪ'nɪʃən] n Definition f; (*Foto*) Schärfe f

defrost [di:'frɒst] vt (*fridge*) abtauen; (*food*) auftauen

degrading [dɪ'greɪdɪŋ] adj erniedrigend

degree [dɪ'griː] n Grad m; (*at university*) akademischer Grad; **a certain/high ~ of** ein gewisses/hohes Maß an +dat; **to a certain ~** einigermaßen; **I have a ~ in chemistry** ≈ ich habe einen Abschluss in Chemie

dehydrated [di:haɪ'dreɪtɪd] adj (*food*) getrocknet, Trocken-; (*person*) ausgetrocknet

de-ice [di:'aɪs] vt enteisen

delay [dɪ'leɪ] vt (*postpone*) verschieben, aufschieben; **to be ~ed** (*event*) sich verzögern; **the train/flight was ~ed** der Zug/die Maschine hatte Verspätung ▷ vi warten; (*hesitate*) zögern ▷ n Verzögerung f; (*of train etc*) Verspätung f; **without ~** unverzüglich; **delayed** adj (*train etc*) verspätet

delegate n ['delɪgət] Delegierte(r) mf ▷ ['delɪgeɪt] vt delegieren; **delegation** [delɪ'geɪʃən] n Abordnung f; (*foreign*) Delegation f

delete [dɪ'liːt] vt (aus)streichen; (*Inform*) löschen; **deletion** n Streichung f; (*Inform*) Löschung f

deli ['delɪ] n (*fam*) Feinkostgeschäft nt

deliberate [dɪ'lɪbərət] adj (*intentional*) absichtlich; **deliberately** adv mit Absicht, extra

delicate ['delɪkɪt] adj (*fine*) fein; (*fragile*) zart; (*a. Med*) empfindlich; (*situation*) heikel

delicatessen [delɪkə'tesn] nsing Feinkostgeschäft nt

delicious [dɪ'lɪʃəs] adj köstlich, lecker

delight [dɪ'laɪt] n Freude f ▷ vt entzücken; **delighted** adj sehr erfreut (*with* über +akk); **delightful** adj entzückend; (*weather, meal etc*) herrlich

deliver [dɪ'lɪvə*] vt (goods) liefern (to sb jdm); (letter, parcel) zustellen; (speech) halten; (baby) entbinden; **delivery** n Lieferung f; (of letter, parcel) Zustellung f; (of baby) Entbindung f; **delivery van** n Lieferwagen m

delude [dɪ'luːd] vt täuschen; **don't ~ yourself** mach dir nichts vor; **delusion** n Irrglaube m

de luxe [dɪ'lʌks] adj Luxus-

demand [dɪ'mɑːnd] vt verlangen (from von); (time, patience etc) erfordern ▷ n (request) Forderung f, Verlangen nt (for nach); (Comm: for goods) Nachfrage f; **on ~** auf Wunsch; **very much in ~** sehr gefragt; **demanding** adj anspruchsvoll

demented [dɪ'mentɪd] adj wahnsinnig

demerara [demə'rɛərə] n: **~ (sugar)** brauner Zucker

demister n Defroster m

demo ['deməʊ] (pl **-s**) n (fam) Demo f

democracy [dɪ'mɒkrəsɪ] n Demokratie f; **democrat**, **Democrat** (US Pol) ['deməkræt] Demokrat(in) m(f); **democratic** adj demokratisch; **the Democratic Party** (US Pol) die Demokratische Partei

demolish [dɪ'mɒlɪʃ] vt abreißen; (fig) zerstören; **demolition** [demə'lɪʃən] n Abbruch m

demonstrate ['demənstreɪt] vt, vi demonstrieren, beweisen; **demonstration** n Demonstration f

demoralize [dɪ'mɒrəlaɪz] vt demoralisieren

denial [dɪ'naɪəl] n Leugnung f; (official ~) Dementi nt

denim ['denɪm] n Jeansstoff m; **denim jacket** n Jeansjacke f; **denims** npl Bluejeans pl

Denmark ['denmɑːk] n Dänemark nt

denomination [dɪnɒmɪ'neɪʃən] n (Rel) Konfession f; (Comm) Nennwert m

dense [dens] adj dicht; (fam: stupid) schwer von Begriff; **density** ['densɪtɪ] n Dichte f

dent [dent] n Beule f, Delle f ▷ vt einbeulen

dental ['dentl] adj Zahn-; **~ care** Zahnpflege f; **~ floss** Zahnseide f; **dentist** ['dentɪst] n Zahnarzt m, Zahnärztin; **dentures** ['dentʃəz] npl Zahnprothese f; (full) Gebiss nt

deny [dɪ'naɪ] vt leugnen, bestreiten; (refuse) ablehnen

deodorant [diː'əʊdərənt] n Deo(dorant) nt

depart [dɪ'pɑːt] vi abreisen; (bus, train) abfahren (for nach, from von); (plane) abfliegen (for nach, from von)

department [dɪ'pɑːtmənt] n Abteilung f; (at university) Institut nt; (Pol: ministry) Ministerium nt; **department store** n Kaufhaus nt

departure [dɪ'pɑːtʃə*] n (of person) Weggang m; (on journey) Abreise f (for nach); (of train etc) Abfahrt f (for nach); (of plane) Abflug m (for nach); **departure lounge** n (Aviat) Abflughalle f; **departure time** n Abfahrtzeit f; (Aviat) Abflugzeit f

depend [dɪ'pend] vi: **it ~s** es kommt darauf an (whether, if ob); **depend on** vt (thing) abhängen von; (person: rely on) sich verlassen auf +akk; (person, area etc) angewiesen sein auf +akk; **it ~s on the weather** es kommt auf das Wetter an; **dependable** adj zuverlässig; **dependence** n Abhängigkeit f (on von); **dependent** adj abhängig (on von)

deport [dɪ'pɔːt] vt ausweisen,

abschieben; **deportation**
[diːpɔːˈteɪʃən] n Abschiebung f
deposit [dɪˈpɒzɪt] n (down
payment) Anzahlung f; (security)
Kaution f; (for bottle) Pfand nt; (to
bank account) Einzahlung f; (in river
etc) Ablagerung f ▷ vt (put down)
abstellen, absetzen; (to bank
account) einzahlen; (sth valuable)
deponieren; **deposit account** n
Sparkonto nt
depot [ˈdepəʊ] n Depot nt
depreciate [dɪˈpriːʃɪeɪt] vi an
Wert verlieren
depress [dɪˈpres] vt (in mood)
deprimieren; **depressed** adj
(person) niedergeschlagen,
deprimiert; **~ area**
Notstandsgebiet nt; **depressing**
adj deprimierend; **depression**
[dɪˈpreʃən] n (mood) Depression f;
(Meteo) Tief nt
deprive [dɪˈpraɪv] vt: **to ~ sb of
sth** jdn einer Sache berauben;
deprived adj (child) (sozial)
benachteiligt
dept abbr = **department** Abt.
depth [depθ] n Tiefe f
deputy [ˈdepjʊtɪ] adj stell-
vertretend, Vize- ▷ n
Stellvertreter(in) m(f); (US Pol)
Abgeordnete(r) mf
derail [dɪˈreɪl] vt entgleisen
lassen; **to be ~ed** entgleisen
deranged [dɪˈreɪndʒd] adj
geistesgestört
derivation [derɪˈveɪʃən] n
Ableitung f; **derive** [dɪˈraɪv] vt
ableiten (from von) ▷ abstammen
(from von)
dermatitis [dɜːməˈtaɪtɪs] n
Hautentzündung f
derogatory [dɪˈrɒɡətərɪ] adj
abfällig
descend [dɪˈsend] vt, vi
hinabsteigen, hinuntergehen;
(person) **to ~ o be ~ed from**

abstammen von; **descendant** n
Nachkomme m; **descent** [dɪˈsent]
n (coming down) Abstieg m; (origin)
Abstammung f
describe [dɪsˈkraɪb] vt beschreiben; **description**
[dɪsˈkrɪpʃən] n Beschreibung f
desert [ˈdezət] n Wüste f
▷ [dɪˈzɜːt] vt verlassen; (abandon)
im Stich lassen; **deserted** adj
verlassen; (empty) menschenleer
deserve [dɪˈzɜːv] vt verdienen
design [dɪˈzaɪn] n (plan) Entwurf
m; (of vehicle, machine)
Konstruktion f; (of object) Design
nt; (planning) Gestaltung f ▷ vt
entwerfen; (machine etc)
konstruieren; **~ed for sb/sth**
(intended) für jdn/etw konzipiert
designate [ˈdezɪgneɪt] vt
bestimmen
designer [dɪˈzaɪnə°] n
Designer(in) m(f); (Tech)
Konstrukteur(in) m(f); **designer
drug** n Designerdroge f
desirable [dɪˈzaɪərəbl] n
wünschenswert; (person)
begehrenswert; **desire** [dɪˈzaɪə°]
n Wunsch m (for nach); (esp sexual)
Begierde f (for nach) ▷ vt
wünschen; (ask for) verlangen; **if
~d** auf Wunsch
desk [desk] n Schreibtisch m;
(reception ~) Empfang m; (at airport
etc) Schalter m; **desktop
publishing** n Desktoppublishing
nt
desolate [ˈdesəlɪt] adj trostlos
despair [dɪsˈpeə°] n Verzweiflung f (at über +akk) ▷ vi
verzweifeln (of an +dat)
despatch [dɪsˈpætʃ] see **dispatch**
desperate [ˈdespərɪt] adj
verzweifelt; (situation)
hoffnungslos; **to be ~ for sth** etw
dringend brauchen, unbedingt
wollen; **desperation**

[despə'reɪʃən] *n* Verzweiflung
f

despicable [dɪ'spɪkəbl] *adj* verachtenswert; **despise** [dɪ'spaɪz]
vt verachten

despite [dɪ'spaɪt] *prep* trotz +*gen*

dessert [dɪ'zɜːt] *n* Nachtisch *m*;
dessert spoon *n* Dessertlöffel *m*

destination [destɪ'neɪʃən] *n* (*of
person*) (Reise)ziel *nt*; (*of goods*)
Bestimmungsort *m*

destiny ['destɪnɪ] *n* Schicksal
nt

destroy [dɪ'strɔɪ] *vt* zerstören;
(*completely*) vernichten;
destruction [dɪ'strʌkʃən] *n* Zerstörung *f*; (*complete*) Vernichtung
f; **destructive** [dɪ'strʌktɪv] *adj*
zerstörerisch; (*esp fig*) destruktiv

detach [dɪ'tætʃ] *vt* abnehmen;
(*from form etc*) abtrennen; (*free*)
lösen (*from* von); **detachable** *adj*
abnehmbar; (*from form etc*)
abtrennbar; **detached** *adj*
(*attitude*) distanziert, objektiv;
~ house Einzelhaus *nt*

detail ['diːteɪl, (*US*) diː'teɪl] *n*
Einzelheit *f*, Detail *nt*; (**further**)
~s from ... Näheres erfahren Sie
bei ...; **to go into ~** ins Detail
gehen; **in ~** ausführlich; **detailed**
adj detailliert, ausführlich

detain [dɪ'teɪn] *vt* aufhalten;
(*police*) in Haft nehmen

detect [dɪ'tekt] *vt* entdecken;
(*notice*) wahrnehmen; **detective**
[dɪ'tektɪv] *n* Detektiv(in) *m(f)*;
detective story *n* Krimi *m*

detention [dɪ'tenʃən] *n* Haft *f*;
(*Sch*) Nachsitzen *nt*

deter [dɪ'tɜː°] *vt* abschrecken
(*from* von)

detergent [dɪ'tɜːdʒənt] *n* Reinigungsmittel *nt*; (*soap powder*)
Waschmittel *nt*

deteriorate [dɪ'tɪərɪəreɪt] *vi* sich
verschlechtern

determination [dɪtɜːmɪ'neɪʃən]
n Entschlossenheit *f*; **determine**
[dɪ'tɜːmɪn] *vt* bestimmen;
determined *adj* (*fest*)
entschlossen

deterrent [dɪ'terənt] *n*
Abschreckungsmittel *nt*

detest [dɪ'test] *vt* verabscheuen;
detestable *adj* abscheulich

detour ['diːtʊə°] *n* Umweg *m*; (*of
traffic*) Umleitung *f*

deuce [djuːs] *n* (*Tennis*) Einstand
m

devalue [diː'væljuː] *vt* abwerten

devastate ['devəsteɪt] *vt* verwüsten; **devastating**
['devəsteɪtɪŋ] *adj* verheerend

develop [dɪ'veləp] *vt* entwickeln; (*illness*) bekommen ▷ *vi* sich
entwickeln; **developing country**
n Entwicklungsland *nt*;
development *n* Entwicklung *f*;
(*of land*) Erschließung *f*

device [dɪ'vaɪs] *n* Vorrichtung *f*,
Gerät *nt*

devil ['devl] *n* Teufel *m*; **devilish**
adj teuflisch

devote [dɪ'vəʊt] *vt* widmen (*to*
dat); **devoted** *adj* liebend; (*servant
etc*) treu ergeben; **devotion** *n*
Hingabe *f*

devour [dɪ'vaʊə°] *vt*
verschlingen

dew [djuː] *n* Tau *m*

diabetes [daɪə'biːtiːz] *n* Diabetes *m*, Zuckerkrankheit *f*;
diabetic [daɪə'betɪk] *adj*
zuckerkrank, für Diabetiker ▷ *n*
Diabetiker(in) *m(f)*

diagnosis (*diagnoses*)
[daɪəg'nəʊsɪs] (*pl* **diagnoses**) *n*
Diagnose *f*

diagonal [daɪ'ægənl] *adj*
diagonal

diagram ['daɪəgræm] *n* Diagramm *nt*

dial ['daɪəl] *n* Skala *f*; (*of clock*)

Zifferblatt *nt* ▷ *vt* (*Tel*) wählen; **dial code** *n* (*US*) Vorwahl *f*
dialect ['daɪəlekt] *n* (*Cards*) Dialekt *m*
dialling code *n* (*Brit*) Vorwahl *f*; **dialling tone** *n* (*Brit*) Amtszeichen *nt*
dialogue, dialog (*US*) ['daɪəlɒg] *n* Dialog *m*
dial tone *n* (*US*) Amtszeichen *nt*
dialysis [daɪˈælɪsɪs] *n* (*Med*) Dialyse *f*
diameter [daɪˈæmɪtə°] *n* Durchmesser *m*
diamond ['daɪəmənd] *n* Diamant *m*; (*Cards*) Karo *nt*
diaper ['daɪpə°] *n* (*US*) Windel *f*
diarrhoea [daɪəˈriːə] *n* Durchfall *m*
diary ['daɪərɪ] *n* (*Taschen*)kalender *m*; (*account*) Tagebuch *nt*
dice [daɪs] *npl* Würfel *pl*; **diced** *adj* in Würfel geschnitten
dictate [dɪkˈteɪt] *vt* diktieren; **dictation** [dɪkˈteɪʃən] *n* Diktat *nt*
dictator [dɪkˈteɪtə°] *n* Diktator(in) *m(f)*; **dictatorship** [dɪkˈteɪtəʃɪp] *n* Diktatur *f*
dictionary ['dɪkʃənrɪ] *n* Wörterbuch *nt*
did [dɪd] *pt of* **do**
didn't ['dɪdnt] *contr of* **did not**
die [daɪ] *vi* sterben (*of an +dat*); (*plant, animal*) eingehen; (*engine*) absterben; **to be dying to do sth** darauf brennen, etw zu tun; **I'm dying for a drink** ich brauche unbedingt was zu trinken; **die away** *vi* schwächer werden; (*wind*) sich legen; **die down** *vi* nachlassen; **die out** *vi* aussterben
diesel ['diːzəl] *n* (*fuel, car*) Diesel *m*; **~ engine** Dieselmotor *m*
diet ['daɪət] *n* Kost *f*; (*special food*) Diät *f* ▷ *vi* eine Diät machen
differ ['dɪfə°] *vi* (*be different*) sich unterscheiden; (*disagree*) anderer Meinung sein; **difference**

['dɪfrəns] *n* Unterschied *m*; **it makes no ~ (to me)** es ist (mir) egal; **it makes a big ~** es macht viel aus; **different** *adj* andere(r, s); (*with pl*) verschieden; **to be quite ~** ganz anders sein (*from* als); (*two people, things*) völlig verschieden sein; **a ~ person** ein anderer Mensch; **differentiate** [dɪfəˈrenʃɪeɪt] *vt, vi* unterscheiden; **differently** ['dɪfrəntlɪ] *adv* anders (*from* als); (*from one another*) unterschiedlich
difficult ['dɪfɪkəlt] *adj* schwierig; **I find it ~** es fällt mir schwer; **difficulty** *n* Schwierigkeit *f*; **with ~** nur schwer; **to have ~ in doing sth** etw nur mit Mühe machen können
dig [dɪg] (**dug, dug**) *vt, vi* (*hole*) graben; **dig in** *vi* (*fam: to food*) reinhauen; **~!** greif(t) zu!; **dig up** *vt* ausgraben
digest [daɪˈdʒest] *vt* (*a. fig*) verdauen; **digestible** [dɪˈdʒestəbl] *adj* verdaulich; **digestion** [dɪˈdʒestʃən] *n* Verdauung *f*; **digestive** [dɪˈdʒestɪv] *adj*: **~ biscuit** (*Brit*) Vollkornkeks *m*
digit ['dɪdʒɪt] *n* Ziffer *f*; **digital** ['dɪdʒɪtəl] *adj* digital; **~ computer** Digitalrechner *m*; **~ watch/clock** Digitaluhr *f*; **digital camera** *n* Digitalkamera *f*; **digital television**, **digital TV** *n* Digitalfernsehen *nt*
dignified ['dɪgnɪfaɪd] *adj* würdevoll; **dignity** ['dɪgnɪtɪ] *n* Würde *f*
dilapidated [dɪˈlæpɪdeɪtɪd] *adj* baufällig
dilemma [daɪˈlemə] *n* Dilemma *nt*
dill [dɪl] *n* Dill *m*
dilute [daɪˈluːt] *vt* verdünnen
dim [dɪm] *adj* (*light*) schwach; (*outline*) undeutlich; (*stupid*)

schwer von Begriff ▷ *vt* verdunkeln; (*US Auto*) abblenden; **~med headlights** (*US*) Abblendlicht *nt*

dime [daɪm] *n* (*US*) Zehncentstück *nt*

dimension [daɪˈmenʃən] *n* Dimension *f*; **~s** *pl* Maße *pl*

diminish [dɪˈmɪnɪʃ] *vt* verringern ▷ *vi* sich verringern

dimple [ˈdɪmpl] *n* Grübchen *nt*

dine [daɪn] *vi* speisen; **dine out** *vi* außer Haus essen; **diner** *n* Gast *m*; (*Rail*) Speisewagen *m*; (*US*) Speiselokal *nt*

dinghy [ˈdɪŋgɪ] *n* Ding(h)i *nt*; (*inflatable*) Schlauchboot *nt*

dingy [ˈdɪndʒɪ] *adj* düster; (*dirty*) schmuddelig

dining car [ˈdaɪnɪŋkɑː*] *n* Speisewagen *m*; **dining room** *n* Esszimmer *nt*; (*in hotel*) Speiseraum *m*; **dining table** *n* Esstisch *m*

dinner [ˈdɪnə*] *n* Abendessen *nt*; (*lunch*) Mittagessen *nt*; (*public*) Diner *nt*; **to be at ~** beim Essen sein; **to have ~** zu Abend/Mittag essen; **dinner jacket** *n* Smoking *m*; **dinner party** *n* Abendgesellschaft *f* (*mit Essen*); **dinnertime** *n* Essenszeit *f*

dinosaur [ˈdaɪnəsɔː*] *n* Dinosaurier *m*

dip [dɪp] *vt* tauchen (*in* in +*akk*); **to ~ (one's headlights)** (*Brit Auto*) abblenden; **~ped headlights** Abblendlicht *nt* ▷ *n* (*in ground*) Bodensenke *f*; (*sauce*) Dip *m*

diploma [dɪˈpləʊmə] *n* Diplom *nt*

diplomat [ˈdɪpləmæt] *n* Diplomat(in) *m(f)*; **diplomatic** [dɪpləˈmætɪk] *adj* diplomatisch

dipstick [ˈdɪpstɪk] *n* Ölmessstab *m*

direct [daɪˈrekt] *adj* direkt;

(*cause, consequence*) unmittelbar; **~ debit** (*mandate*) Einzugsermächtigung *f*; (*transaction*) Abbuchung *f* im Lastschriftverfahren; **~ train** durchgehender Zug ▷ *vt* (*aim, send*) richten (*at, to* an +*akk*); (*film*) die Regie führen bei; (*traffic*) regeln; **direct current** *n* (*Elec*) Gleichstrom *m*

direction [dɪˈrekʃən] *n* (*course*) Richtung *f*; (*Cine*) Regie *f*; **in the ~ of ...** in Richtung ...; **~s** *pl* (*to a place*) Wegbeschreibung *f*

directly [dɪˈrektlɪ] *adv* direkt; (*at once*) sofort

director [dɪˈrektə*] *n* Direktor(in) *m(f)*, Leiter(in) *m(f)*; (*of film*) Regisseur(in) *m(f)*

directory [dɪˈrektərɪ] *n* Adressbuch *nt*; (*Tel*) Telefonbuch *nt*; **~ enquiries** *o* (*US*) **assistance** (*Tel*) Auskunft *f*

dirt [dɜːt] *n* Schmutz *m*, Dreck *m*; **dirt cheap** *adj* spottbillig; **dirt road** *n* unbefestigte Straße; **dirty** *adj* schmutzig

disability [dɪsəˈbɪlɪtɪ] *n* Behinderung *f*; **disabled** [dɪsˈeɪbld] *adj* behindert, Behinderten- ▷ *npl*: **the ~** die Behinderten

disadvantage [dɪsədˈvɑːntɪdʒ] *n* Nachteil *m*; **at a ~** benachteiligt; **disadvantageous** [dɪsædvɑːnˈteɪdʒəs] *adj* unvorteilhaft, ungünstig

disagree [dɪsəˈgriː] *vi* anderer Meinung sein; (*two people*) sich nicht einig sein; (*two reports etc*) nicht übereinstimmen; **to ~ with sb** mit jdm nicht übereinstimmen; (*food*) jdm nicht bekommen; **disagreeable** *adj* unangenehm; (*person*) unsympathisch; **disagreement** *n* Meinungsverschiedenheit *f*

disappear [dɪsə'pɪə*] vi verschwinden; **disappearance** n Verschwinden nt

disappoint [dɪsə'pɔɪnt] vt enttäuschen; **disappointing** adj enttäuschend; **disappointment** n Enttäuschung f

disapproval [dɪsə'pru:vl] n Missbilligung f; **disapprove** [dɪsə'pru:v] vi missbilligen (of akk)

disarm [dɪs'ɑ:m] vt entwaffnen ▷ vi (Pol) abrüsten; **disarmament** n Abrüstung f; **disarming** adj (smile, look) gewinnend

disaster [dɪ'zɑːstə*] n Katastrophe f; **disastrous** [dɪ'zɑːstrəs] adj katastrophal

disbelief [dɪsbə'li:f] n Ungläubigkeit f

disc [dɪsk] n Scheibe f, CD f; see also **disk**; (Anat) Bandscheibe f; **disc brake** n Scheibenbremse f

discharge ['dɪstʃɑːdʒ] n (Med) Ausfluss m ▷ [dɪs'tʃɑːdʒ] vt (person) entlassen; (emit) ausstoßen; (Med) ausscheiden

discipline ['dɪsɪplɪn] n Disziplin f

disc jockey ['dɪskdʒɒkɪ] n Diskjockey m

disclose [dɪs'kləʊz] vt bekannt geben; (secret) enthüllen

disco ['dɪskəʊ] (pl **-s**) n Disko f, Diskomusik f

discomfort [dɪs'kʌmfət] n (slight pain) leichte Schmerzen pl; (unease) Unbehagen nt

disconnect [dɪskə'nekt] vt (electricity, gas, phone) abstellen; (unplug) **to ~ the TV (from the mains)** den Stecker des Fernsehers herausziehen; (Tel) **I've been ~ed** das Gespräch ist unterbrochen worden

discontent [dɪskən'tent] n Unzufriedenheit f; **discontented** adj unzufrieden

discontinue [dɪskən'tɪnjuː] vt einstellen; (product) auslaufen lassen

discount ['dɪskaʊnt] n Rabatt m

discover [dɪs'kʌvə*] vt entdecken; **discovery** n Entdeckung f

discredit [dɪs'kredɪt] vt in Verruf bringen ▷ n Misskredit m

discreet [dɪs'kriːt] adj diskret

discrepancy [dɪs'krepənsɪ] n Unstimmigkeit f, Diskrepanz f

discriminate [dɪs'krɪmɪneɪt] vi unterscheiden; **to ~ against sb** jdn diskriminieren; **discrimination** [dɪskrɪmɪ'neɪʃən] n (different treatment) Diskriminierung f

discus ['dɪskəs] n Diskus m

discuss [dɪs'kʌs] vt diskutieren, besprechen; **discussion** [dɪs'kʌʃən] n Diskussion f

disease [dɪ'ziːz] n Krankheit f

disembark [dɪsɪm'bɑːk] vi von Bord gehen

disentangle ['dɪsɪn'tæŋgl] vt entwirren

disgrace [dɪs'greɪs] n Schande f ▷ vt Schande machen +dat; (family etc) Schande bringen über +akk; (less strong) blamieren; **disgraceful** adj skandalös

disguise [dɪs'gaɪz] vt verkleiden; (voice) verstellen ▷ n Verkleidung f; **in ~** verkleidet

disgust [dɪs'gʌst] n Abscheu m; (physical) Ekel m ▷ vt anekeln, anwidern; **disgusting** adj widerlich; (physically) ekelhaft

dish [dɪʃ] n Schüssel f; (food) Gericht nt; **~es** pl (crockery) Geschirr nt; **to do/wash the ~es** abwaschen; **dishcloth** n (for washing) Spültuch nt; (for drying) Geschirrtuch nt

dishearten [dɪsˈhɑːtən] vt
entmutigen; **don't be ~ed** lass den
Kopf nicht hängen!
dishonest [dɪsˈɒnɪst] adj
unehrlich
dishonour [dɪsˈɒnə*] n Schande
f
dish towel n (US) Geschirrtuch
nt; **dish washer** n
Geschirrspülmaschine f
dishy [ˈdɪʃɪ] adj (Brit fam) gut
aussehend
disillusioned [dɪsɪˈluːʒənd] adj
desillusioniert
disinfect [dɪsɪnˈfekt] vt desinfizieren; **disinfectant** n
Desinfektionsmittel nt
disintegrate [dɪsˈɪntɪgreɪt]
vi zerfallen; (group) sich
auflösen
disjointed [dɪsˈdʒɔɪntɪd] adj
unzusammenhängend
disk [dɪsk] n (Inform: floppy)
Diskette f; **disk drive** n
Diskettenlaufwerk nt; **diskette**
[dɪˈsket] n Diskette f
dislike [dɪsˈlaɪk] n Abneigung f
▷ vt nicht mögen; **to ~ doing sth**
etw ungern tun
dislocate [ˈdɪsləʊkeɪt] vt (Med)
verrenken, ausrenken
dismal [ˈdɪzməl] adj trostlos
dismantle [dɪsˈmæntl] vt
auseinandernehmen; (machine)
demontieren
dismay [dɪsˈmeɪ] n Bestürzung f;
dismayed adj bestürzt
dismiss [dɪsˈmɪs] vt (employee)
entlassen; **dismissal** n
Entlassung f
disobedience [dɪsəˈbiːdɪəns] n
Ungehorsam m; **disobedient** adj
ungehorsam; **disobey** [dɪsəˈbeɪ]
vt nicht gehorchen +dat
disorder [dɪsˈɔːdə*] n (mess)
Unordnung f; (riot) Aufruhr m;
(Med) Störung f, Leiden nt

disorganized [dɪsˈɔːgənaɪzd] adj
chaotisch
disparaging adj geringschätzig
dispatch [dɪˈspætʃ] vt abschicken, abfertigen
dispensable [dɪˈspensəbl] adj
entbehrlich; **dispense** vt
verteilen; **dispense with** vt
verzichten auf +akk; **dispenser** n
Automat m
disperse [dɪˈspɜːs] vi sich
zerstreuen
display [dɪˈspleɪ] n (exhibition)
Ausstellung f, Show f; (of goods)
Auslage f; (Tech) Anzeige f, Display
nt ▷ vt zeigen; (goods) ausstellen
disposable [dɪˈspəʊzəbl] adj
(container, razor etc) Wegwerf-;
~ nappy Wegwerfwindel f;
disposal [dɪˈspəʊzəl] n Loswerden nt; (of waste) Beseitigung f; **to
be at sb's ~** jdm zur Verfügung
stehen; **to have at one's
~** verfügen über; **dispose of** vt
loswerden; (waste etc) beseitigen
dispute [dɪˈspjuːt] n Streit m;
(industrial) Auseinandersetzung f
▷ vt bestreiten
disqualification
[dɪskwɒlɪfɪˈkeɪʃən] n Disquali-
fikation f; **disqualify**
[dɪsˈkwɒlɪfaɪ] vt disqualifizieren
disregard [dɪsrɪˈgɑːd] vt nicht
beachten
disreputable [dɪsˈrepjʊtəbl] adj
verrufen
disrespect [dɪsrɪˈspekt] n
Respektlosigkeit f
disrupt [dɪsˈrʌpt] vt stören;
(interrupt) unterbrechen;
disruption [dɪsˈrʌpʃən] n
Störung f; (interruption)
Unterbrechung f
dissatisfied [dɪsˈsætɪsfaɪd] adj
unzufrieden
dissent [dɪˈsent] n Widerspruch
m

dissolve [dɪ'zɒlv] *vt* auflösen
▷ *vi* sich auflösen
dissuade [dɪ'sweɪd] *vt* (*davon abbringen*) **to ~ sb from doing sth** jdn davon abbringen, etw zu tun
distance ['dɪstəns] *n* Entfernung *f*; **in the/from a ~** in/aus der Ferne; **distant** *adj* (*a. in time*) fern; (*relative etc*) entfernt; (*person*) distanziert
distaste [dɪs'teɪst] *n* Abneigung *f* (*for gegen*)
distil [dɪ'stɪl] *vt* destillieren; **distillery** *n* Brennerei *f*
distinct [dɪ'stɪŋkt] *adj* verschieden; (*clear*) klar, deutlich; **distinction** [dɪ'stɪŋkʃən] *n* (*difference*) Unterschied *m*; (*in exam etc*) Auszeichnung *f*; **distinctive** *adj* unverkennbar; **distinctly** *adv* deutlich
distinguish [dɪ'stɪŋgwɪʃ] *vt* unterscheiden (*sth from sth etw von etw*)
distort [dɪ'stɔːt] *vt* verzerren; (*truth*) verdrehen
distract [dɪ'strækt] *vt* ablenken; **distraction** [dɪ'strækʃən] *n* Ablenkung *f*; (*diversion*) Zerstreuung *f*
distress [dɪ'stres] *n* (*need, danger*) Not *f*; (*suffering*) Leiden *nt*; (*mental*) Qual *f*; (*worry*) Kummer *m* ▷ *vt* mitnehmen, erschüttern; **distressed area** *n* Notstandsgebiet *nt*; **distress signal** *n* Notsignal *nt*
distribute [dɪ'strɪbjuːt] *vt* verteilen; (*Comm: goods*) vertreiben; **distribution** [dɪstrɪ'bjuːʃən] *n* Verteilung *f*; (*Comm: of goods*) Vertrieb *m*; **distributor** [dɪ'strɪbjʊtə°] *n* (*Auto*) Verteiler *m*; (*Comm*) Händler(in) *m(f)*

district ['dɪstrɪkt] *n* Gegend *f*; (*administrative*) Bezirk *m*; **district attorney** *n* (*US*) Staatsanwalt *m*, Staatsanwältin *f*
distrust [dɪs'trʌst] *vt* misstrauen +*dat* ▷ *n* Misstrauen *nt*
disturb [dɪs'tɜːb] *vt* stören; (*worry*) beunruhigen; **disturbance** *n* Störung *f*; **disturbing** *adj* beunruhigend
ditch [dɪtʃ] *n* Graben *m* ▷ *vt* (*fam: person*) den Laufpass geben +*dat*; (*plan etc*) verwerfen
ditto ['dɪtəʊ] *n* dito, ebenfalls
dive [daɪv] *n* (*into water*) Kopfsprung *m*; (*Aviat*) Sturzflug *m*; (*fam*) zwielichtiges Lokal ▷ *vi* (*under water*) tauchen; **diver** *n* Taucher(in) *m(f)*
diverse [daɪ'vɜːs] *adj* verschieden; **diversion** [daɪ'vɜːʃən] *n* (*of traffic*) Umleitung *f*; (*distraction*) Ablenkung *f*; **divert** [daɪ'vɜːt] *vt* ablenken; (*traffic*) umleiten
divide [dɪ'vaɪd] *vt* teilen; (*in several parts, between people*) aufteilen ▷ *vi* sich teilen; **dividend** ['dɪvɪdend] *n* Dividende *f*
divine [dɪ'vaɪn] *adj* göttlich
diving ['daɪvɪŋ] *n* (*Sport*)-tauchen *nt*; (*jumping in*) Springen *nt*; (*Sport: from board*) Kunstspringen *nt*; **diving board** *n* Sprungbrett *nt*; **diving goggles** *npl* Taucherbrille *f*; **diving mask** *n* Tauchmaske *f*
division [dɪ'vɪʒən] *n* Teilung *f*; (*Math*) Division *f*; (*department*) Abteilung *f*; (*Sport*) Liga *f*
divorce [dɪ'vɔːs] *n* Scheidung *f* ▷ *vt* sich scheiden lassen von; **divorced** *adj* geschieden; **to get ~** sich scheiden lassen; **divorcee** [dɪvɔː'siː] *n* Geschiedene(r) *mf*
DIY [diːaɪ'waɪ] *abbr* =

do-it-yourself; **DIY centre** n Baumarkt m

dizzy ['dɪzɪ] adj schwindlig

DJ [diː'dʒeɪ] abbr = **dinner jacket** Smoking m ▷ abbr = **disc jockey** Diskjockey m, DJ m

DNA abbr = **desoxyribonucleic acid** DNS f

 KEYWORD

do [duː] (pt **did**, pp **done**) n (inf) (party etc) Fete f
▷ vb aux **1** (in negative constructions and questions) **I don't understand** ich verstehe nicht; **didn't you know?** wusstest du das nicht?; **what do you think?** was meinen Sie?
2 (for emphasis, in polite phrases) **she does seem rather tired** sie scheint wirklich sehr müde zu sein; **do sit down/help yourself** setzen Sie sich doch hin/greifen Sie doch zu
3 (used to avoid repeating vb) **she swims better than I do** sie schwimmt besser als ich; **she lives in Glasgow — so do I** sie wohnt in Glasgow — ich auch
4 (in tag questions) **you like him, don't you?** du magst/Sie mögen ihn doch, oder?
▷ vt **1** (carry out, perform etc) tun, machen; **what are you doing tonight?** was machst du/machen Sie heute Abend?; **I've got nothing to do** ich habe nichts zu tun; **to do one's hair/nails** sich die Haare/Nägel machen
2 (car etc) fahren
▷ vi **1** (act, behave) **do as I do** mach es wie ich
2 (get on, fare) **he's doing well/badly at school** er ist gut/schlecht in der Schule; **how do you do?** guten Tag

3 (be suitable) gehen; (be sufficient) reichen; **to make do (with)** auskommen mit

do away with vt (kill) umbringen; (abolish: law etc) abschaffen

do up vt (laces, dress, buttons) zumachen; (renovate: room, house) renovieren

do with vt (need) brauchen; (be connected) zu tun haben mit

do without vt, vi auskommen ohne

do up vt (fasten) zumachen; (parcel) verschnüren; (renovate) wiederherrichten

do with vt (need) brauchen; **I could ~ a drink** ich könnte einen Drink gebrauchen

do without vt auskommen ohne; **I can ~ your comments** auf deine Kommentare kann ich verzichten

dock [dɒk] n Dock nt; (Jur) Anklagebank f; **docker** n Hafenarbeiter m; **dockyard** n Werft f

doctor ['dɒktə*] n Arzt m, Ärztin; (in title, also academic) Doktor m

document ['dɒkjʊmənt] n Dokument nt; **documentary** [dɒkjʊ'mentərɪ] n Dokumentarfilm m; **documentation** [dɒkjʊmen'teɪʃən] n Dokumentation f

docusoap ['dɒkjʊsəʊp] n Reality-Serie f, Dokusoap f

doddery ['dɒdərɪ] adj tatterig

dodgem ['dɒdʒəm] n Autoskooter m

dodgy [dɒdʒɪ] adj nicht ganz in Ordnung; (dishonest, unreliable) zwielichtig; **he has a ~ stomach** er hat sich den Magen verdorben

dog [dɒg] n Hund m; **dog food** n Hundefutter nt; **doggie bag**

['dɒgɪ'bæg] n Tüte oder Box, in der Essensreste aus dem Restaurant mit nach Hause genommen werden können

do-it-yourself ['du:ɪtjə'self] n Heimwerken nt, Do-it-yourself nt ▷ adj Heimwerker-;
do-it-yourselfer n Bastler(in) m(f), Heimwerker(in) m(f)

doll [dɒl] n Puppe f

dollar ['dɒlə°] n Dollar m

dolphin ['dɒlfɪn] n Delphin m

domain n Domäne f; (Inform) Domain f

dome [dəʊm] n Kuppel f

domestic [də'mestɪk] adj häuslich; (within country) Innen-, Binnen-; **domestic animal** n Haustier nt; **domesticated** [də'mestɪkeɪtɪd] adj (person) häuslich; (animal) zahm; **domestic flight** n Inlandsflug m

domicile ['dɒmɪsaɪl] n (ständiger) Wohnsitz

dominant ['dɒmɪnənt] adj dominierend, vorherrschend; **dominate** ['dɒmɪneɪt] vt beherrschen

dominoes ['dɒmɪnəʊz] npl Domino(spiel) nt

donate [dəʊ'neɪt] vt spenden; **donation** n Spende f

done [dʌn] pp of **do** ▷ adj (cooked) gar; **well ~** durchgebraten

doner (kebab) ['dɒnəkə'bæb] n Döner (Kebab) m

donkey ['dɒŋkɪ] n Esel m

donor ['dəʊnə] n Spender(in) m(f)

don't [dəʊnt] contr of **do not**

doom [du:m] n Schicksal nt; (downfall) Verderben nt

door [dɔː°] n Tür f; **doorbell** n Türklingel f; **door handle** n Türklinke f; **doorknob** n Türknauf m; **doormat** n Fußabtreter m; **doorstep** n Türstufe f; **right**

on our ~ direkt vor unserer Haustür

dope [dəʊp] (Sport) n (for athlete) Aufputschmittel nt ▷ vt dopen

dormitory ['dɔːmɪtrɪ] n Schlafsaal m; (US) Studentenwohnheim nt

dosage ['dəʊsɪdʒ] n Dosierung f; **dose** [dəʊs] n Dosis f ▷ vt dosieren

dot [dɒt] n Punkt m; **on the ~** auf die Minute genau, pünktlich

dotcom ['dɒtkɒm] n: ~ **(company)** Internetfirma f, Dotcom-Unternehmen nt

dote on [dəʊt ɒn] vt abgöttisch lieben

dotted line n punktierte Linie

double ['dʌbl] adj, adv doppelt; **~ the quantity** die zweifache Menge, doppelt so viel ▷ vt verdoppeln ▷ n (person) Doppelgänger(in) m(f); (Cine) Double nt; **double bass** n Kontrabass m; **double bed** n Doppelbett nt; **double-click** vt (Inform) doppelklicken; **double cream** n Sahne mit hohem Fettgehalt; **doubledecker** n Doppeldecker m; **double glazing** n Doppelverglasung f; **double-park** vi in zweiter Reihe parken; **double room** n Doppelzimmer nt; **doubles** npl (Sport: also match) Doppel nt

doubt [daʊt] n Zweifel m; **no ~** ohne Zweifel, zweifellos, wahrscheinlich; **to have one's ~s** Bedenken haben ▷ vt bezweifeln; (statement, word) anzweifeln; **I ~ it** das bezweifle ich; **doubtful** adj zweifelhaft, zweifelnd; **it is ~ whether ...** es ist fraglich, ob ...; **doubtless** adv ohne Zweifel, sicherlich

dough [dəʊ] n Teig m; **doughnut** n Donut m (rundes Hefegebäck)

dove [dʌv] n Taube f
down [daʊn] n Daunen pl; (fluff)
Flaum m ▷ adv unten; (motion)
nach unten; (towards speaker)
herunter; (away from speaker)
hinunter; **~ here/there** hier/dort
unten; (downstairs) **they came
~ for breakfast** sie kamen zum
Frühstück herunter; (southwards)
he came ~ from Scotland er kam
von Schottland herunter ▷ prep
(towards speaker) herunter; (away
from speaker) hinunter; **to drive
~ the hill/road** den Berg/die
Straße hinunter fahren; (along) **to
walk ~ the street** die Straße
entlang gehen; **he's ~ the pub**
(fam) er ist in der Kneipe ▷ vt
(fam: drink) runterkippen ▷ adj
niedergeschlagen, deprimiert
down-and-out adj
heruntergekommen ▷ n
Obdachlose(r) mf, Penner(in) m(f);
downcast adj niedergeschlagen;
downfall n Sturz m;
down-hearted adj entmutigt;
downhill adv bergab; **he's going
~** (fig) mit ihm geht es bergab

- DOWNING STREET
-
- **Downing Street** ist die Straße
- in London, die von Whitehall
- zum St James's Park führt, und
- in der sich der offizielle
- Wohnsitz des Premierministers
- (Nr. 10) und des Finanzministers
- (Nr. 11) befindet. Im weiteren
- Sinne bezieht sich der Begriff
- „Downing Street" auf die
- britische Regierung.

download [ˈdaʊnləʊd] vt
herunterladen; **downloadable** adj
(Inform) herunterladbar;
downmarket adj für den
Massenmarkt; **down payment** n

Anzahlung f; **downpour** n
Platzregen m; **downs** npl Hügel-
land nt; **downsize** vt verkleinern
▷ vi sich verkleinern
Down's syndrome
[ˈdaʊnzˈsɪndrəʊm] n (Med)
Downsyndrom nt
downstairs [daʊnˈstɛəz] adv
unten; (motion) nach unten;
downstream adv flussabwärts;
downtime n Ausfallzeit f;
downtown adv (be, work etc) in
der Innenstadt; (go) in die
Innenstadt ▷ adj (US) in der
Innenstadt; **~ Chicago** die
Innenstadt von Chicago; **down
under** adv (fam: in/to Australia)
in/nach Australien; (in/to New
Zealand) in/nach Neuseeland;
downwards adv, adj nach unten;
(movement, trend) Abwärts-
doze [dəʊz] vi dösen ▷ n
Nickerchen nt
dozen [ˈdʌzn] n Dutzend nt; **two
~ eggs** zwei Dutzend Eier; **~s of
times** x-mal
DP abbr = **data processing** DV f
drab [dræb] adj trist; (colour)
düster
draft [drɑːft] n (outline) Entwurf
m; (US Mil) Einberufung f
drag [dræg] vt schleppen ▷ n (fam)
to be a ~ (boring) stinklangweilig
sein; (laborious) ein ziemlicher
Schlauch sein; **drag on** vi sich in
die Länge ziehen
dragon [ˈdrægən] n Drache m;
dragonfly n Libelle f
drain [dreɪn] n Abfluss m ▷ vt
(water, oil) ablassen; (vegetables etc)
abgießen; (land) entwässern,
trockenlegen ▷ vi (of water)
abfließen; **drainpipe** n
Abflussrohr nt
drama [ˈdrɑːmə] n (a. fig) Drama
nt; **dramatic** [drəˈmætɪk] adj
dramatisch

drank [dræŋk] *pt of* **drink**

drapes [dreɪps] *npl* (*US*) Vorhänge *pl*

drastic ['dræstɪk] *adj* drastisch

draught [drɑːft] *n* (Luft)zug *m*; **there's a ~** es zieht; **on ~** (*beer*) vom Fass; **draughts** *nsing* Damespiel *nt*; **draughty** *adj* zugig

draw [drɔː] (**drew, drawn**) *vt* (*pull*) ziehen; (*crowd*) anlocken, anziehen; (*picture*) zeichnen ▷ *vi* (*Sport*) unentschieden spielen ▷ *n* (*Sport*) Unentschieden *nt*; (*attraction*) Attraktion *f*; (*for lottery*) Ziehung *f*; **draw out** *vt* herausziehen; (*money*) abheben; **draw up** *vt* (*formulate*) entwerfen; (*list*) erstellen ▷ *vi* (*car*) anhalten; **drawback** *n* Nachteil *m*; **drawbridge** *n* Zugbrücke *f*

drawer ['drɔː*] *n* Schublade *f*

drawing ['drɔːɪŋ] *n* Zeichnung *f*; **drawing pin** *n* Reißzwecke *f*

drawn [drɔːn] *pp of* **draw**

dread [dred] *n* Furcht *f* (*of* vor +*dat*) ▷ *vt* sich fürchten vor +*dat*; **dreadful** *adj* furchtbar; **dreadlocks** *npl* Rastalocken *pl*

dream [driːm] (**dreamed** *o* **dreamt, dreamed** *o* **dreamt**) *vt, vi* träumen (*about* von) ▷ *n* Traum *m*; **dreamt** [dremt] *pt, pp of* **dream**

dreary ['drɪərɪ] *adj* (*weather, place*) trostlos; (*book etc*) langweilig

drench [drentʃ] *vt* durchnässen

dress [dres] *n* Kleidung *f*; (*garment*) Kleid *nt* ▷ *vt* anziehen; (*Med: wound*) verbinden; **to get ~ed** sich anziehen; **dress up** *vi* sich fein machen; (*in costume*) sich verkleiden (*as* als); **dress circle** *n* (*Theat*) erster Rang; **dresser** *n* Anrichte *f*; (*US: dressing table*) (Frisier)kommode *f*; **dressing** *n* (*Gastr*) Dressing *nt*, Soße *f*; (*Med*) Verband *m*; **dressing gown** *n* Bademantel *m*; **dressing room** *n* (*Theat*) Künstlergarderobe *f*; **dressing table** *n* Frisierkommode *f*; **dress rehearsal** *n* (*Theat*) Generalprobe *f*

drew [druː] *pt of* **draw**

dried [draɪd] *adj* getrocknet; (*milk, flowers*) Trocken-; **~ fruit** Dörrobst *nt*; **drier** ['draɪə*] *n see* **dryer**

drift [drɪft] *vi* treiben ▷ *n* (*of snow*) Verwehung *f*; (*fig*) Tendenz *f*; **if you get my ~** wenn du mich richtig verstehst/wenn Sie mich richtig verstehen

drill [drɪl] *n* Bohrer *m* ▷ *vt, vi* bohren

drink [drɪŋk] (**drank, drunk**) *vt, vi* trinken ▷ *n* Getränk *nt*; (*alcoholic*) Drink *m*; **drink-driving** *n* (*Brit*) Trunkenheit *f* am Steuer; **drinking water** *n* Trinkwasser *nt*

drip [drɪp] *n* Tropfen *m* ▷ *vi* tropfen; **drip-dry** *adj* bügelfrei; **dripping** *n* Bratenfett *nt* ▷ *adj*: **~ (wet)** tropfnass

drive [draɪv] (**drove, driven**) *vt* (*car, person in car*) fahren; (*force: person, animal*) treiben; (*Tech*) antreiben; **to ~ sb mad** jdn verrückt machen ▷ *vi* fahren ▷ *n* Fahrt *f*; (*entrance*) Einfahrt *f*, Auffahrt *f*; (*Inform*) Laufwerk *nt*; **to go for a ~** spazieren fahren; **drive away, drive off** *vi* wegfahren ▷ *vt* vertreiben

drive-in *adj* Drive-in-; **~ cinema** (*US*) Autokino *nt*

driven ['drɪvn] *pp of* **drive**

driver ['draɪvə*] *n* Fahrer(in) *m(f)*; (*Inform*) Treiber *m*; **~'s license** (*US*) Führerschein *m*; **~'s seat** Fahrersitz *m*; **driving** ['draɪvɪŋ] *n* (Auto)fahren *nt*; **he likes ~** er fährt gern Auto; **driving lesson** *n*

Fahrstunde f; **driving licence** n (Brit) Führerschein m; **driving school** n Fahrschule f; **driving seat** n (Brit) Fahrersitz m; **to be in the ~** alles im Griff haben; **driving test** n Fahrprüfung f

drizzle ['drɪzl] n Nieselregen m ▷ vi nieseln

drop [drɒp] n (of liquid) Tropfen m; (fall in price etc) Rückgang m ▷ vt (a. fig: give up) fallen lassen ▷ vi (fall) herunterfallen; (figures, temperature) sinken, zurückgehen; **drop by, drop in** vi vorbeikommen; **drop off** vi (to sleep) einnicken; **drop out** vi (withdraw) aussteigen; (university) das Studium abbrechen; **dropout** n Aussteiger(in) m(f)

drought [draʊt] n Dürre f

drove [drəʊv] pt of **drive**

drown [draʊn] vi ertrinken ▷ vt ertränken

drowsy ['draʊzɪ] adj schläfrig

drug [drʌg] n (Med) Medikament nt, Arznei f; (addictive) Droge f; (narcotic) Rauschgift nt; **to be on ~s** drogensüchtig sein ▷ vt (mit Medikamenten) betäuben; **drug addict** n Rauschgiftsüchtige(r) mf; **drug dealer** n Drogenhändler(in) m(f); **druggist** n (US) Drogist(in) m(f); **drugstore** n (US) Drogerie f

drum [drʌm] n Trommel f; **~s** pl Schlagzeug nt; **drummer** n Schlagzeuger(in) m(f)

drunk [drʌŋk] pp of **drink** ▷ adj betrunken; **to get ~** sich betrinken ▷ n Betrunkene(r) mf; (alcoholic) Trinker(in) m(f); **drunk-driving** n (US) Trunkenheit f am Steuer; **drunken** adj betrunken, besoffen

dry [draɪ] adj trocken ▷ vt trocknen; (dishes, oneself, one's hands etc) abtrocknen ▷ vi trocknen, trocken werden; **dry out**

vi trocknen; **dry up** vi austrocknen; **dry-clean** vt chemisch reinigen; **dry-cleaning** n chemische Reinigung; **dryer** n Trockner m; (for hair) Föhn m; (overhead) Trockenhaube f

DTP abbr = **desktop publishing** DTP nt

dual ['djʊəl] adj doppelt; **~ carriageway** (Brit) zweispurige Schnellstraße f; **~ nationality** doppelte Staatsangehörigkeit

dubbed [dʌbd] adj (film) synchronisiert

dubious ['djuːbɪəs] adj zweifelhaft

duchess ['dʌtʃəs] n Herzogin f

duck [dʌk] n Ente f

dude [duːd] n (US fam) Typ m; **a cool ~** ein cooler Typ

due [djuː] adj (time) fällig; (fitting) angemessen; **in ~ course** zu gegebener Zeit; **~ to** infolge +gen, wegen +gen ▷ adv: **~ south/north** etc direkt nach Norden/Süden etc

dug [dʌg] pt, pp of **dig**

duke [djuːk] n Herzog m

dull [dʌl] adj (colour, light, weather) trübe; (boring) langweilig

duly ['djuːlɪ] adv ordnungsgemäß; (as expected) wie erwartet

dumb [dʌm] adj stumm; (fam: stupid) doof, blöde

dumb-bell ['dʌmbel] n Hantel f

dummy ['dʌmɪ] n (sham) Attrappe f; (in shop) Schaufensterpuppe f; (Brit: teat) Schnuller m; (fam: person) Dummkopf m f ▷ adj unecht, Schein-; **~ run** Testlauf m

dump [dʌmp] n Abfallhaufen m; (fam: place) Kaff nt ▷ vt (lit, fig) abladen; (fam) **he ~ed her** er hat mir ihr Schluss gemacht

dumpling ['dʌmplɪŋ] n Kloß m, Knödel m

dune [djuːn] n Düne f

dung [dʌŋ] n (manure) Mist m
dungarees [dʌŋgə'riːz] npl
Latzhose f
dungeon ['dʌndʒən] n Kerker m
duplex ['djuːpleks] n
zweistöckige Wohnung; (US)
Doppelhaushälfte f
duplicate ['djuːplɪkɪt] n Dup-
likat nt ▷ ['djuːplɪkeɪt] vt (make
copies of) kopieren; (repeat)
wiederholen
durable ['djʊərəbl] adj haltbar;
duration [djʊə'reɪʃən] n Dauer f
during ['djʊərɪŋ] prep (time)
während +gen
dusk [dʌsk] n Abenddämmerung f
dust [dʌst] n Staub m ▷ vt
abstauben; **dustbin** n (Brit)
Mülleimer m; **dustcart** n (Brit)
Müllwagen m; **duster** n
Staubtuch nt; **dust jacket** n
Schutzumschlag m; **dustman** n
(Brit) Müllmann m; **dustpan** n
Kehrschaufel f; **dusty** adj staubig
Dutch [dʌtʃ] adj holländisch ▷ n
(language) Holländisch nt; **to
speak/talk double ~** (fam)
Quatsch reden; **the ~** pl die
Holländer; **Dutchman** (pl **-men**)
n Holländer m; **Dutchwoman** (pl
-women) n Holländerin f
duty ['djuːtɪ] n Pflicht f; (task)
Aufgabe f; (tax) Zoll m; **on/off ~** im
Dienst/nicht im Dienst; **to be on
~** Dienst haben; **duty-free** adj
zollfrei; **~ shop** Dutyfreeshop m
duvet ['duːveɪ] n Federbett nt
DVD n abbr = **digital versatile
disk** DVD f; **DVD player** n
DVD-Player m; **DVD recorder** n
DVD-Rekorder m
dwelling ['dwelɪŋ] n Wohnung f
dwindle ['dwɪndl] vi schwinden
dye [daɪ] n Farbstoff m ▷ vt
färben
dynamic [daɪ'næmɪk] adj
dynamisch

dynamo ['daɪnəməʊ] n Dynamo m
dyslexia [dɪs'leksɪə] n Legasthenie
f; **dyslexic** adj legasthenisch; **to
be ~** Legastheniker(in) sein

d

e

E [iː] *abbr* = **east** (*geo*) O; *abbr* = **ecstasy** (*drug*) Ecstasy *nt*

E111 form *n* ≈ Auslandskrankenschein *m*

each [iːtʃ] *adj* jeder/jede/jedes ▷ *pron* jeder/jede/jedes; **I'll have one of ~** ich nehme von jedem eins; **they ~ have a car** jeder von ihnen hat ein Auto; **~ other** einander, sich; **for/against ~ other** füreinander/ gegeneinander ▷ *adv* je; **they cost 10 euros ~** sie kosten je 10 Euro, sie kosten 10 Euro das Stück

eager ['iːgə°] *adj* eifrig; **to be ~ to do sth** darauf brennen, etw zu tun

eagle ['iːgl] *n* Adler *m*

ear [ɪə°] *n* Ohr *nt*; **earache** *n* Ohrenschmerzen *pl*; **eardrum** *n* Trommelfell *nt*

earl [ɜːl] *n* Graf *m*

early ['ɜːlɪ] *adj*, *adv* früh; **to be 10 minutes ~** 10 Minuten zu früh kommen; **at the earliest** frühestens; **in ~ June/2008** Anfang Juni/2008; **~ retirement** vorzeitiger Ruhestand; **~ warning system** Frühwarnsystem *nt*

earn [ɜːn] *vt* verdienen

earnest ['ɜːnɪst] *adj* ernst; **in ~** im Ernst

earnings ['ɜːnɪŋz] *npl* Verdienst *m*, Einkommen *nt*

earplug *n* Ohrenstöpsel *m*, Ohropax® *nt*; **earring** *n* Ohrring *m*

earth [ɜːθ] *n* Erde *f*; **what on ~ ...?** was in aller Welt ...? ▷ *vt* erden; **earthenware** *n* Tonwaren *pl*; **earthquake** *n* Erdbeben *nt*

earwig ['ɪəwɪg] *n* Ohrwurm *m*

ease [iːz] *vt* (*pain*) lindern; (*burden*) erleichtern ▷ *n* (*easiness*) Leichtigkeit *f*; **to feel at ~** sich wohlfühlen; **to feel ill at ~** sich nicht wohlfühlen; **easily** ['iːzɪlɪ] *adv* leicht; **he is ~ the best** er ist mit Abstand der Beste

east [iːst] *n* Osten *m*; **to the ~ of** östlich von ▷ *adv* (*go, face*) nach Osten ▷ *adj* Ost-; **~ wind** Ostwind *m*; **eastbound** *adj* (in) Richtung Osten

Easter ['iːstə°] *n* Ostern *nt*; **at ~** zu Ostern; **Easter egg** *n* Osterei *nt*; **Easter Sunday** *n* Ostersonntag *m*

eastern ['iːstən] *adj* Ost-, östlich; **Eastern Europe** Osteuropa *nt*; **East Germany** *n* Ostdeutschland *nt*; **former ~** die ehemalige DDR, die neuen Bundesländer; **eastwards** ['iːstwədz] *adv* nach Osten

easy ['iːzɪ] *adj* leicht; (*task, solution*) einfach; (*life*) bequem; (*manner*) ungezwungen; **easy-going** *adj* gelassen

eat [iːt] (*ate, eaten*) *vt* essen; (*animal*) fressen; **eat out** *vi* zum

Essen ausgehen; **eat up** vt
aufessen; (animal) auffressen
eaten ['i:tn] pp of **eat**
eavesdrop ['i:vzdrɒp] vi (heimlich) lauschen; **to ~ on sb** jdn
belauschen
eccentric [ɪk'sentrɪk] adj
exzentrisch
echo ['ekəʊ] (pl **-es**) n Echo nt
▷ vi widerhallen
ecological [i:kə'lɒdʒɪkl] adj
ökologisch; **~ disaster**
Umweltkatastrophe f; **ecology**
[ɪ'kɒlədʒɪ] n Ökologie f
economic [i:kə'nɒmɪk] adj
wirtschaftlich, Wirtschafts-; **~ aid**
Wirtschaftshilfe f; **economical** adj
wirtschaftlich; (person) sparsam;
economics nsing o pl
Wirtschaftswissenschaft f;
economist [ɪ'kɒnəmɪst] n
Wirtschaftswissenschaftler(in)
m(f); **economize** [ɪ'kɒnəmaɪz] vi
sparen (on an +dat); **economy**
[ɪ'kɒnəmɪ] n (of state) Wirtschaft
f; (thrift) Sparsamkeit f; **economy
class** n (Aviat) Economyclass f
ecstasy ['ekstəsɪ] n Ekstase f;
(drug) Ecstasy f
eczema ['eksɪmə] n Ekzem nt
edge [edʒ] n Rand m; (of knife)
Schneide f; **on ~** nervös; **edgy**
['edʒɪ] adj nervös
edible ['edɪbl] adj essbar
Edinburgh ['edɪnbərə] n Edin-
burg nt
edit ['edɪt] vt (series, newspaper
etc) herausgeben; (text) redigieren;
(film) schneiden; (Inform)
editieren; **edition** [ɪ'dɪʃən] n
Ausgabe f; **editor** n Redakteur(in)
m(f); (of series etc) Herausgeber(in)
m(f); **editorial** [edɪ'tɔ:rɪəl] adj
Redaktions- ▷ n Leitartikel m
educate ['edjʊkeɪt] vt (child)
erziehen; (at school, university)
ausbilden; (public) aufklären;

educated adj gebildet;
education [edjʊ'keɪʃən] n
Erziehung f; (studies, training)
Ausbildung f; (subject of study)
Pädagogik f; (system) Schulwesen
nt; (knowledge) Bildung f;
educational adj pädagogisch;
(instructive) lehrreich; **~ television**
Schulfernsehen nt
eel [i:l] n Aal m
eerie ['ɪərɪ] adj unheimlich
effect [ɪ'fekt] n Wirkung f (on auf
+akk); **to come into ~** in Kraft
treten; **effective** adj wirksam,
effektiv
effeminate [ɪ'femɪnət] adj (of
man) tuntig
efficiency [ɪ'fɪʃənsɪ] n Leistungsfähigkeit f; (of method)
Wirksamkeit f; **efficient** adj
(Tech) leistungsfähig; (method)
wirksam, effizient
effort ['efət] n Anstrengung f;
(attempt) Versuch m; **to make an
~** sich anstrengen; **effortless** adj
mühelos
e.g. abbr = **exempli gratia (for
example)** z. B.
egg [eg] n Ei nt; **eggcup** n
Eierbecher m; **eggplant** n (US)
Aubergine f; **eggshell** n
Eierschale f
ego ['i:gəʊ] (pl **-s**) n Ich nt;
(self-esteem) Selbstbewusstsein nt;
ego(t)ist ['egəʊ(t)ɪst] n Ego-
zentriker(in) m(f)
Egypt ['i:dʒɪpt] n Ägypten nt;
Egyptian [ɪ'dʒɪpʃən] adj
ägyptisch ▷ n Ägypter(in) m(f)
eiderdown ['aɪdədaʊn] n
Daunendecke f
eight [eɪt] num acht; **at the age
of ~** im Alter von acht Jahren; **it's
~** (**o'clock**) es ist acht Uhr ▷ n (a.
bus etc) Acht f; (boat) Achter m;
eighteen [eɪ'ti:n] num achtzehn
▷ n Achtzehn f; see also **eight**;

eighteenth adj achtzehnte(r, s); see also **eighth**; **eighth** [eɪtθ] adj achte(r, s); **the ~ of June** der achte Juni ⊳ n (fraction) Achtel nt; **an ~ of a litre** ein Achtelliter; **eightieth** ['eɪtɪəθ] adj achtzigste(r, s); see also **eighth**; **eighty** ['eɪtɪ] num achtzig ⊳ n Achtzig f; see also **eight**

Eire ['ɛərə] n die Republik Irland

either ['aɪðə°] conj: **~ ... or** entweder ... oder ⊳ pron: **~ of the two** eine(r, s) von beiden ⊳ adj: **on ~ side** auf beiden Seiten ⊳ adv: **I won't go ~** ich gehe auch nicht

eject [ɪ'dʒekt] vt ausstoßen; (person) vertreiben

elaborate [ɪ'læbərət] adj (complex) kompliziert; (plan) ausgeklügelt; (decoration) kunstvoll ⊳ vi [ɪ'læbəreɪt] **could you ~ on that?** könntest du/könnten Sie mehr darüber sagen?

elastic [ɪ'læstɪk] adj elastisch; **~ band** Gummiband nt

elbow ['elbəʊ] n Ellbogen m; **to give sb the ~** (fam) jdm den Laufpass geben

elder ['eldə°] adj (of two) älter ⊳ n Ältere(r) mf; (Bot) Holunder m; **elderly** adj ältere(r, s) ⊳ n: **the ~** die älteren Leute; **eldest** ['eldɪst] adj älteste(r, s)

elect [ɪ'lekt] vt wählen; **he was ~ed chairman** er wurde zum Vorsitzenden gewählt; **election** [ɪ'lekʃən] n Wahl f; **election campaign** n Wahlkampf m; **electioneering** [ɪlekʃə'nɪərɪŋ] n Wahlpropaganda f; **electorate** [ɪ'lektərɪt] n Wähler pl

electric [ɪ'lektrɪk] adj elektrisch; (car, motor, razor etc) Elektro-; **~ blanket** Heizdecke f; **~ cooker** Elektroherd m; **~ current** elektrischer Strom; **~ shock**

Stromschlag m; **electrical** adj elektrisch; **~ goods/appliances** Elektrogeräte; **electrician** [ɪlek'trɪʃən] n Elektriker(in) m(f); **electricity** [ɪlek'trɪsɪtɪ] n Elektrizität f; **electrocute** [ɪ'lektrəʊkjuːt] vt durch einen Stromschlag töten; **electronic** [ɪlek'trɒnɪk] adj elektronisch

elegance ['elɪgəns] n Eleganz f; **elegant** adj elegant

element ['elɪmənt] n Element nt; **an ~ of truth** ein Körnchen Wahrheit; **elementary** [elɪ'mentərɪ] adj einfach; (basic) grundlegend; **~ stage** Anfangsstadium nt; **~ school** (US) Grundschule f; **~ maths/French** Grundkenntnisse in Mathematik/Französisch

elephant ['elɪfənt] n Elefant m

elevator ['elɪveɪtə°] n (US) Fahrstuhl m

eleven [ɪ'levn] num elf ⊳ n (team, bus etc) Elf f see **eight**; **eleventh** [ɪ'levnθ] adj elfte(r, s) ⊳ n (fraction) Elftel nt see **eighth**

eligible ['elɪdʒəbl] adj infrage kommend; (for grant etc) berechtigt; **~ for a pension/competition** pensions-/teilnahmeberechtigt; **~ bachelor** begehrter Junggeselle

eliminate [ɪ'lɪmɪneɪt] vt ausschließen (from aus), ausschalten; (problem etc) beseitigen; **elimination** n Ausschluss m (from aus); (of problem etc) Beseitigung f

elm [elm] n Ulme f

elope [ɪ'ləʊp] vi durchbrennen (with sb mit jdm)

eloquent ['eləkwənt] adj redegewandt

else [els] adv: **anybody/anything ~** (in addition) sonst (noch) jemand/etwas; (*other*) ein anderer/etwas anderes; **somebody ~** jemand anders; **everyone ~** alle anderen; **or ~** sonst; **elsewhere** *adv* anderswo, woanders; (*direction*) woandershin

ELT *abbr* = **English Language Teaching**

email ['i:meɪl] *vi, vt* mailen (*sth to sb* jdm etw) ▷ *n* E-Mail *f*; **email address** *n* E-Mail-Adresse *f*

emancipated [ɪ'mænsɪpeɪtɪd] *adj* emanzipiert

embankment [ɪm'bæŋkmənt] *n* Böschung *f*; (*for railway*) Bahndamm *m*

embargo [ɪm'bɑ:gəʊ] (*pl* **-es**) *n* Embargo *nt*

embark [ɪm'bɑ:k] *vi* an Bord gehen

embarrass [ɪm'bærəs] *vt* in Verlegenheit bringen; **embarrassed** *adj* verlegen; **embarrassing** *adj* peinlich

embassy ['embəsɪ] *n* Botschaft *f*

embrace [ɪm'breɪs] *vt* umarmen ▷ *n* Umarmung *f*

embroider [ɪm'brɔɪdə°] *vt* besticken; **embroidery** *n* Stickerei *f*

embryo ['embrɪəʊ] (*pl* **-s**) *n* Embryo *m*

emerald ['emərəld] *n* Smaragd *m*

emerge [ɪ'mɜ:dʒ] *vi* auftauchen; **it ~d that ...** es stellte sich heraus, dass ...

emergency [ɪ'mɜ:dʒənsɪ] *n* Notfall *m* ▷ *adj* Not-; **~ exit** Notausgang *m*; **~ landing** Notlandung *f*; **~ room** (US) Unfallstation *f*; **~ service** Notdienst *m*; **~ stop** Vollbremsung *f*

emigrate ['emɪgreɪt] *vi* auswandern

emit [ɪ'mɪt] *vt* ausstoßen; (*heat*) abgeben

emoticon [ɪ'məʊtɪkən] *n* (*Inform*) Emoticon *nt*

emotion [ɪ'məʊʃən] *n* Emotion *f*, Gefühl *nt*; **emotional** *adj* (*person*) emotional; (*experience, moment, scene*) ergreifend

emperor ['empərə°] *n* Kaiser *m*

emphasis ['emfəsɪs] *n* Betonung *f*; **emphasize** ['emfəsaɪz] *vt* betonen; **emphatic**, **emphatically** [ɪm'fætɪk, -lɪ] *adj, adv* nachdrücklich

empire ['empaɪə°] *n* Reich *nt*

employ [ɪm'plɔɪ] *vt* beschäftigen; (*hire*) anstellen; (*use*) anwenden; **employee** [emplɔɪ'i:] *n* Angestellte(r) *mf*; **employer** *n* Arbeitgeber(in) *m(f)*; **employment** *n* Beschäftigung *f*; (*position*) Stellung *f*; **employment agency** *n* Stellenvermittlung *f*

empress ['emprɪs] *n* Kaiserin *f*

empty ['emptɪ] *adj* leer ▷ *vt* (*contents*) leeren; (*container*) ausleeren

enable [ɪ'neɪbl] *vt*: **to ~ sb to do sth** es jdm ermöglichen, etw zu tun

enamel [ɪ'næməl] *n* Email *nt*; (*of teeth*) Zahnschmelz *m*

enchanting [ɪn'tʃɑ:ntɪŋ] *adj* bezaubernd

enclose [ɪn'kləʊz] *vt* einschließen; (*in letter*) beilegen (*in, with dat*); **enclosure** [ɪn'kləʊʒə°] *n* (*for animals*) Gehege *nt*; (*in letter*) Anlage *f*

encore ['ɒŋkɔ:°] *n* Zugabe *f*

encounter [ɪn'kaʊntə°] *n* Begegnung *f* ▷ *vt* (*person*) begegnen +*dat*; (*difficulties*) stoßen auf +*akk*

encourage [ɪn'kʌrɪdʒ] *vt* ermutigen; **encouragement** *n* Ermutigung *f*

encyclopaedia
[ensaɪkləʊ'piːdɪə] n Lexikon nt,
Enzyklopädie f

end [end] n Ende nt; (of film, play
etc) Schluss m; (purpose) Zweck m;
at the ~ of May Ende Mai; **in the
~** schließlich; **to come to an ~** zu
Ende gehen ▷ vt beenden ▷ vi
enden; **end up** vi enden

endanger [ɪn'deɪndʒə°] vt
gefährden; **~ed species** vom
Aussterben bedrohte Art

endeavour [ɪn'devə°] n Bemühung f ▷ vt sich bemühen
(to do sth etw zu tun)

ending ['endɪŋ] n (of book)
Ausgang m; (last part) Schluss m;
(of word) Endung f; **endless**
['endlɪs] adj endlos; (possibilities)
unendlich

endurance [ɪn'djʊərəns] n
Ausdauer f; **endure** [ɪn'djʊə°] vt
ertragen

enemy ['enɪmɪ] n Feind(in) m(f)
▷ adj feindlich

energetic [enə'dʒetɪk] adj
energiegeladen; (active) aktiv;
energy ['enədʒɪ] n Energie f

enforce [ɪn'fɔːs] vt durchsetzen;
(obedience) erzwingen

engage [ɪn'geɪdʒ] vt (employ)
einstellen; (singer, performer)
engagieren; **engaged** adj verlobt;
(toilet, telephone line) besetzt; **to
get ~** sich verloben (to mit);
engaged tone n (Brit Tel)
Belegtzeichen nt; **engagement** n
(to marry) Verlobung f; **~ ring**
Verlobungsring m; **engaging** adj
gewinnend

engine ['endʒɪn] n (Auto) Motor
m; (Rail) Lokomotive f; **~ failure**
(Auto) Motorschaden m; **~ trouble**
(Auto) Defekt m am Motor;
engineer [endʒɪ'nɪə°] n In-
genieur(in) m(f); (US Rail)
Lokomotivführer(in) m(f);

engineering [endʒɪ'nɪərɪŋ] n
Technik f; (mechanical ~)
Maschinenbau m; (subject)
Ingenieurwesen nt; **engine
immobilizer** n (Auto)
Wegfahrsperre f

England ['ɪŋglənd] n England
nt; **English** adj englisch; **he's ~** er
ist Engländer; **the ~ Channel** der
Ärmelkanal ▷ n (language)
Englisch nt; **in ~** auf Englisch; **to
translate into ~** ins Englische
übersetzen; (people) **the ~** pl die
Engländer; **Englishman** (pl **-men**)
n Engländer m; **Englishwoman**
(pl **-women**) n Engländerin f

engrave [ɪn'greɪv] vt ein-
gravieren; **engraving** n Stich
m

engrossed [ɪn'grəʊst] adj
vertieft (in sth in etw akk)

enigma [ɪ'nɪgmə] n Rätsel nt

enjoy [ɪn'dʒɔɪ] vt genießen; **I
~ reading** ich lese gern; **he ~s
teasing her** es macht ihm Spaß,
sie aufzuziehen; **did you ~ the
film?** hat dir der Film gefallen?;
enjoyable adj angenehm;
(entertaining) unterhaltsam;
enjoyment n Vergnügen nt;
(stronger) Freude f (of an +dat)

enlarge [ɪn'lɑːdʒ] vt vergrößern;
(expand) erweitern; **enlargement**
n Vergrößerung f

enormous, **enormously**
[ɪ'nɔːməs, -lɪ] adj, adv riesig,
ungeheuer

enough [ɪ'nʌf] adj genug; **that's
~** das reicht!; (stop it) Schluss
damit!; **I've had ~** das hat mir
gereicht; (to eat) ich bin satt ▷ adv
genug, genügend

enquire [ɪn'kwaɪə°] vi sich
erkundigen (about nach); **enquiry**
[ɪn'kwaɪərɪ] n (question) Anfrage
f; (for information) Erkundigung f
(about über +akk); (investigation)

Untersuchung f; **"Enquiries"** „Auskunft"

enrol [ɪn'rəʊl] vi sich einschreiben; (for course, school) sich anmelden; **enrolment** n Einschreibung f, Anmeldung f

en suite [ɒn'swiːt] adj, n: **room with ~** (**bathroom**) Zimmer nt mit eigenem Bad

ensure [ɪn'ʃʊə°] vt sicherstellen

enter ['entə°] vt eintreten in +akk, betreten; (drive into) einfahren in +akk; (country) einreisen in +akk; (in list) eintragen; (Inform) eingeben; (race, contest) teilnehmen an +dat ▷ vi (towards speaker) hereinkommen; (away from speaker) hineingehen

enterprise ['entəpraɪz] n (Comm) Unternehmen nt

entertain [entə'teɪn] vt (guest) bewirten; (amuse) unterhalten; **entertaining** adj unterhaltsam; **entertainment** n (amusement) Unterhaltung f

enthusiasm [ɪn'θjuːzɪæzəm] n Begeisterung f; **enthusiastic** [ɪnθjuːzɪ'æstɪk] adj begeistert (about von)

entice [ɪn'taɪs] vt locken; (lead astray) verleiten

entire, entirely [ɪn'taɪə°, -lɪ] adj, adv ganz

entitle [ɪn'taɪtl] vt (qualify) berechtigen (to zu); (name) betiteln

entrance ['entrəns] n Eingang m; (for vehicles) Einfahrt f; (entering) Eintritt m; (Theat) Auftritt m; **entrance exam** n Aufnahmeprüfung f; **entrance fee** n Eintrittsgeld nt

entrust [ɪn'trʌst] vt: **to ~ sb with sth** jdm etw anvertrauen

entry ['entrɪ] n (way in) Eingang m; (entering) Eintritt m; (in vehicle) Einfahrt f; (into country) Einreise f;

(admission) Zutritt m; (in diary, accounts) Eintrag m; **"no ~"** „Eintritt verboten"; (for vehicles) „Einfahrt verboten" **entry phone** n Türsprechanlage f

E-number n (food additive) E-Nummer f

envelope ['envələʊp] n (Brief)umschlag m

enviable ['envɪəbl] adj beneidenswert; **envious** ['envɪəs] adj neidisch

environment [ɪn'vaɪərənmənt] n Umgebung f; (ecology) Umwelt f; **environmental** [ɪnvaɪərən'məntəl] adj Umwelt-; **~ pollution** Umweltverschmutzung f; **environmentalist** n Umweltschützer(in) m(f)

envy ['envɪ] n Neid m (of auf +akk) ▷ vt beneiden (sb sth jdn um etw)

epic ['epɪk] n Epos nt; (film) Monumentalfilm m

epidemic [epɪ'demɪk] n Epidemie f

epilepsy [epɪ'lepsɪ] n Epilepsie f; **epileptic** [epɪ'leptɪk] adj epileptisch

episode ['epɪsəʊd] n Episode f; (TV) Folge f

epoch ['iːpɒk] n Zeitalter nt, Epoche f

equal ['iːkwl] adj gleich (to +dat) ▷ n Gleichgestellte(r) mf ▷ vt gleichen; (match) gleichkommen +dat; **two times two ~s four** zwei mal zwei ist gleich vier; **equality** [ɪ'kwɒlɪtɪ] n Gleichheit f; (equal rights) Gleichberechtigung f; **equalize** vi (Sport) ausgleichen; **equalizer** n (Sport) Ausgleichstreffer m; **equally** adv gleich; (on the other hand) andererseits; **equation** [ɪ'kweɪʒən] n (Math) Gleichung f

equator [ɪ'kweɪtə°] n Äquator m

equilibrium [iːkwɪˈlɪbrɪəm] *n*
Gleichgewicht *nt*

equip [ɪˈkwɪp] *vt* ausrüsten;
(*kitchen*) ausstatten; **equipment** *n*
Ausrüstung *f*; (*for kitchen*)
Ausstattung *f*; **electrical**
~ Elektrogeräte *pl*

equivalent [ɪˈkwɪvələnt] *adj*
gleichwertig (*to dat*);
(*corresponding*) entsprechend (*to
dat*) ▷ *n* Äquivalent *nt*; (*amount*)
gleiche Menge; (*in money*)
Gegenwert *m*

era [ˈɪərə] *n* Ära *f*, Zeitalter *nt*

erase [ɪˈreɪz] *vt* ausradieren;
(*tape, disk*) löschen; **eraser** *n*
Radiergummi *m*

erect [ɪˈrekt] *adj* aufrecht ▷ *vt*
(*building, monument*) errichten;
(*tent*) aufstellen; **erection** *n*
Errichtung *f*; (*Anat*) Erektion *f*

erode [ɪˈrəʊd] *vt* zerfressen;
(*land*) auswaschen; (*rights, power*)
aushöhlen; **erosion** [ɪˈrəʊʒən] *n*
Erosion *f*

erotic [ɪˈrɒtɪk] *adj* erotisch

err [ɜː°] *vi* sich irren

errand [ˈerənd] *n* Besorgung *f*

erratic [ɪˈrætɪk] *adj* (*behaviour*)
unberechenbar; (*bus link etc*)
unregelmäßig; (*performance*)
unbeständig

error [ˈerə°] *n* Fehler *m*; **in**
~ irrtümlicherweise; **error
message** *n* (*Inform*)
Fehlermeldung *f*

erupt [ɪˈrʌpt] *vi* ausbrechen

escalator [ˈeskəleɪtə°] *n* Rolltreppe *f*

escalope [ˈeskələp] *n* Schnitzel
nt

escape [ɪˈskeɪp] *n* Flucht *f*; (*from
prison etc*) Ausbruch *m*; **to have a
narrow** ~ gerade noch
davonkommen; **there's no** ~ (*fig*)
es gibt keinen Ausweg ▷ *vt*
(*pursuers*) entkommen +*dat*;

(*punishment etc*) entgehen +*dat* ▷ *vi*
(*from pursuers*) entkommen (*from
dat*); (*from prison etc*) ausbrechen
(*from dat*); (*leak: gas*) ausströmen;
(*water*) auslaufen

escort [ˈeskɔːt] *n* (*companion*)
Begleiter(in) *m(f)*; (*guard*) Eskorte *f*
▷ *vt* [ɪˈskɔːt] (*lady*) begleiten

especially [ɪˈspeʃəlɪ] *adv*
besonders

espionage [ˈespɪɒnɑːʒ] *n* Spio-
nage *f*

Esquire [ɪˈskwaɪə°] *n* (*Brit: in
address*): **J. Brown, Esq** Herrn J.
Brown

essay [ˈeseɪ] *n* Aufsatz *m*;
(*literary*) Essay *m*

essential [ɪˈsenʃəl] *adj* (*necessary*) unentbehrlich,
unverzichtbar; (*basic*) wesentlich
▷ *n* **the ~s** *pl* das Wesentliche;
essentially *adv* im Wesentlichen

establish [ɪˈstæblɪʃ] *vt* (*set up*)
gründen; (*introduce*) einführen;
(*relations*) aufnehmen; (*prove*)
nachweisen; **to ~ that ...**
feststellen, dass ...;
establishment *n* Institution *f*;
(*business*) Unternehmen *nt*

estate [ɪˈsteɪt] *n* Gut *nt*; (*of
deceased*) Nachlass *m*; (*housing* ~)
Siedlung *f*; (*country house*) Landsitz
m; **estate agent** *n* (*Brit*)
Grundstücksmakler(in) *m(f)*,
Immobilienmakler(in) *m(f)*; **estate
car** *n* (*Brit*) Kombiwagen *m*

estimate [ˈestɪmət] *n* Schätzung
f; (*Comm: of price*)
Kostenvoranschlag *m* ▷ [ˈestɪmeɪt]
vt schätzen

Estonia [eˈstəʊnɪə] *n* Estland *nt*;
Estonian [eˈstəʊnɪən] ▷ *adj*
estnisch; ▷ *n* (*person*) Este *m*;
Estin *f*; (*language*) Estnisch *nt*

estuary [ˈestjʊərɪ] *n* Mündung *f*

etching [ˈetʃɪŋ] *n* Radierung *f*

eternal, eternally [ɪˈtɜːnl, -nəlɪ]

adj, adv ewig; **eternity** *n* Ewigkeit *f*

ethical ['eθɪkəl] *adj* ethisch; **ethics** ['eθɪks] *npl* Ethik *f*

Ethiopia [i:θɪ'əʊpɪə] *n* Äthiopien *nt*

ethnic ['eθnɪk] *adj* ethnisch; (*clothes etc*) landesüblich; **~ minority** ethnische Minderheit

e-ticket ['i:tɪkɪt] *n* E-Ticket *nt*

EU *abbr* = **European Union** EU *f*

euphemism ['ju:fɪmɪzəm] *n* Euphemismus *m*

euro ['jʊərəʊ] (*pl* **-s**) *n* (*Fin*) Euro *m*; **Eurocheque** ['jʊərəʊtʃek] *n* Euroscheck *m*; **Europe** ['jʊərəp] *n* Europa *nt*; **European** [jʊərə'pi:ən] *adj* europäisch; **~ Parliament** Europäisches Parlament; **~ Union** Europäische Union ▷ *n* Europäer(in) *m(f)*; **Eurosceptic** ['jʊərəʊskeptɪk] *n* Euroskeptiker(in) *m(f)*; **Eurotunnel** *n* Eurotunnel *m*

evacuate [ɪ'vækjʊeɪt] *vt* (*place*) räumen; (*people*) evakuieren

evade [ɪ'veɪd] *vt* ausweichen +*dat*; (*pursuers*) sich entziehen +*dat*

evaluate [ɪ'væljʊeɪt] *vt* auswerten

evaporate [ɪ'væpəreɪt] *vi* verdampfen; (*fig*) verschwinden; **~d milk** Kondensmilch *f*

even ['i:vən] *adj* (*flat*) eben; (*regular*) gleichmäßig; (*equal*) gleich; (*number*) gerade; **the score is ~** es steht unentschieden ▷ *adv* sogar; **~ you** selbst (*o sogar*) du/Sie; **~ if** selbst wenn, wenn auch; **~ though** obwohl; **not ~** nicht einmal; **~ better** noch besser; **even out** *vi* (*prices*) sich einpendeln

evening ['i:vnɪŋ] *n* Abend *m*; **in the ~** abends, am Abend; **this ~** heute Abend; **evening class** *n* Abendkurs *m*; **evening dress** *n*

(*generally*) Abendkleidung *f*; (*woman's*) Abendkleid *nt*

evenly ['i:vənlɪ] *adv* gleichmäßig

event [ɪ'vent] *n* Ereignis *nt*; (*organized*) Veranstaltung *f*; (*Sport: discipline*) Disziplin *f*; **in the ~ of** im Falle +*gen*; **eventful** *adj* ereignisreich

eventual [ɪ'ventʃʊəl] *adj* (*final*) letztendlich; **eventually** [ɪ'ventʃʊəlɪ] *adv* (*at last*) am Ende; (*given time*) schließlich

ever ['evə*] *adv* (*at any time*) je(mals); **don't ~ do that again** tu das ja nie wieder; **he's the best ~** er ist der Beste, den es je gegeben hat; **have you ~ been to the States?** bist du schon einmal in den Staaten gewesen?; **for ~** (für) immer; **for ~ and ~** auf immer und ewig; **~ so ...** (*fam*) äußerst ...; **~ so drunk** ganz schön betrunken

every ['evrɪ] *adj* jeder/jede/ jedes; **~ day** jeden Tag; **~ other day** jeden zweiten Tag; **~ five days** alle fünf Tage; **I have ~ reason to believe that ...** ich habe allen Grund anzunehmen, dass ...; **everybody** *pron* jeder, alle *pl*; **everyday** *adj* (*commonplace*) alltäglich; (*clothes, language etc*) Alltags-; **everyone** *pron* jeder, alle *pl*; **everything** *pron* alles; **everywhere** *adv* überall; (*with direction*) überallhin

evidence ['evɪdəns] *n* Beweise *pl*; (*single piece*) Beweis *m*; (*testimony*) Aussage *f*; (*signs*) Spuren *pl*; **evident, evidently** *adj, adv* offensichtlich

evil ['i:vl] *adj* böse ▷ *n* Böse(s) *nt*; **an ~** ein Übel

evolution [i:və'lu:ʃən] *n* Entwicklung *f*; (*of life*) Evolution *f*; **evolve** [ɪ'vɒlv] *vi* sich entwickeln

ex- [eks] *pref* Ex-, ehemalig;

~boyfriend Exfreund *m*; **~wife** frühere Frau, Exfrau *f*; **ex** *n* (*fam*) Verflossene(r) *mf*, Ex *mf*

exact [ɪgˈzækt] *adj* genau; **exactly** *adv* genau; **not ~ fast** nicht gerade schnell

exaggerate [ɪgˈzædʒəreɪt] *vt, vi* übertreiben; **exaggerated** *adj* übertrieben; **exaggeration** *n* Übertreibung *f*

exam [ɪgˈzæm] *n* Prüfung *f*; **examination** [ɪgzæmɪˈneɪʃən] *n* (*Med etc*) Untersuchung *f*, Prüfung *f*; (*at university*) Examen *nt*; (*at customs etc*) Kontrolle *f*; **examine** [ɪgˈzæmɪn] *vt* untersuchen (*for* auf *+akk*); (*check*) kontrollieren, prüfen; **examiner** *n* Prüfer(in) *m(f)*

example [ɪgˈzɑːmpl] *n* Beispiel *nt* (*of* für *+akk*); **for ~** zum Beispiel

excavation [ekskəˈveɪʃən] *n* Ausgrabung *f*

exceed [ɪkˈsiːd] *vt* überschreiten, übertreffen; **exceedingly** *adv* äußerst

excel [ɪkˈsel] *vt* übertreffen; **he ~led himself** er hat sich selbst übertroffen ▷ *vi* sich auszeichnen (*in in +dat, at* bei); **excellent, excellently** [ˈeksələnt, -lɪ] *adj, adv* ausgezeichnet

except [ɪkˈsept] *prep*: **~** außer *+dat*; **~ for** abgesehen von ▷ *vt* ausnehmen; **exception** [ɪkˈsepʃən] *n* Ausnahme *f*; **exceptional, exceptionally** [ɪkˈsepʃənl, -nəlɪ] *adj, adv* außergewöhnlich

excess [ekˈses] *n* Übermaß *nt* (*of* an *+dat*); **excess baggage** *n* Übergepäck *nt*; **excesses** *npl* Exzesse *pl*; (*drink, sex*) Ausschweifungen *pl*; **excessive, excessively** *adj, adv* übermäßig; **excess weight** *n* Übergewicht *nt*

exchange [ɪksˈtʃeɪndʒ] *n* Austausch *m* (*for* gegen); (*of bought items*) Umtausch *m* (*for* gegen); (*Fin*) Wechsel *m*; (*Tel*) Vermittlung *f*, Zentrale *f* ▷ *vt* austauschen; (*goods*) tauschen; (*bought items*) umtauschen (*for* gegen); (*money, blows*) wechseln; **exchange rate** *n* Wechselkurs *m*

excite [ɪkˈsaɪt] *vt* erregen; **excited** *adj* aufgeregt; **to get ~** sich aufregen; **exciting** *adj* aufregend; (*book, film*) spannend

exclamation [ekskləˈmeɪʃən] *n* Ausruf *m*; **exclamation mark**, **exclamation point** (*US*) *n* Ausrufezeichen *nt*

exclude [ɪksˈkluːd] *vt* ausschließen; **exclusion** [ɪksˈkluːʒən] *n* Ausschluss *m*; **exclusive** [ɪksˈkluːsɪv] *adj* (*select*) exklusiv; (*sole*) ausschließlich; **exclusively** *adv* ausschließlich

excrement [ˈekskrɪmənt] *n* Kot *m*, Exkremente *pl*

excruciating [ɪksˈkruːʃɪeɪtɪŋ] *adj* fürchterlich, entsetzlich

excursion [ɪksˈkɜːʃən] *n* Ausflug *m*

excusable [ɪksˈkjuːzəbl] *adj* entschuldbar; **excuse** [ɪksˈkjuːz] *vt* entschuldigen; **~ me** Entschuldigung!; **to ~ sb for sth** jdm etw verzeihen; **to ~ sb from sth** jdn von etw befreien ▷ [ɪksˈkjuːs] *n* Entschuldigung *f*, Ausrede *f*

ex-directory [eksdaɪˈrektərɪ] *adj*: **to be ~** (*Brit Tel*) nicht im Telefonbuch stehen

execute [ˈeksɪkjuːt] *vt* (*carry out*) ausführen; (*kill*) hinrichten; **execution** *n* (*killing*) Hinrichtung *f*; (*carrying out*) Ausführung *f*; **executive** [ɪgˈzekjʊtɪv] *n* (*Comm*) leitender Angestellter, leitende Angestellte

exemplary [ɪgˈzemplərɪ] *adj* beispielhaft

exempt [ɪgˈzempt] *adj* befreit (*from* von) ▷ *vt* befreien

exercise [ˈeksəsaɪz] *n* (*in school, sports*) Übung *f*; (*movement*) Bewegung *f*; **to get more ~** mehr Sport treiben; **exercise bike** *n* Heimtrainer *m*; **exercise book** *n* Heft *nt*

exert [ɪgˈzɜːt] *vt* (*influence*) ausüben

exhaust [ɪgˈzɔːst] *n* (*fumes*) Abgase *pl*; (*Auto*) **~ (pipe)** Auspuff *m*; **exhausted** *adj* erschöpft; **exhausting** *adj* anstrengend

exhibit [ɪgˈzɪbɪt] *n* (*in exhibition*) Ausstellungsstück *nt*; **exhibition** [eksɪˈbɪʃən] *n* Ausstellung *f*; **exhibitionist** [eksɪˈbɪʃənɪst] *n* Selbstdarsteller(in) *m(f)*; **exhibitor** *n* Aussteller(in) *m(f)*

exhilarating [ɪgˈzɪləreɪtɪŋ] *adj* belebend, erregend

exile [ˈeksaɪl] *n* Exil *nt*; (*person*) Verbannte(r) *mf* ▷ *vt* verbannen

exist [ɪgˈzɪst] *vi* existieren (*live*) leben (von von); **existence** *n* Existenz *f*; **to come into ~** entstehen; **existing** *adj* bestehend

exit [ˈeksɪt] *n* Ausgang *m*; (*for vehicles*) Ausfahrt *f*; **exit poll** *n* Umfrage direkt nach dem Wahlgang

exorbitant [ɪgˈzɔːbɪtənt] *adj* astronomisch

exotic [ɪgˈzɒtɪk] *adj* exotisch

expand [ɪksˈpænd] *vt* ausdehnen, erweitern ▷ *vi* sich ausdehnen; **expansion** [ɪksˈpænʃən] *n* Expansion *f*, Erweiterung *f*

expect [ɪksˈpekt] *vt* erwarten; (*suppose*) annehmen; **he ~s me to do it** er erwartet, dass ich es mache; **I ~ it'll rain** es wird wohl regnen; **I ~ so** ich denke schon ▷ *vi*: **she's ~ing** sie bekommt ein Kind

expedition [ekspɪˈdɪʃən] *n* Expedition *f*

expenditure [ɪkˈspendɪtʃəˈ] *n* Ausgaben *pl*

expense [ɪkˈspens] *n* Kosten *pl*; (*single cost*) Ausgabe *f*; (**business**) **~s** *pl* Spesen *pl*; **at sb's ~** auf jds Kosten; **expensive** [ɪkˈspensɪv] *adj* teuer

experience [ɪkˈspɪərɪəns] *n* Erfahrung *f*; (*particular incident*) Erlebnis *nt*; **by/from ~** aus Erfahrung ▷ *vt* erfahren, erleben; (*hardship*) durchmachen; **experienced** *adj* erfahren

experiment [ɪkˈsperɪmənt] *n* Versuch *m*, Experiment *nt* ▷ *vi* experimentieren

expert [ˈekspɜːt] *n* Experte *m*, Expertin *f*; (*professional*) Fachmann *m*, Fachfrau *f*; (*Jur*) Sachverständige(r) *mf* ▷ *adj* fachmännisch, Fach-; **expertise** [ekspəˈtiːz] *n* Sachkenntnis *f*

expire [ɪkˈspaɪəˈ] *vi* (*end*) ablaufen; **expiry date** [ɪkˈspaɪərɪdeɪt] *n* Verfallsdatum *nt*

explain [ɪkˈspleɪn] *vt* erklären (*sth to sb* jdm etw); **explanation** [ekspləˈneɪʃən] *n* Erklärung *f*

explicit [ɪkˈsplɪsɪt] *adj* ausdrücklich, eindeutig

explode [ɪkˈspləʊd] *vi* explodieren

exploit [ɪkˈsplɔɪt] *vt* ausbeuten

explore [ɪkˈsplɔːˈ] *vt* erforschen

explosion [ɪkˈspləʊʒən] *n* Explosion *f*; **explosive** [ɪkˈspləʊsɪv] *adj* explosiv ▷ *n* Sprengstoff *m*

export [ekˈspɔːt] *vt, vi* exportieren ▷ [ˈekspɔːt] *n* Export *m* ▷ *adj* (*trade*) Export-

expose [ɪkˈspəʊz] *vt* (*to danger*

etc) aussetzen (*to dat*); (*uncover*)
freilegen; (*imposter*) entlarven;
exposed *adj* (*position*)
ungeschützt; **exposure**
[ɪk'spəʊʒə°] *n* (*Med*)
Unterkühlung *f*; (*Foto: time*)
Belichtung(szeit) *f*; **24 ~s** 24
Aufnahmen
express [ɪk'spres] *adj* (*speedy*)
Express-, Schnell-; **~ delivery**
Eilzustellung *f* ▷ *n* (*Rail*)
Schnellzug *m* ▷ *vt* ausdrücken
▷ *vr*: **to ~ oneself** sich
ausdrücken; **expression**
[ɪk'spreʃən] *n* (*phrase*) Ausdruck
m; (*look*) Gesichtsausdruck *m*;
expressive *adj* ausdrucksvoll;
expressway *n* (*US*) Schnellstraße
f
extend [ɪk'stend] *vt* (*arms*)
ausstrecken; (*lengthen*) verlängern;
(*building*) vergrößern, ausbauen;
(*business, limits*) erweitern;
extension [ɪk'stenʃən] *n*
(*lengthening*) Verlängerung *f*; (*of
building*) Anbau *m*; (*Tel*) Anschluss
m; (*of business, limits*) Erweiterung
f; **extensive** [ɪk'stensɪv] *adj*
(*knowledge*) umfangreich; (*use*)
häufig; **extent** [ɪk'stent] *n*
(*length*) Länge *f*; (*size*) Ausdehnung
f; (*scope*) Umfang *m*, Ausmaß *nt*; **to
a certain/large ~** in
gewissem/hohem Maße
exterior [ek'stɪərɪə°] *n* Äußere(s)
nt
external [ek'stɜːnl] *adj* äußere(r, s), Außen-; **externally** *adv*
äußerlich
extinct [ɪk'stɪŋkt] *adj* (*species*)
ausgestorben
extinguish [ɪk'stɪŋgwɪʃ] *vt*
löschen; **extinguisher** *n*
Löschgerät *nt*
extra ['ekstrə] *adj* zusätzlich;
~ charge Zuschlag *m*; **~ time**
(*Sport*) Verlängerung *f* ▷ *adv*

besonders; **~ large** (*clothing*)
übergroß ▷ *npl*: **~s** zusätzliche
Kosten *pl*; (*food*) Beilagen *pl*;
(*accessories*) Zubehör *nt*; (*for car etc*)
Extras *pl*
extract [ɪk'strækt] *vt* herausziehen (*from aus*); (*tooth*)
ziehen ▷ ['ekstrækt] *n* (*from book
etc*) Auszug *m*
extraordinary [ɪk'strɔːdnrɪ] *adj*
außerordentlich; (*unusual*)
ungewöhnlich; (*amazing*)
erstaunlich
extreme [ɪk'striːm] *adj* äußer-
ste(r, s); (*drastic*) extrem ▷ *n*
Extrem *nt*; **extremely** *adv*
äußerst, höchst; **extreme sports**
npl Extremsportarten *pl*;
extremist [ɪk'striːmɪst] *adj*
extremistisch ▷ *n* Extremist *m*
extricate ['ekstrɪkeɪt] *vt* befreien
(*from aus*)
extrovert ['ekstrəʊvɜːt] *adj*
extrovertiert
exuberance [ɪg'zuːbərəns] *n*
Überschwang *m*; **exuberant** *adj*
überschwänglich
exultation [egzʌl'teɪʃən] *n* Jubel
m
eye [aɪ] *n* Auge *nt*; **to keep an
~ on sb/sth** auf jdn/etw
aufpassen ▷ *vt* mustern;
eyebrow *n* Augenbraue *f*;
eyelash *n* Wimper *f*; **eyelid** *n*
Augenlid *nt*; **eyeliner** *n* Eyeliner
m; **eyeopener** *n*: **that was an
~** das hat mir die Augen geöffnet;
eyeshadow *n* Lidschatten *m*;
eyesight *n* Sehkraft *f*; **eyesore** *n*
Schandfleck *m*; **eye witness** *n*
Augenzeuge *m*, Augenzeugin *f*

f

fabric ['fæbrɪk] *n* Stoff *m*
fabulous ['fæbjʊləs] *adj* sagenhaft
façade [fə'sɑːd] *n* (*a. fig*) Fassade *f*
face [feɪs] *n* Gesicht *nt*; (*of clock*) Zifferblatt *nt*; (*of mountain*) Wand *f*; **in the ~ of** trotz +*gen*; **to be ~ to ~** (*people*) einander gegenüberstehen ▷ *vt, vi* (*person*) gegenüberstehen +*dat*; (*at table*) gegenübersitzen +*dat*; **to ~ north** (*room*) nach Norden gehen; **to ~ (up to) the facts** den Tatsachen ins Auge sehen; **to be ~d with sth** mit etw konfrontiert sein; **face lift** *n* Gesichtsstraffung *f*; (*fig*) Verschönerung *f*; **face powder** *n* Gesichtspuder *m*
facet ['fæsɪt] *n* (*fig*) Aspekt *m*
face value *n* Nennwert *m*
facial ['feɪʃəl] *adj* Gesichts- ▷ *n* (*fam*) (kosmetische) Gesichtsbehandlung

facilitate [fə'sɪlɪteɪt] *vt* erleichtern
facility [fə'sɪlɪtɪ] *n* (*building etc to be used*) Einrichtung *f*, Möglichkeit *f*; (*installation*) Anlage *f*; (*skill*) Gewandtheit *f*
fact [fækt] *n* Tatsache *f*; **as a matter of ~, in ~** eigentlich, tatsächlich
factor ['fæktə*] *n* Faktor *m*
factory ['fæktərɪ] *n* Fabrik *f*; **factory outlet** *n* Fabrikverkauf *m*
factual ['fæktjʊəl] *adj* sachlich
faculty ['fækəltɪ] *n* Fähigkeit *f*; (*at university*) Fakultät *f*; (*US: teaching staff*) Lehrkörper *m*
fade [feɪd] *vi* (*a. fig*) verblassen; **faded** *adj* verblasst, verblichen
faff about ['fæfəbaʊt] *vi* (*Brit fam*) herumwursteln
fag [fæg] *n* (*Brit fam: cigarette*) Kippe *f*; (*US fam pej*) Schwule(r) *m*
Fahrenheit ['færənhaɪt] *n* Fahrenheit
fail [feɪl] *vt* (*exam*) nicht bestehen ▷ *vi* versagen; (*plan, marriage*) scheitern; (*student*) durchfallen; (*eyesight*) nachlassen; **words ~ me** ich bin sprachlos; **failing** *n* Schwäche *f*; **failure** ['feɪljə*] *n* (*person*) Versager(in) *m(f)*; (*act, a. Tech*) Versagen *nt*; (*of engine etc*) Ausfall *m*; (*of plan, marriage*) Scheitern *nt*
faint [feɪnt] *adj* schwach; (*sound*) leise; (*fam*) **I haven't the ~est (idea)** ich habe keinen blassen Schimmer ▷ *vi* ohnmächtig werden (*with* vor +*dat*); **faintness** *n* (*Med*) Schwächegefühl *nt*
fair [feə*] *adj* (*hair*) (dunkel)blond; (*skin*) hell; (*just*) gerecht, fair; (*reasonable*) ganz ordentlich; (*in school*) befriedigend; (*weather*) schön; (*wind*) günstig; **a ~ number/amount of** ziemlich viele/viel ▷ *adv*: **to play ~** fair

spielen; (fig) fair sein; **~ enough** in
Ordnung! ▷ n (fun~) Jahrmarkt m;
(Comm) Messe f; **fair-haired** adj
(dunkel)blond; **fairly** adv
(honestly) fair; (rather) ziemlich

fairy ['fɛərɪ] n Fee f; **fairy tale** n
Märchen nt

faith [feɪθ] n (trust) Vertrauen nt
(in sb zu jdm); (Rel) Glaube m;
faithful, **faithfully** adj, adv treu;
Yours ~ly Hochachtungsvoll

fake [feɪk] n (thing) Fälschung f
▷ adj vorgetäuscht ▷ vt fälschen

falcon ['fɔːlkən] n Falke m

fall [fɔːl] (**fell, fallen**) vi fallen;
(from a height, badly) stürzen; **to
~ ill** krank werden; **to ~ asleep**
einschlafen; **to ~ in love** sich
verlieben ▷ n Fall m; (accident, fig:
of regime) Sturz m; (decrease) Sinken
nt (in +gen); (US: autumn) Herbst m;
fall apart vi auseinanderfallen;
fall behind vi zurückbleiben;
(with work, rent) in Rückstand
geraten; **fall down** vi (person)
hinfallen; **fall off** vi
herunterfallen; (decrease)
zurückgehen; **fall out** vi
herausfallen; (quarrel) sich
streiten; **fall over** vi hinfallen;
fall through vi (plan etc) ins
Wasser fallen

fallen ['fɔːlən] pp of **fall**

fallout ['fɔːlaʊt] n radioaktiver
Niederschlag, Fall-out m

false [fɔːls] adj falsch; (artificial)
künstlich; **false alarm** n blinder
Alarm; **false start** n (Sport)
Fehlstart m; **false teeth** npl
(künstliches) Gebiss

fame [feɪm] n Ruhm m

familiar [fə'mɪlɪə*] adj vertraut,
bekannt; **to be ~ with** vertraut
sein mit, gut kennen; **familiarity**
[fəmɪlɪ'ærɪtɪ] n Vertrautheit f

family ['fæmɪlɪ] n Familie f;
(including relations) Verwandtschaft

f; **family man** n Familienvater m;
family name n Familienname m,
Nachname m; **family practitioner**
n (US) Allgemeinarzt m,
Allgemeinärztin f

famine ['fæmɪn] n Hungersnot f;
famished ['fæmɪʃt] adj
ausgehungert

famous ['feɪməs] adj berühmt

fan [fæn] n (hand-held) Fächer m;
(Elec) Ventilator m; (admirer) Fan m

fanatic [fə'nætɪk] n Fanatiker(in)
m(f)

fancy ['fænsɪ] adj (elaborate)
kunstvoll; (unusual) ausgefallen
▷ vt (like) gernhaben; **he fancies
her** er steht auf sie; **~ that!** stell dir
vor!, so was!; **fancy dress** n
Kostüm nt, Verkleidung f

fan heater ['fænhiːtə*] n
Heizlüfter m; **fanlight** n
Oberlicht nt

fan mail n Fanpost f

fantasise ['fæntəsaɪz] vi träumen (about von); **fantastic**
[fæn'tæstɪk] adj (a. fam)
fantastisch; **that's ~** (fam) das ist
ja toll!; **fantasy** ['fæntəzɪ] n
Fantasie f

far [fɑː*] (**further** o **farther**,
furthest o **farthest**) adj weit; **the
~ end of the room** das andere
Ende des Zimmers; **the Far East**
der Ferne Osten ▷ adv weit;
~ better viel besser; **by ~ the best**
bei weitem der/die/das Beste; **as
~ as ...** bis zum o zur ...; (with place
name) bis nach ...; **as ~ as I'm
concerned** was mich betrifft, von
mir aus; **so ~** soweit, bisher;
faraway adj weit entfernt; (look)
verträumt

fare [fɛə*] n Fahrpreis m; (money)
Fahrgeld nt

farm [fɑːm] n Bauernhof m, Farm
f; **farmer** n Bauer m, Bäuerin f,
Landwirt(in) m(f); **farmhouse** n

Bauernhaus nt; **farming** n
Landwirtschaft f; **farmland** n
Ackerland nt; **farmyard** n Hof m
far-reaching ['fɑːriːtʃɪŋ] adj
weit reichend; **far-sighted** adj
weitsichtig; (fig) weitblickend
fart [fɑːt] n (fam) Furz m; **old
~** (fam: person) alter Sack ▷ vi (fam)
furzen
farther ['fɑːðəʳ] adj, adv
comparative of **far**; see **further**
farthest ['fɑːðɪst] adj, adv
superlative of **far**; see **furthest**
fascinating ['fæsɪneɪtɪŋ] adj
faszinierend; **fascination** n
Faszination f
fascism ['fæʃɪzəm] n Faschismus
m; **fascist** ['fæʃɪst] adj
faschistisch ▷ Faschist(in) m(f)
fashion ['fæʃən] n (clothes) Mode
f; (manner) Art (und Weise) f; **to be
in ~** (in) Mode sein; **out of
~** unmodisch; **fashionable,
fashionably** adj, adv (clothes,
person) modisch; (author, pub etc) in
Mode
fast [fɑːst] adj schnell; **to be
~** (clock) vorgehen ▷ adv schnell;
(firmly) fest; **to be ~ asleep** fest
schlafen ▷ n Fasten nt ▷ vi
fasten; **fastback** n (Auto)
Fließheck nt
fasten ['fɑːsn] vt (attach)
befestigen (to an +dat); (do up)
zumachen; **~ your seatbelts** bitte
anschnallen; **fastener, fastening**
n Verschluss m
fast food n Fast Food nt; **fast
forward** n (for tape)
Schnellvorlauf m; **fast lane** n
Überholspur f
fat [fæt] adj dick; (meat) fett ▷ n
Fett nt
fatal ['feɪtl] adj tödlich
fate [feɪt] n Schicksal nt
fat-free adj (food) fettfrei
father ['fɑːðəʳ] n Vater m; (priest)

Pfarrer m ▷ vt (child) zeugen;
Father Christmas n der
Weihnachtsmann; **father-in-law**
(pl **fathers-in-law**) n
Schwiegervater m
fatigue [fəˈtiːg] n Ermüdung
f
fattening ['fætnɪŋ] adj: **to be
~** dick machen; **fatty** ['fætɪ] adj
(food) fettig
faucet ['fɔːsɪt] n (US)
Wasserhahn m
fault [fɔːlt] n Fehler m; (Tech)
Defekt m; (Elec) Störung f; (blame)
Schuld f; **it's your ~** du bist daran
schuld; **faulty** adj fehlerhaft;
(Tech) defekt
favor (US), **favour** ['feɪvəʳ] n
(approval) Gunst f; (kindness)
Gefallen m; **in ~ of** für; **I'm in ~ (of
going)** ich bin dafür(, dass wir
gehen); **to do sb a ~** jdm einen
Gefallen tun ▷ vt (prefer)
vorziehen; **favourable** adj
günstig (to, for für); **favourite**
['feɪvərɪt] n Liebling m,
Favorit(in) m(f) ▷ adj Lieblings-
fax [fæks] vt faxen ▷ n Fax nt;
fax number n Faxnummer f
faze [feɪz] vt (fam) aus der
Fassung bringen
FBI abbr = **Federal Bureau of
Investigation** FBI nt
fear [fɪəʳ] n Angst f (of vor +dat)
▷ vt befürchten; **fearful** adj
(timid) ängstlich, furchtsam;
(terrible) fürchterlich; **fearless** adj
furchtlos
feasible ['fiːzəbl] adj machbar
feast [fiːst] n Festessen nt
feather ['feðəʳ] n Feder f
feature ['fiːtʃəʳ] n (facial)
(Gesichts)zug m; (characteristic)
Merkmal nt; (of car etc)
Ausstattungsmerkmal nt; (in the
press) (Cine) Feature nt ▷ vt
bringen, (als Besonderheit)

zeigen; **feature film** n Spielfilm m

February ['febrʊərɪ] n Februar m; see also **September**

fed [fed] pt, pp of **feed**

federal ['fedərəl] adj Bundes-; **the Federal Republic of Germany** die Bundesrepublik Deutschland

fed-up [fed'ʌp] adj: **to be ~ with sth** etw satthaben; **I'm ~** ich habe die Nase voll

fee [fiː] n Gebühr f; (of doctor, lawyer) Honorar nt

feeble ['fiːbl] adj schwach

feed [fiːd] (**fed, fed**) vt (baby, animal) füttern; (support) ernähren ▷ n (for baby) Mahlzeit f; (for animals) Futter nt; (Inform: paper ~) Zufuhr f; **feed in** vt (information) eingeben; **feedback** n (information) Feed-back nt

feel [fiːl] (**felt, felt**) vt (sense) fühlen; (pain) empfinden; (touch) anfassen; (think) meinen ▷ vi (person) sich fühlen; **I ~ cold** mir ist kalt; **do you ~ like a walk?** hast du Lust, spazieren zu gehen?; **feeling** n Gefühl nt

feet [fiːt] pl of **foot**

fell [fel] pt of **fall** ▷ vt (tree) fällen

fellow ['feləʊ] n Kerl m, Typ m; **~ citizen** Mitbürger(in) m(f); **~ countryman** Landsmann m; **~ worker** Mitarbeiter(in) m(f)

felt [felt] pt, pp of **feel** ▷ n Filz m; **felt tip**, **felt-tip pen** n Filzstift m

female ['fiːmeɪl] n (of animals) Weibchen nt ▷ adj weiblich; **~ doctor** Ärztin f; **feminine** ['femɪnɪn] adj weiblich; **feminist** ['femɪnɪst] n Feminist(in) m(f) ▷ adj feministisch

fence [fens] n Zaun m

fencing n (Sport) Fechten nt

fender ['fendə°] n (US Auto) Kotflügel m

fennel ['fenl] n Fenchel m

fern [fɜːn] n Farn m

ferocious [fə'rəʊʃəs] adj wild

ferry ['ferɪ] n Fähre f ▷ vt übersetzen

fertile ['fɜːtaɪl] adj fruchtbar; **fertility** [fə'tɪlɪtɪ] n Fruchtbarkeit f; **fertilize** ['fɜːtɪlaɪz] vt (Bio) befruchten; (Agr: land) düngen; **fertilizer** n Dünger m

festival ['festɪvəl] n (Rel) Fest nt; (Art, Mus) Festspiele pl; (pop music) Festival nt; **festive** ['festɪv] adj festlich; **festivities** [fe'stɪvɪtɪz] n Feierlichkeiten pl

fetch [fetʃ] vt holen; (collect) abholen; (in sale, money) einbringen; **fetching** adj reizend

fetish ['fetɪʃ] n Fetisch m

fetus ['fiːtəs] n (US) Fötus m

fever ['fiːvə°] n Fieber nt; **feverish** adj (Med) fiebrig; (fig) fieberhaft

few [fjuː] adj, pron pl wenige pl; **a ~ pl** ein paar; **fewer** adj weniger; **fewest** adj wenigste(r, s)

fiancé [fɪ'ɒnseɪ] n Verlobte(r) m; **fiancée** n Verlobte f

fiasco [fɪ'æskəʊ] (pl **-s** o US **-es**) n Fiasko nt

fiber (US), **fibre** ['faɪbə°] n Faser f; (material) Faserstoff m

fickle ['fɪkl] adj unbeständig

fiction ['fɪkʃən] n (novels) Prosaliteratur f; **fictional**, **fictitious** [fɪk'tɪʃəs] adj erfunden

fiddle ['fɪdl] n Geige f; (trick) Betrug m ▷ vt (accounts, results) frisieren; **fiddle with** vt herumfummeln an +dat; **fiddly** adj knifflig

fidelity [fɪ'delɪtɪ] n Treue f

fidget ['fɪdʒɪt] vi zappeln; **fidgety** adj zappelig

field [fiːld] n Feld nt; (grass-covered) Wiese f; (fig: of work) (Arbeits)gebiet nt

fierce [fɪəs] *adj* heftig; (*animal, appearance*) wild; (*criticism, competition*) scharf

fifteen [fɪfˈtiːn] *num* fünfzehn ▷ *n* Fünfzehn *f*; *see also* **eight**; **fifteenth** *adj* fünfzehnte(r, s); *see also* **eighth**; **fifth** [fɪfθ] *adj* fünfte(r, s) ▷ *n* (*fraction*) Fünftel *nt*; *see also* **eighth**; **fifty** [ˈfɪftɪ] *num* fünfzig ▷ *n* Fünfzig *f*; *see also* **eight**; **fiftieth** *adj* fünfzigste(r, s); *see also* **eighth**

fig [fɪg] *n* Feige *f*

fight [faɪt] (**fought, fought**) *vi* kämpfen (*with, against* gegen, *for, over* um) ▷ *vt* (*person*) kämpfen mit; (*fig: disease, fire etc*) bekämpfen ▷ *n* Kampf *m*; (*brawl*) Schlägerei *f*; (*argument*) Streit *m*; **fight back** *vi* zurückschlagen; **fight off** *vt* abwehren; **fighter** *n* Kämpfer(in) *m(f)*

figurative [ˈfɪgərətɪv] *adj* übertragen

figure [ˈfɪgə*] *n* (*person*) Gestalt *f*; (*of person*) Figur *f*; (*number*) Zahl *f*, Ziffer *f*; (*amount*) Betrag *m*; **a four-figure sum** eine vierstellige Summe ▷ *vt* (*US: think*) glauben ▷ *vi* (*appear*) erscheinen; **figure out** *vt* (*work out*) herausbekommen; **I can't figure him out** ich werde aus ihm nicht schlau; **figure skating** *n* Eiskunstlauf *m*

file [faɪl] *n* (*tool*) Feile *f*; (*dossier*) Akte *f*; (*Inform*) Datei *f*; (*folder*) Aktenordner *m*; **on** ~ in den Akten ▷ *vt* (*metal, nails*) feilen; (*papers*) ablegen (*under* unter) ▷ *vi*: **to** ~ **in/out** hintereinander hereinkommen/hinausgehen; **filing cabinet** *n* Aktenschrank *m*

fill [fɪl] *vt* füllen; (*tooth*) plombieren; (*post*) besetzen; **fill in** *vt* (*hole*) auffüllen; (*form*) ausfüllen; (*tell*) informieren (*on* über); **fill out**

vt (*form*) ausfüllen; **fill up** *vi* (*Auto*) volltanken

fillet [ˈfɪlɪt] *n* Filet *nt*

filling [ˈfɪlɪŋ] *n* (*Gastr*) Füllung *f*; (*for tooth*) Plombe *f*; **filling station** *n* Tankstelle *f*

film [fɪlm] *n* Film *m* ▷ *vt* (*scene*) filmen; **film star** *n* Filmstar *m*; **film studio** *n* Filmstudio *nt*

filter [ˈfɪltə*] *n* Filter *m*; (*traffic lane*) Abbiegespur *f* ▷ *vt* filtern

filth [fɪlθ] *n* Dreck *m*; **filthy** *adj* dreckig

fin [fɪn] *n* Flosse *f*

final [ˈfaɪnl] *adj* letzte(r, s); (*stage, round*) End-; (*decision, version*) endgültig; ~ **score** Schlussstand *m* ▷ *n* (*Sport*) Endspiel *nt*; (*competition*) Finale *nt*; ~**s** *pl* Abschlussexamen *nt*; **finalize** *vt* die endgültige Form geben +*dat*; **finally** *adv* (*lastly*) zuletzt; (*eventually*) schließlich, endlich

finance [faɪˈnæns] *n* Finanzwesen *nt*; ~**s** *pl* Finanzen *pl* ▷ *vt* finanzieren; **financial** [faɪˈnænʃəl] *adj* finanziell; (*adviser, crisis, policy etc*) Finanz-

find [faɪnd] (**found, found**) *vt* finden; **he was found dead** er wurde tot aufgefunden; **I ~ myself in difficulties** ich befinde mich in Schwierigkeiten; **she ~s it difficult/easy** es fällt ihr schwer/leicht; **find out** *vt* herausfinden; **findings** *npl* (*Jur*) Ermittlungsergebnis *nt*; (*of report, Med*) Befund *m*

fine [faɪn] *adj* (*thin*) dünn, fein; (*good*) gut; (*splendid*) herrlich; (*clothes*) elegant; (*weather*) schön; **I'm ~** es geht mir gut; **that's ~** das ist OK ▷ *adv* (*well*) gut ▷ *n* (*Jur*) Geldstrafe *f* ▷ *vt* (*Jur*) mit einer Geldstrafe belegen; **fine arts** *npl*: **the ~** die schönen Künste *pl*;

finely adv (cut) dünn; (ground) fein

finger ['fɪŋgə°] n Finger m ▷ vt herumfingern an +dat; **fingernail** n Fingernagel m; **fingerprint** n Fingerabdruck m; **fingertip** n Fingerspitze f

finicky ['fɪnɪkɪ] adj (person) pingelig; (work) knifflig

finish ['fɪnɪʃ] n Ende nt; (Sport) Finish nt; (line) Ziel nt; (of product) Verarbeitung f ▷ vt beenden; (book etc) zu Ende lesen; (food) aufessen; (drink) austrinken ▷ vi zu Ende gehen; (song, story) enden; (person) fertig sein; (stop) aufhören; **have you ~ed?** bist du fertig?; **to ~ first/second** (Sport) als erster/zweiter durchs Ziel gehen; **finishing line** n Ziellinie f

Finland ['fɪnlənd] n Finnland nt; **Finn** n Finne m, Finnin f; **Finnish** adj finnisch ▷ n (language) Finnisch nt

fir [fɜ:°] n Tanne f

fire [faɪə°] n Feuer nt; (house etc) Brand m; **to set ~ to sth** in Brand stecken; **to be on ~** brennen ▷ vt (bullets, rockets) abfeuern; (fam: dismiss) feuern ▷ vi (Auto: engine) zünden; **to ~ at sb** auf jdn schießen; **fire alarm** n Feuermelder m; **fire brigade** n Feuerwehr f; **fire engine** n Feuerwehrauto nt; **fire escape** n Feuerleiter f; **fire extinguisher** n Feuerlöscher m; **firefighter** n Feuerwehrmann m, Feuerwehrfrau f; **fireman** n Feuerwehrmann m; **fireplace** n (offener) Kamin; **fireproof** adj feuerfest; **fire station** n Feuerwache f; **firewood** n Brennholz nt; **fireworks** npl Feuerwerk nt

firm [fɜ:m] adj fest; (person) **to be ~** entschlossen auftreten ▷ n Firma f

first [fɜ:st] adj erste(r, s) ▷ adv (at first) zuerst; (firstly) erstens; (arrive, finish) als erste(r); (happen) zum ersten Mal; **~ of all** zuallererst ▷ n (person) Erste(r) mf; (Auto: gear) erster Gang; **at ~** zuerst, anfangs; **first aid** n erste Hilfe; **first-class** adj erstklassig; (compartment, ticket) erster Klasse; **~ mail** (Brit) bevorzugt beförderte Post ▷ adv (travel) erster Klasse; **first floor** n (Brit) erster Stock; (US) Erdgeschoss nt; **first lady** n (US) Frau f des Präsidenten; **firstly** adv erstens; **first name** n Vorname m; **first night** n (Theat) Premiere f; **first-rate** adj erstklassig

fir tree n Tannenbaum m

fish [fɪʃ] n Fisch m; **~ and chips** (Brit) frittierter Fisch mit Pommes frites ▷ vi fischen; (with rod) angeln; **to go ~ing** fischen/angeln gehen; **fishbone** n Gräte f; **fishcake** n Fischfrikadelle f; **fish farm** n Fischzucht f; **fish finger** n (Brit) Fischstäbchen nt; **fishing** ['fɪʃɪŋ] n Fischen nt; (with rod) Angeln nt; (as industry) Fischerei f; **fishing boat** n Fischerboot nt; **fishing line** n Angelschnur f; **fishing rod** n Angelrute f; **fishing village** n Fischerdorf nt; **fishmonger** ['fɪʃmʌŋgə°] n Fischhändler(in) m(f); **fish stick** n (US) Fischstäbchen nt; **fish tank** n Aquarium nt

fishy ['fɪʃɪ] adj (fam: suspicious) faul

fist [fɪst] n Faust f

fit [fɪt] adj (Med) gesund; (Sport) in Form, fit; (suitable) geeignet; **to keep ~** sich in Form halten ▷ vt passen +dat; (attach) anbringen (to an +dat); (install) einbauen (in in +akk) ▷ vi passen; (in space, gap) hineinpassen ▷ n (of clothes) Sitz m; (Med) Anfall m; **it's a good ~** es passt gut; **fit in** vt (accommodate) unterbringen; (find time for) einschieben ▷ vi (in space) hineinpassen; (plans, ideas) passen; **he doesn't ~** (here) er passt nicht hierher; **to ~ with sb's plans** sich mit jds Plänen vereinbaren lassen; **fitness** n (Med) Gesundheit f; (Sport) Fitness f; **fitness trainer** n (Sport) Fitnesstrainer(in) m(f); **fitted carpet** n Teppichboden m; **fitted kitchen** n Einbauküche f; **fitting** adj passend ▷ n (of dress) Anprobe f; **~s** pl Ausstattung f

five [faɪv] num fünf ▷ n Fünf f; see also **eight**; **fiver** n (Brit fam) Fünfpfundschein m

fix [fɪks] vt befestigen (to an +dat); (settle) festsetzen; (place, time) ausmachen; (repair) reparieren; **fixer** n (drug addict) Fixer(in) m(f); **fixture** ['fɪkstʃə*] n (Sport) Veranstaltung f; (match) Spiel nt; (in building) Installationsteil nt; **~s** (**and fittings**) pl Ausstattung f

fizzy ['fɪzɪ] adj sprudelnd; **~ drink** Limo f

flabbergasted ['flæbəgɑ:stɪd] adj (fam) platt

flabby ['flæbɪ] adj (fat) wabbelig

flag [flæg] n Fahne f; **flagstone** n Steinplatte f

flake [fleɪk] n Flocke f ▷ vi: **to ~** (**off**) abblättern

flamboyant [flæm'bɔɪənt] adj extravagant

flame [fleɪm] n Flamme f; (person) **an old ~** eine alte Liebe

flan [flæn] n (fruit ~) Obstkuchen m

flannel ['flænl] n Flanell m; (Brit: face ~) Waschlappen m; (fam: waffle) Geschwafel nt ▷ vi herumlabern

flap [flæp] n Klappe f; (fam) **to be in a ~** rotieren ▷ vt (wings) schlagen mit ▷ vi flattern

flared [flɛəd] adj (trousers) mit Schlag; **flares** npl Schlaghose f

flash [flæʃ] n Blitz m; (news ~) Kurzmeldung f; (Foto) Blitzlicht nt; **in a ~** im Nu ▷ vt: **to ~ one's** (**head**)**lights** die Lichthupe betätigen ▷ vi aufblinken; (brightly) aufblitzen; **flashback** n Rückblende f, Flashback m; **flashlight** ['flæʃlaɪt] n (Photo) Blitzlicht nt; (US: torch) Taschenlampe f; **flashy** adj grell, schrill; (pej) protzig

flat [flæt] adj flach; (surface) eben; (drink) abgestanden; (tyre) platt; (battery) leer; (refusal) glatt ▷ n (Brit: rooms) Wohnung f; (Auto) Reifenpanne f; **flat screen** n (Inform) Flachbildschirm m; **flatten** vt platt machen, einebnen

flatter ['flætə*] vt schmeicheln +dat; **flattering** adj schmeichelhaft

flatware ['flætwɛə] n (US) Besteck nt

flavor (US), **flavour** ['fleɪvə*] n Geschmack m ▷ vt Geschmack geben +dat; (with spices) würzen; **flavouring** n Aroma nt

flaw [flɔ:] n Fehler m; **flawless** adj fehlerlos; (complexion) makellos

flea [fli:] n Floh m

fled [fled] pt, pp of **flee**

flee [fli:] (**fled, fled**) vi fliehen

fleece [fli:s] n (of sheep) Vlies nt; (soft material) Fleece m; (jacket) Fleecejacke f

fleet [fli:t] n Flotte f

Flemish ['flemɪʃ] adj flämisch ▷ n (language) Flämisch nt

flesh [fleʃ] n Fleisch nt

flew [flu:] pt of **fly**

flex [fleks] n (Brit Elec) Schnur f

flexibility [fleksɪ'bɪlɪtɪ] n Biegsamkeit f; (fig) Flexibilität f; **flexible** ['fleksɪbl] adj biegsam;

(*plans, person*) flexibel; **flexitime** *n*
gleitende Arbeitszeit, Gleitzeit *f*
flicker ['flɪkə°] *vi* flackern; (*TV*)
flimmern
flies [flaɪz] *pl of* **fly** ▷ *n*
flight [flaɪt] *n* Flug *m*; (*escape*)
Flucht *f*; **~ of stairs** Treppe *f*; **flight
attendant** *n* Flugbegleiter(in)
m(f); **flight recorder** *n*
Flugschreiber *m*
flimsy ['flɪmzɪ] *adj* leicht gebaut,
nicht stabil; (*thin*) hauchdünn;
(*excuse*) fadenscheinig
fling [flɪŋ] (**flung, flung**) *vt*
schleudern ▷ *n*: **to have a ~** eine
(kurze) Affäre haben
flip [flɪp] *vt* schnippen; **to ~ a
coin** eine Münze werfen; **flip
through** *vt* (*book*) durchblättern;
flipchart *n* Flipchart *nt*
flipper ['flɪpə°] *n* Flosse *f*
flirt [flɜːt] *vi* flirten
float [fləʊt] *n* (*for fishing*)
Schwimmer *m*; (*in procession*)
Festwagen *m*; (*money*)
Wechselgeld *nt* ▷ *vi* schwimmen;
(*in air*) schweben
flock [flɒk] *n* (*of sheep*) (*Rel*) Herde
f; (*of birds*) Schwarm *m*; (*of people*)
Schar *f*
flog [flɒg] *vt* auspeitschen; (*Brit
fam*) verscheuern
flood [flʌd] *n* Hochwasser *nt*,
Überschwemmung *f*; (*fig*) Flut *f*
▷ *vt* überschwemmen; **floodlight**
n Flutlicht *nt*; **floodlit** *adj*
(*building*) angestrahlt
floor [flɔː°] *n* Fußboden *m*;
(*storey*) Stock *m*; **ground ~** (*Brit*),
first ~ (*US*) Erdgeschoss *nt*; **first
~** (*Brit*), **second ~** (*US*) erster Stock;
floorboard *n* Diele *f*
flop [flɒp] *n* (*fam: failure*) Reinfall
m, Flop *m* ▷ *vi* misslingen, floppen
floppy disk ['flɒpɪ'dɪsk] *n*
Diskette *f*
Florence ['flɒrəns] *n* Florenz *nt*

florist ['flɒrɪst] *n* Blumenhänd-
ler(in) *m(f)*; **florist's (shop)**
['flɒrɪsts] *n* Blumengeschäft
m(f)
flounder ['flaʊndə°] *n* (*fish*)
Flunder *f*
flour ['flaʊə°] *n* Mehl *nt*
flourish ['flʌrɪʃ] *vi* gedeihen;
(*business*) gut laufen; (*boom*)
florieren ▷ *vt* (*wave about*)
schwenken; **flourishing** *adj*
blühend
flow [fləʊ] *n* Fluss *m*; **to go with
the ~** mit dem Strom schwimmen
▷ *vi* fließen
flower ['flaʊə°] *n* Blume *f* ▷ *vi*
blühen; **flower bed** *n* Blumenbeet
nt; **flowerpot** *n* Blumentopf
m
flown [fləʊn] *pp of* **fly**
flu [fluː] *n* (*fam*) Grippe *f*
fluent *adj* (*Italian etc*) fließend; **to
be ~ in German** fließend Deutsch
sprechen
fluid ['fluːɪd] *n* Flüssigkeit *f* ▷ *adj*
flüssig
flung [flʌŋ] *pt, pp of* **fling**
fluorescent [flʊə'resnt] *adj* flu-
oreszierend, Leucht-
flush [flʌʃ] *n* (*lavatory*)
Wasserspülung *f*; (*blush*) Röte *f*
▷ *vi* (*lavatory*) spülen
flute [fluːt] *n* Flöte *f*
fly [flaɪ] (**flew, flown**) *vt, vi*
fliegen; **how time flies** wie die Zeit
vergeht! ▷ *n* (*insect*) Fliege *f*;
~/flies (*pl*) (*on trousers*)
Hosenschlitz *m*; **fly-drive** *n*
Urlaub *m* mit Flug und
Mietwagen; **flyover** *n* (*Brit*)
Straßenüberführung *f*,
Eisenbahnüberführung *f*; **flysheet**
n Überzelt *nt*
FM *abbr* = **frequency modulation**
≈ UKW
FO *abbr* = **Foreign Office** ≈ AA *nt*
foal [fəʊl] *n* Fohlen *nt*

foam [fəʊm] n Schaum m ▷ vi
schäumen

fob off [fɒb ɒf] vt: **to fob sb off
with sth** jdm etw andrehen

focus ['fəʊkəs] n Brennpunkt m;
in/out of ~ (photo)
scharf/unscharf; (camera)
scharf/unscharf eingestellt ▷ vt
(camera) scharf stellen ▷ vi sich
konzentrieren (on auf +akk)

foetus ['fiːtəs] n Fötus m

fog [fɒg] n Nebel m; **foggy** adj
neblig; **fog light** n (Auto: at rear)
Nebelschlussleuchte f

foil [fɔɪl] vt vereiteln ▷ n Folie f

fold [fəʊld] vt falten ▷ vi (fam:
business) eingehen ▷ n Falte f;
fold up vt (map etc)
zusammenfalten; (chair etc)
zusammenklappen ▷ vi (fam:
business) eingehen; **folder** n
(portfolio) Aktenmappe f;
(pamphlet) Broschüre f; (Inform)
Ordner m; **folding** adj
zusammenklappbar; (bicycle, chair)
Klapp-

folk [fəʊk] n Leute pl; (Mus) Folk
m; **my ~s** pl (fam) meine Leute
▷ adj Volks-

follow ['fɒləʊ] vt folgen +dat;
(pursue) verfolgen; (understand)
folgen können +dat; (career, news
etc) verfolgen; **as ~s** wie folgt ▷ vi
folgen; (result) sich ergeben (from
aus); **follow up** vt (request,
rumour) nachgehen +dat, weiter
verfolgen; **follower** n
Anhänger(in) m(f); **following** adj
folgend; **the ~ day** am
(darauf)folgenden Tag ▷ prep
nach; **follow up** n (event, book etc)
Fortsetzung f

fond [fɒnd] adj: **to be ~ of**
gernhaben; **fondly** adv (with love)
liebevoll; **fondness** n Vorliebe f;
(for people) Zuneigung f

fondue ['fɒnduː] n Fondue nt

font [fɒnt] n Taufbecken nt;
(Typo) Schriftart f

food [fuːd] n Essen nt,
Lebensmittel pl; (for animals)
Futter nt; (groceries) Lebensmittel
pl; **food poisoning** n
Lebensmittelvergiftung f; **food
processor** n Küchenmaschine f;
foodstuff n Lebensmittel nt

fool [fuːl] n Idiot m, Narr m; **to
make a ~ of oneself** sich
blamieren ▷ vt (deceive)
hereinlegen ▷ vi: **to ~ around**
herumalbern; (waste time)
herumtrödeln; **foolish** adj dumm;
foolproof adj idiotensicher

foot [fʊt] (pl **feet** [fiːt]) n Fuß m;
(measure) Fuß m (30,48 cm); **on ~** zu
Fuß ▷ vt (bill) bezahlen;
foot-and-mouth disease n
Maul- und Klauenseuche f;
football n Fußball m; (US:
American ~) Football m; **footballer**
n Fußballspieler(in) m(f);
footbridge n Fußgängerbrücke f;
footing n (hold) Halt m;
footlights npl Rampenlicht nt;
footnote n Fußnote f; **footpath**
n Fußweg m; **footprint** n
Fußabdruck m; **footwear** n
Schuhwerk nt

 KEYWORD

for [fɔː*] prep **1** für; **is this for me?**
ist das für mich?; **the train for
London** der Zug nach London; **he
went for the paper** er ging die
Zeitung holen; **give it to me —
what for?** gib es mir — warum?
2 (because of) wegen; **for this
reason** aus diesem Grunde
3 (referring to distance) **there are
roadworks for 5 km** die Baustelle
ist 5 km lang; **we walked for miles**
wir sind meilenweit gegangen

4 (*referring to time*) seit; (*with future sense*) für; **he was away for 2 years** er war zwei Jahre lang weg **5** (*+infin clauses*) **it is not for me to decide** das kann ich nicht entscheiden; **for this to be possible ...** damit dies möglich wird/wurde ...
6 (*in spite of*) trotz +*gen o* (*inf*) *dat*; **for all his complaints** obwohl er sich ständig beschwert
▷ *conj* denn

forbade [fə'bæd] *pt of* **forbid**
forbid [fə'bɪd] (**forbade, forbidden**) *vt* verbieten

force [fɔːs] *n* Kraft *f*; (*compulsion*) Zwang *m*, Gewalt; **to come into ~** in Kraft treten; **the Forces** *pl* die Streitkräfte ▷ *vt* zwingen; **forced** *adj* (*smile*) gezwungen; **~ landing** Notlandung *f*; **forceful** *adj* kraftvoll
forceps ['fɔːseps] *npl* Zange *f*
forearm ['fɔːrɑːm] *n* Unterarm *m*
forecast ['fɔːkɑːst] *vt* voraussagen; (*weather*) vorhersagen ▷ *n* Vorhersage *f*
forefinger ['fɔːfɪŋɡə*] *n* Zeigefinger *m*
foreground ['fɔːɡraʊnd] *n* Vordergrund *m*
forehand ['fɔːhænd] *n* (*Sport*) Vorhand *f*
forehead ['fɔːhed, 'fɒrɪd] *n* Stirn *f*
foreign ['fɒrən] *adj* ausländisch; **foreigner** *n* Ausländer(in) *m(f)*; **foreign exchange** *n* Devisen *pl*; **foreign language** *n* Fremdsprache *f*; **foreign minister** *n* Außenminister(in) *m(f)*; **Foreign Office** *n* (*Brit*) Außenministerium *nt*; **Foreign Secretary** *n* (*Brit*) Außenminister(in) *m(f)*; **foreign policy** *n* Außenpolitik *f*

foremost ['fɔːməʊst] *adj* erste(r, s); (*leading*) führend
forerunner ['fɔːrʌnə*] *n* Vorläufer(in) *m(f)*
foresee [fɔː'siː] *irr vt* vorhersehen; **foreseeable** *adj* absehbar
forest ['fɒrɪst] *n* Wald *m*; **forestry** ['fɒrɪstrɪ] *n* Forstwirtschaft *f*
forever [fə'revə*] *adv* für immer
forgave [fə'ɡeɪv] *pt of* **forgive**
forge [fɔːdʒ] *n* Schmiede *f* ▷ *vt* schmieden; (*fake*) fälschen; **forger** *n* Fälscher(in) *m(f)*; **forgery** *n* Fälschung *f*
forget [fə'ɡet] (**forgot, forgotten**) *vt, vi* vergessen; **to ~ about sth** etw vergessen; **forgetful** *adj* vergesslich; **forgetfulness** *n* Vergesslichkeit *f*; **forget-me-not** *n* Vergissmeinnicht *nt*
forgive [fə'ɡɪv] (**forgave, forgiven**) *irr vt* verzeihen; **to ~ sb for sth** jdm etw verzeihen
forgot [fə'ɡɒt] *pt of* **forget**
forgotten [fə'ɡɒtn] *pp of* **forget**
fork [fɔːk] *n* Gabel *f*; (*in road*) Gabelung *f* ▷ *vi* (*road*) sich gabeln
form [fɔːm] *n* (*shape*) Form *f*, Klasse *f*; (*document*) Formular *nt*; (*person*) **to be in** (**good**) **~** in Form sein ▷ *vt* bilden
formal ['fɔːməl] *adj* förmlich, formell; **formality** [fɔː'mælɪtɪ] *n* Formalität *f*
format ['fɔːmæt] *n* Format *nt* ▷ *vt* (*Inform*) formatieren
former ['fɔːmə*] *adj* frühere(r, s); (*opposite of latter*) erstere(r, s); **formerly** *adv* früher
formidable ['fɔːmɪdəbl] *adj* gewaltig; (*opponent*) stark
formula ['fɔːmjʊlə] *n* Formel *f*
formulate ['fɔːmjʊleɪt] *vt* formulieren

forth [fɔːθ] adv: **and so ~** und so weiter; **forthcoming** [fɔːθˈkʌmɪŋ] adj kommend, bevorstehend

fortify [ˈfɔːtɪfaɪ] vt verstärken; (for protection) befestigen

fortieth [ˈfɔːtɪəθ] adj vierzigste(r, s); see also **eighth**

fortnight [ˈfɔːtnaɪt] n vierzehn Tage pl

fortress [ˈfɔːtrɪs] n Festung f

fortunate [ˈfɔːtʃənɪt] adj glücklich; **I was ~** ich hatte Glück; **fortunately** adv zum Glück; **fortune** [ˈfɔːtʃən] n (money) Vermögen nt; **good ~** Glück nt; **fortune-teller** n Wahrsager(in) m(f)

forty [ˈfɔːtɪ] num vierzig ▷ n Vierzig f; see also **eight**

forward [ˈfɔːwəd] adv vorwärts ▷ n (Sport) Stürmer(in) m(f) ▷ vt (send on) nachsenden; (Inform) weiterleiten; **forwards** adv vorwärts

foster child [ˈfɒstətʃaɪld] n Pflegekind nt; **foster parents** npl Pflegeeltern pl

fought [fɔːt] pt, pp of **fight**

foul [faʊl] adj (weather) schlecht; (smell) übel ▷ n (Sport) Foul nt

found [faʊnd] pt, pp of **find** ▷ vt (establish) gründen; **foundations** [faʊnˈdeɪʃənz] npl Fundament nt

fountain [ˈfaʊntɪn] n Springbrunnen m; **fountain pen** n Füller m

four [fɔː*] num vier ▷ n Vier f; see also **eight**; **fourteen** [ˈfɔːˈtiːn] num vierzehn ▷ n Vierzehn f; see also **eight**; **fourteenth** adj vierzehnte(r, s); see also **eighth**; **fourth** [fɔːθ] adj vierte(r, s); see also **eighth**

four-wheel drive n Allradantrieb m; (car) Geländewagen m

fowl [faʊl] n Geflügel nt

fox [fɒks] n (a. fig) Fuchs m

fraction [ˈfrækʃən] n (Math) Bruch m; (part) Bruchteil m; **fracture** [ˈfræktʃə*] n (Med) Bruch m ▷ vt brechen

fragile [ˈfrædʒaɪl] adj zerbrechlich

fragment [ˈfrægmənt] n Bruchstück nt

fragrance [ˈfreɪgrəns] n Duft m; **fragrant** adj duftend

frail [freɪl] adj gebrechlich

frame [freɪm] n Rahmen m; (of spectacles) Gestell nt; **~ of mind** Verfassung f ▷ vt einrahmen; **to ~ sb** (fam: incriminate) jdm etwas anhängen; **framework** n Rahmen m, Struktur f

France [frɑːns] n Frankreich nt

frank [fræŋk] adj offen

frankfurter [ˈfræŋkfɛːtə*] n (Frankfurter) Würstchen nt

frankly [ˈfræŋklɪ] adv offen gesagt; **quite ~** ganz ehrlich; **frankness** n Offenheit f

frantic [ˈfræntɪk] adj (activity) hektisch; (effort) verzweifelt; **~ with worry** außer sich vor Sorge

fraud [frɔːd] n (trickery) Betrug m; (person) Schwindler(in) m(f)

freak [friːk] n Anomalie f; (animal, person) Missgeburt f; (fam: fan) Fan m, Freak m ▷ adj (conditions) außergewöhnlich, seltsam; **freak out** vi (fam) ausflippen

freckle [ˈfrekl] n Sommersprosse f

free [friː] adj, adv frei; (without payment) gratis, kostenlos; **for ~** umsonst ▷ vt befreien; **freebie** [ˈfriːbɪ] n (fam) Werbegeschenk nt; **it was a ~** es war gratis; **freedom** [ˈfriːdəm] n Freiheit f; **freefone** [ˈfriːfəʊn] adj: **a ~ number** eine gebührenfreie

Nummer; **free kick** n (Sport)
Freistoß m
freelance ['fri:lɑ:ns] adj
freiberuflich tätig; (artist)
freischaffend ▷ n Freiberufler(in)
m(f)
free-range ['fri:reɪndʒ] adj (hen)
frei laufend; **~ eggs** pl Freilandeier
pl
freeway ['fri:weɪ] n (US)
(gebührenfreie) Autobahn
freeze [fri:z] (**froze, frozen**) vi
(feel cold) frieren; (of lake etc)
zufrieren; (water etc) gefrieren ▷ vt
einfrieren; **freezer** n
Tiefkühltruhe f; (in fridge)
Gefrierfach nt; **freezing** adj
eiskalt; **I'm ~** mir ist eiskalt;
freezing point n Gefrierpunkt m
freight [freɪt] n (goods) Fracht f;
(money charged) Frachtgebühr f;
freight car n (US) Güterwagen m;
freight train n (US) Güterzug m
French [frentʃ] adj französisch
▷ n (language) Französisch nt; **the
~** pl die Franzosen; **French bean** n
grüne Bohne; **French bread** n
Baguette f; **French dressing** n
Vinaigrette f; **French fries** (US)
npl Pommes frites pl; **French kiss**
n Zungenkuss m; **Frenchman** (pl
-men) n Franzose m; **French
toast** n (US) in Ei und Milch
getunktes gebratenes Brot; **French
window(s)** n(pl) Balkontür f,
Terrassentür f; **Frenchwoman** (pl
-women) n Französin f
frequency ['fri:kwənsɪ] n
Häufigkeit f; (Phys) Frequenz f;
frequent ['fri:kwənt] adj häufig;
frequently adv häufig
fresco ['freskəʊ] (pl **-es**) n Fresko
nt
fresh [freʃ] adj frisch; (new) neu;
freshen vi: **to ~ (up)** (person) sich
frisch machen; **fresher, freshman**
(pl **-men**) n Erstsemester nt;

freshwater fish n
Süßwasserfisch m
Fri abbr = **Friday** Fr
friction ['frɪkʃən] n (a. fig)
Reibung f
Friday ['fraɪdeɪ] n Freitag m; see
also **Tuesday**
fridge [frɪdʒ] n Kühlschrank m
fried [fraɪd] adj gebraten;
~ potatoes Bratkartoffeln pl;
~ egg Spiegelei nt; **~ rice**
gebratener Reis
friend [frend] n Freund(in) m(f);
(less close) Bekannte(r) mf; **to make
~s with sb** sich mit jdm
anfreunden; **we're good ~s** wir
sind gut befreundet; **friendly** adj
freundlich; **to be ~ with sb** mit
jdm befreundet sein ▷ n (Sport)
Freundschaftsspiel nt; **friendship**
['frendʃɪp] n Freundschaft f
fright [fraɪt] n Schrecken m;
frighten vt erschrecken; **to be
~ed** Angst haben; **frightening** adj
beängstigend
frill [frɪl] n Rüsche f; **~s** (fam)
Schnickschnack
fringe [frɪndʒ] n (edge) Rand m;
(on shawl etc) Fransen pl; (hair)
Pony m
frivolous ['frɪvələs] adj leichtsinnig; (remark) frivol
frizzy ['frɪzɪ] adj kraus
frog [frɒg] n Frosch m

O KEYWORD

from [frɒm] prep **1** (indicating
starting place) von; (indicating origin
etc) aus +dat; **a letter/telephone
call from my sister** ein
Brief/Anruf von meiner
Schwester; **where do you come
from?** woher kommen Sie?; **to
drink from the bottle** aus der
Flasche trinken

2 (*indicating time*) von ... an; (*past*) seit; **from one o'clock to** o **until** o **till two** von ein Uhr bis zwei; **from January (on)** ab Januar
3 (*indicating distance*) von ... (entfernt)
4 (*indicating price, number etc*) ab +*dat*; **from £10** ab £10; **there were from 20 to 30 people there** es waren zwischen 20 und 30 Leute da
5 (*indicating difference*) **he can't tell red from green** er kann nicht zwischen Rot und Grün unterscheiden; **to be different from sb/sth** anders sein als jd/etw
6 (*because of, based on*) **from what he says** aus dem, was er sagt; **weak from hunger** schwach vor Hunger

front [frʌnt] *n* Vorderseite *f*; (*of house*) Fassade *f*; (*in war, of weather*) Front *f*; (*at seaside*) Promenade *f*; **in ~, at the ~** vorne; **in ~ of** vor; **up ~** (*in advance*) vorher, im Voraus ▷ *adj* vordere(r, s), Vorder-; (*first*) vorderste(r, s); **~ door** Haustür *f*; **~ page** Titelseite *f*; **~ seat** Vordersitz *m*; **~ wheel** Vorderrad *nt*
frontier ['frʌntɪə*] *n* Grenze *f*
front-wheel drive *n* (*Auto*) Frontantrieb *m*
frost [frɒst] *n* Frost *m*; (*white ~*) Reif *m*; **frosting** *n* (*US*) Zuckerguss *m*; **frosty** *adj* frostig
froth [frɒθ] *n* Schaum *m*; **frothy** *adj* schaumig
frown [fraʊn] *vi* die Stirn runzeln
froze [frəʊz] *pt of* **freeze**
frozen [frəʊzn] *pp of* **freeze** ▷ *adj* (*food*) tiefgekühlt, Tiefkühl-
fruit [fruːt] *n* (*as collective, a. type*) Obst *nt*; (*single ~, a. fig*) Frucht *f*;

fruit machine *n* Spielautomat *m*;
fruit salad *n* Obstsalat *m*
frustrated [frʌ'streɪtɪd] *adj* frustriert; **frustratration** *n* Frustration *f*, Frust *m*
fry [fraɪ] *vt* braten; **frying pan** *n* Bratpfanne *f*
fuchsia ['fjuːʃə] *n* Fuchsie *f*
fuck [fʌk] *vt* (*vulg*) ficken; **~ off** verpiss dich!; **fucking** *adj* (*vulg*) Scheiß-
fudge [fʌdʒ] *n* weiche Karamellsüßigkeit
fuel [fjʊəl] *n* Kraftstoff *m*; (*for heating*) Brennstoff *m*; **fuel consumption** *n* Kraftstoffverbrauch *m*; **fuel gauge** *n* Benzinuhr *f*; **fuel oil** *n* Gasöl *nt*; **fuel rod** *n* Brennstab *m*; **fuel tank** *n* Tank *m*; (*for oil*) Öltank *m*
fugitive ['fjuːdʒɪtɪv] *n* Flüchtling *m*
fulfil [fʊl'fɪl] *vt* erfüllen
full [fʊl] *adj* voll; (*person: satisfied*) satt; (*member, employment*) Voll(zeit)-; (*complete*) vollständig; **~ of ...** voller ... *gen*; **full beam** *n* (*Auto*) Fernlicht *nt*; **full moon** *n* Vollmond *m*; **full stop** *n* Punkt *m*; **full-time** *adj*: **~ job** Ganztagsarbeit *f*; **fully** *adv* völlig; (*recover*) voll und ganz; (*discuss*) ausführlich
fumble ['fʌmbl] *vi* herumfummeln (*with, at* an +*dat*)
fumes [fjuːmz] *npl* Dämpfe *pl*; (*of car*) Abgase *pl*
fun [fʌn] *n* Spaß *m*; **for ~** zum Spaß; **it's ~** es macht Spaß; **to make ~ of** sich lustig machen über +*akk*
function ['fʌŋkʃən] *n* Funktion *f*; (*event*) Feier *f*; (*reception*) Empfang *m* ▷ *vi* funktionieren; **function key** *n* (*Inform*) Funktionstaste *f*
fund [fʌnd] *n* Fonds *m*; **~s** *pl* Geldmittel *pl*

fundamental [fʌndə'mentl] *adj* grundlegend; **fundamentally** *adv* im Grunde

funding ['fʌndɪŋ] *n* finanzielle Unterstützung

funeral ['fju:nərəl] *n* Beerdigung *f*

funfair ['fʌnfɛə*] *n* Jahrmarkt *m*

fungus ['fʌŋgəs] (*pl* **fungi** *o* **funguses**) *n* Pilz *m*

funicular [fju:'nɪkjʊlə*] *n* Seilbahn *f*

funnel ['fʌnl] *n* Trichter *m*; (*of steamer*) Schornstein *m*

funny ['fʌnɪ] *adj* (*amusing*) komisch, lustig; (*strange*) seltsam

fur [fɜ:*] *n* Pelz *m*; (*of animal*) Fell *nt*

furious ['fjʊərɪəs] *adj* wütend (*with sb* auf jdn)

furnished ['fɜ:nɪʃd] *adj* möbliert; **furniture** ['fɜ:nɪtʃə*] *n* Möbel *pl*; **piece of ~** Möbelstück *nt*

further ['fɜ:ðə*] *comparative of* **far** ▷ *adj* weitere(r, s); **~ education** Weiterbildung *f*; **until ~ notice** bis auf weiteres ▷ *adv* weiter; **furthest** ['fɜ:ðɪst] *superlative of* **far** ▷ *adj* am weitesten entfernt ▷ *adv* am weitesten

fury ['fjʊərɪ] *n* Wut *f*

fuse [fju:z] *n* (*Elec*) Sicherung *f* ▷ *vi* (*Elec*) durchbrennen; **fuse box** *n* Sicherungskasten *m*

fuss [fʌs] *n* Theater *nt*; **to make a ~** (ein) Theater machen; **fussy** *adj* (*difficult*) schwierig, kompliziert; (*attentive to detail*) pingelig

future ['fju:tʃə*] *adj* künftig ▷ *n* Zukunft *f*

fuze (*US*) *see* **fuse**

fuzzy ['fʌzɪ] *adj* (*indistinct*) verschwommen; (*hair*) kraus

g

gable ['geɪbl] *n* Giebel *m*

gadget ['gædʒɪt] *n* Vorrichtung *f*, Gerät *nt*

Gaelic ['geɪlɪk] *adj* gälisch ▷ *n* (*language*) Gälisch *nt*

gain [geɪn] *vt* (*obtain, win*) gewinnen; (*advantage, respect*) sich verschaffen; (*wealth*) erwerben; (*weight*) zunehmen ▷ *vi* (*improve*) gewinnen (*in an* +*dat*); (*clock*) vorgehen ▷ *n* Gewinn *m* (*in an* +*dat*)

gale [geɪl] *n* Sturm *m*

gall bladder ['gɔ:lblædə*] *n* Gallenblase *f*

gallery ['gælərɪ] *n* Galerie *f*, Museum *nt*

gallon ['gælən] *n* Gallone *f*; ((*Brit*) 4,546 *l*, (*US*) 3,79 *l*)

gallop ['gæləp] *n* Galopp *m* ▷ *vi* galoppieren

gallstone ['gɔ:lstəʊn] *n* Gallenstein *m*

Gambia ['gæmbɪə] *n* Gambia *nt*

gamble ['gæmbl] *vi* um Geld spielen, wetten ▷ *n*: **it's a ~** es ist riskant; **gambling** *n* Glücksspiel *nt*

game [geɪm] *n* Spiel *nt*; *(animals)* Wild *nt*; **a ~ of chess** eine Partie Schach; **~s** *(in school)* Sport *m*; **game show** *n* *(TV)* Gameshow *f*

gammon ['gæmən] *n* geräucherter Schinken

gang [gæŋ] *n* *(of criminals, youths)* Bande *f*, Gang *f*, Clique *f* ▷ *vt*: **to ~ up on** sich verschwören gegen

gangster ['gæŋstə°] *n* Gangster *m*

gangway ['gæŋweɪ] *n* *(for ship)* Gangway *f*; *(Brit: aisle)* Gang *m*, Gangway *f*

gap [gæp] *n* *(hole)* Lücke *f*; *(in time)* Pause *f*; *(in age)* Unterschied *m*

gape [geɪp] *vi* (mit offenem Mund) starren

gap year *n* Jahr zwischen *Schulabschluss und Studium, das oft zu Auslandsaufenthalten genutzt wird*

garage ['gærɑːʒ] *n* Garage *f*; *(for repair)* (Auto)werkstatt *f*; *(for fuel)* Tankstelle *f*

garbage ['gɑːbɪdʒ] *n* *(US)* Müll *m*; *(fam: nonsense)* Quatsch *m*; **garbage can** *n* *(US)* Mülleimer *m*; *(outside)* Mülltonne *f*; **garbage truck** *n* *(US)* Müllwagen *m*

garden ['gɑːdn] *n* Garten *m*; **(public) ~s** Park *m*; **garden centre** *n* Gartencenter *nt*; **gardener** *n* Gärtner(in) *m(f)*; **gardening** *n* Gartenarbeit *f*

gargle ['gɑːgl] *vi* gurgeln

gargoyle ['gɑːgɔɪl] *n* Wasserspeier *m*

garlic ['gɑːlɪk] *n* Knoblauch *m*; **garlic bread** *n* Knoblauchbrot *nt*; **garlic butter** *n* Knoblauchbutter *f*

gas [gæs] *n* Gas *nt*; *(US: petrol)* Benzin *nt*; **to step on the ~** Gas geben; **gas cooker** *n* Gasherd *m*; **gas cylinder** *n* Gasflasche *f*; **gas fire** *n* Gasofen *m*

gasket ['gæskɪt] *n* Dichtung *f*

gas lighter *n* *(for cigarettes)* Gasfeuerzeug *nt*; **gas mask** *n* Gasmaske *f*; **gas meter** *n* Gaszähler *m*

gasoline ['gæsəliːn] *n* *(US)* Benzin *nt*

gasp [gɑːsp] *vi* keuchen; *(in surprise)* nach Luft schnappen

gas pedal *n* *(US)* Gaspedal *nt*; **gas pump** *n* *(US)* Zapfsäule *f*; **gas station** *n* *(US)* Tankstelle *f*; **gas tank** *n* *(US)* Benzintank *m*

gastric ['gæstrɪk] *adj* Magen-; **~ flu** Magen-Darm-Grippe *f*; **~ ulcer** Magengeschwür *nt*

gasworks ['gæswɜːks] *n* Gaswerk *nt*

gate [geɪt] *n* Tor *nt*; *(barrier)* Schranke *f*; *(Aviat)* Gate *nt*, Flugsteig *m*

gateau ['gætəʊ] *(pl* **gateaux***)* *n* Torte *f*

gateway *n* Tor *nt*

gather ['gæðə°] *vt* *(collect)* sammeln; **to ~ speed** beschleunigen ▷ *vi* *(assemble)* sich versammeln; *(understand)* schließen *(from* aus*)*; **gathering** *n* Versammlung *f*

gauge [geɪdʒ] *n* Meßgerät *nt*

gauze [gɔːz] *n* Gaze *f*; *(for bandages)* Mull *m*

gave [geɪv] *pt of* **give**

gay [geɪ] *adj* *(homosexual)* schwul; **~ marriage** *(fam)* Homoehe *f*

gaze [geɪz] *n* Blick *m* ▷ *vi* starren

GCSE *abbr* = **general certificate of secondary education** *(school)* Abschlussprüfung *f* der Sekundarstufe, ≈ mittlere Reife

gear [gɪə°] *n* *(Auto)* Gang *m*; *(equipment)* Ausrüstung *f*; *(clothes)*

Klamotten *pl*; **to change
~** schalten; **gearbox** *n* Getriebe
nt; **gear change, gear shift** (*US*)
n Gangschaltung *f*; **gear lever,
gear stick** (*US*) *n* Schalthebel
m

geese [giːs] *pl of* **goose**

gel [dʒel] *n* Gel *nt* ▷ *vi* gelieren;
they really ~led sie verstanden
sich auf Anhieb

gem [dʒem] *n* Edelstein *m*; (*fig*)
Juwel *nt*

Gemini ['dʒemɪniː] *nsing* (*Astr*)
Zwillinge *pl*

gender ['dʒendə*] *n* Geschlecht
nt

gene [dʒiːn] *n* Gen *nt*

general ['dʒenərəl] *adj* allgemein; **~ knowledge**
Allgemeinbildung *f*; **~ election**
Parlamentswahlen *pl*; **generalize**
['dʒenrəlaɪz] *vi* verallgemeinern;
generally ['dʒenrəlɪ] *adv* im
Allgemeinen

generation [dʒenə'reɪʃən] *n*
Generation *f*; **generation gap** *n*
Generationsunterschied *m*

generator ['dʒenəreɪtə*] *n*
Generator *m*

generosity [dʒenə'rɒsɪtɪ] *n*
Großzügigkeit *f*; **generous**
['dʒenərəs] *adj* großzügig;
(*portion*) reichlich

genetic [dʒɪ'netɪk] *adj* genetisch;
~ research Genforschung *f*;
~ technology Gentechnik *f*;
genetically modified *adj*
gentechnisch verändert,
genmanipuliert; *see also* **GM**

Geneva [dʒɪ'niːvə] *n* Genf *nt*;
Lake ~ der Genfer See

genitals ['dʒenɪtlz] *npl* Ge-
schlechtsteile *pl*

genitive ['dʒenɪtɪv] *n* Genitiv *m*

genius ['dʒiːnɪəs] *n* Genie *nt*

gentle ['dʒentl] *adj* sanft; (*touch*)
zart; **gentleman** (*pl* **-men**) *n*

Herr *m*; (*polite man*) Gentleman *m*

gents [dʒents] *n*: **"~"** (*lavatory*)
„Herren"; **the ~** *pl* die
Herrentoilette

genuine ['dʒenjʊɪn] *adj* echt

geographical [dʒɪə'ɡræfɪkəl]
adj geografisch; **geography**
[dʒɪ'ɒɡrəfɪ] *n* Geografie *f*; (*at
school*) Erdkunde *f*

geological [dʒɪəʊ'lɒdʒɪkəl] *adj*
geologisch; **geology** [dʒɪ'ɒlədʒɪ]
n Geologie *f*

geometry [dʒɪ'ɒmɪtrɪ] *n*
Geometrie *f*

geranium [dʒɪ'reɪnɪəm] *n*
Geranie *f*

gerbil ['dʒɜːbəl] *n* (*Zool*)
Wüstenrennmaus *f*

germ [dʒɜːm] *n* Keim *m*; (*Med*)
Bazillus *m*

German ['dʒɜːmən] *adj* deutsch;
she's ~ sie ist Deutsche;
~ shepherd Deutscher
Schäferhund ▷ *n* (*person*)
Deutsche(r) *mf*; (*language*) Deutsch
nt; **in ~** auf Deutsch; **German
measles** *n sing* Röteln *pl*;
Germany ['dʒɜːmənɪ] *n*
Deutschland *nt*

gesture ['dʒestʃə*] *n* Geste *f*

 KEYWORD

get [ɡet] (*pt, pp* **got,** *pp* **gotten**
(*US*)) *vi* **1** (*become, be*) werden; **to
get old/tired** alt/müde werden;
to get married heiraten
2 (*go*) (an)kommen, gehen
3 (*begin*) **to get to know sb** jdn
kennenlernen; **let's get going** *o*
started! fangen wir an!
4 (*modal vb aux*) **you've got to do it**
du musst/Sie müssen es tun
▷ *vt* **1 to get sth done** (*do*) etw
machen; (*have done*) etw machen
lassen; **to get sth going** *o* **to go**
etw in Gang bringen *o* bekommen;

to get sb to do sth jdn dazu
bringen, etw zu tun
2 (*obtain: money, permission, results*)
erhalten; (*find: job, flat*) finden;
(*fetch: person, object*) holen; **to get
sth for sb** jdm etw besorgen; **get
me Mr Jones, please** (*Tel*)
verbinde/verbinden Sie mich bitte
mit Mr Jones; **get a life!** (*annoyed*)
mach dich mal locker!, reg dich
bloß ab!
3 (*receive: present, letter*)
bekommen, kriegen; (*acquire:
reputation etc*) erwerben
4 (*catch*) bekommen, kriegen; (*hit*)
(*target etc*) treffen, erwischen; **get
him!** (*to dog*) fass!
5 (*take, move*) bringen; **to get sth
to sb** jdm etw bringen
6 (*understand*) verstehen; (*hear*)
mitbekommen; **I've got it!** ich
hab's!
7 (*have, possess*) **to have got sth**
etw haben
get about *vi* herumkommen,
(*news*) sich verbreiten
get across *vi:* **to get sth** über etw *akk*
kommen; *vt:* **to get sth across**
(*communicate*) etw klarmachen
get along *vi* (*people*) (gut)
zurecht-/auskommen (*with*) mit;
(*depart*) sich *akk* auf den Weg
machen
get at *vt* (*reach*) herankommen
an +*akk*; (*facts*) herausbekommen;
what are you getting at? worauf
wollen Sie hinaus?, was meinst du
damit?; **to get at sb** (*nag*) an jdm
herumnörgeln
get away *vi* (*leave*) sich *akk*
davonmachen, wegkommen
(*escape*); **to get away from sth**
von etw *dat* entkommen; **to get
away with sth** mit etw
davonkommen
get back *vi* (*return*)
zurückkommen; (*Tel*) **to get back**

to s.o. jdn zurückrufen
▷ *vt* zurückbekommen
get by *vi* (*pass*) vorbeikommen;
(*manage*) zurecht-/auskommen
(*on*) mit
get down *vi* (her)untergehen; **to
get down to** in Angriff nehmen,
(*find time to do*) kommen zu;
▷ *vt* (*depress*) fertigmachen; **it
gets me down** (*fam*) es macht
mich fertig; **to get sth down**
(*write*) etw aufschreiben
get in *vi* (*train*) ankommen; (*arrive
home*) heimkommen
get into *vt* (*enter*) hinein-/
hereinkommen in +*akk*; (*car, train
etc*) einsteigen in +*akk*; (*clothes*)
anziehen; (*rage, panic etc*) geraten
in +*akk*; **to get into trouble** in
Schwierigkeiten kommen
get off *vi* (*from train etc*)
aussteigen; (*from horse etc*)
absteigen; (*fam: be enthusiastic*) **to
get off on sth** auf etw abfahren;
▷ *vt* (*nail, sticker*)
los-/abbekommen; (*clothes*)
ausziehen
get on *vi* (*progress*)
vorankommen; (*be friends*)
auskommen; (*age*) alt werden;
(*onto train etc*) einsteigen; (*onto
horse etc*) aufsteigen
▷ *vt* etw +*akk* vorantreiben, mit
etw *akk* loslegen
get out *vi* (*of house*)
herauskommen; (*of vehicle*)
aussteigen; **get out!** raus!
▷ *vt* (*take out*) herausholen; (*stain,
nail*) herausbekommen
get out of *vi* (*duty etc*)
herumkommen um
get over *vi* (*illness*) sich *akk*
erholen von; (*surprise*) verkraften;
(*news*) fassen; (*loss*) sich abfinden
mit
get round *vi* herumkommen um;
vt (*fig*) (*person*) herumkriegen

get through vi (*Tel*) durchkommen (*to*) zu
get together vi zusammenkommen
get up vi aufstehen ▷ vt hinaufbringen; (*go up*) hinaufgehen; (*organize*) auf die Beine stellen
get up to vi (*reach*) erreichen; (*prank etc*) anstellen

getaway n Flucht f;
get-together n Treffen nt
Ghana ['gɑːnə] n Ghana nt
gherkin ['gɜːkɪn] n Gewürzgurke f
ghetto ['getəʊ] (pl **-es**) n Ghetto nt
ghost [gəʊst] n Gespenst nt; (*of sb*) Geist m
giant ['dʒaɪənt] n Riese m ▷ adj riesig
giblets ['dʒɪblɪts] npl Geflügelinnereien pl
Gibraltar [dʒɪ'brɔːltə°] n Gibraltar nt
giddy ['gɪdɪ] adj schwindlig
gift [gɪft] n Geschenk nt; (*talent*) Begabung f; **gifted** adj begabt; **giftwrap** vt als Geschenk verpacken
gigantic [dʒaɪ'gæntɪk] adj riesig
giggle ['gɪgl] vi kichern ▷ n Gekicher nt
gill [gɪl] n (*of fish*) Kieme f
gimmick ['gɪmɪk] n (*for sales, publicity*) Gag m
gin [dʒɪn] n Gin m
ginger ['dʒɪndʒə°] n Ingwer m ▷ adj (*colour*) kupferrot; (*cat*) rötlichgelb; **ginger ale** n Gingerale nt; **ginger beer** n Ingwerlimonade f; **gingerbread** n Lebkuchen m (*mit Ingwergeschmack*); **ginger(-haired)** adj rotblond; **gingerly** adv (*move*) vorsichtig

gipsy ['dʒɪpsɪ] n Zigeuner(in) m(f)
giraffe [dʒɪ'rɑːf] n Giraffe f
girl [gɜːl] n Mädchen nt; **girlfriend** n (*feste*) Freundin f; **girl guide** n (*Brit*), **girl scout** (*US*) Pfadfinderin f
gist [dʒɪst] n: **to get the ~** (**of it**) das Wesentliche verstehen
give [gɪv] (**gave, given**) vt geben; (*as present*) schenken (*to sb* jdm); (*state: name etc*) angeben; (*speech*) halten; (*blood*) spenden; **to ~ sb sth** jdm etw geben/schenken ▷ vi (*yield*) nachgeben; **give away** vt (*give free*) verschenken; (*secret*) verraten; **give back** vt zurückgeben; **give in** vi aufgeben; **give up** vt, vi aufgeben; **give way** vi (*collapse, yield*) nachgeben; (*traffic*) die Vorfahrt beachten
given ['gɪvn] pp of **give** ▷ adj (*fixed*) festgesetzt; (*certain*) bestimmt; **~ name** (*US*) Vorname m ▷ conj: **~ that ...** angesichts der Tatsache, dass ...
glacier ['glæsɪə°] n Gletscher m
glad [glæd] adj froh (*about* über); **I was ~ (to hear) that ...** es hat mich gefreut, dass ...; **gladly** ['glædlɪ] adv gerne
glance [glɑːns] n Blick m ▷ vi einen Blick werfen (*at* auf +akk)
gland [glænd] n Drüse f; **glandular fever** n Drüsenfieber nt
glare [glɛə°] n grelles Licht; (*stare*) stechender Blick ▷ vi (*angrily*) **to ~ at sb** jdn böse anstarren; **glaring** adj (*mistake*) krass
glass [glɑːs] n Glas nt; **~es** pl Brille f
glen [glen] n (*Scot*) (enges) Bergtal nt

glide [glaɪd] vi gleiten; (hover)
schweben; **glider** n Segelflugzeug
nt; **gliding** n Segelfliegen nt

glimmer ['glɪmə°] n (of hope)
Schimmer m

glimpse [glɪmps] n flüchtiger
Blick

glitter ['glɪtə°] vi glitzern; (eyes)
funkeln

glitzy ['glɪtsɪ] adj (fam) glanzvoll,
Schickimicki-

global ['gləʊbəl] adj global,
Welt-; **~ warming** die Erwärmung
der Erdatmosphäre; **globe** [gləʊb]
sp2; n (sphere) Kugel f; (world)
Erdball m; (map) Globus m

gloomily ['gluːmɪlɪ] , **gloomy**
adv, adj düster

glorious ['glɔːrɪəs] adj (victory,
past) ruhmreich; (weather, day)
herrlich; **glory** ['glɔːrɪ] n
Herrlichkeit f

gloss [glɒs] n (shine) Glanz m

glossary ['glɒsərɪ] n Glossar nt

glossy ['glɒsɪ] adj (surface)
glänzend ▷ n (magazine)
Hochglanzmagazin nt

glove [glʌv] n Handschuh m;
glove compartment n
Handschuhfach nt

glow [gləʊ] vi glühen

glucose ['gluːkəʊs] n Traubenzucker m

glue [gluː] n Klebstoff m ▷ vt
kleben

glutton ['glʌtn] n Vielfraß m; **a
~ for punishment** (fam) Masochist
m

GM abbr = **genetically modified**
Gen-; **~ foods** gentechnisch
veränderte Lebensmittel

GMT abbr = **Greenwich Mean
Time** WEZ f

go [gəʊ] (**went, gone**) vi gehen;
(in vehicle, travel) fahren; (plane)
fliegen; (road) führen (to nach);
(depart: train, bus) (ab)fahren;

(person) (fort)gehen; (disappear)
verschwinden; (time) vergehen;
(function) gehen, funktionieren;
(machine, engine) laufen; (fit, suit)
passen (with zu); (fail) nachlassen;
**I have to ~ to the doctor/to
London** ich muss zum Arzt/nach
London; **to ~ shopping** einkaufen
gehen; **to ~ for a walk/swim**
spazieren/schwimmen gehen;
has he gone yet? ist er schon
weg?; **the wine ~es in the
cupboard** der Wein kommt in den
Schrank; **to get sth ~ing** etw in
Gang setzen; **to keep ~ing**
weitermachen; (machine etc)
weiterlaufen; **how's the job ~ing?**
was macht der Job?; **his
memory/eyesight is going** sein
Gedächtnis lässt nach/seine
Augen werden schwach; **to
~ deaf/mad/grey**
taub/verrückt/grau werden ▷ vb
aux: **to be ~ing to do sth** etw tun
werden; **I was ~ing to do it** ich
wollte es tun ▷ n (pl **-es**) (attempt)
Versuch m; **can I have another ~?**
darf ich noch mal (probieren)?; **it's
my ~** ich bin dran; **in one ~** auf
einen Schlag; (drink) in einem Zug;
go after vt nachlaufen +dat; (in
vehicle) nachfahren +dat; **go ahead**
vi (in front) vorausgehen; (start)
anfangen; **go away** vi weggehen;
(on holiday, business) verreisen; **go
back** vi (return) zurückgehen; **we
~ a long way** (fam) wir kennen uns
schon ewig; **go by** vi
vorbeigehen; (vehicle)
vorbeifahren; (years, time)
vergehen ▷ vt (judge by) gehen
nach; **go down** vi (sun, ship)
untergehen; (flood, temperature)
zurückgehen; (price) sinken; **to
~ well/badly** gut/schlecht
ankommen; **go in** vi
hineingehen; **go into** vt (enter)

hineingehen in +akk; (crash) fahren gegen, hineinfahren in +akk; **to ~ teaching/politics/the army** Lehrer werden/in die Politik gehen/zum Militär gehen; **go off** vi (depart) weggehen; (in vehicle) wegfahren; (lights) ausgehen; (milk etc) sauer werden; (gun, bomb, alarm) losgehen ▷ vt (dislike) nicht mehr mögen; **go on** vi (continue) weitergehen; (happen) angehen; **to ~ with** o **doing sth** etw weitermachen; **go out** vi (leave house) hinausgehen; (fire, light, person socially) ausgehen; **to ~ for a meal** essen gehen; **go up** vi (temperature, price) steigen; (lift) hochfahren; **go without** vt verzichten auf +akk; (food, sleep) auskommen ohne

go-ahead ['gəʊəhed] adj (progressive) fortschrittlich ▷ n grünes Licht

goal [gəʊl] n (aim) Ziel nt; (Sport) Tor nt; **goalie**, **goalkeeper** n Torwart m, Torfrau f; **goalpost** n Torpfosten m

goat [gəʊt] n Ziege f

gob [gɒb] n (Brit fam) Maul nt; **shut your ~** halt's Maul! ▷ vi spucken; **gobsmacked** (fam: surprised) platt

god [gɒd] n Gott m; **thank God** Gott sei Dank; **godchild** (pl **-children**) n Patenkind nt; **goddaughter** n Patentochter f; **goddess** ['gɒdes] n Göttin f; **godfather** n Pate m; **godmother** n Patin f; **godson** n Patensohn m

goggles npl Schutzbrille f; (for skiing) Skibrille f; (for diving) Taucherbrille f

going ['gəʊɪŋ] adj (rate) üblich; **goings-on** npl Vorgänge pl

go-kart ['gəʊkɑ:t] n Gokart m

gold [gəʊld] n Gold nt; **golden**

adj golden; **goldfish** n Goldfisch m; **gold-plated** adj vergoldet

golf [gɒlf] n Golf nt; **golf ball** n Golfball m; **golf club** n Golfschläger m; (association) Golfklub m; **golf course** n Golfplatz m; **golfer** n Golfspieler(in) m(f)

gone [gɒn] pp of **go**; **he's ~** er ist weg ▷ prep: **just ~ three** kurz nach drei

good [gʊd] n (benefit) Wohl nt; (morally good things) Gute(s) nt; **for the ~ of** zum Wohle +gen; **it's for your own ~** es ist zu deinem/Ihrem Besten o Vorteil; **it's no ~** (doing sth) es hat keinen Sinn o Zweck; (thing) es taugt nichts; **for ~** für immer ▷ adj (better, best) gut; (suitable) passend; (thorough) gründlich; (well-behaved) brav; (kind) nett, lieb; **to be ~ at sport/maths** gut in Sport/Mathe sein; **to be no ~ at sport/maths** schlecht in Sport/Mathe sein; **it's ~ for you** es tut dir gut; **this is ~ for colds** das ist gut gegen Erkältungen; **too ~ to be true** zu schön, um wahr zu sein; **this is just not ~ enough** so geht das nicht; **a ~ three hours** gute drei Stunden; **~ morning/evening** guten Morgen/Abend; **~ night** gute Nacht; **to have a ~ time** sich gut amüsieren

goodbye [gʊd'baɪ] interj auf Wiedersehen

Good Friday n Karfreitag m

good-looking adj gut aussehend

goods [gʊdz] npl Waren pl, Güter pl; **goods train** n (Brit) Güterzug m

goodwill [gʊd'wɪl] n Wohlwollen nt

goose [gu:s] (pl **geese**) n Gans f

▷ vt (fam) **to ~ s.o.** jdn in den Arsch kneifen; **gooseberry** ['gʊzbəri] n Stachelbeere f; **goose bumps** n, **goose pimples** npl Gänsehaut f

gorge [gɔːdʒ] n Schlucht f

gorgeous ['gɔːdʒəs] adj wunderschön; **he's ~** er sieht toll aus

gorilla [gə'rɪlə] n Gorilla m

gossip ['gɒsɪp] n (talk) Klatsch m; (person) Klatschtante f ▷ vi klatschen, tratschen

got [gɒt] pt, pp of **get**

gotten ['gɒtn] (US) pp of **get**

govern ['gʌvən] vt regieren; (province etc) verwalten; **government** n Regierung f; **governor** n Gouverneur(in) m(f); **govt** abbr = **government** Regierung f

gown [gaʊn] n Abendkleid nt; (academic) Robe f

GP abbr = **General Practitioner** Allgemeinarzt, Allgemeinärztin

GPS n abbr = **global positioning system** GPS nt

grab [græb] vt packen; (person) schnappen

grace [greɪs] n Anmut f; (prayer) Tischgebet nt; **5 days' ~** 5 Tage Aufschub; **graceful** adj anmutig

grade [greɪd] n Niveau nt; (of goods) Güteklasse f; (mark) Note f; (US: year) Klasse f; **to make the ~** es schaffen; **grade crossing** n (US) Bahnübergang m; **grade school** n (US) Grundschule f

gradient ['greɪdɪənt] n (upward) Steigung f; (downward) Gefälle nt

gradual, **gradually** ['grædjʊəl, -lɪ] adj, adv allmählich

graduate ['grædjʊɪt] n Uniabsolvent(in) m(f), Hochschulabsolvent(in) m(f) ▷ ['grædjʊeɪt] vi einen akademischen Grad erwerben

grain [greɪn] n (cereals) Getreide nt; (of corn, sand) Korn nt; (in wood) Maserung f

gram [græm] n Gramm nt

grammar ['græmə°] n Grammatik f; **grammar school** n (Brit) ≈ Gymnasium nt

gran [græn] n (fam) Oma f

grand [grænd] adj (pej) hochnäsig; (posh) vornehm ▷ n (fam) 1000 Pfund bzw. 1000 Dollar

grand(d)ad n (fam) Opa m; **granddaughter** n Enkelin f; **grandfather** n Großvater m; **grandma** n (fam) Oma f; **grandmother** n Großmutter f; **grandpa** n (fam) Opa m; **grandparents** npl Großeltern pl; **grandson** n Enkel m

grandstand n (Sport) Tribüne f

granny ['grænɪ] n (fam) Oma f

grant [grɑːnt] vt gewähren (sb sth jdm etw); **to take sb/sth for ~ed** jdn/etw als selbstverständlich hinnehmen ▷ n Subvention f, finanzielle Unterstützung f; (for university) Stipendium nt

grape [greɪp] n Weintraube f; **grapefruit** n Grapefruit f; **grape juice** n Traubensaft m

graph [grɑːf] n Diagramm nt; **graphic** ['græfɪk] adj grafisch; (description) anschaulich

grasp [grɑːsp] vt ergreifen; (understand) begreifen

grass [grɑːs] n Gras nt; (lawn) Rasen m; **grasshopper** n Heuschrecke f

grate [greɪt] n Feuerrost m ▷ vi kratzen ▷ vt (cheese) reiben

grateful, **gratefully** ['greɪtfʊl, -fəlɪ] adj, adv dankbar

grater ['greɪtə°] n Reibe f

gratifying ['grætɪfaɪɪŋ] adj erfreulich

gratitude ['grætɪtjuːd] n Dankbarkeit f

grave [greɪv] n Grab nt ▷ adj
ernst; (mistake) schwer
gravel ['grævəl] n Kies m
graveyard ['greɪvjɑːd] n Friedhof m
gravity ['grævɪtɪ] n Schwerkraft
f; (seriousness) Ernst m
gravy ['greɪvɪ] n Bratensoße
f
gray [greɪ] adj (US) grau
graze [greɪz] vi (of animals)
grasen ▷ vt (touch) streifen; (Med)
abschürfen ▷ n (Med)
Abschürfung f
grease [griːs] n (fat) Fett nt;
(lubricant) Schmiere f ▷ vt
einfetten; (Tech) schmieren;
greasy ['griːsɪ] adj fettig; (hands,
tools) schmierig; (fam: person)
schleimig
great [greɪt] adj groß; (fam: good)
großartig, super; **a ~ deal of** viel;
Great Britain ['greɪt'brɪtn] n
Großbritannien nt;
great-grandfather n Urgroßvater m; **great-grandmother** n
Urgroßmutter f; **greatly** adv sehr;
~ disappointed zutiefst
enttäuscht
Greece [griːs] n Griechenland nt
greed [griːd] n Gier f (for nach);
(for food) Gefräßigkeit f; **greedy**
adj gierig; (for food) gefräßig
Greek [griːk] adj griechisch ▷ n
(person) Grieche m, Griechin f;
(language) Griechisch nt; **it's all
~ to me** ich verstehe nur
Bahnhof
green [griːn] adj grün; **~ with
envy** grün/gelb vor Neid ▷ n
(colour; for golf) Grün nt; (village ~)
Dorfwiese f; **~s** (vegetables) grünes
Gemüse; **the Greens, the Green
Party** (Pol) die Grünen; **green card**
n (US: work permit)
Arbeitserlaubnis f; (Brit: for car)
grüne Versicherungskarte;

greengage n Reneklode f;
greengrocer n Obst- und
Gemüsehändler(in) m(f);
greenhouse n Gewächshaus nt;
~ effect Treibhauseffekt m;
Greenland n Grönland nt; **green
pepper** n grüner Paprika; **green
salad** n grüner Salat
Greenwich Mean Time
['grenɪdʒ'miːntaɪm] n west-
europäische Zeit
greet [griːt] vt grüßen; **greeting**
n Gruß m
grew [gruː] pt of **grow**
grey [greɪ] adj grau; **grey-haired**
adj grauhaarig; **greyhound** n
Windhund m
grid [grɪd] n Gitter nt; **gridlock** n
Verkehrsinfarkt m; **gridlocked** adj
(roads) völlig verstopft; (talks)
festgefahren
grief [griːf] n Kummer m; (over
loss) Trauer f
grievance ['griːvəns] n
Beschwerde f
grieve [griːv] vi trauern (for um)
grill [grɪl] n (on cooker) Grill m ▷ vt
grillen
grim [grɪm] adj (face, humour)
grimmig; (situation, prospects)
trostlos
grin [grɪn] n Grinsen nt ▷ vi
grinsen
grind [graɪnd] (**ground, ground**)
vt mahlen; (sharpen) schleifen; (US:
meat) durchdrehen, hacken
grip [grɪp] n Griff m; **get a
~** nimm dich zusammen!; **to get
to ~s with sth** etw in den Griff
bekommen ▷ vt packen; **gripping**
adj (exciting) spannend
groan [grəʊn] vi stöhnen (with
vor +dat)
grocer ['grəʊsə*] n Lebensmit-
telhändler(in) m(f); **groceries** npl
Lebensmittel pl
groin [grɔɪn] n (Anat) Leiste f;

groin strain n (Med) Leistenbruch m
groom [gruːm] n Bräutigam m
▷ vt: **well ~ed** gepflegt
grope [grəʊp] vi tasten ▷ vt
(sexually harrass) befummeln
gross [grəʊs] adj (coarse) derb;
(extreme: negligence, error) grob;
(disgusting) ekelhaft; (Comm)
brutto; **~ national product**
Bruttosozialprodukt nt; **~ salary**
Bruttogehalt nt
grotty ['grɒtɪ] adj (fam) mies,
vergammelt
ground [graʊnd] pt, pp of **grind**
▷ n Boden m, Erde f; (Sport) Platz
m; **~s** pl (around house)
(Garten)anlagen pl; (reasons)
Gründe pl; (of coffee) Satz m; **on**
(**the**) **~s of** aufgrund von; **ground
floor** n (Brit) Erdgeschoss nt;
ground meat n (US) Hackfleisch
nt
group [gruːp] n Gruppe f ▷ vt
gruppieren
grouse [graʊs] (pl -) n (bird)
Schottisches Moorhuhn;
(complaint) Nörgelei f
grow [grəʊ] (**grew, grown**) vi
wachsen; (increase) zunehmen (in
an); (become) werden; **to ~ old** alt
werden; **to ~ into ...** sich
entwickeln zu ... ▷ vt (crop, plant)
ziehen; (commercially) anbauen;
I'm ~ing a beard ich lasse mir
einen Bart wachsen; **grow up** vi
aufwachsen; (mature) erwachsen
werden; **growing** adj wachsend;
a ~ number of people immer
mehr Leute
growl [graʊl] vi knurren
grown [grəʊn] pp of **grow**
grown-up [grəʊn'ʌp] adj
erwachsen ▷ n Erwachsene(r) mf;
growth [grəʊθ] n Wachstum nt;
(increase) Zunahme f; (Med)
Wucherung f

grubby ['grʌbɪ] adj schmuddelig
grudge [grʌdʒ] n Abneigung f
(against gegen) ▷ vt: **to ~ sb sth**
jdm etw nicht gönnen
gruelling ['grʊəlɪŋ] adj
aufreibend; (pace) mörderisch
gruesome ['gruːsəm] adj
grausig
grumble ['grʌmbl] vi murren
(about über +akk)
grumpy ['grʌmpɪ] adj (fam)
mürrisch, grantig
grunt [grʌnt] vi grunzen
G-string ['dʒiːstrɪŋ] n String m,
Stringtanga m
guarantee [gærən'tiː] n Garantie f (of für); **it's still under ~** es ist
noch Garantie darauf ▷ vt
garantieren
guard [gɑːd] n (sentry) Wache f;
(in prison) Wärter(in) m(f); (Brit
Rail) Schaffner(in) m(f) ▷ vt
bewachen; **a closely ~ed
secret** ein streng gehütetes
Geheimnis
guardian ['gɑːdɪən] n Vormund
m; **~ angel** Schutzengel m
guess [ges] n Vermutung f;
(estimate) Schätzung f; **have a
~** rate mal! ▷ vt, vi raten;
(estimate) schätzen; **I ~ you're
right** du hast wohl recht; **I ~ so** ich
glaube schon
guest [gest] n Gast m; **be my
~** nur zu!; **guest-house** n Pension
f; **guest room** n Gästezimmer
nt
guidance ['gaɪdəns] n (direction)
Leitung f; (advice) Rat m;
(counselling) Beratung f; **for your
~** zu Ihrer Orientierung; **guide**
[gaɪd] n (person) Führer(in) m(f);
(tour) Reiseleiter(in) m(f); (book)
Führer m; (girl ~) Pfadfinderin f
▷ vt führen; **guidebook** n
Reiseführer m; **guide dog** n
Blindenhund m; **guided tour** n

Führung *f* (*of* durch); **guidelines**
npl Richtlinien *pl*
guilt [gɪlt] *n* Schuld *f*; **guilty** *adj*
schuldig (*of gen*); (*look*)
schuldbewusst; **to have a**
~ conscience ein schlechtes
Gewissen haben
guinea pig ['gɪnɪ pɪg] *n*
Meerschweinchen *nt*; (*person*)
Versuchskaninchen *nt*
guitar [gɪ'tɑː°] *n* Gitarre *f*
gulf [gʌlf] *n* Golf *m*; (*gap*) Kluft *f*;
Gulf States *npl* Golfstaaten *pl*
gull [gʌl] *n* Möwe *f*
gullible ['gʌlɪbl] *adj*
leichtgläubig
gulp [gʌlp] *n* (kräftiger) Schluck
▷ *vi* schlucken
gum [gʌm] *n* (*around teeth, usu pl*)
Zahnfleisch *nt*; (*chewing ~*)
Kaugummi *m*
gun [gʌn] *n* Schusswaffe *f*; (*rifle*)
Gewehr *nt*; (*pistol*) Pistole *f*;
gunfire *n* Schüsse *pl*,
Geschützfeuer *nt*; **gunpowder** *n*
Schießpulver *nt*; **gunshot** *n*
Schuss *m*
gush [gʌʃ] *vi* (heraus)strömen
(*from* aus)
gut [gʌt] *n* Darm *m*; **~s** *pl*
(*intestines*) Eingeweide; (*courage*)
Mumm *m*
gutter ['gʌtə°] *n* (*for roof*)
Dachrinne *f*; (*in street*) Rinnstein *m*,
Gosse *f*; **gutter press** *n*
Skandalpresse *f*
guy [gaɪ] *n* (*man*) Typ *m*, Kerl *m*; **~s**
pl (*US*) Leute *pl*
gym [dʒɪm] *n* Turnhalle *f*; (*for*
working out) Fitnesscenter *nt*;
gymnasium [dʒɪm'neɪzɪəm] *n*
Turnhalle *f*; **gymnastics**
[dʒɪm'næstɪks] *nsing* Turnen *nt*;
gym-toned *adj* durchtrainiert
gynaecologist [gaɪnɪ'kɒlədʒɪst]
n Frauenarzt *m*, Frauenärztin *f*,
Gynäkologe *m*, Gynäkologin *f*;

gynaecology *n* Gynäkologie *f*,
Frauenheilkunde *f*
gypsy ['dʒɪpsɪ] *n* Zigeuner(in)
m(f)

h

habit ['hæbɪt] n Gewohnheit f;
habitual [hə'bɪtjʊəl] adj
gewohnt; (drinker, liar)
gewohnheitsmäßig
hack [hæk] vt hacken; **hacker** n
(Inform) Hacker(in) m(f)
had [hæd] pt, pp of **have**
haddock ['hædək] n Schellfisch
m
hadn't ['hædnt] contr of **had not**
haemophiliac, hemophiliac (US)
[hiːməʊ'fɪliæk] n Bluter(in) m(f);
haemorrhage, hemorrhage (US)
['hemərɪdʒ] n Blutung f ▷ vi
bluten; **haemorrhoids**,
hemorrhoids (US) ['hemərɔɪdz]
npl Hämorrhoiden pl
haggis ['hægɪs] n (Scot) mit
gehackten Schafsinnereien und
Haferschrot gefüllter Schafsmagen
Hague [heɪg] n: **the ~** Den Haag
hail [heɪl] n Hagel m ▷ vi hageln
▷ vt: **to ~ sb as sth** jdn als etw

feiern; **hailstone** n Hagelkorn nt;
hailstorm n Hagelschauer m
hair [heə*] n Haar nt, Haare pl; **to
do one's ~** sich frisieren; **to get
one's ~ cut** sich dat die Haare
schneiden lassen; **hairbrush** n
Haarbürste f; **hair conditioner** n
Haarspülung f; **haircut** n
Haarschnitt m; **to have a ~** sich
dat die Haare schneiden lassen;
hairdo (pl **-s**) n Frisur f;
hairdresser n Friseur m, Friseuse
f; **hairdryer** n Haartrockner m;
(hand-held) Fön® m; (over head)
Trockenhaube f; **hair gel** n
Haargel nt; **hairpin** n Haarnadel f;
hair remover n
Enthaarungsmittel nt; **hair spray**
n Haarspray nt; **hair style** n
Frisur f; **hairy** adj haarig,
behaart; (fam: dangerous) brenzlig
hake [heɪk] n Seehecht m
half [hɑːf] (pl **halves**) n Hälfte f;
(Sport: of game) Halbzeit f; **to cut in
~** halbieren ▷ adj halb; **three and
a ~ pounds** dreieinhalb Pfund;
~ an hour, a ~ hour eine halbe
Stunde; **one and a ~** eineinhalb,
anderthalb ▷ adv halb, zur Hälfte;
~ past three, ~ three halb vier; **at
~ past** um halb; **~ asleep** fast
eingeschlafen; **she's ~ German** sie
ist zur Hälfte Deutsche; **~ as big
(as)** halb so groß (wie); **half board**
n Halbpension f; **half fare** n
halber Fahrpreis; **half-hearted**
adj halbherzig; **half-hour** n halbe
Stunde; **half moon** n Halbmond
m; **half pint** n ≈ Viertelliter m o nt;
half price n: (**at**) **~** zum halben
Preis; **half-term** n (at school)
Ferien pl in der Mitte des
Trimesters; **half-time** n Halbzeit
f; **halfway** adv auf halbem Wege;
halfwit n (fam) Trottel m
halibut ['hælɪbət] n Heilbutt m
hall [hɔːl] n (building) Halle f; (for

audience) Saal *m*; (*entrance ~*) Flur *m*; (*large*) Diele *f*; **~ of residence** (*Brit*) Studentenwohnheim *nt*

hallmark ['hɔːlmɑːk] *n* Stempel *m*; (*fig*) Kennzeichen *nt*

hallo [hʌ'ləʊ] *interj* hallo

Hallowe'en [hæləʊ'iːn] *n* Halloween *nt* (*Tag vor Allerheiligen, an dem sich Kinder verkleiden und von Tür zu Tür gehen*)

● **HALLOWE'EN**
●
●
● **Hallowe'en** ist der 31. Oktober,
● der Vorabend von Allerheiligen,
● und nach altem Glauben der
● Abend, an dem man Geister und
● Hexen sehen kann. In
● Großbritannien und vor allem in
● den USA feiern die Kinder
● Hallowe'en, indem sie sich
● verkleiden und mit selbst
● gemachten Laternen aus
● Kürbissen von Tür zu Tür
● ziehen.

halo ['heɪləʊ] (*pl* **-es**) *n* (*of saint*) Heiligenschein *m*

halt [hɔːlt] *n* Pause *f*, Halt *m*; **to come to a ~** zum Stillstand kommen ▷ *vt*, *vi* anhalten

halve [hɑːv] *vt* halbieren

ham [hæm] *n* Schinken *m*; **~ and eggs** Schinken mit Spiegelei

hamburger ['hæmbɜːgə*] *n* (*Gastr*) Hamburger *m*

hammer ['hæmə*] *n* Hammer *m* ▷ *vt*, *vi* hämmern

hammock ['hæmək] *n* Hängematte *f*

hamper ['hæmpə*] *vt* behindern ▷ *n* (*as gift*) Geschenkkorb *m*; (*for picnic*) Picknickkorb *m*

hamster ['hæmstə*] *n* Hamster *m*

hand [hænd] *n* Hand *f*; (*of clock, instrument*) Zeiger *m*; (*in card game*) Blatt *nt*; **to be made by**

~ Handarbeit sein; **~s up!** Hände hoch!; (*at school*) meldet euch!; **~s off!** Finger weg!; **on the one ~ ..., on the other ~...** einerseits ..., andererseits ...; **to give sb a ~** jdm helfen (*with* bei); **it's in his ~s** er hat es in der Hand; **to be in good ~s** gut aufgehoben sein; **to get out of ~** außer Kontrolle geraten ▷ *vt* (*pass*) reichen (*to sb* jdm); **hand down** *vt* (*tradition*) überliefern; (*heirloom*) vererben; **hand in** *vt* einreichen; (*at school, university etc*) abgeben; **hand out** *vt* verteilen; **hand over** *vt* übergeben

handbag *n* Handtasche *f*; **handbook** *n* Handbuch *nt*; **handbrake** *n* (*Brit*) Handbremse *f*; **handcuffs** *npl* Handschellen *pl*; **handful** *n* Handvoll *f*; **handheld PC** *n* Handheld *m*

handicap ['hændɪkæp] *n* Behinderung *f*, Handikap *nt* ▷ *vt* benachteiligen; **handicapped** *adj* behindert; **the ~** die Behinderten

handicraft ['hændɪkrɑːft] *n* Kunsthandwerk *nt*

handkerchief ['hæŋkətʃɪf] *n* Taschentuch *nt*

handle ['hændl] *n* Griff *m*; (*of door*) Klinke *f*; (*of cup etc*) Henkel *m*; (*for winding*) Kurbel *f* ▷ *vt* (*touch*) anfassen; (*deal with: matter*) sich befassen mit; (*people, machine etc*) umgehen mit; (*situation, problem*) fertig werden mit; **handlebars** *npl* Lenkstange *f*

hand luggage ['hændlʌgɪdʒ] *n* Handgepäck *nt*; **handmade** *adj* handgefertigt; **to be ~** Handarbeit sein; **handout** *n* (*sheet*) Handout *nt*, Thesenpapier *nt*; **handset** *n* Hörer *m*; **please replace the ~** bitte legen Sie auf; **hands-free phone** *n* Freisprechanlage *f*; **handshake** *n* Händedruck *m*

handsome ['hænsəm] adj (man) gut aussehend

hands-on [hændz'ɒn] adj praxisorientiert; **~ experience** praktische Erfahrung

handwriting ['hændraɪtɪŋ] n Handschrift f

handy ['hændɪ] adj (useful) praktisch

hang [hæŋ] (**hung, hung**) vt (auf)hängen; (execute: hanged, hanged) hängen; **to ~ sth on sth** etw an etw akk hängen ▷ vi hängen ▷ n: **he's got the ~ of it** er hat den Dreh raus; **hang about** vi sich herumtreiben, rumhängen; **hang on** vi sich festhalten (to an +dat); (fam: wait) warten; **to ~ to sth** etw behalten; **hang up** vi (Tel) auflegen ▷ vt aufhängen

hangar ['hæŋə°] n Flugzeughalle f

hanger ['hæŋə°] n Kleiderbügel m

hang glider ['hæŋglaɪdə°] n (Flug)drachen m; (person) Drachenflieger(in) m(f); **hang-gliding** n Drachenfliegen nt

hangover ['hæŋəʊvə°] n (bad head) Kater m; (relic) Überbleibsel nt

hankie ['hæŋki] n (fam) Taschentuch nt

happen ['hæpən] vi geschehen; (sth strange, unpleasant) passieren; **if anything should ~ to me** wenn mir etwas passieren sollte; **it won't ~ again** es wird nicht wieder vorkommen; **I ~ed to be passing** ich kam zufällig vorbei; **happening** n Ereignis nt, Happening nt

happily ['hæpɪli] adv fröhlich, glücklich; (luckily) glücklicherweise; **happiness** ['hæpɪnəs] n Glück nt; **happy** ['hæpɪ] adj glücklich; (satisfied) **~ with sth** mit etw zufrieden; (willing) **to be ~ to do sth** etw gerne tun; **Happy Christmas** fröhliche Weihnachten!; **Happy New Year** ein glückliches Neues Jahr!; **Happy Birthday** herzlichen Glückwunsch zum Geburtstag!; **happy hour** n Happy Hour f (Zeit, in der man in Bars Getränke zu günstigeren Preisen bekommt)

harass ['hærəs] vt (ständig) belästigen; **harassment** n Belästigung f; (at work) Mobbing nt; **sexual ~** sexuelle Belästigung

harbor (US), **harbour** ['hɑːbə°] n Hafen m

hard [hɑːd] adj hart; (difficult) schwer, schwierig; (harsh) hart(herzig); **don't be ~ on him** sei nicht zu streng zu ihm; **it's ~ to believe** es ist kaum zu glauben ▷ adv (work) schwer; (run) schnell; (rain, snow) stark; **to try ~/~er** sich dat große/mehr Mühe geben; **hardback** n gebundene Ausgabe; **hard-boiled** adj (egg) hart gekocht; **hard copy** n (Inform) Ausdruck m; **hard disk** n (Inform) Festplatte f; **harden** vt härten ▷ vi hart werden; **hardened** adj (person) abgehärtet (to gegen); **hard-hearted** adj hartherzig; **hardliner** n Hardliner(in) m(f); **hardly** ['hɑːdlɪ] adv kaum; **~ ever** fast nie; **hardship** ['hɑːdʃɪp] n Not f; **hard shoulder** n (Brit) Standspur f; **hardware** n (Inform) Hardware f, Haushalts- und Eisenwaren pl; **hard-working** adj fleißig, tüchtig

hare [heə°] n Hase m

harm [hɑːm] n Schaden m; (bodily) Verletzung f; **it wouldn't do any ~** es würde nicht schaden ▷ vt schaden +dat; (person) verletzen; **harmful** adj schädlich; **harmless** adj harmlos

harp [hɑːp] n Harfe f
harsh [hɑːʃ] adj (climate, voice) rau; (light, sound) grell; (severe) hart, streng
harvest ['hɑːvɪst] n Ernte f; (time) Erntezeit f ▷ vt ernten
has [hæz] pres of **have**
hash [hæʃ] n (Gastr) Haschee nt; (fam: hashish) Haschisch nt; **to make a ~ of sth** etw vermasseln; **hash browns** npl (US) ≈ Kartoffelpuffer/Rösti mit Zwiebeln pl
hassle ['hæsl] n Ärger m; (fuss) Theater nt; **no ~** kein Problem ▷ vt bedrängen
hasn't ['hæznt] contr of **has not**
haste [heɪst] n Eile f; **hastily, hasty** adv, adj hastig; (rash) vorschnell
hat [hæt] n Hut m
hatch [hætʃ] n (Naut) Luke f; (in house) Durchreiche f; **hatchback** ['hætʃbæk] n (car) Wagen m mit Hecktür
hate [heɪt] vt hassen; **I ~ doing this** ich mache das sehr ungern ▷ n Hass m (of auf +akk)
haul [hɔːl] vt ziehen, schleppen ▷ n (booty) Beute f; **haulage** ['hɔːlɪdʒ] n Transport m; (trade) Spedition f; **haunted** adj: **a ~ house** ein Haus, in dem es spukt

○ **KEYWORD**

have [hæv] (pt, pp **had**) vb aux **1** haben; (esp with vbs of motion) sein; **to have arrived/slept** angekommen sein/geschlafen haben; **to have been** gewesen sein; **having eaten** o **when he had eaten, he left** nachdem er gegessen hatte, ging er
2 (in tag questions) **you've done it, haven't you?** du hast/Sie haben es doch gemacht, oder nicht?
3 (in short answers and questions) **you've made a mistake — so I have/no I haven't** du hast/Sie haben einen Fehler gemacht — ja, stimmt/nein; **we haven't paid — yes we have!** wir haben nicht bezahlt — doch!; **I've been there before, have you?** ich war schon einmal da, du/Sie auch?
▷ modal vb aux (be obliged): **to have (got) to do sth** etw tun müssen; **you haven't to tell her** du darfst es ihr nicht erzählen
▷ vt **1** (possess) haben; **he has (got) blue eyes** er hat blaue Augen; **I have (got) an idea** ich habe eine Idee
2 (referring to meals etc) **to have breakfast/a cigarette** frühstücken/eine Zigarette rauchen
3 (receive, obtain etc) haben; **may I have your address?** kann ich deine/Ihre Adresse haben?; **to have a baby** ein Kind bekommen
4 (maintain, allow) **he will have it that he is right** er besteht darauf, dass er recht hat; **I won't have it** das lasse ich mir nicht bieten
5 to have sth done etw machen lassen; **to have sb do sth** jdn etw machen lassen; **he soon had them all laughing** er brachte sie alle zum Lachen
6 (experience, suffer) **she had her bag stolen** man hat ihr die Tasche gestohlen; **he had his arm broken** er hat sich den Arm gebrochen
7 (+noun: take, hold etc) **to have a walk/rest** spazieren gehen/sich ausruhen; **to have a meeting/party** eine Besprechung/Party haben;
have on vt (be wearing) anhaben; (have arranged) vorhaben; (Brit) **you're having me on** du verarschst mich doch;

have out vt: **to have it out with sb** (settle problem) etw mit jdm bereden

Hawaii [hə'waɪɪ:] n Hawaii nt
hawk [hɔ:k] n Habicht m
hay [heɪ] n Heu nt; **hay fever** n Heuschnupfen m
hazard ['hæzəd] n Gefahr f; (risk) Risiko nt; **hazardous** adj gefährlich; **~ waste** Sondermüll m; **hazard warning lights** npl Warnblinkanlage f
haze [heɪz] n Dunst m
hazelnut ['heɪzlnʌt] n Haselnuss f
hazy ['heɪzɪ] adj (misty) dunstig; (vague) verschwommen
he [hi:] pron er
head [hed] n Kopf m; (leader) Leiter(in) m(f); (at school) Schulleiter(in) m(f); **~ of state** Staatsoberhaupt nt; **at the ~ of** an der Spitze von; (tossing coin) **~s or tails?** Kopf oder Zahl? ▷ adj (leading) Ober-; **~ boy** Schulsprecher m; **~ girl** Schulsprecherin f ▷ vt anführen; (organization) leiten; **head for** vt zusteuern auf +akk; **he's heading for trouble** er wird Ärger bekommen
headache ['hedeɪk] n Kopfschmerzen pl, Kopfweh nt; **header** n (football) Kopfball m; (dive) Kopfsprung m; **headfirst** adj kopfüber; **headhunt** vt (Comm) abwerben; **heading** n Überschrift f; **headlamp, headlight** n Scheinwerfer m; **headline** n Schlagzeile f; **headmaster** n Schulleiter m; **headmistress** n Schulleiterin f; **head-on collision** adj Frontalzusammenstoß m; **headphones** npl Kopfhörer m; **headquarters** npl (of firm) Zentrale f; **headrest**, **head**

restraint n Kopfstütze f; **headscarf** (pl **-scarves**) n Kopftuch nt; **head teacher** n Schulleiter(in) m(f)
heal [hi:l] vt, vi heilen
health [helθ] n Gesundheit f; **good/bad for one's ~** gesund/ungesund; **your ~!** zum Wohl!; **~ and beauty** Wellness; **health centre** n Ärztezentrum nt; **health club** n Fitnesscenter nt; **health food** n Reformkost f; **~ shop**, **~ store** Bioladen m; **health insurance** n Krankenversicherung f; **health service** n Gesundheitswesen nt; **healthy** adj gesund
heap [hi:p] n Haufen m; **~s of** (fam) jede Menge ▷ vt, vi häufen
hear [hɪə*] (**heard, heard**) vt, vi hören; **to ~ about sth** von etw erfahren; **I've ~d of it/him** ich habe schon davon/von ihm gehört; **hearing** n Gehör nt; (Jur) Verhandlung f; **hearing aid** n Hörgerät nt; **hearsay** n: **from ~** vom Hörensagen
heart [hɑ:t] n Herz nt; **to lose/take ~** den Mut verlieren/Mut fassen; **to learn by ~** auswendig lernen; (cards) **~s** Herz nt; **queen of ~s** Herzdame f; **heart attack** n Herzanfall m; **heartbeat** n Herzschlag m; **heartbreaking** adj herzzerreißend; **heartbroken** adj todunglücklich, untröstlich; **heartburn** n Sodbrennen nt; **heart failure** n Herzversagen nt; **heartfelt** adj tief empfunden; **heartless** adj herzlos; **heart-throb** n (fam) Schwarm m; **heart-to-heart** n offene Aussprache; **hearty** [hɑ:tɪ] adj (meal, appetite) herzhaft; (welcome) herzlich
heat [hi:t] n Hitze f; (pleasant) Wärme f; (temperature) Temperatur

f; (*Sport*) Vorlauf *m* ▷ *vt* (*house, room*) heizen; **heat up** *vi* warm werden ▷ *vt* aufwärmen; **heated** *adj* beheizt; (*fig*) hitzig; **heater** *n* Heizofen *m*; (*Auto*) Heizung f

heath [hi:θ] *n* (*Brit*) Heide f; **heather** ['heðə°] *n* Heidekraut *nt*

heating ['hi:tɪŋ] *n* Heizung f; **heat resistant** *adj* hitzebeständig; **heatwave** *n* Hitzewelle f

heaven ['hevn] *n* Himmel *m*; **heavenly** *adj* himmlisch

heavily ['hevɪlɪ] *adv* (*rain, drink etc*) stark; **heavy** ['hevɪ] *adj* schwer; (*rain, traffic, smoker etc*) stark; **heavy goods vehicle** *n* Lastkraftwagen *m*

Hebrew ['hi:bru:] *adj* hebräisch ▷ *n* (*language*) Hebräisch *nt*

hectic ['hektɪk] *adj* hektisch

he'd [hi:d] *contr of* **he had**; **he would**

hedge [hedʒ] *n* Hecke f

hedgehog ['hedʒhɒg] *n* Igel *m*

heel [hi:l] *n* (*Anat*) Ferse f; (*of shoe*) Absatz *m*

hefty ['heftɪ] *adj* schwer; (*person*) stämmig; (*fine, amount*) saftig

height [haɪt] *n* Höhe f; (*of person*) Größe f

heir [ɛə°] *n* Erbe *m*; **heiress** ['ɛərɪs] *n* Erbin f

held [held] *pt, pp of* **hold**

helicopter ['helɪkɒptə°] *n* Hubschrauber *m*; **heliport** ['helɪpɔːt] *n* Hubschrauberlandeplatz *m*

hell [hel] *n* Hölle f; **go to ~** scher dich zum Teufel ▷ *interj* verdammt; **that's a ~ of a lot of money** das ist verdammt viel Geld

he'll [hi:l] *contr of* **he will**; **he shall**

hello [hʌ'ləʊ] *interj* hallo

helmet ['helmɪt] *n* Helm *m*

help [help] *n* Hilfe f ▷ *vt, vi* helfen +*dat* (with bei); **to ~ sb (to) do sth** jdm helfen, etw zu tun; **can I ~?** kann ich (Ihnen) behilflich sein?; **I couldn't ~ laughing** ich musste einfach lachen; **I can't ~ it** ich kann nichts dafür; **~ yourself** bedienen Sie sich; **helpful** *adj* (*person*) hilfsbereit; (*useful*) nützlich; **helping** *n* Portion f; **helpless** *adj* hilflos

hem [hem] *n* Saum *m*

hemophiliac [hi:məʊ'fɪlɪæk] *n* (*US*) Bluter *m*; **hemorrhage** ['hemərɪdʒ] *n* (*US*) Blutung f; **hemorrhoids** ['hemərɔɪdz] *npl* (*US*) Hämorrhoiden *pl*

hen [hen] *n* Henne f

hen night *n* (*Brit*) Junggesellinnenabschied *m*

hence [hens] *adv* (*reason*) daher

henpecked ['henpekt] *adj*: **to be ~** unter dem Pantoffel stehen

hepatitis [hepə'taɪtɪs] *n* Hepatitis f

her [hɜ:°] *adj* ihr; **she's hurt ~ leg** sie hat sich *dat* das Bein verletzt ▷ *pron* (*direct object*) sie; (*indirect object*) ihr; **do you know ~?** kennst du sie?; **can you help ~?** kannst du ihr helfen?; **it's ~** sie ist's

herb [hɜ:b] *n* Kraut *nt*

herbal medicine ['hɜ:bəl-] *n* Pflanzenheilkunde f; **herbal tea** *n* Kräutertee *m*

herd [hɜ:d] *n* Herde f; **herd instinct** *n* Herdentrieb *m*

here [hɪə°] *adv* hier; (*to this place*) hierher; **come ~** komm her; **I won't be ~ for lunch** ich bin zum Mittagessen nicht da; **~ and there** hier und da, da und dort

hereditary [hɪ'redɪtərɪ] *adj* erblich; **hereditary disease** *n* Erbkrankheit f; **heritage** ['herɪtɪdʒ] *n* Erbe *nt*

hernia ['hɜːnɪə] n Leistenbruch m, Eingeweidebruch m

hero ['hɪərəʊ] (pl -es) n Held m

heroin ['herəʊɪn] n Heroin nt

heroine ['herəʊɪn] n Heldin f; **heroism** ['herəʊɪzəm] n Heldentum nt

herring ['herɪŋ] n Hering m

hers [hɜːz] pron ihre(r, s); **this is ~** das gehört ihr; **a friend of ~** ein Freund von ihr

herself [hɜːˈself] pron (reflexive) sich; **she's bought ~ a flat** sie hat sich eine Wohnung gekauft; **she needs it for ~** sie braucht es für sich (selbst); (emphatic) **she did it ~** sie hat es selbst gemacht; (**all**) **by ~** allein

he's [hiːz] contr of **he is**; **he has**

hesitant ['hezɪtənt] adj zögernd; **hesitate** ['hezɪteɪt] vi zögern; **don't ~ to ask** fragen Sie ruhig; **hesitation** n Zögern nt; **without ~** ohne zu zögern

heterosexual [hetərəʊˈsekʃʊəl] adj heterosexuell ▷ n Heterosexuelle(r) mf

HGV abbr = **heavy goods vehicle** LKW m

hi [haɪ] interj hi, hallo

hiccup ['hɪkʌp] n Schluckauf m; (minor problem) Problemchen nt; **to have** (**the**) **~s** Schluckauf haben

hid [hɪd] pt of **hide**

hidden ['hɪdn] pp of **hide**

hide [haɪd] (**hid, hidden**) vt verstecken (from vor +dat); (feelings, truth) verbergen; (cover) verdecken ▷ vi sich verstecken (from vor +dat)

hideous ['hɪdɪəs] adj scheußlich

hiding ['haɪdɪŋ] n (beating) Tracht f Prügel; (concealment) **to be in ~** sich versteckt halten; **hiding place** n Versteck nt

hi-fi ['haɪfaɪ] n Hi-Fi nt; (system) Hi-Fi-Anlage f

high [haɪ] adj hoch; (wind) stark; (living) im großen Stil; (on drugs) high ▷ adv hoch ▷ n (Meteo) Hoch nt; **highchair** n Hochstuhl m; **higher** adj höher; **higher education** n Hochschulbildung f; **high flier** n Hochbegabte(r) (m)f; **high heels** npl Stöckelschuhe pl; **high jump** n Hochsprung m; **Highlands** npl (schottisches) Hochland nt; **highlight** n (in hair) Strähnchen nt; (fig) Höhepunkt m ▷ vt (with pen) hervorheben; **highlighter** n Textmarker m; **highly** adj hoch, sehr; **~ paid** hoch bezahlt; **I think ~ of him** ich habe eine hohe Meinung von ihm; **high-performance** adj Hochleistungs-; **high school** n (US) Highschool f, ≈ Gymnasium nt; **high-speed** adj Schnell-; **~ train** Hochgeschwindigkeitszug m; **high street** n Hauptstraße f; **high tech** adj Hightech- n Hightech nt; **high tide** n Flut f; **highway** n (US) ≈ Autobahn f; (Brit) Landstraße f

hijack ['haɪdʒæk] vt entführen, hijacken; **hijacker** n Entführer(in) m(f), Hijacker m

hike [haɪk] vi wandern ▷ n Wanderung f; **hiker** n Wanderer m, Wanderin f; **hiking** n Wandern nt

hilarious [hɪˈlɛərɪəs] adj zum Schreien komisch

hill [hɪl] n Hügel m; (higher) Berg m; **hilly** adj hügelig

him [hɪm] pron (direct object) ihn; (indirect object) ihm; **do you know ~?** kennst du ihn?; **can you help ~?** kannst du ihm helfen?; **it's ~** er ist's; **~ too** er auch

himself [hɪmˈself] pron (reflexive) sich; **he's bought ~ a flat** er hat sich eine Wohnung gekauft; **he needs it for ~** er braucht es für sich (selbst); (emphatic) **he did it**

h

~ er hat es selbst gemacht; (**all**) **by** ~ allein

hinder ['hɪndə°] *vt* behindern; **hindrance** ['hɪndrəns] *n* Behinderung *f*

Hindu ['hɪnduː] *adj* hinduistisch ▷ *n* Hindu *m*; **Hinduism** ['hɪnduːɪzəm] *n* Hinduismus *m*

hinge [hɪndʒ] *n* Scharnier *nt*; (*on door*) Angel *f*

hint [hɪnt] *n* Wink *m*, Andeutung *f*; (*trace*) Spur *f* ▷ *vi* andeuten (*at akk*)

hip [hɪp] *n* Hüfte *f*

hippopotamus [hɪpə'pɒtəməs] *n* Nilpferd *nt*

hire ['haɪə°] *vt* (*worker*) anstellen; (*car, bike etc*) mieten ▷ *n* Miete *f*; **for** ~ (*taxi*) frei; **hire car** *n* Mietwagen *m*; **hire charge** *n* Benutzungsgebühr *f*; **hire purchase** *n* Ratenkauf *m*

his [hɪz] *adj* sein; **he's hurt** ~ **leg** er hat sich *dat* das Bein verletzt ▷ *pron* seine(r, s); **it's** ~ es gehört ihm; **a friend of** ~ ein Freund von ihm

historic [hɪ'stɒrɪk] *adj* (*significant*) historisch; **historical** *adj* (*monument etc*) historisch; (*studies etc*) geschichtlich; **history** ['hɪstərɪ] *n* Geschichte *f*

hit [hɪt] *n* (*blow*) Schlag *m*; (*on target*) Treffer *m*; (*successful film, CD etc*) Hit *m* ▷ *vt* (**hit, hit**) schlagen; (*bullet, stone etc*) treffen; **the car** ~ **the tree** das Auto fuhr gegen einen Baum; **to** ~ **one's head on sth** sich *dat* den Kopf an etw *dat* stoßen; **hit (up)on** *vt* stoßen auf +*akk*; **hit-and-run** *adj*: ~ **accident** Unfall *m* mit Fahrerflucht

hitch [hɪtʃ] *vt* (*pull up*) hochziehen ▷ *n* Schwierigkeit *f*; **without a** ~ reibungslos

hitch-hike ['hɪtʃhaɪk] *vi* trampen; **hitch-hiker** *n* Tramper(in)

m(f); **hitchhiking** *n* Trampen *nt*

HIV *abbr* = **human immunodeficiency virus** HIV *nt*; ~ **positive/negative** HIV-positiv/negativ

hive [haɪv] *n* Bienenstock *m*

HM *abbr* = **His/Her Majesty**

HMS *abbr* = **His/Her Majesty's Ship**

hoarse [hɔːs] *adj* heiser

hoax [həʊks] *n* Streich *m*, Jux *m*; (*false alarm*) blinder Alarm

hob [hɒb] *n* (*of cooker*) Kochfeld *nt*

hobble ['hɒbl] *vi* humpeln

hobby ['hɒbɪ] *n* Hobby *nt*

hobo ['həʊbəʊ] (*pl* **-es**) *n* (*US*) Penner(in) *m(f)*

hockey ['hɒkɪ] *n* Hockey *nt*

hold [həʊld] (**held, held**) *vt* halten; (*contain*) enthalten; (*be able to contain*) fassen; (*post, office*) innehaben; (*value*) behalten; (*meeting*) abhalten; (*person as prisoner*) gefangen halten; **to** ~ **one's breath** den Atem anhalten; **to** ~ **hands** Händchen halten; ~ **the line** (*Tel*) bleiben Sie am Apparat ▷ *vi* halten; (*weather*) sich halten ▷ *n* (*grasp*) Halt *m*; (*of ship, aircraft*) Laderaum *m*; **hold back** *vt* zurückhalten; (*keep secret*) verheimlichen; **hold on** *vi* sich festhalten; (*wait*) warten; (*Tel*) dranbleiben; **to** ~ **to sth** etw festhalten; **hold out** *vt* ausstrecken; (*offer*) hinhalten; (*offer*) bieten ▷ *vi* durchhalten; **hold up** *vt* hochhalten; (*support*) stützen; (*delay*) aufhalten; **holdall** *n* Reisetasche *f*; **holder** *n* (*person*) Inhaber(in) *m(f)*; **holdup** *n* (*in traffic*) Stau *m*; (*robbery*) Überfall *m*

hole [həʊl] *n* Loch *nt*; (*of fox, rabbit*) Bau *m*; ~ **in the wall** (*cash dispenser*) Geldautomat *m*

holiday ['hɒlɪdeɪ] *n* (*day off*)
freier Tag; (*public ~*) Feiertag *m*;
(*vacation*) Urlaub *m*; (*at school*)
Ferien *pl*; **on ~** im Urlaub; **to go on
~** Urlaub machen; **holiday camp**
n Ferienlager *nt*; **holiday home** *n*
Ferienhaus *nt*; (*flat*)
Ferienwohnung *f*; **holidaymaker**
n Urlauber(in) *m(f)*; **holiday
resort** *n* Ferienort *m*

Holland ['hɒlənd] *n* Holland *nt*

hollow ['hɒləʊ] *adj* hohl; (*words*)
leer ▷ *n* Vertiefung *f*

holly ['hɒlɪ] *n* Stechpalme *f*

holy ['həʊlɪ] *adj* heilig; **Holy
Week** *n* Karwoche *f*

home [həʊm] *n* Zuhause *nt*;
(*area, country*) Heimat *f*; (*institution*)
Heim *nt*; **at ~** zu Hause; **to make
oneself at ~** es sich *dat* bequem
machen; **away from ~** verreist
▷ *adv*: **to go ~** nach Hause
gehen/fahren; **home address** *n*
Heimatadresse *f*; **home country**
n Heimatland *nt*; **home game** *n*
(*Sport*) Heimspiel *nt*; **homeless** *adj*
obdachlos; **homely** *adj* häuslich;
(*US: ugly*) unscheinbar;
home-made *adj* selbst gemacht;
home movie *n* Amateurfilm *m*;
Home Office *n* (*Brit*)
Innenministerium *nt*

homeopathic *adj* (*US*) *see*
homoeopathic

home page ['həʊmpeɪdʒ] *n*
(*Inform*) Homepage *f*; **Home
Secretary** *n* (*Brit*)
Innenminister(in) *m(f)*; **homesick**
adj: **to be ~** Heimweh haben;
home town *n* Heimatstadt *f*;
homework *n* Hausaufgaben *pl*

homicide ['hɒmɪsaɪd] *n* (*US*)
Totschlag *m*

homoeopathic
[həʊmɪəʊˈpæθɪk] *adj*
homöopathisch

homosexual [hɒməʊˈsekʃʊəl]
adj homosexuell ▷ *n* Homosex-
uelle(r) *mf*

Honduras [hɒnˈdjʊərəs] *n*
Honduras *nt*

honest ['ɒnɪst] *adj* ehrlich;
honesty *n* Ehrlichkeit *f*

honey ['hʌnɪ] *n* Honig *m*;
honeycomb *n* Honigwabe *f*;
honeydew melon *n*
Honigmelone *f*; **honeymoon** *n*
Flitterwochen *pl*

Hong Kong [hɒŋ ˈkɒŋ] *n*
Hongkong *nt*

honor (*US*) *see* **honour**; **honorary**
['ɒnərərɪ] *adj* (*member, title etc*)
Ehren-, ehrenamtlich; **honour**
['ɒnə°] *vt* ehren; (*cheque*) einlösen;
(*contract*) einhalten ▷ *n* Ehre *f*; **in
~ of** zu Ehren von; **honourable** *adj*
ehrenhaft; **honours degree** *n*
*akademischer Grad mit Prüfung im
Spezialfach*

hood [hʊd] *n* Kapuze *f*; (*Auto*)
Verdeck *nt*; (*US Auto*) Kühlerhaube
f

hoof [huːf] (*pl* **hooves**) *n* Huf
m

hook [hʊk] *n* Haken *m*; **hooked**
adj (*keen*) besessen (*on* von);
(*drugs*) abhängig sein (*on* von)

hooligan ['huːlɪgən] *n* Hooligan
m

hoot [huːt] *vi* (*Auto*) hupen

Hoover® ['huːvə] *n* Staubsauger
m; **hoover** *vi, vt* staubsaugen

hop [hɒp] *vi* hüpfen ▷ *n* (*Bot*)
Hopfen *m*

hope [həʊp] *vi, vt* hoffen (*for* auf
+*akk*); **I ~ so/~ not**
hoffentlich/hoffentlich nicht; **I
~ (that) we'll meet** ich hoffe, dass
wir uns sehen werden ▷ *n*
Hoffnung *f*; **there's no ~** es ist
aussichtslos; **hopeful** *adj*
hoffnungsvoll; **hopefully** *adv* (*full
of hope*) hoffnungsvoll; (*I hope so*)
hoffentlich; **hopeless** *adj*

hoffnungslos; (*incompetent*) miserabel

horizon [hə'raɪzn] *n* Horizont *m*; **horizontal** [hɒrɪ'zɒntl] *adj* horizontal

hormone ['hɔ:məʊn] *n* Hormon *nt*

horn [hɔ:n] *n* Horn *nt*; (*Auto*) Hupe *f*

hornet ['hɔ:nɪt] *n* Hornisse *f*

horny ['hɔ:nɪ] *adj* (*fam*) geil

horoscope ['hɒrəskəʊp] *n* Horoskop *nt*

horrible, **horribly** ['hɒrɪbl, -blɪ] *adj*, *adv* schrecklich; **horrid**, **horridly** ['hɒrɪd, -lɪ] *adj*, *adv* abscheulich; **horrify** ['hɒrɪfaɪ] *vt* entsetzen; **horror** ['hɒrə*] *n* Entsetzen *nt*; **~s** (*things*) Schrecken *pl*

hors d'oeuvre [ɔ:'dɜ:vr] *n* Vorspeise *f*

horse [hɔ:s] *n* Pferd *nt*; **horse chestnut** *n* Rosskastanie *f*; **horsepower** *n* Pferdestärke *f*, PS *nt*; **horse racing** *n* Pferderennen *nt*; **horseradish** *n* Meerrettich *m*; **horse riding** *n* Reiten *nt*; **horseshoe** *n* Hufeisen *nt*

horticulture ['hɔ:tɪkʌltʃə*] *n* Gartenbau *m*

hose, **hosepipe** [həʊz, 'həʊzpaɪp] *n* Schlauch *m*

hospitable [hɒ'spɪtəbl] *adj* gastfreundlich

hospital ['hɒspɪtl] *n* Krankenhaus *nt*

hospitality [hɒspɪ'tælɪtɪ] *n* Gastfreundschaft *f*

host [həʊst] *n* Gastgeber *m*; (*TV: of show*) Moderator(in) *m(f)*, Talkmaster(in) *m(f)* ▷ *vt* (*party*) geben; (*TV: TV show*) moderieren

hostage ['hɒstɪdʒ] *n* Geisel *f*

hostel ['hɒstəl] *n* Wohnheim *nt*; (*youth ~*) Jugendherberge *f*

hostess ['həʊstɪs] *n* (*of a party*) Gastgeberin *f*

hostile ['hɒstaɪl] *adj* feindlich; **hostility** [hɒs'tɪlɪtɪ] *n* Feindseligkeit *f*

hot [hɒt] *adj* heiß; (*drink, food, water*) warm; (*spiced*) scharf; **I'm** (**feeling**) **~** mir ist heiß; **hot cross bun** *n* Rosinenbrötchen mit einem Kreuz darauf, hauptsächlich zu Ostern gegessen; **hot dog** *n* Hotdog *m*

hotel [həʊ'tel] *n* Hotel *nt*; **hotel room** *n* Hotelzimmer *nt*

hothouse *n* Treibhaus *nt*; **hotline** *n* Hotline *f*; **hotplate** *n* Kochplatte *f*; **hotspot** *n* (*Inform*) Hotspot *m*; **hot-water bottle** *n* Wärmflasche *f*

hour ['aʊə*] *n* Stunde *f*; **to wait for ~s** stundenlang warten; **~s** *pl* (*of shops etc*) Geschäftszeiten *pl*; **hourly** *adj* stündlich

house [haʊs] (*pl* **houses**) *n* Haus *nt*; **at my ~** bei mir (zu Hause); **to my ~** zu mir (nach Hause); **on the ~** auf Kosten des Hauses; **the House of Commons/Lords** das britische Unterhaus/Oberhaus; **the Houses of Parliament** das britische Parlamentsgebäude ▷ [haʊz] *vt* unterbringen; **houseboat** *n* Hausboot *nt*; **household** *n* Haushalt *m*; **~ appliance** Haushaltsgerät *nt*; **house-husband** *n* Hausmann *m*; **housekeeping** *n* Haushaltung *f*; (*money*) Haushaltsgeld *nt*; **house-trained** *adj* stubenrein; **house-warming (party)** *n* Einzugsparty *f*; **housewife** (*pl* **-wives**) *n* Hausfrau *f*; **house wine** *n* Hauswein *m*; **housework** *n* Hausarbeit *f*

housing ['haʊzɪŋ] *n* (*houses*) Wohnungen *pl*; (*house building*) Wohnungsbau *m*; **housing**

benefit n Wohngeld nt; **housing development, housing estate** (Brit) n Wohnsiedlung f

hover ['hʊvə*] vi schweben; **hovercraft** n Luftkissenboot nt

how [haʊ] adv wie; **~ many** wie viele; **~ much** wie viel; **~ are you?** wie geht es Ihnen?; **~ are things?** wie geht's?; **~'s work?** was macht die Arbeit?; **~ about …?** wie wäre es mit …?; **however** [haʊ'evə*] conj (but) jedoch, aber ▷ adv (no matter how) wie … auch; **~ much it costs** wie viel es auch kostet; **~ you do it** wie man es auch macht

howl [haʊl] vi heulen; **howler** ['haʊlə*] n (fam) grober Schnitzer

HP, hp n (Brit) abbr = **hire purchase** Ratenkauf m ▷ abbr = **horsepower** PS

HQ abbr = **headquarters**

hubcap ['hʌbkæp] n Radkappe f

hug [hʌg] vt umarmen ▷ n Umarmung f

huge [hjuːdʒ] adj riesig

hum [hʌm] vi, vt summen

human ['hjuːmən] adj menschlich; **~ rights** Menschenrechte pl ▷ n: **~ (being)** Mensch m; **humanitarian** [hjuːmænɪ'teərɪən] adj humanitär; **humanity** [hjuː'mænɪtɪ] n Menschheit f; (kindliness) Menschlichkeit f; **humanities** Geisteswissenschaften pl

humble ['hʌmbl] adj demütig; (modest) bescheiden

humid ['hjuːmɪd] adj feucht; **humidity** [hjuː'mɪdɪtɪ] n (Luft)feuchtigkeit f

humiliate [hjuː'mɪlɪeɪt] vt demütigen; **humiliation** [hjuːmɪlɪ'eɪʃn] n Erniedrigung f, Demütigung f

humor (US) see **humour**;

humorous ['hjuːmərəs] adj humorvoll; (story) lustig, witzig;

humour ['hjuːmə*] n Humor m; **sense of ~** Sinn m für Humor

hump [hʌmp] n Buckel m

hunch [hʌntʃ] n Gefühl nt, Ahnung f ▷ vt (back) krümmen; **hunchback** n Bucklige(r) mf

hundred ['hʌndrəd] num: **one ~, a ~** (ein)hundert; **a ~ and one** hundert(und)eins; **two ~** zweihundert; **hundredth** adj hundertste(r, s) ▷ n (fraction) Hundertstel nt; **hundredweight** n Zentner m (50,8 kg)

hung [hʌŋ] pt, pp of **hang**

Hungarian [hʌŋ'geərɪən] adj ungarisch ▷ n (person) Ungar(in) m(f); (language) Ungarisch nt; **Hungary** ['hʌŋɡərɪ] n Ungarn nt

hunger ['hʌŋɡə*] n Hunger m; **hungry** ['hʌŋɡrɪ] adj hungrig; **to be ~** Hunger haben

hunk [hʌŋk] n (fam) gut gebauter Mann; **hunky** ['hʌŋkɪ] adj (fam) gut gebaut

hunt [hʌnt] n Jagd f; (search) Suche f (for nach) ▷ vt, vi jagen; (search) suchen (for nach); **hunting** n Jagen nt, Jagd f

hurdle ['hɜːdl] n (a. fig) Hürde f; **the 400m ~s** der 400m-Hürdenlauf

hurl [hɜːl] vt schleudern

hurricane ['hʌrɪkən] n Orkan m

hurried ['hʌrɪd] adj eilig; **hurry** ['hʌrɪ] n Eile f; **to be in a ~** es eilig haben; **there's no ~** es eilt nicht ▷ vi sich beeilen; **~ (up)** mach schnell! ▷ vt antreiben

hurt [hɜːt] (**hurt, hurt**) vt wehtun +dat; (wound: person, feelings) verletzen; **I've ~ my arm** ich habe mir am Arm wehgetan ▷ vi wehtun; **my arm ~s** mir tut der Arm weh

husband ['hʌzbənd] n Ehemann m

husky ['hʌskɪ] adj rau ▷ n Schlittenhund m

hut [hʌt] n Hütte f

hyacinth ['haɪəsɪnθ] n Hyazinthe f

hybrid ['haɪbrɪd] n Kreuzung f

hydroelectric ['haɪdrəʊɪ'lektrɪk] adj: **~ power station** Wasserkraftwerk nt

hydrofoil ['haɪdrəʊfɔɪl] n Tragflächenboot nt

hydrogen ['haɪdrədʒən] n Wasserstoff m

hygiene ['haɪdʒiːn] n Hygiene f; **hygienic** [haɪ'dʒiːnɪk] adj hygienisch

hymn [hɪm] n Kirchenlied nt

hyperlink ['haɪpəlɪŋk] n Hyperlink m; **hypermarket** n Großmarkt m; **hypersensitive** adj überempfindlich

hyphen ['haɪfən] n Bindestrich m

hypnosis [hɪp'nəʊsɪs] n Hypnose f; **hypnotize** ['hɪpnətaɪz] vt hypnotisieren

hypochondriac [haɪpəʊ'kɒndrɪæk] n eingebildete(r) Kranke(r), eingebildete Kranke

hypocrisy [hɪ'pəkrəsɪ] n Heuchelei f; **hypocrite** ['hɪpəkrɪt] n Heuchler(in) m(f)

hypodermic [haɪpə'dɜːmɪk] adj, n: **~ (needle)** Spritze f

hypothetical [haɪpəʊ'θetɪkəl] adj hypothetisch

hysteria [hɪ'stɪərɪə] n Hysterie f; **hysterical** [hɪ'sterɪkəl] adj hysterisch; (amusing) zum Totlachen

I [aɪ] pron ich

ice [aɪs] n Eis nt ▷ vt (cake) glasieren; **iceberg** n Eisberg m; **iceberg lettuce** n Eisbergsalat m; **icebox** n (US) Kühlschrank m; **icecold** adj eiskalt; **ice cream** n Eis nt; **ice cube** n Eiswürfel m; **iced** adj eisgekühlt; (coffee, tea) Eis-; (cake) glasiert; **ice hockey** n Eishockey nt

Iceland ['aɪslənd] n Island nt; **Icelander** n Isländer(in) m(f); **Icelandic** [aɪs'lændɪk] adj isländisch ▷ n (language) Isländisch nt

ice lolly ['aɪslɒlɪ] n (Brit) Eis nt am Stiel; **ice rink** n Kunsteisbahn f; **ice skating** n Schlittschuhlaufen nt

icing ['aɪsɪŋ] n (on cake) Zuckerguss m

icon ['aɪkɒn] n Ikone f; (Inform) Icon nt, Programmsymbol nt

icy ['aɪsɪ] adj (slippery) vereist; (cold) eisig

I'd [aɪd] contr of **I would**; **I had**

ID abbr = **identification** Ausweis m

idea [aɪ'dɪə] n Idee f; (**I've**) **no ~** (ich habe) keine Ahnung; **that's my ~ of ...** so stelle ich mir ... vor

ideal [aɪ'dɪəl] n Ideal nt ▷ adj ideal; **ideally** adv ideal; (before statement) idealerweise

identical [aɪ'dentɪkəl] adj identisch; **~ twins** eineiige Zwillinge

identify [aɪ'dentɪfaɪ] vt identifizieren; **identity** [aɪ'dentɪtɪ] n Identität f; **identity card** n Personalausweis m

idiom ['ɪdɪəm] n Redewendung f; **idiomatic** adj idiomatisch

idiot ['ɪdɪət] n Idiot(in) m(f)

idle ['aɪdl] adj (doing nothing) untätig; (worker) unbeschäftigt; (machines) außer Betrieb; (lazy) faul; (promise, threat) leer

idol ['aɪdl] n Idol nt; **idolize** ['aɪdəlaɪz] vt vergöttern

idyllic [ɪ'dɪlɪk] adj idyllisch

i.e. abbr = **id est** d.h.

⭕ **KEYWORD**

if [ɪf] conj **1** wenn; (in case also) falls; **if I were you** wenn ich Sie wäre

2 (although) (**even**) **if** (selbst o auch) wenn

3 (whether) ob

4 if so/not wenn ja/nicht; **if only ...** wenn ... doch nur ...; **if only I could** wenn ich doch nur könnte; see also **as**

ignition [ɪg'nɪʃən] n Zündung f; **ignition key** n (Auto) Zündschlüssel m

ignorance ['ɪgnərəns] n Unwissenheit f; **ignorant** adj unwissend; **ignore** [ɪg'nɔː°] vt ignorieren, nicht beachten

I'll [aɪl] contr of **I will**; **I shall**

ill [ɪl] adj krank; **~ at ease** unbehaglich

illegal [ɪ'liːgəl] adj illegal

illegitimate [ɪlɪ'dʒɪtɪmət] adj unzulässig; (child) unehelich

illiterate [ɪ'lɪtərət] adj: **to be ~** Analphabet(in) sein

illness ['ɪlnəs] n Krankheit f

illuminate [ɪ'luːmɪneɪt] vt beleuchten; **illuminating** adj (remark) aufschlussreich

illusion [ɪ'luːʒən] n Illusion f; **to be under the ~ that ...** sich einbilden, dass ...

illustrate ['ɪləstreɪt] vt illustrieren; **illustration** n Abbildung f, Bild nt

I'm [aɪm] contr of **I am**

image ['ɪmɪdʒ] n Bild nt; (public ~) Image nt; **imaginable** [ɪ'mædʒɪnəbl] adj denkbar; **imaginary** [ɪ'mædʒɪnərɪ] adj eingebildet; **~ world** Fantasiewelt f; **imagination** [ɪmædʒɪ'neɪʃən] n Fantasie f; (mistaken) Einbildung f; **imaginative** [ɪ'mædʒɪnətɪv] adj fantasievoll; **imagine** [ɪ'mædʒɪn] vt sich vorstellen; (wrongly) sich einbilden; **~!** stell dir vor!

imbecile ['ɪmbəsiːl] n Trottel m

imitate ['ɪmɪteɪt] vt nachahmen, nachmachen; **imitation** n Nachahmung f ▷ adj imitiert, Kunst-

immaculate [ɪ'mækjʊlɪt] adj tadellos; (spotless) makellos

immature [ɪmə'tjʊə°] adj unreif

immediate [ɪ'miːdɪət] adj unmittelbar; (instant) sofortig; (reply) umgehend; **immediately** adv sofort

immense, **immensely** [ɪ'mens, -lɪ] adj, adv riesig, enorm

immersion heater [ɪˈmɜːʃn
hiːtə] n Boiler m
immigrant [ˈɪmɪgrənt] n Ein-
wanderer m, Einwanderin f;
immigration [ɪmɪˈgreɪʃən] n
Einwanderung f; (facility)
Einwanderungskontrolle f
immobilize [ɪˈməʊbɪlaɪz] vt
lähmen; **immobilizer** n (Auto)
Wegfahrsperre f
immoral [ɪˈmɒrəl] adj
unmoralisch
immortal [ɪˈmɔːtl] adj
unsterblich
immune [ɪˈmjuːn] adj (Med)
immun (from, to gegen); **immune
system** n Immunsystem nt
impact [ˈɪmpækt] n Aufprall m;
(effect) Auswirkung f (on auf +akk)
impatience [ɪmˈpeɪʃəns] n
Ungeduld f; **impatient**,
impatiently adj, adv ungeduldig
impeccable [ɪmˈpekəbl] adj
tadellos
impede [ɪmˈpiːd] vt behindern
imperative [ɪmˈperətɪv] adj
unbedingt erforderlich ▷ n (Ling)
Imperativ m
imperfect [ɪmˈpɜːfɪkt] adj
unvollkommen; (goods) fehlerhaft
▷ n (Ling) Imperfekt nt;
imperfection [ɪmpəˈfekʃən] n
Unvollkommenheit f; (fault) Fehler
m
imperial [ɪmˈpɪərɪəl] adj kaiser-
lich, Reichs-; **imperialism** n
Imperialismus m
impertinence [ɪmˈpɜːtɪnəns] n
Unverschämtheit f, Zumutung f;
impertinent adj unverschämt
implant [ˈɪmplɑːnt] n (Med)
Implantat nt
implausible [ɪmˈplɔːzəbl] adj
unglaubwürdig
implement [ˈɪmplɪmənt] n
Werkzeug nt, Gerät nt
▷ [ɪmplɪˈment] vt durchführen

implication [ɪmplɪˈkeɪʃən] n
Folge f, Auswirkung f; (logical)
Schlussfolgerung f; **implicit**
[ɪmˈplɪsɪt] adj implizit,
unausgesprochen; **imply**
[ɪmˈplaɪ] vt (indicate) andeuten;
(mean) bedeuten; **are you ~ing
that ...** wollen Sie damit sagen,
dass ...
impolite [ɪmpəˈlaɪt] adj
unhöflich
import [ɪmˈpɔːt] vt einführen,
importieren ▷ n [ˈɪmpɔːt] Einfuhr f, Import m
importance [ɪmˈpɔːtəns] n
Bedeutung f; **of no ~** unwichtig;
important adj wichtig (to sb für
jdn); (significant) bedeutend;
(influential) einflussreich
import duty [ˈɪmpɔːt djuːtɪ] n
Einfuhrzoll m; **import licence** n
Einfuhrgenehmigung f
impose [ɪmˈpəʊz] vt (conditions)
auferlegen (on dat); (penalty,
sanctions) verhängen (on gegen);
imposing [ɪmˈpəʊzɪŋ] adj eindrucksvoll, imposant
impossible [ɪmˈpɒsəbl] adj
unmöglich
impotence [ˈɪmpətəns] n
Machtlosigkeit f; (sexual)
Impotenz f; **impotent** adj
machtlos; (sexually) impotent
impractical [ɪmˈpræktɪkəl] adj
unpraktisch; (plan)
undurchführbar
impress [ɪmˈpres] vt beeindrucken; **impression** [ɪmˈpreʃən]
n Eindruck m; **impressive** adj
eindrucksvoll
imprison [ɪmˈprɪzn] vt inhaf-
tieren; **imprisonment** n
Inhaftierung f
improbability [ɪmprɒbəˈbɪlɪtɪ]
n Unwahrscheinlichkeit f;
improbable [ɪmˈprɒbəbl] adj
unwahrscheinlich

improper [ɪm'prɒpə°] *adj*
(*indecent*) unanständig; (*use*)
unsachgemäß
improve [ɪm'pruːv] *vt*
verbessern ▷ *vi* sich verbessern,
besser werden; (*patient*)
Fortschritte machen;
improvement *n* Verbesserung *f*
(*in +gen; on* gegenüber); (*in
appearance*) Verschönerung *f*
improvise ['ɪmprəvaɪz] *vt, vi*
improvisieren
impulse ['ɪmpʌls] *n* Impuls *m*;
impulsive [ɪm'pʌlsɪv] *adj*
impulsiv

⭕ KEYWORD

in [ɪn] *prep* **1** (*indicating place,
position*) in +*dat*; (*with motion*) in
+*akk*; **in here/there** hier/dort; **in
London** in London; **in the United
States** in den Vereinigten Staaten
2 (*indicating time: during*) in +*dat*; **in
summer** im Sommer; **in 1988** (im
Jahre) 1988; **in the afternoon**
nachmittags, am Nachmittag
3 (*indicating time: in the space of*)
innerhalb von; **I'll see you in 2
weeks** *o* **in 2 weeks' time** ich sehe
dich/Sie in zwei Wochen
4 (*indicating manner, circumstances,
state etc*) in +*dat*; **in the sun/rain**
in der Sonne/im Regen; **in
English/French** auf
Englisch/Französisch; **in a
loud/soft voice** mit lauter/leiser
Stimme
5 (*with ratios, numbers*) **1 in 10** jeder
Zehnte; **20 pence in the pound** 20
Pence pro Pfund; **they lined up in
twos** sie stellten sich in
Zweierreihe auf
6 (*referring to people, works*) **the
disease is common in children**
die Krankheit ist bei Kindern
häufig; **in Dickens** bei Dickens;

we have a loyal friend in him er
ist uns ein treuer Freund
7 (*indicating profession etc*) **to be in
teaching/the army** Lehrer,
Lehrerin/beim Militär sein; **to be
in publishing** im Verlagswesen
arbeiten
8 (*with present participle*) **in saying
this, I ...** wenn ich das sage, ... ich;
in accepting this view, he ... weil
er diese Meinung akzeptierte, ...
er
▷ *adv*: **to be in** (*person: at home,
work*) da sein; (*train, ship, plane*)
angekommen sein; (*in fashion*) in
sein; **to ask sb in** jdn hereinbitten;
to run/limp *etc* **in**
hereingerannt/gehumpelt *etc*
kommen
▷ *n*: **the ins and outs** (*of proposal,
situation etc*) die Feinheiten

inability [ɪnə'bɪlɪtɪ] *n* Unfähig-
keit *f*
inaccessible [ɪnæk'sesəbl] *adj*
(*a. fig*) unzugänglich
inaccurate [ɪn'ækjʊrɪt] *adj*
ungenau
inadequate [ɪn'ædɪkwət] *adj*
unzulänglich
inapplicable [ɪnə'plɪkəbl] *adj*
unzutreffend
inappropriate [ɪnə'prəuprɪət]
adj unpassend; (*clothing*)
ungeeignet; (*remark*)
unangebracht
inborn ['ɪn'bɔːn] *adj* angeboren
incapable [ɪn'keɪpəbl] *adj*
unfähig (*of* zu); **to be ~ of doing
sth** nicht imstande sein, etw zu
tun
incense ['ɪnsens] *n* Weihrauch
m
incentive [ɪn'sentɪv] *n* Anreiz *m*
incessant, incessantly [ɪn'sesnt,
-lɪ] *adj, adv* unaufhörlich
incest ['ɪnsest] *n* Inzest *m*

inch [ɪntʃ] n Zoll m (2,54 cm)
incident ['ɪnsɪdənt] n Vorfall m;
(disturbance) Zwischenfall m;
incidentally [ɪnsɪ'dentlɪ]
adv nebenbei bemerkt,
übrigens
inclination [ɪnklɪ'neɪʃən] n
Neigung f; **inclined** ['ɪnklaɪnd]
adj: **to be ~ to do sth** dazu neigen,
etw zu tun
include [ɪn'kluːd] vt einschließen; (on list, in group)
aufnehmen; **including** prep
einschließlich (+gen); **not
~ service** Bedienung nicht
inbegriffen; **inclusive** [ɪn'kluːsɪv]
adj einschließlich (of +gen); (price)
Pauschal-
incoherent [ɪnkəʊ'hɪərənt] adj
zusammenhanglos
income ['ɪnkʌm] n Einkommen
nt; (from business) Einkünfte pl;
income tax n Einkommensteuer
f; (on wages, salary) Lohnsteuer f;
incoming ['ɪnkʌmɪŋ] adj an-
kommend; (mail) eingehend
incompatible [ɪnkəm'pætəbl]
adj unvereinbar; (people)
unverträglich; (Inform) nicht
kompatibel
incompetent [ɪn'kɒmpɪtənt]
adj unfähig
incomplete [ɪnkəm'pliːt] adj
unvollständig
incomprehensible
[ɪnkɒmprɪ'hensəbl] adj
unverständlich
inconceivable [ɪnkən'siːvəbl]
adj unvorstellbar
inconsiderate [ɪnkən'sɪdərət]
adj rücksichtslos
inconsistency [ɪnkən'sɪstənsɪ]
n Inkonsequenz f; (contradictory)
Widersprüchlichkeit f;
inconsistent adj inkonsequent;
(contradictory) widersprüchlich;
(work) unbeständig

inconvenience [ɪnkən'viːnɪəns]
n Unannehmlichkeit f; (trouble)
Umstände pl; **inconvenient** adj
ungünstig, unbequem; (time) **it's
~ for me** es kommt mir
ungelegen; **if it's not too ~ for
you** wenn es dir/Ihnen passt
incorporate [ɪn'kɔːpəreɪt] vt
aufnehmen (into in +akk); (include)
enthalten
incorrect ['ɪnkərekt] adj falsch;
(improper) inkorrekt
increase ['ɪnkriːs] n Zunahme f
(in an +dat); (in amount, speed)
Erhöhung f (in +gen) ▷ [ɪn'kriːs] vt
(price, taxes, salary, speed etc)
erhöhen; (wealth) vermehren;
(number) vergrößern; (business)
erweitern ▷ vi zunehmen (in an
+dat); (prices) steigen; (in size)
größer werden; (in number) sich
vermehren; **increasingly**
[ɪn'kriːsɪŋlɪ] adv zunehmend
incredible, incredibly
[ɪn'kredəbl, -blɪ] adj, adv
unglaublich; (very good)
fantastisch
incredulous [ɪn'kredjʊləs] adj
ungläubig, skeptisch
incriminate [ɪn'krɪmɪneɪt] vt
belasten
incubator ['ɪnkjʊbeɪtə*] n
Brutkasten m
incurable [ɪn'kjʊərəbl] adj
unheilbar
indecent [ɪn'diːsnt] adj
unanständig
indecisive [ɪndɪ'saɪsɪv] adj
(person) unentschlossen; (result)
nicht entscheidend
indeed [ɪn'diːd] adv tatsächlich;
(as answer) allerdings; **very hot
~** wirklich sehr heiß
indefinite [ɪn'defɪnɪt] adj
unbestimmt; **indefinitely** adv
endlos; (postpone) auf
unbestimmte Zeit

independence [ɪndɪ'pendəns]
n Unabhängigkeit f

● **INDEPENDENCE DAY**
●
● Der **Independence Day**, der 4.
● Juli, ist in den USA ein
● gesetzlicher Feiertag zum
● Gedenken an die
● Unabhängigkeitserklärung am
● 4. Juli 1776, mit der die 13
● amerikanischen Kolonien ihre
● Freiheit und Unabhängigkeit
● von Großbritannien erklärten.

independent [ɪndɪ'pendənt]
adj unabhängig (*of* von); (*person*)
selbstständig
indescribable [ɪndɪ'skraɪbəbl]
adj unbeschreiblich
index ['ɪndeks] n Index m,
Verzeichnis nt; **index finger** n
Zeigefinger m
India ['ɪndɪə] n Indien nt; **Indian**
['ɪndɪən] *adj* indisch; (*Native
American*) indianisch ▷ n Inder(in)
m(f); (*Native American*) Indianer(in)
m(f); **Indian Ocean** n Indischer
Ozean; **Indian summer** n Spät-
sommer m, Altweibersommer m
indicate ['ɪndɪkeɪt] vt (*show*)
zeigen; (*instrument*) anzeigen;
(*suggest*) hinweisen auf +akk ▷ vi
(*Auto*) blinken; **indication**
[ɪndɪ'keɪʃn] n (*sign*) Anzeichen nt
(*of* für); **indicator** ['ɪndɪkeɪtə°] n
(*Auto*) Blinker m
indifferent [ɪn'dɪfrənt] *adj* (*not
caring*) gleichgültig (*to, towards*
gegenüber); (*mediocre*)
mittelmäßig
indigestible [ɪndɪ'dʒestəbl] *adj*
unverdaulich; **indigestion**
[ɪndɪ'dʒestʃən] n Verdau-
ungsstörung f
indignity [ɪn'dɪgnɪtɪ] n Demütigung f

indirect, indirectly [ɪndɪ'rekt, -lɪ]
adj, adv indirekt
indiscreet [ɪndɪ'skriːt] *adj*
indiskret
indispensable [ɪndɪ'spensəbl]
adj unentbehrlich
indisposed [ɪndɪ'spəʊzd] *adj*
unwohl
indisputable [ɪndɪ'spjuːtəbl]
adj unbestreitbar; (*evidence*)
unanfechtbar
individual [ɪndɪ'vɪdjʊəl] n
Einzelne(r) mf ▷ *adj* einzeln;
(*distinctive*) eigen, individuell;
~ case Einzelfall m; **individually**
adv (*separately*) einzeln
Indonesia [ɪndəʊ'niːzjə] n
Indonesien nt
indoor ['ɪndɔː°] *adj* (*shoes*)
Haus-; (*plant, games*) Zimmer-;
(*Sport: football, championship, record
etc*) Hallen-; **indoors** *adv* drinnen,
im Haus
indulge [ɪn'dʌldʒ] vi: **to ~ in sth**
sich *dat* etw gönnen; **indulgence**
n Nachsicht f; (*enjoyment*)
(übermäßiger) Genuss; (*luxury*)
Luxus m; **indulgent** *adj*
nachsichtig (*with* gegenüber)
industrial [ɪn'dʌstrɪəl] *adj*
Industrie-, industriell; **~ estate**
Industriegebiet nt; **industry**
['ɪndəstrɪ] n Industrie f
inedible [ɪn'edɪbl] *adj* nicht
essbar, ungenießbar
ineffective [ɪnɪ'fektɪv] *adj*
unwirksam, wirkungslos;
inefficient *adj* unwirksam; (*use,
machine*) unwirtschaftlich; (*method
etc*) unrationell
ineligible [ɪn'elɪdʒəbl] *adj* nicht
berechtigt (*for* zu)
inequality [ɪnɪ'kwɒlɪtɪ] n
Ungleichheit f
inevitable [ɪn'evɪtəbl] *adj*
unvermeidlich; **inevitably** *adv*
zwangsläufig

inexcusable [ɪnɪks'kjuːzəbl] adj unverzeihlich; **that's ~** das kann man nicht verzeihen

inexpensive [ɪnɪks'pensɪv] adj preisgünstig

inexperience [ɪnɪks'pɪərɪəns] n Unerfahrenheit f; **inexperienced** adj unerfahren

inexplicable [ɪnɪks'plɪkəbl] adj unerklärlich

infallible [ɪn'fæləbl] adj unfehlbar

infamous ['ɪnfəməs] adj (person) berüchtigt (for wegen); (deed) niederträchtig

infancy ['ɪnfənsɪ] n frühe Kindheit; **infant** ['ɪnfənt] n Säugling m; (small child) Kleinkind nt; **infant school** n Vorschule f

infatuated [ɪn'fætjʊeɪtɪd] adj vernarrt (with in +akk), verknallt (with in +akk)

infect [ɪn'fekt] vt (person) anstecken; (wound) infizieren; **infection** [ɪn'fekʃən] n Infektion f; **infectious** [ɪn'fekʃəs] adj ansteckend

inferior [ɪn'fɪərɪə*] adj (in quality) minderwertig; (in rank) untergeordnet; **inferiority** [ɪnfɪərɪ'ɒrɪtɪ] n Minderwertigkeit f; **~ complex** Minderwertigkeitskomplex m

infertile [ɪn'fɜːtaɪl] adj unfruchtbar

infidelity [ɪnfɪ'delɪtɪ] n Untreue f

infinite ['ɪnfɪnɪt] adj unendlich

infinitive [ɪn'fɪnɪtɪv] n (Ling) Infinitiv m

infinity [ɪn'fɪnɪtɪ] n Unendlichkeit f

infirmary [ɪn'fɜːmərɪ] n Krankenhaus nt

inflame [ɪn'fleɪm] vt (Med) entzünden; **inflammation** [ɪnflə'meɪʃən] n (Med) Entzündung f

inflatable [ɪn'fleɪtəbl] adj aufblasbar; **~ dinghy** Schlauchboot nt; **inflate** [ɪn'fleɪt] vt aufpumpen; (by blowing) aufblasen; (prices) hochtreiben

inflation [ɪn'fleɪʃən] n Inflation f

inflexible [ɪn'fleksəbl] adj unflexibel

inflict [ɪn'flɪkt] vt: **to ~ sth on sb** jdm etw zufügen; (punishment) jdm etw auferlegen; (wound) jdm etw beibringen

in-flight [ɪn'flaɪt] adj (catering, magazine) Bord-; **~ entertainment** Bordprogramm nt

influence ['ɪnflʊəns] n Einfluss m (on auf +akk) ▷ vt beeinflussen; **influential** [ɪnflʊ'enʃəl] adj einflussreich

influenza [ɪnflʊ'enzə] n Grippe f

inform [ɪn'fɔːm] vt informieren (of, about über +akk); **to keep sb ~ed** jdn auf dem Laufenden halten

informal [ɪn'fɔːməl] adj zwanglos, ungezwungen

information [ɪnfə'meɪʃən] n Auskunft f, Informationen pl; **for your ~** zu deiner/Ihrer Information; **further ~** weitere Informationen, Weiteres; **information desk** n Auskunftsschalter m; **information technology** n Informationstechnik f; **informative** [ɪn'fɔːmətɪv] adj aufschlussreich

infra-red ['ɪnfrə'red] adj infrarot

infrastructure n Infrastruktur f

infuriate [ɪn'fjʊərɪeɪt] vt wütend machen; **infuriating** adj äußerst ärgerlich

infusion [ɪn'fjuːʒən] n (herbal tea) Aufguss m; (Med) Infusion f

ingenious [ɪn'dʒiːnɪəs] *adj (person)* erfinderisch; *(device)* raffiniert; *(idea)* genial

ingredient [ɪn'griːdɪənt] *n (Gastr)* Zutat *f*

inhabit [ɪn'hæbɪt] *vt* bewohnen; **inhabitant** *n* Einwohner(in) *m(f)*

inhale [ɪn'heɪl] *vt* einatmen; *(cigarettes, Med)* inhalieren; **inhaler** *n* Inhalationsgerät *nt*

inherit [ɪn'herɪt] *vt* erben; **inheritance** *n* Erbe *nt*

inhibited [ɪn'hɪbɪtɪd] *adj* gehemmt; **inhibition** [ɪnhɪ'bɪʃən] *n* Hemmung *f*

in-house ['ɪnhaʊs] *adj* intern

inhuman [ɪn'hjuːmən] *adj* unmenschlich

initial [ɪ'nɪʃəl] *adj* anfänglich; **~ stage** Anfangsstadium *nt* ▷ *vt* mit Initialen unterschreiben; **initially** *adv* anfangs; **initials** *npl* Initialen *pl*

initiative [ɪ'nɪʃətɪv] *n* Initiative *f*

inject [ɪn'dʒekt] *vt (drug etc)* einspritzen; **to ~ sb with sth** jdm etw (ein)spritzen; **injection** *n* Spritze *f*, Injektion *f*

in-joke ['ɪndʒəʊk] *n* Insiderwitz *m*

injure ['ɪndʒə*] *vt* verletzen; **to ~ one's leg** sich *dat* das Bein verletzen; **injury** ['ɪndʒərɪ] *n* Verletzung *f*

injustice [ɪn'dʒʌstɪs] *n* Ungerechtigkeit *f*

ink [ɪŋk] *n* Tinte *f*; **ink-jet printer** *n* Tintenstrahldrucker *m*

inland ['ɪnlənd] *adj* Binnen- ▷ *adv* landeinwärts; **inland revenue** *n (Brit)* Finanzamt *nt*

in-laws ['ɪnlɔːz] *npl (fam)* Schwiegereltern *pl*

inline skates ['ɪnlaɪnskeɪts] *npl* Inlineskates *pl*, Inliner *pl*

inmate ['ɪnmeɪt] *n* Insasse *m*

inn [ɪn] *n* Gasthaus *nt*

innate [ɪ'neɪt] *adj* angeboren

inner ['ɪnə*] *adj* innere(r, s); **~ city** Innenstadt *f*

innocence ['ɪnəsns] *n* Unschuld *f*; **innocent** *adj* unschuldig

innovation [ɪnəʊ'veɪʃən] *n* Neuerung *f*

innumerable [ɪ'njuːmərəbl] *adj* unzählig

inoculate [ɪ'nɒkjʊleɪt] *vt* impfen *(against gegen)*; **inoculation** [ɪnɒkjʊ'leɪʃən] *n* Impfung *f*

in-patient ['ɪnpeɪʃənt] *n* stationärer Patient, stationäre Patientin

input ['ɪnpʊt] *n (contribution)* Beitrag *m*; *(Inform)* Eingabe *f*

inquest ['ɪnkwest] *n* gerichtliche Untersuchung (einer Todesursache)

inquire [ɪn'kwaɪə*] *see* **enquire**; **inquiry** [ɪn'kwaɪərɪ] *see* **enquiry**

insane [ɪn'seɪn] *adj* wahnsinnig; *(Med)* geisteskrank; **insanity** [ɪn'sænɪtɪ] *n* Wahnsinn *m*

insatiable [ɪn'seɪʃəbl] *adj* unersättlich

inscription [ɪn'skrɪpʃən] *n (on stone etc)* Inschrift *f*

insect ['ɪnsekt] *n* Insekt *nt*; **insecticide** [ɪn'sektɪsaɪd] *n* Insektenbekämpfungsmittel *nt*; **insect repellent** *n* Insektenschutzmittel *nt*

insecure [ɪnsɪ'kjʊə*] *adj (person)* unsicher; *(shelves)* instabil

insensitive [ɪn'sensɪtɪv] *adj* unempfindlich *(to gegen)*; *(unfeeling)* gefühllos; **insensitivity** [ɪnsensɪ'tɪvɪtɪ] *n* Unempfindlichkeit *f (to gegen)*; *(unfeeling nature)* Gefühllosigkeit *f*

inseparable [ɪn'sepərəbl] *adj* unzertrennlich

insert [ɪn'sɜːt] *vt* einfügen; *(coin)* einwerfen; *(key etc)* hineinstecken

▷ *n* (*in magazine*) Beilage *f*;
insertion *n* (*in text*) Einfügen *nt*

inside ['ɪn'saɪd] *n*: **the ~** das Innere; (*surface*) die Innenseite; **from the ~** von innen ▷ *adj* innere(r, s), Innen-; **~ lane** (*Auto*) Innenspur *f*; (*Sport*) Innenbahn *f* ▷ *adv* (*place*) innen; (*direction*) hinein; **to go ~** hineingehen ▷ *prep* (*place*) in +*dat*; (*into*) in +*akk* ... hinein; (*time, within*) innerhalb +*gen*; **inside out** *adv* verkehrt herum; (*know*) in- und auswendig; **insider** *n* Eingeweihte(r) *mf*, Insider(in) *m(f)*

insight ['ɪnsaɪt] *n* Einblick *m* (*into* in +*akk*)

insignificant [ɪnsɪg'nɪfɪkənt] *adj* unbedeutend

insincere [ɪnsɪn'sɪə°] *adj* unaufrichtig, falsch

insinuate [ɪn'sɪnjʊeɪt] *vt* andeuten; **insinuation** [ɪnsɪnjʊ'eɪʃən] *n* Andeutung *f*

insist [ɪn'sɪst] *vi* darauf bestehen; **to ~ on sth** auf etw *dat* bestehen; **insistent** *adj* hartnäckig

insoluble [ɪn'sɒljʊbl] *adj* unlösbar

insomnia [ɪn'sɒmnɪə] *n* Schlaflosigkeit *f*

inspect [ɪn'spekt] *vt* prüfen, kontrollieren; **inspection** *n* Prüfung *f*; (*check*) Kontrolle *f*; **inspector** *n* (*police ~*) Inspektor(in) *m(f)*; (*senior*) Kommissar(in) *m(f)*; (*on bus etc*) Kontrolleur(in) *m(f)*

inspiration [ɪnspɪ'reɪʃən] *n* Inspiration *f*; **inspire** [ɪn'spaɪə°] *vt* (*respect*) einflößen (*in dat*); (*person*) inspirieren

install [ɪn'stɔːl] *vt* (*software*) installieren; (*furnishings*) einbauen

installment, **instalment** [ɪn'stɔːlmənt] *n* Rate *f*; (*of story*) Folge *f*; **to pay in ~s** auf Raten

zahlen; **installment plan** *n* (*US*) Ratenkauf *m*

instance ['ɪnstəns] *n* (*of discrimination*) Fall *m*; (*example*) Beispiel *nt* (*of* für +*akk*); **for ~** zum Beispiel

instant ['ɪnstənt] *n* Augenblick *m* ▷ *adj* sofortig; **instant coffee** *n* löslicher Kaffee *m*; **instantly** *adv* sofort

instead [ɪn'sted] *adv* stattdessen; **instead of** *prep* (an)statt +*gen*; **~ of me** an meiner Stelle; **~ of going** (an)statt zu gehen

instinct ['ɪnstɪŋkt] *n* Instinkt *m*; **instinctively** [ɪn'stɪŋktɪv, -lɪ] *adj, adv* instinktiv

institute ['ɪnstɪtjuːt] *n* Institut *nt*; **institution** [ɪnstɪ'tjuːʃən] *n* (*organisation*) Institution *f*, Einrichtung *f*; (*home*) Anstalt *f*

instruct [ɪn'strʌkt] *vt* anweisen; **instruction** [ɪn'strʌkʃən] *n* (*teaching*) Unterricht *m*; (*command*) Anweisung *f*; **~s for use** Gebrauchsanweisung *f*; **instructor** *n* Lehrer(in) *m(f)*; (*US*) Dozent(in) *m(f)*

instrument ['ɪnstrʊmənt] *n* Instrument *nt*; **instrument panel** *n* Armaturenbrett *nt*

insufficient [ɪnsə'fɪʃənt] *adj* ungenügend

insulate ['ɪnsjʊleɪt] *vt* (*Elec*) isolieren; **insulating tape** *n* Isolierband *nt*; **insulation** [ɪnsjʊ'leɪʃən] *n* Isolierung *f*

insulin ['ɪnsjʊlɪn] *n* Insulin *nt*

insult ['ɪnsʌlt] *n* Beleidigung *f* ▷ [ɪn'sʌlt] *vt* beleidigen; **insulting** [ɪn'sʌltɪŋ] *adj* beleidigend

insurance [ɪn'ʃʊərəns] *n* Versicherung *f*; **~ company** Versicherungsgesellschaft *f*; **~ policy** Versicherungspolice *f*;

insure [ɪnˈʃʊəʳ] *vt* versichern (*against* gegen)

intact [ɪnˈtækt] *adj* intakt

intake [ˈɪnteɪk] *n* Aufnahme *f*

integrate [ˈɪntɪɡreɪt] *vt* integrieren (*into* in +*akk*); **integration** *n* Integration *f*

integrity [ɪnˈteɡrətɪ] *n* Integrität *f*, Ehrlichkeit *f*

intellect [ˈɪntɪlekt] *n* Intellekt *m*; **intellectual** [ɪntɪˈlektjʊəl] *adj* intellektuell; (*interests etc*) geistig

intelligence [ɪnˈtelɪdʒəns] *n* (*understanding*) Intelligenz *f*; **intelligent** *adj* intelligent

intend [ɪnˈtend] *vt* beabsichtigen; **to ~ to do sth** vorhaben, etw zu tun

intense [ɪnˈtens] *adj* intensiv; (*pressure*) enorm; (*competition*) heftig; **intensity** *n* Intensität *f*; **intensive** *adj* intensiv; **intensive care unit** *n* Intensivstation *f*; **intensive course** *n* Intensivkurs *m*

intent [ɪnˈtent] *adj*: **to be ~ on doing sth** fest entschlossen sein, etw zu tun; **intention** [ɪnˈtenʃən] *n* Absicht *f*; **intentional**, **intentionally** *adj*, *adv* absichtlich

interact [ɪntərˈækt] *vi* aufeinander einwirken; **interaction** *n* Interaktion *f*, Wechselwirkung *f*; **interactive** *adj* interaktiv

interchange [ˈɪntətʃeɪndʒ] *n* (*of motorways*) Autobahnkreuz *nt*; **interchangeable** [ɪntəˈtʃeɪndʒəbl] *adj* austauschbar

intercity [ɪntəˈsɪtɪ] *n* Intercityzug *m*, IC *m*

intercom [ˈɪntəkɒm] *n* (Gegen)sprechanlage *f*

intercourse [ˈɪntəkɔːs] *n* (*sexual*) Geschlechtsverkehr *m*

interest [ˈɪntrest] *n* Interesse *nt*; (*Fin: on money*) Zinsen *pl*; (*Comm: share*) Anteil *m*; **to be of ~** von Interesse sein (*to* für) ▷ *vt* interessieren; **interested** *adj* interessiert (*in* an +*dat*); **to be ~ed in** sich interessieren für; **are you ~ in coming?** hast du Lust, mitzukommen?; **interest-free** *adj* zinsfrei; **interesting** *adj* interessant; **interest rate** *n* Zinssatz *m*

interface [ˈɪntəfeɪs] *n* (*Inform*) Schnittstelle *f*

interfere [ɪntəˈfɪəʳ] *vi* (*meddle*) sich einmischen (*with*, in in +*akk*); **interference** *n* Einmischung *f*; (*TV, Radio*) Störung *f*

interior [ɪnˈtɪərɪəʳ] *adj* Innen- ▷ *n* Innere(s) *nt*; (*of car*) Innenraum *m*; (*of house*) Innenausstattung *f*

intermediate [ɪntəˈmiːdɪət] *adj* Zwischen-; **~ stage** Zwischenstadium *nt*

intermission [ɪntəˈmɪʃən] *n* Pause *f*

intern [ɪnˈtɜːn] *n* Assistent(in) *m(f)*

internal [ɪnˈtɜːnl] *adj* innere(r, s); (*flight*) Inlands-; **~ revenue** (*US*) Finanzamt *nt*; **internally** *adv* innen; (*in body*) innerlich

international [ɪntəˈnæʃnəl] *adj* international; **~ match** Länderspiel *nt*; **~ flight** Auslandsflug *m* ▷ *n* (*Sport: player*) Nationalspieler(in) *m(f)*

Internet [ˈɪntənet] *n* (*Inform*) Internet *nt*; **Internet access** *n* Internetzugang *m*; **Internet auction** *n* Internetauktion *f*; **Internet banking** *n* Onlinebanking *nt*; **Internet café** *n* Internetcafé *nt*; **Internet connection** *n* Internetanschluss *m*; **Internet provider** *n* Internetprovider *m*

interpret [ɪnˈtɜːprɪt] *vi, vt*

(*translate*) dolmetschen; (*explain*) interpretieren; **interpretation** [ɪntɜ:prɪˈteɪʃən] *n* Interpretation *f*; **interpreter** [ɪnˈtɜ:prɪtə°] *n* Dolmetscher(in) *m(f)*

interrogate [ɪnˈterəgeɪt] *vt* verhören; **interrogation** *n* Verhör *nt*

interrupt [ɪntəˈrʌpt] *vt* unterbrechen; **interruption** [ɪntəˈrʌpʃən] *n* Unterbrechung *f*

intersection [ɪntəˈsekʃən] *n* (*of roads*) Kreuzung *f*

interstate [ɪntəˈsteɪt] *n* (US) zwischenstaatlich; **~ highway** ≈ Bundesautobahn *f*

interval [ˈɪntəvəl] *n* (*space, time*) Abstand *m*; (*theatre etc*) Pause *f*

intervene [ɪntəˈviːn] *vi* eingreifen (*in* in); **intervention** [ɪntəˈvenʃən] *n* Eingreifen *nt*; (*Pol*) Intervention *f*

interview [ˈɪntəvjuː] *n* Interview *nt*; (*for job*) Vorstellungsgespräch *nt* ▷ *vt* interviewen; (*job applicant*) ein Vorstellungsgespräch führen mit; **interviewer** *n* Interviewer(in) *m(f)*

intestine [ɪnˈtestɪn] *n* Darm *m*; **~s** *pl* Eingeweide *pl*

intimate [ˈɪntɪmət] *adj* (*friends*) vertraut, eng; (*atmosphere*) gemütlich; (*sexually*) intim

intimidate [ɪnˈtɪmɪdeɪt] *vt* einschüchtern; **intimidation** *n* Einschüchterung *f*

into [ˈɪntʊ] *prep* in +*akk*; (*crash*) gegen; **to change ~ sth** (*turn ~*) zu etw werden; (*put on*) sich *dat* etw anziehen; **to translate ~ French** ins Französische übersetzen; **to be ~ sth** (*fam*) auf etw *akk* stehen

intolerable [ɪnˈtɒlərəbl] *adj* unerträglich

intolerant [ɪnˈtɒlərənt] *adj* intolerant

intoxicated [ɪnˈtɒksɪkeɪtɪd] *adj* betrunken; (*fig*) berauscht

intricate [ˈɪntrɪkət] *adj* kompliziert

intrigue [ɪnˈtriːg] *vt* faszinieren; **intriguing** *adj* faszinierend, fesselnd

introduce [ɪntrəˈdjuːs] *vt* (*person*) vorstellen (*to sb* jdm); (*sth new*) einführen (*to* in +*akk*); **introduction** [ɪntrəˈdʌkʃən] *n* Einführung *f* (*to* in +*akk*); (*to book*) Einleitung *f* (*to* zu); (*to person*) Vorstellung *f*

introvert [ˈɪntrəʊvɜːt] *n* Introvertierte(r) *mf*

intuition [ɪntjuːˈɪʃn] *n* Intuition *f*

invade [ɪnˈveɪd] *vt* einfallen in +*akk*

invalid [ˈɪnvəlɪd] *n* Kranke(r) *mf*; (*disabled*) Invalide *m* ▷ *adj* [ɪnˈvælɪd] (*not valid*) ungültig

invaluable [ɪnˈvæljʊəbl] *adj* äußerst wertvoll, unschätzbar

invariably [ɪnˈvɛərɪəblɪ] *adv* ständig; (*every time*) jedes Mal, ohne Ausnahme

invasion [ɪnˈveɪʒən] *n* Invasion *f* (*of* in +*akk*), Einfall *m* (*of* in +*akk*)

invent [ɪnˈvent] *vt* erfinden; **invention** [ɪnˈvenʃən] *n* Erfindung *f*; **inventor** *n* Erfinder(in) *m(f)*

inverted commas [ɪnˈvɜːtɪd ˈkɒməz] *npl* Anführungszeichen *pl*

invest [ɪnˈvest] *vt, vi* investieren (*in* in +*akk*)

investigate [ɪnˈvestɪgeɪt] *vt* untersuchen; **investigation** [ɪnvestɪˈgeɪʃən] *n* Untersuchung *f* (*into* +*gen*)

investment [ɪnˈvestmənt] *n* Investition *f*; **it's a good ~** es ist eine gute Anlage; (*it'll be useful*) es macht sich bezahlt

invigorating [ɪn'vɪgəreɪtɪŋ] *adj* erfrischend, belebend; (*tonic*) stärkend

invisible [ɪn'vɪzəbl] *adj* unsichtbar

invitation [ɪnvɪ'teɪʃən] *n* Einladung *f*; **invite** [ɪn'vaɪt] *vt* einladen

invoice ['ɪnvɔɪs] *n* (*bill*) Rechnung *f*

involuntary [ɪn'vɒləntərɪ] *adj* unbeabsichtigt

involve [ɪn'vɒlv] *vt* verwickeln (*in sth* in etw *akk*); (*entail*) zur Folge haben; **to be ~d in sth** (*participate in*) an etw *dat* beteiligt sein; **I'm not ~d** (*affected*) ich bin nicht betroffen

inward ['ɪnwəd] *adj* innere(r, s); **inwardly** *adv* innerlich; **inwards** *adv* nach innen

iodine ['aɪədiːn] *n* Jod *nt*

IOU [aɪəʊ'juː] *abbr* = **I owe you** Schuldschein *m*

iPod® ['aɪpɒd] *n* iPod® *m*

IQ *abbr* = **intelligence quotient** IQ *m*

Iran [ɪ'rɑːn] *n* der Iran

Iraq [ɪ'rɑːk] *n* der Irak

Ireland ['aɪələnd] *n* Irland *nt*

iris ['aɪrɪs] *n* (*flower*) Schwertlilie *f*; (*of eye*) Iris *f*

Irish ['aɪrɪʃ] *adj* irisch; **~ coffee** Irish Coffee *m*; **~ Sea** die Irische See ▷ *n* (*language*) Irisch *nt*; **the ~** *pl* die Iren *pl*; **Irishman** (*pl* -**men**) *n* Ire *m*; **Irishwoman** (*pl* -**women**) *n* Irin *f*

iron ['aɪən] *n* Eisen *nt*; (*for ironing*) Bügeleisen *nt* ▷ *adj* eisern ▷ *vt* bügeln

ironic(al) [aɪ'rɒnɪk(əl)] *adj* ironisch

ironing board *n* Bügelbrett *nt*

irony ['aɪrənɪ] *n* Ironie *f*

irrational [ɪ'ræʃənl] *adj* irrational

irregular [ɪ'regjʊlə°] *adj* unregelmäßig; (*shape*) ungleichmäßig

irrelevant [ɪ'reləvənt] *adj* belanglos, irrelevant

irreplaceable [ɪrɪ'pleɪsəbl] *adj* unersetzlich

irresistible [ɪrɪ'zɪstəbl] *adj* unwiderstehlich

irrespective of [ɪrɪ'spektɪv ɒv] *prep* ungeachtet +*gen*

irresponsible [ɪrɪ'spɒnsəbl] *adj* verantwortungslos

irretrievable [ɪrɪ'triːvəbl] *adv* unwiederbringlich; (*loss*) unersetzlich

irritable ['ɪrɪtəbl] *adj* reizbar; **irritate** ['ɪrɪteɪt] *vt* (*annoy*) ärgern; (*deliberately*) reizen; **irritation** [ɪrɪ'teɪʃən] *n* (*anger*) Ärger *m*; (*Med*) Reizung *f*

IRS *abbr* = **Internal Revenue Service** (*US*) Finanzamt *nt*

is [ɪz] *present of* **be** ist

Islam ['ɪzlɑːm] *n* Islam *m*; **Islamic** [ɪz'læmɪk] *adj* islamisch

island ['aɪlənd] *n* Insel *f*; **Isle** [aɪl] *n* (*in names*) **the ~ of Man** die Insel Man; **the ~ of Wight** die Insel Wight; **the British ~s** die Britischen Inseln

isn't ['ɪznt] *contr of* **is not**

isolate ['aɪsəleɪt] *vt* isolieren; **isolated** *adj* (*remote*) abgelegen; (*cut off*) abgeschnitten (*from von*); **an ~ case** ein Einzelfall; **isolation** [aɪsə'leɪʃən] *n* Isolierung *f*

Israel ['ɪzreɪl] *n* Israel *nt*; **Israeli** [ɪz'reɪlɪ] *adj* israelisch ▷ *n* Israeli *m of*

issue ['ɪʃuː] *n* (*matter*) Frage *f*; (*problem*) Problem *nt*; (*subject*) Thema *nt*; (*of newspaper etc*) Ausgabe *f*; **that's not the ~** darum geht es nicht ▷ *vt* ausgeben; (*document*) ausstellen; (*orders*) erteilen; (*book*) herausgeben

◆ KEYWORD

it [ɪt] *pron* **1** (*specific: subject*)
er/sie/es; (*direct object*) ihn/sie/es;
(*indirect object*) ihm/ihr/ihm;
about/from/in/of it
darüber/davon/darin/davon
2 (*impers*) es; **it's raining** es regnet;
it's Friday tomorrow morgen ist
Freitag; **who is it? — it's me** wer ist
da? — ich (bin's)

IT *abbr* = **information technology**
IT *f*

Italian [ɪ'tæljən] *adj* italienisch
▷ *n* Italiener(in) *m(f)*; (*language*)
Italienisch *nt*

italic [ɪ'tælɪk] *adj* kursiv ▷ *npl*: **in
~s** kursiv

Italy ['ɪtəlɪ] *n* Italien *nt*

itch [ɪtʃ] *n* Juckreiz *m*; **I have an
~** mich juckt es ▷ *vi* jucken; **he is
~ing to ...** es juckt ihn, zu ...; **itchy**
adj juckend

it'd ['ɪtd] *contr of* **it would; it had**

item ['aɪtəm] *n* (*article*)
Gegenstand *m*; (*in catalogue*)
Artikel *m*; (*on list, in accounts*)
Posten *m*; (*on agenda*) Punkt *m*; (*in
show programme*) Nummer *f*; (*in
news*) Bericht *m*; (*TV, radio*)
Meldung *f*

itinerary [aɪ'tɪnərərɪ] *n* Reiseroute *f*

it'll ['ɪtl] *contr of* **it will; it shall**

its [ɪts] *pron* sein; (*feminine form*)
ihr

it's [ɪts] *contr of* **it is; it has**

itself [ɪt'self] *pron* (*reflexive*) sich;
(*emphatic*) **the house ~** das Haus
selbst *o* an sich; **by ~** allein; **the
door closes (by) ~** die Tür schließt
sich von selbst

I've [aɪv] *contr of* **I have**

ivory ['aɪvərɪ] *n* Elfenbein *nt*

ivy ['aɪvɪ] *n* Efeu *m*

jab [dʒæb] *vt* (*needle, knife*)
stechen (*into* in +akk) ▷ *n* (*fam*)
Spritze *f*

jack [dʒæk] *n* (*Auto*) Wagenheber
m; (*Cards*) Bube *m*; **jack in** *vt* (*fam*)
aufgeben, hinschmeißen; **jack up**
vt (*car etc*) aufbocken

jacket ['dʒækɪt] *n* Jacke *f*; (*of
man's suit*) Jackett *nt*; (*of book*)
Schutzumschlag *m*; **jacket potato**
(*pl* **-es**) *n* (in der Schale)
gebackene Kartoffel

jack-knife ['dʒæknaɪf] (*pl*
jack-knives) *n* Klappmesser *nt*
▷ *vi* (*truck*) sich quer stellen

jackpot ['dʒækpɒt] *n* Jackpot *m*

jacuzzi® [dʒə'kuːzɪ] *n* (*bath*)
Whirlpool® *m*

jail [dʒeɪl] *n* Gefängnis *nt* ▷ *vt*
einsperren

jam [dʒæm] *n* Konfitüre *f*,
Marmelade *f*; (*traffic ~*) Stau *m* ▷ *vt*
(*street*) verstopfen; (*machine*)

blockieren; **to be ~med** (*stuck*) klemmen; **to ~ on the brakes** eine Vollbremsung machen

Jamaica [dʒə'meɪkə] n Jamaika nt

jam-packed adj proppenvoll

janitor ['dʒænɪtə*] n (US) Hausmeister(in) m(f)

Jan abbr = **January** Jan

January ['dʒænjʊərɪ] n Januar m

Japan [dʒə'pæn] n Japan nt; **Japanese** [dʒæpə'niːz] adj japanisch ▷ n (person) Japaner(in) m(f); (language) Japanisch nt

jar [dʒɑː*] n Glas nt

jaundice ['dʒɔːndɪs] n Gelbsucht f

javelin ['dʒævlɪn] n Speer m; (Sport) Speerwerfen nt

jaw [dʒɔː] n Kiefer m

jazz [dʒæz] n Jazz m

jealous ['dʒeləs] adj eifersüchtig (of auf +akk); **don't make me ~** mach mich nicht neidisch; **jealousy** n Eifersucht f

jeans [dʒiːnz] npl Jeans pl

jeep® [dʒiːp] n Jeep® m

jelly ['dʒelɪ] n Gelee nt; (on meat) Gallert nt; (dessert) Götterspeise f; (US: jam) Marmelade f; **jelly baby** n (sweet) Gummibärchen nt; **jellyfish** n Qualle f

jeopardize ['dʒepədaɪz] vt gefährden

jerk [dʒɜːk] n Ruck m; (fam: idiot) Trottel m ▷ vt ruckartig bewegen ▷ vi (rope) rucken; (muscles) zucken

Jerusalem [dʒə'ruːsələm] n Jerusalem nt

jet [dʒet] n (of water etc) Strahl m; (nozzle) Düse f; (aircraft) Düsenflugzeug nt; **jet foil** n Tragflächenboot nt; **jetlag** n Jetlag m (Müdigkeit nach langem Flug)

Jew [dʒuː] n Jude m, Jüdin f

jewel ['dʒuːəl] n Edelstein m; (esp fig) Juwel nt; **jeweller**, **jeweler** (US) n Juwelier(in) m(f); **jewellery**, **jewelry** (US) n Schmuck m

Jewish ['dʒuːɪʃ] adj jüdisch; **she's ~** sie ist Jüdin

jigsaw (puzzle) ['dʒɪgsɔː(pʌzl)] n Puzzle nt

jilt [dʒɪlt] vt den Laufpass geben +dat

jingle ['dʒɪŋgl] n (advert) Jingle m; (verse) Reim m

jitters ['dʒɪtərz] npl (fam) **to have the ~** Bammel haben; **jittery** adj (fam) ganz nervös

job [dʒɒb] n (piece of work) Arbeit f; (task) Aufgabe f; (occupation) Stellung f, Job m; **what's your ~?** was machen Sie beruflich?; **it's a good ~ you did that** gut, dass du das gemacht hast; **jobcentre** n Arbeitsvermittlungsstelle f, Arbeitsamt nt; **job-hunting** n: **to go ~** auf Arbeitssuche gehen; **jobless** adj arbeitslos; **job seeker** n Arbeitssuchende(r) mf; **jobseeker's allowance** n Arbeitslosengeld nt; **job-sharing** n Arbeitsplatzteilung f

jockey ['dʒɒkɪ] n Jockey m

jog [dʒɒg] vt (person) anstoßen ▷ vi (run) joggen; **jogging** n Jogging nt; **to go ~** joggen gehen

john [dʒɒn] n (US fam) Klo nt

join [dʒɔɪn] vt (put together) verbinden (to mit); (club etc) beitreten +dat; (sit with) sich zu jdm setzen ▷ vi (unite) sich vereinigen; (rivers) zusammenfließen ▷ n Verbindungsstelle f; (seam) Naht f; **join in** vi, vt mitmachen (sth bei etw)

joint [dʒɔɪnt] n (of bones) Gelenk nt; (in pipe etc) Verbindungsstelle f; (of meat) Braten m; (of marijuana)

Joint m ▷ adj gemeinsam; **joint account** n Gemeinschaftskonto nt; **jointly** adv gemeinsam

joke [dʒəʊk] n Witz m; (prank) Streich m; **for a ~** zum Spaß; **it's no ~** das ist nicht zum Lachen ▷ vi Witze machen; **you must be joking** das ist ja wohl nicht dein Ernst!

jolly ['dʒɒlɪ] adj lustig, vergnügt

Jordan ['dʒɔːdən] n (country) Jordanien nt; (river) Jordan m

jot down [dʒɒt daʊn] vt sich notieren; **jotter** n Notizbuch nt

journal ['dʒɜːnl] n (diary) Tagebuch nt; (magazine) Zeitschrift f; **journalism** n Journalismus m; **journalist** n Journalist(in) m(f)

journey ['dʒɜːnɪ] n Reise f; (esp on stage, by car, train) Fahrt f

joy [dʒɔɪ] n Freude f (at über +akk); **joystick** n (Inform) Joystick m; (Aviat) Steuerknüppel m

judge [dʒʌdʒ] n Richter(in) m(f); (Sport) Punktrichter(in) m(f) ▷ vt beurteilen (by nach); **as far as I can ~** meinem Urteil nach ▷ vi urteilen (by nach); **judg(e)ment** n (Jur) Urteil nt; (opinion) Ansicht f; **an error of ~** Fehleinschätzung f

judo ['dʒuːdəʊ] n Judo nt

jug [dʒʌg] n Krug m

juggle ['dʒʌgl] vi (lit, fig) jonglieren (with mit)

juice [dʒuːs] n Saft m; **juicy** adj saftig; (story, scandal) pikant

July [dʒuːˈlaɪ] n Juli m; see also **September**

jumble ['dʒʌmbl] n Durcheinander nt ▷ vt: **to ~ (up)** durcheinanderwerfen; (facts) durcheinanderbringen; **jumble sale** n (for charity) Flohmarkt m; Wohltätigkeitsbasar m

jumbo ['dʒʌmbəʊ] adj (sausage etc) Riesen-; **jumbo jet** n Jumbojet m

jump [dʒʌmp] vi springen; (nervously) zusammenzucken; **to ~ to conclusions** voreilige Schlüsse ziehen; **to ~ from one thing to another** dauernd das Thema wechseln ▷ vt (a. fig: omit) überspringen; **to ~ the lights** bei Rot über die Kreuzung fahren; **to ~ the queue** sich vordrängen ▷ n Sprung m; (for horses) Hindernis nt; **jumper** n Pullover m; (US: dress) Trägerkleid nt; (person, horse) Springer(in) m(f); **jumper cable** n (US), **jump lead** n (Brit Auto) Starthilfekabel nt

junction ['dʒʌŋkʃən] n (of roads) Kreuzung f; (Rail) Knotenpunkt m

June [dʒuːn] n Juni m; see also **September**

jungle ['dʒʌŋgl] n Dschungel m

junior ['dʒuːnɪə°] adj (younger) jünger; (lower position) untergeordnet (to sb jdm) ▷ n: **she's two years my ~** sie ist zwei Jahre jünger als ich; **junior high (school)** n (US) ≈ Mittelschule f; **junior school** n (Brit) Grundschule f

junk [dʒʌŋk] n (trash) Plunder m; **junk food** n Nahrungsmittel pl mit geringem Nährwert, Junkfood nt; **junkie** n (fam) Junkie m, Fixer(in) m(f); (fig: fan) Freak m; **junk mail** n Reklame f; (Inform) Junkmail f; **junk shop** n Trödelladen m

jury ['dʒʊərɪ] n Geschworene pl; (in competition) Jury f

just [dʒʌst] adj gerecht ▷ adv (recently) gerade; (exactly) genau; **~ as expected** genau wie erwartet; **~ as nice** genauso nett; (barely) **~ in time** gerade noch rechtzeitig; (immediately) **~ before/after …** gleich vor/nach …; (small distance) **~ round the corner** gleich um die Ecke; (a little)

~ over an hour etwas mehr als eine Stunde; (*only*) **~ the two of us** nur wir beide; **~ a moment** Moment mal; (*absolutely, simply*) **it was ~ fantastic** es war einfach klasse; **~ about** so etwa; (*more or less*) mehr oder weniger; **~ about ready** fast fertig

justice [ˈdʒʌstɪs] *n* Gerechtigkeit *f*; **justifiable** [dʒʌstɪˈfaɪəbl] *adj* berechtigt; **justifiably** *adv* zu Recht; **justify** [ˈdʒʌstɪfaɪ] *vt* rechtfertigen

jut [dʒʌt] *vi*: **to ~ (out)** herausragen

juvenile [ˈdʒuːvənaɪl] *n adj* Jugend-, jugendlich ▷ *n* Jugendliche(r) *mf*

k

k *abbr* = **thousand**; **15k** 15 000

K *abbr* = **kilobyte** KB

kangaroo [kæŋgəˈruː] *n* Känguru *nt*

karaoke [kærɪˈəʊkɪ] *n* Karaoke *nt*

karate [kəˈrɑːtɪ] *n* Karate *nt*

kart [kɑːt] *n* Gokart *m*

kayak [ˈkaɪæk] *n* Kajak *m o nt*; **kayaking** [ˈkaɪækɪŋ] *n* Kajak-fahren *nt*

Kazakhstan [kæzækˈstɑːn] *n* Kasachstan *nt*

kebab [kəˈbæb] *n* (*shish ~*) Schaschlik *nt o m*; (*doner ~*) Kebab *m*

keel [kiːl] *n* (*Naut*) Kiel *m*; **keel over** *vi* (*boat*) kentern; (*person*) umkippen

keen [kiːn] *adj* begeistert (**on** von); (*hardworking*) eifrig; (*mind, wind*) scharf; (*interest, feeling*) stark; **to be ~ on sb** von jdm angetan sein; **she's ~ on riding** sie reitet

gern; **to be ~ to do sth** darauf erpicht sein, etw zu tun
keep [kiːp] (**kept, kept**) vt (retain) behalten; (secret) für sich behalten; (observe) einhalten; (promise) halten; (run: shop, diary, accounts) führen; (animals) halten; (support, family etc) unterhalten, versorgen; (store) aufbewahren; **to ~ sb waiting** jdn warten lassen; **to ~ sb from doing sth** jdn davon abhalten, etw zu tun; **to ~ sth clean/secret** etw sauber/geheim halten; **"~ clear"** „(bitte) frei halten"; **~ this to yourself** behalten Sie das für sich ▷ vi (food) sich halten; (remain, with adj) bleiben; **~ quiet** sei ruhig!; **~ left** links fahren; **to ~ doing sth** (repeatedly) etw immer wieder tun; **~ at it** mach weiter so!; **it ~s happening** es passiert immer wieder ▷ n (livelihood) Unterhalt m; **keep back** vi zurückbleiben ▷ vt zurückhalten; (information) verschweigen (from sb jdm); **keep off** vt (person, animal) fernhalten; **"~ off the grass"** „Betreten des Rasens verboten"; **keep on** vi weitermachen; (walking) weitergehen; (in car) weiterfahren; **to ~ doing sth** (persistently) etw immer wieder tun ▷ vt (coat etc) anbehalten; **keep out** vt nicht hereinlassen ▷ vi draußen bleiben; **~** (on sign) Eintritt verboten; **keep to** vt (road, path) bleiben auf +dat; (plan etc) sich halten an +akk; **to ~ the point** bei der Sache bleiben; **keep up** vi Schritt halten (with mit) ▷ vt (maintain) aufrechterhalten; (speed) halten; **to ~ appearances** den Schein wahren; **keep it up!** (fam) weiter so!
keeper n (museum etc) Aufseher(in) m(f); (goal~) Torwart

m; (zoo ~) Tierpfleger(in) m(f); **keep-fit** n Fitnesstraining nt; **~ exercises** Gymnastik f
kennel ['kenl] n Hundehütte f; **kennels** n Hundepension f
Kenya ['kenjə] n Kenia nt
kept [kept] pt, pp of **keep**
kerb ['kɜːb] n Randstein m
kerosene ['kerəsiːn] n (US) Petroleum nt
ketchup ['ketʃʌp] n Ketchup nt o m
kettle ['ketl] n Kessel m
key [kiː] n Schlüssel m; (of piano, computer) Taste f; (Mus) Tonart f; (for map etc) Zeichenerklärung f ▷ vt: **to ~ (in)** (Inform) eingeben ▷ adj entscheidend; **keyboard** n (piano, computer) Tastatur f; **keyhole** n Schlüsselloch nt; **keypad** n (Inform) Nummernblock m; **keyring** n Schlüsselring m
kick [kɪk] n Tritt m; (Sport) Stoß m; **I get a ~ out of it** (fam) es turnt mich an ▷ vt, vi treten; **kick out** vt (fam) rausschmeißen (of aus); **kick-off** n (Sport) Anstoß m
kid [kɪd] n (child) Kind nt ▷ vt (tease) auf den Arm nehmen ▷ vi Witze machen; **you're ~ding** das ist doch nicht dein Ernst!; **no ~ding** aber echt!
kidnap ['kɪdnæp] vt entführen; **kidnapper** n Entführer(in) m(f); **kidnapping** n Entführung f
kidney ['kɪdnɪ] n Niere f; **kidney machine** n künstliche Niere
kill [kɪl] vt töten; (esp intentionally) umbringen; (weeds) vernichten; **killer** n Mörder(in) m(f)
kilo ['kiːləʊ] (pl -s) n Kilo nt; **kilobyte** n Kilobyte nt; **kilogramme** n Kilogramm nt; **kilometer** (US), **kilometre** n Kilometer m; **~s per hour**

Stundenkilometer pl; **kilowatt** n Kilowatt nt

kilt [kɪlt] n Schottenrock m

kind [kaɪnd] adj nett, freundlich (to zu) ▷ n Art f; (of coffee, cheese etc) Sorte f; **what ~ of ...?** was für ein(e) ...?; **this ~ of ...** so ein(e) ...; **~ of** (+ adj) irgendwie

kindergarten ['kɪndəgɑːtn] n Kindergarten m

kindly ['kaɪndlɪ] adj nett, freundlich ▷ adv liebenswürdigerweise; **kindness** ['kaɪndnəs] n Freundlichkeit f

king [kɪŋ] n König m; **kingdom** n Königreich nt; **kingfisher** n Eisvogel m; **king-size** adj im Großformat; (bed) extra groß

kipper ['kɪpə°] n Räucherhering m

kiss [kɪs] n Kuss m; **~ of life** Mund-zu-Mund-Beatmung f ▷ vt küssen

kit [kɪt] n (equipment) Ausrüstung f; (fam) Sachen pl; (sports ~) Sportsachen pl; (belongings, clothes) Sachen pl; (for building sth) Bausatz m

kitchen ['kɪtʃɪn] n Küche f; **kitchen foil** n Alufolie f; **kitchen scales** n Küchenwaage f; **kitchen unit** n Küchenschrank m; **kitchenware** n Küchengeschirr nt

kite [kaɪt] n Drachen m

kitten ['kɪtn] n Kätzchen nt

kiwi ['kiːwiː] n (fruit) Kiwi f

km abbr = **kilometres** km

knack [næk] n Dreh m, Trick m; **to get/have got the ~** den Dreh herauskriegen/heraushaben; **knackered** ['nækəd] adj (Brit fam) fix und fertig, kaputt

knee [niː] n Knie nt; **kneecap** n Kniescheibe f; **knee-jerk** adj (reaction) reflexartig; **kneel** [niːl] (**knelt** o **kneeled, knelt** o **kneeled**) vi knien; (action, ~ down) sich hinknien

knelt [nelt] pt, pp of **kneel**

knew [njuː] pt of **know**

knickers ['nɪkəz] npl (Brit fam) Schlüpfer m

knife [naɪf] (pl **knives**) n Messer nt

knight [naɪt] n Ritter m; (in chess) Pferd nt, Springer m

knit [nɪt] vt, vi stricken; **knitting** n (piece of work) Strickarbeit f; (activity) Stricken nt; **knitting needle** n Stricknadel f; **knitwear** n Strickwaren pl

knob [nɒb] n (on door) Knauf m; (on radio etc) Knopf m

knock [nɒk] vt (with hammer etc) schlagen; (accidentally) stoßen; **to ~ one's head** sich dat den Kopf anschlagen ▷ vi klopfen (on, at an +akk) ▷ n (blow) Schlag m; (on door) Klopfen nt; **there was a ~ (at the door)** es hat geklopft; **knock down** vt (object) umstoßen; (person) niederschlagen; (with car) anfahren; (building) abreißen; **knock out** vt (stun) bewusstlos schlagen; (boxer) k.o. schlagen; **knock over** vt umstoßen; (with car) anfahren; **knocker** n Türklopfer m; **knockout** n Knockout m, K.o. m

knot [nɒt] n Knoten m

know [nəʊ] (**knew, known**) vt, vi wissen; (be acquainted with: people, places) kennen; (recognize) erkennen; (language) können; **I'll let you ~** ich sage dir Bescheid; **I ~ some French** ich kann etwas Französisch; **to get to ~ sb** jdn kennenlernen; **to be ~n as** bekannt sein als; **know about** vt Bescheid wissen über +akk; (subject) sich auskennen in +dat; (cars, horses etc) sich auskennen mit; **know of** vt kennen; **not that**

I ~ nicht dass ich wüsste;
know-all n (fam) Klugscheißer m;
know-how n Kenntnis f,
Know-how nt; **knowing** adj
wissend; (look, smile) vielsagend;
knowledge ['nɒlɪdʒ] n Wissen
nt; (of a subject) Kenntnisse pl; **to
(the best of) my ~** meines
Wissens
known [nəʊn] pp of **know**
knuckle ['nʌkl] n (Finger)knöchel m; (Gastr) Hachse f;
knuckle down vi sich an die
Arbeit machen
Koran [kɒˈrɑːn] n Koran m
Korea [kəˈrɪə] n Korea nt
Kosovo ['kɒsɒvəʊ] n der Kosovo
kph abbr = **kilometres per hour**
km/h
Kremlin ['kremlɪn] n: **the ~** der
Kreml
Kurd [kɛːd] n Kurde m, Kurdin f;
Kurdish adj kurdisch
Kuwait [kʊˈweɪt] n Kuwait nt

L abbr (Brit Auto) = **learner**
LA abbr = **Los Angeles**
lab [læb] n (fam) Labor nt
label ['leɪbl] n Etikett nt; (tied)
Anhänger m; (adhesive) Aufkleber
m; (record ~) Label nt ▷ vt
etikettieren; (pej) abstempeln
laboratory [ləˈbɒrətərɪ] n Labor
nt

● LABOR DAY
●
● Der **Labor Day** ist in den USA
● und Kanada der Name für den
● Tag der Arbeit. Er wird dort als
● gesetzlicher Feiertag am ersten
● Montag im September
● begangen.

laborious [ləˈbɔːrɪəs] adj
mühsam; **labor** (US), **labour**
['leɪbə°] n Arbeit f; (Med) Wehen
pl; **to be in ~** Wehen haben ▷ adj

(*Pol*) Labour-; **~ Party** Labour Party f; **labor union** n (*US*) Gewerkschaft f; **labourer** n Arbeiter(in) m(f)

lace [leɪs] n (*fabric*) Spitze f; (*of shoe*) Schnürsenkel m ▷ vt: **to ~ (up)** zuschnüren; **lace-up** n Schnürschuh m

lack [læk] vt, vi: **to be ~ing** fehlen; **sb ~s o is ~ing sth** es fehlt jdm an etw dat; **we ~ the time** uns fehlt die Zeit ▷ n Mangel m (*of* an +dat)

lacquer ['lækə°] n Lack m; (*Brit: hair ~*) Haarspray nt

lad [læd] n Junge m

ladder ['lædə°] n Leiter f; (*in tight*) Laufmasche f

laddish ['lædɪʃ] adj (*Brit*) machohaft

laden ['leɪdn] adj beladen (*with* mit)

ladies ['leɪdɪz], **ladies' room** n Damentoilette f

lad mag n Männerzeitschrift f

lady ['leɪdɪ] n Dame f; (*as title*) Lady f; **ladybird**, **ladybug** (*US*) n Marienkäfer m; **Ladyshave®** n Epiliergerät nt

lag [læg] vi: **to ~ (behind)** zurückliegen ▷ vt (*pipes*) isolieren

lager ['lɑːgə°] n helles Bier; **~ lout** betrunkener Rowdy

lagging ['lægɪŋ] n Isolierung f

laid [leɪd] pt, pp of **lay**; **laid-back** adj (*fam*) cool, gelassen

lain [leɪn] pp of **lie**

lake [leɪk] n See m; **the Lake District** Seengebiet im Nordwesten Englands

lamb [læm] n Lamm nt; (*meat*) Lammfleisch nt; **lamb chop** n Lammkotelett nt

lame [leɪm] adj lahm; (*excuse*) faul; (*argument*) schwach

lament [lə'ment] n Klage f ▷ vt beklagen

laminated ['læmɪneɪtɪd] adj beschichtet

lamp [læmp] n Lampe f; (*in street*) Laterne f; (*in car*) Licht nt, Scheinwerfer m; **lamppost** n Laternenpfahl m; **lampshade** n Lampenschirm m

land [lænd] n Land nt ▷ vi (*from ship*) an Land gehen; (*Aviat*) landen ▷ vt (*passengers*) absetzen; (*goods*) abladen; (*plane*) landen; **landing** n Landung f; (*on stairs*) Treppenabsatz m; **landing stage** n Landesteg m; **landing strip** n Landebahn f

landlady n Hauswirtin f, Vermieterin f; **landlord** n (*of house*) Hauswirt m, Vermieter m; (*of pub*) Gastwirt m; **landmark** n Wahrzeichen nt; (*event*) Meilenstein m; **landowner** n Grundbesitzer(in) m(f); **landscape** n Landschaft f; (*format*) Querformat nt; **landslide** n (*Geo*) Erdrutsch m

lane [leɪn] n (*in country*) enge Landstraße, Weg m; (*in town*) Gasse f; (*of motorway*) Spur f; (*Sport*) Bahn f; **to get in ~** (*in car*) sich einordnen

language ['læŋgwɪdʒ] n Sprache f; (*style*) Ausdrucksweise f

lantern ['læntən] n Laterne f

lap [læp] n Schoß m; (*in race*) Runde f ▷ vt (*in race*) überholen

lapse [læps] n (*mistake*) Irrtum m; (*moral*) Fehltritt m ▷ vi ablaufen

laptop ['læptɒp] n Laptop m

large [lɑːdʒ] adj groß; **by and ~** im Großen und Ganzen; **largely** adv zum größten Teil; **large-scale** adj groß angelegt, Groß-

lark [lɑːk] n (*bird*) Lerche f

laryngitis [lærɪn'dʒaɪtɪs] n Kehlkopfentzündung f; **larynx** ['lærɪŋks] n Kehlkopf m

laser ['leɪzə°] n Laser m; **laser printer** n Laserdrucker m

lash [læʃ] *vt* peitschen; **lash out**
vi (*with fists*) um sich schlagen;
(*spend money*) sich in Unkosten
stürzen (*on* mit)

lass [læs] *n* Mädchen *nt*

last [lɑːst] *adj* letzte(r, s); **the
~ but one** der/die/das vorletzte;
~ night gestern Abend; **~ but not
least** nicht zuletzt ▷ *adv* zuletzt;
(*last time*) das letzte Mal; **at
~** endlich ▷ *n* (*person*) Letzte(r) *mf*;
(*thing*) Letzte(s) *nt*; **he was the
~ to leave** er ging als Letzter ▷ *vi*
(*continue*) dauern; (*remain in good
condition*) durchhalten; (*remain
good*) sich halten; (*money*)
ausreichen; **lasting** *adj*
dauerhaft; (*impression*) nachhaltig;
lastly *adv* schließlich;
last-minute *adj* in letzter
Minute; **last name** *n* Nachname
m

late [leɪt] *adj* spät; (*after proper
time*) zu spät; (*train etc*) verspätet;
(*dead*) verstorben; **to be ~** zu spät
kommen; (*train etc*) Verspätung
haben ▷ *adv* spät; (*after proper
time*) zu spät; **late availibility
flight** *n* Last-Minute-Flug *m*;
lately *adv* in letzter Zeit; **late
opening** *n* verlängerte
Öffnungszeiten *pl*; **later** [leɪtə*]
adj, *adv* später; **see you ~** bis
später; **latest** [leɪtɪst] *adj*
späteste(r, s); (*most recent*)
neueste(r, s) ▷ *n*: **the ~** (*news*) das
Neueste; **at the ~** spätestens

Latin [lætɪn] *n* Latein *nt* ▷ *adj*
lateinisch; **Latin America** *n*
Lateinamerika *nt*;
Latin-American *adj*
lateinamerikanisch ▷ *n* Latein-
amerikaner(in) *m(f)*

latter [lætə*] *adj* (*second of two*)
letztere(r, s); (*last: part, years*)
letzte(r, s), später

Latvia [lætvɪə] *n* Lettland *nt*;

Latvian [lætvɪən] ▷ *adj* lettisch;
▷ *n* (*person*) Lette *m*; Lettin *f*;
(*language*) Lettisch *nt*

laugh [lɑːf] *n* Lachen *nt*; **for a
~** aus Spaß ▷ *vi* lachen (*at, about*
über +*akk*); **to ~ at sb** sich über jdn
lustig machen; **it's no ~ing
matter** es ist nicht zum Lachen;
laughter [lɑːftə*] *n* Gelächter *nt*

launch [lɔːntʃ] *n* (*launching, of
ship*) Stapellauf *m*; (*of rocket*)
Abschuss *m*; (*of product*)
Markteinführung *f*; (*with hype*)
Lancierung *f*; (*event*)
Eröffnungsfeier *f* ▷ *vt* (*ship*) vom
Stapel lassen; (*rocket*) abschießen;
(*product*) einführen; (*with hype*)
lancieren; (*project*) in Gang setzen

launder [lɔːndə*] *vt* waschen
und bügeln; (*fig: money*) waschen;
laundrette [lɔːndret] *n* (*Brit*),
laundromat [lɔːndrəmæt] *n* (*US*)
Waschsalon *m*; **laundry** [lɔːndrɪ]
n (*place*) Wäscherei *f*; (*clothes*)
Wäsche *f*

lavatory [lævətrɪ] *n* Toilette *f*

lavender [lævɪndə*] *n* Lavendel
m

lavish [lævɪʃ] *adj* verschwende-
risch; (*furnishings etc*) üppig; (*gift*)
großzügig

law [lɔː] *n* Gesetz *nt*; (*system*)
Recht *nt*; (*for study*) Jura; (*of sport*)
Regel *f*; **against the
~** gesetzwidrig; **law-abiding** *adj*
gesetzestreu; **law court** *n*
Gerichtshof *m*; **lawful** *adj*
rechtmäßig

lawn [lɔːn] *n* Rasen *m*;
lawnmower *n* Rasenmäher *m*

lawsuit [lɔːsuːt] *n* Prozess *m*;
lawyer [lɔːjə*] *n* Rechtsanwalt
m, Rechtsanwältin *f*

laxative [læksətɪv] *n* Abführ-
mittel *nt*

lay [leɪ] *pt of* **lie** ▷ *vt* (**laid, laid**)
legen; (*table*) decken; (*vulg*)

poppen, bumsen; (*egg*) legen ▷ *adj* Laien-; **lay down** *vt* hinlegen; **lay off** *vt* (*workers*) (vorübergehend) entlassen; (*stop attacking*) in Ruhe lassen; **lay on** *vt* (*provide*) anbieten; (*organize*) veranstalten, bereitstellen; **layabout** *n* Faulenzer(in) *m(f)*; **lay-by** *n* Parkbucht *f*; (*bigger*) Parkplatz *m*

layer ['leɪə°] *n* Schicht *f*

layman ['leɪmən] *n* Laie *m*

layout ['leɪaʊt] *n* Gestaltung *f*; (*of book etc*) Lay-out *nt*

laze [leɪz] *vi* faulenzen; **laziness** ['leɪzɪnɪs] *n* Faulheit *f*; **lazy** ['leɪzɪ] *adj* faul; (*day, time*) gemütlich

lb *abbr* = **pound** Pfd.

lead [led] *n* Blei *nt* ▷ *vt, vi* [li:d] (**led, led**) führen; (*group etc*) leiten; **to ~ the way** vorangehen; **this is ~ing us nowhere** das bringt uns nicht weiter ▷ [li:d] *n* (*race*) Führung *f*; (*distance, time ahead*) Vorsprung *m* (*over* vor +*dat*); (*of police*) Spur *f*; (*Theat*) Hauptrolle *f*; (*dog's lead*) Leine *f*; (*Elec: flex*) Leitung *f*; **lead astray** *vt* irreführen; **lead away** *vt* wegführen; **lead back** *vi* zurückführen; **lead on** *vt* anführen; **lead to** *vt* (*street*) hinführen nach; (*result in*) führen zu; **lead up to** *vt* (*drive*) führen zu

leaded ['ledɪd] *adj* (*petrol*) verbleit

leader ['li:də°] *n* Führer(in) *m(f)*; (*of party*) Vorsitzende(r) *mf*; (*of project, expedition*) Leiter(in) *m(f)*; (*Sport: in race*) der/die Erste; (*in league*) Tabellenführer *m*; **leadership** ['li:dəʃɪp] *n* Führung *f*

lead-free ['led'fri:] *adj* (*petrol*) bleifrei

leading ['li:dɪŋ] *adj* führend, wichtig

leaf [li:f] (*pl* **leaves**) *n* Blatt *nt*;

leaflet ['li:flɪt] *n* Prospekt *m*; (*pamphlet*) Flugblatt *nt*; (*with instructions*) Merkblatt *nt*

league [li:g] *n* Bund *m*; (*Sport*) Liga *f*

leak [li:k] *n* (*gap*) undichte Stelle; (*escape*) Leck *nt*; **to take a ~** (*fam*) pinkeln gehen ▷ *vi* (*pipe etc*) undicht sein; (*liquid etc*) auslaufen; **leaky** *adj* undicht

lean [li:n] *adj* (*meat*) mager; (*face*) schmal; (*person*) drahtig ▷ *vi* (**leant** *o* **leaned, leant** *o* **leaned**) (*not vertical*) sich neigen; (*rest*) **to ~ against sth** sich an etw *akk* lehnen; (*support oneself*) **to ~ on sth** sich auf etw *akk* stützen ▷ *vt* lehnen (*on, against* an +*akk*); **lean back** *vi* sich zurücklehnen; **lean forward** *vi* sich vorbeugen; **lean over** *vi* sich hinüberbeugen; **lean towards** *vt* tendieren zu

leant [lent] *pt, pp of* **lean**

leap [li:p] *n* Sprung *m* ▷ *vi* (**leapt** *o* **leaped, leapt** *o* **leaped**) springen; **leapt** [lept] *pt, pp of* **leap**; **leap year** *n* Schaltjahr *nt*

learn [lɜ:n] (**learnt** *o* **learned, learnt** *o* **learned**) *vt, vi* lernen; (*find out*) erfahren; **to ~ (how) to swim** schwimmen lernen; **learned** ['lɜ:nɪd] *adj* gelehrt; **learner** *n* Anfänger(in) *m(f)*; (*Brit: driver*) Fahrschüler(in) *m(f)*

learnt [lɜ:nt] *pt, pp of* **learn**

lease [li:s] *n* (*of land, premises etc*) Pacht *f*; (*contract*) Pachtvertrag *m*; (*of house, car etc*) Miete *f*; (*contract*) Mietvertrag *m* ▷ *vt* pachten; (*house, car etc*) mieten; **lease out** *vt* vermieten; **leasing** ['li:sɪŋ] *n* Leasing *nt*

least [li:st] *adj* wenigste(r, s); (*slightest*) geringste(r, s) ▷ *adv* am wenigsten; **~ expensive** billigste(r, s) ▷ *n*: **the ~** das Mindeste; **not in the ~** nicht im geringsten; **at ~** wenigstens; (*with number*) mindestens

leather ['leðə°] n Leder nt ▷ adj ledern, Leder-

leave [liːv] n (*time off*) Urlaub m; **on ~** auf Urlaub; **to take one's ~** Abschied nehmen (*of* von) ▷ vt (**left, left**) (*place, person*) verlassen; (*not remove, not change*) lassen; (*~ behind: message, scar etc*) hinterlassen; (*forget*) hinter sich lassen; (*after death*) hinterlassen (*to sb* jdm); (*entrust*) überlassen (*to sb* jdm); **to be left** (*remain*) übrig bleiben; **~ me alone** lass mich in Ruhe!; **don't ~ it to the last minute** warte nicht bis zur letzten Minute ▷ vi (weg)gehen, (weg)fahren; (*on journey*) abreisen; (*bus, train*) abfahren (*for* nach); **leave behind** vt zurücklassen; (*scar etc*) hinterlassen; (*forget*) hinter sich lassen; **leave out** vt auslassen; (*person*) ausschließen (*of* von)

leaves [liːvz] pl of **leaf**

leaving do [ˈliːvɪŋ duː] n Abschiedsfeier f

Lebanon [ˈlebənən] n: **the ~** der Libanon

lecture [ˈlektʃə°] n Vortrag m; (*at university*) Vorlesung f; **to give a ~** einen Vortrag/eine Vorlesung halten; **lecturer** n Dozent(in) m(f); **lecture theatre** n Hörsaal m

led [led] pt, pp of **lead**

LED abbr = **light-emitting diode** Leuchtdiode f

ledge [ledʒ] n Leiste f; (*window ~*) Sims m o nt

leek [liːk] n Lauch m

left [left] pt, pp of **leave** ▷ adj linke(r, s) ▷ adv (*position*) links; (*movement*) nach links ▷ n (*side*) linke Seite; **the Left** (*Pol*) die Linke; **on/to the ~** links (*of* von); **move/fall to the ~** nach links

rücken/fallen; **left-hand** adj linke(r, s); **~ bend** Linkskurve f; **~ drive** Linkssteuerung f; **left-handed** adj linkshändig; **left-hand side** n linke Seite

left-luggage locker n Gepäckschließfach nt; **left-luggage office** n Gepäckaufbewahrung f

leftovers npl Reste pl

left wing n linker Flügel; **left-wing** adj (*Pol*) linksgerichtet

leg [leg] n Bein nt; (*of meat*) Keule f

legacy [ˈlegəsɪ] n Erbe nt, Erbschaft f

legal [ˈliːgəl] adj Rechts-, rechtlich; (*allowed*) legal; (*limit, age*) gesetzlich; **~ aid** Rechtshilfe f; **legalize** vt legalisieren; **legally** adv legal

legend [ˈledʒənd] n Legende f

legible, legibly [ˈledʒəbl, -blɪ] adj, adv leserlich

legislation [ledʒɪsˈleɪʃn] n Gesetze pl

legitimate [lɪˈdʒɪtɪmət] adj rechtmäßig, legitim

legroom [ˈlegrʊm] n Beinfreiheit f

leisure [ˈleʒə°] n (*time*) Freizeit f ▷ adj Freizeit-; **~ centre** Freizeitzentrum nt; **leisurely** [ˈleʒəlɪ] adj gemächlich

lemon [ˈlemən] n Zitrone f; **lemonade** [leməˈneɪd] n Limonade f; **lemon curd** n Brotaufstrich aus Zitronen, Butter, Eiern und Zucker; **lemon juice** n Zitronensaft m; **lemon sole** n Seezunge f

lend [lend] (**lent, lent**) vt leihen; **to ~ sb sth** jdm etw leihen; **to (sb) ~ a hand** (jdm) behilflich sein; **lending library** n Leihbücherei f

length [leŋθ] n Länge f; **4 metres in ~** 4 Meter lang; **what**

~ is it? wie lange ist es?; **for any ~ of time** für längere Zeit; **at ~** (*lengthily*) ausführlich; **lengthen** ['leŋθən] *vt* verlängern; **lengthy** *adj* sehr lange; (*dragging*) langwierig

lenient ['li:nɪənt] *adj* nachsichtig

lens [lenz] *n* Linse *f*; (*Foto*) Objektiv *nt*

lent [lent] *pt, pp of* **lend**

Lent [lent] *n* Fastenzeit *f*

lentil ['lentl] *n* (*Bot*) Linse *f*

Leo ['li:əʊ] (*pl* **-s**) *n* (*Astr*) Löwe *m*

leopard ['lepəd] *n* Leopard *m*

lesbian ['lezbɪən] *adj* lesbisch ▷ *n* Lesbe *f*

less [les] *adj, adv, n* weniger; **~ and ~** immer weniger; (**~ often**) immer seltener; **lessen** ['lesn] *vi* abnehmen, nachlassen ▷ *vt* verringern; (*pain*) lindern; **lesser** ['lesə*] *adj* geringer; (*amount*) kleiner

lesson ['lesn] *n* (*at school*) Stunde *f*; (*unit of study*) Lektion *f*; (*fig*) Lehre *f*; (*Rel*) Lesung *f*; **~s start at 9** der Unterricht beginnt um 9

let [let] (**let, let**) *vt* lassen; (*lease*) vermieten; **to ~ sb have sth** jdm etw geben; **~'s go** gehen wir; **to ~ go** (**of sth**) (etw) loslassen; **let down** *vt* herunterlassen; (*fail to help*) im Stich lassen; (*disappoint*) enttäuschen; **let in** *vt* hereinlassen; **let off** *vt* (*bomb*) hochgehen lassen; (*person*) laufen lassen; **let out** *vt* hinauslassen; (*secret*) verraten; (*scream etc*) ausstoßen; **let up** *vi* nachlassen; (*stop*) aufhören

lethal ['li:θəl] *adj* tödlich

let's *contr* = **let us**

letter ['letə*] *n* (*of alphabet*) Buchstabe *m*; (*message*) Brief *m*; (*official ~*) Schreiben *nt*; **letter**

bomb *n* Briefbombe *f*; **letterbox** *n* Briefkasten *m*

lettuce ['letɪs] *n* Kopfsalat *m*

leukaemia, **leukemia** (*US*) [luː'kiːmɪə] *n* Leukämie *f*

level ['levl] *adj* (*horizontal*) waagerecht; (*ground*) eben; (*two things, two runners*) auf selber Höhe; **to be ~ with sb/sth** mit jdm/etw auf gleicher Höhe sein; **~ on points** punktgleich ▷ *adv* (*run etc*) auf gleicher Höhe, gleich auf; **to draw ~** (*in race*) gleichziehen (**with** mit); (*in game*) ausgleichen ▷ *n* (*altitude*) Höhe *f*; (*standard*) Niveau *nt*; (*amount, degree*) Grad *m*; **to be on a ~ with** auf gleicher Höhe sein mit ▷ *vt* (*ground*) einebnen; **level crossing** *n* (*Brit*) (schienengleicher) Bahnübergang *m*; **level-headed** *adj* vernünftig

lever ['liːvə*, (*US*) 'levə*] *n* Hebel *m*; (*fig*) Druckmittel *nt*; **lever up** *vt* hochstemmen

liability [laɪə'bɪlɪtɪ] *n* Haftung *f*; (*burden*) Belastung *f*; (*obligation*) Verpflichtung *f*; **liable** ['laɪəbl] *adj*: **to be ~ for sth** (*responsible*) für etw haften; **~ for tax** steuerpflichtig

liar ['laɪə*] *n* Lügner(in) *m(f)*

Lib Dem [lɪb'dem] *abbr* = **Liberal Democrat**

liberal ['lɪbərəl] *adj* (*generous*) großzügig; (*broad-minded*) liberal; **Liberal Democrat** *n* (*Brit Pol*) Liberaldemokrat(in) *m(f)* ▷ *adj* liberaldemokratisch

liberate ['lɪbəreɪt] *vt* befreien; **liberation** [lɪbə'reɪʃn] *n* Befreiung *f*

Liberia [laɪ'bɪərɪə] *n* Liberia *nt*

liberty ['lɪbətɪ] *n* Freiheit *f*

Libra ['liːbrə] *n* (*Astr*) Waage *f*

library ['laɪbrərɪ] *n* Bibliothek *f*; (*lending ~*) Bücherei *f*

Libya [ˈlɪbɪə] *n* Libyen *nt*
lice [laɪs] *pl of* **louse**
licence [ˈlaɪsəns] *n* (*permit*)
Genehmigung *f*; (*Comm*) Lizenz *f*;
(*driving ~*) Führerschein *m*; **license**
[ˈlaɪsəns] *n* (*US*) *see* **licence** ▷ *vt*
genehmigen; **licensed** *adj*
(*restaurant etc*) mit
Schankerlaubnis; **license plate** *n*
(*US Auto*) Nummernschild *nt*;
licensing hours *npl*
Ausschankzeiten *pl*
lick [lɪk] *vt* lecken ▷ *n* Lecken
nt
licorice [ˈlɪkərɪs] *n* Lakritze *f*
lid [lɪd] *n* Deckel *m*; (*eye~*) Lid *nt*
lie [laɪ] *n* Lüge *f*; **~ detector**
Lügendetektor *m* ▷ *vi* lügen; **to
~ to sb** jdn belügen ▷ *vi* (**lay, lain**)
(*rest, be situated*) liegen; (*~ down*)
sich legen; (*snow*) liegen bleiben;
to be lying third an dritter Stelle
liegen; **lie about** *vi* herumliegen;
lie down *vi* sich hinlegen
Liechtenstein [ˈlɪktənstaɪn] *n*
Liechtenstein *nt*
lie in [laɪˈɪn] *n*: **to have a
~** ausschlafen
life [laɪf] (*pl* **lives**) *n* Leben *nt*; **to
get ~** lebenslänglich bekommen;
there isn't much ~ here hier ist
nicht viel los; **how many lives
were lost?** wie viele sind ums
Leben gekommen?; **life assurance**
n Lebensversicherung *f*; **lifebelt** *n*
Rettungsring *m*; **lifeboat** *n*
Rettungsboot *nt*; **lifeguard** *n*
Bademeister(in) *m(f)*,
Rettungsschwimmer(in) *m(f)*; **life
insurance** *n* Lebensversicherung
f; **life jacket** *n* Schwimmweste *f*;
lifeless *adj* (*dead*) leblos; **lifelong**
adj lebenslang; **life preserver** *n*
(*US*) Rettungsring *m*; **life-saving**
adj lebensrettend; **life-size(d)** *adj*
in Lebensgröße; **life span** *n*
Lebensspanne *f*; **life style** *n*

Lebensstil *m*; **lifetime** *n*
Lebenszeit *f*
lift [lɪft] *vt* (hoch)heben; (*ban*)
aufheben ▷ *n* (Brit: elevator)
Aufzug *m*, Lift *m*; **to give sb a ~** jdn
im Auto mitnehmen; **lift up** *vt*
hochheben; **lift-off** *n* Start *m*
ligament [ˈlɪgəmənt] *n* Band *nt*
light [laɪt] (**lit** *o* **lighted, lit** *o*
lighted) *vt* beleuchten; (*fire,
cigarette*) anzünden ▷ *n* Licht *nt*;
(*lamp*) Lampe *f*; **~s** *pl* (Auto)
Beleuchtung *f*; (*traffic ~s*) Ampel *f*;
in the ~ of angesichts +*gen* ▷ *adj*
(*bright*) hell; (*not heavy, easy*) leicht;
(*punishment*) milde; (*taxes*) niedrig;
~ blue/green hellblau/hellgrün;
light up *vt* (*illuminate*) beleuchten
▷ *vi* (*a. eyes*) aufleuchten
light bulb *n* Glühbirne *f*
lighten [ˈlaɪtn] *vi* hell werden
▷ *vt* (*give light to*) erhellen; (*make
less heavy*) leichter machen; (*fig*)
erleichtern
lighter [ˈlaɪtə°] *n* (*cigarette ~*)
Feuerzeug *nt*
light-hearted *adj* unbeschwert;
lighthouse *n* Leuchtturm *m*;
lighting *n* Beleuchtung *f*; **lightly**
adv leicht; **light meter** *n* (*Foto*)
Belichtungsmesser *m*
lightning [ˈlaɪtnɪŋ] *n* Blitz *m*
lightweight *adj* leicht
like [laɪk] *vt* mögen, gernhaben;
he ~s swimming er schwimmt
gern; **would you ~ ...?** hättest
du/hätten Sie gern ...?; **I'd ~ to go
home** ich möchte nach Hause
(gehen); **I don't ~ the film** der
Film gefällt mir nicht ▷ *prep* wie;
what's it/he ~? wie ist es/er?; **he
looks ~ you** er sieht dir/Ihnen
ähnlich; **~ that/this** so; **likeable**
[ˈlaɪkəbl] *adj* sympathisch
likelihood [ˈlaɪklɪhʊd] *n* Wahrscheinlichkeit *f*; **likely** [ˈlaɪklɪ]
adj wahrscheinlich; **the bus is**

~ to be late der Bus wird wahrscheinlich Verspätung haben; **he's not (at all) ~ to come** (höchst)wahrscheinlich kommt er nicht

like-minded [laɪkˈmaɪndɪd] *adj* gleich gesinnt

likewise [ˈlaɪkwaɪz] *adv* ebenfalls; **to do ~** das Gleiche tun

liking [ˈlaɪkɪŋ] *n* (*for person*) Zuneigung *f*; (*for type, things*) Vorliebe *f* (*for* für)

lilac [ˈlaɪlək] *n* Flieder *m* ▷ *adj* fliederfarben

lily [ˈlɪlɪ] *n* Lilie *f*; **~ of the valley** Maiglöckchen *nt*

limb [lɪm] *n* Glied *nt*

limbo [ˈlɪmbəʊ] *n*: **in ~** (*plans*) auf Eis gelegt

lime [laɪm] *n* (*tree*) Linde *f*; (*fruit*) Limone *f*; (*substance*) Kalk *m*; **lime juice** *n* Limonensaft *m*; **limelight** *n* (*fig*) Rampenlicht *nt*

limerick [ˈlɪmərɪk] *n* Limerick *m* (*fünfzeiliges komisches Gedicht*)

limestone [ˈlaɪmstəʊn] *n* Kalkstein *m*

limit [ˈlɪmɪt] *n* Grenze *f*; (*for pollution etc*) Grenzwert *m*; **there's a ~ to that** dem sind Grenzen gesetzt; **to be over the ~** (*speed*) das Tempolimit überschreiten; (*alcohol consumption*) fahruntüchtig sein; **that's the ~** jetzt reicht's!, das ist die Höhe! ▷ *vt* beschränken (*to* auf +*akk*); (*freedom, spending*) einschränken; **limitation** [lɪmɪˈteɪʃən] *n* Beschränkung *f*; (*of freedom, spending*) Einschränkung *f*; **limited** *adj* begrenzt; **~ liability company** Gesellschaft *f* mit beschränkter Haftung, GmbH *f*; **public ~ company** Aktiengesellschaft *f*

limousine [ˈlɪməziːn] *n* Limousine *f*

limp [lɪmp] *vi* hinken ▷ *adj* schlaff

line [laɪn] *n* Linie *f*; (*written*) Zeile *f*; (*rope*) Leine *f*; (*on face*) Falte *f*; (*row*) Reihe *f*; (*US: queue*) Schlange *f*; (*Rail*) Bahnlinie *f*; (*between A and B*) Strecke *f*; (*Tel*) Leitung *f*; (*range of items*) Kollektion *f*; **hold the ~** bleiben Sie am Apparat; **to stand in ~** Schlange stehen; **in ~ with** in Übereinstimmung mit; **something along those ~s** etwas in dieser Art; **drop me a ~** schreib mir ein paar Zeilen; **~s** (*Theat*) Text *m* ▷ *vt* (*clothes*) füttern; (*streets*) säumen; **lined** *adj* (*paper*) liniert; (*face*) faltig; **line up** *vi* sich aufstellen; (*US: form queue*) sich anstellen

linen [ˈlɪnɪn] *n* Leinen *nt*; (*sheets etc*) Wäsche *f*

liner [ˈlaɪnə*] *n* Überseedampfer *m*, Passagierschiff *nt*

linger [ˈlɪŋgə*] *vi* verweilen; (*smell*) nicht weggehen

lingerie [ˈlænʒəriː] *n* Damenunterwäsche *f*

lining [ˈlaɪnɪŋ] *n* (*of clothes*) Futter *nt*; (*brake ~*) Bremsbelag *m*

link [lɪŋk] *n* (*connection*) Verbindung *f*; (*of chain*) Glied *nt*; (*relationship*) Beziehung *f* (*with* zu); (*between events*) Zusammenhang *m*; (*Internet*) Link *m* ▷ *vt* verbinden

lion [ˈlaɪən] *n* Löwe *m*; **lioness** *n* Löwin *f*

lip [lɪp] *n* Lippe *f*; **lipstick** *n* Lippenstift *m*

liqueur [lɪˈkjʊə*] *n* Likör *m*

liquid [ˈlɪkwɪd] *n* Flüssigkeit *f* ▷ *adj* flüssig

liquidate [ˈlɪkwɪdeɪt] *vt* liquidieren

liquidizer [ˈlɪkwɪdaɪzə*] *n* Mixer *m*

liquor [ˈlɪkə*] *n* Spirituosen *pl*

liquorice ['lɪkərɪs] *n* Lakritze *f*
Lisbon ['lɪzbən] *n* Lissabon *nt*
lisp [lɪsp] *vt, vi* lispeln
list [lɪst] *n* Liste *f* ▷ *vi* (*ship*)
Schlagseite haben ▷ *vt* auflisten,
aufzählen; **~ed building** unter
Denkmalschutz stehendes
Gebäude
listen ['lɪsn] *vi* zuhören, horchen
(*for sth* auf etw *akk*); **listen to** *vt*
(*person*) zuhören +*dat*; (*radio*)
hören; (*advice*) hören auf; **listener**
n Zuhörer(in) *m(f)*; (*to radio*)
Hörer(in) *m(f)*
lit [lɪt] *pt, pp of* **light**
liter ['liːtə°] *n* (*US*) Liter *m*
literacy ['lɪtərəsɪ] *n* Fähigkeit *f*
zu lesen und zu schreiben; **literal**
['lɪtərəl] *adj* (*translation, meaning*)
wörtlich; (*actual*) buchstäblich;
literally *adv* (*translate, take sth*)
wörtlich; (*really*) buchstäblich,
wirklich; **literary** ['lɪtərərɪ] *adj*
literarisch; (*critic, journal etc*)
Literatur-; (*language*) gehoben;
literature ['lɪtrətʃə°] *n* Literatur
f; (*brochures etc*)
Informationsmaterial *nt*
Lithuania [lɪθjuː'eɪnjə] *n* Litauen
nt; **Lithuanian** [lɪθjuː'eɪnjən]
▷ *adj* litauisch; ▷ *n* (*person*)
Litauer(in) *m(f)*; (*language*)
Litauisch *nt*
litre ['liːtə°] *n* Liter *m*
litter ['lɪtə°] *n* Abfälle *pl*; (*of
animals*) Wurf *m* ▷ *vt*: **to be ~ed
with** übersät sein mit; **litter bin** *n*
Abfalleimer *m*
little ['lɪtl] *adj* (**smaller,
smallest**) klein; (*in quantity*)
wenig; **a ~ while ago** vor kurzer
Zeit ▷ *adv, n* (**fewer, fewest**)
wenig; **a ~** ein bisschen, ein
wenig; **as ~ as possible** so wenig
wie möglich; **for as ~ as £5** ab nur
5 Pfund; **I see very ~ of them** ich
sehe sie sehr selten; **~ by ~** nach

und nach; **little finger** *n* kleiner
Finger
live [laɪv] *adj* lebendig; (*Elec*)
geladen, unter Strom; (*TV, Radio:
event*) live; **~ broadcast**
Direktübertragung *f* ▷ [lɪv] *vi*
leben; (*not die*) überleben; (*dwell*)
wohnen; **you ~ and learn** man
lernt nie aus ▷ *vt* (*life*) führen; **to
~ a life of luxury** im Luxus leben;
live on *vi* weiterleben ▷ *vt*: **to
~ sth** von etw leben; (*feed*) sich von
etw ernähren; **to earn enough to
~** genug verdienen, um davon zu
leben; **live together** *vi*
zusammenleben; **live up to** *vt*
(*reputation*) gerecht werden +*dat*;
(*expectations*) entsprechen +*dat*;
live with *vt* (*parents etc*) wohnen
bei; (*partner*) zusammenleben mit;
(*difficulty*) **you'll just have to ~ it**
du musst dich/Sie müssen sich
eben damit abfinden
liveliness ['laɪvlɪnɪs] *n* Lebhaf-
tigkeit *f*; **lively** ['laɪvlɪ] *adj*
lebhaft
liver ['lɪvə°] *n* Leber *f*
lives [laɪvz] *pl of* **life**
livestock ['laɪvstɒk] *n* Vieh *nt*
living ['lɪvɪŋ] *n* Lebensunterhalt
m; **what do you do for a ~?** was
machen Sie beruflich? ▷ *adj*
lebend; **living room** *n*
Wohnzimmer *nt*
lizard ['lɪzəd] *n* Eidechse *f*
llama ['lɑːmə] *n* (*Zool*) Lama *nt*
load [ləʊd] *n* Last *f*; (*cargo*)
Ladung *f*; (*Tech, fig*) Belastung *f*; **~s
of** (*fam*) massenhaft; **it was a ~ of
rubbish** (*fam*) es war
grottenschlecht ▷ *vt* (*vehicle*)
beladen; (*Inform*) laden; (*film*)
einlegen
loaf [ləʊf] (*pl* **loaves**) *n*: **a ~ of
bread** ein (Laib) Brot *(m)nt*
loan [ləʊn] *n* (*item leant*)
Leihgabe *f*; (*Fin*) Darlehen *nt*; **on**

~ geliehen ▷ vt leihen (to sb jdm)

loathe [ləʊð] vt verabscheuen

loaves [ləʊvz] pl of **loaf**

lobby ['lɒbɪ] n Vorhalle f; (Pol) Lobby f

lobster ['lɒbstə*] n Hummer m

local ['ləʊkəl] adj (traffic, time etc) Orts-; (radio, news, paper) Lokal-; (government, authority) Kommunal-; (anaesthetic) örtlich; **~ call** (Tel) Ortsgespräch nt; **~ elections** Kommunalwahlen pl; **~ time** Ortszeit f; **~ train** Nahverkehrszug m; **the ~ shops** die Geschäfte am Ort ▷ n (pub) Stammlokal nt; **the ~s** pl die Ortsansässigen pl; **locally** adv örtlich, am Ort

locate [ləʊ'keɪt] vt (find) ausfindig machen; (position) legen; (establish) errichten; **to be ~d** sich befinden (in, at in +dat); **location** [ləʊ'keɪʃən] n (position) Lage f; (Cine) Drehort m

loch [lɒx] n (Scot) See m

lock [lɒk] n Schloss nt; (Naut) Schleuse f; (of hair) Locke f ▷ vt (door etc) abschließen ▷ vi (door etc) sich abschließen lassen; (wheels) blockieren; **lock in** vt einschließen, einsperren; **lock out** vt aussperren; **lock up** vt (house) abschließen; (person) einsperren

locker ['lɒkə*] n Schließfach nt; **locker room** n (US) Umkleideraum m

locksmith ['lɒksmɪθ] n Schlosser(in) m(f)

locust ['ləʊkəst] n Heuschrecke f

lodge [lɒdʒ] n (small house) Pförtnerhaus nt; (porter's ~) Pförtnerloge f ▷ vi in Untermiete wohnen (with bei); (get stuck) stecken bleiben; **lodger** n Untermieter(in) m(f); **lodging** n Unterkunft f

loft [lɒft] n Dachboden m

log [lɒg] n Klotz m; (Naut) Log nt; **to keep a ~ of sth** über etw Buch führen; **log in**, **log on** vi (Inform) sich einloggen; **log off**, **log out** vi (Inform) sich ausloggen

logic ['lɒdʒɪk] n Logik f; **logical** adj logisch

login ['lɒgɪn] n (Inform) Log-in nt, Anmeldung f

logo ['lɒgəʊ] (pl **-s**) n Logo nt

loin [lɔɪn] n Lende f

loiter ['lɔɪtə*] vi sich herumtreiben

lollipop ['lɒlɪpɒp] n Lutscher m; **~ man/lady** (Brit) Schülerlotse m, Schülerlotsin f

lolly ['lɒlɪ] n Lutscher m

London ['lʌndən] n London nt; **Londoner** n Londoner(in) m(f)

loneliness ['ləʊnlɪnɪs] n Einsamkeit f; **lonely** ['ləʊnlɪ], (esp US) **lonesome** ['ləʊnsəm] adj einsam

long [lɒŋ] adj lang; (distance) weit; **it's a ~ way** es ist weit (to nach); **for a ~ time** lange; **how ~ is the film?** wie lange dauert der Film?; **in the ~ run** auf die Dauer ▷ adv lange; **not for ~** nicht lange; **~ ago** vor langer Zeit; **before ~** bald; **all day ~** den ganzen Tag; **no ~er** nicht mehr; **as ~ as** solange ▷ vi sich sehnen (for nach); (be waiting) sehnsüchtig warten (for auf); **long-distance call** n Ferngespräch nt; **long drink** n Longdrink m; **long-haul flight** n Langstreckenflug m; **longing** n Sehnsucht f (for nach); **longingly** adv sehnsüchtig; **longitude** ['lɒŋgɪtjuːd] n Länge f; **long jump** n Weitsprung m; **long-life milk** n H-Milch f; **long-range** adj Langstrecken-, Langstrecken-; **~ missile** Langstreckenrakete f; **long-sighted** adj weitsichtig; **long-standing** adj alt, langjährig; **long-term** adj

langfristig; (car park, effect etc)
Langzeit-; **~ unemployment**
Langzeitarbeitslosigkeit f; **long
wave** n Langwelle f
loo [luː] n (Brit fam) Klo nt
look [lʊk] n Blick m; (appearance)
~(s) pl Aussehen nt; **I'll have a
~** ich schau mal nach; **to have a
~ at sth** sich dat etw ansehen; **can
I have a ~?** darf ich mal sehen?
▷ vi schauen, gucken; (with prep)
sehen; (search) nachsehen; (appear)
aussehen; (**I'm) just ~ing** ich
schaue nur; **it ~s like rain** es sieht
nach Regen aus ▷ vt: **~ what
you've done** sieh dir mal an, was
du da angestellt hast; (appear) **he
~s his age** man sieht ihm sein Alter
an; **to ~ one's best** sehr vorteilhaft
aussehen; **look after** vt (care for)
sorgen für; (keep an eye on) aufpassen auf +akk; **look at** vt
ansehen, anschauen; **look back** vi
sich umsehen; (fig) zurückblicken;
look down on vt (fig) herabsehen
auf +akk; **look for** vt suchen; **look
forward to** vt sich freuen auf +akk;
look into vt (investigate) untersuchen; **look out** vi hinaussehen
(of the window zum Fenster); (watch
out) Ausschau halten (for nach); (be
careful) aufpassen, Acht geben (for
auf +akk); **~!** Vorsicht!; **look up** vi
aufsehen ▷ vt (word etc)
nachschlagen; **look up to** vt
aufsehen zu
loony ['luːnɪ] adj (fam) bekloppt
loop [luːp] n Schleife f
loose [luːs] adj locker; (knot,
button) lose; **loosen** vt lockern;
(knot) lösen
loot [luːt] n Beute f
lop-sided ['lɒp'saɪdɪd] adj schief
lord [lɔːd] n (ruler) Herr m; (Brit:
title) Lord m; **the Lord (God)** Gott
der Herr; **the (House of) Lords**
(Brit) das Oberhaus

lorry ['lɒrɪ] n (Brit) Lastwagen m
lose [luːz] (**lost, lost**) vt
verlieren; (chance) verpassen; **to
~ weight** abnehmen; **to ~ one's
life** umkommen ▷ vi verlieren;
(clock, watch) nachgehen; **loser** n
Verlierer(in) m(f); **loss** [lɒs] n
Verlust m; **lost** [lɒst] pt, pp of **lose**;
we're ~ wir haben uns verlaufen
▷ adj verloren; **lost-and-found**
(US), **lost property (office)** n
Fundbüro nt
lot [lɒt] n (fam: batch) Menge f,
Haufen m, Stoß m; **this is the first
~** das ist die erste Ladung; **a
~** viel(e); **a ~ of money** viel Geld;
~s of people viele Leute; **the
(whole) ~** alles; (people) alle
lotion ['ləʊʃən] n Lotion f
lottery ['lɒtərɪ] n Lotterie f
loud [laʊd] adj laut; (colour)
schreiend; **loudspeaker** n
Lautsprecher m; (of stereo) Box f
lounge [laʊndʒ] n Wohnzimmer
nt; (in hotel) Aufenthaltsraum m;
(at airport) Warteraum m ▷ vi sich
herumlümmeln
louse [laʊs] (pl **lice**) n Laus f;
lousy ['laʊzɪ] adj (fam) lausig
lout [laʊt] n Rüpel m
lovable ['lʌvəbl] adj liebenswert
love [lʌv] n Liebe f (of zu); (person,
address) Liebling m, Schatz m;
(Sport) null; **to be in ~** verliebt sein
(with sb in jdn); **to fall in ~** sich
verlieben (with sb in jdn); **to make
~** (sexually) sich lieben; **to make
~ to** (o with) sb mit jdm schlafen;
(in letter) **he sends his ~** er lässt
grüßen; **give her my ~** grüße sie
von mir; **~, Tom** liebe Grüße, Tom
▷ vt (person) lieben; (activity) sehr
gerne mögen; **to ~ to do sth** etw
für sein Leben gerne tun; **I'd ~ a
cup of tea** ich hätte liebend gern
eine Tasse Tee; **love affair** n
(Liebes)verhältnis nt; **love letter** n

Liebesbrief *m*; **love life** *n* Liebesleben *nt*; **lovely** ['lʌvlɪ] *adj* schön, wunderschön; (*charming*) reizend; **we had a ~ time** es war sehr schön; **lover** ['lʌvə] *n* Liebhaber(in) *m(f)*; **loving** *adj* liebevoll

low [ləʊ] *adj* niedrig; (*rank*) niedere(r, s); (*level, note, neckline*) tief; (*intelligence, density*) gering; (*quality, standard*) schlecht; (*not loud*) leise; (*depressed*) niedergeschlagen; **we're ~ on petrol** wir haben kaum noch Benzin ▷ *n* (*Meteo*) Tief *nt*; **low-calorie** *adj* kalorienarm; **lowcut** *adj* (*dress*) tief ausgeschnitten; **low-emission** *adj* schadstoffarm; **lower** ['ləʊə] *adj* niedriger; (*storey, class etc*) untere(r, s) ▷ *vt* herunterlassen; (*eyes, price*) senken; (*pressure*) verringern; **low-fat** *adj* fettarm; **low tide** [ləʊ'taɪd] *n* Ebbe *f*

loyal ['lɔɪəl] *adj* treu; **loyalty** *n* Treue *f*

lozenge ['lɒzɪndʒ] *n* Pastille *f*

- **L-PLATES**

  Als **L-Plates** werden in Großbritannien die weißen Schilder mit einem roten „L" bezeichnet, die vorn und hinten an jedem von einem Fahrschüler gesteuerten Fahrzeug befestigt werden müssen. Fahrschüler müssen einen vorläufigen Führerschein beantragen und dürfen damit unter der Aufsicht eines erfahrenen Autofahrers auf allen Straßen außer Autobahnen fahren.

Ltd *abbr* = **limited** ≈ GmbH *f*
lubricant ['luːbrɪkənt] *n* Schmiermittel *nt*, Gleitmittel *nt*
luck [lʌk] *n* Glück *nt*; **bad ~** Pech

nt; **luckily** *adv* glücklicherweise, zum Glück; **lucky** *adj* (*number, day etc*) Glücks-; **to be ~** Glück haben
ludicrous ['luːdɪkrəs] *adj* grotesk
luggage ['lʌgɪdʒ] *n* Gepäck *nt*; **luggage compartment** *n* Gepäckraum *m*; **luggage rack** *n* Gepäcknetz *nt*
lukewarm ['luːkwɔːm] *adj* lauwarm
lullaby ['lʌləbaɪ] *n* Schlaflied *nt*
lumbago [lʌm'beɪgəʊ] *n* Hexenschuss *m*
luminous ['luːmɪnəs] *adj* leuchtend
lump [lʌmp] *n* Klumpen *m*; (*Med*) Schwellung *f*; (*in breast*) Knoten *m*; (*of sugar*) Stück *nt*; **lump sum** *n* Pauschalsumme *f*; **lumpy** *adj* klumpig
lunacy ['luːnəsɪ] *n* Wahnsinn *m*; **lunatic** ['luːnətɪk] *adj* wahnsinnig ▷ *n* Wahnsinnige(r) *mf*
lunch, luncheon [lʌntʃ, -ən] *n* Mittagessen *nt*; **to have ~** zu Mittag essen; **lunch break, lunch hour** *n* Mittagspause *f*; **lunchtime** *n* Mittagszeit *f*
lung [lʌŋ] *n* Lunge *f*
lurch [lɜːtʃ] *n*: **to leave sb in the ~** jdn im Stich lassen
lurid ['ljʊərɪd] *adj* (*colour*) grell; (*details*) widerlich
lurk [lɜːk] *vi* lauern
lust [lʌst] *n* (sinnliche) Begierde (*for* nach)
Luxembourg ['lʌksəmbɜːg] *n* Luxemburg *nt*; **Luxembourger** [lʌksəm'bɜːgə] *n* Luxemburger(in) *m(f)*
luxurious [lʌg'ʒʊərɪəs] *adj* luxuriös, Luxus-; **luxury** ['lʌkʃərɪ] *n* (*a. luxuries pl*) Luxus *m*; **~ goods** Luxusgüter *pl*
lynx [lɪŋks] *n* Luchs *m*
lyrics ['lɪrɪks] *npl* Liedtext *m*

m

m *abbr* = **metre** m
M *abbr* (*street*) = **Motorway** A; (*size*) = **medium** M
MA *abbr* = **Master of Arts** Magister Artium *m*
ma [maː] *n* (*fam*) Mutti *f*
mac [mæk] *n* (*Brit fam*) Regenmantel *m*
macaroon [mækəˈruːn] *n* Makrone *f*
Macedonia [masɪdəʊnɪə] *n* Mazedonien *nt*
machine [məˈʃiːn] *n* Maschine *f*; **machine gun** *n* Maschinengewehr *nt*; **machinery** [məˈʃiːnərɪ] *n* Maschinen *pl*; (*fig*) Apparat *m*; **machine washable** *adj* waschmaschinenfest
mackerel [ˈmækrəl] *n* Makrele *f*
macro [ˈmækrəʊ] (*pl* **-s**) *n* (*Inform*) Makro *nt*
mad [mæd] *adj* wahnsinnig, verrückt; (*dog*) tollwütig; (*angry*)

wütend, sauer (*at* auf +*akk*); (*fam*) **~ about** (*fond of*) verrückt nach; **to work like ~** wie verrückt arbeiten; **are you ~?** spinnst du/spinnen Sie?
madam [ˈmædəm] *n* gnädige Frau
mad cow disease [mædˈkaʊdɪˈziːz] *n* Rinderwahnsinn *m*; **maddening** *adj* zum Verrücktwerden
made [meɪd] *pt, pp of* **make**
made-to-measure [ˈmeɪdtəˈmeʒə*] *adj* nach Maß; **~ suit** Maßanzug *m*
madly [ˈmædlɪ] *adv* wie verrückt; (*with adj*) wahnsinnig; **madman** [ˈmædmən] (*pl* **-men**) *n* Verrückte(r) *m*; **madwoman** [ˈmædwʊmən] (*pl* **-women**) *n* Verrückte *f*; **madness** [ˈmædnɪs] *n* Wahnsinn *m*
magazine [mægəˈziːn] *n* Zeitschrift *f*
maggot [ˈmægət] *n* Made *f*
magic [ˈmædʒɪk] *n* Magie *f*; (*activity*) Zauberei *f*; (*fig: effect*) Zauber *m*; **as if by ~** wie durch Zauberei ▷ *adj* Zauber-; (*powers*) magisch; **magician** [məˈdʒɪʃən] *n* Zauberer *m*, Zaub(r)erin *f*
magnet [ˈmægnɪt] *n* Magnet *m*; **magnetic** [mægˈnetɪk] *adj* magnetisch; **magnetism** [ˈmægnɪtɪzəm] *n* (*fig*) Anziehungskraft *f*
magnificent, magnificently [mægˈnɪfɪsənt, -lɪ] *adj, adv* herrlich, großartig
magnify [ˈmægnɪfaɪ] *vt* vergrößern; **magnifying glass** *n* Vergrößerungsglas *nt*, Lupe *f*
magpie [ˈmægpaɪ] *n* Elster *f*
maid [meɪd] *n* Dienstmädchen *nt*; **maiden name** *n* Mädchenname *m*; **maiden voyage** *n* Jungfernfahrt *f*

mail [meɪl] n Post f; (e-mail) Mail f ▷ vt (post) aufgeben; (send) mit der Post schicken (to an +akk); **mailbox** n (US) Briefkasten m; (Inform) Mailbox f; **mailing list** n Adressenliste f; **mailman** n (pl -men) (US) Briefträger m; **mail order** n Bestellung f per Post; **mail order firm** n Versandhaus nt; **mailshot** n Mailing nt

main [meɪn] adj Haupt-; ~ **course** Hauptgericht nt; **the ~ thing** die Hauptsache ▷ n (pipe) Hauptleitung f; **mainframe** n Großrechner m; **mainland** n Festland nt; **mainly** adv hauptsächlich; **main road** n Hauptverkehrsstraße f; **main street** n (US) Hauptstraße f

maintain [meɪnˈteɪn] vt (keep up) aufrechterhalten; (machine, roads) instand halten; (service) warten; (claim) behaupten; **maintenance** [ˈmeɪntənəns] n Instandhaltung f; (Tech) Wartung f

maize [meɪz] n Mais m

majestic [məˈdʒestɪk] adj majestätisch; **majesty** [ˈmædʒɪstɪ] n Majestät f; **Your/His/Her Majesty** Eure/Seine/Ihre Majestät

major [ˈmeɪdʒə*] adj (bigger) größer; (important) bedeutend; ~ **part** Großteil m; (role) wichtige Rolle; ~ **road** Hauptverkehrsstraße f; (Mus) **A** ~ A-Dur nt ▷ vi (US) **to ~ in sth** etw als Hauptfach studieren

Majorca [məˈjɔːkə] n Mallorca nt

majority [məˈdʒɒrɪtɪ] n Mehrheit f; **to be in the ~** in der Mehrzahl sein

make [meɪk] n Marke f ▷ vt (made, made) machen; (manufacture) herstellen; (clothes) anfertigen; (dress) nähen; (soup) zubereiten; (bread, cake) backen; (tea, coffee) kochen; (speech) halten; (earn) verdienen; (decision) treffen; **it's made of gold** es ist aus Gold; **to ~ sb do sth** jdn dazu bringen, etw zu tun; (force) jdn zwingen, etw zu tun; **she made us wait** sie ließ uns warten; **what ~s you think that?** wie kommen Sie darauf?; **it ~s the room look smaller** es lässt den Raum kleiner wirken; **to ~ (it to) the airport** (reach) den Flughafen erreichen; (in time) es zum Flughafen schaffen; **he never really made it** er hat es nie zu etwas gebracht; **she didn't ~ it through the night** sie hat die Nacht nicht überlebt; (calculate) **I ~ it £5/a quarter to six** nach meiner Rechnung kommt es auf 5 Pfund/nach meiner Uhr ist es dreiviertel sechs; **he's just made for this job** er ist für diese Arbeit wie geschaffen; **make for** vt zusteuern auf +akk; **make of** vt (think of) halten von; **I couldn't ~ anything of it** ich wurde daraus nicht schlau; **make off** vi sich davonmachen (with mit); **make out** vi zurechtkommen ▷ vt (cheque) ausstellen; (list) aufstellen; (understand) verstehen; (discern) ausmachen; **to ~ (that) ...** es so hinstellen, als ob ...; **make up** vt (team etc) bilden; (face) schminken; (invent: story etc) erfinden; **to ~ one's mind** sich entscheiden; **to make (it) up with sb** sich mit jdm aussöhnen ▷ vi sich versöhnen; **make up for** vt ausgleichen; (time) aufholen

make-believe adj Fantasie-; **makeover** n gründliche Veränderung, Verschönerung f; **maker** n (Comm) Hersteller(in) m(f); **makeshift** adj behelfsmäßig; **make-up** n

Make-up *nt*, Schminke *f*; **making**
['meɪkɪŋ] *n* Herstellung *f*
maladjusted [mælə'dʒʌstɪd] *adj*
verhaltensgestört
malaria [mə'lɛərɪə] *n* Malaria *f*
Malaysia [mə'leɪʒɪə] *n* Malaysia
nt
male [meɪl] *n* Mann *m*; (*animal*)
Männchen *nt* ▷ *adj* männlich;
~ chauvinist Chauvi *m*, Macho *m*;
~ nurse Krankenpfleger *m*
malfunction [mæl'fʌŋkʃən] *vi*
nicht richtig funktionieren ▷ *n*
Defekt *m*
malice ['mælɪs] *n* Bosheit *f*;
malicious [mə'lɪʃəs] *adj* boshaft;
(*behaviour, action*) böswillig;
(*damage*) mutwillig
malignant [mə'lɪgnənt] *adj*
bösartig
mall [mɔːl] *n* (*US*)
Einkaufszentrum *nt*
malnutrition [mælnjʊ'trɪʃən] *n*
Unterernährung *f*
malt [mɔːlt] *n* Malz *nt*
Malta ['mɔːltə] *n* Malta *nt*;
Maltese [mɔːl'tiːz] *adj*
maltesisch ▷ *n* (*person*)
Malteser(in) *m(f)*; (*language*)
Maltesisch *nt*
maltreat [mæl'triːt] *vt* schlecht
behandeln; (*violently*) misshandeln
mammal ['mæməl] *n* Säugetier
nt
mammoth ['mæməθ] *adj*
Mammut-, Riesen-
man [mæn] (*pl* **men**) *n* (*male*)
Mann *m*; (*human race*) der Mensch,
die Menschen *pl*; (*in chess*) Figur *f*
▷ *vt* besetzen
manage ['mænɪdʒ] *vi* zurechtkommen; **can you ~?** schaffst du
es?; **to ~ without sth** ohne etw
auskommen, auf etw verzichten
können ▷ *vt* (*control*) leiten;
(*musician, sportsman*) managen;
(*cope with*) fertig werden mit; (*task,*

portion, climb etc) schaffen; **to ~ to
do sth** es schaffen, etw zu tun;
manageable *adj* (*object*)
handlich; (*task*) zu bewältigen;
management *n* Leitung *f*;
(*directors*) Direktion *f*; (*subject*)
Management *nt*,
Betriebswirtschaft *f*;
management consultant *n*
Unternehmensberater(in) *m(f)*;
manager *n* Geschäftsführer(in)
m(f); (*departmental ~*)
Abteilungsleiter(in) *m(f)*; (*of
branch, bank*) Filialleiter(in) *m(f)*; (*of
musician, sportsman*) Manager(in)
m(f); **managing director** *n*
Geschäftsführer(in) *m(f)*
mane [meɪn] *n* Mähne *f*
maneuver (*US*) *see* **manoeuvre**
mango ['mæŋgəʊ] (*pl* **-es**) *n*
Mango *f*
man-hour *n* Arbeitsstunde *f*
manhunt *n* Fahndung *f*
mania ['meɪnɪə] *n* Manie *f*;
maniac ['meɪnɪæk] *n* Wahnsin-
nige(r) *mf*; (*fan*) Fanatiker(in)
m(f)
manicure ['mænɪkjʊə*] *n*
Maniküre *f*
manipulate [mə'nɪpjʊleɪt] *vt*
manipulieren
mankind [mæn'kaɪnd] *n*
Menschheit *f*
manly ['mænlɪ] *adj* männlich
man-made ['mænmeɪd] *adj*
(*product*) künstlich
manner ['mænə*] *n* Art *f*; **in this
~** auf diese Art und Weise; **~s** *pl*
Manieren *pl*
manoeuvre [mə'nuːvə*] *n*
Manöver *nt* ▷ *vt, vi* manövrieren
manor ['mænə*] *n*: **~ (house)**
Herrenhaus *nt*
manpower ['mænpaʊə*] *n*
Arbeitskräfte *pl*
mansion ['mænʃən] *n* Villa *f*; (*of
old family*) Herrenhaus *nt*

manslaughter ['mænslɔːtə*] n
Totschlag m
mantelpiece ['mæntlpiːs] n
Kaminsims m
manual ['mænjʊəl] adj manuell,
Hand- ▷ n Handbuch nt
manufacture [mænjʊ'fæktʃə*]
vt herstellen ▷ n Herstellung f;
manufacturer n Hersteller m
manure [mə'njʊə*] n Dung m;
(esp artificial) Dünger m
many ['menɪ] (**more, most**) adj,
pron viele; **~ times** oft; **not
~ people** nicht viele Leute; **too
~ problems** zu viele Probleme
map [mæp] n Landkarte f; (of
town) Stadtplan m
maple ['meɪpl] n Ahorn m
marathon ['mærəθən] n Marathon m
marble ['mɑːbl] n Marmor m; (for
playing) Murmel f
march [mɑːtʃ] vi marschieren
▷ n Marsch m; (protest)
Demonstration f
March [mɑːtʃ] n März m; see also
September
mare [meə] n Stute f
margarine [mɑːdʒə'riːn] n
Margarine f
margin ['mɑːdʒɪn] n Rand m;
(extra amount) Spielraum m;
(Comm) Gewinnspanne f;
marginal adj (difference etc)
geringfügig
marijuana [mærɪjʊ'ɑːnə] n
Marihuana nt
marine [mə'riːn] adj Meeres-
marital ['mærɪtl] adj ehelich;
~ status Familienstand m
maritime ['mærɪtaɪm] adj See-
marjoram ['mɑːdʒərəm] n
Majoran m
mark [mɑːk] n (spot) Fleck m; (at
school) Note f; (sign) Zeichen nt
▷ vt (make ~) Flecken machen auf
+akk; (indicate) markieren;

(schoolwork) benoten, korrigieren,
Flecken machen auf +akk;
markedly ['mɑːkɪdlɪ] adv merk-
lich; (with comp adj) wesentlich;
marker n (in book) Lesezeichen nt;
(pen) Marker m
market ['mɑːkɪt] n Markt m;
(stock ~) Börse f ▷ vt (Comm: new
product) auf den Markt bringen;
(goods) vertreiben; **marketing** n
Marketing nt; **market leader** n
Marktführer m; **market place** n
Marktplatz m; **market research** n
Marktforschung f
marmalade ['mɑːməleɪd] n
Orangenmarmelade f
maroon [mə'ruːn] adj rötlich
braun
marquee [mɑː'kiː] n großes Zelt
marriage ['mærɪdʒ] n Ehe f;
(wedding) Heirat f (to mit);
married ['mærɪd] adj (person)
verheiratet
marrow ['mærəʊ] n (bone ~)
Knochenmark nt; (vegetable) Kürbis
m
marry ['mærɪ] vt heiraten; (join)
trauen; (take as husband, wife)
heiraten ▷ vi: **to ~ / to get
married** heiraten
marsh [mɑːʃ] n Marsch f, Sumpf
m
marshal ['mɑːʃəl] n (at rally etc)
Ordner m; (US: police)
Bezirkspolizeichef m
martial arts ['mɑːʃəl'ɑːts] npl
Kampfsportarten pl
martyr ['mɑːtə*] n Märtyrer(in)
m(f)
marvel ['mɑːvəl] n Wunder nt
▷ vi staunen (at über +akk);
marvellous, marvelous (US) adj
wunderbar
marzipan [mɑːzɪ'pæn] n Marzipan nt o m
mascara [mæ'skɑːrə] n Wimperntusche f

m

mascot ['mæskɒt] n Maskottchen nt
masculine ['mæskjʊlɪn] adj
männlich
mashed [mæʃt] adj **~ potatoes**
pl Kartoffelbrei m, Kartoffelpüree
nt
mask [mɑːsk] n (a. Inform) Maske
f ▷ vt (feelings) verbergen
masochist ['mæsəʊkɪst] n
Masochist(in) m(f)
mason ['meɪsn] n (stone~)
Steinmetz(in) m(f); **masonry** n
Mauerwerk nt
mass [mæs] n Masse f; (of people)
Menge f; (Rel) Messe f; **~es of**
massenhaft
massacre ['mæsəkə*] n Blutbad
nt
massage ['mæsɑːʒ] n Massage f
▷ vt massieren
massive ['mæsɪv] adj (powerful)
gewaltig; (very large) riesig
mass media ['mæs'miːdɪə] npl
Massenmedien pl; **mass-produce**
vt in Massenproduktion
herstellen; **mass production** n
Massenproduktion f
master ['mɑːstə*] n Herr m; (of
dog) Besitzer m, Herrchen nt;
(teacher) Lehrer m; (artist) Meister
m ▷ vt meistern; (language etc)
beherrschen; **masterly** adj
meisterhaft; **masterpiece** n
Meisterwerk nt
masturbate ['mæstəbeɪt] vi
masturbieren
mat [mæt] n Matte f; (for table)
Untersetzer m
match [mætʃ] n Streichholz
nt; (Sport) Wettkampf m; (ball
games) Spiel nt; (tennis) Match
nt ▷ vt (be like, suit) passen zu;
(equal) gleichkommen +dat
▷ vi zusammenpassen; **matchbox**
n Streichholzschachtel f;
matching adj (one item)

passend; (two items)
zusammenpassend
mate [meɪt] n (companion)
Kumpel m; (of animal) Weibchen
nt/Männchen nt ▷ vi sich paaren
material [mə'tɪərɪəl] n Material
nt; (for book etc, cloth) Stoff m;
materialistic [mətɪərɪə'lɪstɪk]
adj materialistisch; **materialize**
[mə'tɪərɪəlaɪz] vi zustande
kommen; (hope) wahr werden
maternal [mə'tɜːnl] adj
mütterlich; **maternity**
[mə'tɜːnɪtɪ] adj: **~ dress**
Umstandskleid nt; **~ leave**
Elternzeit f (der Mutter); **~ ward**
Entbindungsstation f
math [mæθ] n (US fam) Mathe f;
mathematical [mæθə'mætɪkəl]
adj mathematisch; **mathematics**
[mæθə'mætɪks] nsing Mathematik
f; **maths** [mæθs] nsing (Brit fam)
Mathe f
matinée ['mætɪneɪ] n Nachmit-
tagsvorstellung f
matter ['mætə*] n (substance)
Materie f; (affair) Sache f; **a
personal ~** eine persönliche
Angelegenheit; **a ~ of taste** eine
Frage des Geschmacks; **no
~ how/what** egal wie/was;
what's the ~? was ist los?; **as a
~ of fact** eigentlich; **a ~ of time**
eine Frage der Zeit ▷ vi darauf
ankommen, wichtig sein; **it
doesn't ~** es macht nichts;
matter-of-fact adj sachlich,
nüchtern
mattress ['mætrəs] n Matratze f
mature [mə'tjʊə*] adj reif ▷ vi
reif werden; **maturity**
[mə'tjʊərɪtɪ] n Reife f
maximum ['mæksɪməm] adj
Höchst-, höchste(r, s); **~ speed**
Höchstgeschwindigkeit f ▷ n
Maximum nt
may [meɪ] (**might**) vb aux (be

possible) können; (*have permission*) dürfen; **it ~ rain** es könnte regnen; **~ I smoke?** darf ich rauchen?; **it ~ not happen** es passiert vielleicht gar nicht; **we ~ as well go** wir können ruhig gehen

May [meɪ] *n* Mai *m*; *see also* **September**

maybe ['meɪbiː] *adv* vielleicht

May Day ['meɪdeɪ] *n* der erste Mai

mayo ['meɪəʊ] (*US fam*), **mayonnaise** [meɪə'neɪz] *n* Mayo *f*, Mayonnaise *f*, Majonäse *f*

mayor [mɛə°] *n* Bürgermeister *m*

maze [meɪz] *n* Irrgarten *m*; (*fig*) Wirrwarr *nt*

MB *abbr* = **megabyte** MB *nt*

O   **KEYWORD**

me [miː] *pron* **1** (*direct*) mich; **it's me** ich bin's
2 (*indirect*) mir; **give them to me** gib sie mir
3 (*after prep*) (+*akk*) mich; (+*dat*) mir; **with/without me** mit mir/ohne mich

meadow ['medəʊ] *n* Wiese *f*
meal [miːl] *n* Essen *nt*, Mahlzeit *f*; **to go out for a ~** essen gehen; **meal pack** *n* (*US*) tiefgekühltes Fertiggericht; **meal time** *n* Essenszeit *f*
mean [miːn] (**meant, meant**) *vt* (*signify*) bedeuten; (*have in mind*) meinen; (*intend*) vorhaben; **I ~ it** ich meine das ernst; **what do you ~ (by that)?** was willst du damit sagen?; **to ~ to do sth** etw tun wollen; **it was ~t for you** es war für dich bestimmt (*o gedacht*); **it was ~t to be a joke** es sollte ein Witz sein ▷ *vi*: **he ~s well** er

meint es gut ▷ *adj* (*stingy*) geizig; (*spiteful*) gemein (*to zu*); **meaning** ['miːnɪŋ] *n* Bedeutung *f*; (*of life, poem*) Sinn *m*; **meaningful** *adj* sinnvoll; **meaningless** *adj* (*text*) ohne Sinn

means [miːnz] (*pl* **means**) *n* Mittel *nt*; (*pl: funds*) Mittel *pl*; **by ~ of** durch, mittels; **by all ~** selbstverständlich; **by no ~** keineswegs; **~ of transport** Beförderungsmittel

meant [ment] *pt, pp of* **mean**

meantime [miːn'taɪm] *adv*: **in the ~** inzwischen; **meanwhile** [miːn'waɪl] *adv* inzwischen

measles ['miːzlz] *nsing* Masern *pl*; **German ~** Röteln *pl*

measure ['meʒə°] *vt, vi* messen ▷ *n* (*unit, device for measuring*) Maß *nt*; (*step*) Maßnahme *f*; **to take ~s** Maßnahmen ergreifen; **measurement** *n* (*amount measured*) Maß *nt*

meat [miːt] *n* Fleisch *nt*; **meatball** *n* Fleischbällchen *nt*

mechanic [mɪ'kænɪk] *n* Mechaniker(in) *m(f)*; **mechanical** *adj* mechanisch; **mechanics** *nsing* Mechanik *f*; **mechanism** ['mekənɪzəm] *n* Mechanismus *m*

medal ['medl] *n* Medaille *f*; (*decoration*) Orden *m*; **medalist** (*US*), **medallist** ['medəlɪst] *n* Medaillengewinner(in) *m(f)*

media ['miːdɪə] *npl* Medien *pl*

median strip ['miːdɪən strɪp] *n* (*US*) Mittelstreifen *m*

mediate ['miːdɪeɪt] *vi* vermitteln

medical ['medɪkəl] *adj* medizinisch; (*treatment etc*) ärztlich; **~ student** *n* Medizinstudent(in) *m(f)* ▷ *n* Untersuchung *f*; **Medicare** ['medɪkɛə°] *n* (*US*) Krankenkasse *f* für ältere Leute; **medication**

m

[medɪ'keɪʃən] n Medikamente pl;
to be on ~ Medikamente nehmen;
medicinal [me'dɪsɪnl] adj Heil-;
~ herbs Heilkräuter pl; **medicine**
['medsɪn] n Arznei f; (science)
Medizin f

medieval [medɪ'iːvəl] adj
mittelalterlich

mediocre [miːdɪ'əʊkə°] adj
mittelmäßig

meditate ['medɪteɪt] vi meditieren; (fig) nachdenken (on über
+akk)

Mediterranean
[medɪtə'reɪnɪən] n (sea)
Mittelmeer nt; (region)
Mittelmeerraum m

medium ['miːdɪəm] adj (quality,
size) mittlere(r, s); (steak)
halbdurch; **~ (dry)** (wine)
halbtrocken; **~ sized** mittelgroß;
~ wave Mittelwelle f ▷ n (pl
media) Medium nt; (means) Mittel
nt

meet [miːt] (**met, met**) vt
treffen; (by arrangement) sich
treffen mit; (difficulties) stoßen auf
+akk; (get to know) kennenlernen;
(requirement, demand) gerecht
werden +dat; (deadline) einhalten;
pleased to ~ you sehr angenehm!;
to ~ sb at the station jdn vom
Bahnhof abholen ▷ vi sich
treffen; (become acquainted) sich
kennenlernen; **we've met**
(before) wir kennen uns schon;
meet up vt sich treffen (with
mit); **meet with** vt (group)
zusammenkommen mit;
(difficulties, resistance etc) stoßen
auf +akk; **meeting** n Treffen nt;
(business ~) Besprechung f; (of
committee) Sitzung f; (assembly)
Versammlung f; **meeting place**,
meeting point n Treffpunkt m

megabyte ['megəbaɪt] n
Megabyte nt

melody ['melədɪ] n Melodie f

melon ['melən] n Melone f

melt [melt] vt, vi schmelzen

member ['membə°] n Mitglied
nt; (of tribe, species) Angehörige(r)
mf; **Member of Parliament**
Parlamentsabgeordnete(r) mf;
membership n Mitgliedschaft f;
membership card n
Mitgliedskarte f

memento [mə'mentəʊ] (pl **-es**)
n Andenken nt (of an +akk)

memo ['meməʊ] (pl **-s**) n
Mitteilung f, Memo nt; **memo pad**
n Notizblock m

memorable ['memərəbl] adj
unvergesslich; **memorial**
[mɪ'mɔːrɪəl] n Denkmal nt (to
für); **memorize** ['meməraɪz] vt
sich einprägen, auswendig lernen;
memory ['memərɪ] n Gedächtnis nt; (Inform: of computer)
Speicher m; (sth recalled)
Erinnerung f; **in ~ of** zur
Erinnerung an +akk; **memory**
stick n (Inform) Memorystick® m

men [men] pl of **man**

menace ['menɪs] n Bedrohung f;
(danger) Gefahr f

mend [mend] vt reparieren;
(clothes) flicken ▷ n. **on the ~** auf
dem Wege der Besserung

meningitis [menɪn'dʒaɪtɪs] n
Hirnhautentzündung f

menopause ['menəʊpɔːz] n
Wechseljahre pl

mental ['mentl] adj geistig;
mentality [men'tælɪtɪ] n Mentalität f; **mentally** ['mentəlɪ] adv
geistig; **~ handicapped** geistig
behindert; **~ ill** geisteskrank

mention ['menʃən] n Erwäh-
nung f ▷ vt erwähnen (to sb jdm
gegenüber); **don't ~ it** bitte sehr,
gern geschehen

menu ['menjuː] n Speisekarte f;
(Inform) Menü nt

merchandise ['mɜːtʃəndaɪz] n
Handelsware f; **merchant**
['mɜːtʃənt] adj Handels-
merciful ['mɜːsɪfʊl] adj gnädig;
mercifully adv glücklicherweise
mercury ['mɜːkjʊrɪ] n Quecksilber nt
mercy ['mɜːsɪ] n Gnade f
mere [mɪə°] adj bloß; **merely**
['mɪəlɪ] adv bloß, lediglich
merge [mɜːdʒ] vi verschmelzen;
(Auto) sich einfädeln; (Comm)
fusionieren; **merger** n (Comm)
Fusion f
meringue [mə'ræŋ] n Baiser nt
merit ['merɪt] n Verdienst nt;
(advantage) Vorzug m
merry ['merɪ] adj fröhlich; (fam:
tipsy) angeheitert; **Merry**
Christmas Fröhliche
Weihnachten!; **merry-go-round** n
Karussell nt
mess [mes] n Unordnung f;
(muddle) Durcheinander nt; (dirty)
Schweinerei f; (trouble)
Schwierigkeiten pl; **in a**
~ (muddled) durcheinander; (untidy)
unordentlich; (fig: person) in der
Klemme; **to make a ~ of sth** etw
verpfuschen; **to look a**
~ unmöglich aussehen; **mess**
about vi (tinker with)
herummurksen (with an +dat);
(play the fool) herumalbern; (do
nothing in particular)
herumgammeln; **mess up** vt
verpfuschen; (make untidy) in
Unordnung bringen; (dirty)
schmutzig machen
message ['mesɪdʒ] n Mitteilung
f, Nachricht f; (meaning) Botschaft
f; **can I give him a ~?** kann ich
ihm etwas ausrichten?; **please**
leave a ~ (on answerphones)
bitte hinterlassen Sie eine
Nachricht; **I get the ~** ich hab's
verstanden

messenger ['mesɪndʒə°] n Bote
m
messy ['mesɪ] adj (untidy)
unordentlich; (situation etc)
verfahren
met [met] pt, pp of **meet**
metal ['metl] n Metall nt;
metallic [mɪ'tælɪk] adj
metallisch
meteorology [miːtɪə'rɒlədʒɪ] n
Meteorologie f
meter ['miːtə°] n Zähler m;
(parking meter) Parkuhr f; (US) see
metre
method ['meθəd] n Methode f;
methodical [mɪ'θɒdɪkəl] adj
methodisch
meticulous [mɪ'tɪkjʊləs] adj
(peinlich) genau
metre ['miːtə°] n Meter m o nt;
metric ['metrɪk] adj metrisch;
~ system Dezimalsystem nt
Mexico ['meksɪkəʊ] n Mexiko nt
mice [maɪs] pl of **mouse**
mickey ['mɪkɪ] n: **to take the**
~ (out of sb) (fam) (jdn) auf den
Arm nehmen
microchip ['maɪkrəʊtʃɪp] n
(Inform) Mikrochip m; **microphone**
n Mikrofon nt; **microscope** n
Mikroskop nt; **microwave (oven)**
n Mikrowelle(nherd) f(m)
mid [mɪd] adj: **in ~ January**
Mitte Januar; **he's in his ~ forties**
er ist Mitte vierzig
midday ['mɪddeɪ] n Mittag m;
at ~ mittags
middle ['mɪdl] n Mitte f; (waist)
Taille f; **in the ~ of** mitten in +dat;
to be in the ~ of doing sth gerade
dabei sein, etw zu tun ▷ adj
mittlere(r, s), Mittel-; **the ~ one**
der/die/das Mittlere;
middle-aged adj mittleren
Alters; **Middle Ages** npl: **the**
~ das Mittelalter; **middle-class**
adj mittelständisch; (bourgeois)

m

bürgerlich; **middle classes** *npl*:
the ~ der Mittelstand; **Middle
East** *n*: **the ~** der Nahe Osten;
middle name *n* zweiter
Vorname
Midlands ['mɪdləndz] *npl*: **the
~** Mittelengland *nt*
midnight ['mɪdnaɪt] *n* Mitternacht *f*
midst [mɪdst] *n*: **in the ~ of**
mitten in +*dat*
midsummer ['mɪdsʌmə°] *n*
Hochsommer *m*; **Midsummer's
Day** Sommersonnenwende *f*
midway [mɪd'weɪ] *adv* auf
halbem Wege; **~ through the film**
nach der Hälfte des Films;
midweek [mɪd'wiːk] *adj, adv* in
der Mitte der Woche
midwife ['mɪdwaɪf] (*pl* **-wives**) *n*
Hebamme *f*
midwinter [mɪd'wɪntə°] *n*
tiefster Winter
might [maɪt] *pt* of **may**;
(*possibility*) könnte; (*permission*)
dürfte; (*would*) würde; **they ~ still
come** sie könnten noch kommen;
he ~ have let me know er hätte
mir doch Bescheid sagen können;
I thought she ~ change her mind
ich dachte schon, sie würde sich
anders entscheiden ▷ *n* Macht *f*,
Kraft *f*
mighty ['maɪtɪ] *adj* gewaltig;
(*powerful*) mächtig
migraine ['miːɡreɪn] *n* Migräne
f
migrant ['maɪɡrənt] *n* (*bird*)
Zugvogel *m*; **~ worker**
Gastarbeiter(in) *m(f)*; Migrant(in)
m(f); **migrate** [maɪ'ɡreɪt] *vi*
abwandern; (*birds*) nach Süden
ziehen
mike [maɪk] *n* (*fam*) Mikro *nt*
Milan [mɪ'læn] *n* Mailand *nt*
mild [maɪld] *adj* mild; (*person*)
sanft; **mildly** *adv*: **to put it**

~ gelinde gesagt; **mildness** *n*
Milde *f*
mile [maɪl] *n* Meile *f* (=1,609 km);
for ~s (and ~s) ≈ kilometerweit; **~s
per hour** Meilen pro Stunde; **~s
better than** hundertmal besser
als; **mileage** *n* Meilen *pl*,
Meilenzahl *f*; **mileometer**
[maɪ'lɒmɪtə°] *n* ≈
Kilometerzähler *m*; **milestone** *n*
(*a. fig*) Meilenstein *m*
militant ['mɪlɪtənt] *adj* militant;
military ['mɪlɪtərɪ] *adj* Militär-,
militärisch
milk [mɪlk] *n* Milch *f* ▷ *vt*
melken; **milk chocolate** *n*
Vollmilchschokolade *f*; **milkman**
(*pl* **-men**) *n* Milchmann *m*; **milk
shake** *n* Milkshake *m*,
Milchmixgetränk *nt*
mill [mɪl] *n* Mühle *f*; (*factory*)
Fabrik *f*
millennium [mɪ'lenɪəm] *n*
Jahrtausend *nt*
milligramme ['mɪlɪɡræm] *n*
Milligramm *nt*; **milliliter** (*US*),
millilitre *n* Milliliter *m*;
millimeter (*US*), **millimetre** *n*
Millimeter *m*
million ['mɪljən] *n* Million *f*; **five
~** fünf Millionen; **~s of people**
Millionen von Menschen;
millionaire [mɪljə'nɛə°] *n* Mil-
lionär(in) *m(f)*
mime [maɪm] *n* Pantomime *f*
▷ *vt, vi* mimen; **mimic** ['mɪmɪk]
n Imitator(in) *m(f)* ▷ *vt, vi*
nachahmen; **mimicry** ['mɪmɪkrɪ]
n Nachahmung *f*
mince [mɪns] *vt* (zer)hacken
▷ *n* (*meat*) Hackfleisch *nt*;
mincemeat *n* süße Gebäckfüllung
aus Rosinen, Äpfeln, Zucker, Gewürzen
und Talg; **mince pie** *n* mit
'mincemeat' gefülltes süßes
Weihnachtsgebäck
mind [maɪnd] *n* (*intellect*)

Verstand m; (also person) Geist m;
out of sight, out of ~ aus den
Augen, aus dem Sinn; **he is out of
his ~** er ist nicht bei Verstand; **to
keep sth in ~** etw im Auge
behalten; **do you have sth in ~?**
denken Sie an etwas Besonderes?;
I've a lot on my ~ mich
beschäftigt so vieles im Moment;
to change one's ~ es sich dat
anders überlegen ▷ vt (look after)
aufpassen auf +akk; (object to)
etwas haben gegen; **~ you, ...**
allerdings ...; **I wouldn't ~ ...** ich
hätte nichts gegen ...; **"~ the
step"** „Vorsicht Stufe!" ▷ vi etwas
dagegen haben; **do you ~ if I ...**
macht es Ihnen etwas aus, wenn
ich ...; **I don't ~** es ist mir egal,
meinetwegen; **never ~** macht
nichts

mine [maɪn] pron meine(r, s);
this is ~ das gehört mir; **a friend
of ~** ein Freund von mir ▷ n
(coalmine) Bergwerk nt; (Mil) Mine
f; **miner** n Bergarbeiter(in) m(f)

mineral ['mɪnərəl] n Mineral nt;
mineral water n Mineralwasser
nt

mingle ['mɪŋgl] vi sich mischen
(with unter +akk)

miniature ['mɪnɪtʃə*] adj
Miniatur-

minibar ['mɪnɪbɑː] n Minibar f;
minibus n Kleinbus m; **minicab** n
Kleintaxi nt

minimal ['mɪnɪml] adj minimal;
minimize ['mɪnɪmaɪz] vt auf ein
Minimum reduzieren; **minimum**
['mɪnɪməm] n Minimum nt ▷ adj
Mindest-

mining ['maɪnɪŋ] n Bergbau m

miniskirt n Minirock m

minister ['mɪnɪstə*] n (Pol)
Minister(in) m(f); (Rel) Pastor(in)
m(f), Pfarrer(in) m(f); **ministry**
['mɪnɪstrɪ] n (Pol) Ministerium nt

minor ['maɪnə*] adj kleiner;
(insignificant) unbedeutend;
(operation, offence) harmlos; **~ road**
Nebenstraße f; (Mus) **A ~** a-Moll nt
▷ n (Brit: under 18)
Minderjährige(r) mf; **minority**
[maɪ'nɒrɪtɪ] n Minderheit f

mint [mɪnt] n Minze f; (sweet)
Pfefferminz(bonbon) nt; **mint
sauce** n Minzsoße f

minus ['maɪnəs] prep minus;
(without) ohne

minute [maɪ'njuːt] adj winzig;
in ~ detail genauestens ▷ ['mɪnɪt]
n Minute f; **just a ~** Moment mal!;
any ~ jeden Augenblick; **~s** pl (of
meeting) Protokoll nt

miracle ['mɪrəkl] n Wunder nt;
miraculous [mɪ'rækjʊləs] adj
unglaublich

mirage ['mɪrɑːʒ] n Fata Morgana
f, Luftspiegelung f

mirror ['mɪrə*] n Spiegel m

misbehave [mɪsbɪ'heɪv] vi sich
schlecht benehmen

miscalculation
['mɪskælkjʊ'leɪʃən] n Fehlkalku-
lation f; (misjudgement)
Fehleinschätzung f

miscarriage [mɪs'kærɪdʒ] n
(Med) Fehlgeburt f

miscellaneous [mɪsɪ'leɪnɪəs]
adj verschieden

mischief ['mɪstʃɪf] n Unfug m;
mischievous ['mɪstʃɪvəs] adj
(person) durchtrieben; (glance)
verschmitzt

misconception [mɪskən'sepʃən]
n falsche Vorstellung

misconduct [mɪs'kɒndʌkt] n
Vergehen nt

miser ['maɪzə*] n Geizhals m

miserable ['mɪzərəbl] adj (person) todunglücklich; (conditions,
life) elend; (pay, weather)
miserabel

miserly ['maɪzəlɪ] adj geizig

m

misery ['mɪzərɪ] n Elend nt; (suffering) Qualen pl

misfit ['mɪsfɪt] n Außenseiter(in) m(f)

misfortune [mɪs'fɔːtʃən] n Pech nt

misguided [mɪs'gaɪdɪd] adj irrig; (optimism) unangebracht

misinform [mɪsɪn'fɔːm] vt falsch informieren

misinterpret [mɪsɪn'tɜːprɪt] vt falsch auslegen

misjudge [mɪs'dʒʌdʒ] vt falsch beurteilen

mislay [mɪs'leɪ] irr vt verlegen

mislead [mɪs'liːd] irr vt irreführen; **misleading** adj irreführend

misprint ['mɪsprɪnt] n Druckfehler m

mispronounce [mɪsprə'naʊns]-vt falsch aussprechen

miss [mɪs] vt (fail to hit, catch) verfehlen; (not notice, hear) nicht mitbekommen; (be too late for) verpassen; (chance) versäumen; (regret the absence of) vermissen; **I ~ you** du fehlst mir ▷ vi nicht treffen; (shooting) danebenschießen; (ball, shot etc) danebengehen; **miss out** vt auslassen ▷ vi: **to ~ on sth** etw verpassen

Miss [mɪs] n (unmarried woman) Fräulein nt

missile ['mɪsaɪl] n Geschoss nt; (rocket) Rakete f

missing ['mɪsɪŋ] adj (person) vermisst; (thing) fehlend; **to be/go ~** vermisst werden, fehlen

mission ['mɪʃən] n (Pol, Mil, Rel) Auftrag m, Mission f; **missionary** ['mɪʃənrɪ] n Missionar(in) m(f)

mist [mɪst] n (feiner) Nebel m; (haze) Dunst m; **mist over, mist up** vi sich beschlagen

mistake [mɪ'steɪk] n Fehler m; **by ~** aus Versehen ▷ irr vt

(**mistook, mistaken**) (misunderstand) falsch verstehen; (mix up) verwechseln (for mit); **there's no mistaking ...** ... ist unverkennbar; (meaning) ... ist unmissverständlich; **mistaken** adj (idea, identity) falsch; **to be ~** sich irren, falschliegen

mistletoe ['mɪsltəʊ] n Mistel f

mistreat [mɪs'triːt] vt schlecht behandeln

mistress ['mɪstrɪs] n (lover) Geliebte f

mistrust [mɪs'trʌst] n Misstrauen nt (of gegen) ▷ vt misstrauen +dat

misty ['mɪstɪ] adj neblig; (hazy) dunstig

misunderstand [mɪsʌndə'stænd] irr vt, vi falsch verstehen; **misunderstanding** n Missverständnis nt; (disagreement) Differenz f

mitten ['mɪtn] n Fausthandschuh m

mix [mɪks] n (mixture) Mischung f ▷ vt mischen; (blend) vermischen (with mit); (drinks, music) mixen; **to ~ business with pleasure** das Angenehme mit dem Nützlichen verbinden ▷ vi (liquids) sich vermischen lassen; **mix up** vt (mix) zusammenmischen; (confuse) verwechseln (with mit); **mixed** adj gemischt; **a ~ bunch** eine bunt gemischte Truppe; **~ grill** Mixed Grill m; **~ vegetables** Mischgemüse nt; **mixer** n (for food) Mixer m; **mixture** ['mɪkstʃə*] n Mischung f; (Med) Saft m; **mix-up** n Durcheinander nt, Missverständnis nt

ml abbr = **millilitre** ml

mm abbr = **millimetre** mm

moan [məʊn] n Stöhnen nt; (complaint) Gejammer nt ▷ vi

stöhnen; (*complain*) jammern, meckern (*about* über +akk)

mobile ['məʊbaɪl] *adj* beweglich; (*on wheels*) fahrbar ▷ *n* (*phone*) Handy *nt*; **mobile phone** *n* Mobiltelefon *nt*, Handy *nt*

mobility [məʊ'bɪlɪtɪ] *n* Beweglichkeit *f*

mock [mɒk] *vt* verspotten ▷ *adj* Schein-; **mockery** *n* Spott *m*

mod cons ['mɒd'kɒnz] *abbr* = **modern conveniences** (moderner) Komfort

mode [məʊd] *n* Art *f*; (*Inform*) Modus *m*

model ['mɒdl] *n* Modell *nt*; (*example*) Vorbild *nt*; (*fashion ~*) Model *nt* ▷ *adj* (*miniature*) Modell-; (*perfect*) Muster- ▷ *vt* (*make*) formen ▷ *vi*: **she ~s for Versace** sie arbeitet als Model bei Versace

modem ['məʊdem] *n* Modem *nt*

moderate ['mɒdərət] *adj* mäßig; (*views, politics*) gemäßigt; (*income, success*) mittelmäßig ▷ *n* (*Pol*) Gemäßigte(r) *mf* ▷ ['mɒdəreɪt] *vt* mäßigen; **moderation** [mɒdə'reɪʃən] *n* Mäßigung *f*; **in ~** mit Maßen

modern ['mɒdən] *adj* modern; **~ history** neuere Geschichte; **~ Greek** Neugriechisch *nt*; **modernize** ['mɒdənaɪz] *vt* modernisieren

modest ['mɒdɪst] *adj* bescheiden; **modesty** *n* Bescheidenheit *f*

modification [mɒdɪfɪ'keɪʃən] *n* Abänderung *f*; **modify** ['mɒdɪfaɪ] *vt* abändern

moist [mɔɪst] *adj* feucht; **moisten** ['mɔɪsn] *vt* befeuchten; **moisture** ['mɔɪstʃə*] *n* Feuchtigkeit *f*; **moisturizer** *n* Feuchtigkeitscreme *f*

molar ['məʊlə*] *n* Backenzahn *m*

mold (*US*) *see* **mould**

mole [məʊl] *n* (*spot*) Leberfleck *m*; (*animal*) Maulwurf *m*

molecule ['mɒlɪkjuːl] *n* Molekül *nt*

molest [məʊ'lest] *vt* belästigen

molt (*US*) *see* **moult**

molten ['məʊltən] *adj* geschmolzen

mom [mɒm] *n* (*US*) Mutti *f*

moment ['məʊmənt] *n* Moment *m*, Augenblick *m*; **just a ~** Moment mall; **at** (*o* **for**) **the ~** im Augenblick; **in a ~** gleich

momentous [məʊ'mentəs] *adj* bedeutsam

Monaco ['mɒnəkəʊ] *n* Monaco *nt*

monarchy ['mɒnəkɪ] *n* Monarchie *f*

monastery ['mɒnəstrɪ] *n* (*for monks*) Kloster *nt*

Monday ['mʌndeɪ] *n* Montag *m*; *see also* **Tuesday**

monetary ['mʌnɪtərɪ] *adj* (*reform, policy, union*) Währungs-; **~ unit** Geldeinheit *f*

money ['mʌnɪ] *n* Geld *nt*; **to get one's ~'s worth** auf seine Kosten kommen; **money order** *n* Postanweisung *f*

mongrel ['mʌŋgrəl] *n* Promenadenmischung *f*

monitor ['mɒnɪtə*] *n* (*screen*) Monitor *m* ▷ *vt* (*progress etc*) überwachen; (*broadcasts*) abhören

monk [mʌŋk] *n* Mönch *m*

monkey ['mʌŋkɪ] *n* Affe *m*; **~ business** Unfug *m*

monopolize [mə'nɒpəlaɪz] *vt* monopolisieren; (*fig: person, thing*) in Beschlag nehmen; **monopoly** [mə'nɒpəlɪ] *n* Monopol *nt*

monotonous [mə'nɒtənəs] *adj* eintönig, monoton

monsoon [mɒn'suːn] *n* Monsun *m*

monster ['mɒnstə*] *n* (*animal,*

thing) Monstrum *nt* ▷ *adj* Riesen-;
monstrosity [mɒnˈstrɒsɪtɪ] *n*
Monstrosität *f*; *(thing)* Ungetüm
nt

Montenegro [mɒntɪˈniːgrəʊ] *n*
Montenegro *nt*

month [mʌnθ] *n* Monat *m*;
monthly *adj* monatlich; *(ticket,
salary)* Monats- ▷ *adv* monatlich
▷ *n (magazine)* Monatsschrift *f*

monty [ˈmɒntɪ] *n*: **to go the full
~** *(fam: strip)* alle Hüllen fallen
lassen; *(go the whole hog)* aufs
Ganze gehen

monument [ˈmɒnjʊmənt] *n*
Denkmal *nt (to* für); **monumental**
[mɒnjʊˈmentl] *adj (huge)*
gewaltig

mood [muːd] *n (of person)*
Laune *f*; *(a. general)* Stimmung *f*;
**to be in a good/bad
~** gute/schlechte Laune haben;
to be in the ~ for sth zu etw
aufgelegt sein; **I'm not in the
~** ich fühle mich nicht danach;
moody *adj* launisch

moon [muːn] *n* Mond *m*; **to be
over the ~** *(fam)* überglücklich
sein; **moonlight** *n* Mondlicht *nt*
▷ *vi* schwarzarbeiten; **moonlit**
adj (night, landscape) mondhell

moor [mɔː*] *n* Moor *nt* ▷ *vt, vi*
festmachen; **moorings** *npl*
Liegeplatz *m*; **moorland** *n*
Moorland *nt*, Heideland *nt*

moose [muːs] *(pl -)* *n* Elch *m*

mop [mɒp] *n* Mopp *m*; **mop up**
vt aufwischen

mope [məʊp] *vi* Trübsal blasen

moped [ˈməʊped] *n (Brit)* Moped
nt

moral [ˈmɒrəl] *adj* moralisch;
(values) sittlich ▷ *n* Moral *f*; **~s** *pl*
Moral *f*; **morale** [mɒˈrɑːl] *n*
Stimmung *f*, Moral *f*; **morality**
[məˈrælɪtɪ] *n* Moral *f*, Ethik *f*

morbid [ˈmɔːbɪd] *adj* krankhaft

○ **KEYWORD**

more [mɔː*] *adj (greater in number
etc)* mehr; *(additional)* noch mehr;
do you want (some) more tea?
möchtest du/möchten Sie noch
etwas Tee?; **I have no** *o* **I don't
have any more money** ich habe
kein Geld mehr
▷ *pron (greater amount)* mehr;
(further o additional amount) noch
mehr; **is there any more?** gibt es
noch mehr?; *(left over)* ist noch
etwas da?; **there's no more** es ist
nichts mehr da
▷ *adv* mehr; **more
dangerous/easily** *etc* **(than)**
gefährlicher/einfacher *etc* (als);
more and more immer mehr;
more and more excited immer
aufgeregter; **more or less** mehr
oder weniger; **more than ever**
mehr denn je; **more beautiful
than ever** schöner denn je

moreish *adj (food)* **these
crisps are really ~** ich kann mit
diesen Chips einfach nicht
aufhören; **moreover** *adv*
außerdem

morgue [mɔːg] *n* Leichen-
schauhaus *nt*

morning [ˈmɔːnɪŋ] *n* Morgen *m*;
in the ~ am Morgen, morgens;
(tomorrow) morgen früh; **this
~** heute morgen ▷ *adj* Morgen-;
(early) Früh-; *(walk etc)*
morgendlich; **morning after pill**
n die Pille danach; **morning
sickness** *n* Schwangerschafts-
übelkeit *f*

Morocco [məˈrɒkəʊ] *n* Marokko
nt

moron [ˈmɔːrɒn] *n* Idiot(in) *m(f)*

morphine [ˈmɔːfiːn] *n* Morphium *nt*

morsel ['mɔːsl] n Bissen m

mortal ['mɔːtl] adj sterblich; (wound) tödlich ▷ n Sterbliche(r) mf; **mortality** [mɔːˈtælɪtɪ] n (death rate) Sterblichkeitsziffer f; **mortally** adv tödlich

mortgage ['mɔːgɪdʒ] n Hypothek f ▷ vt mit einer Hypothek belasten

mortified ['mɔːtɪfaɪd] adj: **I was ~** es war mir schrecklich peinlich

mortuary ['mɔːtjʊərɪ] n Leichenhalle f

mosaic [məʊˈzeɪɪk] n Mosaik nt

Moscow ['mɒskəʊ] n Moskau nt

Moslem ['mɒzlem] adj, n see **Muslim**

mosque [mɒsk] n Moschee f

mosquito [mɒˈskiːtəʊ] (pl **-es**) n (Stech)mücke f; (tropical) Moskito m; **~ net** Moskitonetz nt

moss [mɒs] n Moos nt

most [məʊst] adj meiste pl, die meisten; **in ~ cases** in den meisten Fällen ▷ adv (with verbs) am meisten; (with adj) ...ste; (with adv) am ...sten; (very) äußerst, höchst; **he ate (the) ~** er hat am meisten gegessen; **the ~ beautiful/interesting** der/die/das schönste/interessanteste; **~ interesting** hochinteressant! ▷ n das meiste, der größte Teil; (people) die meisten; **~ of the money/players** das meiste Geld/die meisten Spieler; **for the ~ part** zum größten Teil; **five at the ~** höchstens fünf; **to make the ~ of sth** etw voll ausnützen; **mostly** adv (most of the time) meistens; (mainly) hauptsächlich; (for the most part) größtenteils

MOT abbr = **Ministry of Transport**; **~ (test)** ≈ TÜV m

motel [məʊˈtel] n Motel nt

moth [mɒθ] n Nachtfalter m; (wool-eating) Motte f; **mothball** n Mottenkugel f

mother ['mʌðə°] n Mutter f ▷ vt bemuttern; **mother-in-law** (pl **mothers-in-law**) n Schwiegermutter f; **mother-to-be** (pl **mothers-to-be**) n werdende Mutter

motif [məʊˈtiːf] n Motiv nt

motion ['məʊʃən] n Bewegung f; (in meeting) Antrag m; **motionless** adj bewegungslos

motivate ['məʊtɪveɪt] vt motivieren; **motive** ['məʊtɪv] n Motiv nt

motor ['məʊtə°] n Motor m; (fam: car) Auto nt ▷ adj Motor-; **Motorail train®** n (Brit) Autoreisezug m; **motorbike** n Motorrad nt; **motorboat** n Motorboot nt; **motorcycle** n Motorrad nt; **motor industry** n Automobilindustrie f; **motoring** ['məʊtərɪŋ] n Autofahren nt; **~ organization** Automobilklub m; **motorist** ['məʊtərɪst] n Autofahrer(in) m(f); **motor oil** n Motorenöl nt; **motor racing** n Autorennsport m; **motor scooter** n Motorroller m; **motor show** n Automobilausstellung f; **motor vehicle** n Kraftfahrzeug nt; **motorway** n (Brit) Autobahn f

motto ['mɒtəʊ] (pl **-es**) n Motto nt

mould [məʊld] n Form f; (mildew) Schimmel m ▷ vt (a. fig) formen; **mouldy** ['məʊldɪ] adj schimmelig

moult [məʊlt] vi sich mausern, haaren

mount [maʊnt] vt (horse) steigen auf +akk; (exhibition etc) organisieren; (painting) mit einem Passepartout versehen ▷ vi: **to ~ (up)** (an)steigen ▷ n Passepartout nt

m

mountain ['maʊntɪn] n Berg m;
mountain bike n Mountainbike
nt; **mountaineer** [maʊntɪ'nɪə°]
n Bergsteiger(in) m(f);
mountaineering [maʊntɪ'nɪərɪŋ]
n Bergsteigen nt; **mountainous**
adj bergig; **mountainside** n
Berghang m
mourn [mɔːn] vt betrauern ▷ vi
trauern (for um); **mourner** n
Trauernde(r) mf; **mournful** adj
trauervoll; **mourning** n Trauer f;
to be in ~ trauern (for um)
mouse [maʊs] (pl **mice**) n (a.
Inform) Maus f; **mouse mat**,
mouse pad (US) n Mauspad nt;
mouse trap n Mausefalle f
mousse [muːs] n (Gastr) Creme f;
(styling ~) Schaumfestiger m
moustache [mə'stæʃ] n
Schnurrbart m
mouth [maʊθ] n Mund m; (of
animal) Maul nt; (of cave) Eingang
m; (of bottle etc) Öffnung f; (of river)
Mündung f; **to keep one's ~ shut**
(fam) den Mund halten; **mouthful**
n (of drink) Schluck m; (of food)
Bissen m; **mouth organ** n
Mundharmonika f; **mouthwash** n
Mundwasser nt; **mouthwatering**
adj appetitlich, lecker
move [muːv] n (movement)
Bewegung f; (in game) Zug m; (step)
Schritt m; (moving house) Umzug m;
to make a ~ (in game) ziehen;
(leave) sich auf den Weg machen;
to get a ~ on (with sth) sich (mit
etw) beeilen ▷ vt bewegen;
(object) rücken; (car) wegfahren;
(transport: goods) befördern;
(people) transportieren; (in job)
versetzen; (emotionally) bewegen,
rühren; **I can't ~ it** (stuck, too heavy)
ich bringe es nicht von der Stelle;
to ~ (house) umziehen ▷ vi sich
bewegen; (change place) gehen;
(vehicle, ship) fahren; (move house,

town etc) umziehen; (in game)
ziehen; **move about** vi sich
bewegen; (travel) unterwegs sein;
move away vi weggehen; (move
town) wegziehen; **move in** vi (to
house) einziehen; **move off** vi
losfahren; **move on** vi
weitergehen; (vehicle)
weiterfahren; **move out** vi
ausziehen; **move up** vi (in queue
etc) aufrücken; **movement** n
Bewegung f
movie ['muːvɪ] n Film m; **the ~s**
(the cinema) das Kino; **movie
theatre** n (US) Kino nt
moving ['muːvɪŋ] adj (emotionally) ergreifend, berührend
mow [məʊ] (**mowed, mown** o
mowed) vt mähen; **mower** n
(lawn~) Rasenmäher m
mown [məʊn] pp of **mow**
Mozambique [məʊzæm'biːk] n
Mosambik nt
MP abbr = **Member of Parliament**
Parlamentsabgeordnete(r) mf
mph abbr = **miles per hour** Meilen
pro Stunde
MPV abbr = **multi-purpose
vehicle** Mehrzweckfahrzeug nt
MP3 player [empiː'θriː 'pleɪə°]
n MP3-Player m
Mr [mɪstə°] n (written form of
address) Herr
Mrs ['mɪsɪz] n (written form of
address) Frau
Ms [məz] n (written form of address
for any woman, married or unmarried)
Frau
MS n abbr = **multiple sclerosis** MS
f
Mt abbr = **Mount** Berg m
much [mʌtʃ] (**more, most**) adj
viel; **we haven't got ~ time** wir
haben nicht viel Zeit; **how
~ money?** wie viel Geld? ▷ adv
viel; (with verb) sehr; **~ better** viel
besser; **I like it very ~** es gefällt

mir sehr gut; **I don't like it** ~ ich mag es nicht besonders; **thank you very** ~ danke sehr; **I thought as** ~ das habe ich mir gedacht; ~ **as I like him** so sehr ich ihn mag; **we don't see them** ~ wir sehen sie nicht sehr oft; ~ **the same** fast gleich ▷ n viel; **as** ~ **as you want** so viel du willst; **he's not** ~ **of a cook** er ist kein großer Koch

muck [mʌk] n (fam) Dreck m; **muck about** vi (fam) herumalbern; **muck up** vt (fam) dreckig machen; (spoil) vermasseln; **mucky** adj dreckig

mucus ['mju:kəs] n Schleim m

mud [mʌd] n Schlamm m

muddle ['mʌdl] n Durcheinander nt; **to be in a** ~ durcheinander sein ▷ vt: **to** ~ (**up**) durcheinanderbringen; **muddled** adj konfus

muddy ['mʌdɪ] adj schlammig; (shoes) schmutzig; **mudguard** ['mʌdɡɑːd] n Schutzblech nt

muesli ['mu:zlɪ] n Müsli nt

muffin ['mʌfɪn] n Muffin m; (Brit) weiches, flaches Milchbrötchen aus Hefeteig, das meist getoastet und mit Butter gegessen wird

muffle ['mʌfl] vt (sound) dämpfen; **muffler** n (US) Schalldämpfer m

mug [mʌɡ] n (cup) Becher m; (fam: fool) Trottel m ▷ vt (attack and rob) überfallen; **mugging** n Raubüberfall m

muggy ['mʌɡɪ] adj (weather) schwül

mule [mju:l] n Maulesel m

mull over [mʌl 'əʊvə*] vt nachdenken über +akk

mulled [mʌld] adj: ~ **wine** Glühwein m

multicolored (US), **multicoloured** ['mʌltɪ'kʌləd] adj bunt; **multicultural** adj

multikulturell; **multi-grade** adj: ~ **oil** Mehrbereichsöl nt; **multilingual** adj mehrsprachig; **multinational** n (company) Multi m

multiple ['mʌltɪpl] n Vielfache(s) nt ▷ adj mehrfach; (several) mehrere; **multiple-choice (method)** n Multiple-Choice-Verfahren nt; **multiple sclerosis** ['mʌltɪplskle'rəʊsɪs] n Multiple Sklerose f

multiplex ['mʌltɪpleks] adj, n: ~ (**cinema**) Multiplexkino nt

multiplication [mʌltɪplɪ'keɪʃən] n Multiplikation f; **multiply** ['mʌltɪplaɪ] vt multiplizieren (by mit) ▷ vi sich vermehren

multi-purpose ['mʌltɪ'pɜːpəs]-adj Mehrzweck-; **multistorey (car park)** n Parkhaus nt; **multitasking** n (Inform) Multitasking nt

mum [mʌm] n (fam: mother) Mutti f, Mami f

mumble ['mʌmbl] vt, vi murmeln

mummy ['mʌmɪ] n (dead body) Mumie f; (fam: mother) Mutti f, Mami f

mumps [mʌmps] nsing Mumps m

munch [mʌntʃ] vt, vi mampfen

Munich ['mju:nɪk] n München nt

municipal [mju:'nɪsɪpəl] adj städtisch

mural ['mjʊərəl] n Wandgemälde nt

murder ['mɜːdə*] n Mord m; **the traffic was** ~ der Verkehr war die Hölle ▷ vt ermorden; **murderer** n Mörder(in) m(f)

murky ['mɜːkɪ] adj düster; (water) trüb

murmur ['mɜːmə*] vt, vi murmeln

muscle ['mʌsl] n Muskel m;
  muscular ['mʌskjʊlə°] adj (strong)
  muskulös; (cramp, pain etc) Muskel-
museum [mju:'zɪəm] n Museum
  nt
mushroom ['mʌʃru:m] n (ess-
  barer) Pilz; (button ~) Champignon
  m ▷ vi (fig) emporschießen
mushy ['mʌʃɪ] adj breiig; ~ **peas**
  Erbsenmus nt
music ['mju:zɪk] n Musik f;
  (printed) Noten pl; **musical** adj
  (sound) melodisch; (person)
  musikalisch; ~ **instrument**
  Musikinstrument nt ▷ n (show)
  Musical nt; **musically** adv
  musikalisch; **musician**
  [mju:'zɪʃən] n Musiker(in) m(f)
Muslim ['mʊzlɪm] adj
  moslemisch ▷ n Moslem m,
  Muslime f
mussel ['mʌsl] n Miesmuschel f
must [mʌst] (had to, had to) vb
  aux (need to) müssen; (in negation)
  dürfen; **I ~n't forget that** ich darf
  das nicht vergessen; (certainty) **he
  ~ be there by now** er ist
  inzwischen bestimmt schon da;
  (assumption) **I ~ have lost it** ich
  habe es wohl verloren; ~ **you?**
  muss das sein? ▷ n Muss nt
mustache ['mʌstæʃ] n (US)
  Schnurrbart m
mustard ['mʌstəd] n Senf m; **to
  cut the ~** es bringen
mustn't ['mʌsnt] contr of **must
  not**
mute [mju:t] adj stumm
mutter ['mʌtə°] vt, vi murmeln
mutton ['mʌtn] n Ham-
  melfleisch nt
mutual ['mju:tjʊəl] adj gegenseitig; **by ~ consent** in
  gegenseitigem Einvernehmen
my [maɪ] adj mein; **I've hurt
  ~ leg** ich habe mir das Bein
  verletzt

Myanmar ['maɪænma:] n
  Myanmar nt
myself [maɪ'self] pron (reflexive)
  mich akk, mir dat; **I've hurt ~** ich
  habe mich verletzt; **I've bought
  ~ a flat** ich habe mir eine
  Wohnung gekauft; **I need it for
  ~** ich brauche es für mich (selbst);
  (emphatic) **I did it ~** ich habe es
  selbst gemacht; (all) **by ~** allein
mysterious [mɪ'stɪərɪəs] adj
  geheimnisvoll, mysteriös;
  (inexplicable) rätselhaft; **mystery**
  ['mɪstərɪ] n Geheimnis nt; (puzzle)
  Rätsel nt; **it's a ~ to me** es ist mir
  schleierhaft; **mystify** ['mɪstɪfaɪ]
  vt verblüffen
myth [mɪθ] n Mythos m; (fig:
  untrue story) Märchen nt; **mythical**
  adj mythisch; (fig: untrue)
  erfunden; **mythology**
  [mɪ'θɒlədʒɪ] n Mythologie f

n

N *abbr* = **north** N

nag [næg] *vt, vi* herumnörgeln (*sb* an jdm); **nagging** *n* Nörgelei *f*

nail [neɪl] *n* Nagel *m* ▷ *vt* nageln (*to* an); **nail down** *vt* festnageln; **nailbrush** *n* Nagelbürste *f*; **nail clippers** *npl* Nagelknipser *m*; **nailfile** *n* Nagelfeile *f*; **nail polish** *n* Nagellack *m*; **nail polish remover** *n* Nagellackentferner *m*; **nail scissors** *npl* Nagelschere *f*; **nail varnish** *n* Nagellack *m*

naive [naɪˈiːv] *adj* naiv

naked [ˈneɪkɪd] *adj* nackt

name [neɪm] *n* Name *m*; **his ~ is ...** er heißt ...; **what's your ~?** wie heißen Sie?; (*reputation*) **to have a good/bad ~** einen guten/schlechten Ruf haben ▷ *vt* nennen (*after* nach); (*sth new*) benennen; (*nominate*) ernennen (*as* als/zu); **a boy ~d ...** ein Junge

namens ...; **namely** *adv* nämlich; **name plate** *n* Namensschild *nt*

nan bread [ˈnɑːnˈbred] *n* (*warm serviertes*) *indisches Fladenbrot*

nanny [ˈnænɪ] *n* Kindermädchen *nt*

nap [næp] *n*: **to have/take a ~** ein Nickerchen machen

napkin [ˈnæpkɪn] *n* (*at table*) Serviette *f*

Naples [ˈneɪplz] *n* Neapel *nt*

nappy [ˈnæpɪ] *n* (*Brit*) Windel *f*

narcotic [nɑːˈkɒtɪk] *n* Rauschgift *nt*

narrate [nəˈreɪt] *vt* erzählen; **narration** [nəˈreɪʃən], **narrative** [ˈnærətɪv] *n* Erzählung *f*; **narrator** [nəˈreɪtə*] *n* Erzähler(in) *m(f)*

narrow [ˈnærəʊ] *adj* eng, schmal; (*victory, majority*) knapp; **to have a ~ escape** mit knapper Not davonkommen ▷ *vi* sich verengen; **narrow down** *vt* einschränken (*to sth* auf etw *akk*); **narrow-minded** *adj* engstirnig

nasty [ˈnɑːstɪ] *adj* ekelhaft; (*person*) fies; (*remark*) gehässig; (*accident, wound etc*) schlimm

nation [ˈneɪʃən] *n* Nation *f*; **national** [ˈnæʃənl] *adj* national; **~ anthem** Nationalhymne *f*; **National Health Service** (*Brit*) staatlicher Gesundheitsdienst; **~ insurance** (*Brit*) Sozialversicherung *f*; **~ park** Nationalpark *m*; **~ service** Wehrdienst *m*; **~ socialism** (*Hist*) Nationalsozialismus *m* ▷ *n* Staatsbürger(in) *m(f)*

○ **NATIONAL TRUST**
○
○ Der **National Trust** ist ein 1895
○ gegründeter Natur- und
○ Denkmalschutzverband in
○ Großbritannien, der Gebäude
○ und Gelände von besonderem

- historischen oder ästhetischen
- Interesse erhält und der
- Öffentlichkeit zugänglich
- macht.

nationality [næʃˈnælɪtɪ] *n*
Staatsangehörigkeit *f*,
Nationalität *f*; **nationalize**
[ˈnæʃnəlaɪz] *vt* verstaatlichen;
nationwide *adj, adv* landesweit
native [ˈneɪtɪv] *adj* einheimisch;
(*inborn*) angeboren, natürlich;
Native American Indianer(in)
m(f); **~ country** Heimatland *nt*; **a**
~ German ein gebürtiger
Deutscher, eine gebürtige
Deutsche; **~ language**
Muttersprache *f*; **~ speaker**
Muttersprachler(in) *m(f)* ▷ *n*
Einheimische(r) *mf*; (*in colonial
context*) Eingeborene(r) *mf*
nativity play [nəˈtɪvətɪpleɪ] *n*
Krippenspiel *nt*
NATO [ˈneɪtəʊ] *acr* = **North**
Atlantic Treaty Organization
Nato *f*
natural [ˈnætʃrəl] *adj* natürlich;
(*law, science, forces etc*) Natur-;
(*inborn*) angeboren; **~ gas** Erdgas
nt; **~ resources** Bodenschätze *pl*;
naturally *adv* natürlich; (*by
nature*) von Natur aus; **it comes**
~ to her es fällt ihr leicht
nature [ˈneɪtʃə*] *n* Natur *f*;
(*type*) Art *f*; **it is not in my ~** es
entspricht nicht meiner Art;
by ~ von Natur aus; **nature**
reserve *n* Naturschutzgebiet *nt*
naughty [ˈnɔːtɪ] *adj* (*child*)
ungezogen; (*cheeky*) frech
nausea [ˈnɔːsɪə] *n* Übelkeit *f*
nautical [ˈnɔːtɪkəl] *adj* nautisch;
~ mile Seemeile *f*
nave [neɪv] *n* Hauptschiff *nt*
navel [ˈneɪvəl] *n* Nabel *m*
navigate [ˈnævɪɡeɪt] *vi* navi-
gieren; (*in car*) lotsen, dirigieren;

navigation [nævɪˈɡeɪʃən] *n*
Navigation *f*; (*in car*) Lotsen *nt*
navy [ˈneɪvɪ] *n* Marine *f*; **~ blue**
Marineblau *nt*
Nazi [ˈnɑːtsɪ] *n* Nazi *m*
NB *abbr* = **nota bene** NB
NE *abbr* = **northeast** NO
near [nɪə*] *adj* nahe; **in the**
~ future in nächster Zukunft; **that**
was a ~ miss (*o thing*) das war
knapp; (*with price*) **... or ~est offer**
Verhandlungsbasis ... ▷ *adv* in der
Nähe; **so ~** so nahe; **come ~er**
näher kommen; (*event*) näher
rücken ▷ *prep*: **~ (to)** (*space*) nahe
an +*dat*; (*vicinity*) in der Nähe +*gen*;
~ the sea nahe am Meer; **~ the**
station in der Nähe des Bahnhofs,
in Bahnhofsnähe; **nearby** *adj*
nahe gelegen ▷ *adv* in der Nähe;
nearly *adv* fast; **nearside** *n*
(*Auto*) Beifahrerseite *f*;
near-sighted *adj* kurzsichtig
neat [niːt] *adj* ordentlich; (*work,
writing*) sauber; (*undiluted*) pur
necessarily [nesəˈserəlɪ] *adv*
notwendigerweise; **not ~** nicht
unbedingt; **necessary** [ˈnesəsərɪ]
adj notwendig, nötig; **it's ~ to ...**
man muss ...; **it's not ~ for him to**
come er braucht nicht
mitzukommen; **necessity**
[nɪˈsesɪtɪ] *n* Notwendigkeit *f*; **the**
bare necessities das absolut
Notwendigste; **there is no ~ to ...**
man braucht nicht (zu) ..., man
muss nicht ...
neck [nek] *n* Hals *m*; (*size*)
Halsweite *f*; **back of the ~** Nacken
m; **necklace** [ˈneklɪs] *n*
Halskette *f*; **necktie** *n* (*US*)
Krawatte *f*
nectarine [ˈnektərɪn] *n* Nektarine *f*
née [neɪ] *adj* geborene
need [niːd] *n* (*requirement*)
Bedürfnis *nt* (*for* für); (*necessity*)

Notwendigkeit f; (poverty) Not f; **to be in ~ of sth** etw brauchen; **if ~(s) be nötig; there is no ~ to ...** man braucht nicht (zu) ..., man muss nicht ... ▷ vt brauchen; **I ~ to speak to you** ich muss mit dir reden; **you ~n't go** du brauchst nicht (zu) gehen, du musst nicht gehen

needle ['niːdl] n Nadel f

needless, needlessly ['niːdlɪs, -lɪ] adj, adv unnötig; **~ to say** selbstverständlich

needy ['niːdɪ] adj bedürftig

negative ['negatɪv] n (Ling) Verneinung f; (Foto) Negativ nt ▷ adj negativ; (answer) verneinend

neglect [nɪ'glekt] n Vernachlässigung f ▷ vt vernachlässigen; **to ~ to do sth** es versäumen, etw zu tun; **negligence** ['neglɪdʒəns] n Nachlässigkeit f; **negligent** adj nachlässig

negligible ['neglɪdʒəbl] adj unbedeutend; (amount) geringfügig

negotiate [nɪ'gəʊʃɪeɪt] vi verhandeln; **negotiation** [nɪgəʊʃɪ'eɪʃən] n Verhandlung f

neigh [neɪ] vi (horse) wiehern

neighbor (US), **neighbour** ['neɪbə*] n Nachbar(in) m(f); **neighbo(u)rhood** n Nachbarschaft f; **neighbo(u)ring** adj benachbart

neither ['naɪðə*] adj, pron keine(r, s) von beiden; **~ of you/us** keiner von euch/uns beiden ▷ adv: **~ ... nor ...** weder ... noch ... ▷ conj: **I'm not going - ~ am I** ich gehe nicht - ich auch nicht

neon ['niːɒn] n Neon nt; **~ sign** (advertisement) Leuchtreklame f

nephew ['nefjuː] n Neffe m

nerd [nɜːd] n (fam) Schwachkopf m; **he's a real computer ~** er ist ein totaler Computerfreak

nerve [nɜːv] n Nerv m; **he gets on my ~s** er geht mir auf die Nerven; (courage) **to keep/lose one's ~** die Nerven behalten/verlieren; (cheek) **to have the ~ to do sth** die Frechheit besitzen, etw zu tun; **nerve-racking** adj nervenaufreibend; **nervous** ['nɜːvəs] adj (apprehensive) ängstlich; (on edge) nervös; **nervous breakdown** n Nervenzusammenbruch m

nest [nest] n Nest nt ▷ vi nisten

net [net] n Netz nt; **the Net** (Internet) das Internet; **on the ~** im Netz ▷ adj (price, weight) Netto-; **~ profit** Reingewinn m; **netball** n Netzball m

Netherlands ['neðələndz] npl: **the ~** die Niederlande pl

nettle ['netl] n Nessel f

network ['netwɜːk] n Netz nt; (TV, Radio) Sendenetz nt; (Inform) Netzwerk nt; **networking** n Networking nt (das Knüpfen und Pflegen von Kontakten, das dem beruflichen Fortkommen dienen)

neurosis [njʊə'rəʊsɪs] n Neurose f; **neurotic** [njʊə'rɒtɪk] adj neurotisch

neuter ['njuːtə*] adj (Bio) geschlechtslos; (Ling) sächlich

neutral ['njuːtrəl] adj neutral ▷ n (gear in car) Leerlauf m

never ['nevə*] adv nie(mals); **~ before** noch nie; **~ mind** macht nichts!; **never-ending** adj endlos; **nevertheless** [nevəðə'les] adv trotzdem

new [njuː] adj neu; **this is all ~ to me** das ist für mich noch ungewohnt; **newcomer** n Neuankömmling m; (in job, subject) Neuling m

New England [njuː'ɪŋglənd] n Neuengland nt

n

Newfoundland ['nju:fəndlənd]
n Neufundland *nt*

newly ['nju:lɪ] *adv* neu; **~ made**
(*cake*) frisch gebacken;
newly-weds *npl* Frischvermählte
pl; **new moon** *n* Neumond *m*

news [nju:z] *nsing* (*item of* ~)
Nachricht *f*; (*Radio, TV*)
Nachrichten *pl*; **good ~** ein
erfreuliche Nachricht; **what's the
~?** was gibt's Neues?; **have you
heard the ~?** hast du das Neueste
gehört?; **that's ~ to me** das ist mir
neu; **newsagent**, **news dealer**
(*US*) *n* Zeitungshändler(in) *m(f)*;
news bulletin *n*
Nachrichtensendung *f*; **news flash**
n Kurzmeldung *f*; **newsgroup** *n*
(*Inform*) Diskussionsforum *nt*,
Newsgroup *f*; **newsletter** *n*
Mitteilungsblatt *nt*; **newspaper**
['nju:speɪpə⁰] *n* Zeitung *f*

New Year ['nju:'jɪə⁰] *n* das
neue Jahr; **Happy ~** (ein) frohes
Neues Jahr!; (*toast*) Prosit
Neujahr!; **~'s Day** Neujahr *nt*,
Neujahrstag *m*; **~'s Eve**
Silvesterabend *m*; **~'s resolution**
guter Vorsatz fürs neue Jahr

New York [nju:'jɔːk] *n* New
York *nt*

New Zealand [nju:'ziːlənd] *n*
Neuseeland *nt* ▷ *adj*
neuseeländisch; **New Zealander**
n Neuseeländer(in) *m(f)*

next [nekst] *adj* nächste(r, s);
the week after ~ übernächste
Woche; **~ time I see him** wenn ich
ihn das nächste Mal sehe; **you're
~** du bist jetzt dran ▷ *adv* als
Nächstes; (*then*) dann, darauf; **~ to**
neben +*dat*; **~ to last** vorletzte(r,
s); **~ to impossible** nahezu
unmöglich; **the ~ best thing** das
Nächstbeste; **~ door** nebenan

NHS *abbr* = **National Health
Service**

Niagara Falls [naɪ'ægrə'fɔːlz]
npl Niagarafälle *pl*

nibble ['nɪbl] *vt* knabbern an
+*dat*; **nibbles** *npl* Knabberzeug *nt*

Nicaragua [nɪkə'rægjʊə] *n*
Nicaragua *nt*

nice [naɪs] *adj* nett, sympathisch;
(*taste, food, drink*) gut; (*weather*)
schön; **~ and ...** schön ...; **be ~ to
him** sei nett zu ihm; **have a ~ day**
(*US*) schönen Tag noch!; **nicely** *adv*
nett; (*well*) gut; **that'll do ~** das
genügt vollauf

nick [nɪk] *vt* (*fam: steal*) klauen;
(*capture*) schnappen

nickel ['nɪkl] *n* (*Chem*) Nickel *nt*;
(*US: coin*) Nickel *m*

nickname ['nɪkneɪm] *n*
Spitzname *m*

nicotine ['nɪkətiːn] *n* Nikotin *nt*;
nicotine patch *n* Nikotinpflaster
nt

niece [niːs] *n* Nichte *f*

Nigeria [naɪ'dʒɪərɪə] *n* Nigeria
nt

night [naɪt] *n* Nacht *f*; (*before bed*)
Abend *m*; **good ~** gute Nacht!; **at**
(*o by*) **~** nachts; **to have an early
~** früh schlafen gehen; **nightcap** *n*
Schlummertrunk *m*; **nightclub** *n*
Nachtklub *m*; **nightdress** *n*
Nachthemd *nt*; **nightie** ['naɪtɪ] *n*
(*fam*) Nachthemd *nt*

nightingale ['naɪtɪŋgeɪl] *n*
Nachtigall *f*

night life ['naɪtlaɪf] *n*
Nachtleben *nt*; **nightly** *adv* (*every
evening*) jeden Abend; (*every night*)
jede Nacht; **nightmare**
['naɪtmɛə⁰] *n* Albtraum *m*;
nighttime *n* Nacht *f*; **at ~** nachts

nil [nɪl] *n* (*Sport*) null

Nile [naɪl] *n* Nil *m*

nine [naɪn] *num* neun; **~ times
out of ten** so gut wie immer ▷ *n*
(*a. bus etc*) Neun *f*; *see also* **eight**;
nineteen [naɪn'tiːn] *num*

neunzehn ▷ n (a. bus etc)
Neunzehn f; see also **eight**;
nineteenth adj neunzehnte(r, s);
see also **eighth**; **ninetieth**
['naɪntɪəθ] adj neunzigste(r, s);
see also **eighth**; **ninety** ['naɪntɪ]
num neunzig ▷ n Neunzig f; see
also **eight**; **ninth** [naɪnθ] adj
neunte(r, s) ▷ n (fraction) Neuntel
nt; see also **eighth**

nipple ['nɪpl] n Brustwarze f
nitrogen ['naɪtrədʒən] n Stick-
stoff m

O **KEYWORD**

no [nəʊ] (pl **noes**) adv (opposite of
yes) nein; **to answer no** (to
question) mit Nein antworten; (to
request) Nein o nein sagen; **no
thank you** nein, danke
▷ adj (not any) kein(e); **I have no
money/time** ich habe kein
Geld/keine Zeit; **"no smoking"**
„Rauchen verboten"
▷ n Nein nt; (no vote) Neinstimme f

nobility [nəʊ'bɪlɪtɪ] n Adel m;
noble ['nəʊbl] adj (rank) adlig;
(quality) edel ▷ n Adlige(r)
mf
nobody ['nəʊbədɪ] pron niemand; (emphatic) keiner; **~ knows**
keiner weiß es; **~ else** sonst
niemand, kein anderer ▷ n
Niemand m
no-claims bonus
[nəʊ'kleɪmzbəʊnəs] n Schadenfreiheitsrabatt m
nod [nɒd] vi, vt nicken; **nod off** vi
einnicken
noise [nɔɪz] n (loud) Lärm m;
(sound) Geräusch nt; **noisy** adj
laut; (crowd) lärmend
nominate ['nɒmɪneɪt] vt (in
election) aufstellen; (appoint)
ernennen

nominative ['nɒmɪnətɪv] n
(Ling) Nominativ m
nominee [nɒmɪ'niː] n Kandi-
dat(in) m(f)
non- [nɒn] pref Nicht-; (with adj)
nicht-, un-; **non-alcoholic** adj
alkoholfrei
none [nʌn] pron keine(r, s); **~ of
them** keiner von ihnen; **~ of it is
any use** nichts davon ist
brauchbar; **there are ~ left** es sind
keine mehr da; (with comparative)
to be ~ the wiser auch nicht
schlauer sein; **I was ~ the worse
for it** es hat mir nichts geschadet
nonentity [nɒ'nentɪtɪ] n Null
f
nonetheless [nʌnðə'les] adv
nichtsdestoweniger, dennoch
non-event n Reinfall m;
non-existent adj nicht
vorhanden; **non-fiction** n
Sachbücher pl; **non-iron** adj
bügelfrei; **non-polluting** adj
schadstofffrei; **non-resident** n:
"open to ~s" „auch für
Nichthotelgäste"; **non-returnable**
adj: **~ bottle** Einwegflasche f
nonsense ['nɒnsəns] n Unsinn
m; **don't talk ~** red keinen Unsinn
non-smoker [nɒn'sməʊkə°] n
Nichtraucher(in) m(f);
non-smoking adj Nichtraucher-;
~ area Nichtraucherbereich m;
nonstop adj (train) durchgehend;
(flight) Nonstop- ▷ adv (talk)
ununterbrochen; (travel) ohne
Unterbrechung; (fly) ohne
Zwischenlandung; **non-violent**
adj gewaltfrei
noodles ['nuːdlz] npl Nudeln pl
noon [nuːn] n Mittag m; **at ~** um
12 Uhr mittags
no one ['nəʊwʌn] pron
niemand; (emphatic) keiner; **~ else**
sonst niemand, kein anderer
nor [nɔː] conj: **neither ... ~ ...**

n

weder ... noch ...; **I don't smoke, ~ does he** ich rauche nicht, er auch nicht

norm [nɔːm] n Norm f

normal ['nɔːməl] adj normal; **to get back to ~** sich wieder normalisieren; **normally** adv (usually) normalerweise

north [nɔːθ] n Norden m; **to the ~ of** nördlich von ▷ adv (go, face) nach Norden ▷ adj Nord-; **~ wind** Nordwind m; **North America** n Nordamerika nt; **northbound** adj (in) Richtung Norden; **northeast** n Nordosten m; **to the ~ of** nordöstlich von ▷ adv (go, face) nach Nordosten ▷ adj Nordost-; **northern** ['nɔːðən] adj nördlich; **~ France** Nordfrankreich nt; **Northern Ireland** n Nordirland nt; **North Pole** n Nordpol m; **North Sea** n Nordsee f; **northwards** adv nach Norden; **northwest** n Nordwesten m; **to the ~ of** nordwestlich von ▷ adv (go, face) nach Nordwesten ▷ adj Nordwest-

Norway ['nɔːweɪ] n Norwegen nt; **Norwegian** [nɔː'wiːdʒən] adj norwegisch ▷ n (person) Norweger(in) m(f); (language) Norwegisch nt

nos. abbr = **numbers** Nr.

nose [nəʊz] n Nase f; **nose around** vi herumschnüffeln; **nosebleed** n Nasenbluten nt; **nose-dive** n Sturzflug m; **to take a ~** abstürzen

nosey ['nəʊzɪ] see **nosy**

nostalgia [nɒ'stældʒɪə] n Nostalgie f (for nach); **nostalgic** adj nostalgisch

nostril ['nɒstrɪl] n Nasenloch nt

nosy ['nəʊzɪ] adj neugierig

not [nɒt] adv nicht; **~ a** kein; **~ one of them** kein einziger von ihnen; **he is ~ an expert** er ist kein Experte; **I told him ~ to** (do it) ich sagte ihm, er solle es nicht tun; **~ at all** überhaupt nicht, keineswegs; (don't mention it) gern geschehen; **~ yet** noch nicht

notable ['nəʊtəbl] adj bemerkenswert; **note** [nəʊt] n (written) Notiz f; (short letter) paar Zeilen pl; (on scrap of paper) Zettel m; (comment in book etc) Anmerkung f; (bank~) Schein m; (Mus: sign) Note f; (sound) Ton m; **to make a ~ of sth** sich dat etw notieren; **~s** (of lecture etc) Aufzeichnungen pl; **to take ~s** sich dat Notizen machen (of über +akk) ▷ vt (notice) bemerken (that dass); (write down) notieren; **notebook** n Notizbuch nt; (Inform) Notebook nt; **notepad** n Notizblock m; **notepaper** n Briefpapier nt

nothing ['nʌθɪŋ] n nichts; **~ but ...** lauter ...; **for ~** umsonst; **he thinks ~ of it** er macht sich nichts daraus

notice ['nəʊtɪs] n (announcement) Bekanntmachung f; (on ~ board) Anschlag m; (attention) Beachtung f; (advance warning) Ankündigung f; (to leave job, flat etc) Kündigung f; **at short ~** kurzfristig; **until further ~** bis auf weiteres; **to give sb ~** jdm kündigen; **to hand in one's ~** kündigen; **to take (no) ~ of (sth)** etw (nicht) beachten; **take no ~** kümmere dich darum! ▷ vt bemerken; **noticeable** adj erkennbar; (visible) sichtbar; **to be ~** auffallen; **notice board** n Anschlagtafel f

notification [nəʊtɪfɪ'keɪʃən] n Benachrichtigung f (of von); **notify** ['nəʊtɪfaɪ] vt benachrichtigen (of von)

notion ['nəʊʃən] n Idee f

notorious [nəʊ'tɔːrɪəs] adj berüchtigt

nought [nɔːt] n Null f
noun [naʊn] n Substantiv nt
nourish ['nʌrɪʃ] vt nähren;
nourishing adj nahrhaft;
nourishment n Nahrung f
novel ['nɒvəl] n Roman m ▷ adj
neuartig; **novelist** n
Schriftsteller(in) m(f); **novelty** n
Neuheit f
November [nəʊ'vembə°] n
November m; see also **September**
novice ['nɒvɪs] n Neuling m
now [naʊ] adv (at the moment)
jetzt; (introductory phrase) also;
right ~ jetzt gleich; **just ~** gerade;
by ~ inzwischen; **from ~ on** ab
jetzt; **~ and again** (o **then**) ab und
zu; **nowadays** adv heutzutage
nowhere ['nəʊweə°] adv nirgends; **we're getting ~** wir
kommen nicht weiter; **~ near**
noch lange nicht
nozzle ['nɒzl] n Düse f
nuclear ['njuːklɪə°] adj (energy
etc) Kern-; **~ power station**
Kernkraftwerk nt; **nuclear waste**
n Atommüll m
nude [njuːd] adj nackt ▷ n (person) Nackte(r) mf; (painting etc) Akt
m
nudge [nʌdʒ] vt stupsen; **nudist**
['njuːdɪst] n Nudist(in) m(f),
FKK-Anhänger(in) m(f); **nudist
beach** n FKK-Strand m
nuisance ['njuːsns] n Ärgernis
nt; (person) Plage f; **what a ~** wie
ärgerlich!
nuke [njuːk] (US fam) n (bomb)
Atombombe f ▷ vt eine
Atombombe werfen auf +akk
numb [nʌm] adj taub, gefühllos
▷ vt betäuben
number ['nʌmbə°] n Nummer f;
(Math) Zahl f; (quantity) (An)zahl f;
in small/large ~s in
kleinen/großen Mengen; **a ~ of
times** mehrmals ▷ vt (give a

number to) nummerieren; (count)
zählen (among zu); **his days are
~ed** seine Tage sind gezählt;
number plate n (Brit Auto)
Nummernschild nt
numeral ['njuːmərəl] n Ziffer f;
numerical [njuː'merɪkəl] adj
numerisch; (superiority)
zahlenmäßig; **numerous**
['njuːmərəs] adj zahlreich
nun [nʌn] n Nonne f
Nuremberg ['njuərəmbɜːg] n
Nürnberg nt
nurse [nɜːs] n Krankenschwester
f; (male ~) Krankenpfleger m ▷ vt
(patient) pflegen; (baby) stillen;
nursery n Kinderzimmer nt; (for
plants) Gärtnerei f; (tree)
Baumschule f; **nursery rhyme** n
Kinderreim m; **nursery school** n
Kindergarten m; **~ teacher**
Kindergärtner(in) m(f),
Erzieher(in) m(f); **nursing** n
(profession) Krankenpflege f;
~ home Privatklinik f
nut [nʌt] n Nuss f; (Tech: for bolt)
Mutter f; **nutcase** n (fam)
Spinner(in) m(f); **nutcracker** n,
nutcrackers npl Nussknacker m
nutmeg ['nʌtmeg] n Muskat m,
Muskatnuss f
nutrient ['njuːtrɪənt] n Nährstoff
m
nutrition [njuː'trɪʃən] n Ernährung f; **nutritious** [njuː'trɪʃəs]
adj nahrhaft
nuts [nʌts] (fam) adj verrückt; **to
be ~ about sth** nach etw verrückt
sein ▷ npl (testicles) Eier pl
nutshell ['nʌtʃel] n Nussschale f;
in a ~ kurz gesagt
nutter ['nʌtə°] n (fam)
Spinner(in) m(f); **nutty** ['nʌtɪ]
adj (fam) verrückt
NW abbr = **northwest** NW
nylon® ['naɪlɒn] n Nylon® nt
▷ adj Nylon-

O

O [əʊ] *n* (*Tel*) Null *f*

oak [əʊk] *n* Eiche *f* ▷ *adj* Eichen-

OAP *abbr* = **old-age pensioner** Rentner(in) *m(f)*

oar [ɔːʳ] *n* Ruder *nt*

oasis [əʊˈeɪsɪs] *n* (*pl* **oases**) *n* Oase *f*

oatcake [ˈəʊtkeɪk] *n* Haferkeks *m*

oath [əʊθ] *n* (*statement*) Eid *m*

oats [əʊts] *npl* Hafer *m*; (*Gastr*) Haferflocken *pl*

obedience [əˈbiːdɪəns] *n* Gehorsam *m*; **obedient** *adj* gehorsam; **obey** [əˈbeɪ] *vt*, *vi* gehorchen +*dat*

object [ˈɒbdʒekt] *n* Gegenstand *m*; (*abstract*) Objekt *nt*; (*purpose*) Ziel *nt* ▷ [əbˈdʒekt] *vi* dagegen sein; (*raise objection*) Einwände erheben (*to* gegen); (*morally*) Anstoß nehmen (*to* an +*dat*); **do you ~ to my smoking?** haben Sie etwas dagegen, wenn ich rauche?; **objection** [əbˈdʒekʃən] *n* Einwand *m*

objective [əbˈdʒektɪv] *n* Ziel *nt* ▷ *adj* objektiv; **objectivity** [ɒbdʒekˈtɪvɪtɪ] *n* Objektivität *f*

obligation [ɒblɪˈgeɪʃən] *n* (*duty*) Pflicht *f*; (*commitment*) Verpflichtung *f*; **no ~** unverbindlich; **obligatory** [əˈblɪgətərɪ] *adj* obligatorisch; **oblige** [əˈblaɪdʒ] *vt*: **to ~ sb to do sth** jdn (dazu) zwingen, etw zu tun; **he felt ~d to accept the offer** er fühlte sich verpflichtet, das Angebot anzunehmen

oblique [əˈbliːk] *adj* schräg; (*angle*) schief

oboe [ˈəʊbəʊ] *n* Oboe *f*

obscene [əbˈsiːn] *adj* obszön

obscure [əbˈskjʊəʳ] *adj* unklar; (*unknown*) unbekannt

observant [əbˈzɜːvənt] *adj* aufmerksam; **observation** [ɒbzəˈveɪʃən] *n* (*watching*) Beobachtung *f*; (*remark*) Bemerkung *f*; **observe** [əbˈzɜːv] *vt* (*notice*) bemerken; (*watch*) beobachten; (*customs*) einhalten

obsessed [əbˈsest] *adj* besessen (*with an idea etc* von einem Gedanken etc); **obsession** [əbˈseʃən] *n* Manie *f*

obsolete [ˈɒbsəliːt] *adj* veraltet

obstacle [ˈɒbstəkl] *n* Hindernis *nt* (*to* für); **to be an ~ to sth** einer Sache im Weg stehen

obstinate [ˈɒbstɪnət] *adj* hartnäckig

obstruct [əbˈstrʌkt] *vt* versperren; (*pipe*) verstopfen; (*hinder*) behindern, aufhalten; **obstruction** [əbˈstrʌkʃən] *n* Blockierung *f*; (*of pipe*) Verstopfung *f*; (*obstacle*) Hindernis *nt*

obtain [əbˈteɪn] *vt* erhalten; **obtainable** *adj* erhältlich

obvious [ˈɒbvɪəs] *adj*
offensichtlich; **it was ~ to me
that ...** es war mir klar, dass ...;
obviously *adj* offensichtlich

occasion [əˈkeɪʒən] *n* Gelegenheit *f*; (*special event*) (großes)
Ereignis; **on the ~ of** anlässlich
+*gen*; **special ~** besonderer Anlass;
occasional, occasionally *adj, adv*
gelegentlich

occupant [ˈɒkjʊpənt] *n* (*of
house*) Bewohner(in) *m(f)*; (*of
vehicle*) Insasse *m*, Insassin *f*;
occupation [ɒkjʊˈpeɪʃən] *n*
Beruf *m*; (*pastime*) Beschäftigung *f*;
(*of country etc*) Besetzung *f*;
occupied *adj* (*country, seat, toilet*)
besetzt; (*person*) beschäftigt; **to
keep sb/oneself ~** jdn/sich
beschäftigen; **occupy** [ˈɒkjʊpaɪ]
vt (*country*) besetzen; (*time*)
beanspruchen; (*mind, person*)
beschäftigen

occur [əˈkɜːʳ] *vi* vorkommen;
~ to sb jdm einfallen; **occurrence**
[əˈkʌrəns] *n* (*event*) Ereignis *nt*;
(*presence*) Vorkommen *nt*

ocean [ˈəʊʃən] *n* Ozean *m*; (*US:
sea*) das Meer *nt*

o'clock [əˈklɒk] *adv*: **5 ~** 5 Uhr; **at
10 ~** um 10 Uhr

octagon [ˈɒktəgən] *n* Achteck
nt

October [ɒkˈtəʊbəʳ] *n* Oktober
m; *see also* **September**

octopus [ˈɒktəpəs] *n* Tintenfisch *m*

odd [ɒd] *adj* (*strange*) sonderbar;
(*not even*) ungerade; (*one missing*)
einzeln; **to be the ~ one out** nicht
dazugehören; **~ jobs**
Gelegenheitsarbeiten *pl*; **odds** *npl*
Chancen *pl*; **against all
~** entgegen allen Erwartungen;
~ and ends (*fam*) Kleinkram *pl*

odometer [əʊˈdɒmətəʳ] *n* (*US
Auto*) Meilenzähler *m*

odor (*US*), **odour** [ˈəʊdəʳ] *n*
Geruch *m*

KEYWORD

of [ɒv, əv] *prep* 1 von +*dat* ≈ use of
gen; **the history of Germany** die
Geschichte Deutschlands; **a friend
of ours** ein Freund von uns; **a boy
of 10** ein 10-jähriger Junge;
that was kind of you das war
sehr freundlich von Ihnen
2 (*expressing quantity, amount,
dates etc*) **a kilo of flour** ein Kilo
Mehl; **how much of this do you
need?** wie viel brauchen Sie
(davon)?; **there were 3 of them**
(*people*) sie waren zu dritt; (*objects*)
es gab 3 (davon); **a cup of
tea/vase of flowers** eine
Tasse Tee/Vase mit Blumen;
the 5th of July der 5. Juli
3 (*from, out of*) aus; **a bridge made
of wood** eine Holzbrücke, eine
Brücke aus Holz

off [ɒf] *adv* (*away*) weg, fort; (*free*)
frei; (*switch*) ausgeschaltet; (*milk*)
sauer; **a mile ~** eine Meile
entfernt; **I'll be ~ now** ich gehe
jetzt; **to have the day/Monday
~** heute/Montag freihaben; **the
lights are ~** die Lichter sind aus;
the concert is ~ das Konzert fällt
aus; **I got 10 % ~** ich habe 10 %
Nachlass bekommen ▷ *prep* (*away
from*) von; **to jump/fall ~ the roof**
vom Dach springen/fallen; **to get
~ the bus** aus dem Bus
aussteigen; **he's ~ work/school** er
hat frei/schulfrei; **to take £20
~ the price** den Preis um 20 Pfund
herabsetzen

offence [əˈfens] *n* (*crime*)
Straftat *f*; (*minor*) Vergehen *nt*; (*to
feelings*) Kränkung *f*; **to
cause/take ~** Anstoß

erregen/nehmen; **offend** [ə'fend]
vt kränken; (*eye, ear*) beleidigen;
offender n Straffällige(r) *mf*;
offense (*US*) *see* **offence**;
offensive [ə'fensɪv] *adj* anstößig;
(*insulting*) beleidigend; (*smell*) übel,
abstoßend ▷ n (*Mil*) Offensive f
offer ['ɒfə°] n Angebot *nt*; **on**
~ (*Comm*) im Angebot ▷ vt
anbieten (*to sb* jdm); (*money, a*
chance etc) bieten
offhand [ɒf'hænd] *adj* lässig
▷ *adv* (*say*) auf Anhieb
office ['ɒfɪs] n Büro *nt*; (*position*)
Amt *nt*; **doctor's ~** (*US*) Arztpraxis
f; **office block** n Bürogebäude *nt*;
office hours *npl* Dienstzeit f;
(*notice*) Geschäftszeiten *pl*; **officer**
['ɒfɪsə°] n (*Mil*) Offizier(in) *m(f)*;
(*official*) Polizeibeamte(r) *m*,
Polizeibeamtin f; **office worker**
['ɒfɪswɜːkə°] n Büroangestellte(r)
mf; **official** [ə'fɪʃəl] *adj* offiziell;
(*report etc*) amtlich; **~ language**
Amtssprache f ▷ n Beamte(r) *m*,
Beamtin f, Repräsentant(in)
m(f)
off-licence ['ɒflaɪsəns] n (*Brit*)
Wein- und Spirituosenhandlung f;
off-line *adj* (*Inform*) offline;
off-peak *adj* außerhalb der
Stoßzeiten; (*rate, ticket*) verbilligt;
off-putting *adj* abstoßend,
entmutigend, irritierend;
off-season *adj* außerhalb der
Saison
offshore ['ɒfʃɔː°] *adj* küstennah,
Küsten-; (*oil rig*) im Meer; **offside**
['ɒfsaɪd] n (*Auto*) Fahrerseite f;
(*Sport*) Abseits *nt*
often ['ɒfən] *adv* oft; **every so**
~ von Zeit zu Zeit
oil [ɔɪl] n Öl *nt* ▷ vt ölen; **oil level**
n Ölstand *m*; **oil painting** n
Ölgemälde *nt*; **oil-rig** n
(Öl)bohrinsel f; **oil slick** n
Ölteppich *m*; **oil tanker** n

Öltanker *m*; (*truck*) Tankwagen *m*;
oily *adj* ölig; (*skin, hair*) fettig
ointment ['ɔɪntmənt] n Salbe f
OK, **okay** [əʊ'keɪ] *adj* (*fam*) okay,
in Ordnung; **that's ~ by** (*o* **with**)
me das ist mir recht
old [əʊld] *adj* alt; **old age** n Alter
nt; **~ pension** Rente f; **~ pensioner**
Rentner(in) *m(f)*; **old-fashioned**
adj altmodisch; **old people's**
home n Altersheim *nt*
olive ['ɒlɪv] n Olive f; **olive oil** n
Olivenöl *nt*
Olympic [əʊ'lɪmpɪk] *adj* olympisch; **the ~ Games, the ~s** *pl* die
Olympischen Spiele *pl*, die
Olympiade
omelette ['ɒmlət] n Omelett *nt*
omission [əʊ'mɪʃən] n Auslas-
sung f; **omit** [əʊ'mɪt] vt
auslassen

🔵 **KEYWORD**

on [ɒn] *prep* **1** (*indicating position*)
auf +dat; (*with vb of motion*) auf
+akk; (*on vertical surface, part of*
body) an +dat/akk; **it's on the table**
es ist auf dem Tisch; **she put the**
book on the table sie legte das
Buch auf den Tisch; **on the left**
links
2 (*indicating means, method,*
condition etc) **on foot** (*go, be*) zu
Fuß; **on the train/plane** (*go*) mit
dem Zug/Flugzeug; (*be*) im
Zug/Flugzeug; **on the**
telephone/television am
Telefon/im Fernsehen; **to be on**
drugs Drogen nehmen; **to be on**
holiday/business im Urlaub/auf
Geschäftsreise sein
3 (*referring to time*) **on Friday** (am)
Freitag; **on Fridays** freitags; **on**
June 20th am 20. Juni; **a week on**
Friday Freitag in einer Woche; **on**
arrival he ... als er ankam, ... er ...

4 (*about, concerning*) über +*akk*
▷ *adv* **1** (*referring to dress*) an; **she put her boots/hat on** sie zog ihre Stiefel an/setzte ihren Hut auf
2 (*further, continuously*) weiter; **to walk on** weitergehen
▷ *adj* **1** (*functioning, in operation: machine, TV, light*) an; (*tap*) aufgedreht; (*brakes*) angezogen; **is the meeting still on?** findet die Versammlung noch statt?; **there's a good film on** es läuft ein guter Film
2 that's not on! (*inf*) (*of behaviour*) das ist nicht drin!

once [wʌns] *adv* (*one time, in the past*) einmal; **at ~** sofort; (*at the same time*) gleichzeitig; **~ more** noch einmal; **for ~** ausnahmsweise (einmal); **~ in a while** ab und zu mal ▷ *conj* wenn ... einmal; **~ you've got used to it** sobald Sie sich daran gewöhnt haben

oncoming [ˈɒnkʌmɪŋ] *adj* entgegenkommend; **~ traffic** Gegenverkehr *m*

KEYWORD

one [wʌn] *num* eins; (*with noun, referring back to noun*) ein/eine/ein; **it is one (o'clock)** es ist eins, es ist ein Uhr; **one hundred and fifty** einhundertfünfzig
▷ *adj* **1** (*sole*) einzige(r, s); **the one book which** das einzige Buch, welches
2 (*same*) derselbe/dieselbe/dasselbe; **they came in the one car** sie kamen alle in dem einen Auto
3 (*indef*) **one day I discovered ...** eines Tages bemerkte ich ...
▷ *pron* **1** eine(r, s); **do you have a red one?** haben Sie einen roten/eine rote/ein rotes?; **this one** diese(r, s); **that one** der/die/das; **which one?** welche(r, s)?; **one by one** einzeln
2 one another einander; **do you two ever see one another?** seht ihr beide euch manchmal?
3 (*impers*) man; **one never knows** man kann nie wissen; **to cut one's finger** sich in den Finger schneiden

one-off *adj* einmalig ▷ *n*: **a ~** etwas Einmaliges; **one-parent family** *n* Einelternfamilie *f*; **one-piece** *adj* einteilig; **oneself** *pron* (*reflexive*) sich; **one-way** *adj*: **~ street** Einbahnstraße *f*; **~ ticket** (*US*) einfache Fahrkarte
onion [ˈʌnjən] *n* Zwiebel *f*
on-line [ˈɒnlaɪn] *adj* (*Inform*) online; **~ banking** Homebanking *nt*
only [ˈəʊnlɪ] *adv* nur; (*with time*) erst; **~ yesterday** erst gestern; **he's ~ four** er ist erst vier; **~ just arrived** gerade erst angekommen ▷ *adj* einzige(r, s); **~ child** Einzelkind *nt*
o.n.o. *abbr* = **or nearest offer** VB
onside [ɒnˈsaɪd] *adv* (*Sport*) nicht im Abseits
onto [ˈɒntʊ] *prep* auf +*akk*; (*vertical surface*) an +*akk*; **to be ~ sb** jdm auf die Schliche gekommen sein
onwards [ˈɒnwədz] *adv* voran, vorwärts; **from today ~** von heute an, ab heute
open [ˈəʊpən] *adj* offen; **in the ~ air** im Freien; **~ to the public** für die Öffentlichkeit zugänglich; **the shop is ~ all day** das Geschäft hat den ganzen Tag offen ▷ *vt* öffnen, aufmachen; (*meeting, account, new building*)

eröffnen; (*road*) dem Verkehr
übergeben ▷ *vi* (*door, window etc*)
aufgehen, sich öffnen; (*shop, bank*)
öffnen, aufmachen; (*begin*)
anfangen (*with* mit); **open-air** *adj*
Freiluft-; **open day** *n* Tag *m* der
offenen Tür; **opening** *n* Öffnung
f; (*beginning*) Anfang *m*; (*official, of
exhibition etc*) Eröffnung *f*;
(*opportunity*) Möglichkeit *f*;
~ hours (*o* **times**) Öffnungszeiten
pl; **openly** *adv* offen;
open-minded *adj* aufgeschlossen; **open-plan** *adj*: **~ office**
Großraumbüro *nt*

opera ['ɒpərə] *n* Oper *f*; **opera
glasses** *npl* Opernglas *nt*; **opera
house** *n* Oper *f*, Opernhaus *nt*;
opera singer *n* Opernsänger(in)
m(f)

operate ['ɒpəreɪt] *vt* (*machine*)
bedienen; (*brakes, lights*) betätigen
▷ *vi* (*machine*) laufen; (*bus etc*)
verkehren (*between* zwischen); **to
~** (**on sb**) (*Med*) (jdn) operieren;
operating theatre *n*
Operationssaal *m*; **operation**
[ɒpə'reɪʃən] *n* (*of machine*)
Bedienung *f*; (*functioning*)
Funktionieren *nt*; (*Med*) Operation
f (*on an +dat*); (*undertaking*)
Unternehmen *nt*; **in ~** (*machine*) in
Betrieb; **to have an ~** operiert
werden (*for* wegen); **operator**
['ɒpəreɪtə°] *n*: **to phone the ~** die
Vermittlung anrufen

opinion [ə'pɪnjən] *n* Meinung *f*
(*on* zu); **in my ~** meiner Meinung
nach

opponent [ə'pəʊnənt] *n* Geg-
ner(in) *m(f)*

opportunity [ɒpə'tjuːnɪtɪ] *n*
Gelegenheit *f*

oppose [ə'pəʊz] *vt* sich
widersetzen +*dat*; (*idea*) ablehnen;
opposed *adj*: **to be ~ to sth**
gegen etw sein; **as ~ to** im

Gegensatz zu; **opposing** *adj*
(*team*) gegnerisch; (*points of view*)
entgegengesetzt

opposite ['ɒpəzɪt] *adj* (*house*)
gegenüberliegend; (*direction*)
entgegengesetzt; **the ~ sex** das
andere Geschlecht ▷ *adv*
gegenüber ▷ *prep* gegenüber
+*dat*; **~ me** mir gegenüber ▷ *n*
Gegenteil *nt*

opposition [ɒpə'zɪʃən] *n*
Widerstand *m* (*to* gegen); (*Pol*)
Opposition *f*

oppress [ə'pres] *vt* unterdrücken; **oppressive** *adj* (*heat*)
drückend

opt [ɒpt] *vi*: **to ~ for sth** sich für
etw entscheiden; **to ~ to do sth**
sich entscheiden, etw zu tun

optician [ɒp'tɪʃən] *n* Optiker(in)
m(f)

optimist ['ɒptɪmɪst] *n* Opti-
mist(in) *m(f)*; **optimistic**
[ɒptɪ'mɪstɪk] *adj* optimistisch

option ['ɒpʃən] *n* Möglichkeit *f*;
(*Comm*) Option *f*; **to have no
~** keine Wahl haben; **optional** *adj*
freiwillig; **~ extras** (*Auto*) Extras
pl

or [ɔː°] *conj* oder; (*otherwise*)
sonst; (*after neg*) noch; **hurry up,
~** (**else**) **we'll be late** beeil dich,
sonst kommen wir zu spät

oral ['ɔːrəl] *adj* mündlich; **~ sex**
Oralverkehr *m* ▷ *n* (*exam*)
Mündliche(s) *nt*; **oral surgeon** *n*
Kieferchirurg(in) *m(f)*

orange ['ɒrɪndʒ] *n* Orange *f*
▷ *adj* orangefarben; **orange juice**
n Orangensaft *m*

orbit ['ɔːbɪt] *n* Umlaufbahn *f*; **to
be out of ~** (*fam*) nicht zu
erreichen sein ▷ *vt* umkreisen

orchard ['ɔːtʃəd] *n* Obstgarten *m*

orchestra ['ɔːkɪstrə] *n* Orchester *nt*; (*US Theat*) Parkett *nt*

orchid ['ɔːkɪd] *n* Orchidee *f*

ordeal [ɔːˈdiːl] n Tortur f; (emotional) Qual f

order [ˈɔːdə*] n (sequence) Reihenfolge f; (good arrangement) Ordnung f; (command) Befehl m; (Jur) Anordnung f; (condition) Zustand m; (Comm) Bestellung f; **out of ~** (not functioning) außer Betrieb; (unsuitable) nicht angebracht; **in ~** (items) richtig geordnet; (all right) in Ordnung; **in ~ to do sth** um etw zu tun ▷ vt (arrange) ordnen; (command) befehlen; **to ~ sb to do sth** jdm befehlen, etw zu tun; (food, product) bestellen; **order form** n Bestellschein m

ordinary [ˈɔːdnrɪ] adj gewöhnlich, normal; (average) durchschnittlich

ore [ɔːʳ] n Erz nt

organ [ˈɔːgən] n (Mus) Orgel f; (Anat) Organ nt

organic [ɔːˈgænɪk] adj organisch; (farming, vegetables) Bio-, Öko-; **~ farmer** Biobauer m, Biobäuerin f; **~ food** Biokost f

organization [ɔːgənaɪˈzeɪʃən] n Organisation f; (arrangement) Ordnung f; **organize** [ˈɔːgənaɪz] vt organisieren; **organizer** n (elektronisches) Notizbuch

orgasm [ˈɔːgæzəm] n Orgasmus m

orgy [ˈɔːdʒɪ] n Orgie f

oriental [ɔːrɪˈentəl] adj orientalisch

orientation [ˈɔːrɪenteɪʃən] n Orientierung f

origin [ˈɒrɪdʒɪn] n Ursprung m; (of person) Herkunft f; **original** [əˈrɪdʒɪnl] adj (first) ursprünglich; (painting) original; (idea) originell ▷ n Original nt; **originality** [ərɪdʒɪˈnælɪtɪ] n Originalität f; **originally** adv ursprünglich

Orkneys [ˈɔːknɪz] npl, **Orkney Islands** npl Orkneyinseln pl

ornament [ˈɔːnəmənt] n Schmuckgegenstand m; **ornamental** [ɔːnəˈmentl] adj dekorativ

orphan [ˈɔːfən] n Waise f, Waisenkind nt; **orphanage** [ˈɔːfənɪdʒ] n Waisenhaus nt

orthodox [ˈɔːθədɒks] adj orthodox

orthopaedic, orthopedic (US) [ɔːθəʊˈpiːdɪk] adj orthopädisch

ostentatious [ɒstenˈteɪʃəs] adj protzig

ostrich [ˈɒstrɪtʃ] n (Zool) Strauß m

other [ˈʌðə*] adj, pron andere(r, s); **any ~ questions?** sonst noch Fragen?; **the ~ day** neulich; **every ~ day** jeden zweiten Tag; **any person ~ than him** alle außer ihm; **someone/something or ~** irgendjemand/irgendetwas; **otherwise** adv sonst; (differently) anders

OTT adj abbr = **over the top** übertrieben

otter [ˈɒtə*] n Otter m

ought [ɔːt] vb aux (obligation) sollte; (probability) dürfte; (stronger) müsste; **you ~ to do that** du solltest/Sie sollten das tun; **he ~ to win** er müsste gewinnen; **that ~ to do** das müsste reichen

ounce [aʊns] n Unze f (28,35 g)

our [aʊə*] adj unser; **ours** pron unsere(r, s); **this is ~** das gehört uns; **a friend of ~** ein Freund von uns; **ourselves** pron (reflexive) uns; **we enjoyed ~** wir haben uns amüsiert; **we've got the house to ~** wir haben das Haus für uns; (emphatic) **we did it ~** wir haben es selbst gemacht; **(all) by ~** allein

out [aʊt] adv hinaus/heraus; (not

indoors) draußen; (not at home)
nicht zu Hause; (not alight) aus;
(unconscious) bewusstlos;
(published) herausgekommen;
(results) bekannt gegeben; **have
you been ~ yet?** warst du/waren
Sie schon draußen?; **I was ~ when
they called** ich war nicht da, als
sie vorbeikamen; **to be ~ and
about** unterwegs sein; **the sun is
~** die Sonne scheint; **the fire is
~** das Feuer ist ausgegangen;
(wrong) **the calculation is (way)
~** die Kalkulation stimmt (ganz
und gar) nicht; **they're ~ to get
him** sie sind hinter ihm her ▷ vt
(fam) outen

outback ['autbæk] n (in Australia)
the ~ das Hinterland

outboard ['autbɔːd] adj: **~ motor**
Außenbordmotor m

outbreak ['autbreɪk] n Ausbruch m

outburst ['autbɜːst] n Ausbruch m

outcome ['autkʌm] n Ergebnis
nt

outcry ['autkraɪ] n (public protest)
Protestwelle f (against gegen)

outdo [aut'duː] irr vt übertreffen

outdoor ['autdɔː*] adj Außen-;
(Sport) im Freien; **~ swimming
pool** Freibad nt; **outdoors**
[aut'dɔːz] adv draußen, im Freien

outer ['autə*] adj äußere(r, s);
outer space n Weltraum m

outfit ['autfɪt] n Ausrüstung f;
(clothes) Kleidung f

outgoing ['autgəʊɪŋ] adj
kontaktfreudig

outgrow [aut'grəʊ] irr vt
(clothes) herauswachsen aus

outing ['autɪŋ] n Ausflug m

outlet ['autlet] n Auslass m,
Abfluss m; (US) Steckdose f; (shop)
Verkaufsstelle f

outline ['autlaɪn] n Umriss m;
(summary) Abriss m

outlive [aut'lɪv] vt überleben

outlook ['autlʊk] n Aussicht(en)
f(pl); (prospects) Aussichten pl;
(attitude) Einstellung f
(on zu)

outnumber [aut'nʌmbə*] vt
zahlenmäßig überlegen sein +dat;
~ed zahlenmäßig unterlegen

out of ['autɒv] prep (motion,
motive, origin) aus; (position, away
from) außerhalb +gen;
~ danger/sight/breath außer
Gefahr/Sicht/Atem; **made ~ wood**
aus Holz gemacht; **we are ~ bread**
wir haben kein Brot mehr;
out-of-date adj veraltet;
out-of-the-way adj abgelegen

outpatient ['autpeɪʃənt] n
ambulanter Patient, ambulante
Patientin

output ['autpʊt] n Produktion f;
(of engine) Leistung f; (Inform)
Ausgabe f

outrage ['autreɪdʒ] n (great
anger) Empörung f (at über);
(wicked deed) Schandtat f; (crime)
Verbrechen nt; (indecency) Skandal
m; **outrageous** [aut'reɪdʒəs] adj
unerhört; (clothes, behaviour etc)
unmöglich, schrill

outright ['autraɪt] adv (killed)
sofort ▷ adj total; (denial) völlig;
(winner) unbestritten

outside [aut'saɪd] n Außenseite
f; **on the ~** außen ▷ adj äuße-
re(r, s), Außen-; (chance) sehr
gering ▷ adv außen; **to go ~** nach
draußen gehen ▷ prep außerhalb
+gen; **outsider** n Außenseiter(in)
m(f)

outskirts ['autskɜːts] npl (of
town) Stadtrand m

outstanding [aut'stændɪŋ] adj
hervorragend; (debts etc)
ausstehend

outward ['autwəd] adj äuß-
ere(r, s); **~ journey** Hinfahrt f;

outwardly adv nach außen hin;
outwards adv nach außen
oval ['əʊvəl] adj oval
ovary ['əʊvərɪ] n Eierstock m
ovation [əʊ'veɪʃən] n Ovation f,
Applaus m
oven ['ʌvn] n Backofen m; **oven
glove** n Topfhandschuh m;
ovenproof adj feuerfest;
oven-ready adj bratfertig
over ['əʊvə°] prep (position) über
+dat; (motion) über +akk; **they
spent a long time ~ it** sie haben
lange dazu gebraucht; **from all
~ England** aus ganz England;
~ £20 mehr als 20 Pfund; **~ the
phone/radio** am Telefon/im
Radio; **to talk ~ a glass of wine**
sich bei einem Glas Wein
unterhalten; **~ and above this**
darüber hinaus; **~ the summer**
während des Sommers ▷ adv
(across) hinüber/herüber; (finished)
vorbei; (match, play etc) zu Ende;
(left) übrig; (more) mehr;
~ there/in America da
drüben/drüben in Amerika; **~ to
you** du bist/Sie sind dran; **it's (all)
~ between us** es ist aus zwischen
uns; **~ and ~ again** immer wieder;
to start (all) ~ again noch einmal
von vorn anfangen; **children of 8
and ~** Kinder ab 8 Jahren
over- ['əʊvə°] pref über-
overall ['əʊvərɔ:l] n (Brit) Kittel
m ▷ adj (situation) allgemein;
(length) Gesamt-; **~ majority**
absolute Mehrheit ▷ adv
insgesamt; **overalls** npl Overall
m
overboard ['əʊvəbɔ:d] adv über
Bord
overbooked [əʊvə'bʊkt] adj
überbucht; **overbooking** n
Überbuchung f
overcharge [əʊvə'tʃɑ:dʒ] vt zu
viel verlangen von

overcoat ['əʊvəkəʊt] n Wintermantel m
overcome [əʊvə'kʌm] irr vt
überwinden; **~ by sleep/emotion**
von Schlaf/Rührung übermannt;
we shall ~ wir werden siegen
overcooked [əʊvə'kʊkt] adj
verkocht; (meat) zu lange gebraten
overcrowded [əʊvə'kraʊdɪd]
adj überfüllt
overdo [əʊvə'du:] irr vt übertreiben; **overdone** adj
übertrieben; (food) zu lange
gekocht; (meat) zu lange gebraten
overdose ['əʊvədəʊs] n Über-
dosis f
overdraft ['əʊvədrɑ:ft] n Kon-
toüberziehung f; **overdrawn**
[əʊvə'drɔ:n] adj überzogen
overdue [əʊvə'dju:] adj
überfällig
overestimate [əʊvər'estɪmeɪt]
vt überschätzen
overexpose [əʊvərɪks'pəʊz] vt (Foto)
überbelichten
overflow [əʊvə'fləʊ] vi
überlaufen
overhead ['əʊvəhed] adj (Aviat)
~ locker Gepäckfach nt;
~ projector Overheadprojektor m;
~ railway Hochbahn f
▷ [əʊvə'hed] adv oben;
overhead, (Brit) **overheads** n
(Comm) allgemeine
Geschäftskosten pl
overhear [əʊvə'hɪə°] irr vt zufällig
mit anhören
overheat [əʊvə'hi:t] vi (engine)
heiß laufen
overjoyed [əʊvə'dʒɔɪd] adj
überglücklich (at über)
overland ['əʊvəlænd] adj Über-
land- ▷ [əʊvə'lænd] adv (travel)
über Land
overlap [əʊvə'læp] vi (dates etc)
sich überschneiden; (objects) sich
teilweise decken

overload [əʊvə'ləʊd] *vt* überladen

overlook [əʊvə'lʊk] *vt* (*view from above*) überblicken; (*not notice*) übersehen; (*pardon*) hinwegsehen über +*akk*

overnight [əʊvə'naɪt] *adj* (*journey, train*) Nacht-; **~ bag** Reisetasche *f*; **~ stay** Übernachtung *f* ▷ *adv* über Nacht

overpass ['əʊvəpɑːs] *n* Überführung *f*

overpay [əʊvə'peɪ] *vt* überbezahlen

overrule [əʊvə'ruːl] *vt* verwerfen; (*decision*) aufheben

overseas [əʊvə'siːz] *adj* Übersee-; ausländisch; (*fam*) Auslands- ▷ *adv* (*go*) nach Übersee; (*live, work*) in Übersee

oversee [əʊvə'siː] *irr vt* beaufsichtigen

overshadow [əʊvə'ʃædəʊ] *vt* überschatten

overshoot [əʊvə'ʃuːt] *irr vt* (*runway*) hinausschießen über +*akk*; (*turning*) vorbeifahren +*dat*

oversight ['əʊvəsaɪt] *n* Versehen *nt*

oversimplify [əʊvə'sɪmplɪfaɪ] *vt* zu sehr vereinfachen

oversleep [əʊvə'sliːp] *irr vi* verschlafen

overtake [əʊvə'teɪk] *irr vt, vi* überholen

overtime ['əʊvətaɪm] *n* Überstunden *pl*

overturn [əʊvə'tɜːn] *vt, vi* umkippen

overweight [əʊvə'weɪt] *adj*: **to be ~** Übergewicht haben

overwhelm [əʊvə'welm] *vt* überwältigen; **overwhelming** *adj* überwältigend

overwork [əʊvə'wɜːk] *n* Überarbeitung *f* ▷ *vi* sich überarbeiten; **overworked** *adj* überarbeitet

owe [əʊ] *vt* schulden; **to ~ sth to sb** (*money*) jdm etw schulden; (*favour etc*) jdm etw verdanken; **how much do I ~ you?** was bin ich dir/Ihnen schuldig?; **owing to** *prep* wegen +*gen*

owl [aʊl] *n* Eule *f*

own [əʊn] *vt* besitzen ▷ *adj* eigen; **on one's ~** allein; **he has a flat of his ~** er hat eine eigene Wohung; **own up** *vi*: **to ~ to sth** etw zugeben; **owner** *n* Besitzer(in) *m(f)*; (*of business*) Inhaber(in) *m(f)*; **ownership** *n* Besitz *m*; **under new ~** unter neuer Leitung

ox [ɒks] (*pl* **oxen**) *n* Ochse *m*; **oxtail** ['ɒksteɪl] *n* Ochsenschwanz *m*; **~ soup** Ochsenschwanzsuppe *f*; **oxygen** ['ɒksɪdʒən] *n* Sauerstoff *m*

oyster ['ɔɪstə*] *n* Auster *f*

oz *abbr* = **ounces** Unzen *pl*

Oz ['ɒz] *n* (*fam*) Australien *nt*

ozone ['əʊzəʊn] *n* Ozon *nt*; **~ layer** Ozonschicht *f*

P

p.a. *abbr* = **per annum**

pace [peɪs] *n* (*speed*) Tempo *nt*; (*step*) Schritt *m*; **pacemaker** *n* (*Med*) Schrittmacher *m*

Pacific [pə'sɪfɪk] *n*: **the ~ (Ocean)** der Pazifik; **Pacific Standard Time** *n* pazifische Zeit

pacifier ['pæsɪfaɪə*] *n* (*US: for baby*) Schnuller *m*

pack [pæk] *n* (*of cards*) Spiel *nt*; (*esp US: of cigarettes*) Schachtel *f*; (*gang*) Bande *f*; (*US: backpack*) Rucksack *m* ▷ *vt* (*case*) packen; (*clothes*) einpacken ▷ *vi* (*for holiday*) packen; **pack in** *vt* (*Brit fam: job*) hinschmeißen; **package** ['pækɪdʒ] *n* (*a. Inform, fig*) Paket *nt*; **package deal** *n* Pauschalangebot *nt*; **package holiday**, **package tour** *n* Pauschalreise *f*; **packaging** *n* (*material*) Verpackung *f*; **packed lunch** *n* (*Brit*) Lunchpaket *nt*; **packet** *n* Päckchen *nt*; (*of cigarettes*) Schachtel *f*

pad [pæd] *n* (*of paper*) Schreibblock *m*; (*padding*) Polster *nt*; **padded envelope** *n* wattierter Umschlag; **padding** *n* (*material*) Polsterung *f*

paddle ['pædl] *n* (*for boat*) Paddel *nt* ▷ *vi* (*in boat*) paddeln; **paddling pool** *n* (*Brit*) Planschbecken *nt*

padlock ['pædlɒk] *n* Vorhängeschloss *nt*

page [peɪdʒ] *n* (*of book etc*) Seite *f*

pager ['peɪdʒə*] *n* Piepser *m*

paid [peɪd] *pt, pp of* **pay** ▷ *adj* bezahlt

pain [peɪn] *n* Schmerz *m*; **to be in ~** Schmerzen haben; **she's a (real) ~** sie nervt; **painful** *adj* (*physically*) schmerzhaft; (*embarrassing*) peinlich; **painkiller** *n* schmerzstillendes Mittel

painstaking *adj* sorgfältig

paint [peɪnt] *n* Farbe *f* ▷ *vt* anstreichen; (*picture*) malen; **paintbrush** *n* Pinsel *m*; **painter** *n* Maler(in) *m(f)*; **painting** *n* (*picture*) Bild *nt*, Gemälde *nt*

pair [peə*] *n* Paar *nt*; **a ~ of shoes** ein Paar Schuhe; **a ~ of scissors** eine Schere; **a ~ of trousers** eine Hose

pajamas [pə'dʒɑːməz] *npl* (*US*) Schlafanzug *m*

Pakistan [pɑːkɪ'stɑːn] *n* Pakistan *nt*

pal [pæl] *n* (*fam*) Kumpel *m*

palace ['pæləs] *n* Palast *m*

pale [peɪl] *adj* (*face*) blass, bleich; (*colour*) hell

palm [pɑːm] *n* (*of hand*) Handfläche *f*; **~ (tree)** Palme *f*; **palmtop (computer)** *n* Palmtop(computer) *m*

pamper ['pæmpə*] vt
verhätscheln

pan [pæn] n (saucepan) Topf m;
(frying pan) Pfanne f; **pancake**
['pænkeɪk] n Pfannkuchen m;
Pancake Day n (Brit)
Fastnachtsdienstag m

pandemic [pæn'demɪk] n Pandemie f

panel ['pænl] n (of wood) Tafel f;
(in discussion) Diskussionsteil-
nehmer pl; (in jury) Jurymitglieder
pl

panic ['pænɪk] n Panik f ▷ vi in
Panik geraten; **panicky** ['pænɪkɪ]
adj panisch

pansy ['pænzɪ] n (flower)
Stiefmütterchen nt

panties ['pæntɪz] npl (Damen)-
slip m

pantomime ['pæntəmaɪm] n
(Brit) um die Weihnachtszeit
aufgeführte Märchenkomödie

pants [pænts] npl Unterhose f;
(esp US: trousers) Hose f

pantyhose ['pæntɪhəʊz] npl
(US) Strumpfhose f; **panty-liner** n
Slipeinlage f

paper ['peɪpə*] n Papier nt;
(newspaper) Zeitung f; (exam)
Klausur f; (for reading at conference)
Referat nt; **~s** pl (identity papers)
Papiere pl; **~ bag** Papiertüte f;
~ cup Pappbecher m ▷ vt (wall)
tapezieren; **paperback** n
Taschenbuch nt; **paper clip** n
Büroklammer f; **paper feed** n (of
printer) Papiereinzug m; **paper
round** n: **to do a ~** Zeitungen
austragen; **paperwork** n
Schreibarbeit f

parachute ['pærəʃuːt] n Fallschirm m ▷ vi abspringen

paracetamol [pærə'siːtəmɒl] n
(tablet) Paracetamoltablette
f

parade [pə'reɪd] n (procession)

Umzug m; (Mil) Parade f ▷ vi
vorbeimarschieren

paradise ['pærədaɪs] n Paradies
nt

paragliding ['pærəglaɪdɪŋ] n
Gleitschirmfliegen nt

paragraph ['pærəgrɑːf] n Absatz
m

parallel ['pærəlel] adj parallel
▷ n (Math, fig) Parallele f

paralyze ['pærəlaɪz] vt lähmen;
(fig) lahmlegen

paranoid ['pærənɔɪd] adj
paranoid

paraphrase ['pærəfreɪz] vt
umschreiben; (sth spoken) anders
ausdrücken

parasailing ['pærəseɪlɪŋ] n
Parasailing nt

parasol ['pærəsɒl] n Sonnenschirm m

parcel ['pɑːsl] n Paket nt

pardon ['pɑːdn] n (Jur)
Begnadigung f; **~ me/I beg your
~** verzeih/verzeihen Sie bitte;
(objection) aber ich bitte dich/Sie; **I
beg your ~?/~ me?** wie bitte?

parent ['peərənt] n Elternteil m;
~s pl Eltern pl; **~s-in-law** pl
Schwiegereltern pl; **parental**
[pə'rentl] adj elterlich, Eltern-

parish ['pærɪʃ] n Gemeinde f

park [pɑːk] n Park m ▷ vt, vi
parken; **parking** n Parken nt; **"no
~"** „Parken verboten"; **parking
brake** n (US) Handbremse f;
parking disc n Parkscheibe f;
parking fine n Geldbuße f für
falsches Parken; **parking lights**
npl (US) Standlicht nt; **parking lot**
n (US) Parkplatz m; **parking meter**
n Parkuhr f; **parking place**,
parking space n Parkplatz m;
parking ticket n Strafzettel m

parliament ['pɑːləmənt] n Parlament nt

parrot ['pærət] n Papagei m

parsley ['pɑːslɪ] n Petersilie f
parsnip ['pɑːsnɪp] n Pastinake f (längliches, weißes Wurzelgemüse)
part [pɑːt] n Teil m; (of machine) Teil nt; (Theat) Rolle f; (US: in hair) Scheitel m; **to take ~** teilnehmen (in an +dat); **for the most ~** zum größten Teil ▷ adj Teil- ▷ vt (separate) trennen; (hair) scheiteln ▷ vi (people) sich trennen
partial ['pɑːʃəl] adj (incomplete) teilweise, Teil-
participant [pɑːˈtɪsɪpənt] n Teilnehmer(in) m(f); **participate** [pɑːˈtɪsɪpeɪt] vi teilnehmen (in an +dat)
particular [pəˈtɪkjʊlə°] adj (specific) bestimmt; (exact) genau; (fussy) eigen; **in ~** insbesondere ▷ n **~s** pl (details) Einzelheiten pl; (about person) Personalien pl; **particularly** adv besonders
parting ['pɑːtɪŋ] n (farewell) Abschied m; (Brit: in hair) Scheitel m
partly ['pɑːtlɪ] adv teilweise
partner ['pɑːtnə°] n Partner(in) m(f); **partnership** n Partnerschaft f
partridge ['pɑːtrɪdʒ] n Rebhuhn nt
part-time ['pɑːtˈtaɪm] adj Teilzeit- ▷ adv: **to work ~** Teilzeit arbeiten
party ['pɑːtɪ] n (celebration) Party f; (Pol, Jur) Partei f; (group) Gruppe f ▷ vi feiern
pass [pɑːs] vt (on foot) vorbeigehen an +dat; (in car etc) vorbeifahren an +dat; (time) verbringen; (exam) bestehen; (law) verabschieden; **to ~ sth to sb, to ~ sb sth** jdm etw reichen; **to ~ the ball to sb** jdm den Ball zuspielen ▷ vi (on foot) vorbeigehen; (in car etc) vorbeifahren; (years) vergehen; (in exam) bestehen ▷ n (document) Ausweis m; (Sport) Pass m; **pass**

away vi (die) verscheiden; **pass by** vi (on foot) vorbeigehen; (in car etc) vorbeifahren ▷ vt (on foot) vorbeigehen an +dat; (in car etc) vorbeifahren an +dat; **pass on** vt weitergeben (to an +akk); (disease) übertragen (to auf +akk); **pass out** vi (faint) ohnmächtig werden; **pass round** vt herumreichen
passage ['pæsɪdʒ] n (corridor) Gang m; (in book, music) Passage f; **passageway** n Durchgang m
passenger ['pæsɪndʒə°] n Passagier(in) m(f); (on bus) Fahrgast m; (on train) Reisende(r) mf; (in car) Mitfahrer(in) m(f)
passer-by ['pɑːsəˈbaɪ] (pl **passers-by**) n Passant(in) m(f)
passion ['pæʃən] n Leidenschaft f; **passionate** ['pæʃənɪt] adj leidenschaftlich; **passion fruit** n Passionsfrucht
passive ['pæsɪv] adj passiv; **~ smoking** Passivrauchen nt ▷ n: **~ (voice)** (Ling) Passiv nt
passport ['pɑːspɔːt] n (Reise)-pass m; **passport control** n Passkontrolle f
password ['pɑːswɜːd] n (Inform) Passwort nt
past [pɑːst] n Vergangenheit f ▷ adv (by) vorbei; **it's five ~** es ist fünf nach ▷ adj (years) vergangen; (president etc) ehemalig; (in the ~ **two months** in den letzten zwei Monaten ▷ prep (telling time) nach; **half ~ 10** halb 11; **to go ~ sth** an etw dat vorbeigehen/-fahren
pasta ['pæstə] n Nudeln pl
paste [peɪst] vt (stick) kleben; (Inform) einfügen ▷ n (glue) Kleister m
pastime ['pɑːstaɪm] n Zeitvertreib m
pastry ['peɪstrɪ] n Teig m; (cake) Stückchen
pasty ['pæstɪ] n (Brit) Pastete f

patch [pætʃ] n (area) Fleck m; (for mending) Flicken ▷ vt flicken; **patchy** adj (uneven) ungleichmäßig
pâté ['pæteɪ] n Pastete f
paternal [pə'tɜːnl] adj väterlich; ~ **grandmother** Großmutter f väterlicherseits; **paternity leave** [pə'tɜːnɪtɪliːv] n Elternzeit f (des Vaters)
path [pɑːθ] n (a. Inform) Pfad m; (a. fig) Weg m
pathetic [pə'θetɪk] adj (bad) kläglich, erbärmlich; **it's ~** es ist zum Heulen
patience ['peɪʃəns] n Geduld f; (Brit Cards) Patience f; **patient** adj geduldig ▷ n Patient(in) m(f)
patio ['pætɪəʊ] n Terrasse f
patriotic [pætrɪ'ɒtɪk] adj patriotisch
patrol car [pə'trəʊlkɑːʳ] n Streifenwagen m; **patrolman** (pl -**men**) n (US) Streifenpolizist m
patron ['peɪtrən] n (sponsor) Förderer m, Förderin f; (in shop) Kunde m, Kundin f
patronize ['pætrənaɪz] vt (treat condescendingly) von oben herab behandeln; **patronizing** adj (attitude) herablassend
pattern ['pætən] n Muster nt
pause [pɔːz] n Pause f ▷ vi (speaker) innehalten
pavement n (Brit) Bürgersteig m; (US) Pflaster nt
pay [peɪ] (**paid, paid**) vt bezahlen; **he paid** (**me**) **£20 for it** er hat (mir) 20 Pfund dafür gezahlt; **to ~ attention** Acht geben (to auf +akk); **to ~ sb a visit** jdn besuchen ▷ vi zahlen; (be profitable) sich bezahlt machen; **to ~ for sth** etw bezahlen ▷ n Bezahlung f, Lohn m; **pay back** vt (money) zurückzahlen; **pay in** vt (into account) einzahlen; **payable**

adj zahlbar; (due) fällig; **payday** n Zahltag m; **payee** [peɪ'iː] n Zahlungsempfänger(in) m(f); **payment** n Bezahlung f; (money) Zahlung f; **pay-per-view** adj Pay-per-View-; **pay phone** n Münzfernsprecher m; **pay TV** n Pay-TV nt
PC abbr = **personal computer** PC m; abbr = **politically correct** politisch korrekt
PDA abbr = **personal digital assistant** PDA m
PE abbr = **physical education** (school) Sport m
pea [piː] n Erbse f
peace [piːs] n Frieden m; **peaceful** adj friedlich
peach [piːtʃ] n Pfirsich m
peacock ['piːkɒk] n Pfau m
peak [piːk] n (of mountain) Gipfel m; (fig) Höhepunkt m; **peak period** n Stoßzeit f; (season) Hochsaison
peanut ['piːnʌt] n Erdnuss f; **peanut butter** n Erdnussbutter f
pear [peəʳ] n Birne f
pearl [pɜːl] n Perle f
pebble ['pebl] n Kiesel m
pecan [pɪ'kæn] n Pekannuss
peck [pek] vt, vi picken; **peckish** adj (Brit fam) ein bisschen hungrig
peculiar [pɪ'kjuːlɪəʳ] adj (odd) seltsam; **~ to** charakteristisch für; **peculiarity** [pɪkjʊlɪ'ærɪtɪ] n (singular quality) Besonderheit f; (strangeness) Eigenartigkeit f
pedal ['pedl] n Pedal nt
pedestrian [pɪ'destrɪən] n Fußgänger(in) m(f); **pedestrian crossing** n Fußgängerüberweg m
pee [piː] vi (fam) pinkeln
peel [piːl] n Schale f ▷ vt schälen ▷ vi (paint etc) abblättern; (skin etc) sich schälen
peer [pɪəʳ] n Gleichaltrige(r) mf ▷ vi starren

peg [peg] n (for coat etc) Haken m; (for tent) Hering m; (**clothes**) ~ (Wäsche)klammer f

pelvis ['pelvɪs] n Becken nt

pen [pen] n (ball-point) Kuli m, Kugelschreiber; (fountain ~) Füller m

penalize ['piːnəlaɪz] vt (punish) bestrafen; **penalty** ['penltɪ] n (punishment) Strafe f; (in football) Elfmeter m

pence [pens] pl of **penny**

pencil ['pensl] n Bleistift m; **pencil sharpener** n (Bleistift)spitzer m

penetrate ['penɪtreɪt] vt durchdringen; (enter into) eindringen in +akk

penfriend ['penfrend] n Brief-freund(in) m(f)

penguin ['peŋgwɪn] n Pinguin m

penicillin [penɪˈsɪlɪn] n Penizil-lin nt

peninsula [pɪˈnɪnsjʊlə] n Halbinsel f

penis ['piːnɪs] n Penis m

penknife ['pennaɪf] n (pl **penknives**) n Taschenmesser nt

penny ['penɪ] n (pl **pence** o **pennies**) n (Brit) Penny m; (US) Centstück nt

pension ['penʃən] n Rente f; (for civil servants, executives etc) Pension f; **pensioner** n Rentner(in) m(f); **pension plan, pension scheme** n Rentenversicherung f

penultimate [pɪˈnʌltɪmət] adj vorletzte(r, s)

people ['piːpl] npl (persons) Leute pl; (von Staat) Volk nt; (inhabitants) Bevölkerung f; **people carrier** n Minivan m

pepper ['pepə*] n Pfeffer m; (vegetable) Paprika m; **peppermint** n (sweet) Pfefferminz nt

per [pɜː*] prep pro; ~ **annum** pro Jahr; ~ **cent** Prozent nt

percentage [pəˈsentɪdʒ] n Pro-zentsatz m

perceptible [pəˈseptəbl] adj wahrnehmbar

percolator ['pɜːkəleɪtə*] n Kaf-feemaschine f

percussion [pɜːˈkʌʃən] n (Mus) Schlagzeug nt

perfect ['pɜːfɪkt] adj perfekt; (utter) völlig ⊳ [pəˈfekt] vt vervollkommnen; **perfectly** adv perfekt; (utterly) völlig

perform [pəˈfɔːm] vt (task) ausführen; (play) aufführen; (Med: operation) durchführen ⊳ vi (Theat) auftreten; **performance** n (show) Vorstellung f; (efficiency) Leistung f

perfume ['pɜːfjuːm] n Duft m; (substance) Parfüm nt

perhaps [pəˈhæps] adv vielleicht

period ['pɪərɪəd] n (length of time) Zeit f; (in history) Zeitalter nt; (school) Stunde f; (Med) Periode f; (US: full stop) Punkt m; **for a ~ of three years** für einen Zeitraum von drei Jahren; **periodical** [pɪərɪˈɒdɪkəl] n Zeitschrift f

peripheral [pəˈrɪfərəl] n (Inform) Peripheriegerät nt

perjury ['pɜːdʒərɪ] n Meineid m

perm [pɜːm] n Dauerwelle f

permanent, permanently ['pɜːmənənt, -lɪ] adj, adv ständig

permission [pəˈmɪʃən] n Erlaubnis f; **permit** ['pɜːmɪt] n Genehmigung f ⊳ [pəˈmɪt] vt erlauben, zulassen; **to ~ sb to do sth** jdm erlauben, etw zu tun

persecute ['pɜːsɪkjuːt] vt verfolgen

perseverance [pɜːsɪˈvɪərəns] n Ausdauer f

persist [pəˈsɪst] vi (in belief etc) bleiben (in bei); (rain, smell) andauern; **persistent** adj beharrlich

P

person ['pɜːsn] n Mensch m; (in
official context) Person f; **in ~**
persönlich; **personal** adj
persönlich; (private) privat;
personality [pɜːsə'nælətɪ] n
Persönlichkeit f; **personal
organizer** n Organizer m;
personal stereo (pl **-s**) n
Walkman® m; **personnel**
[pɜːsə'nel] n Personal nt
perspective [pə'spektɪv] n
Perspektive f
persuade [pə'sweɪd] vt überreden; (convince) überzeugen;
persuasive [pə'sweɪsɪv] adj
überzeugend
perverse [pə'vɜːs] adj
eigensinnig; abwegig; **pervert**
['pɜːvɜːt] n Perverse(r) mf
▷ [pə'vɜːt] vt (morally) verderben;
perverted [pə'vɜːtɪd] adj pervers
pessimist ['pesɪmɪst] n Pes-
simist(in) m(f); **pessimistic**
[pesɪ'mɪstɪk] adj pessimistisch
pest [pest] n (insect) Schädling m;
(fig: person) Nervensäge f; (thing)
Plage f; **pester** ['pestə°] vt
plagen; **pesticide** ['pestɪsaɪd] n
Schädlingsbekämpfungsmittel nt
pet [pet] n (animal) Haustier nt;
(person) Liebling m
petal ['petl] n Blütenblatt nt
petition [pə'tɪʃən] n Petition f
petrol ['petrəl] n (Brit) Benzin nt;
petrol pump n (at garage)
Zapfsäule f; **petrol station** n
Tankstelle f; **petrol tank** n
Benzintank m
pharmacy ['fɑːməsɪ] n (shop)
Apotheke f; (science) Pharmazie f
phase [feɪz] n Phase f
PhD abbr = **Doctor of Philosophy**
Dr. phil; (dissertation) Doktorarbeit
f; **to do one's ~** promovieren
pheasant ['feznt] n Fasan m
phenomenon [fɪ'nɒmɪnən] (pl
phenomena) n Phänomen nt

Philippines ['fɪlɪpiːnz] npl
Philippinen pl
philosophical [fɪlə'sɒfɪkəl] adj
philosophisch; (fig) gelassen;
philosophy [fɪ'lɒsəfɪ] n Philosophie f
phone [fəʊn] n Telefon nt ▷ vt, vi
anrufen; **phone book** n
Telefonbuch nt; **phone bill** n
Telefonrechnung f; **phone booth**,
phone box (Brit) n Telefonzelle f;
phonecall n Telefonanruf m;
phonecard n Telefonkarte f;
phone-in n Rundfunkprogramm, bei
dem Hörer anrufen können; **phone
number** n Telefonnummer f
photo ['fəʊtəʊ] (pl **-s**) n Foto nt;
photo booth n Fotoautomat m;
photocopier ['fəʊtəʊ'kɒpɪə°] n
Kopiergerät nt; **photocopy**
['fəʊtəʊkɒpɪ] n Fotokopie f ▷ vt
fotokopieren; **photograph**
['fəʊtəgrɑːf] n Fotografie f,
Aufnahme f ▷ vt fotografieren;
photographer [fə'tɒgrəfə°] n
Fotograf(in) m(f); **photography**
[fə'tɒgrəfɪ] n Fotografie f
phrase [freɪz] n (expression)
Redewendung f, Ausdruck m;
phrase book n Sprachführer m
physical ['fɪzɪkəl] adj (bodily)
körperlich, physisch ▷ n ärztliche
Untersuchung; **physically** adv
(bodily) körperlich, physisch;
~ handicapped körperbehindert
physics ['fɪzɪks] nsing Physik f
physiotherapy [fɪzɪə'θerəpɪ] n
Physiotherapie f
physique [fɪ'ziːk] n Körperbau m
piano ['pjɑːnəʊ] (pl **-s**) n Klavier
nt
pick [pɪk] vt (flowers, fruit)
pflücken; (choose) auswählen;
(team) aufstellen; **pick out** vt
auswählen; **pick up** vt (lift up)
aufheben; (collect) abholen; (learn)
lernen

pickle ['pɪkl] n (food) (Mixed) Pickles pl ▷ vt einlegen

pickpocket ['pɪkpɒkɪt] n Taschendieb(in) m(f)

picnic ['pɪknɪk] n Picknick nt

picture ['pɪktʃə*] n Bild nt; **to go to the ~s** (Brit) ins Kino gehen ▷ vt (visualize) sich vorstellen; **picture book** n Bilderbuch nt; **picturesque** [pɪktʃə'resk] adj malerisch

pie [paɪ] n (meat) Pastete f; (fruit) Kuchen m

piece [piːs] n Stück nt; (part) Teil nt; (in chess) Figur f; (in draughts) Stein m; **a ~ of cake** ein Stück Kuchen; **to fall to ~s** auseinanderfallen

pier [pɪə*] n Pier m

pierce [pɪəs] vt durchstechen, durchbohren; (cold, sound) durchdringen; **pierced** adj (part of body) gepierct; **piercing** adj durchdringend

pig [pɪg] n Schwein nt

pigeon ['pɪdʒən] n Taube f; **pigeonhole** n (compartment) Ablegefach nt

piggy ['pɪgɪ] adj (fam) verfressen; **pigheaded** ['pɪg'hedɪd] adj dickköpfig; **piglet** ['pɪglət] n Ferkel nt; **pigsty** ['pɪgstaɪ] n Schweinestall m; **pigtail** ['pɪgteɪl] n Zopf m

pile [paɪl] n (heap) Haufen m; (one on top of another) Stapel m; **pile up** vi (accumulate) sich anhäufen

piles [paɪlz] npl Hämorr(ho)iden pl

pile-up ['paɪlʌp] n (Auto) Massenkarambolage f

pilgrim ['pɪlgrɪm] n Pilger(in) m(f)

pill [pɪl] n Tablette f; **the ~** die (Antibaby)pille; **to be on the ~** die Pille nehmen

pillar ['pɪlə*] n Pfeiler m

pillow ['pɪləʊ] n (Kopf)kissen nt; **pillowcase** n (Kopf)kissenbezug m

pilot ['paɪlət] n (Aviat) Pilot(in) m(f)

pimple ['pɪmpl] n Pickel m

pin [pɪn] n (for fixing) Nadel f; (in sewing) Stecknadel f; (Tech) Stift m; **I've got ~s and needles in my leg** mein Bein ist mir eingeschlafen ▷ vt (fix with ~) heften (to an +akk)

PIN [pɪn] acr = **personal identification number ~ (number)** PIN f, Geheimzahl f

pinch [pɪntʃ] n (of salt) Prise f ▷ vt zwicken; (fam: steal) klauen ▷ vi (shoe) drücken

pine [paɪn] n Kiefer f

pineapple ['paɪnæpl] n Ananas f

pink [pɪŋk] adj rosa

pinstripe(d) ['pɪnstraɪp(t)] adj Nadelstreifen-

pint [paɪnt] n Pint nt (Brit: 0,57 l, US: 0,473l); (Brit: glass of beer) Bier nt

pious ['paɪəs] adj fromm

pip [pɪp] n (of fruit) Kern m

pipe [paɪp] n (for smoking) Pfeife f; (for water, gas) Rohrleitung f

pirate ['paɪərɪt] n Pirat(in) m(f); **pirated copy** n Raubkopie f

Pisces ['paɪsiːz] nsing (Astr) Fische pl; **she's a ~** sie ist Fisch

piss [pɪs] vi (vulg) pissen ▷ n (vulg) Pisse f; **to take the ~ out of sb** jdn verarschen; **piss off** vi (vulg) sich verpissen; **~!** verpiss dich!; **pissed** adj (Brit fam: drunk) sturzbesoffen; (US fam: annoyed) stocksauer

pistachio [pɪ'stɑːʃɪəʊ] (pl -s) n Pistazie f

piste [piːst] n (Ski) Piste f

pistol ['pɪstl] n Pistole f

pit [pɪt] n (hole) Grube f; (coalmine) Zeche f; **the ~s** (motor racing) die Box; **to be the ~s** (fam) grottenschlecht sein

pitch [pɪtʃ] n (Sport) Spielfeld nt; (Mus: of instrument) Tonlage f; (of voice) Stimmlage f ▷ vt (tent)

P

aufschlagen; (*throw*) werfen;
pitch-black *adj* pechschwarz
pitcher ['pɪtʃə*] *n* (*US: jug*) Krug *m*
pitiful ['pɪtɪfʊl] *adj* (*contemptible*)
jämmerlich
pitta bread ['pɪtə] *n* Pittabrot *nt*
pity ['pɪtɪ] *n* Mitleid *nt*; **what a
~** wie schade; **it's a ~** es ist schade
▷ *vt* Mitleid haben mit
pizza ['piːtsə] *n* Pizza *f*
place [pleɪs] *n* *m* (*spot, in text*)
Stelle *f*; (*town etc*) Ort; (*house*) Haus
nt; (*position, seat, on course*) Platz *m*;
~ of birth Geburtsort *m*; **at my
~** bei mir; **in third ~** auf den dritten
Platz; **to three decimal ~s** bis auf
drei Stellen nach dem Komma; **out
of ~** nicht an der richtigen Stelle;
(*fig: remark*) unangebracht; **in ~ of**
anstelle von; **in the first ~** (*firstly*)
erstens; (*immediately*) gleich; (*in any
case*) überhaupt ▷ *vt* (*put*) stellen,
setzen; (*lay flat*) legen; (*advertisement*) setzen (*in in +akk*); (*Comm:
order*) aufgeben; **place mat** *n* Set *nt*
plague [pleɪg] *n* Pest *f*
plaice [pleɪs] *n* Scholle *f*
plain [pleɪn] *adj* (*clear*) klar,
deutlich; (*simple*) einfach; (*not
beautiful*) unattraktiv; (*yoghurt*)
Natur-; (*Brit: chocolate*)
(Zart)bitter- ▷ *n* Ebene *f*; **plainly**
adv (*frankly*) offen; (*simply*) einfach;
(*obviously*) eindeutig
plait [plæt] *n* Zopf *m* ▷ *vt*
flechten
plan [plæn] *n* Plan *m*; (*for essay
etc*) Konzept *nt* ▷ *vt* planen; **to
~ to do sth, to ~ on doing sth**
vorhaben, etw zu tun ▷ *vi* planen
plane [pleɪn] *n* (*aircraft*)
Flugzeug *nt*; (*tool*) Hobel *m*
planet ['plænɪt] *n* Planet *m*
plank [plæŋk] *n* Brett *nt*
plant [plɑːnt] *n* Pflanze *f*;
(*equipment*) Maschinen *pl*; (*factory*)
Werk *nt* ▷ *vt* (*tree etc*) pflanzen;

plantation [plæn'teɪʃən] *n* Plan-
tage *f*
plaque [plæk] *n* Gedenktafel *f*;
(*on teeth*) Zahnbelag *m*
plaster ['plɑːstə*] *n* (*Brit Med:
sticking ~*) Pflaster *nt*; (*on wall*)
Verputz *m*; **to have one's arm in
~** den Arm in Gips haben
plastered ['plɑːstəd] *adj* (*fam*)
besoffen; **to get (absolutely)
~** sich besaufen
plastic ['plæstɪk] *n* Kunststoff *m*;
to pay with ~ mit Kreditkarte
bezahlen ▷ *adj* Plastik-; **plastic
bag** *n* Plastiktüte *f*; **plastic
surgery** *n* plastische Chirurgie *f*
plate [pleɪt] *n* (*for food*) Teller *m*;
(*flat sheet*) Platte *f*; (*plaque*) Schild
nt
platform ['plætfɔːm] *n* (*Rail*)
Bahnsteig *m*; (*at meeting*) Podium
nt
platinum ['plætɪnəm] *n* Platin *nt*
play [pleɪ] *n* Spiel *nt*; (*Theat*)
(Theater)stück *nt* ▷ *vt* spielen;
(*another player or team*) spielen
gegen; **to ~ the piano** Klavier
spielen; **to ~ a part in** (*fig*) eine
Rolle spielen bei ▷ *vi* spielen;
play at *vt*: **what are you ~ing at?**
was soll das?; **play back** *vt*
abspielen; **play down** *vt*
herunterspielen
playacting *n* Schauspielerei *f*;
playback *n* Wiedergabe *f*; **player**
n Spieler(in) *m(f)*; **playful** *adj*
(*person*) verspielt; (*remark*)
scherzhaft; **playground** *n*
Spielplatz *m*; (*in school*) Schulhof *m*;
playgroup *n* Spielgruppe *f*;
playing card *n* Spielkarte *f*;
playing field *n* Sportplatz *m*;
playmate *n* Spielkamerad(in)
m(f); **playwright** *n*
Dramatiker(in) *m(f)*
plc *abbr* = **public limited company**
AG *f*

plea [pliː] *n* Bitte *f* (*for* um)

plead [pliːd] *vi* dringend bitten (*with sb* jdn); (*Jur*) **to ~ guilty** sich schuldig bekennen

pleasant, pleasantly ['pleznt, -lɪ] *adj, adv* angenehm

please [pliːz] *adv* bitte; **more tea? - yes, ~** noch Tee? - ja, bitte ▷ *vt* (*be agreeable to*) gefallen +*dat*; **~ yourself** wie du willst/Sie wollen; **pleased** *adj* zufrieden; (*glad*) erfreut; **~ to meet you** freut mich, angenehm; **pleasing** *adj* erfreulich; **pleasure** ['pleʒəʳ] *n* Vergnügen *nt*, Freude *f*; **it's a ~** gern geschehen

pledge [pledʒ] *n* Versprechen *nt* ▷ *vt* versprechen

plenty ['plentɪ] *n*: **~ of** eine Menge, viel(e); **to be ~** genug sein, reichen; **I've got ~** ich habe mehr als genug ▷ *adv* (*US fam*) ganz schön

pliable ['plaɪəbl] *adj* biegsam

pliers ['plaɪəz] *npl* (Kombi)zange *f*

plimsoll ['plɪmsəl] *n* (*Brit*) Turnschuh *m*

plonk [plɒŋk] *n* (*Brit fam: wine*) billiger Wein ▷ *vt*: **to ~ sth (down)** etw hinknallen

plot [plɒt] *n* (*of story*) Handlung *f*; (*conspiracy*) Komplott *nt*; (*of land*) Stück *nt* Land, Grundstück *nt* ▷ *vi* ein Komplott schmieden

plough, plow (*US*) [plaʊ] *n* Pflug *m* ▷ *vt, vi* (*Agr*) pflügen; **ploughman's lunch** (*Brit*) in einer Kneipe serviertes Gericht aus Käse, Brot, Mixed Pickles etc

pluck [plʌk] *vt* (*eyebrows, guitar*) zupfen; (*chicken*) rupfen; **pluck up** *vt*: **to ~ (one's) courage** Mut aufbringen

plug [plʌg] *n* (*for sink, bath*) Stöpsel *m*; (*Elec*) Stecker *m*; (*Auto*) (Zünd)kerze *f*; (*fam: publicity*) Schleichwerbung *f* ▷ *vt* (*fam: advertise*) Reklame machen für; **plug in** *vt* anschließen

plum [plʌm] *n* Pflaume *f* ▷ *adj* (*fam: job etc*) Super-

plumber ['plʌməʳ] *n* Klempner(in) *m(f)*; **plumbing** ['plʌmɪŋ] *n* (*fittings*) Leitungen *pl*; (*craft*) Installieren *nt*

plump [plʌmp] *adj* rundlich

plunge [plʌndʒ] *vt* (*knife*) stoßen; (*into water*) tauchen ▷ *vi* stürzen; (*into water*) tauchen

plural ['plʊərəl] *n* Plural *m*

plus [plʌs] *prep* plus; (*as well as*) und ▷ *adj* Plus-; **20 ~** mehr als 20 ▷ *n* (*fig*) Plus *nt*

plywood ['plaɪwʊd] *n* Sperrholz *nt*

pm *abbr* = **post meridiem**; **at 3 ~** um 3 Uhr nachmittags; **at 8 ~** um 8 Uhr abends

pneumonia [njuːˈməʊnɪə] *n* Lungenentzündung *f*

poached [pəʊtʃt] *adj* (*egg*) pochiert, verloren

PO Box *abbr* = **post office box** Postfach *nt*

pocket ['pɒkɪt] *n* Tasche *f* ▷ *vt* (*put in ~*) einstecken; **pocketbook** *n* (*US: wallet*) Brieftasche *f*; **pocket calculator** *n* Taschenrechner *m*; **pocket money** *n* Taschengeld *nt*

podcast ['pɒdkaːst] *n* Podcast *m*

poem ['pəʊəm] *n* Gedicht *nt*; **poet** ['pəʊɪt] *n* Dichter(in) *m(f)*; **poetic** [pəʊˈetɪk] *adj* poetisch; **poetry** ['pəʊɪtrɪ] *n* (*art*) Dichtung *f*; (*poems*) Gedichte *pl*

point [pɔɪnt] *n* Punkt *m*; (*spot*) Stelle *f*; (*sharp tip*) Spitze *f*; (*moment*) Zeitpunkt *m*; (*purpose*) Zweck *m*; (*idea*) Argument *nt*; (*decimal*) Dezimalstelle *f*; **~s** *pl* (*Rail*) Weiche *f*; **~ of view** Standpunkt *m*; **three ~ two** drei Komma zwei; **at some ~** irgendwann (mal); **to get**

to the ~ zur Sache kommen;
there's no ~ es hat keinen Sinn; **I
was on the ~ of leaving** ich wollte
gerade gehen ▷ vt (gun etc)
richten (at auf +akk); **to ~ one's
finger at** mit dem Finger zeigen
auf +akk ▷ vi (with finger etc)
zeigen (at, to auf +akk); **point out**
vt (indicate) aufzeigen; (mention)
hinweisen auf +akk; **pointed** adj
spitz; (question) gezielt; **pointer** n
(on dial) Zeiger m; (tip) Hinweis m;
pointless adj sinnlos
poison ['pɔɪzn] n Gift nt ▷ vt
vergiften; **poisonous** adj giftig
poke [pəʊk] vt (with stick, finger)
stoßen, stupsen; (put) stecken
Poland ['pəʊlənd] n Polen nt
polar ['pəʊlə*] adj Polar-, polar;
~ bear Eisbär m
pole [pəʊl] n Stange f; (Geo, Elec)
Pol m
Pole [pəʊl] n Pole m, Polin f
pole vault n Stabhochsprung m
police [pə'liːs] n Polizei f; **police
car** n Polizeiwagen m; **policeman**
(pl **-men**) n Polizist m; **police
station** n (Polizei)wache f;
policewoman (pl **-women**) n
Polizistin f
policy ['pɒlɪsɪ] n (plan) Politik f;
(principle) Grundsatz m; (insurance
~) (Versicherungs)police f
polio ['pəʊlɪəʊ] n Kinderlähmung f
polish ['pɒlɪʃ] n (for furniture)
Politur f; (for floor) Wachs nt; (for
shoes) Creme f; (shine) Glanz m;
(fig) Schliff m ▷ vt polieren;
(shoes) putzen; (fig) den letzten
Schliff geben +dat
Polish ['pəʊlɪʃ] adj polnisch ▷ n
Polnisch nt
polite [pə'laɪt] adj höflich;
politeness n Höflichkeit f
political, **politically** [pə'lɪtɪkəl, -ɪ]
adj, adv politisch; **~ly correct**
politisch korrekt; **politician**

[pɒlɪ'tɪʃən] n Politiker(in) m(f);
politics ['pɒlɪtɪks] nsing o pl
Politik f
poll [pəʊl] n (election) Wahl f;
(opinion ~) Umfrage f
pollen ['pɒlən] n Pollen m,
Blütenstaub m; **pollen count** n
Pollenflug m
polling station ['pəʊlɪŋsteɪʃən]
n Wahllokal nt
pollute [pə'luːt] vt verschmutzen; **pollution** [pə'luːʃən] n
Verschmutzung f
pompous ['pɒmpəs] adj aufge-
blasen; (language) geschwollen
pond [pɒnd] n Teich m
pony ['pəʊnɪ] n Pony nt;
ponytail n Pferdeschwanz m
poodle ['puːdl] n Pudel m
pool [puːl] n (swimming ~)
Schwimmbad nt; (private)
Swimmingpool m; (of spilt liquid,
blood) Lache f; (game) Poolbillard
nt ▷ vt (money etc)
zusammenlegen
poor [pɔː*] adj arm; (not good)
schlecht ▷ npl: **the ~** die Armen
pl; **poorly** adv (badly) schlecht
▷ adj (Brit) krank
pop [pɒp] n (music) Pop m; (noise)
Knall m ▷ vt (put) stecken;
(balloon) platzen lassen ▷ vi
(balloon) platzen; (cork) knallen; **to
~ in** (person) vorbeischauen; **pop
concert** n Popkonzert nt;
popcorn n Popcorn nt
Pope [pəʊp] n Papst m
pop group ['pɒpɡruːp] n
Popgruppe f; **pop music** n
Popmusik f
poppy ['pɒpɪ] n Mohn m
Popsicle® ['pɒpsɪkl] n (US) Eis
nt am Stiel
pop star ['pɒpstɑː*] n Popstar m
popular ['pɒpjʊlə*] adj (well-
-liked) beliebt (with bei);
(widespread) weit verbreitet

population [pɒpjʊˈleɪʃən] n
Bevölkerung f; (of town) Einwohner
pl

porcelain [ˈpɔːslɪn] n Porzellan
nt

porch [pɔːtʃ] n Vorbau m; (US:
verandah) Veranda f

porcupine [ˈpɔːkjʊpaɪn] n
Stachelschwein nt

pork [pɔːk] n Schweinefleisch nt;
pork chop n Schweinekotelett;
pork pie n Schweinefleischpastete
f

porn [pɔːn] n Porno m;
pornographic [pɔːnəˈgræfɪk] adj
pornografisch; **pornography**
[pɔːˈnɒgrəfɪ] n Pornografie f

porridge [ˈpɒrɪdʒ] n Haferbrei m

port [pɔːt] n (harbour) Hafen m;
(town) Hafenstadt f; (Naut: left side)
Backbord nt; (wine) Portwein m;
(Inform) Anschluss m

portable [ˈpɔːtəbl] adj tragbar;
(radio) Koffer-

portal [ˈpɔːtl] n (Inform) Portal nt

porter [ˈpɔːtə°] n Pförtner(in)
m(f); (for luggage) Gepäckträger m

porthole [ˈpɔːthəʊl] n Bullauge
nt

portion [ˈpɔːʃən] n Teil m; (of
food) Portion f

portrait [ˈpɔːtrɪt] n Porträt nt

portray [pɔːˈtreɪ] vt darstellen

Portugal [ˈpɔːtʃʊgl] n Portugal
nt; **Portuguese** [pɔːtʃʊˈgiːz] adj
portugiesisch ▷ n Portugiese m,
Portugiesin f; (language)
Portugiesisch nt

pose [pəʊz] n Haltung f ▷ vi
posieren ▷ vt (threat, problem)
darstellen

posh [pɒʃ] adj (fam) piekfein

position [pəˈzɪʃən] n Stellung f;
(place) Position f, Lage f; (job) Stelle
f; (opinion) Standpunkt m; **to be in
a ~ to do sth** in der Lage sein, etw
zu tun; **in third ~** auf dem dritten

Platz ▷ vt aufstellen; (Inform:
cursor) positionieren

positive [ˈpɒzɪtɪv] adj positiv;
(convinced) sicher

possess [pəˈzes] vt besitzen;
possession [pəˈzeʃən] n **~(s** pl)
Besitz m; **possessive** adj (person)
besitzergreifend

possibility [pɒsəˈbɪlɪtɪ] n
Möglichkeit f; **possible** [ˈpɒsəbl]
adj möglich; **if ~** wenn möglich; **as
big/soon as ~** so groß/bald wie
möglich; **possibly** adv (perhaps)
vielleicht; **I've done all I ~ can** ich
habe mein Möglichstes getan

post [pəʊst] n (mail) Post f; (pole)
Pfosten m; (job) Stelle f ▷ vt
(letters) aufgeben; **to keep sb ~ed**
jdn auf dem Laufenden halten;
postage [ˈpəʊstɪdʒ] n Porto nt;
~ and packing Porto und
Verpackung; **postal** adj Post-;
(Brit) **~ order** Postanweisung f;
postbox n Briefkasten m;
postcard n Postkarte f; **postcode**
n (Brit) Postleitzahl f

poster [ˈpəʊstə°] n Plakat nt,
Poster nt

postgraduate [pəʊstˈgrædjuɪt]
n jmd, der seine Studien nach dem
ersten akademischen Grad weiterführt

postman [ˈpəʊstmən] (pl -**men**)
n Briefträger m; **postmark** n
Poststempel m

postmortem [pəʊstˈmɔːtəm] n
Autopsie f

post office [ˈpəʊstɒfɪs] n Post® f

postpone [pəˈspəʊn] vt verschieben (till auf +akk)

posture [ˈpɒstʃə°] n Haltung f

pot [pɒt] n Topf m; (tea~, coffee ~)
Kanne f; (fam: marijuana) Pot nt
▷ vt (plant) eintopfen

potato [pəˈteɪtəʊ] (pl -**es**) n
Kartoffel f; **potato chips** (US) npl
Kartoffelchips pl; **potato peeler** n
Kartoffelschäler m

P

potent ['pəʊtənt] adj stark
potential [pəʊ'tenʃəl] adj
potenziell ▷ n Potenzial nt;
potentially adv potenziell
pothole ['pɒthəʊl] n Höhle f; (in road) Schlagloch nt
potter about ['pɒtərəbaʊt] vi herumhantieren
pottery ['pɒtərɪ] n (objects) Töpferwaren pl
potty ['pɒtɪ] adj (Brit fam) verrückt ▷ n Töpfchen nt
poultry ['pəʊltrɪ] n Geflügel nt
pounce [paʊns] vi: **to ~ on** sich stürzen auf +akk
pound [paʊnd] n (money) Pfund nt; (weight) Pfund nt (0,454 kg); **a ~ of cherries** ein Pfund Kirschen; **ten-~ note** Zehnpfundschein m
pour [pɔ:ʳ] vt (liquid) gießen; (rice, sugar etc) schütten; **to ~ sb sth** (drink) jdm etw eingießen; **pouring** adj (rain) strömend
poverty ['pɒvətɪ] n Armut f
powder ['paʊdəʳ] n Pulver nt; (cosmetic) Puder m; **powdered milk** n Milchpulver nt; **powder room** n Damentoilette f
power ['paʊəʳ] n Macht f; (ability) Fähigkeit f; (strength) Stärke f; (Elec) Strom m; **to be in ~** an der Macht sein ▷ vt betreiben, antreiben; **power-assisted steering** n Servolenkung f; **power cut** n Stromausfall m; **powerful** adj (politician etc) mächtig; (engine, government) stark; (argument) durchschlagend; **powerless** adj machtlos; **power station** n Kraftwerk nt
p&p abbr = **postage and packing**
PR abbr = **public relations** ▷ abbr = **proportional representation**
practical, practically ['præktɪkəl,

-ɪ] adj, adv praktisch; **practice** ['præktɪs] n (training) Übung f; (custom) Gewohnheit f; (doctor's, lawyer's) Praxis f; **in ~** (in reality) in der Praxis; **out of ~** außer Übung; **to put sth into ~** etw in die Praxis umsetzen ▷ vt, vi (US) see **practise**; **practise** ['præktɪs] vt (instrument, movement) üben; (profession) ausüben ▷ vi üben; (doctor, lawyer) praktizieren
Prague [prɑ:g] n Prag nt
praise [preɪz] n Lob nt ▷ vt loben
pram [præm] n (Brit) Kinderwagen m
prawn [prɔ:n] n Garnele f, Krabbe f; **prawn crackers** npl Krabbenchips pl
pray [preɪ] vi beten; **to ~ for sth** (fig) stark auf etw akk hoffen; **prayer** ['preəʳ] n Gebet nt
pre- [pri:] pref vor-, prä-
preach [pri:tʃ] vi predigen
prearrange [pri:ə'reɪndʒ] vt im Voraus vereinbaren
precaution [prɪ'kɔ:ʃən] n Vorsichtsmaßnahme f
precede [prɪ'si:d] vt vorausgehen +dat; **preceding** adj vorhergehend
precinct ['pri:sɪŋkt] n (Brit: pedestrian ~) Fußgängerzone f; (Brit: shopping ~) Einkaufsviertel nt; (US: district) Bezirk m
precious ['preʃəs] adj kostbar; **~ stone** Edelstein m
précis ['preɪsi:] n Zusammenfassung f
precise, precisely [prɪ'saɪs, -lɪ] adj, adv genau
precondition [pri:kən'dɪʃən] n Vorbedingung f
predecessor ['pri:dɪsesəʳ] n Vorgänger(in) m(f)
predicament [prɪ'dɪkəmənt] n missliche Lage

predict [prɪ'dɪkt] vt voraussagen; **predictable** adj vorhersehbar; (person) berechenbar

predominant [prɪ'dɒmɪnənt] adj vorherrschend; **predominantly** adv überwiegend

preface ['prefɪs] n Vorwort nt

prefer [prɪ'fɜː'] vt vorziehen (to dat), lieber mögen (to als); **to ~ to do sth** etw lieber tun; **preferably** ['prefrəblɪ] adv vorzugsweise, am liebsten; **preference** ['prefərəns] n (liking) Vorliebe f; **preferential** [prefə'renʃəl] adj: **to get ~ treatment** bevorzugt behandelt werden

prefix ['priːfɪks] n (US Tel) Vorwahl f

pregnancy ['pregnənsɪ] n Schwangerschaft f; **pregnant** ['pregnənt] adj schwanger; **two months ~** im zweiten Monat schwanger

prejudice ['predʒʊdɪs] n Vorurteil nt; **prejudiced** adj (person) voreingenommen

preliminary [prɪ'lɪmɪnərɪ] adj (measures) vorbereitend; (results) vorläufig; (remarks) einleitend

premature ['premətʃʊə'] adj vorzeitig; (hasty) voreilig

premiere ['premɪɛə'] n Premiere f

premises ['premɪsɪz] npl (offices) Räumlichkeiten pl; (of factory, school) Gelände nt

premium-rate ['priːmɪəmreɪt] adj (Tel) zum Höchsttarif

preoccupied [priː'ɒkjʊpaɪd] adj: **to be ~ with sth** mit etw sehr beschäftigt sein

prepaid [priː'peɪd] adj vorausbezahlt; (envelope) frankiert

preparation [prepə'reɪʃən] n Vorbereitung f; **prepare** [prɪ'pɛə'] vt vorbereiten (for auf +akk); (food)

zubereiten; **to be ~d to do sth** bereit sein, etw zu tun ▷ vi sich vorbereiten (for auf +akk)

prerequisite [priː'rekwɪzɪt] n Voraussetzung f

prescribe [prɪ'skraɪb] vt vorschreiben; (Med) verschreiben; **prescription** [prɪ'skrɪpʃən] n Rezept nt

presence ['prezns] n Gegenwart f; **present** ['preznt] adj (in attendance) anwesend (at bei); (current) gegenwärtig; **~ tense** Gegenwart f, Präsens nt ▷ n Gegenwart f; (gift) Geschenk nt; **at ~** zurzeit ▷ [prɪ'zent] vt (TV, Radio) präsentieren; (problem) darstellen; (report etc) vorlegen; **to ~ sb with sth** jdm etw überreichen; **present-day** adj heutig; **presently** adv bald; (at present) zurzeit

preservative [prɪ'zɜːvətɪv] n Konservierungsmittel nt; **preserve** [prɪ'zɜːv] vt erhalten; (food) einmachen, konservieren

president ['prezɪdənt] n Präsident(in) m(f); **presidential** [prezɪ'denʃəl] adj Präsidenten-; (election) Präsidentschafts-

press [pres] n (newspapers, machine) Presse f ▷ vt (push) drücken; **to ~ a button** auf einen Knopf drücken ▷ vi (push) drücken; **pressing** adj dringend; **press-stud** n Druckknopf m; **press-up** n (Brit) Liegestütz m; **pressure** ['preʃə'] n Druck m; **to be under ~** unter Druck stehen; **to put ~ on sb** jdn unter Druck setzen; **pressure cooker** n Schnellkochtopf m; **pressurize** ['preʃəraɪz] vt (person) unter Druck setzen

presumably [prɪ'zjuːməblɪ] adv vermutlich; **presume** [prɪ'zjuːm] vt, vi annehmen

presumptuous [prɪ'zʌmptʃʊəs]
adj anmaßend
presuppose [pri:sə'pəʊz] *vt*
voraussetzen
pretend [prɪ'tend] *vt*: **to ~ that**
so tun als ob; **to ~ to do sth**
vorgeben, etw zu tun ▷ *vi*: **she's
~ing** sie tut nur so
pretentious [prɪ'tenʃəs] *adj*
anmaßend; (*person*)
wichtigtuerisch
pretty ['prɪtɪ] *adj* hübsch ▷ *adv*
ziemlich
prevent [prɪ'vent] *vt* verhindern;
to ~ sb from doing sth jdn daran
hindern, etw zu tun
preview ['pri:vju:] *n* (*Cine*) Vor-
aufführung *f*; (*trailer*) Vorschau *f*
previous, **previously** ['pri:vɪəs,
-lɪ] *adj*, *adv* früher
prey [preɪ] *n* Beute *f*
price [praɪs] *n* Preis *m* ▷ *vt*: **it's ~d
at £10** es ist mit 10 Pfund ausgezeichnet; **priceless** *adj* unbezahl-
bar; **price list** *n* Preisliste *f*; **price
tag** *n* Preisschild *nt*
prick [prɪk] *n* Stich *m*; (*vulg: penis*)
Schwanz *m*; (*vulg: person*) Arsch *m*
▷ *vt* stechen in +*akk*; **to ~ one's
finger** sich *dat* in den Finger
stechen; **prickly** ['prɪklɪ] *adj*
stachelig
pride [praɪd] *n* Stolz *m*; (*arro-
gance*) Hochmut *m* ▷ *vt*: **to ~ oneself on sth** auf etw *akk* stolz sein
priest [pri:st] *n* Priester *m*
primarily ['praɪmərɪlɪ] *adv*
vorwiegend; **primary** ['praɪmərɪ]
adj Haupt-; **~ education**
Grundschulausbildung *f*; **~ school**
Grundschule *f*
prime [praɪm] *adj* Haupt-;
(*excellent*) erstklassig ▷ *n*: **in one's
~** in den besten Jahren; **prime
minister** *n* Premierminister(in)
m(f); **prime time** *n* (*TV*)
Hauptsendezeit *f*

primitive ['prɪmɪtɪv] *adj*
primitiv
primrose ['prɪmrəʊz] *n*
Schlüsselblume *f*
prince [prɪns] *n* Prinz *m*; (*ruler*)
Fürst *m*; **princess** [prɪn'ses] *n*
Prinzessin *f*; Fürstin *f*
principal ['prɪnsɪpəl] *adj*
Haupt-, wichtigste(r, s) ▷ *n*
(*school*) Rektor(in) *m(f)*
principle ['prɪnsəpl] *n* Prinzip *nt*;
in ~ im Prinzip; **on ~** aus Prinzip
print [prɪnt] *n* (*picture*) Druck *m*;
(*Foto*) Abzug *m*; (*made by feet,
fingers*) Abdruck *m*; **out of
~** vergriffen ▷ *vt* drucken; (*photo*)
abziehen; (*write in block letters*) in
Druckschrift schreiben; **print out**
vt (*Inform*) ausdrucken; **printed
matter** *n* Drucksache *f*; **printer** *n*
Drucker *m*; **printout** *n* (*Inform*)
Ausdruck *m*
prior ['praɪə*] *adj* früher; **a
~ engagement** eine vorher
getroffene Verabredung; **~ to sth**
vor etw *dat*; **~ to going abroad,
she had …** bevor sie ins Ausland
ging, hatte sie …
priority [praɪ'ɒrɪtɪ] *n* (*thing
having precedence*) Priorität *f*
prison ['prɪzn] *n* Gefängnis *nt*;
prisoner *n* Gefangene(r) *mf*; **~ of
war** Kriegsgefangene(r) *mf*
privacy ['prɪvəsɪ] *n* Privatleben
nt; **private** ['praɪvɪt] *adj* privat;
(*confidential*) vertraulich ▷ *n*
einfacher Soldat; **in ~** privat;
privately *adv* privat;
(*confidentially*) vertraulich;
privatize ['praɪvətaɪz] *vt*
privatisieren
privilege ['prɪvɪlɪdʒ] *n* Privileg
nt; **privileged** *adj* privilegiert
prize [praɪz] *n* Preis *m*; **prize
money** *n* Preisgeld *nt*;
prizewinner *n* Gewinner(in) *m(f)*;
prizewinning *adj* preisgekrönt

pro [prəʊ] (pl **-s**) n (professional) Profi m; **the ~s and cons** pl das Für und Wider

pro- [prəʊ] pref pro-

probability [prɒbə'bɪlətɪ] n Wahrscheinlichkeit f; **probable**, **probably** ['prɒbəbl, -blɪ] adj, adv wahrscheinlich

probation [prə'beɪʃən] n Probezeit f; (Jur) Bewährung f

probe [prəʊb] n (investigation) Untersuchung f ▷ vt untersuchen

problem ['prɒbləm] n Problem nt; **no ~** kein Problem!

procedure [prə'siːdʒə°] n Verfahren nt

proceed [prə'siːd] vi (continue) fortfahren; (set about sth) vorgehen ▷ vt: **to ~ to do sth** anfangen, etw zu tun; **proceedings** npl (Jur) Verfahren nt; **proceeds** ['prəʊsiːds] npl Erlös m

process ['prəʊses] n Prozess m, Vorgang m; (method) Verfahren nt ▷ vt (application etc) bearbeiten; (food, data) verarbeiten; (film) entwickeln

procession [prə'seʃən] n Umzug m

processor ['prəʊsesə°] n (Inform) Prozessor m; (Gastr) Küchenmaschine f

produce n ['prɒdjuːs] n (Agr) Produkte pl, Erzeugnisse pl ▷ [prə'djuːs] vt (manufacture) herstellen, produzieren; (on farm) erzeugen; (film, play, record) produzieren; (cause) hervorrufen; (evidence, results) liefern; **producer** n (manufacturer) Hersteller(in) m(f); (of film, play, record) Produzent(in) m(f); **product** ['prɒdʌkt] n Produkt nt, Erzeugnis nt; **production** [prə'dʌkʃən] n Produktion f; (Theat) Inszenierung f; **productive** [prə'dʌktɪv] adj produktiv; (land) ertragreich

prof [prɒf] n (fam) Prof m

profession [prə'feʃən] n Beruf m; **professional** [prə'feʃənl] n Profi m ▷ adj beruflich; (expert) fachlich; (sportsman, actor etc) Berufs-

professor [prə'fesə°] n Professor(in) m(f); (US: lecturer) Dozent(in) m(f)

proficient [prə'fɪʃənt] adj kompetent (in in +dat)

profile ['prəʊfaɪl] n Profil nt; **to keep a low ~** sich rarmachen

profit ['prɒfɪt] n Gewinn m ▷ vi profitieren (by, from von); **profitable** adj rentabel

profound [prə'faʊnd] adj tief; (idea, thinker) tiefgründig; (knowledge) profund

program ['prəʊgræm] n (Inform) Programm nt; (US) see **programme** ▷ vt (Inform) programmieren; (US) see **programme**

programme ['prəʊgræm] n Programm nt; (TV, Radio) Sendung f ▷ vt programmieren; **programmer** n Programmierer(in) m(f); **programming** n (Inform) Programmieren nt; **~ language** Programmiersprache f

progress ['prəʊgres] n Fortschritt m; **to make ~** Fortschritte machen ▷ [prə'gres] vi (work, illness etc) fortschreiten; (improve) Fortschritte machen; **progressive** [prə'gresɪv] adj (person, policy) fortschrittlich; **progressively** [prə'gresɪvlɪ] adv zunehmend

prohibit [prə'hɪbɪt] vt verbieten

project ['prɒdʒekt] n Projekt nt

projector [prə'dʒektə°] n Projektor m

prolong [prə'lɒŋ] vt verlängern

prom [prɒm] n (at seaside) Promenade f; (Brit: concert) Konzert nt (bei dem ein Großteil des Publikums im Parkett Stehplätze hat); (US:

P

dance) Ball für die Schüler und
Studenten von Highschools oder
Colleges

prominent ['prɒmɪnənt] *adj*
(*politician, actor etc*) prominent;
(*easily seen*) auffallend

promiscuous [prə'mɪskjʊəs]
adj promisk

promise ['prɒmɪs] *n* Versprechen *nt* ▷ *vt* versprechen; **to
~ sb sth** jdm etw versprechen; **to
~ to do sth** versprechen, etw zu
tun ▷ *vi* versprechen; **promising**
adj vielversprechend

promote [prə'məʊt] *vt* (*in rank*)
befördern; (*help on*) fördern;
(*Comm*) werben für; **promotion**
[prə'məʊʃən] *n* (*in rank*)
Beförderung *f*; (*Comm*) Werbung *f*
(*of* für)

prompt [prɒmpt] *adj* prompt;
(*punctual*) pünktlich ▷ *adv*: **at two
o'clock ~** Punkt zwei Uhr ▷ *vt*
(*Theat: actor*) soufflieren +*dat*

prone [prəʊn] *adj*: **to be ~ to sth**
zu etw neigen

pronounce [prə'naʊns] *vt*
(*word*) aussprechen; **pronounced**
adj ausgeprägt; **pronunciation**
[prənʌnsɪ'eɪʃən] *n* Aussprache *f*

proof [pru:f] *n* Beweis *m*; (*of
alcohol*) Alkoholgehalt *m*

prop [prɒp] *n* Stütze *f*; (*Theat*)
Requisit *nt* ▷ *vt*: **to ~ sth
against sth** etw gegen etw
lehnen; **prop up** *vt* stützen; (*fig*)
unterstützen

proper ['prɒpə*] *adj* richtig;
(*morally correct*) anständig

property ['prɒpətɪ] *n* (*possession*)
Eigentum *nt*; (*house*) Haus *nt*; (*land*)
Grundbesitz *m*; (*characteristic*)
Eigenschaft *f*

proportion [prə'pɔ:ʃən] *n*
Verhältnis *nt*; (*share*) Teil *m*; **~s** *pl*
(*size*) Proportionen *pl*; **in ~ to** im
Verhältnis zu; **proportional** *adj*

proportional; **~ representation**
Verhältniswahlrecht *nt*

proposal [prə'pəʊzl] *n* Vorschlag
m; **~ (of marriage)** (Heirats)antrag
m; **propose** [prə'pəʊz] *vt*
vorschlagen ▷ *vi* (*offer marriage*)
einen Heiratsantrag machen (*to sb*
jdm)

proprietor [prə'praɪətə*] *n*
Besitzer(in) *m(f)*; (*of pub, hotel*)
Inhaber(in) *m(f)*

prose [prəʊz] *n* Prosa *f*

prosecute ['prɒsɪkju:t] *vt* verfolgen (*for* wegen)

prospect ['prɒspekt] *n* Aussicht
f

prosperity [prɒ'sperɪtɪ] *n*
Wohlstand *m*; **prosperous** *adj*
wohlhabend; (*business*) gut
gehend

prostitute ['prɒstɪtju:t] *n* Pros-
tituierte(r) *mf*

protect [prə'tekt] *vt* schützen
(*from, against* vor +*dat*, gegen);
protection [prə'tekʃən] *n* Schutz
m (*from, against* vor +*dat*, gegen);
protective *adj* beschützend;
(*clothing etc*) Schutz-

protein ['prəʊti:n] *n* Protein *nt*

protest ['prəʊtest] *n* Protest *m*;
(*demonstration*)
Protestkundgebung *f* ▷ [prə'test]
vi protestieren (*against* gegen);
(*demonstrate*) demonstrieren

Protestant ['prɒtəstənt] *adj*
protestantisch ▷ *n* Protestant(in)
m(f)

proud, proudly [praʊd, -lɪ] *adj,
adv* stolz (*of* auf +*akk*)

prove [pru:v] *vt* beweisen; (*turn
out to be*) sich erweisen als

proverb ['prɒvɜ:b] *n* Sprichwort
nt

provide [prə'vaɪd] *vt* zur
Verfügung stellen; (*drinks, music
etc*) sorgen für; (*person*) versorgen
(*with* mit); **provide for** *vt* (*family*

etc) sorgen für; **provided** *conj*:
~ (**that**) vorausgesetzt, dass;
provider *n* (*Inform*) Provider *m*
provision [prə'vɪʒən] *n* (*condition*) Bestimmung *f*; **~s** *pl* (*food*) Proviant *m*
provisional, **provisionally**
[prə'vɪʒənl, -ɪ] *adj*, *adv*
provisorisch
provoke [prə'vəʊk] *vt*
provozieren; (*cause*) hervorrufen
proximity [prɒk'sɪmɪtɪ] *n* Nähe *f*
prudent ['pruːdənt] *adj* klug;
(*person*) umsichtig
prudish ['pruːdɪʃ] *adj* prüde
prune [pruːn] *n* Backpflaume *f*
▷ *vt* (*tree etc*) zurechtstutzen
PS *abbr* = **postscript** PS *nt*
psalm [sɑːm] *n* Psalm *m*
pseudo ['sjuːdəʊ] *adj* pseudo-,
Pseudo-; **pseudonym** ['sjuːdə-nɪm] *n* Pseudonym *nt*
PST *abbr* = **Pacific Standard Time**
psychiatric [saɪkɪ'ætrɪk] *adj*
psychiatrisch; (*illness*) psychisch;
psychiatrist [saɪ'kaɪətrɪst] *n*
Psychiater(in) *m(f)*; **psychiatry**
[saɪ'kaɪətrɪ] *n* Psychiatrie *f*;
psychic ['saɪkɪk] *adj* übersinnlich; **I'm not ~** ich kann keine Gedanken lesen; **psychoanalysis**
[saɪkəʊə'næləsɪs] *n* Psychoanalyse *f*; **psychoanalyst**
[saɪkəʊ'ænəlɪst] *n* Psychoanalytiker(in) *m(f)*; **psychological** [saɪkə'lɒdʒɪkəl] *adj* psychologisch; **psychology** [saɪ'kɒlədʒɪ] *n* Psychologie *f*; **psychopath** ['saɪkəʊpæθ] *n* Psychopath(in) *m(f)*
pt *abbr* = **pint**
pto *abbr* = **please turn over** b.w.
pub [pʌb] *n* (*Brit*) Kneipe *f*

● PUB
●
● Ein **pub** ist ein Gasthaus mit
● einer Lizenz zum Ausschank von
● alkoholischen Getränken. Ein
● „Pub" besteht meist aus
● verschiedenen gemütlichen
● (**lounge, snug**) oder
● einfacheren (**public bar**)
● Räumen, in denen oft auch
● Spiele wie Darts, Domino und
● Poolbillard zur Verfügung
● stehen. In „Pubs" werden vor
● allem mittags auch Mahlzeiten
● angeboten (**pub lunch**). Die
● Sperrstunde wurde 2005
● aufgehoben. Dennoch sind
● „Pubs" oft nur von 11 bis 23 Uhr
● geöffnet. Nachmittags bleiben
● sie häufig geschlossen.

puberty ['pjuːbətɪ] *n* Pubertät *f*
public ['pʌblɪk] *n*: **the** (**general**) ~ die (breite) Öffentlichkeit; **in** ~ in der Öffentlichkeit ▷ *adj* öffentlich; (*relating to the State*) Staats-; **~ convenience** (*Brit*) öffentliche Toilette; **~ holiday** gesetzlicher Feiertag; **~ opinion** die öffentliche Meinung; **~ relations** *pl* Öffentlichkeitsarbeit *f*, Public Relations *pl*; **~ school** (*Brit*) Privatschule *f*; **publication** [pʌblɪ'keɪʃən] *n* Veröffentlichung *f*; **publicity** [pʌb'lɪsɪtɪ] *n* Publicity *f*; (*advertisements*) Werbung *f*; **publish** ['pʌblɪʃ] *vt* veröffentlichen; **publisher** *n* Verleger(in) *m(f)*; (*company*) Verlag *m*; **publishing** *n* Verlagswesen *nt*
pub lunch ['pʌb'lʌntʃ] *n* (*oft einfacheres*) Mittagessen in einer Kneipe
pudding ['pʊdɪŋ] *n* (*course*) Nachtisch *m*
puddle ['pʌdl] *n* Pfütze *f*
puff [pʌf] *vi* (*pant*) schnaufen
puffin ['pʌfɪn] *n* Papageientaucher *m*

P

puff paste (US), **puff pastry** ['pʌf'peɪstrɪ] n Blätterteig m
pull [pʊl] n Ziehen nt; **to give sth a ~** an etw dat ziehen ▷ vt (cart, tooth) ziehen; (rope, handle) ziehen an +dat; (fam: date) abschleppen; **to ~ a muscle** sich dat einen Muskel zerren; **to ~ sb's leg** jdn auf den Arm nehmen ▷ vi ziehen; **pull apart** vt (separate) auseinanderziehen; **pull down** vt (blind) herunterziehen; (house) abreißen; **pull in** vi hineinfahren; (stop) anhalten; **pull off** vt (deal etc) zuwege bringen; (clothes) ausziehen; **pull on** vt (clothes) anziehen; **pull out** vi (car from lane) ausscheren; (train) abfahren; (withdraw) aussteigen (of aus) ▷ vt herausziehen; (tooth) ziehen; (troops) abziehen; **pull round, pull through** vi durchkommen; **pull up** vt (raise) hochziehen; (chair) heranziehen ▷ vi anhalten
pullover ['pʊləʊvəʳ] n Pullover m
pulp [pʌlp] n Brei m; (of fruit) Fruchtfleisch nt
pulpit ['pʊlpɪt] n Kanzel f
pulse [pʌls] n Puls m
pump [pʌmp] n Pumpe f; (in petrol station) Zapfsäule f; **pump up** vt (tyre etc) aufpumpen
pumpkin ['pʌmpkɪn] n Kürbis m
pun [pʌn] n Wortspiel nt
punch [pʌntʃ] n (blow) (Faust)schlag m; (tool) Locher m; (hot drink) Punsch m; (cold drink) Bowle f ▷ vt (strike) schlagen; (ticket, paper) lochen
punctual, punctually ['pʌŋktjʊəl, -ɪ] adj, adv pünktlich
punctuation [pʌŋktjʊ'eɪʃən] n Interpunktion f; **punctuation mark** n Satzzeichen nt
puncture ['pʌŋktʃəʳ] n (flat tyre) Reifenpanne f

punish ['pʌnɪʃ] vt bestrafen; **punishment** n Strafe f; (action) Bestrafung f
pupil ['pjuːpl] n (school) Schüler(in) m(f)
puppet ['pʌpɪt] n Marionette f
puppy ['pʌpɪ] n junger Hund
purchase ['pɜːtʃɪs] n Kauf m ▷ vt kaufen
pure [pjʊəʳ] adj rein; (clean) sauber; (utter) pur; **purely** ['pjuːəlɪ] adv rein; **purify** ['pjʊərɪfaɪ] vt reinigen; **purity** ['pjʊərɪtɪ] n Reinheit f
purple ['pɜːpl] adj violett
purpose ['pɜːpəs] n Zweck m; (of person) Absicht f; **on ~** absichtlich
purr [pɜːʳ] vi (cat) schnurren
purse [pɜːs] n Geldbeutel m; (US: handbag) Handtasche f
pursue [pə'sjuː] vt (person, car) verfolgen; (hobby, studies) nachgehen +dat; **pursuit** [pə'sjuːt] n (chase) Verfolgung f; (occupation) Beschäftigung f; (hobby) Hobby nt
pus [pʌs] n Eiter m
push [pʊʃ] n Stoß m ▷ vt (person) stoßen; (car, chair etc) schieben; (button) drücken; (drugs) dealen ▷ vi (in crowd) drängeln; **push in** vi (in queue) sich vordrängeln; **push off** vi (fam: leave) abhauen; **push on** vi (with job) weitermachen; **push up** vt (prices) hochtreiben; **pushchair** n (Brit) Sport(kinder)wagen m; **pusher** n (of drugs) Dealer(in) m(f); **push-up** n (US) Liegestütz m; **pushy** adj (fam) aufdringlich, penetrant
put [pʊt] (**put, put**) vt tun; (upright) stellen; (flat) legen; (express) ausdrücken; (write) schreiben; **he ~ his hand in his pocket** er steckte die Hand in die Tasche; **he ~ his hand on her shoulder** er legte ihr die Hand auf

die Schulter; **to ~ money into one's account** Geld auf sein Konto einzahlen; **put aside** vt (money) zurücklegen; **put away** vt (tidy away) wegräumen; **put back** vt zurücklegen; (clock) zurückstellen; **put down** vt (in writing) aufschreiben; (Brit: animal) einschläfern; (rebellion) niederschlagen; **to put the phone down** (den Hörer) auflegen; **to put one's name down for sth** sich für etw eintragen; **put forward** vt (idea) vorbringen; (name) vorschlagen; (clock) vorstellen; **put in** vt (install) einbauen; (submit) einreichen; **put off** vt (switch off) ausschalten; (postpone) verschieben; **to put sb off doing sth** jdn davon abbringen, etw zu tun; **put on** vt (switch on) anmachen; (clothes) anziehen; (hat, glasses) aufsetzen; (make-up, CD) auflegen; (play) aufführen; **to put the kettle on** Wasser aufsetzen; **to put weight on** zunehmen; **put out** vt (hand, foot) ausstrecken; (light, cigarette) ausmachen; **put up** vt (hand) hochheben; (picture) aufhängen; (tent) aufstellen; (building) errichten; (price) erhöhen; (person) unterbringen; **to ~ with** sich abfinden mit; **I won't ~ with it** das lasse ich mir nicht gefallen

putt [pʌt] vt, vi (Sport) putten
puzzle ['pʌzl] n Rätsel nt; (toy) Geduldsspiel nt; **(jigsaw) ~** Puzzle nt ▷ vt vor ein Rätsel stellen; **it ~s me** es ist mir ein Rätsel; **puzzling** adj rätselhaft
pyjamas [pɪ'dʒɑːməz] npl Schlafanzug m
pylon ['paɪlən] n Mast m
pyramid ['pɪrəmɪd] n Pyramide f

q

quack [kwæk] vi quaken
quaint [kweɪnt] adj (idea, tradition) kurios; (picturesque) malerisch
qualification [kwɒlɪfɪ'keɪʃən] n (for job) Qualifikation f; (from school, university) Abschluss m; **qualified** ['kwɒlɪfaɪd] adj (for job) qualifiziert; **qualify** vt (limit) einschränken; **to be qualified to do sth** berechtigt sein, etw zu tun ▷ vi (finish training) seine Ausbildung abschließen; (contest etc) sich qualifizieren
quality ['kwɒlɪtɪ] n Qualität f; (characteristic) Eigenschaft f
quantity ['kwɒntɪtɪ] n Menge f, Quantität f
quarantine ['kwɒrəntiːn] n Quarantäne f
quarrel ['kwɒrəl] n Streit m ▷ vi sich streiten
quarter ['kwɔːtə*] n Viertel nt;

(of year) Vierteljahr nt; (US: coin) Vierteldollar m; **a ~ of an hour** eine Viertelstunde; **~ to/past** (Brit) (o **~ of/after** (US)) **three** Viertel vor/nach drei ▷ vt vierteln; **quarter final** n Viertelfinale nt; **quarters** npl (Mil) Quartier nt

quartet [kwɔː'tet] n Quartett nt

quay [kiː] n Kai m

queasy ['kwiːzɪ] adj: **I feel ~** mir ist übel

queen [kwiːn] n Königin f; (in cards, chess) Dame f

queer [kwɪə°] adj (strange) seltsam, sonderbar; (pej: homosexual) schwul ▷ n (pej) Schwule(r) m

quench [kwentʃ] vt (thirst) löschen

query ['kwɪərɪ] n Frage f ▷ vt infrage stellen; (bill) reklamieren

question ['kwestʃən] n Frage f; **that's out of the ~** das kommt nicht infrage ▷ vt (person) befragen; (suspect) verhören; (express doubt about) bezweifeln; **questionable** adj zweifelhaft; (improper) fragwürdig; **question mark** n Fragezeichen nt; **questionnaire** [kwestʃə'nɛə°] n Fragebogen m

queue [kjuː] n (Brit) Schlange f; **to jump the ~** sich vordrängeln ▷ vi: **to ~ (up)** Schlange stehen

quibble ['kwɪbl] vi kleinlich sein; (argue) streiten

quiche [kiːʃ] n Quiche

quick [kwɪk] adj schnell; (short) kurz; **be ~** mach schnell!; **quickly** adv schnell

quid [kwɪd] (pl **quid**) n (Brit fam) Pfund nt; **20 ~** 20 Pfund

quiet ['kwaɪət] adj (not noisy) leise; (peaceful, calm) still, ruhig; **be ~** sei still!; **to keep ~ about sth** über etw akk nichts sagen ▷ n

Stille f, Ruhe f; **quiet down** (US), **quieten down** ['kwaɪətən'daʊn] vi sich beruhigen ▷ vt beruhigen; **quietly** adv leise; (calmly) ruhig

quilt [kwɪlt] n (Stepp)decke f

quit [kwɪt] (**quit** o **quitted, quit** o **quitted**) vt (leave) verlassen; (job) aufgeben; **to ~ doing sth** aufhören, etw zu tun ▷ vi aufhören; (resign) kündigen

quite [kwaɪt] adv (fairly) ziemlich; (completely) ganz, völlig; **I don't ~ understand** ich verstehe das nicht ganz; **~ a few** ziemlich viele; **~ so** richtig!

quits [kwɪts] adj: **to be ~ with sb** mit jdm quitt sein

quiver ['kwɪvə°] vi zittern

quiz [kwɪz] n (competition) Quiz nt

quota ['kwəʊtə] n Anteil m; (Comm, Pol) Quote f

quotation [kwəʊ'teɪʃən] n Zitat nt; (price) Kostenvoranschlag m; **quotation marks** npl Anführungszeichen pl; **quote** [kwəʊt] vt (text, author) zitieren; (price) nennen ▷ n Zitat nt; (price) Kostenvoranschlag m; **in ~s** in Anführungszeichen

r

rabbi ['ræbaɪ] n Rabbiner m
rabbit ['ræbɪt] n Kaninchen nt
rabies ['reɪbiːz] nsing Tollwut f
raccoon [rə'kuːn] n Waschbär m
race [reɪs] n (competition) Rennen nt; (people) Rasse f ▷ vt um die Wette laufen/fahren ▷ vi (rush) rennen; **racecourse** n Rennbahn f; **racehorse** n Rennpferd nt; **racetrack** n Rennbahn f
racial ['reɪʃəl] adj Rassen-; **~ discrimination** Rassendiskriminierung f
racing ['reɪsɪŋ] n: (horse) **~** Pferderennen nt; (motor) **~** Autorennen nt; **racing car** n Rennwagen m
racism ['reɪsɪzəm] n Rassismus m; **racist** n Rassist(in) m(f) ▷ adj rassistisch
rack [ræk] n Ständer m, Gestell nt ▷ vt: **to ~ one's brains** sich dat den Kopf zerbrechen

racket ['rækɪt] n (Sport) Schläger m; (noise) Krach m
radar ['reɪdɑː°] n Radar nt o m; **radar trap** n Radarfalle f
radiation [reɪdɪ'eɪʃən] n (radio-active) Strahlung f
radiator ['reɪdɪeɪtə°] n Heiz-körper m; (Auto) Kühler m
radical ['rædɪkəl] adj radikal
radio ['reɪdɪəʊ] (pl **-s**) n Rundfunk m, Radio nt
radioactivity [reɪdɪəʊæk'tɪvɪtɪ] n Radioaktivität f
radio alarm ['reɪdɪəʊə'lɑːm] n Radiowecker m; **radio station** n Rundfunkstation f
radiotherapy [reɪdɪəʊ'θerəpɪ] n Strahlenbehandlung f
radish ['rædɪʃ] n Radieschen nt
radius ['reɪdɪəs] n Radius m; **within a five-mile ~** im Umkreis von fünf Meilen (of um)
raffle ['ræfl] n Tombola f; **raffle ticket** n Los nt
raft [rɑːft] n Floß nt
rag [ræg] n Lumpen m; (for cleaning) Lappen m
rage [reɪdʒ] n Wut f; **to be all the ~** der letzte Schrei sein ▷ vi toben; (disease) wüten
raid [reɪd] n Überfall m (on auf +akk); (by police) Razzia f (on gegen) ▷ vt (bank etc) überfallen; (by police) eine Razzia machen in +dat
rail [reɪl] n (on stairs, balcony etc) Geländer nt; (of ship) Reling f; (Rail) Schiene f; **railcard** n (Brit) ≈ Bahncard® f; **railing** n Geländer nt; **~s** pl (fence) Zaun m; **railroad** n (US) Eisenbahn f; **railroad station** n (US) Bahnhof m; **railway** n (Brit) Eisenbahn f; **railway line** n Bahnlinie f; (track) Gleis m; **railway station** n Bahnhof m
rain [reɪn] n Regen m ▷ vi regnen; **it's ~ing** es regnet; **rainbow** n Regenbogen m;

raincoat n Regenmantel m;
rainfall n Niederschlag m;
rainforest n Regenwald m; **rainy**
adj regnerisch
raise [reɪz] n (US: of wages/salary)
Gehalts-/Lohnerhöhung f ▷ vt
(lift) hochheben; (increase)
erhöhen; (family) großziehen;
(livestock) züchten; (money)
aufbringen; (objection) erheben; **to
~ one's voice** laut werden
raisin ['reɪzən] n Rosine f
rally ['rælɪ] n (Pol) Kundgebung f;
(Auto) Rallye f; (Tennis) Ballwechsel
m
RAM [ræm] acr = **random access
memory** RAM m
ramble ['ræmbl] n Wanderung f
▷ vi (walk) wandern; (talk)
schwafeln
ramp [ræmp] n Rampe f
ran [ræn] pt of **run**
ranch [rɑːntʃ] n Ranch f
rancid ['rænsɪd] adj ranzig
random ['rændəm] adj
willkürlich ▷ n: **at ~** (choose)
willkürlich; (fire) ziellos
rang [ræŋ] pt of **ring**
range [reɪndʒ] n (selection)
Auswahl f (of an +dat); (Comm)
Sortiment nt (of an +dat); (of
missile, telescope) Reichweite f; (of
mountains) Kette f; **in this price
~** in dieser Preisklasse ▷ vi: **to
~ from ... to ...** gehen von ... bis ...;
(temperature, sizes, prices) liegen
zwischen ... und ...
rank [ræŋk] n (Mil) Rang m; (social
position) Stand m ▷ vt einstufen
ransom ['rænsəm] n Lösegeld nt
rap [ræp] n (Mus) Rap m
rape [reɪp] n Vergewaltigung f
▷ vt vergewaltigen
rapid, rapidly ['ræpɪd, -lɪ] adj, adv
schnell
rapist ['reɪpɪst] n Vergewaltiger
m

rare [rɛə*] adj selten, rar;
(especially good) vortrefflich; (steak)
blutig; **rarely** adv selten; **rarity**
['rɛərɪtɪ] n Seltenheit f
rash [ræʃ] adj unbesonnen ▷ n
(Med) (Haut)ausschlag m
rasher ['ræʃə*] n: **~ (of bacon)**
(Speck)scheibe f
raspberry ['rɑːzbərɪ] n Himbeere f
rat [ræt] n Ratte f; (pej: person)
Schwein nt
rate [reɪt] n (proportion, frequency)
Rate f; (speed) Tempo nt; **~ (of
exchange)** (Wechsel)kurs m; **~ of
inflation** Inflationsrate f; **~ of
interest** Zinssatz m; **at any ~** auf
jeden Fall ▷ vt (evaluate)
einschätzen (as als)
rather ['rɑːðə*] adv (in preference)
lieber; (fairly) ziemlich; **I'd ~ stay
here** ich würde lieber hierbleiben;
I'd ~ not lieber nicht; **or ~** (more
accurately) vielmehr
ratio ['reɪʃɪəʊ] (pl **-s**) n Verhältnis
nt
rational ['ræʃənl] adj rational;
rationalize ['ræʃnəlaɪz] vt
rationalisieren
rattle ['rætl] n (toy) Rassel f ▷ vt
(keys, coins) klimpern mit; (person)
durcheinanderbringen ▷ vi (window) klappern; (bottles) klirren;
rattle off vt herunterrasseln;
rattlesnake n Klapperschlange
f
rave [reɪv] vi (talk wildly)
fantasieren; (rage) toben; (enthuse)
schwärmen (about von) ▷ n (Brit:
event) Raveparty f
raven ['reɪvn] n Rabe m
raving ['reɪvɪŋ] adv: **~ mad** total
verrückt
ravishing ['rævɪʃɪŋ] adj
hinreißend
raw [rɔː] adj (food) roh; (skin)
wund; (climate) rau

ray [reɪ] *n* (*of light*) Strahl *m*; **~ of hope** Hoffnungsschimmer *m*

razor ['reɪzə°] *n* Rasierapparat *m*; **razor blade** *n* Rasierklinge *f*

Rd *n abbr* = **road** Str.

re [riː] *prep* (*Comm*) betreffs +*gen*

RE *abbr* = **religious education**

reach [riːtʃ] *n*: **within/out of (sb's) ~** in/außer (jds) Reichweite; **within easy ~ of the shops** nicht weit von den Geschäften ▷ *vt* (*arrive at, contact*) erreichen; (*come down/up as far as*) reichen bis zu; (*contact*) **can you ~ it?** kommst du/kommen Sie dran?; **reach for** *vt* greifen nach; **reach out** *vi* die Hand ausstrecken; **to ~ for** greifen nach

react [riː'ækt] *vi* reagieren (*to* auf +*akk*); **reaction** [riː'ækʃən] *n* Reaktion *f* (*to* auf +*akk*); **reactor** [rɪ'æktə°] *n* Reaktor *m*

read [riːd] (**read, read**) *vt* lesen; (*meter*) ablesen; **to ~ sth to sb** jdm etw vorlesen ▷ *vi* lesen; **to ~ to sb** jdm vorlesen; **it ~s well** es liest sich gut; **it ~s as follows** es lautet folgendermaßen; **read out** *vt* vorlesen; **read through** *vt* durchlesen; **read up on** *vt* nachlesen über +*akk*; **readable** *adj* (*book*) lesenswert; (*handwriting*) lesbar; **reader** *n* Leser(in) *m(f)*; **readership** *n* Leserschaft *f*

readily ['redɪlɪ] *adv* (*willingly*) bereitwillig; **~ available** leicht erhältlich

reading ['riːdɪŋ] *n* (*action*) Lesen *nt*; (*from meter*) Zählerstand *m*; **reading glasses** *npl* Lesebrille *f*; **reading lamp** *n* Leselampe *f*; **reading list** *n* Leseliste *f*; **reading matter** *n* Lektüre *f*

readjust [riːə'dʒʌst] *vt* (*mechanism etc*) neu einstellen ▷ *vi* sich wieder anpassen (*to* an +*akk*)

ready ['redɪ] *adj* fertig, bereit; **to be ~ to do sth** (*willing*) bereit sein, etw zu tun; **are you ~ to go?** bist du so weit?; **to get sth ~** etw fertig machen; **to get (oneself) ~** sich fertig machen; **ready cash** *n* Bargeld *nt*; **ready-made** *adj* (*product*) Fertig-; (*clothes*) Konfektions-; **~ meal** *n* Fertiggericht *nt*

real [rɪəl] *adj* wirklich; (*actual*) eigentlich; (*genuine*) echt; (*idiot etc*) richtig ▷ *adv* (*fam, esp US*) echt; **for ~** echt; **this time it's for ~** diesmal ist es ernst; **get ~** sei realistisch!; **real ale** *n* Ale *nt*; **real estate** *n* Immobilien *pl*

realistic, realistically [rɪə'lɪstɪk, -əlɪ] *adj, adv* realistisch; **reality** [riː'ælɪtɪ] *n* Wirklichkeit *f*; **in ~** in Wirklichkeit; **reality TV** *n* Reality-TV *nt*; **realization** [rɪəlaɪ'zeɪʃən] *n* (*awareness*) Erkenntnis *f*; **realize** ['rɪəlaɪz] *vt* (*understand*) begreifen; (*plan, idea*) realisieren; **I ~d (that) ...** mir wurde klar, dass ...

really ['rɪəlɪ] *adv* wirklich

real time [rɪəl'taɪm] *n* (*Inform*) **in ~** in Echtzeit

realtor ['rɪəltə°] *n* (*US*) Grundstücksmakler(in) *m(f)*

reappear [riːə'pɪə°] *vi* wieder erscheinen

rear [rɪə°] *adj* hintere(r, s), Hinter- ▷ *n* (*of building, vehicle*) hinterer Teil; **at the ~ of** hinter +*dat*; (*inside*) hinten in +*dat*; **rear light** *n* (*Auto*) Rücklicht *nt*

rearm [riː'ɑːm] *vi* wieder aufrüsten

rearrange [riːə'reɪndʒ] *vt* (*furniture, system*) umstellen; (*meeting*) verlegen (*for* auf +*akk*)

rear-view mirror ['rɪəvjuː'mɪrə°] *n* Rückspiegel *m*; **rear window** *n* (*Auto*) Heckscheibe *f*

r

reason ['riːzn] n (cause) Grund m
(for für); (ability to think) Verstand
m; (common sense) Vernunft f; **for
some ~** aus irgendeinem Grund
▷ vi: **to ~ with sb** mit jdm
vernünftig reden; **reasonable** adj
(person, price) vernünftig; (offer)
akzeptabel; (chance) reell; (food,
weather) ganz gut; **reasonably** adv
vernünftig; (fairly) ziemlich

reassure [riːəˈʃʊəʳ] vt beruhigen; **she ~d me that ...** sie
versicherte mir, dass ...

rebel ['rebl] n Rebell(in) m(f)
▷ [rɪˈbel] vi rebellieren; **rebellion**
[rɪˈbelɪən] n Aufstand m

reboot [riːˈbuːt] vt, vi (Inform)
rebooten

rebound [rɪˈbaʊnd] vi (ball etc)
zurückprallen

rebuild [riːˈbɪld] irr vt wieder
aufbauen

recall [rɪˈkɔːl] vt (remember) sich
erinnern an +akk; (call back)
zurückrufen

recap ['riːkæp] vt, vi
rekapitulieren

receipt [rɪˈsiːt] n (document)
Quittung f; (receiving) Empfang m;
~s pl (money) Einnahmen pl

receive [rɪˈsiːv] vt (news etc)
erhalten, bekommen; (visitor)
empfangen; **receiver** n (Tel)
Hörer m; (Radio) Empfänger m

recent ['riːsnt] adj (event) vor
Kurzem stattgefunden; (photo)
neueste(r,s); (invention) neu; **in
~ years** in den letzten Jahren;
recently adv vor Kurzem; (in the
last few days or weeks) in letzter Zeit

reception [rɪˈsepʃən] n Empfang
m; **receptionist** n (in hotel)
Empfangschef m, Empfangsdame
f; (woman in firm) Empfangsdame f;
(Med) Sprechstundenhilfe f

recess [rɪˈses] n (in wall) Nische
f; (US: in school) Pause f

recession [rɪˈseʃən] n Rezession
f

recharge [riːˈtʃɑːdʒ] vt (battery)
aufladen; **rechargeable**
[riːˈtʃɑːdʒəbl] adj wiederaufladbar

recipe ['resɪpɪ] n Rezept nt (for
für)

recipient [rɪˈsɪpɪənt] n
Empfänger(in) m(f)

reciprocal [rɪˈsɪprəkəl] adj
gegenseitig

recite [rɪˈsaɪt] vt vortragen;
(details) aufzählen

reckless ['rekləs] adj leichtsinnig; (driving) gefährlich

reckon ['rekən] vt (calculate)
schätzen; (think) glauben ▷ vi: **to
~ with/on** rechnen mit

reclaim [rɪˈkleɪm] vt (baggage)
abholen; (expenses, tax)
zurückverlangen

recline [rɪˈklaɪn] vi (person) sich
zurücklehnen; **reclining seat** n
Liegesitz m

recognition [rekəgˈnɪʃən] n
(acknowledgement) Anerkennung f;
in ~ of in Anerkennung +gen;
recognize ['rekəgnaɪz] vt
erkennen; (approve officially)
anerkennen

recommend [rekəˈmend] vt
empfehlen; **recommendation**
[rekəmenˈdeɪʃən] n Empfehlung f

reconfirm [riːkənˈfɜːm] vt (flight
etc) rückbestätigen

reconsider [riːkənˈsɪdəʳ] vt noch
einmal überdenken ▷ vi es sich
dat noch einmal überlegen

reconstruct [riːkənˈstrʌkt] vt
wieder aufbauen; (crime)
rekonstruieren

record ['rekɔːd] n (Mus)
(Schall)platte f; (best performance)
Rekord m; **~s** pl (files) Akten pl; **to
keep a ~ of** Buch führen über +akk
▷ adj (time etc) Rekord- ▷ [rɪˈkɔːd]
vt (write down) aufzeichnen; (on

tape etc) aufnehmen; **~ed message** Ansage *f*; **recorded delivery** *n* (*Brit*) **by ~** per Einschreiben

recorder [rɪ'kɔːdə°] *n* (*Mus*) Blockflöte *f*; (**cassette**) **~** (Kassetten)rekorder *m*; **recording** [rɪ'kɔːdɪŋ] *n* (*on tape etc*) Aufnahme *f*; **record player** ['rekɔːdpleɪə°] *n* Plattenspieler *m*

recover [rɪ'kʌvə°] *vt* (*money, item*) zurückbekommen; (*appetite, strength*) wiedergewinnen ▷ *vi* sich erholen

recreation [rekrɪ'eɪʃən] *n* Erholung *f*; **recreational** *adj* Freizeit-; **~ vehicle** (*US*) Wohnmobil *nt*

recruit [rɪ'kruːt] *n* (*Mil*) Rekrut(in) *m(f)*; (*in firm, organization*) neues Mitglied ▷ *vt* (*Mil*) rekrutieren; (*members*) anwerben; (*staff*) einstellen; **recruitment agency** *n* Personalagentur *f*

rectangle ['rektæŋgl] *n* Rechteck *nt*; **rectangular** [rek'tæŋgʊlə°] *adj* rechteckig

rectify ['rektɪfaɪ] *vt* berichtigen

recuperate [rɪ'kuːpəreɪt] *vi* sich erholen

recyclable [riː'saɪkləbl] *adj* recycelbar, wiederverwertbar; **recycle** [riː'saɪkl] *vt* recyceln, wiederverwerten; **~d paper** Recyclingpapier *nt*; **recycling** *n* Recycling *nt*, Wiederverwertung *f*

red [red] *adj* rot ▷ *n*: **in the ~** in den roten Zahlen; **Red Cross** *n* Rotes Kreuz; **red cabbage** *n* Rotkohl *m*; **redcurrant** *n* (rote) Johannisbeere

redeem [rɪ'diːm] *vt* (*Comm*) einlösen

red-handed [red'hændɪd] *adj*: **to catch sb ~** jdn auf frischer Tat ertappen; **redhead** *n* Rothaarige(r) *mf*

redial [riː'daɪəl] *vt, vi* nochmals wählen

redirect [riːdaɪ'rekt] *vt* (*traffic*) umleiten; (*forward*) nachsenden

red light [red'laɪt] *n* (*traffic signal*) rotes Licht; **to go through the ~** bei Rot über die Ampel fahren; **red meat** *n* Rind-, Lamm-, Rehfleisch

redo [riː'duː] *irr vt* nochmals machen

reduce [rɪ'djuːs] *vt* reduzieren (*to* auf +*akk, by* um); **reduction** [rɪ'dʌkʃən] *n* Reduzierung *f*; (*in price*) Ermäßigung *f*

redundant [rɪ'dʌndənt] *adj* überflüssig; **to be made ~** entlassen werden

red wine [red'waɪn] *n* Rotwein *m*

reef [riːf] *n* Riff *nt*

reel [riːl] *n* Spule *f*; (*on fishing rod*) Rolle *f*; **reel off** *vt* herunterrasseln

ref [ref] *n* (*fam: referee*) Schiri *m*

refectory [rɪ'fektərɪ] *n* (*at college*) Mensa *f*

refer [rɪ'fɜː°] *vt*: **to ~ sb to sb/sth** jdn an jdn/etw verweisen; **to ~ sth to sb** (*query, problem*) etw an jdn weiterleiten ▷ *vi*: **to ~ to** (*mention, allude to*) sich beziehen auf +*akk*; (*book*) nachschlagen in +*dat*

referee [refə'riː] *n* Schiedsrichter(in) *m(f)*; (*in boxing*) Ringrichter *m*; (*Brit: for job*) Referenz *f*

reference ['refrəns] *n* (*allusion*) Anspielung *f* (*to* auf +*akk*); (*for job*) Referenz *f*; (*in book*) Verweis *m*; **~ (number)** (*in document*) Aktenzeichen *nt*; **with ~ to** mit Bezug auf +*akk*; **reference book** *n* Nachschlagewerk *nt*

referendum [refə'rendəm] (*pl* **referenda**) *n* Referendum *nt*

refill ['riːfɪl] *vt* [riː'fɪl] nachfüllen ▷ *n* (*for ballpoint pen*) Ersatzmine *f*

refine [rɪ'faɪn] vt (purify) raffinieren; (improve) verfeinern; **refined** adj (genteel) fein

reflect [rɪ'flekt] vt reflektieren; (fig) widerspiegeln ▷ vi nachdenken; (on über +akk); **reflection** [rɪ'flekʃən] n (image) Spiegelbild nt; (thought) Überlegung f; **on ~** nach reiflicher Überlegung

reflex ['riːfleks] n Reflex m

reform [rɪ'fɔːm] n Reform f ▷ vt reformieren; (person) bessern

refrain [rɪ'freɪn] vi: **to ~ from doing sth** es unterlassen, etw zu tun

refresh [rɪ'freʃ] vt erfrischen; **refresher course** n Auffrischungskurs m; **refreshing** adj erfrischend; **refreshments** npl Erfrischungen pl

refrigerator [rɪ'frɪdʒəreɪtə°] n Kühlschrank m

refuel [riː'fjʊəl] vt, vi auftanken

refugee [refjʊ'dʒiː] n Flüchtling m

refund ['riːfʌnd] n (of money) Rückerstattung f; **to get a ~ (on sth)** sein Geld (für etw) zurückbekommen ▷ [rɪ'fʌnd] vt zurückerstatten

refusal [rɪ'fjuːzəl] n (to do sth) Weigerung f; **refuse** ['refjuːs] n Müll m, Abfall m ▷ [rɪ'fjuːz] vt ablehnen; **to ~ sb sth** jdm etw verweigern; **to ~ to do sth** sich weigern, etw zu tun ▷ vi sich weigern

regain [rɪ'geɪn] vt wiedergewinnen, wiedererlangen; **to ~ consciousness** wieder zu Bewusstsein kommen

regard [rɪ'gɑːd] n: **with ~ to** in Bezug auf +akk; **in this ~** in dieser Hinsicht; **~s** (at end of letter) mit freundlichen Grüßen; **give my ~s to ...** viele Grüße an ... +akk ▷ vt:

to ~ sb/sth as sth jdn/etw als etw betrachten; **as ~s ...** was ... betrifft; **regarding** prep bezüglich +gen; **regardless** adj: **~ of** ohne Rücksicht auf +akk ▷ adv trotzdem; **to carry on ~** einfach weitermachen

regime [reɪ'ʒiːm] n (Pol) Regime nt

region ['riːdʒən] n (of country) Region f, Gebiet nt; **in the ~ of** (about) ungefähr; **regional** adj regional

register ['redʒɪstə°] n Register nt; (school) Namensliste f ▷ vt (with an authority) registrieren lassen; (birth, death, vehicle) anmelden ▷ vi (at hotel, for course) sich anmelden; (at university) sich einschreiben; **registered** adj eingetragen; (letter) eingeschrieben; **by ~ post** per Einschreiben; **registration** [redʒɪ'streɪʃən] n (for course) Anmeldung f; (at university) Einschreibung f; (Auto: number) (polizeiliches) Kennzeichen; **registration form** n Anmeldeformular nt; **registration number** n (Auto) (polizeiliches) Kennzeichen; **registry office** ['redʒɪstrɪɒfɪs] n Standesamt nt

regret [rɪ'gret] n Bedauern nt ▷ vt bedauern; **regrettable** adj bedauerlich

regular ['regjʊlə°] adj regelmäßig; (size) normal ▷ n (client) Stammkunde m, Stammkundin f; (in bar) Stammgast m; (petrol) Normalbenzin nt; **regularly** adv regelmäßig

regulate ['regjʊleɪt] vt regulieren; (using rules) regeln; **regulation** [regjʊ'leɪʃən] n (rule) Vorschrift f

rehabilitation [riːəbɪlɪ'teɪʃən] n Rehabilitation f

rehearsal [rɪ'hɜːsəl] n Probe f;
rehearse vt, vi proben

reign [reɪn] n Herrschaft f ▷ vi
herrschen (over über +akk)

reimburse [riːɪmˈbɜːs] vt (person) entschädigen; (expenses)
zurückerstatten

reindeer ['reɪndɪə°] n Rentier nt

reinforce [riːɪnˈfɔːs] vt
verstärken

reinstate [riːɪnˈsteɪt] vt
(employee) wieder einstellen;
(passage in text) wieder aufnehmen

reject ['riːdʒekt] n (Comm)
Ausschussartikel m ▷ [rɪ'dʒekt]
vt ablehnen; **rejection**
[rɪ'dʒekʃən] n Ablehnung f

relapse [rɪ'læps] n Rückfall m

relate [rɪ'leɪt] vt (story) erzählen;
(connect) in Verbindung bringen (to
mit) ▷ vi: **to ~ to** (refer) sich
beziehen auf +akk; **related** adj
verwandt (to mit); **relation**
[rɪ'leɪʃən] n (relative) Verwandte(r)
mf; (connection) Beziehung f; **~s** pl
(dealings) Beziehungen pl;
relationship n (connection)
Beziehung f; (between people)
Verhältnis nt

relative ['relətɪv] n Verwandte(r)
mf ▷ adj relativ; **relatively** adv
relativ, verhältnismäßig

relax [rɪ'læks] vi sich
entspannen; **~!** reg dich nicht auf!
▷ vt (grip, conditions) lockern;
relaxation [riːlækˈseɪʃən] n (rest)
Entspannung f; **relaxed** adj
entspannt; **relaxing** adj
entspannend

release [rɪ'liːs] n (from prison)
Entlassung f; **new/recent ~** (film,
CD) Neuerscheinung f ▷ vt
(animal, hostage) freilassen;
(prisoner) entlassen; (handbrake)
lösen; (news) veröffentlichen;
(film, CD) herausbringen

relent [rɪ'lent] vi nachgeben;

relentless, relentlessly adj, adv
(merciless) erbarmungslos;
(neverending) unaufhörlich

relevance ['reləvəns] n
Relevanz f (to für); **relevant** adj
relevant (to für)

reliable, reliably [rɪ'laɪəbl, -blɪ]
adj, adv zuverlässig; **reliant**
[rɪ'laɪənt] adj: **~ on** abhängig von

relic ['relɪk] n (from past) Relikt nt

relief [rɪ'liːf] n (from anxiety, pain)
Erleichterung f; (assistance) Hilfe f;
relieve [rɪ'liːv] vt (pain) lindern;
(boredom) überwinden; (take over
from) ablösen; **I'm ~d** ich bin
erleichtert

religion [rɪ'lɪdʒən] n Religion f;
religious [rɪ'lɪdʒəs] adj religiös

relish ['relɪʃ] n (for food) würzige
Soße ▷ vt (enjoy) genießen; **I
don't ~ the thought of it** der
Gedanke behagt mir gar nicht

reluctant [rɪ'lʌktənt] adj
widerwillig; **to be ~ to do sth** etw
nur ungern tun; **reluctantly** adv
widerwillig

rely on [rɪ'laɪ ɒn] vt sich
verlassen auf +akk; (depend on)
abhängig sein von

remain [rɪ'meɪn] vi bleiben; (be
left over) übrig bleiben; **remainder**
n (a. Math) Rest m; **remaining** adj
übrig; **remains** npl Überreste pl

remark [rɪ'mɑːk] n Bemerkung f
▷ vt: **to ~ that** bemerken, dass
▷ vi: **to ~ on sth** über etw akk eine
Bemerkung machen; **remarkable,
remarkably** adj, adv
bemerkenswert

remarry [riːˈmærɪ] vi wieder
heiraten

remedy ['remədɪ] n Mittel nt (for
gegen) ▷ vt abhelfen +dat

remember [rɪ'membə°] vt sich
erinnern an +akk; **to ~ to do sth**
daran denken, etw zu tun; **I
~ seeing her** ich erinnere mich

daran, sie gesehen zu haben; **I must ~ that** das muss ich mir merken ▷ *vi* sich erinnern

Remembrance Day [rɪˈmembrənsˈdeɪ] *n* (*Brit*) ≈ Volkstrauertag *m*

● REMEMBRANCE DAY
●
● **Remembrance Sunday/Day** ist
● der britische Gedenktag für die
● Gefallenen der beiden
● Weltkriege und anderer Kriege.
● Er fällt auf einen Sonntag vor
● oder nach dem 11. November
● (am 11.11.1918 endete der Erste
● Weltkrieg) und wird mit einer
● Schweigeminute,
● Kranzniederlegungen an
● Kriegerdenkmälern und dem
● Tragen von Anstecknadeln in
● Form einer Mohnblume
● begangen.

remind [rɪˈmaɪnd] *vt*: **to ~ sb of/about sb/sth** jdn an jdn/etw erinnern; **to ~ sb to do sth** jdn daran erinnern, etw zu tun; **that ~s me** dabei fällt mir ein ...; **reminder** *n* (*to pay*) Mahnung *f*

reminisce [remɪˈnɪs] *vi* in Erinnerungen schwelgen (*about* an +*akk*); **reminiscent** [remɪˈnɪsənt] *adj*: **to be ~ of** erinnern an +*akk*

remittance *n* Überweisung *f* (*to* an +*akk*)

remnant [ˈremnənt] *n* Rest *m*

remote [rɪˈməʊt] *adj* (*place*) abgelegen; (*slight*) gering ▷ *n* (*TV*) Fernbedienung *f*; **remote control** *n* Fernsteuerung *f*; (*device*) Fernbedienung *f*

removal [rɪˈmuːvəl] *n* Entfernung *f*; (*Brit: move from house*) Umzug *m*; **removal firm** *n* (*Brit*) Spedition *f*; **remove** [rɪˈmuːv] *vt* entfernen; (*lid*) abnehmen; (*clothes*) ausziehen; (*doubt, suspicion*) zerstreuen

rename [riːˈneɪm] *vt* umbenennen

renew [rɪˈnjuː] *vt* erneuern; (*licence, passport, library book*) verlängern lassen; **renewable** *adj* (*energy*) erneuerbar

renounce [rɪˈnaʊns] *vt* verzichten auf +*akk*; (*faith, opinion*) abschwören +*dat*

renovate [ˈrenəveɪt] *vt* renovieren

renowned [rɪˈnaʊnd] *adj* berühmt (*for* für)

rent [rent] *n* Miete *f*; **for ~** (*US*) zu vermieten ▷ *vt* (*as hirer, tenant*) mieten; (*as owner*) vermieten; **~ed car** Mietwagen *m*; **rent out** *vt* vermieten; **rental** *n* Miete *f*; (*for car, TV etc*) Leihgebühr *f* ▷ *adj* Miet-

reorganize [riːˈɔːɡənaɪz] *vt* umorganisieren

rep [rep] *n* Vertreter(in) *m(f)*

repair [rɪˈpɛə°] *n* Reparatur *f* ▷ *vt* reparieren; (*damage*) wiedergutmachen; **repair kit** *n* Flickzeug *nt*

repay [riːˈpeɪ] *irr vt* (*money*) zurückzahlen; **to ~ sb for sth** (*fig*) sich bei jdm für etw revanchieren

repeat [rɪˈpiːt] *n* (*Radio, TV*) Wiederholung *f* ▷ *vt* wiederholen; **repetition** [repəˈtɪʃən] *n* Wiederholung *f*; **repetitive** [rɪˈpetɪtɪv] *adj* sich wiederholend

rephrase [riːˈfreɪz] *vt* anders formulieren

replace [rɪˈpleɪs] *vt* ersetzen (*with* durch); (*put back*) zurückstellen, zurücklegen; **replacement** *n* (*thing, person*) Ersatz *m*; (*temporarily in job*) Vertretung *f*; **replacement part** *n* Ersatzteil *nt*

replay [ˈriːpleɪ] *n*: (**action**)

~ Wiederholung f ▷ ['ri:'pleɪ] vt
(*game*) wiederholen
replica ['replɪkə] n Kopie f
reply [rɪ'plaɪ] n Antwort f ▷ vi
antworten; **to ~ to sb/sth**
jdm/auf etw *akk* antworten ▷ vt:
to ~ that antworten, dass
report [rɪ'pɔ:t] n Bericht m;
(*school*) Zeugnis nt ▷ vt (*tell*)
berichten; (*give information against*)
melden; (*to police*) anzeigen ▷ vi
(*present oneself*) sich melden; **to
~ sick** sich krankmelden; **report
card** n (*US: school*) Zeugnis nt;
reporter n Reporter(in) m(f)
represent [reprɪ'zent] vt darstellen; (*speak for*) vertreten;
representation [reprɪzen'teɪʃən]
n (*picture etc*) Darstellung f;
representative [reprɪ'zentətɪv]
n Vertreter(in) m(f); (*US Pol*)
Abgeordnete(r) mf ▷ adj
repräsentativ (*of* für)
reprimand ['reprɪmɑ:nd] n Tadel
m ▷ vt tadeln
reprint ['ri:prɪnt] n Nachdruck m
reproduce [ri:prə'dju:s] vt (*copy*)
reproduzieren ▷ vi (*Bio*) sich
fortpflanzen; **reproduction**
[ri:prə'dʌkʃən] n (*copy*)
Reproduktion f; (*Bio*)
Fortpflanzung f
reptile ['reptaɪl] n Reptil nt
republic [rɪ'pʌblɪk] n Republik f;
republican adj republikanisch
▷ n Republikaner(in) m(f)
repulsive [rɪ'pʌlsɪv] adj
abstoßend
reputable ['repjʊtəbl] adj seriös
reputation [repjʊ'teɪʃən] n Ruf
m; **he has a ~ for being difficult**
er hat den Ruf, schwierig zu sein
request [rɪ'kwest] n Bitte f (*for*
um); **on ~** auf Wunsch ▷ vt bitten
um; **to ~ sb to do sth** jdn bitten,
etw zu tun
require [rɪ'kwaɪə*] vt (*need*)

brauchen; (*desire*) verlangen; **what
qualifications are ~d?** welche
Qualifikationen sind
erforderlich?; **required** adj
erforderlich; **requirement** n
(*condition*) Anforderung f; (*need*)
Bedingung f
rerun ['ri:rʌn] n Wiederholung f
rescue ['reskju:] n Rettung f; **to
come to sb's ~** jdm zu Hilfe
kommen ▷ vt retten; **rescue
party** n Rettungsmannschaft f
research [rɪ'sɜːtʃ] n Forschung f
▷ vi forschen (*into* über +*akk*) ▷ vt
erforschen; **researcher** n
Forscher(in) m(f)
resemblance [rɪ'zembləns] n
Ähnlichkeit f (*to* mit); **resemble**
[rɪ'zembl] vt ähneln +*dat*
resent [rɪ'zent] vt übel nehmen
reservation [rezə'veɪʃən] n
(*booking*) Reservierung f; (*doubt*)
Vorbehalt m; **I have a ~** (*in hotel,
restaurant*) ich habe reserviert;
reserve [rɪ'zɜːv] n (*store*) Vorrat m
(*of* an +*dat*); (*manner*)
Zurückhaltung f; (*Sport*)
Reservespieler(in) m(f); (*game ~*)
Naturschutzgebiet nt ▷ vt (*book in
advance*) reservieren; **reserved** adj
reserviert
reservoir ['resəvwɑ:*] n (*for
water*) Reservoir nt
reside [rɪ'zaɪd] vi wohnen;
residence ['rezɪdəns] n Wohnsitz m; (*living*) Aufenthalt m;
~ permit Aufenthaltsgenehmigung f; **~ hall** Studentenwohnheim nt; **resident**
['rezɪdənt] n (*in house*)
Bewohner(in) m(f); (*in town, area*)
Einwohner(in) m(f)
resign [rɪ'zaɪn] vt (*post*)
zurücktreten von; (*job*) kündigen
▷ vi (*from post*) zurücktreten; (*from
job*) kündigen; **resignation**
[rezɪg'neɪʃən] n (*from post*)

Rücktritt *m*; *(from job)* Kündigung *f*; **resigned** *adj* resigniert; **he is ~ to it** er hat sich damit abgefunden

resist [rɪ'zɪst] *vt* widerstehen +*dat*; **resistance** *n* Widerstand *m* *(to* gegen)

resit [riː'sɪt] *(Brit)* *irr vt* wiederholen ▷ ['riːsɪt] *n* Wiederholungsprüfung *f*

resolution [rezə'luːʃən] *n* *(intention)* Vorsatz *m*; *(decision)* Beschluss *m*

resolve [rɪ'zɒlv] *vt* *(problem)* lösen

resort [rɪ'zɔːt] *n* *(holiday ~)* Urlaubsort *m*; *(health ~)* Kurort *m*; **as a last ~** als letzter Ausweg ▷ *vi*: **to ~ to** greifen zu; *(violence)* anwenden

resources [rɪ'sɔːsɪz] *npl* *(money)* (Geld)mittel *pl*; *(mineral ~)* Bodenschätze *pl*

respect [rɪ'spekt] *n* Respekt *m* *(for* vor +*dat*); *(consideration)* Rücksicht *f (for* auf +*akk*); **with ~ to** in Bezug auf +*akk*; **in this ~** in dieser Hinsicht; **with all due ~** bei allem Respekt ▷ *vt* respektieren; **respectable** [rɪ'spektəbl] *adj* *(person, family)* angesehen; *(district)* anständig; *(achievement, result)* beachtlich; **respected** [rɪ'spektɪd] *adj* angesehen

respective [rɪ'spektɪv] *adj* jeweilig; **respectively** *adv*: **5 % and 10 % ~** 5 % beziehungsweise 10 %

respiratory [rɪ'spɪrətərɪ] *adj*: **~ problems** *(o* **trouble)** Atembeschwerden *pl*

respond [rɪ'spɒnd] *vi* antworten *(to* auf +*akk*); *(react)* reagieren *(to* auf +*akk*); *(to treatment)* ansprechen *(to* auf +*akk*); **response** [rɪ'spɒns] *n* Antwort *f*; *(reaction)* Reaktion *f*; **in ~ to** als Antwort auf +*akk*

responsibility [rɪspɒnsə'bɪlɪtɪ] *n* Verantwortung *f*; **that's her ~** dafür ist sie verantwortlich; **responsible** [rɪ'spɒnsəbl] *adj* verantwortlich *(for* für); *(trustworthy)* verantwortungsbewusst; *(job)* verantwortungsvoll

rest [rest] *n* *(relaxation)* Ruhe *f*; *(break)* Pause *f*; *(remainder)* Rest *m*; **to have** *(o* **take) a ~** sich ausruhen; *(break)* Pause machen; **the ~ of the wine/the people** der Rest des Weins/der Leute ▷ *vi* *(relax)* sich ausruhen; *(lean)* lehnen *(on, against* an +*dat*, gegen)

restaurant ['restərɒnt] *n* Restaurant *nt*; **restaurant car** *n* *(Brit)* Speisewagen *m*

restful ['restfʊl] *adj* *(holiday etc)* erholsam, ruhig; **restless** ['restləs] *adj* unruhig

restore [rɪ'stɔː°] *vt* *(painting, building)* restaurieren; *(order)* wiederherstellen; *(give back)* zurückgeben

restrain [rɪ'streɪn] *vt* *(person, feelings)* zurückhalten; **to ~ oneself** sich beherrschen

restrict [rɪ'strɪkt] *vt* beschränken *(to* auf +*akk*); **restricted** *adj* beschränkt; **restriction** [rɪ'strɪkʃən] *n* Einschränkung *f* *(on* +*gen*)

rest room ['restruːm] *n* *(US)* Toilette *f*

result [rɪ'zʌlt] *n* Ergebnis *nt*; *(consequence)* Folge *f*; **as a ~ of** infolge +*gen* ▷ *vi*: **to ~ in** führen zu; **to ~ from** sich ergeben aus

resume [rɪ'zjuːm] *vt* *(work, negotiations)* wieder aufnehmen; *(journey)* fortsetzen

résumé ['rezjʊmeɪ] *n* Zusammenfassung *f*; *(US: curriculum vitae)* Lebenslauf *m*

resuscitate [rɪˈsʌsɪteɪt] *vt* wiederbeleben

retail [ˈriːteɪl] *adv* im Einzelhandel; **retailer** *n* Einzelhändler(in) *m(f)*

retain [rɪˈteɪn] *vt* behalten; (*heat*) halten

rethink [riːˈθɪŋk] *irr vt* noch einmal überdenken

retire [rɪˈtaɪəʳ] *vi* (*from work*) in den Ruhestand treten; (*withdraw*) sich zurückziehen; **retired** *adj* (*person*) pensioniert; **retirement** *n* (*time of life*) Ruhestand *m*; **retirement age** *n* Rentenalter *nt*

retrace [rɪˈtreɪs] *vt* zurückverfolgen

retrain [riːˈtreɪn] *vi* sich umschulen lassen

retreat [rɪˈtriːt] *n* (*Mil*) Rückzug *m* (*from aus*); (*refuge*) Zufluchtsort *m* ▷ *vi* (*Mil*) sich zurückziehen; (*step back*) zurückweichen

retrieve [rɪˈtriːv] *vt* (*recover*) wiederbekommen; (*rescue*) retten; (*data*) abrufen

retrospect [ˈretrəʊspekt] *n*: **in ~** rückblickend; **retrospective** [retrəʊˈspektɪv] *adj* rückblickend; (*pay rise*) rückwirkend

return [rɪˈtɜːn] *n* (*going back*) Rückkehr *f*; (*giving back*) Rückgabe *f*; (*profit*) Gewinn *m*; (*Brit: ~ ticket*) Rückfahrkarte *f*; (*plane ticket*) Rückflugticket *nt*; (*Tennis*), Return *m*; **in ~** als Gegenleistung (*for* für); **many happy ~s (of the day)** herzlichen Glückwunsch zum Geburtstag! ▷ *vi* (*person*) zurückkehren; (*doubts, symptoms*) wieder auftreten; **to ~ to school/work** wieder in die Schule/die Arbeit gehen ▷ *vt* (*give back*) zurückgeben; **I ~ed his call** ich habe ihn zurückgerufen; **returnable** *adj* (*bottle*) Pfand-;

return flight *n* (*Brit*) Rückflug *m*; (*both ways*) Hin- und Rückflug *m*; **return key** *n* (*Inform*) Eingabetaste *f*; **return ticket** *n* (*Brit*) Rückfahrkarte *f*; (*for plane*) Rückflugticket *nt*

reunification [riːjuːnɪfɪˈkeɪʃən] *n* Wiedervereinigung *f*

reunion [riːˈjuːnjən] *n* (*party*) Treffen *nt*; **reunite** [riːjuːˈnaɪt] *vt* wieder vereinigen

reusable [riːˈjuːzəbl] *adj* wiederverwendbar

reveal [rɪˈviːl] *vt* (*make known*) enthüllen; (*secret*) verraten; (*show*) zeigen; **revealing** *adj* aufschlussreich; (*dress*) freizügig

revenge [rɪˈvendʒ] *n* Rache *f*; (*in game*) Revanche *f*; **to take ~ on sb (for sth)** sich an jdm (für etw) rächen

revenue [ˈrevənjuː] *n* Einnahmen *pl*

reverse [rɪˈvɜːs] *n* (*back*) Rückseite *f*; (*opposite*) Gegenteil *nt*; (*Auto*) **~ (gear)** Rückwärtsgang *m* ▷ *adj*: **in ~ order** in umgekehrter Reihenfolge ▷ *vt* (*order*) umkehren; (*decision*) umstoßen; (*car*) zurücksetzen; **to ~ the charges** (*Brit*) ein R-Gespräch führen ▷ *vi* (*Auto*) rückwärtsfahren

review [rɪˈvjuː] *n* (*of book, film etc*) Rezension *f*; Kritik *f*; **to be under ~** überprüft werden ▷ *vt* (*book, film etc*) rezensieren; (*re-examine*) überprüfen

revise [rɪˈvaɪz] *vt* revidieren; (*text*) überarbeiten; (*Brit: in school*) wiederholen ▷ *vi* (*Brit, in school*) (für eine Prüfung) lernen; **revision** [rɪˈvɪʒən] *n* (*of text*) Überarbeitung *f*; (*Brit, in school*) Wiederholung *f*

revitalize [riːˈvaɪtəlaɪz] *vt* neu beleben

r

revive [rɪ'vaɪv] vt (person) wiederbeleben; (tradition, interest) wieder aufleben lassen ▷ vi (regain consciousness) wieder zu sich kommen

revolt [rɪ'vəʊlt] n Aufstand m; **revolting** adj widerlich

revolution [revə'lu:ʃən] n (Pol, fig) Revolution f; (turn) Umdrehung f; **revolutionary** adj revolutionär ▷ n Revolutionär(in) m(f)

revolve [rɪ'vɒlv] vi sich drehen (around um); **revolver** n Revolver m; **revolving door** n Drehtür f

reward [rɪ'wɔ:d] n Belohnung f ▷ vt belohnen; **rewarding** adj lohnend

rewind [ri:'waɪnd] irr vt (tape) zurückspulen

rewritable [ri:'raɪtəbl] adj (CD, DVD) wiederbeschreibbar; **rewrite** irr vt (write again; recast) umschreiben

rheumatism ['ru:mətɪzəm] n Rheuma nt

Rhine [raɪn] n Rhein m

rhinoceros [raɪ'nɒsərəs] n Nashorn nt

Rhodes [rəʊdz] n Rhodos nt

rhubarb ['ru:bɑ:b] n Rhabarber m

rhyme [raɪm] n Reim m ▷ vi sich reimen (with auf +akk)

rhythm ['rɪðəm] n Rhythmus m

rib [rɪb] n Rippe f

ribbon ['rɪbən] n Band nt

rice [raɪs] n Reis m; **rice pudding** n Milchreis m

rich [rɪtʃ] adj reich; (food) schwer ▷ npl: **the ~** die Reichen pl

rickety ['rɪkɪtɪ] adj wackelig

rid [rɪd] (rid, rid) vt: **to get ~ of sb/sth** jdn/etw loswerden

ridden ['rɪdn] pp of **ride**

riddle ['rɪdl] n Rätsel nt

ride [raɪd] (rode, ridden) vt (horse) reiten; (bicycle) fahren ▷ vi (on horse) reiten; (on bike) fahren ▷ n (in vehicle, on bike) Fahrt f; (on horse) (Aus)ritt m; **to go for a ~** (in car, on bike) spazieren fahren; (on horse) reiten gehen; **to take sb for a ~** (fam) jdn verarschen; **rider** n (on horse) Reiter(in) m(f); (on bike) Fahrer(in) m(f)

ridiculous [rɪ'dɪkjʊləs] adj lächerlich; **don't be ~** red keinen Unsinn!

riding ['raɪdɪŋ] n Reiten nt; **to go ~** reiten gehen ▷ adj Reit-

rifle ['raɪfl] n Gewehr nt

rig [rɪg] n: **oil ~** Bohrinsel f ▷ vt (election etc) manipulieren

right [raɪt] adj (correct, just) richtig; (opposite of left) rechte(r, s); (clothes, job etc) passend; **to be ~** (person) recht haben; (clock) richtig gehen; **that's ~** das stimmt! ▷ n Recht nt (to auf +akk); (side) rechte Seite; **the Right** (Pol) die Rechte; **to take a ~** (Auto) rechts abbiegen; **on the ~** rechts (of von); **to the ~** nach rechts; (on the ~) rechts (of von) ▷ adv (towards the ~) nach rechts; (directly) direkt; (exactly) genau; **to turn ~** (Auto) rechts abbiegen; **~ away** sofort; **~ now** im Moment; (immediately) sofort; **right angle** n rechter Winkel; **right-hand drive** n Rechtssteuerung f ▷ adj rechtsgesteuert; **right-handed** adj: **he is ~** er ist Rechtshänder; **right-hand side** n rechte Seite; **on the ~** auf der rechten Seite; **rightly** adv zu Recht; **right of way** n: **to have ~** (Auto) Vorfahrt haben; **right wing** n (Pol, Sport) rechter Flügel; **right-wing** adj Rechts-; **~ extremist** Rechtsradikale(r) mf

rigid ['rɪdʒɪd] adj (stiff) starr; (strict) streng

rigorous, rigorously ['rɪgərəs, -lɪ]
adj, adv streng
rim [rɪm] *n* (*of cup etc*) Rand *m*; (*of wheel*) Felge *f*
rind [raɪnd] *n* (*of cheese*) Rinde *f*; (*of bacon*) Schwarte *f*; (*of fruit*) Schale *f*
ring [rɪŋ] (**rang, rung**) *vt, vi* (*bell*) läuten; (*Tel*) anrufen ▷ *n* (*on finger, in boxing*) Ring *m*; (*circle*) Kreis *m*; (*at circus*) Manege *f*; **to give sb a ~** (*Tel*) jdn anrufen; **ring back** *vt, vi* zurückrufen; **ring up** *vt, vi* anrufen
ring binder *n* Ringbuch *nt*
ringleader *n* Anführer(in) *m(f)*
ring road *n* (*Brit*) Umgehungsstraße *f*
ringtone *n* Klingelton *m*
rink [rɪŋk] *n* (*ice ~*) Eisbahn *f*; (*for roller-skating*) Rollschuhbahn *f*
rinse [rɪns] *vt* spülen
riot ['raɪət] *n* Aufruhr *m*
rip [rɪp] *n* Riss *m* ▷ *vt* zerreißen; **to ~ sth open** etw aufreißen ▷ *vi* reißen; **rip off** *vt* (*fam: person*) übers Ohr hauen; **rip up** *vt* zerreißen
ripe [raɪp] *adj* (*fruit*) reif; **ripen** *vi* reifen
rip-off ['rɪpɒf] *n*: **that's a ~** (*fam: too expensive*) das ist Wucher
rise [raɪz] (**rose, risen**) *vi* (*from sitting, lying*) aufstehen; (*sun*) aufgehen; (*prices, temperature*) steigen; (*ground*) ansteigen; (*in revolt*) sich erheben ▷ *n* (*increase*) Anstieg *m* (*in +gen*); (*pay ~*) Gehaltserhöhung *f*; (*to power, fame*) Aufstieg *m* (*to zu*); (*slope*) Steigung *f*; **risen** ['rɪzn] *pp of* **rise**
risk [rɪsk] *n* Risiko *nt* ▷ *vt* riskieren; **to ~ doing sth** es riskieren, etw zu tun; **risky** *adj* riskant
risotto [rɪ'zɒtəʊ] (*pl* **-s**) *n* Risotto *nt*

ritual ['rɪtjʊəl] *n* Ritual *nt* ▷ *adj* rituell
rival ['raɪvəl] *n* Rivale *m*, Rivalin *f* (*for um*); (*Comm*) Konkurrent(in) *m(f)*; **rivalry** *n* Rivalität *f*; (*Comm, Sport*) Konkurrenz *f*
river ['rɪvə°] *n* Fluss *m*; **the River Thames** (*Brit*), **the Thames River** (*US*) die Themse; **riverside** *n* Flussufer *nt* ▷ *adj* am Flussufer
road [rəʊd] *n* Straße *f*; (*fig*) Weg *m*; **on the ~** (*travelling*) unterwegs, mit dem Auto/Bus *etc* fahren; **roadblock** *n* Straßensperre *f*; **roadmap** *n* Straßenkarte *f*; **road rage** *n* aggressives Verhalten im Straßenverkehr; **roadside** *n*: **at** (*o by*) **the ~** am Straßenrand; **roadsign** *n* Verkehrsschild *nt*; **road tax** *n* Kraftfahrzeugsteuer *f*; **roadworks** *npl* Bauarbeiten *pl*; **roadworthy** *adj* fahrtüchtig
roar [rɔː°] *n* (*of person, lion*) Brüllen *nt*; (*von Verkehr*) Donnern *nt* ▷ *vi* (*person, lion*) brüllen (*with vor +dat*)
roast [rəʊst] *n* Braten *m* ▷ *adj*: **~ beef** Rinderbraten *m*; **~ chicken** Brathähnchen *nt*; **~ pork** Schweinebraten *m*; **~ potatoes** *pl* im Backofen gebratene Kartoffeln ▷ *vt* (*meat*) braten
rob [rɒb] *vt* bestehlen; (*bank, shop*) ausrauben; **robber** *n* Räuber(in) *m(f)*; **robbery** *n* Raub *m*
robe [rəʊb] *n* (*US: dressing gown*) Morgenrock *m*; (*of judge, priest etc*) Robe *f*, Talar *m*
robin ['rɒbɪn] *n* Rotkehlchen *nt*
robot ['rəʊbɒt] *n* Roboter *m*
robust [rəʊ'bʌst] *adj* robust; (*defence*) stark
rock [rɒk] *n* (*substance*) Stein *m*; (*boulder*) Felsbrocken *m*; (*Mus*) Rock *m*; **stick of ~** (*Brit*) Zuckerstange *f*; **on the ~s** (*drink*)

r

mit Eis; (*marriage*) gescheitert
▷ *vt, vi* (*swing*) schaukeln; (*dance*)
rocken; **rock climbing** *n* Klettern
nt; **to go ~** klettern gehen
rocket ['rɒkɪt] *n* Rakete *f;* (*in salad*) Rucola *m*
rocking chair ['rɒkɪŋtʃeə°] *n*
Schaukelstuhl *m*
rocky ['rɒkɪ] *adj* (*landscape*) felsig;
(*path*) steinig
rod [rɒd] *n* (*bar*) Stange *f;* (*fishing ~*) Rute *f*
rode [rəʊd] *pt of* **ride**
rogue [rəʊg] *n* Schurke *m,*
Gauner *m*
role [rəʊl] *n* Rolle *f;* **role model** *n*
Vorbild *nt*
roll [rəʊl] *n* (*of film, paper etc*)
Rolle *f;* (*bread ~*) Brötchen *nt* ▷ *vt*
(*move by ~ing*) rollen; (*cigarette*)
drehen ▷ *vi* (*move by ~ing*) rollen;
(*ship*) schlingern; (*camera*) laufen;
roll out *vt* (*pastry*) ausrollen; **roll
over** *vi* (*person*) sich umdrehen;
roll up *vi* (*fam: arrive*) antanzen
▷ *vt* (*carpet*) aufrollen; **to roll
one's sleeves up** die Ärmel
hochkrempeln
roller [rəʊlə] *n* (*hair ~*) (Locken)wickler *m;*
Rollerblades® *npl* Inlineskates
pl; **rollerblading** *n* Inlineskaten
nt; **roller coaster** *n* Achterbahn *f;*
roller skates *npl* Rollschuhe *pl;*
roller-skating *n* Rollschuhlaufen
nt; **rolling pin** *n* Nudelholz *nt;*
roll-on (deodorant) *n* Deoroller
m
ROM [rɒm] *acr* = **read only
memory** ROM *m*
Roman ['rəʊmən] *adj* römisch
▷ *n* Römer(in) *m(f);* **Roman
Catholic** *adj* römisch-katholisch
▷ *n* Katholik(in) *m(f)*
romance [rəʊ'mæns] *n* Romantik *f;* (*love affair*) Romanze *f*
Romania [rəʊ'meɪnɪə] *n*
Rumänien *nt;* **Romanian** *adj*

rumänisch ▷ *n* Rumäne *m,*
Rumänin *f;* (*language*) Rumänisch
nt
romantic [rəʊ'mæntɪk] *adj*
romantisch
roof [ruːf] *n* Dach *nt;* **roof rack** *n*
Dachgepäckträger *m*
rook [rʊk] *n* (*in chess*) Turm *m*
room [ruːm] *n* Zimmer *nt,* Raum
m; (*large, for gatherings etc*) Saal *m;*
(*space*) Platz *m;* (*fig*) Spielraum *m;*
to make ~ for Platz machen für;
roommate *n* Zimmergenosse *m,*
Zimmergenossin *f;*
Mitbewohner(in) *m(f);* **room
service** *n* Zimmerservice *m;*
roomy *adj* geräumig; (*garment*)
weit
root [ruːt] *n* Wurzel *f;* **root out** *vt*
(*eradicate*) ausrotten; **root
vegetable** *n* Wurzelgemüse *nt*
rope [rəʊp] *n* Seil *nt;* **to know
the ~s** (*fam*) sich auskennen
rose [rəʊz] *pt of* **rise** ▷ *n* Rose *f*
rosé ['rəʊzeɪ] *n* Rosé(wein) *m*
rot [rɒt] *vi* verfaulen
rota ['rəʊtə] *n* (*Brit*) Dienstplan *m*
rotate [rəʊ'teɪt] *vt* (*turn*) rotieren
lassen ▷ *vi* rotieren; **rotation**
[rəʊ'teɪʃən] *n* (*turning*) Rotation *f;*
in ~ abwechselnd
rotten ['rɒtn] *adj* (*decayed*) faul;
(*mean*) gemein; (*unpleasant*)
scheußlich; (*ill*) elend
rough [rʌf] *adj* (*not smooth*) rau;
(*path*) uneben; (*coarse, violent*)
grob; (*crossing*) stürmisch; (*without
comforts*) hart; (*unfinished,
makeshift*) grob; (*approximate*)
ungefähr; **~ draft** Rohentwurf *m;* **I
have a ~ idea** ich habe eine
ungefähre Vorstellung ▷ *adv:* **to
sleep ~** im Freien schlafen ▷ *vt:*
to ~ it primitiv leben ▷ *n:* **to
write sth in ~** etw ins Unreine
schreiben; **roughly** *adv* grob;
(*approximately*) ungefähr

round [raʊnd] *adj* rund ▷ *adv*: **all ~** (*on all sides*) rundherum; **the long way ~** der längere Weg; **I'll be ~ at 8** ich werde um acht Uhr da sein; **the other way ~** umgekehrt ▷ *prep* (*surrounding*) um (... herum); **~** (**about**) (*approximately*) ungefähr; **~ the corner** um die Ecke; **to go ~ the world** um die Welt reisen; **she lives ~ here** sie wohnt hier in der Gegend ▷ *n* Runde *f*; (*of bread, toast*) Scheibe *f*; **it's my ~** (*of drinks*) die Runde geht auf mich ▷ *vt* (*corner*) biegen um; **round off** *vt* abrunden; **round up** *vt* (*number, price*) aufrunden

roundabout *n* (*Brit Auto*) Kreisverkehr *m*; (*Brit: merry-go-round*) Karussell *nt* ▷ *adj* umständlich; **round-the-clock** *adj* rund um die Uhr; **round trip** *n* Rundreise *f*; **round-trip ticket** *n* (*US*) Rückfahrkarte *f*; (*for plane*) Rückflugticket *nt*

rouse [raʊz] *vt* (*from sleep*) wecken

route [ruːt] *n* Route *f*; (*bus, plane etc service*) Linie *f*; (*fig*) Weg *m*

routine [ruːˈtiːn] *n* Routine *f* ▷ *adj* Routine-

row [rəʊ] *n* (*line*) Reihe *f*; **three times in a ~** dreimal hintereinander ▷ *vt, vi* (*boat*) rudern ▷ [raʊ] *n* (*noise*) Krach *m*; (*dispute*) Streit *m*

rowboat [ˈrəʊbəʊt] *n* (*US*) Ruderboot *nt*

row house [ˈrəʊhaʊs] *n* (*US*) Reihenhaus *nt*

rowing [ˈrəʊɪŋ] *n* Rudern *nt*; **rowing boat** *n* (*Brit*) Ruderboot *nt*; **rowing machine** *n* Rudergerät *nt*

royal [ˈrɔɪəl] *adj* königlich; **royalty** *n* (*family*) Mitglieder *pl* der königlichen Familie; **royalties** *pl* (*from book, music*) Tantiemen *pl*

RSPCA *abbr* = **Royal Society for the Prevention of Cruelty to Animals** britischer Tierschutzverein

RSPCC *abbr* = **Royal Society for the Prevention of Cruelty to Children** britischer Kinderschutzverein

RSVP *abbr* = **répondez s'il vous plaît** u. A. w. g.

rub [rʌb] *vt* reiben; **rub in** *vt* einmassieren; **rub out** *vt* (*with eraser*) ausradieren

rubber [ˈrʌbə°] *n* Gummi *m*; (*Brit: eraser*) Radiergummi *m*; (*US fam: contraceptive*) Gummi *m*; **rubber band** *n* Gummiband *nt*; **rubber stamp** *n* Stempel *m*

rubbish [ˈrʌbɪʃ] *n* Abfall *m*; (*nonsense*) Quatsch *m*; (*poor-quality thing*) Mist *m*; **don't talk ~** red keinen Unsinn!; **rubbish bin** *n* Mülleimer *m*; **rubbish dump** *n* Müllabladeplatz *m*

rubble [ˈrʌbl] *n* Schutt *m*

ruby [ˈruːbɪ] *n* (*stone*) Rubin *m*

rucksack [ˈrʌksæk] *n* Rucksack *m*

rude [ruːd] *adj* (*impolite*) unhöflich; (*indecent*) unanständig

rug [rʌg] *n* Teppich *m*; (*next to bed*) Bettvorleger *m*; (*for knees*) Wolldecke *f*

rugby [ˈrʌgbɪ] *n* Rugby *nt*

rugged [ˈrʌgɪd] *adj* (*coastline*) zerklüftet; (*features*) markant

ruin [ˈruːɪn] *n* Ruine *f*; (*financial, social*) Ruin *m* ▷ *vt* ruinieren

rule [ruːl] *n* Regel *f*; (*governing*) Herrschaft *f*; **as a ~** in der Regel ▷ *vt, vi* (*govern*) regieren; (*decide*) entscheiden; **ruler** *n* Lineal *nt*; (*person*) Herrscher(in) *m(f)*

rum [rʌm] *n* Rum *m*

rumble [ˈrʌmbl] *vi* (*stomach*) knurren; (*train, truck*) rumpeln

rummage [ˈrʌmɪdʒ] *vi*: **~** (**around**) herumstöbern

r

rumor *(US)*, **rumour** ['ruːmə°] *n* Gerücht *nt*

run [rʌn] **(ran, run)** *vt (race, distance)* laufen; *(machine, engine, computer program, water)* laufen lassen; *(manage)* leiten, führen; *(car)* unterhalten; **I ran her home** ich habe sie nach Hause gefahren ▷ *vi (move quickly)* rennen; *(bus, train)* fahren; *(path etc)* verlaufen; *(machine, engine, computer program)* laufen; *(flow)* fließen; *(colours, make-up)* verlaufen; **to ~ for President** für die Präsidentschaft kandidieren; **to be ~ning low** knapp werden; **my nose is ~ning** mir läuft die Nase; **it ~s in the family** es liegt in der Familie ▷ *n (on foot)* Lauf *m*; *(in car)* Spazierfahrt *f*; *(series)* Reihe *f*; *(sudden demand)* Ansturm *m (on auf +akk)*; *(in tights)* Laufmasche *f*; *(in cricket, baseball)* Lauf *m*; **to go for a ~** laufen gehen; *(in car)* eine Spazierfahrt machen; **in the long ~** auf die Dauer; **on the ~** auf der Flucht *(from vor +dat)*; **run about** *vi* herumlaufen; **run away** *vi* weglaufen; **run down** *vt (with car)* umfahren; *(criticize)* heruntermachen; **to be ~** *(tired)* abgespannt sein; **run into** *vt (meet)* zufällig treffen; *(problem)* stoßen auf +akk; **run off** *vi* weglaufen; **run out** *vi (person)* hinausrennen; *(liquid)* auslaufen; *(lease, time)* ablaufen; *(money, supplies)* ausgehen; **he ran ~ of money** ihm ging das Geld aus; **run over** *vt (with car)* überfahren; **run up** *vt (debt, bill)* machen

rung [rʌŋ] *pp of* **ring**

runner ['rʌnə°] *n (athlete)* Läufer(in) *m(f)*; **to do a ~** *(fam)* wegrennen; **runner bean** *n (Brit)* Stangenbohne *f*

running ['rʌnɪŋ] *n (Sport)* Laufen *nt*; *(management)* Leitung *f*, Führung *f* ▷ *adj (water)* fließend; **~ costs** Betriebskosten *pl*; *(for car)* Unterhaltskosten *pl*; **3 days ~** 3 Tage hintereinander

runny ['rʌnɪ] *adj (food)* flüssig; *(nose)* laufend

runway ['rʌnweɪ] *n* Start- und Landebahn *f*

rural ['rʊərəl] *adj* ländlich

rush [rʌʃ] *n* Eile *f*; *(for tickets etc)* Ansturm *m (for auf +akk)*; **to be in a ~** es eilig haben; **there's no ~** es eilt nicht ▷ *vt (do too quickly)* hastig machen; *(meal)* hastig essen; **to ~ sb to hospital** jdn auf dem schnellsten Weg ins Krankenhaus bringen; **don't ~ me** dräng mich nicht ▷ *vi (hurry)* eilen; **don't ~** lass dir Zeit; **rush hour** *n* Hauptverkehrszeit *f*

rusk [rʌsk] *n* Zwieback *m*

Russia ['rʌʃə] *n* Russland *nt*; **Russian** *adj* russisch ▷ *n* Russe *m*, Russin *f*; *(language)* Russisch *nt*

rust [rʌst] *n* Rost *m* ▷ *vi* rosten; **rustproof** ['rʌstpruːf] *adj* rostfrei; **rusty** ['rʌstɪ] *adj* rostig

ruthless ['ruːθləs] *adj* rücksichtslos; *(treatment, criticism)* schonungslos

rye [raɪ] *n* Roggen *m*; **rye bread** *n* Roggenbrot *nt*

S

S *abbr* = **south** S

sabotage ['sæbətɑːʒ] *vt* sabotieren

sachet ['sæʃeɪ] *n* Päckchen *nt*

sack [sæk] *n* (*bag*) Sack *m*; **to get the ~** (*fam*) rausgeschmissen werden ▷ *vt* (*fam*) rausschmeißen

sacred ['seɪkrɪd] *adj* heilig

sacrifice ['sækrɪfaɪs] *n* Opfer *nt* ▷ *vt* opfern

sad [sæd] *adj* traurig

saddle ['sædl] *n* Sattel *m*

sadistic [sə'dɪstɪk] *adj* sadistisch

sadly ['sædlɪ] *adv* (*unfortunately*) leider

safari [sə'fɑːrɪ] *n* Safari

safe [seɪf] *adj* (*free from danger*) sicher; (*out of danger*) in Sicherheit; (*careful*) vorsichtig; **have a ~ journey** gute Fahrt! ▷ *n* Safe *m*; **safeguard** *n* Schutz *m* ▷ *vt* schützen (*against* vor +*dat*); **safely** *adv* sicher; (*arrive*) wohlbehalten;

(*drive*) vorsichtig; **safety** *n* Sicherheit *f*; **safety belt** *n* Sicherheitsgurt *m*; **safety pin** *n* Sicherheitsnadel *f*

Sagittarius [sædʒɪ'tɛərɪəs] *n* (*Astr*) Schütze *m*

Sahara [sə'hɑːrə] *n*: **the ~** (**Desert**) die (Wüste) Sahara

said [sed] *pt, pp of* **say**

sail [seɪl] *n* Segel *nt*; **to set ~** losfahren (*for* nach) ▷ *vi* (*in yacht*) segeln; (*on ship*) mit dem Schiff fahren; (*ship*) auslaufen (*for* nach) ▷ *vt* (*yacht*) segeln mit; (*ship*) steuern; **sailboat** *n* (*US*) Segelboot *nt*; **sailing** *n*: **to go ~** segeln gehen; **sailing boat** *n* (*Brit*) Segelboot *nt*; **sailor** *n* Seemann *m*; (*in navy*) Matrose *m*

saint [seɪnt] *n* Heilige(r) *mf*

sake [seɪk] *n*: **for the ~ of** um +*gen* ... willen; **for your ~** deinetwegen, dir zuliebe

salad ['sæləd] *n* Salat *m*; **salad cream** *n* (*Brit*) *majonäseartige Salatsoße*; **salad dressing** *n* Salatsoße *f*

salary ['sælərɪ] *n* Gehalt *nt*

sale [seɪl] *n* Verkauf *m*; (*at reduced prices*) Ausverkauf *m*; **the ~s** *pl* (*in summer, winter*) der Schlussverkauf; **for ~** zu verkaufen; **sales clerk** *n* (*US*) Verkäufer(in) *m(f)*; **salesman** (*pl* **-men**) *n* Verkäufer *m*; (*rep*) Vertreter *m*; **sales rep** *n* Vertreter(in) *m(f)*; **sales tax** *n* (*US*) Verkaufssteuer *f*; **saleswoman** (*pl* **-women**) *n* Verkäuferin *f*; (*rep*) Vertreterin *f*

salmon ['sæmən] *n* Lachs *m*

saloon [sə'luːn] *n* (*ship's lounge*) Salon *m*; (*US: bar*) Kneipe *f*

salt [sɔːlt] *n* Salz *nt* ▷ *vt* (*flavour*) salzen; (*roads*) mit Salz streuen; **salt cellar**, **salt shaker** (*US*) *n* Salzstreuer *m*; **salty** *adj* salzig

salvage ['sælvɪdʒ] *vt* bergen (*from* aus); (*fig*) retten

same [seɪm] *adj*: **the ~** (*similar*) der/die/das gleiche, die gleichen *pl*; (*identical*) der-/die-/dasselbe, dieselben *pl*; **they live in the ~ house** sie wohnen im selben Haus ▷ *pron*: **the ~** (*similar*) der/die/das Gleiche, die Gleichen *pl*; (*identical*) der-/die-/dasselbe, dieselben *pl*; **all the ~** trotzdem; **the ~ to you** gleichfalls; **it's all the ~ to me** es ist mir egal ▷ *adv*: **the ~** gleich; **they look the ~** sie sehen gleich aus

sample ['sɑːmpl] *n* Probe *f*; (*of fabric*) Muster *nt* ▷ *vt* probieren

sanctions ['sæŋkʃənz] *npl* (*Pol*) Sanktionen *pl*

sanctuary ['sæŋktjʊərɪ] *n* (*refuge*) Zuflucht *f*; (*for animals*) Schutzgebiet *nt*

sand [sænd] *n* Sand *m*

sandal ['sændl] *n* Sandale *f*

sandpaper *n* Sandpapier *nt* ▷ *vt* schmirgeln

sandwich ['sænwɪdʒ] *n* Sandwich *nt*

sandy ['sændɪ] *adj* (*full of sand*) sandig; **~ beach** Sandstrand *m*

sane [seɪn] *adj* geistig gesund, normal; (*sensible*) vernünftig

sang [sæŋ] *pt of* **sing**

sanitary ['sænɪtərɪ] *adj* hygienisch; **sanitary napkin** (*US*), **sanitary towel** *n* Damenbinde *f*

sank [sæŋk] *pt of* **sink**

Santa (Claus) ['sæntə('klɔːz)] *n* der Weihnachtsmann

sarcastic [sɑːˈkæstɪk] *adj* sarkastisch

sardine [sɑːˈdiːn] *n* Sardine *f*

Sardinia [sɑːˈdɪnɪə] *n* Sardinien *nt*

sari [sɑːrɪ] *n* Sari *m* (*von indischen Frauen getragenes Gewand*)

sat [sæt] *pt, pp of* **sit**

Sat *abbr* = **Saturday** Sa.

satellite ['sætəlaɪt] *n* Satellit *m*; **satellite dish** *n* Satellitenschüssel *f*; **satellite TV** *n* Satellitenfernsehen *nt*

satin ['sætɪn] *n* Satin *m*

satisfaction [sætɪsˈfækʃən] *n* (*contentment*) Zufriedenheit *f*; **is that to your ~?** bist du/sind Sie damit zufrieden?; **satisfactory** [sætɪsˈfæktərɪ] *adj* zufriedenstellend; **satisfied** ['sætɪsfaɪd] *adj* zufrieden (*with* mit); **satisfy** ['sætɪsfaɪ] *vt* zufriedenstellen; (*convince*) überzeugen; (*conditions*) erfüllen; (*need, demand*) befriedigen; **satisfying** *adj* befriedigend

Saturday ['sætədeɪ] *n* Samstag *m*, Sonnabend *m*; *see also* **Tuesday**

sauce [sɔːs] *n* Soße *f*; **saucepan** *n* Kochtopf *m*; **saucer** *n* Untertasse *f*

saucy ['sɔːsɪ] *adj* frech

Saudi Arabia ['saʊdɪəˈreɪbɪə] *n* Saudi-Arabien *nt*

sauna ['sɔːnə] *n* Sauna *f*

sausage ['sɒsɪdʒ] *n* Wurst *f*; **sausage roll** *n* mit Wurst gefülltes Blätterteigröllchen

savage ['sævɪdʒ] *adj* (*person, attack*) brutal; (*animal*) wild

save [seɪv] *vt* (*rescue*) retten (*from* vor +dat); (*money, time, electricity etc*) sparen; (*strength*) schonen; (*Inform*) speichern; **to ~ sb's life** jdm das Leben retten ▷ *vi* sparen ▷ *n* (*in football*) Parade *f*; **save up** *vi* sparen (*for* auf +akk); **saving** *n* (*of money*) Sparen *nt*; **~s** *pl* Ersparnisse *pl*; **~s account** Sparkonto *nt*

savory (*US*), **savoury** ['seɪvərɪ] *adj* (*not sweet*) pikant

saw [sɔː] (**sawed, sawn**) *vt, vi* sägen ▷ *n* (*tool*) Säge *f* ▷ *pt of* **see**; **sawdust** *n* Sägemehl *nt*

saxophone ['sæksəfəʊn] n
Saxophon nt

say [seɪ] (**said, said**) vt sagen (to
sb jdm); (prayer) sprechen; **what
does the letter ~?** was steht im
Brief?; **the rules ~ that ...** in den
Regeln heißt es, dass ...; **he's said
to be rich** er soll reich sein ▷ n: **to
have a ~ in sth** bei etw ein
Mitspracherecht haben ▷ adv
zum Beispiel; **saying** n
Sprichwort nt

scab [skæb] n (on cut) Schorf m

scaffolding ['skæfəʊldɪŋ] n
(Bau)gerüst nt

scale [skeɪl] n (of map etc)
Maßstab m; (on thermometer etc)
Skala f; (of pay) Tarifsystem nt;
(Mus) Tonleiter f; (of fish, snake)
Schuppe f; **to ~** maßstabsgerecht;
on a large/small ~ in
großem/kleinem Umfang; **scales**
npl (for weighing) Waage f

scalp [skælp] n Kopfhaut f

scan [skæn] vt (examine) genau
prüfen; (read quickly) überfliegen;
(Inform) scannen ▷ n (Med)
Ultraschall m; **scan in** vt (Inform)
einscannen

scandal ['skændl] n Skandal m;
scandalous adj skandalös

Scandinavia [skændɪ'neɪvɪə] n
Skandinavien nt; **Scandinavian**
adj skandinavisch ▷ n Skandi-
navier(in) m(f)

scanner ['skænə*] n Scanner m

scapegoat ['skeɪpgəʊt] n
Sündenbock m

scar [skɑː*] n Narbe f

scarce ['skɛəs] adj selten; (in
short supply) knapp; **scarcely** adv
kaum

scare ['skɛə*] n (general alarm)
Panik f ▷ vt erschrecken; **to be ~d**
Angst haben (of vor +dat)

scarf [skɑːf] n (pl **-scarves**) n Schal
m; (on head) Kopftuch nt

scarlet ['skɑːlət] adj schar-
lachrot; **scarlet fever** n Scharlach
m

scary ['skɛərɪ] adj (film, story)
gruselig

scatter ['skætə*] vt verstreuen;
(seed, gravel) streuen; (disperse)
auseinandertreiben

scene [siːn] n (location) Ort m;
(division of play) (Theat) Szene f;
(view) Anblick m; **to make a ~** eine
Szene machen; **scenery** ['siːnərɪ]
n (landscape) Landschaft f; (Theat)
Kulissen pl; **scenic** ['siːnɪk] adj
(landscape) malerisch; **~ route**
landschaftlich schöne Strecke

scent [sent] n (perfume) Parfüm
nt; (smell) Duft m

sceptical ['skeptɪkəl] adj (Brit)
skeptisch

schedule ['ʃedjuːl, 'skedʒʊəl] n
(plan) Programm nt; (of work)
Zeitplan m; (list) Liste f; (US: of
trains, buses, air traffic)
Fahr-, Flugplan m; **on
~** planmäßig; **to be behind ~ with
sth** mit etw in Verzug sein ▷ vt:
**the meeting is ~d for next
Monday** die Besprechung ist für
nächsten Montag angesetzt;
scheduled adj (departure, arrival)
planmäßig; **~ flight** Linienflug m

scheme [skiːm] n (plan) Plan m;
(project) Projekt nt; (dishonest)
Intrige f ▷ vi intrigieren

schizophrenic [skɪtsə'frenɪk]
adj schizophren

scholar ['skɒlə*] n Gelehrte(r)
mf; **scholarship** n (grant)
Stipendium nt

school [skuːl] n Schule f;
(university department) Fachbereich
m; (US: university) Universität f;
school bag n Schultasche f;
schoolbook n Schulbuch nt;
schoolboy n Schüler m; **school
bus** n Schulbus m; **schoolgirl** n

Schülerin f; **schoolteacher** n
Lehrer(in) m(f); **schoolwork** n
Schularbeiten pl
sciatica [saɪˈætɪkə] n Ischias m
science [ˈsaɪəns] n Wissenschaft
f; (natural ~) Naturwissenschaft f;
science fiction n Sciencefiction
f; **scientific** [saɪənˈtɪfɪk] adj
wissenschaftlich; **scientist**
[ˈsaɪəntɪst] n Wissenschaftler(in)
m(f); (in natural sciences)
Naturwissenschaftler(in) m(f)
scissors [ˈsɪzəz] npl Schere f
scone [skɒn] n kleines süßes
Hefebrötchen mit oder ohne Rosinen,
das mit Butter oder Dickrahm und
Marmelade gegessen wird
scoop [skuːp] n (exclusive story)
Exklusivbericht m; **a ~ of
ice-cream** eine Kugel Eis ▷ vt: **to
~ (up)** schaufeln
scooter [ˈskuːtə*] n (Motor)-
roller m; (toy) (Tret)roller m
scope [skəup] n Umfang m;
(opportunity) Möglichkeit f
score [skɔː*] n (Sport) Spielstand
m; (final result) Spielergebnis nt; (in
quiz etc) Punktestand m; (Mus)
Partitur f; **to keep (the)
~** mitzählen ▷ vt (goal) schießen;
(points) punkten ▷ vi (keep ~)
mitzählen; **scoreboard** n
Anzeigetafel f
scorn [ˈskɔːn] n Verachtung f;
scornful adj verächtlich
Scorpio [ˈskɔːpɪəu] (pl -**s**) n (Astr)
Skorpion m
scorpion [ˈskɔːpɪən] n Skorpion
m
Scot [skɒt] n Schotte m, Schottin
f; **Scotch** [skɒtʃ] n (whisky)
schottischer Whisky, Scotch m
Scotch tape® n (US) Tesafilm®
m
Scotland [ˈskɒtlənd] n Schottland nt; **Scotsman** (pl -**men**) n
Schotte m; **Scotswoman** (pl

-**women**) n Schottin f; **Scottish**
adj schottisch
scout [skaut] n (boy ~) Pfadfinder
m
scowl [skaul] vi finster blicken
scrambled eggs npl Rührei nt
scrap [skræp] n (bit) Stückchen
nt, Fetzen m; (metal) Schrott m ▷ vt
(car) verschrotten; (plan)
verwerfen; **scrapbook** n
Sammelalbum nt
scrape [skreɪp] n (scratch)
Kratzer m ▷ vt (car) schrammen;
(wall) streifen; **to ~ one's knee**
sich das Knie schürfen; **scrape
through** vi (exam) mit knapper
Not bestehen
scrap heap [ˈskræphiːp] n
Schrotthaufen m; **scrap metal** n
Schrott m; **scrap paper** n
Schmierpapier nt
scratch [ˈskrætʃ] n (mark) Kratzer
m; **to start from ~** von vorne
anfangen ▷ vt kratzen; (car)
zerkratzen; **to ~ one's arm** sich
am Arm kratzen ▷ vi kratzen;
(~ oneself) sich kratzen
scream [skriːm] n Schrei m ▷ vi
schreien (with vor +dat); **to ~ at sb**
jdn anschreien
screen [skriːn] n (TV, Inform)
Bildschirm m; (Cine) Leinwand f
▷ vt (protect) abschirmen; (hide)
verdecken; (film) zeigen;
(applicants, luggage) überprüfen;
screenplay n Drehbuch nt;
screensaver n (Inform)
Bildschirmschoner m
screw [skruː] n Schraube f ▷ vt
(vulg: have sex with) ficken; **to ~ sth
to sth** etw an etw akk schrauben;
to ~ off/on (lid)
ab-/aufschrauben; **screw up** vt
(paper) zusammenknüllen; (make a
mess of) vermasseln; **screwdriver**
n Schraubenzieher m; **screw top**
n Schraubverschluss m

scribble ['skrɪbl] *vt, vi* kritzeln

script [skrɪpt] *n* (*of play*) Text *m*; (*of film*) Drehbuch *nt*; (*style of writing*) Schrift *f*

scroll down ['skrəʊl'daʊn] *vi* (*Inform*) runterscrollen; **scroll up** *vi* (*Inform*) raufscrollen; **scroll bar** *n* (*Inform*) Scrollbar *f*

scrub [skrʌb] *vt* schrubben; **scrubbing brush, scrub brush** (*US*) *n* Scheuerbürste *f*

scruffy ['skrʌfɪ] *adj* vergammelt

scrupulous, scrupulously ['skruːpjʊləs, -lɪ] *adj, adv* gewissenhaft; (*painstaking*) peinlich genau

scuba-diving ['skuːbədaɪvɪŋ] *n* Sporttauchen *nt*

sculptor ['skʌlptə*] *n* Bildhauer(in) *m(f)*; **sculpture** ['skʌlptʃə*] *n* (*Art*) Bildhauerei *f*; (*statue*) Skulptur *f*

sea [siː] *n* Meer *nt*, See *f*; **seafood** *n* Meeresfrüchte *pl*; **sea front** *n* Strandpromenade *f*; **seagull** *n* Möwe *f*

seal [siːl] *n* (*animal*) Robbe *f*; (*stamp, impression*) Siegel *nt*; (*Tech*) Verschluss *m*; (*ring etc*) Dichtung *f* ▷ *vt* versiegeln; (*envelope*) zukleben

seam [siːm] *n* Naht *f*

search [sɜːtʃ] *n* Suche *f* (*for* nach); **to do a ~ for** (*Inform*) suchen nach; **in ~ of** auf der Suche nach ▷ *vi* suchen (*for* nach) ▷ *vt* durchsuchen; **search engine** *n* (*Inform*) Suchmaschine *f*

seashell ['siːʃel] *n* Muschel *f*; **seashore** *n* Strand *m*; **seasick** *adj* seekrank; **seaside** n: **at the ~** am Meer; **to go to the ~** ans Meer fahren; **seaside resort** *n* Seebad *nt*

season ['siːzn] *n* Jahreszeit *f*; (*Comm*) Saison *f*; **high/low**

~ Hoch-/Nebensaison *f* ▷ *vt* (*flavour*) würzen

seasoning *n* Gewürz *nt*

season ticket *n* (*Rail*) Zeitkarte *f*; (*Theat*) Abonnement *nt*; (*Sport*) Dauerkarte *f*

seat [siːt] *n* (*place*) Platz *m*; (*chair*) Sitz *m*; **take a ~** setzen Sie sich ▷ *vt*: **the hall ~s 300** der Saal hat 300 Sitzplätze; **please be ~ed** bitte setzen Sie sich; **to remain ~ed** sitzen bleiben; **seat belt** *n* Sicherheitsgurt *m*

sea view ['siːvjuː] *n* Seeblick *m*; **seaweed** *n* Seetang *m*

secluded [sɪ'kluːdɪd] *adj* abgelegen

second ['sekənd] *adj* zweite(r, s); **the ~ of June** der zweite Juni ▷ *adv* (*in ~ position*) an zweiter Stelle; (*secondly*) zweitens; **he came ~** er ist Zweiter geworden ▷ *n* (*of time*) Sekunde *f*; (*moment*) Augenblick *m*; **~ (gear)** der zweite Gang; (*~ helping*) zweite Portion; **just a ~** (einen) Augenblick!; **secondary** *adj* (*less important*) zweitrangig; **~ education** höhere Schulbildung *f*; **~ school** weiterführende Schule; **second-class** *adj* (*ticket*) zweiter Klasse; **~ stamp** *Briefmarke für nicht bevorzugt beförderte Sendungen* ▷ *adv* (*travel*) zweiter Klasse; **second-hand** *adj, adv* gebraucht; (*information*) aus zweiter Hand; **secondly** *adv* zweitens; **second-rate** *adj* (*pej*) zweitklassig

secret ['siːkrət] *n* Geheimnis *nt* ▷ *adj* geheim; (*admirer*) heimlich

secretary ['sekrətrɪ] *n* Sekretär(in) *m(f)*; (*minister*) Minister(in) *m(f)*; **Secretary of State** *n* (*US*) Außenminister(in) *m(f)*; **secretary's office** *n* Sekretariat *nt*

secretive ['siːkrətɪv] adj (person) geheimnistuerisch; **secretly** ['siːkrətlɪ] adv heimlich

sect [sekt] n Sekte f

section ['sekʃən] n (part) Teil m; (of document) Abschnitt m; (department) Abteilung f

secure [sɪ'kjʊəʳ] adj (safe) sicher (from vor +dat); (firmly fixed) fest ▷ vt (make firm) befestigen; (window, door) fest verschließen; **securely** adv fest; (safely) sicher; **security** [sɪ'kjʊərɪtɪ] n Sicherheit f

sedative ['sedətɪv] n Beruhigungsmittel nt

seduce [sɪ'djuːs] vt verführen; **seductive** [sɪ'dʌktɪv] adj verführerisch; (offer) verlockend

see [siː] (**saw, seen**) vt sehen; (understand) verstehen; (check) nachsehen; (accompany) bringen; (visit) besuchen; (talk to) sprechen; **to ~ the doctor** zum Arzt gehen; **to ~ sb home** jdn nach Hause begleiten; **I saw him swimming** ich habe ihn schwimmen sehen; **~ you** tschüs!; **~ you on Friday** bis Freitag! ▷ vi sehen; (understand) verstehen; (check) nachsehen; **(you) ~** siehst du!; **we'll ~** mal sehen; **see about** vt (attend to) sich kümmern um; **see off** vt (say goodbye to) verabschieden; **see out** vt (show out) zur Tür bringen; **see through** vt: **to see sth through** etw zu Ende bringen; **to ~ sb/sth** jdn/etw durchschauen; **see to** vt sich kümmern um; **~ it that ...** sieh zu, dass ...

seed [siːd] n (of plant) Samen m; (in fruit) Kern m; **seedless** adj kernlos

seedy ['siːdɪ] adj zwielichtig

seek [siːk] (**sought, sought**) vt suchen; (fame) streben nach; **to ~ sb's advice** jdn um Rat fragen

seem [siːm] vi scheinen; **he ~s (to be) honest** er scheint ehrlich zu sein; **it ~s to me that ...** es scheint mir, dass ...

seen [siːn] pp of **see**

seesaw ['siːsɔː] n Wippe f

see-through adj durchsichtig

segment ['segmənt] n Teil m

seize [siːz] vt packen; (confiscate) beschlagnahmen; (opportunity, power) ergreifen

seldom ['seldəm] adv selten

select [sɪ'lekt] adj (exclusive) exklusiv ▷ vt auswählen; **selection** [sɪ'lekʃən] n Auswahl f (of an +dat); **selective** adj (choosy) wählerisch

self [self] (pl **selves**) n Selbst nt, Ich nt; **he's his old ~ again** er ist wieder ganz der Alte; **self-adhesive** adj selbstklebend; **self-assured** n selbstsicher; **self-catering** adj für Selbstversorger; **self-centred** adj egozentrisch; **self-confidence** n Selbstbewusstsein nt; **self-confident** adj selbstbewusst; **self-conscious** adj befangen, verklemmt; **self-contained** adj (flat) separat; **self-control** n Selbstbeherrschung f; **self-defence** n Selbstverteidigung f; **self-employed** adj selbstständig; **self-evident** adj offensichtlich

selfish, selfishly ['selfɪʃ, -lɪ] adj, adv egoistisch, selbstsüchtig; **selfless, selflessly** adj, adv selbstlos

self-pity [self'pɪtɪ] n Selbstmitleid nt; **self-portrait** n Selbstporträt nt; **self-respect** n Selbstachtung f; **self-service** n Selbstbedienung f ▷ adj Selbstbedienungs-

sell [sel] (**sold, sold**) vt verkaufen; **to ~ sb sth, to ~ sth to**

sb jdm etw verkaufen; **do you ~ postcards?** haben Sie Postkarten? ▷ *vi* (*product*) sich verkaufen; **sell out** *vt*: **to be sold ~** ausverkauft sein; **sell-by date** *n* Haltbarkeitsdatum *nt*

Sellotape® ['seləteɪp] *n* (*Brit*) Tesafilm® *m*

semester [sɪ'mestə*] *n* Semester *nt*

semi ['semɪ] *n* (*Brit: house*) Doppelhaushälfte *f*; **semicircle** *n* Halbkreis *m*; **semicolon** *n* Semikolon *nt*; **semidetached (house)** *n* (*Brit*) Doppelhaushälfte *f*; **semifinal** *n* Halbfinale *nt*

seminar ['seminɑː*] *n* Seminar *nt*

semiskimmed milk ['semɪskɪmd'mɪlk] *n* Halbfettmilch *f*

senate ['senət] *n* Senat *m*; **senator** *n* Senator(in) *m(f)*

send [send] (**sent, sent**) *vt* schicken; **to ~ sb sth, to ~ sth to sb** jdm etw schicken; **~ her my best wishes** grüße sie von mir; **send away** *vt* wegschicken ▷ *vi*: **to ~ for** anfordern; **send back** *vt* zurückschicken; **send for** *vt* (*person*) holen lassen; (*by post*) anfordern; **send off** *vt* (*by post*) abschicken; **send out** *vt* (*invitations etc*) verschicken ▷ *vi*: **to ~ for sth** etw holen lassen

sender ['sendə*] *n* Absender(in) *m(f)*

senior ['siːnɪə*] *adj* (*older*) älter; (*high-ranking*) höher; (*pupils*) älter; **he is ~ to me** er ist mir übergeordnet ▷ *n*: **he's eight years my ~** er ist acht Jahre älter als ich; **senior citizen** *n* Senior(in) *m(f)*

sensation [sen'seɪʃən] *n* Gefühl *nt*; (*excitement, person, thing*)

Sensation *f*; **sensational** *adj* sensationell

sense [sens] *n* (*faculty, meaning*) Sinn *m*; (*feeling*) Gefühl *nt*; (*understanding*) Verstand *m*; **~ of smell/taste** Geruchs-/ Geschmackssinn *m*; **to have a ~ of humour** Humor haben; **to make ~** (*sentence etc*) einen Sinn ergeben; (*be sensible*) Sinn machen; **in a ~** gewissermaßen ▷ *vt* spüren; **senseless** *adj* (*stupid*) sinnlos

sensible, sensibly ['sensəbl, -blɪ] *adj, adv* vernünftig

sensitive ['sensɪtɪv] *adj* empfindlich (*to* gegen); (*easily hurt*) sensibel; (*subject*) heikel

sensual ['sensjʊəl] *adj* sinnlich

sensuous ['sensjʊəs] *adj* sinnlich

sent [sent] *pt, pp of* **send**

sentence ['sentəns] *n* (*Ling*) Satz *m*; (*Jur*) Strafe *f* ▷ *vt* verurteilen (*to* zu)

sentiment ['sentɪmənt] *n* (*sentimentality*) Sentimentalität *f*; (*opinion*) Ansicht *f*; **sentimental** [sentɪ'mentl] *adj* sentimental

separate ['seprət] *adj* getrennt, separat; (*individual*) einzeln ▷ ['sepəreɪt] *vt* trennen (*from* von); **they are ~d** (*couple*) sie leben getrennt ▷ *vi* sich trennen; **separately** *adv* getrennt; (*singly*) einzeln

September [sep'tembə*] *n* September *m*; **in ~** im September; **on the 2nd of ~** am 2. September; **at the beginning/in the middle/at the end of ~** Anfang/Mitte/Ende September; **last/next ~** letzten/nächsten September

septic ['septɪk] *adj* vereitert

sequel ['siːkwəl] *n* (*to film, book*) Fortsetzung *f* (*to* von)

sequence ['si:kwəns] n (order)
Reihenfolge f
Serbia ['sɜ:bjə] n Serbien nt
sergeant ['sɑ:dʒənt] n Polizei-
meister(in) m(f); (Mil)
Feldwebel(in) m(f)
serial ['sɪərɪəl] n (TV) Serie f; (in
newspaper etc) Fortsetzungsroman
m ▷ adj (Inform) seriell; **~ number**
Seriennummer f
series ['sɪərɪz] nsing Reihe f; (TV,
Radio) Serie f
serious ['sɪərɪəs] adj ernst;
(injury, illness, mistake) schwer;
(discussion) ernsthaft; **are you ~?**
ist das dein Ernst?; **seriously** adv
ernsthaft; (hurt) schwer; **~?** im
Ernst?; **to take sb ~** jdn ernst
nehmen
sermon ['sɜ:mən] n (Rel) Predigt f
servant ['sɜ:vənt] n Diener(in)
m(f); **serve** [sɜ:v] vt (customer)
bedienen; (food) servieren; (one's
country etc) dienen +dat; (sentence)
verbüßen; **I'm being ~d** ich werde
schon bedient; **it ~s him right** es
geschieht ihm recht ▷ vi dienen
(as als), aufschlagen ▷ n
Aufschlag m
server n (Inform) Server m
service ['sɜ:vɪs] n (in shop, hotel)
Bedienung f; (activity, amenity)
Dienstleistung f; (set of dishes)
Service nt; (Auto) Inspektion f;
(Tech) Wartung f; (Rel)
Gottesdienst m, Aufschlag m;
train/bus ~ Zug-/Busverbindung
f; **"~ not included"** „Bedienung
nicht inbegriffen" ▷ vt (Auto, Tech)
warten; **service area** n (on
motorway) Raststätte f (mit
Tankstelle); **service charge** n
Bedienung f; **service provider** n
(Inform) Provider m; **service
station** n Tankstelle f
session ['seʃən] n (of court,
assembly) Sitzung f

set [set] (**set, set**) vt (place)
stellen; (lay flat) legen; (arrange)
anordnen; (table) decken; (trap,
record) aufstellen; (time, price)
festsetzen; (watch, alarm) stellen
(for auf +akk); **to ~ sb a task** jdm
eine Aufgabe stellen; **to ~ free**
freilassen; **to ~ a good example**
ein gutes Beispiel geben; **the
novel is ~ in London** der Roman
spielt in London ▷ vi (sun)
untergehen; (become hard) fest
werden; (bone)
zusammenwachsen ▷ n (collection
of things) Satz m; (of cutlery,
furniture) Garnitur f; (group of
people) Kreis m; (Radio, TV) Apparat
m, Satz m; (Theat) Bühnenbild nt;
(Cine) (Film)kulisse f ▷ adj (agreed,
prescribed) festgelegt; (ready)
bereit; **~ meal** Menü nt; **set aside**
vt (money) beiseitelegen; (time)
einplanen; **set off** vi aufbrechen
(for nach) ▷ vt (alarm) auslösen;
(enhance) hervorheben; **set out** vi
aufbrechen (for nach) ▷ vt (chairs,
chesspieces etc) aufstellen; (state)
darlegen; **to ~ to do sth** (intend)
beabsichtigen, etw zu tun; **set up**
vt (firm, organization) gründen;
(stall, tent, camera) aufbauen;
(meeting) vereinbaren ▷ vi: **to ~ as
a doctor** sich als Arzt niederlassen
setback n Rückschlag m
settee [se'ti:] n Sofa nt, Couch f
setting ['setɪŋ] n (of novel, film)
Schauplatz m; (surroundings)
Umgebung f
settle ['setl] vt (bill, debt)
begleichen; (dispute) beilegen;
(question) klären; (stomach)
beruhigen ▷ vi: **to ~ (down)** (feel
at home) sich einleben; (calm down)
sich beruhigen; **settle in** vi (in
place) sich einleben; (in job) sich
eingewöhnen; **settle up** vi
(be)zahlen; **to ~ with sb** mit jdm

abrechnen; **settlement** n (*of bill, debt*) Begleichung f; (*colony*) Siedlung f; **to reach a ~** sich einigen

setup ['setʌp] n (*organization*) Organisation f; (*situation*) Situation f

seven ['sevn] num sieben ▷ n Sieben f; *see also* **eight**; **seventeen** ['sevn'ti:n] num siebzehn ▷ n Siebzehn f; *see also* **eight**; **seventeenth** adj siebzehnte(r, s); *see also* **eighth**; **seventh** ['sevnθ] adj siebte(r, s) ▷ n (*fraction*) Siebtel nt; *see also* **eighth**; **seventieth** ['sevntɪɪθ] adj siebzigste(r, s); *see also* **eighth**; **seventy** ['sevntɪ] num siebzig; **~-one** einundsiebzig ▷ n Siebzig f; **to be in one's seventies** in den Siebzigern sein; *see also* **eight**

several ['sevrəl] adj, pron mehrere

severe [sɪ'vɪə°] adj (*strict*) streng; (*serious*) schwer; (*pain*) stark; (*winter*) hart; **severely** adv (*harshly*) hart; (*seriously*) schwer

sew [səʊ] (**sewed, sewn**) vt, vi nähen

sewage ['su:ɪdʒ] n Abwasser nt; **sewer** ['suə°] n Abwasserkanal m

sewing ['səʊɪŋ] n Nähen nt; **sewing machine** n Nähmaschine f

sewn [səʊn] pp of **sew**

sex [seks] n Sex m; (*gender*) Geschlecht nt; **to have ~** Sex haben (**with** mit); **sexism** ['seksɪzəm] n Sexismus m; **sexist** ['seksɪst] adj sexistisch ▷ n Sexist(in) m(f); **sex life** n Sex(ual)leben nt

sexual ['seksjʊəl] adj sexuell; **~ discrimination/harassment** sexuelle Diskriminierung/ Belästigung; **~ intercourse** Geschlechtsverkehr m; **sexuality**

[seksjʊ'ælɪtɪ] n Sexualität f; **sexually** adv sexuell

sexy ['seksɪ] adj sexy, geil

Seychelles ['seɪʃelz] npl Seychellen pl

shabby ['ʃæbɪ] adj schäbig

shack [ʃæk] n Hütte f

shade [ʃeɪd] n (*shadow*) Schatten m; (*for lamp*) (Lampen)schirm m; (*colour*) Farbton m; **~s** (*US: sunglasses*) Sonnenbrille f ▷ vt (*from sun*) abschirmen; (*in drawing*) schattieren

shadow ['ʃædəʊ] n Schatten m

shady ['ʃeɪdɪ] adj schattig; (*fig*) zwielichtig

shake [ʃeɪk] (**shook, shaken**) vt schütteln; (*shock*) erschüttern; **to ~ hands with sb** jdm die Hand geben; **to ~ one's head** den Kopf schütteln ▷ vi (*tremble*) zittern; (*building, ground*) schwanken; **shake off** vt abschütteln; **shaken** ['ʃeɪkn] pp of **shake**; **shaky** ['ʃeɪkɪ] adj (*trembling*) zittrig; (*table, chair, position*) wackelig; (*weak*) unsicher

shall [ʃæl] (**should**) vb aux werden; (*in questions*) sollen; **I ~ do my best** ich werde mein Bestes tun; **~ I come too?** soll ich mitkommen?; **where ~ we go?** wo gehen wir hin?

shallow ['ʃæləʊ] adj (*a. fig*) seicht; (*person*) oberflächlich

shame [ʃeɪm] n (*feeling of ~*) Scham f; (*disgrace*) Schande f; **what a ~!** wie schade!; **~ on you!** schäm dich/schämen Sie sich!; **it's a ~ that ...** schade, dass ...

shampoo [ʃæm'pu:] n Shampoo nt; **to have a ~ and set** sich die Haare waschen und legen lassen ▷ vt (*hair*) waschen; (*carpet*) schamponieren

shandy ['ʃændɪ] n Radler m, Alsterwasser nt

shan't [ʃɑːnt] contr of **shall not**

s

shape [ʃeɪp] n Form f; (unidentified figure) Gestalt f; **in the ~ of** in Form +gen; **to be in good ~** (healthwise) in guter Verfassung sein; **to take ~** (plan, idea) Gestalt annehmen ▷ vt (clay, person) formen; **-shaped** [ʃeɪpt] suf -förmig; **shapeless** adj formlos

share [ʃeə°] n Anteil +dat (in, of an m); (Fin) Aktie f ▷ vt, vi teilen; **shareholder** n Aktionär(in) m(f)

shark [ʃɑːk] n (Zool) Haifisch m

sharp [ʃɑːp] adj scharf; (pin) spitz; (person) scharfsinnig; (pain) heftig; (increase, fall) abrupt; **C/F ~** (Mus) Cis/Dis nt ▷ adv: **at 2 o'clock ~** Punkt 2 Uhr; **sharpen** vt (knife) schärfen; (pencil) spitzen; **sharpener** n (pencil ~) Spitzer m

shatter [ˈʃætə°] vt zerschmettern; (fig) zerstören ▷ vi zerspringen; **shattered** adj (exhausted) kaputt

shave [ʃeɪv] (shaved, shaved o shaven) vt rasieren ▷ vi sich rasieren ▷ n Rasur f; **that was a close ~** (fig) das war knapp; **shave off** vt: **to shave one's beard off** sich den Bart abrasieren; **shaven** [ˈʃeɪvn] pp of **shave** ▷ adj (head) kahl geschoren; **shaver** n (Elec) Rasierapparat m; **shaving brush** n Rasierpinsel m; **shaving foam** n Rasierschaum m; **shaving tackle** n Rasierzeug nt

shawl [ʃɔːl] n Tuch nt

she [ʃiː] pron sie

shed [ʃed] (shed, shed) n Schuppen m ▷ vt (tears, blood) vergießen; (hair, leaves) verlieren

she'd [ʃiːd] contr of **she had; she would**

sheep [ʃiːp] (pl -) n Schaf nt; **sheepdog** n Schäferhund m; **sheepskin** n Schaffell nt

sheer [ʃɪə°] adj (madness) rein; (steep) steil; **by ~ chance** rein zufällig

sheet [ʃiːt] n (on bed) Betttuch nt; (of paper) Blatt nt; (of metal) Platte f; (of glass) Scheibe f; **a ~ of paper** ein Blatt Papier

shelf [ʃelf] (pl shelves) n Bücherbord nt, Regal nt; **shelves** pl (item of furniture) Regal nt

she'll [ʃiːl] contr of **she will; she shall**

shell [ʃel] n (of egg, nut) Schale f; (sea~) Muschel f ▷ vt (peas, nuts) schälen; **shellfish** n (as food) Meeresfrüchte pl

shelter [ˈʃeltə°] n (protection) Schutz m; (accommodation) Unterkunft f; (bus ~) Wartehäuschen nt ▷ vt schützen (from vor +dat) ▷ vi sich unterstellen; **sheltered** adj (spot) geschützt; (life) behütet

shelve [ʃelv] vt (fig) aufschieben; **shelves** pl of **shelf**

shepherd [ˈʃepəd] n Schäfer m; **shepherd's pie** n Hackfleischauflauf mit Decke aus Kartoffelpüree

sherry [ˈʃerɪ] n Sherry m

she's [ʃiːz] contr of **she is; she has**

shield [ʃiːld] n Schild m; (fig) Schutz m ▷ vt schützen (from vor +dat)

shift [ʃɪft] n (change) Veränderung f; (period at work, workers) Schicht f; (on keyboard) Umschalttaste f ▷ vt (furniture etc) verrücken; (stain) entfernen; **to ~ gear(s)** (US Auto) schalten ▷ vi (move) sich bewegen; (move up) rutschen; **shift key** n Umschalttaste f

shin [ʃɪn] n Schienbein nt

shine [ʃaɪn] (shone, shone) vi (be shiny) glänzen; (sun) scheinen; (lamp) leuchten ▷ vt (polish) polieren ▷ n Glanz m

shingles ['ʃɪŋglz] *nsing* (*Med*) Gürtelrose *f*

shiny ['ʃaɪnɪ] *adj* glänzend

ship [ʃɪp] *n* Schiff *nt* ▷ *vt* (*send*) versenden; (*by ship*) verschiffen; **shipment** *n* (*goods*) Sendung *f*; (*sent by ship*) Ladung *f*; **shipwreck** *n* Schiffbruch *m*; **shipyard** *n* Werft *f*

shirt [ʃɜːt] *n* Hemd *nt*

shit [ʃɪt] *n* (*vulg*) Scheiße *f*; (*person*) Arschloch *nt*; **~!** Scheiße!; **shitty** ['ʃɪtɪ] *adj* (*fam*) beschissen

shiver ['ʃɪvə*] *vi* zittern (*with* vor +*dat*)

shock [ʃɒk] *n* (*mental, emotional*) Schock *m*; **to be in ~** unter Schock stehen; **to get a ~** (*Elec*) einen Schlag bekommen ▷ *vt* schockieren; **shock absorber** *n* Stoßdämpfer *m*; **shocked** *adj* schockiert (*by* über +*akk*); **shocking** *adj* schockierend; (*awful*) furchtbar

shoe [ʃuː] *n* Schuh *m*; **shoehorn** *n* Schuhlöffel *m*; **shoelace** *n* Schnürsenkel *m*; **shoe polish** *n* Schuhcreme *f*

shone [ʃɒn] *pt, pp of* **shine**

shook [ʃʊk] *pt of* **shake**

shoot [ʃuːt] (**shot, shot**) *vt* (*wound*) anschießen; (*kill*) erschießen; (*Cine*) drehen; (*fam: heroin*) drücken ▷ *vi* (*with gun, move quickly*) schießen; **to ~ at sb** auf jdn schießen ▷ *n* (*of plant*) Trieb *m*; **shooting** *n* (*exchange of gunfire*) Schießerei *f*; (*killing*) Erschießung *f*

shop [ʃɒp] *n* Geschäft *nt*, Laden *m* ▷ *vi* einkaufen; **shop assistant** *n* Verkäufer(in) *m(f)*; **shopkeeper** *n* Geschäftsinhaber(in) *m(f)*; **shoplifting** *n* Ladendiebstahl *m*; **shopper** *n* Käufer(in) *m(f)*; **shopping** *n* (*activity*) Einkaufen *nt*; (*goods*) Einkäufe *pl*; **to do the** ~ einkaufen; **to go ~** einkaufen gehen; **shopping bag** *n* Einkaufstasche *f*; **shopping cart** *n* (*US*) Einkaufswagen *m*; **shopping center** (*US*), **shopping centre** *n* Einkaufszentrum *nt*; **shopping list** *n* Einkaufszettel *m*; **shopping trolley** *n* (*Brit*) Einkaufswagen *m*; **shop window** *n* Schaufenster *nt*

shore [ʃɔː*] *n* Ufer *nt*; **on ~** an Land

short [ʃɔːt] *adj* kurz; (*person*) klein; **to be ~ of money** knapp bei Kasse sein; **to be ~ of time** wenig Zeit haben; **~ of breath** kurzatmig; **to cut ~** (*holiday*) abbrechen; **we are two ~** wir haben zwei zu wenig; **it's ~ for ...** das ist die Kurzform von ... ▷ *n* (*drink, Elec*) Kurze(r) *m*; **shortage** *n* Knappheit *f* (*of* an +*dat*); **shortbread** *n* Buttergebäck *nt*; **short circuit** *n* Kurzschluss *m*; **shortcoming** *n* Unzulänglichkeit *f*; (*of person*) Fehler *m*; **shortcut** *n* (*quicker route*) Abkürzung *f*; (*Inform*) Shortcut *m*; **shorten** *vt* kürzen; (*in time*) verkürzen; **shorthand** *n* Stenografie *f*; **shortlist** *n*: **to be on the ~** in der engeren Wahl sein; **short-lived** *adj* kurzlebig; **shortly** *adv* bald; **shorts** *npl* Shorts *pl*; **short-sighted** *adj* (*a. fig*) kurzsichtig; **short-sleeved** *adj* kurzärmelig; **short-stay car park** *n* Kurzzeitparkplatz *m*; **short story** *n* Kurzgeschichte *f*; **short-term** *adj* kurzfristig; **short wave** *n* Kurzwelle *f*

shot [ʃɒt] *pt, pp of* **shoot** ▷ *n* (*from gun, in football*) Schuss *m*; (*Foto, Cine*) Aufnahme *f*; (*injection*) Spritze *f*; (*of alcohol*) Schuss *m*

should [ʃʊd] *pt of* **shall** ▷ *vb aux*: **I ~ go now** ich sollte jetzt gehen; **what ~ I do?** was soll ich tun?; **you ~n't have said that** das hättest du/hätten Sie nicht sagen sollen; **that ~ be enough** das müsste reichen

shoulder [ˈʃəʊldə°] n Schulter f

shouldn't [ˈʃʊdnt] contr of **should not**

should've [ˈʃʊdəv] contr of **should have**

shout [ʃaʊt] n Schrei m; (call) Ruf m ▷ vt rufen; (order) brüllen ▷ vi schreien; **to ~ at** anschreien; **to ~ for help** um Hilfe rufen

shove [ʃʌv] vt (person) schubsen; (car, table etc) schieben ▷ vi (in crowd) drängeln

shovel [ˈʃʌvl] n Schaufel f ▷ vt schaufeln

show [ʃəʊ] (showed, shown) vt zeigen; **to ~ sb sth, to ~ sth to sb** jdm etw zeigen; **to ~ sb in** jdn hereinführen; **to ~ sb out** jdn zur Tür bringen ▷ n (Cine, Theat) Vorstellung f; (TV) Show f; (exhibition) Ausstellung f; **show off** vi (pej) angeben; **show round** vt herumführen; **to show sb round the house/the town** jdm das Haus/die Stadt zeigen; **show up** vi (arrive) auftauchen

shower [ˈʃaʊə°] n Dusche f; (rain) Schauer m; **to have** (o **take**) **a ~** duschen ▷ vi (wash) duschen; **shower gel** n Duschgel nt

showing [ˈʃəʊɪŋ] n (Cine) Vorstellung f

shown [ʃəʊn] pp of **show**

showroom [ˈʃəʊruːm] n Ausstellungsraum m

shrank [ʃræŋk] pt of **shrink**

shred [ʃred] n (of paper, fabric) Fetzen m ▷ vt (in shredder) (im Reißwolf) zerkleinern; **shredder** n (for paper) Reißwolf m

shrimp [ʃrɪmp] n Garnele f

shrink [ʃrɪŋk] (**shrank, shrunk**) vi schrumpfen; (clothes) eingehen

shrivel [ˈʃrɪvl] vi: **to ~ (up)** schrumpfen; (skin) runzlig werden; (plant) welken

Shrove Tuesday [ˈʃrəʊvˈtjuːzdeɪ] n Fastnachtsdienstag m

shrub [ʃrʌb] n Busch m, Strauch m

shrug [ʃrʌg] vt, vi: **to ~ (one's shoulders)** die Achseln zucken

shrunk [ʃrʌŋk] pp of **shrink**

shudder [ˈʃʌdə°] vi schaudern; (ground, building) beben

shuffle [ˈʃʌfl] vt, vi mischen

shut [ʃʌt] (**shut, shut**) vt zumachen, schließen; **~ your face!** (fam) halt den Mund! ▷ vi schließen ▷ adj geschlossen; **we're ~** wir haben geschlossen; **shut down** vt schließen; (computer) ausschalten ▷ vi schließen; (computer) sich ausschalten; **shut in** vt einschließen; **shut out** vt (lock out) aussperren; **to shut oneself out** sich aussperren; **shut up** vt (lock up) abschließen; (silence) zum Schweigen bringen ▷ vi (keep quiet) den Mund halten; **~!** halt den Mund!; **shutter** n (on window) (Fenster)laden m; **shutter release** n Auslöser m; **shutter speed** n Belichtungszeit f

shuttle bus [ˈʃʌtlbʌs] n Shuttlebus m

shuttlecock [ˈʃʌtlkɒk] n Federball m

shuttle service [ˈʃʌtlsɜːvɪs] n Pendelverkehr m

shy [ʃaɪ] adj schüchtern; (animal) scheu

Siberia [saɪˈbɪərɪə] n Sibirien nt

Sicily [ˈsɪsɪlɪ] n Sizilien nt

sick [sɪk] adj krank; (joke) makaber; **to be ~** (Brit: vomit) sich übergeben; **to be off ~** wegen Krankheit fehlen; **I feel ~** mir ist schlecht; **to be ~ of sb/sth** jdn/etw satthaben; **it makes me**

~ (fig) es ekelt mich an; **sickbag** n Spucktüte f; **sick leave** n: **to be on ~** krankgeschrieben sein; **sickness** n Krankheit f; (Brit: nausea) Übelkeit f; **sickness benefit** n (Brit) Krankengeld nt

side [saɪd] n Seite f; (of road) Rand m; (of mountain) Hang m; (Sport) Mannschaft f; **by my ~** neben mir; **~ by ~** nebeneinander ▷ adj (door) Seiten-; **sideboard** n Anrichte f; **sideburns** npl Koteletten pl; **side dish** n Beilage f; **side effect** n Nebenwirkung f; **sidelight** n (Brit Auto) Parklicht nt; **side order** n Beilage f; **side road** n Nebenstraße f; **side street** n Seitenstraße f; **sidewalk** n (US) Bürgersteig m; **sideways** adv seitwärts

sieve [sɪv] n Sieb nt

sift [sɪft] vt (flour etc) sieben

sigh [saɪ] vi seufzen

sight [saɪt] n (power of seeing) Sehvermögen nt; (view, thing seen) Anblick m; **~s** pl (of city etc) Sehenswürdigkeiten pl; **to have bad ~** schlecht sehen; **to lose ~ of** aus den Augen verlieren; **out of ~** außer Sicht; **sightseeing** n: **to go ~** Sehenswürdigkeiten besichtigen; **~ tour** Rundfahrt f

sign [saɪn] n Zeichen nt; (notice, road ~) Schild nt ▷ vt unterschreiben ▷ vi unterschreiben; **to ~ for sth** den Empfang einer Sache gen bestätigen; **to ~ in/out** sich ein-/austragen; **sign on** vi (Brit: register as unemployed) sich arbeitslos melden; **sign up** vi (for course) sich einschreiben; (Mil) sich verpflichten

signal ['sɪɡnl] n Signal nt ▷ vi (car driver) blinken

signature ['sɪɡnətʃə°] n Unterschrift f

significant [sɪɡ'nɪfɪkənt] adj

(important) bedeutend, wichtig; (meaning sth) bedeutsam; **significantly** adv (considerably) bedeutend

sign language ['saɪnlæŋɡwɪdʒ] n Zeichensprache f; **signpost** n Wegweiser m

silence ['saɪləns] n Stille f; (of person) Schweigen nt; **~!** Ruhe! ▷ vt zum Schweigen bringen; **silent** adj still; (taciturn) schweigsam; **she remained ~** sie schwieg

silk [sɪlk] n Seide f ▷ adj Seiden-

silly ['sɪlɪ] adj dumm, albern; **don't do anything ~** mach keine Dummheiten; **the ~ season** das Sommerloch

silver ['sɪlvə°] n Silber nt; (coins) Silbermünzen pl ▷ adj Silber-, silbern; **silver-plated** adj versilbert; **silver wedding** n silberne Hochzeit

SIM card ['sɪm-] n (Tel) SIM-Karte f

similar ['sɪmɪlə°] adj ähnlich (to dat); **similarity** [sɪmɪ'lærɪtɪ] n Ähnlichkeit f (to mit); **similarly** adv (equally) ebenso

simple ['sɪmpl] adj einfach; (unsophisticated) schlicht; **simplify** ['sɪmplɪfaɪ] vt vereinfachen; **simply** adv einfach; (merely) bloß; (dress) schlicht

simulate ['sɪmjʊleɪt] vt simulieren

simultaneous, **simultaneously** [sɪməl'teɪnɪəs, -lɪ] adj, adv gleichzeitig

sin [sɪn] n Sünde f ▷ vi sündigen

since [sɪns] adv seitdem; (in the meantime) inzwischen ▷ prep seit +dat; **ever ~ 1995** schon seit 1995 ▷ conj (time) seit, seitdem; (because) da, weil; **ever ~ I've known her** seit ich sie kenne; **it's ages ~ I've seen him** ich habe ihn seit Langem nicht mehr gesehen

sincere [sɪn'sɪə°] adj aufrichtig;
sincerely adv aufrichtig;
Yours ~ mit freundlichen
Grüßen

sing [sɪŋ] (**sang, sung**) vt, vi
singen

Singapore [sɪŋgə'pɔː°] n Singapur nt

singer ['sɪŋə°] n Sänger(in) m(f)

single ['sɪŋgl] adj (one only)
einzig; (not double) einfach; (bed,
room) Einzel-; (unmarried) ledig;
(Brit: ticket) einfach ▷ n (Brit:
ticket) einfache Fahrkarte; (Mus)
Single f; **a ~ to London, please**
(Brit Rail) einfach nach London,
bitte; **single out** vt (choose)
auswählen; **single-handed**,
single-handedly adv im
Alleingang; **single parent** n
Alleinerziehende(r) mf; **single
supplement** n (for hotel room)
Einzelzimmerzuschlag m

singular ['sɪŋgjʊlə°] n Singular
m

sinister ['sɪnɪstə°] adj
unheimlich

sink [sɪŋk] (**sank, sunk**) vt (ship)
versenken ▷ vi sinken ▷ n
Spülbecken nt; (in bathroom)
Waschbecken nt

sip [sɪp] vt nippen an +dat

sir [sɜː°] n: **yes, ~** ja(, mein Herr);
can I help you, ~? kann ich Ihnen
helfen?; **Sir James** (title) Sir James

sister ['sɪstə°] n Schwester f;
(Brit: nurse) Oberschwester f;
sister-in-law (pl **sisters-in-law**) n
Schwägerin f

sit [sɪt] (**sat, sat**) vi (be sitting)
sitzen; (~ down) sich setzen;
(committee, court) tagen ▷ vt (Brit:
exam) machen; **sit down** vi sich
hinsetzen; **sit up** vi (from lying
position) sich aufsetzen

sitcom ['sɪtkɒm] n Situ-
ationskomödie f

site [saɪt] n Platz m; (building ~)
Baustelle f; (web~) Site f

sitting ['sɪtɪŋ] n (meeting, for
portrait) Sitzung f; **sitting room** n
Wohnzimmer nt

situated ['sɪtjʊeɪtɪd] adj: **to be
~** liegen

situation [sɪtjʊ'eɪʃən] n (circum-
stances) Situation f, Lage f; (job)
Stelle f; **"~s vacant/wanted"** (Brit)
„Stellenangebote/Stellengesuche"

six [sɪks] num sechs ▷ n Sechs f;
see also **eight**; **sixpack** n (of beer
etc) Sechserpack nt; **sixteen**
['sɪks'tiːn] num sechzehn ▷ n
Sechzehn f; see also **eight**;
sixteenth adj sechzehnte(r, s); see
also **eighth**; **sixth** [sɪksθ] adj
sechste(r, s); **~ form** (Brit) ≈
Oberstufe f ▷ n (fraction) Sechstel
nt; see also **eighth**; **sixtieth**
['sɪkstɪɪθ] adj sechzigste(r, s); see
also **eighth**; **sixty** ['sɪkstɪ] num
sechzig; **~-one** einundsechzig ▷ n
Sechzig f; **to be in one's sixties** in
den Sechzigern sein; see also **eight**

size [saɪz] n Größe f; **what ~ are
you?** welche Größe hast du/haben
Sie?; **a ~ too big** eine Nummer zu
groß

sizzle ['sɪzl] vi (Gastr) brutzeln

skate [skeɪt] n Schlittschuh m;
(roller ~) Rollschuh m ▷ vi
Schlittschuh laufen; (roller-~)
Rollschuh laufen; **skateboard** n
Skateboard nt; **skating** n Eislauf
m; (roller-~) Rollschuhlauf m;
skating rink n Eisbahn f; (for
roller-skating) Rollschuhbahn f

skeleton ['skelɪtn] n (a. fig)
Skelett nt

skeptical n (US) see **sceptical**

sketch [sketʃ] n Skizze f; (Theat)
Sketch m ▷ vt skizzieren;
sketchbook n Skizzenbuch nt

ski [skiː] n Ski m ▷ vi Ski laufen;
ski boot n Skistiefel m

skid [skɪd] *vi* (*Auto*) schleudern
skier ['skiːə*] *n* Skiläufer(in) *m(f)*;
skiing *n* Skilaufen *nt*; **to go ~** Ski
laufen gehen; **~ holiday** Skiurlaub
m; **skiing instructor** *n*
Skilehrer(in) *m(f)*
skilful, skilfully ['skɪlfʊl, -fəlɪ]
adj, adv geschickt
ski-lift ['skiːlɪft] *n* Skilift *m*
skill [skɪl] *n* Geschick *nt*; (*acquired
technique*) Fertigkeit *f*; **skilled** *adj*
geschickt (*at, in* in +*dat*); (*worker*)
Fach-; (*work*) fachmännisch
skim [skɪm] *vt*: **to ~ (off)** (*fat etc*)
abschöpfen; **to ~ (through)** (*read*)
überfliegen; **skimmed milk** *n*
Magermilch *f*
skin [skɪn] *n* Haut *f*; (*fur*) Fell *nt*;
(*peel*) Schale *f*; **skin diving** *n*
Sporttauchen *nt*; **skinny** *adj* dünn
skip [skɪp] *vi* hüpfen; (*with rope*)
seilspringen ▷ *vt* (*miss out*)
überspringen; (*meal*) ausfallen
lassen; (*school, lesson*) schwänzen
ski pants ['skiːpænts] *npl*
Skihose *f*; **ski pass** *n* Skipass *m*;
ski pole *n* Skistock *m*; **ski resort**
n Skiort *m*
skirt [skɜːt] *n* Rock *m*
ski run ['skiːrʌn] *n* (Ski)abfahrt
f; **ski stick** *n* Skistock *m*; **ski tow**
n Schlepplift *m*
skittle ['skɪtl] *n* Kegel *m*; **~s**
(*game*) Kegeln *nt*
skive [skaɪv] *vi*: **to ~ (off)** (*Brit*)
(*from school*) schwänzen; (*from
work*) blaumachen
skull [skʌl] *n* Schädel *m*
sky [skaɪ] *n* Himmel *m*;
skydiving *n* Fallschirmspringen
nt; **skylight** *n* Dachfenster *nt*;
skyscraper *n* Wolkenkratzer *m*
slam [slæm] *vt* (*door*) zuschlagen;
slam on *vt*: **to slam the brakes
on** voll auf die Bremse treten
slander ['slɑːndə*] *n* Verleumdung *f* ▷ *vt* verleumden

slang [slæŋ] *n* Slang *m*
slap [slæp] *n* Klaps *m*; (*across face*)
Ohrfeige *f* ▷ *vt* schlagen; **to ~ sb's
face** jdn ohrfeigen
slash [slæʃ] *n* (*punctuation mark*)
Schrägstrich *m* ▷ *vt* (*face, tyre*)
aufschlitzen; (*prices*) stark
herabsetzen
slate [sleɪt] *n* (*rock*) Schiefer *m*;
(*roof ~*) Schieferplatte *f*
slaughter ['slɔːtə*] *vt* (*animals*)
schlachten; (*people*) abschlachten
Slav [slɑːv] *adj* slawisch ▷ *n*
Slawe *m*, Slawin *f*
slave [sleɪv] *n* Sklave *m*, Sklavin *f*;
slave away *vi* schuften;
slave-driver *n* (*fam*)
Sklaventreiber(in) *m(f)*; **slavery**
['sleɪvərɪ] *n* Sklaverei *f*
sleaze [sliːz] *n* (*corruption*)
Korruption *f*; **sleazy** *adj* (*bar,
district*) zwielichtig
sledge ['sledʒ] *n* Schlitten *m*
sleep [sliːp] (**slept, slept**) *vi*
schlafen; **to ~ with sb** mit jdm
schlafen ▷ *n* Schlaf *m*; **to put to
~** (*animal*) einschläfern; **sleep in** *vi*
(*lie in*) ausschlafen; **sleeper** *n*
(*Rail: train*) Schlafwagenzug *m*;
(*carriage*) Schlafwagen *m*; **sleeping
bag** *n* Schlafsack *m*; **sleeping car**
n Schlafwagen *m*; **sleeping pill** *n*
Schlaftablette *f*; **sleepless** *adj*
schlaflos; **sleepover** *n* Übernachtung *f* (*bei Freunden etc*); **sleepy** *adj*
schläfrig; (*place*) verschlafen
sleet [sliːt] *n* Schneeregen *m*
sleeve [sliːv] *n* Ärmel *m*;
sleeveless *adj* ärmellos
sleigh [sleɪ] *n* (Pferde)schlitten *m*
slender ['slendə*] *adj* schlank;
(*fig*) gering
slept [slept] *pt, pp of* **sleep**
slice [slaɪs] *n* Scheibe *f*; (*of cake,
tart, pizza*) Stück *nt* ▷ *vt*: **to ~ (up)**
in Scheiben schneiden; **sliced
bread** *n* geschnittenes Brot

slid [slɪd] *pt, pp of* **slide**
slide [slaɪd] (**slid, slid**) *vt* gleiten
lassen; (*push*) schieben ▷ *vi*
gleiten; (*slip*) rutschen ▷ *n* (*Foto*)
Dia *nt*; (*in playground*) Rutschbahn
f; (*Brit: for hair*) Spange *f*
slight [slaɪt] *adj* leicht; (*problem,
difference*) klein; **not in the ~est**
nicht im Geringsten; **slightly** *adv*
etwas; (*injured*) leicht
slim [slɪm] *adj* (*person*) schlank;
(*book*) dünn; (*chance, hope*) gering
▷ *vi* abnehmen
slime [slaɪm] *n* Schleim *m*; **slimy**
adj schleimig
sling [slɪŋ] (**slung, slung**) *vt*
werfen ▷ *n* (*for arm*) Schlinge *f*
slip [slɪp] *n* (*mistake*)
Flüchtigkeitsfehler *m*; **~ of paper**
Zettel *m* ▷ *vt* (*put*) stecken; **to
~ on/off** (*garment*) an-/ausziehen;
it ~ped my mind ich habe es
vergessen ▷ *vi* (*lose balance*)
(aus)rutschen; **slip away** *vi* (*leave*)
sich wegstehlen; **slipper** *n*
Hausschuh *m*; **slippery** *adj* (*path,
road*) glatt; (*soap, fish*) glitschig;
slip-road *n* (*Brit: onto motorway*)
Auffahrt *f*; (*off motorway*) Ausfahrt *f*
slit [slɪt] (**slit, slit**) *vt*
aufschlitzen ▷ *n* Schlitz *m*
slope [sləʊp] *n* Neigung *f*; (*side of
hill*) Hang *m* ▷ *vi* (*be sloping*)
schräg sein; **sloping** *adj* (*floor,
roof*) schräg
sloppy ['slɒpɪ] *adj* (*careless*)
schlampig; (*sentimental*) rührselig
slot [slɒt] *n* (*opening*) Schlitz *m*;
(*Inform*) Steckplatz *m*; **we have a
~ free at 2** (*free time*) um 2 ist noch
ein Termin frei; **slot machine** *n*
Automat *m*; (*for gambling*)
Spielautomat *m*
Slovak ['sləʊvæk] *adj* slowakisch
▷ *n* (*person*) Slowake *m*, Slowakin *f*;
(*language*) Slowakisch *nt*; **Slovakia**
[sləʊ'vækɪə] *n* Slowakei *f*

Slovene ['sləʊviːn], **Slovenian**
[sləʊ'viːnɪən] *adj* slowenisch ▷ *n*
(*person*) Slowene *m*, Slowenin *f*;
(*language*) Slowenisch *nt*; **Slovenia**
[sləʊ'viːnɪə] *n* Slowenien *nt*
slow [sləʊ] *adj* langsam;
(*business*) flau; **to be ~** (*clock*)
nachgehen; (*stupid*) begriffsstutzig
sein; **slow down** *vi* langsamer
werden; (*when driving/walking*)
langsamer fahren/gehen; **slowly**
adv langsam; **slow motion** *n*: **in
~** in Zeitlupe
slug [slʌg] *n* (*Zool*)
Nacktschnecke *f*
slum [slʌm] *n* Slum *m*
slump [slʌmp] *n* Rückgang *m* (*in
an +dat*) ▷ *vi* (*onto chair etc*) sich
fallen lassen; (*prices*) stürzen
slung [slʌŋ] *pt, pp of* **sling**
slur [slɜː°] *n* (*insult*) Verleumdung
f; **slurred** [slɜːd] *adj* undeutlich
slush [slʌʃ] *n* (*snow*)
Schneematsch *m*
slut [slʌt] *n* (*pej*) Schlampe *f*
smack [smæk] *n* Klaps
m ▷ *vt*: **to ~ sb** jdm einen Klaps
geben ▷ *vi*: **to ~ of** riechen nach
small [smɔːl] *adj* klein; **small
ads** *npl* (*Brit*) Kleinanzeigen *pl*;
small change *n* Kleingeld *nt*;
small letters *npl*: **in ~**
Kleinbuchstaben; **smallpox** *n*
Pocken *pl*; **small print** *n*: **the
~** das Kleingedruckte; **small-scale**
adj (*map*) in kleinem Maßstab;
small talk *n* Konversation *f*,
Smalltalk *m*
smart [smɑːt] *adj* (*elegant*)
schick; (*clever*) clever; **smartarse**,
smartass (*US*) *n* (*fam*)
Klugscheißer(in) *m(f)*; **smart card**
n Chipkarte *f*; **smartly** *adv*
(*dressed*) schick; **smartphone** *n*
(*Tel*) Smartphone *nt*
smash [smæʃ] *n* (*car crash*)
Zusammenstoß *m*, Schmetterball

m ▷ vt (break) zerschlagen; (fig: record) brechen, deutlich übertreffen ▷ vi (break) zerbrechen; **to ~ into** (car) krachen gegen

smear [smɪə°] n (mark) Fleck m; (Med) Abstrich m; (fig) Verleumdung f ▷ vt (spread) schmieren; (make dirty) beschmieren; (fig) verleumden

smell [smel] (**smelt** o **smelled, smelt** o **smelled**) vt riechen ▷ vi riechen (of nach); (unpleasantly) stinken ▷ n Geruch m; (unpleasant) Gestank m; **smelly** adj übel riechend; **smelt** [smelt] pt, pp of **smell**

smile [smaɪl] n Lächeln nt ▷ vi lächeln; **to ~ at sb** jdn anlächeln

smock [smɒk] n Kittel m

smog [smɒg] n Smog m

smoke [sməʊk] n Rauch m ▷ vt rauchen; (food) räuchern ▷ vi rauchen; **smoke alarm** n Rauchmelder m; **smoked** adj (food) geräuchert; **smoke-free** adj (zone, building) rauchfrei; **smoker** n Raucher(in) m(f); **smoking** n Rauchen nt; **"no ~"** „Rauchen verboten"

smooth [smuːð] adj glatt; (flight, crossing) ruhig; (movement) geschmeidig; (without problems) reibungslos; (pej: person) aalglatt ▷ vt (hair, dress) glatt streichen; (surface) glätten; **smoothly** adv reibungslos; **to run ~** (engine) ruhig laufen

smudge [smʌdʒ] vt (writing, lipstick) verschmieren

smug [smʌg] adj selbstgefällig

smuggle ['smʌgl] vt schmuggeln; **to ~ in/out** herein-/herausschmuggeln

smutty ['smʌtɪ] adj (obscene) schmutzig

snack [snæk] n Imbiss m; **to have**

a **~** eine Kleinigkeit essen; **snack bar** n Imbissstube f

snail [sneɪl] n Schnecke f; **snail mail** n (fam) Schneckenpost f

snake [sneɪk] n Schlange f

snap [snæp] n (photo) Schnappschuss m ▷ adj (decision) spontan ▷ vt (break) zerbrechen; (rope) zerreißen ▷ vi (break) brechen; (rope) reißen; (bite) schnappen (at nach); **snap off** vt (break) abbrechen; **snap fastener** n (US) Druckknopf m; **snapshot** n Schnappschuss m

snatch [snætʃ] vt (grab) schnappen

sneak [sniːk] vi (move) schleichen; **sneakers** npl (US) Turnschuhe pl

sneeze [sniːz] vi niesen

sniff [snɪf] vi schniefen; (smell) schnüffeln (at an +dat) ▷ vt schnuppern an +dat; (glue) schnüffeln

snob [snɒb] n Snob m; **snobbish** adj versnobt

snog [snɒg] vi, vt knutschen

snooker ['snuːkə°] n Snooker nt

snoop [snuːp] vi: **to ~ (around)** (herum)schnüffeln

snooze [snuːz] n, vi: **to (have a) ~** ein Nickerchen machen

snore [snɔː°] vi schnarchen

snorkel ['snɔːkl] n Schnorchel m; **snorkelling** n Schnorcheln nt; **to go ~** schnorcheln gehen

snout [snaʊt] n Schnauze f

snow [snəʊ] n Schnee m ▷ vi schneien; **snowball** n Schneeball m; **snowboard** n Snowboard nt; **snowboarding** n Snowboarding nt; **snowdrift** n Schneewehe f; **snowdrop** n Schneeglöckchen nt; **snowflake** n Schneeflocke f; **snowman** (pl **-men**) n Schneemann m; **snowplough,**

snowplow (*US*) *n* Schneepflug *m*;
snowstorm *n* Schneesturm *m*;
snowy *adj* (*region*) schneereich;
(*landscape*) verschneit
snug [snʌg] *adj* (*person, place*)
gemütlich
snuggle up ['snʌgl'ʌp] *vi*: **to**
~ to sb sich an jdn ankuscheln

O **KEYWORD**

so [səʊ] *adv* **1** (*thus*) so; (*likewise*)
auch; **so saying he walked away**
indem er das sagte, ging er; **if so**
wenn ja; **I didn't do it — you did**
so! ich hab das nicht gemacht —
hast du wohl!; **so do I, so am I** *etc*
ich auch; **so it is!** tatsächlich!; **I**
hope/think so hoffentlich/ich
glaube schon; **so far** bis jetzt
2 (*in comparisons etc: to such a*
degree) so; **so quickly/big (that)**
so schnell/groß, dass; **I'm so glad**
to see you ich freue mich so,
dich/Sie zu sehen
3 so many so viele; **so much work**
so viel Arbeit; **I love you so much**
ich liebe dich so sehr
4 (*phrases*) **10 or so** etwa 10; **so**
long! (*inf*) (*goodbye*) tschüss!
▷ *conj* **1** (*expressing purpose*) **so as to**
um ... zu; **so (that)** damit
2 (*expressing result*) also; **so I was**
right after all ich hatte also doch
recht; **so you see ...** wie du
siehst/Sie sehen ...

soak [səʊk] *vt* durchnässen;
(*leave in liquid*) einweichen; **I'm ~ed**
ich bin klatschnass; **soaking** *adj*:
~ (wet) klatschnass
soap [səʊp] *n* Seife *f*; **soap**
(opera) *n* Seifenoper *f*; **soap**
powder *n* Waschpulver *nt*
sob [sɒb] *vi* schluchzen
sober ['səʊbə*] *adj* nüchtern;
sober up *vi* nüchtern werden

so-called ['səʊ'kɔːld] *adj*
sogenannt
soccer ['sɒkə*] *n* Fußball *m*
sociable ['səʊʃəbl] *adj* gesellig
social ['səʊʃəl] *adj* sozial;
(*sociable*) gesellig; **socialist** *adj*
sozialistisch ▷ *n* Sozialist(in)
m(f); **socialize** *vi* unter die Leute
gehen; **social networking** *n*
Netzwerken *nt*; **social security** *n*
(*Brit*) Sozialhilfe *f*; (*US*)
Sozialversicherung *f*
society [sə'saɪətɪ] *n* Gesellschaft
f; (*club*) Verein *m*
sock [sɒk] *n* Socke *f*
socket ['sɒkɪt] *n* (*Elec*) Steckdose
f
soda ['səʊdə] *n* (*~ water*) Soda *f*;
(*US: pop*) Limo *f*; **soda water** *n*
Sodawasser *nt*
sofa ['səʊfə] *n* Sofa *nt*; **sofa bed**
n Schlafcouch *f*
soft [sɒft] *adj* weich; (*quiet*) leise;
(*lighting*) gedämpft; (*kind*)
gutmütig; (*weak*) nachgiebig;
~ drink alkoholfreies Getränk;
softly *adv* sanft; (*quietly*) leise;
software *n* (*Inform*) Software *f*
soil [sɔɪl] *n* Erde *f*; (*ground*) Boden
m
solar ['səʊlə*] *adj* Sonnen-, Solar-
solarium [sə'lɛərɪəm] *n*
Solarium *nt*
sold [səʊld] *pt, pp of* sell
soldier ['səʊldʒə*] *n* Soldat(in)
m(f)
sole [səʊl] *n* Sohle *f*; (*fish*)
Seezunge *f* ▷ *vt* besohlen ▷ *adj*
einzig; (*owner, responsibility*)
alleinig; **solely** *adv* nur
solemn ['sɒləm] *adj* feierlich;
(*person*) ernst
solicitor [sə'lɪsɪtə*] *n* (*Brit*)
Rechtsanwalt *m*, Rechtsanwältin *f*
solid ['sɒlɪd] *adj* (*hard*) fest; (*gold,*
oak etc) massiv; (*~ly built*) solide;
(*meal*) kräftig

solitary ['sɒlɪtərɪ] *adj* einsam; (*single*) einzeln; **solitude** ['sɒlɪtjuːd] *n* Einsamkeit *f*
solo ['səʊləʊ] *n* (*Mus*) Solo *nt*
soluble ['sɒljʊbl] *adj* löslich; **solution** [sə'luːʃən] *n* Lösung *f* (*to +gen*); **solve** [sɒlv] *vt* lösen
somber (*US*), **sombre** ['sɒmbə°] *adj* düster

O **KEYWORD**

some [sʌm] *adj* **1** (*a certain amount o number of*) einige; (*a few*) ein paar; (*with singular nouns*) etwas; **some tea/biscuits** etwas Tee/ein paar Kekse; **I've got some money, but not much** ich habe ein bisschen Geld, aber nicht viel
2 (*certain: in contrasts*) manche(r, s); **some people say that ...** manche Leute sagen, dass ...
3 (*unspecified*) irgendein(e); **some woman was asking for you** da hat eine Frau nach dir/Ihnen gefragt; **some day** eines Tages; **some day next week** irgendwann nächste Woche
▷ *pron* **1** (*a certain number*) einige; **have you got some?** hast du/haben Sie welche?
2 (*a certain amount*) etwas; **I've read some of the book** ich habe das Buch teilweise gelesen
▷ *adv*: **some 10 people** etwa 10 Leute

somebody *pron* jemand; **~ (or other)** irgendjemand; **~ else** jemand anders; **someday** *adv* irgendwann; **somehow** *adv* irgendwie; **someone** *pron see* **somebody**; **someplace** *adv* (*US*) *see* **somewhere**; **something** ['sʌmθɪŋ] *pron* etwas; **~ (or other)** irgendetwas; **~ else** etwas anderes; **~ nice** etwas Nettes;

would you like ~ to drink? möchtest du/möchten Sie etwas trinken? ▷ *adv*: **~ like 20** ungefähr 20; **sometime** *adv* irgendwann; **sometimes** *adv* manchmal; **somewhat** *adv* ein wenig; **somewhere** *adv* irgendwo; (*to a place*) irgendwohin; **~ else** irgendwo anders; (*to another place*) irgendwo anders hin
son [sʌn] *n* Sohn *m*
song [sɒŋ] *n* Lied *nt*; Song *m*
son-in-law ['sʌnɪnlɔː] (*pl* **sons-in-law**) *n* Schwiegersohn *m*
soon [suːn] *adv* bald; (*early*) früh; **too ~** zu früh; **as ~ as I ...** sobald ich ...; **as ~ as possible** so bald wie möglich; **sooner** *adv* (*time*) früher; (*for preference*) lieber
soot [sʊt] *n* Ruß *m*
soothe [suːð] *vt* beruhigen; (*pain*) lindern
sophisticated [sə'fɪstɪkeɪtɪd] *adj* (*person*) kultiviert; (*machine*) hoch entwickelt; (*plan*) ausgeklügelt
sophomore ['sɒfəmɔː°] *n* (*US*) College-Student(in) *m(f)* im zweiten Jahr
soppy ['sɒpɪ] *adj* (*fam*) rührselig
soprano [sə'prɑːnəʊ] *n* Sopran *m*
sore [sɔː°] *adj*: **to be ~** wehtun; **to have a ~ throat** Halsschmerzen haben ▷ *n* wunde Stelle
sorrow ['sɒrəʊ] *n* Kummer *m*
sorry ['sɒrɪ] *adj* (*sight, figure*) traurig; (**I'm**) **~** (*excusing*) Entschuldigung!; **I'm ~** (*regretful*) es tut mir leid; **~?** wie bitte?; **I feel ~ for him** er tut mir leid
sort [sɔːt] *n* Art *f*; **what ~ of film is it?** was für ein Film ist das?; **a ~ of** eine Art *+gen*; **all ~s of things** alles Mögliche ▷ *adv*: **~ of** (*fam*) irgendwie ▷ *vt* sortieren; **everything's ~ed** (*dealt with*) alles

s

ist geregelt; **sort out** vt (classify etc) sortieren; (problems) lösen

sought [sɔːt] pt, pp of **seek**

soul [səʊl] n Seele f; (music) Soul m

sound [saʊnd] adj (healthy) gesund; (safe) sicher; (sensible) vernünftig; (theory) stichhaltig; (thrashing) tüchtig ▷ n (noise) Geräusch nt; (Mus) Klang m; (TV) Ton m ▷ vt: **to ~ the alarm** Alarm schlagen; **to ~ one's horn** hupen ▷ vi (seem) klingen (like wie); **soundcard** n (Inform) Soundkarte f; **sound effects** npl Klangeffekte pl; **soundproof** adj schalldicht; **soundtrack** n (of film) Filmmusik f, Soundtrack m

soup [suːp] n Suppe f

sour ['saʊə°] adj sauer; (fig) mürrisch

source [sɔːs] n Quelle f; (fig) Ursprung m

sour cream [saʊə'kriːm] n saure Sahne

south [saʊθ] n Süden m; **to the ~ of** südlich von ▷ adv (go, face) nach Süden ▷ adj Süd-; **South Africa** n Südafrika nt; **South African** adj südafrikanisch ▷ n Südafrikaner(in) m(f); **South America** n Südamerika nt; **South American** adj südamerikanisch ▷ n Südamerikaner(in) m(f); **southbound** adj (in) Richtung Süden; **southern** ['sʌðən] adj Süd-, südlich; **~ Europe** Südeuropa nt; **southwards** ['saʊθwədz] adv nach Süden

souvenir [suːvə'nɪə°] n Andenken nt (of an +akk)

sow [səʊ] (**sowed, sown** o **sowed**) vt (a. fig) säen; (field) besäen ▷ [saʊ] n (pig) Sau f

soya bean ['sɔɪə'biːn] n Sojabohne f

soy sauce ['sɔɪ'sɔːs] n Sojasoße f

spa [spɑː] n (place) Kurort m

space [speɪs] n (room) Platz m, Raum m; (outer ~) Weltraum m; (gap) Zwischenraum m; (for parking) Lücke f; **space bar** n Leertaste f; **spacecraft** (pl -) n Raumschiff nt; **space ship** n Raumschiff nt; **space shuttle** n Raumfähre f

spacing ['speɪsɪŋ] n (in text) Zeilenabstand m; **double ~** zweizeiliger Abstand

spacious ['speɪʃəs] adj geräumig

spade [speɪd] n Spaten m; **~s** Pik nt

spaghetti [spə'getɪ] nsing Spaghetti pl

Spain [speɪn] n Spanien nt

spam [spæm] n (Inform) Spam m

Spaniard ['spænɪəd] n Spanier(in) m(f); **Spanish** ['spænɪʃ] adj spanisch ▷ n (language) Spanisch nt

spanner ['spænə°] n (Brit) Schraubenschlüssel m

spare [speə°] adj (as replacement) Ersatz-; **~ part** Ersatzteil nt; **~ room** Gästezimmer nt; **~ time** Freizeit f; **~ tyre** Ersatzreifen m ▷ n (~ part) Ersatzteil nt ▷ vt (lives, feelings) verschonen; **can you ~ (me) a moment?** hättest du/hätten Sie einen Moment Zeit?

spark [spɑːk] n Funke m; **sparkle** ['spɑːkl] vi funkeln; **sparkling wine** n Schaumwein m, Sekt m; **spark plug** ['spɑːkplʌg] n Zündkerze f

sparrow ['spærəʊ] n Spatz m

sparse [spɑːs] adj spärlich; **sparsely** adv: **~ populated** dünn besiedelt

spasm ['spæzəm] n Krampf m

spat [spæt] pt, pp of **spit**

speak [spiːk] (**spoke, spoken**) vt sprechen; **can you ~ French?** sprechen Sie Französisch?; **to**

~ **one's mind** seine Meinung
sagen ▷ *vi* sprechen (*to* mit, zu);
(*make speech*) reden; **~ing** (*Tel*) am
Apparat; **so to ~** sozusagen; **~ for
yourself** das meinst auch nur du!;
speak up *vi* (*louder*) lauter
sprechen; **speaker** *n* Sprecher(in)
m(f); (*public* ~) Redner(in) *m(f)*;
(*loud*~) Lautsprecher *m*, Box *f*

special ['speʃəl] *adj* besonde-
re(r, s), speziell ▷ *n* (*on menu*)
Tagesgericht *nt*; (*TV, Radio*)
Sondersendung *f*; **special delivery**
n Eilzustellung *f*; **special effects**
npl Spezialeffekte *pl*; **specialist** *n*
Spezialist(in) *m(f)*; (*Tech*)
Fachmann *m*, Fachfrau *f*; (*Med*)
Facharzt *m*, Fachärztin *f*;
speciality [speʃɪ'ælɪtɪ] *n* Spezialität *f*; **specialize** *vi* sich
spezialisieren (*in* auf +*akk*);
specially *adv* besonders;
(*specifically*) extra; **special offer** *n*
Sonderangebot *nt*; **specialty** *n*
(US) *see* **speciality**

species ['spi:ʃi:z] *nsing* Art *f*

specific [spə'sɪfɪk] *adj* spezi-
fisch; (*precise*) genau; **specify**
['spesɪfaɪ] *vt* genau angeben

specimen ['spesɪmən] *n*
(*sample*) Probe *f*; (*example*)
Exemplar *nt*

specs [speks] *npl* (*fam*) Brille *f*

spectacle ['spektəkl] *n*
Schauspiel *nt*

spectacles *npl* Brille *f*

spectacular [spek'tækjʊlə°] *adj*
spektakulär

spectator [spek'teɪtə°] *n*
Zuschauer(in) *m(f)*

sped [sped] *pt, pp of* **speed**

speech [spi:tʃ] *n* (*address*) Rede *f*;
(*faculty*) Sprache *f*; **to make a
~** eine Rede halten; **speechless**
adj sprachlos (*with* vor +*dat*)

speed [spi:d] (**sped** *o* **speeded,
sped** *o* **speeded**) *vi* rasen; (*exceed*

~ *limit*) zu schnell fahren ▷ *n*
Geschwindigkeit *f*; (*of film*)
Lichtempfindlichkeit *f*; **speed up**
vt beschleunigen ▷ *vi* schneller
werden/fahren; (*drive faster*)
schneller fahren; **speedboat** *n*
Rennboot *nt*; **speed bump** *n*
Bodenschwelle *f*; **speed camera** *n*
Blitzgerät *nt*; **speed limit** *n*
Geschwindigkeitsbegrenzung *f*;
speedometer [spɪ'dɒmɪtə°] *n*
Tachometer *m*; **speed trap** *n*
Radarfalle *f*; **speedy** *adj* schnell

spell [spel] (**spelt** *o* **spelled, spelt**
o **spelled**) *vt* buchstabieren; **how
do you ~ ...?** wie schreibt man ...?
▷ *n* (*period*) Weile *f*; (*enchantment*)
Zauber *m*; **a cold/hot ~** (*weather*)
ein Kälteeinbruch/eine
Hitzewelle; **spellchecker** *n*
(*Inform*) Rechtschreibprüfung *f*;
spelling *n* Rechtschreibung *f*; (*of
a word*) Schreibweise *f*; **~ mistake**
n Schreibfehler *m*

spelt [spelt] *pt, pp of* **spell**

spend [spend] (**spent, spent**) *vt*
(*money*) ausgeben (*on* für); (*time*)
verbringen; **spending money** *n*
Taschengeld *nt*

spent [spent] *pt, pp of* **spend**

sperm [spɜ:m] *n* Sperma *nt*

sphere [sfɪə°] *n* (*globe*) Kugel *f*;
(*fig*) Sphäre *f*

spice [spaɪs] *n* Gewürz *nt*; (*fig*)
Würze *f* ▷ *vt* würzen; **spicy**
['spaɪsɪ] *adj* würzig; (*fig*) pikant

spider ['spaɪdə°] *n* Spinne *f*

spike [spaɪk] *n* (*on railing etc*)
Spitze *f*; (*on shoe, tyre*) Spike *m*

spill [spɪl] (**spilt** *o* **spilled, spilt** *o*
spilled) *vt* verschütten

spin [spɪn] (**spun, spun**) *vi* (*turn*)
sich drehen; (*washing*) schleudern;
my head is ~ning mir dreht sich
alles ▷ *vt* (*turn*) drehen; (*coin*)
hochwerfen ▷ *n* (*turn*) Drehung *f*

spinach ['spɪnɪtʃ] *n* Spinat *m*

spin doctor n Spindoktor m
(*Verantwortlicher für die
schönrednerische Öffentlichkeitsarbeit
besonders von Politikern*)

spin-drier ['spɪndraɪə°] n
Wäscheschleuder f; **spin-dry** vt
schleudern

spine [spaɪn] n Rückgrat nt; (*of
animal, plant*) Stachel m; (*of book*)
Rücken m

spiral ['spaɪrəl] n Spirale f ▷ adj
spiralförmig; **spiral staircase** n
Wendeltreppe f

spire ['spaɪə°] n Turmspitze f

spirit ['spɪrɪt] n (*essence, soul*)
Geist m; (*humour, mood*) Stimmung
f; (*courage*) Mut m; (*verve*) Elan m;
~s pl (*drinks*) Spirituosen pl

spiritual ['spɪrɪtjʊəl] adj geistig;
(*Rel*) geistlich

spit [spɪt] (**spat, spat**) vi
spucken ▷ n (*for roasting*)
(Brat)spieß m; (*saliva*) Spucke f;
spit out vt ausspucken

spite [spaɪt] n Boshaftigkeit f; **in
~ of** trotz +gen; **spiteful** adj
boshaft

spitting image ['spɪtɪŋ'ɪmɪdʒ]
n: **he's the ~ of you** er ist
dir/Ihnen wie aus dem Gesicht
geschnitten

splash [splæʃ] vt (*person, object*)
bespritzen ▷ vi (*liquid*) spritzen;
(*play in water*) planschen

splendid ['splendɪd] adj herrlich

splinter ['splɪntə°] n Splitter
m

split [splɪt] (**split, split**) vt (*stone,
wood*) spalten; (*share*) teilen ▷ vi
(*stone, wood*) sich spalten; (*seam*)
platzen ▷ n (*in stone, wood*) Spalt
m; (*in clothing*) Riss m; (*fig*)
Spaltung f; **split up** vi (*couple*) sich
trennen ▷ vt (*divide up*) aufteilen;
split ends npl (Haar)spliss m;
splitting adj (*headache*) rasend

spoil [spɔɪl] (**spoiled** o **spoilt,**

spoiled o **spoilt**) vt verderben;
(*child*) verwöhnen ▷ vi (*food*)
verderben

spoilt [spɔɪlt] pt, pp of **spoil**

spoke [spəʊk] pt of **speak** ▷ n
Speiche f

spoken ['spəʊkən] pp of **speak**

spokesperson ['spəʊkspɜːsən]
(*pl* **-people**) n Sprecher(in) m(f)

sponge [spʌndʒ] n (*for washing*)
Schwamm m; **sponge bag** n
Kulturbeutel m; **sponge cake** n
Biskuitkuchen m

sponsor ['spɒnsə°] n (*of event,
programme*) Sponsor(in) m(f) ▷ vt
unterstützen; (*event, programme*)
sponsern

spontaneous, spontaneously
[spɒn'teɪnɪəs, -lɪ] adj, adv
spontan

spool [spuːl] n Spule f

spoon [spuːn] n Löffel m

sport [spɔːt] n Sport m; **sports
car** n Sportwagen m; **sports
centre** n Sportzentrum nt;
sports club n Sportverein m;
sportsman (*pl* **-men**) n Sportler
m; **sportswear** n Sportkleidung f;
sportswoman (*pl* **-women**) n
Sportlerin f; **sporty** adj sportlich

spot [spɒt] n (*dot*) Punkt m; (*of
paint, blood etc*) Fleck m; (*place*)
Stelle f; (*pimple*) Pickel m; **on the
~** vor Ort; (*at once*) auf der Stelle
▷ vt (*notice*) entdecken; (*difference*)
erkennen; **spotless** adj (*clean*)
blitzsauber; **spotlight** n (*lamp*)
Scheinwerfer m; **spotty** adj
(*pimply*) pickelig

spouse [spaʊs] n Gatte m,
Gattin f

spout [spaʊt] n Schnabel m

sprain [spreɪn] n Verstauchung
f ▷ vt: **to ~ one's ankle** sich den
Knöchel verstauchen

sprang [spræŋ] pt of **spring**

spray [spreɪ] n (*liquid in can*)

Spray nt o m; (~ (can)) Spraydose f
▷ vt (plant, insects) besprühen;
(car) spritzen

spread [spred] (**spread, spread**)
vt (open out) ausbreiten; (news,
disease) verbreiten; (butter, jam)
streichen; (bread, surface)
bestreichen ▷ vi (news, disease,
fire) sich verbreiten ▷ n (of disease,
religion etc) Verbreitung f; (for bread)
Aufstrich m; **spreadsheet** n
(Inform) Tabellenkalkulation f

spring [sprɪŋ] (**sprang, sprung**)
vi (leap) springen ▷ n (season)
Frühling m; (coil) Feder f; (water)
Quelle f; **springboard** n
Sprungbrett nt; **spring onion** n
(Brit) Frühlingszwiebel f; **spring
roll** n (Brit) Frühlingsrolle f;
springy adj (mattress) federnd

sprinkle ['sprɪŋkl] vt streuen;
(liquid) (be)träufeln; **to ~ sth with
sth** etw mit etw bestreuen; (with
liquid) etw mit etw besprengen;
sprinkler n (for lawn)
Rasensprenger m; (for fire)
Sprinkler m

sprint [sprɪnt] vi rennen; (Sport)
sprinten

sprout [spraʊt] n (of plant) Trieb
m; (from seed) Keim m; (**Brussels**)
~s pl Rosenkohl m ▷ vi sprießen

sprung [sprʌŋ] pp of **spring**

spun [spʌn] pt, pp of **spin**

spy [spaɪ] n Spion(in) m(f) ▷ vi
spionieren; **to ~ on sb** jdm
nachspionieren ▷ vt erspähen

squad [skwɒd] n (Sport) Kader m;
(police ~) Kommando nt

square [skweə°] n (shape)
Quadrat nt; (open space) Platz m;
(on chessboard etc) Feld nt ▷ adj (in
shape) quadratisch; **2 ~ metres** 2
Quadratmeter; **2 metres ~** 2 Meter
im Quadrat ▷ vt: **3 ~d** 3 hoch 2;
square root n Quadratwurzel f

squash [skwɒʃ] n (drink)

Fruchtsaftgetränk nt; (Sport)
Squash nt; (US: vegetable) Kürbis m
▷ vt zerquetschen

squat [skwɒt] vi (be crouching)
hocken; **to ~ (down)** sich
(hin)hocken

squeak [skwiːk] vi (door, shoes
etc) quietschen; (animal) quieken

squeal [skwiːl] vi (person)
kreischen (with vor +dat)

squeeze [skwiːz] vt drücken;
(orange) auspressen ▷ vi: **to ~ into
the car** sich in den Wagen
hineinzwängen; **squeeze up** vi
(on bench etc) zusammenrücken

squid [skwɪd] n Tintenfisch m

squint [skwɪnt] vi schielen; (in
bright light) blinzeln

squirrel ['skwɪrəl] n Eichhörnchen nt

squirt [skwɜːt] vt, vi (liquid)
spritzen

Sri Lanka [sriːˈlæŋkə] n Sri
Lanka nt

st abbr = **stone** Gewichtseinheit (6,35
kg)

St abbr = **saint** St.; abbr = **street** Str.

stab [stæb] vt (person) einstechen
auf +akk; (to death) erstechen;
stabbing adj (pain) stechend

stabilize ['steɪbəlaɪz] vt
stabilisieren ▷ vi sich
stabilisieren

stable ['steɪbl] n Stall m ▷ adj
stabil

stack [stæk] n (pile) Stapel m
▷ vt: **to ~ (up)** (auf)stapeln

stadium ['steɪdɪəm] n Stadion
nt

staff [stɑːf] n (personnel) Personal
nt, Lehrkräfte pl

stag [stæg] n Hirsch m

stag night n (Brit)
Junggesellenabschied m

stage [steɪdʒ] n (Theat) Bühne f;
(of project, life etc) Stadium nt; (of
journey) Etappe f; **at this ~** zu

diesem Zeitpunkt ▷ vt (*Theat*) aufführen, inszenieren; (*demonstration*) veranstalten

stagger ['stægə°] vi wanken ▷ vt (*amaze*) verblüffen; **staggering** adj (*amazing*) umwerfend; (*amount, price*) schwindelerregend

stagnate [stæg'neɪt] vi (*fig*) stagnieren

stain [steɪn] n Fleck m; **stained-glass window** n Buntglasfenster nt; **stainless steel** n rostfreier Stahl; **stain remover** n Fleck(en)entferner m

stair [stɛə°] n (Treppen)stufe f; **~s** pl Treppe f; **staircase** n Treppe f

stake [steɪk] n (*post*) Pfahl m; (*in betting*) Einsatz m; (*Fin*) Anteil m (*in* an +dat); **to be at ~** auf dem Spiel stehen

stale [steɪl] adj (*bread*) alt; (*beer*) schal

stalk [stɔːk] n Stiel m ▷ vt (*wild animal*) sich anpirschen an +akk; (*person*) nachstellen +dat

stall [stɔːl] n (*in market*) (Verkaufs)stand m; (*in stable*) Box f; **~s** pl (*Theat*) Parkett nt ▷ vt (*engine*) abwürgen ▷ vi (*driver*) den Motor abwürgen; (*car*) stehen bleiben; (*delay*) Zeit schinden

stamina ['stæmɪnə] n Durchhaltevermögen nt

stammer ['stæmə°] vi, vt stottern

stamp [stæmp] n (*postage ~*) Briefmarke f; (*for document*) Stempel m ▷ vt (*passport etc*) stempeln; (*mail*) frankieren; **stamped addressed envelope** n frankierter Rückumschlag

stand [stænd] (**stood, stood**) vi stehen; (*as candidate*) kandidieren ▷ vt (*place*) stellen; (*endure*) aushalten; **I can't ~ her** ich kann sie nicht ausstehen ▷ n (*stall*)

Stand m; (*seats in stadium*) Tribüne f; (*for coats, bicycles*) Ständer m; (*for small objects*) Gestell nt; **stand around** vi herumstehen; **stand by** vi (*be ready*) sich bereithalten; (*be inactive*) danebenstehen ▷ vt (*fig: person*) halten zu; (*decision, promise*) stehen zu; **stand for** vt (*represent*) stehen für; (*tolerate*) hinnehmen; **stand in for** vt einspringen für; **stand out** vi (*be noticeable*) auffallen; **stand up** vi (*get up*) aufstehen ▷ vt (*girlfriend, boyfriend*) versetzen; **stand up for** vt sich einsetzen für; **stand up to** vt: **to ~ sb** jdm die Stirn bieten

standard ['stændəd] n (*norm*) Norm f; **~ of living** Lebensstandard m ▷ adj Standard-

standardize ['stændədaɪz] vt vereinheitlichen

stand-by ['stændbaɪ] n (*thing in reserve*) Reserve f; **on ~** in Bereitschaft ▷ adj (*flight, ticket*) Stand-by-; **standing order** n (*at bank*) Dauerauftrag m; **standpoint** ['stændpɔɪnt] n Standpunkt m; **standstill** ['stændstɪl] n Stillstand m; **to come to a ~** stehen bleiben; (*fig*) zum Erliegen kommen

stank [stæŋk] pt of **stink**

staple ['steɪpl] n (*for paper*) Heftklammer f ▷ vt heften (*to* an +akk); **stapler** n Hefter m

star [stɑː°] n Stern m; (*person*) Star m ▷ vt: **the film ~s Hugh Grant** der Film zeigt Hugh Grant in der Hauptrolle ▷ vi die Hauptrolle spielen

starch [stɑːtʃ] n Stärke f

stare [stɛə°] vi starren; **to ~ at** anstarren

starfish ['stɑːfɪʃ] n Seestern m

star sign ['stɑːsaɪn] n Sternzeichen nt

start [stɑːt] n (beginning) Anfang m, Beginn m; (Sport) Start m; (lead) Vorsprung m; **from the ~** von Anfang an ▷ vt anfangen; (car, engine) starten; (business, family) gründen; **to ~ to do sth, to ~ doing sth** anfangen, etw zu tun ▷ vi (begin) anfangen; (car) anspringen; (on journey) aufbrechen; (Sport) starten; (jump) zusammenfahren; **~ing from Monday** ab Montag; **start off** vt (discussion, process etc) anfangen, beginnen ▷ vi (begin) anfangen, beginnen; (on journey) aufbrechen; **start over** vi (US) wieder anfangen; **start up** vi (in business) anfangen ▷ vt (car, engine) starten; (business) gründen; **starter** n (Brit: first course) Vorspeise f; (Auto) Anlasser m; **starting point** n (a. fig) Ausgangspunkt m

startle ['stɑːtl] vt erschrecken; **startling** adj überraschend

starve [stɑːv] vi hungern; (to death) verhungern; **I'm starving** ich habe einen Riesenhunger

state [steɪt] n (condition) Zustand m; (Pol) Staat m; **the (United) States** die (Vereinigten) Staaten ▷ adj Staats-; (control, education) staatlich ▷ vt erklären; (facts, name etc) angeben; **stated** adj (fixed) festgesetzt

statement ['steɪtmənt] n (official declaration) Erklärung f; (to police) Aussage f; (from bank) Kontoauszug m

state-of-the-art [steɪtəvðiːˈɑːt] adj hochmodern, auf dem neuesten Stand der Technik

static ['stætɪk] adj (unchanging) konstant

station ['steɪʃən] n (for trains, buses) Bahnhof m; (underground ~) Station f; (police ~, fire ~) Wache f; (TV, Radio) Sender m ▷ vt (Mil) stationieren

stationer's ['steɪʃənəz] n: **~ (shop)** Schreibwarengeschäft nt; **stationery** n Schreibwaren pl

station wagon ['steɪʃənwægən] n (US) Kombiwagen m

statistics [stəˈtɪstɪks] nsing (science) Statistik f; (figures) Statistiken pl

statue ['stætjuː] n Statue f

status ['steɪtəs] n Status m; (prestige) Ansehen nt; **status bar** n (Inform) Statuszeile f

stay [steɪ] n Aufenthalt m ▷ vi bleiben; (with friends, in hotel) wohnen (with bei); **to ~ the night** übernachten; **stay away** vi wegbleiben; **to ~ from sb** sich von jdm fernhalten; **stay behind** vi zurückbleiben; (at work) länger bleiben; **stay in** vi (at home) zu Hause bleiben; **stay out** vi (not come home) wegbleiben; **stay up** vi (at night) aufbleiben

steady ['stedɪ] adj (speed) gleichmäßig; (progress, increase) stetig; (job, income, girlfriend) fest; (worker) zuverlässig; (hand) ruhig; **they've been going ~ for two years** sie sind seit zwei Jahren fest zusammen ▷ vt (nerves) beruhigen; **to ~ oneself** Halt finden

steak [steɪk] n Steak nt; (of fish) Filet nt

steal [stiːl] (**stole, stolen**) vt stehlen; **to ~ sth from sb** jdm etw stehlen

steam [stiːm] n Dampf m ▷ vt (Gastr) dämpfen; **steam up** vi (window) beschlagen; **steamer** n (Gastr) Dampfkochtopf m; (ship) Dampfer m; **steam iron** n Dampfbügeleisen nt

steel [stiːl] n Stahl m ▷ adj Stahl-

steep [stiːp] *adj* steil
steeple ['stiːpl] *n* Kirchturm *m*
steer [stɪə*] *vt, vi* steuern; (*car, bike etc*) lenken; **steering** *n* (*Auto*) Lenkung *f*; **steering wheel** *n* Steuer *nt*, Lenkrad *nt*
stem [stem] *n* (*of plant, glass*) Stiel *m*
step [step] *n* Schritt *m*; (*stair*) Stufe *f*; (*measure*) Maßnahme *f*; **~ by ~** Schritt für Schritt ▷ *vi* treten; **~ this way, please** hier entlang, bitte; **step down** *vi* (*resign*) zurücktreten
stepbrother *n* Stiefbruder *m*; **stepchild** (*pl* **-children**) *n* Stiefkind *nt*; **stepfather** *n* Stiefvater *m*
stepladder *n* Trittleiter *f*
stepmother *n* Stiefmutter *f*; **stepsister** *n* Stiefschwester *f*
stereo ['sterɪəʊ] (*pl* **-s**) *n*: **~ (system)** Stereoanlage *f*
sterile ['steraɪl] *adj* steril; **sterilize** ['sterɪlaɪz] *vt* sterilisieren
sterling ['stɜːlɪŋ] *n* (*Fin*) das Pfund Sterling
stew [stjuː] *n* Eintopf *m*
steward ['stjuːəd] *n* (*on plane, ship*) Steward *m*; **stewardess** *n* Stewardess *f*
stick [stɪk] (**stuck, stuck**) *vt* (*with glue etc*) kleben; (*pin etc*) stecken; (*fam: put*) tun ▷ *vi* (*get jammed*) klemmen; (*hold fast*) haften ▷ *n* Stock *m*; (*hockey ~*) Schläger *m*; (*of chalk*) Stück *nt*; (*of celery, rhubarb*) Stange *f*; **stick out** *vt*: **to stick one's tongue out (at sb)** (jdm) die Zunge herausstrecken ▷ *vi* (*protrude*) vorstehen; (*ears*) abstehen; (*be noticeable*) auffallen; **stick to** *vt* (*rules, plan etc*) sich halten an +*akk*; **sticker** ['stɪkə*] *n* Aufkleber *m*; **sticky** ['stɪkɪ] *adj* klebrig;

(*weather*) schwül; **~ label** Aufkleber *m*; **~ tape** Klebeband *nt*
stiff [stɪf] *adj* steif
stifle ['staɪfl] *vt* (*yawn etc, opposition*) unterdrücken; **stifling** *adj* drückend
still [stɪl] *adj* still; (*drink*) ohne Kohlensäure ▷ *adv* (*yet, even now*) (immer) noch; (*all the same*) immerhin; (*sit, stand*) still; **he ~ doesn't believe me** er glaubt mir immer noch nicht; **keep ~** halt still!; **bigger/better ~** noch größer/besser
still life (*pl* **still lives**) *n* Stillleben *nt*
stimulate ['stɪmjʊleɪt] *vt* anregen, stimulieren; **stimulating** *adj* anregend
sting [stɪŋ] (**stung, stung**) *vt* (*wound with ~*) stechen ▷ *vi* (*eyes, ointment etc*) brennen ▷ *n* (*insect wound*) Stich *m*
stingy ['stɪndʒɪ] *adj* (*fam*) geizig
stink [stɪŋk] (**stank, stunk**) *vi* stinken (*of* nach) ▷ *n* Gestank *m*
stir [stɜː*] *vt* (*mix*) (um)rühren; **stir up** *vt* (*mob*) aufhetzen; (*memories*) wachrufen; **to ~ trouble** Unruhe stiften; **stir-fry** *vt* (unter Rühren) kurz anbraten
stitch [stɪtʃ] *n* (*in sewing*) Stich *m*; (*in knitting*) Masche *f*; **to have a ~** (*pain*) Seitenstechen haben; **he had to have ~es** er musste genäht werden; **she had her ~es out** ihr wurden die Fäden gezogen; **to be in ~es** (*fam*) sich kaputtlachen ▷ *vt* nähen; **stitch up** *vt* (*hole, wound*) nähen
stock [stɒk] *n* (*supply*) Vorrat *m* (*of an* +*dat*); (*of shop*) Bestand *m*; (*for soup etc*) Brühe *f*; **~s and shares** *pl* Aktien und Wertpapiere *pl*; **to be in/out of ~** vorrätig/nicht vorrätig sein; **to**

take ~ Inventur machen; (fig)
Bilanz ziehen ▷ vt (keep in shop)
führen; **stock up** vi sich
eindecken (on, with mit)
stockbroker n Börsenmakler(in)
m(f)
stock cube n Brühwürfel m
stock exchange n Börse f
stocking ['stɒkɪŋ] n Strumpf m
stock market ['stɒkmɑːkɪt] n
Börse f
stole [stəʊl] pt of **steal**; **stolen**
['stəʊlən] pp of **steal**
stomach ['stʌmək] n Magen m;
(belly) Bauch m; **on an empty ~** auf
leeren Magen; **stomach-ache** n
Magenschmerzen pl; **stomach
upset** n Magenverstimmung f
stone [stəʊn] n Stein m; (seed)
Kern m, Stein m; (weight) britische
Gewichtseinheit (6,35 kg) ▷ adj
Stein-, aus Stein; **stony** adj
(ground) steinig
stood [stʊd] pt, pp of **stand**
stool [stuːl] n Hocker m
stop [stɒp] n Halt m; (for bus,
tram, train) Haltestelle f; **to come
to a ~** anhalten ▷ vt (vehicle,
passer-by) anhalten; (put an end to)
ein Ende machen +dat; (cease)
aufhören mit; (prevent from
happening) verhindern; (bleeding)
stillen; (engine, machine) abstellen;
(payments) einstellen; (cheque)
sperren; **to ~ doing sth** aufhören,
etw zu tun; **to ~ sb (from) doing
sth** jdn daran hindern, etw zu tun;
~ it hör auf (damit)! ▷ vi (vehicle)
anhalten; (during journey) Halt
machen; (pedestrian, clock, heart)
stehen bleiben; (rain, noise)
aufhören; (stay) bleiben; **stop by**
vi vorbeischauen; **stop over** vi
Halt machen; (overnight)
übernachten; **stopgap** n
Provisorium nt, Zwischenlösung f;
stopover n (on journey)

Zwischenstation f; **stopper** n
Stöpsel m; **stop sign** n
Stoppschild nt; **stopwatch** n
Stoppuhr f
storage ['stɔːrɪdʒ] n Lagerung f;
store [stɔː°] n (supply) Vorrat m
(of an +dat); (place for storage) Lager
nt; (large shop) Kaufhaus nt; (US:
shop) Geschäft nt ▷ vt lagern;
(Inform) speichern; **storecard** n
Kundenkreditkarte f; **storeroom**
n Lagerraum m
storey ['stɔːrɪ] n (Brit) Stock m,
Stockwerk nt
storm [stɔːm] n Sturm m;
(thunder~) Gewitter nt ▷ vt, vi
(with movement) stürmen; **stormy**
adj stürmisch
story ['stɔːrɪ] n Geschichte f;
(plot) Handlung f; (US: of building)
Stock m, Stockwerk nt
stout [staʊt] adj (fat) korpulent
stove [stəʊv] n Herd m; (for
heating) Ofen m
stow [stəʊ] vt verstauen;
stowaway n blinder Passagier
straight [streɪt] adj (not curved)
gerade; (hair) glatt; (honest) ehrlich
(with zu); (fam: heterosexual) hetero
▷ adv (directly) direkt; (immediately)
sofort; (drink) pur; (think) klar;
~ ahead geradeaus; **to go ~ on**
geradeaus weitergehen/
weiterfahren; **straightaway** adv
sofort; **straightforward** adj
einfach; (person) aufrichtig,
unkompliziert
strain [streɪn] n Belastung f ▷ vt
(eyes) überanstrengen; (rope,
relationship) belasten; (vegetables)
abgießen; **to ~ a muscle** sich
einen Muskel zerren; **strained** adj
(laugh, smile) gezwungen;
(relations) gespannt; **~ muscle**
Muskelzerrung f; **strainer** n Sieb
nt
strand [strænd] n (of wool) Faden

m; (of hair) Strähne f ▷ vt: **to be
(left) ~ed** (person) festsitzen
strange [streɪndʒ] adj seltsam;
(unfamiliar) fremd; **strangely** adv
seltsam; **~ enough**
seltsamerweise; **stranger** n
Fremde(r) mf; **I'm a ~ here** ich bin
hier fremd
strangle ['stræŋgl] vt (kill)
erdrosseln
strap [stræp] n Riemen m; (on
dress etc) Träger m; (on watch) Band
nt ▷ vt (fasten) festschnallen (to an
+dat); **strapless** adj trägerlos
strategy ['strætɪdʒɪ] n Strategie
f
straw [strɔ:] n Stroh nt; (drinking
~) Strohhalm m
strawberry n Erdbeere f
stray [streɪ] n streunendes Tier
▷ adj (cat, dog) streunend ▷ vi
streunen
streak ['stri:k] n (of colour, dirt)
Streifen m; (in hair) Strähne f; (in
character) Zug m
stream [stri:m] n (flow of liquid)
Strom m; (brook) Bach m ▷ vi
strömen; **streamer** n (of paper)
Luftschlange f
street [stri:t] n Straße f;
streetcar n (US) Straßenbahn f;
street lamp, **street light** n
Straßenlaterne f; **street map** n
Stadtplan m
strength [streŋθ] n Kraft f,
Stärke f; **strengthen** vt
verstärken; (fig) stärken
strenuous ['strenjʊəs] adj
anstrengend
stress [stres] n Stress m; (on
word) Betonung f; **to be under
~** im Stress sein ▷ vt betonen;
(put under ~) stressen; **stressed**
adj: **~ (out)** gestresst
stretch [stretʃ] n (of land) Stück
nt; (of road) Strecke f ▷ vt (material,
shoes) dehnen; (rope, canvas)

spannen; (person in job etc) fordern;
to ~ one's legs (walk) sich die
Beine vertreten ▷ vi (person) sich
strecken; (area) sich erstrecken (to
bis zu); **stretch out** vt: **to stretch
one's hand/legs out** die
Hand/die Beine ausstrecken,
ausstrecken ▷ vi (reach) sich
strecken; (lie down) sich
ausstrecken; **stretcher** n
Tragbahre f
strict, **strictly** [strɪkt, -lɪ] adj, adv
(severe(ly)) streng; (exact(ly)) genau;
~ speaking genauer gesagt
strike [straɪk] (struck, struck) vt
(match) anzünden; (hit) schlagen;
(find) finden; **it struck me as
strange** es kam mir seltsam vor
▷ vi (stop work) streiken; (attack)
zuschlagen; (clock) schlagen ▷ n
(by workers) Streik m; **to be on
~** streiken; **strike up** vt
(conversation) anfangen;
(friendship) schließen; **striking** adj
auffallend
string [strɪŋ] n (for tying) Schnur
f; (Mus, Tennis) Saite f; **the ~s** pl
(section of orchestra) die Streicher pl
strip [strɪp] n Streifen m; (Brit: of
footballer etc) Trikot nt ▷ vi
(undress) sich ausziehen, strippen
stripe [straɪp] n Streifen m;
striped adj gestreift
stripper ['strɪpə°] n Stripper(in)
m(f); (paint ~) Farbentferner m
strip-search ['strɪpsɜ:tʃ] n
Leibesvisitation f (bei der man sich
ausziehen muss)
striptease ['strɪpti:z] n Striptease m
stroke [strəʊk] n (Med, Tennis etc)
Schlag m; (of pen, brush) Strich m
▷ vt streicheln
stroll [strəʊl] n Spaziergang m
▷ vi spazieren; **stroller** n (US: for
baby) Buggy m
strong [strɒŋ] adj stark; (healthy)

robust; (wall, table) stabil; (shoes)
fest; (influence, chance) groß;
strongly adv stark; (believe) fest;
(constructed) stabil

struck [strʌk] pt, pp of **strike**

structural, **structurally**
['strʌktʃərəl, -lɪ] adj strukturell;
structure ['strʌktʃə°] n Struktur
f; (building, bridge) Konstruktion f,
Bau m

struggle ['strʌgl] n Kampf m (for
um) ▷ vi (fight) kämpfen (for um);
(do sth with difficulty) sich
abmühen; **to ~ to do sth** sich
abmühen, etw zu tun

stub [stʌb] n (of cigarette) Kippe f;
(of ticket, cheque) Abschnitt m ▷ vt:
to ~ one's toe sich dat den Zeh
stoßen (on an +dat)

stubble ['stʌbl] n Stoppelbart m;
(field) Stoppeln pl

stubborn ['stʌbən] adj (person)
stur

stuck [stʌk] pt, pp of **stick** ▷ adj:
to be ~ (jammed) klemmen; (at a
loss) nicht mehr weiterwissen; **to
get ~** (car in snow etc) stecken
bleiben

student ['stjuːdənt] n Stu-
dent(in) m(f), Schüler(in) m(f)

studio ['stjuːdɪəʊ] (pl **-s**) n
Studio nt

studious ['stjuːdɪəs] adj fleißig

study ['stʌdɪ] n (investigation)
Untersuchung f; (room)
Arbeitszimmer nt ▷ vt, vi
studieren

stuff [stʌf] n Zeug nt, Sachen pl
▷ vt (push) stopfen; (Gastr)
füllen; **to ~ oneself** (fam) sich
vollstopfen; **stuffing** n (Gastr)
Füllung f

stuffy ['stʌfɪ] adj (room) stickig;
(person) spießig

stumble ['stʌmbl] vi stolpern;
(when speaking) stocken

stun [stʌn] vt (shock) fassungslos

machen; **I was ~ned** ich war
fassungslos (o völlig überrascht)

stung [stʌŋ] pt, pp of **sting**

stunk [stʌŋk] pp of **stink**

stunning ['stʌnɪŋ] adj (marvellous) fantastisch; (beautiful)
atemberaubend; (very surprising,
shocking) überwältigend;
unfassbar

stunt [stʌnt] n (Cine) Stunt m

stupid ['stjuːpɪd] adj dumm;
stupidity [stjuːˈpɪdɪtɪ] n
Dummheit f

sturdy ['stɜːdɪ] adj robust;
(building, car) stabil

stutter ['stʌtə°] vi, vt stottern

stye [staɪ] n (Med) Gerstenkorn nt

style [staɪl] n Stil m ▷ vt (hair)
stylen; **styling mousse** n
Schaumfestiger m; **stylish**
['staɪlɪʃ] adj elegant, schick

subconscious [sʌbˈkɒnʃəs] adj
unterbewusst ▷ n: **the ~** das
Unterbewusstsein

subdivide [sʌbdɪˈvaɪd] vt
unterteilen

subject ['sʌbdʒɪkt] n (topic)
Thema nt; (in school) Fach nt;
(citizen) Staatsangehörige(r) mf; (of
kingdom) Untertan(in) m(f);
Subjekt nt; **to change the ~** das
Thema wechseln ▷ adj [səbˈdʒekt]
to be ~ to (dependent on) abhängen
von; (under control of) unterworfen
sein +dat

subjective [səbˈdʒektɪv] adj
subjektiv

sublet [sʌbˈlet] irr vt untervermieten (to an +akk)

submarine [sʌbməˈriːn] n
U-Boot nt

submerge [səbˈmɜːdʒ] vt (put in
water) eintauchen ▷ vi tauchen

submit [səbˈmɪt] vt (application,
claim) einreichen ▷ vi (surrender)
sich ergeben

subordinate [səˈbɔːdɪnət] adj

s

untergeordnet (to +dat) ▷ n
Untergebene(r) mf

subscribe [səb'skraɪb] vi: **to
~ to** (magazine etc) abonnieren;
subscription [səb'skrɪpʃən] n (to
magazine etc) Abonnement nt; (to
club etc) (Mitglieds)beitrag m

subsequent ['sʌbsɪkwənt] adj
nach(folgend); **subsequently** adv
später, anschließend

subside [səb'saɪd] vi (floods)
zurückgehen; (storm) sich legen;
(building) sich senken

substance ['sʌbstəns] n Substanz f

substantial [səb'stænʃəl] adj
beträchtlich; (improvement)
wesentlich; (meal) reichhaltig;
(furniture) solide

substitute ['sʌbstɪtjuːt] n Ersatz
m; (Sport) Ersatzspieler(in) m(f)
▷ vt: **to ~ A for B** B durch A
ersetzen

subtitle ['sʌbtaɪtl] n Untertitel
m

subtle ['sʌtl] adj (difference, taste)
fein; (plan) raffiniert

subtotal ['sʌbtəʊtl] n
Zwischensumme f

subtract [səb'trækt] vt abziehen
(from von)

suburb ['sʌbɜːb] n Vorort m; **in
the ~s** am Stadtrand; **suburban**
[sə'bɜːbən] adj vorstädtisch,
Vorstadt-

subway ['sʌbweɪ] n (Brit)
Unterführung f; (US Rail) U-Bahn f

succeed [sək'siːd] vi erfolgreich
sein; **he ~ed (in doing it)** es gelang
ihm(, es zu tun) ▷ vt nachfolgen
+dat; **succeeding** adj
nachfolgend; **success** [sək'ses] n
Erfolg m; **successful, successfully**
adj, adv erfolgreich

successive [sək'sesɪv] adj
aufeinanderfolgend; **successor** n
Nachfolger(in) m(f)

succulent ['sʌkjʊlənt] adj saftig

succumb [sə'kʌm] vi erliegen (to
+dat)

such [sʌtʃ] adj solche(r, s); **~ a
book** so ein Buch, ein solches
Buch; **it was ~ a success that ...**
es war solch ein Erfolg, dass ...;
~ as wie ▷ adv so; **~ a hot day** so
ein heißer Tag ▷ pron: **as ~** als
solche(r, s)

suck [sʌk] vt (toffee etc) lutschen;
(liquid) saugen; **it ~s** (fam) das ist
beschissen

Sudan [sʊ'dɑːn] n: **(the) ~** der
Sudan

sudden ['sʌdn] adj plötzlich; **all
of a ~** ganz plötzlich; **suddenly**
adv plötzlich

sudoku [sʊ'dəʊkuː] n Sudoku nt

sue [suː] vt verklagen

suede [sweɪd] n Wildleder nt

suffer ['sʌfə°] vt erleiden ▷ vi
leiden; **to ~ from** (Med) leiden an
+dat

sufficient, sufficiently
[sə'fɪʃənt, -lɪ] adj, adv
ausreichend

suffocate ['sʌfəkeɪt] vt, vi
ersticken

sugar ['ʃʊgə°] n Zucker m ▷ vt
zuckern; **sugar bowl** n
Zuckerdose f; **sugary** adj (sweet)
süß

suggest [sə'dʒest] vt vorschlagen; (imply) andeuten; **I ~ saying
nothing** ich schlage vor, nichts zu
sagen; **suggestion** n (proposal)
Vorschlag m; **suggestive** adj
vielsagend; (sexually) anzüglich

suicide ['sʊɪsaɪd] n (act)
Selbstmord m; **suicide bomber** n
Selbstmordattentäter(in) m(f);
suicide bombing n
Selbstmordattentat nt

suit [suːt] n (man's clothes) Anzug
m; (lady's clothes) Kostüm nt; (Cards)
Farbe f ▷ vt (be convenient for)

passen +dat; (clothes, colour) stehen +dat; (climate, food) bekommen +dat; **suitable** adj geeignet (for für); **suitcase** n Koffer m

suite [swiːt] n (of rooms) Suite f; (sofa and chairs) Sitzgarnitur f

sulk [sʌlk] vi schmollen; **sulky** adj eingeschnappt

sultana [sʌl'tɑːnə] n (raisin) Sultanine f

sum [sʌm] n Summe f; (money a.) Betrag m; (calculation) Rechenaufgabe f; **sum up** vt, vi (summarize) zusammenfassen

summarize ['sʌməraiz] vt, vi zusammenfassen; **summary** n Zusammenfassung f

summer ['sʌmə°] n Sommer m; **summer camp** n (US) Ferienlager nt; **summer holidays** n Sommerferien pl; **summertime** n: **in (the)** ~ im Sommer

summit ['sʌmɪt] n (a. Pol) Gipfel m

summon ['sʌmən] vt (doctor, fire brigade etc) rufen; (to one's office) zitieren; **summon up** vt (courage, strength) zusammennehmen

summons ['sʌmənz] nsing (Jur) Vorladung f

sumptuous ['sʌmptjʊəs] adj luxuriös; (meal) üppig

sun [sʌn] n Sonne f ▷ vt: **to ~ oneself** sich sonnen

Sun abbr = **Sunday** So.

sunbathe vi sich sonnen; **sunbathing** n Sonnenbaden nt; **sunbed** n Sonnenbank f; **sunblock** n Sunblocker m; **sunburn** n Sonnenbrand m; **sunburnt** adj: **to be/get** ~ einen Sonnenbrand haben/bekommen

sundae ['sʌndei] n Eisbecher m

Sunday ['sʌndi] n Sonntag m; see also **Tuesday**

sung [sʌŋ] pp of **sing**

sunglasses ['sʌnglɑːsiz] npl

Sonnenbrille f; **sunhat** n Sonnenhut m

sunk [sʌŋk] pp of **sink**

sunlamp ['sʌnlæmp] n Höhensonne f; **sunlight** n Sonnenlicht nt; **sunny** ['sʌni] adj sonnig; **sun protection factor** n Lichtschutzfaktor m; **sunrise** n Sonnenaufgang m; **sunroof** n (Auto) Schiebedach nt; **sunscreen** n Sonnenschutzmittel nt; **sunset** n Sonnenuntergang m; **sunshade** n Sonnenschirm m; **sunshine** n Sonnenschein m; **sunstroke** n Sonnenstich m; **suntan** n (Sonnen)bräune f; **to get/have a** ~ braun werden/sein; ~ **lotion** (o **oil**) Sonnenöl nt

super ['suːpə°] adj (fam) toll

superb, **superbly** [suː'pɜːb, -li] adj, adv ausgezeichnet

superficial, **superficially** [suːpə'fiʃəl, -i] adj, adv oberflächlich

superfluous [sʊ'pɜːflʊəs] adj überflüssig

superglue ['suːpəgluː] n Sekundenkleber m

superior [sʊ'piəriə°] adj (better) besser (to als); (higher in rank) höhergestellt (to als), höher ▷ n (in rank) Vorgesetzte(r) mf

supermarket ['suːpəmɑːkit] n Supermarkt m

supersede [suːpə'siːd] vt ablösen

supersonic [suːpə'sɒnik] adj Überschall-

superstition [suːpə'stiʃən] n Aberglaube m; **superstitious** [suːpə'stiʃəs] adj abergläubisch

superstore ['suːpəstɔː°] n Verbrauchermarkt m

supervise ['suːpəvaiz] vt beaufsichtigen; **supervisor** ['suːpəvaizə] n Aufsicht f; (at university) Doktorvater m

supper ['sʌpə*] n Abendessen nt; (late-night snack) Imbiss

supplement ['sʌplɪmənt] n (extra payment) Zuschlag m; (of newspaper) Beilage f ▷ vt ergänzen; **supplementary** [sʌplɪ'mentərɪ] adj zusätzlich

supplier [sə'plaɪə*] n Lieferant(in) m(f); **supply** [sə'plaɪ] vt (deliver) liefern; (drinks, music etc) sorgen für; **to ~ sb with sth** (provide) jdn mit etw versorgen ▷ n (stock) Vorrat m (of an +dat)

support [sə'pɔ:t] n Unterstützung f; (Tech) Stütze f ▷ vt (hold up) tragen, stützen; (provide for) ernähren, unterhalten; (speak in favour of) unterstützen; **he ~s Manchester United** er ist Manchester-United-Fan

suppose [sə'pəʊz] vt (assume) annehmen; **I ~ so** ich denke schon; **I ~ not** wahrscheinlich nicht; **you're not ~d to smoke here** du darfst/Sie dürfen hier nicht rauchen; **supposedly** [sə'pəʊzɪdlɪ] adv angeblich; **supposing** conj angenommen

suppress [sə'pres] vt unterdrücken

surcharge ['sɜːtʃɑːdʒ] n Zuschlag m

sure [ʃʊə*] adj sicher; **I'm (not) ~** ich bin mir (nicht) sicher; **make ~ you lock up** vergiss/vergessen Sie nicht abzuschließen ▷ adv: **~!** klar!; **~ enough** tatsächlich; **surely** adv: **~ you don't mean it?** das ist nicht dein/Ihr Ernst, oder?

surf [sɜːf] n Brandung f ▷ vi (Sport) surfen ▷ vt: **to ~ the net** im Internet surfen

surface ['sɜːfɪs] n Oberfläche f ▷ vi auftauchen; **surface mail** n: **by ~** auf dem Land-/Seeweg

surfboard ['sɜːfbɔːd] n Surfbrett nt; **surfer** n Surfer(in) m(f);

surfing n Surfen nt; **to go ~** surfen gehen

surgeon ['sɜːdʒən] n Chirurg(in) m(f); **surgery** ['sɜːdʒərɪ] n (operation) Operation f; (room) Praxis f, Sprechzimmer nt; (consulting time) Sprechstunde f; **to have ~** operiert werden

surname ['sɜːneɪm] n Nachname m

surpass [sɜː'pɑːs] vt übertreffen

surplus ['sɜːpləs] n Überschuss m (of an +dat)

surprise [sə'praɪz] n Überraschung f ▷ vt überraschen; **surprising** adj überraschend; **surprisingly** adv überraschenderweise, erstaunlicherweise

surrender [sə'rendə*] vi sich ergeben (to +dat) ▷ vt (weapon, passport) abgeben

surround [sə'raʊnd] vt umgeben; (stand all round) umringen; **surrounding** adj (countryside) umliegend ▷ n **~s** pl Umgebung f

survey ['sɜːveɪ] n (opinion poll) Umfrage f; (of literature etc) Überblick m (of über +akk); (of land) Vermessung f ▷ [sɜː'veɪ] vt (look out over) überblicken; (land) vermessen

survive [sə'vaɪv] vt, vi überleben

susceptible [sə'septəbl] adj empfänglich (to für); (Med) anfällig (to für)

sushi ['suːʃɪ] n Sushi nt

suspect ['sʌspekt] n Verdächtige(r) mf ▷ adj verdächtig ▷ [sə'spekt] vt verdächtigen (of +gen); (think likely) vermuten

suspend [sə'spend] vt (from work) suspendieren; (payment) vorübergehend einstellen; (player) sperren; (hang up) aufhängen; **suspender** n (Brit) Strumpfhalter

m; **~s** pl (US: for trousers)
Hosenträger pl

suspense [sə'spɛns] n Spannung f

suspicious [sə'spɪʃəs] adj misstrauisch (of sb/sth jdm/etw gegenüber); (causing suspicion) verdächtig

SUV abbr = **sport utility vehicle** SUV m, Geländewagen m

swallow ['swɒləʊ] n (bird) Schwalbe f ▷ vt, vi schlucken

swam [swæm] pt of **swim**

swamp [swɒmp] n Sumpf m

swan [swɒn] n Schwan m

swap [swɒp] vt, vi tauschen; **to ~ sth for sth** etw gegen etw eintauschen

sway [sweɪ] vi schwanken

swear [swɛəʳ] (**swore, sworn**) vi (promise) schwören; (curse) fluchen; **to ~ at sb** jdn beschimpfen; **swear by** vt (have faith in) schwören auf +akk; **swearword** n Fluch m

sweat [swɛt] n Schweiß m ▷ vi schwitzen; **sweatband** n Schweißband nt; **sweater** n Pullover m; **sweatshirt** n Sweatshirt nt; **sweaty** adj verschwitzt

swede [swiːd] n Steckrübe f

Swede [swiːd] n Schwede m, Schwedin f; **Sweden** n Schweden nt; **Swedish** adj schwedisch ▷ n (language) Schwedisch nt

sweep [swiːp] (**swept, swept**) vt, vi (with brush) kehren, fegen; **sweep up** vt (dirt etc) zusammenkehren, zusammenfegen

sweet [swiːt] n (Brit: candy) Bonbon nt; (dessert) Nachtisch m ▷ adj süß; (kind) lieb; **sweet-and-sour** adj süßsauer; **sweetcorn** n Mais m; **sweeten** vt (tea etc) süßen; **sweetener** n (substance) Süßstoff m; **sweet**

potato n Süßkartoffel f

swell [swɛl] (**swelled, swollen** o **swelled**) vi: **to ~ (up)** (an)schwellen ▷ adj (US fam) toll; **swelling** n (Med) Schwellung f

sweltering ['swɛltərɪŋ] adj (heat) drückend

swept [swɛpt] pt, pp of **sweep**

swift [swɪft] adj schnell

swig [swɪg] n (fam) Schluck m

swim [swɪm] (**swam, swum**) vi schwimmen ▷ n: **to go for a ~** schwimmen gehen; **swimmer** n Schwimmer(in) m(f); **swimming** n Schwimmen nt; **to go ~** schwimmen gehen; **swimming cap** n (Brit) Badekappe f; **swimming costume** n (Brit) Badeanzug m; **swimming pool** n Schwimmbad nt; (private, in hotel) Swimmingpool m; **swimming trunks** npl (Brit) Badehose f; **swimsuit** n Badeanzug m

swindle ['swɪndl] vt betrügen (out of um)

swine [swaɪn] n (person) Schwein nt

swing [swɪŋ] (**swung, swung**) vt, vi (object) schwingen ▷ n (for child) Schaukel f

swipe [swaɪp] vt (credit card etc) durchziehen; (fam: steal) klauen; **swipe card** n Magnetkarte f

Swiss [swɪs] adj schweizerisch ▷ n Schweizer(in) m(f)

switch [swɪtʃ] n (Elec) Schalter m ▷ vi (change) wechseln (to zu); **switch off** vt abschalten, ausschalten; **switch on** vt anschalten, einschalten; **switchboard** n (Tel) Vermittlung f

Switzerland ['swɪtsələnd] n die Schweiz

swivel ['swɪvl] vi sich drehen ▷ vt drehen; **swivel chair** n Drehstuhl m

swollen ['swəʊlən] pp of **swell**

s

▷ adj (Med) geschwollen; (stomach) aufgebläht

swop [swɒp] *see* **swap**

sword [sɔːd] n Schwert nt

swore [swɔːʳ] pt of **swear**

sworn [swɔːn] pp of **swear**

swot [swɒt] vi (Brit fam) büffeln (for für)

swum [swʌm] pp of **swim**

swung [swʌŋ] pt, pp of **swing**

syllable ['sɪləbl] n Silbe f

syllabus ['sɪləbəs] n Lehrplan m

symbol ['sɪmbəl] n Symbol nt; **symbolic** [sɪm'bɒlɪk] adj symbolisch; **symbolize** vt symbolisieren

symmetrical [sɪ'metrɪkəl] adj symmetrisch

sympathetic [sɪmpə'θetɪk] adj mitfühlend; (understanding) verständnisvoll; **sympathize** ['sɪmpəθaɪz] vi mitfühlen (with sb mit jdm); **sympathy** ['sɪmpəθɪ] n Mitleid nt; (after death) Beileid nt; (understanding) Verständnis nt

symphony ['sɪmfənɪ] n Sinfonie f

symptom ['sɪmptəm] n (a. fig) Symptom nt

synagogue ['sɪnəgɒg] n Synagoge f

synonym ['sɪnənɪm] n Synonym nt; **synonymous** [sɪ'nɒnɪməs] adj synonym (with mit)

synthetic [sɪn'θetɪk] adj (material) synthetisch

syphilis ['sɪfɪlɪs] n Syphilis f

Syria ['sɪrɪə] n Syrien nt

syringe [sɪ'rɪndʒ] n Spritze f

system ['sɪstəm] n System nt; **systematic** [sɪstə'mætɪk] adj systematisch; **system disk** n (Inform) Systemdiskette f; **system(s) software** n (Inform) Systemsoftware f

tab [tæb] n (for hanging up coat etc) Aufhänger m; (Inform) Tabulator m; **to pick up the ~** (fam) die Rechnung übernehmen

table ['teɪbl] n Tisch m; (list) Tabelle f; **~ of contents** Inhaltsverzeichnis nt; **tablecloth** n Tischdecke f; **tablelamp** n Tischlampe f; **tablemat** n Set nt; **tablespoon** n Servierlöffel m; (in recipes) Esslöffel m

tablet ['tæblət] n (Med) Tablette f

table tennis ['teɪbltənɪs] n Tischtennis nt; **table wine** n Tafelwein m

tabloid ['tæblɔɪd] n Boulevardzeitung f

taboo [tə'buː] n Tabu nt ▷ adj tabu

tacit, tacitly ['tæsɪt, -lɪ] adj, adv stillschweigend

tack [tæk] n (small nail) Stift m; (US: thumb~) Reißzwecke f

tackle ['tækl] n (Sport) Angriff m; (equipment) Ausrüstung f ▷ vt (deal with) in Angriff nehmen; (Sport) angreifen; (verbally) zur Rede stellen (about wegen)

tacky ['tækɪ] adj trashig, heruntergekommen

tact [tækt] n Takt m; **tactful, tactfully** adj, adv taktvoll; **tactic(s)** ['tæktɪk(s)] n(pl) Taktik f; **tactless, tactlessly** ['tæktləs, -lɪ] adj, adv taktlos

tag [tæg] n (label) Schild nt; (with maker's name) Etikett nt

Tahiti [tɑːˈhiːtɪ] n Tahiti nt

tail [teɪl] n Schwanz m; **heads or ~s?** Kopf oder Zahl?; **tailback** n (Brit) Rückstau m; **taillight** n (Auto) Rücklicht nt

tailor ['teɪlə*] n Schneider(in) m(f)

tailpipe ['teɪlpaɪp] n (US Auto) Auspuffrohr nt

tainted ['teɪntɪd] adj (US: food) verdorben

Taiwan [taɪˈwæn] n Taiwan nt

take [teɪk] (**took, taken**) vt nehmen; (~ along with one) mitnehmen; (~ to a place) bringen; (subtract) abziehen (from von); (capture: person) fassen; (gain, obtain) bekommen; (Fin, Comm) einnehmen; (train, taxi) nehmen, fahren mit; (trip, walk, holiday, exam, course, photo) machen; (bath) nehmen; (phone call) entgegennehmen; (decision, precautions) treffen; (risk) eingehen; (advice, job) annehmen; (consume) zu sich nehmen; (tablets) nehmen; (heat, pain) ertragen; (react to) aufnehmen; (have room for) Platz haben für; **I'll ~ it** (item in shop) ich nehme es; **how long does it ~?** wie lange dauert es?; **it ~s 4 hours** man braucht 4 Stunden; **do you ~ sugar?** nimmst

du/nehmen Sie Zucker?; **I ~ it that ...** ich nehme an, dass ...; **to ~ part in** teilnehmen an; **to ~ place** stattfinden; **take after** vt nachschlagen +dat; **take along** vt mitnehmen; **take apart** vt auseinandernehmen; **take away** vt (remove) wegnehmen (from sb jdm); (subtract) abziehen (from von); **take back** vt (return) zurückbringen; (retract) zurücknehmen; (remind) zurückversetzen (to in +akk); **take down** vt (picture, curtains) abnehmen; (write down) aufschreiben; **take in** vt (understand) begreifen; (give accommodation to) aufnehmen; (deceive) hereinlegen; (include) einschließen; (show, film etc) mitnehmen; **take off** vi (plane) starten ▷ vt (clothing) ausziehen; (hat, lid) abnehmen; (deduct) abziehen; (Brit: imitate) nachmachen; **to take a day off** sich einen Tag freinehmen; **take on** vt (undertake) übernehmen; (employ) einstellen; (Sport) antreten gegen; **take out** vt (wallet etc) herausnehmen; (person, dog) ausführen; (insurance) abschließen; (money from bank) abheben; (book from library) ausleihen; **take over** vt übernehmen ▷ vi: **he took over (from me)** er hat mich abgelöst; **take to** vt: **I've taken to her/it** ich mag sie/es; **to ~ doing sth** (begin) anfangen, etw zu tun; **take up** vt (carpet) hochnehmen; (space) einnehmen; (time) in Anspruch nehmen; (hobby) anfangen mit; (new job) antreten; (offer) annehmen

takeaway n (Brit: meal) Essen nt zum Mitnehmen

taken ['teɪkn] pp of **take** ▷ adj

(*seat*) besetzt; **to be ~ with**
angetan sein von
takeoff ['teɪkɒf] n (*Aviat*) Start
m; (*imitation*) Nachahmung f;
takeout (*US*) see **takeaway**;
takeover n (*Comm*) Übernahme f
takings ['teɪkɪŋz] npl Einnahmen pl
tale [teɪl] n Geschichte f
talent ['tælənt] n Talent nt;
talented adj begabt
talk [tɔːk] n (*conversation*)
Gespräch nt; (*rumour*) Gerede nt; (*to
audience*) Vortrag m ▷ vi sprechen,
reden; (*have conversation*) sich
unterhalten; **to ~ to** (*o with*) **sb
(about sth)** mit jdm (über etw
akk) sprechen ▷ vt (*language*)
sprechen; (*nonsense*) reden;
(*politics, business*) reden über +akk;
**to ~ sb into doing/out of doing
sth** jdn überreden/jdm ausreden,
etw zu tun; **talk over** vt
besprechen
talkative adj gesprächig; **talk
show** n Talkshow f
tall [tɔːl] adj groß; (*building, tree*)
hoch; **he is 6ft ~** er ist 1,80m groß
tame [teɪm] adj zahm; (*joke,
story*) fade ▷ vt (*animal*) zähmen
tampon ['tæmpɒn] n Tampon m
tan [tæn] n (*on skin*)
(Sonnen)bräune f; **to get/have a
~** braun werden/sein ▷ vi braun
werden
tangerine [tændʒə'riːn] n
Mandarine f
tango ['tæŋɡəʊ] n Tango m
tank [tæŋk] n Tank m; (*for fish*)
Aquarium nt; (*Mil*) Panzer m
tanker ['tæŋkə°] n (*ship*) Tanker
m; (*vehicle*) Tankwagen m
tanned [tænd] adj (*by sun*) braun
tantalizing ['tæntəlaɪzɪŋ] adj
verlockend
Tanzania [tænzə'nɪə] n Tansania
nt

tap [tæp] n (*for water*) Hahn m
▷ vt, vi (*strike*) klopfen; **to ~ sb on
the shoulder** jdm auf die Schulter
klopfen; **tap-dance** vi steppen
tape [teɪp] n (*adhesive ~*)
Klebeband nt; (*for tape recorder*)
Tonband nt; (*cassette*) Kassette f;
(*video*) Video nt ▷ vt (*record*)
aufnehmen; **tape up** vt (*parcel*)
zukleben; **tape measure** n
Maßband nt; **tape recorder** n
Tonbandgerät nt
tapestry ['tæpɪstrɪ] n
Wandteppich m
tap water ['tæpwɔːtə°] n
Leitungswasser nt
target ['tɑːɡɪt] n Ziel nt; (*board*)
Zielscheibe f; **target group** n
Zielgruppe f
tariff ['tærɪf] n (*price list*)
Preisliste f; (*tax*) Zoll m
tarmac ['tɑːmæk] n (*Aviat*)
Rollfeld nt
tart [tɑːt] n (*fruit ~*) (Obst)kuchen
m; (*small*) (Obst)törtchen nt; (*fam,
pej: prostitute*) Nutte f; (*fam:
promiscuous person*) Schlampe f
tartan ['tɑːtən] n Schottenkaro
nt; (*material*) Schottenstoff m
tartar(e) sauce ['tɑːtə'sɔːs] n
Remouladensoße f
task [tɑːsk] n Aufgabe f; (*duty*)
Pflicht f; **taskbar** n (*Inform*)
Taskbar f
Tasmania [tæz'meɪnɪə] n Tas-
manien nt
taste [teɪst] n Geschmack m;
(*sense of ~*) Geschmackssinn m;
(*small quantity*) Kostprobe f; **it has
a strange ~** es schmeckt komisch
▷ vt schmecken; (*try*) probieren
▷ vi (*food*) schmecken (*of nach*); **to
~ good/strange** gut/komisch
schmecken; **tasteful, tastefully**
adj, adv geschmackvoll; **tasteless**,
tastelessly adj, adv
geschmacklos; **tasty** adj lecker

tattered ['tætəd] *adj* (clothes)
zerlumpt; (*fam: person*)
angespannt; **I'm absolutely ~** ich
bin mit den Nerven am Ende
tattoo [tə'tuː] *n* (*on skin*)
Tätowierung *f*
taught [tɔːt] *pt, pp of* **teach**
Taurus ['tɔːrəs] *n* (*Astr*) Stier *m*
tax [tæks] *n* Steuer *f* (*on* auf +*akk*)
▷ *vt* besteuern; **taxable** *adj*
steuerpflichtig; **taxation**
[tæk'seɪʃən] *n* Besteuerung *f*; **tax
bracket** *n* Steuerklasse *f*; **tax disc**
n (*Brit Auto*) Steuermarke *f*;
tax-free *adj* steuerfrei
taxi ['tæksɪ] *n* Taxi *nt* ▷ *vi* (*plane*)
rollen; **taxi driver** *n*
Taxifahrer(in) *m(f)*; **taxi rank**
(*Brit*), **taxi stand** *n* Taxistand *m*
tax return ['tæksrɪ'tɜːn] *n*
Steuererklärung *f*
tea [tiː] *n* Tee *m*; (*afternoon ~*) ≈
Kaffee und Kuchen; (*meal*) frühes
Abendessen; **teabag** *n* Teebeutel
m; **tea break** *n* (Tee)pause *f*
teach [tiːtʃ] (**taught,
taught**) *vt* (*person, subject*)
unterrichten; **to ~ sb** (**how**) **to
dance** jdm das Tanzen
beibringen ▷ *vi* unterrichten;
teacher *n* Lehrer(in) *m(f)*;
teaching *n* (*activity*)
Unterrichten *nt*; (*profession*)
Lehrberuf *m*
teacup ['tiːkʌp] *n* Teetasse *f*
team [tiːm] *n* (*Sport*) Mannschaft
f, Team *nt*; **teamwork** *n*
Teamarbeit *f*
teapot ['tiːpɒt] *n* Teekanne *f*
tear [tɪə°] *n* (*in eye*) Träne *f*
tear [tɛə°] (**tore, torn**) *vt*
zerreißen; **to ~ a muscle** sich
einen Muskel zerren ▷ *n* (*in
material etc*) Riss *m*; **tear down** *vt*
(*building*) abreißen; **tear up** *vt*
(*paper*) zerreißen
tearoom ['tiːrʊm] *n* Teestube *f*,

Café, in dem in erster Linie Tee serviert
wird
tease [tiːz] *vt* (*person*) necken
(*about* wegen)
tea set ['tiːset] *n* Teeservice *nt*;
teashop *n* Teestube *f*; **teaspoon**
n Teelöffel *m*; **tea towel** *n*
Geschirrtuch *nt*
technical ['teknɪkəl] *adj* technisch; (*knowledge, term, dictionary*)
Fach-; **technically** *adv* technisch;
technique [tek'niːk] *n* Technik *f*
techno ['teknəʊ] *n* Techno *f*
technological [teknə'lɒdʒɪkəl]
adj technologisch; **technology**
[tek'nɒlədʒɪ] *n* Technologie *f*,
Technik *f*
tedious ['tiːdɪəs] *adj* langweilig
teen(age) ['tiːn(eɪdʒ)] *adj* (*fash-
ions etc*) Teenager-; **teenager** *n*
Teenager *m*; **teens** [tiːnz] *npl*: **in
one's ~** im Teenageralter
teeth [tiːθ] *pl of* **tooth**
teetotal ['tiː'təʊtl] *adj* abstinent
telegraph pole ['telɪɡrɑːfpəʊl]
n (*Brit*) Telegrafenmast *m*
telephone ['telɪfəʊn] *n* Telefon
nt ▷ *vi* telefonieren ▷ *vt* anrufen;
telephone banking *n*
Telefonbanking *nt*; **telephone
book** *n* Telefonbuch *nt*;
telephone booth, **telephone box**
(*Brit*) *n* Telefonzelle *f*; **telephone
call** *n* Telefonanruf *m*; **telephone
directory** *n* Telefonbuch *nt*;
telephone number *n*
Telefonnummer *f*
telephoto lens ['telɪfəʊtəʊ'lenz]
n Teleobjektiv *nt*
telescope ['telɪskəʊp] *n* Teleskop *nt*
televise ['telɪvaɪz] *vt* im
Fernsehen übertragen; **television**
['telɪvɪʒən] *n* Fernsehen *nt*;
television programme *n*
Fernsehsendung *f*; **television
(set)** *n* Fernseher *m*

t

teleworking ['telɪwɜːkiŋ] n
Telearbeit f
tell [tel] (**told, told**) vt (say,
inform) sagen (sb sth jdm etw);
(story) erzählen; (truth) sagen;
(difference) erkennen; (reveal secret)
verraten; **to ~ sb about sth** jdm
von etw erzählen; **to ~ sth from
sth** etw von etw unterscheiden
▷ vi (be sure) wissen; **tell apart** vt
unterscheiden; **tell off** vt
schimpfen
telling adj aufschlussreich
telly ['telɪ] n (Brit fam) Glotze f; **on
(the) ~** in der Glotze
temp [temp] n Aushilfskraft f
▷ vi als Aushilfskraft arbeiten
temper ['tempə] n (anger) Wut f;
(mood) Laune f; **to lose one's ~** die
Beherrschung verlieren; **to have a
bad ~** jähzornig sein;
temperamental
[tempərə'mentl] adj (moody)
launisch
temperature ['temprɪtʃə] n
Temperatur f; (Med: high ~) Fieber
nt; **to have a ~** Fieber haben
temple ['templ] n Tempel m;
(Anat) Schläfe f
temporarily ['tempərərɪlɪ] adv
vorübergehend; **temporary**
['tempərərɪ] adj vorübergehend;
(road, building) provisorisch
tempt [tempt] vt in Versuchung
führen; **I'm ~ed to accept** ich bin
versucht anzunehmen;
temptation [temp'teɪʃən] n
Versuchung f; **tempting** adj
verlockend
ten [ten] num zehn ▷ n Zehn f;
see also **eight**
tenant ['tenənt] n Mieter(in)
m(f); (of land) Pächter(in) m(f)
tend [tend] vi: **to ~ to do sth**
(person) dazu neigen, etw zu tun;
to ~ towards neigen zu;
tendency ['tendənsɪ] n Tendenz

f; **to have a ~ to do sth** (person)
dazu neigen, etw zu tun
tender ['tendə] adj (loving)
zärtlich; (sore) empfindlich; (meat)
zart
tendon ['tendən] n Sehne f
Tenerife [tenə'riːf] n Teneriffa nt
tenner ['tenə] n (Brit fam: note)
Zehnpfundschein m; (amount) zehn
Pfund
tennis ['tenɪs] n Tennis nt;
tennis ball n Tennisball m; **tennis
court** n Tennisplatz m; **tennis
racket** n Tennisschläger m
tenor ['tenə] n Tenor m
tenpin bowling, tenpins (US)
['tenpɪn'bəʊlɪŋ, 'tenpɪnz] n
Bowling nt
tense [tens] adj angespannt;
(stretched tight) gespannt; **tension**
['tenʃən] n Spannung f; (strain)
Anspannung f
tent [tent] n Zelt nt
tenth [tenθ] adj zehnte(r, s) ▷ n
(fraction) Zehntel nt; see also **eighth**
tent peg ['tentpeg] n Hering m;
tent pole n Zeltstange f
term [tɜːm] n (in school, at
university) Trimester nt; (expression)
Ausdruck m; **~s** pl (conditions)
Bedingungen pl; **to be on good ~s
with sb** mit jdm gut auskommen;
to come to ~s with sth sich mit
etw abfinden; **in the long/short
~** langfristig/kurzfristig; **in ~s
of ...** was ... betrifft
terminal ['tɜːmɪnl] n (bus ~ etc)
Endstation f; (Aviat) Terminal m;
(Inform) Terminal nt; (Elec) Pol m
▷ adj (Med) unheilbar; **terminally**
adv (ill) unheilbar
terminate ['tɜːmɪneɪt] vt (contract) lösen; (pregnancy) abbrechen
▷ vi (train, bus) enden
terminology [tɜːmɪ'nɒlədʒɪ] n
Terminologie f
terrace ['terəs] n (of houses)

Häuserreihe f; (in garden etc)
Terrasse f; **terraced** adj (garden)
terrassenförmig angelegt;
terraced house n (Brit)
Reihenhaus nt
terrible ['terəbl] adj schrecklich
terrific [tə'rɪfɪk] adj (very good)
fantastisch
terrify ['terɪfaɪ] vt erschrecken;
to be terrified schreckliche Angst
haben (of vor +dat)
territory ['terɪtərɪ] n Gebiet nt
terror ['terə*] n Schrecken m;
(Pol) Terror m; **terrorism** n
Terrorismus m; **terrorist** n
Terrorist(in) m(f)
test [test] n Test m, Klassenarbeit
f; (driving ~) Prüfung f; **to put to
the ~** auf die Probe stellen ▷ vt
testen, prüfen; (patience, courage
etc) auf die Probe stellen
Testament ['testəmənt] n: **the
Old/New ~** das Alte/Neue
Testament
test-drive ['testdraɪv] vt Probe
fahren
testicle ['testɪkl] n Hoden m
testify ['testɪfaɪ] vi (Jur)
aussagen
test tube ['testtju:b] n
Reagenzglas nt
tetanus ['tetənəs] n Tetanus m
text [tekst] n Text m; (of
document) Wortlaut m; (sent by
mobile phone) SMS f ▷ vt (message)
simsen, SMSen; **to ~ sb** jdm
simsen, jdm eine SMS schicken;
I'll ~ it to you ich schicke es dir per
SMS
textbook n Lehrbuch nt
texting ['tekstɪŋ] n SMS-
Messaging nt; **text message** n
SMS f; **text messaging** n
SMS-Messaging nt
texture ['tekstʃə*] n
Beschaffenheit f
Thailand ['taɪlænd] n Thailand nt

Thames [temz] n Themse f
than [ðæn] prep, conj als;
bigger/faster ~ me
größer/schneller als ich; **I'd rather
walk ~ drive** ich gehe lieber zu
Fuß als mit dem Auto
thank [θæŋk] vt danken +dat;
~ you danke; **~ you very much**
vielen Dank; **thankful** adj
dankbar; **thankfully** adv (luckily)
zum Glück; **thankless** adj
undankbar; **thanks** npl Dank m;
~ danke!; ~ to dank +gen

● **THANKSGIVING DAY**
●
● **Thanksgiving (Day)** ist ein
● Feiertag in den USA, der auf den
● vierten Donnerstag im
● November fällt. Er soll daran
● erinnern, wie die Pilgerväter die
● gute Ernte im Jahre 1621
● feierten. In Kanada gibt es einen
● ähnlichen Erntedanktag (der
● aber nichts mit den Pilgervätern
● zu tun hat) am zweiten Montag
● im Oktober.

🅞 **KEYWORD**

that [ðæt, ðət] adj (demonstrative)
(pl those) der/die/das, jene(r, s);
that one das da
▷ pron **1** (demonstrative) (pl those)
das; **who's/what's that?** wer ist
da/was ist das?; **is that you?** bist
du/sind Sie das?; **that's what he
said** genau das hat er gesagt;
what happened after that? was
passierte danach?; **that is** das
heißt
2 (relative) (subj) der/die/das, die;
(direct obj) den/die/das, die;
(indirect obj) dem/der/dem, denen;
all (that) I have alles, was ich
habe
3 (relative) (of time); **the day (that)**

an dem Tag, als; **the winter (that) he came** in dem Winter, in dem er kam
▷ *conj* dass; **he thought that I was ill** er dachte, dass ich krank sei, er dachte, ich sei krank
▷ *adv* (*demonstrative*) so; **I can't work that much** ich kann nicht so viel arbeiten

that's [ðæts] *contr of* **that is; that has**

thaw [θɔː] *vi* tauen; (*frozen food*) auftauen ▷ *vt* auftauen lassen

🔵 **KEYWORD**

the [ðə, ðiː] *def art* 1 der/die/das; **to play the piano/violin** Klavier/Geige spielen; **I'm going to the butcher's/the cinema** ich gehe zum Fleischer/ins Kino; **Elizabeth the First** Elisabeth die Erste
2 (+*adj to form noun*) das, die; **the rich and the poor** die Reichen und die Armen
3 (*in comparisons*) **the more he works the more he earns** je mehr er arbeitet, desto mehr verdient er

theater (*US*), **theatre** ['θɪətə°] *n* Theater *nt*; (*for lectures etc*) Saal *m*
theft [θeft] *n* Diebstahl *m*
their [ðɛə°] *adj* ihr; (*unidentified person*) sein; **they cleaned ~ teeth** sie putzten sich die Zähne; **someone has left ~ umbrella here** jemand hat seinen Schirm hier vergessen; **theirs** *pron* ihre(r, s); (*unidentified person*) seine(r, s); **it's ~** es gehört ihnen; **a friend of ~** ein Freund von ihnen; **someone has left ~ here** jemand hat seins hier liegen lassen
them [ðem, ðəm] *pron* (*direct object*) sie; (*indirect object*) ihnen;

(*unidentified person*) ihn/ihm, sie/ihr; **do you know ~?** kennst du/kennen Sie sie?; **can you help ~?** kannst du/können Sie ihnen helfen?; **it's ~** sie sind's; **if anyone has a problem you should help ~** wenn jemand ein Problem hat, solltest du/sollten Sie ihm helfen
theme [θiːm] *n* Thema *nt*; (*Mus*) Motiv *nt*; **~ park** Themenpark *m*; **~ song** Titelmusik *f*
themselves [ðəm'selvz] *pron* sich; **they hurt ~** sie haben sich verletzt; **they ~ were not there** sie selbst waren nicht da; **they did it ~** sie haben es selbst gemacht; **they are not dangerous in ~** an sich sind sie nicht gefährlich; (*all*) **by ~** allein
then [ðen] *adv* (*at that time*) damals; (*next*) dann; (*therefore*) also; (*furthermore*) ferner; **from ~ on** von da an; **by ~** bis dahin
▷ *adj* damalig
theoretical, **theoretically** [θɪə'retɪkəl, -lɪ] *adj, adv* theoretisch
theory ['θɪərɪ] *n* Theorie *f*; **in ~** theoretisch
therapy ['θerəpɪ] *n* Therapie *f*

🔵 **KEYWORD**

there [ðɛə°] *adv* 1 **there is/there are** es o da ist/sind; (*there exists/exist also*) es gibt; **there are 3 of them** (*people, things*) es gibt 3 davon; **there has been an accident** da war ein Unfall
2 (*place*) da, dort; (*direction*) dahin, dorthin; **put it in/on there** leg es dahinein/dorthinauf
3 **there, there** (*esp to child*) na, na

thereabouts *adv* (*approximately*) so ungefähr; **therefore** *adv* daher, deshalb

thermometer [θə'mɒmɪtə*] *n*
Thermometer *nt*

Thermos® ['θɜ:məs] *n*: ~ (**flask**)
Thermosflasche® *f*

these [ði:z] *pron, adj* diese; **I
don't like ~ apples** ich mag diese
Äpfel nicht; ~ **are not my books**
das sind nicht meine Bücher

thesis ['θi:sɪs] (*pl* **theses**) *n* (*for
PhD*) Doktorarbeit *f*

they [ðeɪ] *pron pl* sie; (*people in
general*) man; (*unidentified person*)
er/sie; ~ **are rich** sie sind reich;
~ **say that ...** man sagt, dass ...; **if
anyone looks at this, ~ will see
that ...** wenn sich jemand dies
ansieht, wird er erkennen, dass ...

they'd [ðeɪd] *contr of* **they had;
they would**

they'll [ðeɪl] *contr of* **they will;
they shall**

they've [ðeɪv] *contr of* **they have**

thick [θɪk] *adj* dick; (*fog*) dicht;
(*liquid*) dickflüssig; (*fam: stupid*)
dumm; **thicken** *vi* (*fog*) dichter
werden; (*sauce*) dick werden ▷ *vt*
(*sauce*) eindicken

thief [θi:f] (*pl* **thieves**) *n*
Dieb(in) *m(f)*

thigh [θaɪ] *n* Oberschenkel *m*

thimble ['θɪmbl] *n* Fingerhut *m*

thin [θɪn] *adj* dünn

thing [θɪŋ] *n* Ding *nt*; (*affair*)
Sache *f*; **my ~s** *pl* meine Sachen *pl*;
how are ~s? wie geht's?; **I can't
see a ~** ich kann nichts sehen; **he
knows a ~ or two about cars** er
kennt sich mit Autos aus

think [θɪŋk] (**thought, thought**)
vt, vi denken; (*believe*) meinen; **I
~ so** ich denke schon; **I don't ~ so**
ich glaube nicht; **think about** *vt*
denken an +*akk*; (*reflect on*)
nachdenken über +*akk*; (*have
opinion of*) halten von; **think of** *vt*
denken an +*akk*; (*devise*) sich
ausdenken; (*have opinion of*) halten

von; (*remember*) sich erinnern an
+*akk*; **think over** *vt* überdenken;
think up *vt* sich ausdenken

third [θɜ:d] *adj* dritte(r, s); **the
Third World** die Dritte Welt ▷ *n*
(*fraction*) Drittel *nt*; **in ~** (*gear*) im
dritten Gang; *see also* **eighth**;
thirdly *adv* drittens; **third-party
insurance** *n* Haftpflichtversicherung *f*

thirst [θɜ:st] *n* Durst *m* (*for* nach);
thirsty *adj*: **to be ~** Durst haben

thirteen ['θɜ:'ti:n] *num* dreizehn
▷ *n* Dreizehn *f*; *see also* **eight**;
thirteenth *adj* dreizehnte(r, s);
see also **eighth**; **thirtieth** ['θɜ:tɪɪθ]
adj dreißigste(r, s); *see also* **eighth**;
thirty ['θɜ:tɪ] *num* dreißig;
~-one einunddreißig ▷ *n* Dreißig
f; **to be in one's thirties** in den
Dreißigern sein; *see also* **eight**

KEYWORD

this [ðɪs] *adj* (*demonstrative*) (*pl*
these) diese(r, s); **this evening**
heute Abend; **this one** diese(r, s)
(da)
▷ *pron* (*demonstrative*) (*pl* **these**)
dies, das; **who/what is this?**
wer/was ist das?; **this is where I
live** hier wohne ich; **this is what
he said** das hat er gesagt; **this is
Mr Brown** dies ist Mr Brown; (*on
telephone*) hier ist Mr Brown
▷ *adv* (*demonstrative*) **this
high/long** *etc* so groß/lang *etc*

thistle [θɪsl] *n* Distel *f*

thong [θɒŋ] *n* String *m*

thorn [θɔ:n] *n* Dorn *m*, Stachel *m*

thorough ['θʌrə] *adj* gründlich;
thoroughly *adv* gründlich; (*agree
etc*) völlig

those [ðəʊz] *pron* die da, jene;
~ **who** diejenigen, die ▷ *adj* die,
jene

t

though [ðəʊ] *conj* obwohl; **as ~** als ob ▷ *adv* aber

thought [θɔːt] *pt, pp of* **think** ▷ *n* Gedanke *m*; (*thinking*) Überlegung *f*; **thoughtful** *adj* (*kind*) rücksichtsvoll; (*attentive*) aufmerksam; (*in Gedanken versunken*) nachdenklich; **thoughtless** *adj* (*unkind*) rücksichtslos, gedankenlos

thousand ['θaʊzənd] *num*: (**one**) **~, a ~** tausend; **five ~** fünftausend; **~s of** Tausende von

thrash [θræʃ] *vt* (*hit*) verprügeln; (*defeat*) vernichtend schlagen

thread [θred] *n* Faden *m* ▷ *vt* (*needle*) einfädeln; (*beads*) auffädeln

threat [θret] *n* Drohung *f*; (*danger*) Bedrohung *f* (*to* für); **threaten** *vt* bedrohen; **threatening** *adj* bedrohlich

three [θriː] *num* drei ▷ *n* Drei *f*; *see also* **eight**; **three-dimensional** *adj* dreidimensional; **three-piece suit** *n* Anzug *m* mit Weste; **three-quarters** *npl* drei Viertel *pl*

threshold ['θreʃhəʊld] *n* Schwelle *f*

threw [θruː] *pt of* **throw**

thrifty ['θrɪftɪ] *adj* sparsam

thrilled [θrɪld] *adj*: **to be ~ (with sth)** sich (über etw *akk*) riesig freuen; **thriller** *n* Thriller *m*; **thrilling** *adj* aufregend

thrive [θraɪv] *vi* gedeihen (*on* bei); (*fig, business*) florieren

throat [θrəʊt] *n* Hals *m*, Kehle *f*

throbbing ['θrɒbɪŋ] *adj* (*pain, headache*) pochend

thrombosis [θrɒm'bəʊsɪs] *n* Thrombose *f*; **deep vein ~** tiefe Venenthrombose *f*

throne [θrəʊn] *n* Thron *m*

through [θruː] *prep* durch; (*time*) während +*gen*; (*because of*) aus, durch; (*US: up to and including*) bis;

arranged ~ him durch ihn arrangiert ▷ *adv* durch; **to put sb ~** (*Tel*) jdn verbinden (*to* mit) ▷ *adj* (*ticket, train*) durchgehend; **~ flight** Direktflug *m*; **to be ~ with sb/sth** mit jdm/etw fertig sein;

throughout [θruː'aʊt] *prep* (*place*) überall in +*dat*; (*time*) während +*gen*; **~ the night** die ganze Nacht hindurch ▷ *adv* überall; (*time*) die ganze Zeit

throw [θrəʊ] (**threw, thrown**) *vt* werfen; (*rider*) abwerfen; (*party*) geben; **to ~ sth to sb, to ~ sb sth** jdm etw zuwerfen; **I was ~n by his question** seine Frage hat mich aus dem Konzept gebracht ▷ *n* Wurf *m*; **throw away** *vt* wegwerfen; **throw in** *vt* (*include*) dazugeben; **throw out** *vt* (*unwanted object*) wegwerfen; (*person*) hinauswerfen (*of* aus); **throw up** *vt, vi* (*fam: vomit*) sich übergeben; **throw-in** *n* Einwurf *m*

thrown [θrəʊn] *pp of* **throw**

thru (*US*) *see* **through**

thrush [θrʌʃ] *n* Drossel *f*

thrust [θrʌst] (**thrust, thrust**) *vt, vi* (*push*) stoßen

thruway ['θruːweɪ] *n* (*US*) Schnellstraße *f*

thumb [θʌm] *n* Daumen *m* ▷ *vt*: **to ~ a lift** per Anhalter fahren; **thumbtack** *n* (*US*) Reißzwecke *f*

thunder ['θʌndə°] *n* Donner *m* ▷ *vi* donnern; **thunderstorm** *n* Gewitter *nt*

Thur(s) *abbr* = **Thursday** Do.

Thursday ['θɜːzdɪ] *n* Donnerstag *m*; *see also* **Tuesday**

thus [ðʌs] *adv* (*in this way*) so; (*therefore*) somit, also

thyme [taɪm] *n* Thymian *m*

Tibet [tɪ'bet] *n* Tibet *nt*

tick [tɪk] *n* (*Brit: mark*) Häkchen *nt* ▷ *vt* (*name*) abhaken; (*box, answer*) ankreuzen ▷ *vi* (*clock*) ticken

ticket ['tɪkɪt] *n* (*for train, bus*) (Fahr)karte *f*; (*plane ~*) Flugschein *m*, Ticket *nt*; (*for theatre, match, museum etc*) (Eintritts)karte *f*; (*price ~*) (Preis)schild *nt*; (*raffle ~*) Los *nt*; (*for car park*) Parkschein *m*; (*for traffic offence*) Strafzettel *m*; **ticket collector**, **ticket inspector** (*Brit*) *n* Fahrkartenkontrolleur(in) *m(f)*; **ticket machine** *n* (*for public transport*) Fahrscheinautomat *m*; (*in car park*) Parkscheinautomat *m*; **ticket office** *n* (*Rail*) Fahrkartenschalter *m*; (*Theat*) Kasse *f*

tickle ['tɪkl] *vt* kitzeln; **ticklish** ['tɪklɪʃ] *adj* kitzlig

tide [taɪd] *n* Gezeiten *pl*; **the ~ is in/out** es ist Flut/Ebbe

tidy ['taɪdɪ] *adj* ordentlich ▷ *vt* aufräumen; **tidy up** *vt, vi* aufräumen

tie [taɪ] *n* (*neck~*) Krawatte *f*; (*Sport*) Unentschieden *nt*; (*bond*) Bindung *f* ▷ *vt* (*attach, do up*) binden (*to an +akk*); (*~ together*) zusammenbinden; (*knot*) machen ▷ *vi* (*Sport*) unentschieden spielen; **tie down** *vt* festbinden (*to an +dat*); (*fig*) binden; **tie up** *vt* (*dog*) anbinden; (*parcel*) verschnüren; (*shoelace*) binden; (*boat*) festmachen; **I'm tied up** (*fig*) ich bin beschäftigt

tiger ['taɪgə*] *n* Tiger *m*

tight [taɪt] *adj* (*clothes*) eng; (*knot*) fest; (*screw, lid*) fest sitzend; (*control, security measures*) streng; (*timewise*) knapp; (*schedule*) eng ▷ *adv* (*shut*) fest; (*pull*) stramm; **hold ~** festhalten!; **sleep ~** schlaf gut!; **tighten** *vt* (*knot, rope, screw*) anziehen; (*belt*) enger machen; (*restrictions, control*) verschärfen; **tights** *npl* (*Brit*) Strumpfhose *f*

tile [taɪl] *n* (*on roof*) Dachziegel *m*;

(*on wall, floor*) Fliese *f*; **tiled** *adj* (*roof*) Ziegel-; (*floor, wall*) gefliest

till [tɪl] *n* Kasse *f* ▷ *prep, conj see* **until**

tilt [tɪlt] *vt* kippen; (*head*) neigen ▷ *vi* sich neigen

time [taɪm] *n* Zeit *f*; (*occasion*) Mal *nt*; (*Mus*) Takt *m*; **local ~** Ortszeit; **what ~ is it?, what's the ~?** wie spät ist es?, wie viel Uhr ist es?; **to take one's ~ (over sth)** sich (bei etw) Zeit lassen; **to have a good ~** Spaß haben; **in two weeks' ~** in zwei Wochen; **at ~s** manchmal; **at the same ~** gleichzeitig; **all the ~** die ganze Zeit; **by the ~ he ...** bis er ...; (*in past*) als er ...; **for the ~ being** vorläufig; **in ~** (*not late*) rechtzeitig; **on ~** pünktlich; **the first ~** das erste Mal; **this ~** diesmal; **five ~s** fünfmal; **five ~s six** fünf mal sechs; **four ~s a year** viermal im Jahr; **three at a ~** drei auf einmal ▷ *vt* (*with stopwatch*) stoppen; **you ~d that well** das hast du/haben Sie gut getimt; **time difference** *n* Zeitunterschied *m*; **time limit** *n* Frist *f*; **timer** *n* Timer *m*; (*switch*) Schaltuhr *f*; **time-saving** *adj* zeitsparend; **time switch** *n* Schaltuhr *f*; **timetable** *n* (*for public transport*) Fahrplan *m*; (*school*) Stundenplan *m*; **time zone** *n* Zeitzone *f*

timid ['tɪmɪd] *adj* ängstlich

timing ['taɪmɪŋ] *n* (*coordination*) Timing *nt*, zeitliche Abstimmung

tin [tɪn] *n* (*metal*) Blech *nt*; (*Brit: can*) Dose *f*; **tinfoil** *n* Alufolie *f*; **tinned** [tɪnd] *adj* (*Brit*) aus der Dose; **tin opener** *n* (*Brit*) Dosenöffner *m*

tinsel ['tɪnsəl] *n* ≈ Lametta *nt*

tint [tɪnt] *n* (Farb)ton *m*; (*in hair*) Tönung *f*; **tinted** *adj* getönt

t

tiny ['taɪnɪ] adj winzig
tip [tɪp] n (money) Trinkgeld nt;
(hint) Tipp m; (end) Spitze f; (of
cigarette) Filter m; (Brit: rubbish ~)
Müllkippe f ▷ vt (waiter) Trinkgeld
geben +dat; **tip over** vt, vi
(overturn) umkippen
tipsy ['tɪpsɪ] adj beschwipst
tiptoe ['tɪptəʊ] n: **on ~** auf
Zehenspitzen
tire ['taɪə°] n (US) see **tyre** ▷ vt
müde machen ▷ vi müde werden;
tired adj müde; **to be ~ of sb/sth**
jdn/etw satthaben; **to be ~ of
doing sth** es satthaben, etw zu
tun; **tireless, tirelessly** adv
unermüdlich; **tiresome** adj
lästig; **tiring** adj ermüdend
Tirol [tɪ'rəʊl] see **Tyrol**
tissue ['tɪʃuː] n (Anat) Gewebe nt;
(paper handkerchief)
Tempotaschentuch® nt,
Papier(taschen)tuch nt; **tissue
paper** n Seidenpapier nt
tit [tɪt] n (bird) Meise f; (fam:
breast) Titte f
title ['taɪtl] n Titel m
titter ['tɪtə] vi kichern

⬤ **KEYWORD**

to [tuː, tə] prep **1** (direction) zu,
nach; **I go to France/school** ich
gehe nach Frankreich/zur Schule;
to the left nach links
2 (as far as) bis
3 (with expressions of time) vor; **a
quarter to 5** Viertel vor 5
4 (for, of) für; **secretary to the
director** Sekretärin des Direktors
5 (expressing indirect object) **to give
sth to sb** jdm etw geben; **to talk
to sb** mit jdm sprechen; **I sold it to
a friend** ich habe es einem Freund
verkauft
6 (in relation to) zu; **30 miles to the
gallon** 30 Meilen pro Gallone

7 (purpose, result) zu; **to my
surprise** zu meiner Überraschung
▷ with vb **1** (infin) **to go/eat**
gehen/essen; **to want to do sth**
etw tun wollen; **to try/start to do
sth** versuchen/anfangen, etw zu
tun; **he has a lot to lose** er hat viel
zu verlieren
2 (with vb omitted) **I don't want to**
ich will (es) nicht
3 (purpose, result) um; **I did it to
help you** ich tat es, um dir/Ihnen
zu helfen
4 (after adj etc) **ready to use**
gebrauchsfertig; **too old/young
to ...** zu alt/jung, um ... zu ...
▷ adv: **push/pull the door to** die
Tür zuschieben/zuziehen

toad [təʊd] n Kröte f; **toadstool**
n Giftpilz m
toast [təʊst] n (bread, drink) Toast
m; **a piece** (o slice) **of ~** eine
Scheibe Toast; **to propose a ~ to
sb** einen Toast auf jdn ausbringen
▷ vt (bread) toasten; (person)
trinken auf +akk; **toaster** n
Toaster m
tobacco [tə'bækəʊ] (pl **-es**) n
Tabak m; **tobacconist's**
[tə'bækənɪsts] n: **~ (shop)**
Tabakladen m
toboggan [tə'bɒgən] n Schlitten
m
today [tə'deɪ] adv heute; **a week
~** heute in einer Woche; **~'s
newspaper** die Zeitung von heute
toddler ['tɒdlə°] n Kleinkind
nt
toe [təʊ] n Zehe f, Zeh m; **toenail**
n Zehennagel m
toffee ['tɒfɪ] n (sweet)
Karamellbonbon nt; **toffee apple**
n kandierter Apfel; **toffee-nosed**
adj hochnäsig
tofu ['təʊfuː] n Tofu m
together [tə'geðə°] adv

zusammen; **I tied them ~** ich habe sie zusammengebunden

toilet ['tɔɪlət] n Toilette f; **to go to the ~** auf die Toilette gehen; **toilet bag** n Kulturbeutel m; **toilet paper** n Toilettenpapier nt; **toiletries** ['tɔɪlətrɪz] npl Toilettenartikel pl; **toilet roll** n Rolle f Toilettenpapier

token ['təʊkən] n Marke f; (in casino) Spielmarke f; (voucher, gift ~) Gutschein m; (sign) Zeichen nt

Tokyo ['təʊkɪəʊ] n Tokio nt

told [təʊld] pt, pp of **tell**

tolerant ['tɒlərənt] adj tolerant (of gegenüber); **tolerate** ['tɒləreɪt] vt tolerieren; (noise, pain, heat) ertragen

toll [təʊl] n (charge) Gebühr f; **the death ~** die Zahl der Toten; **toll-free** adj, adv (US Tel) gebührenfrei; **toll road** n gebührenpflichtige Straße

tomato [tə'mɑːtəʊ] (pl **-es**) n Tomate f; **tomato juice** n Tomatensaft m; **tomato ketchup** n Tomatenketchup m o nt; **tomato sauce** n Tomatensoße f; (Brit: ketchup) Tomatenketchup m o nt

tomb [tuːm] n Grabmal nt; **tombstone** n Grabstein m

tomorrow [tə'mɒrəʊ] adv morgen; **~ morning** morgen früh; **~ evening** morgen Abend; **the day after ~** übermorgen; **a week (from) ~/~ week** morgen in einer Woche

ton [tʌn] n (Brit) Tonne f (1016 kg); (US) Tonne f (907 kg); **~s of books** (fam) eine Menge Bücher

tone [təʊn] n Ton m; **tone down** vt mäßigen; **toner** ['təʊnə°] n (for printer) Toner m; **toner cartridge** n Tonerpatrone f

tongs [tɒŋz] npl Zange f; (curling ~) Lockenstab m

tongue [tʌŋ] n Zunge f

tonic ['tɒnɪk] n (Med) Stärkungsmittel nt; **~ (water)** Tonic nt; **gin and ~** Gin m Tonic

tonight [tə'naɪt] adv heute Abend; (during night) heute Nacht

tonsils ['tɒnslz] n Mandeln pl; **tonsillitis** [tɒnsɪ'laɪtɪs] n Mandelentzündung f

too [tuː] adv zu; (also) auch; **~ fast** zu schnell; **~ much/many** zu viel/viele; **me ~** ich auch; **she liked it ~** ihr gefiel es auch

took [tʊk] pt of **take**

tool [tuːl] n Werkzeug nt; **toolbar** n (Inform) Symbolleiste f; **toolbox** n Werkzeugkasten m

tooth [tuːθ] (pl **teeth**) n Zahn m; **toothache** n Zahnschmerzen pl; **toothbrush** n Zahnbürste f; **toothpaste** n Zahnpasta f; **toothpick** n Zahnstocher m

top [tɒp] n (of tower, class, company etc) Spitze f; (of mountain) Gipfel m; (of tree) Krone f; (of street) oberes Ende; (of tube, pen) Kappe f; (of box) Deckel m; (of bikini) Oberteil nt; (sleeveless) Top nt; **at the ~ of the page** oben auf der Seite; **at the ~ of the league** an der Spitze der Liga; **on ~** oben; **on ~ of** auf +dat; (in addition to) zusätzlich +dat; **in ~ (gear)** im höchsten Gang; **over the ~** übertrieben ▷ adj (floor, shelf) oberste(r, s); (price, note) höchste(r, s); (best) Spitzen-; (pupil, school) beste(r, s) ▷ vt (exceed) übersteigen; (be better than) übertreffen; (league) an erster Stelle liegen in +dat; **~ped with cream** mit Sahne obendrauf; **top up** vt auffüllen; **can I top you up?** darf ich dir nachschenken?

topic ['tɒpɪk] n Thema nt; **topical** adj aktuell

topless ['tɒpləs] *adj, adv* oben
ohne

topping ['tɒpɪŋ] *n* (*on top of pizza,
ice-cream etc*) Belag *m*, Garnierung *f*

top-secret ['tɒp'si:krət] *adj*
streng geheim

torch [tɔ:tʃ] *n* (*Brit*)
Taschenlampe *f*

tore [tɔ:°] *pt of* **tear**

torment ['tɔ:ment] *vt* quälen

torn [tɔ:n] *pp of* **tear**

tornado [tɔ:'neɪdəʊ] (*pl* **-es**) *n*
Tornado *m*

torrential [tə'renʃəl] *adj* (*rain*)
sintflutartig

tortoise ['tɔ:təs] *n* Schildkröte
f

torture ['tɔ:tʃə°] *n* Folter *f*; (*fig*)
Qual *f* ▷ *vt* foltern

Tory ['tɔ:rɪ] (*Brit*) *n* Tory *m*,
Konservative(r) *mf* ▷ *adj* Tory-

toss [tɒs] *vt* (*throw*) werfen;
(*salad*) anmachen; **to ~ a coin** eine
Münze werfen ▷ *n*: **I don't give a
~** (*fam*) es ist mir scheißegal

total ['təʊtl] *n* (*of figures, money*)
Gesamtsumme *f*; **a ~ of 30**
insgesamt 30; **in ~** insgesamt
▷ *adj* total; (*sum etc*) Gesamt- ▷ *vt*
(*amount to*) sich belaufen auf +*akk*;
totally *adv* total

touch [tʌtʃ] *n* (*act of ~ing*)
Berührung *f*; (*sense of ~*) Tastsinn
m; (*trace*) Spur *f*; **to be/keep in
~ with sb** mit jdm in Verbindung
stehen/bleiben; **to get in ~ with
sb** sich mit jdm in Verbindung
setzen; **to lose ~ with sb** den
Kontakt zu jdm verlieren ▷ *vt*
(*feel*) berühren; (*emotionally*)
bewegen; **touch on** *vt* (*topic*)
berühren; **touchdown** *n* (*Aviat*)
Landung *f*; (*Sport*) Touchdown *m*;
touching *adj* (*moving*) rührend;
touch screen *n* Touchscreen *m*,
Berührungsbildschirm *m*; **touchy**
adj empfindlich, zickig

tough [tʌf] *adj* hart; (*meat*) zäh;
(*material*) robust; (*meat*) zäh

tour ['tʊə°] *n* Tour *f* (*of* durch); (*of
town, building*) Rundgang *m* (*of*
durch); (*of pop group etc*) Tournee *f*
▷ *vt* eine Tour/einen
Rundgang/eine Tournee machen
durch ▷ *vi* (*on holiday*)
umherreisen; **tour guide** *n*
Reiseleiter(in) *m(f)*

tourism ['tʊərɪzəm] *n* Tourismus *m*, Fremdenverkehr *m*;
tourist *n* Tourist(in) *m(f)*; **tourist
class** *n* Touristenklasse *f*; **tourist
guide** *n* (*book*) Reiseführer *m*;
(*person*) Fremdenführer(in) *m(f)*;
tourist office *n*
Fremdenverkehrsamt *nt*

tournament ['tʊənəmənt] *n*
Turnier *nt*

tour operator ['tʊərɒpəreɪtə°]
n Reiseveranstalter *m*

tow [təʊ] *vt* abschleppen;
(*caravan, trailer*) ziehen; **tow away**
vt abschleppen

towards [tə'wɔ:dz] *prep*: **~ me**
mir entgegen, auf mich zu; **we
walked ~ the station** wir gingen
in Richtung Bahnhof; **my feelings
~ him** meine Gefühle ihm
gegenüber; **she was kind ~ me** sie
war nett zu mir

towel ['taʊəl] *n* Handtuch *nt*

tower ['taʊə°] *n* Turm *m*; **tower
block** *n* (*Brit*) Hochhaus *nt*

town [taʊn] *n* Stadt *f*; **town
center** (*US*), **town centre** *n*
Stadtmitte *f*, Stadtzentrum *nt*;
town hall *n* Rathaus *nt*

towrope ['təʊrəʊp] *n*
Abschleppseil *nt*; **tow truck** *n*
(*US*) Abschleppwagen *m*

toxic ['tɒksɪk] *adj* giftig, Gift-

toy [tɔɪ] *n* Spielzeug *nt*; **toy with**
vt spielen mit; **toyshop** *n*
Spielwarengeschäft *nt*

trace [treɪs] *n* Spur *f*; **without**

~ **spurlos** ▷ vt (find) ausfindig machen; **tracing paper** n Pauspapier nt

track [træk] n (mark) Spur f; (path) Weg m; (Rail) Gleis nt; (on CD, record) Stück nt; **to keep/lose ~ of sb/sth** jdn/etw im Auge behalten/aus den Augen verlieren; **track down** vt ausfindig machen; **trackball** n (Inform) Trackball m; **tracksuit** n Trainingsanzug m

tractor ['træktə*] n Traktor m

trade [treɪd] n (commerce) Handel m; (business) Geschäft nt; (skilled job) Handwerk nt ▷ vi handeln (in mit) ▷ vt (exchange) tauschen (for gegen); **trademark** n Warenzeichen nt; **tradesman** (pl **-men**) n (shopkeeper) Geschäftsmann m; (workman) Handwerker m; **trade(s) union** n (Brit) Gewerkschaft f

tradition [trə'dɪʃən] n Tradition f; **traditional**, **traditionally** adj, adv traditionell

traffic ['træfɪk] n Verkehr m; (pej: trading) Handel m (in mit); **traffic circle** n (US) Kreisverkehr m; **traffic island** n Verkehrsinsel f; **traffic jam** n Stau m; **traffic lights** npl Verkehrsampel f; **traffic warden** n (Brit) ≈ Politesse f

tragedy ['trædʒədɪ] n Tragödie f; **tragic** ['trædʒɪk] adj tragisch

trail [treɪl] n Spur f; (path) Weg m ▷ vt (follow) verfolgen; (drag) schleppen; (drag behind) hinter sich herziehen; (Sport) zurückliegen hinter +dat ▷ vi (hang loosely) schleifen; (Sport) weit zurückliegen; **trailer** n Anhänger m; (US: caravan) Wohnwagen m; (Cine) Trailer m

train [treɪn] n (Rail) Zug m ▷ vt (teach) ausbilden; (Sport) trainieren

▷ vi (Sport) trainieren; **to ~ as** (o **to be**) **a teacher** eine Ausbildung als Lehrer machen; **trained** adj (person, voice) ausgebildet; **trainee** n Auszubildende(r) mf; (academic, practical) Praktikant(in) m(f); **traineeship** n Praktikum nt; **trainer** n (Sport) Trainer(in) m(f); **~s** (Brit: shoes) Turnschuhe pl; **training** n Ausbildung f; (Sport) Training nt; **train station** n Bahnhof m

tram ['træm] n (Brit) Straßenbahn f

tramp [træmp] n Landstreicher(in) m(f) ▷ vi trotten

tranquillizer ['træŋkwɪlaɪzə*] n Beruhigungsmittel nt

transaction n (piece of business) Geschäft nt

transatlantic [trænzət'læntɪk] adj transatlantisch; **~ flight** Transatlantikflug m

transfer ['trænsfə*] n (of money) Überweisung f; (US: ticket) Umsteigekarte f ▷ [træns'fɜː*] vt (money) überweisen (to sb an jdn); (patient) verlegen; (employee) versetzen; (Sport) transferieren ▷ vi (on journey) umsteigen; **transferable** [træns'fɜːrəbl] adj übertragbar

transform [træns'fɔːm] vt umwandeln; **transformation** [trænsfə'meɪʃən] n Umwandlung f

transfusion [træns'fjuːʒən] n Transfusion f

transistor [træn'zɪstə*] n Transistor m; **~ (radio)** Transistorradio nt

transition [træn'zɪʃən] n Übergang m (from ... to von ... zu)

transit lounge ['trænzɪtlaʊndʒ] n Transitraum m; **transit passenger** n Transitreisende(r) mf

t

translate [trænz'leɪt] vt, vi
übersetzen; **translation**
[trænz'leɪʃən] n Übersetzung f;
translator [trænz'leɪtə°] n
Übersetzer(in) m(f)
transmission [trænz'mɪʃən] n
(Auto) Getriebe nt
transparent [træns'pærənt] adj
durchsichtig; (fig) offenkundig
transplant [træns'plɑːnt] (Med)
vt transplantieren ▷ ['trænsplɑːnt]
n (operation) Transplantation f
transport ['trænspɔːt] n (of
goods, people) Beförderung f; **public**
~ öffentliche Verkehrsmittel pl
▷ [træns'pɔːt] vt befördern,
transportieren; **transportation**
[trænspɔː'teɪʃən] n see **transport**
trap [træp] n Falle f ▷ vt: **to be**
~ped (in snow, job etc) festsitzen
trash [træʃ] n (book, film etc)
Schund m; (US: refuse) Abfall m;
trash can n (US) Abfalleimer m;
trashy adj niveaulos; (novel)
Schund-
traumatic [trɔː'mætɪk] adj
traumatisch
travel ['trævl] n Reisen nt ▷ vi
(journey) reisen ▷ vt (distance)
zurücklegen; (country) bereisen;
travel agency, **travel agent** n
(company) Reisebüro nt; **traveler**
(US) see **traveller**; **traveler's**
check (US) see **traveller's cheque**;
travel insurance n
Reiseversicherung f; **traveller** n
Reisende(r) mf; **traveller's cheque**
n (Brit) Reisescheck m; **travelsick**
adj reisekrank
tray [treɪ] n Tablett nt; (for mail
etc) Ablage f; (of printer, photocopier)
Fach nt
tread [tred] n (on tyre) Profil nt;
tread on [tred] (**trod**, **trodden**)
vt treten auf +akk
treasure ['treʒə°] n Schatz m
▷ vt schätzen

treat [triːt] n besondere Freude;
it's my ~ das geht auf meine
Kosten ▷ vt behandeln; **to ~ sb**
(**to sth**) jdn (zu etw) einladen; **to**
~ oneself to sth sich etw leisten;
treatment ['triːtmənt] n
Behandlung f
treaty ['triːtɪ] n Vertrag m
tree [triː] n Baum m
tremble ['trembl] vi zittern
tremendous [trə'mendəs] adj
gewaltig; (fam: very good) toll
trench [trentʃ] n Graben m
trend [trend] n Tendenz f;
(fashion) Mode f, Trend m; **trendy**
adj trendy
trespass ['trespəs] vi: **"no ~ing"**
„Betreten verboten"
trial ['traɪəl] n (Jur) Prozess m;
(test) Versuch m; **by ~ and error**
durch Ausprobieren; **trial period**
n (for employee) Probezeit f
triangle ['traɪæŋgl] n Dreieck nt;
(Mus) Triangel m; **triangular**
[traɪ'æŋgjʊlə°] adj dreieckig
tribe [traɪb] n Stamm m
trick [trɪk] n Trick m; (mischief)
Streich m ▷ vt hereinlegen
tricky ['trɪkɪ] adj (difficult)
schwierig, heikel; (situation)
verzwickt
trifle ['traɪfl] n Kleinigkeit f; (Brit
Gastr) Trifle nt (Nachspeise aus
Biskuit, Wackelpudding, Obst,
Vanillesoße und Sahne)
trigger ['trɪgə°] n (of gun) Abzug
m ▷ vt: **to ~ (off)** auslösen
trim [trɪm] vt (hair, beard)
nachschneiden; (nails) schneiden;
(hedge) stutzen ▷ n: **just a ~,**
please nur etwas nachschneiden,
bitte; **trimmings** npl (decorations)
Verzierungen pl; (extras) Zubehör
nt; (Gastr) Beilagen pl
trip [trɪp] n Reise f; (outing)
Ausflug m ▷ vi stolpern (over über
+akk)

triple ['trɪpl] *adj* dreifach ▷ *adv*:
~ **the price** dreimal so teuer ▷ *vi*
sich verdreifachen; **triplet**
['trɪplɪt] *n* Drilling *m*

tripod ['traɪpɒd] *n* (*Foto*) Stativ
nt

trite [traɪt] *adj* banal

triumph ['traɪʌmf] *n* Triumph *m*

trivial ['trɪvɪəl] *adj* trivial

trod [trɒd] *pt of* **tread**

trodden *pp of* **tread**

trolley ['trɒlɪ] *n* (*Brit: in shop*)
Einkaufswagen *m*; (*for luggage*)
Kofferkuli *m*; (*serving ~*) Teewagen
m

trombone [trɒmˈbəʊn] *n*
Posaune *f*

troops [tru:ps] *npl* (*Mil*) Truppen
pl

trophy ['trəʊfɪ] *n* Trophäe *f*

tropical ['trɒpɪkl] *adj* tropisch

trouble ['trʌbl] *n* (*problems*)
Schwierigkeiten *pl*; (*worry*) Sorgen
pl; (*effort*) Mühe *f*; (*unrest*) Unruhen
pl; (*Med*) Beschwerden *pl*; **to be in**
~ in Schwierigkeiten sein; **to get**
into ~ (*with authority*) Ärger
bekommen; **to make**
~ Schwierigkeiten machen ▷ *vt*
(*worry*) beunruhigen; (*disturb*)
stören; **my back's troubling me**
mein Rücken macht mir zu
schaffen; **sorry to ~ you** ich muss
dich/Sie kurz stören;
troubled *adj* (*worried*)
beunruhigt; **trouble-free** *adj*
problemlos; **troublemaker** *n*
Unruhestifter(in) *m(f)*;
troublesome *adj* lästig

trousers ['traʊzəz] *npl* Hose *f*;
trouser suit *n* (*Brit*) Hosenanzug
m

trout [traʊt] *n* Forelle *f*

truck [trʌk] *n* Lastwagen *m*; (*Brit*
Rail) Güterwagen *m*; **trucker** *n*
(*US: driver*) Lastwagenfahrer(in)
m(f)

true [tru:] *adj* (*factually correct*)
wahr; (*genuine*) echt; **to come**
~ wahr werden

truly ['tru:lɪ] *adv* wirklich; **Yours**
~ (*in letter*) mit freundlichen
Grüßen

trumpet ['trʌmpɪt] *n* Trompete
f

trunk [trʌŋk] *n* (*of tree*) Stamm
m; (*Anat*) Rumpf *m*; (*of elephant*)
Rüssel *m*; (*piece of luggage*)
Überseekoffer *m*; (*US Auto*)
Kofferraum *m*; **trunks** *npl*:
(**swimming**) ~ Badehose *f*

trust [trʌst] *n* (*confidence*)
Vertrauen *nt* (*in zu*) ▷ *vt* vertrauen
+*dat*; **trusting** *adj* vertrauensvoll;
trustworthy *adj*
vertrauenswürdig

truth [tru:θ] *n* Wahrheit *f*;
truthful *adj* ehrlich; (*statement*)
wahrheitsgemäß

try [traɪ] *n* Versuch *m* ▷ *vt*
(*attempt*) versuchen; (~ *out*)
ausprobieren; (*sample*) probieren;
(*Jur: person*) vor Gericht stellen;
(*courage, patience*) auf die Probe
stellen ▷ *vi* versuchen; (*make*
effort) sich bemühen; ~ **and come**
versuch zu kommen; **try on** *vt*
(*clothes*) anprobieren; **try out** *vt*
ausprobieren

T-shirt ['ti:ʃɜ:t] *n* T-Shirt *nt*

tub [tʌb] *n* (*for ice-cream,*
margarine) Becher *m*

tube [tju:b] *n* (*pipe*) Rohr *nt*; (*of*
rubber, plastic) Schlauch *m*; (*for*
toothpaste, glue etc) Tube *f*; **the**
Tube (*in London*) die U-Bahn

tube station ['tju:bsteɪʃən] *n*
U-Bahn-Station *f*

tuck [tʌk] *vt* (*put*) stecken; **tuck**
in *vt* (*shirt*) in die Hose stecken;
(*blanket*) feststecken; (*person*)
zudecken ▷ *vi* (*eat*) zulangen

Tue(s) *abbr* = **Tuesday** Di.

Tuesday ['tju:zdɪ] *n* Dienstag *m*;

on ~ (am) Dienstag; **on ~s** dienstags; **this/last/next ~** diesen/letzten/nächsten Dienstag; **(on) ~ morning/ afternoon/evening** (am) Dienstagmorgen/-nachmittag/ -abend; **every ~** jeden Dienstag; **a week on ~/~ week** Dienstag in einer Woche

tug [tʌg] vt ziehen; **she ~ged his sleeve** sie zog an seinem Ärmel ▷ vi ziehen (at an +dat)

tuition [tju:'ɪʃən] n Unterricht m; (US: fees) Studiengebühren pl; **~ fees** pl Studiengebühren pl

tulip ['tju:lɪp] n Tulpe f

tumble ['tʌmbl] vi (person, prices) fallen; **tumble dryer** n Wäschetrockner m; **tumbler** n (glass) (Becher)glas nt

tummy ['tʌmɪ] n (fam) Bauch m; **tummyache** n (fam) Bauchweh nt

tumor (US), **tumour** ['tju:mə°] n Tumor m

tuna ['tju:nə] n Thunfisch m

tune [tju:n] n Melodie f; **to be in/out of ~** (instrument) gestimmt/verstimmt sein; (singer) richtig/falsch singen ▷ vt (instrument) stimmen; (radio) einstellen (to auf +akk); **tuner** n (in stereo system) Tuner m

Tunisia [tju:'nɪzɪə] n Tunesien nt

tunnel ['tʌnl] n Tunnel m; (under road, railway) Unterführung f

turban ['tɜ:bən] n Turban m

turbulence ['tɜ:bjʊləns] n (Aviat) Turbulenzen pl; **turbulent** adj stürmisch

Turk [tɜ:k] n Türke m, Türkin f

turkey ['tɜ:kɪ] n Truthahn m

Turkey ['tɜ:kɪ] n die Türkei; **Turkish** adj türkisch ▷ n (language) Türkisch nt

turmoil ['tɜ:mɔɪl] n Aufruhr m

turn [tɜ:n] n (rotation) Drehung f; (performance) Nummer f; **to make a left ~** nach links abbiegen; **at the ~ of the century** um die Jahrhundertwende; **it's your ~** du bist/Sie sind dran; **in ~, by ~s** abwechselnd; **to take ~s** sich abwechseln ▷ vt (wheel, key, screw) drehen; (to face other way) umdrehen; (corner) biegen um; (page) umblättern; (transform) verwandeln (into in +akk) ▷ vi (rotate) sich drehen; (to face other way) sich umdrehen; (change direction: driver, car) abbiegen; (become) werden; (weather) umschlagen; **to ~ into sth** (become) sich in etw akk verwandeln; **to ~ cold/green** kalt/grün werden; **to ~ left/right** links/rechts abbiegen; **turn away** vt (person) abweisen; **turn back** vt (person) zurückweisen ▷ vi (go back) umkehren; **turn down** vt (refuse) ablehnen; (radio, TV) leiser stellen; (heating) kleiner stellen; **turn off** vi abbiegen ▷ vt (switch off) ausschalten; (tap) zudrehen; (engine, electricity) abstellen; **turn on** vt (switch on) einschalten; (tap) aufdrehen; (engine, electricity) anstellen; (fam: person) anmachen, antörnen; **turn out** vt (light) ausmachen; (pockets) leeren ▷ vi (develop) sich entwickeln; **as it turned out** wie sich herausstellte; **turn over** vt umdrehen; (page) umblättern ▷ vi (person) sich umdrehen; (car) sich überschlagen; (TV) umschalten (to auf +akk); **turn round** vt (to face other way) umdrehen ▷ vi (person) sich umdrehen; (go back) umkehren; **turn to** vt sich zuwenden +dat; **turn up** vi (person, lost object) auftauchen ▷ vt (radio, TV) lauter stellen; (heating) höher stellen; **turning** n (in road) Abzweigung f; **turning point** n Wendepunkt m

turnip ['tɜːnɪp] n Rübe f

turnover ['tɜːnəʊvə*] n (Fin) Umsatz m

turnpike ['tɜːnpaɪk] n (US) gebührenpflichtige Autobahn

turntable ['tɜːnteɪbl] n (on record player) Plattenteller m

turn-up ['tɜːnʌp] n (Brit: on trousers) Aufschlag m

turquoise ['tɜːkwɔɪz] adj türkis

turtle ['tɜːtl] n (Brit) Wasserschildkröte f; (US) Schildkröte f

tutor ['tjuːtə*] n (private) Privatlehrer(in) m(f); (Brit: at university) Tutor(in) m(f)

tux [tʌks] , **tuxedo** [tʌkˈsiːdəʊ] (pl **-s**) n (US) Smoking m

TV ['tiːˈviː] n Fernsehen nt; (~ set) Fernseher m; **to watch ~** fernsehen; **on ~** im Fernsehen ▷ adj Fernseh-; **~ programme** Fernsehsendung f

tweed [twiːd] n Tweed m

tweezers ['twiːzəz] npl Pinzette f

twelfth [twelfθ] adj zwölfte(r, s); see also **eight**; **twelve** [twelv] num zwölf ▷ n Zwölf f; see also **eight**

twentieth ['twentɪɪθ] adj zwanzigste(r, s); see also **eight**; **twenty** ['twentɪ] num zwanzig; **~-one** einundzwanzig ▷ n Zwanzig f; **to be in one's twenties** in den Zwanzigern sein; see also **eight**

twice [twaɪs] adv zweimal; **~ as much/many** doppelt so viel/viele

twig [twɪg] n Zweig

twilight ['twaɪlaɪt] n (in evening) Dämmerung f

twin [twɪn] n Zwilling m ▷ adj (brother etc) Zwillings-; **~ beds** zwei

Einzelbetten ▷ vt: **York is ~ned with Münster** York ist eine Partnerstadt von Münster

twinge [twɪndʒ] n (pain) stechender Schmerz

twinkle ['twɪŋkl] vi funkeln

twin room ['twɪnˈruːm] n Zweibettzimmer nt; **twin town** n Partnerstadt f

twist [twɪst] vt (turn) drehen, winden; (distort) verdrehen; **I've ~ed my ankle** ich bin mit dem Fuß umgeknickt

two [tuː] num zwei; **to break sth in ~** etw in zwei Teile brechen ▷ n Zwei f; **the ~ of them** die beiden; see also **eight**; **two-dimensional** adj zweidimensional; (fig) oberflächlich; **two-faced** adj falsch, heuchlerisch; **two-piece** adj zweiteilig; **two-way** adj: **~ traffic** Gegenverkehr

type [taɪp] n (sort) Art f; (typeface) Schrift(art) f; **what ~ of car is it?** was für ein Auto ist das?; **he's not my ~** er ist nicht mein Typ; **typeface** n Schrift(art) f; **typewriter** n Schreibmaschine f

typhoid ['taɪfɔɪd] n Typhus m

typhoon [taɪˈfuːn] n Taifun m

typical ['tɪpɪkəl] adj typisch (of für)

typing error ['taɪpɪŋerə*] n Tippfehler m

tyre [taɪə*] n (Brit) Reifen m; **tyre pressure** n Reifendruck m

Tyrol [tɪˈrəʊl] n: **the ~** Tirol nt

t

U

UFO ['juːfəʊ] *acr* = **unidentified flying object** Ufo *nt*
Uganda [juːˈɡændə] *n* Uganda *nt*
ugly ['ʌɡlɪ] *adj* hässlich
UHT *adj abbr* = **ultra-heat treated ~ milk** H-Milch *f*
UK *abbr* = **United Kingdom**
Ukraine [juːˈkreɪn] *n*: **the ~** die Ukraine
ulcer ['ʌlsə°] *n* Geschwür *nt*
ulterior [ʌlˈtɪərɪə°] *adj*: **~ motive** Hintergedanke *m*
ultimate ['ʌltɪmət] *adj* (*final*) letzte(r, s); (*authority*) höchste(r, s); **ultimately** *adv* letzten Endes; (*eventually*) schließlich; **ultimatum** [ʌltɪˈmeɪtəm] *n* Ultimatum *nt*
ultra- ['ʌltrə] *pref* ultra-
ultrasound ['ʌltrəsaʊnd] *n* (*Med*) Ultraschall *m*
umbrella [ʌmˈbrelə] *n* Schirm *m*

umpire ['ʌmpaɪə°] *n* Schiedsrichter(in) *m(f)*
umpteen ['ʌmptiːn] *num* (*fam*) zig; **~ times** zigmal
un- [ʌn] *pref* un-
UN *nsing abbr* = **United Nations** VN, Vereinte Nationen *pl*
unable [ʌnˈeɪbl] *adj*: **to be ~ to do sth** etw nicht tun können
unacceptable [ʌnəˈkseptəbl] *adj* unannehmbar
unaccountably [ʌnəˈkaʊntəblɪ] *adv* unerklärlicherweise
unaccustomed [ʌnəˈkʌstəmd] *adj*: **to be ~ to sth** etw nicht gewohnt sein
unanimous, unanimously [juːˈnænɪməs, -lɪ] *adj, adv* einmütig
unattached [ʌnəˈtætʃt] *adj* (*without partner*) ungebunden
unattended [ʌnəˈtendɪd] *adj* (*luggage, car*) unbeaufsichtigt
unauthorized [ʌnˈɔːθəraɪzd] *adj* unbefugt
unavailable [ʌnəˈveɪləbl] *adj* nicht erhältlich; (*person*) nicht erreichbar
unavoidable [ʌnəˈvɔɪdəbl] *adj* unvermeidlich
unaware [ʌnəˈwɛə°] *adj*: **to be ~ of sth** sich einer Sache *dat* nicht bewusst sein; **I was ~ that ...** ich wusste nicht, dass ...
unbalanced [ʌnˈbælənst] *adj* unausgewogen; (*mentally*) gestört
unbearable [ʌnˈbɛərəbl] *adj* unerträglich
unbeatable [ʌnˈbiːtəbl] *adj* unschlagbar
unbelievable [ʌnbɪˈliːvəbl] *adj* unglaublich
unblock [ʌnˈblɒk] *vt* (*pipe*) frei machen
unbutton [ʌnˈbʌtn] *vt* aufknöpfen

uncertain [ʌnˈsɜːtən] *adj*
unsicher
uncle [ˈʌŋkl] *n* Onkel *m*
uncomfortable [ʌnˈkʌmfətəbl]
adj unbequem
unconditional [ʌnkənˈdɪʃənl]
adj bedingungslos
unconscious [ʌnˈkɒnʃəs] *adj*
(*Med*) bewusstlos; **to be ~ of sth**
sich einer Sache *dat* nicht bewusst
sein; **unconsciously** *adv*
unbewusst
uncork [ʌnˈkɔːk] *vt* entkorken
uncover [ʌnˈkʌvəʳ] *vt*
aufdecken
undecided [ʌndɪˈsaɪdɪd] *adj*
unschlüssig
undeniable [ʌndɪˈnaɪəbl] *adj*
unbestreitbar
under [ˈʌndəʳ] *prep* (*beneath*)
unter +*dat*; (*with motion*) unter
+*akk*; **children ~ eight** Kinder
unter acht; **~ an hour** weniger als
eine Stunde ▷ *adv* (*beneath*)
unten; (*with motion*) darunter;
children aged eight and ~ Kinder
bis zu acht Jahren; **under-age** *adj*
minderjährig
undercarriage [ˈʌndəkærɪdʒ] *n*
Fahrgestell *nt*
underdog [ˈʌndədɒg] *n* (*outsider*)
Außenseiter(in) *m(f)*
underdone [ʌndəˈdʌn] *adj*
(*Gastr*) nicht gar, durch;
(*deliberately*) nicht durchgebraten
underestimate [ʌndərˈestɪmeɪt] *vt* unterschätzen
underexposed [ʌndərɪksˈpəʊzd]
adj (*Foto*) unterbelichtet
undergo [ʌndəˈgəʊ] *irr vt*
(*experience*) durchmachen;
(*operation, test*) sich unterziehen
+*dat*
undergraduate [ʌndəˈgrædjʊət]
n Student(in) *m(f)*
underground [ˈʌndəgraʊnd] *adj*
unterirdisch ▷ *n* (*Brit Rail*) U-Bahn

f; **underground station** *n*
U-Bahn-Station *f*
underlie [ʌndəˈlaɪ] *irr vt*
zugrunde liegen +*dat*
underline [ʌndəˈlaɪn] *vt*
unterstreichen
underlying [ʌndəˈlaɪɪŋ] *adj*
zugrunde liegend
underneath [ʌndəˈniːθ] *prep*
unter; (*with motion*) unter +*akk*
▷ *adv* darunter
underpants [ˈʌndəpænts] *npl*
Unterhose *f*; **undershirt**
[ˈʌndəʃɜːt] *n* (*US*) Unterhemd *nt*;
undershorts [ˈʌndəʃɔːts] *npl* (*US*)
Unterhose *f*
understand [ʌndəˈstænd] *irr vt,
vi* verstehen; **I ~ that ...** (*been told*)
ich habe gehört, dass ...;
(*sympathize*) ich habe Verständnis
dafür, dass ...; **to make oneself
understood** sich verständlich
machen; **understandable** *adj*
verständlich; **understanding** *adj*
verständnisvoll
undertake [ʌndəˈteɪk] *irr vt*
(*task*) übernehmen; **to ~ to do sth**
sich verpflichten, etw zu tun;
undertaker *n* Leichenbestat-
ter(in) *m(f)*; **~'s** (*firm*)
Bestattungsinstitut *nt*
underwater [ʌndəˈwɔːtəʳ] *adv*
unter Wasser ▷ *adj* Unterwasser-
underwear [ˈʌndəweəʳ] *n*
Unterwäsche *f*
undesirable [ʌndɪˈzaɪərəbl] *adj*
unerwünscht
undo [ʌnˈduː] *irr vt* (*unfasten*)
aufmachen; (*work*)
zunichtemachen; (*Inform*)
rückgängig machen
undoubtedly [ʌnˈdaʊtɪdlɪ] *adv*
zweifellos
undress [ʌnˈdres] *vt* ausziehen;
to get ~ed sich ausziehen ▷ *vi*
sich ausziehen
undue [ʌnˈdjuː] *adj* übermäßig

u

unduly [ʌn'dju:lɪ] *adv*
übermäßig

unearth [ʌn'ɜ:θ] *vt (dig up)*
ausgraben; *(find)* aufstöbern

unease [ʌn'i:z] *n* Unbehagen *nt*;
uneasy *adj (person)* unbehaglich;
I'm ~ about it mir ist nicht wohl
dabei

unemployed [ʌnɪm'plɔɪd] *adj*
arbeitslos ▷ ▷ *npl*: **the ~** die
Arbeitslosen *pl*; **unemployment**
[ʌnɪm'plɔɪmənt] *n* Arbeitslosigkeit *f*; **unemployment
benefit** *n* Arbeitslosengeld *nt*

unequal [ʌn'i:kwəl] *adj*
ungleich

uneven [ʌn'i:vən] *adj (surface,
road)* uneben; *(contest)* ungleich

unexpected [ʌnɪk'spektɪd] *adj*
unerwartet

unfair [ʌn'fɛə°] *adj* unfair

unfamiliar [ʌnfə'mɪljə°] *adj*: **to
be ~ with sb/sth** jdn/etw nicht
kennen

unfasten [ʌn'fɑ:sn] *vt*
aufmachen

unfit [ʌn'fɪt] *adj* ungeeignet *(for
für)*; *(in bad health)* nicht fit

unforeseen [ʌnfɔ:'si:n] *adj*
unvorhergesehen

unforgettable [ʌnfə'ɡɪvəbl] *adj*
unvergesslich

unforgivable [ʌnfə'ɡɪvəbl] *adj*
unverzeihlich

unfortunate [ʌn'fɔ:tʃnət] *adj*
(unlucky) unglücklich; **it is ~
that ...** es ist bedauerlich, dass ...;
unfortunately *adv* leider

unfounded [ʌn'faʊndɪd] *adj*
unbegründet

unhappy [ʌn'hæpɪ] *adj (sad)*
unglücklich, unzufrieden; **to be
~ with sth** mit etw unzufrieden
sein

unhealthy [ʌn'helθɪ] *adj*
ungesund

unheard-of [ʌn'hɜ:dɒv] *adj*

(unknown) gänzlich unbekannt;
(outrageous) unerhört

unhelpful [ʌn'helpfʊl] *adj* nicht
hilfreich

unhitch [ʌn'hɪtʃ] *vt (caravan,
trailer)* abkoppeln

unhurt [ʌn'hɜ:t] *adj* unverletzt

uniform ['ju:nɪfɔ:m] *n* Uniform
f ▷ *adj* einheitlich

unify ['ju:nɪfaɪ] *vt* vereinigen

unimportant [ʌnɪm'pɔ:tənt]-
adj unwichtig

uninhabited [ʌnɪn'hæbɪtɪd] *adj*
unbewohnt

uninstall [ʌnɪn'stɔ:l] *vt (Inform)*
deinstallieren

unintentional [ʌnɪn'tenʃənl]
adj unabsichtlich

union ['ju:njən] *n (uniting)*
Vereinigung *f*; *(alliance)* Union *f*;
Union Jack *n* Union Jack *m*
(britische Nationalflagge)

unique [ju:'ni:k] *adj* einzigartig

unit ['ju:nɪt] *n* Einheit *f*; *(of
system, machine)* Teil *nt*; *(in school)*
Lektion *f*

unite [ju:'naɪt] *vt* vereinigen;
the United Kingdom das
Vereinigte Königreich; **the United
Nations** *pl* die Vereinten Nationen
pl; **the United States (of
America)** *pl* die Vereinigten
Staaten (von Amerika) *pl* ▷ *vi* sich
vereinigen

universe ['ju:nɪvɜ:s] *n* Univer-
sum *nt*

university [ju:nɪ'vɜ:sɪtɪ] *n*
Universität *f*

unkind [ʌn'kaɪnd] *adj* unfreundlich *(to zu)*

unknown [ʌn'nəʊn] *adj*
unbekannt *(to +dat)*

unleaded [ʌn'ledɪd] *adj* bleifrei

unless [ən'les] *conj* es sei denn,
wenn ... nicht; **don't do it ~ I tell
you to** mach das nicht, es sei
denn, ich sage es dir; **~ I'm**

mistaken ... wenn ich mich nicht irre ...

unlicensed [ʌn'laɪsənst] adj (to sell alcohol) ohne Lizenz

unlike [ʌn'laɪk] prep (in contrast to) im Gegensatz zu; **it's ~ her to be late** es sieht ihr gar nicht ähnlich, zu spät zu kommen; **unlikely** [ʌn'laɪklɪ] adj unwahrscheinlich

unload [ʌn'ləʊd] vt ausladen

unlock [ʌn'lɒk] vt aufschließen

unlucky [ʌn'lʌkɪ] adj unglücklich; **to be ~** Pech haben

unmistakable [ʌnmɪ'steɪkəbl] adj unverkennbar

unnecessary [ʌn'nesəsərɪ] adj unnötig

unobtainable [ʌnəb'teɪnəbl] adj nicht erhältlich

unoccupied [ʌn'ɒkjʊpaɪd] adj (seat) frei; (building, room) leer stehend

unpack [ʌn'pæk] vt, vi auspacken

unpleasant [ʌn'pleznt] adj unangenehm

unplug [ʌn'plʌg] vt: **to ~ sth** den Stecker von etw herausziehen

unprecedented [ʌn'presɪdəntɪd] adj beispiellos

unpredictable [ʌnprɪ'dɪktəbl] adj (person, weather) unberechenbar

unreasonable [ʌn'ri:znəbl] adj unvernünftig; (demand) übertrieben

unreliable [ʌnrɪ'laɪəbl] adj unzuverlässig

unsafe [ʌn'seɪf] adj nicht sicher; (dangerous) gefährlich

unscrew [ʌn'skru:] vt abschrauben

unsightly [ʌn'saɪtlɪ] adj unansehnlich

unskilled [ʌn'skɪld] adj (worker) ungelernt

unsuccessful [ʌnsək'sesfʊl] adj erfolglos

unsuitable [ʌn'su:təbl] adj ungeeignet (for für)

until [ən'tɪl] prep bis; **not ~** erst; **from Monday ~ Friday** von Montag bis Freitag; **he didn't come home ~ midnight** er kam erst um Mitternacht nach Hause; **~ then** bis dahin ▷ conj bis; **she won't come ~ you invite her** sie kommt erst, wenn du sie einlädst/wenn Sie sie einladen

unusual, unusually [ʌn'ju:ʒʊəl, -ɪ] adj, adv ungewöhnlich

unwanted [ʌn'wɒntɪd] adj unerwünscht, ungewollt

unwell [ʌn'wel] adj krank; **to feel ~** sich nicht wohlfühlen

unwilling [ʌn'wɪlɪŋ] adj: **to be ~ to do sth** nicht bereit sein, etw zu tun

unwind [ʌn'waɪnd] irr vt abwickeln ▷ vi (relax) sich entspannen

unwrap [ʌn'ræp] vt auspacken

unzip [ʌn'zɪp] vt den Reißverschluss aufmachen an +dat; (Inform) entzippen

○ **KEYWORD**

up [ʌp] prep: **to be up sth** oben auf etw dat sein; **to go up sth** (auf) etw akk hinaufgehen; **go up that road** gehen Sie die Straße hinauf

▷ adv **1** (upwards, higher) oben; **put it up a bit higher** stell es etwas weiter nach oben; **up there** da oben, dort oben; **up above** hoch oben

2 to be up (out of bed) auf sein; (prices, level) gestiegen sein; (building, tent) stehen

3 up to (as far as) bis; **up to now** bis jetzt

u

4 to be up to (*depending on*): **it's up to you** das hängt von dir ab; (*equal to*): **he's not up to it** (*job, task etc*) er ist dem nicht gewachsen; (*inf: be doing*) (*showing disapproval, suspicion*) **what is he up to?** was führt er im Schilde?; **his work is not up to the required standard** seine Arbeit entspricht nicht dem geforderten Niveau ▷ *n:* **ups and downs** (*in life, career*) Höhen und Tiefen *pl*

upbringing ['ʌpbrɪŋɪŋ] *n* Erziehung *f*

update [ʌp'deɪt] *n* (*list etc*) Aktualisierung *f;* (*software*) Update *nt* ▷ *vt* (*list etc, person*) auf den neuesten Stand bringen, aktualisieren

upgrade [ʌp'greɪd] *vt* (*computer*) aufrüsten; **we were ~d** das Hotel hat uns ein besseres Zimmer gegeben

upheaval [ʌp'hiːvəl] *n* Aufruhr *m;* (*Pol*) Umbruch *m*

uphill [ʌp'hɪl] *adv* bergauf

upon [ə'pɒn] *prep see* **on**

upper ['ʌpə*ʳ*] *adj* obere(r, s); (*arm, deck*) Ober-

upright ['ʌpraɪt] *adj, adv* aufrecht

uprising ['ʌpraɪzɪŋ] *n* Aufstand *m*

uproar ['ʌprɔː*ʳ*] *n* Aufruhr *m*

upset [ʌp'set] *irr vt* (*overturn*) umkippen; (*disturb*) aufregen; (*sadden*) bestürzen; (*offend*) kränken; (*plans*) durcheinanderbringen ▷ *adj* (*disturbed*) aufgeregt; (*sad*) bestürzt; (*offended*) gekränkt; **~ stomach** ['ʌpset] Magenverstimmung *f*

upside down [ʌpsaɪd'daʊn] *adv* verkehrt herum; (*fig*) drunter und drüber; **to turn sth ~** (*box etc*) etw umdrehen/durchwühlen

upstairs [ʌp'steəz] *adv* oben; (*go, take*) nach oben

up-to-date ['ʌptə'deɪt] *adj* modern; (*fashion, information*) aktuell; **to keep sb ~** jdn auf dem Laufenden halten

upwards ['ʌpwədz] *adv* nach oben

urban ['ɜːbən] *adj* städtisch, Stadt-

urge [ɜːdʒ] *n* Drang *m* ▷ *vt:* **to ~ sb to do sth** jdn drängen, etw zu tun; **urgent, urgently** ['ɜːdʒənt, -lɪ] *adj, adv* dringend

urine ['jʊərɪn] *n* Urin *m*

URL *abbr* = **uniform resource locator** (*Inform*) URL-Adresse *f*

us [ʌs] *pron* uns; **do they know ~?** kennen sie uns?; **can he help ~?** kann er uns helfen?; **it's ~** wir sind's; **both of ~** wir beide

US, USA *nsing abbr* = **United States (of America)** USA *pl*

use [juːs] *n* (*using*) Gebrauch *m;* (*for specific purpose*) Benutzung *f;* **to make ~ of** Gebrauch machen von; **in/out of ~** in/außer Gebrauch; **it's no ~** (*doing that*) es hat keinen Zweck(, das zu tun); **it's (of) no ~ to me** das kann ich nicht brauchen ▷ [juːz] *vt* benutzen, gebrauchen; (*for specific purpose*) verwenden; (*method*) anwenden; **use up** *vt* aufbrauchen

used [juːzd] *adj* (*secondhand*) gebraucht ▷ *vb aux:* **to be ~d to sb/sth** an jdn/etw gewöhnt sein; **to get ~d to sb/sth** sich an jdn/etw gewöhnen; **she ~d to live here** sie hat früher mal hier gewohnt; **useful** *adj* nützlich; **useless** *adj* nutzlos; (*unusable*) unbrauchbar; (*pointless*) zwecklos; **user** ['juːzə*ʳ*] *n* Benutzer(in) *m(f);*

user-friendly *adj* benutzerfreundlich

usual ['juːʒʊəl] *adj* üblich, gewöhnlich; **as ~** wie üblich; **usually** *adv* normalerweise

utensil [juːˈtensl] *n* Gerät *nt*

uterus ['juːtərəs] *n* Gebärmutter *f*

utilize ['juːtɪlaɪz] *vt* verwenden

utmost ['ʌtməʊst] *adj* äußerst; **to do one's ~** sein Möglichstes tun

utter ['ʌtə*] *adj* völlig ▷ *vt* von sich geben; **utterly** *adv* völlig

U-turn ['juːtɜːn] *n* (*Auto*) Wende *f*; **to do a ~** wenden; (*fig*) eine Kehrtwendung machen

vacancy ['veɪkənsɪ] *n* (*job*) offene Stelle; (*room*) freies Zimmer; **vacant** ['veɪkənt] *adj* (*room, toilet*) frei; (*post*) offen; (*building*) leer stehend; **vacate** [vəˈkeɪt] *vt* (*room, building*) räumen; (*seat*) frei machen

vacation [vəˈkeɪʃən] *n* (*US*) Ferien *pl*, Urlaub *m*; (*at university*) (Semester)ferien *pl*; **to go on ~** in Urlaub fahren; **~ course** Ferienkurs *m*

vaccinate ['væksɪneɪt] *vt* impfen; **vaccination** [væksɪˈneɪʃən] *n* Impfung *f*; **~ card** Impfpass *m*

vacuum ['vækjʊm] *n* Vakuum *nt* ▷ *vt, vi* (staub)saugen; **vacuum (cleaner)** *n* Staubsauger *m*

vagina [vəˈdʒaɪnə] *n* Scheide *f*

vague [veɪg] *adj* (*imprecise*) vage; (*resemblance*) entfernt; **vaguely** *adv* in etwa, irgendwie

v

vain [veɪn] adj (attempt)
vergeblich; (conceited) eitel; **in
~** vergeblich, umsonst; **vainly** adv
(in vain) vergeblich
valentine (card)
['væləntaɪn(kɑːd)] n Valentins-
karte f; **Valentine's Day** n
Valentinstag m
valid ['vælɪd] adj (ticket, passport
etc) gültig; (argument) stichhaltig;
(claim) berechtigt
valley ['vælɪ] n Tal nt
valuable ['væljʊəbl] adj wertvoll;
(time) kostbar; **valuables** npl
Wertsachen pl
value ['væljuː] n Wert m ▷ vt
(appreciate) schätzen; **value added
tax** n Mehrwertsteuer f
valve [vælv] n Ventil nt
van [væn] n (Auto) Lieferwagen m
vanilla [vəˈnɪlə] n Vanille f
vanish ['vænɪʃ] vi verschwinden
vanity ['vænɪtɪ] n Eitelkeit f;
vanity case n Schminkkoffer m
vapor (US), **vapour** ['veɪpə*] n
(mist) Dunst m; (steam) Dampf
m
variable ['vɛərɪəbl] adj (weather,
mood) unbeständig; (quality)
unterschiedlich; (speed, height)
regulierbar; **varied** ['vɛərɪd] adj
(interests, selection) vielseitig;
(career) bewegt; (work, diet)
abwechslungsreich; **variety**
[vəˈraɪətɪ] n (diversity)
Abwechslung f; (assortment)
Vielfalt f (of an +dat); (type) Art f;
various ['vɛərɪəs] adj
verschieden
varnish ['vɑːnɪʃ] n Lack m ▷ vt
lackieren
vary ['vɛərɪ] vt (alter) verändern
▷ vi (be different) unterschiedlich
sein; (fluctuate) sich verändern;
(prices) schwanken
vase [vɑːz, ?? veɪz] (US) n Vase f
vast [vɑːst] adj riesig; (area) weit

VAT [væt] abbr = **value added tax**
Mehrwertsteuer f, MwSt.
Vatican ['vætɪkən] n: **the ~** der
Vatikan
VCR [viːsiːˈɑː*] abbr = **video
cassette recorder** Videorekorder
m
VD [viːˈdiː] abbr = **venereal
disease** Geschlechtskrankheit f
VDU [viːdiːˈjuː] abbr = **visual
display unit**
veal [viːl] n Kalbfleisch nt
vegan ['viːgən] n Veganer(in)
m(f)
vegetable ['vedʒtəbl] n Gemüse
nt
vegetarian [vedʒɪˈtɛərɪən] n
Vegetarier(in) m(f) ▷ adj
vegetarisch
veggie ['vedʒɪ] n (fam)
Vegetarier(in) m(f); Gemüse nt
▷ adj vegetarisch; **veggieburger**
n Veggieburger m, Gemüseburger
m
vehicle ['viːɪkl] n Fahrzeug nt
veil [veɪl] n Schleier m
vein [veɪn] n Ader f
Velcro® ['velkrəʊ] n Klettband
nt
velvet ['velvɪt] n Samt m
vending machine
['vendɪŋməʃiːn] n Automat m
venetian blind [vɪˈniːʃənˈblaɪnd]
n Jalousie f
Venezuela [veneˈzweɪlə] n
Venezuela nt
Venice ['venɪs] n Venedig nt
venison ['venɪsn] n Rehfleisch
nt
vent [vent] n Öffnung f
ventilate ['ventɪleɪt] vt lüften;
ventilation [ventɪˈleɪʃən] n
Belüftung f; **ventilator**
['ventɪleɪtə*] n (in room)
Ventilator m; **to be on a ~** (Med)
künstlich beatmet werden
venture ['ventʃə*] n (project)

Unternehmung f; (Comm)
Unternehmen nt ▷ vi (go) (sich)
wagen
venue ['venjuː] n (for concert etc)
Veranstaltungsort m; (Sport)
Austragungsort m
verb [vɜːb] n Verb nt; **verbal** adj
(agreement) mündlich; (skills)
sprachlich; **verbally** adv
mündlich
verdict ['vɜːdɪkt] n Urteil nt
verge [vɜːdʒ] n (of road)
(Straßen)rand m; **to be on the ~ of
doing sth** im Begriff sein, etw zu
tun ▷ vi: **to ~ on** grenzen an +akk
verification [verɪfɪ'keɪʃən] n
(confirmation) Bestätigung f;
(check) Überprüfung f; **verify**
['verɪfaɪ] vt (confirm) bestätigen;
(check) überprüfen
vermin ['vɜːmɪn] npl Schädlinge
pl; (insects) Ungeziefer nt
verruca [ve'ruːkə] n Warze f
versatile ['vɜːsətaɪl] adj
vielseitig
verse [vɜːs] n (poetry) Poesie f;
(stanza) Strophe f
version ['vɜːʃən] n Version f
versus ['vɜːsəs] prep gegen
vertical ['vɜːtɪkəl] adj senkrecht,
vertikal
very ['verɪ] adv sehr; **~ much** sehr
▷ adj: **the ~ book I need** genau
das Buch, das ich brauche; **at that
~ moment** gerade in dem
Augenblick; **at the ~ top** ganz
oben; **the ~ best** der/die/das
Allerbeste
vest [vest] n (Brit) Unterhemd nt;
(US: waistcoat) Weste f
vet [vet] n Tierarzt m, Tierärztin f
veto ['viːtəʊ] n (pl -es) Veto nt
▷ vt sein Veto einlegen gegen
VHF abbr = **very high frequency**
UKW
via ['vaɪə] prep über +akk
viable ['vaɪəbl] adj (plan)

realisierbar; (company) rentabel
vibrate [vaɪ'breɪt] vi vibrieren;
vibration [vaɪ'breɪʃən] n
Vibration f
vicar ['vɪkə*] n Pfarrer(in) m(f)
vice [vaɪs] n (evil) Laster nt; (Tech)
Schraubstock m ▷ pref Vize-;
~-chairman stellvertretender
Vorsitzender; **~-president**
Vizepräsident(in) m(f)
vice versa ['vaɪs'vɜːsə] adv
umgekehrt
vicinity [vɪ'sɪnɪtɪ] n: **in the ~** in
der Nähe (of +gen)
vicious ['vɪʃəs] adj (violent)
brutal; (malicious) gemein; **vicious
circle** n Teufelskreis m
victim ['vɪktɪm] n Opfer nt
Victorian [vɪk'tɔːrɪən] adj
viktorianisch
victory ['vɪktərɪ] n Sieg m
video ['vɪdɪəʊ] (pl -s) adj Video-
▷ n Video nt; (recorder)
Videorekorder m ▷ vt (auf Video)
aufnehmen; **video camera** n
Videokamera f; **video cassette** n
Videokassette f; **video clip** n
Videoclip m; **video game** n
Videospiel nt; **videophone** n
Bildtelefon nt; **video recorder** n
Videorekorder m; **video shop** n
Videothek f; **videotape** n
Videoband nt ▷ vt (auf Video)
aufnehmen
Vienna [vɪ'enə] n Wien nt
Vietnam [vjet'næm] n Vietnam
nt
view [vjuː] n (sight) Blick m (of auf
+akk); (vista) Aussicht f; (opinion)
Ansicht f, Meinung f; **in ~ of**
angesichts +gen ▷ vt (situation,
event) betrachten; (house)
besichtigen; **viewer** n (for slides)
Diabetrachter m; (TV)
Zuschauer(in) m(f); **viewpoint** n
(fig) Standpunkt m
vigilant ['vɪdʒɪlənt] adj wachsam

vile [vaɪl] *adj* abscheulich; (*weather, food*) scheußlich

village ['vɪlɪdʒ] *n* Dorf *nt*; **villager** *n* Dorfbewohner(in) *m(f)*

villain ['vɪlən] *n* Schurke *m*; (*in film, story*) Bösewicht *m*

vine [vaɪn] *n* (Wein)rebe *f*

vinegar ['vɪnɪgə°] *n* Essig *m*

vineyard ['vɪnjəd] *n* Weinberg *m*

vintage ['vɪntɪdʒ] *n* (*of wine*) Jahrgang *m*; **vintage wine** *n* edler Wein

vinyl ['vaɪnɪl] *n* Vinyl *nt*

viola [vɪ'əʊlə] *n* Bratsche *f*

violate ['vaɪəleɪt] *vt* (*treaty*) brechen; (*rights, rule*) verletzen

violence ['vaɪələns] *n* (*brutality*) Gewalt *f*; (*of person*) Gewalttätigkeit *f*; **violent** *adj* (*brutal*) brutal; (*death*) gewaltsam

violet ['vaɪələt] *n* Veilchen *nt*

violin [vaɪə'lɪn] *n* Geige *f*, Violine *f*

VIP *abbr* = **very important person** VIP *mf*

virgin ['vɜːdʒɪn] *n* Jungfrau *f*

Virgo ['vɜːgəʊ] *n* (*Astr*) Jungfrau *f*

virile ['vɪraɪl] *adj* (*man*) männlich

virtual ['vɜːtjʊəl] *adj* (*Inform*) virtuell; **virtually** *adv* praktisch; **virtual reality** *n* virtuelle Realität

virtue ['vɜːtjuː] *n* Tugend *f*; **by ~ of** aufgrund +*gen*; **virtuous** ['vɜːtjʊəs] *adj* tugendhaft

virus ['vaɪrəs] *n* (*Med, Inform*) Virus *nt*

visa ['viːzə] *n* Visum *nt*

visibility [vɪzɪ'bɪlɪtɪ] *n* (*Meteo*) Sichtweite *f*; **good/poor ~** gute/schlechte Sicht; **visible** ['vɪzəbl] *adj* sichtbar; (*evident*) sichtlich; **visibly** *adv* sichtlich

vision ['vɪʒən] *n* (*power of sight*) Sehvermögen *nt*; (*foresight*) Weitblick *m*; (*dream, image*) Vision *f*

visit ['vɪzɪt] *n* Besuch *m*; (*stay*) Aufenthalt *m* ▷ *vt* besuchen; **visiting hours** *npl* Besuchszeiten *pl*; **visitor** *n* Besucher(in) *m(f)*; **~'s book** Gästebuch *nt*; **visitor centre** *n* Informationszentrum *nt*

visor ['vaɪzə°] *n* (*on helmet*) Visier *nt*; (*Auto*) Blende *f*

visual ['vɪzjʊəl] *adj* Seh-; (*image, joke*) visuell; **~ aid** Anschauungsmaterial *nt*; **~ display unit** Monitor *m*; **visualize** *vt* sich vorstelle; **visually** *adv* visuell; **~ impaired** sehbehindert

vital ['vaɪtl] *adj* (*essential*) unerlässlich, wesentlich; (*argument, moment*) entscheidend; **vitality** [vaɪ'tælɪtɪ] *n* Vitalität *f*; **vitally** *adv* äußerst

vitamin ['vɪtəmɪn] *n* Vitamin *nt*

vivacious [vɪ'veɪʃəs] *adj* lebhaft

vivid ['vɪvɪd] *adj* (*description*) anschaulich; (*memory*) lebhaft; (*colour*) leuchtend

V-neck ['viːnek] *n* V-Ausschnitt *m*

vocabulary [vəʊ'kæbjʊlərɪ] *n* Wortschatz *m*, Vokabular *nt*

vocal ['vəʊkəl] *adj* (*of the voice*) Stimm-; (*group*) Gesangs-; (*protest, person*) lautstark

vocation [vəʊ'keɪʃən] *n* Berufung *f*; **vocational** *adj* Berufs-

vodka ['vɒdkə] *n* Wodka *m*

voice [vɔɪs] *n* Stimme *f* ▷ *vt* äußern; **voice mail** *n* Voicemail *f*

void [vɔɪd] *n* Leere *f* ▷ *adj* (*Jur*) ungültig; **~ of** (*ganz*) ohne

volcano [vɒl'keɪnəʊ] *n* (*pl* **-es**) *n* Vulkan *m*

volley ['vɒlɪ] *n* (*Tennis*) Volley *m*; **volleyball** *n* Volleyball *m*

volt [vəʊlt] *n* Volt *nt*; **voltage** *n* Spannung *f*

volume ['vɒljuːm] *n* (*of sound*) Lautstärke *f*; (*space occupied by sth*)

Volumen nt; (size, amount) Umfang m; (book) Band m; **volume control** n Lautstärkeregler m

voluntary, voluntarily ['vɒləntərɪ, -lɪ] adj, adv freiwillig; (unpaid) ehrenamtlich; **volunteer** [vɒlən'tɪə*] n Freiwillige(r) mf ▷ vi sich freiwillig melden ▷ vt: **to ~ to do sth** sich anbieten, etw zu tun

voluptuous [və'lʌptjʊəs] adj sinnlich

vomit ['vɒmɪt] vi sich übergeben

vote [vəʊt] n Stimme f; (ballot) Wahl f; (result) Abstimmungsergebnis nt; (right to vote) Wahlrecht nt ▷ vt (elect) wählen; **they ~d him chairman** sie wählten ihn zum Vorsitzenden ▷ vi wählen; **to ~ for/against sth** für/gegen etw stimmen; **voter** n Wähler(in) m(f)

voucher ['vaʊtʃə*] n Gutschein m

vow [vaʊ] n Gelöbnis nt ▷ vt: **to ~ to do sth** geloben, etw zu tun

vowel ['vaʊəl] n Vokal m

voyage ['vɔɪdʒ] n Reise f

vulgar ['vʌlɡə*] adj vulgär, ordinär

vulnerable ['vʌlnərəbl] adj verwundbar; (sensitive) verletzlich

vulture ['vʌltʃə*] n Geier m

W abbr = **west** W

wade [weɪd] vi (in water) waten

wafer ['weɪfə*] n Waffel f; (Rel) Hostie f; **wafer-thin** adj hauchdünn

waffle ['wɒfl] n Waffel f; (Brit fam: empty talk) Geschwafel nt ▷ vi (Brit fam) schwafeln

wag [wæɡ] vt (tail) wedeln mit

wage [weɪdʒ] n Lohn m

waggon (Brit), **wagon** ['wæɡən] n (horse-drawn) Fuhrwerk nt; (Brit Rail) Waggon m; (US Auto) Wagen m

waist [weɪst] n Taille f; **waistcoat** n (Brit) Weste f; **waistline** n Taille f

wait [weɪt] n Wartezeit f ▷ vi warten (for auf +akk); **to ~ and see** abwarten; **~ a minute** Moment mal!; **wait up** vi aufbleiben

waiter n Kellner m; **~!** Herr Ober!

waiting n: **"no ~"** „Halteverbot";

waiting list n Warteliste f;
waiting room n (Med)
Wartezimmer nt; (Rail) Wartesaal
m
waitress n Kellnerin f
wake [weɪk] (**woke** o **waked,
woken** o **waked**) vt wecken ▷ vi
aufwachen; **wake up** vt
aufwecken ▷ vi aufwachen;
wake-up call n (Tel) Weckruf m
Wales [weɪlz] n Wales nt
walk [wɔːk] n Spaziergang m;
(ramble) Wanderung f; (route) Weg
m; **to go for a ~** spazieren gehen;
it's only a five-minute ~ es sind
nur fünf Minuten zu Fuß ▷ vi
gehen; (stroll) spazieren gehen;
(ramble) wandern ▷ vt (dog)
ausführen; **walking** n: **to go
~** wandern; **walking shoes** npl
Wanderschuhe pl; **walking stick** n
Spazierstock m
Walkman® (pl **-s**) n Walkman®
m
wall [wɔːl] n (inside) Wand f;
(outside) Mauer f
wallet ['wɒlɪt] n Brieftasche f
wallpaper ['wɔːlpeɪpə*] n
Tapete f; (Inform)
Bildschirmhintergrund m ▷ vt
tapezieren
walnut ['wɔːlnʌt] n (nut)
Walnuss f
waltz [wɔːlts] n Walzer m
wander ['wɒndə*] vi (person)
herumwandern
want [wɒnt] n (lack) Mangel m
(of an +dat); (need) Bedürfnis nt; **for
~ of** aus Mangel an +dat ▷ vt
(desire) wollen; (need) brauchen; **I
~ to stay here** ich will hier
bleiben; **he doesn't ~ to** er will
nicht
WAP phone ['wæpfəʊn] n
WAP-Handy nt
war [wɔː*] n Krieg m

ward [wɔːd] n (in hospital)
Station f; (child) Mündel nt
warden ['wɔːdən] n Aufseher(in)
m(f); (in youth hostel) Herbergsvater
m, Herbergsmutter f
wardrobe ['wɔːdrəʊb] n
Kleiderschrank m
warehouse ['wɛəhaʊs] n
Lagerhaus nt
warfare ['wɔːfɛə*] n Krieg m;
(techniques) Kriegsführung f
warm [wɔːm] adj warm;
(welcome) herzlich; **I'm ~** mir ist
warm ▷ vt wärmen; (food)
aufwärmen; **warm over** vt (US:
food) aufwärmen; **warm up** vt
(food) aufwärmen; (room)
erwärmen ▷ vi (food, room) warm
werden; (Sport) sich aufwärmen;
warmly adv warm; (welcome)
herzlich; **warmth** n Wärme f; (of
welcome) Herzlichkeit f
warn [wɔːn] vt warnen (of,
against vor +dat); **to ~ sb not to do
sth** jdn davor warnen, etw zu tun;
warning n Warnung f; **warning
light** n Warnlicht nt; **warning
triangle** n (Auto) Warndreieck nt
warranty ['wɒrəntɪ] n Garantie
f
wart [wɔːt] n Warze f
wary ['wɛərɪ] adj vorsichtig;
(suspicious) misstrauisch
was [wɒz, wəz] pt of **be**
wash [wɒʃ] n: **to have a ~** sich
waschen; **it's in the ~** es ist in der
Wäsche ▷ vt waschen; (plates,
glasses etc) abwaschen; **to ~ one's
hands** sich dat die Hände
waschen; **to ~ the dishes** (das
Geschirr) abwaschen ▷ vi (clean
oneself) sich waschen; **wash off** vt
abwaschen; **wash up** vi (Brit:
wash dishes) abwaschen; (US: clean
oneself) sich waschen; **washable**
adj waschbar; **washbag** n (US)
Kulturbeutel m; **washbasin** n

Waschbecken *nt*; **washcloth** *n*
(US) Waschlappen *m*; **washer** *n*
(Tech) Dichtungsring *m*; (*washing machine*) Waschmaschine *f*;
washing *n* (*laundry*) Wäsche *f*;
washing machine *n*
Waschmaschine *f*; **washing
powder** *n* Waschpulver *nt*;
washing-up *n* (Brit) Abwasch *m*;
to do the ~ abwaschen;
washing-up liquid *n* (Brit)
Spülmittel *nt*; **washroom** *n* (US)
Toilette *f*
wasn't ['wɒznt] *contr of* **was not**
wasp [wɒsp] *n* Wespe *f*
waste [weist] *n* (*materials*) Abfall
m; (*wasting*) Verschwendung *f*; **it's
a ~ of time** das ist
Zeitverschwendung ▷ *adj*
(*superfluous*) überschüssig ▷ *vt*
verschwenden (*on an* +*akk*);
(*opportunity*) vertun; **waste bin** *n*
Abfalleimer *m*; **wastepaper
basket** *n* Papierkorb *m*
watch [wɒtʃ] *n* (*timepiece*)
(Armband)uhr *f* ▷ *vt* (*observe*)
beobachten; (*guard*) aufpassen auf
+*akk*; (*film, play, programme*) sich
dat ansehen; **to ~ TV** fernsehen
▷ *vi* zusehen; (*guard*) Wache
halten; **to ~ for sb/sth** nach
jdm/etw Ausschau halten; **~ out**
pass auf!; **watchdog** *n*
Wachhund *m*; (*fig*)
Aufsichtsbehörde *f*; **watchful** *adj*
wachsam
water ['wɔːtə°] *n* Wasser *nt* ▷ *vt*
(*plant*) gießen ▷ *vi* (*eye*) tränen;
my mouth is ~ing mir läuft das
Wasser im Mund zusammen;
water down *vt* verdünnen;
watercolor (US), **watercolour** *n*
(*painting*) Aquarell *nt*; (*paint*)
Wasserfarbe *f*; **watercress** *n*
(Brunnen)kresse *f*; **waterfall** *n*
Wasserfall *m*; **watering can** *n*
Gießkanne *f*; **water level** *n*

Wasserstand *m*; **watermelon** *n*
Wassermelone *f*; **waterproof** *adj*
wasserdicht; **water-skiing** *n*
Wasserskilaufen *nt*; **water sports**
npl Wassersport *m*; **watertight**
adj wasserdicht; **water wings** *npl*
Schwimmflügel *pl*; **watery** *adj*
wässerig
wave [weiv] *n* Welle *f* ▷ *vt* (*move
to and fro*) schwenken; (*hand, flag*)
winken ▷ *vi* (*person*) winken;
(*flag*) wehen; **wavelength** *n*
Wellenlänge *f*; **to be on the same
~** (*fig*) die gleiche Wellenlänge
haben; **wavy** ['weivi] *adj* wellig
wax [wæks] *n* Wachs *nt*; (*in ear*)
Ohrenschmalz *nt*
way [wei] *n* Weg *m*; (*direction*)
Richtung *f*; (*manner*) Art *f*; **can you
tell me the ~ to ... ?** wie komme
ich (am besten) zu ... ?; **we went
the wrong ~** wir sind in die
falsche Richtung
gefahren/gegangen; **to lose one's
~** sich verirren; **to make ~ for
sb/sth** jdm/etw Platz machen; **to
get one's own ~** seinen Willen
durchsetzen; **"give ~"** (Auto)
„Vorfahrt achten"; **the other
~ round** andersherum; **one ~ or
another** irgendwie; **in a ~** in
gewisser Weise; **in the ~** im Weg;
by the ~ übrigens; **"~ in"**
„Eingang"; **"~ out"** „Ausgang"; **no
~!** (*fam*) kommt nicht infrage!
we [wiː] *pron* wir
weak [wiːk] *adj* schwach;
weaken *vt* schwächen ▷ *vi*
schwächer werden
wealth [welθ] *n* Reichtum *m*;
wealthy *adj* reich
weapon ['wepən] *n* Waffe *f*
wear [weə°] *n* (*have on*) tragen; **what shall I ~?**
was soll ich anziehen? ▷ *vi*
(*become worn*) sich abnutzen ▷ *n*:
~ (and tear) Abnutzung *f*; **wear**

off vi (diminish) nachlassen; **wear out** vt abnutzen; (person) erschöpfen ▷ vi sich abnutzen

weather ['weðə°] n Wetter nt; **I'm feeling under the ~** ich fühle mich nicht ganz wohl; **weather forecast** n Wettervorhersage f

weave [wiːv] (**wove** o **weaved**, **woven** o **weaved**) vt (cloth) weben; (basket etc) flechten

web [web] n (a. fig) Netz nt; **the Web** das Web, das Internet; **webcam** ['webkæm] n Webcam f; **web page** n Webseite f; **website** n Website f

we'd [wiːd] contr of **we had; we would**

Wed abbr = **Wednesday** Mi.

wedding ['wedɪŋ] n Hochzeit f; **wedding anniversary** n Hochzeitstag m; **wedding dress** n Hochzeitskleid nt; **wedding ring** n Ehering m

wedding shower n (US) Party für die zukünftige Braut

wedge [wedʒ] n (under door etc) Keil m; (of cheese etc) Stück nt, Ecke f

Wednesday ['wenzdeɪ] n Mittwoch m; see also **Tuesday**

wee [wiː] adj klein ▷ vi (fam) Pipi machen

weed [wiːd] n Unkraut nt ▷ vt jäten

week [wiːk] n Woche f; **twice a ~** zweimal in der Woche; **a ~ on Friday/Friday ~** Freitag in einer Woche; **a ~ last Friday** letzten Freitag vor einer Woche; **in two ~s' time, in two ~s** in zwei Wochen; **for ~s** wochenlang; **weekday** n Wochentag m; **weekend** n Wochenende nt; **weekend break** n Wochenendurlaub m; **weekly** adj,

adv wöchentlich; (magazine) Wochen-

weep [wiːp] (**wept, wept**) vi weinen

weigh [weɪ] vt, vi wiegen; **it ~s 20 kilos** es wiegt 20 Kilo; **weigh up** vt abwägen; (person) einschätzen; **weight** [weɪt] n Gewicht nt; **to lose/put on ~** abnehmen/zunehmen; **weightlifting** n Gewichtheben nt; **weight training** n Krafttraining nt; **weighty** adj (important) schwerwiegend

weird [wɪəd] adj seltsam; **weirdo** ['wɪədəʊ] n Spinner(in) m(f)

welcome ['welkəm] n Empfang m ▷ adj willkommen; (news) angenehm; **~ to London** willkommen in London! ▷ vt begrüßen; **welcoming** adj freundlich

welfare ['welfeə°] n Wohl nt; (US: social security) Sozialhilfe f; **welfare state** n Wohlfahrtsstaat m

well [wel] n Brunnen m ▷ adj (in good health) gesund; **are you ~?** geht es dir/Ihnen gut?; **to feel ~** sich wohlfühlen; **get ~ soon** gute Besserung! ▷ interj nun; **~, I don't know** nun, ich weiß nicht ▷ adv gut; **~ done** gut gemacht!; **it may ~ be** das kann wohl sein; **as ~** (in addition) auch; **~ over 60** weit über 60

we'll [wiːl] contr of **we will; we shall**

well-behaved [welbɪ'heɪvd] adj brav; **well-being** n Wohl nt; **well-built** adj (person) gut gebaut; **well-done** adj (steak) durchgebraten; **well-earned** adj wohlverdient

wellingtons ['welɪŋtənz] npl Gummistiefel pl

well-known [wel'nəʊn] adj bekannt; **well-off** adj (wealthy)

wohlhabend; **well-paid** *adj* gut
bezahlt

Welsh [welʃ] *adj* walisisch ▷ *n*
(*language*) Walisisch *nt*; **the ~** *pl* die
Waliser *pl*; **Welshman** (*pl* **-men**) *n*
Waliser *m*; **Welshwoman** (*pl*
-women) *n* Waliserin *f*

went [went] *pt of* **go**

wept [wept] *pt, pp of* **weep**

were [wɜː] *pt of* **be**

we're [wɪə*] *contr of* **we are**

weren't [wɜːnt] *contr of* **were not**

west [west] *n* Westen *m*; **the
West** (*Pol*) der Westen ▷ *adv* (*go,
face*) nach Westen ▷ *adj* West-;
westbound *adj* (in) Richtung
Westen; **western** *adj*
West-, westlich; **Western Europe**
Westeuropa *nt* ▷ *n* (*Cine*) Western
m; **West Germany** *n*: (**the
former**) **~** (das ehemalige)
Westdeutschland,
Westdeutschland *n*; **westwards**
['westwədz] *adv* nach Westen

wet [wet] (**wet, wet**) *vt*: **to
~ oneself** in die Hose machen
▷ *adj* nass, feucht; **"~ paint"**
„frisch gestrichen"; **wet suit** *n*
Taucheranzug *m*

we've [wiːv] *contr of* **we have**

whale [weɪl] *n* Wal *m*

wharf [wɔːf] (*pl* **-s** *o* **wharves**) *n*
Kai *m*

○ **KEYWORD**

what [wɒt] *adj* **1** (*in questions*)
welche(r, s) was für ein(e);
what size is it? welche Größe ist
das?
2 (*in exclamations*) was für ein(e);
what a mess! was für ein
Durcheinander!
▷ *pron* (*interrogative/relative*) was;
what are you doing? was machst
du/machen Sie gerade?; **what are
you talking about?** wovon redest

du/reden Sie?; **what's your
name?** wie heißt du/heißen Sie?;
what is it called? wie heißt das?;
what about ...? wie wär's mit ...?;
I saw what you did ich habe
gesehen, was du gemacht
hast/Sie gemacht haben
▷ *excl* (*disbelieving*) wie, was;
what, no coffee! wie, kein
Kaffee?; **I've crashed the car —
what!** ich hatte einen
Autounfall — was!

whatever *pron*: **I'll do ~ you
want** ich tue alles, was du
willst/Sie wollen; **~ he says** egal,
was er sagt

what's [wɒts] *contr of* **what is;
what has**

wheat [wiːt] *n* Weizen *m*

wheel [wiːl] *n* Rad *nt*; (*steering
wheel*) Lenkrad *nt* ▷ *vt* (*bicycle,
trolley*) schieben; **wheelbarrow** *n*
Schubkarren *m*; **wheelchair** *n*
Rollstuhl *m*; **wheel clamp** *n*
Parkkralle *f*

○ **KEYWORD**

when [wen] *adv* wann
▷ *conj* **1** (*at, during, after the time
that*) wenn; (*in past*) als; **she was
reading when I came in** sie las,
als ich hereinkam; **be careful
when you cross the road** sei
vorsichtig, wenn du über die
Straße gehst/seien Sie vorsichtig,
wenn Sie über die Straße gehen
2 (*on, at which*) als; **on the day
when I met him** an dem Tag, an
dem ich ihn traf
3 (*whereas*) wo ... doch

whenever *adv* (*every time*) immer
wenn; **come ~ you like** komm,
wann immer du willst/kommen
Sie, wann immer sie wollen

w

where [wɛə*] *adv* wo; **~ are you going?** wohin gehst du/gehen Sie?; **~ are you from?** woher kommst du/kommen Sie? ▷ *conj* wo; **that's ~ I used to live** da habe ich früher gewohnt; **whereabouts** [wɛərə'baʊts] *adv* wo ▷ *npl* ['wɛərəbaʊts] Aufenthaltsort *m*; **whereas** [wɛər'æz] *conj* während, wohingegen; **whereby** *adv* wodurch; **wherever** [wɛər'evə*] *conj* wo immer; **~ that may be** wo immer das sein mag; **~ I go** überall, wohin ich gehe

whether ['wɛðə*] *conj* ob

🔘 **KEYWORD**

which [wɪtʃ] *adj* **1** (*interrogative*) (*direct, indirect*) welche(r, s); **which one?** welche(r, s)?
2 in which case in diesem Fall; **by which time** zu dieser Zeit
▷ *pron* **1** (*interrogative*) welche(r, s); (*of people also*) wer
2 (*relative*) der/die/das; (*referring to people*) was; **the apple which you ate/which is on the table** der Apfel, den du gegessen hast/der auf dem Tisch liegt; **he said he saw her, which is true** er sagte, er habe sie gesehen, was auch stimmt

whichever *adj, pron* welche(r, s) auch immer
while [waɪl] *n*: **a ~** eine Weile; **for a ~** eine Zeit lang; **a short ~ ago** vor Kurzem ▷ *conj* während; (*although*) obwohl
whine [waɪn] *vi* (*person*) jammern
whip [wɪp] *n* Peitsche *f* ▷ *vt* (*beat*) peitschen; **~ped cream** Schlagsahne *f*
whirl [wɜːl] *vt, vi* herumwirbeln;

whirlpool *n* (*in river, sea*) Strudel *m*; (*pool*) Whirlpool *m*
whisk [wɪsk] *n* Schneebesen *m* ▷ *vt* (*cream etc*) schlagen
whisker ['wɪskə*] *n* (*of animal*) Schnurrhaar *nt*; **~s** *pl* (*of man*) Backenbart *m*
whisk(e)y ['wɪskɪ] *n* Whisky *m*
whisper ['wɪspə*] *vi, vt* flüstern; **to ~ sth to sb** jdm etw zuflüstern
whistle ['wɪsl] *n* Pfiff *m*; (*instrument*) Pfeife *f* ▷ *vt, vi* pfeifen
white [waɪt] *n* (*of egg*) Eiweiß *nt*; (*of eye*) Weiße *nt* ▷ *adj* weiß; (*with fear*) blass; (*coffee*) mit Milch/Sahne; **White House** *n*: **the ~** das Weiße Haus; **white lie** *n* Notlüge *f*; **white meat** *n* helles Fleisch; **white sauce** *n* weiße Soße; **white water rafting** *n* Rafting *nt*; **white wine** *n* Weißwein *m*
Whitsun ['wɪtsn] *n* Pfingsten *nt*

🔘 **KEYWORD**

who [huː] *pron* **1** (*interrogative*) wer; (*akk*) wen; (*dat*) wem; **who is it?, who's there?** wer ist da?
2 (*relative*) der/die/das; **the woman/man who spoke to me** die Frau/der Mann, die/der mit mir sprach

whoever [huː'evə*] *pron* wer auch immer; **~ you choose** wen auch immer du wählst/Sie wählen
whole [həʊl] *adj* ganz ▷ *n* Ganze(s) *nt*; **the ~ of my family** meine ganze Familie; **on the ~** im Großen und Ganzen; **wholefood** *n* (*Brit*) Vollwertkost *f*; **wholeheartedly** *adv* voll und ganz; **wholemeal** *adj* (*Brit*) Vollkorn-; **wholesale** *adv* (*buy, sell*) im Großhandel; **wholesome**

adj gesund; **whole wheat** *adj* Vollkorn-; **wholly** ['həʊlɪ] *adv* völlig

KEYWORD

whom [huːm] *pron* **1** (*interrogative*) (*akk*) wen; (*dat*) wem; **whom did you see?** wen hast du/haben Sie gesehen?; **to whom did you give it?** wem hast du/haben Sie es gegeben?
2 (*relative*) (*akk*) den/die/das; (*dat*) dem/der/dem; **the man whom I saw/to whom I spoke** der Mann, den ich sah/mit dem ich sprach

whooping cough ['huːpɪŋkɒf] *n* Keuchhusten *m*
whose [huːz] *adj* (*in questions*) wessen; (*in relative clauses*) dessen/deren/dessen, deren *pl*; **~ bike is that?** wessen Fahrrad ist das? ▷ *pron* (*in questions*) wessen; **~ is this?** wem gehört das?

KEYWORD

why [waɪ] *adv* warum, weshalb ▷ *conj* warum, weshalb; **that's not why I'm here** ich bin nicht deswegen hier; **that's the reason why** deshalb ▷ *excl* (*expressing surprise, shock*) na so was; (*explaining*) also dann; **why, it's you!** na so was, du bist/Sie sind es!

wicked ['wɪkɪd] *adj* böse; (*fam: great*) geil
wide [waɪd] *adj* breit; (*skirt, trousers*) weit; (*selection*) groß ▷ *adv* weit; **wide-angle lens** *n* Weitwinkelobjektiv *nt*; **wide-awake** *adj* hellwach; **widely** *adv* weit; **~ known**

allgemein bekannt; **widen** *vt* verbreitern; (*fig*) erweitern; **wide-open** *adj* weit offen; **widescreen TV** *n* Breitbildfernseher *m*; **widespread** *adj* weit verbreitet
widow ['wɪdəʊ] *n* Witwe *f*; **widowed** *adj* verwitwet; **widower** *n* Witwer *m*
width [wɪdθ] *n* Breite *f*
wife [waɪf] (*pl* **wives**) *n* (Ehe)frau *f*
Wi-Fi ['waɪfaɪ] *n* Wi-Fi *nt*
wig [wɪg] *n* Perücke *f*
wiggle ['wɪgl] *vt* wackeln mit
wild [waɪld] *adj* wild; (*violent*) heftig; (*plan, idea*) verrückt ▷ *n*: **in the ~** in freier Wildbahn; **wildlife** *n* Tier- und Pflanzenwelt *f*; **wildly** *adv* wild; (*exaggerated*) maßlos

KEYWORD

will [wɪl] *vb aux* **1** (*forms future tense*) werden; **I will finish it tomorrow** ich mache es morgen zu Ende
2 (*in conjectures, predictions*) **he will** *o* **he'll be there by now** er dürfte jetzt da sein; **that will be the postman** das wird der Postbote sein
3 (*in commands, requests, offers*) **will you be quiet!** sei/seien Sie endlich still!; **will you help me?** hilfst du/helfen Sie mir?; **will you have a cup of tea?** trinkst du/trinken Sie eine Tasse Tee?; **I won't put up with it!** das lasse ich mir nicht gefallen!
▷ *vt* wollen
▷ *n* Wille *m*; (*jur*) Testament *nt*

willing *adj* bereitwillig; **to be ~ to do sth** bereit sein, etw zu tun; **willingly** *adv* gern(e)
willow ['wɪləʊ] *n* Weide *f*

w

willpower ['wɪlpauə°] n Willenskraft f

wimp [wɪmp] n Weichei nt

win [wɪn] (**won, won**) vt, vi gewinnen ▷ n Sieg m; **win over**, **win round** vt für sich gewinnen

wind [waɪnd] (**wound, wound**) vt (rope, bandage) wickeln; **wind down** vt (car window) herunterkurbeln; **wind up** vt (clock) aufziehen; (car window) hochkurbeln; (meeting, speech) abschließen; (person) aufziehen, ärgern

wind [wɪnd] n Wind m; (Med) Blähungen pl; **wind farm** n Windpark m; **wind instrument** n Blasinstrument nt; **windmill** n Windmühle f

window ['wɪndəu] n Fenster nt; (counter) Schalter m; **~ of opportunity** Chance f, Gelegenheit f; **window box** n Blumenkasten m; **windowpane** n Fensterscheibe f; **window-shopping** n: **to go ~** einen Schaufensterbummel machen; **windowsill** n Fensterbrett nt

windpipe ['wɪndpaɪp] n Luftröhre f; **windscreen** n (Brit) Windschutzscheibe f; **windscreen wiper** n (Brit) Scheibenwischer m; **windshield** n (US) Windschutzscheibe f; **windshield wiper** n (US) Scheibenwischer m; **windsurfer** n Windsurfer(in) m(f); (board) Surfbrett nt; **windsurfing** n Windsurfen nt

windy ['wɪndɪ] adj windig

wine [waɪn] n Wein m; **wine bar** n Weinlokal nt; **wineglass** n Weinglas nt; **wine list** n Weinkarte f; **wine tasting** n (event) Weinprobe f

wing [wɪŋ] n Flügel m; (Brit Auto) Kotflügel m; **~s** pl (Theat) Kulissen pl

wink [wɪŋk] vi zwinkern; **to ~ at sb** jdm zuzwinkern

winner ['wɪnə°] n Gewinner(in) m(f); (Sport) Sieger(in) m(f); **winning** adj (team, horse etc) siegreich; **~ number** Gewinnzahl f ▷ n **~s** pl Gewinn m

winter ['wɪntə°] n Winter m; **winter sports** npl Wintersport m; **wint(e)ry** ['wɪntrɪ] adj winterlich

wipe [waɪp] vt abwischen; **to ~ one's nose** sich dat die Nase putzen; **to ~ one's feet** (on mat) sich dat die Schuhe abtreten; **wipe off** vt abwischen; **wipe out** vt (destroy) vernichten; (data, debt) löschen; (epidemic etc) ausrotten

wire ['waɪə°] n Draht m; (Elec) Leitung f; (US: telegram) Telegramm nt ▷ vt (plug in) anschließen; (US Tel) telegrafieren (sb sth jdm etw); **wireless** ['waɪələs] adj drahtlos

wisdom ['wɪzdəm] n Weisheit f; **wisdom tooth** n Weisheitszahn m

wise, wisely [waɪz, -lɪ] adj, adv weise

wish [wɪʃ] n Wunsch m (for nach); **with best ~es** (in letter) herzliche Grüße ▷ vt wünschen, wollen; **to ~ sb good luck/Merry Christmas** jdm viel Glück/frohe Weihnachten wünschen; **I ~ I'd never seen him** ich wünschte, ich hätte ihn nie gesehen

witch [wɪtʃ] n Hexe f

⭕ **KEYWORD**

with [wɪð] prep **1** (accompanying, in the company of) mit; **we stayed with friends** wir übernachteten bei Freunden; **I'll be with you in a minute** einen Augenblick, ich bin sofort da; **I'm not with you** (I don't understand) das verstehe ich nicht; **to be with it** (inf) (up-to-date) auf dem Laufenden sein; (alert) (voll) da sein inf **2** (descriptive, indicating manner etc) mit; **the man with the grey hat** der Mann mit dem grauen Hut; **red with anger** rot vor Wut

withdraw [wɪðˈdrɔː] irr vt zurückziehen; (money) abheben; (comment) zurücknehmen ▷ vi sich zurückziehen

wither [ˈwɪðə°] vi (plant) verwelken

withhold [wɪðˈhəʊld] irr vt vorenthalten (from sb jdm)

within [wɪðˈɪn] prep innerhalb +gen; **~ walking distance** zu Fuß erreichbar

without [wɪðˈaʊt] prep ohne; **~ asking** ohne zu fragen

withstand [wɪðˈstænd] irr vt standhalten +dat

witness [ˈwɪtnəs] n Zeuge m, Zeugin f ▷ vt Zeuge sein; **witness box**, **witness stand** (US) n Zeugenstand m

witty [ˈwɪtɪ] adj geistreich

wives [waɪvz] pl of **wife**

WMD abbr = **weapon of mass destruction** Massenvernichtungswaffe

wobble [ˈwɒbl] vi wackeln; **wobbly** adj wackelig

wok [wɒk] n Wok m

woke [wəʊk] pt of **wake**

woken [ˈwəʊkn] pp of **wake**

wolf [wʊlf] (pl **wolves**) n Wolf m

woman [ˈwʊmən] (pl **women**) n Frau f

womb [wuːm] n Gebärmutter f

women [ˈwɪmɪn] pl of **woman**

won [wʌn] pt, pp of **win**

wonder [ˈwʌndə°] n (marvel) Wunder nt; (surprise) Staunen nt ▷ vt, vi (speculate) sich fragen; **I ~ what/if ...** ich frage mich, was/ob ...; **wonderful**, **wonderfully** adj, adv wunderbar

won't [wəʊnt] contr of **will not**

wood [wʊd] n Holz nt; **~s** Wald m; **wooden** adj Holz-; (fig) hölzern; **woodpecker** n Specht m; **woodwork** n (wooden parts) Holzteile pl; (in school) Werken nt

wool [wʊl] n Wolle f; **woollen**, **woolen** (US) adj Woll-

word [wɜːd] n Wort nt; (promise) Ehrenwort nt; **~s** pl (of song) Text m; **to have a ~ with sb** mit jdm sprechen; **in other ~s** mit anderen Worten ▷ vt formulieren; **wording** n Wortlaut m, Formulierung f; **word processing** n Textverarbeitung f; **word processor** n (program) Textverarbeitungsprogramm nt

wore [wɔː°] pt of **wear**

work [wɜːk] n Arbeit f; (of art, literature) Werk nt; **~ of art** Kunstwerk nt; **he's at ~** er ist in/auf der Arbeit; **out of ~** arbeitslos ▷ vi arbeiten (at, on an +dat); (machine, plan) funktionieren; (medicine) wirken; (succeed) klappen ▷ vt (machine) bedienen; (plan) aufgehen; **work out** vi (plan) klappen; (sum) aufgehen; (person) trainieren ▷ vt (price, speed etc) ausrechnen; (plan) ausarbeiten; **work up: to get worked up** sich aufregen; **workaholic** [wɜːkəˈhɒlɪk] n Arbeitstier nt; **worker** n Arbeiter(in) m(f); **working class** n Arbeiterklasse f; **workman** (pl **-men**) n Handwerker m; **workout** n (Sport) Fitnesstraining nt, Konditionstraining nt; **work permit** n Arbeitserlaubnis f;

w

workplace n Arbeitsplatz m;
workshop n Werkstatt f;
(meeting) Workshop m; **work
station** n (Inform) Workstation
f
world [wɜːld] n Welt f; **world
championship** n Weltmeisterschaft f; **World War** n: ~ I/II, the
First/Second ~ der Erste/Zweite
Weltkrieg; **world-wide** adj, adv
weltweit; **World Wide Web** n
World Wide Web nt
worm [wɜːm] n Wurm m
worn [wɔːn] pp of **wear** ▷ adj
(clothes) abgetragen; (tyre)
abgefahren; **worn-out** adj
abgenutzt; (person) erschöpft
worried ['wʌrɪd] adj besorgt; **be
~ about** sth dat Sorgen machen
um; **worry** ['wʌrɪ] n Sorge f ▷ vt
Sorgen machen +dat ▷ vi sich
Sorgen machen (about um); **don't
~!** keine Sorge!; **worrying** adj
beunruhigend
worse [wɜːs] adj comparative of
bad; schlechter; (pain, mistake etc)
schlimmer ▷ adv comparative of
badly; schlechter; **worsen** vt
verschlechtern ▷ vi sich
verschlechtern
worship ['wɜːʃɪp] vt anbeten,
anhimmeln
worst [wɜːst] adj superlative of
bad; schlechteste(r, s); (pain,
mistake etc) schlimmste(r, s) ▷ adv
superlative of **badly**; am
schlechtesten ▷ n: **the ~ is over**
das Schlimmste ist vorbei; **at (the)
~** schlimmstenfalls
worth [wɜːθ] n Wert m; **£10 ~ of
food** Essen für 10 Pfund ▷ adj: **it is
~ £50** es ist 50 Pfund wert;
~ seeing sehenswert; **it's ~ it**
(rewarding) es lohnt sich;
worthless adj wertlos;
worthwhile adj lohnend,
lohnenswert; **worthy** ['wɜːðɪ]

adj (deserving respect) würdig; **to
be ~ of sth** etw verdienen

○ **KEYWORD**

would [wʊd] vb aux **1** (conditional
tense) **if you asked him he would
do it** wenn du ihn fragtest/Sie ihn
fragten, würde er es tun; **if you
had asked him he would have
done it** wenn du ihn gefragt
hättest/Sie ihn gefragt hätten,
hätte er es getan
2 (in offers, invitations, requests)
would you like a biscuit?
möchtest du/möchten Sie einen
Keks?; **would you ask him to
come in?** würdest du/würden Sie
ihn bitte hereinbitten?
3 (in indirect speech) **I said I would
do it** ich sagte, ich würde es tun
4 (emphatic) **it WOULD have to
snow today!** es musste ja
ausgerechnet heute schneien!
5 (insistence) **she wouldn't behave**
sie wollte sich partout nicht
anständig benehmen
6 (conjecture) **it would have been
midnight** es mag ungefähr
Mitternacht gewesen sein; **it
would seem so** es sieht wohl so
aus
7 (indicating habit) **he would go
there on Mondays** er ging jeden
Montag dorthin

wouldn't ['wʊdnt] contr of
would not
would've ['wʊdəv] contr of
would have
wound [wuːnd] n Wunde f ▷ vt
verwunden; (fig) verletzen
▷ [waʊnd] pt, pp of **wind**
wove [wəʊv] pt of **weave**
woven ['wəʊvn] pp of **weave**
wrap [ræp] vt (parcel, present)
einwickeln; **to ~ sth round sth**

etw um etw wickeln; **wrap up** vt
(parcel, present) einwickeln ▷ vi
(dress warmly) sich warm anziehen;
wrapper n (of sweet) Papier nt;
wrapping paper n Packpapier nt;
(giftwrap) Geschenkpapier nt
wreath [riːθ] n Kranz m
wreck [rek] n (ship, plane, car)
Wrack nt; **a nervous ~** ein
Nervenbündel m ▷ vt (car) zu
Schrott fahren; (fig) zerstören;
wreckage ['rekɪdʒ] n Trümmer pl
wrench [rentʃ] n (tool)
Schraubenschlüssel m
wrestling ['reslɪŋ] n Ringen nt
wring out ['rɪŋ'aʊt] (**wrung,
wrung**) vt auswringen
wrinkle ['rɪŋkl] n Falte f
wrist [rɪst] n Handgelenk nt;
wristwatch n Armbanduhr f
write [raɪt] (**wrote, written**) vt
schreiben; (cheque) ausstellen ▷ vi
schreiben; **to ~ to sb** jdm
schreiben; **write down** vt
aufschreiben; **write off** vt (debt,
person) abschreiben; (car) zu
Schrott fahren ▷ vi: **to ~ off for
sth** etw anfordern; **write out** vt
(name etc) ausschreiben; (cheque)
ausstellen; **write-protected** adj
(Inform) schreibgeschützt; **writer**
n Verfasser(in) m(f); (author)
Schriftsteller(in) m(f); **writing** n
Schrift f; (profession) Schreiben nt;
in ~ schriftlich; **writing paper** n
Schreibpapier nt
written ['rɪtən] pp of **write**
wrong [rɒŋ] adj (incorrect) falsch;
(morally) unrecht; **you're ~** du
hast/Sie haben unrecht; **what's
~ with your leg?** was ist mit
deinem/Ihrem Bein los?; **you've
got the ~ number** du bist/Sie sind
falsch verbunden; **I dialled the
~ number** ich habe mich
verwählt; **don't get me
~** versteh/verstehen Sie mich

nicht falsch; **to go ~** (plan)
schiefgehen; **wrongly** adv falsch;
(unjustly) zu Unrecht
wrote [rəʊt] pt of **write**
WWW abbr = **World Wide Web**
WWW

xenophobia [zenə'fəʊbɪə] *n*
Ausländerfeindlichkeit *f*
XL *abbr* = **extra large** XL, übergroß
Xmas ['krɪsməs] *n* Weihnachten
nt
X-ray ['eksreɪ] *n* (*picture*)
Röntgenaufnahme *f* ▷ *vt* röntgen
xylophone ['zaɪləfəʊn] *n* Xylo

yacht [jɒt] *n* Jacht *f*; **yachting** *n*
Segeln *nt*; **to go ~** segeln gehen
yam [jæm] *n* (*US*) Süßkartoffel
f
yard [jɑːd] *n* Hof *m*; (*US: garden*)
Garten *m*; (*measure*) Yard *nt* (0,91 m)
yawn [jɔːn] *vi* gähnen
yd *abbr* = **yard(s)**
year ['jɪə*] *n* Jahr *nt*; **this/last/
next ~** dieses/letztes/nächstes
Jahr; **he is 28 ~s old** er ist 28 Jahre
alt; **~s ago** vor Jahren; **a
five-year-old** ein(e)
Fünfjährige(r); **yearly** *adj, adv*
jährlich
yearn [jɜːn] *vi* sich sehnen (*for*
nach +*dat*); **to ~ to do sth** sich
danach sehnen, etw zu tun
yeast [jiːst] *n* Hefe *f*
yell [jel] *vi, vt* schreien; **to ~ at sb**
jdn anschreien
yellow ['jeləʊ] *adj* gelb; **~ card**

(Sport) gelbe Karte; **~ fever** Gelbfieber nt; **~ line** (Brit) ≈ Halteverbot nt; **double ~ line** (Brit) ≈ absolutes Halteverbot; **the Yellow Pages®** pl die Gelben Seiten pl

yes [jes] adv ja; (answering negative question) doch; **to say ~ to sth** ja zu etw sagen ▷ n Ja nt

yesterday ['jestədeɪ] adv gestern; **~ morning/evening** gestern Morgen/Abend; **the day before ~** vorgestern; **~'s newspaper** die Zeitung von gestern

yet [jet] adv (still) noch; (up to now) bis jetzt; (in a question: already) schon; **he hasn't arrived ~** er ist noch nicht gekommen; **have you finished ~?** bist du/sind Sie schon fertig?; **~ again** schon wieder; **as ~** bis jetzt ▷ conj doch

yield [jiːld] n Ertrag m ▷ vt (result, crop) hervorbringen; (profit, interest) bringen ▷ vi nachgeben (to +dat); (Mil) sich ergeben (to +dat); **"~"** (US Auto) „Vorfahrt beachten"

yoga ['jəʊgə] n Yoga nt

yog(h)urt [ˈjɒgət] n Jog(h)urt m

yolk [jəʊk] n Eigelb nt

Yorkshire pudding ['jɔːkʃəˈpʊdɪŋ] n gebackener Eierteig, der meist zum Roastbeef gegessen wird

O KEYWORD

you [juː] pron **1** (subj, in comparisons) (familiar form) (sg) du; (pl) ihr; (in letters) Du, Ihr; (polite form) Sie; **you Germans** ihr Deutschen; **she's younger than you** sie ist jünger als du/ihr/Sie
2 (direct object, after prep +akk) (familiar form) (sg) dich; (pl) euch; (in letters) Dich, Euch; (polite form) Sie; **I know you** ich kenne dich/euch/Sie
3 (indirect object, after prep +dat) (familiar form) (sg) dir; (pl) euch; (in letters) Dir, Euch; (polite form) Ihnen; **I gave it to you** ich gab es dir/euch/Ihnen
4 (impers) (one) (subj) man; (direct object) einen; (indirect object) einem; **fresh air does you good** frische Luft tut (einem) gut

you'd [juːd] contr of **you had; you would**; **~ better leave** du solltest/Sie sollten gehen

you'll [juːl] contr of **you will; you shall**

young [jʌŋ] adj jung ▷ n **the ~** pl (~ people) die jungen Leute pl; (animals) die Jungen pl; **youngster** ['jʌŋstə°] n Jugendliche(r) mf

your ['jɔː°] adj sing dein; polite form Ihr; pl euer; polite form Ihr; **have you hurt ~ leg?** hast du dir/haben Sie sich das Bein verletzt?

you're ['jʊə°] contr of **you are**

yours ['jɔːz] pron sing deine(r, s); polite form Ihre(r, s); pl eure(r, s); polite form Ihre(r, s); **is this ~?** gehört das dir/Ihnen?; **a friend of ~** ein Freund von dir/Ihnen

yourself [jɔːˈself] pron sing dich; polite form sich; **have you hurt ~?** hast du dich/haben Sie sich verletzt?; **did you do it ~?** hast du/haben Sie es selbst gemacht?; **(all) by ~** allein; **yourselves** pron pl euch; polite form sich; **have you hurt ~?** habt ihr euch/haben Sie sich verletzt?; **did you do it ~?** habt ihr/haben Sie es selbst gemacht?; **(all) by ~** allein

youth [juːθ] n (period) Jugend f; (young man) junger Mann; (young people) Jugend f; **youth group** n

Y

Jugendgruppe *f*; **youth hostel** *n* Jugendherberge *f*
you've [ju:v] *contr of* **you have**
yucky ['jʌkɪ] *adj* (*fam*) eklig
yummy ['jʌmɪ] *adj* (*fam*) lecker
yuppie, **yuppy** ['jʌpɪ] *n* Yuppie *m*

Z

zap [zæp] *vt* (*Inform*) löschen; (*in computer game*) abknallen ▷ *vi* (*TV*) zappen; **zapper** *n* (*TV*) Fernbedienung *f*; **zapping** *n* (*TV*) ständiges Umschalten, Zapping *nt*
zebra ['zebrə, ?? 'zi:brə] (*US*) *n* Zebra *nt*; **zebra crossing** *n* (*Brit*) Zebrastreifen *m*
zero [zɪərəʊ] (*pl* **-es**) *n* Null *f*; **10 degrees below ~** 10 Grad unter null
zest [zest] *n* (*enthusiasm*) Begeisterung *f*
zigzag ['zɪgzæg] *n* Zickzack *m* ▷ *vi* (*person, vehicle*) im Zickzack gehen/fahren; (*path*) im Zickzack verlaufen
zinc [zɪŋk] *n* Zink *nt*
zip [zɪp] *n* (*Brit*) Reißverschluss *m* ▷ *vt*: **to ~ (up)** den Reißverschluss zumachen; (*Inform*) zippen; **zip code** *n* (*US*) Postleitzahl *f*; **Zip disk®** *n* (*Inform*) ZIP-Diskette® *f*;

Zip drive® *n* (*Inform*)
ZIP-Laufwerk® *nt*; **Zip file®** *n*
(*Inform*) ZIP-Datei® *f*; **zipper** *n*
(*US*) Reißverschluss *m*
zit [zɪt] *n* (*fam*) Pickel *m*
zodiac [ˈzəʊdɪæk] *n* Tierkreis *m*;
sign of the ~ Tierkreiszeichen
nt
zone [zəʊn] *n* Zone *f*; (*area*)
Gebiet *nt*; (*in town*) Bezirk *m*
zoo [zuː] *n* Zoo *m*
zoom [zuːm] *vi* (*move fast*)
brausen, sausen ▷ *n*: **~ (lens)**
Zoomobjektiv *nt*; **zoom in** *vi*
(*Foto*) heranzoomen (*on an +akk*)
zucchini [zuːˈkiːnɪ] (*pl* **-(s)**) *n*
(*US*) Zucchini *f*

VERB TABLES

Introduction

The **Verb Tables** in the following section contain 31 tables of German verbs in alphabetical order. Each table shows you the following forms: **Present**, **Perfect**, **Future**, **Subjunctive**, **Imperfect**, **Conditional**, **Imperative** and the **Present** and **Past Participles**.

In order to help you use the verbs shown in the Verb Tables correctly, there are also a number of example phrases at the bottom of each page to show the verb as it is used in context.

In German there are **regular** verbs or **weak** verbs (their forms follow the normal rules) and **irregular** or **strong** verbs (their forms do not follow the normal rules) and **mixed** verbs (their forms have features of both **weak** and **strong** verbs).

The **Verb Tables** given show one **weak** verb – machen, Verb Table 19 and three **mixed** verbs – bringen, Verb Table 2; denken, Verb Table 3 and kennen Verb Table 13. The rest of the verbs shown are **strong** verbs.

▶ **bleiben** (to remain)

PRESENT

ich	bleibe
du	bleibst
er	bleibt
wir	bleiben
ihr	bleibt
sie	bleiben

PRESENT SUBJUNCTIVE

ich	bleibe
du	bleibest
er	bleibe
wir	bleiben
ihr	bleibet
sie	bleiben

PERFECT

ich	bin geblieben
du	bist geblieben
er	ist geblieben
wir	sind geblieben
ihr	seid geblieben
sie	sind geblieben

IMPERFECT

ich	blieb
du	bliebst
er	blieb
wir	blieben
ihr	bliebt
sie	blieben

FUTURE

ich	werde bleiben
du	wirst bleiben
er	wird bleiben
wir	werden bleiben
ihr	werdet bleiben
sie	werden bleiben

CONDITIONAL

ich	würde bleiben
du	würdest bleiben
er	würde bleiben
wir	würden bleiben
ihr	würdet bleiben
sie	würden bleiben

IMPERATIVE

bleib(e)!/bleiben wir!/bleibt!
bleiben Sie!

PAST PARTICIPLE

geblieben

PRESENT PARTICIPLE

bleibend

EXAMPLE PHRASES

*Hoffentlich **bleibt** das Wetter schön.* I hope the weather will stay fine.
*Vom Kuchen **ist** nur noch ein Stück **geblieben**.* There's only one piece of cake left.
*Dieses Erlebnis **blieb** in meiner Erinnerung.* This experience stayed with me.

---

ich = I **du** = you **er** = he **wir** = we/one **ihr** = you **sie** = they

▶ **bringen** (to bring)

PRESENT

ich	bringe
du	bringst
er	bringt
wir	bringen
ihr	bringt
sie	bringen

PRESENT SUBJUNCTIVE

ich	bringe
du	bringest
er	bringe
wir	bringen
ihr	bringet
sie	bringen

PERFECT

ich	habe gebracht
du	hast gebracht
er	hat gebracht
wir	haben gebracht
ihr	habt gebracht
sie	haben gebracht

IMPERFECT

ich	brachte
du	brachtest
er	brachte
wir	brachten
ihr	brachtet
sie	brachten

FUTURE

ich	werde bringen
du	wirst bringen
er	wird bringen
wir	werden bringen
ihr	werdet bringen
sie	werden bringen

CONDITIONAL

ich	würde bringen
du	würdest bringen
er	würde bringen
wir	würden bringen
ihr	würdet bringen
sie	würden bringen

IMPERATIVE

bring(e)!/bringen wir!/bringt!
bringen Sie!

PAST PARTICIPLE

gebracht

PRESENT PARTICIPLE

bringend

EXAMPLE PHRASES

*Kannst du mich zum Flughafen **bringen**?* Can you take me to the airport?
*Max **hat** mir Blumen **gebracht**.* Max brought me flowers.
*Das **brachte** mich auf eine Idee.* It gave me an idea.

ich = I **du** = you **er** = he **wir** = we/one **ihr** = you **sie** = they

▶ **denken** (to think)

PRESENT		**PRESENT SUBJUNCTIVE**	
ich	denke	ich	denke
du	denkst	du	denkest
er	denkt	er	denke
wir	denken	wir	denken
ihr	denkt	ihr	denket
sie	denken	sie	denken

PERFECT		**IMPERFECT**	
ich	habe gedacht	ich	dachte
du	hast gedacht	du	dachtest
er	hat gedacht	er	dachte
wir	haben gedacht	wir	dachten
ihr	habt gedacht	ihr	dachtet
sie	haben gedacht	sie	dachten

FUTURE		**CONDITIONAL**	
ich	werde denken	ich	würde denken
du	wirst denken	du	würdest denken
er	wird denken	er	würde denken
wir	werden denken	wir	würden denken
ihr	werdet denken	ihr	würdet denken
sie	werden denken	sie	würden denken

IMPERATIVE

denk(e)!/denken wir!/denkt!
denken Sie!

PAST PARTICIPLE

gedacht

PRESENT PARTICIPLE

denkend

EXAMPLE PHRASES

*Wie **denken** Sie darüber?* What do you think about it?
*Das war für ihn **gedacht**.* It was meant for him.
*Es war das Erste, woran ich **dachte**.* It was the first thing I thought of.

---

ich = I **du** = you **er** = he **wir** = we/one **ihr** = you **sie** = they

► dürfen (to be allowed to)

PRESENT

ich	darf
du	darfst
er	darf
wir	dürfen
ihr	dürft
sie	dürfen

PRESENT SUBJUNCTIVE

ich	dürfe
du	dürfest
er	dürfe
wir	dürfen
ihr	dürfet
sie	dürfen

PERFECT

ich	habe gedurft/dürfen
du	hast gedurft/dürfen
er	hat gedurft/dürfen
wir	haben gedurft/dürfen
ihr	habt gedurft/dürfen
sie	haben gedurft/dürfen

IMPERFECT

ich	durfte
du	durftest
er	durfte
wir	durften
ihr	durftet
sie	durften

FUTURE

ich	werde dürfen
du	wirst dürfen
er	wird dürfen
wir	werden dürfen
ihr	werdet dürfen
sie	werden dürfen

CONDITIONAL

ich	würde dürfen
du	würdest dürfen
er	würde dürfen
wir	würden dürfen
ihr	würdet dürfen
sie	würden dürfen

IMPERATIVE

PAST PARTICIPLE

gedurft/dürfen*

PRESENT PARTICIPLE

dürfend

The second form is used when combined with an infinitive construction.

EXAMPLE PHRASES

Darf ich ins Kino? Can I go to the cinema?
Das würde ich zu Hause nicht dürfen. I wouldn't be allowed to do that at home.
Das dürfen Sie mir glauben. You can take my word for it.

ich = I **du** = you **er** = he **wir** = we/one **ihr** = you **sie** = they

▶ **fahren** (to drive/to go)

PRESENT			PRESENT SUBJUNCTIVE	
ich	fahre		ich	fahre
du	fährst		du	fahrest
er	fährt		er	fahre
wir	fahren		wir	fahren
ihr	fahrt		ihr	fahret
sie	fahren		sie	fahren

PERFECT			IMPERFECT	
ich	bin gefahren*		ich	fuhr
du	bist gefahren		du	fuhrst
er	ist gefahren		er	fuhr
wir	sind gefahren		wir	fuhren
ihr	seid gefahren		ihr	fuhrt
sie	sind gefahren		sie	fuhren

FUTURE			CONDITIONAL	
ich	werde fahren		ich	würde fahren
du	wirst fahren		du	würdest fahren
er	wird fahren		er	würde fahren
wir	werden fahren		wir	würden fahren
ihr	werdet fahren		ihr	würdet fahren
sie	werden fahren		sie	würden fahren

IIMPERATIVE

fahr(e)!/fahren wir!/fahrt!
fahren Sie!
OR: ich habe/hätte gefahren
etc (*when transitive*).

PAST PARTICIPLE

gefahren

PRESENT PARTICIPLE

fahrend

EXAMPLE PHRASES

*Sie **fahren** mit dem Bus in die Schule*. They go to school by bus.
*Rechts **fahren**!* Drive on the right!
*Ich **bin** mit der Familie nach Spanien **gefahren**.* I went to Spain with my family.

---

ich = I **du** = you **er** = he **wir** = we/one **ihr** = you **sie** = they

▶ **fallen** (to fall)

PRESENT

ich	falle
du	fällst
er	fällt
wir	fallen
ihr	fallt
sie	fallen

PRESENT SUBJUNCTIVE

ich	falle
du	fallest
er	falle
wir	fallen
ihr	fallet
sie	fallen

PERFECT

ich	bin gefallen
du	bist gefallen
er	ist gefallen
wir	sind gefallen
ihr	seid gefallen
sie	sind gefallen

IMPERFECT

ich	fiel
du	fielst
er	fiel
wir	fielen
ihr	fielt
sie	fielen

FUTURE

ich	werde fallen
du	wirst fallen
er	wird fallen
wir	werden fallen
ihr	werdet fallen
sie	werden fallen

CONDITIONAL

ich	würde fallen
du	würdest fallen
er	würde fallen
wir	würden fallen
ihr	würdet fallen
sie	würden fallen

IMPERATIVE

fall(e)!/fallen wir!/fallt!
fallen Sie!

PAST PARTICIPLE

gefallen

PRESENT PARTICIPLE

fallend

EXAMPLE PHRASES

*Er **fiel** vom Fahrrad.* He fell off his bike.
*Ich **bin** durch die Prüfung **gefallen**.* I failed my exam.
*Die Aktien **fielen** im Kurs.* Share prices went down.

---

ich = I **du** = you **er** = he **wir** = we/one **ihr** = you **sie** = they

▶ finden (to find)

PRESENT

ich	finde
du	findest
er	findet
wir	finden
ihr	findet
sie	finden

PRESENT SUBJUNCTIVE

ich	finde
du	findest
er	finde
wir	finden
ihr	findet
sie	finden

PERFECT

ich	habe gefunden
du	hast gefunden
er	hat gefunden
wir	haben gefunden
ihr	habt gefunden
sie	haben gefunden

IMPERFECT

ich	fand
du	fand(e)st
er	fand
wir	fanden
ihr	fandet
sie	fanden

FUTURE

ich	werde finden
du	wirst finden
er	wird finden
wir	werden finden
ihr	werdet finden
sie	werden finden

CONDITIONAL

ich	würde finden
du	würdest finden
er	würde finden
wir	würden finden
ihr	würdet finden
sie	würden finden

IMPERATIVE

find(e)!/finden wir!/findet!
finden Sie!

PAST PARTICIPLE

gefunden

PRESENT PARTICIPLE

findend

EXAMPLE PHRASES

*Hast du deine Brieftasche **gefunden?*** Have you found your wallet?
*Er **fand** den Mut, sie zu fragen.* He found the courage to ask her.
*Ich **finde**, sie ist eine gute Lehrerin.* I think she's a good teacher.

ich = I **du** = you **er** = he **wir** = we/one **ihr** = you **sie** = they

▶ **geben** (to give)

PRESENT

ich	gebe
du	gibst
er	gibt
wir	geben
ihr	gebt
sie	geben

PRESENT SUBJUNCTIVE

ich	gebe
du	gebest
er	gebe
wir	geben
ihr	gebet
sie	geben

PERFECT

ich	habe gegeben
du	hast gegeben
er	hat gegeben
wir	haben gegeben
ihr	habt gegeben
sie	haben gegeben

IMPERFECT

ich	gab
du	gabst
er	gab
wir	gaben
ihr	gabt
sie	gaben

FUTURE

ich	werde geben
du	wirst geben
er	wird geben
wir	werden geben
ihr	werdet geben
sie	werden geben

CONDITIONAL

ich	würde geben
du	würdest geben
er	würde geben
wir	würden geben
ihr	würdet geben
sie	würden geben

IMPERATIVE

gib!/geben wir!/gebt!
geben Sie!

PAST PARTICIPLE

gegeben

PRESENT PARTICIPLE

gebend

EXAMPLE PHRASES

*Er **gab** mir das Geld für die Bücher.* He gave me the money for the books.
*Was **gibt** es im Kino?* What's on at the cinema?
*Wir **würden** alles darum **geben**, ins Finale zu kommen.* We would give anything
  to reach the finals.

ich = I **du** = you **er** = he **wir** = we/one **ihr** = you **sie** = they

▶ gehen (to go)

PRESENT

ich	gehe
du	gehst
er	geht
wir	gehen
ihr	geht
sie	gehen

PRESENT SUBJUNCTIVE

ich	gehe
du	gehest
er	gehe
wir	gehen
ihr	gehet
sie	gehen

PERFECT

ich	bin gegangen
du	bist gegangen
er	ist gegangen
wir	sind gegangen
ihr	seid gegangen
sie	sind gegangen

IMPERFECT

ich	ging
du	gingst
er	ging
wir	gingen
ihr	gingt
sie	gingen

FUTURE

ich	werde gehen
du	wirst gehen
er	wird gehen
wir	werden gehen
ihr	werdet gehen
sie	werden gehen

CONDITIONAL

ich	würde gehen
du	würdest gehen
er	würde gehen
wir	würden gehen
ihr	würdet gehen
sie	würden gehen

IMPERATIVE

geh(e)!/gehen wir!/geht!
gehen Sie!

PAST PARTICIPLE

gegangen

PRESENT PARTICIPLE

gehend

EXAMPLE PHRASES

*Die Kinder **gingen** ins Haus.* The children went into the house.
*Wie **geht** es dir?* How are you?
*Wir **sind** gestern schwimmen **gegangen**.* We went swimming yesterday.

---

ich = I   **du** = you   **er** = he   **wir** = we/one   **ihr** = you   **sie** = they

▶ **haben** (to have)

PRESENT

ich	habe
du	hast
er	hat
wir	haben
ihr	habt
sie	haben

PRESENT SUBJUNCTIVE

ich	habe
du	habest
er	habe
wir	haben
ihr	habet
sie	haben

PERFECT

ich	habe gehabt
du	hast gehabt
er	hat gehabt
wir	haben gehabt
ihr	habt gehabt
sie	haben gehabt

IMPERFECT

ich	hatte
du	hattest
er	hatte
wir	hatten
ihr	hattet
sie	hatten

FUTURE

ich	werde haben
du	wirst haben
er	wird haben
wir	werden haben
ihr	werdet haben
sie	werden haben

CONDITIONAL

ich	würde haben
du	würdest haben
er	würde haben
wir	würden haben
ihr	würdet haben
sie	würden haben

IMPERATIVE

hab(e)!/haben wir!/habt!
haben Sie!

PAST PARTICIPLE

gehabt

PRESENT PARTICIPLE

habend

EXAMPLE PHRASES

Hast du eine Schwester? Have you got a sister?
*Er **hatte** Hunger.* He was hungry.
*Ich **hätte** gern ein Eis.* I'd like an ice cream.
*Sie **hat** heute Geburtstag.* It's her birthday today.

ich = I **du** = you **er** = he **wir** = we/one **ihr** = you **sie** = they

▶ halten (to hold)

PRESENT

ich	halte
du	hältst
er	hält
wir	halten
ihr	haltet
sie	halten

PRESENT SUBJUNCTIVE

ich	halte
du	haltest
er	halte
wir	halten
ihr	haltet
sie	halten

PERFECT

ich	habe gehalten
du	hast gehalten
er	hat gehalten
wir	haben gehalten
ihr	habt gehalten
sie	haben gehalten

IMPERFECT

ich	hielt
du	hielt(e)st
er	hielt
wir	hielten
ihr	hieltet
sie	hielten

FUTURE

ich	werde halten
du	wirst halten
er	wird halten
wir	werden halten
ihr	werdet halten
sie	werden halten

CONDITIONAL

ich	würde halten
du	würdest halten
er	würde halten
wir	würden halten
ihr	würdet halten
sie	würden halten

IMPERATIVE

halt(e)!/halten wir!/haltet!
halten Sie!

PAST PARTICIPLE

gehalten

PRESENT PARTICIPLE

haltend

EXAMPLE PHRASES

*Kannst du das mal **halten**?* Can you hold that for a moment?
*Der Bus **hielt** vor dem Rathaus.* The bus stopped in front of the town hall.
*Ich **habe** sie für deine Mutter **gehalten**.* I took her for your mother.

ich = I   **du** = you   **er** = he   **wir** = we/one   **ihr** = you   **sie** = they

▶ helfen (to help)

PRESENT

ich	helfe
du	hilfst
er	hilft
wir	helfen
ihr	helft
sie	helfen

PRESENT SUBJUNCTIVE

ich	helfe
du	helfest
er	helfe
wir	helfen
ihr	helfet
sie	helfen

PERFECT

ich	habe geholfen
du	hast geholfen
er	hat geholfen
wir	haben geholfen
ihr	habt geholfen
sie	haben geholfen

IMPERFECT

ich	half
du	halfst
er	half
wir	halfen
ihr	halft
sie	halfen

FUTURE

ich	werde helfen
du	wirst helfen
er	wird helfen
wir	werden helfen
ihr	werdet helfen
sie	werden helfen

CONDITIONAL

ich	würde helfen
du	würdest helfen
er	würde helfen
wir	würden helfen
ihr	würdet helfen
sie	würden helfen

IMPERATIVE

hilf!/helfen wir!/helft!
helfen Sie!

PAST PARTICIPLE

geholfen

PRESENT PARTICIPLE

helfend

EXAMPLE PHRASES

*Er **hat** mir dabei **geholfen**.* He helped me with it.
*Diese Arznei **hilft** gegen Kopfschmerzen.* This medicine is good for headaches.
*Sein Vorschlag **half** mir wenig.* His suggestion was not much help to me.

ich = I **du** = you **er** = he **wir** = we/one **ihr** = you **sie** = they

▶ **kennen** (to know) *(be acquainted with)*

PRESENT		PRESENT SUBJUNCTIVE	
ich	kenne	ich	kenne
du	kennst	du	kennest
er	kennt	er	kenne
wir	kennen	wir	kennen
ihr	kennt	ihr	kennet
sie	kennen	sie	kennen

PERFECT		IMPERFECT	
ich	habe gekannt	ich	kannte
du	hast gekannt	du	kanntest
er	hat gekannt	er	kannte
wir	haben gekannt	wir	kannten
ihr	habt gekannt	ihr	kanntet
sie	haben gekannt	sie	kannten

FUTURE		CONDITIONAL	
ich	werde kennen	ich	würde kennen
du	wirst kennen	du	würdest kennen
er	wird kennen	er	würde kennen
wir	werden kennen	wir	würden kennen
ihr	werdet kennen	ihr	würdet kennen
sie	werden kennen	sie	würden kennen

IMPERATIVE

kenn(e)!/kennen wir!/kennt!
kennen Sie!

PAST PARTICIPLE

gekannt

PRESENT PARTICIPLE

kennend

EXAMPLE PHRASES

*Ich **kenne** ihn nicht.* I don't know him.
*Er **kannte** kein Erbarmen.* He knew no mercy.
***Kennst** du mich noch?* Do you remember me?

ich = I **du** = you **er** = he **wir** = we/one **ihr** = you **sie** = they

▶ **kommen** (to come)

PRESENT

ich	komme
du	kommst
er	kommt
wir	kommen
ihr	kommt
sie	kommen

PRESENT SUBJUNCTIVE

ich	komme
du	kommest
er	komme
wir	kommen
ihr	kommet
sie	kommen

PERFECT

ich	bin gekommen
du	bist gekommen
er	ist gekommen
wir	sind gekommen
ihr	seid gekommen
sie	sind gekommen

IMPERFECT

ich	kam
du	kamst
er	kam
wir	kamen
ihr	kamt
sie	kamen

FUTURE

ich	werde kommen
du	wirst kommen
er	wird kommen
wir	werden kommen
ihr	werdet kommen
sie	werden kommen

CONDITIONAL

ich	würde kommen
du	würdest kommen
er	würde kommen
wir	würden kommen
ihr	würdet kommen
sie	würden kommen

IMPERATIVE

komm(e)!/kommen wir!
kommt!/kommen Sie!

PAST PARTICIPLE

gekommen

PRESENT PARTICIPLE

kommend

EXAMPLE PHRASES

*Er **kam** die Straße entlang.* He was coming along the street.
*Ich **komme** zu deiner Party.* I'm coming to your party.
*Woher **kommst** du?* Where do you come from?

ich = I **du** = you **er** = he **wir** = we/one **ihr** = you **sie** = they

▶ **können** (to be able to)

PRESENT

ich	kann
du	kannst
er	kann
wir	können
ihr	könnt
sie	können

PRESENT SUBJUNCTIVE

ich	könne
du	könnest
er	könne
wir	können
ihr	könnet
sie	können

PERFECT

ich	habe gekonnt/können
du	hast gekonnt/können
er	hat gekonnt/können
wir	haben gekonnt/können
ihr	habt gekonnt/können
sie	haben gekonnt/können

IMPERFECT

ich	konnte
du	konntest
er	konnte
wir	konnten
ihr	konntet
sie	konnten

FUTURE

ich	werde können
du	wirst können
er	wird können
wir	werden können
ihr	werdet können
sie	werden können

CONDITIONAL

ich	würde können
du	würdest können
er	würde können
wir	würden können
ihr	würdet können
sie	würden können

IMPERATIVE

PAST PARTICIPLE

gekonnt/können*

PRESENT PARTICIPLE

könnend

The second form is used when combined with an infinitive construction.

EXAMPLE PHRASES

*Er **kann** gut schwimmen.* He can swim well.
*Sie **konnte** kein Wort Deutsch.* She couldn't speak a word of German.
***Kann** ich gehen?* Can I go?

ich = I **du** = you **er** = he **wir** = we/one **ihr** = you **sie** = they

▶ **lassen** (to leave; to allow)

PRESENT

ich	lasse
du	lässt
er	lässt
wir	lassen
ihr	lasst
sie	lassen

PRESENT SUBJUNCTIVE

ich	lasse
du	lassest
er	lasse
wir	lassen
ihr	lasset
sie	lassen

PERFECT

ich	habe gelassen
du	hast gelassen
er	hat gelassen
wir	haben gelassen
ihr	habt gelassen
sie	haben gelassen

IMPERFECT

ich	ließ
du	ließest
er	ließ
wir	ließen
ihr	ließt
sie	ließen

FUTURE

ich	werde lassen
du	wirst lassen
er	wird lassen
wir	werden lassen
ihr	werdet lassen
sie	werden lassen

CONDITIONAL

ich	würde lassen
du	würdest lassen
er	würde lassen
wir	würden lassen
ihr	würdet lassen
sie	würden lassen

IMPERATIVE

lass!/lassen wir!/lasst!
lassen Sie!

PAST PARTICIPLE

gelassen/lassen*

PRESENT PARTICIPLE

lassend

*The second form is used when combined with an infinitive construction.

EXAMPLE PHRASES

Sie *ließ* uns warten. She kept us waiting.
Ich *lasse* den Hund nicht auf das Sofa. I won't let the dog get up on the sofa.
Sie *haben* ihn allein im Auto *gelassen*. They left him alone in the car.

ich = I **du** = you **er** = he **wir** = we/one **ihr** = you **sie** = they

▶ laufen (to run)

PRESENT

ich	laufe
du	läufst
er	läuft
wir	laufen
ihr	lauft
sie	laufen

PRESENT SUBJUNCTIVE

ich	laufe
du	laufest
er	laufe
wir	laufen
ihr	laufet
sie	laufen

PERFECT

ich	bin gelaufen
du	bist gelaufen
er	ist gelaufen
wir	sind gelaufen
ihr	seid gelaufen
sie	sind gelaufen

IMPERFECT

ich	lief
du	liefst
er	lief
wir	liefen
ihr	lieft
sie	liefen

FUTURE

ich	werde laufen
du	wirst laufen
er	wird laufen
wir	werden laufen
ihr	werdet laufen
sie	werden laufen

CONDITIONAL

ich	würde laufen
du	würdest laufen
er	würde laufen
wir	würden laufen
ihr	würdet laufen
sie	würden laufen

IIMPERATIVE

lauf(e)!/laufen wir!/lauft!
laufen Sie!

PAST PARTICIPLE

gelaufen

PRESENT PARTICIPLE

laufend

EXAMPLE PHRASES

*Er **lief** so schnell er konnte.* He ran as fast as he could.
*Sie **läuft** ständig zur Polizei.* She's always going to the police.
*Das Schiff **ist** auf Grund **gelaufen**.* The ship ran aground.

ich = I   **du** = you   **er** = he   **wir** = we/one   **ihr** = you   **sie** = they

▶ **liegen** (to lie)

PRESENT

ich	liege
du	liegst
er	liegt
wir	liegen
ihr	liegt
sie	liegen

PRESENT SUBJUNCTIVE

ich	liege
du	liegest
er	liege
wir	liegen
ihr	lieget
sie	liegen

PERFECT

ich	habe gelegen
du	hast gelegen
er	hat gelegen
wir	haben gelegen
ihr	habt gelegen
sie	haben gelegen

IMPERFECT

ich	lag
du	lagst
er	lag
wir	lagen
ihr	lagt
sie	lagen

FUTURE

ich	werde liegen
du	wirst liegen
er	wird liegen
wir	werden liegen
ihr	werdet liegen
sie	werden liegen

CONDITIONAL

ich	würde liegen
du	würdest liegen
er	würde liegen
wir	würden liegen
ihr	würdet liegen
sie	würden liegen

IMPERATIVE

lieg(e)!/liegen wir!/liegt!
liegen Sie!

PAST PARTICIPLE

gelegen

PRESENT PARTICIPLE

liegend

EXAMPLE PHRASES

*Wir **lagen** den ganzen Tag am Strand.* We lay on the beach all day.
*Köln **liegt** am Rhein.* Cologne is on the Rhine.
*Es **hat** daran **gelegen**, dass ich krank war.* It was because I was ill.

ich = I **du** = you **er** = he **wir** = we/one **ihr** = you **sie** = they

▶ machen (to do *or* to make)

PRESENT

ich	mache
du	machst
er	macht
wir	machen
ihr	macht
sie	machen

PRESENT SUBJUNCTIVE

ich	mache
du	machest
er	mache
wir	machen
ihr	machet
sie	machen

PERFECT

ich	habe gemacht
du	hast gemacht
er	hat gemacht
wir	haben gemacht
ihr	habt gemacht
sie	haben gemacht

IMPERFECT

ich	machte
du	machtest
er	machte
wir	machten
ihr	machtet
sie	machten

FUTURE

ich	werde machen
du	wirst machen
er	wird machen
wir	werden machen
ihr	werdet machen
sie	werden machen

CONDITIONAL

ich	würde machen
du	würdest machen
er	würde machen
wir	würden machen
ihr	würdet machen
sie	würden machen

IMPERATIVE

mach!/macht!/machen Sie!

PAST PARTICIPLE

gemacht

PRESENT PARTICIPLE

machend

EXAMPLE PHRASES

*Was **machst** du?* What are you doing?
*Ich **habe** die Betten **gemacht**.* I made the beds.
*Ich **werde** es morgen **machen**.* I'll do it tomorrow.

---

ich = I **du** = you **er** = he **wir** = we/one **ihr** = you **sie** = they

▶ **mögen** (to like)

PRESENT

ich	mag
du	magst
er	mag
wir	mögen
ihr	mögt
sie	mögen

PRESENT SUBJUNCTIVE

ich	möge
du	mögest
er	möge
wir	mögen
ihr	möget
sie	mögen

PERFECT

ich	habe gemocht/mögen
du	hast gemocht/mögen
er	hat gemocht/mögen
wir	haben gemocht/mögen
ihr	habt gemocht/mögen
sie	haben gemocht/mögen

IMPERFECT

ich	mochte
du	mochtest
er	mochte
wir	mochten
ihr	mochtet
sie	mochten

FUTURE

ich	werde mögen
du	wirst mögen
er	wird mögen
wir	werden mögen
ihr	werdet mögen
sie	werden mögen

CONDITIONAL

ich	würde mögen
du	würdest mögen
er	würde mögen
wir	würden mögen
ihr	würdet mögen
sie	würden mögen

IMPERATIVE

PAST PARTICIPLE

gemocht/mögen*

PRESENT PARTICIPLE

mögend

*The second form is used when combined with an infinitive construction.

EXAMPLE PHRASES

*Ich **mag** gern Vanilleeis.* I like vanilla ice cream.
*Er **mochte** sie nicht danach fragen.* He didn't want to ask her about it.
*Ich **habe** ihn noch nie **gemocht**.* I never liked him.

ich = I **du** = you **er** = he **wir** = we/one **ihr** = you **sie** = they

▶ **müssen** (to have to)

PRESENT		PRESENT SUBJUNCTIVE	
ich	muss	ich	müsse
du	musst	du	müssest
er	muss	er	müsse
wir	müssen	wir	müssen
ihr	müsst	ihr	müsset
sie	müssen	sie	müssen

PERFECT		IMPERFECT	
ich	habe gemusst/müssen	ich	musste
du	hast gemusst/müssen	du	musstest
er	hat gemusst/müssen	er	musste
wir	haben gemusst/müssen	wir	mussten
ihr	habt gemusst/müssen	ihr	musstet
sie	haben gemusst/müssen	sie	mussten

FUTURE		CONDITIONAL	
ich	werde müssen	ich	würde müssen
du	wirst müssen	du	würdest müssen
er	wird müssen	er	würde müssen
wir	werden müssen	wir	würden müssen
ihr	werdet müssen	ihr	würdet müssen
sie	werden müssen	sie	würden müssen

IMPERATIVE

PAST PARTICIPLE

gemusst/müssen*

PRESENT PARTICIPLE

müssend

The second form is used when combined with an infinitive construction.

EXAMPLE PHRASES

*Ich **muss** aufs Klo.* I must go to the loo.
*Wir **müssen** jeden Abend unsere Hausaufgaben machen.* We have to do our homework
  every night.
*Sie **hat** abwaschen **müssen**.* She had to wash up.

ich = I **du** = you **er** = he **wir** = we/one **ihr** = you **sie** = they

▶ **nehmen** (to take)

PRESENT

ich	nehme
du	nimmst
er	nimmt
wir	nehmen
ihr	nehmt
sie	nehmen

PRESENT SUBJUNCTIVE

ich	nehme
du	nehmest
er	nehme
wir	nehmen
ihr	nehmet
sie	nehmen

PERFECT

ich	habe genommen
du	hast genommen
er	hat genommen
wir	haben genommen
ihr	habt genommen
sie	haben genommen

IMPERFECT

ich	nahm
du	nahmst
er	nahm
wir	nahmen
ihr	nahmt
sie	nahmen

FUTURE

ich	werde nehmen
du	wirst nehmen
er	wird nehmen
wir	werden nehmen
ihr	werdet nehmen
sie	werden nehmen

CONDITIONAL

ich	würde nehmen
du	würdest nehmen
er	würde nehmen
wir	würden nehmen
ihr	würdet nehmen
sie	würden nehmen

IMPERATIVE

nimm!/nehmen wir!/nehmt!
nehmen Sie!

PAST PARTICIPLE

genommen

PRESENT PARTICIPLE

nehmend

EXAMPLE PHRASES

Hast du den Bus in die Stadt genommen? Did you take the bus into town?
Wie viel nimmst du dafür? How much will you take for it?
Er nahm sich vom Brot. He helped himself to bread.

ich = I du = you er = he wir = we/one ihr = you sie = they

▶ **sein** (to be)

PRESENT

ich	bin
du	bist
er	ist
wir	sind
ihr	seid
sie	sind

PRESENT SUBJUNCTIVE

ich	sei
du	sei(e)st
er	sei
wir	seien
ihr	seiet
sie	seien

PERFECT

ich	bin gewesen
du	bist gewesen
er	ist gewesen
wir	sind gewesen
ihr	seid gewesen
sie	sind gewesen

IMPERFECT

ich	war
du	warst
er	war
wir	waren
ihr	wart
sie	waren

FUTURE

ich	werde sein
du	wirst sein
er	wird sein
wir	werden sein
ihr	werdet sein
sie	werden sein

CONDITIONAL

ich	würde sein
du	würdest sein
er	würde sein
wir	würden sein
ihr	würdet sein
sie	würden sein

IMPERATIVE

sei!/seien wir!/seid!/seien Sie!

PAST PARTICIPLE

gewesen

PRESENT PARTICIPLE

seiend

EXAMPLE PHRASES

*Er **ist** zehn Jahre alt.* He is ten years old.
*Mir **ist** kalt.* I'm cold.
*Wir **waren** gestern im Theater.* We were at the theatre yesterday.
***Seid** ruhig!* Be quiet!

---

ich = I   **du** = you   **er** = he   **wir** = we/one   **ihr** = you   **sie** = they

▶ **sitzen** (to sit)

PRESENT

ich	sitze
du	sitzt
er	sitzt
wir	sitzen
ihr	sitzt
sie	sitzen

PRESENT SUBJUNCTIVE

ich	sitze
du	sitzest
er	sitze
wir	sitzen
ihr	sitzet
sie	sitzen

PERFECT

ich	habe gesessen
du	hast gesessen
er	hat gesessen
wir	haben gesessen
ihr	habt gesessen
sie	haben gesessen

IMPERFECT

ich	saß
du	saßest
er	saß
wir	saßen
ihr	saßt
sie	saßen

FUTURE

ich	werde sitzen
du	wirst sitzen
er	wird sitzen
wir	werden sitzen
ihr	werdet sitzen
sie	werden sitzen

CONDITIONAL

ich	würde sitzen
du	würdest sitzen
er	würde sitzen
wir	würden sitzen
ihr	würdet sitzen
sie	würden sitzen

IMPERATIVE

sitz(e)!/sitzen wir!/sitzt!
sitzen Sie!

PAST PARTICIPLE

gesessen

PRESENT PARTICIPLE

sitzend

EXAMPLE PHRASES

Er saß auf meinem Stuhl. He was sitting on my chair.
*Deine Krawatte **sitzt** nicht richtig.* Your tie isn't straight.
*Ich **habe** zwei Jahre über dieser Arbeit **gesessen**.* I've spent two years on this piece
   of work.

ich = I **du** = you **er** = he **wir** = we/one **ihr** = you **sie** = they

▶ **sprechen** (to speak)

PRESENT

ich	spreche
du	sprichst
er	spricht
wir	sprechen
ihr	sprecht
sie	sprechen

PRESENT SUBJUNCTIVE

ich	spreche
du	sprechest
er	spreche
wir	sprechen
ihr	sprechet
sie	sprechen

PERFECT

ich	habe gesprochen
du	hast gesprochen
er	hat gesprochen
wir	haben gesprochen
ihr	habt gesprochen
sie	haben gesprochen

IMPERFECT

ich	sprach
du	sprachst
er	sprach
wir	sprachen
ihr	spracht
sie	sprachen

FUTURE

ich	werde sprechen
du	wirst sprechen
er	wird sprechen
wir	werden sprechen
ihr	werdet sprechen
sie	werden sprechen

CONDITIONAL

ich	würde sprechen
du	würdest sprechen
er	würde sprechen
wir	würden sprechen
ihr	würdet sprechen
sie	würden sprechen

IMPERATIVE

sprich!/sprechen wir!/sprecht!
sprechen Sie!

PAST PARTICIPLE

gesprochen

PRESENT PARTICIPLE

sprechend

EXAMPLE PHRASES

*Er **spricht** kein Italienisch.* He doesn't speak Italian.
*Ich **würde** dich gern privat **sprechen**.* I would like to speak to you privately.
***Hast** du mit ihr **gesprochen**?* Have you spoken to her?

ich = I **du** = you **er** = he **wir** = we/one **ihr** = you **sie** = they

▶ **stehen** (to stand)

PRESENT

ich	stehe
du	stehst
er	steht
wir	stehen
ihr	steht
sie	stehen

PRESENT SUBJUNCTIVE

ich	stehe
du	stehest
er	stehe
wir	stehen
ihr	stehet
sie	stehen

PERFECT

ich	habe gestanden
du	hast gestanden
er	hat gestanden
wir	haben gestanden
ihr	habt gestanden
sie	haben gestanden

IMPERFECT

ich	stand
du	stand(e)st
er	stand
wir	standen
ihr	standet
sie	standen

FUTURE

ich	werde stehen
du	wirst stehen
er	wird stehen
wir	werden stehen
ihr	werdet stehen
sie	werden stehen

CONDITIONAL

ich	würde stehen
du	würdest stehen
er	würde stehen
wir	würden stehen
ihr	würdet stehen
sie	würden stehen

IMPERATIVE

steh(e)!/stehen wir!/steht!
stehen Sie!

PAST PARTICIPLE

gestanden

PRESENT PARTICIPLE

stehend

EXAMPLE PHRASES

*Wir **standen** an der Bushaltestelle.* We stood at the bus stop.
*Es **hat** in der Zeitung **gestanden**.* It was in the newspaper.
*Dieses Kleid **würde** dir gut **stehen**.* This dress would suit you.

---

ich = I **du** = you **er** = he **wir** = we/one **ihr** = you **sie** = they

▶ **tragen** (to wear, to carry)

PRESENT

ich	trage
du	trägst
er	trägt
wir	tragen
ihr	tragt
sie	tragen

PRESENT SUBJUNCTIVE

ich	trage
du	tragest
er	trage
wir	tragen
ihr	traget
sie	tragen

PERFECT

ich	habe getragen
du	hast getragen
er	hat getragen
wir	haben getragen
ihr	habt getragen
sie	haben getragen

IMPERFECT

ich	trug
du	trugst
er	trug
wir	trugen
ihr	trugt
sie	trugen

FUTURE

ich	werde tragen
du	wirst tragen
er	wird tragen
wir	werden tragen
ihr	werdet tragen
sie	werden tragen

CONDITIONAL

ich	würde tragen
du	würdest tragen
er	würde tragen
wir	würden tragen
ihr	würdet tragen
sie	würden tragen

IMPERATIVE

trag(e)!/tragen wir!/tragt!
tragen Sie!

PAST PARTICIPLE

getragen

PRESENT PARTICIPLE

tragend

EXAMPLE PHRASES

*Ich **trug** ihren Koffer zum Bahnhof.* I carried her case to the station.
*Du **trägst** die ganze Verantwortung dafür.* You bear the full responsibility for it.
*Ich **würde** meine Haare gern länger **tragen**.* I'd like to wear my hair longer.

---

ich = I   **du** = you   **er** = he   **wir** = we/one   **ihr** = you   **sie** = they

▶ **tun** (to do)

PRESENT

ich	tue
du	tust
er	tut
wir	tun
ihr	tut
sie	tun

PRESENT SUBJUNCTIVE

ich	tue
du	tuest
er	tue
wir	tuen
ihr	tuet
sie	tuen

PERFECT

ich	habe getan
du	hast getan
er	hat getan
wir	haben getan
ihr	habt getan
sie	haben getan

IMPERFECT

ich	tat
du	tat(e)st
er	tat
wir	taten
ihr	tatet
sie	taten

FUTURE

ich	werde tun
du	wirst tun
er	wird tun
wir	werden tun
ihr	werdet tun
sie	werden tun

CONDITIONAL

ich	würde tun
du	würdest tun
er	würde tun
wir	würden tun
ihr	würdet tun
sie	würden tun

IMPERATIVE

tu(e)!/tun wir!/tut!/tun Sie!

PAST PARTICIPLE

getan

PRESENT PARTICIPLE

tuend

EXAMPLE PHRASES

*Ich **werde** das auf keinen Fall **tun**.* There is no way I'll do that.
*So etwas **tut** man nicht!* That is just not done!
*Sie **tat**, als ob sie schliefe.* She pretended to be sleeping.

ich = I **du** = you **er** = he **wir** = we/one **ihr** = you **sie** = they

▶ **werden** (to become)

PRESENT

ich	werde
du	wirst
er	wird
wir	werden
ihr	werdet
sie	werden

PRESENT SUBJUNCTIVE

ich	werde
du	werdest
er	werde
wir	werden
ihr	werdet
sie	werden

PERFECT

ich	bin geworden/worden
du	bist geworden/worden
er	ist geworden/worden
wir	sind geworden/worden
ihr	seid geworden/worden
sie	sind geworden/worden

IMPERFECT

ich	wurde
du	wurdest
er	wurde
wir	wurden
ihr	wurdet
sie	wurden

FUTURE

ich	werde werden
du	wirst werden
er	wird werden
wir	werden werden
ihr	werdet werden
sie	werden werden

CONDITIONAL

ich	würde werden
du	würdest werden
er	würde werden
wir	würden werden
ihr	würdet werden
sie	würden werden

IMPERATIVE

werde!/werden wir!/werdet!
werden Sie!

PAST PARTICIPLE

geworden/worden*

PRESENT PARTICIPLE

werdend

The second form is used when combined with an infinitive construction.

EXAMPLE PHRASES

*Mir **wird** schlecht.* I feel ill.
*Ich will Lehrerin **werden**.* I want to be a teacher.
*Der Kuchen **ist** gut **geworden**.* The cake turned out well.

---

ich = I **du** = you **er** = he **wir** = we/one **ihr** = you **sie** = they

▶ **wissen** (to know)

PRESENT

ich	weiß
du	weißt
er	weiß
wir	wissen
ihr	wisst
sie	wissen

PRESENT SUBJUNCTIVE

ich	wisse
du	wissest
er	wisse
wir	wissen
ihr	wisset
sie	wissen

PERFECT

ich	habe gewusst
du	hast gewusst
er	hat gewusst
wir	haben gewusst
ihr	habt gewusst
sie	haben gewusst

IMPERFECT

ich	wusste
du	wusstest
er	wusste
wir	wussten
ihr	wusstet
sie	wussten

FUTURE

ich	werde wissen
du	wirst wissen
er	wird wissen
wir	werden wissen
ihr	werdet wissen
sie	werden wissen

CONDITIONAL

ich	würde wissen
du	würdest wissen
er	würde wissen
wir	würden wissen
ihr	würdet wissen
sie	würden wissen

IMPERATIVE

wisse!/wissen wir!/wisset!
wissen Sie!

PAST PARTICIPLE

gewusst

PRESENT PARTICIPLE

wissend

EXAMPLE PHRASES

*Ich **weiß** nicht.* I don't know.
*Er **hat** nichts davon **gewusst**.* He didn't know anything about it.
*Sie **wussten**, wo das Kino war.* They knew where the cinema was.

ich = I **du** = you **er** = he **wir** = we/one **ihr** = you **sie** = they

▶ **wollen** (to want)

PRESENT

ich	will
du	willst
er	will
wir	wollen
ihr	wollt
sie	wollen

PRESENT SUBJUNCTIVE

ich	wolle
du	wollest
er	wolle
wir	wollen
ihr	wollet
sie	wollen

PERFECT

ich	habe gewollt/wollen
du	hast gewollt/wollen
er	hat gewollt/wollen
wir	haben gewollt/wollen
ihr	habt gewollt/wollen
sie	haben gewollt/wollen

IMPERFECT

ich	wollte
du	wolltest
er	wollte
wir	wollten
ihr	wolltet
sie	wollten

FUTURE

ich	werde wollen
du	wirst wollen
er	wird wollen
wir	werden wollen
ihr	werdet wollen
sie	werden wollen

CONDITIONAL

ich	würde wollen
du	würdest wollen
er	würde wollen
wir	würden wollen
ihr	würdet wollen
sie	würden wollen

IMPERATIVE

wolle!/wollen wir!/wollt!
wollen Sie!

PAST PARTICIPLE

gewollt/wollen*

PRESENT PARTICIPLE

wollend

*The second form is used when combined with an infinitive construction.

EXAMPLE PHRASES

*Er **will** nach London gehen.* He wants to go to London.
*Das **habe** ich nicht **gewollt**.* I didn't want this to happen.
*Sie **wollten** nur mehr Geld.* All they wanted was more money.

ich = I **du** = you **er** = he **wir** = we/one **ihr** = you **sie** = they